GREAT BOOKS OF THE WESTERN WORLD

GREAT BOOKS
OF THE WESTERN WORLD

ROBERT MAYNARD HUTCHINS, *EDITOR IN CHIEF*

14.

PLUTARCH

PLUTARCH

The Lives of the Noble Grecians
and Romans

The Dryden Translation

William Benton, *Publisher*

ENCYCLOPÆDIA BRITANNICA, INC.

CHICAGO · LONDON · TORONTO · GENEVA

THE UNIVERSITY OF CHICAGO

The Great Books
is published with the editorial advice of the faculties
of The University of Chicago

BIOGRAPHICAL NOTE

PLUTARCH, c. 46–c. 120

PLUTARCH lived in the time of the emperors Nerva, Trajan, and Hadrian, a time usually thought of as the beginning of the best age of the Roman imperial period and as the last great era of Greek and Roman literature. He is not quoted nor even mentioned by his celebrated contemporaries, Juvenal, Quintilian, Martial, Tacitus, and the younger Pliny. He never wrote directly of himself, and the sources for his life are the many scattered passages where some reminiscence appears incidentally.

Later, when his fame became widespread, legends grew up to supplement the little extant knowledge. The legends tended to confirm the impression made by his works that he was to an exceptional degree representative of his time. Plutarch was pictured as tutor to Trajan, to whom he was supposed to have dedicated a treatise on the good of a prince after the manner of Plato's epistle to Dion. He was supposed to have lived for a long period in Rome, where he was held in great esteem, honored with consular rank, and later appointed governor of Greece by the Emperor, who had been his pupil.

These legendary titles and distinctions apparently have no basis in fact. The truth seems to be that the man who wrote of the fall of Athens, of the growth of Roman dominion over the East, of the overthrow of the Roman republic, was a Theban provincial, fortunate in his ancestors and in his education, contented with his family and his friends, and loyal in a spirited way to his town. He did go to Rome on several occasions. His visits were short. He himself records that he had "no leisure while there to study and exercise the Latin tongue, as well for the business I had then to do, as also to satisfy them that came to learn philosophy of me." He adds, however, that he had familiar conversation with many of the highest men in Rome; his lack of Latin would not prevent that in the "Greek city,"as Juvenal indignantly called it. From this "great place, containing plenty of all sorts of books" he returned to "his poor little town and remained there willingly, being loath to make it less by the withdrawal of even one."

The place of his birth was Chaeronea in Boeotia. It was a town not incapable of stirring the imagination by the contrast of its memories with its present obscurity. Plutarch relates that long ago Epaminondas had called it "the playfield of Mars." Not as long ago as that, Macedon and the allied armies of Thebes and Athens had fought on its plains a battle "fatal to Greek liberty." Chaeronea appears in Plutarch's life of Antony, where he recalls the story he had from his great-grandfather Nicarchus. The citizens of the town, Nicarchus among them, had been forced by Antony's supply officers to carry corn like beasts of burden. They were starting out in file on their second trip to the sea when news came of Antony's defeat at Actium. "Antony's purveyors and soldiers fled upon the news, and the citizens of Chaeronea divided the corn among themselves."

Among the sons of Nicarchus was Lamprias, Plutarch's grandfather. Plutarch remembers him with joy as a man whose wit was affected by wine as incense by fire. Lamprias too figures in the life of Antony as able to pass on, from a friend who had lived in Alexandria, tales of the luxurious revels of Antony and Cleopatra. Plutarch's father is mentioned by him a number of times, once with vivid gratitude for the way in which he taught his son to share honor and avoid envy.

As a young man, Plutarch studied at Athens with Ammonius, reputedly an Egyptian who taught at Alexandria before settling in Athens. Plutarch boarded in his teacher's house and records that one of his fellow students was a descendant of Themistocles.

It is not known when he wrote the series of treatises collected under the title *Moralia*. Many of them, he tells us, were expansions of his notes for lectures at Rome. It was after his return to Chaeronea that he compiled his *Symposiacs,* or *Table Talk,* wherein a variety of personages are depicted in discussion of a wide variety of lively, often trivial, problems. According to most opinion, he began work on the *Parallel Lives* towards the end of his life. He states that his original intention had been to instruct others, but in the course of writing he discovered that more and more it was he himself who was deriving profit and stimulation from "lodging these men one after the other in his house."

In his native Chaeronea, Plutarch seems to have held many municipal offices. When he was ridiculed on one occasion for his patience in discharging trivial duties, he said: "You remember what Antisthenes said, when someone was surprised that he carried some pickled fish home from the market: 'But it is for myself.' When you reproach me for watching tiles measured out and stone and mortar brought up, I give you the converse answer: 'It is not for myself, but for the city.'" He filled the position of Archon a number of times and served as a priest of Apollo at Delphi. His term in this last office seems to have lasted to the end of his life, for in one of his *Symposiacs* he argues on the question *Whether an Old Man should continue in Public Life* by submitting that no one would say to him: "You have served for many pythiads, you have taken part enough in the sacrifices, processions, and dances, and it is high time, Plutarch, now you are an old man, to lay aside your garland and retire as superannuated from the oracle."

There is much testimony in his writing of the tenderness and warmth in the smaller circle of his family. Plutarch wrote affectionate descriptions of his little girl, Timoxena, and a famous letter of consolation to his wife at the time of this child's death. In another letter to his wife he writes that he finds "scarcely an erasure, as in a book well-written" in the happiness of his long life. Legend reports that the people of Rome requested after his death that a statue be erected to honor his virtue.

This translation was made by many hands, but is commonly called the Dryden Translation.

CONTENTS

CONTENTS

THESEUS

LEGENDARY

As GEOGRAPHERS, Sosius, crowd into the edges of their maps parts of the world which they do not know about, adding notes in the margin to the effect, that beyond this lies nothing but the sandy deserts full of wild beasts, unapproachable bogs, Scythian ice, or a frozen sea, so in this work of mine, in which I have compared the lives of the greatest men with one another, after passing through those periods which probable reasoning can reach to and real history find a footing in, I might very well say of those that are farther off: "Beyond this there is nothing but prodigies and fictions, the only inhabitants are the poets and inventors of fables; there is no credit, or certainty any farther."

Yet, after publishing an account of Lycurgus the lawgiver and Numa the king, I thought I might, not without reason, ascend as high as to Romulus, being brought by my history so near to his time. Considering therefore with myself—

Whom shall I set so great a man to face?
Or whom oppose? Who's equal to the place?

(as Æschylus expresses it), I found none so fit as him that peopled the beautiful and far-famed city of Athens, to be set in opposition with the father of the invincible and renowned city of Rome. Let us hope that Fable may, in what shall follow, so submit to the purifying processes of Reason as to take the character of exact history. In any case, however, where it shall be found contumaciously slighting credibility and refusing to be reduced to anything like probable fact, we shall beg that we may meet with candid readers, and such as will receive with indulgence the stories of antiquity.

Theseus seemed to me to resemble Romulus in many particulars. Both of them, born out of wedlock and of uncertain parentage, had the repute of being sprung from the gods.

Both warriors; that by all the world's allowed.

Both of them united with strength of body an equal vigour of mind; and of the two most famous cities of the world, the one built

Rome, and the other made Athens be inhabited. Both stand charged with the rape of women; neither of them could avoid domestic misfortunes nor jealousy at home; but towards the close of their lives are both of them said to have incurred great odium with their countrymen, if, that is, we may take the stories least like poetry as our guide to the truth.

The lineage of Theseus, by his father's side, ascends as high as to Erechtheus and the first inhabitants of Attica. By his mother's side he was descended of Pelops. For Pelops was the most powerful of all the kings of Peloponnesus, not so much by the greatness of his riches as the multitude of his children, having married many daughters to chief men, and put many sons in places of command in the towns round about him. One of whom named Pittheus, grandfather to Theseus, was governor of the small city of the Trœzenians and had the repute of a man of the greatest knowledge and wisdom of his time; which then, it seems, consisted chiefly in grave maxims, such as the poet Hesiod got his great fame by, in his book of Works and Days. And, indeed, among these is one that they ascribe to Pittheus,—

Unto a friend suffice
A stipulated price;

which, also, Aristotle mentions. And Euripides, by calling Hippolytus "scholar of the holy Pittheus," shows the opinion that the world had of him.

Ægeus, being desirous of children, and consulting the oracle of Delphi, received the celebrated answer which forbade him the company of any woman before his return to Athens. But the oracle being so obscure as not to satisfy him that he was clearly forbid this, he went to Trœzen, and communicated to Pittheus the voice of the god, which was in this manner,—

Loose not the wine-skin foot, thou chief of men,
Until to Athens thou art come again.

Pittheus, therefore, taking advantage from the obscurity of the oracle, prevailed upon him, it is uncertain whether by persuasion or deceit, to lie with his daughter Æthra. Ægeus afterwards, knowing her whom he had lain with to be Pittheus's daughter, and suspecting her to be with child by him, left a sword and a pair of shoes, hiding them under a great stone that had a hollow in it exactly fitting them; and went away making her only privy to it, and commanding her, if she brought forth a son who, when he came to man's estate, should be able to lift up the stone and take away what he had left there, she should send him away to him with those things with all secrecy, and with injunctions to him as much as possible to conceal his journey from every one; for he greatly feared the Pallantidæ, who were continually mutinying against him, and despised him for his want of children, they themselves being fifty brothers, all sons of Pallas.

When Æthra was delivered of a son, some say that he was immediately named Theseus, from the tokens which his father had *put* under the stone; others that he had received his name afterwards at Athens, when Ægeus *acknowledged* him for his son. He was brought up under his grandfather Pittheus, and had a tutor and attendant set over him named Connidas, to whom the Athenians even to this time, the day before the feast that is dedicated to Theseus, sacrifice a ram, giving this honour to his memory upon much juster grounds than to Silanio and Parrhasius for making pictures and statues of Theseus. There being then a custom for the Grecian youth, upon their first coming to man's estate, to go to Delphi and offer first-fruits of their hair to the god, Theseus also went thither, and a place there to this day is yet named Thesea, as it is said, from him. He clipped only the fore part of his head, as Homer says the Abantes did. And this sort of tonsure was from him named Theseus. The Abantes first used it, not in imitation of the Arabians, as some imagine, nor of the Mysians, but because they were a warlike people, and used to close fighting, and above all other nations accustomed to engage hand to hand; as Archilochus testifies in these verses:—

Slings shall not whirl, nor many arrows fly,
  When on the plain the battle joins; but swords,
Man against man, the deadly conflict try
    As is the practice of Eubœa's lords
Skilled with the spear.—

Therefore that they might not give their enemies a hold by their hair, they cut it in this manner. They write also that this was the reason why Alexander gave command to his captains that all the beards of the Macedonians should be shaved, as being the readiest hold for an enemy.

Æthra for some time concealed the true parentage of Theseus, and a report was given out by Pittheus that he was begotten by Neptune; for the Trœzenians pay Neptune the highest veneration. He is their tutelar god; to him they offer all their first-fruits, and in his honour stamp their money with a trident.

Theseus displaying not only great strength of body, but equal bravery, and a quickness alike and force of understanding, his mother Æthra, conducting him to the stone, and informing him who was his true father, commanded him to take from thence the tokens that Ægeus had left, and sail to Athens. He without any difficulty set himself to the stone and lifted it up; but refused to take his journey by sea, though it was much the safer way, and though his mother and grandfather begged him to do so. For it was at that time very dangerous to go by land on the road to Athens, no part of it being free from robbers and murderers. That age produced a sort of men, in force of hand, and swiftness of foot, and strength of body, excelling the ordinary rate and wholly incapable of fatigue; making use, however, of these gifts of nature to no good or profitable purpose for mankind, but rejoicing and priding themselves in insolence, and taking the benefit of their superior strength in the exercise of inhumanity and cruelty, and in seizing, forcing, and committing all manner of outrages upon everything that fell into their hands; all respect for others, all justice, they thought, all equity and humanity, though naturally lauded by common people, either out of want of courage to commit injuries or fear to receive them, yet no way concerned those who were strong enough to win for themselves. Some of these, Hercules destroyed and cut off in his passage through these countries; but some escaping his notice while he was passing by, fled and hid themselves, or else were spared by him in contempt of their abject submission. After that Hercules fell into misfortune, and, having slain Iphitus, retired to Lydia, and for a long time was there slave to Omphale, a punishment which he had imposed upon himself for the murder: then, indeed, Lydia enjoyed high peace and security, but in Greece and the countries about it the like villainies again revived and broke out, there being none to repress or chastise them. It was therefore a very hazardous journey to travel by land from Athens to Peloponnesus; and Pittheus, giving him an exact account of each of the robbers and villains, their strength, and the cruelty they used to all strangers, tried to persuade Theseus to go by sea. But he, it seems, had long since been secretly fired by the glory of Hercules, held him in the highest estimation, and was never more satisfied than in listening to any that gave an account of him; especially those that had seen him, or had been present at any action or saying of his. So that he was altogether in the same state of feeling as, in after ages, Themistocles was, when he said that he could not sleep for the trophy of Miltiades; entertaining such admiration for the virtue of Hercules, that in the night his dreams were all of that hero's actions, and in the day a continual emulation stirred him up to perform the like. Besides, they were related, being born of cousins-german. For Æthra was daughter of Pittheus, and Alcmena of Lysidice; and Lysidice and Pittheus were brother and sister, children of Hippodamia and Pelops. He thought it therefore a dishonourable thing, and not to be endured, that Hercules should go out everywhere, and purge both land and sea from wicked men, and he himself should fly from the like adventures that actually came in his way; disgracing his reputed father by a mean flight by sea, and not showing his true one as good evidence of the greatness of his birth by noble and worthy actions, as by the token that he brought with him the shoes and the sword.

With this mind and these thoughts, he set forward with a design to do injury to nobody, but to repel and revenge himself of all those that should offer any. And first of all, in a set combat, he slew Periphetes, in the neighbourhood of Epidaurus, who used a club for his arms, and from thence had the name of Corynetes, or the club-bearer; who seized upon him, and forbade him to go forward in his journey. Being pleased with the club, he took it, and made it his weapon, continuing to use it as Hercules did the lion's skin, on whose shoulders that served to prove how huge a beast he had killed; and to the same end Theseus carried about him this club; overcome indeed by him, but now, in his hands, invincible.

Passing on farther towards the Isthmus of Peloponnesus, he slew Sinnis, often surnamed the Bender of Pines, after the same manner in which he himself had destroyed many others before. And this he did without having either practised or ever learnt the art of bending these trees, to show that natural strength is above all art. This Sinnis had a daughter of remarkable beauty and stature, called Perigune, who, when her father was killed, fled, and was sought after everywhere by Theseus; and coming into a place overgrown with brushwood, shrubs, and asparagus-thorn, there, in a childlike innocent manner, prayed and begged them, as if they understood her, to give her shelter, with vows that if she escaped she would never cut them down nor burn them. But Theseus calling upon her, and giving her his promise that he would use her with respect, and offer her no injury, she came forth, and in due time bore him a son, named Melanippus; but afterwards was married to Deioneus, the son of Eurytus, the Œchalian, Theseus himself giving her to him. Ioxus, the son of this Melanippus, who was born to Theseus, accompanied Ornytus in the colony that he carried with him into Caria, whence it is a family usage amongst the people called Ioxids, both male and female, never to burn either shrubs or asparagus-thorn, but to respect and honour them.

The Crommyonian sow, which they called Phæa, was a savage and formidable wild beast, by no means an enemy to be despised. Theseus killed her, going out of his way on purpose to meet and engage her, so that he might not seem to perform all his great exploits out of mere necessity; being also of opinion that it was the part of a brave man to chastise villainous and wicked men when attacked by them, but to seek out and overcome the more noble wild beasts. Others relate that Phæa was a woman, a robber full of cruelty and lust, that lived in Crommyon, and had the name of Sow given her from the foulness of her life and manners, and afterwards was killed by Theseus. He slew also Sciron, upon the borders of Megara, casting him down from the rocks, being, as most report, a notorious robber of all passengers, and, as others add, accustomed, out of insolence and wantonness, to stretch forth his feet to strangers commanding them to wash them, and then while they did it, with a kick to send them down the rock into the sea.

The writers of Megara, however, in contradiction to the received report, and, as Simonides, expresses it, "fighting with all antiquity," contend that Sciron was neither a robber nor doer of violence, but a punisher of all such, and the relative and friend of good and just men; for Æacus, they say, was ever esteemed a man of the greatest sanctity of all the Greeks; and Cychreus, the Salaminian, was honoured at Athens with divine worship; and the virtues of Peleus and Telamon were not unknown to any one. Now Sciron was son-in-law to Cychreus, father-in-law to Æacus, and grandfather to Peleus and Telamon, who were both of them sons of Endeis, the daughter of Sciron and Chariclo; it was not probable, therefore, that the best of men should make these alliances with one who was worst, giving and receiving mutually what was of greatest value and most dear to them. Theseus, by their account, did not slay Sciron in his first journey to Athens, but afterwards, when he took Eleusis, a city of the Megarians, having circumvented Diocles, the governor. Such are the contradictions in this story.

In Eleusis he killed Cercyon, the Arcadian, in a wrestling match. And going on a little farther, in Erineus, he slew Damastes, otherwise called Procrustes, forcing his body to the size of his own bed, as he himself was used to do with all strangers; this he did in imitation of Hercules, who always returned upon his assailants the same sort of violence that they offered to him; sacrificed Busiris, killed Antæus in wrestling, and Cycnus in single combat, and Termerus by breaking his skull in pieces (whence, they say, comes the proverb of "a Termerian mischief"), for it seems Termerus killed passengers that he met by running with his head against them. And so also Theseus proceeded in the punishment of evil men, who underwent the same violence from him which they had inflicted upon others, justly suffering after the manner of their own injustice.

As he went forward on his journey, and was come as far as the river Cephisus, some of the race of the Phytalidæ met him and saluted him, and upon his desire to use the purifications, then in custom, they performed them with all the usual ceremonies, and, having offered propitiatory sacrifices to the gods, invited him and entertained him at their house, a kindness which, in all his journey hitherto, he had not met.

On the eighth day of Cronius, now called Hecatombæon, he arrived at Athens, where he found the public affairs full of all confusion, and divided into parties and factions, Ægeus also, and his whole private family, labouring under the same distemper; for Medea, having fled from Corinth, and promised Ægeus to make him, by her art, capable of having children, was living with him. She first was aware of Theseus, whom as yet Ægeus did not know, and he being in years, full of jealousies and suspicions, and fearing everything by reason of the faction that was then in the city, she easily persuaded Theseus to kill him by poison at a feast, to which he was to be invited as a stranger. He, coming to the entertainment, thought it not fit to discover himself at once, but willing to give his father the occasion of first finding him out, the meat being on the table, he drew his sword as if he designed to cut with it; Ægeus, at once recognising the token, threw down the cup of poison, and, questioning his son, embraced him, and having gathered together all his citizens, owned him publicly before them, who, on their part, received him gladly for the fame of his greatness and bravery; and it is said, that when the cup fell, the poison was spilt there where now is the enclosed space in the Delphinium; for in that place stood Ægeus's house, and the figure of Mercury on the east side of the temple is called the Mercury of Ægeus's gate.

The sons of Pallas, who before were quiet, upon expectation of recovering the kingdom after Ægeus's death, who was without issue, as soon as Theseus appeared and was acknowledged the successor, highly resenting that Ægeus first, an adopted son only of Pandion, and not at all related to the family of Erechtheus, should be holding the kingdom, and that after him, Theseus, a visitor and stranger, should be destined to succeed to it, broke out into open war. And dividing themselves into two companies, one part of them marched openly from Sphettus, with their father, against the city, the other, hiding themselves in the village of Gargettus, lay in ambush, with a design to set upon the enemy on both sides. They had with them a crier of the township of Agnus, named Leos, who discovered to Theseus all the designs of the Pallantidæ. He immediately fell upon those that lay in ambuscade, and cut them all off; upon tidings of which Pallas and his company fled and were dispersed.

From hence they say is derived the custom among the people of the township of Pallene to have no marriages or any alliance with the people of Agnus, nor to suffer the criers to pronounce in their proclamations the words used in all other parts of the country, *Accouëtĕ Leoi* (Hear ye people), hating the very sound of Leo, because of the treason of Leos.

Theseus, longing to be in action, and desirous also to make himself popular, left Athens to fight with the bull of Marathon, which did no small mischief to the inhabitants of Tetrapolis. And having overcome it, he brought it alive in triumph through the city, and afterwards sacrificed it to the Delphinian Apollo. The story of Hecale, also, of her receiving and entertaining Theseus in this expedition, seems to be not altogether void of truth; for the townships round about, meeting upon a certain day, used to offer a sacrifice which they called Hecalesia, to Jupiter Hecaleius, and to pay honour to Hecale, whom, by a diminutive name, they called Hecalene, because she, while entertaining Theseus, who was quite a youth, addressed him, as old people do, with similar endearing diminutives; and having made a vow to Jupiter for him as he was going to the fight, that, if he returned in safety, she would offer sacrifices in thanks of it, and dying before he came back, she had these honours given her by way of return for her hospitality, by the command of Theseus, as Philochorus tells us.

Not long after arrived the third time from Crete the collectors of the tribute which the Athenians paid them upon the following occasion. Androgeus having been treacherously murdered in the confines of Attica, not only Minos, his father, put the Athenians to extreme distress by a perpetual war, but the gods also laid waste their country; both famine and pestilence lay heavy upon them, and even their rivers were dried up. Being told by the oracle that, if they appeased and reconciled Minos, the anger of the gods would cease and they should enjoy rest from the miseries they laboured under, they sent heralds, and with much supplication were at last reconciled, entering into an agreement to send to Crete every nine years a tribute of seven young men and as many virgins, as most writers agree in stating; and the most poetical story adds, that the Minotaur destroyed them, or that, wandering in the labyrinth, and finding no possible means of getting out, they miserably ended their lives there; and that this Minotaur was (as Euripides hath it)—

A mingled form where two strange shapes combined,
And different natures, bull and man, were joined.

But Philochorus says that the Cretans will by no means allow the truth of this, but say that the labyrinth was only an ordinary prison, having no other bad quality but that it secured the prisoners from escaping, and that Minos, having instituted games in honour of Androgeus, gave, as a reward to the victors, these youths, who in the meantime were kept in the labyrinth; and that the first that overcame in those games was one of the greatest power and command among them, named Taurus, a man of no merciful or gentle disposition, who treated the Athenians that were made his prize in a proud and cruel manner. Also Aristotle himself, in the account that he gives of the form of government of the Bottiæans, is manifestly of opinion that the youths were not slain by Minos, but spent the remainder of their days in slavery in Crete; that the Cretans, in former times, to acquit themselves of an ancient vow which they had made, were used to send an offering of the first-fruits of their men to Delphi, and that some descendants of these Athenian slaves were mingled with them and sent amongst them, and, unable to get their living there, removed from thence, first into Italy, and settled about Japygia; from thence again, that they removed to Thrace, and were named Bottiæans; and that this is the reason why, in a certain sacrifice, the Bottiæan girls sing a hymn beginning *Let us go to Athens.* This may show us how dangerous it is to incur the hostility of a city that is mistress of eloquence and song. For Minos was always ill spoken of, and represented ever as a very wicked man, in the Athenian theatres; neither did Hesiod avail him by calling him "the most royal Minos," nor Homer, who styles him "Jupiter's familiar friend"; the tragedians got the better, and from the vantage ground of the stage showered down obloquy upon him, as a man of cruelty and violence; whereas, in fact, he appears to have been a king and a law-giver, and Rhadamanthus, a judge under him, administering the statutes that he ordained.

Now, when the time of the third tribute was come, and the fathers who had any young men for their sons were to proceed by lot to the choice of those that were to be sent, there arose fresh discontents and accusations against Ægeus among the people, who were full of grief and indignation that he who was the cause of all their miseries was the only person exempt from the punishment; adopting and settling his kingdom upon a bastard and foreign son, he took no thought, they said, of their destitution and loss, not of bastards, but lawful children. These things sensibly affected Theseus, who, thinking it but just not to disregard, but rather partake of, the sufferings of his fellow-citizens, offered himself for one without any lot. All else were struck with admiration for the nobleness and with love for the goodness of the act; and Ægeus, after prayers and entreaties, finding him inflexible and not to be persuaded, proceeded to the choosing of the rest by lot. Hollanicus, however, tells us that the Athenians did not send the young men and virgins by lot, but that Minos himself used to come and make his own choice, and pitched upon Theseus before all others; according to the conditions agreed upon between them, namely, that the Athenians should furnish them with a ship and that the young men that were to sail with him should carry no weapons of war; but that if the Minotaur was destroyed, the tribute should cease.

On the two former occasions of the payment of the tribute, entertaining no hopes of safety or return, they sent out the ship with a black sail, as to unavoidable destruction; but now, Theseus encouraging his father, and speaking greatly of himself, as confident that he should kill the Minotaur, he gave the pilot another sail, which was white, commanding him, as he returned, if Theseus were safe, to make use of that; but if not, to sail with the black one, and to hang out that sign of his misfortune. Simonides says that the sail which Ægeus delivered to the pilot was not white, but—

> Scarlet, in the juicy bloom
> Of the living oak-tree steeped,

and that this was to be the sign of their escape. Phereclus, son of Amarsyas, according to Simonides, was pilot of the ship. But Philochorus says Theseus had sent him by Scirus, from Salamis, Nausithoüs to be his steersman, and Phæax his look-out-man in the prow, the Athenians having as yet not applied themselves to navigation; and that Scirus did this because one of the young men, Menesthes, was his daughter's son; and this the chapels of Nausithoüs and Phæax, built by Theseus near the temple of Scirus, confirm. He adds, also, that the feast named Cybernesia was in honour of them. The lot being cast, and Theseus having received out of the Prytaneüm those upon whom it fell, he went to the Delphinium, and made an offering for them to Apollo of his suppliant's badge, which was a bough of a consecrated olive tree, with white wool tied about it.

Having thus performed his devotion, he went to sea, the sixth day of Munychion, on which day even to this time the Athenians send their virgins to the same temple to make supplication to the gods. It is further reported that he was commanded by the oracle of Delphi to make Venus his guide, and to invoke her as the companion and conductress of his voyage, and that, as he was sacrificing a she goat to her by the sea-side, it was suddenly changed into a he, and for this cause that goddess had the name of Epitragia.

When he arrived at Crete, as most of the ancient historians as well as poets tell us, having a clue of thread given him by Ariadne, who had fallen in love with him, and being instructed by her how to use it so as to conduct him through the windings of the labyrinth, he escaped out of it and slew the Minotaur, and sailed back, taking along with him Ariadne and the young Athenian captives. Pherecydes adds that he bored holes in the bottom of the Cretan ships to hinder their pursuit. Demon writes that Taurus, the chief captain of Minos, was slain by Theseus at the mouth of the port, in a naval combat as he was sailing out for Athens.

But Philochorus gives us the story thus: That at the setting forth of the yearly games by King Minos, Taurus was expected to carry away the prize, as he had done before; and was much grudged the honour. His character and manners made his power hateful, and he was accused moreover of too near familiarity with Pasiphae, for which reason, when Theseus desired the combat, Minos readily complied. And as it was a custom in Crete that the women also should be admitted to the sight of these games, Ariadne, being present, was struck with admiration of the manly beauty of Theseus, and the vigour and address which he showed in the combat, overcoming all that encountered with him. Minos, too, being extremely pleased with him, especially because he had overthrown and disgraced Taurus, voluntarily gave up the young captives to Theseus, and remitted the tribute to the Athenians.

Clidemus gives an account peculiar to himself, very ambitiously, and beginning a great way back: That it was a decree consented to by all Greece, that no vessel from any place, containing above five persons, should be permitted to sail, Jason only excepted, who was made captain of the great ship Argo, to sail about and scour the sea of pirates. But Dædalus having escaped from Crete, and flying by sea to Athens, Minos, contrary to this decree, pursued him with his ships of war, was forced by a storm upon Sicily, and there ended his life. After his decease, Deucalion, his son, desiring a quarrel with the Athenians, sent to them, demanding that they should deliver up Dædalus to him, threatening upon their refusal to put to death all the young Athenians whom his father had received as hostages from the city. To this angry message Theseus returned a very gentle answer excusing himself that he could not deliver up Dædalus, who was nearly related to him, being his cousin-german, his mother being Merope, the daughter of Erechtheus. In the meanwhile he secretly prepared a navy, part of it at home near the village of the Thymœtadæ, a place of no resort, and far from any common roads, the other part by his grandfather Pittheus's means at Trœzen, that so his design might be carried on with the greatest secrecy. As soon as ever his fleet was in readiness, he set sail, having with him Dædalus and other exiles from Crete for his guides; and none of the Cretans having any knowledge of his coming, but imagining when they saw his fleet that they were friends and vessels of their own, he soon made himself master of the port, and immediately making a descent, reached Gnossus before any notice of his coming, and, in a battle before the gates of the labyrinth, put Deucalion and all his guards to the sword. The government by this means falling to Ariadne, he made a league with her, and received the captives of her, and ratified a perpetual friendship between the Athenians and the Cretans, whom he engaged under an oath never again to commence any war with Athens.

There are yet many other traditions about these things, and as many concerning Ariadne, all inconsistent with each other. Some relate that she hung herself, being deserted by Theseus. Others that she was carried away by his sailors to the isle of Naxos, and married to Œnarus, priest of Bacchus; and that Theseus left her because he fell in love with another—

For Ægle's love was burning in his breast;

a verse which Hereas, the Megarian, says was formerly in the poet Hesiod's works, but put out by Pisistratus, in like manner as he added in Homer's Raising of the Dead, to gratify the Athenians, the line—

Theseus, Pirithous, mighty son of gods.

Others say Ariadne had sons also by Theseus, Œnopion and Staphylus; and among these is the poet Ion of Chios, who writes of his own native city—

Which once Œnopion, son of Theseus built.

But the more famous of the legendary stories everybody (as I may say) has in his mouth.

In Pæon, however, the Amathusian, there is a story given, differing from the rest. For he writes that Theseus, being driven by a storm upon the isle of Cyprus, and having aboard with him Ariadne, big with child, and extremely discomposed with the rolling of the sea, set her on shore, and left her there alone, to return himself and help the ship, when, on a sudden, a violent wind carried him again out to sea. That the women of the island received Ariadne very kindly, and did all they could to console and alleviate her distress at being left behind. That they counterfeited kind letters, and delivered them to her, as sent from Theseus, and, when she fell in labour, were diligent in performing to her every needful service; but that she died before she could be delivered, and was honourably interred. That soon after Theseus returned, and was greatly afflicted for her loss, and at his departure left a sum of money among the people of the island, ordering them to do sacrifice to Ariadne; and caused two little images to be made and dedicated to her, one of silver and the other of brass. Moreover, that on the second day of Gorpiæus, which is sacred to Ariadne, they have this ceremony among their sacrifices, to have a youth lie down and with his voice and gesture represent the pains of a woman in travail; and that the Amathusians call the grove in which they show her tomb, the grove of Venus Ariadne.

Differing yet from this account, some of the Naxians write that there were two Minoses and two Ariadnes, one of whom, they say, was married to Bacchus, in the isle of Naxos, and bore the children Staphylus and his brother; but that the other, of a later age, was carried off by Theseus, and, being afterwards deserted by him, retired to Naxos, with her nurse Corcyna, whose grave they yet show. That this Ariadne also died there, and was worshipped by the island, but in a different manner from the former; for her day is celebrated with general joy and revelling, but all the sacrifices performed to the latter are attended with mourning and gloom.

Now Theseus, in his return from Crete, put in at Delos, and having sacrificed to the god of the island, dedicated to the temple the image of Venus which Ariadne had given him, and danced with the young Athenians a dance that, in memory of him, they say is still preserved among the inhabitants of Delos, consisting in certain measured turnings and returnings, imitative of the windings and twistings of the labyrinth. And this dance, as Dicæarchus writes, is called among the Delians the Crane. This he danced around the Ceratonian Altar, so called from its consisting of horns taken from the left side of the head. They say also that he instituted games in Delos, where he was the first that began the custom of giving a palm to the victors.

When they were come near the coast of Attica, so great was the joy for the happy success of their voyage, that neither Theseus himself nor the pilot remembered to hang out the sail which should have been the token of their safety to Ægeus, who, in despair at the sight, threw himself headlong from a rock, and perished in the sea. But Theseus being arrived at the port of Phalerum, paid there the sacrifices which he had vowed to the gods at his setting out to sea, and sent a herald to the city to carry the news of his safe return. At his entrance, the herald found the people for the most part full of grief for the loss of their king; others, as may well be believed, as full of joy for the tidings that he brought, and eager to welcome him and crown him with garlands for his good news, which he indeed accepted of, but hung them upon his herald's staff; and thus returning to the seaside before Theseus had finished his libation to the gods, he stayed apart for fear of disturbing the holy rites; but, as soon as the libation was ended, went up and related the king's death, upon the hearing of which, with great lamentations and a confused tumult of grief, they ran with all haste to the city. And from hence, they say, it comes that at this day, in the feast of Oschophoria, the herald is not crowned, but his staff, and all who are present at the libation cry out *eleleu, iou, iou,* the first of which confused sounds is commonly used by men in haste, or at a triumph, the other is proper to people in consternation or disorder of mind.

Theseus, after the funeral of his father, paid his vows to Apollo the seventh day of Pyanepsion; for on that day the youth that returned with him safe from Crete made their entry into the city. They say, also, that the custom of boiling pulse at this feast is derived from hence; because the young men that escaped put all that was left of their provision together, and, boiling it in one common pot, feasted themselves with it, and ate it all up

together. Hence, also, they carry in procession an olive branch bound about with wool (such as they then made use of in their supplications), which they call Eiresione, crowned with all sorts of fruits, to signify that scarcity and barrenness was ceased, singing in their procession this song:—

Eiresione bring figs, and Eiresione bring loaves;
Bring us honey in pints, and oil to rub on our
*   bodies,*
And a strong flagon of wine, for all to go mellow
*   to bed on.*

Although some hold opinion that this ceremony is retained in memory of the Heraclidæ, who were thus entertained and brought up by the Athenians, most are of the opinion which we have given above.

The ship wherein Theseus and the youth of Athens returned had thirty oars, and was preserved by the Athenians down even to the time of Demetrius Phalereus, for they took away the old planks as they decayed, putting in new and stronger timber in their place, insomuch that this ship became a standing example among the philosophers, for the logical question of things that grow; one side holding that the ship remained the same, and the other contending that it was not the same.

The feast called Oschophoria, or the feast of boughs, which to this day the Athenians celebrate, was then first instituted by Theseus. For he took not with him the full number of virgins which by lot were to be carried away, but selected two youths of his acquaintance, of fair and womanish faces, but of a manly and forward spirit, and having, by frequent baths, and avoiding the heat and scorching of the sun, with a constant use of all the ointments and washes and dresses that serve to the adorning of the head or smoothing the skin or improving the complexion, in a manner changed them from what they were before, and having taught them farther to counterfeit the very voice and carriage and gait of virgins so that there could not be the least difference perceived, he, undiscovered by any, put them into the number of the Athenian maids designed for Crete. At his return, he and these two youths led up a solemn procession, in the same habit that is now worn by those who carry the vine-branches. These branches they carry in honour of Bacchus and Ariadne, for the sake of their story before related; or rather because they happened to return in autumn, the time of gathering the grapes.

The women, whom they call Deipnopheræ, or supper-carriers, are taken into these ceremonies, and assist at the sacrifice, in remembrance and imitation of the mothers of the young men and virgins upon whom the lot fell, for thus they ran about bringing bread and meat to their children; and because the women then told their sons and daughters many tales and stories, to comfort and encourage them under the danger they were going upon, it has still continued a custom that at this feast old fables and tales should be told. For these particularities we are indebted to the history of Demon. There was then a place chosen out, and a temple erected in it to Theseus, and those families out of whom the tribute of the youth was gathered were appointed to pay a tax to the temple for sacrifices to him. And the house of the Phytalidæ had the overseeing of these sacrifices, Theseus doing them that honour in recompense of their former hospitality.

Now, after the death of his father Ægeus, forming in his mind a great and wonderful design, he gathered together all the inhabitants of Attica into one town, and made them one people of one city, whereas before they lived dispersed, and were not easy to assemble upon any affair for the common interest. Nay, differences and even wars often occurred between them, which he by his persuasions appeased, going from township to township, and from tribe to tribe. And those of a more private and mean condition readily embracing such good advice, to those of greater power he promised a commonwealth without monarchy, a democracy, or people's government, in which he should only be continued as their commander in war and the protector of their laws, all things else being equally distributed among them;—and by this means brought a part of them over to his proposal. The rest, fearing his power, which was already grown very formidable, and knowing his courage and resolution, chose rather to be persuaded than forced into a compliance. He then dissolved all the distinct state-houses, council halls, and magistracies, and built one common statehouse and council hall on the site of the present upper town, and gave the name of Athens to the whole state, ordaining a common feast and sacrifice, which he called Panathenæa, or the sacrifice of all the united Athenians. He instituted also another sacrifice called Metœcia, or Feast of Migration, which is yet celebrated on the sixteenth day of Hecatombæon.

Then, as he had promised, he laid down his regal power and proceeded to order a commonwealth, entering upon this great work not without advice from the gods. For having sent to consult the oracle of Delphi concerning the fortune of his new government and city, he received this answer:—

> Son of the Pitthean maid,
> To your town the terms and fates,
> My father gives of many states.
> Be not anxious nor afraid;
> The bladder will not fail to swim
> On the waves that compass him.

Which oracle, they say, one of the Sibyls long after did in a manner repeat to the Athenians, in this verse:—

> The bladder may be dipt, but not be drowned.

Farther yet designing to enlarge his city, he invited all strangers to come and enjoy equal privileges with the natives, and it is said that the common form, Come hither, all ye people, was the words that Theseus proclaimed when he thus set up a commonwealth, in a manner, for all nations. Yet he did not suffer his state, by the promiscuous multitude that flowed in, to be turned into confusion and be left without any order or degree, but was the first that divided the Commonwealth into three distinct ranks, the noblemen, the husbandmen, and artificers. To the nobility he committed the care of religion, the choice of magistrates, the teaching and dispensing of the laws, and interpretation and direction in all sacred matters; the whole city being, as it were, reduced to an exact equality, the nobles excelling the rest in honour, the husbandmen in profit, and the artificers in number. And that Theseus was the first, who, as Aristotle says, out of an inclination to popular government, parted with the regal power, Homer also seems to testify, in his catalogue of the ships, where he gives the name of People to the Athenians only.

He also coined money, and stamped it with the image of an ox, either in memory of the Marathonian bull, or of Taurus, whom he vanquished, or else to put his people in mind to follow husbandry; and from this coin came the expression so frequent among the Greeks, of a thing being worth ten or a hundred oxen.

After this he joined Megara to Attica, and erected that famous pillar on the Isthmus, which bears an inscription of two lines, showing the bounds of the two countries that meet there. On the east side the inscription is,—

Peloponnesus there, Ionia here

and on the west side,—

Peloponnesus here, Ionia there.

He also instituted the games, in emulation of Hercules, being ambitious that as the Greeks, by that hero's appointment, celebrated the Olympian games to the honour of Jupiter, so by his institution, they should celebrate the Isthmian to the honour of Neptune. For those that were observed there before, dedicated to Melicerta, were performed privately in the night, and had the form rather of a religious rite than of an open spectacle or public feast. There are some who say that the Isthmian games were first instituted in memory of Sciron, Theseus thus making expiation for his death, upon account of the nearness of kindred between them, Sciron being the son of Canethus and Heniocha, the daughter of Pittheus; though others write that Sinnis, not Sciron, was their son, and that to his honour, and not to the other's, these games were ordained by Theseus. At the same time he made an agreement with the Corinthians, that they should allow those that came from Athens to the celebration of the Isthmian games as much space of honour before the rest to behold the spectacle in, as the sail of the ship that brought them thither, stretched to its full extent, could cover; so Hellanicus and Andro of Halicarnassus have established.

Concerning his voyage into the Euxine Sea, Philochorus and some others write that he made it with Hercules, offering him his service in the war against the Amazons, and had Antiope given him for the reward of his valour; but the greater number, of whom are Pherecydes, Hellanicus, and Herodorus, write that he made this voyage many years after Hercules, with a navy under his own command, and took the Amazon prisoner—the more probable story, for we do not read that any other, of all those that accompanied him in this action, took any Amazon prisoner. Bion adds, that, to take her, he had to use deceit and fly away; for the Amazons, he says, being naturally lovers of men, were so far from avoiding Theseus when he touched upon their coasts, that they sent him presents to his ship; but he, having invited Antiope, who brought them, to come aboard, immediately set sail and carried her away.

An author named Menecrates, that wrote the history of Nicæ in Bithynia, adds, that Theseus, having Antiope aboard his vessel, cruised for some time about those coasts, and that there were in the same ship three young men of Athens, that accompanied him in this voyage, all brothers, whose names were Euneos, Thoas, and Soloon. The last of these fell desperately in love with Antiope, and, escaping the notice of the rest, revealed the secret only to one of his most intimate acquaintances, and employed him to disclose his passion to Antiope; she rejected his pretences with a very positive denial, yet treated the matter with much gentleness and discretion, and made no complaint to Theseus of anything that had happened; but Soloon, the thing being desperate, leaped into a river near the seaside and drowned himself.

As soon as Theseus was acquainted with his death, and his unhappy love that was the cause of it, he was extremely distressed, and, in the height of his grief, an oracle which he had formerly received at Delphi came into his mind; for he had been commanded by the priestess of Apollo Pythius, that wherever in a strange land he was most sorrowful and under the greatest affliction, he should build a city there, and leave some of his followers to be governors of the place. For this cause he there founded a city, which he called, from the name of Apollo, Pythopolis, and, in honour of the unfortunate youth, he named the river that runs by it Soloon, and left the two surviving brothers intrusted with the care of the government and laws, joining with them Hermus, one of the nobility of Athens, from whom a place in the city is called the House of Hermus; though by an error in the accent it has been taken for the House of Hermes, or Mercury, and the honour that was designed to the hero, transferred to the god.

This was the origin and cause of the Amazonian invasion of Attica, which would seem to have been no slight or womanish enterprise. For it is impossible that they should have placed their camp in the very city, and joined battle close by the Pnyx and the hill called Museum, unless, having first conquered the country round about, they had thus with impunity advanced to the city. That they made so long a journey by land, and passed the Cimmerian Bosphorus, when frozen, as Hellanicus writes, is difficult to be believed. That they encamped all but in the city is certain, and may be sufficiently confirmed by the names that the places hereabout yet retain, and the graves and monuments of those that fell in the battle.

Both armies being in sight, there was a long pause and doubt on each side which should give the first onset; at last Theseus, having sacrificed to Fear, in obedience to the command of an oracle he had received, gave them battle; and this happened in the month of Boedromion, in which to this very day the Athenians celebrate the Feast Boedromia. Clidemus, desirous to be very circumstantial, writes that the left wing of the Amazons moved towards the place which is yet called Amazonium and the right towards the Pnyx, near Chrysa, that with this wing the Athenians, issuing from behind the Museum, engaged, and that the graves of those that were slain are to be seen in the street that leads to the gate called the Piraic, by the chapel of the hero Chalcodon; and that here the Athenians were routed, and gave way before the women, as far as to the temple of the Furies, but, fresh supplies coming in from the Palladium, Ardettus, and the Lyceum, they charged their right wing, and beat them back into their tents, in which action a great number of the Amazons were slain. At length, after four months, a peace was concluded between them by the mediation of Hippolyta (for so this historian calls the Amazon whom Theseus married, and not Antiope), though others write that she was slain with a dart by Molpadia, while fighting by Theseus's side, and that the pillar which stands by the temple of Olympian Earth was erected to her honour.

Nor is it to be wondered at, that in events of such antiquity, history should be in disorder. For indeed we are also told that those of the Amazons that were wounded were privately sent away by Antiope to Chalcis, where many by her care recovered, but some that died were buried there in the place that is to this time called Amazonium. That this war, however, was ended by a treaty is evident, both from the name of the place adjoining to the temple of Theseus, called, from the solemn oath there taken, Horcomosium; and also from the ancient sacrifice which used to be celebrated to the Amazons the day before the Feast of Theseus. The Megarians also show a spot in their city where some Amazons were buried, on the way from the market to a place called Rhus, where the building in the shape of a lozenge stands. It is said, likewise, that others of them were slain near Chæronea, and buried near the little rivulet formerly called

Thermodon, but now Hæmon, of which an account is given in the life of Demosthenes. It appears further that the passage of the Amazons through Thessaly was not without opposition, for there are yet shown many tombs of them near Scotussa and Cynoscephalæ.

This is as much as is worth telling concerning the Amazons. For the account which the author of the poem called the *Theseid* gives of this rising of the Amazons, how Antiope, to revenge herself upon Theseus for refusing her and marrying Phædra, came down upon the city with her train of Amazons, whom Hercules slew, is manifestly nothing else but fable and invention. It is true, indeed, that Theseus married Phædra, but that was after the death of Antiope, by whom he had a son called Hippolytus, or, as Pindar writes, Demophon. The calamities which befell Phædra and this son, since none of the historians have contradicted the tragic poets that have written of them, we must suppose happened as represented uniformly by them.

There are also other traditions of the marriages of Theseus, neither honourable in their occasions nor fortunate in their events, which yet were never represented in the Greek plays. For he is said to have carried off Anaxo, a Trœzenian, and having slain Sinnis and Cercyon, to have ravished their daughters; to have married Periboea, the mother of Ajax, and then Phereboea, and then Iope, the daughter of Iphicles. And further, he is accused of deserting Ariadne (as is before related), being in love with Ægle, the daughter of Panopeus, neither justly nor honourably; and lastly, of the rape of Helen, which filled all Attica with war and blood, and was in the end the occasion of his banishment and death, as will presently be related.

Herodorus is of opinion, that though there were many famous expeditions undertaken by the bravest men of his time, yet Theseus never joined in any of them, once only excepted, with the Lapithæ, in their war against the Centaurs; but others say that he accompanied Jason to Colchis and Meleager to the slaying of the Calydonian boar, and that hence it came to be a proverb, *Not without Theseus;* that he himself, however, without aid of any one, performed many glorious exploits, and that from him began the saying, *He is a second Hercules.* He also joined Adrastus in recovering the bodies of those that were slain before Thebes, but not as Euripides in his tragedy says, by force of

arms, but by persuasion and mutual agreement and composition, for so the greater part
of the historians write; Philochorus adds further that this was the first treaty that ever
was made for the recovering the bodies of the
dead, but in the history of Hercules, it is
shown that it was he who first gave leave to
his enemies to carry off their slain. The bury-
ing-places of the most part are yet to be seen
in the village called Eleutheræ; those of the
commanders, at Eleusis, where Theseus allotted them a place, to oblige Adrastus. The
story of Euripides in his suppliants is disproved by Æschylus in his Eleusinians, where
Theseus himself relates the facts as here told.

The celebrated friendship between Theseus
and Pirithoüs is said to have been thus begun: the fame of the strength and valour of
Theseus being spread through Greece, Pirithoüs was desirous to make a trial and
proof of it himself, and to this end seized
a herd of oxen which belonged to Theseus,
and was driving them away from Marathon,
and, when the news was brought that Theseus pursued him in arms, he did not fly, but
turned back and went to meet him. But as
soon as they had viewed one another, each
so admired the gracefulness and beauty, and
was seized with such respect for the courage
of the other, that they forgot all thoughts
of fighting; and Pirithoüs, first stretching out
his hand to Theseus, bade him be judge in
this case himself, and promised to submit
willingly to any penalty he should impose.
But Theseus not only forgave him all, but
entreated him to be his friend and brother
in arms; and they ratified their friendship by
oaths.

After this Pirithoüs married Deidamia, and
invited Theseus to the wedding, entreating
him to come and see his country, and make
acquaintance with the Lapithæ; he had at the
same time invited the Centaurs to the feast,
who growing hot with wine and beginning
to be insolent and wild, and offering violence
to the women, the Lapithæ took immediate
revenge upon them, slaying many of them
upon the place, and afterwards, having overcome them in battle, drove the whole race of
them out of their country, Theseus all along
taking their part and fighting on their side.
But Herodorus gives a different relation of
these things; that Theseus came not to the
assistance of the Lapithæ till the war was already begun; and that it was in this journey
that he had the first sight of Hercules, having

made it his business to find him out at
Trachis, where he had chosen to rest himself
after all his wanderings and his labours; and
that this interview was honourably performed
on each part, with extreme respect, and good-
will, and admiration of each other. Yet it is
more credible, as others write, that there were,
before, frequent interviews between them,
and that it was by the means of Theseus that
Hercules was initiated at Eleusis, and purified
before initiation, upon account of several rash
actions of his former life.

Theseus was now fifty years old, as Hellanicus states, when he carried off Helen, who
was yet too young to be married. Some writers,
to take away this accusation of one of the
greatest crimes laid to his charge, say, that he
did not steal away Helen himself, but that
Idas and Lynceus were the ravishers, who
brought her to him, and committed her to his
charge, and that, therefore, he refused to restore her at the demand of Castor and Pollux;
or, indeed, they say her own father, Tyndarus,
had sent her to be kept by him, for fear of
Enarophorus, the son of Hippocoön, who
would have carried her away by force when
she was yet a child.

But the most probable account, and that
which has most witnesses on its side, is this:
Theseus and Pirithoüs went both together to
Sparta, and, having seized the young lady as
she was dancing in the temple Diana Orthia,
fled away with her. There were presently men
sent in arms to pursue, but they followed no
further than to Tegea; and Theseus and Pirithoüs, being now out of danger, having
passed through Peloponnesus, made an agreement between themselves, that he to whom
the lot should fall should have Helen to his
wife, but should be obliged to assist in procuring another for his friend. The lot fell
upon Theseus, who conveyed her to Aphidnæ,
not being yet marriageable, and delivered her
to one of his allies, called Aphidnus, and,
having sent his mother, Æthra, after to take
care of her, desired him to keep them so
secretly, that none might know where they
were; which done, to return the same service
to his friend Pirithoüs, he accompanied him
in his journey to Epirus, in order to steal
away the king of the Molossians' daughter.
The king, his own name being Aidoneus, or
Pluto, called his wife Proserpina, and his
daughter Cora, and a great dog, which he
kept, Cerberus, with whom he ordered all
that came as suitors to his daughter to fight,

and promised her to him that should over-come the beast. But having been informed that the design of Pirithoüs and his com-panion was not to court his daughter, but to force her away, he caused them both to be seized, and threw Pirithoüs to be torn in pieces by his dog, and put Theseus into prison, and kept him.

About this time, Menestheus, the son of Peteus, grandson of Orneus, and great-grand-son to Erechtheus, the first man that is re-corded to have affected popularity and in-gratiated himself with the multitude, stirred up and exasperated the most eminent men of the city, who had long borne a secret grudge to Theseus, conceiving that he had robbed them of their several little kingdoms and lordships, and having pent them all up in one city, was using them as his subjects and slaves. He put also the meaner people into commotion, telling them, that, deluded with a mere dream of liberty, though indeed they were deprived of both that and of their proper homes and religious usages, instead of many good and gracious kings of their own, they had given themselves up to be lorded over by a new-comer and a stranger.

Whilst he was thus busied in infecting the minds of the citizens, the war that Castor and Pollux brought against Athens came very op-portunely to further the sedition he had been promoting, and some say that by his persua-sions was wholly the cause of their invading the city. At their first approach, they com-mitted no acts of hostility, but peaceably de-manded their sister Helen; but the Athenians returning answer that they neither had her there nor knew where she was disposed of, they prepared to assault the city, when Acad-emus, having, by whatever means, found it out, disclosed to them that she was secretly kept at Aphidnæ. For which reason he was both highly honoured during his life by Castor and Pollux, and the Lacedæmonians, when often in aftertimes they made incur-sions into Attica, and destroyed all the coun-try round about, spared the Academy for the sake of Academus. But Dicæarchus writes that there were two Arcadians in the army of Castor and Pollux, the one called Echede-mus, and the other Marathus; from the first that which is now called Academia was then named Echedemia, and the village Marathon had its name from the other, who, to fulfil some oracle, voluntarily offered himself to be made a sacrifice before battle.

As soon as they were arrived at Aphidnæ, they overcame their enemies in a set battle, and then assaulted and took the town. And here, they say, Alycus, the son of Sciron, was slain, of the party of the Dioscuri (Castor and Pollux), from whom a place in Megara, where he was buried, is called Alycus to this day. And Hereas writes that it was Theseus himself that killed him, in witness of which he cites these verses concerning Alycus—

And Alycus upon Aphidnæ's plain,
By Theseus in the cause of Helen slain.

Though it is not at all probable that Theseus himself was there when both the city and his mother were taken.

Aphidnæ being won by Castor and Pollux, and the city of Athens being in consterna-tion, Menestheus persuaded the people to open their gates, and receive them with all manner of friendship, for they were, he told them, at enmity with none but Theseus, who had first injured them, and were benefac-tors and saviours to all mankind beside. And their behaviour gave credit to those promises; for, having made themselves absolute masters of the place, they demanded no more than to be initiated, since they were as nearly related to the city as Hercules was, who had received the same honour. This their desire they easily obtained, and were adopted by Aphidnus, as Hercules had been by Pylius. They were hon-oured also like gods, and were called by a new name, Anaces, either from the *cessation* of the war, or from the *care* they took that none should suffer any injury, though there was so great an army within the walls; for the phrase *anākōs ĕkhein* is used of those who look to or care for anything; kings for this reason, per-haps, are called *anactes*. Others say, that from the appearance of their star in the heavens, they were thus called, for in the Attic dialect this name comes very near the words that signify *above*.

Some say that Æthra, Theseus's mother, was here taken prisoner, and carried to Lacedæ-mon, and from thence went away with Helen to Troy, alleging this verse of Homer to prove that she waited upon Helen—

Æthra of Pittheus born, and large eyed Clymene.

Others reject this verse as none of Homer's, as they do likewise the whole fable of Mu-nychus, who, the story says, was the son of Demophon and Laodice, born secretly, and brought up by Æthra at Troy. But Ister, in the thirteenth book of his Attic History, gives us an account of Æthra, different yet from all the rest: that Achilles and Patroclus overcame Paris in Thessaly, near the river Sperchius, but that Hector took and plundered the city of the Trœzenians, and made Æthra prisoner there. But this seems a groundless tale.

Now Hercules, passing by the Molossians, was entertained in his way to Aidoneus the king, who, in conversation, accidentally spoke of the journey of Theseus and Pirithoüs into his country, of what they had designed to do, and what they were forced to suffer. Hercules was much grieved for the inglorious death of the one and the miserable condition of the other. As for Pirithoüs, he thought it useless to complain; but begged to have Theseus released for his sake, and obtained that favour from the king.

Theseus, being thus set at liberty, returned to Athens, where his friends were not yet wholly suppressed, and dedicated to Hercules all the sacred places which the city had set apart for himself, changing their names from Thesea to Heraclea, four only excepted, as Philochorus writes. And wishing immediately to resume the first place in the commonwealth, and manage the state as before, he soon found himself involved in factions and troubles; those who long had hated him had now added to their hatred contempt; and the minds of the people were so generally corrupted, that, instead of obeying commands with silence, they expected to be flattered into their duty. He had some thoughts to have reduced them by force, but was overpowered by demagogues and factions. And at last, despairing of any good success of his affairs in Athens, he sent away his children privately to Eubœa, commending them to the care of Elephenor, the son of Chalcodon; and he himself having solemnly cursed the people of Athens in the village of Gargettus, in which there yet remains the place called Araterion, or the place of cursing, sailed to Scyros, where he had lands left him by his father, and friendship, as he thought, with those of the island.

Lycomedes was then king of Scyros. Theseus, therefore, addressed himself to him and desired to have his lands put into his possession, as designing to settle and to dwell there, though others say that he came to beg his assistance against the Athenians. But Lycomedes, either jealous of the glory of so great a man, or to gratify Menestheus, having led him up to the highest cliff of the island, on pretence of showing him from thence the lands that he desired, threw him headlong down from the rock, and killed him. Others say he fell down of himself by a slip of his foot, as he was walking there, according to his custom, after supper. At that time there was no notice taken, nor were any concerned for his death, but Menestheus quietly possessed the kingdom of Athens. His sons were brought up in a private condition, and accompanied Elephenor to the Trojan war, but, after the decease of Menestheus in that expedition, returned to Athens, and recovered the government.

But in succeeding ages, besides several other circumstances that moved the Athenians to honour Theseus as a demigod, in the battle which was fought at Marathon against the Medes, many of the soldiers believed they saw an apparition of Theseus in arms, rushing on at the head of them against the barbarians. And after the Median war, Phædo being archon of Athens, the Athenians, consulting the oracle at Delphi, were commanded to gather together the bones of Theseus, and, laying them in some honourable place, keep them as sacred in the city. But it was very difficult to recover these relics, or so much as to find out the place where they lay, on account of the inhospitable and savage temper of the barbarous people that inhabited the island. Nevertheless, afterwards, when Cimon took the island (as is related in his life), and had a great ambition to find out the place where Theseus was buried, he, by chance, spied an eagle upon a rising ground pecking with her beak and tearing up the earth with her talons, when on the sudden it came into his mind, as it were by some divine inspiration, to dig there, and search for the bones of Theseus. There were found in that place a coffin of a man of more than ordinary size, and a brazen spear-head, and a sword lying by it, all which he took aboard his galley and brought with him to Athens. Upon which the Athenians, greatly delighted, went out to meet and receive the relics with splendid processions and sacrifices, as if it were Theseus himself returning alive to the city.

He lies interred in the middle of the city, near the present gymnasium. His tomb is a sanctuary and refuge for slaves, and all those of mean condition that fly from the persecution of men in power, in memory that Theseus while he lived was an assister and protector of the distressed, and never refused the petitions of the afflicted that fled to him. The chief and most solemn sacrifice which they celebrate to him is kept on the eighth day of Pyanepsion, on which he returned with the Athenian young men from Crete. Besides which they sacrifice to him on the eighth day of every month, either because he returned from Trœzen the eighth day of Hecatombæon, as Diodorus the geographer writes, or else thinking that number to be proper to him, because he was reputed to be born of Neptune, because they sacrifice to Neptune on the eighth day of every month. The number eight being the first cube of an even number, and the double of the first square, seemed to be an emblem of the steadfast and immovable power of this god, who from thence has the names of Asphalius and Gæiochus, that is, the establisher and stayer of the earth.

ROMULUS

LEGENDARY, 8TH CENTURY B.C.

FROM whom, and for what reason, the city of Rome, a name so great in glory, and famous in the mouths of all men, was so first called, authors do not agree. Some are of opinion that the Pelasgians, wandering over the greater part of the habitable world, and subduing numerous nations, fixed themselves here, and, from their own great *strength* in war, called the city Rome. Others, that at the taking of Troy, some few that escaped and met with shipping, put to sea, and driven by winds, were carried upon the coasts of Tuscany, and came to anchor off the mouth of the river Tiber, where their women, out of heart and weary with the sea, on its being proposed by one of the highest birth and best understanding amongst them, whose name was Roma, burnt the ships. With which act the men at first were angry, but afterwards, of necessity, seating themselves near Palatium, where things in a short while succeeded far better than they could hope, in that they found the country very good, and the people courteous, they not only did the lady Roma other honours, but added also this, of calling after her name the city which she had been the occasion of their founding. From this, they say, has come down that custom at Rome for women to salute their kinsmen and husbands with kisses; because these women, after they had burnt the ships, made use of such endearments when entreating and pacifying their husbands.

Some again say that Roma, from whom this city was so called, was daughter of Italus and Leucaria; or, by another account, of Telaphus, Hercules's son, and that she was married to Æneas, or, according to others again, to Ascanius, Æneas's son. Some tell us that Romanus, the son of Ulysses and Circe, built it; some, Romus, the son of Emathion, Diomede having sent him from Troy; and others, Romus, king of the Latins, after driving out the Tyrrhenians, who had come from Thessaly into Lydia, and from thence into Italy. Those very authors, too, who, in accordance with the safest account, make Romulus give the name of the city, yet differ concerning his birth and family. For some say, he was son to Æneas and Dexithea, daughter of Phorbas, and was, with his brother Remus, in their infancy, carried into Italy, and being on the river when the waters came down in a flood, all the vessels were cast away except only that where the young children were, which being gently landed on a level bank of the river, they were both unexpectedly saved, and from them the place was called Rome.

Some say, Roma, daughter of the Trojan lady above mentioned, was married to Latinus, Telemachus's son, and became mother to Romulus; others, that Æmilia, daughter of Æneas and Lavinia, had him by the god Mars; and others give you mere fables of his origin. For to Tarchetius, they say, king of Alba, who was a most wicked and cruel man, there appeared in his own house a strange vision, a male figure that rose out of a hearth, and stayed there for many days. There was an oracle of Tethys in Tuscany which Tarchetius consulted, and received an answer that a virgin should give herself to the apparition, and that a son should be born of her, highly renowned, eminent for valour, good fortune, and strength of body. Tarchetius told the prophecy to one of his own daughters, and commanded her to do this thing; which she avoiding as an indignity, sent her handmaid.

Tarchetius, hearing this, in great anger imprisoned them both, purposing to put them to death, but being deterred from murder by the goddess Vesta in a dream, enjoined them for their punishment the working a web of cloth, in their chains as they were, which when they finished, they should be suffered to marry; but whatever they worked by day, Tarchetius commanded others to unravel in the night.

In the meantime, the waiting-woman was delivered of two boys, whom Tarchetius gave into the hands of one Teratius, with command to destroy them; he, however, carried and laid them by the river side, where a wolf came and continued to suckle them, while birds of various sorts brought little morsels of food, which they put into their mouths; till a cowherd, spying them, was first strangely surprised, but, venturing to draw nearer, took the children up in his arms. Thus they were saved, and when they grew up, set upon Tarchetius and overcame him. This one Promathion says, who compiled a history of Italy.

But the story which is most believed and has the greatest number of vouchers was first published, in its chief particulars, amongst the Greeks by Diocles of Peparethus, whom Fabius Pictor also follows in most points. Here again there are variations, but in general outline it runs thus: the kings of Alba reigned in lineal descent from Æneas, and the succession devolved at length upon two brothers, Numitor and Amulius. Amulius proposed to divide things into two equal shares, and set as equivalent to the kingdom the treasure and gold that were brought from Troy. Numitor chose the kingdom; but Amulius, having the money, and being able to do more with that than Numitor, took his kingdom from him with great ease, and, fearing lest his daughter might have children, made her a Vestal, bound in that condition forever to live a single and maiden life. This lady some call Ilia, others Rhea, and others Silvia.

However, not long after, she was, contrary to the established laws of the Vestals, discovered to be with child, and should have suffered the most cruel punishment, had not Antho, the king's daughter, mediated with her father for her; nevertheless, she was confined, and debarred all company, that she might not be delivered without the king's knowledge. In time she brought forth two boys, of more than human size and beauty, whom Amulius, becoming yet more alarmed, commanded a servant to take and cast away; this man some call Faustulus, others say Faustulus was the man who brought them up. He put the children, however, in a small trough, and went towards the river with a design to cast them in; but, seeing the waters much swollen and coming violently down, was afraid to go nearer, and dropping the children near the bank, went away. The river overflowing, the flood at last bore up the trough, and, gently wafting it, landed them on a smooth piece of ground, which they now called Cermanus, formerly Germanus, perhaps from *Germani,* which signifies brothers.

Near this place grew a wild fig-tree, which they called Ruminalis, either from Romulus (as it is vulgarly thought), or from *ruminating,* because cattle did usually in the heat of the day seek cover under it, and there chew the cud; or, better, from the suckling of these children there, for the ancients called the dug or teat of any creature *ruma;* and there is a tutelar goddess of the rearing of children whom they still call Rumilia, in sacrificing to whom they use no wine, but make libations of milk. While the infants lay here, history tells us, a she-wolf nursed them, and a woodpecker constantly fed and watched them; these creatures are esteemed holy to the god Mars; the woodpecker the Latins still especially worship and honour. Which things, as much as any, gave credit to what the mother of the children said, that their father was the god Mars; though some say that it was a mistake put upon her by Amulius, who himself had come to her dressed up in armour.

Others think that the first rise of this fable came from the children's nurse, through the ambiguity of her name; for the Latins not only called wolves *lupæ,* but also women of loose life; and such an one was the wife of Faustulus, who nurtured these children, Acca Larentia by name. To her the Romans offer sacrifices, and in the month of April the priest of Mars makes libations there; it is called the Larentian Feast.

They honour also another Larentia, for the following reason: the keeper of Hercules's temple having, it seems, little else to do, proposed to his deity a game at dice, laying down that, if he himself won, he would have something valuable of the god; but if he were beaten, he would spread him a noble table, and procure him a fair lady's company. Upon these terms, throwing first for the god and then for himself, he found himself beaten. Wishing to pay his stakes honourably, and holding himself bound by what he had said, he both provided the deity a good supper, and giving money to Larentia, then in her beauty, though not publicly known, gave her a feast in the temple, where he had also laid a bed, and after supper locked her in, as if the god were really to come to her. And indeed, it is said, the deity did truly visit her, and commanded her in the morning to walk to the market-place, and, whatever man she met first, to salute him, and make him her friend. She met one named Tarrutius, who was a man advanced in years, fairly rich, without children, and had always lived a single life. He received Larentia, and loved her well, and at his death left her sole heir of all his large and fair possessions, most of which she, in her last will and testament, bequeathed to the people. It was reported of her, being now celebrated and esteemed the mistress of a god, that she suddenly disappeared near the place where the first Larentia lay buried; the spot is at this day called Velabrum, because, the river frequently overflowing, they went over in ferry-boats somewhere hereabouts to the forum, the Latin word for ferrying being *velatura*. Others derive the name from *velum,* a sail; because the exhibitors of public shows used to hang the road that leads from the forum to the Circus Maximus with sails, beginning at this spot. Upon these accounts the second Larentia is honoured at Rome.

Meantime Faustulus, Amulius's swineherd, brought up the children without any man's knowledge; or, as those say who wish to keep closer to probabilities, with the knowledge and secret assistance of Numitor; for it is said, they went to school at Gabii, and were well instructed in letters, and other accomplishments befitting their birth. And they were called Romulus and Remus (from *ruma,* the dug), as we had before, because they were found sucking the wolf.

In their very infancy, the size and beauty of their bodies intimated their natural superiority; and when they grew up, they both proved brave and manly, attempting all enterprises that seemed hazardous, and showing in them a courage altogether undaunted. But Romulus seemed rather to act by counsel, and to show the sagacity of a

statesman, and in all his dealings with their neighbours, whether relating to feeding of flocks or to hunting, gave the idea of being born rather to rule than to obey. To their comrades and inferiors they were therefore dear; but the king's servants, his bailiffs and overseers, as being in nothing better than themselves, they despised and slighted, nor were the least concerned at their commands and menaces. They used honest pastimes and liberal studies, not esteeming sloth and idleness honest and liberal, but rather such exercises as hunting and running, repelling robbers, taking of thieves, and delivering the wronged and oppressed from injury. For doing such things they became famous.

A quarrel occurring betwixt Numitor's and Amulius's cowherds, the latter, not enduring the driving away of their cattle by the others, fell upon them and put them to flight, and rescued the greatest part of the prey. At which Numitor being highly incensed, they little regarded it, but collected and took into their company a number of needy men and runaway slaves—acts which looked like the first stages of rebellion.

It so happened, that when Romulus was attending a sacrifice, being fond of sacred rites and divination, Numitor's herdsmen, meeting with Remus on a journey with few companions, fell upon him, and after some fighting, took him prisoner, carried him before Numitor, and there accused him. Numitor would not punish him himself, fearing his brother's anger, but went to Amulius, and desired justice, as he was Amulius's brother and was affronted by Amulius's servants. The men of Alba likewise resenting the thing, and thinking he had been dishonourably used, Amulius was induced to deliver Remus up into Numitor's hands, to use him as he thought fit.

He therefore took and carried him home, and, being struck with admiration of the youth's person, in stature and strength of body exceeding all men, and perceiving in his very countenance the courage and force of his mind, which stood unsubdued and unmoved by his present circumstances, and hearing further that all the enterprises and actions of his life were answerable to what he saw of him, but chiefly, as it seemed, a divine influence aiding and directing the first steps that were to lead to great results, out of the mere thought of his mind, and casually, as it were, he put his hand upon the fact, and, in gentle terms and with a kind aspect, to inspire him with confidence and hope, asked him who he was, and whence he was derived. He, taking heart, spoke thus: "I will hide nothing from you, for you seem to be of a more princely temper than Amulius, in that you give a hearing and examine before you punish, while he condemns before the cause is heard. Formerly, then, we (for we are twins) thought ourselves the sons of Faustulus and Larentia, the king's servants; but since we have been accused and aspersed with calumnies, and brought in peril of our lives here before you, we hear great things of ourselves, the truth of which my present danger is likely to bring to the test. Our birth is said to have been secret, our fostering and nurture in our infancy still more strange; by birds and beasts, to whom we were cast out, we were fed, by the milk of a wolf and the morsels of a woodpecker, as we lay in a little trough by the side of the river. The trough is still in being, and is preserved, with brass plates round it, and an inscription in letters almost effaced, which may prove hereafter unavailing tokens to our parents when we are dead and gone." Numitor, upon these words, and computing the dates by the young man's looks, slighted not the hope that flattered him, but considered how to come at his daughter privately (for she was still kept under restraint), to talk with her concerning these matters.

Faustulus, hearing Remus was taken and delivered up, called on Romulus to assist in his rescue, informing him then plainly of the particulars of his birth, not but he had before given hints of it, and told as much as an attentive man might make no small conclusions from; he himself, full of concern and fear of not coming in time, took the trough, and ran instantly to Numitor; but giving a suspicion to some of the king's sentries at his gate, and being gazed upon by them and perplexed with their questions, he let it be seen that he was hiding the trough under his cloak. By chance there was one among them who was at the exposing of the children, and was employed in the office; he, seeing the trough and knowing it by its make and inscription, guessed at the business, and, without further delay, telling the king of it, brought in the man to be examined, Faustulus, hard beset, did not show himself altogether proof against terror; nor yet was he wholly forced out of all; confessed indeed the children were alive, but lived, he said, as shepherds, a great way from

Alba; he himself was going to carry the trough to Ilia, who had often greatly desired to see and handle it, for a confirmation of her hopes of her children.

As men generally do who are troubled in mind and act either in fear or passion, it so fell out Amulius now did; for he sent in haste as a messenger, a man, otherwise honest, and friendly to Numitor, with commands to learn from Numitor whether any tidings were come to him of the children being alive. He, coming and seeing how little Remus wanted of being received into the arms and embraces of Numitor, both gave him surer confidence in his hope, and advised them, with all expedition, to proceed to action; himself too joining and assisting them, and indeed, had they wished it, the time would not have let them demur. For Romulus was now come very near, and many of the citizens, out of fear and hatred of Amulius, were running out to join him; besides, he brought great forces with him, divided into companies each of an hundred men, every captain carrying a small bundle of grass and shrubs tied to a pole. The Latins call such bundles *manipuli,* and from hence it is that in their armies they still call their captains *manipulares.* Remus rousing the citizens within to revolt, and Romulus making attacks from without, the tyrant, not knowing either what to do, or what expedient to think of for his security, in this perplexity and confusion was taken and put to death.

This narrative for the most part given by Fabius and Diocles of Peparethus, who seem to be the earliest historians of the foundation of Rome, is suspected by some, because of its dramatic and fictitious appearance; but it would not wholly be disbelieved, if men would remember what a poet fortune sometimes shows herself, and consider that the Roman power would hardly have reached so high a pitch without a divinely ordered origin, attended with great and extraordinary circumstances.

Amulius now being dead and matters quietly disposed, the two brothers would neither dwell in Alba without governing there, nor take the government into their own hands during the life of their grandfather. Having therefore delivered the dominion up into his hands, and paid their mother befitting honour, they resolved to live by themselves, and build a city in the same place where they were in their infancy brought up. This seems the most honourable reason for their departure; though perhaps it was necessary, having such a body of slaves and fugitives collected about them, either to come to nothing by dispersing them, or if not so, then to live with them elsewhere. For that the inhabitants of Alba did not think fugitives worthy of being received and incorporated as citizens among them plainly appears from the matter of the women, an attempt made not wantonly but of necessity, because they could not get wives by goodwill. For they certainly paid unusual respect and honour to those whom they thus forcibly seized.

Not long after the first foundation of the city, they opened a sanctuary of refuge for all fugitives, which they called the temple of the god Asylæus, where they received and protected all, delivering none back, neither the servant to his master, the debtor to his creditor, nor the murderer into the hands of the magistrate, saying it was a privileged place, and they could so maintain it by an order of the holy oracle; insomuch that the city grew presently very populous, for they say, it consisted at first of no more than a thousand houses. But of that hereafter.

Their minds being full bent upon building, there arose presently a difference about the place. Romulus chose what was called Roma Quadrata, or the Square Rome, and would have the city there. Remus laid out a piece of ground on the Aventine Mount, well fortified by nature, which was from him called Remonium, but now Rignarium. Concluding at last to decide the contest by a divination from a flight of birds, and placing themselves apart at some distance, Remus, they say, saw six vultures, and Romulus double that number. Others say, Remus did truly see his number, and that Romulus feigned his, but when Remus came to him, that then he did indeed see twelve.

Hence it is that the Romans, in their divinations from birds, chiefly regard the vulture, though Herodorus Ponticus relates that Hercules was always very joyful when a vulture appeared to him upon any action. For it is a creature the least hurtful of any, pernicious neither to corn, fruit-tree, nor cattle; it preys only upon carrion, and never kills or hurts any living thing; and as for birds, it touches not them, though they are dead, as being of its own species, whereas eagles, owls, and hawks mangle and kill their own fellow-creatures; yet, as Æschylus says,—

What bird is clean that preys on fellow bird?

Besides, all other birds are, so to say, never out of our eyes; they let themselves be seen of us continually; but a vulture is a very rare sight, and you can seldom meet with a man that has seen their young; their rarity and infrequency has raised a strange opinion in some, that they come to us from some other world; as soothsayers ascribe a divine origination to all things not produced either of nature or of themselves.

When Remus knew the cheat, he was much displeased; and as Romulus was casting up a ditch, where he designed the foundation of the city-wall, he turned some pieces of the work to ridicule, and obstructed others; at last, as he was in contempt leaping over it, some say Romulus himself struck him, others Celer, one of his companions; he fell, however, and in the scuffle Faustulus also was slain, and Plistinus, who, being Faustulus's brother, story tells us, helped to bring up Romulus. Celer upon this fled instantly into Tuscany, and from him the Romans call all men that are swift of feet Celeres; and because Quintus Metellus, at his father's funeral, in a few days' time gave the people a show of gladiators, admiring his expedition in getting it ready, they gave him the name of Celer.

Romulus, having buried his brother Remus, together with his two foster-fathers, on the mount Remonia, set to building his city; and sent for men out of Tuscany, who directed him by sacred usages and written rules in all the ceremonies to be observed, as in a religious rite. First, they dug a round trench about that which is now the Comitium, or Court of Assembly, and into it solemnly threw the first-fruits of all things either good by custom or necessary by nature; lastly, every man taking a small piece of earth of the country from whence he came, they all threw in promiscuously together. This trench they call, as they do the heavens, Mundus; making which their centre, they described the city in a circle round it. Then the founder fitted to a plough a brazen ploughshare, and, yoking together a bull and a cow, drove himself a deep line or furrow round the bounds; while the business of those that followed after was to see that whatever earth was thrown up should be turned all inwards towards the city; and not to let any clod lie outside. With this line they described the wall, and called it, by a contraction, Pomœrium, that is, *postmurum,* after or beside the wall; and where they designed to make a gate, there they took out the share, carried the plough over, and left a space; for which reason they consider the whole wall as holy, except where the gates are; for had they adjudged them also sacred, they could not, without offence to religion, have given free ingress and egress for the necessaries of human life, some of which are in themselves unclean.

As for the day they began to build the city, it is universally agreed to have been the twenty-first of April, and that day the Romans annually keep holy, calling it their country's birthday. At first, they say, they sacrificed no living creature on this day, thinking it fit to preserve the feast of their country's birthday pure and without stain of blood. Yet before ever the city was built, there was a feast of herdsmen and shepherds kept on this day, which went by the name of Palilia. The Roman and Greek months have now little or no agreement; they say, however, the day on which Romulus began to build was quite certainly the thirtieth of the month, at which time there was an eclipse of the sun which they conceived to be that seen by Antimachus, the Teian poet, in the third year of the sixth Olympiad.

In the times of Varro the philosopher, a man deeply read in Roman history, lived one Tarrutius, his familiar acquaintance, a good philosopher and mathematician, and one, too, that out of curiosity had studied the way of drawing schemes and tables, and was thought to be a proficient in the art; to him Varro propounded to cast Romulus's nativity, even to the first day and hour, making his deductions from the several events of the man's life which he should be informed of, exactly as in working back a geometrical problem; for it belonged, he said, to the same science both to foretell a man's life by knowing the time of his birth, and also to find out his birth by the knowledge of his life. This task Tarrutius undertook, and first looking into the actions and casualties of the man, together with the time of his life and manner of his death, and then comparing all these remarks together, he very confidently and positively pronounced that Romulus was conceived in his mother's womb the first year of the second Olympiad, the twenty-third day of the month the Ægyptians call Chœac, and the third hour after sunset, at which time there was a total eclipse of the sun; that he was born the twenty-first day of the month Thoth, about sunrising; and that the first stone of Rome was laid by him the ninth day of the month

Pharmuthi, between the second and third hour. For the fortunes of cities as well as of men, they think, have their certain periods of time prefixed, which may be collected and foreknown from the position of the stars at their first foundation. But these and the like relations may perhaps not so much take and delight the reader with their novelty and curiosity, as offend him by their extravagance.

The city now being built, Romulus enlisted all that were of age to bear arms into military companies, each company consisting of three thousand footmen and three hundred horse. These companies were called legions, because they were the choicest and most select of the people for fighting men. The rest of the multitude he called the people; an hundred of the most eminent he chose for counsellors; these he styled patricians, and their assembly the senate, which signifies a council of elders.

The patricians, some say, were so called because they were the fathers of lawful children; others, because they could give a good account who their own fathers were, which not every one of the rabble that poured into the city at first could do; others, from patronage, their word for protection of inferiors, the origin of which they attribute to Patron, one of those that came over with Evander, who was a great protector and defender of the weak and needy.

But perhaps the most probable judgment might be, that Romulus, esteeming it the duty of the chiefest and wealthiest men, with a fatherly care and concern to look after the meaner, and also encouraging the commonalty not to dread or be aggrieved at the honours of their superiors, but to love and respect them, and to think and call them their fathers, might from hence give them the name of patricians. For at this very time all foreigners give senators the style of lords; but the Romans, making use of a more honourable and less invidious name, call them *Patres Conscripti;* at first, indeed, simply *Patres,* but afterwards, more being added, *Patres Conscripti.* By this more imposing title he distinguished the senate from the populace; and in other ways also separated the nobles and the commons,—calling them patrons, and these their clients,—by which means he created wonderful love and amity betwixt them, productive of great justice in their dealings. For they were always their clients' counsellors in law cases, their advocates in courts of justice; in fine, their advisers and supporters in all affairs whatever. These again faithfully served their patrons, not only paying them all respect and deference, but also, in case of poverty, helping them to portion their daughters and pay off their debts; and for a patron to witness against his client, or a client against his patron, was what no law nor magistrate could enforce. In aftertimes, all other duties subsisting still between them, it was thought mean and dishonourable for the better sort to take money from their inferiors. And so much of these matters.

In the fourth month, after the city was built, as Fabius writes, the adventure of stealing the women was attempted; and some say Romulus himself, being naturally a martial man, and predisposed too, perhaps by certain oracles, to believe the fates had ordained the future growth and greatness of Rome should depend upon the benefit of war, upon these accounts first offered violence to the Sabines, since he took away only thirty virgins, more to give an occasion of war than out of any want of women.

But this is not very probable; it would seem rather that, observing his city to be filled by a confluence of foreigners, few of whom had wives, and that the multitude in general, consisting of a mixture of mean and obscure men, fell under contempt, and seemed to be of no long continuance together, and hoping farther, after the women were appeased, to make this injury in some measure an occasion of confederacy and mutual commerce with the Sabines, he took in hand this exploit after this manner.

First, he gave it out as if he had found an altar of a certain god hid under ground; the god they called Consus, either the god of counsel (for they still call a consultation *consilium,* and their chief magistrates *consules,* namely, counsellors), or else the equestrian Neptune, for the altar is kept covered in the Circus Maximus at all other times, and only at horse-races is exposed to public view; others merely say that this god had his altar hid under ground because counsel ought to be secret and concealed.

Upon discovery of this altar, Romulus, by proclamation, appointed a day for a splendid sacrifice, and for public games and shows, to entertain all sorts of people: many flocked thither, and he himself sat in front, amidst his nobles clad in purple. Now the signal for their falling on was to be whenever he rose and gathered up his robe and threw it over his body; his men stood all ready armed, with their eyes intent upon him, and when the sign was given, drawing their swords and falling on with a great shout, they ravished away the daughters of the Sabines, they themselves flying without any let or hindrance.

They say there were but thirty taken, and from them the *Curiæ* or Fraternities were named; but Valerius Antias says five hundred and twenty-seven, Juba, six hundred and eighty-three virgins: which was indeed the greatest excuse Romulus could allege, namely, that they had taken no married woman, save one only, Hersilia by name, and her too unknowingly; which showed that they did not commit this rape wantonly, but with a design purely of forming alliance with their neighbours by the greatest and surest bonds.

This Hersilia some say Hostilius married, a most eminent man among the Romans; others, Romulus himself, and that she bore two children to him,—a daughter, by reason of primogeniture called Prima, and one only son, whom, from the great concourse of citizens to him at that time, he called Aollius, but after ages Abillius. But Zenodotus the Trœzenian, in giving this account, is contradicted by many.

Among those who committed this rape upon the virgins, there were, they say, as it so then happened, some of the meaner sort of men, who were carrying off a damsel, excelling all in beauty and comeliness and stature, whom when some of superior rank that met them, attempted to take away, they cried out they were carrying her to Talasius, a young man, indeed, but brave and worthy; hearing that, they commended and applauded them loudly, and also some, turning back, accompanied them with good-will and pleasure, shouting out the name of Talasius.

Hence the Romans to this very time, at their weddings, sing *Talasius* for their nuptial word, as the Greeks do *Hymenæus,* because they say Talasius was very happy in his marriage. But Sextius Sulla the Carthaginian, a man wanting neither learning nor ingenuity, told me Romulus gave this word as a sign when to begin the onset; everybody, therefore, who made prize of a maiden, cried out, "Talasius"; and for that reason the custom continues so now at marriages.

But most are of opinion (of whom Juba particularly is one) that this word was used to new-married women by way of incitement to good housewifery and *talasia* (spinning), as we say in Greek, Greek words at that time not being as yet overpowered by Italian.

But if this be the case, and if the Romans did at the time use the word *talasia* as we do, a man might fancy a more probable reason of the custom. For when the Sabines, after the war against the Romans, were reconciled, conditions were made concerning their women, that they should be obliged to do no other servile offices to their husbands but what concerned spinning; it was customary, therefore, ever after, at weddings, for those that gave the bride or escorted her or otherwise were present, sportingly to say "Talasius," intimating that she was henceforth to serve in spinning and no more.

It continues also a custom at this very day for the bride not of herself to pass her husband's threshold, but to be lifted over, in memory that the Sabine virgins were carried in by violence, and did not go in of their own will. Some say, too, the custom of parting the bride's hair with the head of a spear was in token their marriages began at first by war and acts of hostility, of which I have spoken more fully in my book of Questions.

This rape was committed on the eighteenth day of the month Sextilis, now called August, on which the solemnities of the Consualia are kept.

The Sabines were a numerous and martial people, but lived in small, unfortified villages, as it befitted, they thought, a colony of the Lacedæmonians to be bold and fearless; nevertheless, seeing themselves bound by such hostages to their good behaviour, and being solicitous for their daughters, they sent ambassadors to Romulus with fair and equitable requests, that he would return their young women and recall that act of violence, and afterwards, by persuasion and lawful means, seek friendly correspondence between both nations. Romulus would not part with the young women, yet proposed to the Sabines to enter into an alliance with them; upon which point some consulted and demurred long, but Acron, king of the Ceninenses, a man of high spirit and a good warrior, who had all along a jealousy of Romulus's bold attempts, and considering particularly, from this exploit upon the women, that he was growing formidable to all people, and indeed insufferable, were he not chastised, first rose up in arms, and with a powerful army advanced against him.

Romulus likewise prepared to receive him; but when they came within sight and viewed each other, they made a challenge to fight a single duel, the armies standing by under arms, without participation. And Romulus, making a vow to Jupiter, if he should conquer, to carry, himself, and dedicate his adversary's armour to his honour, overcame him in combat, and a battle ensuing, routed his army also, and then took his city; but did those he found in it no injury, only commanded them to demolish the place and attend him to Rome, there to be admitted to all the privileges of citizens. And indeed there was nothing did more advance the greatness of Rome, than that she did always unite and incorporate those whom she conquered into herself.

Romulus, that he might perform his vow in the most acceptable manner to Jupiter, and withal make the pomp of it delightful to the eye of the city, cut down a tall oak which he saw growing in the camp, which he trimmed to the shape of a trophy, and fastened on it Acron's whole suit of armour disposed in proper form; then he himself, girding his clothes about him, and crowning his head with a laurel garland, his hair gracefully flowing, carried the trophy resting erect upon his right shoulder, and so marched on, singing songs of triumph, and his whole army following after, the citizens all receiving him with acclamations of joy and wonder.

The procession of this day was the origin and model of all after triumphs. This trophy was styled an offering to Jupiter Feretrius, from *ferire,* which in Latin is to smite; for Romulus prayed he might smite and overthrow his enemy; and the spoils were called *opima,* or royal spoils, says Varro, from their richness, which the word *opes* signifies; though one would more probably conjecture from *opus,* an act; for it is only to the general of an army who with his own hand kills his enemies' general that this honour is granted of offering the *opima spolia.* And three only of the Roman captains have had it conferred on them: first, Romulus, upon killing Acron the Ceninensian; next, Cornelius Cossus, for slaying Tolumnius the Tuscan; and lastly, Claudius Marcellus, upon his conquering Viridomarus, king of the Gauls. The two latter, Cossus and Marcellus, made their entries in triumphant chariots, bearing their trophies themselves; but that Romulus made use of a chariot, Dionysius is wrong in asserting. History says, Tarquinius, Damaratus's son, was the first that brought triumphs to this great pomp and grandeur; others, that Publicola was the first that rode in triumph. The statues of Romulus in triumph are, as may be seen in Rome, all on foot.

After the overthrow of the Ceninensians, the other Sabines still protracting the time in preparations, the people of Fidenæ, Crustumerium, and Antemna joined their forces against the Romans; they in like manner were defeated in battle, and surrendered up to Romulus their cities to be seized, their lands and territories to be divided, and themselves to be transplanted to Rome. All the lands which Romulus acquired, he distributed among the citizens, except only what the parents of the stolen virgins had; these he suffered to possess their own.

The rest of the Sabines, enraged hereat, choosing Tatius their captain, marched straight against Rome. The city was almost inaccessible, having for its fortress that which is now the Capitol, where a strong guard was placed, and Tarpeius their captain; not Tarpeia the virgin, as some say who would make Romulus a fool. But Tarpeia, daughter to the captain, coveting the golden bracelets she saw them wear, betrayed the fort into the Sabines' hands, and asked, in reward of her treachery, the things they wore on their left arms. Tatius conditioning thus with her, in the night she opened one of the gates, and received the Sabines.

And truly Antigonus, it would seem, was not solitary in saying he loved betrayers, but hated those who had betrayed; nor Cæsar, who told Rhymitalces the Thracian, that he loved the treason, but hated the traitor; but it is the general feeling of all who have occasion for wicked men's service, as people have for the poison of venomous beasts; they are glad of them while they are of use, and abhor their baseness when it is over. And so then did Tatius behave towards Tarpeia, for he commanded the Sabines, in regard to their contract, not to refuse her the least part of what they wore on their left arms; and he himself first took his bracelet off his arm, and threw that, together with his buckler, at her; and all the rest following, she, being borne down and quite buried with the multitude of gold and their shields, died under the weight and pressure of them; Tarpeius also himself, being prosecuted by Romulus, was found guilty of treason, as Juba says Sulpicius Galba relates.

Those who write otherwise concerning Tarpeia, as that she was the daughter of Tatius, the Sabine captain, and being forcibly

detained by Romulus, acted and suffered thus by her father's contrivance, speak very absurdly, of whom Antigonus is one. And Simylus, the poet, who thinks Tarpeia betrayed the Capitol, not to the Sabines, but the Gauls, having fallen in love with their king, talks mere folly, saying thus:—

Tarpeia 'twas, who, dwelling close thereby,
Laid open Rome unto the enemy,
She, for the love of the besieging Gaul,
Betrayed the city's strength, the Capitol.

And a little after, speaking of her death:—

The numerous nations of the Celtic foe
Bore her not living to the banks of Po;
Their heavy shields upon the maid they threw,
And with their splendid gifts entombed at once
and slew.

Tarpeia afterwards was buried there, and the hill from her was called Tarpeius, until the reign of King Tarquin, who dedicated the place to Jupiter, at which time her bones were removed, and so it lost her name, except only that part of the Capitol which they still called the Tarpeian Rock, from which they used to cast down malefactors.

The Sabines being possessed of the hill, Romulus, in great fury, bade them battle, and Tatius was confident to accept it, perceiving, if they were overpowered, that they had behind them a secure retreat. The level in the middle, where they were to join battle, being surrounded with many little hills seemed to enforce both parties to a sharp and desperate conflict, by reason of the difficulties of the place, which had but a few outlets, inconvenient either for refuge or pursuit. It happened, too, the river having overflowed not many days before, there was left behind in the plain, where now the Forum stands, a deep blind mud and slime, which, though it did not appear much to the eye, and was not easily avoided, at bottom was deceitful and dangerous; upon which the Sabines being unwarily about to enter, met with a piece of good fortune; for Curtius, a gallant man, eager of honour, and of aspiring thoughts, being mounted on horseback, was galloping on before the rest, and mired his horse here, and, endeavouring for a while, by whip and spur and voice to disentangle him, but finding it impossible, quitted him and saved himself; the place from him to this very time is called the Curtian Lake. The Sabines, having avoided this danger, began the fight very smartly, the fortune of the day being very dubious, though many were slain; amongst whom was Hostilius, who, they say, was husband to Hersilia, and grandfather to that Hostilius who reigned after Numa.

There were many other brief conflicts, we may suppose, but the most memorable was the last, in which Romulus having received a wound on his head by a stone, and being almost felled to the ground by it, and disabled, the Romans gave way, and, being driven out of the level ground, fled towards the Palatium. Romulus, by this time recovering from his wound a little, turned about to renew the battle, and, facing the fliers, with a loud voice encouraged them to stand and fight. But being overborne with numbers, and nobody daring to face about, stretching out his hands to heaven, he prayed to Jupiter to stop the army, and not to neglect, but maintain the Roman cause, now in extreme danger. The prayer was no sooner made, than shame and respect for their king checked many; the fears of the fugitives changed suddenly into confidence. The place they first stood at was where now is the temple of Jupiter Stator (which may be translated the Stayer); there they rallied again into ranks and repulsed the Sabines to the place called now Regia, and to the temple of Vesta; where both parties, preparing to begin a second battle, were prevented by a spectacle, strange to behold, and defying description. For the daughters of the Sabines, who had been carried off, came running, in great confusion, some on this side, some on that, with miserable cries and lamentations, like creatures possessed, in the midst of the army and among the dead bodies, to come at their husbands and their fathers, some with their young babes in their arms, others their hair loose about their ears, but all calling, now upon the Sabines, now upon the Romans, in the most tender and endearing words. Hereupon both melted into compassion, and fell back, to make room for them betwixt the armies. The sight of the women carried sorrow and commiseration upon both sides into the hearts of all, but still more their words, which began with expostulation and upbraiding, and ended with entreaty and supplication.

"Wherein," say they, "have we injured or offended you, as to deserve such sufferings past and present? We were ravished away unjustly and violently by those whose now we are; that being done, we were so long neglected by our fathers, our brothers and countrymen, that time, having now by the strictest bonds united us to those we once mortally hated, has made it impossible for us not to tremble at the danger and weep at the death of the very men who once used violence to us. You did not come to vindicate our honour, while we were virgins, against our assailants; but do come now to force away wives from their husbands and mothers from their children, a succour more grievous to its wretched objects than the former betrayal and neglect of them. Which shall we call the worst, their love-making or your compassion? If you were making war upon any other occasion, for our sakes you ought to withhold your hands from those to whom we have made you fathers-in-law and grandsires. If it be for our own cause, then take us, and with us your sons-in-law and grandchildren. Restore to us our parents and kindred, but do not rob us of our children and husbands. Make us not, we entreat you, twice captives."

Hersilia having spoken many such words as these, and the others earnestly praying, a truce was made, and the chief officers came to a parley; the women, in the meantime, brought and presented their husbands and children to their fathers and brothers; gave those that wanted meat and drink, and carried the wounded home to be cured, and showed also how much they governed within doors, and how indulgent their husbands were to them, in demeaning themselves towards them with all kindness and respect imaginable. Upon this, conditions were agreed, that what women pleased might stay where they were, exempt, as aforesaid, from all drudgery and labour but spinning; that the Romans and Sabines should inhabit the city together; that the city should be called Rome from Romulus; but the Romans, Quirites, from the country of Tatius; and that they both should govern and command in common. The place of the ratification is still called Comitium, from *coire,* to meet.

The city being thus doubled in number, an hundred of the Sabines were elected senators, and the legions were increased to six thousand foot and six hundred horse; then they divided the people into three tribes: the first, from Romulus, named Ramnenses; the second from Tatius, Tatienses; the third Luceres, from the *lucus,* or grove, where the Asylum stood, whither many fled for sanctuary, and were received into the city. And that they were just three, the very name of *tribe* and *tribune* seems to show; each tribe contained ten *curiæ,* or brotherhoods, which, some say, took their names from the Sabine women; but that seems to be false, because many had their names from various places. Though it is true, they then constituted many things in honour to the women; as to give them the way wherever they met them; to speak no ill word in their presence; not to appear naked before them, or else be liable to prosecution before the judge, of homicide; that their children should wear an ornament about their necks called the *bulla* (because it was like a bubble), and the *prætexta,* a gown edged with purple.

The princes did not immediately join in council together, but at first each met with his own hundred; afterwards all assembled together. Tatius dwelt where now the temple of Moneta stands, and Romulus, close by the steps, as they call them, of the Fair Shore, near the descent from the Mount Palatine to the Circus Maximus. There, they say, grew the holy cornel tree, of which they report, that Romulus once, to try his strength, threw a dart from the Aventine Mount, the staff of which was made of cornel, which struck so deep into the ground, that no one of many that tried could pluck it up, and the soil, being fertile, gave nourishment to the wood, which sent forth branches, and produced a cornel stock of considerable bigness. This did posterity preserve and worship as one of the most sacred things; and therefore walled it about; and if to any one it appeared not green nor flourishing, but inclining to pine and wither, he immediately made outcry to all he met, and they, like people hearing of a house on fire, with one accord would cry for water, and run from all parts with buckets full to the place. But when Caius Cæsar, they say, was repairing the steps about it, some of the labourers digging too close, the roots were destroyed, and the tree withered.

The Sabines adopted the Roman months, of which whatever is remarkable is mentioned in the Life of Numa. Romulus, on the other hand, adopted their long shields, and changed his own armour and that of all the Romans, who before wore round targets of the Argive pattern. Feasts and sacrifices they partook of in common, not abolishing any which either nation observed before, and instituting several new ones; of which one was the Matronalia, instituted in honour of the women, for their extinction of the war; likewise the Carmentalia. This Carmenta some think a deity presiding over human birth; for which reason she is much honoured by mothers. Others say she was the wife of Evander, the Arcadian, being

a prophetess, and wont to deliver her oracles in verse, and from *carmen,* a verse, was called Carmenta; her proper name being Nicostrata. Others more probably derive Carmenta from *carens mente,* or insane, in allusion to her prophetic frenzies. Of the feast of Palilia we have spoken before.

The Lupercalia, by the time of its celebration, may seem to be a feast of purification, for it is solemnised on the *dies nefasti,* or noncourt days, of the month February, which name signifies purification, and the very day of the feast was anciently called Februata; but its name is equivalent to the Greek Lycæa; and it seems thus to be of great antiquity, and brought in by the Arcadians who came with Evander. Yet this is but dubious, for it may come as well from the wolf that nursed Romulus; and we see the Luperci, the priests, begin their course from the place where they say Romulus was exposed. But the ceremonies performed in it render the origin of the thing more difficult to be guessed at; for there are goats killed, then, two young noblemen's sons being brought, some are to stain their foreheads with the bloody knife, others presently to wipe it off with wool dipped in milk; then the young boys must laugh after their foreheads are wiped; that done, having cut the goats' skins into thongs, they run about naked, only with something about their middle, lashing all they meet; and the young wives do not avoid their strokes, fancying they will help conception and childbirth. Another thing peculiar to this feast is for the Luperci to sacrifice a dog.

But, as a certain poet who wrote fabulous explanations of Roman customs in elegiac verses, asserts, Romulus and Remus, after the conquest of Amulius, ran joyfully to the place where the wolf gave them suck; and thus, in imitation of that, this feast was held, and two young noblemen ran—

Striking at all, as when from Alba town,
With sword in hand, the twins came hurrying down;

and there the bloody knife applied to their foreheads was a sign of the danger and bloodshed of that day; the cleansing of them in milk, a remembrance of their food and nourishment. Caius Acilius writes, that, before the city was built, the cattle of Romulus and Remus one day going astray, they, praying to the god Faunus, ran out to seek them naked, wishing not to be troubled with sweat, and that this is why the Luperci run naked. If the sacrifice be by way of purification, a dog might very well be sacrificed, for the Greeks, in their illustrations, carry out young dogs, and frequently use this ceremony of *periscylacismus,* as they call it. Or if again it is a sacrifice of gratitude to the wolf that nourished and preserved Romulus, there is good reason in killing a dog, as being an enemy to wolves. Unless, indeed, after all, the creature is punished for hindering the Luperci in their running.

They say, too, Romulus was the first that consecrated holy fire, and instituted holy virgins to keep it, called vestals; others ascribe it to Numa Pompilius; agreeing, however, that Romulus was otherwise eminently religious, and skilled in divination, and for that reason carried the *lituus,* a crooked rod with which soothsayers describe the quarters of the heavens, when they sit to observe the flights of birds. This of his, being kept in the Palatium, was lost when the city was taken by the Gauls; and afterwards, that barbarous people being driven out, was found in the ruins, under a great heap of ashes, untouched by the fire, all things about it being consumed and burnt.

He instituted also certain laws, one of which is somewhat severe, which suffers not a wife to leave her husband, but grants a husband power to turn off his wife, either upon poisoning her children, or counterfeiting his keys, or for adultery; but if the husband upon any other occasion put her away, he ordered one moiety of his estate to be given to the wife, the other to fall to the goddess Ceres; and whoever cast off his wife, to make an atonement by sacrifice to the gods of the dead.

This, too, is observable as a singular thing in Romulus, that he appointed no punishment for real parricide, but called all murder so, thinking the one an accursed thing, but the other a thing impossible; and, for a long time, his judgment seemed to have been right; for in almost six hundred years together, nobody committed the like in Rome; and Lucius Hostius, after the wars of Hannibal, is recorded to have been the first parricide. Let this much suffice concerning these matters.

In the fifth year of the reign of Tatius, some of his friends and kinsmen, meeting ambassadors coming from Laurentum to Rome, attempted on the road to take away their money by force, and, upon their resistance, killed them. So great a villainy having been committed Romulus thought the malefactors ought at once to be punished, but Tatius shuffled off and deferred the execution of it; and

this one thing was the beginning of open quarrel betwixt them; in all other respects they were very careful of their conduct, and administered affairs together with great unanimity. The relations of the slain, being debarred of lawful satisfaction by reason of Tatius, fell upon him as he was sacrificing with Romulus at Lavinium and slew him; but escorted Romulus home, commending and extolling him for a just prince. Romulus took the body of Tatius, and buried it very splendidly in the Aventine Mount, near the place called Armilustrium, but altogether neglected revenging his murder. Some authors write, that the city of Laurentum, fearing the consequences, delivered up the murderers of Tatius; but Romulus dismissed them, saying, one murder was requited with another. This gave occasion of talk and jealousy, as if he were well pleased at the removal of his co-partner in the government.

Nothing of these things, however, raised any sort of feud or disturbance among the Sabines; but some out of love to him, others out of fear of his power, some again reverencing him as a god, they all continued living peacefully in admiration and awe of him; many foreign nations, too, showed respect to Romulus; the Ancient Latins sent and entered into league and confederacy with him. Fidenæ he took, a neighbouring city to Rome, by a party of horse, as some say, whom he sent before with commands to cut down the hinges of the gates, himself afterwards unexpectedly coming up. Others say, they having first made the invasion, plundering and ravaging the country and suburbs, Romulus lay in ambush for them, and having killed many of their men, took the city; but, nevertheless, did not raze or demolish it, but made it a Roman colony, and sent thither, on the Ides of April, two thousand five hundred inhabitants.

Soon after a plague broke out, causing sudden death without any previous sickness; it infected also the corn with unfruitfulness, and cattle with barrenness; there rained blood, too, in the city; so that, to their actual sufferings, fear of the wrath of the gods was added. But when the same mischiefs fell upon Laurentum, then everybody judged it was divine vengeance that fell upon both cities, for the neglect of executing justice upon the murder of Tatius and the ambassadors. But the murderers on both sides being delivered up and punished, the pestilence visibly abated; and Romulus purified the cities with lustrations, which, they say, even now, are performed at the wood called Ferentina. But before the plague ceased, the Camertines invaded the Romans and overran the country, thinking them, by reason of the distemper, unable to resist; but Romulus at once made head against them, and gained the victory, with the slaughter of six thousand men, then took their city, and brought half of those he found there to Rome, sending from Rome to Camerium double the number he left there. This was done on the first of August. So many citizens had he to spare, in sixteen years' time from his first founding Rome. Among other spoils he took a brazen four-horse chariot from Camerium, which he placed in the temple of Vulcan, setting on it his own statue, with a figure of victory crowning him.

The Roman cause thus daily gathering strength, their weaker neighbours shrunk away, and were thankful to be left untouched; but the stronger, out of fear or envy, thought they ought not to give way to Romulus, but to curb and put a stop to his growing greatness. The first were the Veientes, a people of Tuscany, who had large possessions, and dwelt in a spacious city; they took occasion to commence a war, by claiming Fidenæ as belonging to them; a thing not only very unreasonable, but very ridiculous, that they, who did not assist them in the greatest extremities, but permitted them to be slain, should challenge their lands and houses when in the hands of others. But being scornfully retorted upon by Romulus in his answers, they divided themselves into two bodies; with one they attacked the garrison of Fidenæ, the other marched against Romulus; that which went against Fidenæ got the victory, and slew two thousand Romans; the other was worsted by Romulus, with the loss of eight thousand men.

A fresh battle was fought near Fidenæ, and here all men acknowledge the day's success to have been chiefly the work of Romulus himself, who showed the highest skill as well as courage, and seemed to manifest a strength and swiftness more than human. But what some write, that of fourteen thousand that fell that day, above half were slain by Romulus's own hand, verges too near to fable, and is, indeed, simply incredible; since even the Messenians are thought to go too far in saying that Aristomenes three times offered sacrifice for the death of a hundred enemies, Lacedæmonians, slain by himself. The army being thus routed, Romulus, suffering those that were left to make their escape, led his forces against the city; they, having suffered such great losses, did not venture to oppose, but, humbly suing to him, made a league and friendship for an hundred years; surrendering also a large district of land called Septempagium, that is, the seven parts, as also their salt-works upon the river, and fifty noblemen for hostages. He made his triumph for this on the Ides of October, leading, among the rest of his many captives, the general of the Veientes, an elderly man, but who had not, it seemed, acted with the prudence of age; whence even now, in sacrifices for victories, they lead an old man through the marketplace to the Capitol, apparelled in purple, with a *bulla*, or child's toy, tied to it, and the crier cries, *Sardians to be sold;* for the Tuscans are said to be a colony of the Sardians, and the Veientes are a city of Tuscany.

This was the last battle Romulus ever fought; afterwards he, as most, nay all men, very few excepted, do, who are raised by great and miraculous good-haps of fortune to power and greatness, so, I say, did he; relying upon his own great actions, and growing of an haughtier mind, he forsook his popular behaviour for kingly arrogance, odious to the people; to whom in particular the state which he assumed was hateful. For he dressed in scarlet, with the purple-bordered robe over it; he gave audience on a couch of state, having always about him some young men called *Celeres*, from their swiftness in doing commissions; there went before him others with staves, to make room, with leather thongs tied on their bodies, to bind on the moment whoever he commanded. The Latins formerly used *ligare* in the same sense as now *alligare,* to bind, whence the name *lictors*, for these officers, and *bacula,* or staves, for their rods, because staves were then used. It is probable, however, they were first called *litores,* afterwards, by putting in a *c, lictores,* or, in Greek, *liturgi,* or people's officers, for *leïtos* is still Greek for the commons, and *laös* for the people in general.

But when, after the death of his grandfather Numitor in Alba, the throne devolving upon Romulus, he, to court the people, put the government into their own hands, and appointed an annual magistrate over the Albans, this taught the great men of Rome to seek after a free and anti-monarchical state, wherein all might in turn be subjects and rulers. For neither were the patricians any longer admitted to state affairs, only had the name and title left them, convening in council rather for fashion's sake than advice, where they heard in silence the king's commands, and so departed, exceeding the commonalty only in hearing first what was done.

These and the like were matters of small moment; but when he of his own accord parted among his soldiers what lands were acquired by war, and restored the Veientes their hostages, the senate neither consenting nor approving of it, then, indeed, he seemed to put a great affront upon them; so that, on his sudden and strange disappearance a short while after, the senate fell under suspicion and calumny. He disappeared on the Nones of July, as they now call the month which was then Quintilis, leaving nothing of certainty to be related of his death, only the time, as just mentioned, for on that day many ceremonies are still performed in representation of what happened.

Neither is this uncertainty to be thought strange, seeing the manner of the death of Scipio Africanus, who died at his own home after supper, has been found capable neither of proof or disproof; for some say he died a natural death, being of a sickly habit; others, that he poisoned himself; others again, that his enemies, breaking in upon him in the night, stifled him. Yet Scipio's dead body lay open to be seen of all, and any one, from his own observation, might form his suspicions and conjectures, whereas Romulus, when he vanished, left neither the least part of his body, nor any remnant of his clothes to be seen.

So that some fancied the senators, having fallen upon him in the temple of Vulcan, cut his body into pieces, and took each a part away in his bosom; others think his disappearance was neither in the temple of Vulcan, nor with the senators only by, but that it came to pass that, as he was haranguing the people without the city, near a place called the Goat's Marsh, on a sudden strange and unaccountable disorders and alterations took place in the air; the face of the sun was darkened, and the day turned into night, and that, too, no quiet, peaceable night, but with terrible thunderings, and boisterous winds from all quarters; during which the common people dispersed and fled, but the senators kept close together. The tempest being over and the light breaking out, when the people gathered again, they missed and inquired for their king; the senators suffered them not to search, or busy themselves about the matter, but commanded them to honour and worship Romulus as one taken up to the gods, and about to be to them, in the place of a good prince, now a propitious god. The multitude, hearing this, went away believing and rejoicing in hopes of good things from him; but there were some, who, canvassing the matter in a hostile temper, accused and aspersed the patricians, as men that persuaded the people to believe ridiculous tales, when they themselves were the murderers of the king.

Things being in this disorder, one, they say, of the patricians, of noble family and approved good character, and a faithful and familiar friend of Romulus himself, having come with him from Alba, Julius Proculus by name, presented himself in the Forum; and, taking a most sacred oath, protested before them all, that, as he was travelling on the road, he had seen Romulus coming to meet him, looking taller and comelier than ever, dressed in shining and flaming armour; and he, being affrighted at the apparition, said, "Why, O king, or for what purpose have you abandoned us to unjust and wicked surmises, and the whole city to bereavement and endless sorrow?" and that he made answer, "It pleased the gods, O Proculus, that we, who came from them, should remain so long a time amongst men as we did; and, having built a city to be the greatest in the world for empire and glory, should again return to heaven. But farewell; and tell the Romans, that, by the exercise of temperance and fortitude, they shall attain the height of human power; we will be to you the propitious god Quirinus." This seemed credible to the Romans, upon the honesty and oath of the relater, and indeed, too, there mingled with it a certain divine passion, some preternatural influence similar to possession by a divinity; nobody contradicted it, but, laying aside all jealousies and detractions, they prayed to Quirinus and saluted him as a god.

This is like some of the Greek fables of Aristeas the Proconnesian, and Cleomedes the Astypalæan; for they say Aristeas died in a fuller's work-shop, and his friends coming to look for him, found his body vanished; and that some presently after, coming from abroad, said they met him travelling towards Croton. And that Cleomedes, being an extraordinarily strong and gigantic man, but also wild and mad, committed many desperate freaks; and at last, in a school-house, striking a pillar that sustained the roof with his fist, broke it in the middle, so that the house fell and destroyed the children in it; and being pursued, he fled into a great chest, and, shutting to the lid, held it so fast, that many men, with their united strength, could not force it open; afterwards, breaking the chest to pieces, they found no man in it alive or dead; in astonishment at which, they sent to consult the oracle at Delphi; to whom the prophetess made this answer,—

Of all the heroes Cleomede is last.

They say, too, the body of Alcmena, as they were carrying her to her grave, vanished, and a stone was found lying on the bier.

And many such improbabilities do your fabulous writers relate, deifying creatures naturally mortal; for though altogether to disown a divine nature in human virtue were impious and base, so again, to mix heaven with earth is ridiculous. Let us believe with Pindar, that—

All human bodies yield to Death's decree,
The soul survives to all eternity.

For that alone is derived from the gods, thence comes, and thither returns; not with the body, but when most disengaged and separated from it, and when most entirely pure and clean and free from the flesh: for the most perfect soul, says Heraclitus, is a dry light, which flies out of the body as lightning breaks from a cloud; but that which is clogged and surfeited with body is like gross and humid incense, slow to kindle and ascend. We must not, therefore, contrary to nature, send the bodies, too, of good men to heaven; but we must really believe that, according to their divine nature and law, their virtue and their souls are translated out of men into heroes, out of heroes into demi-gods, out of demi-gods, after passing, as in the rite of initiation, through a final cleansing and sanctification, and so freeing themselves from all that pertains to mortality and sense, are thus, not by human decree, but really and according to right reason, elevated into gods admitted thus to the greatest and most blessed perfection.

Romulus's surname Quirinus, some say, is equivalent to Mars; others, that he was so called because the citizens were called Quirites; others, because the ancients called a dart or spear Quiris; thus, the statue of Juno resting on a spear is called Quiritis, and the dart in the Regia is addressed as Mars, and those that were distinguished in war were usually presented with a dart; that, therefore, Romulus being a martial god, or a god of darts, was called Quir-

inus. A temple is certainly built to his honour on the mount called from him Quirinalis.

The day he vanished on is called the Flight of the People and the Nones of the Goats, because they go then out of the city and sacrifice at the Goat's Marsh, and, as they go, they shout out some of the Roman names, as Marcus, Lucius, Caius, imitating the way in which they then fled and called upon one another in that fright and hurry.

Some, however, say this was not in imitation of a flight, but of a quick and hasty onset, referring it to the following occasion: After the Gauls who had taken Rome were driven out by Camillus, and the city was scarcely as yet recovering her strength, many of the Latins, under the command of Livius Postumius, took this time to march against her. Postumius halting not far from Rome, sent a herald, signifying that the Latins were desirous to renew their former alliance and affinity (that was now almost decayed) by contracting new marriages between both nations; if, therefore, they would send forth a good number of their virgins and widows, they should have peace and friendship, such as the Sabines had formerly had on the like conditions.

The Romans, hearing this, dreaded a war, yet thought a surrender of their women little better than mere captivity. Being in this doubt, a servant-maid called Philotis (or, as some say, Tutola), advised them to do neither, but, by a stratagem, avoid both fighting and the giving up of such pledges. The stratagem was this, that they should send herself, with other well-looking servant-maids, to the enemy, in the dress of free-born virgins, and she should in the night light up a fire signal, at which the Romans should come armed and surprise them asleep.

The Latins were thus deceived, and accordingly Philotis set up a torch in a wild fig-tree, screening it behind with curtains and coverlets from the sight of the enemy, while visible to the Romans. They, when they saw it, eagerly ran out of the gates, calling in their haste to each other as they went out, and so, falling in unexpectedly upon the enemy, they defeated them, and upon that made a feast of triumph, called the Nones of the Goats, because of the wild fig-tree called by the Romans *caprificus,* or the goat-fig. They feast the women without the city in arbours made of fig-tree boughs, and the maid-servants gather together and run about playing; afterwards they fight in sport, and throw stones one at another, in memory that they then aided and assisted the Roman men in fight.

This only a few authors admit for true; for the calling upon one another's names by day and the going out to the Goat's Marsh to do sacrifice seem to agree more with the former story, unless, indeed, we shall say that both the actions might have happened on the same day in different years.

It was in the fifty-fourth year of his age and the thirty-eighth of his reign that Romulus, they tell us, left the world.

ROMULUS and THESEUS
Compared

THIS is what I have learnt of Romulus and Theseus, worthy of memory. It seems, first of all, that Theseus, out of his own free-will, without any compulsion, when he might have reigned in security at Trœzen in the enjoyment of no inglorious empire, of his own motion affected great actions, whereas the other, to escape present servitude and a punishment that threatened him (according to Plato's phrase), grew valiant purely out of fear, and dreading the extremest inflictions, attempted great enterprises out of mere necessity.

Again, his greatest action was only the killing of one King of Alba; while, as mere by-adventures and preludes, the other can name Sciron, Sinnis, Procrustes, and Corynetes; by reducing and killing of whom, he rid Greece of terrible oppressors, before any of them that were relieved knew who did it; moreover, he might without any trouble as well have gone to Athens by sea, considering he himself never was in the least injured by those robbers; whereas Romulus could not but be in trouble whilst Amulius lived. Add to this, the fact that Theseus, for no wrong done to himself, but for the sake of others, fell upon these villains; but Romulus and Remus, as long as they themselves suffered no ill by the tyrant, permitted him to oppress all others. And if it be a great thing to have been wounded in battle by the Sabines, to have killed King Acron, and to have conquered many enemies, we may oppose to these actions the battle with the Centaurs and the feats done against the Amazons.

But what Theseus adventured, in offering himself voluntarily with young boys and virgins, as part of the tribute unto Crete, either to be a prey to a monster or a victim upon the tomb of Androgeus, or, according to the mildest form of the story, to live vilely and dishonourably in slavery to insulting and cruel men; it is not to be expressed what an act of courage, magnanimity, or justice to the public, or of love for honour and bravery, that was. So what methinks the philosophers did not ill define love to be the provision of the gods for the care and preservation of the young; for the love of Ariadne, above all, seems to have been the proper work and design of some god in order to preserve Theseus; and, indeed, we ought not to blame her for loving him, but rather wonder all men and women were not alike affected towards him; and if she alone were so, truly I dare pronounce her worthy of the love of a god, who was herself so great a lover of virtue and goodness, and the bravest man.

Both Theseus and Romulus were by nature meant for governors; yet neither lived up to the true character of a king, but fell off, and ran, the one into popularity, the other into tyranny, falling both into the same fault out of different passions. For a ruler's first aim is to maintain his office, which is done no less by avoiding what is unfit than by observing what is suitable. Whoever is either too remiss or too strict is no more a king or a governor, but either a demagogue or a despot, and so becomes either odious or contemptible to his subjects. Though certainly the one seems to be the fault of easiness and good-nature, the other of pride and severity.

If men's calamities, again, are not to be wholly imputed to fortune, but refer themselves to differences of character, who will acquit either Theseus of rash and unreasonable anger against his son, or Romulus against his brother? Looking at motives, we more easily excuse the anger which a stronger cause, like a severer blow, provoked. Romulus, having disagreed with his brother advisedly and deliberately on public matters, one would think could not on a sudden have been put into so great a passion; but love and jealousy and the complaints of his wife, which few men can avoid being moved by, seduced Theseus to commit that outrage upon his son. And what is more, Romulus, in his anger, committed an action of unfortunate consequence; but that of Theseus ended only in words, some evil speaking, and an old man's curse; the rest of the youth's disasters seem to have proceeded from fortune; so that, so far, a man would give his vote on Theseus's part.

But Romulus has, first of all one great plea, that his performances proceeded from very small beginnings; for both the brothers being thought servants and the sons of swine-herds, before becoming freemen themselves, gave liberty to almost all the Latins, obtaining at once all the most honourable titles, as destroyers of their country's enemies, preservers of their friends and kindred, princes of the people, founders of cities, not removers, like Theseus, who raised and compiled only one house out of many, demolishing many cities bearing the names of ancient kings and heroes. Romulus, indeed, did the same afterwards, forcing his enemies to deface and ruin their own dwellings, and to sojourn with their conquerors; but at first, not by removal, or increase of an existing city, but by foundation of a new one, he obtained himself lands, a country, a kingdom, wives, children, and relations. And, in so doing, he killed or destroyed nobody, but benefited those that wanted houses and homes and were willing to be of a society and become citizens. Robbers and malefactors he slew not; but he subdued nations, he overthrew cities, he triumphed over kings and commanders.

As to Remus, it is doubtful by whose hand he fell; it is generally imputed to others. His mother he clearly retrieved from death, and placed his grandfather, who was brought under base and dishonourable vassalage, on the ancient throne of Æneas, to whom he did voluntarily many good offices, but never did him harm even inadvertently. But Theseus, in his forgetfulness, and neglect of the command concerning the flag, can scarcely, methinks, by any excuses, or before the most indulgent judges, avoid the imputation of parricide. And, indeed, one of the Attic writers, perceiving it to be very hard to make an excuse for this, feigns that Ægeus, at the approach of the ship, running hastily to the Acropolis to see what news, slipped and fell down, as if he had no servants, or none would attend him on his way to the shore.

And, indeed, the faults committed in the rapes of women admit of no plausible excuse in Theseus. First, because of the often repetition of the crime; for he stole Ariadne, Antiope, Anaxo the Trœzenian, at last Helen, when he was an old man, and she not marriageable; she a child, and he at an age past even lawful wedlock. Then, on account of the cause; for the Trœzenian, Lacedæmonian, and Amazonian virgins, beside that they were not betrothed to him, were not worthier to raise children by than the Athenian women, derived from Erechtheus and Cecrops; but it is to be suspected these things were done out of wantonness and lust. Romulus, when he had taken near eight hundred women, chose not all, but only Hersilia, as they say, for himself; the rest he divided among the chief of the city; and afterwards, by the respect and tenderness and justice shown towards them, he made it clear that this violence and injury was a commendable and politic exploit to establish a society; by which he intermixed and united both nations, and made it the fountain of after friendship and public stability.

And to the reverence and love and constancy he established in matrimony, time can witness, for in two hundred and thirty years, neither any husband deserted his wife, nor any wife her husband; but, as the curious among the Greeks can name the first case of parricide or matricide, so the Romans all well know that Spurius Carvilius was the first who put away his wife, accusing her of barrenness.

The immediate results were similar; for upon those marriages the two princes shared in the dominion, and both nations fell under the same government. But from the marriages of Theseus proceeded nothing of friendship or correspondence for the advantage of commerce, but enmities and wars and the slaughter of citizens, and, at last, the loss of the city Aphidnæ, when only out of the compassion of the enemy, whom they entreated and caressed like gods, they escaped suffering what Troy did by Paris. Theseus's mother, however, was not only in danger, but suffered actually what Hecuba did, deserted and neglected by her son, unless her captivity be not a fiction, as I could wish both that and other things were.

The circumstances of the divine intervention, said to have preceded or accompanied their births, are also in contrast; for Romulus was preserved by the special favour of the gods; but the oracle given to Ægeus commanding him to abstain, seems to demonstrate that the birth of Theseus was not agreeable to the will of the gods.

LYCURGUS

LEGENDARY, 9TH CENTURY B.C.

THERE is so much uncertainty in the accounts which historians have left us of Lycurgus, the lawgiver of Sparta, that scarcely anything is asserted by one of them which is not called into question or contradicted by the rest. Their sentiments are quite different as to the family he came of, the voyages he undertook, the place and manner of his death, but most of all when they speak of the laws he made and the commonwealth which he founded. They cannot, by any means, be brought to an agreement as to the very age in which he lived; for some of them say that he flourished in the time of Iphitus, and that they two jointly contrived the ordinance for the cessation of arms during the solemnity of the Olympic games. Of this opinion was Aristotle; and for confirmation of it, he alleges an inscription upon one of the copper quoits used in those sports, upon which the name of Lycurgus continued uneffaced to his time. But Eratosthenes and Apollodorus and other chronologers, computing the time by the successions of the Spartan kings, pretend to demonstrate that he was much more ancient than the institution of the Olympic games. Timæus conjectures that there were two of this name, and in diverse times, but that the one of them being much more famous than the other, men gave to him the glory of the exploits of both; the elder of the two, according to him, was not long after Homer; and some are so particular as to say that he had seen him. But that he was of great antiquity may be gathered from a passage in Xenophon, where he makes him contemporary with the Heraclidæ. By descent, indeed, the very last kings of Sparta were Heraclidæ too; but he seems in that place to speak of the first and more immediate successors of Hercules. But notwithstanding this confusion and obscurity, we shall endeavour to compose the history of his life, adhering to those statements which are least contradicted, and depending upon those authors who are most worthy of credit.

The poet Simonides will have it that Lycurgus was the son of Prytanis, and not of Eunomus; but in this opinion he is singular, for all the rest deduce the genealogy of them both as follows:—

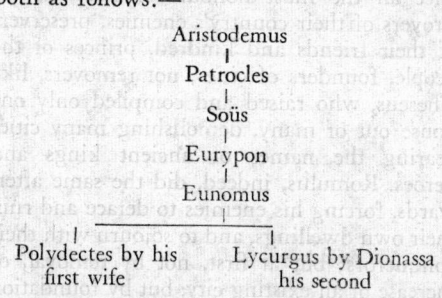

Aristodemus
|
Patrocles
|
Soüs
|
Eurypon
|
Eunomus
_____|_____
| |
Polydectes by his   Lycurgus by Dionassa
first wife   his second

Dieuchidas says he was the sixth from Patrocles and the eleventh from Hercules. Be this as it will, Soüs certainly was the most renowned of all his ancestors, under whose conduct the Spartans made slaves of the Helots, and added to their dominions, by conquest, a good part of Arcadia. There goes a story of this king Soüs, that, being besieged by the Clitorians in a dry and stony place so that he could come at no water, he was at last constrained to agree with them upon these terms, that he would restore to them all his conquests, provided that himself and all his men should drink of the nearest spring. After the usual oaths and ratifications, he called his soldiers together, and offered to him that would forbear drinking his kingdom for a reward; and when not a man of them was able to forbear, in short, when they had all drunk their fill, at last comes King Soüs himself to the spring, and, having sprinkled his face only, wihout swallowing one drop, marches off in the face of his enemies, refusing to yield up his conquests, because himself and all his men had not, according to the articles, drunk of their water.

Although he was justly had in admiration on this account, yet his family was not surnamed from him, but from his son Eurypon (of whom they were called Eurypontids); the reason of which was that Eurypon relaxed the rigour of the monarchy, seeking favour and popularity with the many. They, after this first step, grew bolder; and the succeeding kings partly incurred hatred with their people by trying to use force, or, for popularity's sake and through weakness, gave way; and anarchy and confusion long prevailed in Sparta, causing, moreover, the death of the father of Lycurgus. For as he was endeavouring to quell a riot, he was stabbed with a butcher's knife, and left the title of king to his eldest son, Polydectes.

He, too, dying soon after, the right of succession (as every one thought) rested in Lycurgus; and reign he did, until it was found that the queen, his sister-in-law, was with child; upon which he immediately declared that the kingdom belonged to her issue, provided it were male, and that he himself exercised the regal jurisdiction only as his guardian; the Spartan name for which office is *prodicus*. Soon after, an overture was made to him by the queen, that she would herself in some way destroy the infant, upon condition that he would marry her when he came to the crown. Abhorring the woman's wickedness, he nevertheless did not reject her proposal, but, making show of closing with her, despatched the messenger with thanks and expressions of joy, but dissuaded her earnestly from procuring herself to miscarry, which would impair her health, if not endanger her life; he himself, he said, would see to it, that the child, as soon as born, should be taken out of the way.

By such artifices having drawn on the woman to the time of her lying-in, as soon as he heard that she was in labour, he sent persons to be by and observe all that passed, with orders that if it were a girl they should deliver it to the women, but if a boy, should bring it to him wheresoever he were, and whatsoever doing. It so fell out that when he was at supper with the principal magistrates the queen was brought to bed of a boy, who was soon after presented to him as he was at the table; he, taking him into his arms, said to those about him, "Men of Sparta, here is a king born unto us"; this said, he laid him down in the king's place, and named him Charilaus, that is, the joy of the people; because that all were transported with joy and with wonder at his noble and just spirit.

His reign had lasted only eight months, but he was honoured on other accounts by the citizens, and there were more who obeyed him because of his eminent virtues, than because he was regent to the king and had the royal power in his hands. Some, however, envied and sought to impede his growing influence while he was still young; chiefly the kindred and friends of the queen-mother, who pretended to have been dealt with injuriously. Her brother Leonidas, in a warm debate which fell out betwixt him and Lycurgus, went so far as to tell him to his face that he was well assured that ere long he should see him king; suggesting suspicions and preparing the way for an accusation of him, as though he had made away with his nephew, if the child should chance to fail, though by a natural death. Words of the like import were designedly cast abroad by the queen-mother and her adherents.

Troubled at this, and not knowing what it might come to, he thought it his wisest course to avoid their envy by a voluntary exile, and to travel from place to place until his nephew came to marriageable years, and, by having a son, had secured the succession; setting sail, therefore, with this resolution, he first arrived at Crete, where, having considered their several forms of government, and got an acquaintance with the principal men among them, some of their laws he very much approved of, and resolved to make use of them in his own country; a good part he rejected as useless. Among the persons there the most renowned for their learning and their wisdom in state matters was one Thales, whom Lycurgus, by importunities and assurances of friendship, persuaded to go over to Lacedæmon; where, though by his outward appearance and his own profession he seemed to be no other than a lyric poet, in reality he performed the part of one of the ablest lawgivers in the world. The very songs which he composed were exhortations to obedience and concord, and the very measure and cadence of the verse, conveying impressions of order and tranquillity, had so great an influence on the minds of the listeners, that they were insensibly softened and civilised, insomuch that they renounced their private feuds and animosities, and were reunited in a common admiration of virtue. So that it may truly be said that Thales prepared the way for the discipline introduced by Lycurgus.

From Crete he sailed to Asia, with design, as is said, to examine the difference betwixt the manners and rules of life of the Cretans, which were very sober and temperate, and those of the Ionians, a people of sumptuous and delicate habits, and so to form a judgment; just as physicians do by comparing healthy and diseased bodies. Here he had the first sight of Homer's works, in the hands, we may suppose, of the posterity of Creophylus; and, having observed that the few loose expressions and actions of ill example which are to be found in his poems were much outweighed by serious lessons of state and rules of morality, he set himself eagerly to transcribe and digest them into order, as thinking they would be of good use in his own country. They had, indeed, already obtained some slight repute among the Greeks, and scattered portions, as chance conveyed them, were in the hands of individuals; but Lycurgus first made them really known.

The Egyptians say that he took a voyage into Egypt, and that, being much taken with their way of separating the soldiery from the rest of the nation, he transferred it from them to Sparta, a removal from contact with those employed in low and mechanical occupations giving high refinement and beauty to the state. Some Greek writers also record this. But as for his voyages into Spain, Africa and the Indies, and his conferences there with the Gymnosophists, the whole relation, as far as I can find, rests on the single credit of the Spartan Aristocrates, the son of Hipparchus.

Lycurgus was much missed at Sparta, and often sent for, "for kings indeed we have," they said, "who wear the marks and assume the titles of royalty, but as for the qualities of their minds, they have nothing by which they are to be distinguished from their subjects"; adding, that in him alone was the true foundation of sovereignty to be seen, a nature made to rule, and a genius to gain obedience. Nor were the kings themselves averse to see him back, for they looked upon his presence as a bulwark against the insolence of the people.

Things being in this posture at his return, he applied himself, without loss of time, to a thorough reformation, and resolved to change the whole face of the commonwealth; for what could a few particular laws and a partial alteration avail? He must act as wise physicians do, in the case of one who labours under a complication of diseases, by force of medicines reduce and exhaust him, change his whole temperament, and then set him upon a totally new regimen of diet.

Having thus projected things, away he goes to Delphi to consult Apollo there; which having done, and offered his sacrifice, he returned with that renowned oracle, in which he is called beloved of God, and rather God than man; that his prayers were heard, that his laws should be the best, and the commonwealth which observed them the most famous in the world. Encouraged by these things he set himself to bring over to his side the leading men of Sparta, exhorting them to give him a helping hand in his great undertaking; he broke it first to his particular friends, and then by degrees gained others, and animated them all to put his design in execution.

When things were ripe for action, he gave orders to thirty of the principal men of Sparta to be ready armed at the market-place by break of day, to the end that he might strike a terror into the opposite party. Hermippus hath set down the names of twenty of the most eminent of them; but the name of him whom Lycurgus most confided in, and who was of most use to him, both in making his laws and putting them in execution was Arthmiadas. Things growing to a tumult, King Charilaus, apprehending that it was a conspiracy against his person, took sanctuary in the temple of Minerva of the Brazen House; but, being soon after undeceived, and having taken an oath of them that they had no designs against him, he quitted his refuge, and himself also entered into the confederacy with them; of so gentle and flexible a disposition he was, to which Archelaus, his brother-king, alluded, when, hearing him extolled for his goodness, he said, "Who can say he is anything but good? He is so even to the bad."

Amongst the many changes and alterations which Lycurgus made, the first and of greatest importance was the establishment of the senate, which having a power equal to the king's in matters of great consequence, and, as Plato expresses it, allaying and qualifying the fiery genius of the royal office, gave steadiness and safety to the commonwealth. For the state, which before had no firm basis to stand upon, but leaned one while towards an absolute monarchy, when the kings had the upper hand, and another while towards a pure democracy, when the people had the better, found in this establishment of the senate a central weight, like ballast in a ship, which always kept things in a just equilibrium; the twenty-eight always adhering to the kings so far as to resist democracy, and on the other hand, supporting the people against the establishment of absolute monarchy.

As for the determinate number of twenty-eight, Aristotle states, that it so fell out because two of the original associates, for want of courage, fell off from the enterprise; but Sphærus assures us that there were but twenty-eight of the confederates at first; perhaps there is some mystery in the number, which consists of seven multiplied by four, and is the first of perfect numbers after six, being, as that is, equal to all its parts. For my part, I believe Lycurgus fixed upon the number of twenty-eight, that, the two kings being reckoned amongst them, they might be thirty in all. So eagerly set was he upon this establishment, that he took the trouble to obtain an oracle about it from Delphi, the Rhetra, which runs thus: "After that you have built a temple to Jupiter Helianius, and to Minerva Hellania, and after that you have *phyle'd* the people into *phyles,* and *obe'd* them into *obes,* you shall establish a council of thirty elders, the leaders included, and shall, from time to time, *apellazein* the people betwixt Babyca and Cnacion, there propound and put to the vote. The commons have the final voice and decision." By *phyles* and *obes* are meant the divisions of the people; by the *leaders,* the two kings; *apellazein,* referring to the Pythian Apollo, signifies to assemble; Babyca and Cnacion they now call Œnus; Aristotle says Cnacion is a river, and Babyca a bridge.

Betwixt this Babyca and Cnacion, their assemblies were held, for they had no council-house or building to meet in. Lycurgus was of opinion that ornaments were so far from advantaging them in their counsels, that they were rather an hindrance, by diverting their attention from the business before them to statues and pictures, and roofs curiously fretted, the usual embellishments of such places amongst the other Greeks.

The people then being thus assembled in the open air, it was not allowed to any one of their order to give his advice, but only either to ratify or reject what should be propounded to them by the king or senate. But because it fell out afterwards that the people, by adding or omitting words, distorted and perverted the sense of propositions, Kings Polydorus and Theopompus inserted into the Rhetra, or grand covenant, the following clause: "That if the people decide crookedly it should be lawful for the elders and leaders to dissolve"; that is to say, refuse ratification, and dismiss the people as depravers and per-

verters of their counsel. It passed among the people, by their management, as being equally authentic with the rest of the Rhetra, as appears by these verses of Tyrtæus,—

These oracles they from Apollo heard,
And brought from Pytho home the perfect word:
The heaven-appointed kings, who love the land,
Shall foremost in the nation's council stand;
The elders next to them; the commons last;
Let a straight Rhetra *among all be passed.*

Although Lycurgus had, in this manner, used all the qualifications possible in the constitution of his commonwealth, yet those who succeeded him found the oligarchical element still too strong and dominant, and to check its high temper and its violence, put, as Plato says, a bit in its mouth, which was the power of the ephori, established an hundred and thirty years after the death of Lycurgus. Elatus and his colleagues were the first who had this dignity conferred upon them in the reign of King Theopompus, who, when his queen upbraided him one day that he would leave the regal power to his children less than he had received it from his ancestors, said in answer, "No, greater; for it will last longer." For, indeed, their prerogative being thus reduced within reasonable bounds, the Spartan kings were at once freed from all further jealousies and consequent danger, and never experienced the calamities of their neighbours at Messene and Argos, who, by maintaining their prerogative too strictly, for want of yielding a little to the populace, lost it all.

Indeed, whosoever shall look at the sedition and misgovernment which befell these bordering nations to whom they were as near related in blood as situation, will find in them the best reason to admire the wisdom and foresight of Lycurgus. For these three states, in their first rise, were equal, or, if there were any odds, they lay on the side of the Messenians and Argives, who, in the first allotment, were thought to have been luckier than the Spartans; yet was their happiness of but small continuance, partly the tyrannical temper of their kings and partly the ungovernableness of the people quickly bringing upon them such disorders, and so complete an overthrow of all existing institutions, as clearly to show how truly divine a blessing the Spartans had had in that wise lawgiver who gave their government its happy balance and temper. But of this I shall say more in its due place.

After the creation of the thirty senators, his next task, and, indeed, the most hazardous he ever undertook, was the making a new division of their lands. For there was an extreme inequality amongst them, and their state was overloaded with a multitude of indigent and necessitous persons, while its whole wealth had centred upon a very few. To the end, therefore, that he might expel from the state arrogance and envy, luxury and crime, and those yet more inveterate diseases of want and superfluity, he obtained of them to renounce their properties, and to consent to a new division of the land, and that they should live all together on an equal footing; merit to be their only road to eminence, and the disgrace of evil, and credit of worthy acts, their one measure of difference between man and man.

Upon their consent to these proposals, proceeding at once to put them into execution, he divided the country of Laconia in general into thirty thousand equal shares, and the part attached to the city of Sparta into nine thousand; these he distributed among the Spartans, as he did the others to the country citizens. Some authors say that he made but six thousand lots for the citizens of Sparta, and that King Polydorus added three thousand more. Others say that Polydorus doubled the number Lycurgus had made, which, according to them, was but four thousand five hundred. A lot was so much as to yield, one year with another, about seventy bushels of grain for the master of the family, and twelve for his wife, with a suitable proportion of oil and wine. And this he thought sufficient to keep their bodies in good health and strength; superfluities they were better without. It is reported, that, as he returned from a journey shortly after the division of the lands, in harvest time, the ground being newly reaped, seeing the stacks all standing equal and alike, he smiled, and said to those about him, "Methinks all Laconia looks like one family estate just divided among a number of brothers."

Not contented with this, he resolved to make a division of their movables too, that there might be no odious distinction or inequality left amongst them; but finding that it would be very dangerous to go about it openly, he took another course, and defeated their avarice by the following stratagem: he commanded that all gold and silver coin should be called in, and that only a sort of money made of iron should be current, a great weight and quantity of which was very little worth; so that to lay up twenty or thirty pounds there was required a pretty large closet, and, to remove it, nothing less than a yoke of oxen. With the diffusion of this money, at once a number of vices were banished from Lacedæmon; for who would rob another of such a coin? Who would unjustly detain or take by force, or accept as a bribe, a thing which it was not easy to hide, nor a credit to have, nor indeed of any use to cut in pieces? For when it was just red hot, they quenched it in vinegar, and by that means spoilt it, and made it almost incapable of being worked.

In the next place, he declared an outlawry of all needless and superfluous arts; but here he might almost have spared his proclamation; for they of themselves would have gone after the gold and silver, the money which remained being not so proper payment for curious work; for, being of iron, it was scarcely portable, neither, if they should take the means to export it, would it pass amongst the other Greeks, who ridiculed it. So there was now no more means of purchasing foreign goods and small wares; merchants sent no shiploads into Laconian ports; no rhetoric-master, no itinerant fortune-teller, no harlot-monger, or gold or silversmith, engraver, or jeweller, set foot in a country which had no money; so that luxury, deprived little by little of that which fed and fomented it, wasted to nothing and died away of itself. For the rich had no advantage here over the poor, as their wealth and abundance had no road to come abroad by but were shut up at home doing nothing. And in this way they became excellent artists in common, necessary things; bedsteads, chairs, and tables, and such like staple utensils in a family, were admirably well made there; their cup, particularly, was very much in fashion, and eagerly bought up by soldiers, as Critias reports; for its colour was such as to prevent water, drunk upon necessity and disagreeable to look at, from being noticed; and the shape of it was such that the mud stuck to the sides, so that only the purer part came to the drinker's mouth. For this, also, they had to thank their lawgiver, who, by relieving the artisans of the trouble of making useless things, set them to show their skill in giving beauty to those of daily and indispensable use.

The third and most masterly stroke of this great lawgiver, by which he struck a yet more effectual blow against luxury and the desire of riches, was the ordinance, he made, that they should all eat in common, of the same bread and same meat, and of kinds that were specified, and should not spend their lives at home, laid on costly couches at splendid tables, delivering themselves up into the hands of their tradesmen and cooks, to fatten them in corners, like greedy brutes, and to ruin not their minds only but their very bodies which, enfeebled by indulgence and excess, would stand in need of long sleep, warm bathing, freedom from work, and, in a word, of as much care and attendance as if they were continually sick.

It was certainly an extraordinary thing to have brought about such a result as this, but a greater yet to have taken away from wealth, as Theophrastus observes, not merely the property of being coveted, but its very nature of being wealth. For the rich, being obliged to go to the same table with the poor, could not make use of or enjoy their abundance, nor so much as please their vanity by looking at or displaying it. So that the common proverb, that Plutus, the god of riches, is blind, was nowhere in all the world literally verified but in Sparta. There, indeed, he was not only blind, but like a picture, without either life or motion. Nor were they allowed to take food at home first, and then attend the public tables, for every one had an eye upon those who did not eat and drink like the rest, and reproached them with being dainty and effeminate.

This last ordinance in particular exasperated the wealthier men. They collected in a body against Lycurgus, and from ill words came to throwing stones, so that at length he was forced to run out of the market-place, and make to sanctuary to save his life; by good-hap he outran all, excepting one Alcander, a young man otherwise not ill accomplished, but hasty and violent, who came up so close to him, that when he turned to see who was so near him, he struck him upon the face with his stick, and put out one of his eyes. Lycurgus, so far from being daunted and discouraged by this accident, stopped short and showed his disfigured face and eye beat out to his countrymen; they, dismayed and ashamed at the sight, delivered Alcander into his hands to be punished, and escorted him home, with expressions of great concern for his ill-usage. Lycurgus, having thanked them for their care of his person, dismissed them all, excepting only Alcander; and, taking him with him into his house, neither did nor said anything severely to him, but, dismissing those whose place it was, bade Alcander to wait upon him at table. The young man, who was of an ingenuous temper, without murmuring did as he was commanded; and being thus admitted to live with Lycurgus, he had an opportunity to observe in him, besides his gentleness and calmness of temper, an extraordinary sobriety and an indefatigable industry, and so, from an enemy, became one of his most zealous admirers, and told his friends and relations that Lycurgus was not that morose and ill-natured man they had formerly taken him for, but the one mild and gentle character of the world. And thus did Lycurgus, for chastisement of his fault, make of a wild and passionate young man one of the discreetest citizens of Sparta.

In memory of this accident, Lycurgus built a temple to Minerva, surnamed Optilĕtis; optilus being the Doric of these parts for ophthalmus, the eye. Some authors, however, of whom Dioscorides is one (who wrote a treatise on the commonwealth of Sparta), say that he was wounded, indeed, but did not lose his eye with the blow; and that he built the temple in gratitude for the cure. Be this as it will, certain it is, that, after this misadventure, the Lacedæmonians made it a rule never to carry so much as a staff into their public assemblies.

But to return to their public repasts;— these had several names in Greek; the Cretans called them andria, because the men only came to them. The Lacedæmonians called them phiditia, that is, by changing l into d, the same as philitia, love feasts, because that, by eating and drinking together, they had opportunity of making friends. Or perhaps from phido, parsimony, because they were so many schools of sobriety; or perhaps the first letter is an addition, and the word at first was editia, from edode, eating. They met by companies of fifteen, more or less, and each of them stood bound to bring in monthly a bushel of meal, eight gallons of wine, five pounds of cheese, two pounds and a half of figs, and some very small sum of money to buy flesh or fish with. Besides this, when any of them made sacrifice to the gods, they always sent a dole to the common hall; and, likewise, when any of them had been a hunting, he sent thither a part of the venison he had killed; for these two occasions were the only excuses allowed for supping at home. The custom of eating together was observed strictly for a great while afterwards; insomuch that

King Agis himself, after having vanquished the Athenians, sending for his commons at his return home, because he desired to eat privately with his queen, was refused them by the polemarchs; which refusal when he resented so much as to omit next day the sacrifice due for a war happily ended, they made him pay a fine.

They used to send their children to these tables as to schools of temperance; here they were instructed in state affairs by listening to experienced statesmen; here they learned to converse with pleasantry, to make jests without scurrility and take them without ill humour. In this point of good breeding, the Lacedæmonians excelled particularly, but if any man were uneasy under it, upon the least hint given, there was no more to be said to him. It was customary also for the eldest man in the company to say to each of them, as they came in, "Through this" (pointing to the door), "no words go out."

When any one had a desire to be admitted into any of these little societies, he was to go through the following probation: each man in the company took a little ball of soft bread, which they were to throw into a deep basin, which a waiter carried round upon his head; those that liked the person to be chosen dropped their ball into the basin without altering its figure, and those who disliked him pressed it betwixt their fingers, and made it flat; and this signified as much as a negative voice. And if there were but one of these flattened pieces in the basin, the suitor was rejected, so desirous were they that all the members of the company should be agreeable to each other. The basin was called *caddichus,* and the rejected candidate had a name thence derived. Their most famous dish was the black broth, which was so much valued that the elderly men fed only upon that, leaving what flesh there was to the younger.

They say that a certain king of Pontus, having heard much of this black broth of theirs, sent for a Lacedæmonian cook on purpose to make him some, but had no sooner tasted it than he found it extremely bad, which the cook observing, told him, "Sir, to make this broth relish, you should have bathed yourself first in the river Eurotas."

After drinking moderately, every man went to his home without lights, for the use of them was, on all occasions, forbid, to the end that they might accustom themselves to march boldly in the dark. Such was the common fashion of their meals.

Lycurgus would never reduce his laws into writing; nay there is a Rhetra expressly to forbid it. For he thought that the most material points, and such as most directly tended to the public welfare, being imprinted on the hearts of their youth by a good discipline, would be sure to remain, and would find a stronger security, than any compulsion would be, in the principles of action formed in them by their best lawgiver, education. And as for things of lesser importance, as pecuniary contracts, and such like, the forms of which have to be changed as occasion requires, he thought it the best way to prescribe no positive rule or inviolable usage in such cases, willing that their manner and form should be altered according to the circumstances of time, and determinations of men of sound judgment. Every end and object of law and enactment it was his design education should effect.

One, then, of the Rhetras was, that their laws should not be written; another is particularly levelled against luxury and expensiveness, for by it it was ordained that the ceilings of their houses should only be wrought by the axe, and their gates and doors smoothed only by the saw. Epaminondas's famous dictum about his own table, that "Treason and a dinner like this do not keep company together," may be said to have been anticipated by Lycurgus. Luxury and a house of this kind could not well be companions. For a man might have a less than ordinary share of sense that would furnish such plain and common rooms with silver-footed couches and purple coverlets and gold and silver plate. Doubtless he had good reason to think that they would proportion their beds to their houses, and their coverlets to their beds, and the rest of their goods and furniture to these. It is reported that king Leotychides, the first of that name, was so little used to the sight of any other kind of work, that, being entertained at Corinth in a stately room, he was much surprised to see the timber and ceiling so finely carved and panelled, and asked his host whether the trees grew so in his country.

A third ordinance or Rhetra was, that they should not make war often, or long, with the same enemy, lest that they should train and instruct them in war, by habituating them to defend themselves. And this is what Agesilaus was much blamed for, a long time after; it being thought, that, by his continual incursions into Bœotia, he made the Thebans a match for the Lacedæmonians; and therefore Antalcidas, seeing him wounded one day, said to him, that he was very well paid for taking such pains to make the Thebans good soldiers, whether they would or no. These laws were called the Rhetras, to intimate that they were divine sanctions and revelations.

In order to the good education of their youth (which, as I said before, he thought the most important and noblest work of a lawgiver), he went so far back as to take into consideration their very conception and birth, by regulating their marriages. For Aristotle is wrong in saying, that, after he had tried all ways to reduce the women to more modesty and sobriety, he was at last forced to leave them as they were, because that in the absence of their husbands, who spent the best part of their lives in the wars, their wives, whom they were obliged to leave absolute mistresses at home, took great liberties and assumed the superiority; and were treated with overmuch respect and called by the title of lady or queen. The truth is, he took in their case, also, all the care that was possible; he ordered the maidens to exercise themselves with wrestling, running, throwing the quoit, and casting the dart, to the end that the fruit they conceived might, in strong and healthy bodies, take firmer root and find better growth, and withal that they, with this greater vigour, might be the more able to undergo the pains of child-bearing.

And to the end he might take away their overgreat tenderness and fear of exposure to the air, and all acquired womanishness, he ordered that the young women should go naked in the processions, as well as the young men, and dance, too, in that condition, at certain solemn feasts, singing certain songs, whilst the young men stood around, seeing and hearing them. On these occasions they now and then made, by jests, a befitting reflection upon those who had misbehaved themselves in the wars; and again sang encomiums upon those who had done any gallant action, and by these means inspired the younger sort with an emulation of their glory. Those that were thus commended went away proud, elated, and gratified with their honour among the maidens; and those who were rallied were as sensibly touched with it as if they had been formally reprimanded; and so much the more, because the kings and the elders, as well as the rest of the city, saw and heard all that passed. Nor was there anything shameful in this nakedness of the young women; modesty attended them,

and all wantonness was excluded. It taught them simplicity and a care for good health, and gave them some taste of higher feelings, admitted as they thus were to the field of noble action and glory. Hence it was natural for them to think and speak as Gorgo, for example, the wife of Leonidas, is said to have done, when some foreign lady, as it would seem, told her that the women of Lacedæmon were the only women in the world who could rule men; "With good reason," she said, "for we are the only women who bring forth men."

These public processions of the maidens, and their appearing naked in their exercises and dancings, were incitements to marriage, operating upon the young with the rigour and certainty, as Plato says, of love, if not of mathematics. But besides all this, to promote it yet more effectually, those who continued bachelors were in a degree disfranchised by law; for they were excluded from the sight of those public processions in which the young men and maidens danced naked, and, in winter-time, the officers compelled them to march naked themselves round the market-place, singing as they went a certain song to their own disgrace, that they justly suffered this punishment for disobeying the laws. Moreover, they were denied that respect and observance which the younger men paid their elders; and no man, for example, found fault with what was said to Dercyllidas, though so eminent a commander; upon whose approach one day, a young man, instead of rising, retained his seat, remarking, "No child of yours will make room for me."

In their marriages, the husband carried off his bride by a sort of force; nor were their brides ever small and of tender years, but in their full bloom and ripeness. After this, she who superintended the wedding comes and clips the hair of the bride close round her head, dresses her up in man's clothes, and leaves her upon a mattress in the dark; afterwards comes the bridegroom, in his everyday clothes, sober and composed, as having supped at the common table, and, entering privately into the room where the bride lies, unties her virgin zone, and takes her to himself; and, after staying some time together, he returns composedly to his own apartment, to sleep as usual with the other young men.

And so he continues to do, spending his days, and, indeed, his nights, with them, visiting his bride in fear and shame, and with circumspection, when he thought he should not be observed; she, also, on her part, using her wit to help and find favourable opportunities for their meeting, when company was out of the way. In this manner they lived a long time, insomuch that they sometimes had children by their wives before ever they saw their faces by daylight. Their interviews, being thus difficult and rare, served not only for continual exercise of their self-control, but brought them together with their bodies healthy and vigorous, and their affections fresh and lively, unsated and undulled by easy access and long continuance with each other; while their partings were always early enough to leave behind unextinguished in each of them some remaining fire of longing and mutual delight.

After guarding marriage with this modesty and reserve, he was equally careful to banish empty and womanish jealousy. For this object, excluding all licentious disorders, he made it, nevertheless, honourable for men to give the use of their wives to those whom they should think fit, that so they might have children by them; ridiculing those in whose opinion such favours are so unfit for participation as to fight and shed blood and go to war about it. Lycurgus allowed a man who was advanced in years and had a young wife to recommend some virtuous and approved young man, that she might have a child by him, who might inherit the good qualities of the father, and be a son to himself.

On the other side, an honest man who had love for a married woman upon account of her modesty and the well-favouredness of her children, might, without formality, beg her company of her husband, that he might raise, as it were, from this plot of good ground, worthy and well-allied children for himself. And indeed, Lycurgus was of a persuasion that children were not so much the property of their parents as of the whole commonwealth, and, therefore, would not have his citizens begot by the first-comers, but by the best men that could be found; the laws of other nations seemed to him very absurd and inconsistent, where people would be so solicitous for their dogs and horses as to exert interest and to pay money to procure fine breeding, and yet kept their wives shut up, to be made mothers only by themselves, who might be foolish, infirm, or diseased; as if it were not apparent that children of a bad breed would prove their bad qualities first upon those who kept and were rearing them, and well-born children, in like manner, their good qualities.

These regulations, founded on natural and social grounds, were certainly so far from that scandalous liberty which was afterwards charged upon their women, that they knew not what adultery meant. It is told, for instance, of Geradas, a very ancient Spartan, that, being asked by a stranger what punishment their law had appointed for adulterers, he answered, "There are no adulterers in our country." "But," replied the stranger, "suppose there were?" "Then," answered he, "the offender would have to give the plaintiff a bull with a neck so long as that he might drink from the top of Taygetus of the Eurotas river below it." The man, surprised at this, said, "Why, 'tis impossible to find such a bull." Geradas smilingly replied, " 'Tis as possible as to find an adulterer in Sparta." So much I had to say of their marriages.

Nor was it in the power of the father to dispose of the child as he thought fit; he was obliged to carry it before certain triers at a place called Lesche; these were some of the elders of the tribe to which the child belonged; their business it was carefully to view the infant, and, if they found it stout and well made, they gave order for its rearing, and allotted to it one of the nine thousand shares of land above mentioned for its maintenance, but, if they found it puny and ill-shaped, ordered it to be taken to what was called the Apothetæ, a sort of chasm under Taygetus; as thinking it neither for the good of the child itself, nor for the public interest, that it should be brought up, if it did not, from the very outset, appear made to be healthy and vigorous.

Upon the same account, the women did not bathe the new-born children with water, as is the custom in all other countries, but with wine, to prove the temper and complexion of their bodies; from a notion they had that epileptic and weakly children faint and waste away upon their being thus bathed, while, on the contrary, those of a strong and vigorous habit acquire firmness and get a temper by it, like steel.

There was much care and art, too, used by the nurses; they had no swaddling bands; the children grew up free and unconstrained in limb and form, and not dainty and fanciful about their food; not afraid in the dark, or of being left alone; and without peevishness, or ill-humour, or crying. Upon this account, Spartan nurses were often bought up, or hired by people of other countries; and it is recorded that she who suckled Alcibiades was a Spartan; who, however, if fortunate in his nurse, was not so in his preceptor; his guardian, Pericles, as Plato tells us, chose a servant for that office called Zopyrus, no better than any common slave.

Lycurgus was of another mind; he would not have masters bought out of the market for his young Spartans, nor such as should sell their pains; nor was it lawful, indeed, for the father himself to breed up the children after his own fancy; but as soon as they were seven years old they were to be enrolled in certain companies and classes, where they all lived under the same order and discipline, doing their exercises and taking their play together. Of these, he who showed the most conduct and courage was made captain; they had their eyes always upon him, obeyed his orders, and underwent patiently whatsoever punishment he inflicted; so that the whole course of their education was one continued exercise of a ready and perfect obedience. The old men, too, were spectators of their performances, and often raised quarrels and disputes among them, to have a good opportunity of finding out their different characters, and of seeing which would be valiant, which a coward, when they should come to more dangerous encounters. Reading and writing they gave them, just enough to serve their turn; their chief care was to make them good subjects, and to teach them to endure pain and conquer in battle. To this end, as they grew in years, their discipline was proportionately increased; their heads were close-clipped, they were accustomed to go barefoot, and for the most part to play naked.

After they were twelve years old, they were no longer allowed to wear any undergarment; they had one coat to serve them a year; their bodies were hard and dry, with but little acquaintance of baths and unguents; these human indulgences they were allowed only on some few particular days in the year. They lodged together in little bands upon beds made of the rushes which grew by the banks of the river Eurotas, which they were to break off with their hands without a knife; if it were winter, they mingled some thistle-down with their rushes, which it was thought had the property of giving warmth. By the time they were come to this age there was not any of the more hopeful boys who had not a lover to bear him company. The old men, too, had an eye upon them, coming often to the grounds to hear and see them contend either in wit or strength with one another, and this as seriously and with as much concern as if they were their fathers, their tutors, or their magistrates; so that there scarcely was any time or place without some one present to put them in mind of their duty, and punish them if they had neglected it.

Besides all this, there was always one of the best and honestest men in the city appointed to undertake the charge and governance of them; he again arranged them into their several bands, and set over each of them for their captain the most temperate and boldest of those they called Irens, who were usually twenty years old, two years out of the boys; and the oldest of the boys, again, were Mell-Irens, as much as to say, who would shortly be men. This young man, therefore, was their captain when they fought and their master at home, using them for the offices of his house; sending the eldest of them to fetch wood, and the weaker and less able to gather salads and herbs, and these they must either go without or steal; which they did by creeping into the gardens, or conveying themselves cunningly and closely into the eating-houses; if they were taken in the act, they were whipped without mercy, for thieving so ill and awkwardly. They stole, too, all other meat they could lay their hands on, looking out and watching all opportunities, when people were asleep or more careless than usual. If they were caught, they were not only punished with whipping, but hunger, too, being reduced to their ordinary allowance, which was but very slender, and so contrived on purpose, that they might set about to help themselves, and be forced to exercise their energy and address.

This was the principal design of their hard fare; there was another not inconsiderable, that they might grow taller; for the vital spirits, not being overburdened and oppressed by too great a quantity of nourishment; which necessarily discharges itself into thickness and breadth, do, by their natural lightness, rise; and the body, giving and yielding because it is pliant, grows in height. The same thing seems, also, to conduce to beauty of shape; a dry and lean habit is a better subject for nature's configuration, which the gross and over-fed are too heavy to submit to properly. Just as we find that women who take physic whilst they are with child, bear leaner and smaller but better-shaped and prettier children; the material they come of having been more pliable and easily moulded. The reason, however, I leave others to determine.

To return from whence we have digressed. So seriously did the Lacedæmonian children go about their stealing, that a youth, having stolen a young fox and hid it under his coat, suffered it to tear out his very bowels with its teeth and claws and died upon the place, rather than let it be seen. What is practised to this very day in Lacedæmon is enough to gain credit to this story, for I myself have seen several of the youths endure whipping to death at the foot of the altar of Diana surnamed Orthia.

The Iren, or under-master, used to stay a little with them after supper, and one of them he bade to sing a song, to another he put a question which required an advised and deliberate answer; for example, Who was the best man in the city? What he thought of such an action of such a man? They used them thus early to pass a right judgment upon persons and things, and to inform themselves of the abilities or defects of their countrymen. If they had not an answer ready to the question, Who was a good or who an ill-reputed citizen, they were looked upon as of a dull and careless disposition, and to have little or no sense of virtue and honour; besides this, they were to give a good reason for what they said, and in as few words and as comprehensive as might be; he that failed of this, or answered not to the purpose, had his thumb bit by the master. Sometimes the Iren did this in the presence of the old men and magistrates, that they might see whether he punished them justly and in due measure or not, and when he did amiss, they would not reprove him before the boys, but, when they were gone, he was called to an account and underwent correction, if he had run far into either of the extremes of indulgence or severity.

Their lovers and favourers, too, had a share in the young boy's honour or disgrace; and there goes a story that one of them was fined by the magistrate, because the lad whom he loved cried out effeminately as he was fighting. And though this sort of love was so approved among them, that the most virtuous matrons would make professions of it to young girls, yet rivalry did not exist, and if several men's fancies met in one person, it was rather the beginning of an intimate friendship, whilst they all jointly conspired to render the object of their affection as accomplished as possible.

They taught them, also, to speak with a natural and graceful raillery, and to comprehend much matter of thought in few words. For Lycurgus, who ordered, as we saw, that a great piece of money should be but of an inconsiderable value, on the contrary would allow no discourse to be current which did not contain in few words a great deal of useful and curious sense; children in Sparta, by a habit of long silence, came to give just and sententious answers; for, indeed, as loose and incontinent livers are seldom fathers of many children, so loose and incontinent talkers seldom originate many sensible words. King Agis, when some Athenian laughed at their short swords, and said that the jugglers on the stage swallowed them with ease, answered him, "We find them long enough to reach our enemies with"; and as their swords were short and sharp, so, it seems to me, were their sayings. They reach the point and arrest the attention of the hearers better than any.

Lycurgus himself seems to have been short and sententious, if we may trust the anecdotes of him; as appears by his answer to one who by all means would set up a democracy in Lacedæmon. "Begin, friend," said he, "and set it up in your family." Another asked him why he allowed of such mean and trivial sacrifices to the gods. He replied, "That we may always have something to offer to them." Being asked what sort of martial exercises or combats he approved of, he answered, "All sorts, except that in which you stretch out your hands." Similar answers, addressed to his countrymen by letter, are ascribed to him; as, being consulted how they might best oppose an invasion of their enemies, he returned this answer, "By continuing poor, and not coveting each man to be greater than his fellow." Being consulted again whether it were requisite to enclose the city with a wall, he sent them word, "The city is well fortified which hath a wall of men instead of brick." But whether these letters are counterfeit or not is not easy to determine.

Of their dislike to talkativeness, the following apophthegms are evidence. King Leonidas said to one who held him in discourse upon some useful matter, but not in due time and place, "Much to the purpose, Sir, elsewhere." King Charilaus, the nephew of Lycurgus, being asked why his uncle had made so few laws, answered, "Men of few words require but few laws." When one, named Hecatæus the sophist, because that, being invited to the public table, he had not spoken one word all supper-time, Archidamidas answered in his vindication, "He who knows how to speak, knows also when."

The sharp and yet not ungraceful retorts which I mentioned may be instanced as follows. Demaratus, being asked in a troublesome manner by an importunate fellow, Who was the best man in Lacedæmon? answered at last, "He, Sir, that is the least like you." Some, in company where Agis was, much extolled the Eleans for their just and honourable management of the Olympic games; "Indeed," said Agis, "they are highly to be commended if they can do justice one day in five years." Theopompus answered a stranger who talked much of his affection to the Lacedæmonians, and said that his countrymen called him Philolacon (a lover of the Lacedæmonians), that it had been more for his honour if they had called him Philopolites (a lover of his own countrymen). And Plistoanax, the son of Pausanias, when an orator of Athens said the Lacedæmonians had no learning, told him, "You say true, Sir; we alone of all the Greeks have learned none of your bad qualities." One asked Archidamidas what number there might be of the Spartans, he answered: "Enough, Sir, to keep out wicked men."

We may see their character, too, in their very jests. For they did not throw them out at random, but the very wit of them was grounded upon something or other worth thinking about. For instance, one, being asked to go hear a man who exactly counterfeited the voice of a nightingale, answered, "Sir, I have heard the nightingale itself." Another, having read the following inscription upon a tomb—

Seeking to quench a cruel tyranny,
They, at Selinus, did in battle die,

said, it served them right; for instead of trying to quench the tyranny, they should have let it burn out. A lad, being offered some game-cocks that would die upon the spot, said that he cared not for cocks that would die, but for such that would live and kill others. Another, seeing people easing themselves on seats, said, "God forbid I should sit where I could not get up to salute my elders." In short, their answers were so sententious and pertinent, that one said well that intellectual much more truly than athletic exercise was the Spartan characteristic.

Nor was their instruction in music and verse less carefully attended to than their habits of grace and good-breeding in conversation. And their very songs had a life and spirit in them that inflamed and possessed men's minds with an enthusiasm and ardour for action; the style of them was plain and without affectation; the subject always serious and moral; most usually, it was in praise of such men as had died in defence of their country, or in derision of those that had been cowards; the former they declared happy and glorified; the life of the latter they described as most miserable and abject. There were also vaunts of what they would do, and boasts of what they had done, varying with the various ages, as, for example, they had three choirs in their solemn festivals, the first of the old men, the second of the young men, and the last of the children; the old men began thus:—

We once were young, and brave, and strong;

the young men answered them, singing:—
And we're so now, come on and try;

the children came last and said:—
But we'll be strongest by and by.

Indeed, if we will take the pains to consider their compositions, some of which were still extant in our days, and the airs on the flute to which they marched when going to battle, we shall find that Terpander and Pindar had reason to say that musing and valour were allied. The first says of Lacedæmon—

The spear and song in her do meet,
And Justice walks about her street;

And Pindar—

Councils of wise elders here,
And the young men's conquering spear,
And dance, and song, and joy appear;

both describing the Spartans as no less musical than warlike; in the words of one of their own poets—

With the iron stern and sharp,
Comes the playing on the harp.

For, indeed, before they engaged in battle, the king first did sacrifice to the Muses, in all likelihood to put them in mind of the manner of their education, and of the judgment that would be passed upon their actions, and thereby to animate them to the performance of exploits that should deserve a record. At such times, too, the Lacedæmonians abated a little the severity of their manners in favour of their young men, suffering them to curl and adorn their hair, and to have costly arms and fine clothes; and were well pleased to see them, like proud horses, neighing and pressing to the course. And, therefore, as soon as they came to be well-grown, they took a great deal of care of their hair, to have it parted and trimmed, especially against a day of battle, pursuant to a saying recorded of their lawgiver, that a large head of hair added beauty to a good face, and terror to an ugly one.

When they were in the field, their exercises were generally more moderate, their fare not so hard, nor so strict a hand held over them by their officers, so that they were the only people in the world to whom war gave repose. When their army was drawn up in battle array, and the enemy near, the king sacrificed a goat, commanded the soldiers to set their garlands upon their heads, and the pipers to play the tune of the hymn to Castor, and himself began the pæan of advance. It was at once a magnificent and a terrible sight to see them march on to the tune of their flutes, without any disorder in their ranks, any discomposure in their minds, or change in their countenances, calmly and cheerfully moving with the music to the deadly fight. Men, in this temper, were not likely to be possessed with fear or any transport of fury, but with the deliberate valour of hope and assurance, as if some divinity were attending and conducting them.

The king had always about his person some one who had been crowned in the Olympic games; and upon this account a Lacedæmonian is said to have refused a considerable present, which was offered to him upon condition that he would not come into the lists; and when he had with much to-do thrown his antagonist, some of the spectators saying to him, "And now, Sir Lacedæmonian, what are you the better for your victory?" he answered, smiling, "I shall fight next the king."

After they had routed an enemy, they pursued him till they were well assured of the victory, and then they sounded a retreat, thinking it base and unworthy of a Grecian people to cut men in pieces, who had given up and abandoned all resistance. This manner of dealing with their enemies did not only show magnanimity, but was politic too; for, knowing that they killed only those who made resistance, and gave quarter to the rest, men generally thought it their best way to consult their safety by flight.

Hippius the sophist says that Lycurgus himself was a great soldier and an experienced commander. Philostephanus attributes to him the first division of the cavalry into troops of fifties in a square body; but Demetrius the Phalerian says quite the contrary, and that he made all his laws in a continued peace. And, indeed, the Olympic holy truce, or cessation of arms, that was procured by his means and management, inclines me to think him a kind-natured man, and one that loved quietness and peace. Notwithstanding all this Hermippus tells us that he had no hand in the ordinance, that Iphitus made it, and Lycurgus came only as a spectator, and that by mere accident too. Being there, he heard as it were a man's voice behind him, blaming and wondering at him that he did not encourage his countrymen to resort to the assembly, and, turning about and seeing no man, concluded that it was a voice from heaven, and upon this immediately went to Iphitus and assisted him in ordering the ceremonies of that feast, which, by his means, were better established, and with more repute than before.

To return to the Lacedæmonians. Their discipline continued still after they were full-grown men. No one was allowed to live after his own fancy; but the city was a sort of camp, in which every man had his share of provisions and business set out, and looked upon himself not so much born to serve his own ends as the interest of his country. Therefore if they were commanded nothing else, they went to see the boys perform their exercises, to teach them something useful or to learn it themselves of those who knew better. And indeed one of the greatest and highest blessings Lycurgus procured his people was the abundance of leisure which proceeded from his forbidding to them the exercise of any mean and mechanical trade. Of the money-making that depends on troublesome going about and seeing people and doing business, they had no need at all in a state where wealth obtained no honour or respect. The Helots tilled their ground for them, and paid them yearly in kind the appointed quantity, without any trouble of theirs. To this purpose there goes a story of a Lacedæmonian who, happening to be at Athens when the courts were sitting, was told of a citizen that had been fined for living an idle life, and was being escorted home in much distress of mind by his condoling friends; the Lacedæmonian was much surprised at it and desired his

friend to show him the man who was condemned for living like a freeman. So much beneath them did they esteem the frivolous devotion of time and attention to the mechanical
arts and to money-making.

It need not be said that upon the prohibition of gold and silver, all lawsuits immediately ceased, for there was now neither avarice nor poverty amongst them, but equality,
where every one's wants were supplied, and independence, because those wants were so small.
All their time, except when they were in the
field, was taken up by the choral dances and
the festivals, in hunting, and in attendance on
the exercise-grounds and the places of public
conversation.

Those who were under thirty years of age
were not allowed to go into the market-place,
but had the necessaries of their family supplied by the care of their relations and lovers;
nor was it for the credit of elderly men to be
seen too often in the market-place; it was
esteemed more suitable for them to frequent
the exercise-grounds and places of conversation, where they spent their leisure rationally
in conversation, not on money-making and
market-prices, but for the most part in passing
judgment on some action worth considering;
extolling the good, and censuring those who
were otherwise, and that in a light and sportive manner, conveying, without too much
gravity, lessons of advice and improvement.
Nor was Lycurgus himself unduly austere; it
was he who dedicated, says Sosibius, the little
statue of Laughter. Mirth, introduced seasonably at their suppers and places of common
entertainment, was to serve as a sort of sweet-
meat to accompany their strict and hard life.
To conclude, he bred up his citizens in such
a way that they neither would nor could live
by themselves; they were to make themselves
one with the public good, and, clustering like
bees around their commander, be by their
zeal and public spirit carried all but out of
themselves, and devoted wholly to their country.

What their sentiments were will better appear by a few of their sayings. Pædaretus, not
being admitted into the list of the three hundred, returned home with a joyful face, well
pleased to find that there were in Sparta
three hundred better men than himself. And
Polycratidas, being sent with some others ambassador to the lieutenants of the king of
Persia, being asked by them whether they
came in a private or in a public character,

answered, "In a public, if we succeed; if not,
in a private character." Argileonis, asking
some who came from Amphipolis if her son
Brasidas died courageously and as became a
Spartan, on their beginning to praise him to
a high degree, and saying there was not such
another left in Sparta, answered, "Do not
say so; Brasidas was a good and brave man,
but there are in Sparta many better than he."

The senate, as I said before, consisted of
those who were Lycurgus's chief aiders and
assistants in his plans. The vacancies he ordered to be supplied out of the best and most
deserving men past sixty years old, and we
need not wonder if there was much striving
for it; for what more glorious competition
could there be amongst men, than one in
which it was not contested who was swiftest
among the swift or strongest of the strong,
but who of many wise and good was wisest
and best, and fittest to be intrusted for ever
after, as the reward of his merits, with the
supreme authority of the commonwealth, and
with power over the lives, franchises, and highest interests of all his countrymen?

The manner of their election was as follows: The people being called together, some
selected persons were locked up in a room
near the place of election, so contrived that
they could neither see nor be seen, but could
only hear the noise of the assembly without;
for they decided this, as most other affairs
of moment, by the shouts of the people. This
done, the competitors were not brought in
and presented all together, but one after
another by lot, and passed in order through
the assembly without speaking a word. Those
who were locked up had writing-tables with
them, in which they recorded and marked
each shout by its loudness, without knowing
in favour of which candidate each of them
was made, but merely that they came first,
second, third, and so forth. He who was found
to have the most and loudest acclamations
was declared senator duly elected.

Upon this he had a garland set upon his
head, and went in procession to all the
temples to give thanks to the gods; a great
number of young men followed him with
applauses, and women, also, singing verses in
his honour, and extolling the virtue and happiness of his life. As he went round the city
in this manner, each of his relations and
friends set a table before him, saying, "The
city honours you with this banquet"; but he,
instead of accepting, passed round to the

common table where he formerly used to eat, and was served as before, excepting that now he had a second allowance, which he took and put by. By the time supper was ended, the women who were of kin to him had come about the door; and he, beckoning to her whom he most esteemed, presented to her the portion he had saved, saying, that it had been a mark of esteem to him, and was so now to her; upon which she was triumphantly waited upon home by the women.

Touching burials, Lycurgus made very wise regulations; for first of all, to cut off all superstition, he allowed them to bury their dead within the city, and even round about their temples, to the end that their youth might be accustomed to such spectacles, and not be afraid to see a dead body, or imagine that to touch a corpse or to tread upon a grave would defile a man. In the next place, he commanded them to put nothing into the ground with them, except, if they pleased, a few olive leaves, and the scarlet cloth that they were wrapped in. He would not suffer the names to be inscribed, except only of men who fell in the wars, or women who died in a sacred office. The time, too, appointed for mourning, was very short, eleven days; on the twelfth, they were to do sacrifice to Ceres, and leave it off; so that we may see, that as he cut off all superfluity, so in things necessary there was nothing so small and trivial which did not express some homage of virtue or scorn of vice.

He filled Lacedæmon all through with proofs and examples of good conduct; with the constant sight of which from their youth up the people would hardly fail to be gradually formed and advanced in virtue. And this was the reason why he forbade them to travel abroad, and go about acquainting themselves with foreign rules of morality, the habits of ill-educated people, and different views of government. Withal he banished from Lacedæmon all strangers who would not give a very good reason for their coming thither; not because he was afraid lest they should inform themselves of and imitate his manner of government (as Thucydides says), or learn anything to their good; but rather lest they should introduce something contrary to good manners. With strange people, strange words must be admitted; these novelties produce novelties in thought; and on these follow views and feelings whose discordant character destroys the harmony of the state. He was as careful to save his city from the infection of foreign bad hab-

its, as men usually are to prevent the introduction of a pestilence.

Hitherto I, for my part, see no sign of injustice or want of equity in the laws of Lycurgus, though some who admit them to be well contrived to make good soldiers, pronounce them defective in point of justice. The Cryptia, perhaps (if it were one of Lycurgus's ordinances, as Aristotle says it was), gave both him and Plato, too, this opinion alike of the lawgiver and his government. By this ordinance, the magistrates despatched privately some of the ablest of the young men into the country, from time to time, armed only with their daggers, and taking a little necessary provision with them; in the daytime, they hid themselves in out-of-the-way places, and there lay close, but in the night issued out into the highways, and killed all the Helots they could light upon; sometimes they set upon them by day, as they were at work in the fields, and murdered them. As, also, Thucydides, in his history of the Peloponnesian war, tells us, that a good number of them, after being singled out for their bravery by the Spartans, garlanded, as enfranchised persons, and led about to all the temples in token of honours, shortly after disappeared all of a sudden, being about the number of two thousand; and no man either then or since could give an account how they came by their deaths. And Aristotle, in particular, adds, that the ephori, so soon as they were entered into their office, used to declare war against them, that they might be massacred without a breach of religion.

It is confessed, on all hands, that the Spartans dealt with them very hardly; for it was a common thing to force them to drink to excess, and to lead them in that condition into their public halls, that the children might see what a sight a drunken man is; they made them to dance low dances, and sing ridiculous songs, forbidding them expressly to meddle with any of a better kind. And accordingly, when the Thebans made their invasion into Laconia, and took a great number of the Helots, they could by no means persuade them to sing the verses of Terpander, Alcman, or Spendon, "For," said they, "the masters do not like it." So that it was truly observed by one, that in Sparta he who was free was most so, and he that was a slave there, the greatest slave in the world. For my part, I am of opinion that these outrages and cruelties began to be exercised in Sparta at a later time, especially after the great earthquake, when the Helots made a general insurrection, and, joining with the Messenians, laid the country waste, and brought the greatest danger upon the city. For I cannot persuade myself to ascribe to Lycurgus so wicked and barbarous a course, judging of him from the gentleness of his disposition and justice upon all other occasions; to which the oracle also testified.

When he perceived that his more important institutions had taken root in the minds of his countrymen, that custom had rendered them familiar and easy, that his commonwealth was now grown up and able to go alone, then, as Plato somewhere tells us, the Maker of the world, when first he saw it existing and beginning its motion, felt joy, even so Lycurgus, viewing with joy and satisfaction the greatness and beauty of his political structure, now fairly at work and in motion, conceived the thought to make it immortal too, and, as far as human forecast could reach, to deliver it down unchangeable to posterity. He called an extraordinary assembly of all the people, and told them that he now thought everything reasonably well established, both for the happiness and the virtue of the state; but that there was one thing still behind, of the greatest importance, which he thought not fit to impart until he had consulted the oracle; in the meantime, his desire was that they would observe the laws without any the least alteration until his return, and then he would do as the god should direct him. They all consented readily, and bade him hasten his journey; but, before he departed, he administered an oath to the two kings, the senate, and the whole commons, to abide by and maintain the established form of polity until Lycurgus should be come back.

This done, he set out for Delphi, and, having sacrificed to Apollo, asked him whether the laws he had established were good, and sufficient for a people's happiness and virtue. The oracle answered that the laws were excellent, and that the people, while it observed them, should live in the height of renown. Lycurgus took the oracle in writing, and sent it over to Sparta; and, having sacrificed the second time to Apollo, and taken leave of his friends and his son, he resolved that the Spartans should not be released from the oath they had taken, and that he would, of his own act, close his life where he was.

He was now about that age in which life was still tolerable, and yet might be quitted without regret. Everything, moreover, about him was in a sufficiently prosperous condition. He therefore made an end of himself by a total abstinence from food, thinking it a statesman's duty to make his very death, if possible, an act of service to the state, and even in the end of his life to give some example of virtue and effect some useful purpose. He would, on the one hand, crown and consummate his own happiness by a death suitable to so honourable a life, and on the other hand, would secure to his countrymen the enjoyment of the advantages he had spent his life in obtaining for them, since they had solemnly sworn the maintenance of his institutions until his return.

Nor was he deceived in his expectations, for the city of Lacedæmon continued the chief city of all Greece for the space of five hundred years, in strict observance of Lycurgus's laws; in all which time there was no manner of alteration made, during the reign of fourteen kings down to the time of Agis, the son of Archidamus. For the new creation of the ephori, though thought to be in favour of the people, was so far from diminishing, that it very much heightened, the aristocratical character of the government.

In the time of Agis, gold and silver first flowed into Sparta, and with them all those mischiefs which attend the immoderate desire of riches. Lysander promoted this disorder; for by bringing in rich spoils from the wars, although himself incorrupt, he yet by this means filled his country with avarice and luxury, and subverted the laws and ordinances of Lycurgus; so long as which were in force, the aspect presented by Sparta was rather that of a rule of life followed by one wise and temperate man, than of the political government of a nation. And as the poets feign of Hercules, that, with his lion's skin and his club, he went over the world, punishing lawless and cruel tyrants, so may it be said of the Lacedæmonians, that, with a common staff and a coarse coat, they gained the willing and joyful obedience of Greece, through whose whole extent they suppressed unjust usurpations and despotisms, arbitrated in war, and composed civil dissensions; and this often without so much as taking down one buckler, but barely by sending some one single deputy to whose direction all at once submitted, like bees swarming and taking their places around their prince. Such a fund of order and equity, enough and to spare for others, existed in their state.

And therefore I cannot but wonder at those who say that the Spartans were good subjects, but bad governors, and for proof of it allege a saying of King Theopompus, who when one said that Sparta held up so long because their kings could command so well, replied, "Nay, rather because the people know so well how to obey." For people do not obey, unless rulers know how to command; obedience is a lesson taught by commanders. A true leader himself creates the obedience of his own followers; as it is the last attainment in the art of riding to make a horse gentle and tractable, so is it of the science of government, to inspire men with a willingness to obey. The Lacedæmonians inspired men not with a mere willingness, but with an absolute desire to be their subjects. For they did not send petitions to them for ships or money, or a supply of armed men, but only for a Spartan commander; and, having obtained one, used him with honour and reverence; so the Sicilians behaved to Gylippus, the Chalcidians to Brasidas, and all the Greeks in Asia to Lysander, Callicratidas, and Agesilaus; they styled them the composers and chasteners of each people or prince they were sent to, and had their eyes always fixed upon the city of Sparta itself, as the perfect model of good manners and wise government.

The rest seemed as scholars, they the masters of Greece; and to this Stratonicus pleasantly alluded, when in jest he pretended to make a law that the Athenians should conduct religious processions and the mysteries, the Eleans should preside at the Olympic games, and, if either did amiss, the Lacedæmonians be beaten. Antisthenes, too, one of the scholars of Socrates, said, in earnest, of the Thebans, when they were elated by their victory at Leuctra, that they looked like schoolboys who had beaten their master.

However, it was not the design of Lycurgus that his city should govern a great many others; he thought rather that the happiness of a state, as a private man, consisted chiefly in the exercise of virtue, and in the concord of the inhabitants; his aim, therefore, in all his arrangements, was to make and keep them free-minded, self-dependent, and temperate. And therefore all those who have written well on politics, as Plato, Diogenes, and Zeno, have taken Lycurgus for their model, leaving behind them, however, mere projects and words; whereas Lycurgus was the author, not in writing but in reality, of a government which none else could so much as copy; and while men in general have treated the individual philosophic character as unattainable, he, by the example of a complete philosophic state, raised himself high above all other lawgivers of Greece. And so Aristotle says they did him less honour at Lacedæmon after his death than he deserved, although he has a temple there, and they offer sacrifices yearly to him as to a god.

It is reported that when his bones were brought home to Sparta his tomb was struck with lightning, an accident which befell no eminent person but himself and Euripides, who was buried at Arethusa in Macedonia; and it may serve that poet's admirers as a testimony in his favour, that he had in this the same fate with that holy man and favourite of the gods. Some say Lycurgus died in Cirrha; Apollothemis says, after he had come to Elis; Timæus and Aristoxenus, that he ended his life in Crete; Aristoxenus adds that his tomb is shown by the Cretans in the district of Pergamus, near the strangers' road. He left an only son, Antiorus, on whose death without issue his family became extinct. But his relations and friends kept up an annual commemoration of him down to a long time after; and the days of the meeting were called Lycurgides. Aristocrates, the son of Hipparchus, says that he died in Crete, and that his Cretan friends, in accordance with his own request, when they had burned his body, scattered the ashes into the sea; for fear lest, if his relics should be transported to Lacedæmon, the people might pretend to be released from their oaths, and make innovations in the government. Thus much may suffice for the life and actions of Lycurgus.

NUMA POMPILIUS

LEGENDARY, 8TH–7TH CENTURY B.C.

Though the pedigrees of noble families of Rome go back in exact form as far as Numa Pompilius, yet there is great diversity amongst historians concerning the time in which he reigned; a certain writer called Clodius, in a book of his entitled *Strictures on Chronology,* avers that the ancient registers of Rome were lost when the city was sacked by the Gauls, and that those which are now extant were conterfeited, to flatter and serve the humour of some men who wished to have themselves derived from some ancient and noble lineage, though in reality with no claim to it. And though it be commonly reported that Numa was a scholar and a familiar acquaintance of Pythagoras, yet it is again contradicted by others, who affirm that he was acquainted with neither the Greek language nor learning, and that he was a person of that natural talent and ability as of himself to attain to virtue, or else that he found some barbarian instructor superior to Pythagoras. Some affirm, also, that Pythagoras was not contemporary with Numa, but lived at least five generations after him; and that some other Pythagoras, a native of Sparta, who, in the sixteenth Olympiad, in the third year of which Numa became king, won a prize at the Olympic race, might, in his travel through Italy, have gained acquaintance with Numa, and assisted him in the constitution of his kingdom; whence it comes that many Laconian laws and customs appear amongst the Roman institutions. Yet, in any case, Numa was descended of the Sabines, who declare themselves to be a colony of the Lacedæmonians. And chronology, in general, is uncertain; especially when fixed by the lists of victors in the Olympic games, which were published at a late period by Hippias the Elean, and rest on no positive authority. Commencing, however, at a convenient point, we will proceed to give the most noticeable events that are recorded of the life of Numa.

It was the thirty-seventh year, counted from the foundation of Rome, when Romulus, then reigning, did, on the fifth day of the month of July, called the Caprotine Nones, offer a public sacrifice at the Goat's Marsh, in presence of the senate and people of Rome. Suddenly the sky was darkened, a thick cloud of storm and rain settled on the earth; the common people fled in affright, and were dispersed; and in this whirlwind Romulus disappeared, his body being never found either living or dead. A foul suspicion presently attached to the patricians, and rumours were current among the people as if that they, weary of kingly government, and exasperated of late by the imperious deportment of Romulus towards them, had plotted against his life and made him away, that so they might assume the authority and government into their own hands. This suspicion they sought to turn aside by decreeing divine honours to Romulus, as to one not dead but translated to a higher condition. And Proculus, a man of note, took oath that he saw Romulus caught up into heaven in his arms and vestments, and heard him, as he ascended, cry out that they should hereafter style him by the name of Quirinus.

This trouble, being appeased, was followed by another, about the election of a new king; for the minds of the original Romans and the new inhabitants were not as yet grown into that perfect unity of temper, but that there were diversities of factions amongst the commonalty, and jealousies and emulations amongst the senators; for though all agreed that it was necessary to have a king, yet what person or of which nation was matter of dispute. For those who had been builders of the city with Romulus, and had already yielded a share of their lands and dwellings to the Sabines, were indignant at any pretension on their part to rule over their benefactors. On the other side, the Sabines could plausibly allege, that, at their king Tatius's decease, they had peaceably submitted to the sole command of Romulus; so now their turn was come to have a king chosen out of their own nation; nor did they esteem themselves to have combined with the Romans as inferiors, nor to have contributed less than they to the increase of Rome, which without their numbers and association, could scarcely have merited the name of a city.

Thus did both parties argue and dispute their cause; but lest meanwhile discord, in the absence of all command, should occasion general confusion, it was agreed that the hundred and fifty senators should interchangeably execute the office of supreme magistrate, and each in succession, with the ensigns of royalty, should offer the solemn sacrifices and despatch public business for the space of six hours by day and six by night; which vicissitude and equal distribution of power would preclude all rivalry amongst the senators and envy from the people, when they should behold one, elevated to the degree of a king, levelled within the space of a day to the condition of a private citizen. This form of government is termed, by the Romans, *interregnum*.

Nor yet could they, by this plausible and modest way of rule, escape suspicion and clamour of the vulgar, as though they were changing the form of government to an oligarchy, and designing to keep the supreme power in a sort of wardship under themselves, without ever proceeding to choose a king. Both parties came at length to the conclusion that the one should choose a king out of the body of the other; the Romans make a choice of a Sabine, or the Sabines name a Roman; this was esteemed the best expedient to put an end to all party spirit, and the prince who should be chosen would have an equal affection to the one party as his electors and to the other as his kinsmen. The Sabines remitted the choice to the original Romans, and they, too, on their part, were more inclinable to receive a Sabine king elected by themselves than to see a Roman exalted by the Sabines. Consultations being accordingly held, they named Numa Pompilius, of the Sabine race, a person of that high reputation for excellence, that, though he were not actually residing at Rome, yet he was no sooner nominated than accepted by the Sabines, with acclamation almost greater than that of the electors themselves.

The choice being declared and made known to the people, principal men of both parties were appointed to visit and entreat him, that he would accept the administration of the government. Numa resided at a famous city of the Sabines called Cures, whence the Romans and Sabines gave themselves the joint name of Quirites. Pomponius, an illustrious person, was his father, and he the youngest of his four sons, being (as it had been divinely ordered) born on the twenty-first day of April, the day of the foundation of Rome. He was endued with a soul rarely tempered by nature, and disposed to virtue, which he had yet more subdued by discipline, a severe life, and the study of philosophy; means which had not only succeeded in expelling the baser passions, but also the violent and rapacious temper which barbarians are apt to think highly of; true bravery, in his judgment, was regarded as consisting in the subjugation of our passions by reason.

He banished all luxury and softness from his own home, and while citizens alike and strangers found in him an incorruptible judge and counsellor, in private he devoted himself not to amusement or lucre, but to the worship of the immortal gods, and rational contemplation of their divine power and nature. So famous was he, that Tatius, the colleague of Romulus, chose him for his son-in-law, and gave him his only daughter, which, however, did not stimulate his vanity to desire to dwell with his father-in-law at Rome; he rather chose to inhabit with his Sabines, and cherish his own father in his old age; and Tatia, also, preferred the private condition of her husband before the honours and splendour she might have enjoyed with her father. She is said to have died after she had been married thirteen years, and then Numa, leaving the conversation of the town, betook himself to a country life, and in a solitary manner frequented the groves and fields consecrated to the gods, passing his life in desert places. And this in particular gave occasion to the story about the goddess, namely, that Numa did not retire from human society out of any melancholy or disorder of mind, but because he had tasted the joys of more elevated intercourse, and, admitted to celestial wedlock in the love and converse of the goddess Egeria, had attained to blessedness, and to a divine wisdom.

The story evidently resembles those very ancient fables which the Phrygians have received and still recount of Attis, the Bithynians of Herodotus, the Arcadians of Endymion, not to mention several others who were thought blessed and beloved of the gods; nor does it seem strange if God, a lover, not of horses or birds, but men, should not disdain to dwell with the virtuous and converse with the wise and temperate soul, though it be altogether hard, indeed, to believe, that any god or dæmon is capable of a sensual or bodily love and passion for any human form or beauty. Though, indeed, the wise Egyptians do not plausibly make the distinction, that it may be possible for a divine spirit so to apply itself to the nature of a woman, as to imbreed in her the first beginnings of generation, while on the other side they conclude it impossible for the male kind to have any intercourse or mixture by the body with any divinity, not considering, however, that what takes place on the one side must also take place on the other; intermixture, by force of terms, is reciprocal. Not that it is otherwise than befitting to suppose that the gods feel towards men affection, and love, in the sense of affection, and in the form of care and solicitude for their virtue and their good dispositions. And, therefore, it was no error of those who feigned, that Phorbas, Hyacinthus, and Admetus were beloved by Apollo; or that Hippolytus the Sicyonian was so much in his favour, that, as often as he sailed from Sicyon to Cirrha, the Pythian prophetess uttered this heroic verse, expressive of the god's attention and joy:

Now doth Hippolytus return again,
And venture his dear life upon the main.

It is reported, also, that Pan became enamoured of Pindar for his verses, and the divine power rendered honour to Hesiod and Archilochus after their death for the sake of the Muses; there is a statement, also, that Æsculapius sojourned with Sophocles in his lifetime, of which many proofs still exist, and that, when he was dead, another deity took care for his funeral rites. And so if any credit may be given to these instances, why should we judge it incongruous, that a like spirit of the gods should visit Zaleucus, Minos, Zoroaster, Lycurgus, and Numa, the controllers of kingdoms, and the legislators for commonwealths? Nay, it may be reasonable to believe, that the gods, with a serious purpose, assist at the councils and serious debates of such men, to inspire and direct them; and visit poets and musicians, if at all, in their more sportive moods; but, for difference of opinion here, as Bacchylides said, "the road is broad." For there is no absurdity in the account also given, that Lycurgus and Numa, and other famous lawgivers, having the task of subduing perverse and refractory multitudes, and of introducing great innovations, themselves made this pretension to divine authority, which, if not true, assuredly was expedient for the interests of those it imposed upon.

Numa was about forty years of age when the ambassadors came to make him offers of the kingdom; the speakers were Proculus and Velesus, one or other of whom it had been thought the people would elect as their new king; the original Romans being for Proculus, and the Sabines for Velesus. Their speech was very short, supposing that, when they came to tender a kingdom, there needed little to persuade to an acceptance; but, contrary to their expectations, they found that they had to use many reasons and entreaties to induce one, that lived in peace and quietness, to accept the government of a city whose foundation and increase had been made, in a manner, in war.

In presence of his father and his kinsman Marcius, he returned answer that "Every alteration of a man's life is dangerous to him; but madness only could induce one who needs nothing, and is satisfied with everything, to quit a life he is accustomed to; which, whatever else it is deficient in, at any rate has the advantage of certainty over one wholly doubtful and unknown. Though, indeed, the difficulties of this government cannot even be called unknown; Romulus, who first held it, did not escape the suspicion of having plotted against the life of his colleague Tatius; nor the senate the like accusation, of having treasonably murdered Romulus. Yet Romulus had the advantage to be thought divinely born and miraculously preserved and nurtured. My birth was mortal; I was reared and instructed by men that are known to you. The very points of my character that are most commended mark me as unfit to reign,—love of retirement and of studies inconsistent with business, a passion that has become inveterate in me for peace, for unwarlike occupations, and for the society of men whose meetings are but those of worship and of kindly intercourse, whose lives in general are spent upon their farms and their pastures. I should but be, methinks, a laughing-stock, while I should go about to inculcate the worship of the gods and give lessons in the love of justice and the abhorrence of violence and war, to a city whose needs are rather for a captain than for a king."

The Romans, perceiving by these words that he was declining to accept the kingdom, were the more instant and urgent with him that he would not forsake and desert them in this condition, and suffer them to relapse, as they must, into their former sedition and civil discord, there being no person on whom both parties could accord but on himself. And, at length, his father and Marcius, taking him aside, persuaded him to accept a gift so noble in itself, and tendered to him rather from heaven than from men. "Though," said they, "you neither desire riches, being content with what you have, nor court the fame of authority, as having already the more valuable fame of virtue, yet you will consider that government itself is a service of God, who now calls out into action your qualities of justice and wisdom, which were not meant to be left useless and unemployed. Cease, therefore, to avoid and turn your back upon an office which, to a wise man, is a field for great and honourable actions, for the magnificent worship of the gods, and for the introduction of habits of piety, which authority alone can effect amongst a people. Tatius, though a foreigner, was beloved, and the memory of Romulus has received divine honours; and who knows but that this people, being victorious, may be satiated with war, and, content with the trophies and spoils they have acquired, may be, above all things, desirous to have a pacific and justice-loving prince to lead them to good order and quiet? But, if, indeed, their desires are uncontrollably and madly set on war, were it not better, then, to have the reins held by such a moderating hand as is able to divert the fury another way, and that your native city and the whole Sabine nation should possess in you a bond of goodwill and friendship with this young and growing power?"

With these reasons and persuasions several auspicious omens are said to have concurred, and the zeal, also, of his fellow-citizens, who, on understanding what message the Roman ambassadors had brought him, entreated him to accompany them, and to accept the kingdom as a means to unanimity and concord between the nations.

Numa, yielding to these inducements, having first performed divine sacrifice, proceeded to Rome, being met on his way by the senate and people, who, with an impatient desire, came forth to receive him; the women, also, welcomed him with joyful acclamations, and sacrifices were offered for him in all the temples, and so universal was the joy, that they seemed to be receiving, not a new king, but a new kingdom. In this manner he descended into the forum, where Spurius Vettius, whose turn it was to be *interrex* at that hour, put it to the vote; and all declared him king.

Then the regalities and robes of authority were brought to him; but he refused to be invested with them until he had first consulted and been confirmed by the gods; so being accompanied by the priests and augurs, he ascended the Capitol, which at that time the Romans called the Tarpeian Hill. Then the chief of the augurs covered Numa's head, and turned his face towards the south, and, standing behind him, laid his right hand on his head, and prayed, turning his eyes every way, in expectation of some auspicious signal from the gods. It was wonderful, meantime, with what silence and devotion the multitude stood assembled in the forum, in similar expectation and suspense, till auspicious birds appeared and passed on the right. Then Numa, apparelling himself in his royal robes, descended from the hill to the people, by whom he was received and congratulated with shouts and acclamations of welcome, as a holy king, and beloved of all the gods.

The first thing he did at his entrance into government was to dismiss the band of three hundred men which had been Romulus's life-guard, called by him Celeres, saying that he would not distrust those who put confidence in him; nor rule over a people that distrusted him. The next thing he did was to add to the two priests of Jupiter and Mars a third, in honour of Romulus, whom he called the Flamen Quirinalis. The Romans anciently called their priests *flamines,* by corruption of the word *pilamines,* from a certain cap which they wore, called *pileus.* In those times Greek words were more mixed with the Latin than at present; thus also the royal robe, which is called *læna,* Juba says, is the same as the Greek *chlæna;* and that the name of Camillus, given to the boy with both his parents living, who serves in the temple of Jupiter, was taken from the name given by some Greeks to Mercury, denoting his office of attendance on the gods.

When Numa had, by such measures, won the favour and affection of the people, he set himself without delay to the task of bringing the hard and iron Roman temper to somewhat more of gentleness and equity. Plato's expression of a city in high fever was never more applicable than to Rome at that time; in its origin formed by daring and warlike spirits, whom bold and desperate adventure brought thither from every quarter, it had found in perpetual wars and incursions on its neighbours its after sustenance and means of growth, and in conflict with danger the source of new strength; like piles, which the blows of the hammer serve to fix into the ground. Wherefore Numa, judging it no slight undertaking to mollify and bend to peace the presumptuous and stubborn spirits of this people, began to operate upon them with the sanctions of religion. He sacrificed often and used processions and religious dances, in which most commonly he officiated in person; by such combinations of solemnity with refined and humanising pleasures, seeking to win over and mitigate their fiery and warlike tempers. At times, also, he filled their imaginations with religious terrors, professing that strange apparitions had been seen, and dreadful voices heard; thus subduing and humbling their minds by a sense of supernatural fears.

This method which Numa used made it believed that he had been much conversant with Pythagoras; for in the philosophy of the one, as in the policy of the other, man's relations to the deity occupy a great place. It is said, also, that the solemnity of his exterior garb and gestures was adopted by him from the same feeling with Pythagoras. For it is said of Pythagoras, that he had taught an eagle to come at his call, and stoop down to him in his flight; and that, as he passed among the people assembled at the Olympic games, he showed them his golden thigh; besides many other strange and miraculous seeming practices, on which Timon the Philasian wrote the distich—

Who, of the glory of a juggler proud,
With solemn talk imposed upon the crowd.

In like manner Numa spoke of a certain goddess or mountain nymph that was in love with him, and met him in secret, as before related; and professed that he entertained familiar conversation with the Muses, to whose teaching he ascribed the greatest part of his revelations; and amongst them, above all, he recommended to the veneration of the Romans one in particular, whom he named Tacita, the silent; which he did perhaps in imitation and honour of the Pythagorean silence. His opinion, also, of images is very agreeable to the doctrine of Pythagoras; who conceived of the first principle of being as transcending sense and passion, invisible and incorrupt, and only to be apprehended by abstract intelligence. So Numa forbade the Romans to represent God in the form of man or beast, nor was there any painted or graven image of a deity admitted amongst them for the space of the first hundred and seventy years, all which time their temples and chapels were kept free and pure from images; to such baser objects they deemed it impious to liken the highest, and all access to God impossible, except by the pure act of the intellect. His sacrifices, also, had great similitude to the ceremonial of Pythagoras, for they were not celebrated with effusion of blood, but consisted of flour, wine, and the least costly offerings.

Other external proofs, too, are urged to show the connection Numa had with Pythagoras. The comic writer Epicharmus, an ancient author, and of the school of Pythagoras, in a book of his dedicated to Antenor, records that Pythagoras was made a freeman of Rome. Again, Numa gave to one of his four sons the name of Mamercus, which was the name of one of the sons of Pythagoras; from whence, as they say, sprang that ancient patrician family of the Æmilli, for that the king gave him in sport the surname of Æmilius, for his engaging and graceful manner in speaking. I remember, too, that when I was at Rome, I heard many say, that, when the oracle directed two statues to be raised, one to the wisest and another to the most valiant man in Greece, they erected two of brass, one representing Alcibiades, and the other Pythagoras.

But to pass by these matters, which are full of uncertainty and not so important as to be worth our time to insist on them, the original constitution of the priests, called Pontifices, is ascribed unto Numa, and he himself was, it is said, the first of them; and that they have the name of Pontifices from *potens*, powerful, because they attend the service of the gods, who have power and command over all. Others make the word refer to exceptions of impossible cases; the priests were to perform all the duties possible to them; if anything lay beyond their power, the exception was not to be cavilled at. The most common opinion is the most absurd, which derives this word from *pons*, and assigns the priests the title of bridge-makers. The sacrifices performed on the bridge were amongst the most sacred and ancient, and the keeping and repairing of the bridge attached, like any other public sacred office, to the priesthood. It was accounted not simply unlawful, but a positive sacrilege, to pull down the wooden bridge; which moreover is said, in obedience to an oracle, to have been built entirely of timber and fastened with wooden pins, without nails or cramps of iron. The stone bridge was built a very long time after when Æmilius was quæstor, and they do, indeed, say also that the wooden bridge was not so old as Numa's time, but was finished by Ancus Marcius, when he was king, who was the grandson of Numa by his daughter.

The office of Pontifex Maximus, or chief priest, was to declare and interpret the divine law, or, rather, to preside over sacred rites; he not only prescribed rules for public ceremony, but regulated the sacrifices of private persons, not suffering them to vary from established custom, and giving information to every one of what was requisite for purposes of worship or supplication. He was also guardian of the vestal virgins, the institution of whom, and of their perpetual fire, was attributed to Numa, who, perhaps, fancied the charge of pure and uncorrupted flames would be fitly intrusted to chaste and unpolluted persons, or that fire, which consumes, but produces nothing, bears an analogy to the virgin estate.

In Greece, wherever a perpetual holy fire is kept, as at Delphi and Athens, the charge of it is committed, not to virgins, but widows past the time of marriage. And in case by any accident it should happen that this fire became extinct, as the holy lamp was at Athens under the tyranny of Aristion, and at Delphi, when that temple was burnt by the Medes, as also in the time of the Mithridatic and Roman civil war, when not only the fire was extinguished, but the altar demolished, then, afterwards, in kindling this fire again, it was esteemed an impiety to light it from common sparks or flame, or from anything but the pure and unpolluted rays of the sun, which they usually effect by concave mirrors, of a figure formed by the revolution of an isosceles rectangular triangle, all the lines from the circumference of which meeting in a centre, by holding it in the light of the sun they can collect and concentrate all its rays at this one point of convergence; where the air will now become rarefied, and any light, dry, combustible matter will kindle as soon as applied, under the effect of the rays, which here acquired the substance and active force of fire.

Some are of opinion that these vestals had no other business than the preservation of this fire; but others conceive that they were keepers of other divine secrets concealed from all but themselves, of which we have told all that may lawfully be asked or told, in the life of Camillus. Gegania and Verenia, it is re-corded, were the names of the first two virgins consecrated and ordained by Numa; Canuleia and Tarpeia succeeded; Servius afterwards added two, and the number of four has continued to the present time.

The statutes prescribed by Numa for the vestals were these: that they should take a vow of virginity for the space of thirty years, the first ten of which they were to spend in learning their duties, the second ten in performing them, and the remaining ten in teaching and instructing others. Thus the whole term being completed, it was lawful for them to marry, and, leaving the sacred order, to choose any condition of life that pleased them; but this permission few, as they say, made use of; and in cases where they did so, it was observed that their change was not a happy one, but accompanied ever after with regret and melancholy; so that the greater number, from religious fears and scruples, forbore, and continued to old age and death in the strict observance of a single life.

For this condition he compensated by great privileges and prerogatives; as that they had power to make a will in the lifetime of their father; that they had a free administration of their own affairs without guardian or tutor, which was the privilege of women who were the mothers of three children; when they go abroad, they have the fasces carried before them; and if in their walks they chance to meet a criminal on his way to execution, it saves his life, upon oath made that the meeting was an accidental one, and not concerted or of set purpose. Any one who presses upon the chair on which they are carried, is put to death.

If these vestals commit any minor fault, they are punishable by the high priest only, who scourges the offender, sometimes with her clothes off, in a dark place, with a curtain drawn between; but she that has broken her vow is buried alive near the gate called Collina, where a little mound of earth stands, inside the city, reaching some little distance, called in Latin *agger*, under it a narrow room is constructed, to which a descent is made by stairs; here they prepare a bed, and light a lamp, and leave a small quantity of victuals, such as bread, water, a pail of milk, and some oil; that so that body which had been consecrated and devoted to the most sacred service of religion might not be said to perish by such a death as famine. The culprit herself is put in a litter, which they cover over, and tie her down with cords on it, so that nothing she utters may be heard. They then take her to the Forum; all people silently go out of the way as she passes, and such as follow accompany the bier with solemn and speechless sorrow; and indeed, there is not any spectacle more appalling, nor any day observed by the city with greater appearance of gloom and sadness. When they come to the place of execution, the officers loose the cords, and then the high priest, lifting his hands to heaven, pronounces certain prayers to himself before the act; then he brings out the prisoner, being still covered, and placing her upon the steps that lead down to the cell, turns away his face with the rest of the priests; the stairs are drawn up after she has gone down, and a quantity of earth is heaped up over the entrance to the cell, so as to prevent it from being distinguished from the rest of the mound. This is the punishment of those who break their vow of virginity.

It is said, also, that Numa built the temple of Vesta, which was intended for a repository of the holy fire, of a circular form, not to represent the figure of the earth, as if that were the same as Vesta, but that of the general universe, in the centre of which the Pythagoreans place the element of fire; and give it the name of Vesta and the unit; and do not hold that the earth is immovable, or that it is situated in the centre of the globe, but that it keeps a circular motion about the seat of fire, and is not in the number of the primary elements; in this agreeing with the opinion of Plato, who, they say, in his later life, conceived that the earth held a lateral position, and that the central and sovereign space was reserved for some nobler body.

There was yet a further use of the priests, and that was to give people directions in the national usages at funeral rites. Numa taught them to regard these offices, not as a pollution, but as a duty paid to the gods below, into whose hands the better part of us is transmitted; especially they were to worship the goddess Libitina, who presided over all the ceremonies performed at burials; whether they meant hereby Proserpina, or, as the most learned of the Romans conceive, Venus, not inaptly attributing the beginning and end of man's life to the agency of one and the same deity. Numa also prescribed rules for regulating the days of mourning, according to certain times and ages. As, for example, a child of three years was not to be mourned for at all; one older, up to ten years, for as many months as it was years old; and the longest time of mourning for any person whatsoever was not to exceed the term of ten months; which was the time appointed for women that lost their husbands to continue in widowhood. If any married again before that time, by the laws of Numa, she was to sacrifice a cow big with calf.

Numa, also, was founder of several other orders of priests, two of which I shall mention, the Salii and the Feciales, which are among the clearest proofs of the devoutness and sanctity of his character. These Fecials, or guardians of peace, seem to have had their name from their office, which was to put a stop to disputes by conference and speech; for it was not allowable to take up arms until they had declared all hopes of accommodation to be at an end, for in Greek, too, we call it peace when disputes are settled by words, and not by force. The Romans commonly despatched the Fecials, or heralds, to those who had offered them injury, requesting satisfaction; and, in case they refused, they then called the gods to witness, and, with imprecations upon themselves and their country should they be acting unjustly, so declared war; against their will, or without their consent, it was lawful neither for soldier nor king to take up arms; the war was begun with them, and when they had first handed it over to the commander as a just quarrel, then his business was to deliberate of the manner and ways to carry it on.

It is believed that the slaughter and destruction which the Gauls made of the Romans was a judgment on the city for neglect of this religious proceeding; for that when these barbarians besieged the Clusinians, Fabius Ambustus was despatched to their camp to negotiate peace for the besieged; and, on their returning a rude refusal, Fabius imagined that his office of ambassador was at an end, and, rashly engaging on the side of the Clusinians, challenged the bravest of the enemy to a single combat. It was the fortune of Fabius to kill his adversary, and to take his spoils; but when the Gauls discovered it, they sent a herald to Rome to complain against him; since, before war was declared, he had, against the law of nations, made a breach of the peace. The matter being debated in the senate, the Fecials were of opinion that Fabius ought to be consigned into the hands of the Gauls; but he, being forewarned of their judgment, fled to the people, by whose protection and favour he escaped the sentence. On this, the Gauls marched with their army to Rome, where, having taken the capitol, they sacked the city. The particulars of all which are fully given in the history of Camillus.

The origin of the Salii is this. In the eighth year of the reign of Numa, a terrible pestilence, which traversed all Italy, ravaged likewise the city of Rome; and the citizens being in distress and despondent, a brazen target, they say, fell from heaven into hands of Numa, who gave them this marvellous account of it; that Egeria and the Muses had assured him it was sent from heaven for the cure and safety of the city, and that, to keep it secure, he was ordered by them to make eleven others, so like in dimensions and form to the original that no thief should be able to distinguish the true from the counterfeit. He farther declared, that he was commanded to consecrate to the Muses the place, and the fields about it, where they had been chiefly wont to meet with him, and that the spring which watered the fields should be hallowed for the use of the vestal virgins, who were to wash and cleanse the penetralia of their sanctuary with those holy waters. The truth of all this was speedily verified by the cessation of the pestilence. Numa displayed the target to the artificers and bade them show their skill in making others like it; all despaired, until at length one Marmurius Veturius, an excellent workman, happily hit upon it, and made all so exactly the same that Numa himself was at a loss and could not distinguish.

The keeping of these targets was committed to the charge of certain priests, called Salii, who did not receive their name, as some tell the story, from Salius, a dancing-master, born in Samothrace, or at Mantinea, who taught the way of dancing in arms; but more truly from that jumping dance which the Salii themselves use, when in the month of March they carry the sacred targets through the city; at which procession they are habited in short frocks of purple, girt with a broad belt studded with brass; on their heads they wear a brass helmet, and carry in their hands short daggers, which they clash every now and then against the targets. But the chief thing is the dance itself. They move with much grace, performing, in quick time and close order, various intricate figures, with a great display of strength and agility.

The targets were called Ancilia from their form; for they are not made round, nor like proper targets, of a complete circumference, but are cut out into a wavy line, the ends of which are rounded off and turned in at the thickest part towards each other; so that their shape is curvilinear, or, in Greek, *ancylon;* or the name may come from *ancon,* the elbow, on which they are carried. Thus Juba writes, who is eager to make it Greek. But it might be, for that matter, from its having come down *anecathen,* from above; or from its *akesis,* or cure of diseases; or *auchmon lysis,* because it put an end to a drought; or from its *anaschesis,* or relief from calamities, which is the origin of the Athenian name Anaces, given to Castor and Pollux; if we must, that is, reduce it to Greek.

The reward which Mamurius received for his art was to be mentioned and commemorated in the verses which the Salii sang, as they danced in their arms through the city though some will have it that they do not say *Veturium Mamuium,* but *Veterem Memoriam,* ancient remembrance.

After Numa had in this manner instituted these several orders of priests, he erected, near the temple of Vesta, what is called to this day Regia, or king's house, where he spent the most part of his time, performing divine service, instructing the priests, or conversing with them on sacred subjects. He had another house upon the Mount Quirinalis, the site of which they show to this day.

In all public processions and solemn prayers, criers were sent before to give notice to the people that they should forbear their work, and rest. They say that the Pythagoreans did not allow people to worship and pray to their gods by the way, but would have them go out from their houses direct, with their minds set upon the duty, and so Numa, in like manner, wished that his citizens should neither see nor hear any religious service in a perfunctory and inattentive manner, but, laying aside all other occupations, should apply their minds to religion as to a most serious business; and that the streets should be free from all noises and cries that accompany manual labour, and clear for the sacred solemnity. Some traces of this custom remain at Rome to this day, for when the consul begins to take auspices or do sacrifice, they call out to the people, *Hoc age,* Attend to this, whereby the auditors then present are admonished to compose and recollect themselves.

Many other of his precepts resemble those of the Pythagoreans. The Pythagoreans said, for example, "Thou shalt not make a peck-measure thy seat to sit on. Thou shalt not stir the fire with a sword. When thou goest out upon a journey, look not behind thee. When thou sacrificest to the celestial gods, let it be with an odd number, and when to the terrestrial, with even." The significance of each of which precepts they would not commonly disclose. So some of Numa's traditions have no obvious meaning. "Thou shalt not make libation to the gods of wine from an unpruned vine. No sacrifices shall be performed without meal. Turn round to pay adoration to the gods; sit after you have worshipped." The first two directions seem to denote the cultivation and subduing of the earth as a part of religion; and as to the turning which the worshippers are to use in divine adoration, it is said to represent the rotatory motion of the world. But, in my opinion, the meaning rather is, that the worshipper, since the temples front the east, enters with his back to the rising sun; there, faces round to the east, and so turns back to the god of the temple, by this circular movement referring the fulfillment of his prayers to both divinities. Unless, indeed, this change of posture may have a mystical meaning, like the Egyptian wheels, and signify to us the instability of human fortune, and that, in whatever way God changes and turns our lot and condition, we should rest contented, and accept it as right and fitting. They say, also, that the sitting after worship was to be by way of omen of their petitions being granted, and the blessing they asked assured to them. Again, as different courses of actions are divided by intervals of rest, they might seat themselves after the completion of what they had done, to seek favour of the gods for beginning something else. And this would very well suit with what we had before; the lawgiver wants to habituate us to make our petitions to the deity not by the way, and, as it were, in a hurry, when we have other things to do, but with time and leisure to attend to it.

By such discipline and schooling in religion, the city passed insensibly into such a submissiveness of temper, and stood in such awe and reverence of the virtue of Numa, that they received, with an undoubted assurance, whatever he delivered though never so fabulous, and thought nothing incredible or impossible from him.

There goes a story that he once invited a great number of citizens to an entertainment, at which the dishes in which the meat was served were very homely and plain, and the repast itself poor and ordinary fare; the guests seated, he began to tell them that the goddess that consulted with him was then at that time come to him; when on a sudden the room was furnished with all sorts of costly drinking-vessels, and the tables loaded with rich meats, and a most sumptuous entertainment.

But the dialogue which is reported to have passed between him and Jupiter surpasses all the fabulous legends that were ever invented. They say that before Mount Aventine was inhabited or enclosed within the walls of the city, two demigods, Picus and Faunus, frequented the springs and thick shades of that place; which might be two satyrs, or Pans, except that they went about Italy playing the same sorts of tricks, by skill in drugs and magic, as are ascribed by the Greeks to the Dactyli of Mount Ida. Numa contrived one day to surprise these demigods, by mixing wine and honey in the waters of the spring of which they usually drank. On finding themselves ensnared, they changed themselves into various shapes, dropping their own form and assuming every kind of unusual and hideous appearance; but when they saw they were safely entrapped, and in no possibility of getting free, they revealed to him many secrets and future events; and particularly a charm for thunder and lightning, still in use, performed with onions and hair and pilchards.

Some say they did not tell him the charm, but by their magic brought down Jupiter out of heaven; and that he then, in an angry manner answering the inquiries, told Numa that, if he would charm the thunder and lightning, he must do it with heads. "How," said Numa, "with the heads of onions?" "No," replied Jupiter, "of men." But Numa, willing to elude the cruelty of this receipt, turned it another way, saying, "Your meaning is, the hairs of men's heads." "No," replied Jupiter, "with living"—"pilchards," said Numa interrupting him. These answers he had learnt from Egeria. Jupiter returned again to heaven, pacified and *ileos*, or propitious. The place was, in remembrance of him, called Ilicium, from this Greek word; and the spell in this manner effected.

These stories, laughable as they are, show us the feelings which people then, by force of habit, entertained towards the deity. And Numa's own thoughts are said to have been fixed to that degree on divine objects, that he once, when a message was brought to him that "Enemies are approaching," answered with a smile, "And I am sacrificing." It was he, also, that built the temples of Faith and Terminus, and taught the Romans that the name of Faith was the most solemn oath that they could swear. They still use it.

To the god Terminus, or Boundary, they offer to this day both public and private sacrifices, upon the borders and stone-marks of their land; living victims now, though anciently those sacrifices were solemnised without blood; for Numa reasoned that the god of boundaries, who watched over peace, and testified to fair dealing, should have no concern with blood. It is very clear that it was this king who first prescribed bounds to the territory of Rome; for Romulus would but have openly betrayed how much he had encroached on his neighbours' lands, had he ever set limits to his own; for boundaries are, indeed, a defence to those who choose to observe them, but are only a testimony against the dishonesty of those who break through them. The truth is, the portion of lands which the Romans possessed at the beginning was very narrow, until Romulus enlarged them by war; all those acquisitions Numa now divided amongst the indigent commonalty, wishing to do away with that extreme want which is a compulsion to dishonesty, and, by turning the people to husbandry, to bring them, as well as their lands, into better order.

For there is no employment that gives so keen and quick a relish for peace as husbandry and a country life, which leave in men all that kind of courage that makes them ready to fight in defence of their own, while it destroys the licence that breaks out into acts of injustice and rapacity. Numa, therefore, hoping agriculture would be a sort of charm to captivate the affections of his people to peace, and viewing it rather as a means to moral than to economical profit, divided all the lands into several parcels, to which he gave the name of *pagus,* or parish, and over every one of them he ordained chief overseers; and, taking a delight sometimes to inspect his colonies in person, he formed his judgment of every man's habits by the results; of which being witness himself, he preferred those to honours and employments who had done well, and by rebukes and reproaches incited the indolent and careless to improvement.

But of all his measures the most commended was his distribution of the people by their trades into companies or guilds; for as the city consisted, or rather did not consist of, but was divided into, two different tribes, the diversity between which could not be effaced and in the meantime prevented all unity and caused perpetual tumult and ill-blood, reflecting how hard substances that do not readily mix when in the lump may, by being beaten into powder, in that minute form be combined, he resolved to divide the whole population into a number of small divisions, and thus hoped, by introducing other distinctions, to obliterate the original and great distinction, which would be lost among the smaller. So, distinguishing the whole people by the several arts and trades, he formed the companies of musicians, goldsmiths, carpenters, dyers, shoemakers, skinners, braziers, and potters; and all other handicraftsmen he composed and reduced into a single company, appointing every one their proper courts, councils, and religious observances. In this manner all factious distinctions began, for the first time, to pass out of use, no person any longer being either thought of or spoken of under the notion of a Sabine or a Roman, a Romulian or a Tatian; and the new division became a source of general harmony and intermixture.

He is also much to be commended for the repeal, or rather amendment, of that law which gives power to fathers to sell their children; he exempted such as were married, conditionally that it had been with the liking and consent of their parents; for it seemed a hard thing that a woman who had given herself in marriage to a man whom she judged free should afterwards find herself living with a slave.

He attempted, also, the formation of a calendar, not with absolute exactness, yet not without some scientific knowledge. During the reign of Romulus, they had let their months run on without any certain or equal term; some of them contained twenty days, others thirty-five, others more; they had no sort of knowledge of the inequality in the motions of the sun and moon; they only kept to the one rule that the whole course of the year contained three hundred and sixty days. Numa, calculating the difference between the lunar and the solar year at eleven days, for that the moon completed her anniversary course in three hundred and fifty-four days, and the sun in three hundred and sixty-five, to remedy this incongruity doubled the eleven days, and every other year added an intercalary month, to follow February, consisting of twenty-two days, and called by the Romans the month Mercedinus. This amendment, however, itself, in course of time, came to need other amendments.

He also altered the order of the months; for March, which was reckoned the first, he put into the third place; and January, which was the eleventh, he made the first; and February, which was the twelfth and last, the second. Many will have it, that it was Numa, also, who added the two months of January and February; for in the beginning they had had a year of ten months; as there are barbarians who count only three; the Arcadians, in Greece, had but four; the Acarnanians, six. The Egyptian year at first, they say, was of one month; afterwards, of four; and so, though they live in the newest of all countries, they have the credit of being a more ancient nation than any, and reckon, in their genealogies, a prodigious number of years, counting months, that is, as years.

That the Romans, at first, comprehended the whole year within ten, and not twelve months, plainly appears by the name of the last, December, meaning the tenth month; and that March was the first is likewise evident, for the fifth month after it was called Quintilis, and the sixth Sextilis, and so the rest; whereas, if January and February had, in this account, preceded March, Quintilis would have been fifth in name and seventh in reckoning. It was also natural that March, dedicated to Mars, should be Romulus's first, and April, named from Venus, or Aphrodite, his second month; in it they sacrifice to Venus, and the women bathe on the calends, or first day of it, with myrtle garlands on their heads. But others, because of its being *p* and not *ph*, will not allow of the derivation of this word from Aphrodite, but say it is called April from *aperio*, Latin for to open, because that this month is high spring, and opens and discloses the buds and flowers. The next is called May, from Maia, the mother of Mercury, to whom it is sacred; then June follows, so called from Juno; some, however, derive them from the two ages, old and young, *majores*, being their name for older, and *juniores* for younger men. To the other months they gave denominations according to their order; so the fifth was called Quintilis, Sextilis the

sixth, and the rest, September, October, November, and December.

Afterwards Quintilis received the name of Julius, from Cæsar, who defeated Pompey; as also Sextilis that of Augustus, from the second Cæsar, who had that title. Domitian, also, in imitation, gave the two other following months his own names, of Germanicus and Domitianus; but, on his being slain, they recovered their ancient denominations of September and October. The two last are the only ones that have kept their names throughout without any alteration.

Of the months which were added or transposed in their order by Numa, February comes from *februa;* and is as much a Purification month; in it they make offerings to the dead, and celebrate the Lupercalia, which, in most points, resembles a purification. January was so called from Janus, and precedence given to it by Numa before March, which was dedicated to the god Mars; because, as I conceive, he wished to take every opportunity of intimating that the arts and studies of peace are to be preferred before those of war.

For this Janus, whether in remote antiquity he were a demigod or a king, was certainly a great lover of civil and social unity, and one who reclaimed men from brutal and savage living; for which reason they figure him with two faces, to represent the two states and conditions out of the one of which he brought mankind, to lead them into the other. His temple at Rome has two gates, which they call the gates of war, because they stand open in the time of war, and shut in the times of peace; of which latter there was very seldom an example, for, as the Roman empire was enlarged and extended, it was so encompassed with barbarous nations and enemies to be resisted, that it was seldom or never at peace. Only in the time of Augustus Cæsar, after he had overcome Antony, this temple was shut; as likewise once before, when Marcus Atilius and Titus Manlius were consuls; but then it was not long before, wars breaking out, the gates were again opened.

But, during the reign of Numa, those gates were never seen open a single day, but continued constantly shut for a space of forty-three years together; such an entire and universal cessation of war existed. For not only had the people of Rome itself been softened and charmed into a peaceful temper by the just and mild rule of a pacific prince, but even the neighbouring cities, as if some

salubrious and gentle air had blown from
Rome upon them, began to experience a
change of feeling, and partook in the general
longing for the sweets of peace and order,
and for life employed in the quiet tillage of
soil, bringing up of children, and worship of
the gods. Festival days and sports, and the
secure and peaceful interchange of friendly
visits and hospitalities prevailed all through
the whole of Italy. The love of virtue and
justice flowed from Numa's wisdom as from a
fountain, and the serenity of his spirit diffused itself, like a calm, on all sides; so that
the hyperboles of poets were flat and tame to
express what then existed; as that—

Over the iron shield the spiders hang their
*   threads,*

or that—

Rust eats the pointed spear and double-edged
*   sword.*
No more is heard the trumpet's brazen roar,
Sweet sleep is banished from our eyes no more.

For during the whole reign of Numa, there
was neither war, nor sedition, nor innovation
in the state, nor any envy or ill-will to his
person, nor plot or conspiracy from views of
ambition. Either fear of the gods that were
thought to watch over him, or reverence for
his virtue, or a divine felicity of fortune that
in his days preserved human innocence, made
his reign, by whatever means, a living example and verification of that saying which
Plato, long afterwards, ventured to pronounce,
that the sole and only hope of respite or remedy for human evils was in some happy conjunction of events which should unite in a single person the power of a king and the wisdom
of a philosopher, so as to elevate virtue to control and mastery over vice.

The wise man is blessed in himself, and
blessed also are the auditors who can hear
and receive those words which flow from his
mouth; and perhaps, too, there is no need of
compulsion or menaces to affect the multitude,
for the mere sight itself of a shining and conspicuous example of virtue in the life of their
prince will bring them spontaneously to virtue,
and to a conformity with that blameless and
blessed life of good-will and mutual concord,
supported by temperance and justice, which is
the highest benefit that human means can confer; and he is the truest ruler who can best introduce it into the hearts and practice of his
subjects. It is the praise of Numa that no one
seems ever to have discerned this so clearly as
he.

As to his children and wives, there is a
diversity of reports by several authors; some
will have it that he never had any other wife
than Tatia; nor more children than one
daughter called Pompilia; others will have it
that he left also four sons, namely, Pompo,
Pinus, Calpus, and Mamercus, every one of
whom had issue, and from them descended
the noble and illustrious families of Pomponii,
Pinarii, Calpurnii, and Mamerci, which for
this reason took also the surname of Rex, or
King.

But there is a third set of writers who say
that these pedigrees are but a piece of flattery
used by writers who, to gain favour with these
great families, made them fictitious genealogies from the lineage of Numa; and that
Pompilia was not the daughter of Tatia, but
Lucretia, another wife whom he married after
he came to his kingdom; however, all of
them agree in opinion that she was married
to the son of that Marcius who persuaded him
to accept the government, and accompanied
him to Rome, where, as a mark of honour, he
was chosen into the senate, and after the death
of Numa, standing in competition with Tullus
Hostilius for the kingdom, and being disappointed of the election, in discontent killed
himself; his son Marcius, however, who had
married Pompilia, continuing at Rome, was
the father of Ancus Marcius, who succeeded
Tullus Hostilius in the kingdom, and was but
five years of age when Numa died.

Numa lived something above eighty years,
and then, as Piso writes, was not taken out
of the world by a sudden or acute disease,
but died of old age and by a gradual and
gentle decline. At his funeral all the glories
of his life were consummated, when all the
neighbouring states in alliance and amity with
Rome met to honour and grace the rites of
his interment with garlands and public presents; the senators carried the bier on which
his corpse was laid, and the priests followed
and accompanied the solemn procession;
while a general crowd, in which women and
children took part, followed with such cries
and weeping as if they had bewailed the
death and loss of some most dear relation
taken away in the flower of age, and not an
old and worn-out king.

It is said that his body, by his particular
command, was not burnt, but that they made,
in conformity with his order, two stone
coffins, and buried both under the hill Janiculum, in one of which his body was laid, and

the other his sacred books, which, as the Greek legislators their tables, he had written out for himself, but had so long inculcated the contents of them, whilst he lived, into the minds and hearts of the priests, that their understandings became fully possessed with the whole spirit and purpose of them; and he therefore bade that they should be buried with his body, as though such holy precepts could not without irreverence be left to circulate in mere lifeless writings.

For this very reason, they say, the Pythagoreans bade that their precepts should not be committed to paper, but rather preserved in the living memories of those who were worthy to receive them; and when some of their out-of-the-way and abstruse geometrical processes had been divulged to an unworthy person, they said the gods threatened to punish this wickedness and profanity by a signal and wide-spreading calamity. With these several instances concurring to show a similarity in the lives of Numa and Pythagoras, we may easily pardon those who seek to establish the fact of a real acquaintance between them.

Valerius Antias writes that the books which were buried in the aforesaid chest or coffin of stone were twelve volumes of holy writ and twelve others of Greek philosophy, and that about four hundred years afterwards, when P. Cornelius and M. Bæbius were consuls, in a time of heavy rains, a violent torrent washed away the earth, and dislodged the chests of

stone; and, their covers falling off, one of them was found wholly empty, without the least relic of any human body; in the other were the books before mentioned, which the prætor Petilius having read and perused, made oath in the senate, that, in his opinion, it was not fit for their contents to be made public to the people; whereupon the volumes were all carried to the Comitium, and there burnt.

It is the fortune of all good men that their virtue rises in glory after their deaths, and that the envy which evil men conceive against them never outlives them long; some have the happiness even to see it die before them; but in Numa's case, also, the fortunes of the succeeding kings served as foils to set off the brightness of his reputation. For after him there were five kings, the last of whom ended his old age in banishment, being deposed from his crown; of the other four, three were assassinated and murdered by treason; the other, who was Tullus Hostilius, that immediately succeeded Numa, derided his virtues, and especially his devotion to religious worship, as a cowardly and mean-spirited occupation, and diverted the minds of the people to war; but was checked in these youthful insolences, and was himself driven by an acute and tormenting disease into superstitions, wholly different from Numa's piety, and left others also to participate in these terrors when he died by the stroke of a thunderbolt.

LYCURGUS and NUMA
Compared

Having thus finished the lives of Lycurgus and Numa, we shall now, though the work be difficult, put together their points of difference as they lie here before our view. Their points of likeness are obvious; their moderation, their religion, their capacity of government and discipline, their both deriving their laws and constitutions from the gods.

Yet in their common glories there are circumstances of diversity; for first Numa accepted and Lycurgus resigned a kingdom; Numa received without desiring it, Lycurgus had it and gave it up; the one from a private person and a stranger was raised by others to be their king; the other from the condition of a prince voluntarily descended to the state of privacy. It was glorious to acquire a throne by justice, yet more glorious to prefer justice

before a throne; the same virtue which made the one appear worthy of regal power exalted the other to the disregard of it. Lastly, as the musicians tune their harps, so the one let down the high-flown spirits of the people at Rome to a lower key, as the other screwed them up at Sparta to a higher note, when they were sunken low by dissoluteness and riot.

The harder task was that of Lycurgus; for it was not so much his business to persuade his citizens to put off their armour or ungird their swords, as to cast away their gold or silver, and abandon costly furniture and rich tables; nor was it necessary to preach to them, that, laying aside their arms, they should observe the festivals, and sacrifice to the gods, but rather, that, giving up feasting and drinking, they should employ their time in laborious and martial exercises; so that while the one effected all by persuasions and his people's love for him, the other, with danger and hazard of his person, scarcely in the end succeeded.

Numa's muse was a gentle and loving inspiration, fitting him well to turn and soothe his people into peace and justice out of their violent and fiery tempers; whereas, if we must admit the treatment of the Helots to be a part of Lycurgus's legislation, a most cruel and iniquitous proceeding, we must own that Numa was by a great deal the more humane and Greek-like legislator, granting even to actual slaves a licence to sit at meat with their masters at the feast of Saturn, that they also might have some taste and relish of the sweets of liberty. For this custom, too, is ascribed to Numa, whose wish was, they conceive, to give a place in the enjoyment of the yearly fruits of the soil to those who had helped to produce them. Others will have it to be in remembrance of the age of Saturn, when there was no distinction between master and slave, but all lived as brothers and as equals in a condition of equality.

In general, it seems that both aimed at the same design and intent, which was to bring their people to moderation and frugality; but of other virtues, the one set his affection most on fortitude, and the other on justice; unless we will attribute their different ways to the different habits and temperaments which they had to work upon by their enactments; for Numa did not out of cowardice or fear affect peace, but because he would not be guilty of injustice; nor did Lycurgus promote a spirit of war in his people that they might do injustice to others, but that they might protect themselves by it.

In bringing the habits they formed in their people to a just and happy mean, mitigating them where they exceeded, and strengthening them where they were deficient, both were compelled to make great innovations. The frame of government which Numa formed was democratic and popular to the last extreme, goldsmiths and flute-players and shoemakers constituting his promiscuous, many-colored commonalty. Lycurgus was rigid and aristocratical, banishing all the base and mechanic arts to the company of servants and strangers, and allowing the true citizens no implements but the spear and shield, the trade of war only, and the service of Mars, and no other knowledge or study, but that of obedience to their commanding officers, and

victory over their enemies. Every sort of money-making was forbid them as freemen; and to make them thoroughly so and keep them so through their whole lives, every conceivable concern with money was handed over, with the cooking and the waiting at table, to slaves and Helots.

But Numa made none of these distinctions; he only suppressed military rapacity, allowing free scope to every other means of obtaining wealth; nor did he endeavour to do away with inequality in this respect, but permitted riches to be amassed to any extent, and paid no attention to the gradual and continual augmentation and influx of poverty; which it was his business at the outset, whilst there was no great disparity in the estates of men, and whilst people still lived much in one manner, to obviate, as Lycurgus did, and take measures of precaution against the mischiefs of avarice, mischiefs not of small importance, but the real seed and first beginning of all the great and extensive evils of after-times. The redivision of estates, Lycurgus is not, it seems to me, to be blamed for making, nor Numa for omitting; this equality was the basis and foundation of the one commonwealth; but at Rome, where the lands had been lately divided, there was nothing to urge any redivision or any disturbance of the first arrangement, which was probably still in existence.

With respect to wives and children, and that community which both, with a sound policy, appointed, to prevent all jealousy, their methods, however, were different. For when a Roman thought himself to have a sufficient number of children, in case his neighbour who had none should come and request his wife of him, he had a lawful power to give her up to him who desired her, either for a certain time, or for good. The Lacedæmonian husband, on the other hand, might allow the use of his wife to any other that desired to have children by her, and yet still keep her in his house, the original marriage obligation still subsisting as at first. Nay, many husbands, as we have said, would invite men whom they thought likely to procure them fine and good-looking children into their houses. What is the difference, then, between the two customs? Shall we say that the Lacedæmonian system is one of an extreme and entire unconcern about their wives, and would cause most people endless disquiet and annoyance with pangs and jealousies; the Roman course wears an air of a more delicate acquiescence, draws the veil of a new contract over the change, and concedes the general insupportableness of mere community?

Numa's directions, too, for the care of young women, are better adapted to the female sex and to propriety; Lycurgus's are altogether unreserved and unfeminine, and have given a great handle to the poets, who call them (Ibycus, for example) *Phænomerides,* barethighed; and give them the character (as does Euripides) of being wild after husbands—

These with the young men from the house go out,
With thighs that show, and robes that fly about.

For in fact the skirts of the frock worn by unmarried girls were not sewn together at the lower part, but used to fly back and show the whole thigh bare as they walked. The thing is most distinctly given by Sophocles—

> *—She, also, the young maid,*
> *Whose frock, no robe yet o'er it laid,*
> *Folding back, leaves her bare thigh free,*
> *Hermione.*

And so their women, it is said, were bold and masculine, overbearing to their husbands in the first place, absolute mistresses in their houses, giving their opinions about public matters freely, and speaking openly even on the most important subjects.

But the matrons, under the government of Numa, still indeed received from their husbands all that high respect and honour which had been paid them under Romulus as a sort of atonement for the violence done to them; nevertheless, great modesty was enjoined upon them; all busy intermeddling forbidden, sobriety insisted on, and silence made habitual. Wine they were not to touch at all, nor to speak, except in their husband's company, even on the most ordinary subjects. So that once when a woman had the confidence to plead her own cause in a court of judicature, the senate, it is said, sent to inquire of the oracle what the prodigy did portend; and, indeed, their general good behaviour and submissiveness is justly proved by the record of those that were otherwise; for as the Greek historians record in their annals the names of those who first unsheathed the sword of civil war, or murdered their brothers, or were parricides, or killed their mothers, so the Roman writers report it as the first example, that Spurius Carvilius divorced his wife, being a case that never before happened, in the space of two hundred and thirty years

from the foundation of the city; and that one Thalæa, the wife of Pinarius, had a quarrel (the first instance of the kind) with her mother-in-law, Gegania, in the reign of Tarquinius Superbus; so successful was the legislator in securing order and good conduct in the marriage relation.

Their respective regulations for marrying the young women are in accordance with those for their education. Lycurgus made them brides when they were of full age and inclination for it. Intercourse, where nature was thus consulted, would produce, he thought, love and tenderness, instead of the dislike and fear attending an unnatural compulsion; and their bodies, also, would be better able to bear the trials of breeding and of bearing children, in his judgment the one end of marriage.

The Romans, on the other hand, gave their daughters in marriage as early as twelve years old, or even under; thus they thought their bodies and minds alike would be delivered to the future husband pure and undefiled. The way of Lycurgus seems the more natural with a view to the birth of children; the other, looking to a life to be spent together, is more moral. However, the rules which Lycurgus drew up for superintendence of children, their collection into companies, their discipline and association, as also his exact regulations for their meals, exercises, and sports, argue Numa no more than an ordinary lawgiver. Numa left the whole matter simply to be decided by the parent's wishes or necessities; he might, if he pleased, make his son a husbandman or carpenter, coppersmith or musician; as if it were of no importance for them to be directed and trained up from the beginning to one and the same common end, or as though it would do for them to be like passengers on shipboard, brought thither each for his own ends and by his own choice, uniting to act for the common good only in time of danger upon occasion of their private fears, in general looking simply to their own interest.

We may forbear, indeed, to blame common legislators, who may be deficient in power or knowledge. But when a wise man like Numa had received the sovereignty over a new and docile people, was there anything that would better deserve his attention than the education of children, and the training up of the young, not to contrariety and discordance of character, but to the unity of the common model of virtue, to which from their cradle they should have been formed and moulded? One benefit among many that Lycurgus obtained by his course was the permanence which it secured to his laws. The obligation of oaths to preserve them would have availed but little, if he had not, by discipline and education, infused them into the children's characters, and imbued their whole early life with a love of his government. The result was that the main points and fundamentals of his legislation continued for above five hundred years, like some deep and thoroughly ingrained tincture, retaining their hold upon the nation.

But Numa's whole design and aim, the continuance of peace and goodwill, on his death vanished with him; no sooner did he expire his last breath than the gates of Janus's temple flew wide open, and, as if war had, indeed, been kept and caged up within those walls, it rushed forth to fill all Italy with blood and slaughter; and thus that best and justest fabric of things was of no long continuance, because it wanted that cement which should have kept all together, education. What, then, some may say, has not Rome been advanced and bettered by her wars? A question

that will need a long answer, if it is to be one to satisfy men who take the *better* to consist in riches, luxury, and dominion, rather than in security, gentleness, and that independence which is accompanied by justice. However, it makes much for Lycurgus, that, after the Romans had deserted the doctrine and discipline of Numa, their empire grew and their power increased so much; whereas so soon as the Lacedæmonians fell from the institutions of Lycurgus, they sank from the highest to the lowest state, and, after forfeiting their supremacy over the rest of Greece, were themselves in danger of absolute extirpation.

Thus much, meantime, was peculiarly signal and almost divine in the circumstances of Numa, that he was an alien, and yet courted to come and accept a kingdom, the frame of which though he entirely altered, yet he performed it by mere persuasion, and ruled a city that as yet had scarce become one city, without recurring to arms or any violence (such as Lycurgus used, supporting himself by the aid of the nobler citizens against the commonalty), but, by mere force of wisdom and justice, established union and harmony amongst all.

SOLON

638–539 B.C.

DIDYMUS, the grammarian, in his answer to Asclepiades concerning Solon's Tables of Law, mentions a passage of one Philocles, who states that Solon's father's name was Euphorion, contrary to the opinion of all others who have written concerning him; for they generally agree that he was the son of Execestides, a man of moderate wealth and power in the city, but of a most noble stock, being descended from Codrus; his mother, as Heraclides Ponticus affirms, was cousin to Pisistratus's mother, and the two at first were great friends, partly because they were akin, and partly because of Pisistratus's noble qualities and beauty. And they say Solon loved him; and that is the reason, I suppose, that when afterwards they differed about the government, their enmity never produced any hot and violent passion; they remembered their old kindnesses, and retained—

Still in its embers living the strong fire

of their love and dear affection. For that Solon was not proof against beauty, nor of courage to stand up to passion and meet it—

Hand to hand as in the ring,

we may conjecture by his poems, and one of his laws, in which there are practices forbidden to slaves, which he would appear, therefore, to recommend to freemen. Pisistratus, it is stated, was similarly attached to one Charmus; he it was who dedicated the figure of Love in the Academy, where the runners in the sacred torch race light their torches.

Solon, as Hermippus writes, when his father had ruined his estate in doing benefits and kindnesses to other men, though he had friends enough that were willing to contribute to his relief, yet was ashamed to be beholden to others, since he was descended from a family who were accustomed to do kindnesses rather than receive them; and therefore applied himself to merchandise in his youth;

though others assure us that he travelled rather to get learning and experience than to make money. It is certain that he was a lover of knowledge, for when he was old he would say, that he—
Each day grew older, and learnt something new;
and yet no admirer of riches, esteeming as equally wealthy the man—
Who hath both gold and silver in his hand,
Horses and mules, and acres of wheat-land,
And him whose all is decent food to eat,
Clothes to his back and shoes upon his feet,
And a young wife and child, since so 'twill be,
And no more years than will with that agree;
and in another place—
Wealth I would have, but wealth by wrong
procure
I would not; justice, e'en if slow, is sure.
And it is perfectly possible for a good man and a statesman, without being solicitous for superfluities, to show some concern for competent necessaries.

In his time, as Hesiod says,—"Work was a shame to none," nor was distinction made with respect to trade, but merchandise was a noble calling, which brought home the good things which the barbarous nations enjoyed, was the occasion of friendship with their kings, and a great source of experience. Some merchants have built great cities, as Protis, the founder of Massilia, to whom the Gauls, near the Rhone, were much attached. Some report also, that Thales and Hippocrates the mathematician traded; and that Plato defrayed the charges of his travels by selling oil in Egypt. Solon's softness and profuseness, his popular rather than philosophical tone about pleasure in his poems, have been ascribed to his trading life; for, having suffered a thousand dangers, it was natural they should be recompensed with some gratifications and enjoyments; but that he accounted himself rather poor than rich is evident from the lines—
Some wicked men are rich, some good are poor,
We will not change our virtue for their store:
Virtue's a thing that none can take away;
But money changes owners all the day.

At first he used his poetry only in trifles, not for any serious purpose, but simply to pass away his idle hours; but afterwards he introduced moral sentences and state matters, which he did, not to record them merely as an historian, but to justify his own actions, and sometimes to correct, chastise, and stir up the Athenians to noble performances.

Some report that he designed to put his laws into heroic verse, and that they began thus:—
We humbly beg a blessing on our laws
From mighty Jove, and honour, and applause.

In philosophy, as most of the wise men then, he chiefly esteemed the political part of morals; in physics, he was very plain and antiquated, as appears by this:—
It is the clouds that make the snow and hail,
And thunder comes from lightning without fail;
The sea is stormy when the winds have blown,
But it deals fairly when 'tis left alone.
And, indeed, it is probable that at that time Thales alone had raised philosophy above mere practice into speculation; and the rest of the wise men were so called from prudence in political concerns.

It is said, that they had an interview at Delphi, and another at Corinth, by the procurement of Periander, who made a meeting for them, and a supper. But their reputation was chiefly raised by sending the tripod to them all, by their modest refusal, and complaisant yielding to one another. For, as the story goes, some of the Coans fishing with a net, some strangers, Milesians, bought the draught at a venture; the net brought up a golden tripod, which, they say, Helen, at her return from Troy, upon the remembrance of an old prophecy, threw in there. Now, the strangers at first contesting with the fishers about the tripod, and the cities espousing the quarrel so far as to engage themselves in a war, Apollo decided the controversy by commanding to present it to the wisest man; and first it was sent to Miletus to Thales, the Coans freely presenting him with that for which they fought against the whole body of the Milesians; but Thales declaring Bias the wiser person, it was sent to him; from him to another; and so, going round them all, it came to Thales a second time; and, at last, being carried from Miletus to Thebes, was there dedicated to Apollo Ismenius. Theophrastus writes that it was first presented to Bias at Priene; and next to Thales at Miletus, and so through all it returned to Bias, and was afterwards sent to Delphi. This is the general report, only some, instead of a tripod, say this present was a cup sent by Crœsus; others, a piece of plate that one Bathycles had left.

It is stated, that Anacharsis and Solon, and Solon and Thales, were familiarly acquainted, and some have delivered parts of their discourse; for, they say, Anacharsis, coming to Athens, knocked at Solon's door, and told him, that he, being a stranger, was come to be his guest, and contract a friendship with him; and Solon replying, "It is better to make friends at home," Anacharsis replied, "Then you that are at home make friendship with me." Solon, somewhat surprised at the readiness of the repartee, received him kindly, and kept him some time with him, being already engaged in public business and the compilation of his laws; which, when Anacharsis understood, he laughed at him for imagining the dishonesty and covetousness of his countrymen could be restrained by written laws, which were like spiders' webs, and would catch, it is true, the weak and poor, but easily be broken by the mighty and rich. To this Solon rejoined that men keep their promises when neither side can get anything by the breaking of them; and he would so fit his laws to the citizens, that all should understand it was more eligible to be just than to break the laws. But the event rather agreed with the conjecture of Anacharsis than Solon's hope. Anacharsis, being once at the Assembly, expressed his wonder at the fact that in Greece wise men spoke and fools decided.

Solon went, they say, to Thales, at Miletus, and wondered that Thales took no care to get him a wife and children. To this, Thales made no answer for the present; but a few days after procured a stranger to pretend that he had left Athens ten days ago; and Solon inquiring what news there, the man, according to his instructions, replied, "None but a young man's funeral, which the whole city attended; for he was the son, they said, of an honourable man, the most virtuous of the citizens, who was not then at home, but had been travelling a long time." Solon replied, "What a miserable man is he! But what was his name?" "I have heard it," says the man, "but have now forgotten it, only there was a great talk of his wisdom and his justice." Thus Solon was drawn on by every answer, and his fears heightened, till at last, being extremely concerned, he mentioned his own name, and asked the stranger if that young man was called Solon's son; and the stranger assenting, he began to beat his head, and to do and say all that is usual with men in transports of grief. But Thales took his hand, and with a smile, said, "These things, Solon, keep me from marriage and rearing children, which are too great for even your

constancy to support; however, be not concerned at the report, for it is a fiction." This Hermippus relates, from Patæcus, who boasted that he had Æsop's soul.

However, it is irrational and poor-spirited not to seek conveniences for fear of losing them, for upon the same account we should not allow ourselves to like wealth, glory, or wisdom, since we may fear to be deprived of all these; nay, even virtue itself, than which there is no greater nor more desirable possession, is often suspended by sickness or drugs. Now Thales, though unmarried, could not be free from solicitude unless he likewise felt no care for his friends, his kinsman, or his country; yet we are told he adopted Cybisthus, his sister's son.

For the soul, having a principle of kindness in itself, and being born to love, as well as perceive, think, or remember, inclines and fixes upon some stranger, when a man has none of his own to embrace. And alien or illegitimate objects insinuate themselves into his affections, as into some estate that lacks lawful heirs; and with affection come anxiety and care; insomuch that you may see men that use the strongest language against the marriage-bed and the fruit of it, when some servant's or concubine's child is sick or dies, almost killed with grief, and abjectly lamenting. Some have given way to shameful and desperate sorrow at the loss of a dog or horse; others have borne the death of virtuous children without any extravagant or unbecoming grief, have passed the rest of their lives like men, and according to the principles of reason. It is not affection, it is weakness that brings men, unarmed against fortune by reason, into these endless pains and terrors; and they indeed have not even the present enjoyment of what they dote upon, the possibility of the future loss causing them continual pangs, tremors, and distresses. We must not provide against the loss of wealth by poverty, or of friends by refusing all acquaintance, or of children by having none, but by morality and reason. But of this too much.

Now, when the Athenians were tired with a tedious and difficult war that they conducted against the Megarians for the island Salamis, and made a law that it should be death for any man, by writing or speaking, to assert that the city ought to endeavour to recover it, Solon, vexed at the disgrace, and perceiving thousands of the youth wished for somebody to begin, but did not dare to stir first for fear of the law, counterfeited a distraction, and by his own family it was spread about the city that he was mad. He then secretly composed some elegiac verses, and getting them by heart, that it might seem extempore, ran out into the market-place with a cap upon his head, and, the people gathering about him, got upon the herald's stand, and sang that elegy which begins thus:—

I am a herald come from Salamis the fair,
My news from thence my verses shall declare.

The poem is called *Salamis;* it contains an hundred verses very elegantly written; when it had been sung, his friends commended it, and especially Pisistratus exhorted the citizens to obey his directions; insomuch that they recalled the law, and renewed the war under Solon's conduct.

The popular tale is, that with Pisistratus he sailed to Colias, and, finding the women, according to the custom of the country there, sacrificing to Ceres, he sent a trusty friend to Salamis, who should pretend himself a renegade, and advise them, if they desired to seize the chief Athenian women, to come with him at once to Colias; the Megarians presently sent off men in the vessel with him; and Solon, seeing it put off from the island, commanded the women to be gone, and some beardless youths, dressed in their clothes, their shoes and caps, and privately armed with daggers, to dance and play near the shore till the enemies had landed and the vessel was in their power. Things being thus ordered, the Megarians were lured with the appearance, and, coming to the shore, jumped out, eager who should first seize a prize, so that not one of them escaped; and the Athenians set sail for the island and took it.

Others say that it was not taken this way, but that he first received this oracle from Delphi:—

Those heroes that in fair Asopia rest,
All buried with their faces to the west,
Go and appease with offerings of the best;

and that Solon, sailing by night to the island, sacrificed to the heroes Periphemus and Cychreus, and then taking five hundred Athenian volunteers (a law having passed that those that took the island should be highest in the government), with a number of fisherboats and one thirty-oared ship, anchored in a bay of Salamis that looks towards Nisæa; and the Megarians that were then in the island, hearing only an uncertain report, hurried to their arms, and sent a ship to rec-

onnoitre the enemies. This ship Solon took, and, securing the Megarians, manned it with Athenians, and gave them orders to sail to the island with as much privacy as possible; meantime he, with the other soldiers, marched against the Megarians by land, and whilst they were fighting, those from the ship took the city. And this narrative is confirmed by the following solemnity, that was afterwards observed: An Athenian ship used to sail silently at first to the island, then, with noise and a great shout, one leapt out armed, and with a loud cry ran to the promontory Sciradium to meet those that approached upon the land. And just by there stands a temple which Solon dedicated to Mars. For he beat the Megarians, and as many as were not killed in the battle he sent away upon conditions.

The Megarians, however, still contending, and both sides having received considerable losses, they chose the Spartans for arbitrators. Now, many affirm that Homer's authority did Solon a considerable kindness, and that, introducing a line into the Catalogue of Ships, when the matter was to be determined, he read the passage as follows:—

Twelve ships from Salamis stout Ajax brought,
And ranked his men where the Athenians fought.

The Athenians, however, call this but an idle story, and report that Solon made it appear to the judges, that Philæus and Eurysaces, the sons of Ajax, being made citizens of Athens, gave them the island, and that one of them dwelt at Brauron in Attica, the other at Melite; and they have a township of Philaidæ, to which Pisistratus belonged, deriving its name from this Philæus. Solon took a further argument against the Megarians from the dead bodies, which, he said, were not buried after their fashion, but according to the Athenian; for the Megarians turn the corpse to the east, the Athenians to the west. But Hereas the Megarian denies this, and affirms that they likewise turn the body to the west, and also that the Athenians have a separate tomb for everybody, but the Megarians put two or three into one. However, some of Apollo's oracles, where he calls Salamis Ionian, made much for Solon. This matter was determined by five Spartans, Critolaidas, Amompharetus, Hypsechidas, Anaxilas, and Cleomenes.

For this, Solon grew famed and powerful; but his advice in favour of defending the oracle at Delphi, to give aid, and not to suffer the Cirrhæans to profane it, but to maintain the honour of the god, got him most repute among the Greeks; for upon his persuasion the Amphictyons undertook the war, as amongst others, Aristotle affirms, in his enumeration of the victors at the Pythian games, where he makes Solon the author of this counsel. Solon, however, was not general in that expedition, as Hermippus states, out of Evanthes the Samian; for Æschines the orator says no such thing, and, in the Delphian register, Alcmæon, not Solon, is named as commander of the Athenians.

Now the Cylonian pollution had a long while disturbed the commonwealth, ever since the time when Megacles the archon persuaded the conspirators with Cylon that took sanctuary in Minerva's temple to come down and stand to a fair trial. And they, tying a thread to the image, and holding one end of it, went down to the tribunal; but when they came to the temple of the Furies, the thread broke of its own accord, upon which, as if the goddess had refused them protection, they were seized by Megacles and the other magistrates; as many as were without the temples were stoned, these that fled for sanctuary were butchered at the altar, and only those escaped who made supplication to the wives of the magistrates. But they from that time were considered under pollution, and regarded with hatred.

The remainder of the faction of Cylon grew strong again, and had continual quarrels with the family of Megacles; and now the quarrel being at its height, and the people divided, Solon, being in reputation, interposed with the chiefest of the Athenians, and by entreaty and admonition persuaded the polluted to submit to a trial and the decision of three hundred noble citizens. And Myron of Phlya being their accuser, they were found guilty, and as many as were then alive were banished, and the bodies of the dead were dug up, and scattered beyond the confines of the country.

In the midst of these distractions, the Megarians falling upon them, they lost Nisæa and Salamis again; besides, the city was disturbed with superstitious fears and strange appearances, and the priests declared that the sacrifices intimated some villainies and pollutions that were to be expiated. Upon this, they sent for Epimenides the Phæstian from Crete, who is counted the seventh wise man by those that will not admit Periander into the number. He seems to have been thought a favourite of heaven, possessed of knowledge in all the supernatural and ritual parts of religion; and, therefore, the men of his age called him a new Curies, and son of a nymph named Balte. When he came to Athens, and grew acquainted with Solon, he served him in many instances, and prepared the way for his legislation. He made them moderate in their forms of worship, and abated their mourning by ordering some sacrifices presently after the funeral, and taking off those severe and barbarous ceremonies which the women usually practised; but the greatest benefit was his purifying and sanctifying the city, by certain propitiatory and expiatory lustrations, and foundations of sacred buildings, by that means making them more submissive to justice, and more inclined to harmony. It is reported that, looking upon Munychia, and considering a long while, he said to those that stood by, "How blind is man in future things! for did the Athenians foresee what mischief this would do their city, they would even eat it with their own teeth to be rid of it." A similar anticipation is ascribed to Thales; they say he commanded his friends to bury him in an obscure and contemned quarter of the territory of Miletus, saying that it should some day be the market-place of the Milesians. Epimenides, being much honoured, and receiving from the city rich offers of large gifts and privileges, requested but one branch of the sacred olive, and, on that being granted, returned.

The Athenians, now the Cylonian sedition was over and the polluted gone into banishment, fell into their old quarrels about the government, there being as many different parties as there were diversities in the country. The Hill quarter favoured democracy, the Plain, oligarchy, and those that lived by the Seaside stood for a mixed sort of government, and so hindered either of the other parties from prevailing. And the disparity of fortune between the rich and the poor, at that time, also reached its height; so that the city seemed to be in a truly dangerous condition, and no other means for freeing it from disturbances and settling it to be possible but a despotic power. All the people were indebted to the rich; and either they tilled their land for their creditors, paying them a sixth part of the increase, and were, therefore, called Hectemorii and Thetes, or else they engaged their body for the debt, and might be seized, and either sent into slavery at home, or sold to strangers; some (for no law forbade it) were forced to sell their children, or fly their country to avoid the cruelty of their creditors; but the most part and the bravest of them began to combine together and encourage one another to stand to it, to choose a leader, to liberate the condemned debtors, divide the land, and change the government.

Then the wisest of the Athenians, perceiving Solon was of all men the only one not implicated in the troubles, that he had not joined in the exactions of the rich, and was not involved in the necessities of the poor, pressed him to succour the commonwealth and compose the differences. Though Phanias the Lesbian affirms, that Solon, to save his country, put a trick upon both parties, and privately promised the poor a division of the lands, and the rich security for their debts. Solon, however, himself says, that it was reluctantly at first that he engaged in state affairs, being afraid of the pride of one party and the greediness of the other; he was chosen archon, however, after Philombrotus, and empowered to be an arbitrator and lawgiver; the rich consenting because he was wealthy, the poor because he was honest. There was a saying of his current before the election, that when things are *even* there never can be war, and this pleased both parties, the wealthy and the poor; the one conceiving him to mean, when all have their fair proportion; the others, when all are absolutely equal.

Thus, there being great hopes on both sides, the chief men pressed Solon to take the government into his own hands, and, when he was once settled, manage the business freely and according to his pleasure; and many of the commons, perceiving it would be a difficult change to be effected by law and reason, were willing to have one wise and just man set over the affairs; and some say that Solon had this oracle from Apollo—

Take the mid-seat, and be the vessel's guide;
Many in Athens are upon your side.

But chiefly his familiar friends chid him for disaffecting monarchy only because of the name, as if the virtue of the ruler could not make it a lawful form; Euboea had made this experiment when it chose Tynnondas, and Mitylene, which had made Pittacus its prince; yet this could not shake Solon's resolution; but, as they say, he replied to his friends, that it was true a tyranny was a very fair spot, but it had no way down from it; and in a copy of verses to Phocus he writes—

that I spared my land,
And withheld from usurpation and from violence
my hand,
And forbore to fix a stain and a disgrace on my
good name,
I regret not; I believe that it will be my chiefest
fame.

From which it is manifest that he was a man of great reputation before he gave his laws. The several mocks that were put upon him for refusing the power, he records in these words:—

Solon surely was a dreamer, and a man of simple
mind;
When the gods would give him fortune, he of his
own will declined;
When the net was full of fishes, over-heavy
thinking it,
He declined to haul it up, through want of heart
and want of wit.
Had but I that chance of riches and of kingship,
for one day,
I would give my skin for flaying, and my house
to die away.

Thus he makes the many and the low people speak of him. Yet, though he refused the government, he was not too mild in the affair; he did not show himself mean and submissive to the powerful, nor make his laws to pleasure those that chose him. For where it was well before, he applied no remedy, nor altered anything, for fear lest—

Overthrowing altogether and disordering the
state,

he should be too weak to new-model and recompose it to a tolerable condition; but what he thought he could effect by persuasion upon the pliable, and by force upon the stubborn, this he did, as he himself says—

With force and justice working both in one.

And, therefore, when he was afterwards asked if he had left the Athenians the best laws that could be given, he replied, "The best they could receive." The way which, the moderns say, the Athenians have of softening the badness of a thing, by ingeniously giving it some pretty and innocent appellation, calling harlots, for example, mistresses, tributes customs, a garrison a guard, and the jail the chamber, seems originally to have been Solon's contrivance, who called cancelling debts Seisacthea, a relief, or disencumbrance. For the first thing which he settled was, that what debts remained should be forgiven, and no man, for the future, should engage the body of his debtor for security. Though some, as Androtion, affirm that the debts were not cancelled, but the interest only lessened, which sufficiently pleased the people; so that they named this benefit the Seisacthea, together with the enlarging their measures, and raising the value of their money; for he made a pound, which before passed for seventy-three drachmas, go for a hundred; so that, though the number of pieces in the payment was equal, the value was less; which proved a considerable benefit to those that were to discharge great debts, and no loss to the creditors. But most agree that it was the taking off the debts that was called Seisacthea, which is confirmed by some places in his poem, where he takes honour to himself, that—

The mortgage-stones that covered her, by me
Removed,—the land that was a slave is free:

that some who had been seized for their debts he had brought back from other countries, where—

—so far their lot to roam,
They had forgot the language of their home;

and some he had set at liberty—

Who here in shameful servitude were held.

While he was designing this, a most vexatious thing happened; for when he had resolved to take off the debts, and was considering the proper form and fit beginning for it, he told some of his friends, Conon, Clinias, and Hipponicus, in whom he had a great deal of confidence, that he would not meddle with the lands, but only free the people from their debts; upon which they, using their advantage, made haste and borrowed some considerable sums of money, and purchased some large farms; and when the law was enacted, they kept the possessions, and would not return the money; which brought Solon into great suspicion and dislike, as if he himself had not been abused, but was concerned in the contrivance. But he presently stopped this suspicion, by releasing his debtors of five talents (for he had lent so much), according to the law; others, as Polyzelus the Rhodian, say fifteen; his friends, however, were ever afterward called Chreocopidæ, repudiators.

In this he pleased neither party, for the rich were angry for their money, and the poor that the land was not divided, and, as Lycurgus ordered in his commonwealth, all men reduced to equality. He, it is true, being the eleventh from Hercules, and having reigned many years in Lacedæmon, had got a great reputation and friends and power, which he could use in modelling his state;

and applying force more than persuasion, insomuch that he lost his eye in the scuffle, was able to employ the most effectual means for the safety and harmony of a state, by not permitting any to be poor or rich in his commonwealth. Solon could not rise to that in his polity, being but a citizen of the middle classes; yet he acted fully up to the height of his power, having nothing but the goodwill and good opinion of his citizens to rely on; and that he offended the most part, who looked for another result, he declares in the words—

Formerly they boasted of me vainly; with averted eyes
Now they look askance upon me; friends no more, but enemies.

And yet had any other man, he says, received the same power—

He would not have forborne, nor let alone,
But made the fattest of the milk his own.

Soon, however, becoming sensible of the good that was done, they laid by their grudges, made a public sacrifice, calling it Seisacthea, and chose Solon to new-model and make laws for the commonwealth, giving him the entire power over everything, their magistracies, their assemblies, courts, and councils; that he should appoint the number, times of meeting, and what estate they must have that could be capable of these, and dissolve or continue any of the present constitutions, according to his pleasure.

First, then, he repealed all Draco's laws, except those concerning homicide, because they were too severe, and the punishments too great; for death was appointed for almost all offences, insomuch that those that were convicted of idleness were to die, and those that stole a cabbage or an apple to suffer even as villains that committed sacrilege or murder. So that Demades, in after time, was thought to have said very happily, that Draco's laws were written not with ink but blood; and he, himself, being once asked why he made death the punishment of most offences, replied, "Small ones deserve that, and I have no higher for the greater crimes."

Next, Solon, being willing to continue the magistracies in the hands of the rich men, and yet receive the people into the other part of the government, took an account of the citizens' estates, and those that were worth five hundred measures of fruit, dry and liquid, he placed in the first rank, calling them Pentacosiomedimni; those that could keep an horse, or were worth three hundred measures, were named Hippada Teluntes, and made the second class; the Zeugitæ, that had two hundred measures, were in the third; and all the others were called Thetes, who were not admitted to any office, but could come to the assembly, and act as jurors; which at first seemed nothing, but afterwards was found an enormous privilege, as almost every matter of dispute came before them in this latter capacity. Even in the cases which he assigned to the archon's cognisance, he allowed an appeal to the courts.

Besides, it is said that he was obscure and ambiguous in the wording of his laws, on purpose to increase the honour of his courts; for since their differences could not be adjusted by the letter, they would have to bring all their causes to the judges, who thus were in a manner masters of the laws. Of this equalisation he himself makes mention in this manner:—

Such power I gave the people as might do,
Abridged not what they had, now lavished new,
Those that were great in wealth and high in place
My counsel likewise kept from all disgrace.
Before them both I held my shield of might,
And let not either touch the other's right.

And for the greater security of the weak commons, he gave general liberty of indicting for an act of injury; if any one was beaten, maimed, or suffered any violence, any man that would and was able might prosecute the wrong-doer; intending by this to accustom the citizens, like members of the same body, to resent and be sensible of one another's injuries. And there is a saying of his agreeable to his law, for, being asked what city was best modelled, "That," said he, "where those that are not injured try and punish the unjust as much as those that are."

When he had constituted the Areopagus of those who had been yearly archons, of which he himself was a member therefore, observing that the people, now free from their debts, were unsettled and imperious, he formed another council of four hundred, a hundred out of each of the four tribes, which was to inspect all matters before they were propounded to the people, and to take care that nothing but what had been first examined should be brought before the general assembly. The upper council, or Areopagus, he made inspectors and keepers of the laws, conceiving that the commonwealth, held by these two councils, like anchors, would be less liable

to be tossed by tumults, and the people be more quiet.

Such is the general statement, that Solon instituted the Areopagus; which seems to be confirmed, because Draco makes no mention of the Areopagites, but in all causes of blood refers to the Ephetæ; yet Solon's thirteenth table contains the eighth law set down in these very words: "Whoever before Solon's archonship were disfranchised, let them be restored, except those that, being condemned by the Areopagus, Ephetæ, or in the Prytaneum by the kings, for homicide, murder, or designs against the government, were in banishment when this law was made"; and these words seem to show that the Areopagus existed before Solon's laws, for who could be condemned by that council before his time, if he was the first that instituted the court? Unless, which is probable, there is some ellipsis, or want of precision in the language, and it should run thus:—"Those that are convicted of such offences as belong to the cognisance of the Areopagites, Ephetæ, or the Prytanes, when this law was made," shall remain still in disgrace, whilst others are restored; of this the reader must judge.

Amongst his other laws, one is very peculiar and surprising, which disfranchises all who stand neuter in a sedition; for it seems he would not have any one remain insensible and regardless of the public good, and securing his private affairs, glory that he has no feeling of the distempers of his country; but at once join with the good party and those that have the right upon their side, assist and venture with them, rather than keep out of harm's way and watch who would get the better. It seems an absurd and foolish law which permits an heiress, if her lawful husband fail her, to take his nearest kinsman; yet some say this law was well contrived against those who, conscious of their own unfitness, yet, for the sake of the portion, would match with heiresses, and make use of law to put a violence upon nature; for now, since she can quit him for whom she pleases, they would either abstain from such marriages, or continue them with disgrace, and suffer for their covetousness and designed affront; it is well done, moreover, to confine her to her husband's nearest kinsman, that the children may be of the same family. Agreeable to this is the law that the bride and bridegroom shall be shut into a chamber, and eat a quince together; and that the husband of an heiress shall consort with her thrice a month; for though there be no children, yet it is an honour and due affection which an husband ought to pay to a virtuous, chaste wife; it takes off all petty differences, and will not permit their little quarrels to proceed to a rupture.

In all other marriages he forbade dowries to be given; the wife was to have three suits of clothes, a little inconsiderable household stuff, and that was all; for he would not have marriages contracted for gain or an estate, but for pure love, kind affection, and birth of children. When the mother of Dionysius desired him to marry her to one of his citizens, "Indeed," said he, "by my tyranny I have broken my country's laws, but cannot put a violence upon those of nature by an unseasonable marriage." Such disorder is never to be suffered in a commonwealth, nor such unseasonable and unloving and unperforming marriages, which attain no due end or fruit; any provident governor or lawgiver might say to an old man that takes a young wife what is said to Philoctetes in the tragedy—

Truly, in a fit state thou to marry!
and if he find a young man, with a rich and elderly wife, growing fat in his place, like the partridges, remove him to a young woman of proper age. And of this enough.

Another commendable law of Solon's is that which forbids men to speak evil of the dead; for it is pious to think the deceased sacred, and just, not to meddle with those that are gone, and politic, to prevent the perpetuity of discord. He likewise forbade them to speak evil of the living in the temples, the courts of justice, the public offices, or at the games, or else to pay three drachmas to the person, and two to the public. For never to be able to control passion shows a weak nature and ill-breeding; and always to moderate it is very hard, and to some impossible. And laws must look to possibilities, if the maker designs to punish few in order to their amendment, and not many to no purpose.

He is likewise much commended for his law concerning wills; for before him none could be made, but all the wealth and estate of the deceased belonged to his family; but he by permitting them, if they had no children, to bestow it on whom they pleased, showed that he esteemed friendship a stronger tie than kindred, and affection than necessity; and made every man's estate truly his own. Yet he allowed not all sorts of legacies, but those only which were not extorted by the

frenzy of a disease, charms, imprisonment, force, or the persuasions of a wife; with good reason thinking that being seduced into wrong was as bad as being forced, and that between deceit and necessity, flattery and compulsion, there was little difference, since both may equally suspend the exercise of reason.

He regulated the walks, feasts, and mourning of the women, and took away everything that was either unbecoming or immodest; when they walked abroad, no more than three articles of dress were allowed them; an obol's worth of meat and drink; and no basket above a cubit high; and at night they were not to go about unless in a chariot with a torch before them. Mourners tearing themselves to raise pity, and set wailings, and at one man's funeral to lament for another, he forbade. To offer an ox at the grave was not permitted, nor to bury above three pieces of dress with the body, or visit the tombs of any besides their own family, unless at the very funeral; most of which are likewise forbidden by our laws, but this is further added in ours, that those that are convicted of extravagance in their mournings are to be punished as soft and effeminate by the censors of women.

Observing the city to be filled with persons that flocked from all parts into Attica for security of living, and that most of the country was barren and unfruitful, and that traders at sea import nothing to those that could give them nothing in exchange, he turned his citizens to trade, and made a law that no son be obliged to relieve a father who had not bred him up to any calling. It is true, Lycurgus, having a city free from all strangers, and land, according to Euripides—

Large for large hosts, for twice their number much,
and, above all, an abundance of labourers about Sparta, who should not be left idle, but be kept down with continual toil and work, did well to take off his citizens from laborious and mechanical occupations, and keep them to their arms, and teach them only the art of war.

But Solon, fitting his laws to the state of things, and not making things to suit his laws, and finding the ground scarce rich enough to maintain the husbandmen, and altogether incapable of feeding an unoccupied and leisured multitude, brought trades into credit, and ordered the Areopagites to examine how every man got his living, and chastise the idle. But that law was yet more rigid which, as Heraclides Ponticus delivers, declared the sons of unmarried mothers not obliged to relieve their fathers; for he that avoids the honourable form of union shows that he does not take a woman for children, but for pleasure, and thus gets his just reward, and has taken away from himself every title to upbraid his children, to whom he has made their very birth a scandal and reproach.

Solon's laws in general about women are his strangest; for he permitted any one to kill an adulterer that found him in the act; but if any one forced a free woman, a hundred drachmas was the fine, if he enticed her, twenty; except those that sell themselves openly, that is, harlots, who go openly to those that hire them. He made it unlawful to sell a daughter or a sister, unless, being yet unmarried, she was found wanton. Now it is irrational to punish the same crime sometimes very severely and without remorse, and sometimes very lightly, and as it were in sport, with a trivial fine; unless there being little money then in Athens, scarcity made those mulcts the more grievous punishment.

In the valuation for sacrifices, a sheep and a bushel were both estimated at a drachma; the victor in the Isthmian games was to have for reward an hundred drachmas; the conqueror in the Olympian, five hundred; he that brought a wolf, five drachmas; for a whelp, one; the former sum, as Demetrius the Phalerian asserts, was the value of an ox, the latter, of a sheep. The prices which Solon, in his sixteenth table, sets on choice victims, were naturally far greater; yet they, too, are very low in comparison of the present. The Athenians were, from the beginning, great enemies to wolves, their fields being better for pasture than corn. Some affirm their tribes did not take their names from the sons of Ion, but from the different sorts of occupation that they followed; the soldiers were called Hoplitæ, the craftsmen Ergades, and, of the remaining two, the farmers Gedeontes, and the shepherds and graziers Ægicores.

Since the country has but few rivers, lakes, or large springs, and many used wells which they had dug, there was a law made, that, where there was a public well within a *hippicon,* that is, four furlongs, all should draw at that; but when it was farther off, they should try and procure a well of their own; and if they had dug ten fathoms deep and could find no water, they had liberty to fetch a pitcherful of four gallons and a half in a day from their neighbours'; for he thought it prudent to make provision against want, but not to supply laziness. He showed skill in his orders about planting, for any one that would plant another tree was not to set it within five feet of his neighbour's field; but if a fig or an olive, not within nine; for their roots spread farther, nor can they be planted near all sorts of trees without damage, for they draw away the nourishment, and in some cases are noxious by their effluvia. He that would dig a pit or a ditch was to dig it at the distance of its own depth from his neighbour's ground; and he that would raise stocks of bees was not to place them within three hundred feet of those which another had already raised.

He permitted only oil to be exported, and those that exported any other fruit, the archon was solemnly to curse, or else pay an hundred drachmas himself; and this law was written in his first table, and, therefore, let none think it incredible, as some affirm, that the exportation of figs was once unlawful, and the informer against the delinquents called a sycophant. He made a law, also, concerning hurts and injuries from beasts, in which he commands the master of any dog that bit a man to deliver him up with a log about his neck, four and a half feet long; a happy device for men's security. The law concerning naturalising strangers is of doubtful character, he permitted only those to be made free of Athens who were in perpetual exile from their own country, or came with their whole family to trade there; this he did, not to discourage strangers, but rather to invite them to a permanent participation in the privileges of the government; and, besides, he thought those would prove the more faithful citizens who had been forced from their own country, or voluntarily forsook it. The law of public entertainment (*parasitein* is his name for it) is also peculiarly Solon's; for if any man came often, or if he that was invited refused, they were punished, for he concluded that one was greedy, the other a contemner of the state.

All his laws he established for an hundred years, and wrote them on wooden tables or rollers, named *axones,* which might be turned round in oblong cases; some of their relics were in my time still to be seen in the Prytaneum, or common hall, at Athens. These, as Aristotle states, were called *cyrbes,* and there is a passage of Cratinus the comedian—

By Solon, and by Draco, if you please,
Whose Cyrbes make the fires that parch our peas.

But some say those are properly *cyrbes,* which contain laws concerning sacrifices and the rites of religion, and all the other *axones.* The council all jointly swore to confirm the laws, and every one of the Thesmothetæ vowed for himself at the stone in the marketplace, that if he broke any of the statutes, he would dedicate a golden statue, as big as himself, at Delphi.

Observing the irregularity of the months, and that the moon does not always rise and set with the sun, but often in the same day overtakes and gets before him, he ordered the day should be named the Old and New, attributing that part of it which was before the conjunction to the old moon, and the rest to the new, he being the first, it seems, that understood that verse of Homer—

The end and the beginning of the month,—

and the following day he called the new moon. After the twentieth he did not count by addition, but, like the moon itself in its wane, by subtraction; thus up to the thirtieth.

Now when these laws were enacted, and some came to Solon every day, to commend or dispraise them, and to advise, if possible, to leave out or put in something, and many criticised and desired him to explain, and tell the meaning of such and such a passage, he, knowing that to do it was useless, and not to do it would get him ill-will, and desirous to bring himself out of all straits, and to escape all displeasure and exceptions, it being a hard thing, as he himself says—

In great affairs to satisfy all sides,

as an excuse for travelling, bought a trading vessel, and, having leave for ten years' absence, departed, hoping that by that time his laws would have become familiar.

His first voyage was for Egypt, and he lived, as he himself says—

Near Nilus' mouth, by fair Canopus' shore,

and spent some time in study with Psenophis of Heliopolis, and Sonchis the Saite, the most learned of all the priests; from whom, as Plato says, getting knowledge of the Atlantic story, he put it into a poem, and proposed to bring it to the knowledge of the Greeks. From thence he sailed to Cyprus, where he was made much of by Philocyprus, one of the kings there, who had a small city built by Demophon, Theseus's son, near the river Clarius, in a strong situation, but incommodius and uneasy of access. Solon persuaded him, since there lay a fair plain below, to remove, and build there a pleasanter and more spacious city. And he stayed himself, and assisted in gathering inhabitants, and in fitting it both for defence and convenience of living; insomuch that many flocked to Philocyprus, and the other kings imitated the design; and, therefore, to honour Solon, he called the city Soli, which was formerly named Æpea. And Solon himself, in his Elegies, addressing Philocyprus, mentions this foundation in these words:—

Long may you live, and fill the Solian throne,
Succeeded still by children of your own;
And from your happy island while I sail,
Let Cyprus send for me a favouring gale;
May she advance, and bless your new command,
Prosper your town, and send me safe to land.

That Solon should discourse with Crœsus, some think not agreeable with chronology; but I cannot reject so famous and well-attested a narrative, and, what is more, so agreeable to Solon's temper, and so worthy his wisdom and greatness of mind, because, forsooth, it does not agree with some chronological canons, which thousands have endeavoured to regulate, and yet, to this day, could never bring their differing opinions to any agreement. They say, therefore, that Solon, coming to Crœsus at his request, was in the same condition as an inland man when first he goes to see the sea; for as he fancies every river he meets with to be the ocean, so Solon, as he passed through the court, and saw a great many nobles richly dressed, and proudly attended with a multitude of guards and footboys, thought every one had been the king, till he was brought to Crœsus, who was decked with every possible rarity and curiosity, in ornaments of jewels, purple, and gold, that could make a grand and gorgeous spectacle of him.

Now when Solon came before him, and seemed not at all surprised, nor gave Crœsus those compliments he expected, but showed himself to all discerning eyes to be a man that despised the gaudiness and petty ostentation of it, he commanded them to open all his treasure houses, and carry him to see his sumptuous furniture and luxuries, though he did not wish it; Solon could judge of him well enough by the first sight of him; and, when he returned from viewing all, Crœsus asked him if ever he had known a happier man than he. And when Solon answered that he had known one Tellus, a fellow-citizen of his own, and told him that this Tellus had been an honest man, had had good children, a competent estate, and died bravely in battle for his country, Crœsus took him for an ill-bred fellow and a fool, for not measuring happiness by the abundance of gold and silver, and preferring the life and death of a private and mean man before so much power and empire.

He asked him, however, again, if, besides Tellus, he knew any other man more happy. And Solon replying, Yes, Cleobis and Biton, who were loving brothers, and extremely dutiful sons to their mother, and, when the oxen delayed her, harnessed themselves to the waggon, and drew her to Juno's temple, her neighbours all calling her happy, and she herself rejoicing; then, after sacrificing and feasting, they went to rest, and never rose again, but died in the midst of their honour a painless and tranquil death.

"What," said Crœsus, angrily, "and dost not thou reckon us amongst the happy men at all?" Solon, unwilling either to flatter or exasperate him more, replied, "The gods, O king, have given the Greeks all other gifts in moderate degree; and so our wisdom, too, is a cheerful and a homely, not a noble and kingly wisdom; and this, observing the numerous misfortunes that attend all conditions, forbids us to grow insolent upon our present enjoyments, or to admire any man's happiness that may yet, in course of time, suffer change. For the uncertain future has yet to come, with every possible variety of fortune; and him only to whom the divinity has continued happiness unto the end we call happy; to salute as happy one that is still in the midst of life and hazard, we think as little safe and conclusive as to crown and proclaim as victorious the wrestler that is yet in the ring." After this, he was dismissed, having given Crœsus some pain, but no instruction.

Æsop, who wrote the fables, being then at Sardis upon Crœsus's invitation, and very much esteemed, was concerned that Solon was so ill received, and gave him this advice: "Solon, let your converse with kings be either short or seasonable." "Nay, rather," replied Solon, "either short or reasonable." So at this time Crœsus despised Solon; but when he was overcome by Cyrus, had lost his city, was taken alive, condemned to be burnt, and laid bound upon the pile before all the Persians and Cyrus himself, he cried out as loud as possibly he could three times, "O Solon!" and Cyrus being surprised, and sending some to inquire what man or god this Solon was, who alone he invoked in this extremity, Crœsus told him the whole story, saying, "He was one of the wise men of Greece, whom I sent for, not to be instructed, or to learn anything that I wanted, but that he should see and be a witness of my happiness; the loss of which was, it seems, to be a greater evil than the enjoyment was a good; for when I had them they were goods only in opinion, but now the loss of them has brought upon me intolerable and real evils. And he, conjecturing from what then was, this that now is, bade look to the end of my life, and not rely and grow proud upon uncertainties." When this was told Cyrus, who was a wiser man than Crœsus, and saw in the present example Solon's Maxim confirmed, he not only freed Crœsus from punishment, but honoured him as long as he lived; and Solon had the glory, by the same saying, to save one king and instruct another.

When Solon was gone, the citizens began to quarrel; Lycurgus headed the Plain; Megacles, the son of Alcmæon, those to the Seaside; and Pisistratus the Hill-party, in which were the poorest people, the Thetes, and greatest enemies to the rich; insomuch that, though the city still used the new laws, yet all looked for and desired a change of government, hoping severally that the change would be better for them, and put them above the contrary faction.

Affairs standing thus, Solon returned, and was reverenced by all, and honoured; but his old age would not permit him to be as active, and to speak in public, as formerly; yet, by privately conferring with the heads of the factions, he endeavoured to compose the differences, Pisistratus appearing the most tractable; for he was extremely smooth and engaging in his language, a great friend to the poor, and moderate in his resentments; and what nature had not given him, he had the skill to imitate; so that he was trusted more than the others, being accounted a prudent and orderly man, one that loved equality, and would be an enemy to any that moved against the present settlement. Thus he deceived the majority of people; but Solon quickly discovered his character, and found out his design before any one else; yet did not hate him upon this, but endeavoured to humble him, and bring him off from his ambition, and often told him and others, that if any one could banish the passion for pre-eminence from his mind, and cure him of his desire of absolute power, none would make a more virtuous man or a more excellent citizen.

Thespis, at this time, beginning to act tragedies, and the thing, because it was new, taking very much with the multitude, though it was not yet made a matter of competition, Solon, being by nature fond of hearing and learning something new, and now, in his old age, living idly, and enjoying himself, indeed, with music and with wine, went to see Thespis himself, as the ancient custom was, act: and after the play was done, he addressed him, and asked him if he was not ashamed to tell so many lies before such a number of people; and Thespis replying that it was no harm to say or do so in play, Solon vehemently struck his staff against the ground: "Ah," said he, "if we honour and commend such play as this, we shall find it some day in our business."

Now when Pisistratus, having wounded himself, was brought into the market-place in a chariot, and stirred up the people, as if he had been thus treated by his opponents because of his political conduct, and a great many were enraged and cried out, Solon, coming close to him, said, "This, O son of Hippocrates, is a bad copy of Homer's Ulysses; you do, to trick your countrymen, what he did to deceive his enemies." After this, the people were eager to protect Pisistratus, and met in an assembly, where one Ariston making a motion that they should allow Pisistratus fifty clubmen for a guard to his person, Solon opposed it, and said much to the same purport as what he has left us in his poems—

You dote upon his words and taking phrase;

and again—

True, you are singly each a crafty soul,
But all together make one empty fool.

But observing the poor men bent to gratify Pisistratus, and tumultuous, and the rich fearful and getting out of harm's way, he departed, saying he was wiser than some and stouter than others; wiser than those that did not understand the design, stouter than those that, though they understood it, were afraid to oppose the tyranny.

Now, the people, having passed the law, were not nice with Pisistratus about the number of his clubmen, but took no notice of it, though he enlisted and kept as many as he would, until he seized the Acropolis. When that was done, and the city in an uproar, Megacles, with all his family, at once fled; but Solon, though he was now very old, and had none to back him, yet came into the market-place and made a speech to the citizens, partly

blaming their inadvertency and meanness of spirit, and in part urging and exhorting them not thus tamely to lose their liberty; and likewise then spoke that memorable saying, that, before, it was an easier task to stop the rising tyranny, but now the great and more glorious action to destroy it, when it was begun already, and had gathered strength.

But all being afraid to side with him, he returned home, and, taking his arms, he brought them out and laid them in the porch before his door, with these words: "I have done my part to maintain my country and my laws," and then he busied himself no more. His friends advising him to fly, he refused, but wrote poems, and thus reproached the Athenians in them:—

If now you suffer, do not blame the Powers,
For they are good, and all the fault was ours.
All the strongholds you put into his hands,
And now his slaves must do what he commands.

And many telling him that the tyrant would take his life for this, and asking what he trusted to, that he ventured to speak so boldly, he replied, "To my old age."

But Pisistratus, having got the command, so extremely courted Solon, so honoured him, obliged him, and sent to see him, that Solon gave him his advice, and approved many of his actions; for he retained most of Solon's laws, observed them himself, and compelled his friends to obey. And he himself, though already absolute ruler, being accused of murder before the Areopagus, came quietly to clear himself; but his accuser did not appear.

And he added other laws, one of which is that the maimed in the wars should be maintained at the public charge; this Heraclides Ponticus records, and that Pisistratus followed Solon's example in this, who had decreed it in the case of one Thersippus, that was maimed; and Theophrastus asserts that it was Pisistratus, not Solon, that made that law against laziness, which was the reason that the country was more productive, and the city tranquiller.

Now Solon, having begun the great work in verse, the history or fable of the Atlantic Island, which he had learned from the wise men in Sais, and thought convenient for the Athenians to know, abandoned it; not, as Plato says, by reason of want of time, but because of his age, and being discouraged at the greatness of the task; for that he had leisure enough, such verses testify, as—

Each day grow older, and learn something new;

and again—
But now the Powers, of Beauty, Song, and Wine,
Which are most men's delights, are also mine.

Plato, willing to improve the story of the Atlantic Island, as if it were a fair estate that wanted an heir and came with some title to him, formed, indeed, stately entrances, noble enclosures, large courts, such as never yet introduced any story, fable, or poetic fiction; but, beginning it late, ended his life before his work; and the reader's regret for the unfinished part is the greater, as the satisfaction he takes in that which is complete is extraordinary. For as the city of Athens left only the temple of Jupier Olympius unfinished, so Plato, amongst all his excellent works, left this only piece about the Atlantic Island imperfect.

Solon lived after Pisistratus seized the government, as Heraclides Ponticus asserts, a long time; but Phanias the Eresian says not two full years; for Pisistratus began his tyranny when Comias was archon, and Phanias says Solon died under Hegestratus, who succeeded Comias. The story that his ashes were scattered about the island Salamis is too strange to be easily believed, or be thought anything but a mere fable; and yet it is given, amongst other good authors, by Aristotle, the philosopher.

POPLICOLA

[*Publicola*]

FLOURISHED 500 B.C.

Such was Solon. To him we compare Poplicola, who received this later title from the Roman people for his merit, as a noble accession to his former name, Publius Valerius. He descended from Valerius, a man amongst the early citizens, reputed the principal reconciler of the differences betwixt the Romans and Sabines, and one that was most instrumental in persuading their kings to assent to peace and union.

Thus descended, Publius Valerius, as it is said, whilst Rome remained under its kingly government, obtained as great a name from his eloquence as from his riches, charitably employing the one in liberal aid to the poor, the other with integrity and freedom in the service of justice; thereby giving assurance, that, should the government fall into a republic, he would become a chief man in the community. The illegal and wicked accession of Tarquinius Superbus to the crown, with his making it, instead of kingly rule, the instrument of insolence and tyranny, having inspired the people with a hatred to his reign, upon the death of Lucretia (she killing herself after violence had been done to her), they took an occasion of revolt; and Lucius Brutus, engaging in the change, came to Valerius before all others, and, with his zealous assistance, deposed the kings.

And whilst the people inclined towards the electing one leader instead of their king, Valerius acquiesced, that to rule was rather Brutus's due, as the author of the democracy. But when the name of monarchy was odious to the people, and a divided power appeared more grateful in the prospect, and two were chosen to hold it, Valerius, entertaining hopes that he might be elected consul with Brutus, was disappointed; for, instead of Valerius, notwithstanding the endeavours of Brutus, Tarquinius Collatinus was chosen, the husband of Lucretia, a man noways his superior in merit. But the nobles, dreading the return of their kings, who still used all endeavours abroad and solicitations at home, were resolved upon a chieftain of an intense hatred to them, and noways likely to yield.

Now Valerius was troubled that his desire to serve his country should be doubted, because he had sustained no private injury from the insolence of the tyrants. He withdrew from the senate and practice of the bar, quitting all public concerns; which gave an occasion of discourse, and fear, too, lest his anger should reconcile him to the king's side, and he should prove the ruin of the state, tottering as yet under the uncertainties of a change. But Brutus being doubtful of some others, and determined to give the test to the senate upon the altars, upon the day appointed Valerius came with cheerfulness into the Forum, and was the first man that took the oath, in no way to submit or yield to Tarquin's propositions, but rigorously to maintain liberty; which gave great satisfaction to the senate and assurance to the consuls, his action soon after showing the sincerity of his oath.

For ambassadors came from Tarquin, with popular and specious proposals, whereby they thought to seduce the people, as though the king had cast off all insolence, and made moderation the only measure of his desires. To this embassy the consuls thought fit to give public audience, but Valerius opposed it, and would not permit that the poorer people, who entertained more fear of war than of tyranny, should have any occasion offered them, or any temptations to new designs. Afterwards other ambassadors arrived, who declared their king would recede from his crown, and lay down his arms, only capitulating for a restitution to himself, his friends, and allies, of their moneys and estates to support them in their banishment. Now, several inclining to the request, and Collatinus in particular favouring it, Brutus, a man of vehement and unbending nature, rushed into the Forum, there proclaiming his fellow-consul to be a traitor, in granting subsidies to tyranny, and supplies for a war to those to whom it was monstrous to allow so much as subsistence in exile. This caused an assembly of the citizens, amongst whom the first that spake was Caius Minucius, a private man, who advised Brutus, and urged the Romans to keep the property, and employ it against the tyrants, rather than to remit it to the tyrants, to be used against themselves. The Romans, however, decided that whilst they had enjoyed the liberty they had fought for, they should not sacrifice peace for the sake of money; but send out the tyrants' property after them.

This question, however, of his property was the least part of Tarquin's design; the demand sounded the feelings of the people, and was preparatory to a conspiracy which the ambassadors endeavoured to excite, delaying their return, under pretence of selling some of the goods and reserving others to be sent away, till, in fine they corrupted two of the most eminent families in Rome, the Aquillian, which had three, and the Vitellian, which had two senators. Those all were, by the mother's side, nephews to Collatinus; besides which Brutus had a special alliance to the Vitellii from his marriage with their sister, by whom he had several children; two of whom, of their own age, their near relations and daily companions, the Vitellii seduced to join in the plot, to ally themselves to the great house and royal hopes of the Tarquins, and gain emancipation from the violence and imbecility united of their father, whose austerity to offenders they termed violence, while the imbecility which he had long feigned, to protect himself from the tyrants, still, it appears, was, in name at least, ascribed to him.

Upon these considerations the youths came to confer with the Aquillii, and thought it convenient to bind themselves in a solemn and dreadful oath, by tasting the blood of a murdered man, and touching his entrails. For which design they met at the house of the Aquillii. The building chosen for the transaction was, as was natural, dark and unfrequented, and a slave named Vindicius had, as it chanced, concealed himself there, not out of design or any intelligence of the affair, but, accidentally being within, seeing with how much haste and concern they came in, he was afraid to be discovered, and placed himself behind a chest, where he was able to observe their actions and overhear their debates. Their resolutions were to kill the consuls, and they wrote letters to Tarquin to this effect, and gave them to the ambassadors, who were lodging upon the spot with the Aquillii, and were present at the consultation.

Upon their departure, Vindicius secretly quitted the house, but was at a loss what to do in the matter, for to arraign the sons before the father Brutus, or the nephews before the uncle Collatinus, seemed equally (as indeed it was) shocking; yet he knew no private Roman to whom he could intrust secrets of such importance. Unable, however, to keep silence, and burdened with his knowledge, he went and addressed himself to Valerius, whose known freedom and kindness of temper were an inducement; as he was a person to whom the needy had easy access, and who never shut his gates against the petitions or indigences of humble people. But when Vindicius came and made a complete discovery to him, his brother Marcus and his own wife being present, Valerius was struck with amazement, and by no means would dismiss the discoverer, but confined him to the room, and placed his wife as a guard to the door, sending his brother in the interim to beset the king's palace, and seize, if possible, the writings there, and secure the domestics, whilst he, with his constant attendance of clients and friends, and a great retinue of attendants, repaired to the house of the Aquillii, who were, as it chanced, absent from home; and so, forcing an entrance through the gates, they lit upon the letters then lying in the lodgings of the ambassadors.

Meantime the Aquillii returned in all haste, and, coming to blows about the gate, endeavoured a recovery of the letters. The other party made a resistance, and throwing their gowns around their opponents' necks, at last, after much struggling on both sides, made their way with their prisoners through the streets into the Forum. The like engagement happened about the king's palace, where Marcus seized some other letters which it was designed should be conveyed away in the goods, and, laying hands on such of the king's people as he could find, dragged them also into the Forum.

When the consuls had quieted the tumult, Vindicius was brought out by the orders of Valerius, and the accusation stated, and the letters were opened, to which the traitors could make no plea. Most of the people standing mute and sorrowful, some only, out of kindness to Brutus, mentioning banishment, the tears of Collatinus, attended with Valerius's silence, gave some hopes of mercy. But Brutus, calling his two sons by their names, "Canst not thou," said he, "O Titus, or thou, Tiberius, make any defence against the indictment?" The question being thrice proposed, and no reply made, he turned himself to the lictors and cried, "What remains is your duty." They immediately seized the youths, and, stripping them of their clothes, bound their hands behind them and scourged their bodies with their rods; too tragical a scene for others to look at; Brutus, however, is said not to have turned aside his face, nor allowed the least glance of pity to soften and smooth his aspect of rigour and austerity, but sternly watched his children suffer, even till the lictors, extending them on the ground, cut off their heads with an axe; then departed, committing the rest to the judgment of his colleague.

An action truly open alike to the highest commendation and the strongest censure; for either the greatness of his virtue raised him above the impressions of sorrow, or the extravagance of his misery took away all sense of it; but neither seemed common, or the result of humanity, but either divine or brutish. Yet it is more reasonable that our judgment should yield to his reputation, than that his merit should suffer detraction by the weakness of our judgment; in the Roman's opinion, Brutus did a greater work in the establishment of the government than Romulus in the foundation of the city.

Upon Brutus's departure out of the Forum, consternation, horror, and silence for some time possessed all that reflected on what was done; the easiness and tardiness, however, of Collatinus gave confidence to the Aquillii to request some time to answer their charge, and that Vindicius, their servant, should be remitted into their hands, and no longer harboured amongst their accusers. The consul seemed inclined to their proposal, and was proceeding to dissolve the assembly; but Valerius would not suffer Vindicius, who was surrounded by his people, to be surrendered, nor the meeting to withdraw without punishing the traitors; and at length laid violent hands upon the Aquillii, and, calling Brutus to his assistance, exclaimed against the unreasonable course of Collatinus, to impose upon his colleague the necessity of taking away the lives of his own sons, and yet have thoughts of gratifying some women with the lives of traitors and public enemies.

Collatinus, displeased at this, and commanding Vindicius to be taken away, the lictors made their way through the crowd and seized their man, and struck all who endeavoured a rescue. Valerius's friends headed the resistance, and the people cried out for Brutus, who, returning, on silence being made, told them he had been competent to pass sentence by himself upon his own sons, but left the rest to the suffrages of the free citizens: "Let every man speak that wishes, and persuade whom he can." But there was no need of oratory, for, it being referred to the vote, they were returned condemned by all the suffrages, and were accordingly beheaded.

Collatinus's relationship to the kings had, indeed, already rendered him suspicious, and his second name, too, had made him obnoxious to the people, who were loth to hear the very sound of Tarquin; but after this had happened, perceiving himself an offence to every one, he relinquished his charge and departed from the city. At the new elections in his room, Valerius obtained, with high honour, the consulship, as a just reward of his zeal; of which he thought Vindicius deserved a share, whom he made, first of all freedmen, a citizen of Rome, and gave him the privilege of voting in what tribe soever he was pleased to be enrolled; other freedmen, received the right of suffrage a long time after from Appius, who thus courted popularity; and from this Vindicius, a perfect manumission is called to this day *vindicta*. This done, the goods of the kings were exposed to plunder, and the palace to ruin.

The pleasantest part of the field of Mars, which Tarquin had owned, was devoted to the service of that god; but, it happening to be harvest season, and the sheaves yet being on the ground, they thought it not proper to commit them to the flail, or unsanctify them with any use; and, therefore, carrying them to the river-side, and trees withal that were cut down, they cast all into the water, dedicating the soil, free from all occupation, to the deity. Now, these thrown in, one upon another, and closing together, the stream did not bear them far, but where the first were carried down and came to a bottom, the remainder, finding no farther conveyance, were stopped and interwoven one with another; the stream working the mass into a firmness, and washing down fresh mud. This, settling there, became an accession of matter, as well as cement, to the rubbish, insomuch that the violence of the waters could not remove it, but forced and compressed it all together. Thus its bulk and solidity gained it new subsidies, which gave it extension enough to stop on its way most of what the stream brought down. This is now a sacred island, lying by the city, adorned with the temples of the gods, and walks, and is called in the Latin tongue *inter duos pontes*.[1] Though some say this did not happen at the dedication of Tarquin's field, but in aftertimes, when Tarquinia, a vestal priestess, gave an adjacent field to the public, and obtained great honours in consequence, as, amongst the rest, that of all women her testimony alone should be received; she had also the liberty to marry, but refused it; thus some tell the story.

Tarquin, despairing of a return to his kingdom by the conspiracy, found a kind reception amongst the Tuscans, who, with a great army, proceeded to restore him. The consuls headed the Romans against them, and made their rendezvous in certain holy places, the one called the Arsian grove, the other the Æsuvian meadow. When they came into action, Aruns, the son of Tarquin, and Brutus, the Roman

[1] Between two bridges.

consul, not accidentally encountering each other, but out of hatred and rage, the one to avenge tyranny and enmity to his country, the other his banishment, set spurs to their horses, and, engaging with more fury than forethought, disregarding their own security, fell together in the combat. This dreadful onset hardly was followed by a more favourable end; both armies, doing and receiving equal damage, were separated by a storm.

Valerius was much concerned, not knowing what the result of the day was, and seeing his men as well dismayed at the sight of their own dead, as rejoiced at the loss of the enemy; so apparently equal in the number was the slaughter on either side. Each party, however, felt surer of defeat from the actual sight of their own dead, than they could feel of victory from conjecture about those of their adversaries. The night being come (and such as one may presume must follow such a battle), and the armies laid to rest, they say that the grove shook, and uttered a voice, saying that the Tuscans had lost one man more than the Romans; clearly a divine announcement; and the Romans at once received it with shouts and expressions of joy; whilst the Tuscans, through fear and amazement, deserted their tents, and were for the most part dispersed. The Romans, falling upon the remainder, amounting to nearly five thousand, took them prisoners, and plundered the camp; when they numbered the dead, they found on the Tuscans' side eleven thousand and three hundred, exceeding their own loss but by one man.

This fight happened upon the last of February, and Valerius triumphed in honour of it, being the first consul that drove in with a four-horse chariot; which sight both appeared magnificent, and was received with an admiration free from envy or offence (as some suggest) on the part of the spectators; it would not otherwise have been continued with so much eagerness and emulation through all the after ages. The people applauded likewise the honours he did to his colleague, in adding to his obsequies a funeral oration, which was so much liked by the Romans, and found so good a reception, that it became customary for the best men to celebrate the funerals of great citizens with speeches in their commendation; and their antiquity in Rome is affirmed to be greater than in Greece, unless, with the orator Anaximenes, we make Solon the first author. Yet some part of Valerius's behavior did give offence and disgust to the people, because Brutus, whom they esteemed the father of their liberty, had not presumed to rule without a colleague, but united one and then another to him in his commission; while Valerius, they said, centring all authority in himself, seemed not in any sense a successor to Brutus in the consulship, but to Tarquin in the tyranny; he might make verbal harangues to Brutus's memory, yet, when he was attended with all the rods and axes, proceeding down from a house than which the king's house that he had demolished had not been statelier, those actions showed him an imitator of Tarquin. For, indeed, his dwelling-house on the Velia was somewhat imposing in appearance, hanging over the forum, and overlooking all transactions there; the access to it was hard, and to see him far off coming down, a stately and royal spectacle.

But Valerius showed how well it were for men in power and great offices to have ears that give admittance to truth before flattery; for upon his friends telling him that he displeased the people, he contended not, neither resented it, but while it was still night, sending for a number of work-people, pulled down his house and levelled it with the ground; so that in the morning the people, seeing and flocking together, expressed their wonder and their respect for his magnanimity, and their sorrow, as though it had been a human being, for the large and beautiful house which was thus lost to them by an unfounded jealousy, while its owner, their consul, without a roof of his own, had to beg a lodging with his friends. For his friends received him, till a place the people gave him was furnished with a house, though less stately than his own, where now stands the temple, as it is called, of Vica Pota.

He resolved to render the government, as well as himself, instead of terrible, familiar and pleasant to the people, and parted the axes from the rods, and always, upon his entrance into the assembly, lowered these also to the people, to show, in the strongest way, the republican foundation of the government; and this the consuls observe to this day. But the humility of the man was but a means, not, as they thought, of lessening himself, but merely to abate their envy by this moderation; for whatever he detracted from his authority he added to his real power, the people still submitting with satisfaction, which they expressed by calling him Poplicola, or people-lover,

which name had the pre-eminence of the rest, and, therefore, in the sequel of his narrative we shall use no other.

He gave free leave to any to sue for the consulship; but before the admittance of a colleague, mistrusting the chances, lest emulation or ignorance should cross his designs, by his sole authority enacted his best and most important measures. First, he supplied the vacancies of the senators, whom either Tarquin long before had put to death, or the war lately cut off; those that he enrolled, they write, amounted to a hundred and sixty-four; afterwards he made several laws which added much to the people's liberty, in particular one granting offenders the liberty of appealing to the people from the judgment of the consuls; a second, that made it death to usurp any magistracy without the people's consent; a third, for the relief of poor citizens, which, taking off their taxes, encouraged their labours; another, against disobedience to the consuls, which was no less popular than the rest, and rather to the benefit of the commonalty than to the advantage of the nobles, for it imposed upon disobedience the penalty of ten oxen and two sheep; the price of a sheep being ten obols, of an ox, an hundred. For the use of money was then infrequent amongst the Romans, but their wealth in cattle great; even now pieces of property are called *peculia*, from *pecus*, cattle; and they had stamped upon their most ancient money an ox, a sheep, or a hog; and surnamed their sons Suillii, Bubulci, Caprarii, and Porcii, from *capræ*, goats, and *porci*, hogs.

Amidst this mildness and moderation, for one excessive fault he instituted one excessive punishment; for he made it lawful without trial to take away any man's life that aspired to a tyranny, and acquitted the slayer, if he produced evidence of the crime; for though it was not probable for a man, whose designs were so great, to escape all notice; yet because it was possible he might, although observed, by force anticipate judgment, which the usurpation itself would then preclude, he gave a licence to any to anticipate the usurper.

He was honoured likewise for the law touching the treasury; for because it was necessary for the citizens to contribute out of their estates to the maintenance of wars, and he was unwilling himself to be concerned in the care of it, or to permit his friends, or indeed to let the public money pass into any private house, he allotted the temple of Saturn for the treasury, in which to this day they deposit the tribute-money, and granted the people the liberty of choosing two young men as quæstors, or treasurers. The first were Publius Veturius and Marcus Minucius; and a large sum was collected, for they assessed one hundred and thirty thousand, excusing orphans and widows from the payment.

After these dispositions, he admitted Lucretius, the father of Lucretia, as his colleague, and gave him the precedence in the government, by resigning the fasces to him, as due to his years, which privilege of seniority continued to our time. But within a few days Lucretius died, and in a new election Marcus Horatius succeeded in that honour, and continued consul for the remainder of the year.

Now, whilst Tarquin was making preparations in Tuscany for a second war against the Romans, it is said a great portent occurred. When Tarquin was king, and had all but completed the buildings of the Capitol, designing, whether from oracular advice or his own pleasure, to erect an earthen chariot upon the top, he intrusted the workmanship to Tuscans of the city Veii, but soon after lost his kingdom. The work thus modelled, the Tuscans set in a furnace, but the clay showed not those passive qualities which usually attend its nature, to subside and be condensed upon the evaporation of the moisture, but rose and swelled out to that bulk, that, when solid and firm, notwithstanding the removal of the roof and opening the walls of the furnace, it could not be taken out without much difficulty. The soothsayers looked upon this as a divine prognostic of success and power to those that should possess it; and the Tuscans resolved not to deliver it to the Romans, who demanded it, but answered that it rather belonged to Tarquin than to those who had sent him into exile. A few days after, they had a horserace there, with the usual shows and solemnities, and as the charioteer with his garland on his head was quietly driving the victorious chariot out of the ring, the horses, upon no apparent occasion, taking fright, either by divine instigation or by accident, hurried away their driver at full speed to Rome; neither did his holding them in prevail, nor his voice, but he was forced along with violence till, coming to the Capitol, he was thrown out by the gate called Ratumena. This occurrence raised wonder and fear in the Veientines, who now permitted the delivery of the chariot.

The building of the temple of the Capito-line Jupiter had been vowed by Tarquin, the son of Demaratus, when warring with the Sabines; Tarquinius Superbus, his son or grandson, built, but could not dedicate it, because he lost his kingdom before it was quite finished. And now that it was completed with all its ornaments, Poplicola was ambitious to dedicate it; but the nobility envied him that honour, as, indeed, also, in some degree, those his prudence in making laws and conduct in wars entitled him to. Grudging him, at any rate, the addition of this, they urged Horatius to sue for the dedication, and, whilst Poplicola was engaged in some military expedition, voted it to Horatius, and conducted him to the Capitol, as though, were Poplicola present, they could not have carried it.

Yet, some write, Poplicola was by lot destined against his will to the expedition, the other to the dedication; and what happened in the performance seems to intimate some ground for this conjecture; for, upon the Ides of September, which happens about the full moon of the month Metagitnion, the people having assembled at the Capitol and silence being enjoined, Horatius, after the performance of other ceremonies, holding the doors, according to custom, was proceeding to pronounce the words of dedication, when Marcus, the brother of Poplicola, who had got a place on purpose beforehand near the door, observing his opportunity, cried, "O consul, thy son lies dead in the camp"; which made a great impression upon all others who heard it, yet in nowise discomposed Horatius, who returned merely the reply, "Cast the dead out whither you please; I am not a mourner"; and so completed the dedication. The news was not true, but Marcus thought the lie might avert him from his performance; but it argues him a man of wonderful self-possession, whether he at once saw through the cheat, or, believing it as true, showed no discomposure.

The same fortune attended the dedication of the second temple; the first, as has been said, was built by Tarquin, and dedicated by Horatius; it was burnt down in the civil wars. The second, Sulla built, and, dying before the dedication, left that honour to Catulus; and when this was demolished in the Vitellian sedition, Vespasian, with the same success that attended him in other things, began a third and lived to see it finished, but did not live to see it again destroyed, as it presently was; but was as fortunate in dying before its destruction, as Sulla was the reverse in dying before the dedication of his. For immediately after Vespasian's death it was consumed by fire. The fourth, which now exists, was both built and dedicated by Domitian.

It is said Tarquin expended forty thousand pounds of silver in the very foundations; but the whole wealth of the richest private man in Rome would not discharge the cost of the gilding of this temple in our days, it amounting to above twelve thousand talents; the pillars were cut out of Pentelican marble, of a length most happily proportioned to their thickness; these we saw at Athens; but when they were cut anew at Rome and polished, they did not gain so much in embellishment as they lost in symmetry, being rendered too taper and slender. Should any one who wonders at the costliness of the Capitol visit any one gallery in Domitian's palace, or hall, or bath, or the apartments of his concubines, Epicharmus's remark upon the prodigal, that—

'Tis not beneficence, but, truth to say,
A mere disease of giving things away;

would be in his mouth in application to Domitian. It is neither piety, he would say, nor magnificence, but, indeed, a mere disease of building, and a desire, like Midas, of converting everything into gold or stone. And thus much for this matter.

Tarquin, after the great battle wherein he lost his son in combat with Brutus, fled to Clusium, and sought aid from Lars Porsenna, then one of those most powerful princes of Italy, and a man of worth and generosity; who assured him of assistance, immediately sending his commands to Rome that they should receive Tarquin as their king, and, upon the Romans' refusal, proclaimed war, and, having signified the time and place where he intended his attack, approached with a great army.

Poplicola was, in his absence, chosen consul a second time, and Titus Lucretius his colleague, and, returning to Rome, to show a spirit yet loftier than Porsenna's, built the city Sigliura when Porsenna was already in the neighbourhood; and walling it at great expense, there placed a colony of seven hundred men, as being little concerned at the war. Nevertheless, Porsenna, making a sharp assault, obliged the defendants to retire to Rome, who had almost in their entrance admitted the enemy into the city with them; only Poplicola by sallying out at the gate prevented them, and, joining battle by Tiber side, opposed the enemy, that pressed on with their multitude, but at last, sinking under desperate wounds, was carried out of the fight.

The same fortune fell upon Lucretius, so that the Romans, being dismayed, retreated into the city for their security, and Rome was in great hazard of being taken, the enemy forcing their way on to the wooden bridge, where Horatius Cocles, seconded by two of the first men in Rome, Herminius and Lartius, made head against them. Horatius obtained this name from the loss of one of his eyes in the wars, or, as others write, from the depressure of his nose, which, leaving nothing in the middle to separate them, made both eyes appear but as one; and hence, intending to say Cyclops, by a mispronunciation they called him Cocles. This Cocles kept the bridge, and held back the enemy, till his own party broke it down behind, and then with his armour dropped into the river, and swam to the hither side, with a wound in his hip from a Tuscan spear. Poplicola, admiring his courage, proposed at once that the Romans should every one make him a present of a day's provisions, and afterwards give him as much land as he could plough round in one day, and besides erected a brazen statue to his honour in the temple of Vulcan, as a requital for the lameness caused by his wound.

But Porsenna laying close siege to the city, and a famine raging amongst the Romans, also a new army of the Tuscans making incursions into the country, Poplicola, a third time chosen consul, designed to make, without sallying out, his defence against Porsenna, but, privately stealing forth against the new army of the Tuscans, put them to flight and slew five thousand.

The story of Mucius is variously given; we, like others, must follow the commonly received statement. He was a man endowed with every virtue, but most eminent in war; and, resolving to kill Porsenna, attired himself in the Tuscan habit, and using the Tuscan language, came to the camp, and approaching the seat where the king sat amongst his nobles, but not certainly knowing the king, and fearful to inquire, drew out his sword, and stabbed one who he thought had most the appearance of king. Mucius was taken in the act, and whilst he was under examination, a pan of fire was brought to the king, who intended to sacrifice; Mucius thrust his right hand into the flame, and whilst it burnt stood looking at Porsenna with a steadfast and undaunted countenance; Porsenna at last in admiration dismissed him, and returned his sword, reaching it from his seat; Mucius received it in his left hand, which occasioned the name of Scævola, left-handed, and said, "I have overcome the terrors of Porsenna, yet am vanquished by his generosity, and gratitude obliges me to disclose what no punishment could extort"; and assured him then, that three hundred Romans, all of the same resolution, lurked about his camp, only waiting for an opportunity; he, by lot appointed to the enterprise, was not sorry that he had miscarried in it, because so brave and good a man deserved rather to be a friend to the Romans than an enemy. To this Porsenna gave credit, and thereupon expressed an inclination to a truce, not, I presume, so much out of fear of the three hundred Romans, as in admiration of the Roman courage. All other writers call this man Mucius Scævola, yet Athendorus, son of Sandon, in a book addressed to Octavia, Cæsar's sister, avers he was also called Postumus.

Poplicola, not so much esteeming Porsenna's enmity dangerous to Rome as his friendship and alliance serviceable, was induced to refer the controversy with Tarquin to his arbitration, and several times undertook to prove Tarquin the worst of men, and justly deprived of his kingdom. But Tarquin proudly replied he would admit no judge, much less Porsenna, that had fallen away from his engagements; and Porsenna, resenting this answer, and mistrusting the equity of his cause, moved also by the solicitations of his son Aruns, who was earnest for the Roman interest, made a peace on these conditions, that they should resign the land they had taken from the Tuscans, and restore all prisoners and receive back their deserters. To confirm the peace, the Romans gave as hostages ten sons of patrician parents, and as many daughters, amongst whom was Valeria, the daughter of Poplicola.

Upon these assurances, Porsenna ceased from all acts of hostility, and the young girls went down to the river to bathe, at that part where the winding of the bank formed a bay and made the waters stiller and quieter; and, seeing no guard, nor any one coming or going over, they were encouraged to swim over, notwithstanding the depth and violence of the stream. Some affirm that one of them, by name Clœlia, passing over on horseback, persuaded the rest to swim after; but, upon their safe arrival, presenting themselves to Poplicola, he neither praised nor approved their return, but was concerned lest he should appear less faithful than Porsenna, and this boldness in the maidens should argue treachery in the Romans; so that, apprehending them, he sent them back to Porsenna.

But Tarquin's men, having intelligence of this, laid a strong ambuscade on the other side for those that conducted them; and while these were skirmishing together, Valeria, the daughter of Poplicola, rushed through the enemy, and fled, and with the assistance of three of her attendants made good her escape, whilst the rest were dangerously hedged in by the soldiers; but Aruns, Porsenna's son, upon tidings of it, hastened to their rescue, and, putting the enemy to flight, delivered the Romans.

When Porsenna saw the maidens returned, demanding who was the author and adviser of the act, and understanding Clœlia to be the person, he looked on her with a cheerful and benignant countenance, and commanding one of his horses to be brought, sumptuously adorned, made her a present of it. This is produced as evidence by those who affirm that only Clœlia passed the river on horseback; those who deny it call it only the honour the Tuscan did to her courage; a figure, however, on horseback, stands in the Via Sacra, as you go to the Palatium, which some say is the statue of Clœlia, others of Valeria. Porsenna, thus reconciled to the Romans, gave them a fresh instance of his generosity, and commanded his soldiers to quit the camp merely with their arms, leaving their tents, full of corn and other stores, as a gift to the Romans. Hence even down to our time, when there is a public sale of goods, they cry Porsenna's first, by way of perpetual commemoration of his kindness. There stood also, by the senate-house, a brazen statue of him, of plain and antique workmanship.

Afterwards, the Sabines, making incursions upon the Romans, Marcus Valerius, brother to Poplicola, was made consul, and with him Postumius Tubertus. Marcus, through the management of affairs by the conduct and direct assistance of Poplicola, obtained two great victories, in the latter of which he slew thirteen thousand Sabines without the loss of one Roman, and was honoured, as an accession to his triumph, with a house built in the Palatium at the public charge; and whereas the doors of other houses opened inward into the house, they made this to open outward into the street, to intimate their perpetual public recognition of his merit by thus continually making way for him. The same fashion in their doors the Greeks, they say, had of old universally, which appears from their comedies, where those that are going out make a noise at the door within, to give notice to those that pass by or stand near the door, that the opening the door into the street might occasion no surprisal.

The year after, Poplicola was made consul the fourth time, when a confederacy of the Sabines and Latins threatened a war; a superstitious fear also overran the city on the occasion of general miscarriages of their women, no single birth coming to its due time. Poplicola, upon consultation of the Sibylline books, sacrificing to Pluto, and renewing certain games commanded by Apollo, restored the city to more cheerful assurance in the gods, and then prepared against the menaces of men.

There were appearances of great preparation, and of a formidable confederacy. Amongst the Sabines there was one Appius Clausus, a man of a great wealth and strength of body, but most eminent for his high character and for his eloquence; yet, as is usually the fate of great men, he could not escape the envy of others, which was much occasioned by his dissuading the war, and seeming to promote the Roman interest, with a view, it is thought, to obtaining absolute power in his own country for himself. Knowing how welcome these reports would be to the multitude, and how offensive to the army and the abettors of the war, he was afraid to stand a trial, but, having a considerable body of friends and allies to assist him, raised a tumult amongst the Sabines, which delayed the war.

Neither was Poplicola wanting, not only to understand the grounds of the sedition, but to promote and increase it, and he despatched emissaries with instructions to Clausus, that Poplicola was assured of his goodness and justice, and thought it indeed unworthy in any man, however injured, to seek revenge upon his fellow-citizens; yet if he pleased, for his own security, to leave his enemies and come to Rome, he should be received, both in public and private, with the honour his merit deserved, and their own glory required. Appius, seriously weighing the matter, came to the conclusion that it was the best resource which necessity left him, and advising with his friends, and they inviting again others in the same manner, he came to Rome, bringing five thousand families, with their wives and children, people of the quietest and steadiest temper of all the Sabines. Poplicola, informed of their approach, received them with all the kind offices of a friend, and admitted them at once to the franchise, allotting to every one two acres of land by the river Anio, but to Clausus twenty-five acres, and gave him a place in the senate; a commencement of political power which he used so wisely, that he rose to the highest reputation, was very influential, and left the Claudian house behind him, inferior to none in Rome.

The departure of these men rendered things quiet amongst the Sabines; yet the chief of the community would not suffer them to settle into peace, but resented that Clausus now, by turning deserter, should disappoint that revenge upon the Romans, which, while at home, he had unsuccessfully opposed. Coming with a great army, they sat down before Fidenæ, and placed an ambuscade of two thousand men near Rome, in wooded and hollow spots, with a design that some few horsemen, as soon as it was day, should go out and ravage the country, commanding them upon their approach to the town so to retreat as to draw the enemy into the ambush.

Poplicola, however, soon advertised of these designs by deserters, disposed his forces to their respective charges. Postumius Balbus, his son-in-law, going out with three thousand men in the evening, was ordered to take the hills, under which the ambush lay, there to observe their motions; his colleague, Lucretius, attended with a body of the lightest and boldest men, was appointed to meet the Sabine horse; whilst he, with the rest of the army, encompassed the enemy. And a thick mist rising accidentally, Postumius, early in the morning, with shouts from the hills, assailed the ambuscade, Lucretius charged the light-horse, and Poplicola besieged the camp; so that on all sides defeat and ruin came upon the Sabines, and without any resistance the Romans killed them in their flight, their very hopes leading them to their death, for each division, presuming that the other was safe, gave up all thought of fighting or keeping their ground; and these quitting the camp to retire to the ambuscade, and the ambuscade flying to the camp, fugitives thus met fugitives, and found those from whom they expected succour as much in need of succour from themselves.

The nearness, however, of the city Fidenæ was the preservation of the Sabines, especially those that fled from the camp; those that could not gain the city either perished in the field, or were taken prisoners. This victory, the Romans, though usually ascribing such success to some god, attributed to the conduct of one captain; and it was observed to be heard amongst the soldiers, that Poplicola had delivered their enemies lame and blind, and only not in chains, to be despatched by their swords. From the spoil and prisoners great wealth accrued to the people.

Poplicola, having completed his triumph, and bequeathed the city to the care of the succeeding consuls, died; thus closing a life which, so far as human life may be, had been full of all that is good and honourable. The people, as though they had not duly rewarded his deserts when alive, but still were in his debt, decreed him a public interment, every one contributing his quadrans towards the charge; the women, besides, by private consent, mourned a whole year, a signal mark of honour to his memory. He was buried, by the people's desire, within the city, in the part called Velia, where his posterity had likewise privilege of burial; now, however, none of the family are interred there, but the body is carried thither and set down, and some one places a burning torch under it and immediately takes it away, as an attestation of the deceased's privilege, and his receding from his honour, after which the body is removed.

POPLICOLA and SOLON
Compared

THERE is something singular in the present parallel which has not occurred in any other of the lives; that the one should be the imitator of the other, and the other his best evidence. Upon the survey of Solon's sentence to Crœsus in favour of Tellus's happiness, it seems more applicable to Poplicola; for Tellus, whose virtuous life and dying well had gained him the name of the happiest man, yet was never celebrated in Solon's poems for a good man, nor have his children or any magistracy of his deserved a memorial; but Poplicola's life was the most eminent amongst the Romans, as well for the greatness of his virtue as his power, and also since his death many amongst the distinguished families, even in our days, the Poplicolæ, Messalæ, and Valerii, after a lapse of six hundred years, acknowledge him as the fountain of their honour. Besides, Tellus, though keeping his post and fighting like a valiant soldier, was yet slain by his enemies; but Poplicola, the better fortune, slew his, and saw his country victorious under his command. And his honours and triumphs brought him, which was Solon's ambition, to a happy end; the ejaculation which, in his verses against Mimnermus about the continuance of man's life, he himself made—

Mourned let me die; and may I, when life ends,
Occasion sighs and sorrows to my friends,

is evidence to Poplicola's happiness; his death did not only draw tears from his friends and acquaintance, but was the object of universal regret and sorrow through the whole city; the women deplored his loss as that of a son, brother, or common father. "Wealth I would have," said Solon, "but wealth by wrong procure would not," because punishment would follow. But Poplicola's riches were not only justly his, but he spent them nobly in doing good to the distressed. So that if Solon was reputed the wisest man, we must allow Poplicola to be the happiest; for what Solon wished for as the greatest and most perfect good, this Poplicola had, and used and enjoyed to his death.

And as Solon may thus be said to have contributed to Poplicola's glory, so did also Poplicola to his, by his choice of him as his model in the formation of republican institutions; in reducing, for example, the excessive powers and assumption of the consulship. Several of his laws, indeed, he actually transferred to Rome, as his empowering the people to elect their officers, and allowing offenders the liberty of appealing to the people, as Solon did to the jurors. He did not, indeed, create a new senate, as Solon did, but augmented the old to almost double its number. The appointment of treasurers again, the quæstors, has a like origin; with the intent that the chief magistrate should not, if of good character, be withdrawn from greater matters; or, if bad, have the greater temptation to injustice, by holding both the government and treasury in his hands.

The aversion to tyranny was stronger in Poplicola; any one who attempted usurpation could, by Solon's law, only be punished upon conviction; but Poplicola made it death before a trial. And though Solon justly gloried, that, when arbitrary power was absolutely offered to him by circumstances, and when his countrymen would have willingly seen him accept it, he yet declined it; still Poplicola merited no less, who, receiving a despotic command, converted it to a popular office, and did not employ the whole legal power which he held. We must allow, indeed, that Solon was before Poplicola in observing that—

A people always minds its rulers best
When it is neither humoured nor oppressed.

The remission of debts was peculiar to Solon; it was his great means for confirming the citizens' liberty; for a mere law to give all men equal rights is but useless, if the poor must sacrifice those rights to their debts, and, in the very seats and sanctuaries of equality, the courts of justice, the offices of state, and the public discussions, be more than anywhere at the beck and bidding of the rich. A yet more extraordinary success was, that, although usually civil violence is caused by any remission of debts, upon this one occasion this dangerous but powerful remedy actually put an end to civil violence already existing, Solon's own private worth and reputation overbalancing all the ordinary ill-repute and discredit of the change.

The beginning of his government was more glorious, for he was entirely original, and followed no man's example, and, without the aid of any ally, achieved his most important measures by his own conduct; yet the close of Poplicola's life was more happy and desirable, for Solon saw the dissolution of his own commonwealth. Poplicola maintained the state in good order down to the civil wars. Solon, leaving his laws, as soon as he had made them, engraven in wood, but destitute of a defender, departed from Athens; whilst Poplicola, remaining both in and out of office, laboured to establish the government. Solon, though he actually knew of Pisistratus's ambition, yet was not able to suppress it, but had to yield to usurpation in its infancy; whereas Poplicola utterly subverted and dissolved a potent monarchy, strongly settled by long continuance, uniting thus to virtues equal to those, and purposes identical with those of Solon, the good fortune and the power that alone could make them effective.

In military exploits, Daimachus of Platæa will not even allow Solon the conduct of the war against the Megarians, as was before intimated; but Poplicola was victorious in the most important conflicts, both as a private soldier and commander. In domestic politics, also, Solon, in play, as it were, and by counterfeiting madness induced the enterprise against Salamis; whereas Poplicola, in the very beginning, exposed himself to the greatest risk, took arms against Tarquin, detected the conspiracy, and, being principally concerned both in preventing the escape of and afterwards punishing the traitors, not only expelled the tyrants from the city, but extirpated their very hopes. And as, in cases calling for contest and resistance and manful opposition, he behaved with courage and resolution, so, in instances where peaceable language, persuasion, and concession were requisite, he was yet more to be commended; and succeeded in gaining happily to reconciliation and friendship, Porsenna, a terrible and invincible enemy.

Some may, perhaps, object that Solon recovered Salamis, which they had lost, for the Athenians; whereas Poplicola receded from part of what the Romans were at that time possessed of; but judgment is to be made of actions according to the times in which they were performed. The conduct of a wise politician is ever suited to the present posture of affairs; often by foregoing a part he saves the whole, and by yielding in a small matter secures a greater; and so Poplicola, by restoring what the Romans had lately usurped, saved their undoubted patrimony, and procured, moreover, the stores of the enemy for those who were only too thankful to secure their city. Permitting the decision of the controversy to his adversary, he not only got the victory, but likewise what he himself would willingly have given to purchase the victory, Porsenna putting an end to the war, and leaving them all the provision of his camp, from the sense of the virtue and gallant disposition of the Romans which their consul had impressed upon him.

THEMISTOCLES

527?–?460 B.C.

THE birth of Themistocles was somewhat too obscure to do him honour. His father, Neocles, was not of the distinguished people of Athens, but of the township of Phrearrhi, and of the tribe Leontis; and by his mother's side, as it is reported, he was base-born—

I am not of the noble Grecian race,
I'm poor Abrotonon, and born in Thrace;
Let the Greek women scorn me, if they please,
I was the mother of Themistocles.

Yet Phanias writes that the mother of Themistocles was not of Thrace, but of Caria, and that her name was not Abrotonon, but Euterpe; and Neanthes adds farther that she was of Halicarnassus in Caria. And, as illegitimate children, including those that were of half-blood or had but one parent an Athenian, had to attend at the Cynosarges (a wrestling-place outside the gates, dedicated to Hercules, who was also of half-blood amongst the gods, having had a mortal woman for his mother), Themistocles persuaded several of the young men of high birth to accompany him to anoint and exercise themselves together at Cynosarges; an ingenious device for destroying the distinction between the noble and the base-born, and between those of the whole and those of the half-blood of Athens. However, it is certain that he was related to the house of the Lycomedæ; for Simonides records that he rebuilt the chapel of Phlya, belonging to that family, and beautified it with pictures and other ornaments, after it had been burnt by the Persians.

It is confessed by all that from his youth he was of a vehement and impetuous nature, of a quick apprehension, and a strong and aspiring bent for action and great affairs. The holidays and intervals in his studies he did not spend in play or idleness, as other children, but would be always inventing or arranging some oration or declamation to himself, the subject of which was generally the excusing or accusing his companions, so that his master would often say to him, "You, my boy, will be nothing small, but great one way or other, for good or else for bad." He received reluctantly and carelessly instructions given him to improve his manners and behaviour, or to teach him any pleasing or graceful accomplishment, but whatever was said to improve him in sagacity, or in management of affairs, he would give attention to, beyond one of his years, from confidence in his natural capacities for such things.

And thus afterwards, when in company where people engaged themselves in what are commonly thought the liberal and elegant amusements, he was obliged to defend himself against the observations of those who considered themselves highly accomplished, by the somewhat arrogant retort, that he certainly could not make use of any stringed instrument, could only, were a small and obscure city put into his hands, make it great and glorious.

Notwithstanding this, Stesimbrotus says that Themistocles was a hearer of Anaxagoras, and that he studied natural philosophy under Melissus, contrary to chronology; Melissus commanded the Samians in the siege by Pericles, who was much Themistocles's junior; and with Pericles, also, Anaxagoras was intimate. They, therefore, might rather be credited who report, that Themistocles was an admirer of Mnesiphilus the Phrearrhian, who was neither rhetorician nor natural philosopher, but a professor of that which was then called wisdom, consisting in a sort of political shrewdness and practical sagacity, which had begun and continued, almost like a sect of philosophy, from Solon: but those who came afterwards, and mixed it with pleadings and legal artifices, and transformed the practical part of it into a mere art of speaking and an exercise of words, were generally called sophists. Themistocles resorted to Mnesiphilus when he had already embarked in politics.

In the first essays of his youth he was not regular nor happily balanced; he allowed himself to follow mere natural character, which, without the control of reason and instruction, is apt to hurry, upon either side, into sudden

88

and violent courses, and very often to break away and determine upon the worst; as he afterwards owned himself, saying, that the wildest colts make the best horses, if they only get properly trained and broken in. But those who upon this fasten stories of their own invention, as of his being disowned by his father, and that his mother died for grief of her son's ill-fame, certainly calumniate him; and there are others who relate, on the contrary, how that to deter him from public business, and to let him see how the vulgar behave themselves towards their leaders when they have at last no further use of them, his father showed him the old galleys as they lay forsaken and cast about upon the sea-shore.

Yet it is evident that his mind was early imbued with the keenest interest in public affairs, and the most passionate ambition for distinction. Eager from the first to obtain the highest place, he unhesitatingly accepted the hatred of the most powerful and influential leaders in the city, but more especially of Aristides, the son of Lysimachus, who always opposed him. And yet all this great enmity between them arose, it appears, from a very boyish occasion, both being attached to the beautiful Stesilaus of Ceos, as Ariston the philosopher tells us; ever after which they took opposite sides, and were rivals in politics. Not but that the incompatibility of their lives and manners may seem to have increased the difference, for Aristides was of a mild nature, and of a nobler sort of character, and, in public matters, acting always with a view, not to glory or popularity, but to the best interest of the state consistent with security and honesty, he was often forced to oppose Themistocles, and interfere against the increase of his influence, seeing him stirring up the people to all kinds of enterprises, and introducing various innovations.

For it is said that Themistocles was so transported with the thoughts of glory, and so inflamed with the passion for great actions, that, though he was still young when the battle of Marathon was fought against the Persians, upon the skilful conduct of the general, Miltiades, being everywhere talked about, he was observed to be thoughtful and reserved, alone by himself; he passed the nights without sleep, and avoided all his usual places of recreation, and to those who wondered at the change, and inquired the reason of it, he gave the answer, that "the trophy of Miltiades would not let him sleep." And when others were of opinion that the battle of Marathon would be an end to the war, Themistocles thought that it was but the beginning of far greater conflicts, and for these, to the benefit of all Greece, he kept himself in continual readiness, and his city also in proper training, foreseeing from far before what would happen.

And, first of all, the Athenians being accustomed to divide amongst themselves the revenue proceeding from the silver mines at Laurium, he was the only man that durst propose to the people that this distribution should cease, and that with the money ships should be built to make war against the Æginetans, who were the most flourishing people in all Greece, and by the number of their ships held the sovereignty of the sea; and Themistocles thus was more easily able to persuade them, avoiding all mention of danger from Darius or the Persians, who were at a great distance, and their coming very uncertain, and at that time not much to be feared; but by a seasonable employment of the emulation and anger felt by the Athenians against the Æginetans, he induced them to preparation. So that with this money an hundred ships were built, with which they afterwards fought against Xerxes.

And henceforward, little by little, turning and drawing the city down towards the sea, in the belief that, whereas by land they were not a fit match for their next neighbours, with their ships they might be able to repel the Persians and command Greece, thus, as Plato says, from steady soldiers he turned them into mariners and seamen tossed about the sea, and gave occasion for the reproach against him, that he took away from the Athenians the spear and the shield, and bound them to the bench and the oar. These measures he carried in the assembly, against the opposition, as Stesimbrotus relates, of Miltiades; and whether or no he hereby injured the purity and true balance of government may be a question for philosophers, but that the deliverance of Greece came at that time from the sea, and that these galleys restored Athens again after it was destroyed, were others wanting, Xerxes himself would be sufficient evidence, who, though his land-forces were still entire, after his defeat at sea, fled away, and thought himself no longer able to encounter the Greeks; and, as it seems to me, left Mardonius behind him, not out of any hopes he could have to bring them into subjection, but to hinder them from pursuing him.

Themistocles is said to have been eager in the acquisition of riches, according to some, that he might be the more liberal; for loving to sacrifice often, and to be splendid in his entertainment of strangers, he required a plentiful revenue; yet he is accused by others of having been parsimonious and sordid to that degree that he would sell provisions which were sent to him as a present. He desired Diphilides, who was a breeder of horses, to give him a colt, and when he refused it, threatened that in a short time he would turn his house into a wooden horse, intimating that he would stir up dispute and litigation between him and some of his relations.

He went beyond all men in the passion for distinction. When he was still young and unknown in the world, he entreated Episcles of Hermione, who had a good hand at the lute and was much sought after by the Athenians, to come and practise at home with him, being ambitious of having people inquire after his house and frequent his company. When he came to the Olympic games, and was so splendid in his equipage and entertainments, in his rich tents and furniture, that he strove to outdo Cimon, he displeased the Greeks, who thought that such magnificence might be allowed in one who was a young man and of a great family, but was a great piece of insolence in one as yet undistinguished, and without title or means for making any such display. In a dramatic contest, the play he paid for won the prize, which was then a matter that excited much emulation; he put up a tablet in record of it, with the inscription: "Themistocles of Phrearrhi was at the charge of it; Phrynichus made it; Adimantus was archon."

He was well liked by the common people, would salute every particular citizen by his own name, and always show himself a just judge in questions of business between private men; he said to Simonides, the poet of Ceos, who desired something of him, when he was commander of the army, that was not reasonable, "Simonides, you would be no good poet if you wrote false measure, nor should I be a good magistrate if for favour I made false law." And at another time, laughing at Simonides, he said that he was a man of little judgment to speak against the Corinthians, who were inhabitants of a great city, and to have his own picture drawn so often, having so ill-looking a face.

Gradually growing to be great, and win-

ning the favour of the people, he at last gained the day with his faction over that of Aristides, and procured his banishment by ostracism. When the king of Persia was now advancing against Greece, and the Athenians were in consultation who should be general, and many withdrew themselves of their own accord, being terrified with the greatness of the danger, there was one Epicydes, a popular speaker, son to Euphemides, a man of an elegant tongue but of a faint heart, and a slave to riches, who was desirous of the command, and was looked upon to be in a fair way to carry it by the number of votes; but Themistocles, fearing that, if the command should fall into such hands, all would be lost, bought off Epicydes and his pretensions, it is said, for a sum of money.

When the king of Persia sent messengers into Greece, with an interpreter, to demand earth and water, as an acknowledgment of subjection, Themistocles, by the consent of the people, seized upon the interpreter, and put him to death, for presuming to publish the barbarian orders and decrees in the Greek language; this is one of the actions he is commended for, as also for what he did to Arthmius of Zelea, who brought gold from the king of Persia to corrupt the Greeks, and was, by an order from Themistocles, degraded and disfranchised, he and his children and his posterity; but that which most of all redounded to his credit was, that he put an end to all the civil wars of Greece, composed their differences, and persuaded them to lay aside all enmity during the war with the Persians; and in this great work, Chileus the Arcadian was, it is said, of great assistance to him.

Having taken upon himself the command of the Athenian forces, he immediately endeavoured to persuade the citizens to leave the city, and to embark upon their galleys, and meet with the Persians at a great distance from Greece; but many being against this, he led a large force, together with the Lacedæmonians, into Tempe, that in this pass they might maintain the safety of Thessaly, which had not as yet declared for the king; but when they returned without performing anything, and it was known that not only the Thessalians, but all as far as Bœotia, was going over to Xerxes, then the Athenians more willingly hearkened to the advice of Themistocles to fight by sea, and sent him with a fleet to guard the straits of Artemisium.

When the contingents met here, the Greeks would have the Lacedæmonians to command, and Eurybiades to be their admiral; but the Athenians, who surpassed all the rest together in number of vessels, would not submit to come after any other, till Themistocles, perceiving the danger of the contest, yielded his own command to Eurybiades, and got the Athenians to submit, extenuating the loss by persuading them that if in this war they behaved themselves like men, he would answer for it after that, that the Greeks, of their own will, would submit to their command. And by this moderation of his, it is evident that he was the chief means of the deliverance of Greece, and gained the Athenians the glory of alike surpassing their enemies in valour, and their confederates in wisdom.

As soon as the Persian armada arrived at Aphetæ, Eurybiades was astonished to see such a vast number of vessels before him, and being informed that two hundred more were sailing around behind the island of Sciathus, he immediately determined to retire farther into Greece, and to sail back into some part of Peloponnesus, where their land army and their fleet might join, for he looked upon the Persian forces to be altogether unassailable by sea. But the Eubœans, fearing that the Greeks would forsake them, and leave them to the mercy of the enemy, sent Pelagon to confer privately with Themistocles, taking with him a good sum of money, which, as Herodotus reports, he accepted and gave to Eurybiades.

In this affair none of his own countrymen opposed him so much as Architeles, captain of the sacred galley, who, having no money to supply his seamen, was eager to go home; but Themistocles so incensed the Athenians against them, that they set upon him and left him not so much as his supper, at which Architeles was much surprised, and took it very ill; but Themistocles immediately sent him in a chest a service of provisions, and at the bottom of it a talent of silver, desiring him to sup to-night, and to-morrow provide for his seamen; if not, he would report it among the Athenians that he had received money from the enemy. So Phanias the Lesbian tells the story.

Though the fights between the Greeks and Persians in the straits of Eubœa were not so important as to make any final decision of the war, yet the experience which the Greeks obtained in them was of great advantage; for thus, by actual trial and in real danger, they found out that neither number of ships, nor riches and ornaments, nor boasting shouts, nor barbarous songs of victory, were any way terrible to men that knew how to fight and were resolved to come hand to hand with their enemies; these things they were to despise, and to come up close and grapple with their foes.

This Pindar appears to have seen, and says justly enough of the fight at Artemisium, that—

> There the sons of Athens set
> The stone that freedom stands on yet.

For the first step towards victory undoubtedly is to gain courage. Artemisium is in Eubœa, beyond the city of Histiæa, a sea-beach open to the north; most nearly opposite to it stands Olizon, in the country which formally was under Philoctetes; there is a small temple there, dedicated to Diana, surnamed of the Dawn, and trees about it, around which again stand pillars of white marble; and if you rub them with your hand, they send forth both the smell and colour of saffron. On one of these pillars these verses are engraved:—

> With numerous tribes from Asia's region brought
> The sons of Athens on these waters fought;
> Erecting, after they had quelled the Mede,
> To Artemis this record of the deed.

There is a place still to be seen upon this shore, where, in the middle of a great heap of sand, they take out from the bottom a dark powder like ashes, or something that has passed the fire; and here, it is supposed, the shipwrecks and bodies of the dead were burnt.

But when news came from Thermopylæ to Artemisium informing them that king Leonidas was slain, and that Xerxes had made himself master of all the passages by land, they returned back to the interior of Greece, the Athenians having the command of the rear, the place of honour and danger, and much elated by what had been done.

As Themistocles sailed along the coasts, he took notice of the harbours and fit places for the enemy's ships to come to land at, and engraved large letters in such stones as he found there by chance, as also in others which he set up on purpose near to the landing-places, or where they were to water; in which inscriptions he called upon the Ionians to forsake the Medes, if it were possible, and to come over to the Greeks, who were their proper founders and fathers, and were now hazarding all for their liberties; but, if this could not be done, at any rate to impede and disturb the Persians in all engagements. He hoped that these writings would prevail with the Ionians to revolt, or raise some trouble by making their fidelity doubtful to the Persians.

Now, though Xerxes had already passed through Doris and invaded the country of Phocis, and was burning and destroying the cities of the Phocians, yet the Greeks sent them no relief; and, though the Athenians earnestly desired them to meet the Persians in Bœotia, before they could come into Attica, as they themselves had come forward by sea at Artemisium, they gave no ear to their requests, being wholly intent upon Peloponnesus, and resolved to gather all their forces together within the Isthmus, and to build a wall from sea to sea in that narrow neck of land; so that the Athenians were enraged to see themselves betrayed, and at the same time afflicted and dejected at their own destitution. For to fight alone against such a numerous army was to no purpose, and the only expedient now left them was to leave their city and cling to their ships; which the people were very unwilling to submit to, imagining that it would signify little now to gain a victory, and not understanding how there could be deliverance any longer after they had once forsaken the temples of their gods and exposed the tombs and monuments of their ancestors to the fury of their enemies.

Themistocles, being at a loss, and not able to draw the people over to his opinion by any human reason, set his machines to work, as in a theatre, and employed prodigies and oracles. The serpent of Minerva, kept in the inner part of her temple, disappeared; the priest gave it out to the people that the offerings which were set for it were found untouched, and declared, by the suggestion of Themistocles, that the goddess had left the city, and taken her flight before them towards the sea. And he often urged them with the oracle which bade them trust to walls of wood, showing them that walls of wood could signify nothing else but ships; and that the island of Salamis was termed in it, not miserable or unhappy, but had the epithet of divine, for that it should one day be associated with a great good fortune of the Greeks.

At length his opinion prevailed, and he obtained a decree that the city should be committed to the protection of Minerva, "Queen of Athens"; that they who were of age to bear arms should embark, and that each should see to sending away his children, women, and slaves where he could. This decree being confirmed, most of the Athenians removed their parents, wives, and children to Trœzen, where they were received with eager good-will by the Trœzenians, who passed a vote that they should be maintained at the public charge, by a daily payment of two obols to every one, and leave be given to the children to gather fruit where they pleased, and schoolmasters paid to instruct them. This vote was proposed by Nicagoras.

There was no public treasure at that time in Athens; but the council of Areopagus, as Aristotle says, distributed to every one that served eight drachmas, which was a great help to the manning of the fleet; but Clidemus ascribes this also to the art of Themistocles. When the Athenians were on their way down to the haven of Piræus, the shield with the head of Medusa was missing; and he, under the pretext of searching for it, ransacked all places, and found among their goods considerable sums of money concealed, which he applied to the public use; and with this the soldiers and seamen were well provided for their voyage.

When the whole city of Athens were going on board, it afforded a spectacle worthy alike of pity and admiration, to see them thus send away their fathers and children before them, and, unmoved with their cries and tears, passed over into the island. But that which stirred compassion most of all was, that many old men, by reason of their great age, were left behind; and even the tame domestic animals could not be seen without some pity, running about the town and howling, as desirous to be carried along with their masters that had kept them; among which it is reported that Xanthippus, the father of Pericles, had a dog that would not endure to stay behind, but leaped into the sea, and swam along by the galley's side till he came to the island of Salamis, where he fainted away and died, and that spot in the island, which is still called the Dog's Grave, is said to be his.

Among the great actions of Themistocles at this crisis, the recall of Aristides was not the least, for, before the war, he had been ostracised by the party which Themistocles headed, and was in banishment; but now, perceiving that the people regretted his absence, and were fearful that he might go over to the Persians to revenge himself, and thereby ruin the affairs of Greece, Themistocles proposed a decree that those who were banished for a time might return again, to give assistance by word and deed to the cause of Greece with the rest of their fellow-citizens.

Eurybiades, by reason of the greatness of Sparta, was admiral of the Greek fleet, but yet was faint-hearted in time of danger, and willing to weigh anchor and set sail for the isthmus of Corinth, near which the land army lay encamped; which Themistocles resisted; and this was the occasion of the well-known words, when Eurybiades, to check his impatience, told him that at the Olympic games they that start up before the rest are lashed; "And they," replied Themistocles, "that are left behind are not crowned." Again, Eurybiades, lifting up his staff as if he were going to strike, Themistocles said, "Strike if you will, but hear"; Eurybiades, wondering much at his moderation, desired him to speak, and Themistocles now brought him to a better understanding.

And when one who stood by him told him that it did not become those who had neither city nor house to lose, to persuade others to relinquish their habitations and forsake their countries, Themistocles gave this reply: "We have indeed left our houses and our walls, base fellow, not thinking it fit to become slaves for the sake of things that have no life nor soul; and yet our city is the greatest of all Greece, consisting of two hundred galleys, which are here to defend you, if you please; but if you run away and betray us, as you did once before, the Greeks shall soon hear news of the Athenians possessing as fair a country, and as large and free a city, as that they have lost." These expressions of Themistocles made Eurybiades suspect that if he retreated the Athenians would fall off from him.

When one of Eretria began to oppose him, he said, "Have you anything to say of war, that are like an inkfish? You have a sword, but no heart." Some say that while Themistocles was thus speaking upon the deck, an owl was seen flying to the right hand of the fleet, which came and sate upon the top of the mast; and this happy omen so far disposed the Greeks to follow his advice, that they presently prepared to fight. Yet, when the enemy's fleet was arrived at the haven of Phalerum, upon the coast of Attica, and with the number of their ships concealed all the shore, and when they saw the king himself in person come down with his land army to the seaside, with all his forces united, then the good counsel of Themistocles

was soon forgotten, and the Peloponnesians cast their eyes again towards the isthmus, and took it very ill if any one spoke against their returning home; and, resolving to depart that night, the pilots had orders what course to steer.

Themistocles, in great distress that the Greeks should retire, and lose the advantage of the narrow seas and strait passage, and slip home every one to his own city, considered with himself, and contrived that stratagem that was carried out by Sicinnus. This Sicinnus was a Persian captive, but a great lover of Themistocles, and the attendant of his children. Upon this occasion, he sent him privately to Xerxes, commanding him to tell the king that Themistocles, the admiral of the Athenians, having espoused his interest, wished to be the first to inform him that the Greeks were ready to make their escape, and that he counselled him to hinder their flight, to set upon them while they were in this confusion and at a distance from their land army, and hereby destroy all their forces by sea.

Xerxes was very joyful at this message, and received it as from one who wished him all that was good, and immediately issued instructions to the commanders of his ships, that they should instantly set out with two hundred galleys to encompass all the islands, and enclose all the straits and passages, that none of the Greeks might escape, and that they should afterwards follow with the rest of their fleet at leisure. This being done, Aristides, the son of Lysimachus, was the first man that perceived it, and went to the tent of Themistocles, not out of any friendship, for he had been formerly banished by his means, as has been related, but to inform him how they were encompassed by their enemies. Themistocles, knowing the generosity of Aristides, and much struck by his visit at that time, imparted to him all that he had transacted by Sicinnus, and entreated him that, as he would be more readily believed among the Greeks, he would make use of his credit to help to induce them to stay and fight their enemies in the narrow seas. Aristides applauded Themistocles, and went to the other commanders and captains of the galleys, and encouraged them to engage; yet they did not perfectly assent to him, till a galley of Tenos, which deserted from the Persians, of which Panætius was commander, came in, while they were still doubting, and confirmed the news that all the straits and passages were beset; and then their rage and fury, as well as their necessity, provoked them all to fight.

As soon as it was day, Xerxes placed himself high up, to view his fleet, and how it was set in order. Phanodemus says, he sat upon a promontory above the temple of Hercules, where the coast of Attica is separated from the island by a narrow channel; but Acestodorus writes, that it was in the confines of Megara, upon those hills which are called the Horns, where he sat in a chair of gold, with many secretaries about him to write down all that was done in the fight.

When Themistocles was about to sacrifice, close to the admiral's galley, there were three prisoners brought to him, fine looking men, and richly dressed in ornamented clothing and gold, said to be the children of Artayctes and Sandauce, sister to Xerxes. As soon as the prophet Euphrantides saw them, and observed that at the same time the fire blazed out from the offerings with a more than ordinary flame, and a man sneezed on the right, which was an intimation of a fortunate event, he took Themistocles by the hand, and bade him consecrate the three young men for sacrifice, and offer them up with prayers for victory to Bacchus the Devourer; so should the Greeks not only save themselves, but also obtain victory. Themistocles was much disturbed at this strange and terrible prophecy, but the common people, who in any difficult crisis and great exigency ever look for relief rather to strange and extravagant than to reasonable means, calling upon Bacchus with one voice, led the captives to the altar, and compelled the execution of the sacrifice as the prophet had commanded. This is reported by Phanias the Lesbian, a philosopher well read in history.

The number of the enemy's ships the poet Æschylus gives in his tragedy called *The Persians,* as on his certain knowledge, in the following words:—

Xerxes, I know, did into battle lead
One thousand ships; of more than usual speed
Seven and two hundred. So it is agreed.

The Athenians had a hundred and eighty; in every ship eighteen men fought upon the deck, four of whom were archers and the rest men at arms.

As Themistocles had fixed upon the most advantageous place, so, with no less sagacity, he chose the best time of fighting; for he would not run the prows of his galleys against the Persians, nor begin the fight till the time of day was come, when there regularly blows in a fresh breeze from the open sea, and brings in with it a strong swell into the channel; which was no inconvenience to the Greek ships, which were low-built, and little above the water, but did much to hurt the Persians, which had high sterns and lofty decks, and were heavy and cumbrous in their movements, as it presented them broadside to the quick charges of the Greeks, who kept their eyes upon the motions of Themistocles, as their best example, and more particularly because, opposed to his ship, Ariamenes, admiral to Xerxes, a brave man and by far the best and worthiest of the king's brothers, was seen throwing darts and shooting arrows from his huge galley, as from the walls of a castle. Aminias the Decelean and Sosicles the Pedian, who sailed in the same vessel, upon the ships meeting stem to stem, and transfixing each the other with their brazen prows, so that they were fastened together, when Ariamenes attempted to board theirs, ran at him with their pikes, and thrust him into the sea; his body, as it floated amongst other shipwrecks, was known to Artemisia, and carried to Xerxes.

It is reported that, in the middle of the fight, a great flame rose into the air above the city of Eleusis, and that sounds and voices were heard through all the Thriasian plain, as far as the sea, sounding like a number of men accompanying and escorting the mystic Iacchus, and that a mist seemed to form and rise from the place from whence the sounds came, and, passing forward, fell upon the galleys. Others believed that they saw apparitions, in the shape of armed men, reaching out their hands from the island of Ægina before the Grecian galleys; and supposed they were the Æacidæ, whom they had invoked to their aid before the battle. The first man that took a ship was Lycomedes the Athenian, captain of the galley, who cut down its ensign, and dedicated it to Apollo the Laurelcrowned. And as the Persians fought in a narrow arm of the sea, and could bring but part of their fleet to fight, and fell foul of one another, the Greeks thus equalled them in strength, and fought with them till the evening forced them back, and obtained, as says Simonides, that noble and famous victory, than which neither amongst the Greeks nor barbarians was ever known more glorious exploit on the seas; by the joint valour, indeed, and zeal of all who fought, but by the wisdom and sagacity of Themistocles.

After this sea-fight, Xerxes, enraged at his ill-fortune, attempted, by casting great heaps of earth and stones into the sea, to stop up the channel and to make a dam, upon which he might lead his land-forces over into the island of Salamis.

Themistocles, being desirous to try the opinion of Aristides, told him that he proposed to set sail for the Hellespont, to break the bridge of ships, so as to shut up, he said, Asia a prisoner within Europe; but Aristides, disliking the design, said: "We have hitherto fought with an enemy who has regarded little else but his pleasure and luxury; but if we shut him up within Greece, and drive him to necessity, he that is master of such great forces will no longer sit quietly with an umbrella of gold over his head, looking upon the fight for his pleasure; but in such a strait will attempt all things; he will be resolute, and appear himself in person upon all occasions, he will soon correct his errors, and supply what he has formerly omitted through remissness, and will be better advised in all things. Therefore, it is noways our interest, Themistocles," he said, "to take away the bridge that is already made, but rather to build another, if it were possible, that he might make his retreat with the more expedition." To which Themistocles answered: "If this be requisite, we must immediately use all diligence, art, and industry, to rid ourselves of him as soon as may be"; and to this purpose he found out among the captives one of the King of Persia's eunuchs, named Arnaces, whom he sent to the king, to inform him that the Greeks, being now victorious by sea, had decreed to sail to the Hellespont, where the boats were fastened together, and destroy the bridge; but that Themistocles, being concerned for the king, revealed this to him, that he might hasten towards the Asiatic seas, and pass over into his own dominions; and in the meantime would cause delays and hinder the confederates from pursuing him. Xerxes no sooner heard this, but, being very much terrified, he proceeded to retreat out of Greece with all speed. The prudence of Themistocles and Aristides in this was afterwards more fully understood at the battle of Platæa, where Mardonimus, with a very small fraction of the forces of Xerxes, put the Greeks in danger of losing all.

Herodotus writes, that of all the cities of Greece, Ægina was held to have performed the best service in the war; while all single men yielded to Themistocles, though, out of envy, unwillingly; and when they returned to the entrance of Peloponnesus, where the several commanders delivered their suffrages at the altar, to determine who was most worthy, every one gave the first vote for himself and the second for Themistocles. The Lacedæmonians carried him with them to Sparta, where, giving the rewards of valour to Eurybiades, and of wisdom and conduct to Themistocles, they crowned him with olive, presented him with the best chariot in the city, and sent three hundred young men to accompany him to the confines of their country. And at the next Olympic games, when Themistocles entered the course, the spectators took no further notice of those who were contesting the prizes, but spent the whole day in looking upon him, showing him to the strangers, admiring him, and applauding him by clapping their hands, and other expressions of joy, so that he himself, much gratified, confessed to his friends that he then reaped the fruit of all his labours for the Greeks.

He was, indeed, by nature, a great lover of honour, as is evident from the anecdotes recorded of him. When chosen admiral by the Athenians, he would not quite conclude any single matter of business, either public or private, but deferred all till the day they were to set sail, that, by despatching a great quantity of business all at once, and having to meet a great variety of people, he might make an appearance of greatness and power. Viewing the dead bodies cast up by the sea, he perceived bracelets and necklaces of gold about them, yet passed on, only showing them to a friend that followed him, saying, "Take you these things, for you are not Themistocles." He said to Antiphates, a handsome young man, who had formerly avoided, but now in his glory courted him, "Time, young man, has taught us both a lesson." He said that the Athenians did not honour him or admire him, but made, as it were, a sort of plane-tree of him; sheltered themselves under him in bad weather, and as soon as it was fine, plucked his leaves and cut his branches. When the Seriphian told him that he had not obtained this honour by himself, but by the greatness of the city, he replied, "You speak truth; I should never have been famous if I had been of Seriphus; nor you, had you been of Athens."

When another of the generals, who thought

he had performed considerable service for the Athenians, boastingly compared his actions with those of Themistocles, he told him that once upon a time the Day after the Festival found fault with the Festival: "On you there is nothing but hurry and trouble and preparation, but, when I come, everybody sits down quietly and enjoys himself"; which the Festival admitted was true, but "if I had not come first, you would not have come at all." "Even so," he said, "if Themistocles had not come before, where had you been now?" Laughing at his own son, who got his mother, and, by his mother's means, his father also, to indulge him, he told him that he had the most power of any one in Greece: "For the Athenians command the rest of Greece, I command the Athenians, your mother commands me, and you command your mother." Loving to be singular in all things, when he had land to sell, he ordered the crier to give notice that there were good neighbours near it. Of two who made love to his daughter, he preferred the man of worth to the one who was rich, saying he desired a man without riches, rather than riches without a man. Such was the character of his sayings.

After these things, he began to rebuild and fortify the city of Athens, bribing, as Theopompus reports, the Lacedæmonian ephors not to be against it, but, as most relate it, overreaching and deceiving them. For, under the pretext of an embassy, he went to Sparta, whereupon the Lacedæmonians charging him with rebuilding the walls, and Poliarchus coming on purpose from Ægina to denounce it, he denied the fact, bidding them to send people to Athens to see whether it were so or no; by which delay he got time for the building of the wall, and also placed these ambassadors in the hands of his countrymen as hostages for him; and so, when the Lacedæmonians knew the truth, they did him no hurt, but, suppressing all display of their anger for the present, sent him away.

Next he proceeded to establish the harbour of Piræus, observing the great natural advantages of the locality, and desirous to unite the whole city with the sea, and to reverse, in a manner, the policy of ancient Athenian kings, who, endeavouring to withdraw their subjects from the sea, and to accustom them to live, not by sailing about, but by planting and tilling the earth, spread the story of the dispute between Minerva and Neptune for the sovereignty of Athens, in which Minerva, by pro-

ducing to the judges an olive-tree, was declared to have won; whereas Themistocles did not only knead up, as Aristophanes says, the port and the city into one, but made the city absolutely the dependent and the adjunct of the port, and the land of the sea, which increased the power and confidence of the people against the nobility; the authority coming into the hands of sailors and boatswains and pilots. Thus it was one of the orders of the thirty tyrants, that the hustings in the assembly, which had faced towards the sea, should be turned round towards the land; implying their opinion that the empire by sea had been the origin of the democracy, and that the farming population were not so much opposed to oligarchy.

Themistocles, however, formed yet higher designs with a view to naval supremacy. For, after the departure of Xerxes, when the Grecian fleet was arrived at Pagasæ, where they wintered, Themistocles, in a public oration to the people of Athens, told them that he had a design to perform something that would tend greatly to their interests and safety, but was of such a nature that it could not be made generally public. The Athenians ordered him to impart it to Aristides only; and, if he approved of it, to put it in practice. And when Themistocles had discovered to him that his design was to burn the Grecian fleet in the haven of Pagasæ, Aristides coming out to the people, gave this report of the stratagem contrived by Themistocles, that no proposal could be more politic, or more dishonourable; on which the Athenians commanded Themistocles to think no further of it.

When the Lacedæmonians proposed, at the general council of the Amphictyonians, that the representatives of those cities which were not in the league, nor had fought against the Persians, should be excluded, Themistocles, fearing that the Thessalians, with those of Thebes, Argos, and others, being thrown out of the council, the Lacedæmonians would become wholly masters of the votes, and do what they pleased, supported the deputies of the cities, and prevailed with the members then sitting to alter their opinion on this point, showing them that there were but one-and-thirty cities which had partaken in the war, and that most of these, also, were very small; how intolerable would it be, if the rest of Greece should be excluded, and the general council should come to be ruled by two or three great cities. By this, chiefly, he incurred the displeasure of the Lacedæmonians, whose honours and favours were now shown to Cimon, with a view to making him the opponent of the state policy of Themistocles.

He was also burdensome to the confederates, sailing about the islands and collecting money from them. Herodotus says, that, requiring money of those of the island of Andros, he told them that he had brought with him two goddesses, Persuasion and Force; and they answered him that they had also two great goddesses, which prohibited them from giving him any money, Poverty and Impossibility. Timocreon, the Rhodian poet, reprehends him somewhat bitterly for being wrought upon by money to let some who were banished return, while abandoning himself, who was his guest and friend. The verses are these:—

Pausanias you may praise, and Xanthippus, he be
  for,
For Leutychidas, a third; Aristides, I proclaim,
From the sacred Athens came.
The one true man of all; for Themistocles
  Latona doth abhor,
The liar, traitor, cheat, who to gain his filthy pay,
Timocreon, his friend, neglected to restore
To his native Rhodian shore;
Three silver talents took, and departed (curses
  with him) on his way,
Restoring people here, expelling there, and killing
  here,
Filling evermore his purse: and at the Isthmus
  gave a treat,
To be laughed at, of cold meat,
Which they ate, and prayed the gods some one
  else might give the feast another year.

But after the sentence and banishment of Themistocles, Timocreon reviles him yet more immoderately and wildly in a poem that begins thus:—

Unto all the Greeks repair,
O Muse, and tell these verses there,
As is fitting and is fair.

The story is, that it was put to the question whether Timocreon should be banished for siding with the Persians, and Themistocles gave his vote against him. So when Themistocles was accused of intriguing with the Medes, Timocreon made these lines upon him:—

So now Timocreon, indeed, is not the sole friend
  of the Mede,
There are some knaves besides; nor is it only
  mine that fails,
But other foxes have lost tails.—

When the citizens of Athens began to listen willingly to those who traduced and reproached him, he was forced, with somewhat obnoxious frequency, to put them in mind of the great services he had performed, and ask those who were offended with him whether they were weary with receiving benefits often from the same person, so rendering himself more odious. And he yet more provoked the people by building a temple to Diana with the epithet of Aristobule, or Diana of Best Counsel; intimating thereby, that he had given the best counsel, not only to the Athenians, but to all Greece. He built this temple near his own house, in the district called Melite, where now the public officers carry out the bodies of such as are executed, and throw the halters and clothes of those that are strangled or otherwise put to death. There is to this day a small figure of Themistocles in the temple of Diana of Best Counsel, which represents him to be a person not only of a noble mind, but also of a most heroic aspect.

At length the Athenians banished him, making use of the ostracism to humble his eminence and authority, as they ordinarily did with all whom they thought too powerful, or, by their greatness, disproportionable to the equality thought requisite in a popular government. For the ostracism was instituted, not so much to punish the offender, as to mitigate and pacify the violence of the envious, who delighted to humble eminent men, and who, by fixing this disgrace upon them, might vent some part of their rancour.

Themistocles being banished from Athens, while he stayed at Argos the detection of Pausanias happened, which gave such advantage to his enemies, that Leobotes of Agraule, son of Alcmæon, indicted him of treason, the Spartans supporting him in the accusation.

When Pausanias went about this treasonable design, he concealed it at first from Themistocles, though he were his intimate friend; but when he saw him expelled out of the commonwealth, and how impatiently he took his banishment, he ventured to communicate it to him, and desired his assistance, showing him the king of Persia's letters, and exasperating him against the Greeks, as a villainous, ungrateful people. However, Themistocles immediately rejected the proposals of Pausanias, and wholly refused to be a party in the enterprise, though he never revealed his communications, nor disclosed the conspiracy to any man, either hoping that Pausanias would desist from his intentions, or expecting that so inconsiderate an attempt after such chimerical objects would be discovered by other means.

After that Pausanias was put to death, letters and writings being found concerning this matter, which rendered Themistocles suspected, the Lacedæmonians were clamorous against him, and his enemies among the Athenians accused him; when, being absent from Athens, he made his defence by letters, especially against the points that had been previously alleged against him. In answer to the malicious detractions of his enemies, he merely wrote to the citizens, urging that he who was always ambitious to govern, and not of a character or a disposition to serve, would never sell himself and his country into slavery to a barbarous and hostile nation.

Notwithstanding this, the people, being persuaded by his accusers, sent officers to take him and bring him away to be tried before a council of the Greeks, but, having timely notice of it, he passed over into the island of Corcyra, where the state was under obligations to him; for, being chosen as arbitrator in a difference between them and the Corinthians, he decided the controversy by ordering the Corinthians to pay down twenty talents, and declaring the town and island of Leucas a joint colony from both cities. From thence he fled into Epirus, and, the Athenians and Lacedæmonians still pursuing him, he threw himself upon chances of safety that seemed all but desperate.

For he fled for refuge to Admetus, king of the Molossians, who had formerly made some request to the Athenians, when Themistocles was in the height of his authority, and had been disdainfully used and insulted by him, and had let it appear plain enough, that, could he lay hold of him, he would take his revenge. Yet in this misfortune, Themistocles, fearing the recent hatred of his neighbours and fellow-citizens more than the old displeasure of the king, put himself at his mercy and became an humble suppliant to Admetus, after a peculiar manner different from the custom of other countries. For taking the king's son, who was then a child, in his arms, he laid himself down at his hearth, this being the most sacred and only manner of supplication among the Molossians, which was not to be refused. And some say that his wife, Phthia, intimated to Themistocles this way of petitioning, and placed her young son with him before the hearth; others, that king Admetus, that he might be under a religious obligation not to deliver him up to his pursuers, prepared and enacted with him a sort of stage-play to this effect.

At this time Epicrates of Acharnæ privately conveyed his wife and children out of Athens, and sent them hither, for which afterwards Cimon condemned him and put him to death, as Stesimbrotus reports, and yet somehow, either forgetting this himself, or making Themistocles to be little mindful of it, says presently that he sailed into Sicily, and desired in marriage the daughter of Hiero, tyrant of Syracuse, promising to bring the Greeks under his power; and, on Hiero refusing him, departed thence into Asia; but this is not probable.

For Theophrastus writes, in his work on Monarchy, that when Hiero sent race-horses to the Olympian games, and erected a pavilion sumptuously furnished, Themistocles made an oration to the Greeks, inciting them to pull down the tyrant's tent, and not to suffer his horses to run. Thucydides says, that, passing overland to the Ægæan Sea, he took ship at Pydna in the bay Therme, not being known to any one in the ship, till, being terrified to see the vessel driven by the winds near to Naxos, which was then besieged by the Athenians, he made himself known to the master and pilot, and partly entreating them, partly threatening that if they went on shore he would accuse them, and make the Athenians to believe that they did not take him in out of ignorance, but that he had corrupted them with money from the beginning, he compelled them to bear off and stand out to sea, and sail forward towards the coast of Asia.

A great part of his estate was privately conveyed away by his friends, and sent after him by sea into Asia; besides which, there was discovered and confiscated to the value of fourscore talents, as Theophrastus writes; Theopompus says an hundred; though Themistocles was never worth three talents before he was concerned in public affairs.

When he arrived at Cyme, and understood that all along the coast there were many laid wait for him, and particularly Ergoteles and Pythodorus (for the game was worth the hunting for such as were thankful to make money by any means, the king of Persia having offered by public proclamation two hundred talents to him that should take him), he fled to Ægæ, a small city of the Æolians, where no one knew him but only his host Nicogenes, who was the richest man in Æolia, and well known to the great men of Inner Asia. While Themistocles lay hid for some days in his house, one night, after a sacrifice and supper ensuing, Olbius, the attendant upon Nicogenes's children, fell into a sort of frenzy and fit of inspiration, and cried out in verse—

Night shall speak, and night instruct thee,
By the voice of night conduct thee.

After this, Themistocles, going to bed, dreamed that he saw a snake coil itself up upon his belly, and so creep to his neck; then, as soon as it touched his face, it turned into an eagle, which spread its wings over him, and took him up and flew away with him a great distance; then there appeared a herald's golden wand, and upon this at last it set him down securely, after infinite terror and disturbance.

His departure was effected by Nicogenes by the following artifice: the barbarous nations, and amongst them the Persians especially, are extremely jealous, severe, and suspicious about their women, not only their wives, but also their bought slaves and concubines, whom they keep so strictly that no one ever sees them abroad; they spend their lives shut up within doors, and, when they take a journey, are carried in close tents, curtained in on all sides, and set upon a waggon. Such a travelling carriage being prepared for Themistocles, they hid him in it, and carried him on his journey, and told those whom they met or spoke with upon the road that they were conveying a young Greek woman out of Ionia to a nobleman at court.

Thucydides and Charon of Lampsacus say that Xerxes was dead, and that Themistocles had an interview with his son; but Ephorus, Dinon, Clitarchus, Heraclides, and many others, write that he came to Xerxes. The chronological tables better agree with the account of Thucydides, and yet neither can their statements be said to be quite set at rest.

When Themistocles was come to the critical point, he applied himself first to Artabanus, commander of a thousand men, telling him that he was a Greek, and desired to speak with the king about important affairs concerning which the king was extremely solicitous. Artabanus answered him: "O stranger, the laws of men are different, and one thing is honourable to one man, and to others another; but it is honourable for all to honour and observe their own laws. It is the habit of the Greeks, we are told, to honour, above all things, liberty and equality; but amongst our many excellent laws, we account this the most excellent, to honour the king, and to worship him, as the image of the great preserver of the universe; if, then, you shall consent to our laws, and fall down before the king and worship him, you may both see him and speak to him; but if your mind be otherwise, you must make use of others to intercede for you, for it is not the national custom here for the king to give audience to any one that doth not fall down before him."

Themistocles, hearing this, replied: "Artabanus, I, that come hither to increase the power and glory of the king, will not only submit myself to his laws, since so it hath pleased the god who exalteth the Persian empire to this greatness, but will also cause many more to be worshippers and adorers of the king. Let not this, therefore, be an impediment why I should not communicate to the king what I have to impart." Artabanus asking him, "Who must we tell him that you are? For your words signify you to be no ordinary person." Themistocles answered, "No man, O Artabanus, must be informed of this before the king himself." Thus Phanias relates; to which Eratosthenes, in his treatise on Riches, adds, that it was by the means of a woman of Eretria, who was kept by Artabanus, that he obtained this audience and interview with him.

When he was introduced to the king, and had paid his reverence to him, he stood silent, till the king commanding the interpreter to ask him who he was, he replied, "O king, I am Themistocles the Athenian, driven into banishment by the Greeks. The evils that I have done to the Persians are numerous; but my benefits to them yet greater, in withholding the Greeks from pursuit, so soon as the deliverance of my own country allowed me to show kindness also to you. I come with a mind suited to my present calamities, prepared alike for favours and for anger, to welcome your gracious reconciliation, and to deprecate your wrath. Take my own countrymen for witnesses of the services I have done for Persia, and make use of this occasion to show the world your virtue, rather than to satisfy your indignation. If you save me, you will save your suppliant; if otherwise, will destroy an enemy of the Greeks." He talked also of divine admonitions, such as the vision which he saw at Nicogenes's house, and the direction given him by the oracle of Dodona, where Jupiter commanded him to go to him that had a name like his, by which he understood that he was sent from Jupiter to him, seeing that they both were great, and had the name of kings.

The king heard him attentively, and, though he admired his temper and courage, gave him no answer at that time; but, when he was with his intimate friends, rejoiced in his great good fortune, and esteemed himself very happy in this, and prayed to his god Arimanius, that all his enemies might be ever of the same mind with the Greeks, to abuse and expel the bravest men amongst them. Then he sacrificed to the gods, and presently fell to drinking, and was so well pleased, that in the night, in the middle of his sleep, he cried out for joy three times, "I have Themistocles the Athenian."

In the morning, calling together the chief of his court, he had Themistocles brought before him, who expected no good of it, when he saw, for example, the guards fiercely set against him as soon as they learnt his name, and giving him ill language. As he came forward towards the king, who was seated, the rest keeping silence, passing by Roxanes, a commander of a thousand men, he heard him, with a slight groan, say, without stirring out of his place, "You subtle Greek serpent, the king's good genius hath brought thee hither." Yet, when he came into the presence, and again fell down, the king saluted him, and spake to him kindly, telling him he was now indebted to him two hundred talents; for it was just and reasonable that he should receive the reward which was proposed to whosoever should bring Themistocles; and promising much more, and encouraging him, he commanded him to speak freely what he would concerning the affairs of Greece. Themistocles replied, that a man's discourse was like to a rich Persian carpet, the beautiful figures and patterns of which can only be shown by spreading and extending it out; when it is contracted and folded up, they are obscure and lost; and, therefore, he desired time. The king being pleased with the comparison, and bidding him take what time he would, he desired a year.

In which time, having learnt the Persian language sufficiently, he spoke with the king by himself without the help of an interpreter, it being supposed that he discoursed only about the affairs of Greece; but there happening, at the same time, great alterations at court, and removals of the king's favourites, he drew upon himself the envy of the great people, who imagined that he had taken the boldness to speak concerning them. For the favours shown to other strangers were nothing in comparison with the honours conferred on him; the king invited him to partake of his own pastimes and recreations both at home and abroad, carrying him with him a-hunting, and made him his intimate so far that he permitted him to see the queen-mother, and converse frequently with her. By the king's command, he also was made acquainted with the Magian learning.

When Demaratus the Lacedæmonian, being ordered by the king to ask whatsoever he pleased, that it should immediately be granted him, desired that he might make his public entrance, and be carried in state through the city of Sardis, with the tiara set in the royal manner upon his head, Mithropaustes, cousin to the king, touched him on the head, and told him that he had no brains for the royal tiara to cover, and if Jupiter should give him his lightning and thunder, he would not any the more be Jupiter for that; the king also repulsed him with anger, resolving never to be reconciled to him, but to be inexorable to all supplications on his behalf. Yet Themistocles pacified him, and prevailed with him to forgive him.

And it is reported that the succeeding kings, in whose reigns there was a greater communication between the Greeks and Persians, when they invited any considerable Greek into their service, to encourage him, would write and promise him that he should be as great with them as Themistocles had been. They relate, also, how Themistocles, when he was in great prosperity, and courted by many, seeing himself splendidly served at his table, turned to his children and said, "Children, we had been undone if we had not been undone." Most writers say that he had three cities given him, Magnesia, Myus, and Lampsacus, to maintain him in bread, meat, and wine. Neanthes of Cyzicus, and Phanias, add two more, the city of Palæscepsis, to provide him with clothes, and Percote, with bedding and furniture for his house.

As he was going down towards the sea-coast to take measures against Greece, a Persian whose name was Epixyes, governor of the upper Phrygia, laid wait to kill him, having for that purpose provided a long time before a number of Pisidians, who were to set upon him when he should stop to rest at a city that is called Lion's-head. But Themistocles, sleeping in the middle of the day, saw the Mother of the gods appear to him in a dream and say unto him, "Themistocles, keep back from the Lion's-head, for fear you fall into the lion's jaws; for this advice I expect that your daughter Mnesiptolema should be my servant."

Themistocles was much astonished, and when he had made his vows to the goddess, left the broad road, and, making a circuit, went another way, changing his intended station to avoid that place, and at night took up his rest in the fields. But one of the sumpter-horses, which carried the furniture for his tent, having fallen that day into the river, his servants spread out the tapestry, which was wet, and hung it up to dry; in the meantime the Pisidians made towards them with their swords drawn, and, not discerning exactly by the moon what it was that was stretched out, thought it to be the tent of Themistocles, and that they should find him resting himself within it; but when they came near, and lifted up the hangings, those who watched there fell upon them and took them. Themistocles, having escaped this great danger, in admiration of the goodness of the goddess that appeared to him, built, in memory of it, a temple in the city of Magnesia, which is dedicated to Dindymene, Mother of the gods, in which he consecrated and devoted his daughter Mnesiptolema to her service.

When he came to Sardis, he visited the temples of the gods, and observing, at his leisure, their buildings, ornaments, and the number of their offerings, he saw in the temple of the Mother of the gods the statue of a virgin in brass, two cubits high, called the water-bringer. Themistocles had caused this to be made and set up when he was surveyor of the waters at Athens, out of the fines of those whom he detected in drawing off and diverting the public water by pipes for their private use; and whether he had some regret to see this image in captivity, or was desirous to let the Athenians see in what great credit and authority he was with the king, he entered into a treaty with the governor to persuade him to send this statue back to Athens, which so enraged the Persian officer, that he told him he would write the king word of it. Themistocles, being affrighted hereat, got access to his wives and concubines, by presents of money to whom he appeased the fury of the governor; and afterwards behaved with more reserve and circumspection, fearing the envy of the Persians, and did not, as Theopompus writes, continue to travel about Asia, but lived quietly in his own house in Magnesia, where for a long time he passed his days in great security, being courted by all, and enjoying rich presents, and honoured equally with the greatest persons in the Persian empire; the king, at that time, not minding his concerns with Greece, being taken up with the affairs of inner Asia.

But when Egypt revolted, being assisted by the Athenians, and the Greek galleys roved about as far as Cyprus and Cilicia, and Cimon had made himself master of the seas, the king turned his thoughts thither, and, bending his mind chiefly to resist the Greeks, and to check the growth of their power against him, began to raise forces, and send out commanders, and to despatch messengers to Themistocles at Magnesia, to put him in mind of his promise, and to summon him to act against the Greeks.

Yet this did not increase his hatred nor exasperate him against the Athenians, neither was he in any way elevated with the thoughts of the honour and powerful command he was to have in this war; but judging, perhaps, that the object would not be attained, the Greeks having at that time, beside other great commanders, Cimon, in particular, who was gaining wonderful military successes; but chiefly being ashamed to sully the glory of his former great actions, and of his many victories and trophies, he determined to put a conclusion to his life, agreeable to its previous course. He sacrificed to the gods, and invited his friends; and, having entertained them and shaken hands with them, drank bull's blood, as is the usual story; as others state, a poison producing instant death; and ended his days in the city of Magnesia, having lived sixty-five years, most of which he had spent in politics and in wars, in government and command. The king being informed of the cause and manner of his death, admired him more than ever, and continued to show kindness to his friends and relations.

Themistocles left three sons by Archippe, daughter to Lysander of Alopece,—Archeptolis, Poleuctus, and Cleophantus. Plato, the philosopher, mentions the last as a most excellent horseman, but otherwise insignificant person; of two sons yet older than these, Neocles and Diocles, Neocles died when he was young by the bite of a horse, and Diocles was adopted by his grandfather, Lysander.

He had many daughters, of whom Mnesiptolema, whom he had by a second marriage, was wife to Archeptolis, her brother by another mother; Italia was married to Panthoides, of the island of Chios; Sybaris to Nicomedes the Athenian. After the death of Themistocles, his nephew, Phrasicles, went to Magnesia, and married, with her brothers' consent, another daughter, Nicomache, and took charge of her sister Asia, the youngest of all the children.

The Magnesians possess a splendid sepulchre of Themistocles, placed in the middle of their market-place. It is not worth while taking notice of what Andocides states in his address to his friends concerning his remains, how the Athenians robbed his tomb, and threw his ashes into the air; for he feigns this, to exasperate the oligarchical faction against the people; and there is no man living but knows that Phylarchus simply invents in his history, where he all but uses an actual stage machine, and brings in Neocles and Demopolis as the sons of Themistocles, to incite

or move compassion, as if he were writing a tragedy. Diodorus, the cosmographer, says, in his work on Tombs, but by conjecture rather than of certain knowledge, that near to the haven of Piræus where the land runs out like an elbow from the promontory of Alcimus, when you have doubled the cape and passed inward where the sea is always calm, there is a large piece of masonry, and upon this the Tomb of Themistocles, in the shape of an altar; and Plato the comedian confirms this, he believes, in these verses:—

Thy tomb is fairly placed upon the strand,
Where merchants still shall greet it with the
*   land;*
Still in and out 'twill see them come and go,
And watch the galleys as they race below.

Various honours also and privileges were granted to the kindred of Themistocles at Magnesia, which were observed down to our times, and were enjoyed by another Themistocles of Athens, with whom I had an intimate acquaintance and friendship in the house of Ammonius the philosopher.

CAMILLUS

445?–365 B.C.

AMONG the many remarkable things that are related of Furius Camillus, it seems singular and strange above all, that he, who continually was in the highest commands, and obtained the greatest successes, was five times chosen dictator, triumphed four times, and was styled a second founder of Rome, yet never was so much as once consul. The reason of which was the state and temper of the commonwealth at that time; for the people, being at dissension with the senate, refused to return consuls, but in their stead elected other magistrates, called military tribunes, who acted, indeed, with full consular power, but were thought to exercise a less obnoxious amount of authority, because it was divided among a large number; for to have the management of affairs intrusted to the hands of six persons rather than two was some satisfaction to the opponents of oligarchy.

This was the condition of the times when Camillus was in the height of his actions and glory, and, although the government in the meantime had often proceeded to consular

elections, yet he could never persuade himself to be consul against the inclination of the people. In all his other administrations, which were many and various, he so behaved himself, that, when alone in authority, he exercised his power as in common, but the honour of all actions redounded entirely to himself, even when in joint commission with others; the reason of the former was his moderation in command; of the latter, his great judgment and wisdom, which gave him without controversy the first place.

The house of the Furii was not, at that time, of any considerable distinction; he, by his own acts, first raised himself to honour, serving under Postumius Tubertis, dictator, in the great battle against the Æquians and Volscians. For riding out from the rest of the army, and in the charge receiving a wound in his thigh, he for all that did not quit the fight, but, letting the dart drag in the wound, and engaging with the bravest of the enemy, put them to flight; for which action, among other rewards bestowed on him, he was created censor, an office in those days of great repute and authority. During his censorship one very good act of his is recorded, that, whereas the wars had made many widows, he obliged such as had no wives, some by fair persuasion, others by threatening to set fines on their heads, to take them in marriage; another necessary one, in causing orphans to be rated, who before were exempted from taxes, the frequent wars requiring more than ordinary expenses to maintain them.

What, however, pressed them most was the siege of Veii. Some call this people Veientani. This was the head city of Tuscany, not inferior to Rome, either in number of arms or multitude of soldiers, insomuch that, presuming on her wealth and luxury, and priding herself upon her refinement and sumptuousness, she engaged in many honourable contests with the Romans for glory and empire. But now they abandoned their former ambitious hopes, having been weakened by great defeats, so that, having fortified themselves with high and strong walls, and furnished the city with all sorts of weapons offensive and defensive, as likewise with corn and all manner of provisions, they cheerfully endured a siege, which, though tedious to them, was no less troublesome and distressing to the besiegers. For the Romans, having never been accustomed to stay away from home except in summer, and for no great length of time, and constantly to winter at home, were then first compelled by the tribunes to build forts in the enemy's country, and raising strong works about their camp, to join winter and summer together.

And now, the seventh year of the war drawing to an end, the commanders began to be suspected as too slow and remiss in driving on the siege, insomuch that they were discharged and others chosen for the war, among whom was Camillus, then second time tribune. But at present he had no hand in the siege, the duties that fell by lot to him being to make war upon the Faliscans and Capenates, who, taking advantage of the Romans being occupied on all hands, had carried ravages into their country, and, through all the Tuscan war, given them much annoyance, but were now reduced by Camillus, and with great loss shut up within their walls.

And now, in the very heat of the war, a strange phenomenon in the Alban lake, which, in the absence of any known cause and explanation by natural reasons, seemed as great a prodigy as the most incredible that are reported, occasioned great alarm. It was the beginning of autumn, and the summer now ending had, to all observation, been neither rainy nor much troubled with southern winds; and of the many lakes, brooks, and springs of all sorts with which Italy abounds, some were wholly dried up, others drew very little water with them; all the rivers, as is usual in summer, ran in a very low and hollow channel. But the Alban lake, that is fed by no other waters but its own, and is on all sides encircled with fruitful mountains, without any cause, unless it were divine, began visibly to rise and swell, increasing to the feet of the mountains, and by degrees reaching the level of the very tops of them, and all this without any waves or agitation. At first it was the wonder of shepherds and herdsmen; but when the earth, which, like a great dam, held up the lake from falling into the lower grounds, through the quantity and weight of water was broken down, and in a violent stream it ran through the ploughed fields and plantations to discharge itself in the sea, it not only struck terror into the Romans, but was thought by all the inhabitants of Italy to portend some extraordinary event. But the greatest talk of it was in the camp that besieged Veii, so that in the town itself, also, the occurrence became known.

As in long sieges it commonly happens that parties on both sides meet often and converse with one another, so it chanced that a Roman had gained much confidence and familiarity with one of the besieged, a man versed in ancient prophecies, and of repute for more than ordinary skill in divination. The Roman, observing him to be overjoyed at the story of the lake, and to mock at the siege, told him that this was not the only prodigy that of late had happened to the Romans; others more wonderful yet than this had befallen them, which he was willing to communicate to him, that he might the better provide for his private interests in these public distempers. The man greedily embraced the proposal, expecting to hear some wonderful secrets; but when, by little and little, he had led him on in conversation and insensibly drawn him a good way from the gates of the city, he snatched him up by the middle, being stronger than he, and, by the assistance of others that came running from the camp, seized and delivered him to the commanders.

The man, reduced to this necessity, and

sensible now that destiny was not to be avoided, discovered to them the secret oracles of Veii; that it was not possible the city should be taken, until the Alban lake, which now broke forth and had found out new passages, was drawn back from that course, and so diverted that it could not mingle with the sea. The senate, having heard and satisfied themselves about the matter, decreed to send to Delphi, to ask counsel of the god. The messengers were persons of the highest repute, Licinius Cossus, Valerius Potitus, and Fabius Ambustus; who, having made their voyage by sea and consulted the god, returned with other answers, particularly that there had been a neglect of some of their national rites relating to the Latin feasts; but the Alban water the oracle commanded, if it were possible, they should keep from the sea, and shut it up in its ancient bounds; but if that was not to be done, then they should carry it off by ditches and trenches into the lower grounds, and so dry it up; which message being delivered, the priests performed what related to the sacrifices, and the people went to work and turned the water.

And now the senate, in the tenth year of the war, taking away all other commands, created Camillus dictator, who chose Cornelius Scipio for his general of horse. And in the first place he made vows unto the gods, that, if they would grant a happy conclusion of the war, he would celebrate to their honour the great games, and dedicate a temple to the goddess whom the Romans call Matuta, the Mother, though, from the ceremonies which are used, one would think she was Leucothea. For they take a servant-maid into the secret part of the temple, and there cuff her, and drive her out again, and they embrace their brothers' children in place of their own; and, in general, the ceremonies of the sacrifice remind one of the nursing of Bacchus by Ino, and the calamities occasioned by her husband's concubine.

Camillus, having made these vows, marched into the country of the Faliscans, and in a great battle overthrew them and the Capenates, their confederates; afterwards he turned to the siege of Veii, and, finding that to take it by assault would prove a difficult and hazardous attempt, proceeded to cut mines underground, the earth about the city being easy to break up, and allowing such depth for the works as would prevent their being discovered by the enemy. This design going on in a hopeful way, he openly gave assaults to the enemy to keep them to the walls, whilst they that worked underground in the mines were, without being perceived, arrived within the citadel, close to the temple of Juno, which was the greatest and most honoured in all the city.

It is said that the prince of the Tuscans was at that very time at sacrifice, and that the priest, after he had looked into the entrails of the beast, cried out with a loud voice that the gods would give the victory to those that should complete those offerings; and that the Romans who were in the mines, hearing the words, immediately pulled down the floor, and, ascending with noise and clashing of weapons, frightened away the enemy, and, snatching up the entrails, carried them to Camillus. But this may look like a fable.

The city, however, being taken by storm, and the soldiers busied in pillaging and gathering an infinite quantity of riches and spoils, Camillus, from the high tower, viewing what was done, at first wept for pity; and when they that were by congratulated his success, he lifted up his hands to heaven, and broke out into this prayer: "O most mighty Jupiter, and ye gods that are judges of good and evil actions, ye know that not without just cause, but constrained by necessity, we have been forced to revenge ourselves on the city of our unrighteous and wicked enemies. But if, in the vicissitude of things, there may be any calamity due, to counterbalance this great felicity, I beg that it may be diverted from the city and army of the Romans, and fall, with as little hurt as may be, upon my own head." Having said these words, and just turning about (as the custom of the Romans is to turn to the right after adoration or prayer), he stumbled and fell, to the astonishment of all that were present. But, recovering himself presently from the fall, he told them that he had received what he had prayed for, a small mischance, in compensation for the greatest good fortune.

Having sacked the city, he resolved, according as he had vowed, to carry Juno's image to Rome; and, the workmen being ready for that purpose, he sacrificed to the goddess, and made his supplications that she would be pleased to accept of their devotion toward her, and graciously vouchsafe to accept of a place among the gods that presided at Rome; and the statue, they say, answered in a low voice that she was ready and willing to go. Livy writes, that, in praying, Camillus touched the goddess, and invited her, and that some of the standers-by cried out that she was willing and would come.

They who stand up for the miracle and endeavour to maintain it have one great advocate on their side in the wonderful fortune of the city, which, from a small and contemptible beginning, could never have attained to that greatness and power without many signal manifestations of the divine presence and co-operation. Other wonders of the like nature, drops of sweat seen to stand on statues, groans heard from them, the figures seen to turn round and to close their eyes, are recorded by many ancient historians; and we ourselves could relate divers wonderful things, which we have been told by men of our own time, that are not lightly to be rejected; but to give too easy credit to such things, or wholly to disbelieve them, is equally dangerous, so incapable is human infirmity of keeping any bounds, or exercising command over itself, running off sometimes to superstition and dotage, at other times to the contempt and neglect of all that is supernatural. But moderation is best, and to avoid all extremes.

Camillus, however, whether puffed up with the greatness of his achievement in conquering a city that was the rival of Rome, and had held out a ten years' siege, or exalted with the felicitations of those that were about him, assumed to himself more than became a civil and legal magistrate; among other things, in the pride and haughtiness of his triumph, driving through Rome in a chariot drawn with four white horses, which no general either before or since ever did; for the Romans consider such a mode of conveyance to be sacred, and specially set apart to the king and father of the gods. This alienated the hearts of his fellow-citizens, who were not accustomed to such pomp and display.

The second pique they had against him was his opposing the law by which the city was to be divided; for the tribunes of the people brought forward a motion that the people and senate should be divided into two parts, one of which should remain at home, the other, as the lot should decide, remove to the new-taken city. By which means they should not only have much more room, but, by the advantage of two great and magnificent cities, be better able to maintain their territories and their fortunes in general. The people, therefore, who were numerous and indigent, greedily embraced it, and crowded continually to the forum, with tumultuous demands to have

it put to the vote. But the senate and the noblest citizens, judging the proceedings of the tribunes to tend rather to a destruction than a division of Rome, greatly averse to it, went to Camillus for assistance, who, fearing the result if it came to a direct contest, contrived to occupy the people with other business, and so staved it off. He thus became unpopular.

But the greatest and most apparent cause of their dislike against him arose from the tenths of the spoil; the multitude having here, if not a just, yet a plausible case against him. For it seems, as he went to the siege of Veii, he had vowed to Apollo that if he took the city he would dedicate to him the tenth of the spoil. The city being taken and sacked, whether he was loath to trouble the soldiers at that time, or that through the multitude of business he had forgotten his vow, he suffered them to enjoy that part of the spoils also. Some time afterwards, when his authority was laid down, he brought the matter before the senate, and the priests, at the same time, reported, out of the sacrifices, that there were intimations of divine anger, requiring propitiations and offerings. The senate decreed the obligations to be in force.

But seeing it was difficult for every one to produce the very same things they had taken, to be divided anew, they ordained that every one upon oath should bring into the public the tenth part of his gains. This occasioned many annoyances and hardships to the soldiers, who were poor men, and had endured much in the war, and now were forced, out of what they had gained and spent, to bring in so great a proportion. Camillus, being assaulted by their clamour and tumults, for want of a better excuse, betook himself to the poorest of defences, confessing he had forgotten his vow; they in turn complained that he had vowed the tenth of the enemy's goods, and now levied it out of the tenth of the citizens'. Nevertheless, every one having brought in his due proportion, it was decreed that out of it a bowl of massy gold should be made, and sent to Delphi. And when there was great scarcity of gold in the city, and the magistrates were considering where to get it, the Roman ladies, meeting together and consulting among themselves, out of the golden ornaments they wore contributed as much as went to the making of the offering, which in weight came to eight talents of gold. The senate, to give them the honour they had deserved, ordained that funeral orations should be used at the obsequies of women as well as men, it having never before been a custom that any women after death should receive any public eulogy. Choosing out, therefore, three of the noblest citizens as a deputation, they sent them in a vessel of war, well manned and sumptuously adorned. Storm and calm at sea may both, they say, alike be dangerous; as they at this time experienced, being brought almost to the very brink of destruction, and, beyond all expectation, escaping. For near the isles of Æolus the wind slacking, galleys of the Lipareans came upon them, taking them for pirates; and, when they held up their hands as suppliants, forbore indeed from violence, but took their ship in tow, and carried her into the harbour, where they exposed to sale their goods and persons as lawful prize, they being pirates; and scarcely, at last, by the virtue and interest of one man, Timasitheus by name, who was in office as general, and used his utmost persuasion, they were, with much ado, dismissed. He, however, himself sent out some of his own vessels with them, to accompany them in their voyage and assist them at the dedication; for which he received honours at Rome, as he had deserved.

And now the tribunes of the people again resuming their motion for the division of the city, the war against the Faliscans luckily broke out, giving liberty to the chief citizens to choose what magistrates they pleased, and to appoint Camillus military tribune, with five colleagues; affairs then requiring a commander of authority and reputation, as well as experience. And when the people had ratified the election, he marched with his forces into the territories of the Faliscans, and laid siege to Falerii, a well-fortified city, and plentifully stored with all necessaries of war. And although he perceived it would be no small work to take it, and no little time would be required for it, yet he was willing to exercise the citizens and keep them abroad, that they might have no leisure, idling at home, to follow the tribunes in factions and seditions; a very common remedy, indeed, with the Romans, who thus carried off, like good physicians, the ill humours of their commonwealth. The Falerians, trusting in the strength of their city, which was well fortified on all sides, made so little account of the siege, that all, with the exception of those that guarded the walls, as in times of peace, walked about the streets in their common dress, the boys went to school, and were led by their master to play and exercise about the town walls; for

the Falerians, like the Greeks, used to have a single teacher for many pupils, wishing their children to live and be brought up from the beginning in each other's company.

This schoolmaster, designing to betray the Falerians by their children, led them out every day under the town wall, at first but a little way, and, when they had exercised, brought them home again. Afterwards by degrees he drew them farther and farther, till by practice he had made them bold and fearless, as if no danger was about them; and at last, having got them all together, he brought them to the outposts of the Romans, and delivered them up, demanding to be led to Camillus. Where being come, and standing in the middle, he said that he was the master and teacher of these children, but preferring his favour before all other obligations, he was come to deliver up his charge to him, and, in that, the whole city. When Camillus had heard him out, he was astounded at the treachery of the act, and, turning to the standers-by, observed that, "War, indeed, is of necessity attended with much injustice and violence! Certain laws, however, all good men observe even in war itself, nor is victory so great an object as to induce us to incur for its sake obligations for base and impious acts. A great general should rely on his own virtue, and not on other men's vices." Which said, he commanded the officers to tear off the man's clothes, and bind his hands behind him, and give the boys rods and scourges to punish the traitor and drive him back to the city.

By this time the Falerians had discovered the treachery of the schoolmaster, and the city, as was likely, was full of lamentations and cries for their calamity, men and women of worth running in distraction about the walls and gates; when, behold, the boys came whipping their master on, naked and bound, calling Camillus their preserver and god and father. Insomuch that it struck not only into the parents, but the rest of the citizens that saw what was done, such admiration and love of Camillus's justice, that, immediately meeting in assembly, they sent ambassadors to him, to resign whatever they had to his disposal. Camillus sent them to Rome, where, being brought into the senate, they spoke to this purpose: that the Romans, preferring justice before victory, had taught them rather to embrace submission than liberty; they did not so much confess themselves to be inferior in strength, as they must acknowledge them to be superior in virtue. The senate remitted the whole matter to Camillus, to judge and order as he thought fit; who, taking a sum of money of the Falerians, and, making a peace with the whole nation of the Faliscans, returned home.

But the soldiers, who had expected to have the pillage of the city, when they came to Rome empty-handed, railed against Camillus among their fellow-citizens, as a hater of the people, and one that grudged all advantage to the poor. Afterwards, when the tribunes of the people again brought their motion for dividing the city to the vote, Camillus appeared openly against it, shrinking from no unpopularity, and inveighing boldly against the promoters of it, and so urging and constraining the multitude that, contrary to their inclinations, they rejected the proposal, but yet hated Camillus. Insomuch that though a great misfortune befell him in his family (one of his two sons dying of a disease), commiseration for this could not in the least make them abate their malice. And, indeed, he took this loss with immoderate sorrow, being a man naturally of a mild and tender disposition, and, when the accusation was preferred against him, kept his house, and mourned amongst the women of his family.

His accuser was Lucius Apuleius; the charge, appropriation of the Tuscan spoils; certain brass gates, part of those spoils, were said to be in his possession. The people were exasperated against him, and it was plain they would take hold of any occasion to condemn him. Gathering, therefore, together his friends and fellow-soldiers, and such as had borne command with him, a considerable number in all, he besought them that they would not suffer him to be unjustly overborne by shameful accusations, and left the mock and scorn of his enemies. His friends, having advised and consulted among themselves, made answer, that, as to the sentence, they did not see how they could help him, but that they would contribute to whatsoever fine should be set upon him. Not able to endure so great an indignity, he resolved, in his anger, to leave the city, and go into exile; and so, having taken leave of his wife and his son, he went silently to the gate of the city, and there stopping and turning round, stretched out his hands to the Capitol, and prayed to the gods, that if, without any fault of his own, but merely through the malice and violence of the people, he was driven out into banishment, the Romans might quickly repent of it; and that all mankind might witness their need for the assistance, and desire for the return of Camillus.

Thus, like Achilles, having left his imprecations on the citizens, he went into banishment; so that, neither appearing nor making defence, he was condemned in the sum of fifteen thousand asses, which, reduced to silver, make one thousand five hundred drachmas; for the as was the money of the time, ten of such copper pieces making the denarius, or piece of ten. And there is not a Roman but believes that immediately upon the prayers of Camillus, a sudden judgment followed, and that he received a revenge for the injustice done unto him; which though we cannot think was pleasant, but rather grievous and bitter to him, yet was very remarkable, and noised over the whole world. Such a punishment visited the city of Rome, an era of such loss and danger and disgrace so quickly succeeded; whether it thus fell out by fortune, or it be the office of some god not to see injured virtue go unavenged.

The first token that seemed to threaten some mischief to ensue was the death of the censor Julius; for the Romans have a religious reverence for the office of a censor, and esteem it sacred. The second was, that, just before Camillus went into exile, Marcus Cædicius, a person of no great distinction, nor of the rank of senator, but esteemed a good and respectable man, reported to the military tribunes a thing worthy their consideration: that, going along the night before in the street called the New Way, and being called by somebody in a loud voice, he turned about, but could see no one, but heard a voice greater than human, which said these words, "Go, Marcus Cædicius, and early in the morning tell the military tribunes that they are shortly to expect the Gauls." But the tribunes made a mock and sport with the story, and a little after came Camillus's banishment.

The Gauls are of the Celtic race, and are reported to have been compelled by their numbers to leave their country, which was insufficient to sustain them all, and to have gone in search of other homes. And being, many thousands of them, young men and able to bear arms, and carrying with them a still greater number of women and young children, some of them, passing the Riphæan mountains, fell upon the Northern Ocean, and possessed themselves of the farthest parts of Europe; others, seating themselves between the Pyrenean mountains and the Alps, lived there a considerable time, near to the Senones and Celtorii; but, afterwards tasting wine which was then first brought them out of Italy, they were all so much taken with the liquor, and transported with the hitherto unknown delight, that, snatching up their arms and taking their families along with them, they marched directly to the Alps, to find out the country which yielded such fruit, pronouncing all others barren and useless.

He that first brought wine among them and was the chief instigator of their coming into Italy is said to have been one Aruns, a Tuscan, a man of noble extraction, and not of bad natural character, but involved in the following misfortune. He was guardian to an orphan, one of the richest of the country, and much admired for his beauty, whose name was Lucumo. From his childhood he had been bred up with Aruns in his family, and when now grown up did not leave his house, professing to wish for the enjoyment of his society. And thus for a great while he secretly enjoyed Aruns's wife, corrupting her, and himself corrupted by her. But when they were both so far gone in their passion that they could neither refrain their lust nor conceal it, the young man seized the woman and openly sought to carry her away. The husband, going to law, and finding himself overpowered by the interest and money of his opponent, left his country and, hearing of the state of the Gauls, went to them, and was the conductor of their expedition into Italy.

At their first coming they at once possessed themselves of all that country which anciently the Tuscans inhabited, reaching from the Alps to both the seas, as the names themselves testify; for the North or Adriatic Sea is named from the Tuscan city, Adria, and that to the south the Tuscan Sea simply. The whole country is rich in fruit-trees, has excellent pasture, and is well watered with rivers. It had eighteen large and beautiful cities, well provided with all the means for industry and wealth, and all the enjoyments and pleasures of life. The Gauls cast out the Tuscans, and seated themselves in them. But this was long before.

The Gauls at this time were besieging Clusium, a Tuscan city. The Clusinians sent to the Romans for succour, desiring them to interpose with the barbarians by letters and ambassadors. There were sent three of the family of the Fabii, persons of high rank and distinction in the city. The Gauls received them courteously, from respect to the name of Rome, and, giving over the assault which was then making upon the walls, came to conference with them; when the ambassadors asking what injury they had received of the Clusinians that they thus invaded their city, Brennus, King of the Gauls, laughed and made answer: "The Clusinians do us injury, in that, being able only to till a small parcel of ground, they must needs possess a great territory, and will not yield any part to us who are strangers, many in number, and poor. In the same nature, O Romans, formerly the Albans, Fidenates, and Ardeates, and now lately the Veientines and Capenates, and many of the Faliscans and Volscians, did you injury; upon whom ye make war if they do not yield you part of what they possess, make slaves of them, waste and spoil their country, and ruin their cities; neither in so doing are cruel or unjust, but follow that most ancient of all laws, which gives the possessions of the feeble to the strong; which begins with God and ends in the beasts; since all these, by nature, seek the stronger to have advantage over the weaker. Cease, therefore, to pity the Clusinians whom we besiege, lest ye teach the Gauls to be kind and compassionate to those that are oppressed by you."

By this answer the Romans, perceiving that Brennus was not to be treated with, went into Clusium, and encouraged and stirred up the inhabitants to make a sally with them upon the barbarians, which they did either to try their strength or to show their own. The sally being made, and the fight growing hot about the walls, one of the Fabii, Quintus Ambustus, being well mounted, and setting spurs to his horse, made full against a Gaul, a man of huge bulk and stature, whom he saw riding out at a distance from the rest. At the first he was not recognised, through the quickness of the conflict and the glittering of his armour, that precluded any view of him; but when he had overthrown the Gaul, and was going to gather the spoils, Brennus knew him; and, invoking the gods to be witnesses, that, contrary to the known and common law of nations, which is holily observed by all mankind, he who had come as an ambassador had now engaged in hostility against him, he drew off his men, and bidding Clusium farewell, led his army directly to Rome. But not wishing that it should look as if they took advantage of that injury, and were ready to embrace any occasion of quarrel, he sent a herald to demand the man in punishment, and in the meantime marched leisurely on.

The senate being met at Rome, among many others that spoke against the Fabii, the priests called fecials were the most decided, who, on the religious ground, urged the senate that they should lay the whole guilt and penalty of the fact upon him that committed it, and so exonerate the rest. These fecials Numa Pompilius, the mildest and justest of kings, constituted guardians of peace, and the judges and determiners of all causes by which war may justifiably be made. The senate referring the whole matter to the people, and the priests there, as well as in the senate, pleading against Fabius, the multitude, however, so little regarded their authority, that in scorn and contempt of it they chose Fabius and the rest of his brothers military tribunes.

The Gauls, on hearing this, in great rage threw aside every delay, and hastened on with all the speed they could make. The places through which they marched, terrified with their numbers and the splendour of their preparations for war, and in alarm at their violence and fierceness, began to give up their territories as already lost, with little doubt but their cities would quickly follow; contrary, however, to expectation, they did no injury as they passed, nor took anything from the fields; and, as they went by any city, cried out that they were going to Rome; that the Romans only were their enemies, and that they took all others for their friends.

Whilst the barbarians were thus hastening with all speed, the military tribunes brought the Romans into the field to be ready to engage them, being not inferior to the Gauls in number (for they were no less than forty thousand foot), but most of them raw soldiers, and such as never handled a weapon before. Besides, they had wholly neglected all religious usages, had not obtained favourable sacrifices, nor made inquiries of the prophets, natural in danger and before battle. No less did the multitude of commanders distract and confound their proceedings; frequently before, upon less occasions, they had chosen a single leader, with the title of dictator, being sensible of what great importance it is in critical times to have the soldiers united under one general with the entire and absolute control placed in his hands. Add to all, the remembrance of Camillus's treatment, which made it now seem a dangerous thing for officers to command without humouring their soldiers.

In this condition they left the city, and encamped by the river Allia, about ten miles from Rome, and not far from the place where it falls into the Tiber; and here the Gauls came upon them, and, after a disgraceful resistance, devoid of order and discipline, they were miserably defeated. The left wing was immediately driven into the river, and there destroyed; the right had less damage by declining the shock, and from the low grounds getting to the tops of the hills, from whence most of them afterwards dropped into the city; the rest, as many as escaped, the enemy being weary of the slaughter, stole by night to Veii, giving up Rome and all that was in it for lost.

This battle was fought about the summer solstice, the moon being at full, the very same day in which the sad disaster of the Fabii had happened, when three hundred of that name were at one time cut off by the Tuscans. But from this second loss and defeat the day got the name of Alliensis from the river Allia, and still retains it. The question of unlucky days, whether we should consider any to be so, and whether Heraclitus did well in upbraiding Hesiod for distinguishing them into fortunate and unfortunate, as ignorant that the nature of every day is the same, I have examined in another place; but upon occasion of the present subject, I think it will not be amiss to annex a few examples relating to this matter.

On the fifth of their month Hippodromius, which corresponds to the Athenian Hecatombæon, the Bœotians gained two signal victories, the one at Leuctra, the other at Ceressus, about three hundred years before, when they overcame Lattamyas and the Thessalians, both which asserted the liberty of Greece. Again, on the sixth of Boëdromion, the Persians were worsted by the Greeks at Marathon; on the third, at Platæa, as also at Mycale; on the twenty-fifth, at Arbela. The Athenians, about the full moon in Boëdromion, gained their sea-victory at Naxos under the conduct of Chabrias; on the twentieth, at Salamis, as we have shown in our treatise on Days. Thargelion was a very unfortunate month to the barbarians, for in it Alexander overcame Darius's generals on the Granicus; and the Carthaginians, on the twenty-fourth, were beaten by Timoleon in Sicily, on which same day and month Troy seems to have been taken, as Ephorus, Callisthenes, Damastes, and Phylarchus state. On the other hand, the month Metagitnion, which in Bœotia is called Panemus, was not very lucky to the Greeks; for on its seventh day they were defeated by Antipater, at the battle in Cranon, and utterly ruined; and before, at Chæronea, were defeated by Philip; and on the very same day, same month, and same year, those that went with Archidamus into Italy were there cut off by the barbarians. The Carthaginians also observe the twenty-first of the same month, as bringing with it the largest number and the severest of their losses. I am not ignorant that, about the Feast of Mysteries, Thebes was destroyed the second time by Alexander; and after that, upon the very twentieth of Boëdromion, on which day they lead forth the mystic Iacchus, the Athenians received a garrison of the Macedonians. On the selfsame day the Romans lost their army under Cæpio by the Cimbrians, and in a subsequent year, under the conduct of Lucullus, overcame the Armenians and Tigranes. King Attalus and Pompey died both on their birthdays. One could reckon up several that have had variety of fortune on the same day. This day, meantime, is one of the unfortunate ones to the Romans, and for its sake two others in every month; fear and superstition, as the custom of it is, more and more prevailing. But I have discussed this more accurately in my *Roman Questions*.

And now, after the battle, had the Gauls immediately pursued those that fled, there had been no remedy but Rome must have wholly been ruined, and those who remained in it utterly destroyed; such was the terror that those who escaped the battle brought with them into the city, and with such distraction and confusion were themselves in turn infected. But the Gauls, not imagining their victory to be so considerable, and overtaken with the present joy, fell to feasting and dividing the spoil, by which means they gave leisure to those who were for leaving the city to make their escape, and to those that remained to anticipate and prepare for their coming. For they who resolved to stay at Rome, abandoning the rest of the city, betook themselves to the Capitol, which they fortified with the help of missiles and new works. One of their principal cares was of their holy things, most of which they conveyed into the Capitol.

But the consecrated fire the vestal virgins took, and fled with it, as likewise their other sacred things. Some write that they have nothing in their charge but the ever-living fire which Numa had ordained to be worshipped as the principle of all things; for fire is the most active thing in nature, and all produc-

tion is either motion, or attended with motion; all the other parts of matter, so long as they are without warmth, lie sluggish and dead, and require the accession of a sort of soul or vitality in the principle of heat; and upon that accession, in whatever way, immediately receive a capacity either of acting or being acted upon. And thus Numa, a man curious in such things, and whose wisdom made it thought that he conversed with the Muses, consecrated fire, and ordained it to be kept ever burning, as an image of that eternal power which orders and actuates all things.

Others say that this fire was kept burning in front of the holy things, as in Greece, for purification, and that there were other things hid in the most secret part of the temple, which were kept from the view of all, except those virgins whom they call vestals. The most common opinion was, that the image of Pallas, brought into Italy by Æneas, was laid up there; others say that the Samothracian images lay there, telling a story how that Dardanus carried them to Troy, and, when he had built the city, celebrated those rites, and dedicated those images there; that after Troy was taken, Æneas stole them away, and kept them till his coming into Italy. But they who profess to know more of the matter affirm that there are two barrels, not of any great size, one of which stands open and has nothing in it, the other full and sealed up; but that neither of them may be seen but by the most holy virgins. Others think that they who say this are misled by the fact that the virgins put most of their holy things into two barrels at this time of the Gaulish invasion, and hid them underground in the temple of Quirinus; and that from hence that place to this day bears the name of Barrels.

However it be, taking the most precious and important things they had, they fled away with them, shaping their course along the river-side, where Lucius Albinius, a simple citizen of Rome, who among others was making his escape, overtook them, having his wife, children, and goods in a cart; and, seeing the virgins, dragging along in their arms the holy things of the gods, in a helpless and weary condition, he caused his wife and children to get down, and, taking out his goods, put the virgins in the cart, that they might make their escape to some of the Greek cities. This devout act of Albinius, and the respect he showed thus signally to the gods at a time of such extremity, deserved not to be passed over in silence. But the priests that belonged to other gods, and the most elderly of the senators, men who had been consuls and had enjoyed triumphs, could not endure to leave the city; but, putting on their sacred and splendid robes, Fabius the high priest performing the office, they made their prayers to the gods, and, devoting themselves, as it were, for their country, sate themselves down in their ivory chairs in the forum, and in that posture expected the event.

On the third day after the battle, Brennus appeared with his army at the city, and, finding the gates wide open and no guards upon the walls, first began to suspect it was some design or stratagem, never dreaming that the Romans were in so desperate a condition. But when he found it to be so indeed, he entered at the Colline gate, and took Rome, in the three hundred and sixtieth year, or a little more, after it was built; if, indeed, it can be supposed probable that an exact chronological statement has been preserved of events which were themselves the cause of chronological difficulties about things of later date. Of the calamity itself, however, and of the fact of the capture, some faint rumours seem to have passed at the time into Greece. Heraclides Ponticus, who lived not long after these times, in his book upon the Soul, relates that a certain report came from the west, that an army, proceeding from the Hyperboreans, had taken a Greek city called Rome, seated somewhere upon the great sea. But I do not wonder that so fabulous and high-flown an author as Heraclides should embellish the truth of the story with expressions about Hyperboreans and the great sea. Aristotle the philosopher appears to have heard a correct statement of the taking of the city by the Gauls, but he calls its deliverer Lucius; whereas Camillus's surname was not Lucius, but Marcus. But this is a matter of conjecture.

Brennus, having taken possession of Rome, set a strong guard about the Capitol, and, going himself down into the forum, was there struck with amazement at the sight of so many men sitting in that order and silence, observing that they neither rose at his coming, nor so much as changed colour or countenance, but remained without fear or concern leaning upon their staves, and sitting quietly, looking at each other. The Gauls, for a great while, stood wondering at the strangeness of the sight, not daring to approach or touch them, taking them for an assembly of superior beings. But when one, bolder than the rest, drew near to Marcus Papirius, and, putting forth his hand, gently touched his chin and stroked his long beard, Papirius with his staff struck him a severe blow on the head; upon which the barbarian drew his sword and slew him. This was the introduction to the slaughter; for the rest, following his example, set upon them all and killed them, and despatched all others that came in their way; and so went on to the sacking and pillaging the houses, which they continued for many days ensuing. Afterwards, they burnt them down to the ground and demolished them, being incensed at those who kept the Capitol, because they would not yield to summons; but, on the contrary, when assailed, had repelled them, with some loss, from their defences. This provoked them to ruin the whole city, and to put to the sword all that came to their hands, young and old, men, women, and children.

And now, the siege of the Capitol having lasted a good while, the Gauls began to be in want of provision; and dividing their forces, part of them stayed with their king at the siege, the rest went to forage the country, ravaging the towns and villages where they came, but not all together in a body, but in different squadrons and parties; and to such a confidence had success raised them, that they carelessly rambled about without the least fear or apprehension of danger.

But the greatest and best ordered body of their forces went to the city of Ardea, where Camillus then sojourned, having, ever since his leaving Rome, sequestered himself from all business, and taken to a private life; but now he began to rouse up himself, and consider not how to avoid or escape the enemy, but to find out an opportunity to be revenged upon them. And perceiving that the Ardeatians wanted not men, but rather enterprise, through the inexperience and timidity of their officers, he began to speak with the young men, first to the effect that they ought not to ascribe the misfortune of the Romans to the courage of their enemy, nor attribute the losses they sustained by rash counsel to the conduct of men who had no title to victory; the event had been only an evidence of the power of fortune; that it was a brave thing even with danger to repel a foreign and barbarous invader whose end in conquering was, like fire, to lay waste and destroy, but if they would be courageous and resolute he was ready to put an opportunity into their hands to gain a victory, without hazard at all.

When he found the young men embraced the thing, he went to the magistrates and council of the city, and, having persuaded them also, he mustered all that could bear arms, and drew them up within the walls, that they might not be perceived by the enemy, who was near; who, having scoured the country, and now returned heavy-laden with booty, lay encamped in the plains in a careless and negligent posture, so that, with the night ensuing upon debauch and drunkenness, silence prevailed through all the camp.

When Camillus learned this from his scouts, he drew out the Ardeatians, and in the dead of the night, passing in silence over the ground that lay between, came up to their works, and, commanding his trumpets to sound and his men to shout and halloo, he struck terror into them from all quarters; while drunkenness impeded and sleep retarded their movements. A few, whom fear had sobered, getting into some order, for a while resisted; and so died with their weapons in their hands. But the greatest part of them, buried in wine and sleep, were surprised without their arms, and despatched; and as many of them as by the advantage of the night got out of the camp were the next day found scattered abroad and wandering in the fields, and were picked up by the horse that pursued them.

The fame of this action soon flew through the neighbouring cities, and stirred up the young men from various quarters to come and join themselves with him. But none were so much concerned as those Romans who escaped in the battle of Allia, and were now at Veii, thus lamenting with themselves, "O heavens, what a commander has Providence bereaved Rome of, to honour Ardea with his actions! And that city, which brought forth and nursed so great a man, is lost and gone, and we, destitute of a leader and shut up within strange walls, sit idle, and see Italy ruined before our eyes. Come, let us send to the Ardeatians to have back our general, or else, with weapons in our hands, let us go thither to him; for he is no longer a banished man, nor we citizens, having no country but what is in the possession of the enemy." To this they all agreed, and sent to Camillus to desire him to take the command; but he answered, that he would not, until they that were in the Capitol should legally appoint

him; for he esteemed them, so long as they were in being, to be his country; that if they should command him he would readily obey; but against their consent he would intermeddle with nothing.

When this answer was returned, they admired the modesty and temper of Camillus; but they could not tell how to find a messenger to carry the intelligence to the Capitol, or rather, indeed, it seemed altogether impossible for any one to get to the citadel whilst the enemy was in full possession of the city. But among the young men there was one Pontius Cominius, of ordinary birth, but ambitious of honour, who proffered himself to run the hazard, and took no letters with him to those in the Capitol, lest, if he were intercepted, the enemy might learn the intentions of Camillus; but, putting on a poor dress and carrying corks under it, he boldly travelled the greatest part of the way by day, and came to the city when it was dark. The bridge he could not pass, as it was guarded by the barbarians; so that taking his clothes, which were neither many nor heavy, and binding them about his head, he laid his body upon the corks, and swimming with them, got over to the city. And avoiding those quarters where he perceived the enemy was awake, which he guessed at by the lights and noise, he went to the Carmental gate, where there was greatest silence, and where the hill of the Capitol is steepest and rises with craggy and broken rock.

By this way he got up, though with much difficulty, by the hollow of the cliff, and presented himself to the guards, saluting them, and telling them his name; he was taken in, and carried to the commanders. And a senate being immediately called, he related to them in order the victory of Camillus, which they had not heard of before, and the proceedings of the soldiers, urging them to confirm Camillus in the command, as on him alone all their fellow-countrymen outside the city would rely. Having heard and consulted of the matter, the senate declared Camillus dictator, and sent back Pontius the same way that he came, who, with the same success as before, got through the enemy without being discovered, and delivered to the Romans outside the decision of the senate, who joyfully received it. Camillus, on his arrival, found twenty thousand of them ready in arms; with which forces, and those confederates he brought along with him, he prepared to set upon the enemy.

But at Rome some of the barbarians, passing by chance near the place at which Pontius by night had got into the Capitol, spied in several places marks of feet and hands, where he had laid hold and clambered, and places where the plants that grew to the rock had been rubbed off, and the earth had slipped, and went accordingly and reported it to the king, who, coming in person, and viewing it, for the present said nothing, but in the evening, picking out such of the Gauls as were nimblest of body, and by living in the mountains were accustomed to climb, he said to them, "The enemy themselves have shown us a way how to come at them, which we knew not of before, and have taught us that it is not so difficult and impossible but that men may overcome it. It would be a great shame, having begun well, to fail in the end, and to give up a place as impregnable, when the enemy himself lets us see the way by which it may be taken; for where it was easy for one man to get up, it will not be hard for many, one after another; nay, when many shall undertake it, they will be aid and strength to each other. Rewards and honours shall be bestowed on every man as he shall acquit himself."

When the king had thus spoken, the Gauls cheerfully undertook to perform it, and in the dead of night a good party of them together, with great silence, began to climb the rock, clinging to the precipitous and difficult ascent, which yet upon trial offered a way to them, and proved less difficult than they had expected. So that the foremost of them having gained the top of all, and put themselves into order, they all but surprised the outworks, and mastered the watch, who were fast asleep; for neither man nor dog perceived their coming.

But there were sacred geese kept near the temple of Juno, which at other times were plentifully fed, but now, by reason that corn and other provisions were grown scarce for all, were but in a poor condition. The creature is by nature of quick sense, and apprehensive of the least noise, so that these, being moreover watchful through hunger, and restless, immediately discovered the coming of the Gauls, and, running up and down with their noise and cackling, they raised the whole camp, while the barbarians on the other side, perceiving themselves discovered, no longer endeavoured to conceal their attempt, but with shouting and violence advanced to the assault.

The Romans, every one in haste snatching up the next weapon that came to hand, did what they could on the sudden occasion. Manlius, a man of consular dignity, of strong body and great spirit, was the first that made head against them, and, engaging with two of the enemy at once, with his sword cut off the right arm of one just as he was lifting up his blade to strike, and, running his target full in the face of the other, tumbled him headlong down the steep rock; then mounting the rampart, and there standing with others that came running to his assistance, drove down the rest of them, who, indeed, to begin, had not been many, and did nothing worthy of so bold an attempt.

The Romans, having thus escaped this danger, early in the morning took the captain of the watch and flung him down the rock upon the heads of their enemies, and to Manlius for his victory voted a reward, intended more for honour than advantage, bringing him, each man of them as much as he received for his daily allowance, which was half a pound of bread and one eighth of a pint of wine.

Henceforward, the affairs of the Gauls were daily in a worse and worse condition; they wanted provisions, being withheld from foraging through fear of Camillus, and sickness also was amongst them, occasioned by the number of carcases that lay in heaps unburied. Being lodged among the ruins, the ashes, which were very deep, blown about by the winds and combining with the sultry heats, breathed up, so to say, a dry and searching air, the inhalation of which was destructive to their health. But the chief cause was the change from their natural climate, coming as they did out of shady and hilly countries, abounding in means of shelter from the heat, to lodge in low, and, in the autumn season, very unhealthy ground; added to which was the length and tediousness of the siege, as they had now sate seven months before the Capitol. There was, therefore, a great destruction among them, and the number of the dead grew so great that the living gave up burying them. Neither, indeed, were things on that account any better with the besieged, for famine increased upon them, and despondency with not hearing anything of Camillus, it being impossible to send any one to him, the city was so guarded by the barbarians.

Things being in this sad condition on both sides, a motion of treaty was made at first by some of the outposts, as they happened to speak with one another; which being embraced by the leading men, Sulpicius, tribune of the Romans, came to a parley with Brennus, in which it was agreed, that the Romans laying down a thousand weight of gold, the Gauls upon the receipt of it should immediately quit the city and territories. The agreement being confirmed by oath on both sides, and the gold brought forth, the Gauls used false dealing in the weights, secretly at first, but afterwards openly pulled back and disturbed the balance; at which the Romans indignantly complaining, Brennus, in a scoffing and insulting manner, pulled off his sword and belt, and threw them both into the scales; and when Sulpicius asked what that meant, "What should it mean," says he, "but woe to the conquered?" which afterwards became a proverbial saying.

As for the Romans, some were so incensed that they were for taking their gold back again and returning to endure the siege. Others were for passing by and dissembling a petty injury, and not to account that the indignity of the thing lay in paying more than was due, since the paying anything at all was itself a dishonour only submitted to as a necessity of the times.

Whilst this difference remained still unsettled, both amongst themselves and with the Gauls, Camillus was at the gates with his army; and having learned what was going on, commanded the main body of his forces to follow slowly after him in good order, and himself with the choicest of his men hastening on, went at once to the Romans; where all giving way to him, and receiving him as their sole magistrate, with profound silence and order, he took the gold out of the scales, and delivered it to his officers, and commanded the Gauls to take their weights and scales and depart; saying that it was customary with the Romans to deliver their country with iron, not with gold.

And when Brennus began to rage, and say that he was unjustly dealt with in such a breach of contract, Camillus answered that it was never legally made, and the agreement of no force or obligation; for that himself being declared dictator, and there being no other magistrate by law, the engagement had been made with men who had no power to enter into it; but now they might say anything they had to urge, for he was come with full power by law to grant pardon to such as should ask it, or inflict punishment on the guilty, if they did not repent.

At this, Brennus broke into violent anger, and an immediate quarrel ensued; both sides drew their swords and attacked, but in confusion, as could not be otherwise amongst houses, and in narrow lanes and places where it was impossible to form in any order. But Brennus, presently recollecting himself, called off his men, and, with the loss of a few only, brought them to their camp; and rising in the night with all his forces, left the city, and, advancing about eight miles, encamped upon the way to Gabii.

As soon as day appeared, Camillus came up with him, splendidly armed himself, and his soldiers full of courage and confidence; and there engaging with him in a sharp conflict, which lasted a long while, overthrew his army with great slaughter, and took their camp. Of those that fled, some were presently cut off by the pursuers; others, and these were the greatest number, dispersed hither and thither, and were despatched by the people that came sallying out from the neighbouring towns and villages.

Thus Rome was strangely taken, and more strangely recovered, having been seven whole months in the possession of the barbarians, who entered her a little after the Ides of July, and were driven out about the Ides of February following. Camillus triumphed, as he deserved, having saved his country that was lost, and brought the city, so to say, back again to itself. For those that had fled abroad, together with their wives and children, accompanied him as he rode in; and those who had been shut up in the Capitol, and were reduced almost to the point of perishing with hunger, went out to meet him, embracing each other as they met, and weeping for joy, and, through the excess of the present pleasure, scarce believing in its truth. And when the priests and ministers of the gods appeared bearing the sacred things, which in their flight they had either hid on the spot, or conveyed away with them, and now openly showed in safety, the citizens who saw the blessed sight felt as if with these the gods themselves were again returned unto Rome. After Camillus had sacrificed to the gods, and purified the city according to the directions of those properly instructed, he restored the existing temples, and erected a new one to Rumour, or Voice, informing himself of the spot in which that voice from heaven came by night to Marcus Cædicius, foretelling the coming of the barbarian army.

It was a matter of difficulty, and a hard task, amidst so much rubbish, to discover and re-determine the consecrated places; but by the zeal of Camillus, and the incessant labour of the priests, it was at last accomplished. But when it came also to rebuilding the city, which was wholly demolished, despondency seized the multitude, and a backwardness to engage in a work for which they had no materials; at a time, too, when they rather needed relief and repose from their past labours, than any new demands upon their exhausted strength and impaired fortunes. Thus insensibly they turned their thoughts again towards Veii, a city ready-built and well-provided, and gave an opening to the arts of flatterers eager to gratify their desires, and lent their ears to seditious language flung out against Camillus; as that, out of ambition and self-glory, he withheld them from a city fit to receive them, forcing them to live in the midst of ruins, and to re-erect a pile of burnt rubbish, that he might be esteemed not the chief magistrate only and general of Rome, but, to the exclusion of Romulus, its founder also. The senate, therefore, fearing a sedition, would not suffer Camillus, though desirous, to lay down his authority within the year, though no dictator had ever held it above six months.

They themselves, meantime, used their best endeavours, by kind persuasions and familiar addresses, to encourage and appease the people, showing them the shrines and tombs of their ancestors, calling to their remembrance the sacred spots and holy places which Romulus and Numa or any other of their kings had consecrated and left to their keeping; and among the strongest religious arguments, urged the head, newly separated from the body, which was found in laying the foundation of the Capitol, marking it as a place destined by fate to be the head of all Italy; and the holy fire which had just been rekindled again, since the end of the war, by the vestal virgins; "What a disgrace it would be to them to lose and extinguish this, leaving the city it belonged to, to be either inhabited by strangers and new-comers, or left a wild pasture for cattle to graze on?" Such reasons as these, urged with complaint and expostulation, sometimes in private upon individuals, and sometimes in their public assemblies, were met, on the other hand, by laments and protestations of distress and helplessness; entreaties that, reunited as they just were, after a sort of shipwreck, naked and destitute, they would not constrain them to patch up the pieces of a ruined and shattered city, when they had another at hand ready-built and prepared.

Camillus thought good to refer it to general deliberation, and himself spoke largely and earnestly in behalf of his country, as also many others. At last, calling to Lucius Lucretius, whose place it was to speak first, he commanded him to give his sentence, and the rest as they followed, in order. Silence being made, and Lucretius just about to begin, by chance a centurion passing by outside with his company of the day-guard called out with a loud voice to the ensign-bearer to halt and fix his standard, for this was the best place to stay in. This voice, coming in that moment of time, and at that crisis of uncertainty and anxiety for the future, was taken as a direction what was to be done; so that Lucretius, assuming an attitude of devotion, gave sentence in concurrence with the gods, as he said, as likewise did all that followed.

Even among the common people it created a wonderful change of feeling; every one now cheered and encouraged his neighbour, and set himself to the work, proceeding in it, however, not by any regular lines or divisions, but every one pitching upon that plot of ground which came next to hand, or best pleased his fancy; by which haste and hurry in building, they constructed their city in narrow and ill-designed lanes, and with houses huddled together one upon another; for it is said that within the compass of the year the whole city was built up anew, both in its public walls and private buildings.

The persons, however, appointed by Camillus to resume and mark out, in this general confusion, all consecrated places, coming, in their way round the Palatium, to the chapel of Mars, found the chapel itself indeed destroyed and burnt to the ground, like everything else, by the barbarians; but whilst they were clearing the place, and carrying away the rubbish, lit upon Romulus's augural staff, buried under a great heap of ashes. This sort of staff is crooked at one end, and is called *lituus;* they make use of it in quartering out the regions of the heavens when engaged in divination from the flight of birds; Romulus, who was himself a great diviner, made use of it. But when he disappeared from the earth, the priests took his staff and kept it, as other holy things, from the touch of man; and when they now found that, whereas all other things were consumed, this staff had altogether escaped the flames, they began to conceive happier hopes of Rome, and to augur from this token its future everlasting safety.

And now they had scarcely got a breathing time from their trouble, when a new war came upon them; and the Æquians, Volscians, and Latins all at once invaded their territories, and the Tuscans besieged Sutrium, their confederate city. The military tribunes who commanded the army, and were encamped about the hill Mæcius, being closely besieged by the Latins, and the camp in danger to be lost, sent to Rome, where Camillus was a third time chosen dictator.

Of this war two different accounts are given; I shall begin with the more fabulous. They say that the Latins (whether out of pretence, or a real design to revive the ancient relationship of the two nations) sent to desire of the Romans some free-born maidens in marriage; that when the Romans were at a loss how to determine (for on one hand they dreaded a war, having scarcely yet settled and recovered themselves, and on the other side suspected that this asking of wives was, in plain terms, nothing else but a demand for hostages, though covered over with the specious name of intermarriage and alliance), a certain handmaid, by name Tutula, or, as some call her, Philotis, persuaded the magistrates to send with her some of the most youthful and best-looking maid-servants, in the bridal dress of noble virgins, and leave the rest to her care and management; that the magistrates, consenting, chose out as many as she thought necessary for her purpose, and adorning them with gold and rich clothes, delivered them to the Latins, who were encamped not far from the city; that at night the rest stole away the enemy's swords, but Tutula or Philotis, getting to the top of a wild fig-tree, and spreading out a thick woollen cloth behind her, held out a torch towards Rome, which was the signal concerted between her and the commanders, without the knowledge, however, of any other of the citizens, which was the reason that their issuing out from the city was tumultuous, the officers pushing their men on, and they calling upon one another's names, and scarce able to bring themselves into order; that setting upon the enemy's works, who either were asleep or expected no such matter, they took the camp and destroyed most of them; and that this was done on the Nones of July, which was

then called Quintilis, and that the feast that is observed on that day is a commemoration of what was then done.

For in it, first, they run out of the city in great crowds, and call out aloud several familiar and common names, Caius, Marcus, Lucius, and the like, in representation of the way in which they called to one another when they went out in such haste. In the next place, the maid-servants, gaily dressed, run about, playing and jesting upon all they meet, and amongst themselves, also, use a kind of skirmishing, to show they ·helped in the conflict against the Latins; and while eating and drinking, they sit shaded over with boughs of wild fig-tree, and the day they call Nonæ Caprotinæ, as some think from that wild fig-tree on which the maid-servant held up her torch, the Roman name for a wild fig-tree being *caprificus*. Others refer most of what is said or done at this feast to the fate of Romulus, for, on this day, he vanished outside the gates in a sudden darkness and storm (some think it an eclipse of the sun), and from this the day was caller Nonæ Caprotinæ, the Latin for a goat being *capra,* and the place where he disappeared having the name of Goat's Marsh, as is stated in his life.

But the general stream of writers prefer the other account of this war, which they thus relate. Camillus, being the third time chosen dictator, and learning that the army under the tribunes was besieged by the Latins and Volscians, was constrained to arm, not only those under, but also those over, the age of service; and taking a large circuit round the mountain Mæcius, undiscovered by the enemy, lodged his army on their rear, and then by many fires gave notice of his arrival. The besieged, encouraged by this, prepared to sally forth and join battle; but the Latins and Volscians, fearing this exposure to an enemy on both sides, drew themselves within their works, and fortified their camp with a strong palisade of trees on every side, resolving to wait for more supplies from home, and expecting, also, the assistance of the Tuscans, their confederates.

Camillus, detecting their object, and fearing to be reduced to the same position to which he had brought them, namely, to be besieged himself, resolved to lose no time: and finding their rampart was all of timber, and observing that a strong wind constantly at sun-rising blew off from the mountains, after having prepared a quantity of combustibles, about break of day he drew forth his forces, commanding a part with their missiles to assault the enemy with noise and shouting on the other quarter, whilst he, with those that were to fling in the fire, went to that side of the enemy's camp to which the wind usually blew, and there waited his opportunity. When the skirmish was begun, and the sun risen, and a strong wind set in from the mountains, he gave the signal of onset; and heaving in an infinite quantity of fiery matter, filled all their rampart with it, so that the flame being fed by the close timber and wooden palisades, went on and spread into all quarters. The Latins, having nothing ready to keep it off or extinguish it, when the camp was now almost full of fire, were driven back within a very small compass, and at last forced by necessity to come into their enemy's hands, who stood before the works ready armed and prepared to receive them; of these very few escaped, while those that stayed in the camp were all a prey to the fire, until the Romans, to gain the pillage, extinguished it.

These things performed, Camillus, leaving his son Lucius in the camp to guard the prisoners and secure the booty, passed into the enemy's country, where, having taken the city of the Æquians and reduced the Volscians to obedience, he then immediately led his army to Sutrium, not having heard what had befallen the Sutrians, but making haste to assist them, as if they were still in danger and besieged by the Tuscans. They, however, had already surrendered their city to their enemies, and destitute of all things, with nothing left but their clothes, met Camillus on the way, leading their wives and children, and bewailing their misfortune. Camillus himself was struck with compassion, and perceiving the soldiers weeping, and commiserating their case, while the Sutrians hung about and clung to them, resolved not to defer revenge, but that very day to lead his army to Sutrium; conjecturing that the enemy, having just taken a rich and plentiful city, without an enemy left within it, nor any from without to be expected, would be found abandoned to enjoyment and unguarded.

Neither did his opinion fail him; he not only passed through their country without discovery, but came up to their very gates and possessed himself of the walls, not a man being left to guard them, but their whole army scattered about in the houses, drinking and making merry. Nay, when at last they did perceive that the enemy had seized the city,

they were so overloaded with meat and wine, that few were able so much as to endeavour to escape, but either waited shamefully for their death within doors, or surrendered themselves to the conqueror. Thus the city of the Sutrians was twice taken in one day; and they who were in possession lost it, and they who had lost regained it, alike by the means of Camillus. For all which actions he received a triumph, which brought him no less honour and reputation than the two former ones; for those citizens who before most regarded him with an evil eye, and ascribed his successes to a certain luck rather than real merit, were compelled by these last acts of his to allow the whole honour to his great abilities and energy.

Of all the adversaries and enviers of his glory, Marcus Manlius was the most distinguished, he who first drove back the Gauls when they made their night attack upon the Capitol, and who for that reason had been named Capitolinus. This man, affecting the first place in the commonwealth, and not able by noble ways to outdo Camillus's reputation, took that ordinary course towards usurpation of absolute power, namely, to gain the multitude, those of them especially that were in debt; defending some by pleading their causes against their creditors, rescuing others by force, and not suffering the law to proceed against them; insomuch that in a short time he got great numbers of indigent people about him, whose tumults and uproars in the forum struck terror into the principal citizens. After that Quintius Capitolinus, who was made dictator to suppress these disorders, had committed Manlius to prison, the people immediately changed their apparel, a thing never done but in great and public calamities, and the senate, fearing some tumult, ordered him to be released.

He, however, when set at liberty, changed not his course, but was rather the more insolent in his proceedings, filling the whole city with faction and sedition. They chose, therefore, Camillus again military tribune; and a day being appointed for Manlius to answer to his charge, the prospect from the place where his trial was held proved a great impediment to his accusers, for the very spot where Manlius by night fought with the Gauls overlooked the Forum from the Capitol, so that, stretching forth his hands that way, and weeping, he called to their remembrance his past actions, raising compassion in all that beheld him. Insomuch that the judges were at a loss what to do, and several times adjourned the trial, unwilling to acquit him of the crime, which was sufficiently proved, and yet unable to execute the law while his noble action remained, as it were, before their eyes. Camillus, considering this, transferred the court outside the gate to the Peteline Grove, from whence there is no prospect of the Capitol. Here his accuser went on with his charge, and his judges were capable of remembering and duly resenting his guilty deeds. He was convicted, carried to the Capitol, and flung headlong from the rock; so that one and the same spot was thus the witness of his greatest glory, and monument of his most unfortunate end. The Romans, besides, razed his house, and built there a temple to the goddess they call Moneta, ordaining for the future that none of the patrician order should ever dwell on the Capitoline.

And now Camillus, being called to his sixth tribuneship, desired to be excused, as being aged, and perhaps not unfearful of the malice of fortune, and those reverses which seem to ensue upon great prosperity. But the most apparent pretence was the weakness of his body, for he happened at that time to be sick; the people, however, would admit of no excuses, but, crying that they wanted not his strength for horse or for foot service, but only his counsel and conduct, constrained him to undertake the command, and with one of his fellow-tribunes to lead the army immediately against the enemy. These were the Prænestines and Volscians, who, with large forces, were laying waste the territory of the Roman confederates. Having marched out with his army, he sat down and encamped near the enemy, meaning himself to protract the war, or if there should come any necessity or occasion of fighting, in the meantime to regain his strength.

But Lucius Furius, his colleague, carried away with the desire of glory, was not to be held in, but, impatient to give battle, inflamed the inferior officers of the army with the same eagerness; so that Camillus, fearing he might seem out of envy to be wishing to rob the young men of the glory of a noble exploit, consented, though unwillingly, that he should draw out the forces, whilst himself, by reason of weakness, stayed behind with a few in the camp. Lucius, engaging rashly, was discomfited, when Camillus, perceiving the Romans to give ground and fly, could not contain himself, but, leaping from his bed, with those he had about him ran to meet them at the gates

of the camp, making his way through the flyers to oppose the pursuers; so that those who had got within the camp turned back at once and followed him, and those that came flying from without made head again and gathered about him, exhorting one another not to forsake their general. Thus the enemy, for that time, was stopped in his pursuit. The next day Camillus, drawing out his forces and joining battle with them, overthrew them by main force, and following close upon them, entered pell-mell with them into their camp, and took it, slaying the greatest part of them.

Afterwards, having heard that the city Satricum was taken by the Tuscans, and the inhabitants, all Romans, put to the sword, he sent home to Rome the main body of his forces and heaviest-armed, and taking with him the lightest and most vigorous soldiers, set suddenly upon the Tuscans, who were in the possession of the city, and mastered them, slaying some and expelling the rest; and so, returning to Rome with great spoils, gave signal evidence of their superior wisdom, who, not mistrusting the weakness and age of a commander endued with courage and conduct, had rather chosen him who was sickly and desirous to be excused, than younger men who were forward and ambitious to command.

When, therefore, the revolt of the Tusculans was reported, they gave Camillus the charge of reducing them, choosing one of his five colleagues to go with him. And when every one was eager for the place, contrary to the expectation of all, he passed by the rest and chose Lucius Furius, the very same man who lately, against the judgment of Camillus, had rashly hazarded and nearly lost a battle; willing, as it should seem, to dissemble that miscarriage, and free him from the shame of it.

The Tusculans, hearing of Camillus's coming against them, made a cunning attempt at revoking their act of revolt; their fields, as in times of highest peace, were full of ploughmen and shepherds; their gates stood wide open, and their children were being taught in the schools; of the people, such as were tradesmen, he found in their workshops, busied about their several employments, and the better sort of citizens walking in the public places in their ordinary dress; the magistrates hurried about to provide quarters for the Romans, as if they stood in fear of no danger and were conscious of no fault. Which arts, though they could not dispossess Camillus of the conviction he had of their treason, yet induced some compassion for their repentance; he commanded them to go to the senate and deprecate their anger, and joined himself as an intercessor in their behalf, so that their city was acquitted of all guilt and admitted to Roman citizenship. These were the most memorable actions of his sixth tribuneship.

After these things, Licinius Stolo raised a great sedition in the city, and brought the people to dissension with the senate, contending, that of two consuls one should be chosen out of the commons, and not both out of the patricians. Tribunes of the people were chosen, but the election of consuls was interrupted and prevented by the people. And as this absence of any supreme magistrate was leading to yet further confusion, Camillus was the fourth time created dictator by the senate, sorely against the people's will, and not altogether in accordance with his own; he had little desire for a conflict with men whose past services entitled them to tell him that he had achieved far greater actions in war along with them than in politics with the patricians, who, indeed, had only put him forward now out of envy; that, if successful, he might crush the people, or failing, be crushed himself.

However, to provide as good a remedy as he could for the present, knowing the day on which the tribunes of the people intended to prefer the law, he appointed it by proclamation for a general muster, and called the people from the Forum into the Campus, threatening to set heavy fines upon such as should not obey. On the other side, the tribunes of the people met his threats by solemnly protesting they would fine him in fifty thousand drachmas of silver, if he persisted in obstructing the people from giving their suffrages for the law. Whether it were, then, that he feared another banishment or condemnation, which would ill become his age and past great actions, or found himself unable to stem the current of the multitude, which ran strong and violent, he betook himself, for the present, to his house, and afterwards, for some days together professing sickness, finally laid down his dictatorship. The senate created another dictator; who, choosing Stolo, leader of the sedition, to be his general of horse, suffered that law to be enacted and ratified, which was most grievous to the patricians, namely, that no person whatsoever should possess above five hundred acres of land. Stolo was much distinguished by the victory he had gained; but, not long after, was found himself to possess more than he had allowed to others, and suffered the penalties of his own law.

And now the contention about election of consuls coming on (which was the main point and original cause of the dissension, and had throughout furnished most matter of division between the senate and the people), certain intelligence arrived, that the Gauls again, proceeding from the Adriatic Sea, were marching in vast numbers upon Rome. On the very heels of the report followed manifest acts also of hostility; the country through which they marched was all wasted, and such as by flight could not make their escape to Rome were dispersing and scattering among the mountains.

The terror of this war quieted the sedition; nobles and commons, senate and people together unanimously chose Camillus the fifth time dictator; who, though very aged, not wanting much of fourscore years, yet, considering the danger and necessity of his country, did not, as before, pretend sickness, or depreciate his own capacity, but at once undertook the charge and enrolled soldiers. And, knowing that the great force of the barbarians lay chiefly in their swords, with which they laid about them in a rude and inartificial manner, hacking and hewing the head and shoulders, he caused head-pieces entire of iron to be made for most of his men, smoothing and polishing the outside, that the enemy's swords, lighting upon them, might either slide off or be broken; and fitted also their shields with a little rim of brass, the wood itself not being sufficient to bear off the blows. Besides, he taught his soldiers to use their long javelins in close encounter, and, by bringing them under their enemy's swords, to receive their strokes upon them.

When the Gauls drew near, about the river Anio, dragging a heavy camp after them, and loaded with infinite spoil, Camillus drew forth his forces, and planted himself upon a hill of easy ascent, and which had many dips in it, with the object that the greatest part of his army might lie concealed, and those who appeared might be thought to have betaken themselves, through fear, to those upper grounds. And the more to increase this opinion in them, he suffered them, without any disturbance, to spoil and pillage even to his very trenches, keeping himself quiet within his works, which were well fortified; till, at last, perceiving that part of the enemy were scattered about the country foraging, and that those that were in the camp did nothing day and night but drink and revel, in the nighttime he drew up his lightest-armed men, and sent them out before to impede the enemy while forming into order, and to harass them when they should first issue out of their camp; and early in the morning brought down his main body, and set them in battle array in the lower grounds, a numerous and courageous army, not, as the barbarians had supposed, an inconsiderable and fearful division.

The first thing that shook the courage of the Gauls was, that their enemies had, contrary to their expectation, the honour of being aggressors. In the next place, the light-armed men, falling upon them before they could get into their usual order or range themselves in their proper squadrons, so disturbed and pressed upon them, that they were obliged to fight at random, without any order at all. But at last, when Camillus brought on his heavy-armed legions, the barbarians, with their swords drawn, went vigorously to engage them; the Romans, however, opposing their javelins and receiving the force of their blows on those parts of their defences which were well guarded with steel, turned the edge of their weapons, being made of soft and ill-tempered metal, so that their swords bent and doubled up in their hands; and their shields were pierced through and through, and grew heavy with the javelins that stuck upon them. And thus forced to quit their own weapons, they endeavoured to take advantage of those of their enemies, laid hold of the javelins with their hands, and tried to pluck them away. But the Romans, perceiving them now naked and defenceless, betook themselves to their swords, which they so well used, that in a little time great slaughter was made in the foremost ranks, while the rest fled over all parts of the level country; the hills and upper grounds Camillus had secured beforehand, and their camp they knew it would not be difficult for the enemy to take, as, through confidence of victory, they had left it unguarded.

This fight, it is stated, was thirteen years after the sacking of Rome; and from henceforward the Romans took courage, and surmounted the apprehensions they had hitherto entertained of the barbarians, whose previous defeat they had attributed rather to pestilence and a concurrence of mischances than to their own superior valour. And, indeed, this fear had been formerly so great that they made a law that priests should be excused from service in war, unless in an invasion from the Gaul.

This was the last military action that ever Camillus performed; for the voluntary surrender of the city of the Velitrani was but a mere accessory to it. But the greatest of all civil contests, and the hardest to be managed, was still to be fought out against the people; who, returning home full of victory and success, insisted, contrary to established law, to have one of the consuls chosen out of their own body. The senate strongly opposed it, and would not suffer Camillus to lay down his dictatorship, thinking that, under the shelter of his great name and authority, they should be better able to contend for the power of his aristocracy.

But when Camillus was sitting upon the tribunal, despatching public affairs, an officer, sent by the tribunes of the people, commanded him to rise and follow him, laying his hand upon him, as ready to seize and carry him away; upon which, such a noise and tumult as was never heard before filled the whole Forum, some that were about Camillus thrusting the officer from the bench, and the multitude below calling out to him to bring Camillus down. Being at a loss what to do in these difficulties, he yet laid not down his authority, but, taking the senators along with him, he went to the senate-house; but before he entered, besought the gods that they would bring these troubles to a happy conclusion, solemnly vowing, when the tumult was ended, to build a temple to Concord. A great conflict of opposite opinions arose in the senate; but, at last, the most moderate and most acceptable to the people prevailed, and consent was given, that of two consuls, one should be chosen from the commonalty.

When the dictator proclaimed this determination of the senate to the people, at the moment pleased and reconciled with the senate, as indeed could not otherwise be, they accompanied Camillus home, with all expressions and acclamations of joy; and the next day, assembling together, they voted a temple of Concord to be built, according to Camillus's vow, facing the assembly and the forum; and to the feasts, called the Latin holidays, they added one day more, making four in all;

and ordained that, on the present occasion, the whole people of Rome should sacrifice with garlands on their heads.

In the election of consuls held by Camillus, Marcus Æmilius was chosen of the patricians, and Lucius Sextius the first of the commonalty; and this was the last of all Camillus's actions. In the year following, a pestilential sickness infected Rome, which, besides an infinite number of the common people, swept away most of the magistrates, among whom was Camillus; whose death cannot be called immature, if we consider his great age, or greater actions, yet was he more lamented than all the rest put together that then died of that distemper.

PERICLES

490?–429 B.C.

CÆSAR once, seeing some wealthy strangers at Rome, carrying up and down with them in their arms and bosoms young puppy-dogs and monkeys, embracing and making much of them, took occasion not unnaturally to ask whether the women in their country were not used to bear children; by that prince-like reprimand gravely reflecting upon persons who spend and lavish upon brute beasts that affection and kindness which nature has implanted in us to be bestowed on those of our own kind. With like reason may we blame those who misuse that love of inquiry and observation which nature has implanted in our souls, by expending it on objects unworthy of the attention either of their eyes or their ears, while they disregard such as are excellent in themselves, and would do them good.

The mere outward sense, being passive in responding to the impression of the objects that come in its way and strike upon it, perhaps cannot help entertaining and taking notice of everything that addresses it, be it what it will, useful or unuseful; but, in the exercise of his mental perception, every man, if he chooses, has a natural power to turn himself upon all occasions, and to change and shift with the greatest ease to what he shall himself judge desirable. So that it becomes a man's duty to pursue and make after the best and choicest of everything, that he may not only employ his contemplation, but may also be improved by it. For as that colour is most suitable to the eye whose freshness and pleasantness stimulates and strengthens the sight, so a man ought to apply his intellectual perception to such objects as, with the sense of delight, are apt to call it forth, and allure it to its own proper good and advantage.

Such objects we find in the acts of virtue, which also produce in the minds of mere readers about them an emulation and eagerness that may lead them on to imitation. In other things there does not immediately follow upon the admiration and liking of the thing done any strong desire of doing the like. Nay, many times, on the very contrary, when we are pleased with the work, we slight and set little by the workman or artist himself, as, for instance, in perfumes and purple dyes, we are taken with the things themselves well enough, but do not think dyers and perfumers otherwise than low and sordid people. It was not said amiss by Antisthenes, when people told him that one Ismenias was an excellent piper. "It may be so," said he, "but he is but a wretched human being, otherwise he would not have been an excellent piper." And King Philip, to the same purpose, told his son Alexander, who once at a merry-meeting played a piece of music charmingly and skilfully, "Are you not ashamed, son, to play so well?" For it is enough for a king or prince to find leisure sometimes to hear others sing, and he does the muses quite honour enough when he pleases to be but present, while others engage in such exercises and trials of skill.

He who busies himself in mean occupations produces, in the very pains he takes about things of little or no use, an evidence against himself of his negligence and indisposition to what is really good. Nor did any generous and ingenuous young man, at the sight of the statue of Jupiter at Pisa, ever desire to be a Phidias, or on seeing that of Juno at Argos, long to be a Polyclitus, or feel induced by his pleasure in their poems to wish to be an Anacreon or Philetas or Archilochus. For it does not necessarily follow, that, if a piece of work please for its gracefulness, therefore he that wrought it deserves our admiration. Whence it is that neither do such things really profit or advantage the beholders, upon the sight of which no zeal arises for the imitation of them, nor any impulse or inclination, which may prompt any desire or endeavour of doing the like.

But virtue, by the bare statement of its actions, can so affect men's minds as to create at once both admiration of the things done and desire to imitate the doers of them. The goods of fortune we would possess and would enjoy; those of virtue we long to practise and exercise. We are content to receive the former from others, the latter we wish others to experience from us. Moral good is a practical stimulus; it is no sooner seen, than it inspires an impulse to practice, and influences the mind and character not by a mere imitation which we look at, but by the statement of the fact creates a moral purpose which we form.

And so we have thought fit to spend our time and pains in writing of the lives of famous persons; and have composed this tenth book upon that subject, containing the life of Pericles, and that of Fabius Maximus, who carried on the war against Hannibal, men alike, as in their other virtues and good parts, so especially in their mild and upright temper and demeanour, and in that capacity to bear the cross-grained humours of their fellow-citizens and colleagues in office, which made them both most useful and serviceable to the interests of their countries. Whether we take a right aim at our intended purpose, it is left to the reader to judge by what he shall here find.

Pericles was of the tribe Acamantis, and the township Cholargus, of the noblest birth both on his father's and mother's side. Xanthippus, his father, who defeated the King of Persia's generals in the battle at Mycale, took to wife Agariste, the grandchild of Clisthenes, who drove out the sons of Pisistratus, and nobly put an end to their tyrannical usurpation, and, moreover, made a body of laws, and settled a model of government admirably tempered and suited for the harmony and safety of the people.

His mother, being near her time, fancied in a dream that she was brought to bed of a lion, and a few days after was delivered of Pericles, in other respects perfectly formed, only his head was somewhat longish and out of proportion. For which reason almost all the images and statues that were made of him have the head covered with a helmet, the workmen apparently being willing not to expose him. The poets of Athens called him *Schinocephalos,* or squill-head, from *schinos,* a squill, or sea-onion. One of the comic poets, Cratinus, in the *Chirons,* tells us that—

Old Chronos once took queen Sedition to wife:
Which two brought to life
That tyrant far-famed
Whom the gods the supreme skull-compeller have
* named;*

and, in the *Nemesis,* addresses him—

Come, Jove, thou head *of Gods.*

And a second, Teleclides, says, that now, in embarrassment with political difficulties, he sits in the city—

Fainting underneath the load
Of his own head: and now abroad
From his huge gallery of a pate
Sends forth trouble to the state.

And a third, Eupolis, in the comedy called the *Demi,* in a series of questions about each of the demagogues, whom he makes in the play to come up from hell, upon Pericles being named last, exclaims—

And here by way of summary, now we've done,
Behold, in brief, the heads of all in one.

The master that taught him music, most authors are agreed, was Damon (whose name, they say, ought to be pronounced with the first syllable short). Though Aristotle tells us that he was thoroughly practised in all accomplishments of this kind by Pythoclides. Damon, it is not unlikely, being a sophist, out of policy sheltered himself under the profession of music to conceal from people in general his skill in other things, and under this pretence attended Pericles, the young athlete of politics, so to say, as his training-master in these exercises. Damon's lyre, however, did not prove altogether a successful blind; he was banished the country by ostracism for ten years, as a dangerous intermeddler and a favourer of arbitrary power, and, by this means, gave the stage occasion to play upon him. As, for instance, Plato, the comic poet, introduces a character who questions him—

Tell me, if you please,
Since you're the Chiron who taught Pericles.

Pericles, also, was a hearer of Zeno, the Eleatic, who treated of natural philosophy in the same manner as Parmenides did, but had also perfected himself in an art of his own for refuting and silencing opponents in argument; as Timon of Phlius describes it—

Also the two-edged tongue of mighty Zeno, who,
Say what one would, could argue it untrue.

But he that saw most of Pericles, and furnished him most especially with a weight and grandeur of sense, superior to all arts of popularity, and in general gave him his elevation and sublimity of purpose and of character, was Anaxagoras of Clazomenæ; whom the men of those times called by the name of Nous, that is, mind, or intelligence, whether in admiration of the great and extraordinary gift he had displayed for the science of nature, or because that he was the first of the philosophers who did not refer the first ordering of the world to fortune or chance, nor to necessity or compulsion, but to a pure, unadulterated intelligence, which in all other existing mixed and compound things acts as a principle of discrimination, and of combination of like with like.

For this man, Pericles entertained an extraordinary esteem and admiration, and filling himself with this lofty and, as they call it, up-in-the-air sort of thought, derived hence not merely, as was natural, elevation of purpose and dignity of language, raised far above the base and dishonest buffooneries of mob-eloquence, but, besides this, a composure of countenance, and a serenity and calmness in all his movements, which no occurrence whilst he was speaking could disturb, a sustained and even tone of voice, and various other advantages of a similar kind, which produced the greatest effect on his hearers. Once, after being reviled and ill-spoken of all day long in his own hearing by some vile and abandoned fellow in the open market-place, where he was engaged in the despatch of some urgent affair, he continued his business in perfect silence, and in the evening returned home composedly, the man still dogging him at the heels, and pelting him all the way with abuse and foul language; and stepping into his house, it being by this time dark, he ordered one of his servants to take a light, and to go along with the man and see him safe home.

Ion, it is true, the dramatic poet, says that Pericles's manner in company was somewhat over-assuming and pompous; and that into his high-bearing there entered a good deal of slightingness and scorn of others; he reserves his commendation for Cimon's ease and pliancy and natural grace in society. Ion, however, who must needs make virtue, like a show of tragedies, include some comic scenes, we shall not altogether rely upon; Zeno used to bid those who called Pericles's gravity the affectation of a charlatan, to go and affect the like themselves; inasmuch as this mere counterfeiting might in time insensibly instil into them a real love and knowledge of those noble qualities.

Nor were these the only advantages which Pericles derived from Anaxagoras's acquaintance; he seems also to have become, by his instructions, superior to that superstition with which an ignorant wonder at appearances, for example, in the heavens, possesses the minds of people unacquainted with their causes, eager for the supernatural, and excitable through an inexperience which the knowledge of natural causes removes, replacing wild and timid superstition by the good hope and assurance of an intelligent piety.

There is a story, that once Pericles had brought to him from a country farm of his a ram's head with one horn, and that Lampon, the diviner, upon seeing the horn grow strong and solid out of the midst of the forehead, gave it as his judgment, that, there being at that time two potent factions, parties, or interests in the city, the one of Thucydides and the other of Pericles, the government would come about to that one of them in whose ground or estate this token or indication of fate had shown itself. But that Anaxagoras, cleaving the skull in sunder, showed to the bystanders that the brain had not filled up its natural place, but being oblong, like an egg, had collected from all parts of the vessel which contained it in a point to that place from whence the root of the horn took its rise. And that, for that time, Anaxagoras was much admired for his explanation by those that were present; and Lampon no less a little while after, when Thucydides was over-powered, and the whole affairs of the state and government came into the hands of Pericles.

And yet, in my opinion, it is no absurdity to say that they were both in the right, both natural philosopher and diviner, one justly detecting the cause of this event, by which it was produced, the other the end for which it was designed. For it was the business of the one to find out and give an account of what it was made, and in what manner and by what means it grew as it did; and of the other to foretell to what end and purpose it was so made, and what it might mean or portend. Those who say that to find out the cause of a prodigy is in effect to destroy its supposed signification as such, do not take notice, that, at the same time, together with divine prodigies, they also do away with signs and signals of human art and concert, as, for instance, the clashings of quoits, fire-beacons, and the shadows of sun-dials, every one of which has its cause, and by that cause and contrivance is a sign of something else. But these are subjects, perhaps, that would better befit another place.

Pericles, while yet but a young man, stood in considerable apprehension of the people, as he was thought in face and figure to be very like the tyrant Pisistratus, and those of great age remarked upon the sweetness of his voice, and his volubility and rapidity in speaking, and were struck with amazement at the resemblance. Reflecting, too, that he had a considerable estate, and was descended of a noble family, and had friends of great influence, he was fearful all this might bring him to be banished as a dangerous person; and for this reason meddled not at all with state affairs, but in military service showed himself of a brave and intrepid nature.

But when Aristides was now dead, and Themistocles driven out, and Cimon was for the most part kept abroad by the expeditions he made in parts out of Greece, Pericles, seeing things in this posture, now advanced and took his side, not with the rich and few, but with the many and poor, contrary to his natural bent, which was far from democratical; but, most likely fearing he might fall under suspicion of aiming at arbitrary power, and seeing Cimon on the side of the aristocracy, and much beloved by the better and more distinguished people, he joined the party of the people, with a view at once both to secure himself and procure means against Cimon.

He immediately entered, also, on quite a new course of life and management of his time. For he was never seen to walk in any street but that which led to the market-place and council-hall, and he avoided invitations of friends to supper, and all friendly visiting and intercourse whatever; in all the time he had to do with the public, which was not a little, he was never known to have gone to any of his friends to a supper, except that once when his near kinsman, Euryptolemus, married, he remained present till the ceremony of the drink-offering, and then immediately rose from table and went his way. For

these friendly meetings are very quick to defeat any assumed superiority, and in intimate familiarity an exterior of gravity is hard to maintain. Real excellence, indeed, is most recognised when most openly looked into; and in really good men, nothing which meets the eyes of external observers so truly deserves their admiration, as their daily common life does that of their nearer friends.

Pericles, however, to avoid any feeling of commonness, or any satiety on the part of the people, presented himself at intervals only, not speaking to every business, nor at all times coming into the assembly, but, as Critolaus says, reserving himself, like the Salaminian galley, for great occasions, while matters of lesser importance were despatched by friends or other speakers under his direction. And of this number we are told Ephialtes made one, who broke the power of the council of Areopagus, giving the people, according to Plato's expression, so copious and so strong a draught of liberty, that growing wild and unruly, like an unmanageable horse, it, as the comic poets say—

—got beyond all keeping in,
Champing at Euboea, and among the islands
    leaping in.

The style of speaking most consonant to his form of life and the dignity of his views he found, so to say, in the tones of that instrument with which Anaxagoras had furnished him; of his teaching he continually availed himself, and deepened the colours of rhetoric with the dye of natural science. For having, in addition to his great natural genius, attained, by the study of nature, to use the words of the divine Plato, this height of intelligence, and this universal consummating power, and drawing hence whatever might be of advantage to him in the art of speaking, he showed himself far superior to all others. Upon which account, they say, he had his nickname given him, though some are of opinion he was named the Olympian from the public buildings with which he adorned the city, and others, again, from his great power in public affairs, whether of war or peace. Nor is it unlikely that the confluence of many attributes may have conferred it on him. However, the comedies represented at the time, which, both in good earnest and in merriment, let fly many hard words at him, plainly show that he got that appellation especially from his speaking; they speak of his "thundering and lightning" when he harangued the people, and of his wielding a dreadful thunderbolt in his tongue.

A saying also of Thucydides, the son of Melesias, stands on record, spoken by him by way of pleasantry upon Pericles's dexterity. Thucydides was one of the noble and distinguished citizens, and had been his greatest opponent; and, when Archidamus, the King of the Lacedæmonians, asked him whether he or Pericles were the better wrestler, he made this answer: "When I," said he, "have thrown him and given him a fair fall, by persisting that he had no fall, he gets the better of me, and makes the bystanders, in spite of their own eyes, believe him." The truth, however, is, that Pericles himself was very careful what and how he was to speak, insomuch that, whenever he went up to the hustings, he prayed the gods that no one word might unawares slip from him unsuitable to the matter and the occasion.

He has left nothing in writing behind him, except some decrees; and there are but very few of his sayings recorded; one, for example, is, that he said Ægina must, like a gathering in a man's eye, be removed from Piræus; and another, that he said he saw already war moving on its way towards them out of Peloponnesus. Again, when on a time Sophocles, who was his fellow-commissioner in the generalship, was going on board with him, and praised the beauty of a youth they met with in the way to the ship, "Sophocles," said he, "a general ought not only to have clean hands but also clean eyes." And Stesimbrotus tells us, that, in his encomium on those who fell in battle at Samos, he said they were become immortal, as the gods were. "For," said he, "we do not see them themselves, but only by the honours we pay them, and by the benefits they do us, attribute to them immortality; and the like attributes belong also to those that die in the service of their country."

Since Thucydides describes the rule of Pericles as an aristocratical government, that went by the name of a democracy, but was, indeed, the supremacy of a single great man, while many others say, on the contrary, that by him the common people were first encouraged and led on to such evils as appropriations of subject territory, allowances for attending theatres, payments for performing public duties, and by these bad habits were, under the influence of his public measures, changed from a sober, thrifty people, that maintained themselves by their own labours, to lovers of expense, intemperance, and licence, let us examine the cause of this change by the actual matters of fact.

At the first, as has been said, when he set himself against Cimon's great authority, he did caress the people. Finding himself come short of his competitor in wealth and money, by which advantages the other was enabled to take care of the poor, inviting every day some one or other of the citizens that was in want to supper, and bestowing clothes on the aged people, and breaking down the hedges and enclosures of his grounds, that all that would might freely gather what fruit they pleased, Pericles, thus outdone in popular arts, by the advice of one Damonides of Œa, as Aristotle states, turned to the distribution of the public moneys; and in a short time having bought the people over, what with moneys allowed for shows and for service on juries, and what with other forms of pay and largess, he made use of them against the council of Areopagus, of which he himself was no member, as having never been appointed by lot either chief archon, or lawgiver, or king, or captain. For from of old these offices were conferred on persons by lot, and they who had acquitted themselves duly in the discharge of them were advanced to the court of Areopagus.

And so Pericles, having secured his power in interest with the populace, directed the exertions of his party against this council with such success, that most of these causes and matters which had been used to be tried there were, by the agency of Ephialtes, removed from its cognisance; Cimon, also, was banished by ostracism as a favourer of the Lacedæmonians and a hater of the people, though in wealth and noble birth he was among the first, and had won several most glorious victories over the barbarians, and had filled the city with money and spoils of war; as is recorded in the history of his life. So vast an authority had Pericles obtained among the people.

The ostracism was limited by law to ten years; but the Lacedæmonians, in the meantime, entering with a great army into the territory of Tanagra, and the Athenians going out against them, Cimon, coming from his banishment before his time was out, put himself in arms and array with those of his fellow-citizens that were of his own tribe, and desired by his deeds to wipe off the suspicion of his favouring the Lacedæmonians, by venturing his own person along with his countrymen. But Pericles' friends, gathering in a body, forced him to retire as a banished man.

For which cause also Pericles seems to have exerted himself more in that than in any battle, and to have been conspicuous above all for his exposure of himself to danger. All Cimon's friends, also, to a man, fell together side by side, whom Pericles had accused with him of taking part with the Lacedæmonians. Defeated in this battle on their own frontiers, and expecting a new and perilous attack with return of spring, the Athenians now felt regret and sorrow for the loss of Cimon, and repentance for their expulsion of him. Pericles, being sensible of their feelings, did not hesitate or delay to gratify it, and himself made the motion for recalling him home. He, upon his return, concluded a peace betwixt the two cities; for the Lacedæmonians entertained as kindly feelings towards him as they did the reverse towards Pericles and the other popular leaders.

Yet some there are who say that Pericles did not propose the order for Cimon's return till some private articles of agreement had been made between them, and this by means of Elpinice, Cimon's sister; that Cimon, namely, should go out to sea with a fleet of two hundred ships, and be commander-in-chief abroad, with a design to reduce the King of Persia's territories, and that Pericles should have the power at home.

This Elpinice, it was thought, had before this time procured some favour for her brother Cimon at Pericles's hands, and induced him to be more remiss and gentle in urging the charge when Cimon was tried for his life; for Pericles was one of the committee appointed by the commons to plead against him. And when Elpinice came and besought him in her brother's behalf, he answered, with a smile, "O Elpinice, you are too old a woman to undertake such business as this." But, when he appeared to impeach him, he stood up but once to speak, merely to acquit himself of his commission, and went out of court, having done Cimon the least prejudice of any of his accusers.

How, then, can one believe Idomeneus, who charges Pericles as if he had by treachery procured the murder of Ephialtes, the popular statesman, one who was his friend, and of his own party in all his political course, out of jealousy, forsooth, and envy of his great reputation? This historian, it seems, having raked up these stories, I know not whence, has befouled with them a man who, per-

chance, was not altogether free from fault or blame, but yet had a noble spirit, and a soul that was bent on honour; and where such qualities are, there can no such cruel and brutal passion find harbour or gain admittance. As to Ephialtes, the truth of the story, as Aristotle has told it, is this; that having made himself formidable to the oligarchical party, by being an uncompromising asserter of the people's rights in calling to account and prosecuting those who any way wronged them, his enemies, lying in wait for him, by the means of Aristodicus the Tanagræan, privately despatched him.

Cimon, while he was admiral, ended his days in the Isle of Cyprus. And the aristocratical party, seeing that Pericles was already before this grown to be the greatest and foremost man of all the city, but nevertheless wishing there should be somebody set up against him, to blunt and turn the edge of his power, that it might not altogether prove a monarchy, put forward Thucydides of Alopece, a discreet person, and a near kinsman of Cimon's, to conduct the opposition against him; who, indeed, though less skilled in warlike affairs than Cimon was, yet was better versed in speaking and political business and keeping close guard in the city, and, engaging with Pericles on the hustings, in a short time brought the government to an equality of parties. For he would not suffer those who were called the honest and good (persons of worth and distinction) to be scattered up and down and mix themselves and be lost among the populace, as formerly, diminishing and obscuring their superiority amongst the masses; but taking them apart by themselves and uniting them in one body, by their combined weight he was able, as it were upon the balance, to make a counterpoise of the other party.

For, indeed, there was from the beginning a sort of concealed split, or seam, as it might be in a piece of iron, marking the different popular and aristocratical tendencies; but the open rivalry and contention of these two opponents made the gash deep, and severed the city into the two parties of the People and the Few. And so Pericles, at that time, more than at any other, let loose the reins to the people, and made his policy subservient to their pleasure, contriving continually to have some great public show or solemnity, some banquet, or some procession or other in the town to please them, coaxing his countrymen like children with such delights and pleasures as were not, however, unedifying. Besides that every year he sent out three-score galleys, on board of which there were numbers of the citizens, who were in pay eight months, learning at the same time and practising the art of seamanship.

He sent, moreover, a thousand of them into the Chersonese as planters, to share the land among them by lot, and five hundred more into the isle of Naxos, and half that number to Andros, a thousand into Thrace to dwell among the Bisaltæ, and others into Italy, when the city Sybaris, which now was called Thurii, was to be repeopled. And this he did to ease and discharge the city of an idle, and, by reason of their idleness, a busy, meddling crowd of people; and at the same time to meet the necessities and restore the fortunes of the poor townsmen, and to intimidate, also, and check their allies from attempting any change, by posting such garrisons, as it were, in the midst of them.

That which gave most pleasure and ornament to the city of Athens, and the greatest admiration and even astonishment to all strangers, and that which now is Greece's only evidence that the power she boasts of and her ancient wealth are no romance or idle story, was his construction of the public and sacred buildings. Yet this was that of all his actions in the government which his enemies most looked askance upon and cavilled at in the popular assemblies, crying out how that the commonwealth of Athens had lost its reputation and was ill-spoken of abroad for removing the common treasure of the Greeks from the isle of Delos into their own custody; and how that their fairest excuse for so doing, namely, that they took it away for fear the barbarians should seize it, and on purpose to secure it in a safe place, this Pericles had made unavailable, and how that "Greece cannot but resent it as an insufferable affront, and consider herself to be tyrannised over openly, when she sees the treasure, which was contributed by her upon a necessity for the war, wantonly lavished out by us upon our city, to gild her all over, and to adorn and set her forth, as it were some vain woman, hung round with precious stones and figures and temples, which cost a world of money."

Pericles, on the other hand, informed the people, that they were in no way obliged to give any account of those moneys to their allies, so long as they maintained their defence, and kept off the barbarians from attacking them; while in the meantime they did not so much as supply one horse or man or ship, but only found money for the service; "which money," said he, "is not theirs that give it, but theirs that receive it, if so be they perform the conditions upon which they receive it." And that it was good reason, that, now the city was sufficiently provided and stored with all things necessary for the war, they should convert the overplus of its wealth to such undertakings as would hereafter, when completed, give them eternal honour, and, for the present, while in process, freely supply all the inhabitants with plenty. With their variety of workmanship and of occasions for service, which summon all arts and trades and require all hands to be employed about them, they do actually put the whole city, in a manner, into state-pay; while at the same time she is both beautified and maintained by herself.

For as those who are of age and strength for war are provided for and maintained in the armaments abroad by their pay out of the public stock, so, it being his desire and design that the undisciplined mechanic multitude that stayed at home should not go without their share of public salaries, and yet should not have them given them for sitting still and doing nothing, to that end he thought fit to bring in among them, with the approbation of the people, these vast projects of buildings and designs of work that would be of some continuance before they were finished, and would give employment to numerous arts, so that the part of the people that stayed at home might, no less than those that were at sea or in garrisons or on expeditions, have a fair and just occasion of receiving the benefit and having their share of the public moneys.

The materials were stone, brass, ivory, gold, ebony, cypress-wood; and the arts or trades that wrought and fashioned them were smiths and carpenters, moulders, founders and braziers, stone-cutters, dyers, goldsmiths, ivory-workers, painters, embroiderers, turners; those again that conveyed them to the town for use, merchants and mariners and ship-masters by sea, and by land, cartwrights, cattle-breeders, waggoners, ropemakers, flax-workers, shoemakers and leather-dressers, roadmakers, miners. And every trade in the same nature, as a captain in an army has his particular company of soldiers under him, had its own hired company of journeymen and labourers belonging to it banded together as in array, to be as it were the instrument and body for the performance of the service. Thus, to say all in a word, the occasions and services of these public works distributed plenty through every age and condition.

As then grew the works up, no less stately in size than exquisite in form, the workmen striving to outvie the material and the design with the beauty of their workmanship, yet the most wonderful thing of all was the rapidity of their execution.

Undertakings, any one of which singly might have required, they thought, for their completion, several successions and ages of men, were every one of them accomplished in the height and prime of one man's political service. Although they say, too, that Zeuxis once, having heard Agatharchus, the painter, boast of despatching his work with speed and ease, replied, "I take a long time." For ease and speed in doing a thing do not give the work lasting solidity or exactness of beauty; the expenditure of time allowed to a man's pains beforehand for the production of a thing is repaid by way of interest with a vital force for the preservation when once produced. For which reason Pericles's works are especially admired, as having been made quickly, to last long. For every particular piece of his work was immediately, even at that time, for its beauty and elegance, antique; and yet in its vigour and freshness looks to this day as if it were just executed. There is a sort of bloom of newness upon those works of his, preserving them from the touch of time, as if they had some perennial spirit and undying vitality mingled in the composition of them.

Phidias had the oversight of all the works, and was surveyor-general, though upon the various portions other great masters and workmen were employed. For Callicrates and Ictinus built the Parthenon; the chapel at Eleusis, where the mysteries were celebrated, was begun by Corœbus, who erected the pillars that stand upon the floor or pavement, and joined them to the architraves; and after his death Metagenes of Xypete added the frieze and the upper line of columns; Xenocles of Cholargus roofed or arched the lantern on top of the temple of Castor and Pollux; and the long wall, which Socrates says he himself heard Pericles propose to the people, was undertaken by Callicrates. This work Cratinus ridicules, as long in finishing—

'Tis long since Pericles, if words would do it,
Talked up the wall; yet adds not one mite to it.

The Odeum, or music-room, which in its interior was full of seats and ranges of pillars, and outside had its roof made to slope and descend from one single point at the top, was constructed, we are told, in imitation of the King of Persia's Pavilion; this likewise by Pericles's order; which Cratinus again, in his comedy called *The Thracian Women,* made an occasion of raillery—

So, we see here,
Jupiter Long-pate Pericles appear,
Since ostracism time, he's laid aside his head,
And wears the new Odeum in its stead.

Pericles, also eager for distinction, then first obtained the decree for a contest in musical skill to be held yearly at the Panathenæa, and he himself, being chosen judge, arranged the order and method in which the competitors should sing and play on the flute and on the harp. And both at that time, and at other times also, they sat in this music-room to see and hear all such trials of skill.

The propylæa, or entrances to the Acropolis, were finished in five years' time, Mnesicles being the principal architect. A strange accident happened in the course of building, which showed that the goddess was not averse to the work, but was aiding and co-operating to bring it to perfection. One of the artificers, the quickest and the handiest workman among them all, with a slip of his foot fell down from a great height, and lay in a miserable condition, the physicians having no hope of his recovery. When Pericles was in distress about this, Minerva appeared to him at night in a dream, and ordered a course of treatment, which he applied, and in a short time and with great ease cured the man. And upon this occasion it was that he set up a brass statue of Minerva, surnamed Health, in the citadel near the altar, which they say was there before.

But it was Phidias who wrought the goddess's image in gold, and he has his name inscribed on the pedestal as the workman of it; and indeed the whole work in a manner was under his charge, and he had, as we have said already, the oversight over all the artists and workmen, through Pericles's friendship for him; and this, indeed, made him much envied, and his patron shamefully slandered with stories, as if Phidias were in the habit of receiving, for Pericles's use, freeborn women that came to see the works.

The comic writers of the town, when they had got hold of this story, made much of it, and bespattered him with all the ribaldry they could invent, charging him falsely with the wife of Menippus, one who was his friend and served as lieutenant under him in the wars; and with the birds kept by Pyrilampes, an acquaintance of Pericles, who, they pretended, used to give presents of peacocks to Pericles's female friends. And how can one wonder at any number of strange assertions from men whose whole lives were devoted to mockery, and who were ready at any time to sacrifice the reputation of their superiors to vulgar envy and spite, as to some evil genius, when even Stesimbrotus the Thracian has dared to lay to the charge of Pericles a monstrous and fabulous piece of criminality with his son's wife? So very difficult a matter is it to trace and find out the truth of anything by history, when, on the one hand, those who afterwards write it find long periods of time intercepting their view, and, on the other hand, the contemporary records of any actions and lives, partly through envy and ill-will, partly through favour and flattery, pervert and distort truth.

When the orators, who sided with Thucydides and his party, were at one time crying out, as their custom was, against Pericles, as one who squandered away the public money, and made havoc of the state revenues, he rose in the open assembly and put the question to the people, whether they thought that he had laid out much; and they saying, "Too much, a great deal," "Then," said he, "since it is so, let the cost not go to your account, but to mine; and let the inscription upon the buildings stand in my name." When they heard him say thus, whether it were out of a surprise to see the greatness of his spirit or out of emulation of the glory of the works, they cried aloud, bidding him to spend on, and lay out what he thought fit from the public purse, and to spare no cost, till all were finished.

At length, coming to a final contest with Thucydides which of the two should ostracise the other out of the country, and having gone through this peril, he threw his antagonist out, and broke up the confederacy that had been organised against him. So that now all schism and division being at an end, and the city brought to evenness and unity, he got all Athens and all affairs that pertained to the Athenians into his own hands, their tributes, their armies, and their galleys, the islands, the sea, and their wide-extended power, partly over other Greeks and partly over barbarians, and all that empire, which they possessed, founded and fortified upon subject nations and royal friendships and alliances.

After this he was no longer the same man he had been before, nor as tame and gentle and familiar as formerly with the populace, so as readily to yield to their pleasures and to comply with the desires of the multitude, as a steersman shifts with the winds. Quitting that loose, remiss, and, in some cases, licentious court of the popular will, he turned those soft and flowery modulations to the austerity of aristocratical and regal rule; and employing this uprightly and undeviatingly for the country's best interests, he was able generally to lead the people along, with their own wills and consents, by persuading and showing them what was to be done; and sometimes, too, urging and pressing them forward extremely against their will, he made them, whether they would or no, yield submission to what was for their advantage.

In which, to say the truth, he did but like a skilful physician, who, in a complicated and chronic disease, as he sees occasion, at one while allows his patient the moderate use of such things as please him, at another while gives him keen pains and drugs to work the cure. For there arising and growing up, as was natural, all manner of distempered feelings among a people which had so vast a command and dominion, he alone, as a great master, knowing how to handle and deal fitly with each one of them, and, in an especial manner, making that use of hopes and fears, as his two chief rudders, with the one to check the career of their confidence at any time, with the other to raise them up and cheer them when under any discouragement, plainly showed by this, that rhetoric, or the art of speaking, is, in Plato's language, the government of the souls of men, and that her chief business is to address the affections and passions, which are as it were the strings and keys to the soul, and require a skilful and careful touch to be played on as they should be.

The source of this predominance was not barely his power of language, but, as Thucydides assures us, the reputation of his life, and the confidence felt in his character; his manifest freedom from every kind of corruption, and superiority to all considerations of money. Notwithstanding, he had made the city of Athens, which was great of itself, as great and rich as can be imagined, and though he were himself in power and interest more than equal to many kings and absolute rulers, who some of them also bequeathed by will their power to their children, he, for his part, did not make the patrimony his father left him greater than it was by one drachma.

Thucydides, indeed, gives a plain statement of the greatness of his power; and the comic poets, in their spiteful manner, more than hint at it, styling his companions and friends the new Pisistratidæ, and calling on him to abjure any intention of usurpation, as one whose eminence was too great to be any longer proportionable to and compatible with a democracy or popular government. And Teleclides says the Athenians had surrendered up to him—

The tribute of the cities, and with them, the cities
*   too, to do with them as he pleases, and undo;*
To build up, if he likes, stone walls around a
*   town; and again, if so he likes, to pull them*
*   down;*
Their treaties and alliances, power, empire, peace,
*   and war, their wealth and their success forever*
*   more.*

Nor was all this the luck of some happy occasion; nor was it the mere bloom and grace of a policy that flourished for a season; but having for forty years together maintained the first place among statesmen such as Ephialtes and Leocrates and Myronides and Cimon and Tolmides and Thucydides were; after the defeat and banishment of Thucydides, for no less than fifteen years longer, in the exercise of one continuous unintermitted command in the office, to which he was annually re-elected, of General, he preserved his integrity unspotted; though otherwise he was not altogether idle or careless in looking after his pecuniary advantage. His paternal estate, which of right belonged to him, he so ordered that it might neither through negligence be wasted or lessened, nor yet, being so full of business as he was, cost him any great trouble or time with taking care of it; and put it into such a way of management as he thought to be the most easy for himself, and the most exact. All his yearly products and profits he sold together in a lump, and supplied his household needs afterwards by buying everything that he or his family wanted out of the market.

Upon which account, his children, when they grew to age, were not well pleased with his management, and the women that lived with him were treated with little cost, and complained of his way of housekeeping, where everything was ordered and set down from day to day, and reduced to the greatest exact-

ness; since there was not there, as is usual in a great family and a plentiful estate, anything to spare, or over and above; but all that went out or came in, all disbursements and all receipts, proceeded as it were by number and measure. His manager in all this was a single servant, Evangelus by name, a man either naturally gifted or instructed by Pericles so as to excel every one in this art of domestic economy.

All this, in truth, was very little in harmony with Anaxagoras's wisdom; if, indeed, it be true that he, by a kind of divine impulse and greatness of spirit, voluntarily quitted his house, and left his land to lie fallow and to be grazed by sheep like a common. But the life of a contemplative philosopher and that of an active statesman are, I presume, not the same thing; for the one merely employs, upon great and good objects of thought, an intelligence that requires no aid of instruments nor supply of any external materials; whereas the other, who tempers and applies his virtue to human uses, may have occasion for affluence, not as a matter of necessity, but as a noble thing; which was Pericles's case, who relieved numerous poor citizens.

However, there is a story that Anaxagoras himself, while Pericles was taken up with public affairs, lay neglected, and that, now being grown old, he wrapped himself up with a resolution to die for want of food; which being by chance brought to Pericles's ear, he was horror-struck, and instantly ran thither, and used all the arguments and entreaties he could to him, lamenting not so much Anaxagoras's condition as his own, should he lose such a counsellor as he had found him to be; and that, upon this, Anaxagoras unfolded his robe, and showing himself, made answer: "Pericles," said he, "even those who have occasion for a lamp supply it with oil."

The Lacedæmonians beginning to show themselves troubled at the growth of the Athenian power, Pericles, on the other hand, to elevate the people's spirit yet more, and to raise them to the thought of great actions, proposed a decree, to summon all the Greeks in what part soever, whether of Europe or Asia, every city, little as well as great, to send their deputies to Athens to a general assembly, or convention, there to consult and advise concerning the Greek temples which the barbarians had burnt down, and the sacrifices which were due from them upon vows they had made to their gods for the safety of Greece when they fought against the barbarians; and also concerning the navigation of the sea, that they might henceforward pass to and fro and trade securely and be at peace among themselves.

Upon this errand there were twenty men, of such as were above fifty years of age, sent by commission; five to summon the Ionians and Dorians in Asia, and the islanders as far as Lesbos and Rhodes; five to visit all the places in the Hellespont and Thrace, up to Byzantium; and other five besides these to go to Bœotia and Phocis and Peloponnesus, and from hence to pass through the Locrians over to the neighbouring continent as far as Acarnania and Ambracia; and the rest to take their course through Eubœa to the Œtæans and the Malian Gulf, and to the Achæans of Phthiotis and the Thessalians; all of them to treat with the people as they passed, and to persuade them to come and take their part in the debates for settling the peace and jointly regulating the affairs of Greece.

Nothing was effected, nor did the cities meet by their deputies, as was desired; the Lacedæmonians, as it is said, crossing the design underhand, and the attempt being disappointed and baffled first in Peloponnesus. I thought fit, however, to introduce the mention of it, to show the spirit of the man and the greatness of his thoughts.

In his military conduct, he gained a great reputation for wariness; he would not by his good-will engage in any fight which had much uncertainty or hazard; he did not envy the glory of generals whose rash adventures fortune favoured with brilliant success, however they were admired by others, nor did he think them worthy his imitation, but always used to say to his citizens that, so far as lay in his power, they should continue immortal, and live for ever.

Seeing Tolmides, the son of Tolmæus, upon the confidence of his former successes, and flushed with the honour his military actions had procured him, making preparations to attack the Bœotians in their own country when there was no likely opportunity, and that he had prevailed with the bravest and most enterprising of the youth to enlist themselves as volunteers in the service, who besides his other force made up a thousand, he endeavoured to withhold him and to advise him from it in the public assembly, telling him in a memorable saying of his, which still goes about, that, if he would not take Pericles's advice, yet he would not do amiss to wait and be ruled by

time, the wisest counsellor of all. This saying, at that time, was but slightly commended; but within a few days after, when news was brought that Tolmides himself had been defeated and slain in battle near Coronea, and that many brave citizens had fallen with him, it gained him great repute as well as goodwill among the people, for wisdom and for love of his countrymen.

But of all his expeditions, that to the Chersonese gave most satisfaction and pleasure, having proved the safety of the Greeks who inhabited there. For not only by carrying along with him a thousand fresh citizens of Athens he gave new strength and vigour to the cities, but also by belting the neck of land, which joins the peninsula to the continent, with bulwarks and forts from sea to sea, he put a stop to the inroads of the Thracians, who lay all about the Chersonese, and closed the door against a continual and grievous war, with which that country had been long harassed, lying exposed to the encroachments and influx of barbarous neighbors, and groaning under the evils of a predatory population both upon and within its borders.

Nor was he less admired and talked of abroad for his sailing around the Peloponnesus, having set out from Pegæ, or The Fountains, the port of Megara, with a hundred galleys. For he not only laid waste the sea-coast, as Tolmides had done before, but also, advancing far up into the mainland with the soldiers he had on board, by the terror of his appearance drove many within their walls; and at Nemea, with main force, routed and raised a trophy over the Sicyonians, who stood their ground and joined battle with him. And having taken on board a supply of soldiers into the galleys out of Achaia, then in league with Athens, he crossed with the fleet to the opposite continent, and, sailing along by the mouth of the river Achelous, overran Acarnania and shut up the Œniadæ within their city walls, and having ravaged and wasted their country, weighed anchor for home with the double advantage of having shown himself formidable to his enemies, and at the same time safe and energetic to his fellow-citizens; for there was not so much as any chance miscarriage that happened, the whole voyage through, to those who were under his charge.

Entering also the Euxine Sea with a large and finely equipped fleet, he obtained for the Greek cities any new arrangements they wanted, and entered into friendly relations with them; and to the barbarous nations, and kings and chiefs round about them, displayed the greatness of the power of the Athenians, their perfect ability and confidence to sail wherever they had a mind, and to bring the whole sea under their control. He left the Sinopians thirteen ships of war, with soldiers under the command of Lamachus, to assist them against Timesileus the tyrant; and when he and his accomplices had been thrown out, obtained a decree that six hundred of the Athenians that were willing should sail to Sinope and plant themselves there with the Sinopians, sharing among them the houses and land which the tyrant and his party had previously held.

But in other things he did not comply with the giddy impulses of the citizens, nor quit his own resolutions to follow their fancies, when, carried away with the thought of their strength and great success, they were eager to interfere again in Egypt, and to disturb the King of Persia's maritime dominions. Nay, there were a good many who were, even then, possessed with that unblest and inauspicious passion for Sicily, which afterward the orators of Alcibiades's party blew up into a flame. There were some also who dreamt of Tuscany and Carthage, and not without plausible reason in their present large dominion and prosperous course of their affairs.

But Pericles curbed this passion for foreign conquest, and unsparingly pruned and cut down their ever busy fancies for a multitude of undertakings; and directed their power for the most part to securing and consolidating what they had already got, supposing it would be quite enough for them to do, if they could keep the Lacedæmonians in check; to whom he entertained all along a sense of opposition; which, as upon many other occasions, so he particularly showed by what he did in the time of the holy war. The Lacedæmonians, having gone with an army to Delphi, restored Apollo's temple, which the Phocians had got into their possession, to the Delphians; immediately after their departure, Pericles, with another army, came and restored the Phocians. And the Lacedæmonians, having engraven the record of their privilege of consulting the oracle before others, which the Delphians gave them, upon the forehead of the brazen wolf which stands there, he, also, having received from the Phocians the like privilege for the Athenians, had it cut upon the same wolf of brass on his right side.

That he did well and wisely in thus re-straining the exertions of the Athenians within the compass of Greece, the events themselves that happened afterward bore sufficient witness. For, in the first place, the Eubœans revolted, against whom he passed over with forces; and then, immediately after, news came that the Megarians were turned their enemies; and a hostile army was upon the borders of Attica, under the conduct of Plistoanax, King of the Lacedæmonians. Wherefore Pericles came with his army back again in all haste out of Eubœa, to meet the war which threatened at home, and did not venture to engage a numerous and brave army eager for battle; but perceiving that Plistoanax was a very young man, and governed himself mostly by the counsel and advice of Cleandrides, whom the ephors had sent with him, by reason of his youth, to be a kind of guardian and assistant to him, he privately made trial of this man's integrity, and, in a short time, having corrupted him with money, prevailed with him to withdraw the Peloponnesians out of Attica.

When the army had retired and dispersed into their several states, the Lacedæmonians in anger fined their king in so large a sum of money, that, unable to pay it, he quitted Lacedæmon; while Cleandrides fled, and had sentence of death passed upon him in his absence. This was the father of Gylippus, who overpowered the Athenians in Sicily. And it seems that this covetousness was an hereditary disease transmitted from father to son; for Gylippus also afterwards was caught in foul practices, and expelled from Sparta for it. But this we have told at large in the account of Lysander.

When Pericles, in giving up his accounts of this expedition, stated a disbursement of ten talents, as laid out upon fit occasion, the people, without any question, nor troubling themselves to investigate the mystery, freely allowed of it. And some historians, in which number is Theophrastus, the philosopher, have given it as a truth that Pericles every year used to send privately the sum of ten talents to Sparta, with which he complimented those in office, to keep off the war; not to purchase peace neither, but time, that he might prepare at leisure, and be the better able to carry on war hereafter.

Immediately after this, turning his forces against the revolters, and passing over into the island of Eubœa with fifty sail of ships and five thousand men in arms, he reduced their cities, and drove out the citizens of the Chalcidians, called Hippobotæ, horse-feeders, the chief persons for wealth and reputation among them; and removing all the Histiæans out of the country, brought in a plantation of Athenians in their room; making them his one example of severity, because they had captured an Attic ship and killed all on board.

After this, having made a truce between the Athenians and Lacedæmonians for thirty years, he ordered, by public decree, the expedition against the isle of Samos, on the ground, that, when they were bid to leave off their war with the Milesians they had not complied.

And as these measures against the Samians are thought to have been taken to please Aspasia, this may be a fit point for inquiry about the woman, what art or charming faculty she had that enabled her to captivate, as she did, the greatest statesmen, and to give the philosophers occasion to speak so much about her, and that, too, not to her disparagement. That she was a Milesian by birth, the daughter of Axiochus, is a thing acknowledged. And they say it was in emulation of Thargelia, a courtesan of the old Ionian times, that she made her addresses to men of great power. Thargelia was a great beauty, extremely charming, and at the same time sagacious; she had numerous suitors among the Greeks, and brought all who had to do with her over to the Persian interest, and by their means, being men of the greatest power and station, sowed the seeds of the Median faction up and down in several cities.

Aspasia, some say, was courted and caressed by Pericles upon account of her knowledge and skill in politics. Socrates himself would sometimes go to visit her, and some of his acquaintance with him; and those who frequented her company would carry their wives with them to listen to her. Her occupation was anything but creditable, her house being a home for young courtesans. Æschines tells us, also, that Lysicles, a sheep-dealer, a man of low birth and character, by keeping Aspasia company after Pericles's death, came to be a chief man in Athens. And in Plato's *Menexenus*, though we do not take the introduction as quite serious, still thus much seems to be historical, that she had the repute of being resorted to by many of the Athenians for instruction in the art of speaking. Pericles's inclination for her seems, however, to have rather proceeded from the passion of love. He had a wife that was near of kin to him, who had been married first to Hipponicus, by whom she had Callias, surnamed the Rich; and also she brought Pericles, while she lived with him, two sons, Xanthippus and Paralus. Afterwards, when they did not well agree, nor like to live together, he parted with her, with her own consent, to another man, and himself took Aspasia, and loved her with wonderful affection; every day, both as he went out and as he came in from the market-place, he saluted and kissed her.

In the comedies she goes by the nicknames of the new Omphale and Deianira, and again is styled Juno. Cratinus, in downright terms, calls her a harlot.

> To find him a Juno the goddess of lust
> Bore that harlot past shame,
> Aspasia by name.

It should seem also that he had a son by her; Eupolis, in his *Demi*, introduced Pericles asking after his safety, and Myronides replying—

> My son? He lives: a man he had been long,
> But that the harlot-mother did him wrong.

Aspasia, they say, became so celebrated and renowned, that Cyrus, also who made war against Artaxerxes for the Persian monarchy, gave her whom he loved the best of all his concubines the name of Aspasia, who before that was called Milto. She was a Phocæan by birth, the daughter of one Hermotimus, and, when Cyrus fell in battle, was carried to the king, and had great influence at court. These things coming into my memory as I am writing this story, it would be unnatural for me to omit them.

Pericles, however, was particularly charged with having proposed to the assembly the war against the Samians, from favour to the Milesians, upon the entreaty of Aspasia. For the two states were at war for the possession of Priene; and the Samians, getting the better, refused to lay down their arms and to have the controversy betwixt them decided by arbitration before the Athenians. Pericles, therefore, fitting out a fleet, went and broke up the oligarchical government at Samos, and taking fifty of the principal men of the town as hostages, and as many of their children, sent them to the isle of Lemnos, there to be kept, though he had offers, as some relate, of a talent apiece for himself from each one of the hostages, and of many other presents from those who were anxious not to have a democracy. Moreover, Pisuthnes the Persian, one of the king's lieutenants, bearing some good-will to the Samians, sent him ten thousand pieces of gold to excuse the city. Pericles, however, would receive none of all this; but after he had taken that course with the Samians which he thought fit and set up a democracy among them, sailed back to Athens.

But they, however, immediately revolted, Pisuthnes having privily got away their hostages for them, and provided them with means for the war. Whereupon Pericles came out with a fleet a second time against them, and found them not idle nor slinking away, but manfully resolved to try for the dominion of the sea. The issue was, that after a sharp sea-fight about the island called Tragia, Pericles obtained a decisive victory, having with forty-four ships routed seventy of the enemy's, twenty of which were carrying soldiers.

Together with his victory and pursuit, having made himself master of the port, he laid siege to the Samians, and blocked them up, who yet, one way or another, still ventured to make sallies, and fight under the city walls. But after that another greater fleet from Athens was arrived, and that the Samians were now shut up with a close leaguer on every side, Pericles, taking with him sixty galleys, sailed out into the main sea, with the intention, as most authors give the account, to meet a squadron of Phœnecian ships that were coming for the Samians' relief, and to fight them at as great distance as could be from the island; but, as Stesimbrotus says, with a design of putting over to Cyprus, which does not seem to be probable.

But, whichever of the two was his intention, it seems to have been a miscalculation. For on his departure, Melissus, the son of Ithagenes, a philosopher, being at that time the general in Samos, despising either the small number of the ships that were left or the inexperience of the commanders, prevailed with the citizens to attack the Athenians. And the Samians having won the battle, and taken several of the men prisoners, and disabled several of the ships, were masters of the sea, and brought into port all necessaries they wanted for the war, which they had not before. Aristotle says, too, that Pericles had been once before this worsted by this Melissus in a sea-fight.

The Samians, that they might requite an affront which had before been put upon them, branded the Athenians, whom they took prisoners, in their foreheads, with the figure of an owl. For so the Athenians had marked them before with a Samæna, which is a sort of ship, low and flat in the prow, so as to look snub-nosed, but wide and large and well-spread in

the hold, by which it both carries a large cargo and sails well. And it was so called, because the first of that kind was seen at Samos, having been built by order of Polycrates, the tyrant. These brands upon the Samians' foreheads, they say, are the allusion in the passage of Aristophanes, where he says—

For, oh, the Samians are a lettered people.

Pericles, as soon as news was brought him of the disaster that had befallen his army, made all the haste he could to come in to their relief, and having defeated Melissus, who bore up against him, and put the enemy to flight, he immediately proceeded to hem them in with a wall, resolving to master them and take the town, rather with some cost and time than with the wounds and hazards of his citizens. But as it was a hard matter to keep back the Athenians, who were vexed at the delay, and were eagerly bent to fight, he divided the whole multitude into eight parts, and arranged by lot that that part which had the white bean should have leave to feast and take their ease while the other seven were fighting. And this is the reason, they say, that people, when at any time they have been merry, and enjoyed themselves, called it white day, in allusion to this white bean.

Ephorus the historian tells us besides, that Pericles made use of engines of battery in this siege, being much taken with the curiousness of the invention, with the aid and presence of Artemon himself, the engineer, who, being lame, used to be carried about in a litter, where the works required his attendance, and for that reason was called Periphoretus. But Heraclides Ponticus disproves this out of Anacreon's poems, where mention is made of this Artemon Periphoretus several ages before the Samian war, or any of these occurrences. And he says that Artemon, being a man who loved his ease, and had a great apprehension of danger, for the most part kept close within doors, having two of his servants to hold a brazen shield over his head, that nothing might fall upon him from above; and if he were at any time forced upon necessity to go abroad, that he was carried about in a little hanging bed, close to the very ground, and that for this reason he was called Periphoretus.

In the ninth month, the Samians surrendering themselves and delivering up the town, Pericles pulled down their walls, and seized their shipping, and set a fine of a large sum of money upon them, part of which they paid down at once, and they agreed to bring in the rest by a certain time, and gave hostages for security. Duris, the Samian, makes a tragical drama out of these events, charging the Athenians and Pericles with a great deal of cruelty, which neither Thucydides, nor Ephorus, nor Aristotle have given any relation of, and probably with little regard to truth; how, for example, he brought the captains and soldiers of the galleys into the market-place at Miletus, and there having bound them fast to boards for ten days, then, when they were already all but half dead, gave order to have them killed by beating out their brains with clubs, and their dead bodies to be flung out into the open streets and fields, unburied. Duris, however, who, even where he has no private feeling concerned, is not wont to keep his narrative within the limits of truth, is the more likely upon this occasion to have exaggerated the calamities which befell his country, to create odium against the Athenians.

Pericles, however, after the reduction of Samos, returning back to Athens, took care that those who died in the war should be honourably buried, and made a funeral harangue, as the custom is, in their commendation at their graves, for which he gained great admiration. As he came down from the stage on which he spoke, the rest of the women came and complimented him, taking him by the hand, and crowning him with garlands and ribbons, like a victorious athlete in the games; but Elpinice, coming near to him, said, "These are brave deeds, Pericles, that you have done, and such as deserve our chaplets; who have lost us many a worthy citizen, not in a war with Phœnicians or Medes, like my brother Cimon, but for the overthrow of an allied and kindred city." As Elpinice spoke these words, he, smiling quietly, as it is said, returned her answer with this verse:—

Old women should not seek to be perfumed.

Ion says of him, that upon this exploit of his, conquering the Samians, he indulged very high and proud thoughts of himself: whereas Agamemnon was ten years taking a barbarous city, he had in nine months' time vanquished and taken the greatest and most powerful of the Ionians. And indeed it was not without reason that he assumed this glory to himself, for, in real truth, there was much uncertainty and great hazard in this great war, if so be, as Thucydides tells us, the Samian state were within a very little of wresting the whole power and dominion of the sea out of the Athenians' hands.

After this was over, the Peloponnesian war beginning to break out in full tide, he advised the people to send help to the Corcyræans, who were attacked by the Corinthians, and to secure to themselves an island possessed of great naval resources, since the Peloponnesians were already all but in actual hostilities against them.

The people readily consenting to the motion, and voting an aid and succour for them, he despatched Lacedæmonius, Cimon's son, having only ten ships with him, as it were out of a design to affront him; for there was a great kindness and friendship betwixt Cimon's family and the Lacedæmonians; so, in order that Lacedæmonius might lie the more open to a charge, or suspicion at least, of favouring the Lacedæmonians and playing false, if he performed no considerable exploit in this service, he allowed him a small number of ships, and sent him out against his will; and indeed he made it somewhat his business to hinder Cimon's sons from rising in the state, professing that by their very names they were not to be looked upon as native and true Athenians, but foreigners and strangers, one being called Lacedæmonius, another Thessalus, and the third Eleus; and they were all three of them, it was thought, born of an Arcadian woman. Being, however, ill spoken of on account of these ten galleys, as having afforded but a small supply to the people that were in need, and yet given a great advantage to those who might complain of the act of intervention, Pericles sent out a larger force afterwards to Corcyra, which arrived after the fight was over.

And when now the Corinthians, angry and indignant with the Athenians, accused them publicly at Lacedæmon, the Megarians joined with them, complaining that they were, contrary to common right and the articles of peace sworn to among the Greeks, kept out and driven away from every market and from all ports under the control of the Athenians. The Æginetans, also, professing to be ill-used and treated with violence, made supplications in private to the Lacedæmonians for redress, though not daring openly to call the Athenians in question. In the meantime, also, the city Potidæa, under the dominion of the Athenians, but a colony formerly of the Corinthians, had revolted, and was beset with a formal siege, and was a further occasion of precipitating the war.

Yet notwithstanding all this, there being

embassies sent to Athens, and Archidamus, the King of the Lacedæmonians, endeavouring to bring the greater part of the complaints and matters in dispute to a fair determination, and to pacify and allay the heats of the allies, it is very likely that the war would not upon any other grounds of quarrel have fallen upon the Athenians, could they have been prevailed with to repeal the ordinance against the Megarians, and to be reconciled to them. Upon which account, since Pericles was the man who mainly opposed it, and stirred up the people's passions to persist in their contention with the Megarians, he was regarded as the sole cause of the war.

They say, moreover, that ambassadors went, by order, from Lacedæmon to Athens about this very business, and that when Pericles was urging a certain law which made it illegal to take down or withdraw the tablet of the decree, one of the ambassadors, Polyalces by name, said, "Well, do not take it down then, but *turn* it; there is no law, I suppose, which forbids that"; which, though prettily said, did not move Pericles from his resolution.

There may have been, in all likelihood, something of a secret grudge and private animosity which he had against the Megarians. Yet, upon a public and open charge against them, that they had appropriated part of the sacred land on the frontier, he proposed a decree that a herald should be sent to them, and the same also to the Lacedæmonians, with an accusation of the Megarians; an order which certainly shows equitable and friendly proceeding enough. And after that the herald who was sent, by name Anthemocritus, died, and it was believed that the Megarians had contrived his death, then Charinus proposed a decree against them, that there should be an irreconcilable and implacable enmity thenceforward betwixt the two commonwealths; and that if any one of the Megarians should but set his foot in Attica, he should be put to death; and that the commanders, when they take the usual oath, should, over and above that, swear that they will twice every year make an inroad into the Megarian country; and that Anthemocritus should be buried near the Thracian Gates, which are now called the Dipylon, or Double Gate.

On the other hand, the Megarians, utterly denying and disowning the murder of Anthemocritus, throw the whole matter upon Aspasia and Pericles, availing themselves of the famous verses in the Acharnians—

To Megara some of our madcaps ran,
And stole Simætha thence, their courtesan.
Which exploit the Megarians to outdo,
Came to Aspasia's house, and took off two.

The true occasion of the quarrel is not so easy to find out. But of inducing the refusal to annul the decree, all alike charge Pericles. Some say he met the request with a positive refusal, out of high spirit and a view of the state's best interest, accounting that the demand made in those embassies was designed for a trial of their compliance, and that a concession would be taken for a confession of weakness as if they durst not do otherwise; while some others there are who say that it was rather out of arrogance and a wilful spirit of contention, to show his own strength, that he took occasion to slight the Lacedæmonians.

The worst motive of all, which is confirmed by most witnesses, is to the following effect: Phidias the Moulder had, as has before been said, undertaken to make the statue of Minerva. Now he, being admitted to friendship with Pericles, and a great favourite of his, had many enemies upon this account, who envied and maligned him; who also, to make trial in a case of his, what kind of judges the commons would prove, should there be occasion to bring Pericles himself before them, having tampered with Menon, one who had been a workman with Phidias, stationed him in the market-place, with a petition desiring public security upon his discovery and impeachment of Phidias. The people admitting the man to tell his story, and the prosecution proceeding in the assembly, there was nothing of theft or cheat proved against him; for Phidias, from the very first beginning, by the advice of Pericles, had so wrought and wrapt the gold that was used in the work about the statue, that they might take it all off, and make out the just weight of it, which Pericles at that time bade the accusers do. But the reputation of his works was what brought envy upon Phidias, especially that where he represents the fight of the Amazons upon the goddess's shield; he had introduced a likeness of himself as a bald old man holding up a great stone with both hands, and had put in a very fine representation of Pericles fighting with an Amazon. And the position of the hand which holds out the spear in front of the face, was ingeniously contrived to conceal in some degree the likeness, which meantime showed itself on either side.

Phidias then was carried away to prison,

and there died of a disease; but, as some say, of poison, administered by the enemies of Pericles, to raise a slander, or a suspicion at least, as though he had procured it. The informer Menon, upon Glycon's proposal, the people made free from payment of taxes and customs, and ordered the generals to take care that nobody should do him any hurt.

About the same time, Aspasia was indicted of impiety, upon the complaint of Hermippus, the comedian, who also laid further to her charge that she received into her house freeborn women for the uses of Pericles. And Diopithes proposed a decree, that public accusations should be laid against persons who neglected religion, or taught new doctrines about things above, directing suspicion, by means of Anaxagoras, against Pericles himself. The people receiving and admitting these accusations and complaints, at length, by this means, they came to enact a decree, at the motion of Dracontides, that Pericles should bring in the accounts of the moneys he had expended, and lodge them with the Prytanes; and that the judges, carrying their suffrage from the altar in the Acropolis, should examine and determine the business in the city. This last clause Hagnon took out of the decree, and moved that the causes should be tried before fifteen hundred jurors, whether they should be styled prosecutions for robbery, or bribery, or any kind of malversation.

Aspasia, Pericles begged off, shedding, as Æschines says, many tears at the trial, and personally entreating the jurors. But fearing how it might go with Anaxagoras, he sent him out of the city. And finding that in Phidias's case he had miscarried with the people, being afraid of impeachment, he kindled the war, which hitherto had lingered and smothered, and blew it up into a flame; hoping, by that means, to disperse and scatter these complaints and charges, and to allay their jealousy; the city usually throwing herself upon him alone, and trusting to his sole conduct, upon the urgency of great affairs and public dangers, by reason of his authority and the sway he bore.

These are given out to have been the reasons which induced Pericles not to suffer the people of Athens to yield to the proposals of the Lacedæmonians; but their truth is uncertain.

The Lacedæmonians, for their part, feeling sure that if they could once remove him, they might be at what terms they pleased with the

Athenians, sent them word that they should expel the "Pollution" with which Pericles on the mother's side was tainted, as Thucydides tells us. But the issue proved quite contrary to what those who sent the message expected; instead of bringing Pericles under suspicion and reproach, they raised him into yet greater credit and esteem with the citizens, as a man whom their enemies most hated and feared. In the same way, also, before Archidamus, who was at the head of the Peloponnesians, made his invasion into Attica, he told the Athenians beforehand, that if Archidamus, while he laid waste the rest of the country, should forbear and spare his estate, either on the ground of friendship or right of hospitality that was betwixt them, or on purpose to give his enemies an occasion of traducing him; that then he did freely bestow upon the state all his land and the buildings upon it for the public use.

The Lacedæmonians, therefore, and their allies, with a great army, invaded the Athenian territories, under the conduct of King Archidamus, and laying waste the country, marched on as far as Acharnæ, and there pitched their camp, presuming that the Athenians would never endure that, but would come out and fight them for their country's and their honour's sake. But Pericles looked upon it as dangerous to engage in battle, to the risk of the city itself, against sixty thousand men-at-arms of Peloponnesians and Bœotians; for so many they were in number that made the inroad at first; and he endeavoured to appease those who were desirous to fight, and were grieved and discontented to see how things went, and gave them good words, saying, that "trees, when they are lopped and cut, grow up again in a short time, but men, being once lost, cannot easily be recovered."

He did not convene the people into an assembly, for fear lest they should force him to act against his judgment; but, like a skilful steersman or pilot of a ship, who, when a sudden squall comes on, out at sea, makes all his arrangements, sees that all is tight and fast, and then follows the dictates of his skill, and minds the business of the ship, taking no notice of the tears and entreaties of the sea-sick and fearful passengers, so he, having shut up the city gates, and placed guards at all posts for security, followed his own reason and judgment, little regarding those that cried out against him and were angry at his management, although there were a great many of his friends that urged him with requests, and many of his enemies threatened and accused him for doing as he did, and many made songs and lampoons upon him, which were sung about the town to his disgrace, reproaching him with the cowardly exercise of his office of general, and the tame abandonment of everything to the enemy's hands.

Cleon, also, already was among his assailants, making use of the feeling against him as a step to the leadership of the people, as appears in the anapæstic verses of Hermippus—

> Satyr-king, instead of swords,
> Will you always handle words?
> Very brave indeed we find them,
> But a Teles lurks behind them.
>
> Yet to gnash your teeth you're seen,
> When the little dagger keen,
> Whetted every day anew,
> Of sharp Cleon touches you.

Pericles, however, was not at all moved by any attacks, but took all patiently, and submitted in silence to the disgrace they threw upon him and the ill-will they bore him; and, sending out a fleet of a hundred galleys to Peloponnesus, he did not go along with it in person, but stayed behind, that he might watch at home and keep the city under his own control, till the Peloponnesians broke up their camp and were gone. Yet to soothe the common people, jaded and distressed with the war, he relieved them with distributions of public moneys, and ordained new divisions of subject land. For having turned out all the people of Ægina, he parted the island among the Athenians according to lot. Some comfort, also, and ease in their miseries, they might receive from what their enemies endured. For the fleet, sailing round the Peloponnese, ravaged a great deal of the country, and pillaged and plundered the towns and smaller cities; and by land he himself entered with an army the Megarian country, and made havoc of it all. Whence it is clear that the Peloponnesians, though they did the Athenians much mischief by land, yet suffering as much themselves from them by sea, would not have protracted the war to such a length, but would quickly have given it over, as Pericles at first foretold they would, had not some divine power crossed human purposes.

In the first place, the pestilential disease, or plague, seized upon the city, and ate up all the flower and prime of their youth and strength. Upon occasion of which, the people, distempered and afflicted in their souls, as well as in their bodies, were utterly enraged like madmen against Pericles, and, like patients grown delirious, sought to lay violent hands on their physician, or, as it were, their father. They had been possessed, by his enemies, with the belief that the occasion of the plague was the crowding of the country people together into the town, forced as they were now, in the heat of the summer-weather, to dwell many of them together even as they could, in small tenements and stifling hovels, and to be tied to a lazy course of life within doors, whereas before they lived in a pure, open, and free air. The cause and author of all this, said they, is he who on account of the war has poured a multitude of people from the country in upon us within the walls, and uses all these men that he has here upon no employ or service, but keeps them pent up like cattle, to be overrun with infection from one another, affording them neither shift of quarters nor any refreshment.

With the design to remedy these evils, and do the enemy some inconvenience, Pericles got a hundred and fifty galleys ready, and having embarked many tried soldiers, both foot and horse, was about to sail out, giving great hope to his citizens, and no less alarm to his enemies, upon the sight of so great a force. And now the vessels having their complement of men, and Pericles being gone aboard his own galley, it happened that the sun was eclipsed, and it grew dark on a sudden, to the affright of all, for this was looked upon as extremely ominous. Pericles, therefore, perceiving the steersman seized with fear and at a loss what to do, took his cloak and held it up before the man's face, and screening him with it so that he could not see, asked him whether he imagined there was any great hurt, or the sign of any great hurt in this, and he answering No, "Why," said he, "and what does that differ from this, only that what has caused that darkness there, is something greater than a cloak?" This is a story which philosophers tell their scholars.

Pericles, however, after putting out to sea, seems not to have done any other exploit befitting such preparations, and when he had laid siege to the holy city Epidaurus, which gave him some hope of surrender, miscarried in his design by reason of the sickness. For it not only seized upon the Athenians, but upon all others, too, that held any sort of communication with the army.

Finding after this the Athenians ill-affected and highly displeased with him, he tried and endeavoured what he could to appease and re-encourage them. But he could not pacify or allay their anger, nor persuade or prevail with them any way, till they freely passed their votes upon him, resumed their power, took away his command from him, and fined him in a sum of money; which by their account that say least, was fifteen talents, while they who reckon most, name fifty. The name prefixed to the accusation was Cleon, as Idomeneus tells us; Simmias, according to Theophrastus; and Heraclides Ponticus gives it as Lacratidas.

After this, public troubles were soon to leave him unmolested; the people, so to say, discharged their passion in their stroke, and lost their stings in the wound. But his domestic concerns were in an unhappy condition, many of his friends and acquaintance having died in the plague time, and those of his family having long since been in disorder and in a kind of mutiny against him. For the eldest of his lawfully begotten sons, Xanthippus by name, being naturally prodigal, and marrying a young and expensive wife, the daughter of Tisander, son of Epilycus, was highly offended at his father's economy in making him but a scanty allowance, by little and little at a time. He sent, therefore, to a friend one day and borrowed some money of him in his father Pericles's name, pretending it was by his order. The man coming afterward to demand the debt, Pericles was so far from yielding to pay it, that he entered an action against him.

Upon which the young man, Xanthippus, thought himself so ill-used and disobliged that he openly reviled his father; telling first, by way of ridicule, stories about his conversations at home, and the discourses he had with the sophists and scholars that came to his house. As, for instance, how one who was a practiser of the five games of skill, having with a dart or javelin unawares against his will struck and killed Epitimus the Pharsalian, his father spent a whole day with Protagoras in a serious dispute, whether the javelin, or the man that threw it, or the masters of the games who appointed these sports, were, according to the strictest and best reason, to be accounted the cause of this mischance. Besides this, Stesimbrotus tells us that it was Xanthippus who spread abroad among the people the infamous story concerning his own wife; and in general that this difference of the young man's with his father, and the breach betwixt

them, continued never to be healed or made up till his death. For Xanthippus died in the plague time of the sickness.

At which time Pericles also lost his sister, and the greatest part of his relations and friends, and those who had been most useful and serviceable to him in managing the affairs of state. However, he did not shrink or give in upon these occasions, nor betray or lower his high spirit and the greatness of his mind under all his misfortunes; he was not even so much as seen to weep or to mourn, or even attend the burial of any of his friends or relations, till at last he lost his only remaining legitimate son. Subdued by this blow, and yet striving still, as far as he could, to maintain his principle, and to preserve and keep up the greatness of his soul, when he came, however, to perform the ceremony of putting a garland of flowers upon the head of the corpse, he was vanquished by his passion at the sight, so that he burst into exclamations, and shed copious tears, having never done any such thing in all his life before.

The city having made trial of other generals for the conduct of war, and orators for business of state, when they found there was no one who was of weight enough for such a charge, or of authority sufficient to be trusted with so great a command, regretted the loss of him, and invited him again to address and advise them, and to reassume the office of general. He, however, lay at home in dejection and mourning; but was persuaded by Alcibiades and others of his friends to come abroad and show himself to the people; who having, upon his appearance, made their acknowledgments, and apologised for their untowardly treatment of him, he undertook the public affairs once more; and, being chosen general, requested that the statute concerning base-born children, which he himself had formerly caused to be made, might be suspended; that so the name and race of his family might not, for absolute want of a lawful heir to succeed, be wholly lost and extinguished.

The case of the statute was thus: Pericles, when long ago at the height of his power in the state, having then, as has been said, children lawfully begotten, proposed a law that those only should be reputed true citizens of Athens who were born of such parents as were both Athenians. After this, the King of Egypt having sent to the people, by way of present, forty thousand bushels of wheat, which were to be shared out among the citizens, a great many actions and suits about legitimacy occurred, by virtue of that edict; cases which, till that time, had not been known nor taken notice of; and several persons suffered by false accusations. There were little less than five thousand who were convicted and sold for slaves; those who, enduring the test, remained in the government and passed muster for true Athenians were found upon the poll to be fourteen thousands and forty persons in number.

It looked strange, that a law, which had been carried so far against so many people, should be cancelled again by the same man that made it; yet the present calamity and distress which Pericles laboured under in his family broke through all objections, and prevailed with the Athenians to pity him, as one whose losses and misfortunes had sufficiently punished his former arrogance and haughtiness. His sufferings deserved, they thought, their pity, and even indignation, and his request was such as became a man to ask and men to grant; they gave him permission to enrol his son in the register of his fraternity, giving him his own name. This son afterward, after having defeated the Peloponnesians at Arginusæ, was, with his fellow-generals, put to death by the people.

About the time when his son was enrolled, it should seem the plague seized Pericles, not with sharp and violent fits, as it did others that had it, but with a dull and lingering distemper, attended with various changes and alterations, leisurely, by little and little, wasting the strength of his body, and undermining the noble faculties of his soul. So that Theophrastus, in his *Morals,* when discussing whether men's characters change with their circumstances, and their moral habits, disturbed by the ailings of their bodies, start aside from the rules of virtue, has left it upon record, that Pericles, when he was sick, showed one of his friends that came to visit him an amulet or charm that the women had hung about his neck; as much as to say, that he was very sick indeed when he would admit of such a foolery as that was.

When he was now near his end, the best of the citizens and those of his friends who were left alive, sitting about him, were speaking of the greatness of his merit, and his power, and reckoning up his famous actions and the number of his victories; for there were no less than nine trophies, which, as their chief commander and conqueror of their enemies, he had set up for the honour of the city. They

talked thus together among themselves, as though he were unable to understand or mind what they said, but had now lost his consciousness. He had listened, however, all the while, and attended to all, and, speaking out among them, said that he wondered they should commend and take notice of things which were as much owing to fortune as to anything else, and had happened to many other commanders, and, at the same time, should not speak or make mention of that which was the most excellent and greatest thing of all. "For," said he, "no Athenian, through my means, ever wore mourning."

He was indeed a character deserving our high admiration not only for his equitable and mild temper, which all along in the many affairs of his life, and the great animosities which he incurred, he constantly maintained; but also for the high spirit and feeling which made him regard it the noblest of all his honours that, in the exercise of such immense power, he never had gratified his envy or his passion, nor ever had treated any enemy as irreconcilably opposed to him.

And to me it appears that this one thing gives that otherwise childish and arrogant title a fitting and becoming significance; so dispassionate a temper, a life so pure and unblemished, in the height of power and place, might well be called Olympian, in accordance with our conceptions of the divine beings, to whom, as the natural authors of all good and of nothing evil, we ascribe the rule and government of the world. Not as the poets represent, who, while confounding us with their ignorant fancies, are themselves confuted by their own poems and fictions, and call the place, indeed, where they say the gods make their abode, a secure and quiet seat, free from all hazards and commotions, untroubled with winds or with clouds, and equally through all time illumined with a soft serenity and a pure light as though such were a home most agreeable for a blessed and immortal nature; and yet, in the meanwhile, affirm that the gods themselves are full of trouble and enmity and anger and other passions, which no way become or belong to even men that have any understanding. But this will, perhaps, seem a subject fitter for some other consideration, and that ought to be treated of in some other place.

The course of public affairs after his death produced a quick and speedy sense of the loss of Pericles. Those who, while he lived, resented his great authority, as that which eclipsed themselves, presently after his quitting the stage, making trial of other orators and demagogues, readily acknowledged that there never had been in nature such a disposition as his was, more moderate and reasonable in the height of that state he took upon him, or more grave and impressive in the mildness which he used. And that invidious arbitrary power, to which formerly they gave the name of monarchy and tyranny, did then appear to have been the chief bulwark of public safety; so great a corruption and such a flood of mischief and vice followed which he, by keeping weak and low, had withheld from notice, and had prevented from attaining incurable height through a licentious impunity.

FABIUS

c. 270–203 B.C.

HAVING related the memorable actions of Pericles, our history now proceeds to the life of Fabius. A son of Hercules and a nymph, or some woman of that country, who brought him forth on the banks of Tiber, was, it is said, the first Fabius, the founder of the numerous and distinguished family of the name. Others will have it that they were first called Fodii, because the first of the race delighted in digging pitfalls for wild beasts, *fodere* being still the Latin for to dig, and *fossa* for a ditch, and that in process of time, by the change of the two letters, they grew to be called Fabii. But be these things true or false, certain it is that this family for a long time yielded a great number of eminent persons.

Our Fabius, who was fourth in descent from that Fabius Rullus who first brought the honourable surname of Maximus into his family, was also, by way of personal nickname, called Verrucosus, from a wart on his upper lip; and in his childhood they in like manner named him Ovicula, or The Lamb, on account of his extreme mildness of temper. His slowness in speaking, his long labour and pains in learning, his deliberation in entering into the sports of other children, his easy submission to everybody, as if he had no will of his own, made those who judge superficially of him, the greater number, esteem him insensible and stupid; and few only saw that this tardiness proceeded from stability, and discerned the greatness of his mind, and the lionlikeness of his temper. But as soon as he came into employments, his virtues exerted and showed themselves; his reputed want of energy then was recognised by people in general as a freedom of passion; his slowness in words and actions, the effect of a true prudence; his want of rapidity and his sluggishness, as constancy and firmness.

Living in a great commonwealth, surrounded by many enemies, he saw the wisdom of inuring his body (nature's own weapon) to warlike exercises, and disciplining his tongue for public oratory in a style conformable to his life and character. His eloquence, indeed, had not much of popular ornament, nor empty artifice, but there was in it great weight of sense; it was strong and sententious, much after the way of Thucydides. We have yet extant his funeral oration upon the death of his son, who died consul, which he recited before the people.

He was five times consul, and in his first consulship had the honour of a triumph for the victory he gained over the Ligurians, whom he defeated in a set battle, and drove them to take shelter in the Alps, from whence they never after made any inroad or depredation upon their neighbours.

After this, Hannibal came into Italy, who, at his first entrance, having gained a great battle near the river Trebia, traversed all Tuscany with his victorious army, and, desolating the country round about, filled Rome itself with astonishment and terror. Besides the more common signs of thunder and lightning then happening, the report of several unheard-of and utterly strange portents much increased the popular consternation. For it was said that some targets sweated blood; that at Antium, when they reaped their corn, many of the ears were filled with blood; that it had rained red-hot stones; that the Falerians had seen the heavens open and several scrolls falling down, in one of which was plainly written, "Mars himself stirs his arms."

But these prodigies had no effect upon the

impetuous and fiery temper of the consul Flaminius, whose natural promptness had been much heightened by his late unexpected victory over the Gauls, when he fought them contrary to the order of the senate and the advice of his colleague. Fabius, on the other side, thought it not seasonable to engage with the enemy; not that he much regarded the prodigies, which he thought too strange to be easily understood, though many were alarmed by them; but in regard that the Carthaginians were but few, and in want of money and supplies, he deemed it best not to meet in the field a general whose army had been tried in many encounters, and whose object was a battle, but to send aid to their allies, control the movements of the various subject cities, and let the force and vigour of Hannibal waste away and expire, like a flame, for want of the aliment.

These weighty reasons did not prevail with Flaminius, who protested he would never suffer the advance of the enemy to the city, nor be reduced, like Camillus in former time, to fight for Rome within the walls of Rome. Accordingly he ordered the tribunes to draw out the army into the field; and though he himself, leaping on horseback to go out, was no sooner mounted but the beast, without any apparent cause, fell into so violent a fit of trembling and bounding that he cast his rider headlong on the ground, he was no ways deterred; but proceeded as he had begun, and marched forward up to Hannibal, who was posted near the Lake Thrasymene in Tuscany. At the moment of this engagement, there happened so great an earthquake, that it destroyed several towns, altered the course of rivers, and carried off parts of high cliffs, yet such was the eagerness of the combatants, that they were entirely insensible of it.

In this battle Flaminius fell, after many proofs of his strength and courage, and round about him all the bravest of the army; in the whole fifteen thousand were killed, and as many made prisoners. Hannibal, desirous to bestow funeral honours upon the body of Flaminius, made diligent search after it, but could not find it among the dead, nor was it ever known what became of it.

Upon the former engagement near Trebia, neither the general who wrote, nor the express who told the news, used straightforward and direct terms, nor related it otherwise than as a drawn battle, with equal loss on either side; but on this occasion as soon as Pomponius, the prætor, had the intelligence, he caused the people to assemble, and, without disguising or dissembling the matter, told them plainly, "We are beaten, O Romans, in a great battle; the consul Flaminius is killed; think, therefore, what is to be done for your safety." Letting loose his news like a gate of wind upon an open sea, he threw the city into utter confusion: in such consternation, their thoughts found no support or stay. The danger at hand at last awakened their judgments into a resolution to choose a dictator, who by the sovereign authority of his office, and by his personal wisdom and courage, might be able to manage the public affairs. Their choice unanimously fell upon Fabius, whose character seemed equal to the greatness of the office, whose age was so far advanced as to give him experience, without taking from him the vigour of action; his body could execute what his soul designed, and his temper was a happy compound of confidence and cautiousness.

Fabius, being thus installed in the office of dictator, in the first place gave the command of the horse to Lucius Minucius; and next asked leave of the senate for himself, that in time of battle he might serve on horseback, which by an ancient law amongst the Romans was forbid to their generals; whether it were, that, placing their greatest strength in their foot, they would have their commanders-in-chief posted amongst them, or else to let them know, that, how great and absolute soever their authority were, the people and senate were still their masters, of whom they must ask leave. Fabius, however, to make the authority of his charge more observable, and to render the people more submissive and obedient to him, caused himself to be accompanied with the full body of four-and-twenty lictors; and, when the surviving consul came to visit him, sent him word to dismiss his lictors with their fasces, the ensigns of authority, and appear before him as a private person.

The first solemn action of his dictatorship was very fitly a religious one: an admonition to the people, that their late overthrow had not befallen them through want of courage in their soldiers, but through the neglect of divine ceremonies in the general. He therefore exhorted them not to fear the enemy, but by extraordinary honour to propitiate the gods. This he did, not to fill their minds with superstition, but by religious feeling to raise their courage, and lessen their fear of the enemy by inspiring the belief that Heaven was on their side.

With this view, the secret prophecies called

the Sibylline Books were consulted; sundry predictions found in them were said to refer to the fortunes and events of the time; but none except the consulter was informed. Presenting himself to the people, the dictator made a vow before them to offer in sacrifice the whole product of the next season, all Italy over, of the cows, goats, swine, sheep, both in the mountains and the plains; and to celebrate musical festivities with an expenditure of the precise sum of 333 sestertia and 333 denarii, with one-third of a denarius over. The sum total of which is, in our money, 83,583 drachmas and 2 obols. What the mystery might be in that exact number is not easy to determine, unless it were in honour of the perfection of the number three, as being the first of odd numbers, the first that contains in itself multiplication, with all other properties whatsoever belonging to numbers in general.

In this manner Fabius, having given the people better heart for the future, by making them believe that the gods took their side, for his own part placed his whole confidence in himself, believing that the gods bestowed victory and good fortune by the instrumentality of valour and of prudence; and thus prepared he set forth to oppose Hannibal, not with intention to fight him, but with the purpose of wearing out and wasting the vigour of his arms by lapse of time, of meeting his want of resources by superior means, by large numbers the smallness of his forces. With this design, he always encamped on the highest grounds, where the enemy's horse could have no access to him. Still he kept pace with them; when they marched he followed them; when they encamped he did the same, but at such a distance as not to be compelled to an engagement, and always keeping upon the hills, free from the insults of their horse; by which means he gave them no rest, but kept them in a continual alarm.

But this his dilatory way gave occasion in his own camp for suspicion of want of courage; and this opinion prevailed yet more in Hannibal's army. Hannibal was himself the only man who was not deceived, who discerned his skill and detected his tactics, and saw, unless he could by art or force bring him to battle, that the Carthaginians, unable to use the arms in which they were superior, and suffering the continual drain of lives and treasure in which they were inferior, would in the end come to nothing. He resolved, therefore, with all the arts and subtleties of war to break his

measures, and to bring Fabius to an engagement; like a cunning wrestler, watching every opportunity to get good hold and close with his adversary. He at one time attacked, and sought to distract his attention, tried to draw him off in various directions, and endeavoured in all ways to tempt him from his safe policy.

All this artifice, though it had no effect upon the firm judgment and conviction of the dictator, yet upon the common soldier, and even upon the general of the horse himself, it had too great an operation: Minucius, unseasonably eager for action, bold and confident, humoured the soldiery, and himself contributed to fill them with wild eagerness and empty hopes, which they vented in reproaches upon Fabius, calling him Hannibal's pedagogue, since he did nothing else but follow him up and down and wait upon him. At the same time, they cried up Minucius for the only captain worthy to command the Romans; whose vanity and presumption rose so high in consequence, that he insolently jested at Fabius's encampment upon the mountains, saying that he seated them there as on a theatre, to behold the flames and desolation of their country. And he would sometimes ask the friends of the general, whether it were not his meaning, by thus leading them from mountain to mountain, to carry them at last (having no hopes on earth) up into heaven, or to hide them in the clouds from Hannibal's army?

When his friends reported these things to the dictator, persuading him that, to avoid the general obloquy, he should engage the enemy, his answer was, "I should be more faint-hearted than they make me, if, through fear of idle reproaches, I should abandon my own convictions. It is no inglorious thing to have fear for the safety of our country, but to be turned from one's course by men's opinions, by blame, and by misrepresentation, shows a man unfit to hold an office such as this, which, by such conduct, he makes the slave of those whose errors it is his business to control."

An oversight of Hannibal occurred soon after. Desirous to refresh his horse in some good pasture-grounds, and to draw off his army, he ordered his guides to conduct him to the district of Casinum. They, mistaking his bad pronunciation, led him and his army to the town of Casilinum, on the frontier of Campania which the river Lothronus, called by the Romans Vulturnus, divides in two parts. The country around is enclosed by mountains, with a valley opening towards the sea, in which the river overflowing forms a quantity of marsh lands with deep banks of sand, and discharges itself into the sea on a very unsafe and rough shore. While Hannibal was proceeding hither, Fabius, by his knowledge of the roads, succeeded in making his way around before him, and despatched four thousand choice men to seize the exit from it and stop him up, and lodged the rest of his army upon the neighbouring hills, in the most advantageous places; at the same time detaching a party of his lightest armed men to fall upon Hannibal's rear; which they did with such success, that they cut off eight hundred of them, and put the whole army in disorder. Hannibal, finding the error and the danger he was fallen into, immediately crucified the guides; but considered the enemy to be so advantageously posted, that there was no hope of breaking through them; while his soldiers began to be despondent and terrified, and to think themselves surrounded with embarrassments too difficult to be surmounted.

Thus reduced, Hannibal had recourse to stratagem; he caused two thousand head of oxen which he had in his camp to have torches or dry fagots well fastened to their horns, and lighting them in the beginning of the night, ordered the beasts to be driven on towards the heights commanding the passages out of the valley and the enemy's posts; when this was done, he made his army in the dark leisurely march after them. The oxen at first kept a slow orderly pace, and with their lighted heads resembled an army marching by night, astonishing the shepherds and herdsmen of the hills about. But when the fire burnt down the horns of the beasts to the quick, they no longer observed their sober pace, but, unruly and wild with their pain, ran dispersed about, tossing their heads and scattering the fire round about them upon each other and setting light as they passed to the trees.

This was a surprising spectacle to the Romans on guard upon the heights. Seeing flames which appeared to come from men advancing with torches, they were possessed with the alarm that the enemy was approaching in various quarters, and that they were being surrounded; and, quitting their post, abandoned the pass, and precipitately retired to their camp on the hills. They were no sooner gone, but the light-armed of Hannibal's men, according to his order, immediately seized the heights, and soon after the whole army, with all the baggage, came up and safely marched through the passes.

Fabius, before the night was over, quickly found out the trick; for some of the beasts fell into his hands; but for fear of an ambush in the dark, he kept his men all night to their arms in the camp. As soon as it was day, he attacked the enemy in the rear, where, after a good deal of skirmishing in the uneven ground, the disorder might have become general, but that Hannibal detached from his van a body of Spaniards, who, of themselves active and nimble, were accustomed to the climbing of mountains. These briskly attacked the Roman troops, who were in heavy armour, killed a good many, and left Fabius no longer in condition to follow the enemy. This action brought the extreme of obloquy and contempt upon the dictator; they said it was now manifest that he was not only inferior to his adversary, as they had always thought, in courage, but even in that conduct, foresight, and generalship, by which he had proposed to bring the war to an end.

And Hannibal, to enhance their anger against him, marched with his army close to the lands and possessions of Fabius, and, giving orders to his soldiers to burn and destroy all the country about, forbade them to do the least damage in the estates of the Roman general, and placed guards for their security. This, when reported at Rome, had the effect with the people which Hannibal desired. Their tribunes raised a thousand stories against him, chiefly at the instigation of Metilius, who, not so much out of hatred to him as out of friendship to Minucius, whose kinsman he was, thought by depressing Fabius to raise his friend.

The senate on their part were also offended with him for the bargain he had made with Hannibal about the exchange of prisoners, the conditions of which were, that, after exchange made of man for man, if any on either side remained, they should be redeemed at the price of two hundred and fifty drachmas a head. Upon the whole account, there remained two hundred and forty Romans unexchanged, and the senate now not only refused to allow money for the ransoms, but also reproached Fabius for making a contract, contrary to the honour and interest of the commonwealth, for redeeming men whose cowardice had put them in the hands of the enemy. Fabius heard and endured all this with invincible patience; and, having no money by him, and on the other side being resolved to keep his word with Hannibal and not to abandon the captives, he despatched his son to Rome to sell land, and to bring with him the price, sufficient to discharge the ransoms; which was punctually performed by his son and delivery accordingly made to him of the prisoners, amongst whom many, when they were released, made proposals to repay the money; which Fabius in all cases declined.

About this time, he was called to Rome by the priests, to assist, according to the duty of his office, at certain sacrifices, and was thus forced to leave the command of the army with Minucius; but before he parted, not only charged him as his commander-in-chief, but besought and entreated him not to come, in his absence, to a battle with Hannibal.

His commands, entreaties, and advice were lost upon Minucius, for his back was no sooner turned but the new general immediately sought occasions to attack the enemy. And notice being brought him that Hannibal had sent out a great party of his army to forage, he fell upon a detachment of the remainder, doing great execution, and driving them to their very camp, with no little terror to the rest, who apprehended their breaking in upon them; and when Hannibal had recalled his scattered forces to the camp, he, nevertheless, without any loss, made his retreat, a success which aggravated his boldness and presumption, and filled the soldiers with rash confidence.

The news spread to Rome, where Fabius, on being told it, said that what he most feared was Minucius's success; but the people, highly elated, hurried to the Forum to listen to an address from Metilius, the tribune, in which he infinitely extolled the valour of Minucius, and fell bitterly upon Fabius, accusing him for want not merely of courage, but even of loyalty; and not only him, but also many other eminent and considerable persons; saying that it was they that had brought the Carthaginians into Italy, with the design to destroy the liberty of the people; for which end they had at once put the supreme authority into the hands of a single person, who by his slowness and delays might give Hannibal leisure to establish himself in Italy, and the people of Carthage time and opportunity to supply him with fresh succours to complete his conquest.

Fabius came forward with no intention to answer the tribune, but only said that they should expedite the sacrifices, that so he might speedily return to the army to punish Minucius, who had presumed to fight contrary to his orders; words which immediately possessed the people with the belief that Minucius stood in danger of his life. For it was in the power of the dictator to imprison and to put to death, and they feared that Fabius, of a mild temper in general, would be as hard to be appeased when once irritated, as he was slow to be provoked.

Nobody dared to raise his voice in opposition; Metilius alone, whose office of tribune gave him security to say what he pleased (for in the time of a dictatorship that magistrateal one preserves his authority), boldly applied himself to the people in the behalf of Minucius: that they should not suffer him to be made a sacrifice to the enmity of Fabius, nor permit him to be destroyed, like the son of Manlius Torquatus, who was beheaded by his father for a victory fought and triumphantly won against order; he exhorted them to take away from Fabius that absolute power of a dictator, and to put it into more worthy hands, better able and more inclined to use it for the public good.

These impressions very much prevailed upon the people, though not so far as wholly to dispossess Fabius of the dictatorship. But they decreed that Minucius should have an equal authority with the dictator in the conduct of the war; which was a thing then without precedent, though a little later it was again practised after the disaster at Cannæ; when the dictator, Marcus Junius, being with the army, they chose at Rome Fabius Buteo dictator, that he might create new senators, to supply the numerous places of those who were killed. But as soon as, once acting in public, he had filled those vacant places with a sufficient number, he immediately dismissed his lictors, and withdrew from all his attendance, and mingling like a common person with the rest of the people, quietly went about his own affairs in the Forum.

The enemies of Fabius thought they had sufficiently humiliated and subdued him by raising Minucius to be his equal in authority; but they mistook the temper of the man, who looked upon their folly as not his loss, but like Diogenes, who, being told that some persons derided him, made answer, "But I am not derided," meaning that only those were really insulted on whom such insults made an impression, so Fabius, with great tranquillity and unconcern, submitted to what happened, and contributed a proof to the argument of the philosophers that a just and good man is not capable of being dishonoured. His only vexation arose from his fear lest this ill counsel, by supplying opportunities to the diseased military ambition of his subordinate, should damage the public cause.

Lest the rashness of Minucius should now at once run headlong into some disaster, he returned back with all privacy and speed to the army; where he found Minucius so elevated with his new dignity, that, a joint-authority not contenting him, he required by turns to have the command of the army every other day. This Fabius rejected, but was contented that the army should be divided; thinking each general singly would better command his part, than partially command the whole. The first and fourth legion he took for his own division, the second and third he delivered to Minucius; so also of the auxiliary forces each had an equal share.

Minucius, thus exalted, could not contain himself from boasting of his success in humiliating the high and powerful office of the dictatorship. Fabius quietly reminded him that it was, in all wisdom, Hannibal, and not Fabius, whom he had to combat; but if he must needs contend with his colleague, it had best be in diligence and care for the preservation of Rome; that it might not be said, a man so favoured by the people served them worse than he who had been ill-treated and disgraced by them.

The young general, despising these admonitions as the false humility of age, immediately removed with the body of his army, and encamped by himself. Hannibal, who was not ignorant of all these passages, lay watching his advantage from them. It happened that between his army and that of Minucius there was a certain eminence, which seemed a very advantageous and not difficult post to encamp upon; the level field around it appeared, from a distance, to be all smooth and even, though it had many inconsiderable ditches and dips in it, not discernible to the eye. Hannibal, had he pleased, could easily have possessed himself of this ground; but he had reserved it for a bait, or train, in proper season, to draw the Romans to an engagement. Now that Minucius and Fabius were divided, he thought the opportunity fair for his purpose; and, therefore, having in the night-time lodged a convenient number of his men in these ditches and hollow places, early in the morning he sent forth a small detachment, who, in the

sight of Minucius, proceeded to possess themselves of the rising ground.

According to his expectation, Minucius swallowed the bait, and first sent out his light troops, and after them some horse, to dislodge the enemy; and, at last, when he saw Hannibal in person advancing to the assistance of his men, marched down with his whole army drawn up. He engaged with the troops on the eminence, and sustained their missiles; the combat for some time was equal; but as soon as Hannibal perceived that the whole army was now sufficiently advanced within the toils he had set for them, so that their backs were open to his men whom he had posted in the hollows, he gave the signal; upon which they rushed forth from various quarters, and with loud cries furiously attacked Minucius in the rear. The surprise and the slaughter was great, and struck universal alarm and disorder through the whole army. Minucius himself lost all his confidence; he looked from officer to officer, and found all alike unprepared to face the danger, and yielding to a flight, which, however, could not end in safety. The Numidian horsemen were already in full victory riding about the plain, cutting down the fugitives.

Fabius was not ignorant of this danger of his countrymen; he foresaw what would happen from the rashness of Minucius, and the cunning of Hannibal; and, therefore, kept his men to their arms, in readiness to wait the event; nor would he trust to the reports of others, but he himself, in front of his camp, viewed all that passed. When, therefore, he saw the army of Minucius encompassed by the enemy, and that by their countenance and shifting their ground they appeared more disposed to flight than to resistance, with a great sigh, striking his hand upon his thigh, he said to those about him, "O Hercules! how much sooner than I expected, though later than he seemed to desire, hath Minucius destroyed himself!" He then commanded the ensigns to be led forward, and the army to follow, telling them, "We must make haste to rescue Minucius, who is a valiant man, and a lover of his country; and if he hath been too forward to engage the enemy, at another time we will tell him of it."

Thus, at the head of his men, Fabius marched up to the enemy, and first cleared the plain of the Numidians; and next fell upon those who were charging the Romans in the rear, cutting down all that made opposition, and obliging the rest to save themselves by a hasty retreat, lest they should be environed as the Romans had been. Hannibal, seeing so sudden a change of affairs, and Fabius, beyond the force of his age, opening his way through the ranks up the hillside, that he might join Minucius, warily forbore, sounded a retreat, and drew off his men into their camp; while the Romans on their part were no less contented to retire in safety. It is reported that upon this occasion Hannibal said jestingly to his friends: "Did not I tell you, that this cloud which always hovered upon the mountains would, at some time or other, come down with a storm upon us?"

Fabius, after his men had picked up the spoils of the field, retired to his own camp, without saying any harsh or reproachful thing to his colleague; who, also, on his part, gathering his army together, spoke and said to them: "To conduct great matters and never commit a fault is above the force of human nature; but to learn and improve by the faults we have committed, is that which becomes a good and sensible man. Some reasons I may have to accuse fortune, but I have many more to thank her; for in a few hours she hath cured a long mistake, and taught me that I am not the man who should command others, but have need of another to command me; and that we are not to contend for victory over those to whom it is our advantage to yield. Therefore in everything else henceforth the dictator must be your commander; only in showing gratitude towards him I will still be your leader, and always be the first to obey his orders."

Having said this, he commanded the Roman eagles to move forward, and all his men to follow him to the camp of Fabius. The soldiers, then, as he entered, stood amazed at the novelty of the sight, and were anxious and doubtful what the meaning might be. When he came near the dictator's tent, Fabius went forth to meet him, on which he at once laid his standards at his feet, calling him with a loud voice his father; while the soldiers with him saluted the soldiers here as their patrons, the term employed by freedmen to those who gave them their liberty. After silence was obtained, Minucius said, "You have this day, O dictator, obtained two victories; one by your valour and conduct over Hannibal, and another by your wisdom and goodness over your colleague; by one victory you preserved, and by the other instructed us; and when we were

already suffering one shameful defeat from Hannibal, by another welcome one from you we were restored to honour and safety. I can address you by no nobler name than that of a kind father, though a father's beneficence falls short of that I have received from you. From a father I individually received the gift of life; to you I owe its preservation not for myself only, but for all these who are under me." After this, he threw himself into the arms of the dictator; and in the same manner the soldiers of each army embraced one another with gladness and tears of joy.

Not long after, Fabius laid down the dictatorship, and consuls were again created. Those who immediately succeeded observed the same method in managing the war, and avoided all occasions of fighting Hannibal in a pitched battle; they only succoured their allies, and preserved the towns from falling off to the enemy.

But afterwards, when Terentius Varro, a man of obscure birth, but very popular and bold, had obtained the consulship, he soon made it appear that by his rashness and ignorance he would stake the whole commonwealth on the hazard. For it was his custom to declaim in all assemblies, that, as long as Rome employed generals like Fabius, there never would be an end of the war; vaunting that whenever he should get sight of the enemy, he would that same day free Italy from the strangers. With these promises he so prevailed, that he raised a greater army than had ever yet been sent out of Rome. There were enlisted eighty-eight thousand fighting men; but what gave confidence to the populace, only terrified the wise and experienced, and none more than Fabius; since if so great a body, and the flower of the Roman youth, should be cut off, they could not see any new resource for the safety of Rome.

They addressed themselves, therefore, to the other consul, Æmilius Paulus, a man of great experience in war, but unpopular, and fearful also of the people, who once before upon some impeachment had condemned him; so that he needed encouragement to withstand his colleague's temerity. Fabius told him, if he would profitably serve his country, he must no less oppose Varro's ignorant eagerness than Hannibal's conscious readiness, since both alike conspired to decide the fate of Rome by a battle. "It is more reasonable," he said to him, "that you should believe me than Varro, in matters relating to Hannibal, when I tell you that if for this year you abstain from fighting with him, either his army will perish of itself, or else he will be glad to depart of his own will. This evidently appears, inasmuch as, notwithstanding his victories, none of the countries or towns of Italy come in to him, and his army is not now the third part of what it was at first." To this Paulus is said to have replied, "Did I only consider myself, I should rather choose to be exposed to the weapons of Hannibal than once more to the suffrages of my fellow-citizens, who are urgent for what you disapprove; yet since the cause of Rome is at stake, I will rather seek in my conduct to please and obey Fabius than all the world besides."

These good measures were defeated by the importunity of Varro; whom, when they were both come to the army, nothing would content but a separate command, that each consul should have his day; and when his turn came, he posted his army close to Hannibal, at a village called Cannæ, by the river Aufidus. It was no sooner day, but he set up the scarlet coat flying over his tent, which was the signal of battle. This boldness of the consul, and the numerousness of his army, double theirs, startled the Carthaginians; but Hannibal commanded them to their arms, and with a small train rode out to take a full prospect of the enemy as they were now forming in their ranks, from a rising ground not far distant. One of his followers, called Gisco, a Carthaginian of equal rank with himself, told him that the numbers of the enemy were astonishing; to which Hannibal replied with a serious countenance, "There is one thing, Gisco, yet more astonishing, which you take no notice of"; and when Gisco inquired what, answered, that "in all those great numbers before us, there is not one man called Gisco." This unexpected jest of their general made all the company laugh, and as they came down from the hill they told it to those whom they met, which caused a general laughter amongst them all, from which they were hardly able to recover themselves. The army, seeing Hannibal's attendants come back from viewing the enemy in such a laughing condition, concluded that it must be profound contempt of the enemy, that made their general at this moment indulge in such hilarity.

According to his usual manner, Hannibal employed stratagems to advantage himself. In the first place, he so drew up his men that the wind was at their backs, which at that time blew with a perfect storm of violence, and, sweeping over the great plains of sand, carried before it a cloud of dust over the Carthaginian army into the faces of the Romans, which much disturbed them in the fight. In the next place, all his best men he put into his wings; and in the body which was somewhat more advanced than the wings, placed the worst and the weakest of his army. He commanded those in the wings, that, when the enemy had made a thorough charge upon that middle advance body, which he knew would recoil, as not being able to withstand their shock, and when the Romans in their pursuit should be far enough engaged within the two wings, they should, both on the right and the left, charge them in the flank, and endeavour to encompass them.

This appears to have been the chief cause of the Roman loss. Pressing upon Hannibal's front, which gave ground, they reduced the form of his army into a perfect half-moon, and gave ample opportunity to the captains of the chosen troops to charge them right and left on their flanks, and to cut off and destroy all who did not fall back before the Carthaginian wings united in their rear. To this general calamity, it is also said, that a strange mistake among the cavalry much contributed. For the horse of Æmilius receiving a hurt and throwing his master, those about him immediately alighted to aid the consul; and the Roman troops, seeing their commanders thus quitting their horses, took it for a sign that they should all dismount and charge the enemy on foot. At the sight of this, Hannibal was heard to say, "This pleases me better than if they had been delivered to me bound hand and foot." For the particulars of this engagement, we refer our readers to those authors who have written at large upon the subject.

The consul Varro, with a thin company, fled to Venusia; Æmilius Paulus, unable any longer to oppose the flight of his men, or the pursuit of the enemy, his body all covered with wounds, and his soul no less wounded with grief, sat himself down upon a stone, expecting the kindness of a despatching blow. His face was so disfigured, and all his person so stained with blood, that his very friends and domestics passing by knew him not. At last Cornelius Lentulus, a young man of patrician race, perceiving who he was, alighted from his horse, and, tendering it to him, desired him to get up and save a life so necessary to the safety of the commonwealth, which, at this time, would dearly want so great a captain. But nothing could prevail upon him to accept of the offer; he obliged young Lentulus, with tears in his eyes, to remount his horse; then standing up, he gave him his hand, and commanded him to tell Fabius Maximus that Æmilius Paulus had followed his directions to his very last, and had not in the least deviated from those measures which were agreed between them; but that it was his hard fate to be overpowered by Varro in the first place, and secondly by Hannibal. Having despatched Lentulus with this commission, he marked where the slaughter was greatest, and there threw himself upon the swords of the enemy. In this battle it is reported that fifty thousand Romans were slain, four thousand prisoners taken in the field, and ten thousand in the camp of both consuls.

The friends of Hannibal earnestly persuaded him to follow up his victory, and pursue the flying Romans into the very gates of Rome, assuring him that in five days' time he might sup in the Capitol; nor is it easy to imagine what consideration hindered him from it. It would seem rather that some supernatural or divine intervention caused the hesitation and timidity which he now displayed, and which made Barcas, a Carthaginian, tell him with indignation, "You know, Hannibal, how to gain a victory, but not how to use it." Yet it produced a marvellous revolution in his affairs; he, who hitherto had not one town, market, or seaport in his possession, who had nothing for the subsistence of his men but what he pillaged from day to day, who had no place of retreat or basis of operation, but was roving, as it were, with a huge troop of banditti, now became master of the best provinces and towns of Italy, and of Capua itself, next to Rome the most flourishing and opulent city, all which came over to him, and submitted to his authority.

It is the saying of Euripides, that "a man is in ill-case when he must try a friend," and so neither, it would seem, is a state in a good one, when it needs an able general. And so it was with the Romans; the counsels and actions of Fabius, which, before the battle, they had branded as cowardice and fear, now, in the other extreme, they accounted to have been more than human wisdom; as though nothing but a divine power of intellect could have seen so far, and foretold contrary to the judgment of all others, a result which, even now it had arrived, was hardly credible. In

him, therefore, they placed their whole remaining hopes; his wisdom was the sacred altar and temple to which they fled for refuge, and his counsels, more than anything, preserved them from dispersing and deserting their city, as in the time when the Gauls took possession of Rome. He, whom they esteemed fearful and pusillanimous when they were, as they thought, in a prosperous condition, was now the only man, in this general and unbounded dejection and confusion, who showed no fear, but walked the streets with an assured and serene countenance, addressed his fellow-citizens, checked the women's lamentations, and the public gatherings of those who wanted thus to vent their sorrows. He caused the senate to meet, he heartened up the magistrates, and was himself as the soul and life of every office.

He placed guards at the gates of the city to stop the frightened multitude from flying; he regulated and confined their mournings for their slain friends, both as to time and place; ordering that each family should perform such observances within private walls, and that they should continue only the space of one month, and then the whole city should be purified. The feast of Ceres happening to fall within this time, it was decreed that the solemnity should be intermitted, lest the fewness, and the sorrowful countenance of those who should celebrate it, might too much expose to the people the greatness of their loss; besides that, the worship most acceptable to the gods is that which comes from cheerful hearts. But those rites which were proper for appeasing their anger, and procuring auspicious signs and presages, were by the direction of the augurs carefully performed. Fabius Pictor, a near kinsman to Maximus, was sent to consult the oracle of Delphi; and about the same time, two vestals having been detected to have been violated, the one killed herself, and the other, according to custom, was buried alive.

Above all, let us admire the high spirit and equanimity of this Roman commonwealth; that when the consul Varro came beaten and flying home, full of shame and humiliation, after he had so disgracefully and calamitously managed their affairs, yet the whole senate and people went forth to meet him at the gates of the city, and received him with honour and respect. And, silence being commanded, the magistrates and chief of the senate, Fabius amongst them, commended him before the people, because he did not despair of the safety of the commonwealth, after so great a loss, but was come to take the government into his hands, to execute the laws, and aid his fellow-citizens in their prospect of future deliverance.

When word was brought to Rome that Hannibal, after the fight, had marched with his army into other parts of Italy, the hearts of the Romans began to revive, and they proceeded to send out generals and armies. The most distinguished commands were held by Fabius Maximus and Claudius Marcellus, both generals of great fame, though upon opposite grounds. For Marcellus, as we have set forth in his life, was a man of action and high spirit, ready and bold with his own hand, and, as Homer describes his warriors, fierce, and delighting in fights. Boldness, enterprise, and daring to match those of Hannibal, constituted his tactics, and marked his engagements. But Fabius adhered to his former principles, still persuaded that, by following close and not fighting him, Hannibal and his army would at least be tired out and consumed, like a wrestler in too high condition, whose very excess of strength makes him the more likely suddenly to give way and lose it.

Posidonius tells us that the Romans called Marcellus their sword, and Fabius their buckler; and that the vigour of the one, mixed with the steadiness of the other, made a happy compound that proved the salvation of Rome. So that Hannibal found by experience that encountering the one, he met with a rapid, impetuous river, which drove him back, and still made some breach upon him; and by the other, though silently and quietly passing by him, he was insensibly washed away and consumed; and, at last, was brought to this, that he dreaded Marcellus when he was in motion, and Fabius when he sat still.

During the whole course of this war, he had still to do with one or both of these generals; for each of them was five times consul, and, as prætors or proconsuls or consuls, they had always a part in the government of the army, till, at last, Marcellus fell into the trap which Hannibal had laid for him, and was killed in his fifth consulship.

But all his craft and subtlety were unsuccessful upon Fabius, who only once was in some danger of being caught, when counterfeit letters came to him from the principal inhabitants of Metapontum, with promises to deliver up their town if he would come before

it with his army, and intimations that they should expect him. This train had almost drawn him in; he resolved to march to them with part of his army, and was diverted only by consulting the omens of the birds, which he found to be inauspicious; and not long after it was discovered that the letters had been forged by Hannibal, who, for his reception, had laid an ambush to entertain him. This, perhaps, we must rather attribute to the favour of the gods than to the prudence of Fabius.

In preserving the towns and allies from revolt by fair and gentle treatment, and in not using rigour, or showing a suspicion upon every light suggestion, his conduct was remarkable. It is told of him, that being informed of a certain Marsian, eminent for courage and good birth, who had been speaking underhand with some of the soldiers about deserting, Fabius was so far from using severity against him, that he called for him, and told him he was sensible of the neglect that had been shown to his merit and good service, which, he said, was a great fault in the commanders who reward more by favour than by desert; "but, henceforth, whenever you are aggrieved," said Fabius, "I shall consider it your fault, if you apply yourself to any one but to me"; and when he had so spoken, he bestowed an excellent horse, and other presents upon him; and, from that time forwards, there was not a faithfuller and more trusty man in the whole army.

With good reason he judged, that, if those who have the government of horses and dogs endeavour by gentle usage to cure their angry and untractable tempers, rather than by cruelty and beating, much more should those who have the command of men try to bring them to order and discipline by the mildest and fairest means, and not treat them worse than gardeners do those wild plants, which, with care and attention, lose gradually the savageness of their nature, and bear excellent fruit.

At another time, some of his officers informed him that one of their men was very often absent from his place, and out at nights; he asked them what kind of man he was; they all answered, that the whole army had not a better man, that he was a native of Lucania, and proceeded to speak of several actions which they had seen him perform. Fabius made strict inquiry, and discovered at last that these frequent excursions which he ventured upon were to visit a young girl, with whom he was in love. Upon which he gave private order to some of his men to find out the woman and secretly convey her into his own tent; and then sent for the Lucanian, and, calling him aside, told him, that he very well knew how often he had been out away from the camp at night, which was a capital transgression against military discipline and the Roman laws, but he knew also how brave he was, and the good services he had done; therefore, in consideration of them, he was willing to forgive him his fault; but to keep him in good order, he was resolved to place one over him to be his keeper, who should be accountable for his good behaviour. Having said this, he produced the woman, and told the soldier, terrified and amazed at the adventure, "This is the person who must answer for you; and by your future behaviour we shall see whether your night rambles were on account of love, or for any other worse design."

Another passage there was, something of the same kind, which gained him possession of Tarentum. There was a young Tarentine in the army that had a sister in Tarentum, then in possession of the enemy, who entirely loved her brother, and wholly depended upon him. He, being informed that a certain Bruttian, whom Hannibal had made a commander of the garrison, was deeply in love with his sister, conceived hopes that he might possibly turn it to the advantage of the Romans. And having first communicated his design to Fabius, he left the army as a deserter in show, and went over to Tarentum. The first days passed, and the Bruttian abstained from visiting the sister; for neither of them knew that the brother had notice of the amour between them. The young Tarentine, however, took an occasion to tell his sister how he had heard that a man of station and authority had made his addresses to her, and desired her, therefore, to tell him who it was; "for," said he, "if he be a man that has bravery and reputation, it matters not what countryman he is, since at this time the sword mingles all nations, and makes them equal; compulsion makes all things honourable; and in a time when right is weak, we may be thankful if might assumes a form of gentleness."

Upon this the woman sent for her friend, and made the brother and him acquainted; and whereas she henceforth showed more countenance to her lover than formerly, in the same degrees that her kindness increased,

his friendship, also, with the brother advanced. So that at last our Tarentine thought this Bruttian officer well enough prepared to receive the offers he had to make him, and that it would be easy for a mercenary man, who was in love, to accept, upon the terms proposed, the large rewards promised by Fabius. In conclusion, the bargain was struck, and the promise made of delivering the town. This is the common tradition, though some relate the story otherwise, and say, that this woman, by whom the Bruttian was inveigled to betray the town, was not a native of Tarentum, but a Bruttian born, and was kept by Fabius as his concubine; and being a country-woman and an acquaintance of the Bruttian governor, he privately sent her to him to corrupt him.

Whilst these matters were thus in process, to draw off Hannibal from scenting the design, Fabius sends orders to the garrison in Rhegium, that they should waste and spoil the Bruttian country, and should also lay siege to Caulonia, and storm the place with all their might. These were a body of eight thousand men, the worst of the Roman army, who had most of them been runaways, and had been brought home by Marcellus from Sicily, in dishonour, so that the loss of them would not be any great grief to the Romans. Fabius, therefore, threw out these men as a bait for Hannibal, to divert him from Tarentum; who instantly caught at it, and led his forces to Caulonia; in the meantime, Fabius sat down before Tarentum. On the sixth day of the siege, the young Tarentine slips by night out of the town, and, having carefully observed the place where the Bruttian commander, according to agreement, was to admit the Romans, gave an account of the whole matter to Fabius; who thought it not safe to rely wholly upon the plot, but, while proceeding with secrecy to the post, gave order for a general assault to be made on the other side of the town, both by land and sea. This being accordingly executed, while the Tarentines hurried to defend the town on the side attacked, Fabius received the signal from the Bruttian, scaled the walls, and entered the town unopposed.

Here, we must confess, ambition seems to have overcome him. To make it appear to the world that he had taken Tarentum by force and his own prowess, and not by treachery, he commanded his men to kill the Bruttians before all others; yet he did not succeed in establishing the impression he desired, but merely gained the character of perfidy and cruelty. Many of the Tarentines were also killed, and thirty thousand of them were sold for slaves; the army had the plunder of the town, and there was brought into the treasury three thousand talents. Whilst they were carrying off everything else as plunder, the officer who took the inventory asked what should be done with their gods, meaning the pictures and statues; Fabius answered, "Let us leave their angry gods to the Tarentines." Nevertheless, he removed the colossal statue of Hercules, and had it set up in the capitol, with one of himself on horseback, in brass, near it; proceedings very different from those of Marcellus on a like occasion, and which, indeed, very much set off in the eyes of the world his clemency and humanity, as appears in the account of his life.

Hannibal, it is said, was within five miles of Tarentum, when he was informed that the town was taken. He said openly, "Rome then has also got a Hannibal; as we won Tarentum, so have we lost it." And, in private with some of his confidants, he told them, for the first time, that he always thought it difficult, but now he held it impossible, with the forces he then had, to master Italy.

Upon this success, Fabius had a triumph decreed him at Rome, much more splendid than his first; they looked upon him now as a champion who had learned to cope with his antagonist, and could now easily foil his arts and prove his best skill ineffectual. And, indeed, the army of Hannibal was at this time partly worn away with continual action, and partly weakened and become dissolute with overabundance and luxury. Marcus Livius, who was governor of Tarentum when it was betrayed to Hannibal, and then retired into the citadel, which he kept till the town was retaken, was annoyed at these honours and distinctions, and, on one occasion, openly declared in the senate, that by his resistance, more than by any action of Fabius, Tarentum had been recovered; on which Fabius laughingly replied, "You say very true, for if Marcus Livius had not lost Tarentum, Fabius Maximus had never recovered it."

The people, amongst other marks of gratitude, gave his son the consulship of the next year; shortly after whose entrance upon his office, there being some business on foot about provision for the war, his father, either by reason of age and infirmity, or perhaps out of design to try his son, came up to him on horseback. While he was still at a distance, the young consul observed it, and bade one of his lictors command his father to alight, and tell him if he had any business with the consul, he should come on foot. The standers-by seemed offended at the imperiousness of the son towards a father so venerable for his age and his authority, and turned their eyes in silence towards Fabius. He, however, instantly alighted from his horse, and with open arms came up, almost running, and embraced his son, saying, "Yes, my son, you do well, and understand well what authority you have received, and over whom you are to use it. This was the way by which we and our forefathers advanced the dignity of Rome, preferring ever her honour and service to our own fathers and children."

And, in fact, it is told that the great-grandfather of our Fabius, who was undoubtedly the greatest man of Rome in his time, both in reputation and authority, who had been five times consul, and had been honoured with several triumphs for victories obtained by him, took pleasure in serving as lieutenant under his own son, when he went as consul to his command. And when afterwards his son had a triumph bestowed upon him for his good service, the old man followed, on horseback, his triumphant chariot, as one of his attendants; and made it his glory, that while he really was, and was acknowledged to be, the greatest man in Rome, and held a father's full power over his son, he yet submitted himself to the laws and the magistrate.

But the praises of our Fabius are not bounded here. He afterwards lost his son, and was remarkable for bearing the loss with the moderation becoming a pious father and a wise man, and as it was the custom amongst the Romans, upon the death of any illustrious person, to have a funeral oration recited by some of the nearest relations, he took upon himself that office, and delivered a speech in the Forum, which he committed afterwards to writing.

After Cornelius Scipio, who was sent into Spain, had driven the Carthaginians, defeated by him in many battles, out of the country, and had gained over to Rome many towns and nations with large resources, he was received at his coming home with unexampled joy and acclamation of the people; who, to show their gratitude, elected him consul for the year ensuing. Knowing what high expectation they had of him, he thought the occupation of contesting Italy with Hannibal a mere old man's employment, and proposed no less a task to himself than to make Carthage the seat of the war, fill Africa with arms and devastation, and so oblige Hannibal, instead of invading the countries of others, to draw back and defend his own. And to this end he proceeded to exert all the influence he had with the people.

Fabius, on the other side, opposed the undertaking with all his might, alarming the city, and telling them that nothing but the temerity of a hot young man could inspire them with such dangerous counsels, and sparing no means, by word or deed, to prevent it. He prevailed with the senate to espouse his sentiments; but the common people thought that he envied the fame of Scipio, and that he was afraid lest this young conqueror should achieve some great and noble exploit, and have the glory, perhaps, of driving Hannibal out of Italy, or even of ending the war, which had for so many years continued and been protracted under his management.

To say the truth, when Fabius first opposed this project of Scipio, he probably did it out of caution and prudence, in consideration only of the public safety, and of the danger which the commonwealth might incur; but when he found Scipio every day increasing in the esteem of the people, rivalry and ambition led him further, and made him violent and personal in his opposition. For he even applied to Crassus, the colleague of Scipio, and urged him not to yield the command to Scipio, but that, if his inclinations were for it, he should himself in person lead the army to Carthage. He also hindered the giving of money to Scipio for the war; so that he was forced to raise it upon his own credit and interest from the cities of Etruria, which were extremely attached to him. On the other side, Crassus would not stir against him, nor remove out of Italy, being, in his own nature, averse to all contention, and also having, by his office of high priest, religious duties to retain him.

Fabius, therefore, tried other ways to oppose the design; he impeded the levies, and he declaimed, both in the senate and to the people, that Scipio was not only himself flying from Hannibal, but was also endeavouring to drain Italy of all its forces, and to spirit away the youth of the country to a foreign war, leaving behind them their parents, wives, and children, and the city itself, a defenceless prey to the conquering and undefeated enemy at their doors. With this he so far alarmed the people, that at last they would only allow Scipio for the war the legions which were in Sicily, and three hundred, whom he particularly trusted, of those men who had served with him in Spain. In these transactions, Fabius seems to have followed the dictates of his own wary temper.

But, after that Scipio was gone over into Africa, when news almost immediately came to Rome of wonderful exploits and victories, of which the fame was confirmed by the spoils he sent home; of a Numidian king taken prisoner; of a vast slaughter of their men; of two camps of the enemy burnt and destroyed, and in them a great quantity of arms and horses; and when, hereupon, the Carthaginians were compelled to send envoys to Hannibal to call him home, and leave his idle hopes in Italy, to defend Carthage; when, for such eminent and transcending services, the whole people of Rome cried up and extolled the actions of Scipio; even then, Fabius contended that a successor should be sent in his place, alleging for it only the old reason of the mutability of fortune, as if she would be weary of long favouring the same person.

With this language many did begin to feel offended; it seemed to be morosity and ill-will, the pusillanimity of old age, or a fear, that had now become exaggerated, of the skill of Hannibal. Nay, when Hannibal had put his army on shipboard, and taken his leave of Italy, Fabius still could not forbear to oppose and disturb the universal joy of Rome, expressing his fears and apprehensions, telling them that the commonwealth was never in more danger than now, and that Hannibal was a more formidable enemy under the walls of Carthage than ever he had been in Italy; that it would be fatal to Rome whenever Scipio should encounter his victorious army, still warm with the blood of so many Roman generals, dictators, and consuls slain. And the people were, in some degree, startled with these declamations, and were brought to believe that the further off Hannibal was, the nearer was their danger. Scipio, however, shortly afterwards fought Hannibal, and utterly defeated him, humbled the pride of Carthage beneath his feet, gave his countrymen joy and exultation beyond all their hopes, and—

Long shaken on the seas restored the state.

Fabius Maximus, however, did not live to see the prosperous end of this war, and the final overthrow of Hannibal, nor to rejoice in the re-established happiness and security of the commonwealth; for about the time that Hannibal left Italy, he fell sick and died. At Thebes, Epaminondas died so poor that he was buried at the public charge; one small iron coin was all, it is said, that was found in his house. Fabius did not need this, but the people, as a mark of their affection, defrayed the expenses of his funeral by a private contribution from each citizen of the smallest piece of coin; thus owning him their common father, and making his end no less honourable than his life.

FABIUS and PERICLES
Compared

WE have here had two lives rich in examples, both of civil and military excellence. Let us first compare the two men in their warlike capacity.

Pericles presided in his commonwealth when it was in its most flourishing and opulent condition, great and growing in power; so that it may be thought it was rather the common success and fortune that kept him from any fall or disaster. But the task of Fabius, who undertook the government in the worst and most difficult times, was not to preserve and maintain the well-established felicity of a prosperous state, but to raise and uphold a sinking and ruinous commonwealth. Besides, the victories of Cimon, the trophies of Myronides and Leocrates, with the many famous exploits of Tolmides, were employed by Pericles rather to fill the city with festive entertainments and solemnities than to enlarge and secure its empire. Whereas, Fabius, when he took upon him the government, had the frightful object before his eyes of Roman armies destroyed, of their generals and consuls slain, of lakes and plains and forests strewed with the dead bodies, and rivers stained with the blood of his fellow-citizens; and yet, with his mature and solid counsels, with the firmness of his resolution, he, as it were, put his shoulder to the falling commonwealth, and kept it up from foundering through the failings and weakness of others.

Perhaps it may be more easy to govern a city broken and tamed with calamities and adversity, and compelled by danger and necessity to listen to wisdom, than to set a bridle on wantonness and temerity, and rule a people pampered and restive with long prosperity as were the Athenians when Pericles held the reins of government. But then again, not to be daunted nor discomposed with the vast heap of calamities under which the people of Rome at that time groaned and succumbed, argues a courage in Fabius and a strength of purpose more than ordinary.

We may set Tarentum retaken against Samos won by Pericles, and the conquest of Euboea we may well balance with the towns of Campania; though Capua itself was reduced by the consuls Fulvius and Appius. I do not find that Fabius won any set battle but that against the Ligurians, for which he had his triumph; whereas Pericles erected nine trophies for as many victories obtained by land and by sea. But no action of Pericles can be compared to that memorable rescue of Minucius, when Fabius redeemed both him and his army from utter destruction, a noble act combining the highest valour, wisdom and humanity.

On the other side, it does not appear that Pericles was ever so overreached as Fabius was by Hannibal with his flaming oxen. His enemy there had, without his agency, put himself accidentally into his power, yet Fabius let him slip in the night, and, when day came, was worsted by him, was anticipated in the moment of success, and mastered by his prisoner.

If it is the part of a good general, not only to provide for the present, but also to have a clear foresight of things to come, in this point Pericles is the superior; for he admonished the Athenians, and told them beforehand the ruin the war would bring upon them, by their grasping more than they were able to manage. But Fabius was not so good a prophet, when he denounced to the Romans that the undertaking of Scipio would be the destruction of the commonwealth. So that Pericles was a good prophet of bad success, and Fabius was a bad prophet of success that was good. And, indeed, to lose an advantage through diffidence is no less blamable in a general than to fall into danger for want of foresight; for both these faults, though of a contrary nature, spring from the same root, want of judgment and experience.

As for their civil policy, it is imputed to

Pericles that he occasioned the war, since no terms of peace, offered by the Lacedæmonians, would content him. It is true, I presume, that Fabius, also, was not for yielding any point to the Carthaginians, but was ready to hazard all, rather than lessen the empire of Rome. The mildness of Fabius towards his colleague Minucius does, by way of comparison, rebuke and condemn the exertions of Pericles to banish Cimon and Thucydides, noble, aristocratic men, who by his means suffered ostracism. The authority of Pericles in Athens was much greater than that of Fabius in Rome. Hence it was more easy for him to prevent miscarriages arising from the mistakes and insufficiency of other officers; only Tolmides broke loose from him, and, contrary to his persuasions, unadvisedly fought with the Bœotians, and was slain. The greatness of his influence made all others submit and conform themselves to his judgment. Whereas Fabius, sure and unerring himself, for want of that general power,

had not the means to obviate the miscarriages of others; but it had been happy for the Romans if his authority had been greater, for so, we may presume, their disasters had been fewer.

As to liberality and public spirit, Pericles was eminent in never taking any gifts, and Fabius, for giving his own money to ransom his soldiers, though the sum did not exceed six talents. Than Pericles, meantime, no man had ever greater opportunities to enrich himself, having had presents offered him from so many kings and princes and allies, yet no man was ever more free from corruption. And for the beauty and magnificence of temples and public edifices with which he adorned his country, it must be confessed, that all the ornaments and structures of Rome, to the time of the Cæsars, had nothing to compare, either in greatness of design or of expense, with the lustre of those which Pericles only erected at Athens.

ALCIBIADES

C. 450–404 B.C.

ALCIBIADES, as it is supposed, was anciently descended from Eurysaces, the son of Ajax, by his father's side; and by his mother's side from Alcmæon. Dinomache, his mother, was the daughter of Megacles. His father, Clinias, having fitted out a galley at his own expense, gained great honour in the sea-fight at Artemisium, and was afterwards slain in the battle of Coronea, fighting against the Bœotians. Pericles and Ariphron, the sons of Xanthippus, nearly related to him, became the guardians of Alcibiades. It has been said not untruly that the friendship which Socrates felt for him has much contributed to his fame; and certain it is, that, though we have no account from any writer concerning the mother of Nicias or Demosthenes, of Lamachus or Phormion, of Thrasybulus or Theramenes, notwithstanding these were all illustrious men of the same period, yet we know even the nurse of Alcibiades, that her country was Lacedæmon, and her name Amycla, and that Zopyrus was his teacher and attendant; the one being recorded by Antisthenes, and the other by Plato.

It is not, perhaps, material to say anything of

the beauty of Alcibiades, only that it bloomed with him in all the ages of his life, in his infancy, in his youth, and in his manhood; and, in the peculiar character becoming to each of these periods, gave him, in every one of them, a grace and a charm. What Euripides says, that—

Of all fair things the autumn, too, is fair,

is by no means universally true. But it happened so with Alcibiades, amongst few others, by reason of his happy constitution and natural vigour of body. It is said that his lisping, when he spoke, became him well, and gave a grace and persuasiveness to his rapid speech. Aristophanes takes notice of it in the verses in which he jests at Theorus: "How like a *colax* he is," says Alcibiades, meaning a *corax;* on which it is remarked,—

How very happily he lisped the truth.

Archippus also alludes to it in a passage where he ridicules the son of Alcibiades:—

That people may believe him like his father,
He walks like one dissolved in luxury,
Lets his robe trail behind him on the ground,
Carelessly leans his head, and in his talk
Affects to lisp.

His conduct displayed many great inconsistencies and variations, not unnaturally, in accordance with the many and wonderful vicissitudes of his fortunes; but among the many strong passions of his real character, the one most prevailing of all was his ambition and desire of superiority, which appears in several anecdotes told of his sayings whilst he was a child. Once being hard pressed in wrestling, and fearing to be thrown, he got the hand of his antagonist to his mouth, and bit it with all his force; and when the other loosed his hold presently, he said, "You bite, Alcibiades, like a woman!" "No," replied he, "like a lion." Another time as he played at dice in the street, being then but a child, a loaded cart came that way, when it was his turn to throw; at first he called to the driver to stop, because he was to throw in the way over which the cart was to pass; but the man giving him no attention and driving on, when the rest of the boys divided and gave way, Alcibiades threw himself on his face before the cart and, stretching himself out, bade the carter pass on now if he would; which so startled the man, that he put back his horses, while all that saw it were terrified, and, crying out, ran to assist Alcibiades.

When he began to study, he obeyed all his other masters fairly well, but refused to learn upon the flute, as a sordid thing, and not becoming a free citizen; saying that to play on the lute or the harp does not in any way disfigure a man's body or face, but one is hardly to be known by the most intimate friends when playing on the flute. Besides, one who plays on the harp may speak or sing at the same time; but the use of the flute stops the mouth, intercepts the voice, and prevents all articulation. "Therefore," said he, "let the Theban youths pipe, who do not know how to speak, but we Athenians, as our ancestors have told us, have Minerva for our patroness, and Apollo for our protector, one of whom threw away the flute, and the other stripped the flute-player of his skin."

Thus, between raillery and good earnest, Alcibiades kept not only himself but others from learning, as it presently became the talk of the young boys, how Alcibiades despised playing on the flute, and ridiculed those who studied it. In consequence of which, it ceased to be reckoned amongst the liberal accomplishments, and became generally neglected.

It is stated in the invective which Antiphon wrote against Alcibiades, that once, when he was a boy, he ran away to the house of Democrates, one of those who made a favourite of him, and that Ariphon had determined to cause proclamation to be made for him, had not Pericles diverted him from it, by saying, that if he were dead, the proclaiming of him could only cause it to be discovered one day sooner, and if he were safe, it would be a reproach to him as long as he lived. Antiphon also says, that he killed one of his own servants with the blow of a staff in Sibyrtius's wrestling ground. But it is unreasonable to give credit to all that is objected by an enemy, who makes open profession of his design to defame him.

It was manifest that the many well-born persons who were continually seeking his company, and making their court to him, were attracted and captivated by his brilliant and extraordinary beauty only. But the affection which Socrates entertained for him is a great evidence of the natural noble qualities and good disposition of the boy, which Socrates, indeed, detected both in and under his personal beauty; and, hearing that his wealth and station, and the great number both of strangers and Athenians who flattered and caressed him, might at last corrupt him, resolved, if possible, to interpose, and preserve so hopeful a plant from perishing in the flower, before its fruit came to perfection.

For never did fortune surround and enclose a man with so many of those things which we vulgarly call goods, or so protect him from every weapon of philosophy, and fence him from every access of free and searching words, as she did Alcibiades; who, from the beginning, was exposed to the flatteries of those who sought merely his gratification, such as might well unnerve him, and indispose him to listen to any real adviser or instructor. Yet such was the happiness of his genius, that he discerned Socrates from the rest, and admitted him, whilst he drove away the wealthy and the noble who made court to him. And, in a little time, they grew intimate, and Alcibiades, listening now to language entirely free from every thought of unmanly fondness and silly displays of affection, finding himself with one who sought to lay open to him the deficiencies of his mind, and repress his vain and foolish arrogance—

Dropped like the craven cock his conquered wing.

He esteemed these endeavours of Socrates as most truly a means which the gods made use of for the care and preservation of youth, and began to think meanly of himself and to admire him; to be pleased with his kindness, and to stand in awe of his virtue; and, unawares to himself, there became formed in his mind that reflex image and reciprocation of Love, or Anteros, that Plato talks of. It was a matter of general wonder, when people saw him joining Socrates in his meals and his exercises, living with him in the same tent, whilst he was reserved and rough to all others who made their addresses to him, and acted, indeed, with great insolence to some of them.

As in particular to Anytus, the son of Anthemion, one who was very fond of him, and invited him to an entertainment which he had prepared for some strangers. Alcibiades refused the invitation; but, having drunk to excess at his own house with some of his companions, went thither with them to play some frolic; and, standing at the door of the room where the guests were enjoying themselves, and seeing the tables covered with gold and silver cups, he commanded his servants to take away the one-half of them, and carry them to his own house; and then, disdaining so much as to enter into the room himself, as soon as he had done this, went away. The company was indignant, and exclaimed at his rude and insulting conduct; Anytus, however, said, on the contrary, he had shown great consideration and tenderness in taking only a part when he might have taken all.

He behaved in the same manner to all others who courted him except only one stranger, who, as the story is told, having but a small estate, sold it all for about a hundred staters, which he presented to Alcibiades, and besought him to accept. Alcibiades, smiling and well pleased at the thing, invited him to supper, and, after a very kind entertainment, gave him his gold again, requiring him, moreover, not to fail to be present the next day, when the public revenue was offered to farm, and to outbid all others. The man would have excused himself, because the contract was so large, and would cost many talents; but Alcibiades, who had at that time a private pique against the existing farmers of the revenue, threatened to have him beaten if he refused.

The next morning, the stranger, coming to the market-place, offered a talent more than the existing rate; upon which the farmers, enraged and consulting together, called upon him to name his sureties, concluding that he could find none. The poor man, being startled at the proposal, began to retire; but Alcibiades, standing at a distance, cried out to the magistrates: "Set my name down; he is a friend of mine; I will be security for him." When the other bidders heard this, they perceived that all their contrivance was defeated; for their way was, with the profits of the second year to pay the rent for the year preceding; so that, not seeing any other way to extricate themselves out of the difficulty, they began to entreat the stranger, and offered him a sum of money. Alcibiades would not suffer him to accept of less than a talent; but when that was paid down, he commanded him to relinquish the bargain, having by this device relieved his necessity.

Though Socrates had many and powerful rivals, yet the natural good qualities of Alcibiades gave his affection the mastery. His words overcame him so much, as to draw tears from his eyes, and to disturb his very soul. Yet sometimes he would abandon himself to flatterers, when they proposed to him varieties of pleasure, and would desert Socrates; who, then, would pursue him, as if he had been a fugitive slave. He despised every one else, and had no reverence or awe for any one but him. Cleanthes, the philosopher, speaking of one to whom he was attached, says his only hold on him was by his ears, while his rivals had all the others offered them; and there is no question that Alcibiades was very easily caught by pleasure; and the expression used by Thucydides about the excesses of his habitual course of living gives occasion to believe so.

But those who endeavoured to corrupt Alcibiades took advantage chiefly of his vanity and ambition, and thrust him on unseasonably to undertake great enterprises, persuading him, that as soon as he began to concern himself in public affairs, he would not only obscure the rest of the generals and statesmen, but outdo the authority and the reputation which Pericles himself had gained in Greece. But in the same manner as iron which is softened by the fire grows hard with the cold and all its parts are closed again, so, as often as Socrates observed Alcibiades to be misled by luxury or pride, he reduced and corrected him by his addresses, and made him humble and modest, by showing him in how many things he was deficient, and how very far from perfection in virtue.

When he was past his childhood, he went once to a grammar-school, and asked the master for one of Homer's books; and he making answer that he had nothing of Homer's, Alcibiades gave him a blow with his fist, and went away. Another schoolmaster telling him that he had Homer corrected by himself; "How?" said Alcibiades, "And do you employ your time in teaching children to read? You, who are able to amend Homer, may well undertake to instruct men." Being once desirous to speak with Pericles, he went to his house and was told there that he was not at leisure, but busied in considering how to give up his accounts to the Athenians; Alcibiades, as he went away, said, "It were better for him to consider how he might avoid giving up his accounts at all."

Whilst he was very young, he was a soldier in the expedition against Potidæa, where Socrates lodged in the same tent with him, and stood next to him in battle. Once there happened a sharp skirmish, in which they both behaved with signal bravery; but Alcibiades receiving a wound, Socrates threw himself before him to defend him, and beyond any question saved him and his arms from the enemy, and so in all justice might have challenged the prize of valour. But the generals appearing eager to adjudge the honour of Alcibiades, because of his rank, Socrates, who desired to increase his thirst after glory of a noble kind, was the first to give evidence for him, and pressed them to crown him, and to decree to him the complete suit of armour. Afterwards, in the battle of Delium, when the Athenians were routed, and Socrates with a few others was retreating on foot, Alcibiades, who was on horseback, observing it, would not pass on, but stayed to shelter him from the danger, and brought him safe off, though the enemy pressed hard upon them, and cut off many. But this happened some time after.

He gave a box on the ear to Hipponicus, the father of Callias, whose birth and wealth made him a person of great influence and repute. And this he did unprovoked by any passion or quarrel between them, but only because, in a frolic, he had agreed with his companions to do it. People were justly offended at this insolence when it became known through the city; but early the next morning, Alcibiades went to his house and knocked at the door, and being admitted to him, took off his outer garment, and presenting his naked body, desired him to scourge and chastise him as he pleased. Upon this Hipponicus forgot all his resentment, and not only pardoned him, but

soon after gave him his daughter Hipparete in marriage.

Some say that it was not Hipponicus, but his son, Callias, who gave Hipparete to Alcibiades, together with a portion of ten talents, and that after, when she had a child, Alcibiades forced him to give ten talents more, upon pretence that such was the agreement if she brought him any children. Afterwards, Callias, for fear of coming to his death by his means, declared, in a full assembly of the people, that, if he should happen to die without children, the state should inherit his house and all his goods.

Hipparete was a virtuous and dutiful wife, but, at last, growing impatient of the outrages done to her by her husband's continual entertaining of courtesans, as well strangers as Athenians, she departed from him and retired to her brother's house. Alcibiades seemed not at all concerned at this, and lived on still in the same luxury; but the law requiring that she should deliver to the archon in person, and not by proxy, the instrument by which she claimed a divorce, when, in obedience to the law, she presented herself before him to perform this, Alcibiades came in, caught her up, and carried her home through the market-place, no one daring to oppose him nor to take her from him. She continued with him till her death, which happened not long after, when Alcibiades had gone to Ephesus. Nor is this violence to be thought so very enormous or unmanly. For the law, in making her who desires to be divorced appear in public, seems to design to give her husband an opportunity of treating with her, and endeavouring to retain her.

Alcibiades had a dog which cost him seventy minas, and was a very large one, and very handsome. His tail, which was his principal ornament, he caused to be cut off, and his acquaintances exclaiming at him for it, and telling him that all Athens was sorry for the dog, and cried out upon him for this action, he laughed, and said, "Just what I wanted has happened then. I wished the Athenians to talk about this, that they might not say something worse of me."

It is said that the first time he came into the assembly was upon occasion of a largess of money which he made to the people. This was not done by design, but as he passed along he heard a shout, and inquiring the cause, and having learned that there was a donative making to the people, he went in amongst them and gave money also. The multitude thereupon applauding him, and shouting, he was so transported at it, that he forgot a quail which he had under his robe, and the bird, being frighted with the noise, flew off; upon which the people made louder acclamations than before, and many of them started up to pursue the bird; and one Antiochus, a pilot, caught it and restored it to him, for which he was ever after a favourite with Alcibiades.

He had great advantages for entering public life; his noble birth, his riches, the personal courage he had shown in divers battles, and the multitude of his friends and dependants, threw open, so to say, folding-doors for his admittance. But he did not consent to let his power with the people rest on anything, rather than on his own gift of eloquence. That he was a master in the art of speaking, the comic poets bear him witness; and the most eloquent of public speakers, in his oration against Midias, allows that Alcibiades, among other perfections, was a most accomplished orator. If, however, we give credit to Theophrastus, who of all philosophers was the most curious inquirer, and the greatest lover of history, we are to understand that Alcibiades had the highest capacity for inventing, for discerning what was the right thing to be said for any purpose, and on any occasion; but aiming not only at saying what was required, but also at saying it well, in respect, that is, of words and phrases, when these did not readily occur, he would often pause in the middle of his discourse for want of the apt word, and would be silent and stop till he could recollect himself, and had considered what to say.

His expenses in horses kept for the public games, and in the number of his chariots, were matter of great observation; never did any one but he, either private person or king, send seven chariots to the Olympic games. And to have carried away at once the first, the second, and the fourth prize, as Thucydides says, or the third, as Euripides relates it, outdoes far away every distinction that ever was known or thought of in that kind. Euripides celebrates his success in this manner:—

—But my song to you,
Son of Clinias, is due.
Victory is noble; how much more
To do as never Greek before;
To obtain in the great chariot race
The first, the second, and third place;
With easy step advanced to fame

To bid the herald three times claim
The olive for one victor's name.

The emulation displayed by the deputations of various states in the presents which they made to him, rendered this success yet more illustrious. The Ephesians erected a tent for him, adorned magnificently; the city of Chios furnished him with provender for his horses and with great numbers of beasts for sacrifice; and the Lesbians sent him wine and other provisions for the many great entertainments which he made.

Yet in the midst of all this he escaped not without censure, occasioned either by the ill-nature of his enemies or by his own misconduct. For it is said, that one Diomedes, an Athenian, a worthy man and a friend to Alcibiades, passionately desiring to obtain the victory at the Olympic games, and having heard much of a chariot which belonged to the state at Argos, where he knew that Alcibiades had great power and many friends, prevailed with him to undertake to buy the chariot. Alcibiades did indeed buy it, but then claimed it for his own, leaving Diomedes to rage at him, and to call upon the gods and men to bear witness to the injustice. It would seem there was a suit at law commenced upon this occasion, and there is yet extant an oration concerning the chariot, written by Isocrates in defence of the son of Alcibiades. But the plaintiff in this action is named Tisias, and not Diomedes.

As soon as he began to intermeddle in the government, which was when he was very young, he quickly lessened the credit of all who aspired to the confidence of the people except Phæax, the son of Erasistratus, and Nicias, the son of Niceratus, who alone could contest it with him. Nicias was arrived at a mature age, and was esteemed their first general. Phæax was but a rising statesman like Alcibiades; he was descended from noble ancestors, but was his inferior, as in many other things, so, principally, in eloquence. He possessed rather the art of persuading in private conversation than of debate before the people, and was, as Eupolis said of him—

The best of talkers, and of speakers worst.

There is extant an oration written by Phæax against Alcibiades, in which, amongst other things, it is said, that Alcibiades made daily use at his table of many gold and silver vessels, which belonged to the commonwealth, as if they had been his own.

There was a certain Hyperbolus, of the township of Perithœdæ, whom Thucydides also speaks of as a man of bad character, a general butt for the mockery of all the comic writers of the time, but quite unconcerned at the worst things they could say, and, being careless of glory, also insensible of shame; a temper which some people call boldness and courage, whereas it is indeed impudence and recklessness. He was liked by nobody, yet the people made frequent use of him, when they had a mind to disgrace or calumniate any persons in authority.

At this time, the people, by his persuasions, were ready to proceed to pronounce the sentence of ten years' banishment, called ostracism. This they made use of to humiliate and drive out of the city such citizens as outdid the rest in credit and power, indulging not so much perhaps their apprehensions as their jealousies in this way. And when, at this time, there was no doubt but that the ostracism would fall upon one of those three, Alcibiades contrived to form a coalition of parties, and, communicating his project to Nicias, turned the sentence upon Hyperbolus himself. Others say, that it was not with Nicias, but Phæax, that he consulted, and by help of his party procured the banishment of Hyperbolus, when he least suspected it. For, before that time, no mean or obscure person had ever fallen under that punishment, so that Plato, the comic poet, speaking of Hyperbolus, might well say—

The man deserved the fate; deny't who can?
Yes, but the fate did not deserve the man;
Not for the like of him and his slave-brands
Did Athens put the sherd into our hands.

But we have given elsewhere a fuller statement of what is known to us of the matter.

Alcibiades was not less disturbed at the distinctions which Nicias gained amongst the enemies of Athens than at the honours which the Athenians themselves paid to him. For though Alcibiades was the proper appointed person to receive all Lacedæmonians when they came to Athens, and had taken particular care of those that were made prisoners at Pylos, yet, after they had obtained the peace and restitution of the captives, by the procurement chiefly of Nicias, they paid him very special attentions. And it was commonly said in Greece, that the war was begun by Pericles, and that Nicias made an end of it, and the peace was generally called the peace of Nicias. Alcibiades was extremely annoyed at this,

and being full of envy, set himself to break the league. First, therefore, observing that the Argives, as well out of fear as hatred to the Lacedæmonians, sought for protection against them, he gave them a secret assurance of alliance with Athens. And communicating, as well in person as by letters, with the chief advisers of the people there, he encouraged them not to fear the Lacedæmonians, nor make concessions to them, but to wait a little, and keep their eyes on the Athenians, who, already, were all but sorry they had made peace, and would soon give it up.

And afterwards, when the Lacedæmonians had made a league with the Bœotians and had not delivered up Panactum entire, as they ought to have done by the treaty, but only after first destroying it, which gave great offence to the people of Athens, Alcibiades laid hold of that opportunity to exasperate them more highly. He exclaimed fiercely against Nicias, and accused him of many things, which seemed probable enough: as that, when he was general, he made no attempt himself to capture their enemies that were shut up in the isle of Sphacteria, but, when they were afterwards made prisoners by others, he procured their release and sent them back to the Lacedæmonians, only to get favour with them; that he would not make use of his credit with them to prevent their entering into this confederacy with the Bœotians and Corinthians, and yet, on the other side, that he sought to stand in the way of those Greeks who were inclined to make an alliance and friendship with Athens, if the Lacedæmonians did not like it.

It happened, at the very time when Nicias was by these arts brought into disgrace with the people, that ambassadors arrived from Lacedæmon, who, at their first coming, said what seemed very satisfactory, declaring that they had full powers to arrange all matters in dispute upon fair and equal terms. The council received their propositions, and the people were to assemble on the morrow to give them audience. Alcibiades grew very apprehensive of this, and contrived to gain a secret conference with the ambassadors. When they were met, he said: "What is it you intend, you men of Sparta? Can you be ignorant that the council always acts with moderation and respect towards ambassadors, but that the people are full of ambition and great designs? So that, if you let them know what full powers your commission gives you, they will urge and press you to unreasonable conditions. Quit, therefore, this indiscreet simplicity, if you expect to obtain equal terms from the Athenians, and would not have things extorted from you contrary to your inclinations, and begin to treat with the people upon some reasonable articles, not avowing yourselves plenipotentiaries; and I will be ready to assist you, out of good-will to the Lacedæmonians." When he had said thus, he gave them his oath for the performance of what he promised, and by this way drew them from Nicias to rely entirely upon himself, and left them full of admiration of the discernment and sagacity they had seen in him.

The next day, when the people were assembled and the ambassadors introduced, Alcibiades, with great apparent courtesy, demanded of them, with what powers they were come. They made answer that they were not come as plenipotentiaries. Instantly upon that, Alcibiades, with a loud voice, as though he had received and not done the wrong, began to call them dishonest prevaricators, and to urge that such men could not possibly come with a purpose to say or do anything that was sincere. The council was incensed, the people were in a rage, and Nicias, who knew nothing of the deceit and the imposture, was in the greatest confusion, equally surprised and ashamed at such a change in the men. So thus the Lacedæmonian ambassadors were utterly rejected, and Alcibiades was declared general, who presently united the Argives, the Eleans, and the people of Mantinea, into a confederacy with the Athenians.

No man commended the method by which Alcibiades effected all this, yet it was a great political feat thus to divide and shake almost all Peloponnesus, and to combine so many men in arms against the Lacedæmonians in one day before Mantinea; and, moreover, to remove the war and the danger so far from the frontier of the Athenians, that even success would profit the enemy but little, should they be conquerors, whereas, if they were defeated, Sparta itself was hardly safe.

After this battle at Mantinea, the select thousand of the army of the Argives attempted to overthrow the government of the people in Argos, and make themselves masters of the city; and the Lacedæmonians came to their aid and abolished the democracy. But the people took arms again, and gained the advantage, and Alcibiades came in to their aid and completed the victory, and persuaded them to build long walls, and by that means

to join their city to the sea, and so to bring it wholly within the reach of the Athenian power. To this purpose he procured them builders and masons from Athens, and displayed the greatest zeal for their service, and gained no less honour and power to himself than to the commonwealth of Athens.

He also persuaded the people of Patræ to join their city to the sea, by building long walls; and when some one told them, by way of warning, that the Athenians would swallow them up at last, Alcibiades made answer, "Possibly it may be so, but it will be by little and little, and beginning at the feet, whereas the Lacedæmonians will begin at the head and devour you all at once."

Nor did he neglect either to advise the Athenians to look to their interests by land, and often put the young men in mind of the oath which they had made at Agraulos, to the effect that they would account wheat and barley, and vines and olives, to be the limits of Attica; by which they were taught to claim a title to all land that was cultivated and productive.

But with all these words and deeds, and with all this sagacity and eloquence, he intermingled exorbitant luxury and wantonness, in his eating and drinking and dissolute living; wore long purple robes like a woman, which dragged after him as he went through the market-place; caused the planks of his galley to be cut away, that so he might lie the softer, his bed not being placed on the boards, but hanging upon girths. His shield, again, which was richly gilded, had not the usual ensigns of the Athenians, but a Cupid, holding a thunderbolt in his hand, was painted upon it. The sight of all this made the people of good repute in the city feel disgust and abhorrence, and apprehension also, at his free living, and his contempt of law, as things monstrous in themselves, and indicating designs of usurpation. Aristophanes has well expressed the people's feeling towards him—

They love, and hate, and cannot do without him.

And still more strongly, under a figurative expression,—

Best rear no lion in your state, 'tis true;
But treat him like a lion if you do.

The truth is, his liberalities, his public shows, and other munificence to the people, which were such as nothing could exceed, the glory of his ancestors, the force of his eloquence, the grace of his person, his strength of body, joined with his great courage and knowledge in military affairs, prevailed upon the Athenians to endure patiently his excesses, to indulge many things to him, and, according to their habit, to give the softest names to his faults, attributing them to youth and good nature.

As, for example, he kept Agatharcus, the painter, a prisoner till he had painted his whole house, but then dismissed him with a reward. He publicly struck Taureas, who exhibited certain shows in opposition to him and contended with him for the prize. He selected for himself one of the captive Mehan women, and had a son by her, whom he took care to educate. This the Athenians styled great humanity, and yet he was the principal cause of the slaughter of all the inhabitants of the isle of Melos who were of age to bear arms, having spoken in favour of that decree. When Aristophon, the painter, had drawn Nemea sitting and holding Alcibiades in her arms, the multitude seemed pleased with the piece, and thronged to see it, but older people disliked and disrelished it, and looked on these things as enormities, and movements towards tyranny. So that it was not said amiss by Archestratus, that Greece could not support a second Alcibiades.

Once, when Alcibiades succeeded well in an oration which he made, and the whole assembly attended upon him to do him honour, Timon, the misanthrope, did not pass slightly by him, nor avoid him, as did others, but purposely met him, and taking him by the hand, said, "Go on boldly, my son, and increase in credit with the people, for thou wilt one day bring them calamities enough." Some that were present laughed at the saying, and some reviled Timon; but there were others upon whom it made a deep impression; so various was the judgment which was made of him, and so irregular his own character.

The Athenians, even in the lifetime of Pericles, had already cast a longing eye upon Sicily; but did not attempt anything till after his death. Then, under pretence of aiding their confederates, they sent succours upon all occasions to those who were oppressed by the Syracusans, preparing the way for sending over a greater force. But Alcibiades was the person who inflamed this desire of theirs to the height, and prevailed with them no longer to proceed secretly, and by little and little, in their design, but to sail out with a great fleet, and undertake at once to make themselves masters of the island. He possessed the people with great hopes, and he himself entertained

yet greater; and the conquest of Sicily, which was the utmost bound of their ambition, was but the mere outset of his expectation.

Nicias endeavoured to divert the people from the expedition, by representing to them that the taking of Syracuse would be a work of great difficulty; but Alcibiades dreamed of nothing less than the conquest of Carthage and Libya, and by the accession of these conceiving himself at once made master of Italy and Peloponnesus, seemed to look upon Sicily as little more than a magazine for the war. The young men were soon elevated with these hopes, and listened gladly to those of riper years, who talked wonders of the countries they were going to; so that you might see great numbers sitting in the wrestling grounds and public places, drawing on the ground the figure of the island and the situation of Libya and Carthage.

Socrates, the philosopher, and Meton, the astrologer, are said, however, never to have hoped for any good to the commonwealth from this war; the one, it is to be supposed, presaging what would ensue, by the intervention of his attendant Genius; and the other, either upon rational consideration of the project or by use of the art of divination, conceived fears for its issue, and, feigning madness, caught up a burning torch, and seemed as if he would have set his own house on fire. Others report, that he did not take upon him to act the madman, but secretly in the night set his house on fire, and the next morning besought the people, that for his comfort, after such a calamity, they would spare his son from the expedition. By which artifice he deceived his fellow-citizens, and obtained of them what he desired.

Together with Alcibiades, Nicias, much against his will, was appointed general; and he endeavoured to avoid the command, not the less on account of his colleague. But the Athenians thought the war would proceed more prosperously, if they did not send Alcibiades free from all restraint, but tempered his heat with the caution of Nicias. This they chose the rather to do, because Lamachus, the third general, though he was of mature years, yet in several battles had appeared no less hot and rash than Alcibiades himself. When they began to deliberate of the number of forces, and of the manner of making the necessary provisions, Nicias made another attempt to oppose the design, and to prevent the war; but Alcibiades contradicted him, and carried his point with the people. And one Demostratus, an orator, proposing to give the generals absolute power over the preparations and the whole management of the war, it was presently decreed so.

When all things were fitted for the voyage, many unlucky omens appeared. At that very time the feast of Adonis happened in which the women were used to expose, in all parts of the city, images resembling dead men carried out to their burial, and to represent funeral solemnities by lamentations and mournful songs. The mutilation, however, of the images of Mercury, most of which, in one night, had their faces all disfigured, terrified many persons who were wont to despise most things of that nature. It was given out that it was done by the Corinthians, for the sake of the Syracusans, who were their colony, in hopes that the Athenians, by such prodigies, might be induced to delay or abandon the war.

But the report gained no credit with the people, nor yet the opinion of those who would not believe that there was anything ominous in the matter, but that it was only an extravagant action, committed, in that sort of sport which runs into licence, by wild young men coming from a debauch. Alike enraged and terrified at the thing, looking upon it to proceed from a conspiracy of persons who designed some commotions in the state, the council, as well as the assembly of the people, which were held frequently in a few days' space, examined diligently everything that might administer ground for suspicion.

During this examination, Androcles, one of the demagogues, produced certain slaves and strangers before them, who accused Alcibiades and some of his friends of defacing other images in the same manner, and of having profanely acted the sacred mysteries at a drunken meeting, where one Theodorus represented the herald, Polytion the torch-bearer, and Alcibiades the chief priest, while the rest of the party appeared as candidates for initiation, and received the title of Initiates. These were the matters contained in the articles of information which Thessalus, the son of Cimon, exhibited against Alcibiades, for his impious mockery of the goddesses Ceres and Proserpine. The people were highly exasperated and incensed against Alcibiades upon this accusation, which being aggravated by Androcles, the most malicious of all his enemies, at first disturbed his friends exceedingly.

But when they perceived that all the seamen designed for Sicily were for him, and the soldiers also, and when the Argive and Mantinean auxiliaries, a thousand men at arms, openly declared that they had undertaken this distant maritime expedition for the sake of Alcibiades, and that, if he was ill-used, they would all go home, they recovered their courage, and became eager to make use of the present opportunity for justifying him. At this his enemies were again discouraged, fearing lest the people should be more gentle to him in their sentence, because of the occasion they had for his service. Therefore, to obviate this, they contrived that some other orators, who did not appear to be enemies to Alcibiades, but really hated him no less than those who avowed it, should stand up in the assembly and say that it was a very absurd thing that one who was created general of such an army with absolute power, after his troops were assembled, and the confederates were come, should lose the opportunity, whilst the people were choosing his judges by lot, and appointing times for the hearing of the cause. And, therefore, let him set sail at once, good fortune attend him; and when the war should be at an end, he might then in person make his defence according to the laws.

Alcibiades perceived the malice of this postponement, and, appearing in the assembly, represented that it was monstrous for him to be sent with the command of so large an army, when he lay under such accusations and calumnies; that he deserved to die, if he could not clear himself of the crimes objected to him; but when he had so done, and had proved his innocence, he should then cheerfully apply himself to the war, as standing no longer in fear of false accusers. But he could not prevail with the people, who commanded him to sail immediately. So he departed, together with the other generals, having with them near 140 galleys, 5100 men at arms, and about 1300 archers, slingers, and light-armed men, and all the other provisions corresponding.

Arriving on the coast of Italy, he landed at Rhegium, and there stated his views of the manner in which they ought to conduct the war. He was opposed by Nicias; but Lamachus being of his opinion, they sailed for Sicily forthwith, and took Catana. This was all that was done while he was there, for he was soon after recalled by the Athenians to abide his trial.

At first, as we before said, there were only some slight suspicions advanced against Alcibiades, and accusations by certain slaves and strangers. But afterwards, in his absence, his enemies attacked him more violently, and confounded together the breaking of the images with the profanation of the mysteries, as though both had been committed in pursuance of the same conspiracy for changing the government. The people proceeded to imprison all that were accused, without distinction, and without hearing them, and repented now, considering the importance of the charge, that they had not immediately brought Alcibiades to his trial, and given judgment against him. Any of his friends or acquaintance who fell into the people's hands, whilst they were in this fury, did not fail to meet with very severe usage. Thucydides has omitted to name the informers, but others mention Dioclides and Teucer. Amongst whom is Phrynichus, the comic poet, in whom we find the following:—

O dearest Hermes! only do take care,
And mind you do not miss your footing there;
Should you get hurt, occasion may arise
For a new Dioclides to tell lies.

To which he makes Mercury return this answer:—

will so, for I feel no inclination
To reward Teucer for more information.

The truth is, his accusers alleged nothing that was certain or solid against him. One of them, being asked how he knew the men who defaced the images, replying, that he saw them by the light of the moon, made a palpable misstatement, for it was just new moon when the fact was committed. This made all men of understanding cry out upon the thing; but the people were as eager as ever to receive further accusations, nor was their first heat at all abated, but they instantly seized and imprisoned every one that was accused.

Amongst those who were detained in prison for their trials was Andocides, the orator, whose descent the historian Hellanicus deduces from Ulysses. He was always supposed to hate popular government, and to support oligarchy. The chief ground of his being suspected of defacing the images was because the great Mercury, which stood near his house, and was an ancient monument of the tribe Ægeïs, was almost the only statue of all the remarkable ones which remained entire. For this cause, it is now called the Mercury of Andocides, all men giving it that name, though the inscription is evidence to the contrary.

It happened that Andocides, amongst the rest who were prisoners upon the same account, contracted particular acquaintance and intimacy with one Timæus, a person inferior to him in repute, but of remarkable dexterity and boldness. He persuaded Andocides to ac-

cuse himself and some few others of this crime, urging to him that, upon his confession, he would be, by the decree of the people, secure of his pardon, whereas the event of judgment is uncertain to all men, but to great persons, such as he was, most formidable. So that it was better for him, if he regarded himself, to save his life by a falsity, than to suffer an infamous death, as really guilty of the crime. And if he had regard to the public good, it was commendable to sacrifice a few suspected men, by that means to rescue many excellent persons from the fury of the people. Andocides was prevailed upon, and accused himself and some others, and, by the terms of the decree, obtained his pardon, while all the persons named by him, except some few who had saved themselves by flight, suffered death. To gain the greater credit to his information, he accused his own servants amongst others. But notwithstanding this, the people's anger was not wholly appeased; and being now no longer diverted by the mutilators, they were at leisure to pour out their whole rage upon Alcibiades. And, in conclusion, they sent the galley named Salaminian to recall him.

But they expressly commanded those that were sent to use no violence, nor seize upon his person, but address themselves to him in the mildest terms, requiring him to follow them to Athens in order to abide his trial, and clear himself before the people. For they feared mutiny and sedition in the army in an enemy's country, which indeed it would have been easy for Alcibiades to effect, if he had wished it. For the soldiers were dispirited upon his departure, expecting for the future tedious delays, and that the war would be drawn out into a lazy length by Nicias, when Alcibiades, who was the spur to action, was taken away. For though Lamachus was a soldier, and a man of courage, poverty deprived him of authority and respect in the army.

Alcibiades, just upon his departure, prevented Messena from falling into the hands of the Athenians. There were some in that city who were upon the point of delivering it up, but he, knowing the persons, gave information to some friends of the Syracusans, and so defeated the whole contrivance. When he arrived at Thurii, he went on shore, and, concealing himself there, escaped those who searched after him. But to one who knew him, and asked him if he durst not trust his own native country, he made answer, "In everything else, yes; but in a matter that touches my life, I would not even my own mother, lest she might by mistake throw in the black ball instead of the white." When, afterwards, he was told that the assembly had pronounced judgment of death against him, all he said was, "I will make them feel that I am alive."

The information against him was conceived in this form:—

"Thessalus, the son of Cimon, of the township of Lacia, lays information that Alcibiades, the son of Clinias of the township of the Scambonidæ, has committed a crime against the goddess Ceres and Proserpine, by representing in derision the holy mysteries, and showing them to his companions in his own house. Where, being habited in such robes as are used by the chief priest when he shows the holy things, he named himself the chief priest, Polytion the torch-bearer, and Theodorus, of the township of Phegæa, the herald; and saluted the rest of his company as Initiates and Novices, all which was done contrary to the laws and institutions of the Eumolpidæ, and the heralds and priests of the temple at Eleusis."

He was condemned as contumacious upon his not appearing, his property confiscated, and it was decreed that all the priests and priestesses should solemnly curse him. But one of them, Theano, the daughter of Menon, of the township of Agraule, is said to have opposed that part of the decree, saying that her holy office obliged her to make prayers, but not execrations.

Alcibiades, lying under these heavy decrees and sentences, when first he fled from Thurii, passed over into Peloponnesus and remained some time at Argos. But being there in fear of his enemies, and seeing himself utterly hopeless of return to his native country, he sent to Sparta, desiring safe conduct, and assuring them that he would make them amends by his future services for all the mischief he had done them while he was their enemy. The Spartans giving him the security he desired, he went eagerly, was well received, and, at his very first coming, succeeded in inducing them, without any further caution or delay, to send aid to the Syracusans; and so roused and excited them, that they forthwith despatched Gylippus into Sicily to crush the forces which the Athenians had in Sicily. A second point was to renew the war upon the Athenians at home. But the third thing, and the most important of all, was to make them fortify Decelea, which above everything reduced and wasted the resources of the Athenians.

The renown which he earned by these public services was equalled by the admiration he attracted to his private life; he captivated and won over everybody by his conformity to Spartan habits. People who saw him wearing his hair close cut, bathing in cold water, eating coarse meal, and dining on black broth, doubted, or rather could not believe, that he ever had a cook in his house, or had ever seen a perfumer, or had worn a mantle of Milesian purple.

For he had, as it was observed, this peculiar talent and artifice for gaining men's affections, that he could at once comply with and really embrace and enter into their habits and ways of life, and change faster than the chameleon. One colour, indeed, they say the chameleon cannot assume: it cannot itself appear white; but Alcibiades, whether with good men or with bad, could adapt himself to his company, and equally wear the appearance of virtue or vice. At Sparta, he was devoted to athletic exercises, was frugal and reserved; in Ionia, luxurious, gay, and indolent; in Thrace, always drinking; in Thessaly, ever on horseback; and when he lived with Tisaphernes, the Persian satrap, he exceeded the Persians themselves in magnificence and pomp. Not that his natural disposition changed so easily, nor that his real character was so variable, but, whenever he was sensible that by pursuing his own inclinations he might give offence to those with whom he had occasion to converse, he transformed himself into any shape, and adopted any fashion, that he observed to be most agreeable to them.

So that to have seen him at Lacedæmon, a man, judging by the outward appearance, would have said, " 'Tis not Achilles's son, but he, himself; the very man that Lycurgus designed to form"; while his real feeling and acts would have rather provoked the exclamation, " 'Tis the same woman still." For while king Agis was absent, and abroad with the army, he corrupted his wife, Timæa, and had a child born by her. Nor did she even deny it, but when she was brought to bed of a son, called him in public Leotychides, but, amongst her confidants and attendants, would whisper that his name was Alcibiades. To such a degree was she transported by her passion for him. He, on the other side, would say, in his vain way, he had not done this thing out of mere wantonness of insult, nor to gratify a passion, but that his race might one day be kings over the Lacedæmonians.

There were many who told Agis that this was so, but time itself gave the greatest confirmation to the story. For Agis, alarmed by an earthquake, had quitted his wife, and for ten months after was never with her; Leotychides, therefore, being born after these ten months, he would not acknowledge him for his son; which was the reason that afterwards he was not admitted to the succession.

After the defeat which the Athenians received in Sicily, ambassadors were despatched to Sparta at once from Chios and Lesbos and Cyzicus, to signify their purpose of revolting from the Athenians. The Bœotians interposed in favour of the Lesbians, and Pharnabazus of the Cyzicenes, but the Lacedæmonians, at the persuasion of Alcibiades, chose to assist Chios before all others. He himself, also, went instantly to sea, procured the immediate revolt of almost all Ionia, and, co-operating with the Lacedæmonian generals, did great mischief to the Athenians.

But Agis was his enemy, hating him for having dishonoured his wife, and also impatient of his glory, as almost every enterprise and every success was ascribed to Alcibiades. Others, also, of the most powerful and ambitious amongst the Spartans were possessed with jealousy of him, and at last prevailed with the magistrates in the city to send orders into Ionia that he should be killed. Alcibiades, however, had secret intelligence of this, and in apprehension of the result, while he communicated all affairs to the Lacedæmonians, yet took care not to put himself into their power.

At last he retired to Tisaphernes, the King of Persia's satrap, for his security, and immediately became the first and most influential person about him. For this barbarian, not being himself sincere, but a lover of guile and wickedness, admired his address and wonderful subtlety. And, indeed, the charm of daily intercourse with him was more than any character could resist or any disposition escape. Even those who feared and envied him could not but take delight, and have a sort of kindness for him, when they saw him and were in his company. So that Tisaphernes, otherwise a cruel character, and, above all other Persians, a hater of the Greeks, was yet so won by the flatteries of Alcibiades, that he set himself even to exceed him in responding to them. The most beautiful of his parks, containing salubrious streams and meadows, where he had built pavilions, and places of retirement royally and exquisitely adorned, received by his direction

the name of Alcibiades, and was always so called and so spoken of.

Thus Alcibiades, quitting the interests of the Spartans, whom he could no longer trust, because he stood in fear of Agis, endeavoured to do them ill offices, and render them odious to Tisaphernes, who by his means was hindered from assisting them vigorously, and from finally ruining the Athenians. For his advice was to furnish them but sparingly with money, and so wear them out, and consume them insensibly; when they had wasted their strength upon one another, they would both become ready to submit to the king. Tisaphernes readily pursued his counsel, and so openly expressed the liking and admiration which he had for him, that Alcibiades was looked up to by the Greeks of both parties, and the Athenians, now in their misfortunes, repented them of their severe sentence against him. And he, on the other side, began to be troubled for them, and to fear lest, if that commonwealth were utterly destroyed, he should fall into the hands of the Lacedæmonians, his enemies.

At that time the whole strength of the Athenians was in Samos. Their fleet maintained itself here, and issued from these headquarters to reduce such as had revolted, and protect the rest of their territories; in one way or other still contriving to be a match for their enemies at sea. What they stood in fear of was Tisaphernes and the Phœnician fleet of one hundred and fifty galleys, which was said to be already under sail; if those came, there remained then no hopes for the commonwealth of Athens.

Understanding this, Alcibiades sent secretly to the chief men of the Athenians, who were then at Samos, giving them hopes that he would make Tisaphernes their friend; he was willing, he implied, to do some favour, not to the people, not in reliance upon them, but to the better citizens, if only, like brave men, they would make the attempt to put down the insolence of the people, and, by taking upon them the government, would endeavour to save the city from ruin. All of them gave a ready ear to the proposal made by Alcibiades, except only Phrynichus, of the township of Dirades, one of the generals, who suspected, as the truth was, that Alcibiades concerned not himself whether the government were in the people or the better citizens, but only sought by any means to make way for his return into his native country, and to that end inveighed against the people, thereby to gain the others, and to insinuate himself into their good opinion.

But when Phrynichus found his counsel to be rejected and that he was himself become a declared enemy of Alcibiades, he gave secret intelligence to Astyochus, the enemy's admiral, cautioning him to beware of Alcibiades and to seize him as a double dealer, unaware that one traitor was making discoveries to another. For Astyochus, who was eager to gain the favour of Tisaphernes, observing the credit Alcibiades had with him, revealed to Alcibiades all that Phrynichus had said against him. Alcibiades at once despatched messengers to Samos, to accuse Phrynichus of the treachery. Upon this, all the commanders were enraged with Phrynichus, and set themselves against him, and he, seeing no other way to extricate himself from the present danger, attempted to remedy one evil by a greater. He sent to Astyochus to reproach him for betraying him, and to make an offer to him at the same time to deliver into his hands both the army and the navy of the Athenians.

This occasioned no damage to the Athenians, because Astyochus repeated his treachery and revealed also this proposal to Alcibiades. But this again was foreseen by Phrynichus, who, expecting a second accusation from Alcibiades to anticipate him, advertised the Athenians beforehand that the enemy was ready to sail in order to surprise them, and therefore advised them to fortify their camp, and be in a readiness to go aboard their ships. While the Athenians were intent upon doing these things, they received other letters from Alcibiades, admonishing them to beware of Phrynichus, as one who designed to betray their fleet to the enemy, to which they then gave no credit at all, conceiving that Alcibiades, who knew perfectly the counsels and preparations of the enemy, was merely making use of that knowledge, in order to impose upon them in this false accusation of Phrynichus. Yet, afterwards, when Phrynichus was stabbed with a dagger in the market-place by Hermon, one of the guards, the Athenians, entering into an examination of the cause, solemnly condemned Phrynichus of treason, and decreed crowns to Hermon and his associates.

And now the friends of Alcibiades, carrying all before them at Samos, despatched Pisander to Athens, to attempt a change of government, and to encourage the aristocratical citizens to take upon themselves the government, and overthrow the democracy, representing to them, that upon these terms, Alcibiades would procure them the friendship and alliance of Tisaphernes.

This was the colour and pretence made use of by those who desired to change the government of Athens to an oligarchy. But as soon as they prevailed, and had got the administration of affairs into their hands, under the name of the Five Thousand (whereas, indeed, they were but four hundred), they slighted Alcibiades altogether, and prosecuted the war with less vigour; partly because they durst not yet trust the citizens, who secretly detested this change, and partly because they thought the Lacedæmonians, who always befriended the government of the few, would be inclined to give them favourable terms.

The people in the city were terrified into submission, many of those who had dared openly to oppose the four hundred having been put to death. But those who were at Samos, indignant when they heard this news, were eager to set sail instantly for the Piræus; sending for Alcibiades, they declared him general, requiring him to lead them on to put down the tyrants.

He, however, in that juncture, did not, as it might have been thought a man would, on being suddenly exalted by the favour of a multitude, think himself under an obligation to gratify and submit to all the wishes of those who, from a fugitive and an exile, had created him general of so great an army, and given him the command of such a fleet. But, as became a great captain, he opposed himself to the precipitate resolutions which their rage led them to, and, by restraining them from the great error they were about to commit, unequivocally saved the commonwealth. For if they then sailed to Athens, all Ionia and the islands and the Hellespont would have fallen into the enemies' hands without opposition, while the Athenians, involved in civil war, would have been fighting with one another within the circuit of their own walls.

It was Alcibiades alone, or, at least, principally, who prevented all this mischief; for he not only used persuasion to the whole army, and showed them the danger, but applied himself to them, one by one, entreating some, and constraining others. He was much assisted, however, by Thrasybulus of Stiria, who having the loudest voice, as we are told, of all the Athenians, went along with him, and cried out to those who were ready to be gone.

A second great service which Alcibiades did for them was his undertaking that the Phœnician fleet, which the Lacedæmonians expected to be sent to them by the King of Persia, should either come in aid of the Athenians or otherwise should not come at all. He sailed off with all expedition in order to perform this, and the ships, which had already been seen as near as Aspendus, were not brought any further by Tisaphernes, who thus deceived the Lacedæmonians; and it was by both sides believed that they had been diverted by the procurement of Alcibiades. The Lacedæmonians, in particular, accused him, that he had advised the Barbarian to stand still, and suffer the Greeks to waste and destroy one another, as it was evident that the accession of so great a force to either party would enable them to take away the entire dominion of the sea from the other side.

Soon after this, the four hundred usurpers were driven out, the friends of Alcibiades vigorously assisting those who were for the popular government. And now the people in the city not only desired, but commanded Alcibiades to return home from his exile. He, however, desired not to owe his return to the mere grace and commiseration of the people, and resolved to come back, not with empty hands, but with glory, and after some service done.

To this end, he sailed from Samos with a few ships, and cruised on the sea of Cnidos, and about the isle of Cos; but receiving intelligence there that Mindarus, the Spartan admiral, had sailed with his whole army into the Hellespont, and that the Athenians had followed him, he hurried back to succour the Athenian commanders, and, by good fortune, arrived with eighteen galleys at a critical time. For both the fleets having engaged near Abydos, the fight between them had lasted till night, the one side having the advantage on one quarter, and the other on another. Upon his first appearance, both sides formed a false impression; the enemy was encouraged and the Athenians terrified. But Alcibiades suddenly raised the Athenian ensign in the admiral ship, and fell upon those galleys of the Peloponnesians which had the advantage and were in pursuit. He soon put these to flight, and followed them so close that he forced them on shore, and broke the ships in pieces, the sailors abandoning them and swimming away in spite of all the efforts of Pharnabazus, who had come down to their assistance by land and did what he could to protect them from the shore. In fine, the Athenians, having taken thirty of the enemy's ships, and recovered all their own, erected a trophy.

After the gaining of so glorious a victory, his vanity made him eager to show himself to Tisaphernes, and, having furnished himself with gifts and presents, and an equipage suitable to his dignity, he set out to visit him. But the thing did not succeed as he had imagined, for Tisaphernes had been long suspected by the Lacedæmonians, and was afraid to fall into disgrace with his king upon that account, and therefore thought that Alcibiades arrived very opportunely, and immediately caused him to be seized, and sent away prisoner to Sardis, fancying, by this act of injustice, to clear himself from all former imputations. But about thirty days after, Alcibiades escaped from his keeping, and having got a horse, fled to Clazomenæ, where he procured Tisaphernes additional disgrace by professing he was a party to his escape.

From there he sailed to the Athenian camp, and, being informed there that Mindarus and Pharnabazus were together at Cyzicus, he made a speech to the soldiers, telling them that sea-fighting, land-fighting, and, by the gods, fighting against fortified cities too, must be all one for them, as unless they conquered everywhere, there was no money for them. As soon as ever he got them on shipboard, he hastened to Proconnesus, and gave command to seize all the small vessels they met, and guard them safely in the interior of the fleet, that the enemy might have no notice of his coming; and a great storm of rain, accompanied with thunder and darkness, which happened at the same time, contributed much to the concealment of his enterprise. Indeed, it was not only undiscovered by the enemy, but the Athenians themselves were ignorant of it, for he commanded them suddenly on board, and set sail when they had abandoned all intention of it.

As the darkness presently passed away, the Peloponnesian fleet was seen riding out at sea in front of the harbour of Cyzicus. Fearing, if they discovered the number of his ships, they might endeavour to save themselves by land, he commanded the rest of the captains to slacken, and follow him slowly, whilst he, advancing with forty ships, showed himself to the enemy, and provoked them to fight. The enemy, being deceived as to their numbers, despised them, and, supposing they were to contend with those only, made themselves ready and began the fight. But as soon as they were engaged, they perceived the other part of the fleet coming down upon them, at which they were so terrified that they fled immediately. Upon that, Alcibiades, breaking through the midst of them with twenty of his best ships, hastened to the shore, disembarked, and pursued those who abandoned their ships and fled to land, and made a great slaughter of them.

Mindarus and Pharnabazus, coming to their succour, were utterly defeated. Mindarus was slain upon the place, fighting valiantly; Pharnabazus saved himself by flight. The Athenians slew great numbers of their enemies, won much spoil, and took all their ships. They also made themselves masters of Cyzicus, which was deserted by Pharnabazus, and destroyed its Peloponnesian garrison, and thereby not only secured to themselves the Hellespont, but by force drove the Lacedæmonians from out of all the rest of the sea. They intercepted some letters written to the ephors, which gave an account of this fatal overthrow, after their short laconic manner. "Our hopes are at an end. Mindarus is slain. The men starve. We know not what to do."

The soldiers who followed Alcibiades in this last fight were so exalted with their success, and felt that degree of pride, that, looking on themselves as invincible, they disdained to mix with the other soldiers, who had been often overcome. For it happened not long before, Thrasyllus had received a defeat near Ephesus, and, upon that occasion, the Ephesians erected their brazen trophy to the disgrace of the Athenians. The soldiers of Alcibiades reproached those who were under the command of Thrasyllus with this misfortune, at the same time magnifying themselves and their own commander, and it went so far that they would not exercise with them, nor lodge in the same quarters. But soon after, Pharnabazus, with a great force of horse and foot, falling upon the soldiers of Thrasyllus, as they were laying waste the territory of Abydos, Alcibiades came to their aid, routed Pharnabazus, and together with Thrasyllus pursued him till it was night; and in this action the troops united, and returned together to the camp, rejoicing and congratulating one another.

The next day he erected a trophy, and then proceeded to lay waste with fire and sword the whole province which was under Pharnabazus, where none ventured to resist; and he took divers priests and priestesses, but released them without ransom. He prepared next to attack the Chalcedonians, who had revolted from the Athenians, and had received a Lacedæmonian governor and garrison. But having intelligence that they had removed their corn and cattle out of the fields, and were conveying it all to the Bithynians, who were their friends, he drew down his army to the frontier of the Bithynians, and then sent a herald to charge them with this proceeding. The Bithynians, terrified at his approach, delivered up to him the booty, and entered into alliance with him.

Afterwards he proceeded to the siege of Chalcedon, and enclosed it with a wall from sea to sea. Pharnabazus advanced with his forces to raise the siege, and Hippocrates, the governor of the town, at the same time, gathering together all the strength he had, made a sally upon the Athenians. Alcibiades divided his army so as to engage both at once, and not only forced Pharnabazus to a dishonourable flight, but defeated Hippocrates, and killed him and a number of the soldiers with him.

After this he sailed into the Hellespont, in order to raise supplies of money, and took the city of Selymbria, in which action, through his precipitation, he exposed himself to great danger. For some within the town had undertaken to betray it into his hands, and, by agreement, were to give him a signal by a lighted torch about midnight. But one of the conspirators beginning to repent himself of the design, the rest, for fear of being discovered, were driven to give the signal before the appointed hour. Alcibiades, as soon as he saw the torch lifted up in the air, though his army was not in readiness to march, ran instantly towards the walls, taking with him about thirty men only, and commanding the rest of the army to follow him with all possible speed. When he came thither, he found the gate opened for him and entered with his thirty men, and about twenty more light-armed men, who were come up to them. They were no sooner in the city, but he perceived the Selymbrians all armed, coming down upon him; so that there was no hope of escaping if he stayed to receive them; and, on the other hand, having been always successful till that day, wherever he commanded, he could not endure to be defeated and fly. So, requiring silence by sound of a trumpet, he commanded one of his men to make proclamation that the Selymbrians should not take arms against the Athenians. This cooled such of the inhabitants as were fiercest for the fight, for they supposed that all their enemies were within the walls, and it raised the hopes of others who were disposed to an accommodation. Whilst they were parleying, and propositions making on one side and the other, Alcibiades's whole army came up to the town. And now, conjecturing rightly that the Selymbrians were well inclined to peace, and fearing lest the city might be sacked by the Thracians, who came in great numbers to his army to serve as volunteers, out of kindness for him, he commanded them all to retreat without the walls. And upon the submission of the Selymbrians, he saved them from being pillaged, only taking of them a sum of money, and, after placing an Athenian garrison in the town, departed.

During this action, the Athenian captains who besieged Chalcedon concluded a treaty with Pharnabazus upon these articles: That he should give them a sum of money; that the Chalcedonians should return to the subjection of Athens, and that the Athenians should make no inroad into the province whereof Pharnabazus was governor; and Pharnabazus was also to provide safe conducts for the Athenian ambassadors to the King of Persia. Afterwards, when Alcibiades returned thither, Pharnabazus required that he also should be sworn to the treaty; but he refused it, unless Pharnabazus would swear at the same time.

When the treaty was sworn to on both sides, Alcibiades went against the Byzantines, who had revolted from the Athenians, and drew a line of circumvallation about the city. But Anaxilaus and Lycurgus, together with some others, having undertaken to betray the city to him upon his engagement to preserve the lives and property of the inhabitants, he caused a report to be spread abroad, as if by reason of some unexpected movement in Ionia, he should be obliged to raise the siege. And, accordingly, that day he made a show to depart with his whole fleet; but returned the same night, and went ashore with all his men at arms, and, silently and undiscovered, marched up to the walls. At the same time, his ships rowed into the harbour with all possible violence, coming on with much fury, and with great shouts and outcries. The Byzantines, thus surprised and astonished, while they all hurried to the defence of their port and shipping, gave opportunity to those who favoured the Athenians securely to receive Alcibiades into the city.

Yet the enterprise was not accomplished without fighting, for the Peloponnesians, Bœotians, and Megarians, not only repulsed those who came out of the ships, and forced them on board again, but, hearing that the Athenians were entered on the other side, drew up in order, and went to meet them. Alcibiades, however, gained the victory after some sharp fighting, in which he himself had the command of the right wing, and Theramenes of the left, and took about three hundred, who survived of the enemy, prisoners of war.

After the battle, not one of the Byzantines was slain, or driven out of the city, according to the terms upon which the city was put into his hands, that they should receive no prejudice in life or property. And thus Anaxilaus, being afterwards accused at Lacedæmon for this treason, neither disowned nor professed to be ashamed of the action; for he urged that he was not a Lacedæmonian, but a Byzantine, and saw not Sparta, but Byzantium, in extreme danger, the city so blockaded that it was not possible to bring in any new provisions, and the Peloponnesians and Bœotians, who were in garrison, devouring the old stores, whilst the Byzantines, with their wives and children, were starving; that he had not, therefore, betrayed his country to enemies, but had delivered it from the calamities of war, and had but followed the example of the most worthy Lacedæmonians, who esteemed nothing to be honourable and just, but what was profitable for their country. The Lacedæmonians, upon hearing his defence, respected it, and discharged all that were accused.

And now Alcibiades began to desire to see his native country again, or rather to show his fellow-citizens a person who had gained so many victories for them. He set sail for Athens, the ships that accompanied him being adorned with great numbers of shields and other spoils, and towing after them many galleys taken from the enemy, and the ensigns and ornaments of many others which he had sunk and destroyed, all of them together amounting to two hundred.

Little credit, perhaps, can be given to what Duris the Samian, who professed to be descended from Alcibiades, adds, that Chrysogonus, who had gained a victory at the Pythian games, played upon his flute for the galleys, whilst the oars kept time with the music; and that Callippides, the tragedian, attired in his buskins, his purple robes, and other ornaments used in the theatre, gave the word to the rowers, and that the admiral galley entered into the port with a purple sail. Neither Theopompus, nor Ephorus, nor Xenophon, mention them. Nor indeed, is it credible that one who returned from so long an exile, and such variety of misfortunes, should come home to his countrymen in the style of revellers breaking up from a drinking-party. On the contrary, he ventured the harbour full of fear, nor would he venture to go on shore, till, standing on the deck, he saw Euryptolemus, his cousin, and others of his friends and acquaintance, who were ready to receive him, and invited him to land.

As soon as he was landed, the multitude who came out to meet him scarcely seemed so much as to see any of the other captains, but came in throngs about Alcibiades, and saluted him with loud acclamations, and still followed him; those who could press near him crowned him with garlands, and they who could not come up so close yet stayed to behold him afar off, and the old men pointed him out, and showed him to the young ones.

Nevertheless, this public joy was mixed with some tears, and the present happiness was alloyed by the remembrance of the miseries they had endured. They made reflections, that they could not have so unfortunately miscarried in Sicily, or been defeated in any of their other expectations, if they had left the management of their affairs formerly, and the command of their forces, to Alcibiades, since, upon his undertaking the administration, when they were in a manner driven from the sea, and could scarce defend the suburbs of their city by land, and, at the same time, were miserably distracted with intestine factions, he had raised them up from this low and deplorable condition, and had not only restored them to their ancient dominion of the sea, but had also made them everywhere victorious over their enemies on land.

There had been a decree for recalling him from his banishment already passed by the people, at the instance of Critias, the son of Callæschrus, as appears by his elegies, in which he puts Alcibiades in mind of this service:—

From my proposal did that edict come,
Which from your tedious exile brought you
  home.
The public vote at first was moved by me,
And my voice put the seal to the decree.

The people being summoned to an assembly, Alcibiades came in amongst them, and first bewailed and lamented his own sufferings, and, in gentle terms complaining of the usage he had received, imputed all to his hard fortune, and some ill-genius that attended him: then he spoke at large of their prospects, and exhorted them to courage and good hope. The people crowned him with crowns of gold, and created him general, both at land and sea, with absolute power. They also made a decree that his estate should be restored to him, and that the Eumolpidæ and the holy herald should absolve him from the curses which they had solemnly pronounced against him by sentence of the people. Which when all the rest obeyed, Theodorus, the high priest, excused himself, "For," said he, "if he is innocent, I never cursed him."

But notwithstanding the affairs of Alcibiades went so prosperously, and so much to his glory, yet many were still somewhat disturbed, and looked upon the time of his arrival to be ominous. For on the day that he came into the port, the feast of the goddess Minerva, which they call the Plynteria, was kept. It is the twenty-fifth day of Thargelion, when the Praxiergidæ solemnise their secret rites, taking all the ornaments from off her image, and keeping the part of the temple where it stands close covered. Hence the Athenians esteem this day most inauspicious, and never undertake anything of importance upon it; and, therefore, they imagined that the goddess did not receive Alcibiades graciously and propitiously, thus hiding her face and rejecting him.

Yet, notwithstanding, everything succeeded according to his wish. When the one hundred galleys, that were to return with him, were fitted out and ready to sail, an honourable zeal detained him till the celebration of the mysteries was over. For ever since Decelea had been occupied, as the enemy commanded the roads leading from Athens to Eleusis, the procession, being conducted by sea, had not been performed with any proper solemnity; they were forced to omit the sacrifices and dances and other holy ceremonies, which had usually been performed in the way, when they led forth Iacchus.

Alcibiades, therefore, judged it would be a glorious action, which would do honour to the gods and gain him esteem with men, if he restored the ancient splendour to these rites, escorting the procession again by land, and protecting it with his army in the face of the enemy. For either, if Agis stood still and did not oppose, it would very much diminish and obscure his reputation, or, in the other alternative, Alcibiades would engage in a holy war, in the cause of the gods, and in defence of the most sacred and solemn ceremonies; and this in the sight of his country, where he should have all his fellow-citizens witnesses of his valour.

As soon as he had resolved upon this design, and had communicated it to the Eumolpidæ and heralds, he placed sentinels on the tops of the hills, and at the break of day sent forth his scouts. And then taking with him the priests and Initiates and the Initiators, and encompassing them with his soldiers, he conducted them with great order and profound silence; an august and venerable procession, wherein all who did not envy him said he performed at once the office of a high priest and of a general. The enemy did not dare to attempt anything against them, and thus he brought them back to safety to the city.

Upon which, as he was exalted in his own thought, so the opinion which the people had of his conduct was raised to that degree, that they looked upon their armies as irresistible and invincible while he commanded them; and he so won, indeed, upon the lower and meaner sort of people, that they passionately desired to have him "tyrant" over them, and some of them did not scruple to tell him so, and to advise him to put himself out of the reach of envy, by abolishing the laws and ordinances of the people, and suppressing the idle talkers that were ruining the state, that so he might act and take upon him the management of affairs, without standing in fear of being called to an account.

How far his own inclinations led him to usurp sovereign power is uncertain, but the most considerable persons in the city were so much afraid of it, that they hastened him on shipboard as speedily as they could, appointing the colleagues whom he chose, and allowing him all other things as he desired. Thereupon he set sail with a fleet of one hundred ships, and, arriving at Andros, he there fought with and defeated as well the inhabitants as the Lacedæmonians who assisted them.

He did not, however, take the city; which gave the first occasion to his enemies for all their accusations against him. Certainly, if ever man was ruined by his own glory, it was Alcibiades. For his continual success had produced such an idea of his courage and conduct, that if he failed in anything he undertook, it was imputed to his neglect, and no one would believe it was through want of power. For they thought nothing was too hard for him, if he went about it in good earnest. They fancied, every day, that they should hear news of the reduction of Chios, and of the rest of Ionia, and grew impatient that things were not effected as fast and as rapidly as they could wish for them. They never considered how extremely money was wanting, and that, having to carry on war with an enemy who had supplies of all things from a great king, he was often forced to quit his armament in order to procure money and provisions for the subsistence of his soldiers.

This it was which gave occasion for the last accusation which was made against him. For Lysander, being sent from Lacedæmon with a commission to be admiral of their fleet, and being furnished by Cyrus with a great sum of money, gave every sailor four obols a day, whereas before they had but three. Alcibiades could hardly allow his men three obols, and therefore was constrained to go into Caria to furnish himself with money. He left the care of the fleet, in his absence, to Antiochus, an experienced seaman, but rash and inconsiderate, who had express orders from Alcibiades not to engage, though the enemy provoked him. But he slighted and disregarded these directions to that degree, that, having made ready his own galley and another, he stood for Ephesus, where the enemy lay, and, as he sailed before the heads of their galleys, used every provocation possible, both in words and deeds. Lysander at first manned out a few ships, and pursued him. But all the Athenian ships coming in to his assistance, Lysander, also, brought up his whole fleet, which gained an entire victory. He slew Antiochus himself, took many men and ships, and erected a trophy.

As soon as Alcibiades heard this news, he returned to Samos, and loosing from hence with his whole fleet, came and offered battle to Lysander. But Lysander, content with the victory he had gained, would not stir. Amongst others in the army who hated Alcibiades, Thrasybulus, the son of Thrason, was his particular enemy, and went purposely to Athens to accuse him, and to exasperate his enemies in the city against him. Addressing the people, he represented that Alcibiades had ruined their affairs and lost their ships by mere self-conceited neglect of his duties, committing the government of the army, in his absence, to men who gained his favour by drinking and scurrilous talking, whilst he wandered up and down at pleasure to raise money, giving himself up to every sort of luxury and excess amongst the courtesans of Abydos and Ionia at a time when the enemy's navy were on the watch close at hand. It was also objected to him, that he had fortified a castle near Bisanthe in Thrace, for a safe retreat for himself, as one that either could not, or would not, live in his own country. The Athenians gave credit to these informations, and showed the resentment and displeasure which they had conceived against him by choosing other generals.

As soon as Alcibiades heard of this, he immediately forsook the army, afraid of what might follow; and, collecting a body of mercenary soldiers, made war upon his own account against those Thracians who called themselves free, and acknowledged no king. By this means he amassed to himself a considerable treasure, and, at the same time, secured the bordering Greeks from the incursions of the barbarians.

Tydeus, Menander, and Adimantus, the new-made generals, were at that time posted at Ægospotami, with all the ships which the Athenians had left. From whence they were used to go out to sea every morning, and offer battle to Lysander, who lay near Lampsacus; and when they had done so, returning back again, lay, all the rest of the day, carelessly and without order, in contempt of the enemy.

Alcibiades, who was not far off, did not think so slightly of their danger, nor neglect to let them know it, but, mounting his horse, came to the generals, and represented to them that they had chosen a very inconvenient station, where there was no safe harbour, and where they were distant from any town; so that they were constrained to send for their necessary provisions as far as Sestos. He also pointed out to them their carelessness in suffering the soldiers, when they went ashore, to disperse and wander up and down at their pleasure, while the enemy's fleet, under the command of one general, and strictly obedient to discipline, lay so very near them. He advised them to remove the fleet to Sestos. But the admirals not only disregarded what he said, but Tydeus, with insulting expressions, commanded him to be gone, saying, that now not he, but others, had the command of the forces.

Alcibiades, suspecting something of treachery in them, departed, and told his friends, who accompanied him out of the camp, that if the generals had not used him with such insupportable contempt, he would within a few days have forced the Lacedæmonians, however unwilling, either to have fought the Athenians at sea or to have deserted their ships. Some looked upon this as a piece of ostentation only; others said, the thing was probable, for that he might have brought down by land great numbers of the Thracian cavalry and archers, to assault and disorder them in their camp. The event, however, soon made it evident how rightly he had judged of the errors which the Athenians committed. For Lysander fell upon them on a sudden, when they least suspected it, with such fury that Conon alone, with eight galleys, escaped him; all the rest, which were about two hundred, he took and carried away, together with three thousand prisoners, whom he put to death. And within a short time after, he took Athens itself, burnt all the ships which he found there, and demolished their long walls.

After this, Alcibiades, standing in dread of the Lacedæmonians, who were now masters both at sea and land, retired into Bithynia. He sent thither great treasure before him, took much with him, but left much more in the castle where he had before resided. But he lost great part of his wealth in Bithynia, being robbed by some Thracians who lived in those parts, and thereupon determined to go to the court of Artaxerxes, not doubting but that the king, if he would make trial of his abilities, would find him not inferior to Themistocles, besides that he was recommended by a more honourable cause. For he went not, as Themistocles did, to offer his service against his fellow-citizens, but against their enemies, and to implore the king's aid for the defence of his country. He concluded that Pharnabazus would most readily procure him a safe conduct, and therefore went into Phrygia to him, and continued to dwell there some time, paying him great respect, and being honourably treated by him.

The Athenians, in the meantime, were miserably afflicted at their loss of empire; but when they were deprived of liberty also, and Lysander set up thirty despotic rulers in the city, in their ruin now they began to turn to those thoughts which, while safety was yet possible, they would not entertain; they acknowledged and bewailed their former errors and follies, and judged this second ill-usage of Alcibiades to be of all the most inexcusable. For he was rejected without any fault committed by himself, and only because they were incensed against his subordinate for having shamefully lost a few ships, they much more shamefully deprived the commonwealth of its most valiant and accomplished general.

Yet in this sad state of affairs they had still some faint hopes left them, nor would they utterly despair of the Athenian commonwealth while Alcibiades was safe. For they persuaded themselves that if before, when he was an exile, he could not content himself to live idly and at ease, much less now, if he could find any favourable opportunity, would he endure the insolence of the Lacedæmonians, and the outrages of the Thirty. Nor was it an absurd thing in the people to entertain such imaginations, when the Thirty themselves were so very solicitous to be informed and to get intelligence of all his actions and designs. In fine, Critias represented to Lysander that the Lacedæmonians could never securely enjoy the dominion of Greece till the Athenian democracy was absolutely destroyed; and, though now the people of Athens seemed quietly and patiently to submit to so small a number of governors, yet so long as Alcibiades lived, the knowledge of this fact would never suffer them to acquiesce in their present circumstances.

Yet Lysander would not be prevailed upon by these representations, till at last he received secret orders from the magistrates of Lacedæmon, expressly requiring him to get Alcibiades despatched: whether it was that they feared his energy and boldness in enterprising what was hazardous, or that it was done to gratify King Agis. Upon receipt of this order, Lysander sent away a messenger to Pharnabazus, desiring him to put it in execution. Pharnabazus committed the affair to Magæus, his brother, and to his uncle, Susamithres.

Alcibiades resided at that time in a small village in Phrygia, together with Timandra, a mistress of his. As he slept, he had this dream: he thought himself attired in his mistress's habit, and that she, holding him in her arms, dressed his head and painted his face as if he had been a woman; others say, he dreamed that he saw Magæus cut off his head and burn his body; at any rate, it was but a little while before his death that he had these visions.

Those who were sent to assassinate him had not courage enough to enter the house, but surrounded it first, and set it on fire. Alcibiades, as soon as he perceived it, getting together great quantities of clothes and furniture, threw them upon the fire to choke it, and, having wrapped his cloak about his left arm, and holding his naked sword in his right, he cast himself into the middle of the fire, and escaped securely through it before his clothes were burnt. The barbarians, as soon as they saw him, retreated, and none of them durst stay to wait for him, or to engage with him, but, standing at a distance, they slew him with their darts and arrows. When he was dead the barbarians departed, and Timandra took up his dead body, and, covering and wrapping it up in her own robes, she buried it as decently and as honourably as her circumstances would allow.

It is said, that the famous Lais, who was called the Corinthian, though she was a native of Hyccara, a small town in Sicily, from whence she was brought a captive, was the daughter of this Timandra.

There are some who agree with this account of Alcibiades's death in all points, except that they impute the cause of it neither to Pharnabazus, nor Lysander, nor the Lacedæmonians; but they say he was keeping with him a young lady of a noble house, whom he had debauched, and that her brothers, not being able to endure the indignity, set fire by night to the house where he was living, and, as he endeavoured to save himself from the flames, slew him with their darts, in the manner just related.

CORIOLANUS

LEGENDARY, 5TH CENTURY B.C.

THE patrician house of the Marcii in Rome produced many men of distinction, and among the rest, Ancus Marcius, grandson to Numa by his daughter, and king after Tullus Hostilius; of the same family were also Publius and Quintus Marcius, which two conveyed into the city the best and most abundant supply of water they have at Rome. As likewise Censorinus, who, having been twice chosen censor by the people, afterwards himself induced them to make a law that nobody should bear that office twice.

But Caius Marcius, of whom I now write,

being left an orphan, and brought up under the widowhood of his mother, has shown us by experience, that, although the early loss of a father may be attended with other disadvantages, yet it can hinder none from being either virtuous or eminent in the world, and that it is no obstacle to true goodness and excellence; however bad men may be pleased to lay the blame of their corruptions upon that misfortune and the neglect of them in their minority.

Nor is he less an evidence to the truth of their opinion who conceive that a generous and worthy nature without proper discipline, like a rich soil without culture, is apt with its better fruits to produce also much that is bad and faulty. While the force and vigour of his soul, and a persevering constancy in all he undertook, led him successfully into many noble achievements, yet, on the other side, also, by indulging the vehemence of his passion, and through an obstinate reluctance to yield or accommodate his humours and sentiments to those of a people about him, he rendered himself incapable of acting and associating with others. Those who saw with admiration how proof his nature was against all the softnesses of pleasure, the hardships of service, and the allurements of gain, while allowing to that universal firmness of his the respective names of temperance, fortitude, and justice, yet, in the life of the citizen and the statesman, could not choose but be disgusted at the severity and ruggedness of his deportment, and with his overbearing, haughty, and imperious temper. Education and study, and the favours of the muses, confer no greater benefit on those that seek them than these humanising and civilising lessons, which teach our natural qualities to submit to the limitations prescribed by reason, and to avoid the wildness of extremes.

Those were times at Rome in which that kind of worth was most esteemed which displayed itself in military achievements; one evidence of which we find in the Latin word for virtue, which is properly equivalent to manly courage. As if valour and all virtue had been the same thing, they used as the common term the name of the particular excellence. But Marcius, having a more passionate inclination than any of that age for feats of war, began at once, from his very childhood, to handle arms; and feeling that adventitious implements and artificial arms would effect little, and be of small use to such as have not their native and natural weapons well fixed and prepared for service, he so exercised and inured his body to all sorts of activity and encounter, that besides the lightness of a racer, he had a weight in close seizures and wrestlings with an enemy, from which it was hard for any to disengage himself; so that his competitors at home in displays of bravery, loth to own themselves inferior in that respect, were wont to ascribe their deficiencies to his strength of body, which they said no resistance and no fatigue could exhaust.

The first time he went out to the wars, being yet a stripling, was when Tarquinius Superbus, who had been King of Rome and was afterwards expelled, after many unsuccessful attempts, now entered upon his last effort, and proceeded to hazard all as it were upon a single throw. A great number of the Latins and other people of Italy joined their forces, and were marching with him toward the city, to procure his restoration; not, however, so much out of a desire to serve and oblige Tarquin, as to gratify their own fear and envy at the increase of the Roman greatness; which they were anxious to check and reduce. The armies met and engaged in a decisive battle, in the vicissitudes of which, Marcius, while fighting bravely in the dictator's presence, saw a Roman soldier struck down at a little distance, and immediately stepped in and stood before him, and slew his assailant.

The general, after having gained the victory, crowned him for this act, one of the first, with a garland of oaken branches, it being the Roman custom thus to adorn those who had saved the life of a citizen; whether that the law intended some special honour to the oak, in memory of the Arcadians, a people the oracle had made famous by the name of acorn-eaters; or whether the reason of it was because they might easily, and in all places where they fought, have plenty of oak for that purpose; or, finally, whether the oaken wreath, being sacred to Jupiter, the guardian of the city, might, therefore, be thought a proper ornament for one who preserved a citizen. And the oak, in truth, is the tree which bears the most and the prettiest fruit of any that grow wild, and is the strongest of all that are under cultivation; its acorns were the principal diet of the first mortals, and the honey found in it gave them drink. I may say, too, it furnished fowl and other creatures as dainties, in producing mistletoe for bird-lime to ensnare them.

In this battle, meantime, it is stated that Castor and Pollux appeared, and immediately after the battle were seen at Rome just by the fountain where their temple now stands, with their horses foaming with sweat, and told the news of the victory to the people in the Forum. The fifteenth of July, being the day of this conquest, became consequently a solemn holiday sacred to the Twin Brothers.

It may be observed, in general, that when young men arrive early at fame and repute, if they are of a nature but slightly touched with emulation, this early attainment is apt to extinguish their thirst and satiate their small appetite; whereas the first distinctions of more solid and weighty characters do but stimulate and quicken them and take them away like a wind in the pursuit of honour; they look upon these marks and testimonies to their virtue not as a recompense received for what they have already done, but as a pledge given by themselves of what they will perform hereafter, ashamed now to forsake or underlive the credit they have won, or, rather, not to exceed and obscure all that is gone before by the lustre of their following actions.

Marcius, having a spirit of this noble make, was ambitious always to surpass himself, and did nothing, how extraordinary soever, but he thought he was bound to outdo it at the next occasion; and ever desiring to give continual fresh instances of his prowess, he added one exploit to another, and heaped up trophies upon trophies, so as to make it matter of contest also among his commanders, the latter still vying with the earlier, which should pay him the greatest honour and speak highest in his commendation. Of all the numerous wars and conflicts in those days there was not one from which he returned without laurels and rewards.

And, whereas others made glory the end of their daring, the end of his glory was his mother's gladness; the delight she took to hear him praised and to see him crowned, and her weeping for joy in his embraces rendered him in his own thoughts the most honoured and most happy person in the world. Epaminondas is similarly said to have acknowledged his feeling, that it was the greatest felicity of his whole life that his father and mother survived to hear of his successful generalship and his victory at Leuctra. And he had the advantage, indeed, to have both his parents partake with him, and enjoy the pleasure of his good fortune. But Marcius, believing himself bound to pay his mother, Volumnia, all that gratitude and duty which would have belonged to his father, had he also been alive, could never satiate himself in his tenderness and respect to her. He took a wife, also, at her request and wish, and continued, even after he had children, to live still with his mother, without parting families.

The repute of his integrity and courage had, by this time, gained him a considerable influence and authority in Rome, when the senate, favouring the wealthier citizens, began to be at variance with the common people, who made sad complaints of the rigorous and inhuman usage they received from the money-lenders. For as many as were behind with them, and had any sort of property, they stripped of all they had, by the way of pledges and sales; and

such as through former exactions were reduced already to extreme indigence, and had nothing more to be deprived of, these they led away in person and put their bodies under constraint, notwithstanding the scars and wounds that they could show in attestation of their public services in numerous campaigns; the last of which had been against the Sabines, which they undertook upon a promise made by their rich creditors that they would treat them with more gentleness for the future, Marcus Valerius, the consul, having, by order from the senate, engaged also for the performance of it.

But when, after they had fought courageously and beaten the enemy, there was, nevertheless, no moderation or forbearance used, and the senate also professed to remember nothing of that agreement, and sat without testifying the least concern to see them dragged away like slaves and their goods seized upon as formerly, there began now to be open disorders and dangerous meetings in the city; and the enemy, also, aware of the popular confusion, invaded and laid waste the country.

And when the consuls now gave notice, that all who were of an age to bear arms should make their personal appearance, but found no one regard the summons, the members of the government, then coming to consult what course should be taken, were themselves again divided in opinion; some thought it most advisable to comply a little in favour of the poor, by relaxing their overstrained rights, and mitigating the extreme rigour of the law, while others withstood this proposal; Marcius in particular, with more vehemence than the rest, alleging that the business of money on either side was not the main thing in question, urged that this disorderly proceeding was but the first insolent step towards open revolt against the laws, which it would become the wisdom of the government to check at the earliest moment.

There had been frequent assemblies of the whole senate, within a small compass of time, about this difficulty, but without any certain issue; the poor commonalty, therefore, perceiving there was likely to be no redress of their grievances, on a sudden collected in a body, and, encouraging each other in their resolution, forsook the city, with one accord, and seizing the hill which is now called the Holy Mount, sat down by the river Anio, without committing any sort of violence or seditious outrage, but merely exclaiming, as they went along, that they had this long time past been, in fact, expelled and excluded from the city by the cruelty of the rich; that Italy would everywhere afford them the benefit of air and water and a place of burial, which was all they could expect in the city, unless it were, perhaps, the privilege of being wounded and killed in time of war for the defence of their creditors. The senate, apprehending the consequences, sent the most moderate and popular men of their own order to treat with them.

Menenius Agrippa, their chief spokesman, after much entreaty to the people, and much plain-speaking on behalf of the senate, concluded, at length, with the celebrated fable. "It once happened," he said, "that all the other members of a man mutinied against the stomach, which they accused as the only idle, uncontributing part in the whole body, while the rest were put to hardships and the expense of much labour to supply and minister to its appetites. The stomach, however, merely ridiculed the silliness of the members, who appeared not to be aware that the stomach certainly does receive the general nourishment, but only to return it again, and redistribute it amongst the rest. Such is the case," he said, "ye citizens, between you and the senate. The counsels and plans that are there duly digested, convey and secure to all of you your proper benefit and support."

A reconciliation ensued, the senate acceding to the request of the people for the annual election of five protectors for those in need of succour, the same that are now called the tribunes of the people; and the first two they pitched upon were Junius Brutus and Sicinnius Vellutus, their leaders in the secession.

The city being thus united, the commons stood presently to their arms, and followed their commanders to the war with great alacrity. As for Marcius, though he was not a little vexed himself to see the populace prevail so far, and gain ground of the senators, and might observe many other patricians have the same dislike of the late concessions, he yet besought them not to yield at least to the common people in the zeal and forwardness they now showed for their country's service, but to prove that they were superior to them, not so much in power and riches, as in merit and worth.

The Romans were now at war with the Volscian nation, whose principal city was Corioli; when, therefore, Cominius, the consul, had invested this important place, the rest of the Volscians, fearing it would be taken, mustered up whatever force they could from all parts, to re-

lieve it, designing to give the Romans battle before the city, and so attack them on both sides. Cominius, to avoid this inconvenience, divided his army, marching himself with one body to encounter the Volscians on their approach from without and leaving Titus Lartius, one of the bravest Romans of his time, to command the other and continue the siege.

Those within Corioli, despising now the smallness of their number, made a sally upon them, and prevailed at first, and pursued the Romans into their trenches. Here it was that Marcius, flying out with a slender company, and cutting those in pieces that first engaged him, obliged the other assailants to slacken their speed; and then, with loud cries, called upon the Romans to renew the battle. For he had, what Cato thought a great point in a soldier, not only strength of hand and stroke, but also a voice and look that of themselves were a terror to an enemy.

Divers of his own party now rallying and making up to him, the enemies soon retreated; but Marcius, not content to see them draw off and retire, pressed hard upon the rear, and drove them, as they fled away in haste, to the very gates of their city; where, perceiving the Romans to fall back from their pursuit, beaten off by the multitude of darts poured in upon them from the walls, and that none of his followers had the hardiness to think of falling in pell-mell among the fugitives and so entering a city full of enemies in arms, he, nevertheless, stood and urged them to the attempt, crying out, that fortune had now set open Corioli, not so much to shelter the vanquished, as to receive the conquerors. Seconded by a few that were willing to venture with him, he bore along through the crowd, made good his passage, and thrust himself into the gate through the midst of them, nobody at first daring to resist him.

But when the citizens on looking about saw that a very small number had entered, they now took courage, and came up and attacked them. A combat ensued of the most extraordinary description, in which Marcius, by strength of hand, and swiftness of foot, and daring of soul, overpowering every one that he assailed, succeeded in driving the enemy to seek refuge, for the most part, in the interior of the town, while those remaining submitted, and threw down their arms, thus affording Lartius abundant opportunity to bring in the rest of the Romans with ease and safety.

Corioli being thus surprised and taken, the

greater part of the soldiers employed themselves in spoiling and pillaging it, while Marcius indignantly reproached them, and exclaimed that it was a dishonourable and unworthy thing, when the consul and their fellow-citizens had now perhaps encountered the other Volscians, and were hazarding their lives in battle, basely to misspend the time in running up and down for booty, and, under a pretence of enriching themselves, keep out of danger. Few paid him any attention, but, putting himself at the head of these, he took the road by which the consul's army had marched before him, encouraging his companions, and beseeching them, as they went along, not to give up, and praying often to the gods, too, that he might be so happy as to arrive before the fight was over, and come seasonably up to assist Cominius, and partake in the peril of the action.

It was customary with the Romans of that age, when they were moving into battle array, and were on the point of taking up their bucklers, and girding their coats about them, to make at the same time an unwritten will, or verbal testament, and to name who should be their heirs, in the hearing of three or four witnesses. In this precise posture Marcius found them at his arrival, the enemy being advanced within view.

They were not a little disturbed by his first appearance, seeing him covered with blood and sweat, and attended with a small train; but when he hastily made up to the consul with gladness in his looks, giving him his hand, and recounting to him how the city had been taken, and when they saw Cominius also embrace and salute him, every one took fresh heart; those that were near enough hearing, and those that were at a distance guessing, what had happened; and all cried out to be led to battle. First, however, Marcius desired to know of him how the Volscians had arrayed their army, and where they had placed their best men, and on his answering that he took the troops of the Antiates in the centre to be their prime warriors, that would yield to none in bravery, "Let me demand and obtain of you," said Marcius, "that we may be posted against them." The consul granted the request, with much admiration for his gallantry.

And when the conflict began by the soldiers darting at each other, and Marcius sallied out before the rest, the Volscians opposed to him were not able to make head against him; wherever he fell in, he broke their ranks, and made a lane through them; but the parties turning again, and enclosing him on each side with their weapons, the consul, who observed the danger he was in, despatched some of the choicest men he had for his rescue. The conflict then growing warm and sharp about Marcius, and many falling dead in a little space, the Romans bore so hard upon their enemies, and pressed them with such violence, that they forced them at length to abandon their ground, and to quit the field. And going now to prosecute the victory, they besought Marcius, tired out with his toils, and faint and heavy through the loss of blood, that he would retire to the camp. He replied, however, that weariness was not for conquerors, and joined with them in the pursuit. The rest of the Volscian army was in like manner defeated, great numbers killed, and no less taken captive.

The day after, when Marcius, with the rest of the army, presented themselves at the consul's tent, Cominius rose, and having rendered all due acknowledgement to the gods for the success of that enterprise, turned next to Marcius, and first of all delivered the strongest encomium upon his rare exploits, which he had partly been an eye-witness of himself, in the late battle, and had partly learned from the testimony of Lartius. And then he required him to choose a tenth part of all the treasure and horses and captives that had fallen into their hands, before any division should be made to others; besides which, he made him the special present of a horse with trappings and ornaments, in honour of his actions.

The whole army applauded; Marcius, however, stepped forth, and declaring his thankful acceptance of the horse, and his gratification at the praises of his general, said that all other things, which he could only regard rather as mercenary advantages than any significations of honour, he must waive, and should be content with the ordinary proportion of such rewards. "I have only," said he, "one special grace to beg, and this I hope you will not deny me. There was a certain hospitable friend of mine among the Volscians, a man of probity and virtue, who is become a prisoner, and from former wealth and freedom is now reduced to servitude. Among his many misfortunes let my intercession redeem him from the one of being sold as a common slave."

Such a refusal and such a request on the part of Marcius were followed with yet louder acclamations; and he had many more admirers of this generous superiority to avarice, than of the bravery he had shown in battle. The very persons who conceived some envy and despite to see him so specially honoured, could not but acknowledge that one who so nobly could refuse reward was beyond others worthy to receive it; and were more charmed with that virtue which made him despise advantage, than with any of those former actions that have gained him his title to it. It is the higher accomplishment to use money well than to use arms; but not to need it is more noble than to use it.

When the noise of approbation and applause ceased, Cominius, resuming, said: "It is idle, fellow-soldiers, to force and obtrude those other gifts of ours on one who is unwilling to accept them; let us, therefore, give him one of such a kind that he cannot well reject it; let us pass a vote, I mean, that he shall hereafter be called Coriolanus, unless you think that his performance at Corioli has itself anticipated any such resolution." Hence, therefore, he had this third name of Coriolanus, making it all the plainer that Caius was a personal proper name, and the second, or surname, Marcius, one common to his house and family; the third being a subsequent addition which used to be imposed either from some particular act, or fortune, bodily characteristic, or good quality of the bearer.

Just as the Greeks, too, gave additional names in old time, in some cases from some achievement, Soter, for example, and Callinicus; or personal appearance, as Physcon and Grypus; good qualities, Euergetes and Philadelphus; good fortune, Eudæmon, the title of the second Battus. Several monarchs have also had names given them in mockery, as Antigonus was called Doson, and Ptolemy, Lathyrus.

This sort of title was yet more common among the Romans. One of the Metelli was surnamed Diadematus, because he walked about for a long time with a bandage on his head to conceal a scar; and another, of the same family, got the name of Celer, from the rapidity he displayed in giving a funeral entertainment of gladiators within a few days after his father's death, his speed and energy in doing which was thought extraordinary. There are some, too, who even at this day take names from certain casual incidents at their nativity: a child that is born when his father is away from home is called Proculus; or Postumus, if after his decease; and when twins come into the world, and one dies at the birth, the survivor has the name of Vopiscus. From bodily peculiarities they derive not only their Sullas and Nigers, but their Cæci and Claudii, wisely endeavouring to accustom their people not to reckon either the loss of sight, or any other bodily misfortune, as a matter of disgrace to them, but to answer to such names without shame, as if they were really their own. But this discussion better befits another place.

The war against the Volscians was no sooner at an end, than the popular orators revived domestic troubles, and raised another sedition, without any new cause or complaint or just grievance to proceed upon, but merely turning the very mischiefs that unavoidably ensued from their former contests into a pretext against the patricians. The greatest part of their arable land had been left unsown and without tillage, and the time of war allowing them no means or leisure to import provision from other countries, there was an extreme scarcity. The movers of the people then observing that there was no corn to be bought, and that if there had been they had no money to buy it, began to calumniate the wealthy with false stories and whisper it about, as if they, out of their malice, had purposely contrived the famine.

Meanwhile, there came an embassy from the Velitrani, proposing to deliver up their city to the Romans, and desiring they would send some new inhabitants to people it, as a late pestilential disease had swept away so many of the natives, that there was hardly a tenth part remaining of their whole community. This necessity of the Velitrani was considered by all more prudent people as most opportune in the present state of affairs; since the dearth made it needful to ease the city of its superfluous members, and they were in hope also, at the same time, to dissipate the gathering sedition by ridding themselves of the more violent and heated partisans, and discharging, so to say, the elements of disease and disorder in the state. The consuls, therefore, singled out such citizens to supply the desolation at Velitræ, and gave notice to others, that they should be ready to march against the Volscians, with the politic design of preventing intestine broils by employment abroad, and in the hope that when rich as well as poor, plebeians and patricians, should be mingled again in the same army and the same camp, and engage in one common service for the public, it would mutually dispose them to reconciliation and friendship.

But Sicinnius and Brutus, the popular orators, interposed, crying out that the consuls disguised the most cruel and barbarous action in the world under that mild and plausible name of a colony, and were simply precipitating so many poor citizens into a mere pit of destruction, bidding them settle down in a country where the air was charged with disease, and the ground covered with dead bodies, and expose themselves to the evil influence of a strange and angered deity. And then, as if it would not satisfy their hatred to destroy some by hunger, and offer others to the mercy of a plague, they must proceed to involve them also in a needless war of their own making, that no calamity might be wanting to complete the punishment of the citizens for refusing to submit to that of slavery to the rich.

By such addresses, the people were so possessed, that none of them would appear upon the consular summons to be enlisted for the war; and they showed entire aversion to the proposal for a new plantation; so that the senate was at a loss what to say or do. But Marcius, who began now to bear himself higher and to feel confidence in his past actions, conscious, too, of the admiration of the best and greatest men of Rome, openly took the lead in opposing the favourers of the people. The colony was despatched to Velitræ, those that were chosen by lot being compelled to depart upon high penalties; and when they obstinately persisted in refusing to enrol themselves for the Volscian service, he mustered up his own clients, and as many others as could be wrought upon by persuasion, and with these made inroad into the territories of the Antiates, where, finding a considerable quantity of corn, and collecting much booty, both of cattle and prisoners, he reserved nothing for himself in private, but returned safe to Rome, while those that ventured out with him were seen laden with pillage, and driving their prey before them. This sight filled those that had stayed at home with regret for their perverseness, with envy at their fortunate fellow-citizens, and with feelings of dislike to Marcius, and hostility to his growing reputation and power, which might probably be used against the popular interest.

Not long after he stood for the consulship; when, however, the people began to relent and incline to favour him, being sensible what a shame it would be to repulse and affront a man of his birth and merit, after he had done them so many signal services.

It was usual for those who stood for offices among them to solicit and address themselves personally to the citizens, presenting themselves in the Forum with the toga on alone, and no tunic under it; either to promote their supplications by the humility of their dress, or that such as had received wounds might more readily display those marks of their fortitude. Certainly, it was not out of suspicion of bribery and corruption that they required all such petitioners for their favour to appear ungirt and open, without any close garment; as it was much later, and many ages after this, that buying and selling crept in at their elections, and money became an ingredient in the public suffrages; proceeding thence to attempt their tribunals, and even attack their camps, till, by hiring the valiant, and enslaving iron to silver, it grew master of the state, and turned their commonwealth into a monarchy.

For it was well and truly said that the first destroyer of the liberties of a people is he who first gave them bounties and largesses. At Rome the mischief seems to have stolen secretly in, and by little and little, not being at once discerned and taken notice of. It is not certainly known who the man was that did there first either bribe the citizens, or corrupt the courts; whereas, in Athens, Anytus, the son of Anthemion, is said to have been the first that gave money to the judges, when on his trial, toward the latter end of the Peloponnesian war, for letting the fort of Pylos fall into the hands of the enemy, in a period while the pure and golden race of men were still in possession of the Roman Forum.

Marcius, therefore, as the fashion of candidates was, showing the scars and gashes that were still visible on his body, from the many conflicts in which he had signalised himself during a service of seventeen years together, they were, so to say, put out of countenance at this display of merit, and told one another that they ought in common modesty to create him consul.

But when the day of election was now come, and Marcius appeared in the Forum, with a pompous train of senators attending him, and the patricians all manifested greater concern, and seemed to be exerting greater efforts, than they had ever done before on the like occasion, the commons then fell off again from the kindness they had conceived for him, and in the place of their late benevolence, began to feel something of indignation and envy; passions assisted by the fear they entertained, that if a man of such aristocratic temper and so influential among the patricians should be invested with the power which that office would give him, he might employ it to deprive the people of all that liberty which was yet left them. In conclusion, they rejected Marcius.

Two other names were announced, to the great mortification of the senators, who felt as if the indignity reflected rather upon themselves than on Marcius. He, for his part, could not bear the affront with any patience. He had always indulged his temper, and had regarded the proud and contentious element of human nature as a sort of nobleness and magnanimity; reason and discipline had not imbued him with that solidity and equanimity which enters so largely into the virtues of the statesman. He had never learned how essential it is for any one who undertakes public business, and desires to deal with mankind, to avoid above all things that self-will, which, as Plato says, belongs to the family of solitude; and to pursue, above all things, that capacity so generally ridiculed, of submission to ill-treatment.

Marcius, straightforward and direct, and possessed with the idea that to vanquish and overbear all opposition is the true part of bravery, and never imagining that it was the weakness and womanishness of his nature that broke out, so to say, in these ulcerations of anger, retired, full of fury and bitterness against the people. The young patricians, too, all that were proudest and most conscious of their noble birth, had always been devoted to his interest, and, adhering to him now, with a fidelity that did him no good, aggravated his resentment with the expression of their indignation and condolence. He had been their captain, and their willing instructor in the arts of war, when out upon expeditions, and their model in that true emulation and love of excellence which makes men extol, without envy, or jealousy, each other's brave achievements.

In the midst of these distempers, a large quantity of corn reached Rome, a great part bought up in Italy, but an equal amount sent as a present from Syracuse, from Gelo, then reigning there. Many began now to hope well of their affairs, supposing the city, by this means, would be delivered at once, both of its want and discord. A council, therefore, being presently held, the people came flocking about the senate-house, eagerly awaiting the issue of that deliberation, expecting that the market-prices would now be less cruel, and that what had come as gift would be distributed as such. There were some within who so advised the senate; but Marcius, standing up, sharply inveighed against those who spoke in favour of

the multitude, calling them flatterers of the rabble, traitors to the nobility, and alleging that, by such gratifications, they did but cherish those ill seeds of boldness and petulance that had been sown among the people, to their own prejudice, which they should have done well to observe and stifle at their first appearance, and not have suffered the plebeians to grow so strong, by granting them magistrates of such authority as the tribunes. They were, indeed, even now formidable to the state since everything they desired was granted them; no constraint was put on their will; they refused obedience to the consuls and, overthrowing all law and magistracy, gave the title of magistrate to their private factious leaders.

"When things are come to such a pass for us to sit here and decree largesses and bounties for them, like those Greeks where the populace is supreme and absolute, what would it be else," said he, "but to take their disobedience into pay and maintain it for the common ruin of us all? They certainly cannot look upon these liberalities as a reward of public service, which they know they have so often deserted; nor yet of those secessions, by which they openly renounced their country; much less of the calumnies and slanders they have been always so ready to entertain against the senate; but will rather conclude that a bounty, which seems to have no other visible cause or reason, must needs be the effect of our fear and flattery; and will, therefore, set no limit to their disobedience, nor ever cease from disturbances and sedition. Concession is mere madness; if we have any wisdom and resolution at all, we shall, on the contrary, never rest till we have recovered from them that tribunician power they have extorted from us; as being a plain subversion of the consulship, and a perpetual ground of separation in our city that is no longer one, as heretofore, but has in this received such a wound and rupture as is never likely to close and unite again, or suffer us to be of one mind, and to give over inflaming our distempers, and being a torment to each other."

Marcius, with much more to this purpose, succeeded, to an extraordinary degree, in inspiring the younger men with the same furious sentiments, and had almost all the wealthy on his side, who cried him up as the only person their city had, superior alike to force and flattery; some of the older men, however, opposed him, suspecting the consequences.

As, indeed, there came no good of it; for the

tribunes, who were present, perceiving how the proposal of Marcius took, ran out into the crowd with exclamations, calling on the plebeians to stand together, and come in to their assistance. The assembly met, and soon became tumultuous. The sum of what Marcius had spoken, having been reported to the people, excited them to such fury that they were ready to break in upon the senate. The tribunes prevented this, by laying all the blame on Coriolanus, whom, therefore, they cited by their messengers to come before them and defend himself. And when he contemptuously repulsed the officers who brought him the summons, they came themselves, with the Ædiles, or overseers of the market, proposing to carry him away by force, and, accordingly, began to lay hold on his person. The patricians, however, coming to his rescue, not only thrust off the tribunes, but also beat the Ædiles, that were their seconds in the quarrel; night approaching, put an end to the contest.

But, as soon as it was day, the consuls, observing the people to be highly exasperated, and that they ran from all quarters and gathered in the Forum, were afraid for the whole city, so that, convening the senate afresh, they desired them to advise how they might best compose and pacify the incensed multitude by equitable language and indulgent decrees; since, if they wisely considered the state of things, they would find that it was no time to stand upon terms of honour and a mere point of glory; such a critical conjuncture called for gentle methods, and for temperate and humane counsels. The majority, therefore, of the senators giving way, the consuls proceeded to pacify the people in the best manner they were able, answering gently to such imputations and charges as had been cast upon the senate, and using much tenderness and moderation in the admonitions and reproofs they gave them. On the point of the price of provisions, they said there should be no difference at all between them.

When a great part of the commonalty was grown cool, and it appeared from their orderly and peaceful behaviour that they had been very much appeased by what they had heard, the tribunes, standing up, declared, in the name of the people, that since the senate was pleased to act soberly and do them reason, they, likewise, should be ready to yield in all that was fair and equitable on their side; they must insist, however, that Marcius should give in his answer to the several charges as follows: first,

could he deny that he instigated the senate to overthrow the government and annul the privileges of the people? And, in the next place, when called to account for it, did he not disobey the summons? And, lastly, by the blows and other public affronts to the Ædiles, had he not done all he could to commence a civil war?

These articles were brought in against him, with a design either to humble Marcius, and show his submission, if, contrary to his nature, he should now court and sue the people; or, if he should follow his natural disposition, which they rather expected from their judgment of his character, then that he might thus make the breach final between himself and the people.

He came, therefore, as it were, to make his apology, and clear himself; in which belief the people kept silence, and gave him a quiet hearing. But when, instead of the submissive and deprecatory language expected from him, he began to use not only an offensive kind of freedom, seeming rather to accuse than apologise, but, as well by the tone of his voice as the air of his countenance, displayed a security that was not far from disdain and contempt of them, the whole multitude then became angry, and gave evident signs of impatience and disgust; and Sicinnius, the most violent of the tribunes, after a little private conference with his colleagues, proceeded solemnly to pronounce before them all, that Marcius was condemned to die by the tribunes of the people, and bid the Ædiles take him to the Tarpeian rock, and without delay throw him headlong from the precipice.

When they, however, in compliance with the order, came to seize upon his body, many, even of the plebeian party, felt it to be a horrible and extravagant act; the patricians, meantime, wholly beside themselves with distress and horror, hurried up with cries to the rescue; and while some made actual use of their hands to hinder the arrest, and surrounding Marcius, got him in among them, others, as in so great a tumult no good could be done by words, stretched out theirs, beseeching the multitude that they would not proceed to such furious extremities; and at length, the friends and acquaintance of the tribunes, wisely perceiving how impossible it would be to carry off Marcius to punishment without much bloodshed and slaughter of the nobility, persuaded them to forbear everything unusual and odious; not to despatch him by any sudden violence, or without regular process, but refer the cause to the general suffrage of the people.

Sicinnius then, after a little pause, turning to the patricians, demanded what their meaning was, thus forcibly to rescue Marcius out of the people's hands, as they were going to punish him; when it was replied by them, on the other side, and the question put, "Rather, how came it into your minds, and what is it you design, thus to drag one of the worthiest men of Rome, without trial, to a barbarous and illegal execution?" "Very well," said Sicinnius, "you shall have no ground in this respect for quarrel or complaint against the people. The people grant your request, and your partisan shall be tried. We appoint you, Marcius," directing his speech to him, "the third market-day ensuing, to appear and defend yourself, and to try if you can satisfy the Roman citizens of your innocence, who will then judge your case by vote." The patricians were content with such a truce and respite for that time, and gladly returned home, having for the present brought off Marcius in safety.

During the interval before the appointed time (for the Romans hold their sessions every ninth day, which from that cause are called *mundinæ* in Latin), a war fell out with the Antiates, likely to be of some continuance, which gave them hope they might one way or other elude the judgment. The people, they presumed, would become tractable, and their indignation lessen and languish by degrees in so long a space, if occupation and war did not wholly put it out of their mind.

But when, contrary to expectation, they made a speedy agreement with the people of Antium, and the army came back to Rome, the patricians were again in great perplexity, and had frequent meetings to consider how things might be arranged, without either abandoning Marcius, or yet giving occasion to the popular orators to create new disorders. Appius Claudius, whom they counted among the senators most averse to the popular interest, made a solemn declaration, and told them beforehand, that the senate would utterly destroy itself and betray the government, if they should once suffer the people to assume the authority of pronouncing sentence upon any of the patricians; but the oldest senators and most favourable to the people maintained, on the other side, that the people would not be so harsh and severe upon them as some were pleased to imagine, but rather become more gentle and humane upon the concession of that power,

since it was not contempt of the senate, but the impression of being contemned by it, which made them pretend to such a prerogative. Let that be once allowed them as a mark of respect and kind feeling, and the mere possession of this power of voting would at once dispossess them of their animosity.

When, therefore, Marcius saw that the senate was in pain and suspense upon his account, divided, as it were, betwixt their kindness for him and their apprehensions from the people, he desired to know of the tribunes what the crimes were they intended to charge him with, and what the heads of the indictment they would oblige him to plead to before the people; and being told by them that he was to be impeached for attempting usurpation, and that they would prove him guilty of designing to establish arbitrary government, stepping forth upon this, "Let me go then," he said, "to clear myself from that imputation before an assembly of them; I freely offer myself to any sort of trial, nor do I refuse any kind of punishment whatsoever; only," he continued, "let what you now mention be really made my accusation, and do not you play false with the senate." On their consenting to these terms, he came to his trial.

But when the people met together, the tribunes, contrary to all former practice, extorted first, that votes should be taken, not by centuries, but tribes; a change by which the indigent and factious rabble, that had no respect for honesty and justice, would be sure to carry it against those who were rich and well known, and accustomed to serve the state in war.

In the next place, whereas they had engaged to prosecute Marcius upon no other head but that of tyranny, which could never be made out against him, they relinquished this plea, and urged instead, his language in the senate against an abasement of the price of corn, and for the overthrow of the tribunician power; adding further, as a new impeachment, the distribution that was made by him of the spoil and booty he had taken from the Antiates, when he overran their country, which he had divided among those that had followed him, whereas it ought rather to have been brought into the public treasury; which last accusation did, they say, more discompose Marcius than all the rest, as he had not anticipated he should ever be questioned on that subject, and, therefore, was less provided with any satisfactory answer to it on the sudden. And when, by way of excuse, he began to magnify the merits of those who had been partakers with him in the action, those that had stayed at home, being more numerous than the other, interrupted him with outcries. In conclusion, when they came to vote, a majority of three tribes condemned him; the penalty being perpetual banishment.

The sentence of his condemnation being pronounced, the people went away with greater triumph and exultation than they had ever shown for any victory over enemies; while the senate was in grief and deep dejection, repenting now and vexed to the soul that they had not done and suffered all things rather than give way to the insolence of the people, and permit them to assume and abuse so great an authority. There was no need then to look at men's dresses, or other marks of distinction, to know one from another; any one who was glad was, beyond all doubt, a plebeian, any one who looked sorrowful, a patrician.

Marcius alone, himself, was neither stunned nor humiliated. In mien, carriage, and countenance he bore the appearance of entire composure, and, while all his friends were full of distress, seemed the only man that was not touched with his misfortune. Not that either reflection taught him, or gentleness of temper made it natural for him, to submit; he was wholly possessed, on the contrary, with a profound and deep-seated fury, which passes with many for no pain at all. And pain, it is true, transmuted, so to say, by its own fiery heat into anger, loses every appearance of depression and feebleness; the angry man makes a show of energy, as the man in a high fever does of natural heat, while, in fact, all this action of the soul is but mere diseased palpitation, distension, and inflammation. That such was his distempered state appeared presently plainly enough in his actions.

On his return home, after saluting his mother and his wife, who were all in tears and full of loud lamentations, and exhorting them to moderate the sense they had of his calamity, he proceeded at once to the city gates, whither all the nobility came to attend him; and so not so much as taking anything with him, or making any request to the company, he departed from them, having only three or four clients with him. He continued solitary for a few days in a place in the country, distracted with a variety of counsels, such as rage and indignation suggested to him; and proposing to himself no honourable or useful end, but only how he might best satisfy his revenge on the Ro-

mans, he resolved at length to raise up a heavy war against them from their nearest neighbours. He determined, first to make trial of the Volscians, whom he knew to be still vigorous and flourishing, both in men and treasure, and he imagined their force and power was not so much abated as their spite and anger increased by the late overthrows they had received from the Romans.

There was a man of Antium, called Tullus Aufidius, who, for his wealth and bravery and the splendour of his family, had the respect and privilege of a king among the Volscians, but whom Marcius knew to have a particular hostility to himself, above all other Romans. Frequent menaces and challenges had passed in battle between them, and those exchanges of defiance to which their hot and eager emulation is apt to prompt young soldiers had added private animosity to their national feelings of opposition. Yet for all this, considering Tullus to have a certain generosity of temper, and knowing that no Volscian, so much as he, desired an occasion to requite upon the Romans the evils they had done, he did what much confirms the saying, that—

Hard and unequal is with wrath the strife,
Which makes us buy its pleasure with our life.

Putting on such a dress as would make him appear to any whom he might meet most unlike what he really was, like Ulysses—

The town he entered of his mortal foes.

His arrival at Antium was about evening, and, though several met him in the streets, yet he passed along without being known to any and went directly to the house of Tullus, and, entering undiscovered, went up to the fire-hearth, and seated himself there without speaking a word, covering up his head. Those of the family could not but wonder, and yet they were afraid either to raise or question him, for there was a certain air of majesty both in his posture and silence, but they recounted to Tullus, being then at supper, the strangeness of this accident.

He immediately rose from table and came in, and asked who he was, and for what business he came thither; and then Marcius, unmuffling himself, and pausing awhile, "If," said he, "you cannot call me to mind, Tullus, or do not believe your eyes concerning me, I must of necessity be my own accuser. I am Caius Marcius, the author of so much mischief to the Volscians; of which, were I seeking to deny it, the surname of Coriolanus I now bear would be a sufficient evidence against me. The one recompense I have received for all the hardships and perils I have gone through was the title that proclaims my enmity to your nation, and this is the only thing which is still left me. Of all other advantages, I have been stripped and deprived by the envy and outrage of the Roman people, and the cowardice and treachery of the magistrates and those of my own order. I am driven out as an exile, and become an humble suppliant at your hearth, not so much for safety and protection (should I have come hither, had I been afraid to die?) as to seek vengeance against those that expelled me; which, methinks, I have already obtained, by putting myself into your hands. If, therefore, you have really a mind to attack your enemies, come then, make use of that affliction you see me in to assist the enterprise, and convert my personal felicity into a common blessing to the Volscians; as, indeed, I am likely to be more serviceable in fighting for than against you, with the advantage which I now possess, of knowing all the secrets of the enemy that I am attacking. But if you decline to make any further attempts I am neither desirous to live myself, nor will it be well in you to preserve a person who has been your rival and adversary of old, and now, when he offers you his service, appears unprofitable and useless to you."

Tullus, on hearing this, was extremely rejoiced, and giving him his right hand, exclaimed, "Rise, Marcius, and be of good courage; it is a great happiness you bring to Antium, in the present use you make of yourself; expect everything that is good from the Volscians." He then proceeded to feast and entertain him with every display of kindness, and for several days after they were in close deliberation together on the prospects of a war.

While this design was forming, there were great troubles and commotions at Rome, from the animosity of the senators against the people, heightened just now by the late condemnation of Marcius.

Besides that their soothsayers and priests, and even private persons, reported signs and prodigies not to be neglected; one of which is stated to have occurred as follows: Titus Latinus, a man of ordinary condition, but of a quiet and virtuous character, free from all superstitious fancies, and yet more from vanity and exaggeration, had an apparition in his sleep, as if Jupiter came and bade him tell the senate, that it was with a bad and unacceptable dancer that they had headed his procession. Having beheld the vision, he said, he did not much attend to it at the first appearance; but after he had seen and slighted it a second and third time, he had lost a hopeful son, and was himself struck with a palsy. He was brought into the senate on a litter to tell this, and the story goes that he had no sooner delivered his message there, but he at once felt his strength return and got upon his legs, and went home alone without need of any support.

The senators, in wonder and surprise, made a diligent search into the matter. That which his dream alluded to was this: some citizen had, for some heinous offence, given up a servant of his to the rest of his fellows with charge to whip him first through the market, and then to kill him; and while they were executing this command, and scourging the wretch, who screwed and turned himself into all manner of shapes and unseemly motions, through the pain he was in, the solemn procession in honour of Jupiter chanced to follow at their heels. Several of the attendants on which were, indeed, scandalised at the sight, yet no one of them interfered, or acted further in the matter than merely to utter some common reproaches and execrations on a master who inflicted so cruel a punishment.

For the Romans treated their slaves with great humanity in these times, when, working and labouring themselves, and living together among them, they naturally were more gentle and familiar with them. It was one of the severest punishments for a slave who had committed a fault to have to take the piece of wood which supports the pole of a waggon, and carry it about through the neighbourhood; a slave who had once undergone the shame of this, and been thus seen by the household and the neighbours, had no longer any trust or credit among them, and had the name of *furcifer; furca* being the Latin word for a prop, or support.

When, therefore, Latinus had related his dream, and the senators were considering who this disagreeable and ungainly dancer could be, some of the company, having been struck with the strangeness of the punishment, called to mind and mentioned the miserable slave who was lashed through the streets and afterwards put to death. The priests, when consulted, confirmed the conjecture; the master was punished; and orders given for a new celebration of the procession and the spectacles in honour of the god.

Numa, in other respects also a wise arranger of religious offices, would seem to have been especially judicious in his direction, with a view to the attentiveness of the people, that, when the magistrates or priests performed any divine worship, a herald should go before, and proclaim with a loud voice, *Hoc age,* Do this you are about, and so warn them to mind whatever sacred action they were engaged in, and not suffer any business or worldly avocation to disturb and interrupt it; most of the things which men do of this kind being in a manner forced from them, and effected by constraint.

It is usual with the Romans to recommence their sacrifices and processions and spectacles, not only upon such a cause as this, but for any slighter reason. If but one of the horses which drew the chariots called Tensæ, upon which the images of their gods were placed, happened to fail and falter, or if the driver took hold of the reins with his left hand, they would decree that the whole operation should commence anew; and, in later ages, one and the same sacrifice was performed thirty times over, because of the occurrence of some defect or mistake or accident in the service. Such was the Roman reverence and caution in religious matters.

Marcius and Tullus were now secretly discoursing of their project with the chief men of Antium, advising them to invade the Romans while they were at variance among themselves. And when shame appeared to hinder them from embracing the motion, as they had sworn to a truce and cessation of arms for the space of two years, the Romans themselves soon furnished them with a pretence, by making proclamation, out of some jealousy or slanderous report, in the midst of the spectacles, that all the Volscians who had come to see them should depart the city before sunset. Some affirm that this was a contrivance of Marcius, who sent a man privately to the consuls, falsely to accuse the Volscians of intending to fall upon the Romans during the games, and to set the city on fire.

This public affront roused and inflamed their hostility to the Romans; and Tullus, perceiving it, made his advantage of it, aggravating the fact, and working on their indignation, till he persuaded them, at last, to despatch ambassadors to Rome, requiring the Romans to restore that part of their country and those towns which they had taken from the Volscians in the late war. When the Romans heard the message, they indignantly replied that the Volscians were the first that took up arms, but the Romans would be the last to lay them down.

This answer being brought back, Tullus called a general assembly of the Volscians; and the vote passing for a war, he then proposed that they should call in Marcius, laying aside the remembrance of former grudges, and assuring themselves that the services they should now receive from him as a friend and associate would abundantly outweigh any harm or damage he had done them when he was their enemy.

Marcius was accordingly summoned, and having made his entrance, and spoken to the people, won their good opinion of his capacity, his skill, counsel, and boldness, not less by his present words than by his past actions. They joined him in commission with Tullus, to have full power as the general of their forces in all that related to the war. And he, fearing lest the time that would be requisite to bring all the Volscians together in full preparation might be so long as to lose him the opportunity of action, left order with the chief persons and magistrates of the city to provide other things, while he himself, prevailing upon the most forward to assemble and march out with him as volunteers without staying to be enrolled, made a sudden inroad into the Roman confines, when nobody expected him, and possessed himself of so much booty, that the Volscians found they had more than they could either carry away or use in the camp.

The abundance of provision which he gained, and the waste and havoc of the country which he made, were, however, of themselves and in his account, the smallest results of that invasion; the great mischief he intended, and his special object in all, was to increase at Rome the suspicions entertained of the patricians, and to make them upon worse terms with the people. With this view, while spoiling all the fields and destroying the property of other men, he took special care to preserve their farms and lands untouched, and would not allow his soldiers to ravage there, or seize upon anything which belonged to them.

From hence their invectives and quarrels against one another broke out afresh, and rose to a greater height than ever; the senators reproaching those of the commonalty with their late injustice to Marcius; while the plebeians, on their side, did not hesitate to accuse them of having, out of spite and revenge, solicited him to this enterprise, and thus, when others were involved in the miseries of a war by their means, they sat like unconcerned spectators, as being furnished with a guardian and protector abroad of their wealth and fortunes, in the very person of the public enemy. After this incursion and exploit, which was of great advantage to the Volscians, as they learned by it to grow more hardy and to contemn their enemy, Marcius drew them off, and returned in safety.

But when the whole strength of the Volscians was brought together in the field, with great expedition and alacrity, it appeared so considerable a body, that they agreed to leave part in garrison, for the security of their towns, and with the other part to march against the Romans. Marcius now desired Tullus to choose which of the two charges would be most agreeable to him. Tullus answered that since he knew Marcius to be equally valiant with himself, and far more fortunate, he would have him take the command of those that were going out to the war, while he made it his care to defend their cities at home, and provide all conveniences for the army abroad.

Marcius thus reinforced, and much stronger than before, moved first towards the city called Circæum, a Roman colony. He received its surrender and did the inhabitants no injury; passing thence, he entered and laid waste the country of the Latins, where he expected the Romans would meet him, as the Latins were their confederates and allies, and had often sent to demand succours from them. The people, however, on their part, showing little inclination for the service, and the consuls themselves being unwilling to run the hazard of a battle when the time of their office was almost ready to expire, they dismissed the Latin ambassadors without any effect; so that Marcius, finding no army to oppose him, marched up to their cities, and having taken by force Toleria, Lavici, Peda, and Bola, all of which offered resistance, not only plundered their houses, but made a prey likewise of their persons. Meantime he showed particular regard for all such as came over to his party, and, for fear they might sustain any damage against his will, encamped at the greatest distance he could, and wholly abstained from the lands of their property.

After, however, that he had made himself master of Bola, a town not above ten miles from Rome, where he found great treasure, and put almost all the adults to the sword; and when on this, the other Volscians that were ordered to stay behind and protect their cities,

hearing of his achievements and success, had not patience to remain any longer at home, but came hastening in their arms to Marcius, saying that he alone was their general and the sole commander they would own; with all this, his name and renown spread throughout all Italy, and universal wonder prevailed at the sudden and mighty revolution in the fortunes of two nations which the loss and the accession of a single man had effected.

All at Rome was in great disorder; they were utterly averse from fighting, and spent their whole time in cabals and disputes and reproaches against each other; until news was brought that the enemy had laid close siege to Lavinium, where were the images and sacred things of their tutelar gods, and from whence they derived the origin of their nation, that being the first city which Æneas built in Italy.

These tidings produced a change as universal as it was extraordinary in the thoughts and inclinations of the people, but occasioned a yet stranger revulsion of feelings among the patricians. The people now were for repealing the sentence against Marcius, and calling him back into the city; whereas the senate, being assembled to preconsider the decree, opposed and finally rejected the proposal, either out of the mere humour of contradicting and withstanding the people in whatever they should desire, or because they were unwilling, perhaps, that he should owe his restoration to their kindness; or having now conceived a displeasure against Marcius himself, who was bringing distress upon all alike, though he had not been ill-treated by all, and was become a declared enemy to his whole country, though he knew well enough that the principal and all the better men condoled with him and suffered in his injuries.

This resolution of theirs being made public, the people could proceed no further, having no authority to pass anything by suffrage, and enact it for a law, without a previous decree from the senate. When Marcius heard of this, he was more exasperated than ever, and, quitting the siege of Lavinium, marched furiously towards Rome, and encamped at a place called the Cluilian ditches, about five miles from the city.

The nearness of his approach did, indeed, create much terror and disturbance, yet it also ended their dissensions for the present; as nobody now, whether consul or senator, durst any longer contradict the people in their design of recalling Marcius; but, seeing their women running affrighted up and down the streets, and the old men at prayer in every temple with tears and supplications, and that, in short, there was a general absence among them both of courage and wisdom to provide for their own safety, they came at last to be all of one mind, that the people had been in the right to propose as they did a reconciliation with Marcius, and that the senate was guilty of a fatal error to begin a quarrel with him when it was a time to forget offences, and they should have studied rather to appease him. It was, therefore, unanimously agreed by all parties that ambassadors should be despatched, offering him return to his country, and desiring he would free them from the terrors and distresses of the war.

The persons sent by the senate with this message were chosen out of his kindred and acquaintance, who naturally expected a very kind reception at their first interview, upon the score of that relation and their old familiarity and friendship with him; in which, however, they were much mistaken. Being led through the enemy's camp, they found him sitting in state amidst the chief men of the Volscians, looking insupportably proud and arrogant. He bade them declare the cause of their coming, which they did in the most gentle and tender terms, and with a behaviour suitable to their language. When they had made an end of speaking, he returned them a sharp answer, full of bitterness and angry resentment, as to what concerned himself and the ill-usage he had received from them; but as general of the Volscians, he demanded restitution of the cities and the lands which had been seized upon during the late war, and that the same rights and franchises should be granted them at Rome, which had been before accorded to the Latins; since there could be no assurance that a peace would be firm and lasting without fair and just conditions on both sides. He allowed them thirty days to consider and resolve.

The ambassadors being departed, he withdrew his forces out of the Roman territory. This, those of the Volscians who had long envied his reputation, and could not endure to see the influence he had with the people, laid hold of, as the first matter of complaint against him. Among them was also Tullus himself, not for any wrong done him personally by Marcius, but through the weakness incident to human nature. He could not help feeling mortified to find his own glory thus totally obscured, and himself overlooked and neglected now by the Volscians, who had so great an

opinion of their new leader, that he alone was all to them, while other captains, they thought, should be content with that share of power which he might think fit to accord.

From hence the first seeds of complaint and accusation were scattered about in secret, and the malcontents met and heightened each other's indignation, saying, that to retreat as he did was in effect to betray and deliver up, though not their cities and their arms, yet what was as bad, the critical times and opportunities for action, on which depend the preservation or the loss of everything else; since in less than thirty days' space, for which he had given a respite for the war, there might happen the greatest changes in the world. Yet Marcius spent not any part of the time idly, but attacked the confederates of the enemy, ravaged their land, and took from them seven great and populous cities in that interval.

The Romans, in the meanwhile, durst not venture out to their relief; but were utterly fearful, and showed no more disposition or capacity for action than if their bodies had been struck with a palsy, and became destitute of sense and motion. But when the thirty days were expired, and Marcius appeared again with his whole army, they sent another embassy, to beseech him that he would moderate his displeasure and would withdraw the Volscian army, and then make any proposals he thought best for both parties; the Romans would make no concessions to menaces, but if it were his opinion that the Volscians ought to have any favour shown them, upon laying down their arms they might obtain all they could in reason desire.

The reply of Marcius was, that he should make no answer to this as general of the Volscians, but, in the quality still of a Roman citizen, he would advise and exhort them, as the case stood, not to carry it so high, but think rather of just compliance, and return to him, before three days were at an end, with a ratification of his previous demands; otherwise, they must understand that they could not have any further freedom of passing through his camp upon idle errands.

When the ambassadors were come back, and had acquainted the senate with the answer, seeing the whole state now threatened as it were by a tempest, and the waves ready to overwhelm them, they were forced, as we say in extreme perils, to let down the sacred anchor.

A decree was made, that the whole order of their priests, those who initiated in the mysteries or had the custody of them, and those who, according to the ancient practice of the country, divined from birds, should all and every one of them go in full procession to Marcius with their pontifical array, and the dress and habit which they respectively used in their several functions, and should urge him, as before, to withdraw his forces, and then treat with his countrymen in favour of the Volscians. He consented so far, indeed, as to give the deputation an admittance into his camp, but granted nothing at all, nor so much as expressed himself more mildly; but without capitulating or receding, bade them once for all choose whether they would yield or fight, since the old terms were the only terms of peace.

When this solemn application proved ineffectual, the priests, too, returning unsuccessful, they determined to sit still within the city and keep watch about their walls, intending only to repulse the enemy, should he offer to attack them, and placing their hopes chiefly in time and in extraordinary accidents of fortune; as to themselves, they felt incapable of doing anything for their own deliverance; mere confusion and terror and ill-boding reports possessed the whole city; till at last a thing happened not unlike what we so often find represented, without, however, being accepted as true by people in general, in Homer.

On some great and unusual occasion we find him say—

But him the blue-eyed goddess did inspire,

and elsewhere—

But some immortal turned my mind away,
To think what others of the deed would say;

and again—

Were't his own thought or were't a god's
command?

People are apt, in such passages, to censure and disregard the poet, as if, by the introduction of mere impossibilities and idle fictions, he were denying the action of a man's own deliberate thought and free choice; which is not in the least the case in Homer's representation, where the ordinary, probable, and habitual conclusions that common reason leads to are continually ascribed to our own direct agency. He certainly says frequently enough—

But I consulted with my own great soul;

or, as in another passage—

He spoke. Achilles, with quick pain possessed,
Resolved two purposes in his strong breast;

and in a third—

—Yet never to her wishes won
The just mind of the brave Bellerophon.

But where the act is something out of the way and extraordinary, and seems in a manner to demand some impulse of divine possession and sudden inspiration to account for it, here he does introduce divine agency, not to destroy, but to prompt the human will; not to create in us another agency, but offering images to stimulate our own; images that in no sort or kind make our action involuntary, but give occasion rather to spontaneous action, aided and sustained by feelings of confidence and hope. For either we must totally dismiss and exclude divine influences from every kind of causality and origination in what we do, or else what other way can we conceive in which divine aid and co-operation can act? Certainly we cannot suppose that the divine beings actually and literally turn our bodies and direct our hands and our feet this way or that, to do what is right: it is obvious that they must actuate the practical and elective element of our nature, by certain initial occasions, by images presented to the imagination, and thoughts suggested to the mind, such either as to excite it to, or avert and withhold it from, any particular course.

In the perplexity which I have described, the Roman women went, some to other temples, but the greater part, and the ladies of highest rank, to the altar of Jupiter Capitolinus. Among these suppliants was Valeria, sister to the great Poplicola, who did the Romans eminent service both in peace and war. Poplicola himself was now deceased, as is told in the history of his life; but Valeria lived still, and enjoyed great respect and honour at Rome, her life and conduct no way disparaging her birth. She, suddenly seized with the sort of instinct or emotion of mind which I have described, and happily lighting, not without divine guidance, on the right expedient, both rose herself, and bade the others rise, and went directly with them to the house of Volumnia, the mother of Marcius. And coming in and finding her sitting with her daughter-in-law, and with her little grandchildren on her lap, Valeria, then surrounded by her female companions, spoke in the name of them all:—

"We that now make our appearance, O Volumnia, and you, Vergilia, are come as mere women to women, not by direction of the senate, or an order from the consuls, or the appointment of any other magistrate; but the divine being himself, as I conceive, moved to compassion by our prayers, prompted us to visit you in a body, and request a thing on which our own and the common safety depends, and which, if you consent to it, will raise your glory above that of the daughters of the Sabines, who won over their fathers and their husbands from mortal enmity to peace and friendship. Arise and come with us to Marcius; join in our supplication, and bear for your country this true and just testimony on her behalf; that, notwithstanding the many mischiefs that have been done her, yet she has never outraged you, nor so much as thought of treating you ill, in all her resentment, but does now restore you safe into his hands, though there be small likelihood she should obtain from him any equitable terms."

The words of Valeria were seconded by the acclamations of the other women, to which Volumnia made answer:—

"I and Vergilia, my countrywomen, have an equal share with you all in the common miseries, and we have the additional sorrow, which is wholly ours, that we have lost the merit and good fame of Marcius, and see his person confined, rather than protected, by the arms of the enemy. Yet I account this the greatest of all misfortunes, if indeed the affairs of Rome be sunk to so feeble a state as to have their last dependence upon us. For it is hardly imaginable he should have any consideration left for us, when he has no regard for the country which he was wont to prefer before his mother and wife and children. Make use, however, of our service; and lead us, if you please, to him; we are able, if nothing more, at least to spend our last breath in making suit to him for our country."

Having spoken thus, she took Vergilia by the hand, and the young children, and so accompanied them to the Volscian camp. So lamentable a sight much affected the enemies themselves, who viewed them in respectful silence. Marcius was then sitting in his place, with his chief officers about him, and, seeing the party of women advance toward them, wondered what should be the matter; but perceiving at length that his mother was at the head of them, he would fain have hardened himself in his former inexorable temper, but, overcome by his feelings, and confounded at what he saw, he did not endure they should approach him sitting in state, but came down hastily to meet them, saluting his mother first, and embracing her a long time, and then his

wife and children, sparing neither tears nor caresses, but suffering himself to be borne away and carried headlong, as it were, by the impetuous violence of his passion.

When he had satisfied himself, and observed that his mother, Volumnia, was desirous to say something, the Volscian council being first called in, he heard her to the following effect: "Our dress and our very persons, my son, might tell you, though we should say nothing ourselves, in how forlorn a condition we have lived at home since your banishment and absence from us; and now consider with yourself, whether we may not pass for the most unfortunate of all women, to have that sight, which should be the sweetest that we could see, converted, through I know not what fatality, to one of all others the most formidable and dreadful—Volumnia to behold her son, and Vergilia her husband, in arms against the walls of Rome.

"Even prayer itself, whence others gain comfort and relief in all manner of misfortunes, is that which most adds to our confusion and distress; since our best wishes are inconsistent with themselves, nor can we at the same time petition the gods for Rome's victory and your preservation, but what the worst of our enemies would imprecate as a curse, is the very object of our vows. Your wife and children are under the sad necessity, that they must either be deprived of you or of their native soil.

"As for myself, I am resolved not to wait till war shall determine this alternative for me; but if I cannot prevail with you to prefer amity and concord to quarrel and hostility, and to be the benefactor to both parties rather than the destroyer of one of them, be assured of this from me, and reckon steadfastly upon it, that you shall not be able to reach your country, unless you trample first upon the corpse of her that brought you into life. For it will be ill in me to wait and loiter in the world till the day come wherein I shall see a child of mine, either led in triumph by his own countrymen, or triumphing over them.

"Did I require you to save your country by ruining the Volscians, then, I confess, my son, the case would be hard for you to solve. It is base to bring destitution on our fellow-citizens; it is unjust to betray those who have placed their confidence in us. But, as it is, we do but desire a deliverance equally expedient for them and us; only more glorious and honourable on the Volscian side, who, as superior in arms, will be thought freely to bestow the two greatest of blessings, peace and friendship, even when they themselves receive the same.

"If we obtain these, the common thanks will be chiefly due to you as the principal cause; but if they be not granted, you alone must expect to bear the blame from both nations. The chance of all war is uncertain, yet thus much is certain in the present, that you, by conquering Rome, will only get the reputation of having undone your country; but if the Volscians happen to be defeated under your conduct, then the world will say, that, to satisfy a revengeful humour, you brought misery on your friends and patrons."

Marcius listened to his mother while she spoke without answering her a word; and Volumnia, seeing him stand mute also for a long time after she had ceased, resumed: "O my son," said she, "what is the meaning of this silence? Is it a duty to postpone everything to a sense of injuries, and wrong to gratify a mother in a request like this? Is it the characteristic of a great man to remember wrongs that have been done him, and not the part of a great and good man to remember benefits such as those that children receive from parents, and to requite them with honour and respect? You, methinks, who are so relentless in the punishment of the ungrateful, should not be more careless than others to be grateful yourself. You have punished your country already; you have not yet paid your debt to me. Nature and religion, surely, unattended by any constraint, should have won your consent to petitions so worthy and so just as these; but if it must be so, I will even use my last resource."

Having said this, she threw herself down at his feet, as did also his wife and children; upon which Marcius, crying out, "O mother! what is it you have done to me!" raised her up from the ground, and pressing her right hand with more than ordinary vehemence, "You have gained a victory," said he, "fortunate enough for the Romans, but destructive to your son; whom you, though none else, have defeated." After which, and a little private conference with his mother and his wife, he sent them back again to Rome, as they desired of him.

The next morning he broke up his camp, and led the Volscians homeward, variously affected with what he had done; some of them complaining of him and condemning his act, others, who were inclined to a peaceful conclusion, unfavourable to neither. A third party, while much disliking his proceedings, yet could not look upon Marcius as a treacherous person, but thought it pardonable in him to be thus shaken and driven to surrender at last, under such compulsion. None, however, opposed his commands; they all obediently followed him, though rather from admiration of his virtue, than any regard they now had to his authority.

The Roman people, meantime, more effectually manifested how much fear and danger they had been in while the war lasted, by their deportment after they were freed from it. Those that guarded the walls had no sooner given notice that the Volscians were dislodged and drawn off, but they set open all their temples in a moment, and began to crown themselves with garlands and prepare for sacrifice, as they were wont to do upon tidings brought of any signal victory.

But the joy and transport of the whole city was chiefly remarkable in the honours and marks of affection paid to the women, as well by the senate as the people in general; every one declaring that they were, beyond all question, the instruments of the public safety. And the senate having passed a decree that whatsoever they would ask in the way of any favour or honour should be allowed and done for them by the magistrates, they demanded simply that a temple might be erected to Female Fortune, the expense of which they offered to defray out of their own contributions, if the city would pay the cost of sacrifices, and other matters pertaining to the due honour of the gods, out of the common treasury.

The senate, much commending their public spirit, caused the temple to be built and a statue set up in it at the public charge; they, however, made up a sum among themselves for a second image of Fortune, which the Romans say uttered, as it was putting up, words to this effect, "Blessed of the gods, O women, is your gift."

These words, they profess, were repeated a second time, expecting our belief for what seems pretty nearly an impossibility. It may be possible enough that statues may seem to sweat, and to run with tears, and to stand with certain dewy drops of a sanguine colour; for timber and stones are frequently known to contract a kind of scurf and rottenness, productive of moisture; and various tints may form on the surfaces, both from within and from the action of the air outside; and by these signs it is not absurd to imagine that the deity may forewarn us. It may happen, also, that images and statues may sometimes make a noise not unlike that of a moan or groan, through a rupture or violent internal separation of the parts; but that an articulate voice, and such express words, and language so clear and exact and elaborate, should proceed from inanimate things is, in my judgment, a thing utterly out of possibility. For it was never known that either the soul of man, or the deity himself, uttered vocal sounds and language, alone, without an organised body and members fitted for speech.

But where history seems in a manner to force our assent by the concurrence of numerous and credible witnesses, we are to conclude that an impression distinct from sensation affects the imaginative part of our nature, and then carries away the judgment, so as to believe it to be a sensation; just as in sleep we fancy we see and hear, without really doing either. Persons, however, whose strong feelings of reverence to the deity, and tenderness for religion, will not allow them to deny or invalidate anything of this kind, have certainly a strong argument for their faith, in the wonderful and transcendent character of the divine power; which admits no manner of comparison with ours, either in its nature or its action, the modes or the strength of its operations. It is no contradiction to reason that it should do things that we cannot do, and effect what for us is impracticable: differing from us in all respects, in its acts yet more than in other points we may well believe it to be unlike us and remote from us. Knowledge of divine things for the most part, as Heraclitus says, is lost to us by incredulity.

When Marcius came back to Antium, Tullus, who thoroughly hated and greatly feared him, proceeded at once to contrive how he might immediately despatch him, as, if he escaped now, he was never likely to give him such another advantage. Having therefore got together and suborned several partisans against him, he required Marcius to resign his charge, and give the Volscians an account of his administration. He, apprehending the danger of a private condition, while Tullus held the office of general and exercised the greatest power among his fellow-citizens, made answer, that he was ready to lay down his commission whenever those from whose common authority he had received it should think fit to recall it, and that in the meantime he was ready to give the Antiates satisfaction, as to all particulars of his conduct, if they were desirous of it.

An assembly was called, and popular speakers, as had been concerted, came forward to exasperate and incense the multitude; but when Marcius stood up to answer, the more unruly and tumultuous part of the people became quiet on a sudden, and out of reverence allowed him to speak without the least disturbance; while all the better people, and such as were satisfied with a peace, made it evident by their whole behaviour, that they would give him a favourable hearing, and judge and pronounce according to equity.

Tullus, therefore, began to dread the issue of the defence he was going to make for himself; for he was an admirable speaker, and the former services he had done the Volscians had procured and still preserved for him greater kindness than could be outweighed by any blame for his late conduct. Indeed, the very accusation itself was a proof and testimony of the greatness of his merits, since people could never have complained or thought themselves wronged, because Rome was not brought into their power, but that by his means they had come so near to taking it.

For these reasons, the conspirators judged it prudent not to make any further delays, nor to test the general feeling; but the boldest of their faction, crying out that they ought not to listen to a traitor, nor allow him still to retain office and play the tyrant among them, fell upon Marcius in a body, and slew him there, none of those that were present offering to defend him. But it quickly appeared that the action was in nowise approved by the majority of the Volscians, who hurried out of their several cities to show respect to his corpse; to which they gave honourable interment, adorning his sepulchre with arms and trophies, as the monument of a noble hero and a famous general.

When the Romans heard tidings of his death, they gave no other signification either of honour or of anger towards him, but simply granted the request of the women, that they might put themselves into mourning and bewail him for ten months, as the usage was upon the loss of a father or a son or a brother; that being the period fixed for the longest lamentation by the laws of Numa Pompilius, as is more amply told in the account of him.

Marcius was no sooner deceased, but the Volscians felt the need of his assistance. They quarrelled first with the Æquians, their confederates and their friends, about the appointment of the general of their joint forces, and carried their dispute to the length of bloodshed and slaughter; and were then defeated by the Romans in a pitched battle, where not only Tullus lost his life, but the principal flower of their whole army was cut in pieces; so that they were forced to submit and accept of peace upon very dishonourable terms, becoming subjects of Rome, and pledging themselves to submission.

ALCIBIADES and CORIOLANUS
Compared

HAVING described all their actions that seem to deserve commemoration, their military ones, we may say, incline the balance very decidedly upon neither side. They both, in pretty equal measure, displayed on numerous occasions the daring and courage of the soldier, and the skill and foresight of the general; unless, indeed, the fact that Alcibiades was victorious and successful in many contests both by sea and land, ought to gain him the title of a more complete commander. That so long as they remained and held command in their respective countries they eminently sustained, and when they were driven into exile yet more eminently damaged, the fortunes of those countries, is common to both.

All the sober citizens felt disgust at the petulance, the low flattery, and base seductions which Alcibiades, in his public life, allowed himself to employ with the view of winning the people's favour; and the ungraciousness, pride, and oligarchical haughtiness which Marcius, on the other hand, displayed in his, were the abhorrence of the Roman populace. Neither of these courses can be called commendable; but a man who ingratiates himself by indulgence and flattery is hardly so censurable as one who, to avoid the appearance of flattering, insults. To seek power by servility to the people is a disgrace, but to maintain it by terror, violence, and oppression is not a disgrace only, but an injustice.

Marcius, according to our common conceptions of his character, was undoubtedly simple and straightforward; Alcibiades, unscrupulous as a public man, and false. He is more especially blamed for the dishonourable and treacherous way in which, as Thucydides relates, he imposed upon the Lacedæmonian ambassadors, and disturbed the continuance of the peace. Yet this policy, which engaged the city again in war, nevertheless placed it in a powerful and formidable position, by the accession, which Alcibiades obtained for it, of the alliance of Argos and Mantinea. And Coriolanus also, Dionysius relates, used unfair means to excite war between the Romans and the Volscians, in the false report which he spread about the visitors at the Games; and the motive of this action seems to make it the worse of the two; since it was not done, like the other, out of ordinary political jealousy, strife, and competition. Simply to gratify anger from which, as Ion says, no one ever yet got any return, he threw whole districts of Italy into confusion, and sacrificed to his passion against his country numerous innocent cities.

It is true, indeed, that Alcibiades also, by his resentment, was the occasion of great disasters to his country, but he relented as soon as he found their feelings to be changed; and after he was driven out a second time, so far from taking pleasure in the errors and inadvertencies of their commanders, or being indifferent to the danger they were thus incurring, he did the very thing that Aristides is so highly commended for doing to Themistocles; he came to the generals who were his enemies, and pointed out to them what they ought to do. Coriolanus, on the other hand, first of all attacked the whole body of his countrymen, though only one portion of them had done him any wrong, while the other, the better and nobler portion, had actually suffered, as well as sympathised, with him. And, secondly, by the obduracy with which he resisted numerous embassies and supplications, addressed in propitiation of his single anger and offence, he showed that it had been to destroy and overthrow, not to recover and regain his country, that he had excited bitter and implacable hostilities against it.

There is, indeed, one distinction that may be drawn. Alcibiades, it may be said, was not safe among the Spartans, and had the inducements at once of fear and of hatred to lead him again to Athens; whereas Marcius could not honourably have left the Volscians, when they were behaving so well to him: he, in the command of their forces and the enjoyment of their entire confidence, was in a very different position from Alcibiades, whom the Lacedæmonians did not so much wish to adopt into their service, as to use and then abandon. Driven about from house to house in the city, and from general to general in the camp, the latter had no resort but to place himself in the hands of Tisaphernes; unless, indeed, we are to suppose that his object in courting favour with him was to avert the entire destruction of his native city, whither he wished himself to return.

As regards money, Alcibiades, we are told, was often guilty of procuring it by accepting bribes, and spent it ill in luxury and dissipation. Coriolanus declined to receive it, even when pressed upon him by his commanders as an honour; and one great reason for the odium he incurred with the populace in the discussions about their debts was, that he trampled upon the poor, not for money's sake, but out of pride and insolence.

Antipater, in a letter written upon the death of Aristotle, the philosopher, observes, "Amongst his other gifts he had that of persuasiveness"; and the absence of this in the character of Marcius made all his great actions and noble qualities unacceptable to those whom they benefited: pride, and self-will, the consort, as Plato calls it, of solitude, made him insufferable. With the skill which Alcibiades, on the contrary, possessed to treat every one in the way most agreeable to him, we cannot wonder that all his successes were attended with the most exuberant favour and honour; his very errors, at times, being accompanied by something of grace and felicity. And so in spite of great and frequent hurt that he had done the city, he was repeatedly appointed to office and command; while Coriolanus stood in vain for a place which his great services had made his due. The one, in spite of the harm he occasioned, could not make himself hated, nor the other, with all the admiration he attracted, succeed in being beloved by his countrymen.

Coriolanus, moreover, it should be said, did not as a general obtain any successes for his country, but only for his enemies against his country. Alcibiades was often of service to Athens, both as a soldier and as a commander. So long as he was personally present, he had the perfect mastery of his political adversaries; calumny only succeeded in his absence.

Coriolanus was condemned in person at Rome; and in like manner killed by the Volscians, not indeed with any right or justice, yet not without some pretext occasioned by his own acts; since, after rejecting all conditions of peace in public, in private he yielded to the solicitations of the women and, without establishing peace, threw up the favourable chances of war. He ought, before retiring, to have obtained the consent of those who had placed their trust in him; if indeed he considered their claims on him to be the strongest.

Or, if we say that he did not care about the Volscians, but merely had prosecuted the war, which he now abandoned, for the satisfaction of his own resentment, then the noble thing would have been, not to spare his country for his mother's sake, but his mother in and with his country; since both his mother and his wife were part and parcel of that endangered country. After harshly repelling public supplications, the entreaties of ambassadors, and the prayers of priests, to concede all as a private favour to his mother was less an honour to her than a dishonour to the city which thus escaped, in spite, it would seem, of its own demerits through the intercession of a single woman. Such a grace could, indeed, seem merely invidious, ungracious, and unreasonable in the eyes of both parties; he retreated without listening to the persuasions of his opponents or asking the consent of his friends.

The origin of all lay in his unsociable, supercilious, and self-willed disposition, which, in all cases, is offensive to most people; and when combined with a passion for distinction passes into absolute savageness and mercilessness. Men decline to ask favours of the people, professing not to need any honours from them; and then are indignant if they do not obtain them. Metellus, Aristides, and Epaminondas certainly did not beg favours of the multitude; but that was because they, in real truth, did not value the gifts which a popular body can either confer or refuse; and when they were more than once driven into exile, rejected at elections, and condemned in courts of justice, they showed no resentment at the ill-humour of their fellow-citizens, but were willing and contented to return and be reconciled when the feeling altered and they were wished for. He who least likes courting favour, ought also least to think of resenting neglect; to feel wounded at being refused a distinction can only arise from an overweening appetite to have it.

Alcibiades never professed to deny that it was pleasant to him to be honoured, and distasteful to him to be overlooked; and, accordingly, he always tried to place himself upon good terms with all that he met; Coriolanus's pride forbade him to pay attentions to those who could have promoted his advancement, and yet his love of distinction made him feel hurt and angry when he was disregarded.

Such are the faulty parts of his character, which in all other respects was a noble one. For his temperance, continence, and probity he claims to be compared with the best and purest of the Greeks; not in any sort or kind with Alcibiades, the least scrupulous and most entirely careless of human beings in all these points.

TIMOLEON

411?–337 B.C.

IT was for the sake of others that I first commenced writing biographies; but I find myself proceeding and attaching myself to it for my own; the virtues of these great men serving me as a sort of looking-glass, in which I may see how to adjust and adorn my own life. Indeed, it can be compared to nothing but daily living and associating together; we receive, as it were, in our inquiry, and entertain each successive guest, view—

Their stature and their qualities,

and select from their actions all that is noblest and worthiest to know.

Ah, and what greater pleasure could one have? or what more effective means to one's moral improvement?

Democritus tells us we ought to pray that of the phantasms appearing in the circumambient air, such may present themselves to us as are propitious, and that we may rather meet with those that are agreeable to our natures and are good than the evil and unfortunate; which is simply introducing into philosophy a doctrine untrue in itself, and leading to endless superstitions. My method, on the contrary, is, by the study of history, and by the familiarity acquired in writing, to habituate my memory to receive and retain images of the best and worthiest characters. I thus am enabled to free myself from any ignoble, base, or vicious impressions, contracted from the contagion of ill company that I may be unavoidably engaged in, by the remedy of turning my thoughts in a happy and calm temper to view these noble examples. Of this kind are those of Timoleon the Corinthian and Paulus Æmilius, to write whose lives is my present business; men equally famous, not only for their virtues, but success; insomuch that they have left it doubtful whether they owe their greatest achievements to good fortune, or their own prudence and conduct.

The affairs of the Syracusans, before Timoleon was sent into Sicily, were in this posture: after Dion had driven out Dionysius the tyrant, he was slain by treachery, and those that had assisted him in delivering Syracuse were divided among themselves; and thus the city by a continual change of governors, and a train of mischiefs that succeeded each other, became almost abandoned; while of the rest of Sicily, part was now utterly depopulated and desolate through long continuance of war, and most of the cities that had been left standing were in the hands of barbarians and soldiers out of employment, that were ready to embrace every turn of government.

Such being the state of things, Dionysius takes the opportunity, and in the tenth year of his banishment, by the help of some mercenary troops he had got together, forces out Nysæus, then master of Syracuse, recovers all afresh, and is again settled in his dominion; and as at first he had been strangely deprived of the greatest and most absolute power that ever was by a very small party, so now, in a yet stranger manner, when in exile and of mean condition, he became the sovereign of those who had ejected him. All, therefore, that remained in Syracuse had to serve under a tyrant, who at the best was of an ungentle nature, and exasperated now to a degree of savageness by the late misfortunes and calamities he had suffered.

The better and more distinguished citizens, having timely retired thence to Hicetes, ruler of the Leontines, put themselves under his protection, and chose him for their general in the war; not that he was much preferable to any open and avowed tyrant, but they had no other sanctuary at present, and it gave them some ground of confidence that he was of a Syracusan family, and had forces able to encounter those of Dionysius.

In the meantime the Carthaginians appeared before Sicily with a great navy, watching when and where they might make a descent upon the island; and terror at this fleet made the Sicilians incline to send an embassy into Greece to demand succours from the Corinthians, whom they confided in rather than others, not only upon the account of their near kindred, and the great benefits they had often received by trusting them, but because Corinth had ever shown herself attached to freedom and averse from tyranny and had engaged in many noble wars, not for empire or aggrandisement, but for the sole liberty of the Greeks.

But Hicetes, who made it the business of his command not so much to deliver the Syracusans from other tyrants, as to enslave them to himself, had already entered into some secret conferences with those of Carthage, while in public he commended the design of his Syracusan clients, and despatched ambassadors from himself, together with theirs, into Peloponnesus; not that he really desired any relief to come from there, but in case the Corinthians, as was likely enough, on account of the troubles of Greece and occupation at home, should refuse their assistance, hoping then he should be able with less difficulty to dispose and incline things for the Carthaginian interest, and so make use of these foreign pretenders, as instruments and auxiliaries for himself, either against the Syracusans or Dionysius, as occasion served. This was discovered a while after.

The ambassadors being arrived, and their request known, the Corinthians, who had always a great concern for all their colonies and plantations, but especially for Syracuse, since by good fortune there was nothing to molest them in their own country, where they were enjoying peace and leisure at that time, readily and with one accord passed a vote for their assistance. And when they were deliberating about the choice of a captain for the expedition, and the magistrates were urging the claims of various aspirants for reputation, one of the crowd stood up and named Timoleon, son of Timodemus, who had long absented himself from public business, and had neither any thoughts of, nor the least pretensions to, an employment of that nature.

Some god or other, it might rather seem, had put it in the man's heart to mention him; such favour and good-will on the part of Fortune seemed at once to be shown in his election, and to accompany all his following actions, as though it were on purpose to commend his worth, and add grace and ornament to his personal virtues.

As regards his parentage, both Timodemus, his father, and his mother, Demariste, were of high rank in the city; and as for himself, he was noted for his love of his country, and his gentleness of temper, except in his extreme hatred to tyrants and wicked men. His natural abilities for war were so happily tempered, that while a rare prudence might be seen in all the enterprises of his younger years, an equal courage showed itself in the last exploits of his declining age.

He had an elder brother, whose name was Timophanes, who was every way unlike him, being indiscreet and rash, and infected by the suggestions of some friends and foreign soldiers, whom he kept always about him, with a passion for absolute power. He seemed to have a certain force and vehemence in all military service, and even to delight in dangers, and thus he took much with the people, and was advanced to the highest charges, as a vigorous and effective warrior; in the obtaining of which offices and promotions, Timoleon much assisted him, helping to conceal or at least to extenuate his errors, embellishing by his praise whatever was commendable in him, and setting off his good qualities to the best advantage.

It happened once in the battle fought by the Corinthians against the forces of Argos and Cleonæ, that Timoleon served among the infantry, when Timophanes, commanding their cavalry, was brought into extreme danger; as his horse being wounded fell forward and threw him headlong amidst the enemies, while part of his companions dispersed at once in a panic, and the small number that remained, bearing up against a great multitude, had much ado to maintain any resistance. As soon, therefore, as Timoleon was aware of the accident, he ran hastily in to his brother's rescue, and covering the fallen Timophanes with his buckler, after having received abundance of darts, and several strokes by the sword upon his body and his armour, he at length with much difficulty obliged the enemies to retire, and brought off his brother alive and safe.

But when the Corinthians, for fear of losing their city a second time, as they had once before, by admitting their allies, made a decree to maintain four hundred mercenaries for its security, and gave Timophanes the command over them, he, abandoning all regard to honour and equity, at once proceeded to put into execution his plans for making himself absolute, and bringing the place under his own power; and having cut off many principal citizens, uncondemned and without trial, who were most likely to hinder his designs, he declared himself tyrant of Corinth; a procedure that infinitely afflicted Timoleon, to whom the wickedness of such a brother appeared to be his own reproach and calamity. He undertook to persuade him by reasoning, that desisting from that wild and unhappy ambition, he would bethink himself how he should make the Corinthians some amends, and find out an expedient to remedy and correct the evils he had done them.

When his single admonition was rejected and contemned by him, he makes a second attempt, taking with him Æschylus his kinsman, brother to the wife of Timophanes, and a certain diviner, that was his friend, whom Theopompus in his history calls Satyrus, but Ephorus and Timæus mention in theirs by the name of Orthagoras. After a few days, then, he returns to his brother with this company, all three of them surrounding and earnestly importuning him upon the same subject, that now at length he would listen to reason, and be of another mind. But when Timophanes began first to laugh at the men's simplicity, and presently broke out into rage and indignation against them, Timoleon stepped aside from him and stood weeping with his face covered, while the other two, drawing out their swords, despatched him in a moment.

On the rumour of this act being soon scattered about, the better and more generous of the Corinthians highly applauded Timoleon for the hatred of wrong and the greatness of soul that had made him, though of a gentle disposition and full of love and kindness for his family, think the obligations to his country stronger than the ties of consanguinity, and prefer that which is good and just before gain and interest and his own particular advantage. For the same brother, who with so much bravery had been saved by him when he fought valiantly in the cause of Corinth, he had now as nobly sacrificed for enslaving her afterwards by a base usurpation.

But then, on the other side, those that knew not how to live in a democracy, and had been used to make their humble court to the men of power, though they openly professed to rejoice at the death of the tyrant, nevertheless, secretly reviling Timoleon, as one that had committed an impious and abominable act, drove him into melancholy and dejection.

And when he came to understand how heavily his mother took it, and that she likewise uttered the saddest complaints and most terrible imprecations against him, he went to satisfy and comfort her as to what had happened; and finding that she would not endure so much as to look upon him, but caused her doors to be shut, that he might have no admission into her presence, with grief at this he grew so disordered in his mind and so disconsolate, that he determined to put an end to his perplexity with his life, by abstaining from all manner of sustenance.

But through the care and diligence of his friends, who were every instant with him, and added force to their entreaties, he came to resolve and promise at last, that he would endure living, provided it might be in solitude, and remote from company; so that, quitting all civil transactions and commerce with the world for a long while after his first retirement, he never came into Corinth, but wandered up and down the fields, full of anxious and tormenting thoughts, and spent his time in desert places, at the farthest distance from society and human intercourse.

So true it is that the minds of men are easily shaken and carried off from their own sentiments through the casual commendation or reproof of others, unless the judgments that we make, and the purposes we conceive, be confirmed by reason and philosophy, and thus obtain strength and steadiness. An action must not only be just and laudable in its own nature, but it must proceed likewise from solid motives and a lasting principle, that so we may fully and constantly approve the thing, and be perfectly satisfied in what we do; for otherwise, after having put our resolution into practice, we shall out of pure weakness come to be troubled at the performance, when the grace and godliness, which rendered it before so amiable and pleasing to us, begin to decay and wear out of our fancy; like greedy people, who, seizing on the more delicious morsels of any dish with a keen appetite, are presently disgusted when they grow full, and find themselves oppressed and uneasy now by what they before so greedily desired. For a succeeding dislike spoils the best of actions, and repentance makes that which was never so well done become base and faulty; whereas the choice that is founded upon knowledge and wise reasoning does not change by disappointment, or suffer us to repent, though it happen perchance to be less prosperous in the issue.

And thus, Phocion, of Athens, having always vigorously opposed the measures of Leosthenes, when success appeared to attend them,

and he saw his countrymen rejoicing and offering sacrifice in honour of their victory, "I
should have been as glad," said he to them,
"that I myself had been the author of what
Leosthenes has achieved for you, as I am that I
gave you my own counsel against it."

A more vehement reply is recorded to have
been made by Aristides the Locrian, one of
Plato's companions, to Dionysius the elder,
who demanded one of his daughters in marriage: "I had rather," said he to him, "see the
virgin in her grave than in the palace of a tyrant." And when Dionysius, enraged at the
affront, made his sons be put to death a while
after, and then again insultingly asked, whether he were still in the same mind as to the disposal of his daughters, his answer was, "I cannot but grieve at the cruelty of your deeds, but
am not sorry for the freedom of my own
words." Such expressions as these may belong
perhaps to a more sublime and accomplished
virtue.

The grief, however, of Timoleon at what
had been done, whether it arose from commiseration of his brother's fate or the reverence he
bore his mother, so shattered and broke his
spirits that for the space of almost twenty years
he had not offered to concern himself in any
honourable or public action. When, therefore,
he was pitched upon for a general, and, joyfully accepted as such by the suffrages of the people, Teleclides, who was at that time the most
powerful and distinguished man in Corinth,
began to exhort him that he would act now
like a man of worth and gallantry: "For,"
said he, "if you do bravely in this service we
shall believe that you delivered us from a
tyrant; but if otherwise that you killed your
brother."

While he was yet preparing to set sail, and
enlisting soldiers to embark with him, there
came letters to the Corinthians from Hicetes,
plainly disclosing his revolt and treachery. For
his ambassadors had no sooner gone for Corinth, but he openly joined the Carthaginians,
negotiating that they might assist him to throw
out Dionysius, and become master of Syracuse
in his room. And fearing he might be disappointed of his aim if troops and a commander
should come from Corinth before this were effected, he sent a letter of advice thither, in all
haste, to prevent their setting out, telling them
they need not be at any cost and trouble upon
his account, or run the hazard of a Sicilian voyage, especially since the Carthaginians, alliance
with whom against Dionysius the slowness of

their motions had compelled him to embrace,
would dispute their passage, and lay in wait to
attack them with a numerous fleet. This letter
being publicly read, if any had been cold and
indifferent before as to the expedition in hand,
the indignation they now conceived against
Hicetes so exasperated and inflamed them all
that they willingly contributed to supply Timoleon, and endeavoured with one accord to
hasten his departure.

When the vessels were equipped, and his soldiers every way provided for, the female priest
of Proserpina had a dream or vision wherein
she and her mother Ceres appeared to them in
a travelling garb, and were heard to say that
they were going to sail with Timoleon into
Sicily; whereupon the Corinthians, having
built a sacred galley, devoted it to them, and
called it the galley of the goddesses.

Timoleon went in person to Delphi, where
he sacrificed to Apollo, and, descending into
the place of prophecy, was surprised with the
following marvellous occurrence. A riband,
with crowns and figures of victory embroidered upon it, slipped off from among the gifts
that were there consecrated and hung up in the
temple, and fell directly down upon his head;
so that Apollo seemed already to crown him
with success, and send him thence to conquer
and triumph.

He put to sea only with seven ships of Corinth, two of Corcyra, and a tenth which was
furnished by the Leucadians; and when he was
now entered into the deep by night, and carried with a prosperous gale, the heaven seemed
all on a sudden to break open, and a bright
spreading flame to issue forth from it, and
hover over the ship he was in; and, having
formed itself into a torch, not unlike those that
are used in the mysteries, it began to steer the
same course, and run along in their company,
guiding them by its light to that quarter of
Italy where they designed to go ashore. The
soothsayers affirmed that this apparition agreed
with the dream of the holy woman, since the
goddesses were now visibly joining in the expedition, and sending this light from heaven
before them, Sicily being thought sacred to
Proserpina, as poets feign that the rape was
committed there, and that the island was given
her in dowry when she married Pluto.

These early demonstrations of divine favour
greatly encouraged his whole army; so that
making all the speed they were able, by a voyage across the open sea, they were soon passing
along the coast of Italy. But the tidings that

came from Sicily much perplexed Timoleon, and disheartened his soldiers.

For Hicetes, having already beaten Dionysius out of the field, and reduced most of the quarters of Syracuse itself, now hemmed him in and besieged him in the citadel and what is called the Island, whither he was fled for his last refuge; while the Carthaginians, by agreement, were to make it their business to hinder Timoleon from landing in any port of Sicily; so that he and his party being driven back, they might with ease and at their own leisure divide the island among themselves.

In pursuance of which design the Carthaginians sent away twenty of their galleys to Rhegium, having aboard them certain ambassadors from Hicetes to Timoleon, who carried instructions suitable to these proceedings, specious amusements, and plausible stories, to colour and conceal dishonest purposes. They had order to propose and demand that Timoleon himself, if he liked the offer, should come and advise with Hicetes and partake of all his conquests, but that he might send back his ships and forces to Corinth, since the war was in a manner finished, and the Carthaginians had blocked up the passage, determined to oppose them if they should try to force their way towards the shore.

When, therefore, the Corinthians met with these envoys at Rhegium, and received their message, and saw the Phœnician vessels riding at anchor in the bay, they became keenly sensible of the abuse that was put upon them, and felt a general indignation against Hicetes, and great apprehensions for the Siceliots, whom they now plainly perceived to be as it were a prize and recompense to Hicetes on one side for his perfidy, and to the Carthaginians on the other for the sovereign power they secured to him. For it seemed utterly impossible to force and overbear the Carthaginian ships that lay before them and were double their number, as also to vanquish the victorious troops which Hicetes had with him in Syracuse, to take the lead of which very troops they had undertaken their voyage.

The case being thus, Timoleon, after some conference with the envoys of Hicetes and the Carthaginian captains, told them he should readily submit to their proposals (to what purpose would it be to refuse compliance?): he was desirous only, before his return to Corinth, that what had passed between them in private might be solemnly declared before the people of Rhegium, a Greek city, and a common friend to the parties; this, he said, would very much conduce to his own security and discharge; and they likewise would more strictly observe articles of agreement, on behalf of the Syracusans, which they had obliged themselves to in the presence of so many witnesses. The design of all which was only to divert their attention, while he got an opportunity of slipping away from their fleet; a contrivance that all the principal Rhegians were privy and assisting to, who had a great desire that the affairs of Sicily should fall into Corinthian hands, and dreaded the consequences of having barbarian neighbours.

An assembly was therefore called, and the gates shut, that the citizens might have no liberty to turn to other business; and a succession of speakers came forward, addressing the people at great length, to the same effect, without bringing the subject to any conclusion, making way each for another and purposely spinning out the time, till the Corinthian galleys should get clear of the haven; the Carthaginian commanders being detained there without any suspicion, as also Timoleon still remained present, and gave signs as if he were just preparing to make an oration.

But upon secret notice that the rest of the galleys were already gone off, and that his alone remained waiting for him, by the help and concealment of those Rhegians that were about the hustings and favoured his departure, he made shift to slip away through the crowd, and running down to the port, set sail with all speed; and having reached his other vessels, they came all safe to Tauromenium in Sicily, whither they had been formerly invited, and where they were now kindly received by Andromachus, then ruler of the city. This man was father of Timæus, the historian, and incomparably the best of all those that bore sway in Sicily at that time, governing his citizens according to law and justice and openly professing an aversion and enmity to all tyrants; upon which account he gave Timoleon leave to muster up his troops there, and to make that city the seat of war, persuading the inhabitants to join their arms with the Corinthian forces, and assist them in the design of delivering Sicily.

But the Carthaginians who were left in Rhegium perceiving, when the assembly was dissolved, that Timoleon had given them the go-by, were not a little vexed to see themselves outwitted, much to the amusement of the Rhegians, who could not but smile to find Phœnicians complain of being cheated. However, they despatched a messenger aboard one of their galleys to Tauromenium, who, after much blustering in the insolent barbaric way, and many menaces to Andromachus if he did not forthwith send the Corinthians off, stretched out his hand with the inside upward, and then turning it down again, threatened he would handle their city even so, and turn it topsy-turvy in as little time, and with as much ease. Andromachus, laughing at the man's confidence, made no other reply, but, imitating his gesture, bid him hasten his own departure, unless he had a mind to see that kind of dexterity practised first upon the galley which brought him hither.

Hicetes, informed that Timoleon had made good his passage, was in great fear of what might follow, and sent to desire the Carthaginians that a large number of galleys might be ordered to attend and secure the coast. And now it was that the Syracusans began wholly to despair of safety, seeing the Carthaginians possessed of their haven, Hicetes master of the town, and Dionysius supreme in the citadel; while Timoleon had as yet but a slender hold of Sicily, as it were by the fringe or border of it, in the small city of the Tauromenians, with a feeble hope and a poor company, having but a thousand soldiers at the most, and no more provisions, either of corn or money, than were just necessary for the maintenance and the pay of that inconsiderable number.

Nor did the other towns of Sicily confide in him, overpowered as they were with violence and outrage, and embittered against all that should offer to lead armies by the treacherous conduct chiefly of Callipus, an Athenian, and Pharax, a Lacedæmonian captain, both of whom, after giving out that the design of their coming was to introduce liberty and to depose tyrants, so tyrannised themselves, that the reign of former oppressors seemed to be a golden age in comparison, and the Sicilians began to consider those more happy who had expired in servitude, than any that had lived to see such a dismal freedom.

Looking, therefore, for no better usage from the Corinthian general, but imagining that it was only the same old course of things once more, specious pretences and false professions to allure them by fair hopes and kind promises into the obedience of a new master, they all, with one accord, unless it were the people of Adranum, suspected the exhortations, and rejected the overtures that were made them in his name.

These were inhabitants of a small city, consecrated to Adranus, a certain god that was in high veneration throughout Sicily, and, as it happened, they were then at variance among themselves, insomuch that one party called in Hicetes and the Carthaginians to assist them, while the other sent proposals to Timoleon. It so fell out that these auxiliaries, striving which should be soonest, both arrived at Adranum about the same time; Hicetes bringing with him at least five thousand men, while all the force Timoleon could make did not exceed twelve hundred.

With these he marched out of Tauromenium, which was about three hundred and forty furlongs distant from that city. The first day he moved but slowly, and took up his quarters betimes after a short journey; but the day following he quickened his pace, and, having passed through much difficult ground, towards evening received advice that Hicetes was just approaching Adranum, and pitching his camp before it; upon which intelligence, his captains and other officers caused the vanguard to halt, that the army being refreshed, and having reposed a while, might engage the enemy with better heart.

But Timoleon, coming up in haste, desired them not to stop for that reason, but rather use all possible diligence to surprise the enemy, whom probably they would now find in disorder, as having lately ended their march and being taken up at present in erecting tents and preparing supper; which he had no sooner said, but laying hold of his buckler and putting himself in the front, he led them on as it were to certain victory. The braveness of such a leader made them all follow him with like courage and assurance.

They were now within less than thirty furlongs of Adranum, which they quickly traversed, and immediately fell in upon the enemy, who were seized with confusion, and began to retire at their first approaches; one consequence of which was that, amidst so little opposition, and so early and general a flight, there were not many more than three hundred slain, and about twice the number made prisoners. Their camp and baggage, however, was all taken.

The fortune of this onset soon induced the Adranitans to unlock their gates, and to embrace the interest of Timoleon, to whom they recounted, with a mixture of affright and admiration, how, at the very minute of the encounter, the doors of their temple flew open of their own accord, that the javelin also, which their god held in his hand, was observed to tremble at the point, and that drops of sweat had been seen running down his face; prodigies that not only presaged the victory then obtained, but were an omen, it seems, of all his future exploits, to which this first happy action gave the occasion.

For now the neighbouring cities and potentates sent deputies, one upon another, to seek his friendship and make offer of their service. Among the rest Mamercus, the tyrant of Catana, an experienced warrior and a wealthy prince, made proposals of alliance with him, and what was of greater importance still, Dionysius himself, being now grown desperate, and well-nigh forced to surrender, despising Hicetes who had been thus shamefully baffled, and admiring the valour of Timoleon, found means to advertise him and his Corinthians that he should be content to deliver up himself and the citadel into their hands.

Timoleon, gladly embracing this unlooked-for advantage, sends away Euclides and Telemachus, two Corinthian captains, with four hundred men, for the seizure and custody of the castle, with directions to enter not all at once, or in open view, that being impracticable so long as the enemy kept guard, but by stealth, and in small companies. And so they took possession of the fortress and the palace of Dionysius, with all the stores and ammunition he had prepared and laid up to maintain the war. They found a good number of horses, every variety of engines, a multitude of darts, and weapons to arm seventy thousand men (a magazine that had been formed from ancient time), besides two thousand soldiers that were then with him, whom he gave up with the rest for Timoleon's service.

Dionysius himself, putting his treasure aboard, and taking a few friends, sailed away unobserved by Hicetes, and being brought to the camp of Timoleon, there first appeared in the humble dress of a private person, and was shortly after sent to Corinth with a single ship and a small sum of money. Born and educated in the most splendid court and the most absolute monarchy that ever was, which he held and kept up for the space of ten years succeeding his father's death, he had, after Dion's expedition, spent twelve other years in a continual agitation of wars and contests, and great variety of fortune, during which time all the mischiefs he had committed in his former reign were more than repaid by the ills

he himself then suffered, since he lived to see the deaths of his sons in the prime and vigour of their age, and the rape of his daughters in the flower of their virginity, and the wicked abuse of his sister and his wife, who, after being first exposed to all the lawless insults of the soldiery, was then murdered with her children, and cast into the sea; the particulars of which are more exactly given in the life of Dion.

Upon the news of his landing at Corinth, there was hardly a man in Greece who had not the curiosity to come and view the late formidable tyrant, and say some words to him; part, rejoicing at his disasters, were led thither out of mere spite and hatred, that they might have the pleasure of trampling, as it were, on the ruins of his broken fortune; but others, letting their attention and their sympathy turn rather to the changes and revolutions of his life, could not but see in them a proof of the strength and potency with which divine and unseen causes operate amidst the weakness of human and visible things.

For neither art nor nature did in that age produce anything comparable to this work and wonder of fortune which showed the very same man, that was not long before supreme monarch of Sicily, loitering about perhaps in the fish-market, or sitting in a perfumer's shop drinking the diluted wine of taverns, or squabbling in the street with common women, or pretending to instruct the singing women of the theatre, and seriously disputing with them about the measure and harmony of pieces of music that were performed there.

Such behaviour on his part was variously criticised. He was thought by many to act thus out of pure compliance with his own natural indolent and vicious inclinations; while finer judges were of the opinion, that in all this he was playing a politic part, with a design to be contemned among them, and that the Corinthians might not feel any apprehension or suspicion of his being uneasy under his reverse of fortune, or solicitous to retrieve it; to avoid which danger, he purposely and against his true nature affected an appearance of folly and want of spirit in his private life and amusements.

However it be, there are sayings and repartees of his left still upon record, which seem to show that he not ignobly accommodated himself to his present circumstances; as may appear in part from the ingenuousness of the avowal he made on coming to Leucadia, which, as well as Syracuse, was a Corinthian colony, where he told the inhabitants that he found himself not unlike boys who had been in fault, who can talk cheerfully with their brothers, but are ashamed to see their father; so likewise he, he said, could gladly reside with them in that island, whereas he felt a certain awe upon his mind which made him averse to the sight of Corinth, that was a common mother to them both.

The thing is further evident from the reply he once made to a stranger in Corinth, who, deriding him in a rude and scornful manner about the conferences he used to have with philosophers, whose company had been one of his pleasures while yet a monarch, and demanding, in fine, what he was the better now for all those wise and learned discourses of Plato, "Do you think," said he, "I have made no profit of his philosophy when you see me bear my change of fortune as I do?"

And when Aristoxenus, the musician, and several others, desired to know how Plato offended him, and what had been the ground of his displeasure with him, he made answer that, of the many evils attaching to the condition of sovereignty, the one greatest infelicity was that none of those who were accounted friends would venture to speak freely, or tell the plain truth; and that by means of such he had been deprived of Plato's kindness.

At another time, when one of those pleasant companions that are desirous to pass for wits, in mockery to Dionysius, as if he were still the tyrant, shook out the folds of his cloak, as he was entering into a room where he was, to show there were no concealed weapons about him, Dionysius, by way of retort, observed, that he would prefer he would do so on leaving the room, as a security that he was carrying nothing off with him.

And when Philip of Macedon, at a drinking party, began to speak in banter about the verses and tragedies which his father, Dionysius the elder, had left behind him, and pretended to wonder how he could get any time from his other business to compose such elaborate and ingenious pieces, he replied, very much to the purpose, "It was at those leisurable hours, which such as you and I, and those we call happy men, bestow upon our cups."

Plato had not the opportunity to see Dionysius at Corinth, being already dead before he came thither; but Diogenes of Sinope, at their first meeting in the street there, saluted him with the ambiguous expression, "O Dionysius, how little you deserve your present life!" Upon which Dionysius stopped and replied, "I thank you, Diogenes, for your condolence." "Condole with you!" replied Diogenes; "Do you not suppose that, on the contrary, I am indignant that such a slave as you, who, if you had your due, should have been let alone to grow old and die in the state of tyranny, as your father did before you, should now enjoy the ease of private persons, and be here to sport and frolic in our society?"

So that when I compare those sad stories of Philistus, touching the daughters of Leptines, where he makes pitiful moan on their behalf, as fallen from all the blessings and advantages of powerful greatness to the miseries of an humble life, they seem to me like the lamentations of a woman who has lost her box of ointment, her purple dresses, and her golden trinkets. Such anecdotes will not, I conceive, be thought either foreign to my purpose of writing Lives, or unprofitable in themselves, by such readers as are not in too much haste, or busied and taken up with other concerns.

But if the misfortune of Dionysius appears strange and extraordinary, we shall have no less reason to wonder at the good fortune of Timoleon, who, within fifty days after his landing in Sicily, both recovered the citadel of Syracuse and sent Dionysius an exile into Peloponnesus. This lucky beginning so animated the Corinthians, that they ordered him a supply of two thousand foot and two hundred horse, who, reaching Thurii, intended to cross over thence into Sicily; but finding the whole sea beset with Carthaginian ships, which made their passage impracticable, they were constrained to stop there, and watch their opportunity; which time, however, was employed in a noble action. For the Thurians, going out to war against their Bruttian enemies, left their city in charge with these Corinthian strangers, who defended it as carefully as if it had been their own country, and faithfully resigned it up again.

Hicetes, in the interim, continued still to besiege the castle of Syracuse, and hindered all provisions from coming in by sea to relieve the Corinthians that were in it.

He had engaged also, and despatched towards Adranum, two unknown foreigners to assassinate Timoleon, who at no time kept any standing guard about his person, and was then altogether secure, diverting himself, without any apprehension, among the citizens of the place, it being a festival in honour of their gods. The two men that were sent, having casually heard that Timoleon was about to sacrifice, came directly into the temple with poniards under their cloaks, and pressing in among the crowd, by little and little got up close to the altar; but, as they were just looking for a sign from each other to begin the attempt, a third person struck one of them over the head with a sword, upon whose sudden fall, neither he that gave the blow, nor the partisan of him that received it, kept their stations any longer; but the one, making way with his bloody sword, put no stop to his flight, till he gained the top of a certain lofty precipice, while the other, laying hold of the altar, besought Timoleon to spare his life, and he would reveal to him the whole conspiracy. His pardon being granted, he confessed that both himself and his dead companion were sent thither purposely to slay him.

While this discovery was made, he that killed the other conspirator had been fetched down from his sanctuary of the rock, loudly and often protesting, as he came along, that there was no injustice in the fact, as he had only taken righteous vengeance for his father's blood, whom this man had murdered before in the city of Leontini; the truth of which was attested by several there present, who could not choose but wonder too at the strange dexterity of Fortune's operations, the facility with which she makes one event the spring and motion to something wholly different, uniting every scattered accident and loose particular and remote action, and interweaving them together to serve her purpose; so that things that in themselves seem to have no connection or interdependence whatsoever, become in her hands, so to say, the end and the beginning of each other.

The Corinthians, satisfied as to the innocence of this seasonable feat, honoured and rewarded the author with a present of ten pounds in their money, since he had, as it were, lent the use of his just resentment to the tutelar genius that seemed to be protecting Timoleon, and had not pre-expended this anger, so long ago conceived, but had reserved and deferred, under fortune's guidance, for his preservation, the revenge of a private quarrel.

But this fortunate escape had effects and consequences beyond the present, as it inspired the highest hopes and future expectations of Timoleon, making people reverence and protect him as a sacred person sent by heaven to revenge and redeem Sicily.

Hicetes, having missed his aim in this enterprise, and perceiving, also, that many went off and sided with Timoleon, began to chide himself for his foolish modesty, that, when so considerable a force of the Carthaginians lay ready to be commanded by him, he had employed them hitherto by degrees and in small numbers, introducing their reinforcements by stealth and clandestinely, as if he had been ashamed of the action. Therefore, now laying aside his former nicety, he called in Mago, their admiral, with his whole navy, who presently set sail, and seized upon the port with a formidable fleet of at least a hundred and fifty vessels, landing there sixty thousand foot, which were all lodged within the city of Syracuse; so that, in all men's opinion, the time anciently talked of and long expected, wherein Sicily should be subjugated by barbarians, was now come to its fatal period. For in all their preceding wars and many desperate conflicts with Sicily, the Carthaginians had never been able, before this, to take Syracuse; whereas Hicetes now receiving them and putting them into their hands, you might see it become now, as it were, a camp of barbarians.

By this means, the Corinthian soldiers that kept the castle found themselves brought into great danger and hardship; as, besides that their provision grew scarce, and they began to be in want, because the havens were strictly guarded and blocked up, the enemy exercised them still with skirmishes and combats about their walls, and they were not only obliged to be continually in arms, but to divide and prepare themselves for assaults and encounters of every kind, and to repel every variety of the means of offence employed by a besieging army.

Timoleon made shift to relieve them in these straits, sending corn from Catana by small fishing-boats and little skiffs, which commonly gained a passage through the Carthaginian galleys in times of storm, stealing up when the blockading ships were driven apart and dispersed by the stress of weather; which Mago and Hicetes observing, they agreed to fall upon Catana, from whence these supplies were brought in to the besieged, and accordingly put off from Syracuse, taking with them the best soldiers in their whole army.

Upon this Neon, the Corinthian, who was

captain of those that kept the citadel, taking notice that the enemies who stayed there behind were very negligent and careless in keeping guard, made a sudden sally upon them as they lay scattered, and, killing some and putting others to flight, he took and possessed himself of that quarter which they call Acradina, and was thought to be the strongest and most impregnable part of Syracuse, a city made up and compacted, as it were, of several towns put together. Having thus stored himself with corn and money, he did not abandon the place, nor retire again into the castle, but fortifying the precincts of Acradina, and joining it by works to the citadel, he undertook the defence of both.

Mago and Hicetes were now come near to Catana, when a horseman, despatched from Syracuse, brought them tidings that Acradina was taken; upon which they returned, in all haste, with great disorder and confusion, having neither been able to reduce the city they went against, nor to preserve that they were masters of.

These successes, indeed, were such as might leave foresight and courage a pretence still of disputing it with fortune, which contributed most to the result. But the next following event can scarcely be ascribed to anything but pure felicity. The Corinthian soldiers who stayed at Thurii, partly for fear of the Carthaginian galleys which lay in wait for them under the command of Hanno, and partly because of tempestuous weather which had lasted for many days, and rendered the sea dangerous, took a resolution to march by land over the Bruttian territories, and what with persuasion and force together, made good their passage through those barbarians to the city of Rhegium, the sea being still rough and raging as before.

But Hanno, not expecting the Corinthians would venture out, and supposing it would be useless to wait there any longer, bethought himself, as he imagined, of a most ingenious and clever stratagem apt to delude and ensnare the enemy; in pursuance of which he commanded the seamen to crown themselves with garlands, and adorning his galleys with bucklers both of the Greek and Carthaginian make, he sailed away for Syracuse in this triumphant equipage, and using all his oars as he passed under the castle with much shouting and laughter, cried out, on purpose to dishearten the besieged, that he was come from vanquishing and taking the Corinthian suc-

cours, which he fell upon at sea as they were passing over into Sicily.

While he was thus trifling and playing his tricks before Syracuse, the Corinthians, now come as far as Rhegium, observing the coast clear, and that the wind was laid, as it were by miracle, to afford them in all appearance a quiet and smooth passage, went immediately aboard on such little barks and fishing boats as were then at hand, and got over to Sicily with such complete safety and in such an extraordinary calm, that they drew their horses by the reins, swimming along by them as the vessels went across. When they were all landed, Timoleon came to receive them, and by their means at once obtained possession of Messena, from whence he marched in good order to Syracuse, trusting more to his late prosperous achievements than his present strength, as the whole army he had then with him did not exceed the number of four thousand.

Mago, however, was troubled and fearful at the first notice of his coming, and grew more apprehensive and jealous still upon the following occasion. The marshes about Syracuse, that receive a great deal of fresh water, as well from springs as from lakes and rivers discharging themselves into the sea, breed abundance of eels, which may be always taken there in great quantities by any that will fish for them. The mercenary soldiers that served on both sides were wont to follow the sport together at their vacant hours, and upon any cessation of arms; who being all Greeks, and having no cause of private enmity to each other, as they would venture bravely in fight, so in times of truce used to meet and converse amicably together.

And at this present time, while engaged about this common business of fishing, they fell into talk together; and some expressing their admiration of the neighbouring sea, and others telling how much they were taken with the convenience and commodiousness of the buildings and public works, one of the Corinthian party took occasion to demand of the others: "And is it possible that you who are Grecians born should be so forward to reduce a city of this greatness, and enjoying so many rare advantages, into the state of barbarism; and lend your assistance to plant Carthaginians, that are the worst and bloodiest of men, so much the nearer to us? Whereas you should rather wish there were many more Sicilies to lie between them and Greece. Have you so little sense as to believe, that they come hither with an army, from the Pillars of Hercules and the Atlantic Sea, to hazard themselves for the establishment of Hicetes? who, if he had had the consideration which becomes a general, would never have thrown out his ancestors and founders to bring in the enemies of his country in the room of them, when he might have enjoyed all suitable honour and command, with consent of Timoleon and the rest of Corinth."

The Greeks that were in pay with Hicetes, noising these discourses about their camp, gave Mago some ground to suspect, as indeed he had long sought for a pretence to be gone, that there was treachery contrived against him; so that, although Hicetes entreated him to tarry, and made it appear how much stronger they were than the enemy, yet, conceiving they came far more short of Timoleon in respect of courage and fortune than they surpassed him in number, he presently went aboard and set sail for Africa, letting Sicily escape out of his hands with dishonour to himself, and for such uncertain causes, that no human reason could give an account of his departure.

The day after he went away, Timoleon came up before the city in array for a battle. But when he and his company heard of this sudden flight, and saw the docks all empty, they could not forbear laughing at the cowardice of Mago, and in mockery caused proclamation to be made through the city that a reward would be given to any one who could bring them tidings whither the Carthaginian fleet had conveyed itself from them.

However, Hicetes resolving to fight it out alone, and not quitting his hold of the city, but sticking close to the quarters he was in possession of, places that were well fortified and not easy to be attacked, Timoleon divided his forces into three parts, and fell himself upon the side where the river Anapas ran, which was most strong and difficult of access; and he commanded those that were led by Isias, a Corinthian captain, to make their assault from the post of Acradina, while Dinarchus and Demaretus, that brought him the last supply from Corinth, were, with a third division, to attempt the quarter called Epipolæ. A considerable impression being made from every side at once, the soldiers of Hicetes were beaten off and put to flight; and this—that the city came to be taken by storm, and fall suddenly into their hands, upon the defeat and rout of the enemy—we must in all justice ascribe to the valour of the assailants and the wise conduct of their general; but that not so much as a man of the Corinthians was either slain or wounded in the action, this the good fortune of Timoleon seems to challenge for her own work, as though, in a sort of rivalry with his own personal exertions, she made it her aim to exceed and obscure his actions by her favours, that those who heard him commended for his noble deeds might rather admire the happiness than the merit of them.

For the fame of what was done not only passed through all Sicily, and filled Italy with wonder, but even Greece itself, after a few days, came to ring with the greatness of his exploit; insomuch that those of Corinth, who had as yet no certainty that their auxiliaries were landed on the island, had tidings brought them at the same time that they were safe and were conquerors. In so prosperous a course did affairs run, and such was the speed and celerity of execution with which fortune, as with a new ornament, set off the native lustres of the performance.

Timoleon, being master of the citadel, avoided the error which Dion had been guilty of. He spared not the place for the beauty and sumptuousness of its fabric, and, keeping clear of those suspicions which occasioned first the unpopularity and afterwards the fall of Dion, made a public crier give notice that all the Syracusans who were willing to have a hand in the work should bring pick-axes and mattocks, and other instruments, and help him to demolish the fortifications of the tyrants. When they all came up with one accord, looking upon that order and that day as the surest foundation of their liberty, they not only pulled down the castle, but overturned the palaces and monuments adjoining, and whatever else might preserve any memory of former tyrants. Having soon levelled and cleared the place, he there presently erected courts for administration of justice, ratifying the citizens by this means, and building popular government on the fall and ruin of tyranny.

But since he had recovered a city destitute of inhabitants, some of them dead in civil wars and insurrections, and others being fled to escape tyrants, so that through solitude and want of people the great market-place of Syracuse was overgrown with such quantity of rank herbage that it became a pasture for their horses, the grooms lying along in the grass as they fed by them; while also other towns, very few excepted, were become full of stags and wild boars, so that those who had nothing else to do went frequently a-hunting, and found game in the suburbs and about the walls; and not one of those who possessed themselves of castles, or made garrisons in the country, could be persuaded to quit their present abode, or would accept an invitation to return back into the city, so much did they all dread and abhor the very name of assemblies and forms of government and public speaking, that had produced the greater part of those usurpers who had successively assumed a dominion over them—Timoleon, therefore, with the Syracusans that remained, considering this vast desolation, and how little hope there was to have it otherwise supplied, thought good to write to the Corinthians, requesting that they would send a colony out of Greece to repeople Syracuse, for else the land about it would lie unimproved.

Besides this, they expected to be involved in a greater war from Africa, having news brought them that Mago had killed himself, and that the Carthaginians, out of rage for his ill-conduct in the late expedition, had caused his body to be nailed upon a cross, and that they were raising a mighty force, with design to make their descent upon Sicily the next summer.

These letters from Timoleon being delivered at Corinth, and the ambassadors of Syracuse beseeching them at the same time that they would take upon them the care of their poor city, and once again become the founders of it, the Corinthians were not tempted by any feeling of cupidity to lay hold of the advantage. Nor did they seize and appropriate the city to themselves, but going about first to the games that are kept as sacred in Greece, and to the most numerously attended religious assemblages, they made publication by heralds, that the Corinthians, having destroyed the usurpation at Syracuse and driven out the tyrant, did thereby invite the Syracusan exiles, and any other Siceliots, to return and inhabit the city, with full enjoyment of freedom under their own laws, the land being divided among them in just and equal proportions.

And after this, sending messengers into Asia and the several islands where they understood that most of the scattered fugitives were then residing, they bade them all repair to Corinth, engaging that the Corinthians would afford them vessels and commanders, and a safe convoy, at their own charges, to Syracuse.

Such generous proposals, being thus spread about, gained them the just and honourable recompense of general praise and benediction, for delivering the country from oppressors, and saving it from barbarians, and restoring it at length to the rightful owners of the place.

These, when they were assembled at Corinth, and found how insufficient their company was, besought the Corinthians that they might have a supplement of other persons, as well out of their city as the rest of Greece, to go with them as joint colonists; and so raising themselves to the number of ten thousand, they sailed together to Syracuse. By this time great multitudes, also, from Italy and Sicily had flocked in to Timoleon, so that, as Athanis reports, their entire body amounted now to sixty thousand men.

Among these he divided the whole territory, and sold the houses for a thousand talents; by which method he both left it in the power of the old Syracusans to redeem their own, and made it a means also for raising a stock for the community, which had been so much impoverished of late and was so unable to defray other expenses, and especially those of a war, that they exposed their very statues to sale, a regular process being observed, and sentence of auction passed upon each of them by majority of votes, as if they had been so many criminals taking their trial; in the course of which it is said that while condemnation was pronounced upon all other statues, that of the ancient usurper Gelo was exempted, out of admiration and honour and for the sake of the victory he gained over the Carthaginian forces at the river Himera.

Syracuse being thus happily revived, and replenished again by the general concourse of inhabitants from all parts, Timoleon was desirous now to rescue other cities from the like bondage, and wholly and once for all to extirpate arbitrary government out of Sicily. And for this purpose, marching in to the territories of those that used it, he compelled Hicetes first to renounce the Carthaginian interest, and, demolishing the fortresses which were held by him, to live henceforth among the Leontinians as a private person. Leptines, also, the tyrant of Apollonia and divers other little towns, after some resistance made, seeing the danger he was in of being taken by force, surrendered himself; upon which Timoleon spared his life, and sent him away to Corinth, counting it a glorious thing that the mother city should expose to the view of other

Greeks these Sicilian tyrants, living now in an exiled and a low condition.

After this he returned to Syracuse, that he might have leisure to attend to the establishment of the new constitution, and assist Cephalus and Dionysius, who were sent from Corinth to make laws, in determining the most important points of it.

In the meanwhile, desirous that his hired soldiers should not want action, but might rather enrich themselves by some plunder from the enemy, he despatched Dinarchus and Demaretus with a portion of them into the part of the island belonging to the Carthaginians, where they obliged several cities to revolt from the barbarians, and not only lived in great abundance themselves, but raised money from their spoil to carry on the war.

Meantime, the Carthaginians landed at the promontory of Lilybæum, bringing with them an army of seventy thousand men on board two hundred galleys, besides a thousand other vessels laden with engines of battery, chariots, corn, and other military stores, as if they did not intend to manage the war by piecemeal and in parts as heretofore, but to drive the Greeks altogether and at once out of all Sicily. And indeed it was a force sufficient to overpower the Siceliots, even though they had been at perfect union among themselves, and had never been enfeebled by intestine quarrels.

Hearing that part of their subject territory was suffering devastation, they forthwith made toward the Corinthians with great fury, having Hasdrubal and Hamilcar for their generals; the report of whose numbers and strength coming suddenly to Syracuse, the citizens were so terrified, that hardly three thousand, among so many myriads of them, had the courage to take up arms and join Timoleon. The foreigners, serving for pay, were not above four thousand in all, and about a thousand of these grew faint-hearted by the way, and forsook Timoleon in his march towards the enemy, looking on him as frantic and distracted, destitute of the sense which might have been expected from his time of life, thus to venture out against an army of seventy thousand men, with no more than five thousand foot and a thousand horse; and, when he should have kept those forces to defend the city, choosing rather to remove them eight days' journey from Syracuse, so that if they were beaten from the field, they would have no retreat, nor any burial if they fell upon it. Timoleon, however, reckoned it some

kind of advantage, that these had thus discovered themselves before the battle, and encouraging the rest, led them with all speed to the river Crimesus, where it was told him the Carthaginians were drawn together.

As he was marching up an ascent, from the top of which they expected to have a view of the army and of the strength of the enemy, there met him by chance a train of mules loaded with parsley; which his soldiers conceived to be an ominous occurrence or illboding token, because this is the herb with which we not unfrequently adorn the sepulchres of the dead; and there is a proverb derived from the custom, used of one who is dangerously sick, that he has need of nothing but parsley. So to ease their minds, and free them from any superstitious thoughts or forebodings of evil, Timoleon halted, and concluded an address suitable to the occasion, by saying, that a garland of triumph was here luckily brought them, and had fallen into their hands of its own accord, as an anticipation of victory, the same with which the Corinthians crown the victors in the Isthmian games, accounting chaplets of parsley the sacred wreath proper to their country; parsley being at that time still the emblem of victory at the Isthmian, as it is now at the Nemean sports; and it is not so very long ago that the pine first began to be used in its place.

Timoleon, therefore, having thus bespoke his soldiers, took part of the parsley, and with it made himself a chaplet first, his captains and their companies all following the example of their leader. The soothsayers then, observing also two eagles on the wing towards them, one of which bore a snake struck through with her talons, and the other, as she flew, uttered a loud cry indicating boldness and assurance, at once showed them to the soldiers, who with one consent fell to supplicate the gods, and call them in to their assistance.

It was now about the beginning of summer, and conclusion of the month called Thargelion, not far from the solstice; and the river sending up a thick mist, all the adjacent plain was at first darkened with the fog, so that for a while they could discern nothing from the enemy's camp; only a confused buzz and undistinguished mixture of voices came up to the hill from the distant motions and clamours of so vast a multitude. When the Corinthians had mounted, and stood on the top, and had laid down their bucklers to take breath and repose themselves, the sun coming

round and drawing up the vapours from below, the gross foggy air that was now gathered and condensed above formed in a cloud
upon the mountains; and, all the under places
being clear and open, the river Crimesus appeared to them again, and they could descry
the enemies passing over it, first with their
formidable four-horse chariots of war, and
then ten thousand footmen bearing white
shields, whom they guessed to be all Carthaginians, from the splendour of their arms,
and the slowness and order of their march.

And when now the troops of various other
nations, flowing in behind them, began to
throng for passage in a tumultuous and unruly manner, Timoleon, perceiving that the
river gave them opportunity to single off
whatever number of their enemies they had
a mind to engage at once, and bidding his
soldiers observe how their forces were divided
into two separate bodies by the intervention
of the stream, some being already over, and
others still to ford it, gave Demaretus command to fall in upon the Carthaginians with
his horse, and disturb their ranks before they
should be drawn up into form of battle; and
coming down into the plain himself, forming
his right and left wing of other Sicilians, in-
termingling only a few strangers in each, he
placed the natives of Syracuse in the middle,
with the stoutest mercenaries he had about
his own person; and waiting a little to observe
the action of his horse, when he saw they
were not only hindered from grappling with
the Carthaginians by the armed chariots that
ran to and fro before the army, but forced
continually to wheel about to escape having
their ranks broken, and so to repeat their
charges anew, he took his buckler in his hand,
and crying out to the foot that they should
follow him with courage and confidence, he
seemed to speak with a more than human accent, and a voice stronger than ordinary;
whether it were that he naturally raised it so
high in the vehemence and ardour with his
mind to assault the enemy, or else, as many
then thought, some god or other spoke with
him.

When his soldiers quickly gave an echo to
it, and besought him to lead them on without
any further delay, he made a sign to the horse,
that they should draw off from the front
where the chariots were, and pass sidewards
to attack their enemies in the flank; then,
making his vanguard firm by joining man to
man and buckler to buckler, he caused the

trumpet to sound, and so bore in upon the
Carthaginians. They, for their part, stoutly
received and sustained his first onset; and
having their bodies armed with breast-plates
of iron, and helmets of brass on their heads,
besides great bucklers to cover and secure
them, they could easily repel the charge of the
Greek spears.

But when the business came to a decision
by the sword, where mastery depends no less
upon art than strength, all on a sudden from
the mountain-tops violent peals of thunder
and vivid flashes of lightning broke out; following upon which the darkness, that had
been hovering about the higher grounds and
the crests of the hills, descending to the place
of battle and bringing a tempest of rain and
of wind and hail along with it, was driven
upon the Greeks behind, and fell only at their
backs, but discharged itself in the very faces of
the barbarians, the rain beating on them, and
the lightning dazzling them without cessation; annoyances that in many ways distressed
at any rate the inexperienced, who had not
been used to such hardships, and, in particular, the claps of thunder, and the noise of the
rain and hail beating on their arms, kept
them from hearing the commands of their
officers.

Besides which, the very mud also was a
great hindrance to the Carthaginians, who
were not lightly equipped, but, as I said before, loaded with heavy armour; and then
their shirts underneath getting drenched, the
foldings about the bosom filled with water,
grew unwieldy and cumbersome to them as
they fought, and made it easy for the Greeks
to throw them down, and, when they were
once down, impossible for them, under that
weight, to disengage themselves and rise again
with weapons in their hands.

The river Crimesus, too, swollen partly by
the rain, and partly by the stoppage of its
course with the numbers that were passing
through, overflowed its banks; and the level
ground by the side of it, being so situated as
to have a number of small ravines and hollows of the hillside descending upon it, was
now filled with rivulets and currents that had
no certain channel, in which the Carthaginians stumbled and rolled about, and found
themselves in great difficulty. So that, in fine,
the storm bearing still upon them, and the
Greeks having cut in pieces four hundred
men of their first ranks, the whole body of
their army began to fly.

Great numbers were overtaken in the plain, and put to the sword there; and many of them, as they were making their way back through the river, falling foul upon others that were yet coming over, were borne away and overwhelmed by the waters; but the major part, attempting to get up the hill so as to make their escape, were intercepted and destroyed by the light-armed troops. It is said that, of ten thousand who lay dead after the fight, three thousand, at least, were Carthaginian citizens; a heavy loss and great grief to their countrymen; those that fell being men inferior to none among them as to birth, wealth, or reputation. Nor do their records mention that so many native Carthaginians were ever cut off before in any one battle; as they usually employed Africans, Spaniards, and Numidians in their wars, so that if they chanced to be defeated, it was still at the cost and damage of other nations.

The Greeks easily discovered of what condition and account the slain were by the richness of their spoils; for when they came to collect the booty, there was little reckoning made either of brass or iron, so abundant were better metals, and so common were silver and gold. Passing over the river they became masters of their camp and carriages. As for captives, a great many of them were stolen away and sold privately by the soldiers, but about five thousand were brought in and delivered up for the benefit of the public; two hundred of their chariots of war were also taken. The tent of Timoleon then presented a most glorious and magnificent appearance, being heaped up and hung round with every variety of spoils and military ornaments, among which were a thousand breastplates of rare workmanship and beauty, and bucklers to the number of ten thousand. The victors being but few to strip so many that were vanquished, and having such valuable booty to occupy them, it was the third day after the fight before they could erect and finish the trophy of their conquest.

Timoleon sent tidings of his victory to Corinth, with the best and goodliest arms he had taken as a proof of it; that he thus might render his country an object of emulation to the whole world, when, of all the cities of Greece, men should there alone behold the chief temples adorned, not with Grecian spoils, nor offerings obtained by the bloodshed and plunder of their own countrymen and kindred, and attended, therefore, with sad and unhappy remembrances, but with such as had been stripped from barbarians and enemies to their nation, with the noblest titles inscribed upon them, titles telling of the justice as well as fortitude of the conquerors; namely, that the people of Corinth, and Timoleon their general, having redeemed the Greeks of Sicily from Carthaginian bondage, made oblation of these to the gods, in grateful acknowledgment of their favour.

Having done this, he left his hired soldiers in the enemy's country to drive and carry away all they could throughout the subject-territory of Carthage, and so marched with the rest of his army to Syracuse, where he issued an edict for banishing the thousand mercenaries who had basely deserted him before the battle, and obliged them to quit the city before sunset. They, sailing into Italy, lost their lives there by the hands of the Bruttians, in spite of a public assurance of safety previously given them; thus receiving, from the divine power, a just reward of their own treachery.

Mamercus, however, the tyrant of Catana, and Hicetes, after all, either envying Timoleon the glory of his exploits, or fearing him as one that would keep no agreement, or have any peace with tyrants, made a league with the Carthaginians, and pressed them much to send a new army and commander into Sicily, unless they would be content to hazard all and to be wholly ejected out of that island.

And in consequence of this, Gisco was despatched with a navy of seventy sail. He took numerous Greek mercenaries also into pay, that being the first time they had ever been enlisted for the Carthaginian service; but then it seems the Carthaginians began to admire them, as the most irresistible soldiers of all mankind.

Uniting their forces in the territory of Messena, they cut off four hundred of Timoleon's paid soldiers, and within the dependencies of Carthage, at a place called Hieræ, destroyed, by an ambuscade, the whole body of mercenaries that served under Euthymus the Leucadian; which accidents, however, made the good fortune of Timoleon accounted all the more remarkable, as these were the men that, with Philomelus of Phocis and Onomarchus, had forcibly broken into the temple of Apollo at Delphi, and were partakers with them in the sacrilege; so that being hated and shunned by all, as persons under a curse, they were constrained to wander about in Peloponnesus; when, for want of others, Timoleon was glad to take them into service in his expedition for Sicily, where they were successful in whatever enterprise they attempted under his conduct.

But now, when all the important dangers were past, on his sending them out for the relief and defence of his party in several places, they perished and were destroyed at a distance from him, not all together, but in small parties; and the vengeance which was destined for them accommodated itself to the good fortune which guarded Timoleon so as not to allow any harm or prejudice for good men to arise from the punishment of the wicked. The benevolence and kindness which the gods had for Timoleon was thus as distinctly recognised in his disasters as in his successes.

What most annoyed the Syracusans was their being insulted and mocked by the tyrants; as, for example, by Mamercus, who valued himself much upon his gift for writing poems and tragedies, and took occasion, when coming to present the gods with the bucklers of the hired soldiers whom he had killed, to make a boast of his victory in an insulting elegiac inscription:—

*These shields with purple, gold, and ivory
    wrought,
Were won by us that but with poor ones fought.*

After this, while Timoleon marched to Calauria, Hicetes made an inroad into the borders of Syracuse, where he met with considerable booty, and having done much mischief and havoc, returned back by Calauria itself, in contempt of Timoleon and the slender force he had then with him. He, suffering Hicetes to pass forward, pursued him with his horsemen and light infantry; which Hicetes perceiving, crossed the river Damyrias, and then stood in a posture to receive him; the difficulty of the passage, and the height and steepness of the bank on each side, giving advantage enough to make him confident.

A strange contention and dispute, meantime, among the officers of Timoleon a little retarded the conflict; no one of them was willing to let another pass over before him to engage the enemy; each man claiming it as a right to venture first and begin the onset; so that their fording was likely to be tumultuous and without order, a mere general struggle which should be the foremost.

Timoleon, therefore, desiring to decide the quarrel by lot, took a ring from each of the pretenders, which he cast into his own cloak, and, after he had shaken all together, the first he drew out had, by good fortune, the figure of a trophy engraved as a seal upon it; at the sight of which the young captains all shouted for joy, and, without waiting any longer to see how chance would determine it for the rest, took every man his way through the river with all the speed they could make, and fell to blows with the enemies, who were not able to bear up against the violence of their attack, but fled in haste and left their arms behind them all alike, and a thousand dead upon the place.

Not long after, Timoleon, marching up to the city of the Leontines, took Hicetes alive, and his son Eupolemus, and Euthymus, the commander of his horse, who were bound and brought to him by their own soldiers. Hicetes and the stripling his son were then executed as tyrants and traitors; and Euthymus, though a brave man, and one of singular courage, could obtain no mercy, because he was charged with contemptuous language in disparagement of the Corinthians when they first sent their forces into Sicily; it is said that he told the Leontini in a speech that the news did not sound terrible, nor was any great danger to be feared because of—

Corinthian women coming out of doors.

So true it is that men are usually more stung and galled by reproachful words than hostile actions; and they bear an affront with less patience than an injury; to do harm and mischief by deeds is counted pardonable from enemies, as nothing less can be expected in a state of war; whereas virulent and contumelious words appear to be the expression of needless hatred, and to proceed from an excess of rancour.

When Timoleon came back to Syracuse, the citizens brought the wives and daughters of Hicetes and his son to a public trial, and condemned and put them to death. This seems to be the least pleasing action of Timoleon's life; since if he had interposed, the unhappy women would have been spared. He would appear to have disregarded the thing, and to have given them up to the citizens, who were eager to take vengeance for the wrongs done to Dion, who expelled Dionysius; since it was this very Hicetes who took Arete the wife and Aristomache the sister of Dion, with a son that had not yet passed his childhood, and threw them all together into the sea alive, as related in the life of Dion.

After this, he moved towards Catana against Mamercus, who gave him battle near the river Abolus, and was overthrown and put to flight, losing above two thousand men, a considerable part of whom were the Phœnician troops sent by Gisco to his assistance. After this defeat the Carthaginians sued for peace; which was granted on the conditions that they should confine themselves to the country within the river Lycus, that those of the inhabitants who wished to remove to the Syracusan territories should be allowed to depart with their whole families and fortunes, and, lastly, that Carthage should renounce all engagements to the tyrants.

Mamercus, now forsaken and despairing of success, took ship for Italy with the design of bringing in the Lucanians against Timoleon and the people of Syracuse; but the men in his galleys turning back and landing again and delivering up Catana to Timoleon, thus obliged him to fly for his own safety to Messena, where Hippo was tyrant. Timoleon, however, coming up against them, and besieging the city both by sea and land, Hippo, fearful of the event, endeavoured to slip away in a vessel; which the people of Messena surprised as it was putting off, and seizing on his person, and bringing all their children from school into the theatre to witness the glorious spectacle of a tyrant punished, they first publicly scourged and then put him to death.

Mamercus made surrender of himself to Timoleon, with the proviso that he should be tried at Syracuse and Timoleon should take no part in his accusation. Thither he was brought accordingly, and presenting himself to plead before the people, he essayed to pronounce an oration he had long before composed in his own defence; but finding himself interrupted by noise and clamours, and observing from their aspect and demeanour that the assembly was inexorable, he threw off his upper garment, and running across the theatre as hard as he could, dashed his head against one of the stones under the seats with intention to have killed himself; but he had not the fortune to perish as he designed, but was taken up alive, and suffered the death of a robber.

Thus did Timoleon cut the nerves of tyranny and put a period to the wars; and, whereas, at his first entering upon Sicily, the island was as it were become wild again, and was hateful to the very natives on account of the evils and miseries they suffered there, he so civilised and restored it, and rendered it so desirable to all men, that even strangers now came by sea to inhabit those towns and places which their own citizens had formerly forsaken and left desolate.

Agrigentum and Gela, two famous cities that had been ruined and laid waste by the Carthaginians after the Attic war, were then peopled again, the one by Megellus and Pheristus from Elea, the other by Gorgus, from the island of Ceos, partly with new settlers, partly with the old inhabitants whom they collected again from various parts; to all of whom Timoleon not only afforded a secure and peaceful abode after so obstinate a war, but was further so zealous in assisting and providing for them that he was honoured among them as their founder.

Similar feelings also possessed to such a degree all the rest of the Sicilians that there was no proposal for peace, nor reformation of laws, nor assignation of land, nor reconstitution of government, which they could think well of, unless he lent his aid as a chief architect, to finish and adorn the work, and superadd some touches from his own hand, which might render it pleasing both to God and man.

Although Greece had in his time produced several persons of extraordinary worth, and much renowned for their achievements, such as Timotheus and Agesilaus and Pelopidas and (Timoleon's chief model) Epaminondas, yet the lustre of their best actions was obscured by a degree of violence and labour, insomuch that some of them were matter of blame and of repentance; whereas there is not any one act of Timoleon's, setting aside the necessity he was placed under in reference to his brother, to which, as Timæus observes, we may not fitly apply that exclamation of Sophocles—

O gods! what Venus, or what grace divine,
Did here with human workmanship combine?

For as the poetry of Antimachus, and the painting of Dionysius, the artists of Colophon, though full of force and vigour, yet appeared to be strained and elaborate in comparison with the pictures of Nicomachus and the verses of Homer, which, besides their general strength and beauty, have the peculiar charm of seeming to have been executed with perfect ease and readiness; so the expeditions and acts of Epaminondas or Agesilaus, that were full of toil and effort, when compared with the easy and natural as well as noble and glorious achievements of Timoleon, compel our fair and unbiased judgment to pronounce the latter not indeed the effect of fortune, but the success of fortunate merit. Though he himself indeed ascribed that success to the sole favour of fortune; and both in the letters which he wrote to his friends at Corinth, and in the speeches he made to the people of Syracuse, he would say, that he was thankful unto God, who, designing to save Sicily, was pleased to honour him with the name and title of the deliverance he vouchsafed it.

And having built a chapel in his house, he there sacrificed to Good Hap, as a deity that had favoured him, and devoted the house itself to the Sacred Genius; it being a house which the Syracusans had selected for him, as a special reward and monument of his brave exploits, granting him together with it the most agreeable and beautiful piece of land in the whole country, where he kept his residence for the most part, and enjoyed a private life with his wife and children, who came to him from Corinth. For he returned thither no more, unwilling to be concerned in the broils and tumults of Greece, or to expose himself to public envy (the fatal mischief which great commanders continually run into, from the insatiable appetite for honours and authority); but wisely chose to spend the remainder of his days in Sicily, and there partake of the blessings he himself had procured, the greatest of which was to behold so many cities flourish, and so many thousands of people live happy through his means.

As, however, not only, as Simonides says, "on every lark must grow a crest," but also in every democracy there must spring up a false accuser, so was it at Syracuse: two of their popular spokesmen, Laphystius and Demænetus by name, fell to slander Timoleon. The former of whom requiring him to put in sureties that he would answer to an indictment that would be brought against him, Timoleon would not suffer the citizens, who were incensed at this demand, to oppose it or hinder the proceeding, since he of his own accord had been, he said, at all that trouble, and run so many dangerous risks for this very end and purpose, that every one who wished to try matters by law should freely have recourse to it. And when Demænetus, in a full audience of the people, laid several things to his charge which had been done while he was general, he made no other reply to him, but only said he was much indebted to the gods for granting the request he had so often made them, namely, that he might live to see the Syracusans enjoy that liberty of speech which they now seemed to be masters of.

Timoleon, therefore, having by confession of all done the greatest and the noblest things of any Greek of his age, and alone distinguished himself in those actions to which their orators and philosophers, in their harangues and panegyrics at their solemn national assemblies, used to exhort and incite the Greeks, and being withdrawn beforehand by happy fortune, unspotted and without blood, from the calamities of civil war, in which ancient Greece was soon after involved; having also given full proof, as of his sage conduct and manly courage to the barbarians and tyrants, so of his justice and gentleness to the Greeks, and his friends in general; having raised, too, the greater part of those trophies he won in battle without any tears shed or any mourning worn by the citizens either of Syracuse or Corinth, and within less than eight years' space delivered Sicily from its inveterate grievances and intestine distempers, and given it up free to the native inhabitants, began, as he was now growing old, to find his eyes fail, and awhile after became perfectly blind.

Not that he had done anything himself which might occasion this defect, or was deprived of his sight by any outrage of fortune; it seems rather to have been some inbred and hereditary weakness that was founded in natural causes, which by length of time came to discover itself. For it is said, that several of his kindred and family were subject to the like gradual decay, and lost all use of their eyes, as he did, in their declining years. Athanis, the historian, tells us that even during the war against Hippo and Mamercus, while he was in his camp at Mylæ, there appeared a white speck within his eye, from whence all could foresee the deprivation that was coming on him; this, however, did not hinder him then from continuing the siege, and prosecuting the war, till he got both the tyrants into his power; but upon his coming back to Syracuse, he presently resigned the authority of sole commander, and besought the citizens to excuse him from any further service, since things were already brought to so fair an issue.

Nor is it so much to be wondered that he himself should bear the misfortune without any marks of trouble; but the respect and gratitude which the Syracusans showed him when he was entirely blind may justly deserve our admiration. They used to go themselves to visit him in troops, and brought all the strangers that travelled through their country to his house and manor, that they also might have the pleasure to see their noble benefactor; making it the great matter of their joy and exultation, that when, after so many brave and happy exploits, he might have returned with triumph into Greece, he should disregard all the glorious preparations that were there made to receive him, and choose rather to stay here and end his days among them.

Of the various things decreed and done in honour of Timoleon, I consider one most signal testimony to have been the vote which they passed, that, whenever they should be at war with any foreign nation, they should make use of none but a Corinthian general.

The method, also, of their proceeding in council was a noble demonstration of the same deference for his person. For, determining matters of less consequence themselves, they always called him to advise in the more difficult cases, and such as were of greater moment. He was, on these occasions, carried through the market-place in a litter, and brought in, sitting, into the theatre, where the people with one voice saluted him by his name; and then, after returning the courtesy, and pausing for a time, till the noise of their gratulations and blessings began to cease, he heard the business in debate, and delivered his opinion. This being confirmed by a general suffrage, his servants went back with the litter through the midst of the assembly, the people waiting on him with acclamations and applauses, and then returning to consider other public matters, which they could despatch in his absence.

Being thus cherished in his old age, with all the respect and tenderness due to a common father, he was seized with a very slight indisposition, which, however, was sufficient, with the aid of time, to put a period to his life. There was an allotment then of certain days given, within the space of which the Syracusans were to provide whatever should be necessary for his burial, and all the neighbouring country people and strangers were to make their appearance in a body; so that the funeral pomp was set out with great splendour and magnificence in all other respects, and the bier, decked with ornaments and trophies, was borne by a select body of young men over that ground where the palace and castle of Dionysius stood before they were demolished by Timoleon. There attended on the solemnity several thousands of men and women, all crowned with flowers, and arrayed in fresh and clean attire, which made it look like the procession of a public festival; while the language of all, and their tears mingling with their praise and benediction of the dead Timoleon, manifestly showed that it was not any superficial honour, or commanded homage, which they paid him, but the testimony of a just sorrow for his death, and the expression of true affection.

The bier at length being placed upon the pile of wood that was kindled to consume his corpse, Demetrius, one of their loudest criers, proceeded to read a proclamation to the following purpose: "The people of Syracuse have made a special decree to inter Timoleon, the son of Timodemus, the Corinthian, at the common expense of two hundred minæ, and to honour his memory for ever, by the establishment of annual prizes to be competed for in music, and horse-races, and all sorts of bodily exercise; and this, because he suppressed the tyrants, overthrew the barbarians, replenished the principal cities, that were desolate, with new inhabitants, and then restored the Sicilian Greeks to the privilege of living by their own laws."

Besides this, they made a tomb for him in the market-place, which they afterwards built round with colonnades, and attached to it places of exercise for the young men, and gave it the name of the Timoleonteum. And keeping to that form and order of civil policy and observing those laws and constitutions which he left them, they lived themselves a long time in great prosperity.

ÆMILIUS PAULUS

c. 229–160 b.c.

ALMOST all historians agree that the Æmilii were one of the ancient and patrician houses in Rome; and those authors who affirm that King Numa was pupil to Pythagoras tell us that the first who gave name to his posterity was Mamercus, the son of Pythagoras, who, for his grace and address in speaking, was called Æmilius. Most of this race that have risen through their merit to reputation also enjoyed good fortune; and even the misfortune to Lucius Paulus at the battle of Cannæ gave testimony to his wisdom and valour. For not being able to persuade his colleague not to hazard the battle, he, though against his judgment, joined with him in the contest, but was no companion in his flight; on the contrary, when he that was so resolute to engage deserted him in the midst of danger he kept the field and died fighting. This Æmilius had a daughter named Æmilia, who was married to Scipio the Great, and a son Paulus, who is the subject of my present history.

In his early manhood, which fell at a time when Rome was flourishing with illustrious characters, he was distinguished for not attaching himself to the studies usual with the young men of mark of that age, nor treading the same paths to fame. For he did not practise oratory with a view to pleading causes, nor would he stoop to salute, embrace, and entertain the vulgar, which were the usual insinuating arts by which many grew popular. Not that he was incapable of either, but he chose to purchase a much more lasting glory by his valour, justice, and integrity, and in these virtues he soon outstripped all his equals.

The first honourable office he aspired to was that of ædile, which he carried against twelve competitors of such merit that all of them in process of time were consuls. Being afterwards chosen into the number of priests called augurs, appointed amongst the Romans to observe and register divinations made by the flight of birds or prodigies in the air, he so carefully studied the ancient customs of his country, and so thoroughly understood the religion of his ancestors, that this office, which was before only esteemed a title of honour and merely upon that account sought after, by his means rose to the rank of one of the highest arts, and gave a confirmation to the correctness of the definition, which some philosophers have given of religion, that it is the science of worshipping the gods.

When he performed any part of his duty, he did it with great skill and utmost care, making it, when he was engaged in it, his only business, not omitting any one ceremony, or adding the least circumstance, but always insisting, with his companions of the same order, even on points that might seem inconsiderable, and urging upon them, that though they might think the Deity was easily pacified, and ready to forgive faults of inadvertency, yet any such laxity was a very dangerous thing for a commonwealth to allow; because no man ever began the disturbance of his country's peace by a notorious breach of its laws; and those who are careless in trifles give a precedent for remissness in important duties.

Nor was he less severe in requiring and observing the ancient Roman discipline in military affairs; not endeavouring, when he had the command, to ingratiate himself with his soldiers by popular flattery, though this custom prevailed at that time amongst many, who, by favour and gentleness to those that were under them in their first employment, sought to be promoted to a second; but, by instructing them in the laws of military discipline with the same care and exactness a priest would use in teaching ceremonies and dreadful mysteries, and by severity to such as transgressed and contemned those laws, he maintained his country in its former greatness, esteeming victory over enemies itself but as an accessory to the proper training and disciplining of the citizens.

Whilst the Romans were engaged in war with Antiochus the Great, against whom their most experienced commanders were employed, there arose another war in the west, and they were all up in arms in Spain.

Thither they sent Æmilius, in the quality of prætor, not with six axes, which number other prætors were accustomed to have carried before them, but with twelve; so that in his prætorship he was honoured with the dignity of a consul. He twice overcame the barbarians in battle, thirty thousand of whom were slain: successes chiefly to be ascribed to the wisdom and conduct of the commander, who by his great skill in choosing the advantage of the ground, and making the onset at the passage of a river, gave his soldiers an easy victory. Having made himself master of two hundred and fifty cities, whose inhabitants voluntarily yielded, and bound themselves by oath to fidelity, he left the province in peace, and returned to Rome, not enriching himself a drachma by the war. And, indeed, in general, he was but remiss in making money; though he always lived freely and generously on what he had, which was so far from being excessive, that after his death there was barely enough left to answer his wife's dowry.

His first wife was Papiria, the daughter of Maso, who had formerly been consul. With her he lived a considerable time in wedlock, and then divorced her, though she had made him the father of noble children, being mother of the renowned Scipio and Fabius Maximus. The reason of this separation has not come to our knowledge; but there seems to be a truth conveyed in the account of another Roman's being divorced from his wife, which may be applicable here. This person being highly blamed by his friends, who demanded, "Was she not chaste? was she not fair? was she not fruitful?" holding out his shoe, asked them, whether it was not new and well made. "Yet," added he, "none of you can tell where it pinches me." Certain it is, that great and open faults have often led to no separation; while mere petty repeated annoyances, arising from unpleasantness or incongruity of character, have been the occasion of such estrangement as to make it impossible for man and wife to live together with any content.

Æmilius, having thus put away Papiria, married a second wife, by whom he had two sons, whom he brought up in his own house, transferring the two former into the greatest and the most noble families of Rome. The elder was adopted into the house of Fabius Maximus, who was five times consul; the younger by the son of Scipio Africanus, his cousin-german, and was by him named Scipio.

Of the daughters of Æmilius, one was married to the son of Cato, the other to Ælius Tubero, a most worthy man, and the one Roman who best succeeded in combining liberal habits with poverty. For there were sixteen near relations, all of them of the family of the Ælii, possessed of but one farm, which sufficed them all, whilst one small house, or rather cottage, contained them, their numerous offspring, and their wives; amongst whom was the daughter of our Æmilius, who, although her father had been twice consul, and had twice triumphed, was not ashamed of her husband's poverty, but proud of his virtue that kept him poor. Far otherwise it is with the brothers and relations of this age, who, unless whole tracts of land, or at least walls and rivers, part their inheritances, and keep them at a distance, never cease from mutual quarrels. History suggests a variety of good counsel of this sort, by the way, to those who desire to learn and improve.

To proceed: Æmilius, being chosen consul, waged war with the Ligurians, or Ligustines, a people near the Alps. They were a bold and warlike nation, and their neighbourhood to the Romans had begun to give them skill in the arts of war. They occupy the further parts of Italy ending under the Alps, and those parts of the Alps themselves which are washed by the Tuscan sea and face toward Africa, mingled there with Gauls and Iberians of the coast. Besides, at that time they had turned their thoughts to the seas, and sailing as far as the Pillars of Hercules in light vessels fitted for that purpose, robbed and destroyed all that trafficked in those parts. They, with an army of forty thousand, waited the coming of Æmilius, who brought with him not above eight thousand, so that the enemy was five to one when they engaged; yet he vanquished and put them to flight, forcing them to retire into their walled towns, and in this condition offered them fair conditions of accommodation; it being the policy of the Romans not utterly to destroy the Ligurians, because they were a sort of guard and bulwark against the frequent attempts of the Gauls to overrun Italy. Trusting wholly therefore to Æmilius, they delivered up their towns and shipping into his hands. He, at the utmost, razed only the fortifications and delivered their towns to them again, but took away all their shipping with him, leaving them no vessels bigger than those of three oars, and set at liberty great numbers of prisoners they had taken both by sea and land, strangers as well as Romans. These were the acts most worthy of remark in his first consulship.

Afterwards he frequently intimated his desire of being a second time consul, and was once candidate; but meeting with a repulse and being passed by, he gave up all thought of it, and devoted himself to his duties as augur, and to the education of his children, whom he not only brought up, as he himself had been, in the Roman and ancient discipline, but also with unusual zeal in that of Greece. To this purpose he not only procured masters to teach them grammar, logic and rhetoric, but had for them also preceptors in modelling and drawing, managers of horses and dogs, and instructors in field sports, all from Greece. And, if he was not hindered by public affairs, he himself would be with them at their studies, and see them perform their exercises, being the most affectionate father in Rome.

This was the time, in public matters, when the Romans were engaged in war with Perseus, King of the Macedonians, and great complaints were made of their commanders, who, either through their want of skill or courage, were conducting matters so shamefully, that they did less hurt to the enemy than they received from him. They that not long before had forced Antiochus the Great to quit the rest of Asia, to retire beyond Mount Taurus, and confine himself to Syria, glad to buy his peace with fifteen thousand talents; they that not long since had vanquished King Philip in Thessaly, and freed the Greeks from the Macedonian yoke; nay, had overcome Hannibal himself, who far surpassed all kings in daring and power—thought it scorn that Perseus should think himself an enemy fit to match the Romans, and to be able to wage war with them so long on equal terms, with the remainder only of his father's routed forces; not being aware that Philip after his defeat had greatly improved both the strength and discipline of the Macedonian army. To make which appear, I shall briefly recount the story from the beginning.

Antigonus, the most powerful amongst the captains and successors of Alexander, having obtained for himself and his posterity the title of king, had a son named Demetrius, father to Antigonus, called Gonatas, and he had a son Demetrius, who, reigning some short time, died and left a young son called Philip. The chief men of Macedon, fearing great confusion might arise in his minority, called in Antigonus, cousin-german to the late king, and married him to the widow, the mother of Philip. At first they only styled him regent and general, but when they found by experience that he governed the kingdom with moderation and to general advantage, gave him the title of king. This was he that was surnamed Doson, as if he was a great promiser and a bad performer.

To him succeeded Philip, who in his youth gave great hopes of equalling the best of kings, and that he one day would restore Macedon to its former state and dignity, and prove himself the one man able to check the power of the Romans, now rising and extending over the whole world. But, being vanquished in a pitched battle by Titus Flamininus near Scotussa, his resolution failed, and he yielded himself and all that he had to the mercy of the Romans, well contented that he could escape with paying a small tribute.

Yet afterwards, recollecting himself, he bore it with great impatience, and thought he lived rather like a slave that was pleased with ease, than a man of sense and courage, whilst he held his kingdom at the pleasure of his conquerors; which made him turn his whole mind to war, and prepare himself with as much cunning and privacy as possible. To this end, he left his cities on the high roads and sea-coast ungarrisoned, and almost desolate, that they might seem inconsiderable; in the meantime, collecting large forces up the country, and furnishing his inland posts, strongholds, and towns, with arms, money, and men fit for service, he thus provided himself for war, and yet kept his preparations close. He had in his armoury arms for thirty thousand men; in granaries, in places of strength, eight millions of bushels of corn, and as much ready money as would defray the charge of maintaining ten thousand mercenary soldiers for ten years in defence of the country. But before he could put these things into motion, and carry his designs into effect, he died for grief and anguish of mind, being sensible he had put his innocent son Demetrius to death, upon the calumnies of one that was far more guilty.

Perseus, his son that survived, inherited his hatred of the Romans as well as his kingdom, but was incompetent to carry out his designs, through want of courage and the viciousness of a character in which, among faults and diseases of various sorts, covetousness bore the chief place. There is a statement also of his not being true-born; that the wife of King Philip took him from his mother, Gnathænion (a woman of Argos, that earned her living as a seamstress), as soon as he was born, and passed him upon her husband as her own. And this might be the chief cause of his contriving the death of Demetrius; as he might well fear that, so long as there was a lawful successor in the family, there was no security that his spurious birth might not be revealed.

Notwithstanding all this, and though his spirit was so mean and temper so sordid, yet trusting to the strength of his resources, he engaged in a war with the Romans, and for a long time maintained it; repulsing and even vanquishing some generals of consular dignity, and some great armies and fleets. He routed Publius Licinius, who was the first that invaded Macedonia, in a cavalry battle, slew twenty-five hundred practiced soldiers, and took six hundred prisoners; and surprising their fleet as they rode at anchor before Orens, he took twenty ships of burden with all their lading, sunk the rest that were freighted with corn, and, besides this, made himself master of four galleys with five banks of oars.

He fought a second battle with Hostilius, a consular officer, as he was making his way into the country at Elimiæ, and forced him to retreat; and, when he afterwards by stealth designed an invasion through Thessaly, challenged him to fight, which the other feared to accept. Nay more, to show his contempt to the Romans, and that he wanted employment, as an incidental war, he made an expedition against the Dardanians, in which he slew ten thousand of those barbarian people, and brought a great spoil away. He privately, moreover, solicited the Gauls (also called Basternæ), a warlike nation, and famous for horsemen, dwelling near the Danube; and incited the Illyrians, by the means of Genthius, their king, to join with him in the war. It was also reported that the barbarians, allured by promise of rewards, were to make an irruption into Italy, through the lower Gaul by the shore of the Adriatic Sea.

The Romans, being advertised of these things, thought it necessary no longer to choose their commanders by favour or solicitation, but of their own motion to select a general of wisdom and capacity for the management of great affairs. And such was Paulus Æmilius, advanced in years, being nearly threescore, yet vigorous in his own person, and rich in valiant sons and sons-in-law, besides a great number of influential relations and friends, all of whom joined in urging him to yield to the desires of the people, who called him to the consulship. He at first manifested some shyness of the people and withdrew himself from their importunity, professing reluctance to hold office; but, when they daily came to his doors, urging him to come forth to the place of election, and pressing him with noise and clamour, he acceded to their request.

When he appeared amongst the candidates, it did not look as if it were to sue for the consulship, but to bring victory and success, that he came down into the Campus; they all received him there with such hopes and such gladness, unanimously choosing him a second time consul; nor would they suffer the lots to be cast, as was usual, to determine which province should fall to his share, but immediately decreed him the command of the Macedonian war.

It is told, that when he had been proclaimed general against Perseus, and was honourably accompanied home by great numbers of people, he found his daughter Tertia, a very little girl, weeping, and taking her to him asked her why she was crying. She, catching him about the neck and kissing him, said, "O father, do you not know that Perseus is dead?" meaning a little dog of that name that was brought up in the house with her; to which Æmilius replied, "Good fortune, my daughter; I embrace the omen." This Cicero, the orator, relates in his book *On Divination*.

It was the custom for such as were chosen consuls, from a stage designed for such purposes, to address the people, and return them thanks for their favour. Æmilius, therefore, having gathered an assembly, spoke and said that he sued for the first consulship, because he himself stood in need of such honour; but for the second, because they wanted a general; upon which account he thought there was no thanks due: if they judged they could manage the war by any other to more advantage, he would willingly yield up his charge; but, if they confided in him, they were not to make themselves his colleagues in his office, or raise reports, and criticise his actions, but, without talking, supply him with means and assistance necessary to the carrying on of the war; for if they proposed to command their own commander they would render this expedition more ridiculous than the former.

By this speech he inspired great reverence

for him amongst the citizens and great expectations of future success; all were well pleased that they had passed by such as sought to be preferred by flattery, and fixed upon a commander endued with wisdom and courage to tell them the truth. So entirely did the people of Rome, that they might rule, and become masters of the world, yield obedience and service to reason and superior virtue.

That Æmilius, setting forward to the war, by a prosperous voyage and successful journey, arrived with speed and safety at his camp I attribute to good fortune; but, when I see how the war under his command was brought to a happy issue, partly by his own daring boldness, partly by his good counsel, partly by the ready administration of his friends, partly by his presence of mind and skill to embrace the most proper advice in the extremity of danger, I cannot ascribe any of his remarkable and famous actions (as I can those of other commanders) to his so much celebrated good fortune; unless you will say that the covetousness of Perseus was the good fortune of Æmilius.

The truth is, Perseus's fear of spending his money was the destruction and utter ruin of all those splendid and great preparations with which the Macedonians were in high hopes to carry on the war with success. For there came at his request ten thousand horsemen of the Basternæ, and as many foot, who were to keep pace with them, and supply their places in case of failure; all of them professed soldiers, men skilled neither in tilling of land, nor in navigation of ships, nor able to get their living by grazing, but whose only business and single art and trade it was to fight and conquer all that resisted them.

When these came into the district of Mædica, and encamped and mixed with the king's soldiers, being men of great stature, admirable at their exercises, great boasters, and loud in their threats against their enemies, they gave new courage to the Macedonians, who were ready to think the Romans would not be able to confront them, but would be struck with terror at their looks and motions, they were so strange and so formidable to behold. When Perseus had thus encouraged his men, and elevated them with these great hopes, as soon as a thousand gold pieces were demanded for each captain, he was so amazed and beside himself at the vastness of the amount, that out of mere stinginess he drew back and let himself lose their assistance, as if he had been some steward, not the enemy of the Romans,

and would have to give an exact account of the expenses of the war to those with whom he waged it. Nay, when he had his foes as tutors, to instruct him what he had to do, who, besides their other preparations, had a hundred thousand men drawn together and in readiness for their service; yet he that was to engage against so considerable a force, and in a war that was maintaining such numbers as this, nevertheless doled out his money, and put seals on his bags, and was as fearful of touching it, as if it had belonged to some one else.

And all this was done by one, not descended from Lydians or Phœnicians, but who could pretend to some share of the virtues of Alexander and Philip, whom he was allied to by birth; men who conquered the world by judging that empire was to be purchased by money, not money by empire. Certainly it became a proverb, that not Philip, but his gold, took the cities of Greece. And Alexander, when he undertook his expedition against the Indians, and found his Macedonians encumbered and appear to march heavily with their Persian spoils, first set fire to his own carriages, and thence persuaded the rest to imitate his example, that thus freed they might proceed to the war without hindrance.

Whereas Perseus, abounding in wealth, would not preserve himself, his children, and his kingdom, at the expense of a small part of his treasure; but chose rather to be carried away with numbers of his subjects with the name of the wealthy captive, and show the Romans what great riches he had husbanded and preserved for them. For he not only played false with the Gauls, and sent them away, but also, after alluring Genthius, King of the Illyrians, by the hopes of three hundred talents, to assist him in the war, he caused the money to be counted out in the presence of his messengers, and to be sealed up. Upon which Genthius, thinking himself possessed of what he desired, committed a wicked and shameful act: he seized and imprisoned the ambassadors sent to him from the Romans. Whence Perseus, concluding that there was no need of money to make Genthius an enemy to the Romans, but that he had given a lasting earnest of his enmity, and by his flagrant injustice sufficiently involved himself in the war, defrauded the unfortunate king of his three hundred talents, and without any concern beheld him, his wife, and children, in a short time after, carried out of their kingdom, as from their nest, by Lucius Anicius, who was sent against him with an army.

Æmilius, coming against such an adversary, made light indeed of him, but admired his preparation and power. For he had four thousand horse, and not much fewer than forty thousand full-armed foot of the phalanx; and planting himself along the seaside, at the foot of Mount Olympus, in ground with no access on any side, and on all sides fortified with fences and bulwarks of wood, remained in great security, thinking by delay and expense to weary out Æmilius.

But he, in the meantime, busy in thought, weighed all counsels and all means of attack, and perceiving his soldiers, from their former want of discipline, to be impatient of delay, and ready on all occasions to teach their general his duty, rebuked them, and bade them not meddle with what was not their concern, but only take care that they and their arms were in readiness, and to use their swords like Romans when their commander should think fit to employ them. Further, he ordered that the sentinels by night should watch without javelins, that thus they might be more careful and surer to resist sleep, having no arms to defend themselves against any attacks of an enemy.

What most annoyed the army was the want of water; for only a little, and that foul, flowed out, or rather came by drops from a spring adjoining the sea; but Æmilius, considering that he was at the foot of the high and woody Mount Olympus, and conjecturing by the flourishing growth of the trees that there were springs that had their course underground, dug a great many holes and wells along the foot of the mountain, which were presently filled with pure water escaping from its confinement into the vacuum they afforded. Although there are some, indeed, who deny that there are reservoirs of water lying ready provided out of sight, in the places from whence springs flow, and that when they appear, they merely issue and run out; on the contrary, they say, they are then formed and come into existence for the first time, by the liquefaction of the surrounding matter; and that this change is caused by density and cold, when the moist vapour, by being closely pressed together, becomes fluid.

As women's breasts are not like vessels full of milk always prepared and ready to flow from them; but their nourishment being changed in their breasts, is there made milk, and from thence is pressed out. In like manner, places of the earth that are cold and full of springs, do not contain any hidden waters or receptacles which are capable, as from a source always ready and furnished, of supplying all the brooks and deep rivers; but by compressing and condensing the vapours and air they turn them into that substance. And thus places that are dug open flow by that pressure, and afford the more water (as the breasts of women do milk by their being sucked), the vapour thus moistening and becoming fluid; whereas ground that remains idle and undug is not capable of producing any water, whilst it wants the motion which is the cause of liquefaction.

But those that assert this opinion give occasion to the doubtful to argue, that on the same ground there should be no blood in living creatures, but that it must be formed by the wound, some sort of spirit or flesh being changed into a liquid and flowing matter. Moreover, they are refuted by the fact that men who dig mines, either in sieges or for metals, meet with rivers, which are not collected by little and little (as must necessarily be, if they had their being at the very instant the earth was opened), but break out at once with violence; and upon the cutting through a rock, there often gush out great quantities of water, which then as suddenly cease. But of this enough.

Æmilius lay still for some days, and it is said that there were never two great armies so nigh that enjoyed so much quiet. When he had tried and considered all things, he was informed that there was yet one passage left unguarded, through Perrhæbia by the temple of Apollo and the Rock Gathering; therefore, conceiving more hope from the place being left defenceless than fear from the roughness and difficulty of the passage, he proposed it for consultation.

Amongst those that were present at the council, Scipio, surnamed Nasica, son-in-law to Scipio Africanus, who afterwards was so powerful in the senate-house, was the first that offered himself to command those that should be sent to encompass the enemy. Next to him, Fabius Maximus, eldest son of Æmilius, although yet very young, offered himself with great zeal. Æmilius, rejoicing, gave them, not so many as Polybius states, but, as Nasica himself tells us in a brief letter which he wrote to one of the kings with an account of the expedition, three thousand Italians that were not Romans, and his left wing consisting of five thousand.

Taking with him, besides these, one hundred and twenty horsemen, and two hundred Thracians and Cretans intermixed that Harpalus had sent, he began his journey towards the sea, and encamped near the temple of Hercules, as if he designed to embark, and so to sail round and environ the enemy. But when the soldiers had supped and it was dark, he made the captains acquainted with his real intentions, and marching all night in the opposite direction away from the sea, till he came under the temple of Apollo, there rested his army. At this place Mount Olympus rises in height more than ten furlongs, as appears by the epigram made by the man that measured it:—

The summit of Olympus, at the site
Where stands Apollo's temple, has a height
Of full ten furlongs by the line, and more,
Ten furlongs, and one hundred feet, less four.
Eumelus's son, Xenagoras, reached the place.
Adieu, O king, and do thy pilgrim grace.

It is allowed, say the geometricians, that no mountain in height or sea in depth exceeds ten furlongs, and yet it seems probable that Xenagoras did not take his admeasurement carelessly, but according to the rules of art, and with instruments for the purpose. Here it was that Nasica passed the night.

A Cretan deserted, who fled to the enemy during the march, discovered to Perseus the design which the Romans had to encompass him; for he, seeing that Æmilius lay still, had not suspected any such attempt. He was startled at the news, yet did not put his army in motion, but sent ten thousand mercenary soldiers, and two thousand Macedonians, under command of Milo, with order to hasten and possess themselves of the passes. Polybius relates that the Romans found these men asleep when they attacked them; but Nasica says there was a sharp and severe conflict on the top of the mountain, that he himself encountered a mercenary Thracian, pierced him through with his javelin, and slew him; and that the enemy being forced to retreat, Milo stripped to his coat and fled shamefully without his armour, while he followed without danger, and conveyed the whole army down into the country.

After this event, Perseus, now grown fearful, and fallen from his hopes, removed his camp in all haste; he was under the necessity either to stop before Pydna, and there run the hazard of a battle, or disperse his army into cities, and there expect the event of the war, which, having once made its way into his country, could not be driven out without great slaughter and bloodshed. But Perseus, being told by his friends that he was much superior in number, and that men fighting in the defence of their wives and children must needs feel all the more courage, especially when all was done in the sight of their king, who himself was engaged in equal danger, was thus again encouraged; and, pitching his camp, prepared himself to fight, viewed the country, and gave out the commands, as if he designed to set upon the Romans as soon as they approached. The place was a field fit for the action of a phalanx, which requires smooth standing and even ground, and also had divers little hills, one joining another, fit for the motions whether in retreat or advance of light troops and skirmishers. Through the middle ran the rivers Æson and Leucus, which though not very deep, it being the latter end of summer, yet were likely enough to give the Romans some trouble.

As soon as Æmilius had rejoined Nasica, he advanced in battle array against the enemy; but when he found how they were drawn up, and the number of their forces, he regarded them with admiration and surprise, and halted, considering within himself. The young commanders, eager to fight, riding along by his side, pressed him not to delay, and most of all Nasica, flushed with his late success on Olympus. To whom Æmilius answered with a smile: "So would I do were I of your age; but many victories have taught me the ways in which men are defeated, and forbid me to engage soldiers weary with a long march against an army drawn up and prepared for battle."

Then he gave command that the front of his army, and such as were in sight of the enemy, should form as if ready to engage, and those in the rear should cast up the trenches and fortify the camp; so that the hindmost in succession wheeling off by degrees and withdrawing, their whole order was insensibly broken up, and the army encamped without noise or trouble.

When it was night, and, supper being over, all were turning to sleep and rest, on a sudden the moon, which was then at full and high in the heavens, grew dark, and by degrees losing her light, passed through various colours, and at length was totally eclipsed. The Romans, according to their custom, clattering brass pans and lifting up fire-brands and torches into the air, invoked the return of her light; the Macedonians behaved far otherwise; terror and amazement seized their whole army, and a rumour crept by degrees into their camp that this eclipse portended even that of their king.

Æmilius was no novice in these things, nor was ignorant of the nature of the seeming irregularities of eclipses—that in a certain revolution of time, the moon in her course enters the shadow of the earth and is there obscured, till, passing the region of darkness, she is again enlightened by the sun. Yet being a devout man, a religious observer of sacrifices and the art of divination, as soon as he perceived the moon beginning to regain her former lustre, he offered up to her eleven heifers. At the break of day he sacrificed as many as twenty in succession to Hercules, without any token that his offering was accepted; but at the one-and-twentieth, the signs promised victory to defenders. He then vowed a hecatomb and solemn sports to Hercules, and commanded his captains to make ready for battle, staying only till the sun should decline and come round to the west, lest, being in their faces in the morning, it should dazzle the eyes of his soldiers. Thus he whiled away the time in his tent, which was open towards the plain where his enemies were encamped.

When it grew towards evening, some tell us, Æmilius himself used a stratagem to induce the enemy to begin the fight; that he turned loose a horse without a bridle, and sent some of the Romans to catch him, upon whose following the beast the battle began. Others relate that the Thracians, under the command of one Alexander, set upon the Roman beasts of burden that were bringing forage to the camp; that to oppose these, a party of seven hundred Ligurians were immediately detached; and that, relief coming still from both armies, the main bodies at last engaged. Æmilius, like a wise pilot, foreseeing by the present waves and motion of the armies the greatness of the following storm, came out of his tent, went through the legions, and encouraged his soldiers.

Nasica, in the meantime, who had ridden out to the skirmishers, saw the whole force of the enemy on the point of engaging. First marched the Thracians, who, he himself tells us, inspired him with most terror; they were of great stature, with bright and glittering shields and black frocks under them, their legs armed with greaves, and they brandished, as they moved, straight and heavily-ironed spears over their right shoulders. Next the Thracians marched the mercenary soldiers, armed after different fashions; with these the Pæonians were mingled. These were succeeded by a third division, of picked men, native Macedonians, the choicest for courage and strength, in the prime of life, gleaming with gilt armour and scarlet coats. As these were taking their places they were followed from the camp by the troops in phalanx called the Brazen Shields, so that the whole plain seemed alive with the flashing of steel and the glistening of brass; and the hills also with their shouts, as they cheered each other on. In this order they marched, and with such boldness and speed, that those that were first slain died at but two furlongs distance from the Roman camp.

The battle being begun, Æmilius came in and found that the foremost of the Macedonians had already fixed the ends of their spears into the shields of his Romans, so that it was impossible to come near them with their swords. When he saw this, and observed that the rest of the Macedonians took the targets that hung on their left shoulders, and brought them round before them, and all at once stooped their pikes against their enemies' shields, and considered the great strength of this wall of shields, and the formidable appearance of a front thus bristling with arms, he was seized with amazement and alarm; nothing he had ever seen before had been equal to it; and in aftertimes he frequently used to speak both of the sight and of his own sensations. These, however, he dissembled, and rode through his army without either breastplate or helmet, with a serene and cheerful countenance.

On the contrary, as Polybius relates, no sooner was the battle begun, but the Macedonian king basely withdrew to the city Pydna, under a pretence of sacrificing to Hercules; a god that is not wont to regard the faint offerings of cowards, or to fulfil unsanctioned vows. For truly it can hardly be a thing that heaven would sanction, that he that never shoots should carry away the prize, he triumph that slinks from the battle, he that takes no pains to meet with success, or the wicked man prosper. But to Æmilius's petitions the god listened; he prayed for victory with his sword in his hand, and fought while entreating divine assistance.

A certain Posidonius, who has at some length written a history of Perseus, and professes to have lived at the time, and to have been himself engaged in these events, denies that Perseus left the field either through fear or pretence of sacrificing, but that, the very day before the fight, he received a kick from a horse on his thigh; that though very much disabled, and dissuaded by all his friends, he commanded one of his riding-horses to be brought, and entered the field unarmed; that amongst an infinite number of darts that flew about on all sides, one of iron lighted on him, and though not with the point, yet by a glance struck him with such force on his left side that it tore his clothes and so bruised his flesh that the mark remained a long time after. This is what Posidonius says in defence of Perseus.

The Romans not being able to make a breach in the phalanx, one Salius, a commander of the Pelignians, snatched the ensign of his company and threw it amongst the enemies; on seeing which, the Pelignians (as amongst the Italians it is always thought the greatest breach of honour to abandon a standard) rushed with great violence towards the place, where the conflict grew very fierce and the slaughter terrible on both sides. For these endeavoured to cut the spears asunder with their swords, or to beat them back with their shields, or put them by with their hands; and, on the other side, the Macedonians held their long sarissas in both hands, and pierced those that came in their way quite through their armour, no shield or corslet being able to resist the force of that weapon. The Pelignians and Marrucinians were thrown headlong to the ground, having without consideration, with mere animal fury, rushed upon a certain death. Their first ranks being slain, those that were behind were forced to give back; it cannot be said they fled, but they retreated towards Mount Olocrus. When Æmilius saw this, Posidonius relates, he rent his clothes, some of his men being ready to fly, and the rest not willing to engage with a phalanx into which they could not hope to make any entrance—a sort of palisade, as it were, impregnable and unapproachable, with its close array of long spears everywhere meeting the assailant.

Nevertheless, the unequalness of the ground would not permit a widely extended front to be so exactly drawn up as to have their shields everywhere joined; and Æmilius perceived that there were a great many interstices and breaches in the Macedonian phalanx; as it usually happens in all great armies, according to the different efforts of the combatants, who in one part press forward with eagerness, and in another are forced to fall back. Taking, therefore, this occasion, with all speed he broke up his men into their cohorts, and gave them order to fall into the intervals and openings of the enemy's body, and not to make one general attack upon them all, but to engage, as they were divided, in several partial battles. These commands Æmilius gave to his captains, and they to their soldiers; and no sooner had they entered the spaces and separated their enemies, but they charged them, some on their sides where they were naked and exposed, and others, making a circuit, behind; and thus destroyed the force of the phalanx, which consists in common action and close union. And now, come to fight man to man, or in small parties, the Macedonians smote in vain upon firm and long shields with their little swords, whilst their slight bucklers were not able to sustain the weight and force of the Roman swords, which pierced through all their armour to their bodies; they turned, in fine, and fled.

The conflict was obstinate. And here Marcus, the son of Cato, and son-in-law of Æmilius, whilst he showed all possible courage, let fall his sword. Being a young man carefully brought up and disciplined, and, son of so renowned a father, bound to give proof of more than ordinary virtue, he thought his life but a burden, should he live and permit his enemies to enjoy this spoil. He hurried hither and thither, and wherever he espied a friend or companion, declared his misfortune, and begged their assistance; a considerable number of brave men being thus collected, with one accord they made their way through their fellows after their leader, and fell upon the enemy; whom after a sharp conflict, many wounds, and much slaughter, they repulsed, possessed the place that was now deserted and free, and set themselves to search for the sword, which at last they found covered with a great heap of arms and dead bodies. Overjoyed with this success, they raised the song of triumph, and, with more eagerness than ever, charged the foes that yet remained firm and unbroken.

In the end, three thousand of the chosen

men, who kept their ground and fought valiantly to the last, were all cut in pieces, while the slaughter of such as fled was also very great. The plain and the lower part of the hills were filled with dead bodies, and the water of the river Leucus, which the Romans did not pass till the next day after the battle, was then mingled with blood. For it is said there fell more than twenty-five thousand of the enemy; of the Romans, as Posidonius relates, a hundred; as Nasica, only fourscore. This battle, though so great, was very quickly decided, it being three in the afternoon when they first engaged, and not four when the enemy was vanquished; the rest of the day was spent in pursuit of the fugitives, whom they followed about thirteen or fourteen miles, so that it was far in the night when they returned.

All the others were met by their servants with torches, and brought back with joy and great triumph to their tents, which were set out with lights, and decked with wreaths of ivy and laurel. But the general himself was in great grief. Of the two sons that served under him in the war, the youngest was missing, whom he held most dear, and whose courage and good qualities he perceived much to excel those of his brothers. Bold and eager for distinction, and still a mere child in age, he concluded that he had perished whilst for want of experience he had engaged himself too far amongst his enemies. His sorrow and fears became known to the army; the soldiers, quitting their suppers, ran about with lights, some to Æmilius's tent, some out of the trenches, to seek him amongst such as were slain in the first onset. There was nothing but grief in the camp, and the plain was filled with the cries of men calling out for Scipio; for from his very youth, he was an object of admiration; endowed above any of his equals with the good qualities requisite either for command or counsel. At length, when it was late, and they almost despaired, he returned from the pursuit with only two or three of his companions all covered with the fresh blood of his enemies, having been, like some dog of noble breed, carried away by the pleasure, greater than he could control, of his first victory. This was that Scipio that afterwards destroyed Carthage and Numantia, and was without dispute the first of the Romans in merit, and had the greatest authority amongst them. Thus Fortune, deferring her displeasure and jealousy of such great success to some other time, let Æmilius at present enjoy this victory, without any detraction or diminution.

As for Perseus, from Pydna he fled to Pella with his cavalry, which was as yet almost entire. But when the foot came up with them, and, upbraiding them as cowards and traitors, tried to pull them off their horses, and fell to blows, Perseus, fearing the tumult, forsook the common road, and, lest he should be known, pulled off his purple, and carried it before him, and took his crown in his hand and, that he might the better converse with his friends, alighted from his horse and led him.

Of those that were about him, one stopped, pretending to tie his shoe that was loose, another to water his horse, a third to drink himself; and thus lagging behind, by degrees left him, they having not so much reason to fear their enemies as his cruelty; for he, disordered by his misfortune, sought to clear himself by laying the cause of the overthrow upon everybody else.

He arrived at Pella in the night, where Euctus and Eudæus, two of his treasurers, came to him, and, what with their reflecting on his former faults, and their free and ill-timed admonitions and counsels, so exasperated him, that he killed them both, stabbing them with his own dagger. After this, nobody stuck to him but Evander the Cretan, Archedemus the Ætolian, and Neon the Bœotian. Of the common soldiers there followed him only those from Crete, not out of any good-will, but because they were as constant to his riches as the bees to their hive. For he carried a great treasure with him, out of which he had suffered them to take cups, bowls, and other vessels of silver and gold, to the value of fifty talents.

But when he was come to Amphipolis, and afterwards to Galepsus, and his fears were a little abated, he relapsed into his old and constitutional disease of covetousness, and lamented to his friends that he had, through inadvertency, allowed some gold plate which had belonged to Alexander the Great to go into the hands of the Cretans, and besought those that had it, with tears in his eyes, to exchange with him again for money. Those that understood him thoroughly knew very well that he only played the Cretan with the Cretans, but those that believed him, and restored what they had, were cheated; as he not only did not pay the money, but by craft got thirty talents more of his friends into his hands (which in a short time after fell to the enemy), and with them sailed to Samothrace, and there fled to the temple of Castor and Pollux for refuge.

The Macedonians were always accounted great lovers of their kings, but now, as if their chief prop was broken, they all gave way together, and submitted to Æmilius, and in two days made him master of their whole country. This seems to confirm the opinion which ascribes whatever he did to good fortune. The omen, also, that happened at Amphipolis has a supernatural character. When he was sacrificing there, and the holy rites were just begun, on a sudden, lightning fell upon the altar, set the wood on fire, and completed the immolation of the sacrifice.

The most signal manifestation, however, of preternatural agency appears in the story of the rumour of his success. For on the fourth day after Perseus was vanquished at Pydna, whilst the people at Rome were seeing the horse-races, a report suddenly rose at the entrance of the theatre that Æmilius had defeated Perseus in a great battle, and was reducing all Macedonia under his power; and from thence it spread amongst the people, and created general joy, with shoutings and acclamations for that whole day through the city. But when no certain author was found of the news, and every one alike had taken it at random, it was abandoned for the present and thought no more of, until, a few days after, certain intelligence came, and then the first was looked upon as no less than a miracle, having, under an appearance of fiction, contained what was real and true.

It is reported also, that the news of the battle fought in Italy, near the river Sagra, was conveyed into Peloponnesus the same day, and of that at Mycale against the Medes, to Platæa. When the Romans had defeated the Tarquins, who were combined with the Latins, a little after there were seen at Rome two tall and comely men, who professed to bring the news from the camp. They were conjectured to be Castor and Pollux. The first man that spoke to them in the Forum, near the fountain where they were cooling their horses, which were all of a foam, expressed surprise at the report of the victory, when, it is said, they smiled, and gently touched his beard with their hands, the hair of which from being black was, on the spot, changed to yellow. This gave credit to what they said, and fixed the name of Ahenobarbus, or Brazen-beard, on the man.

And a thing which happened in our own time will make all these credible. For when Antonius rebelled against Domitian, and Rome was in consternation, expecting great wars from the quarter of Germany, all on a sudden, and nobody knows upon what account, the people spontaneously gave out a rumour of victory, and the news ran current through the city, that Antonius himself was slain, his whole army destroyed, and not so much as a part of it escaped; nay, this belief was so strong and positive, that many of the magistrates offered up sacrifice. But when, at length, the author was sought for, and none was to be found, it vanished by degrees, every one shifting it off from himself to another, and, at last, was lost in the numberless crowd, as in a vast ocean, and, having no solid ground to support its credit, was in a short time not so much as named in the city. Nevertheless, when Domitian marched out with his forces to the war, he met with messengers and letters that gave him a relation of the victory; and the rumour, it was found, had come the very day it was gained, though the distance between the places was more than twenty-five hundred miles. The truth of this no man of our time is ignorant of.

But to proceed. Cnæus Octavius, who was joined in command with Æmilius, came to an anchor with his fleet under Samothrace, where, out of respect to the gods, he permitted Perseus to enjoy the benefit of refuge, but took care that he should not escape by sea. Notwithstanding, Perseus secretly persuaded Oroandes of Crete, master of a small vessel, to convey him and his treasure away. He, however, playing the true Cretan, took in the treasure, and bade him come, in the night, with his children and most necessary attendants, to the port by the temple of Ceres; but, as soon as it was evening, set sail without him.

It had been sad enough for Perseus to be forced to let down himself, his wife, and children through a narrow window by a wall—people altogether unaccustomed to hardship and fleeing; but that which drew a far sadder sigh from his heart was, when he was told by a man, as he wandered on the shore, that he had seen Oroandes under sail in the main sea; it being now about daybreak. So, there being no hopes left of escaping, he fled back again to the wall, which he and his wife recovered, though they were seen by the Romans, before they could reach them. His children he himself had delivered into the hands of Ion, one that had been his favourite, but now proved his betrayer, and was the chief cause that forced him (beasts themselves will do so when their young ones are taken) to come and yield himself up to those that had them in their power. His greatest confidence was in Nasica, and it was for him he called, but he not being there, he bewailed his misfortune, and, seeing there was no possible remedy, surrendered himself to Octavius.

And here, in particular, he made it manifest that he was possessed with a vice more sordid than covetousness itself, namely, the fondness of life; by which he deprived himself even of pity, the only thing that fortune never takes away from the most wretched. He desired to be brought to Æmilius, who arose from his seat, and, accompanied with his friends, went to receive him, with tears in his eyes, as a great man fallen by the anger of the gods and his own ill-fortune; when Perseus—the most shameful of sights—threw himself at his feet, embraced his knees, and uttered unmanly cries and petitions, such as Æmilius was not able to bear, nor would vouchsafe to hear; but looking on him with a sad and angry countenance he said, "Why, unhappy man, do you thus take pains to exonerate fortune of your heaviest charge against her, by conduct that will make it seem that you are not unjustly in calamity, and that it is not your present condition, but your former happiness, that was more than your deserts? And why depreciate also my victory, and make my conquests insignificant, by proving yourself a coward, and a foe beneath a Roman? Distressed valour challenges great respect, even from enemies; but cowardice, though never so successful, from the Romans has always met with scorn." Yet for all this he took him up, gave him his hand, and delivered him into the custody of Tubero.

Meantime, he himself carried his sons, his sons-in-law, and others of chief rank, especially of the younger sort, back with him into his tent, where for a long time he sat down without speaking one word, insomuch that they all wondered at him. At last, he began to discourse of fortune and human affairs. "Is it meet," said he, "for him that knows he is but man, in his greatest prosperity to pride himself, and be exalted at the conquest of a city, nation, or kingdom, and not, rather, well to weigh this change of fortune, in which all warriors may see an example of their common frailty, and learn a lesson that there is nothing durable or constant? For what time

can men select to think themselves secure, when that of victory itself forces us more than any to dread our own fortune? And a very little consideration on the law of things, and how all are hurried round, and each man's station changed, will introduce sadness in the midst of the greatest joy. Or can you, when you see before your eyes the succession of Alexander himself, who arrived at the height of power and ruled the greatest empire, in the short space of an hour trodden underfoot— when you behold a king, that was but even now surrounded with so numerous an army, receiving nourishment to support his life from the hands of his conquerors—can you, I say, believe there is any certainty in what we now possess, whilst there is such a thing as chance? No, young men, cast off that vain pride and empty boast of victory; sit down with humility, looking always for what is yet to come, and the possible future reverses which the divine displeasure may eventually make the end of our present happiness." It is said that Æmilius, having spoken much more to the same purpose, dismissed the young men properly humbled, and with their vainglory and insolence thoroughly chastened and curbed by his address.

When this was done, he put his army into garrisons, to refresh themselves, and went himself to visit Greece, and to spend a short time in relaxations equally honourable and humane. For as he passed, he eased the people's grievances, reformed their governments, and bestowed gifts upon them; to some corn, to others oil out of the king's storehouses, in which, they report, there were such vast quantities laid up, that receivers and petitioners were lacking before they could be exhausted.

In Delphi he found a great square pillar of white marble, designed for the pedestal of King Perseus's golden statue, on which he commanded his own to be placed, alleging that it was but just that the conquered should give place to the conquerors. In Olympia he is said to have uttered the saying everybody has heard, that Phidias had carved Homer's Jupiter.

When the ten commissioners arrived from Rome, he delivered up again to the Macedonians their cities and country, granting them to live at liberty, and according to their own laws, only paying the Romans the tribute of a hundred talents, double which sum they had been wont to pay to their kings.

Then he celebrated all manner of shows and

games, and sacrifices to the gods, and made great entertainments and feasts; the charge of all which he liberally defrayed out of the king's treasury; and showed that he understood the ordering and placing of his guests, and how every man should be received, answerably to their rank and quality, with such nice exactness, that the Greeks were full of wonder, finding the care of these matters of pleasure did not escape him, and that though involved in such important business, he could observe correctness in these trifles. Nor was it least gratifying to him, that, amidst all the magnificent and splendid preparations, he himself was always the most grateful sight, and greatest pleasure to those he entertained. And he told those that seemed to wonder at his diligence, that there was the same spirit shown in marshalling a banquet as an army; in rendering the one formidable to the enemy, the other acceptable to the guests.

Nor did men less praise his liberality, and the greatness of his soul, than his other virtues; for he would not so much as see those great quantities of silver and gold, which were heaped together out of the king's palaces, but delivered them to the quæstors, to be put into the public treasury. He only permitted his own sons, who were great lovers of learning, to take the king's books; and when he distributed rewards due to extraordinary valour, he gave his son-in-law, Ælius Tubero, a bowl that weighed five pounds. This is that Tubero we have already mentioned, who was one of sixteen relations that lived together, and were all maintained out of one little farm; and it is said that this was the first plate that ever entered the house of the Ælii, brought thither as an honour and reward of virtue; before this time, neither they nor their wives ever made use either of silver or gold.

Having thus settled everything well, taking his leave of the Greeks, and exhorting the Macedonians, that, mindful of the liberty they had received from the Romans, they should endeavour to maintain it by their obedience to the laws, and concord amongst themselves, he departed for Epirus, having orders from the senate to give the soldiers that followed him in the war against Perseus the pillage of the cities of that country.

That he might set upon them all at once by surprise and unawares, he summoned ten of the principal men out of each, whom he commanded, on such an appointed day, to bring all the gold and silver they had either in their private houses or temples; and, with every one of these, as if it were for this very purpose, and under a pretence of searching for and receiving the gold, he sent a centurion and a guard of soldiers; who, the set day being come, rose all at once, and at the very self-same time fell upon them, and proceeded to ransack the cities; so that in one hour a hundred and fifty thousand persons were made slaves, and threescore and ten cities sacked. Yet what was given to each soldier, out of so vast a destruction and utter ruin, amounted to no more than eleven drachmas; so that men could only shudder at the issue of a war, where the wealth of a whole nation thus divided turned to so little advantage and profit to each particular man.

When Æmilius had done this—an action perfectly contrary to his gentle and mild nature—he went down to Oricus, where he embarked his army for Italy. He sailed up the river Tiber in the king's galley, that had sixteen banks of oars, and was richly adorned with captured arms and with cloths of purple and scarlet; so that, the vessel rowing slowly against the stream, the Romans that crowded on the shore to meet him had a foretaste of his following triumph.

But the soldiers, who had cast a covetous eye on the treasures of Perseus, when they did not obtain as much as they thought they deserved, were secretly enraged and angry with Æmilius for this, but openly complained that he had been a severe and tyrannical commander over them; nor were they ready to show their desire of his triumph. When Servius Galba, who was Æmilius's enemy, though he commanded as tribune under him, understood this, he had the boldness plainly to affirm that a triumph was not to be allowed him; and sowed various calumnies amongst the soldiers, which yet further increased their ill-will.

Nay more, he desired the tribunes of the people, because the four hours that were remaining of the day could not suffice for the accusation, to let him put it off till another. But when the tribunes commanded him to speak then, if he had anything to say, he began a long oration, filled with all manner of reproaches, in which he spent the remaining part of the time, and the tribunes, when it was dark, dismissed the assembly. The soldiers growing more vehement on this, thronged all to Galba, and entering into a conspiracy, early in the morning beset the capitol, where the tribunes had appointed the following assembly to be held.

As soon as it was day it was put to the vote, and the first tribe was proceeding to refuse the triumph; and the news spread amongst the people and to the senate. The people were indeed much grieved that Æmilius should meet with such ignominy; but this was only in words, which had no effect. The chief of the senate exclaimed against it as a base action, and excited one another to repress the boldness and insolence of the soldiers, which would ere long become altogether ungovernable and violent, were they now permitted to deprive Æmilius of his triumph. Forcing a passage through the crowd, they came up in great numbers, and desired the tribunes to defer polling till they had spoken what they had to say to the people.

All things thus suspended, and silence being made, Marcus Servilius stood up, a man of consular dignity, and who had killed twenty-three of his enemies that had challenged him in single combat. "It is now more than ever," said he, "clear to my mind how great a commander our Æmilius Paulus is, when I see he was able to perform such famous and great exploits with an army so full of sedition and baseness; nor can I sufficiently wonder, that a people that seemed to glory in the triumphs over Illyrians and Ligurians, should now through envy refuse to see the Macedonian king led alive, and all the glory of Philip and Alexander, in captivity to the Roman power. For is it not a strange thing for you, who upon a slight rumour of victory that came by chance into the city, did offer sacrifices and put up your requests unto the gods that you might see the report verified, now, when the general is returned with an undoubted conquest, to defraud the gods of honour, and yourselves of joy, as if you feared to behold the greatness of his warlike deed, or were resolved to spare your enemy? And of the two, much better were it to put a stop to the triumph, out of pity to him, than out of envy to your general; yet to such a height of power is malice arrived amongst you, that a man without one scar to show on his skin, that is smooth and sleek with ease and homekeeping habits, will undertake to define the office and duties of a general before us, who with our own wounds have been taught how to judge of the valour or the cowardice of commanders."

And, at the same time, putting aside his garment, he showed an infinite number of scars upon his breast, and, turning about, he exposed some parts of his person which it is usual to conceal; and, addressing Galba, said: "You deride me for these, in which I glory before my fellow-citizens, for it is in their service, in which I have ridden night and day, that I received them; but go collect the votes, whilst I follow after, and note the base and ungrateful, and such as choose rather to be flattered and courted than commanded by their general." It is said this speech so stopped the soldiers' mouths, and altered their minds, that all the tribes decreed a triumph for Æmilius; which was performed after this manner.

The people erected scaffolds in the Forum, in the circuses, as they call their buildings for horse-races, and in all other parts of the city where they could best behold the show. The spectators were clad in white garments; all the temples were open, and full of garlands and perfumes; the ways were cleared and kept open by numerous officers, who drove back all who crowded into or ran across the main avenue. This triumph lasted three days.

On the first, which was scarcely long enough for the sight, were to be seen the statues, pictures, and colossal images which were taken from the enemy, drawn upon two hundred and fifty chariots.

On the second was carried in a great many waggons the finest and richest armour of the Macedonians, both of brass and steel, all newly polished and glittering; the pieces of which were piled up and arranged purposely with the greatest art, so as to seem to be tumbled in heaps carelessly and by chance; helmets were thrown upon shields, coats of mail upon greaves; Cretan targets, and Thracian bucklers and quivers of arrows, lay huddled amongst horses' bits, and through these there appeared the points of naked swords, intermixed with long Macedonian sarissas. All these arms were fastened together with just so much looseness that they struck against one another as they were drawn along, and made a harsh and alarming noise, so that, even as spoils of a conquered enemy, they could not be beheld without dread. After these waggons loaded with armour there followed three thousand men who carried the silver that was coined, in seven hundred and fifty vessels, each of which weighed three talents, and was carried by four men. Others brought silver bowls and goblets and cups, all disposed in such order as to make the best show, and all curious as well for their size as the solidity of their embossed work.

On the third day, early in the morning, first came the trumpeters, who did not sound as they were wont in a procession or solemn entry, but such a charge as the Romans use when they encourage the soldiers to fight. Next followed young men wearing frocks with ornamented borders, who led to the sacrifice a hundred and twenty stalled oxen, with their horns gilded, and their heads adorned with ribbons and garlands; and with these were boys that carried basins for libation, of silver and gold. After this was brought the gold coin, which was divided into vessels that weighed three talents, like those that contained the silver; they were in number seventy-seven. These were followed by those that brought the consecrated bowl which Æmilius had caused to be made, that weighed ten talents, and was set with precious stones. Then were exposed to view the cups of Antigonus and Seleucuse, and those of the Thericlean make, and all the gold plate that was used at Perseus's table. Next to these came Perseus's chariot, in which his armour was placed, and on that his diadem.

And, after a little intermission, the king's children were led captives, and with them a train of their attendants, masters, and teachers, all shedding tears, and stretching out hands to the spectators, and making the children themselves also beg and entreat their compassion. There were two sons and a daughter, whose tender age made them but little sensible of the greatness of their misery, which very insensibility of their condition rendered it the more deplorable; insomuch that Perseus himself was scarcely regarded as he went along, whilst pity fixed the eyes of the Romans upon the infants; and many of them could not forbear tears, and all beheld the sight with a mixture of sorrow and pleasure, until the children were passed.

After his children and their attendants came Perseus himself, clad all in black, and wearing the boots of his country, and looking like one altogether stunned and deprived of reason, through the greatness of his misfortunes. Next followed a great company of his friends and familiars, whose countenances were disfigured with grief and who let the spectators see, by their tears and their continual looking upon Perseus, that it was his fortune they so

much lamented, and that they were regardless of their own.

Perseus sent to Æmilius to entreat that he might not be led in pomp, but be left out of the triumph; who, deriding, as was but just, his cowardice and fondness of life, sent him this answer, that as for that, it had been before, and was now, in his own power, giving him to understand that the disgrace could be avoided by death; which the faint-hearted man not having the spirit for, and made effeminate by I know not what hopes, allowed himself to appear as a part of his own spoils.

After these were carried four hundred crowns, all made of gold, sent from the cities by their respective deputations to Æmilius, in honour of his victory. Then he himself came, seated on a chariot magnificently adorned (a man well worthy to be looked at, even without these ensigns of power), dressed in a robe of purple, interwoven with gold, and holding a laurel branch in his right hand. All the army, in like manner, with boughs of laurel in their hands, divided into their bands and companies, followed the chariot of their commander; some singing verses, according to the usual custom, mingled with raillery; others, songs of triumph and the praise of Æmilius's deeds; who, indeed, was admired and accounted happy by all men, and unenvied by every one that was good; except so far as it seems the province of some god to lessen that happiness which is too great and inordinate, and so to mingle the affairs of human life that no one should be entirely free and exempt from calamities; but, as we read in Homer, that those should think themselves truly blessed to whom fortune has given an equal share of good and evil.

Æmilius had four sons, of whom Scipio and Fabius, as is already related, were adopted into other families; the other two, whom he had by a second wife, and who were yet but young, he brought up in his own house. One of these died at fourteen years of age, five days before his father's triumph, the other at twelve, three days after; so that there was no Roman without a deep sense of his suffering, and who did not shudder at the cruelty of fortune, that had not scrupled to bring so much sorrow into a house replenished with happiness, rejoicing, and sacrifices, and to intermingle tears and laments with songs of victory and triumph.

Æmilius, however, reasoning justly that courage and resolution was not merely to resist armour and spears, but all the shocks of ill-fortune, so met and so adapted himself to these mingled and contrasting circumstances, as to outbalance the evil with the good, and his private concerns with those of the public; and thus did not allow anything either to take away from the grandeur, or sully the dignity of his victory. For as soon as he had buried the first of his sons (as we have already said), he triumphed; and the second dying almost as soon as his triumph was over, he gathered together an assembly of the people, and made an oration to them, not like a man that stood in need of comfort from others, but one that undertook to support his fellow-citizens in their grief for the sufferings he himself underwent.

"I," he said, "who never yet feared anything that was human, have, amongst such as were divine, always had a dread of Fortune as faithless and inconstant; and, for the very reason that in this war she had been as a favourable gale in all my affairs, I still expected some change and reflux of things. In one day I passed the Ionian sea, and reached Corcyra from Brundisium; thence in five more I sacrificed at Delphi, and in other five days came to my forces in Macedonia, where, after I had finished the usual sacrifices for the purifying of the army, I entered on my duties, and, in the space of fifteen days, put an honourable period to the war.

"Still retaining a jealousy of Fortune, even from the smooth current of my affairs, and seeing myself secure and free from the danger of any enemy, I chiefly dreaded the change of the goddess at sea, whilst conveying home my victorious army, vast spoils, and a captive king. Nay, indeed, after I was returned to you safe, and saw the city full of joy, congratulating, and sacrifices, yet still I distrusted, well knowing that Fortune never conferred any great benefits that were unmixed and unattended with probabilities of reverse. Nor could my mind, that was still, as it were, in labour, and always foreseeing something to befall this city, free itself from this fear, until this great misfortune befell me in my own family, and till, in the midst of those days set apart for triumph, I carried two of the best of sons, my only destined successors, one after another to their funerals.

"Now, therefore, I am myself safe from danger, at least as to what was my greatest care; and I trust and am verily persuaded that for the time to come Fortune will prove constant and harmless unto you; since she has sufficiently wreaked her jealousy at our great successes on me and mine, and has made the conqueror as marked an example of human instability as the captive whom he led in triumph, with this only difference, that Perseus, though conquered, does yet enjoy his children, while the conqueror, Æmilius, is deprived of his." This was the generous and magnanimous oration Æmilius is said to have spoken to the people, from a heart truly sincere and free from all artifice.

Although he very much pitied the condition of Perseus, and studied to befriend him in what he was able, yet he could procure no other favour than his removal from the common prison, the *carcer*, into a more cleanly and humane place of security, where, whilst he was guarded, it is said, he starved himself to death.

Others state his death to be of the strangest and most unusual character: that the soldiers who were his guard, having conceived a spite and hatred against him for some reason, and finding no other way to grieve and afflict him, kept him from sleep, took pains to disturb him when he was disposed to rest, and found out contrivances to keep him continually awake, by which means at length he was utterly worn out, and expired.

Two of his children, also, died soon after him; the third, who was named Alexander, they say proved an exquisite artist in turning and graving small figures, and learned so perfectly to speak and write the Roman language, that he became clerk to the magistrates, and behaved himself in his office with great skill and conduct.

They ascribed to Æmilius's conquest of Macedonia this most acceptable benefit to the people, that he brought so vast a quantity of money into the public treasury, that they never paid any taxes, until Hirtius and Pansa were consuls, which was in the first war between Antony and Cæsar.

This also was peculiar and remarkable in Æmilius, that though he was extremely beloved and honoured by the people, yet he always sided with the nobles; nor would he either say or do anything to ingratiate himself with the multitude, but constantly adhered to the nobility, in all political matters, which in aftertimes was cast in Scipio Africanus's teeth by Appius; these two being in their time the most considerable men in the city, and standing in competition for the office of censor. The one had on his side the nobles and the senate, to which party the Appii were always attached; the other, although his own interest was great, yet made use of the favour and love of the people.

When, therefore, Appius saw Scipio come to the market-place, surrounded with men of mean rank, and such as were but newly made free, yet were very fit to manage a debate, to gather together the rabble, and to carry whatsoever they designed by importunity and noise, crying out with a loud voice: "Groan now," said he, "O Æmilius Paulus, if you have knowledge in your grave of what is done above, that your son aspires to be censor, by the help of Æmilius, the common crier, and Licinius Philonicus."

Scipio always had the good-will of the people, because he was constantly heaping favours on them; but Æmilius, although he still took part with the nobles, yet was as much the people's favourite as those who most sought popularity and used every art to obtain it. This they made manifest, when, amongst other dignities, they thought him worthy of the office of censor, a trust accounted most sacred and of great authority, as well in other things, as in the strict examination into men's lives. For the censors had power to expel a senator, and enrol whom they judged most fit in his room, and to disgrace such young men as lived licentiously, by taking away their horses. Besides this, they were to value and assess each man's estate, and register the number of the people.

There were numbered by Æmilius 347,452 men. He declared Marcus Æmilius Lepidus first senator, who had already four times held that honour, and he removed from their office three of the senators of the least note. The same moderation he and his fellow-censor, Marcius Philippus, used at the muster of the knights.

Whilst he was thus busy about many and weighty affairs he fell sick of a disease, which at first seemed hazardous; and although after a while it proved without danger, yet was troublesome and difficult to be cured; so that by the advice of his physicians he sailed to Velia, in south Italy, and there dwelt a long

time near the sea, where he enjoyed all possible quietness.

The Romans, in the meanwhile, longed for his return, and oftentimes by their expressions in the theatres gave public testimony of their great desire and impatience to see him. When, therefore, the time drew nigh that a solemn sacrifice was of necessity to be offered, and he found, as he thought, his body strong enough, he came back again to Rome, and there performed the holy rites with the rest of the priests, the people in the meantime crowding about him and congratulating his return.

The next day he sacrificed again to the gods for his recovery; and, having finished the sacrifice, returned to his house and sat down to dinner, when, all on a sudden and when no change was expected, he fell into a fit of delirium, and, being quite deprived of his senses, the third day after ended a life in which he had wanted no manner of thing which is thought to conduce to happiness.

Nay, his very funeral pomp had something in it remarkable and to be admired, and his virtue was graced with the most solemn and happy rites at his burial; consisting, not in gold and ivory, or in the usual sumptuousness and splendour of such preparations, but in the good-will, honour, and love, not only of his fellow-citizens, but of his enemies themselves. For as many Spaniards, Ligurians, and Macedonians as happened to be present at the solemnity, that were young and of vigorous bodies, took up the bier and carried it; whilst the more aged followed, called Æmilius the benefactor and preserver of their countries.

For not only at the time of his conquest had he acted to all with kindness and clemency, but, through the whole course of his life, he continued to do them good and look after their concerns, as if they had been his familiars and relations. They report that the whole of his estate scarce amounted to three hundred and seventy thousand drachmas; to which he left his two sons co-heirs; but Scipio, who was the youngest, being adopted into the more wealthy family of Africanus, gave it all to his brother. Such are said to have been the life and manners of Æmilius.

ÆMILIUS PAULUS and TIMOLEON Compared

SUCH being the story of these two great men's lives, without doubt in the comparison very little difference will be found between them. They made war with two powerful enemies: the one against the Macedonians, and the other with the Carthaginians, and the success was in both cases glorious. One conquered Macedon from the seventh succeeding heir of Antigonus; the other freed Sicily from usurping tyrants, and restored the island to its former liberty. Unless, indeed, it be made a point of Æmilius's side, that he engaged with Perseus when his forces were entire, and composed of men that had often successfully fought with the Romans; whereas Timoleon found Dionysius in a despairing condition, his affairs being reduced to the last extremity; or, on the contrary, it be urged in favour of Timoleon, that he vanquished several tyrants, and a powerful Carthaginian army, with an inconsiderable number of men gathered together from all parts, not with such an army as Æmilius had, of well-disciplined soldiers, experienced in war, and accustomed to obey; but with such as through the hopes of gain restored to him, unskilled in fighting and ungovernable. And when actions are equally glorious, and the means to compass them unequal, the greater esteem is certainly due to that general who conquers with the smaller power.

Both have the reputation of having behaved themselves with an uncorrupted integrity in all the affairs they managed; but Æmilius had the advantage of being, from his infancy, by the laws and customs of his country brought up to the proper management of public affairs, which Timoleon brought himself to by his own efforts. And this is plain; for at that time all the Romans were uniformly orderly and obedient, respectful to the laws and to their fellow-citizens: whereas it is remarkable that not one of the Greek generals commanding in Sicily could keep himself uncorrupted, except Dion, and of him many entertained a jealousy that he would establish a monarchy there, after the Lacedæmonian manner. Timæus writes, that the Syracusans sent even Gylippus home dishonourably, and with a reputation lost by the unsatiable covetousness he displayed when he commanded the army. And numerous historians tell us of the wicked and perfidious acts committed by Pharax the Spartan and Callippus the Athenian, with

the view of making themselves kings of Sicily. Yet what were these men, and what strength had they, to entertain such a thought? The first of them was a follower of Dionysius, when he was expelled from Syracuse, and the other a hired captain of foot under Dion, and came into Sicily with him. But Timoleon, at the request and prayers of the Syracusans, was sent to be their general, and had no need to seek for power, but had a perfect title, founded on their own offers, to hold it; and yet no sooner had he freed Sicily from her oppressors, but he willingly surrendered it.

It is truly worthy our admiration in Æmilius, that though he conquered so great and so rich a realm as that of Macedon, yet he would not touch, nor see any of the money, nor did he advantage himself one farthing by it, though he was very generous of his own to others. I would not intend any reflection on Timoleon for accepting of a house and handsome estate in the country, which the Syracusans presented him with; there is no dishonour in accepting; but yet there is greater glory in a refusal, and the supremest virtue is shown in not wanting what it might fairly take.

And as that body is, without doubt, the most strong and healthful which can the easiest support extreme cold and excessive heat in the change of seasons, and that the most firm and collected mind which is not puffed up with prosperity nor dejected with adversity; so the virtue of Æmilius was eminently seen in his countenance and behaviour, continuing as noble and lofty upon the loss of two dear sons, as when he achieved his greatest victories and triumphs. But Timoleon, after he had justly punished his brother, a truly heroic action, let his reason yield to a causeless sorrow, and, humiliated with grief and remorse, forbore for twenty years to appear in any public place, or meddle with any affairs of the commonwealth. It is truly very commendable to abhor and shun the doing any base action; but to stand in fear of every kind of censure or disrepute may argue a gentle and open-hearted, but not an heroic temper.

PELOPIDAS

410?–364 B.C.

CATO MAJOR, hearing some commend one that was rash, and inconsiderately daring in a battle, said, "There is a difference between a man's prizing valour at a great rate, and valuing life at little," a very just remark. Antigonus, we know, at least, had a soldier, a venturous fellow, but of wretched health and constitution; the reason of whose ill-look he took the trouble to inquire into; and, on understanding from him that it was a disease, commanded his physicians to employ their utmost skill, and if possible recover him; which brave hero, when once cured, never afterwards sought danger or showed himself venturous in battle; and, when Antigonus wondered and upbraided him with his change, made no secret of the reason, and said, "Sir, you are the cause of my cowardice, by freeing me from those miseries which made me care little for life."

With the same feeling, the Sybarite seems to have said of the Spartans, that it was no commendable thing in them to be so ready to die in the wars, since by that they were freed from such hard labour and miserable living. In truth, the Sybarites, a soft and dissolute people, might well imagine they hated life, because in their eager pursuit of virtue and glory they were not afraid to die; but, in fact, the Lacedæmonians found their virtue secured them happiness alike in living or in dying; as we see in the epitaph that says—

They died, but not as lavish of their blood,
Or thinking death itself was simply good;
Their wishes neither were to live nor die,
But to do both alike commendably.

An endeavour to avoid death is not blamable, if we do not basely desire to live; nor a willingness to die good and virtuous, if it proceeds from a contempt of life. And, therefore, Homer always takes care to bring his bravest and most daring heroes well armed into battle; and the Greek law-givers punished those that threw away their shields, but not him that lost his sword or spear, intimating that self-defence is more a man's business than offence. This is especially true of a governor of a city, or a general; for if, as Iphicrates divides it out, the light-armed are the hands, the horse the feet, the infantry the breast, and the general the head, he, when he puts himself upon danger, not only ventures his own person, but all those whose safety depends on his; and so on the contrary. Callicratidas, therefore, though otherwise a great man, was wrong in his answer to the augur who advised him, the sacrifice being unlucky, to be careful of his life; "Sparta," said he, "will not miss one man." It is true, Callicratidas, when simply serving in any engagement either at sea or land, was but a single person, but as a general, he united in his life the lives of all, and could hardly be called one when his death involved the ruin of so many.

The saying of old Antigonus was better, who, when he was to fight at Andros, and one told him, "The enemy's ships are more than ours"; replied, "For how many then wilt thou reckon me?" intimating that a brave and experienced commander is to be highly valued, one of the first duties of whose office indeed it is to save him on whose safety depends that of others. And, therefore, I applaud Timotheus, who, when Chares showed the wounds he had received, and his shield pierced by a dart, told him, "Yet how ashamed I was, at the siege of Samos, when a dart fell near me, for exposing myself, more like a boy than like a general in command of a large army." Indeed, where the general's hazarding himself will go far to decide the result, there he must fight and venture his person, and not mind their maxims, who would have a general die, if not *of,* at least *in* old age; but when the advantage will be but small if he gets the better, and the loss considerable if he falls, who then would desire, at the risk of the commander's life, a piece of success which a common soldier might obtain?

This I thought fit to premise before the lives of Pelopidas and Marcellus, who were both great men, but who both fell by their own rashness. For, being gallant men, and having gained their respective countries great glory and reputation by their conduct in war against terrible enemies, the one, as history relates, overthrowing Hannibal, who was till then invincible; the other, in a set battle beating the Lacedæmonians, then supreme both at sea and land; they ventured at last too far, and were heedlessly prodigal of their lives, when there was the greatest need of men and commanders such as they. And this agreement in their characters and their deaths is the reason why I compare their lives.

Pelopidas, the son of Hippoclus, was descended, as likewise Epaminondas was, from an honourable family in Thebes; and, being brought up to opulence, and having a fair estate left him whilst he was young, he made it his business to relieve the good and deserving amongst the poor, that he might show himself lord and not slave of his estate. For amongst men, as Aristotle observes, some are too narrow-minded to use their wealth, and some are loose and abuse it; and these live perpetual slaves to their pleasures, as the others to their gain.

Others permitted themselves to be obliged by Pelopidas, and thankfully made use of his liberality and kindness; but amongst all his friends he could never persuade Epaminondas to be a sharer in his wealth. He, however, stepped down into his poverty, and took pleasure in the same poor attire, spare diet, unwearied endurance of hardships, and unshrinking boldness in war; like Capaneus in Euripides, who had—

Abundant wealth and in that wealth no pride,
he was ashamed any one should think that he spent more upon his person than the meanest Theban.

Epaminondas made his familiar and hereditary poverty more light and easy by his philosophy and single life; but Pelopidas married a woman of good family, and had children; yet still thinking little of his private interests, and devoting all his time to the public, he ruined his estate; and, when his friends admonished and told him how necessary that money which he neglected was: "Yes," he replied, "necessary to Nicodemus," pointing to a blind cripple.

Both seemed equally fitted by nature for all sorts of excellence; but bodily exercises chiefly delighted Pelopidas, learning Epaminondas; and the one spent his spare hours in hunting and the Palæstra, the other in hearing lectures or philosophising. And, amongst a thousand points for praise in both, the judicious esteem

nothing equal to that constant benevolence and friendship, which they inviolably preserved in all their expeditions, public actions, and administration of the commonwealth. For if any one looks on the administrations of Aristides and Themistocles, of Cimon and Pericles, of Nicias and Alcibiades, what confusion, what envy, what mutual jealousy appears? And if he then casts his eye on the kindness and reverence that Pelopidas showed Epaminondas, he must needs confess that these are more truly and more justly styled colleagues in government and command than the others, who strove rather to overcome one another than their enemies.

The true cause of this was their virtue; whence it came that they did not make their actions aim at wealth and glory, an endeavour sure to lead to bitter and contentious jealousy; but both from the beginning being inflamed with a divine desire of seeing their country glorious by their exertions, they used to that end one another's excellences as their own. Many, indeed, think this strict and entire affection is to be dated from the battle at Mantinea, where they both fought, being part of the succours that were sent from Thebes to the Lacedæmonians, their then friends and allies. For, being placed together amongst the infantry, and engaging the Arcadians, when the Lacedæmonian wing, in which they fought, gave ground, and many fled, they closed their shields together and resisted the assailants.

Pelopidas, having received seven wounds in the forepart of his body, fell upon an heap of slain friends and enemies; but Epaminondas, though he thought him past recovery, advanced to defend his arms and body, and singly fought a multitude, resolving rather to die than forsake his helpless Pelopidas. And now, he being much distressed, being wounded in the breast by a spear, and in the arm by a sword, Agesipolis, the King of the Spartans, came to his succour from the other wing, and beyond hope delivered both.

After this the Lacedæmonians pretended to be friends to Thebes, but in truth looked with jealous suspicions on the designs and power of the city, and chiefly hated the party of Ismenias and Androclides, in which Pelopidas also was an associate, as tending to liberty and the advancement of the commonalty. Therefore Archias, Leontidas, and Philip, all rich men, and of oligarchical principles, and immoderately ambitious, urged Phœbidas the

Spartan, as he was on his way past the city with a considerable force, to surprise the Cadmea, and, banishing the contrary faction, to establish an oligarchy, and by that means subject the city to the supremacy of the Spartans. He, accepting the proposal, at the festival of Ceres unexpectedly fell on the Thebans, and made himself master of the citadel. Ismenias was taken, carried to Sparta, and in a short time murdered; but Pelopidas, Pherenicus, Androclides, and many more that fled were publicly proclaimed outlaws. Epaminondas stayed at home, being not much looked after, as one whom philosophy had made inactive and poverty incapable.

The Lacedæmonians cashiered Phœbidas, and fined him one hundred thousand drachmas, yet still kept a garrison in the Cadmea; which made all Greece wonder at their inconsistency, since they punished the doer, but approved the deed. And though the Thebans, having lost their polity, and being enslaved by Archias and Leontidas, had no hopes to get free from this tyranny, which they saw guarded by the whole military power of the Spartans, and had no means to break the yoke, unless these could be deposed from their command of sea and land; yet Leontidas and his associates, understanding the exiles lived at Athens in favour with the people, and with honour from all the good and virtuous, formed secret designs against their lives, and, suborning some unknown fellows, despatched Androclides, but were not successful on the rest.

Letters, besides, were sent from Sparta to the Athenians, warning them neither to receive nor countenance the exiles, but expel them as declared common enemies of the confederacy. But the Athenians, from their natural hereditary inclination to be kind, and also to make a grateful return to the Thebans, who had very much assisted them in restoring their democracy, and had publicly enacted, that if any Athenian would march armed through Bœotia against the tyrants, that no Bœotian should either see or hear it, did the Thebans no harm.

Pelopidas, though one of the youngest, was active in privately exciting each single exile; and often told them at their meetings that it was both dishonourable and impious to neglect their enslaved and engarrisoned country, and, lazily contented with their own lives and safety, depend on the decree of the Athenians, and through fear fawn on every smooth-tongued orator that was able to work upon

the people: no, they must venture for this great prize, taking Thrasybulus's bold courage for example, and as he advanced from Thebes and broke the power of the Athenian tyrants, so they should march from Athens and free Thebes. When by this method he had persuaded them, they privately despatched some persons to those friends they had left at Thebes, and acquainted them with their designs.

Their plans being approved, Charon, a man of the greatest distinction, offered his house for their reception; Phillidas contrived to get himself made secretary to Archias and Philip, who then held the office of polemarch or chief captain; and Epaminondas had already inflamed the youth. For, in their exercises, he had encouraged them to challenge and wrestle with the Spartans, and again, when he saw them puffed up with victory and success, sharply told them that it was the greater shame to be such cowards as to serve those whom in strength they so much excelled.

The day for action being fixed, it was agreed upon by the exiles that Pherenicus with the rest should stay at the Thriasian plain, while some few of the younger men tried the first danger by endeavouring to get into the city; and, if they were surprised by their enemies, the others should take care to provide for their children and parents. Pelopidas first offered to undertake the business; then Melon, Damoclides, and Theopompus, men of noble families, who, in other things loving and faithful to one another, were rivals constant only in glory and courageous exploits.

They were twelve in all, and having taken leave of those that stayed behind, and sent a messenger to Charon, they went forward, clad in short coats, and carrying hounds and hunting-poles with them, that they might be taken for hunters beating over the fields, and prevent all suspicion in those that met them on the way. When the messenger came to Charon, and told him they were approaching, he did not change his resolution at the sight of danger, but, being a man of his word, offered them his house.

But one Hipposthenidas—a man of no ill principles, a lover of his country, and a friend to the exiles, but not of as much resolution as the shortness of time and the character of the action required, being as it were dizzied at the greatness of the approaching enterprise and beginning now for the first time to comprehend that, relying on that weak assistance which could be expected from the exiles, they were undertaking no less a task than to shake the government, and overthrow the whole power of Sparta,—went privately to his house and sent a friend to Melon and Pelopidas, desiring them to forbear for the present, to return to Athens and expect a better opportunity.

The messenger's name was Chlidon, who, going home in haste and bringing out his horse, asked for the bridle; but, his wife not knowing where it was, and, when it could not be found, telling him she had lent it to a friend, first they began to chide, then to curse one another, and his wife wished the journey might prove ill to him and those that sent him; insomuch that Chlidon's passion made him waste a great part of the day in this quarrelling, and then, looking on this chance as an omen, he laid aside all thoughts of his journey, and went away to some other business. So nearly had these great and glorious designs, even in their very birth, lost their opportunity.

But Pelopidas and his companions, dressing themselves like countrymen, divided, and, whilst it was yet day, entered at different quarters of the city. It was, besides, a windy day, and now it just began to snow, which contributed much to their concealment, because most people were gone indoors to avoid the weather. Those, however, that were concerned in the design received them as they came, and conducted them to Charon's house, where the exiles and others made up forty-eight in number. The tyrant's affairs stood thus: the secretary, Phillidas, as I have already observed, was an accomplice in and privy to all the contrivance of the exiles, and he a while before had invited Archias, with others, to an entertainment on that day, to drink freely, and meet some women of the town, on purpose that when they were drunk, and given up to their pleasures, he might deliver them over to the conspirators. But before Archias was thoroughly heated notice was given him that the exiles were privately in the town; a true report indeed, but obscure, and not well confirmed; nevertheless, though Phillidas endeavoured to divert the discourse, Archias sent one of his guards to Charon, and commanded him to attend immediately.

It was evening, and Pelopidas and his friends with him in the house were putting themselves into a fit posture for action, having their breastplates on already, and their swords girt; but at the sudden knocking at the door, one stepping forth to inquire the matter, and learning from the officer that Charon was sent for by the polemarch, returned in great confusion and acquainted those within; and immediately conjectured that the whole plot was discovered, and they should be cut in pieces, before so much as achieving any action to do credit to their bravery; yet all agreed that Charon should obey and attend the polemarch to prevent suspicion. Charon was, indeed, a man of courage and resolution in all dangers, yet in this case he was extremely concerned, lest any should suspect that he was the traitor and the death of so many brave citizens be laid on him. And, therefore, when he was ready to depart, he brought his son out of the women's apartment, a little boy as yet, but one of the best looking and strongest of all those of his age, and delivered him to Pelopidas with these words: "If you find me a traitor, treat the boy as an enemy without any mercy."

The concern which Charon showed drew tears from many; but all protested vehemently against his supposing any one of them so mean-spirited and base, at the appearance of approaching danger, as to suspect or blame him; and therefore desired him not to involve his son, but to set him out of harm's way: that so he, perhaps escaping the tyrant's power, might live to revenge the city and his friends. Charon, however, refused to remove him, and asked, "What life, what safety could be more honourable, than to die bravely with his father and such generous companions?" Thus, imploring the protection of the gods, and saluting and encouraging them all, he departed, considering with himself, and composing his voice and countenance, that he might look as little like as possible to what in fact he really was.

When he was come to the door, Archias with Phillidas came out to him, and said, "I have heard, Charon, that there are some men just come, and lurking in the town, and that some of the citizens are resorting to them." Charon was at first disturbed, but asking, "Who are they, and who conceals them?" and finding Archias did not thoroughly understand the matter, he concluded that none of those privy to the design had given this information, and replied, "Do not disturb yourself for an empty rumour; I will look into it, however, for no report in such a case is to be neglected."

Phillidas, who stood by, commended him, and leading back Archias, got him deep in drink, still prolonging the entertainment with the hopes of the women's company at last. But when Charon returned, and found the men prepared, not as if they hoped for safety and success, but to die bravely and with the slaughter of their enemies, he told Pelopidas and his friends the truth, but pretended to others in the house that Archias talked to him about something else, inventing a story for the occasion.

This storm was just blowing over, when fortune brought another; for a messenger came with a letter from one Archias, the Hierophant at Athens, to his namesake Archias, who was his friend and guest. This did not merely contain a vague conjectural suspicion, but, as it appeared afterwards, disclosed every particular of the design. The messenger being brought in to Archias, who was now pretty well drunk, and delivering the letter, said to him, "The writer of this desired it might be read at once; it is on urgent business." Archias, with a smile, replied, "Urgent business tomorrow," and so receiving the letter, he put it under his pillow, and returned to what he had been speaking of with Phillidas, and these words of his are a proverb to this day amongst the Greeks.

Now when the opportunity seemed convenient for action, they set out in two companies; Pelopidas and Damoclides with their party went against Leontidas and Hypates, that lived near together; Charon and Melon against Archias and Philip, having put on women's apparel over their breastplates, and thick garlands of fir and pine to shade their faces; and so, as soon as they came to the door, the guests clapped and gave an huzza, supposing them to be the women they expected. But when the conspirators had looked about the room, and carefully marked all that were at the entertainment, they drew their swords, and making at Archias and Philip amongst the tables, disclosed who they were. Phillidas persuaded some few of his guests to sit still, and those that got up and endeavoured to assist the polemarch, being drunk, were easily despatched. But Pelopidas and his party met with a harder task; as they attempted Leontidas, a sober and formidable man, and when they came to his house found his door shut, he being already gone to bed. They knocked a long time before any one would answer, but at last, a servant that heard

them, came out and unbarred the door. As soon as the gate gave way, they rushed in, and, overturning the man, made all haste to Leontidas's chamber. But Leontidas, guessing at the matter by the noise and running, leaped from his bed and drew his dagger, but forgot to put out the lights, and by that means make them fall foul of one another in the dark. As it was, being easily seen by reason of the light, he received them at his chamber door and stabbed Cephisodorus, the first man that entered: on his falling the next that he engaged was Pelopidas; and the passage being narrow and Cephisodorus's body lying in the way, there was a fierce and dangerous conflict. At last Pelopidas prevailed, and having killed Leontidas, he and his companions went in pursuit of Hypates, and after the same manner broke into his house. He perceived the design, and fled to his neighbours; but they closely followed, and caught and killed him.

This done they joined Melon, and sent to hasten the exiles they had left in Attica; and called upon the citizens to maintain their liberty, and taking down the spoils from the porches, and breaking open all the armourers' shops that were near, equipped those that came to their assistance. Epaminondas and Gorgidas came in already armed, with a gallant train of young men and the best of the old.

Now the city was in a great excitement and confusion, a great noise and hurry, lights set up in every house, men running here and there; however, the people did not as yet gather into a body, but, amazed at the proceedings, and not clearly understanding the matter, waited for the day. And, therefore, the Spartan officers were thought to have been in fault for not falling on at once, since their garrison consisted of about fifteen hundred men, and many of the citizens ran to them; but, alarmed with the noise, the fires, and the confused running of the people, they kept quietly within the Cadmea. As soon as day appeared, the exiles from Attica came in armed, and there was a general assembly of the people.

Epaminondas and Gorgidas brought forth Pelopidas and his party, encompassed by the priests, who held out garlands, and exhorted the people to fight for their country and their gods. The assembly, at their appearance, rose up in a body and with shouts and acclamations received the men as their deliverers and benefactors.

Then Pelopidas, being chosen chief captain of Bœotia, together with Melon and Charon, proceeded at once to blockade the citadel, and stormed it on all sides, being extremely desirous to expel the Lacedæmonians, and free the Cadmea, before an army could come from Sparta to their relief. And he just so narrowly succeeded, that they, having surrendered on terms and departed, on their way home met Cleombrotus at Megara marching towards Thebes with a considerable force. The Spartans condemned and executed Herippidas and Arcissus, two of their governors, at Thebes, and Lysanoridas the third, being severely fined, fled to Peloponnesus.

This action so closely resembling that of Thrasybulus, in the courage of the actors, the danger, the encounters, and equally crowned with success, was called the sister of it by the Greeks. For we can scarcely find any other examples where so small and weak a party of men by bold courage overcame such numerous and powerful enemies, or brought greater blessings to their country by so doing. But the subsequent change of affairs made this action the more famous; for the war which forever ruined the pretensions of Sparta to command, and put an end to the supremacy she then exercised alike by sea and by land, proceeded from that night, in which Pelopidas not surprising any fort, or castle, or citadel, but coming, the twelfth man, to a private house, loosed and broke, if we may speak truth in metaphor, the chains of the Spartan sway, which before seemed of adamant and indissoluble.

But now the Lacedæmonians invading Bœotia with a great army, the Athenians, affrighted at the danger, declared themselves no allies to Thebes, and prosecuting those that stood for the Bœotian interest, executed some, and banished and fined others; and the cause of Thebes, destitute of allies, seemed in a desperate condition. But Pelopidas and Gorgidas, holding the office of captains of Bœotia, designing to breed a quarrel between the Lacedæmonians and Athenians, made this contrivance.

One Sphodrias, a Spartan, a man famous indeed for courage in battle, but of no sound judgment, full of ungrounded hopes and foolish ambition, was left with an army at Thespiæ, to receive and succour the Theban renegades. To him Pelopidas and his colleagues privately sent a merchant, one of their friends, with money, and, what proved more

efficient, advice—that it more became a man of his worth to set upon some great enterprise, and that he should, making a sudden incursion on the unprotected Athenians, surprise the Piræus; since nothing could be so grateful to Sparta as to take Athens; and the Thebans, of course, would not stir to the assistance of men whom they now hated and looked upon as traitors.

Sphodrias, being at last wrought upon, marched into Attica by night with his army, and advanced as far as Eleusis; but there his soldiers' hearts failing, after exposing his project and involving the Spartans in a dangerous war, he retreated to Thespiæ. After this the Athenians zealously sent supplies to Thebes, and putting to sea, sailed to many places, and offered support and protection to all those of the Greeks who were willing to revolt.

The Thebans, meantime, singly, having many skirmishes with the Spartans in Bœotia, and fighting some battles, not great indeed, but important as training and instructing them, thus had their minds raised, and their bodies inured to labour, and gained both experience and courage by these frequent encounters, insomuch that we have it related that Antalcidas, the Spartan, said to Agesilaus, returning wounded from Bœotia, "Indeed, the Thebans have paid you handsomely for instructing them in the art of war, against their wills."

In real truth, however, Agesilaus was not their master in this, but those that prudently and opportunely, as men do young dogs, set them on their enemies, and brought them safely off after they had tasted the sweets of victory and resolution. Of all those leaders, Pelopidas deserves the most honour; as after they had once chosen him general, he was every year in command as long as he lived; either captain of the sacred band, or, what was most frequent, chief captain of Bœotia. About Platæa and Thespiæ the Spartans were routed and put to flight, and Phœbidas, that surprised the Cadmea, slain; and at Tanagra a considerable force was worsted, and the leader, Panthoides, killed. But these encounters, though they raised the victors' spirits, did not thoroughly dishearten the unsuccessful; for there was no set battle, or regular fighting, but mere incursions on advantage, in which, according to occasion, they charged, retired again, or pursued.

But the battle at Tegyræ, which seemed a

prelude to Leuctra, won Pelopidas great reputation; for none of the other commanders could claim any hand in the design, nor the enemies any show of victory. The city of the Orchomenians siding with the Spartans, and having received two companies for its guard, he kept a constant eye upon it, and watched his opportunity. Hearing that the garrison had moved into Locris, and hoping to find Orchomenus defenceless, he marched with his sacred band and some few horsemen. But when he approached the city, and found that a reinforcement of the garrison was on its march from Sparta, he made a circuit round the foot of the mountains, and retreated with his little army through Tegyræ, that being the only way he could pass.

For the river Melas, almost as soon as it rises, spreads itself into marshes and navigable pools, and makes all the plain between impassable. A little below the marshes stands the temple and oracle of Apollo Tegyræus, forsaken not long before that time, having flourished till the Median wars, Echecrates then being priest. Here they profess that the god was born; the neighbouring mountain is called Delos, and there the river Melas comes again into a channel; behind the temple rise two springs, admirable for the sweetness, abundance, and coolness of the streams; one they called Phœnix, the other Elæa, even to the present time, as if Lucina had not been delivered between two trees, but fountains. A place hard by, called Ptoum, is shown, where they say she was affrighted by the appearance of a boar; and the stories of the Python and Tityus are in like manner appropriated by these localities.

I omit many of the points that are used as arguments. For our tradition does not rank this god amongst those that were born, and then made immortal, as Hercules and Bacchus, whom their virtue raised above a mortal and passible condition; but Apollo is one of the eternal unbegotten deities, if we may collect any certainty concerning these things, from the statements of the oldest and wisest in such subjects.

As the Thebans were retreating from Orchomenus towards Tegyræ, the Spartans, at the same time marching from Locris, met them. As soon as they came in view, advancing through the straits, one told Pelopidas, "We are fallen into our enemy's hands." He replied, "And why not they into ours?" and immediately commanded his horse to come up from the rear and charge, while he himself drew his infantry, being three hundred in number, into a close body, hoping by that means, at whatsoever point he made the attack, to break his way through his more numerous enemies.

The Spartans had two companies (the company consisting, as Ephorus states, of five hundred; Callisthenes says seven hundred; others, as Polybius, nine hundred); and their leaders Gorgoleon and Theopompus, confident of success, advanced upon the Thebans. The charge being made with much fury, chiefly where the commanders were posted, the Spartan captains that engaged Pelopidas were first killed; and those immediately around them suffering severely, the whole army was thus disheartened, and opened a lane for the Thebans as if they desired to pass through and escape.

But when Pelopidas entered, and turning against those that stood their ground, still went on with a bloody slaughter, an open flight ensued amongst the Spartans. The pursuit was carried but a little way, because they feared the neighbouring Orchomenians and the reinforcements from Lacedæmon; they had succeeded, however, in fighting a way through their enemies, and overpowering their whole force; and, therefore, erecting a trophy, and spoiling the slain, they returned home extremely encouraged with their achievements.

For in all the great wars there had ever been against Greeks or barbarians, the Spartans were never before beaten by a smaller company than their own; nor, indeed, in a set battle, when their number was equal. Hence their courage was thought irresistible, and their high repute before the battle made a conquest already of enemies, who thought themselves no match for the men of Sparta even on equal terms. But this battle first taught the other Greeks, that not only Eurotas, or the country between Babyce and Cnacion, breeds men of courage and resolution, but that where the youth are ashamed of baseness, and ready to venture in a good cause, where they fly disgrace more than danger, there, wherever it be, are found the bravest and most formidable opponents.

Gorgidas, according to some, first formed the Sacred Band of three hundred chosen men, to whom, as being a guard for the citadel, the State allowed provision, and all things necessary for exercise: and hence they were called the city band, as citadels of old were usually called cities. Others say that it was composed of young men attached to each other by personal affection, and a pleasant saying of Pammenes is current, that Homer's Nestor was not well skilled in ordering an army, when he advised the Greeks to rank tribe and tribe, and family and family together, that—

So tribe might tribe, and kinsmen kinsmen aid.

but that he should have joined lovers and their beloved.

For men of the same tribe or family little value one another when dangers press; but a band cemented by friendship grounded upon love is never to be broken, and invincible; since the lovers, ashamed to be base in sight of their beloved, and the beloved before their lovers, willingly rush into danger for the relief of one another. Nor can that be wondered at since they have more regard for their absent lovers than for others present; as in the instance of the man who, when his enemy was going to kill him, earnestly requested him to run him through the breast, that his lover might not blush to see him wounded in the back.

It is a tradition likewise that Iolaüs, who assisted Hercules in his labours and fought at his side, was beloved of him; and Aristotle observes that, even in his time, lovers plighted their faith at Iolaüs's tomb. It is likely, therefore, that this band was called sacred on this account, as Plato calls a lover a divine friend. It is stated that it was never beaten till the battle at Chæronea; and when Philip, after the fight, took a view of the slain, and came to the place where the three hundred that fought his phalanx lay dead together, he wondered, and understanding that it was the band of lovers, he shed tears and said, "Perish any man who suspects that these men either did or suffered anything that was base."

It was not the disaster of Laius, as the poets imagine, that first gave rise to this form of attachment amongst the Thebans, but their lawgivers, designing to soften whilst they were young their natural fierceness, brought, for example, the pipe into great esteem, both in serious and sportive occasions, and gave great encouragement to these friendships in the Palæstra, to temper the manners and characters of the youth. With a view to this they did well, again, to make Harmony, the daughter of Mars and Venus, their tutelar deity; since, where force and courage is joined with gracefulness and winning behaviour, a harmony ensues that combines all the elements of society in perfect consonance and order.

Gorgidas distributed this Sacred Band all through the front ranks of the infantry, and thus made their gallantry less conspicuous; not being united in one body, but mingled with so many others of inferior resolution, they had no fair opportunity of showing what they could do. But Pelopidas, having sufficiently tried their bravery at Tegyræ, where they had fought alone and around his own person, never afterward divided them, but, keeping them entire, and as one man, gave them the first duty in the greatest battles. For as horses run brisker in a chariot than singly, not that their joint force divides the air with greater ease, but because being matched one against the other emulation kindles and inflames their courage; thus he thought brave men, provoking one another to noble actions, would prove most serviceable, and most resolute, where all were united together.

Now when the Lacedæmonians had made peace with the other Greeks, and united all their strength against the Thebans only, and their king, Cleombrotus, had passed the frontier with ten thousand foot and one thousand horse, and not only subjection, as heretofore, but total dispersion and annihilation threatened, and Bœotia was in a greater fear than ever—Pelopidas, leaving his house, when his wife followed him on his way, and with tears begged him to be careful of his life, made answer, "Private men, my wife, should be advised to look to themselves, generals to save others." And when he came to the camp, and found the chief captains disagreeing, he, first, joined the side of Epaminondas, who advised to fight the enemy; though Pelopidas himself was not then in office as chief captain of Bœotia, but in command of the Sacred Band, and trusted as it was fit a man should be, who had given his country such proofs of his zeal for its freedom.

And so when a battle was agreed on, and they encamped in front of the Spartans at Leuctra, Pelopidas saw a vision, which much discomposed him. In that plain lie the bodies of the daughters of one Scedasus, called from the place Leuctridæ, having been buried there after having been ravished by some Spartan strangers. When this base and lawless deed was done, and their father could get no satisfaction at Lacedæmon, with bitter imprecations on the Spartans, he killed himself at his daughters' tombs; and from that time the

prophecies and oracles still warned them to
have a great care of the divine vengeance at
Leuctra. Many, however, did not understand
the meaning, being uncertain about the place,
because there was a little maritime town of
Laconia called Leuctron, and near Megalopolis in Arcadia a place of the same name;
and the villainy was committed long before
this battle.

Now Pelopidas, being asleep in the camp,
thought he saw the maidens weeping about
their tombs, and cursing the Spartans, and
Scedasus commanding, if they desired the victory, to sacrifice a virgin with chestnut hair
to his daughters. Pelopidas looked on this as
an harsh and impious injunction, but rose
and told it to the prophets and commanders
of the army, some of whom contended that
it was fit to obey, and adduced as examples
from the ancients, Menœceus, son of Creon;
Macaria, daughter of Hercules; and from later
times, Pherecydes, the philosopher, slain by
the Lacedæmonians, and his skin, as the oracles advised, still kept by their kings. Leonidas, again, warned by the oracle, did as it
were sacrifice himself for the good of Greece;
Themistocles offered human victims to Bacchus Omestes, before the engagement at Salamis; and success showed their actions to be
good. On the contrary, Agesilaus, going from
the same place, and against the same enemies
that Agamemnon did, and being commanded
in a dream at Aulis to sacrifice his daughter,
was so weak as to disobey; the consequence
of which was, that his expedition was unsuccessful and inglorious.

But some on the other side urged that such
a barbarous and impious obligation could not
be pleasing to any Superior Beings; that ty-
phons and giants did not preside over the
world, but the general father of gods and
men; that it was absurd to imagine any divinities or powers delighted in slaughter and sacrifices of men; or, if there were such, they
were to be neglected as weak and unable to
assist; such unreasonable and cruel desires
could only proceed from, and live in, weak
and depraved minds.

The commanders thus disputing, and Pelopidas being in a great perplexity, a mare colt
breaking from the herd, ran through the
camp, and when she came to the place where
they were stood still; and whilst some admired
her bright chestnut colour, others her mettle,
or the strength and fury of her neighing,
Theocritus, the augur, took thought, and cried

out to Pelopidas, "O good friend! look, the
sacrifice is come; expect no other virgin, but
use that which the gods have sent thee."
With that they took the colt, and, leading her
to the maidens' sepulchres, with the usual
solemnity and prayers, offered her with joy,
and spread through the whole army the account of Pelopidas's dream, and how they
had given the required sacrifice.

In the battle, Epaminondas, bending his
phalanx to the left, that, as much as possible,
he might divide the right wing, composed of
Spartans, from the other Greeks, and distress
Cleombrotus by a fierce charge in column on
that wing, the enemies perceived the design,
and began to change their order, to open and
extend their right wing, and, as they far exceeded him in number, to encompass Epaminondas. But Pelopidas with the three hundred came rapidly up, before Cleombrotus
could extend his line, and close up his divisions, and so fell upon the Spartans while in
disorder; though the Lacedæmonians, the expertest and most practised soldiers of all mankind, used to train and accustom themselves
to nothing so much as to keep themselves
from confusion upon any change of position,
and to follow any leader, or right-hand man,
and form in order, and fight on what part
soever dangers press.

In this battle, however, Epaminondas with
his phalanx, neglecting the other Greeks, and
charging them alone, and Pelopidas coming
up with such incredible speed and fury, so
broke their courage and baffled their art that
there began such a flight and slaughter
amongst the Spartans as was never before
known. And so Pelopidas, though in no high
office, but only captain of a small band, got as
much reputation by the victory as Epaminondas, who was general and chief captain of
Bœotia.

Into Peloponnesus, however, they both advanced together as colleagues in supreme command, and gained the greater part of the nations there from the Spartan confederacy; Elis,
Argos, all Arcadia, and much of Laconia itself. It was the dead of winter, and but few
of the last days of the month remained, and,
in the beginning of the next, new officers were
to succeed, and whoever failed to deliver up
his charge forfeited his head. Therefore, the
other chief captains fearing the law, and to
avoid the sharpness of the winter, advised a
retreat. But Pelopidas joined with Epaminondas, and, encouraging his countrymen, led

them against Sparta, and, passing the Eurotas, took many of the towns, and wasted the country as far as the sea.

This army consisted of seventy thousand Greeks, of which number the Thebans could not make the twelfth part; but the reputation of the men made all their allies contented to follow them as leaders, though no articles to that effect had been made. For, indeed, it seems the first and paramount law, that he that wants a defender is naturally a subject to him that is able to defend: as mariners, though in a calm or in the port they grow insolent, and brave the pilot, yet when a storm comes, and danger is at hand, they all attend, and put their hopes in him.

So the Argives, Eleans, and Arcadians, in their congresses, would contend with the Thebans for superiority in command, yet in a battle, or any hazardous undertaking, of their own will followed their Theban captains. In this expedition they united all Arcadia into one body, and expelling the Spartans that inhabited Messenia, they called back the old Messenians, and established them in Ithome in one body; and, returning through Cenchreæ, they dispersed the Athenians, who designed to set upon them in the straits, and hinder their march.

For these exploits, all the other Greeks loved their courage and admired their success; but among their own citizens, envy, still increasing with their glory, prepared them no pleasing nor agreeable reception. Both were tried for their lives, because they did not deliver up their command in the first month, Bucatius, as the law required, but kept it four months longer, in which time they did these memorable actions in Messenia, Arcadia, and Laconia.

Pelopidas was first tried, and therefore in greatest danger, but both were acquitted. Epaminondas bore the accusation and trial very patiently, esteeming it a great and essential part of courage and generosity not to resent injuries in political life. But Pelopidas, being a man of a fiercer temper, and stirred on by his friends to revenge the affront, took the following occasion.

Meneclidas, the orator, was one of those that had met with Melon and Pelopidas at Charon's house; but not receiving equal honour, and being powerful in his speech, but loose in his manners, and ill-natured, he abused his natural endowments, even after this trial, to accuse and calumniate his betters. He excluded Epaminondas from the chief captaincy, and for a long time kept the upper hand of him, but he was not powerful enough to bring Pelopidas out of the people's favour, and therefore endeavoured to raise a quarrel between him and Charon. And since it is some comfort to the envious to make those men, whom themselves cannot excel, appear worse than others, he studiously enlarged upon Charon's actions in his speeches to the people, and made panegyrics on his expeditions and victories; and, of the victory which the horsemen won at Platæa, before the battle at Leuctra, under Charon's command, he endeavoured to make the following sacred memorial.

Androcydes, the Cyzicenian, had undertaken to paint a previous battle for the city, and was at work in Thebes; and when the revolt began, and the war came on, the Thebans kept the picture that was then almost finished. This picture Meneclidas persuaded them to dedicate, inscribed with Charon's name, designing by that means to obscure the glory of Epaminondas and Pelopidas. This was a ludicrous piece of pretension, to set a single victory, where only one Gerandas, an obscure Spartan, and forty more were slain, above such numerous and important battles. This motion Pelopidas opposed, as contrary to law, alleging that it was not the custom of the Thebans to honour any single man, but to attribute the victory to their country; yet in all the contest he extremely commended Charon, and confined himself to showing Meneclidas to be a troublesome and envious fellow, asking the Thebans, if they had done nothing that was excellent themselves. The result was that Meneclidas was severely fined; and he, being unable to pay, endeavoured afterwards to disturb the government. These things give us some light into Pelopidas's life.

Now when Alexander, the tyrant of Pheræ, made open war against some of the Thessalians, and had designs against all, the cities sent an embassy to Thebes, to desire succours and a general; and Pelopidas, knowing that Epaminondas was detained by the Peloponnesian affairs, offered himself to lead the Thessalians, being unwilling to let his courage and skill lie idle, and thinking it unfit that Epaminondas should be withdrawn from his present duties.

When he came into Thessaly with his army, he presently took Larissa, and endeavoured to reclaim Alexander, who submitted, and bring him, from being a tyrant, to govern gently, and according to law; but finding him untractable and brutish, and hearing great complaints of his lust and cruelty, Pelopidas began to be severe, and used him roughly, insomuch that the tyrant stole away privately with his guard.

But Pelopidas, leaving the Thessalians fearless of the tyrant, and friends amongst themselves, marched into Macedonia, where Ptolemy was then at war with Alexander, the King of Macedon; both parties having sent for him to hear and determine their differences, and assist the one that appeared injured. When he came, he reconciled them, calling back the exiles; and receiving for hostages Philip, the king's brother, and thirty children of the nobles, he brought them to Thebes; showing the other Greeks how wide a reputation the Thebans had gained for honesty and courage.

This was that Philip who afterwards endeavoured to enslave the Greeks: then he was a boy, and lived with Pammenes in Thebes; and hence some conjecture that he took Epaminondas's actions for the rule of his own; and perhaps, indeed, he did take example from his activity and skill in war, which, however, was but a small portion of his virtues; of his temperance, justice, generosity, and mildness, in which he was truly great, Philip enjoyed no share either by nature or imitation.

After this, upon a second complaint of the Thessalians against Alexander of Pheræ, as a disturber of the cities, Pelopidas was joined with Ismenias, in an embassy to him; but led no forces from Thebes, not expecting any war, and therefore was necessitated to make use of the Thessalians upon the emergency. At the same time, also, Macedon was in confusion again, as Ptolemy had murdered the king, and seized the government; but the king's friends sent for Pelopidas, and he being willing to interpose in the matter, but having no soldiers of his own, enlisted some mercenaries in the country, and with them marched against Ptolemy.

When they faced one another Ptolemy corrupted these mercenaries with a sum of money, and persuaded them to revolt to him; but yet fearing the very name and reputation of Pelopidas, he came to him as his superior, submitted, begged his pardon, and protested that he kept the government only for the brothers of the dead king, and would prove a friend to the friends, and an enemy to the enemies of Thebes; and, to confirm this, he gave his son, Philoxenus, and fifty of his companions, for hostages. These Pelopidas sent to Thebes; but he himself, being vexed at the treachery of the mercenaries, and understanding that most of their goods, their wives, and children lay at Pharsalus, so that if he could take them the injury would be sufficiently revenged, got together some of the Thessalians, and marched to Pharsalus.

When he just entered the city, Alexander, the tyrant, appeared before it with an army; but Pelopidas and his friends, thinking that he came to clear himself from those crimes that were laid to his charge, went to him; and though they knew very well that he was profligate and cruel, yet they imagined that the authority of Thebes, and their own dignity and reputation, would secure them from violence. But the tyrant, seeing them come unarmed and alone, seized them, and made himself master of Pharsalus. Upon this his subjects were much intimidated, thinking that after so great and so bold an iniquity he would spare none, but behave himself toward all, and in all matters, as one despairing of his life.

The Thebans, when they heard of this, were very much enraged, and despatched an army, Epaminondas being then in disgrace, under the command of other leaders. When the tyrant brought Pelopidas to Pheræ, at first he permitted those that desired it to speak with him, imagining that this disaster would break his spirit, and make him appear contemptible. But when Pelopidas advised the complaining Pheræans to be comforted, as if the tyrant was now certain in a short time to smart for his injuries, and sent to tell him, "that it was absurd daily to torment and murder his wretched innocent subjects, and yet spare him, who, he well knew, if ever he got his liberty, would be bitterly revenged"; the tyrant, wondering at his boldness and freedom of speech, replied, "And why is Pelopidas in haste to die?" He, hearing of it, rejoined, "That you may be the sooner ruined, being then more hated by the gods than now."

From that time he forbade any to converse with him; but Thebe, the daughter of Jason and wife to Alexander, hearing from the keepers of the bravery and noble behaviour of Pelopidas, had a great desire to see and speak with him. Now when she came into the prison, and, as a woman, could not at once discern his greatness in his calamity, only judging by the meanness of his attire and general appearance, that he was used basely and not befitting a man of his reputation, she wept.

Pelopidas, at first not knowing who she was, stood amazed; but when he understood, saluted her by her father's name—Jason and he having been friends and familiars—and she saying, "I pity your wife, sir," he replied, "And I you, that though not in chains, can endure Alexander." This touched the woman, who already hated Alexander for his cruelty and injustice, for his general debaucheries, and for his abuse of her youngest brother. She, therefore, often went to Pelopidas, and, speaking freely of the indignities she suffered, grew more enraged and more exasperated against Alexander.

The Theban generals that were sent into Thessaly did nothing, but, being either unskilful or unfortunate, made a dishonourable retreat, for which the city fined each of them ten thousand drachmas, and sent Epaminondas with their forces. The Thessalians, inspirited by the fame of this general, at once began to stir, and the tyrant's affairs were at the verge of destruction; so great was the fear that possessed his captains and his friends, and so eager the desire of his subjects to revolt, in hope of his speedy punishment.

But Epaminondas, more solicitous for the safety of Pelopidas than his own glory, and fearing that if things came to extremity Alexander would grow desperate, and, like a wild beast, turn and worry him, did not prosecute the war to the utmost; but, hovering still over him with his army, he so handled the tyrant as not to leave him any confidence, and yet not to drive him to despair and fury. He was aware of his savageness, and the little value he had for right and justice, insomuch that sometimes he buried men alive, and sometimes dressed them in bears' and boars' skins, and then baited them with dogs, or shot at them for his divertisement.

At Melibœa and Scotussa, two cities, his allies, he called all the inhabitants to an assembly, and then surrounded them and cut them to pieces with his guards. He consecrated the spear with which he killed his uncle Polyphron, and, crowning it with garlands, sacrificed to it as a god, and called it Tychon. And once seeing a tragedian act Euripides's *Troades,* he left the theatre; but sending for the actor, bade him not to be con-

cerned at his departure, but act as he had been used to do, as it was not in contempt of him that he departed, but because he was ashamed that his citizens should see him, who never pitied any man that he murdered, weep at the sufferings of Hecuba and Andromache. This tyrant, however, alarmed at the very name, report, and appearance of an expedition under the conduct of Epaminondas, presently—

Dropped like a craven cock his conquered wing, and sent an embassy to entreat and offer satisfaction. Epaminondas refused to admit such a man as an ally to the Thebans, but granted him a truce of thirty days, and, Pelopidas and Ismenias being delivered up, returned home.

Now the Thebans, understanding that the Spartans and Athenians had sent an embassy to the Persians for assistance, themselves, likewise, sent Pelopidas; an excellent design to increase his glory, no man having ever before passed through the dominions of the king with greater fame and reputation.

For the glory that he won against the Spartans did not creep slowly or obscurely; but, after the fame of the first battle at Leuctra was gone abroad, the report of new victories continually following, exceedingly increased, and spread his celebrity far and near. Whatever satraps or generals or commanders he met, he was the object of their wonder and discourse. "This is the man," they said, "who hath beaten the Lacedæmonians from sea and land, and confined that Sparta within Taygetus and Eurotas, which, but a little before, under the conduct of Agesilaus, was entering upon a war with the great king about Susa and Ecbatana."

This pleased Artaxerxes, and he was the more inclined to show Pelopidas attention and honour, being desirous to seem reverenced, and attended by the greatest. But when he saw him and heard his discourse, more solid than the Athenians, and not so haughty as the Spartans, his regard was heightened, and, truly acting like a king, he openly showed the respect that he felt for him; and this the other ambassadors perceived.

Of all other Greeks he had been thought to have done Antalcidas, the Spartan, the greatest honour, by sending him that garland dipped in an unguent, which he himself had worn at an entertainment. Indeed, he did not deal so delicately with Pelopidas, but, according to the custom, gave him the most splendid and considerable presents, and granted him his desires—that the Grecians should be free, Messenia inhabited, and the Thebans accounted the king's hereditary friends.

With these answers, but not accepting one of the presents, except what was a pledge of kindness and good-will, he returned. This behaviour of Pelopidas ruined the other ambassadors; the Athenians condemned and executed their Timagoras, and, indeed, if they did it for receiving so many presents from the king, their sentence was just and good; as he not only took gold and silver, but a rich bed, and slaves to make it, as if the Greeks were unskilful in that art; besides eighty cows and herdsmen, professing he needed cows' milk for some distemper; and, lastly, he was carried in a litter to the seaside, with a present of four talents for his attendants.

But the Athenians, perhaps, were not so much irritated at his greediness for the presents. For Epicrates, the baggage-carrier, not only confessed to the people that he had received gifts from the king, but made a motion, that instead of nine archons, they should yearly choose nine poor citizens to be sent ambassadors to the king, and enriched by his presents, and the people only laughed at the joke. But they were vexed that the Thebans obtained their desires, never considering that Pelopidas's fame was more powerful than all their rhetorical discourse, with a man who still inclined to the victorious in arms. This embassy, having obtained the restitution of Messenia, and the freedom of the other Greeks, got Pelopidas a great deal of good-will at his return.

At this time, Alexander, the Pheræan, falling back to his old nature, and having seized many of the Thessalian cities, and put garrisons upon the Achæans of Phthiotis, and the Magnesians, the cities, hearing that Pelopidas was returned, sent an embassy to Thebes requesting succours, and him for their leader. The Thebans willingly granted their desire; and now when all things were prepared, and the general beginning to march, the sun was eclipsed, and darkness spread over the city at noonday.

Now when Pelopidas saw them startled at the prodigy, he did not think it fit to force on men who were afraid and out of heart, nor to hazard seven thousand of his citizens; and therefore with only three hundred horse volunteers, set forward himself to Thessaly, much against the will of the augurs and his fellow-citizens in general, who all imagined

this marked portent to have reference to this great man. But he was heated against Alexander for the injuries he had received, and hoped likewise, from the discourse which formerly he had with Thebe, that his family by this time was divided and in disorder. But the glory of the expedition chiefly excited him; for he was extremely desirous at this time, when the Lacedæmonians were sending out military officers to assist Dionysius, the Sicilian tyrant, and the Athenians took Alexander's pay, and honoured him with a brazen statue as a benefactor, that the Thebans should be seen, alone, of all the Greeks, undertaking the cause of those who were oppressed by tyrants, and destroying the violent and illegal forms of government in Greece.

When Pelopidas was come to Pharsalus, he formed an army, and presently marched against Alexander; and Alexander, understanding that Pelopidas had few Thebans with him, and that his own infantry was double the number of the Thessalians, faced him at Thetidium. Some one told Pelopidas, "The tyrant meets us with a great army." "So much the better," he replied, "for then we shall overcome the more."

Between the two armies lay some steep high hills about Cynoscephalæ, which both parties endeavoured to take by their foot. Pelopidas commanded his horse, which were good and many, to charge that of the enemies; they routed and pursued them through the plain. But Alexander meantime took the hills, and charging the Thessalian foot that came up later and strove to climb the steep and craggy ascent, killed the foremost, and the others, much distressed, could do the enemies no harm.

Pelopidas, observing this, sounded a retreat to his horse, and gave orders that they should charge the enemies that kept their ground; and he himself, taking his shield, quickly joined those that fought about the hills, and advancing to the front, filled his men with such courage and alacrity, that the enemies imagined they came with other spirits and other bodies to the onset. They stood two or three charges, but finding these come on stoutly, and the horse, also, returning from the pursuit, gave ground, and retreated in order.

Pelopidas, now perceiving from the rising ground that the enemy's army was, though not yet routed, full of disorder and confusion, stood and looked about for Alexander; and when he saw him in the right wing, encouraging and ordering his mercenaries, he could not moderate his anger, but inflamed at the sight, and blindly following his passion, regardless alike of his own life and his command, advanced far before his soldiers, crying out and challenging the tyrant who did not dare to receive him, but retreating, hid himself amongst his guard. The foremost of the mercenaries that came hand to hand were driven back by Pelopidas, and some killed; but many at a distance shot through his armour and wounded him, till the Thessalians, in anxiety for the result, ran down from the hill to his relief, but found him already slain. The horse came up also, and routed the phalanx, and following the pursuit a great way filled the whole country with the slain, which were above three thousand.

No one can wonder that the Thebans then present should show great grief at the death of Pelopidas, calling him their father, deliverer, and instructor in all that was good and commendable. But the Thessalians and the allies, outdoing in their public edicts all the just honours that could be paid to human courage, gave, in their display of feeling, yet stronger demonstrations of the kindness they had for him. It is stated that none of the soldiers, when they heard of his death, would put off their armour, unbridle their horses, or dress their wounds, but still hot and with their arms on, ran to the corpse, and, as if he had been yet alive and could see what they did, heaped up spoils about his body. They cut off their horses' manes and their own hair, many kindled no fire in their tents, took no supper, and silence and sadness was spread over all the army; as if they had not gained the greatest and most glorious victory, but were overcome by the tyrant and enslaved.

As soon as it was known in the cities, the magistrates, youths, children, and priests came out to meet the body, and brought trophies, crowns, and suits of golden armour; and, when he was to be interred, the elders of the Thessalians came and begged the Thebans that they might give the funeral; and one of them said, "Friends, we ask a favour of you, that will prove both an honour and comfort to us in this our great misfortune. The Thessalians shall never again wait on the living Pelopidas, shall never give honours of which he can be sensible, but if we may have his body, adorn his funeral, and inter him, we shall hope to show that we esteem his death a greater loss to the Thessalians than to the

Thebans. You have lost only a good general, we both a general and our liberty. For how shall we dare to desire from you another captain, since we cannot restore Pelopidas?"

The Thebans granted their request, and there was never a more splendid funeral in the opinion of those who do not think the glory of such solemnities consists only in gold, ivory, and purple; as Philistus did, who extravagantly celebrates the funeral of Dionysius, in which his tyranny concluded like the pompous exit of some great tragedy. Alexander the Great, at the death of Hephæstion, not only cut off the manes of his horses and his mules, but took down the battlements from the city walls, that even the towns might seem mourners, and instead of their former beauteous appearance, look bald at his funeral.

But such honours, being commanded and forced from the mourners, attended with feelings of jealousy towards those who received them, and of hatred towards those who exacted them, were no testimonies of love and respect, but of the barbaric pride, luxury, and insolence of those who lavished their wealth in these vain and undesirable displays. But that a man of common rank, dying in a strange country, neither his wife, children, nor kinsmen present, none either asking or compelling it, should be attended, buried, and crowned by so many cities that strove to exceed one another in the demonstrations of their love, seems to be the sum and completion of happy fortune. For the death of happy men is not, as Æsop observes, most grievous, but most blessed, since it secures their felicity, and puts it out of fortune's power. And that Spartan advised well, who, embracing Diagoras, that had himself been crowned in the Olympic Games, and saw his sons and grandchildren victors, said, "Die, Diagoras, for thou canst not be a god."

And yet who would compare all the victories in the Pythian and Olympian Games put together with one of those enterprises of Pelopidas, of which he successfully performed so many? Having spent his life in brave and glorious actions, he died at last in the chief command, for the thirteenth time, of the Bœotians, fighting bravely and in the act of slaying a tyrant, in defence of the liberty of the Thessalians.

His death, as it brought grief, so likewise it produced advantage to the allies; for the Thebans, as soon as they heard of his fall, delayed not their revenge, but presently sent seven thousand foot and seven hundred horse, under the command of Malcitas and Diogiton. And they, finding Alexander weak and without forces, compelled him to restore the cities he had taken, to withdraw his garrisons from the Magnesians and Achæans of Phthiotis, and swear to assist the Thebans against whatsoever enemies they should require.

This contented the Thebans, but punishment overtook the tyrant for his wickedness, and the death of Pelopidas was revenged by Heaven in the following manner. Pelopidas, as I have already mentioned, had taught his wife, Thebe, not to fear the outward splendour and show of the tyrant's defences, since she was admitted within them. She, of herself, too, dreaded his inconstancy, and hated his cruelty; and therefore, conspiring with her three brothers, Tisiphonus, Pytholaus, and Lycophron, made the following attempt upon him.

All the other apartments were full of the tyrant's night guards, but their bed-chamber was an upper room, and before the door lay a chained dog to guard it, which would fly at all but the tyrant and his wife and one servant that fed him. When Thebe, therefore, designed to kill her husband, she hid her brothers all day in a room hard by, and she, going in alone, according to her usual custom, to Alexander, who was asleep already, in a little time came out again, and commanded the servant to lead away the dog, for Alexander wished to rest quietly. She covered the stairs with wool, that the young men might make no noise as they came up; and then, bringing up her brothers with their weapons, and leaving them at the chamber door, she went in, and brought away the tyrant's sword that hung over his head, and showed it them for confirmation that he was fast asleep. The young men appearing fearful, and unwilling to do the murder, she chid them, and angrily vowed she would wake Alexander and discover the conspiracy; and so, with a lamp in her hand, she conducted them in, they being both ashamed and afraid, and brought them to the bed; when one of them caught him by the feet, the other pulled him backwards by the hair, and the third ran him through. The death was more speedy, perhaps, than was fit; but, in that he was the first tyrant that was killed by the contrivance of his wife, and as his corpse was abused, thrown out, and trodden under foot by the Pheræans, he seems to have suffered what his villainies deserved.

MARCELLUS

268?–208 B.C.

THEY say that Marcus Claudius, who was five times consul of the Romans, was the son of Marcus; and that he was the first of his family called Marcellus, that is, *martial,* as Posidonius affirms. He was, indeed, by long experience, skilful in the art of war, of a strong body, valiant of hand, and by natural inclinations addicted to war. This high temper and heat he showed conspicuously in battle; in other respects he was modest and obliging, and so far studious of Greek learning and discipline, as to honour and admire those that excelled in it, though he did not himself attain a proficiency in them equal to his desire, by reason of his employments. For if ever there were any men whom, as Homer says, Heaven

From their first youth unto their utmost age
Appointed the laborious wars to wage,

certainly they were the chief Romans of that time; who in their youth had war with the Carthaginians in Sicily; in their middle age with the Gauls in the defence of Italy itself; and at last, when now grown old, struggled again with Hannibal and the Carthaginians, and wanted in their latest years what is granted to most men, exemption from military toils, their rank and their great qualities still making them be called upon to undertake the command.

Marcellus, ignorant or unskilful of no kind of fighting, in single combat surpassed himself; he never declined a challenge, and never accepted without killing his challenger. In Sicily, he protected and saved his brother Otacilius when surrounded in battle, and slew the enemies that pressed upon him; for which act he was by the generals, while he was yet but young, presented with crowns and other honourable rewards; and, his good qualities more and more displaying themselves, he was created Curule Ædile by the people and by the high priests Augur; which is that priesthood to which chiefly the law assigns the observation of auguries.

In his ædileship, a certain mischance brought him to the necessity of bringing an impeachment into the senate. He had a son named Marcus, of great beauty, in the flower of his age, and no less admired for the goodness of his character. This youth, Capitolinus, a bold and ill-mannered man, Marcellus's colleague, sought to abuse. The boy at first himself repelled him; but when the other again persecuted him, told his father. Marcellus, highly indignant, accused the man in the senate, where he, having appealed to the tribunes of the people, endeavoured by various shifts and exceptions to elude the impeachment; and, when the tribunes refused their protection, by flat denial rejected the charge. As there was no witness of the fact, the senate thought fit to call the youth himself before them; on witnessing whose blushes and tears, and shame mixed with the highest indignation, seeking no further evidence of the crime, they condemned Capitolinus, and set a fine upon him; of the money of which Marcellus caused silver vessels for libation to be made, which he dedicated to the gods.

After the end of the first Punic war, which lasted one-and-twenty years, the seed of Gallic tumults sprang up, and began again to trouble Rome. The Insubrians, a people inhabiting the subalpine region of Italy, strong in their own forces, raised from among the other Gauls aids of mercenary soldiers, called Gæsatæ. And it was a sort of miracle, and special good fortune for Rome, that the Gallic war was not coincident with the Punic, but that the Gauls had with fidelity stood quiet as spectators while the Punic war continued, as though they had been under engagement to await and attack the victors, and now only were at liberty to come forward. Still the position itself, and the ancient renown of the Gauls, struck no little fear into the minds of the Romans, who were about to undertake a war so near home and upon their own borders; and regarded the Gauls, because they had once taken their city, with more apprehension than any people, as is apparent from the enactment which from that time forth provided that the high priests should enjoy an exemption from all military duty, except only in Gallic insurrections.

The great preparations, also, made by the Romans for war (for it is not reported that the people of Rome ever had at one time so many legions in arms, either before or since), and their extraordinary sacrifices, were plain arguments of their fear. For though they were most averse to barbarous and cruel rites, and entertained more than any nation the same pious and reverent sentiments of the gods with the Greeks; yet, when this war was coming upon them, they then, from some prophecies in the Sibyls' books, put alive underground a pair of Greeks, one male, the other female; and likewise two Gauls, one of each sex, in the market called the beast market. They continue even to this day to offer to these Greeks and Gauls certain ceremonial observances in the month of November.

In the beginning of this war, in which the Romans sometimes obtained remarkable victories, sometimes were shamefully beaten, nothing was done toward the determination of the contest until Flaminius and Furius, being consuls, led large forces against the Insubrians.

At the time of their departure, the river that runs through the country of Picenum was seen flowing with blood; there was a report that three moons had been seen at once at Ariminum; and, in the consular assembly, the augurs declared that the consuls had been unduly and inauspiciously created. The senate, therefore, immediately sent letters to the camp, recalling the consuls to Rome with all possible speed, and commanding them to forbear from acting against the enemies, and to abdicate the consulship on the first opportunity. These letters being brought to Flaminius, he deferred to open them till, having defeated and put to flight the enemy's forces, he wasted and ravaged their borders.

The people, therefore, did not go forth to meet him when he returned with huge spoils; nay, because he had not instantly obeyed the command in the letters, by which he was recalled, but slighted and contemned them, they were very near denying him the honour of a triumph. Nor was the triumph sooner passed than they deposed him, with his colleague, from the magistracy, and reduced them to the state of private citizens.

So much were all things at Rome made to depend upon religion; they would not allow any contempt of the omens and the ancient rites, even though attended with the highest success, thinking it to be of more importance to the public safety that the magistrates should reverence the gods, than that they should overcome their enemies.

Thus Tiberius Sempronius, whom for his probity and virtue the citizens highly esteemed, created Scipio Nasica and Caius Marcius consuls to succeed him; and when they were gone into their provinces, lit upon books concerning the religious observances, where he found something he had not known before; which was this: when the consul took his auspices, he sat without the city in a house, or tent, hired for that occasion; but, if it happened that he, for any urgent cause, returned into the city, without having yet seen any certain signs, he was obliged to leave that first building, or tent, and to seek another to repeat the survey from.

Tiberius, it appears, in ignorance of this, had twice used the same building before announcing the new consuls. Now, understanding his error, he referred the matter to the senate; nor did the senate neglect this minute fault, but soon wrote expressly of it to Scipio Nasica and Caius Marcius; who, leaving their provinces and without delay returning to Rome, laid down their magistracy. This happened at a later period.

About the same time, too, the priesthood was taken away from two men of very great honour, Cornelius Cethegus and Quintus Sulpicius: from the former, because he had not rightly held out the entrails of a beast slain for sacrifice; from the latter, because, while he was immolating, the tufted cap which the Flamens wear had fallen from his head. Minucius, the dictator, who had already named Caius Flaminius master of the horse, they deposed from his command, because the squeak of a mouse was heard, and put others into their places. And yet, notwithstanding, by observing so anxiously these little niceties they did not run into any superstition, because they never varied from nor exceeded the observances of their ancestors.

So soon as Flaminius with his colleague had resigned the consulate, Marcellus was declared consul by the presiding officers called Interrexes; and, entering into the magistracy, chose Cnæus Cornelius his colleague. There was a report that, the Gauls proposing a pacification, and the senate also inclining to peace, Marcellus inflamed the people to war; but a peace appears to have been agreed upon, which the Gæsatæ broke; who, passing the Alps, stirred up the Insubrians (they being thirty thousand in number, and the Insubrians more numerous by far); and, proud of their strength, marched directly to Acerræ, a city seated on the north of the river Po. From thence Britomartus, king of the Gæsatæ, taking with him ten thousand soldiers, harassed the country round about.

News of which being brought to Marcellus, leaving his colleague at Acerræ with the foot and all the heavy arms and a third part of the horse, and carrying with him the rest of the horse and six hundred light-armed foot, marching night and day without remission, he stayed not till he came up to these ten thousand near a Gaulish village called Clastidium, which not long before had been reduced under the Roman jurisdiction. Nor had he time to refresh his soldiers or to give them rest. For the barbarians, that were then present, immediately observed his approach, and contemned him, because he had very few foot with him. The Gauls were singularly skilful in horsemanship, and thought to excel in it; and as at present they also exceeded Marcellus in number, they made no account of him. They, therefore, with their king at their head, instantly charged upon him, as if they would trample him under their horses' feet, threatening all kinds of cruelties.

Marcellus, because his men were few, that they might not be encompassed and charged on all sides by the enemy, extended his wings of horse, and, riding about, drew out his wings of foot in length, till he came near to the enemy. Just as he was in the act of turning round to face the enemy, it so happened that his horse, startled with their fierce look and their cries, gave back, and carried him forcibly aside. Fearing lest this accident, if converted into an omen, might discourage his soldiers, he quickly brought his horse round to confront the enemy, and made a gesture of adoration to the sun, as if he had wheeled about not by chance, but for a purpose of devotion. For it was customary to the Romans, when they offered worship to the gods, to turn round; and in this moment of meeting the enemy, he is said to have vowed the best of the arms to Jupiter Feretrius.

The king of the Gauls beholding Marcellus, and from the badges of his authority conjecturing him to be the general, advanced some way before his embattled army, and with a loud voice challenged him, and, brandishing his lance; fiercely ran in full career at him; exceeding the rest of the Gauls in stature, and with his armour, that was adorned with gold and silver and various colours, shining like lightning. These arms seeming to Marcellus, while he viewed the enemy's army drawn up in battalia, to be the best and fairest, and thinking them to be those he had vowed to Jupiter, he instantly ran upon the king, and pierced through his breastplate with his lance; then pressing upon him with the weight of his horse, threw him to the ground, and with two or three strokes more slew him.

Immediately he leapt from his horse, laid his hand upon the dead king's arms, and, looking up towards Heaven, thus spoke: "O Jupiter Feretrius, arbiter of the exploits of captains, and of the acts of commanders in war and battles, be thou witness that I, a general, have slain a general; I, a consul, have slain a king with my own hand, third of all the Romans; and that to thee I consecrate these first and most excellent of the spoils. Grant to us to despatch the relics of the war with the same course of fortune."

Then the Roman horse joining battle not only with the enemy's horse, but also with the foot who attacked them, obtained a singular and unheard-of victory. For never before or since have so few horse defeated such numerous forces of horse and foot together. The enemies being to a great number slain, and the spoils collected, he returned to his colleague, who was conducting the war with ill-success against the enemies near the greatest and most populous of the Gallic cities, Milan. This was their capital, and, therefore, fighting valiantly in defence of it, they were not so much besieged by Cornelius, as they besieged him. But Marcellus having returned, and the Gæsatæ retiring as soon as they were certified of the death of the king and the defeat of his army, Milan was taken. The rest of their towns, and all they had, the Gauls delivered up of their own accord to the Romans, and had peace upon equitable conditions granted to them.

Marcellus alone, by a decree of the senate, triumphed. The triumph was in magnificence, opulence, spoils, and the gigantic bodies of the captives most remarkable. But the most grateful and most rare spectacle of all was the general himself, carrying the arms of the barbarian king to the god to whom he had vowed them.

He had taken a tall and straight stock of an oak, and had lopped and formed it to a trophy. Upon this he fastened and hung about the arms of the king, arranging all the pieces in their suitable places. The procession advancing solemnly, he, carrying this trophy, ascended the chariot; and thus, himself the fairest and most glorious triumphant image, was conveyed into the city. The army adorned with shining armour followed in order, and with verses composed for the occasion, and with songs of victory celebrated the praises of Jupiter and of their general. Then entering the temple of Jupiter Feretrius, he dedicated his gift; the third, and to our memory the last, that ever did so. The first was Romulus, after having slain Acron, king of the Cæninenses; the second, Cornelius Cossus, who slew Tolumnius, the Etruscan; after them Marcellus, having killed Britomartus, king of the Gauls; after Marcellus, no man.

The god to whom these spoils were consecrated is called Jupiter Feretrius, from the trophy carried on the *feretrum,* one of the Greek words which at that time still existed in great numbers in Latin; or, as others say, it is the surname of the Thundering Jupiter derived from *ferire,* to strike. Others there are who would have the name to be deduced from the *strokes* that are given in fight; since even now in battles, when they press upon their enemies, they constantly call out to each other, "Strike," in Latin *feri.*

Spoils in general they call *spolia,* and these in particular *opima;* though, indeed, they say that Numa Pompilius, in his commentaries, makes mention of first, second, and third Spolia Opima; and that he prescribes that the first taken be consecrated to Jupiter Feretrius, the second to Mars, the third to Quirinus; as also that the reward of the first be three hundred asses; of the second, two hundred; of the third, one hundred. The general account, however, prevails, that those spoils only are *opima* which the general first takes in set battle, and takes from the enemy's chief captain whom he has slain with his own hand. But of this enough.

The victory and the ending of the war was so welcome to the people of Rome, that they sent to Apollo of Delphi, in testimony of their gratitude, a present of a golden cup of an hundred pound weight, and gave a great part of the spoil to their associate cities, and took care that many presents should be sent also to Hiero, King of the Syracusans, their friend and ally.

When Hannibal invaded Italy, Marcellus was despatched with a fleet to Sicily. And when the army had been defeated at Cannæ, and many thousands of them perished, and few had saved themselves by flying to Canusium, and all feared lest Hannibal, who had destroyed the strength of the Roman army, should advance at once with his victorious troops to Rome, Marcellus first sent for the protection of the city fifteen hundred soldiers from the fleet. Then, by decree of the senate, going to Canusium, having heard that many of the soldiers had come together in that place, he led them out of the fortifications to prevent the enemy from ravaging the country. The chief Roman commanders had most of them fallen in battles; and the citizens complained that the extreme caution of Fabius Maximus, whose integrity and wisdom gave him the highest authority, verged upon timidity and inaction. They confided in him to keep them out of danger, but could not expect that he would enable them to retaliate. Fixing, therefore, their thoughts upon Marcellus, and hoping to combine his boldness, confidence, and promptitude with Fabius's caution and prudence, and to temper the one by the other, they sent, sometimes both with consular command, sometimes one as consul, the other as proconsul, against the enemy. Posidonius writes that Fabius was called the buckler, Marcellus the sword of Rome. Certainly, Hannibal himself confessed that he feared Fabius as a schoolmaster, Marcellus as an adversary: the former, lest he should be hindered from doing mischief; the latter, lest he should receive harm himself.

And first, when among Hannibal's soldiers, proud of their victory, carelessness and boldness had grown to a great height, Marcellus, attacking all their stragglers and plundering parties, cut them off, and by little and little diminished their forces. Then carrying aid to the Neapolitans and Nolans, he confirmed the minds of the former, who, indeed, were of their own accord faithful enough to the Romans; but in Nola he found a state of discord, the senate not being able to rule and keep in the common people, who were generally favourers of Hannibal.

There was in the town one Bantius, a man renowned for his high birth and courage. This man, after he had fought most fiercely at Cannæ, and had killed many of the enemies, at last was found lying in a heap of dead bodies, covered with darts, and was brought to Hannibal, who so honoured him, that he not only dismissed him without ransom, but also contracted friendship with him,

and made him his guest. In gratitude for this great favour, he became one of the strongest partisans of Hannibal, and urged the people to revolt.

Marcellus could not be induced to put to death a man of such eminence, and who had endured such dangers in fighting on the Roman side; but, knowing himself able, by the general kindliness of his disposition, and in particular by the attractiveness of his address, to gain over a character whose passion was for honour, one day when Bantius saluted him, he asked him who he was; not that he knew him not before, but seeking an occasion of further conference. When Bantius had told who he was, Marcellus, seeming surprised with joy and wonder, replied: "Are you that Bantius whom the Romans commend above the rest that fought at Cannæ, and praise as the one man that not only did not forsake the consul Paulus Æmilius, but received in his own body many darts thrown at him?" Bantius owning himself to be that very man, and showing his scars: "Why, then," said Marcellus, "did not you, having such proofs to show of your affection to us, come to me at my first arrival here? Do you think that we are unwilling to requite with favour those who have well deserved, and who are honoured even by our enemies?" He followed up his courtesies by a present of a war-horse and five hundred drachmas in money. From that time Bantius became the most faithful assistant and ally of Marcellus, and a most keen discoverer of those that attempted innovation and sedition.

These were many, and had entered into a conspiracy to plunder the baggage of the Romans, when they should make an irruption against the enemy. Marcellus, therefore, having marshalled his army within the city, placed the baggage near to the gates, and, by an edict, forbade the Nolans to go to the walls. Thus, outside the city, no arms could be seen; by which prudent device he allured Hannibal to move with his army in some disorder to the city, thinking that things were in a tumult there.

Then Marcellus, the nearest gate being, as he had commanded, thrown open, issuing forth with the flower of his horse in front, charged the enemy. By and by the foot, sallying out of another gate, with a loud shout joined in the battle. And while Hannibal opposes part of his forces to these, the third gate also is opened, out of which the rest break forth, and on all quarters fall upon the enemies, who were dismayed at this unexpected encounter, and did but feebly resist those with whom they had been first engaged, because of their attack by these others who sallied out later. Here Hannibal's soldiers, with much bloodshed and many wounds, were beaten back to their camp, and for the first time turned their backs to the Romans. There fell in this action, as it is related, more than five thousand of them; of the Romans, not above five hundred. Livy does not affirm that either the victory or the slaughter of the enemy was so great; but certain it is that the adventure brought great glory to Marcellus, and to the Romans, after their calamities, a great revival of confidence, as they began now to entertain a hope that the enemy with whom they contended was not invincible, but liable like themselves to defeats.

Therefore, the other consul being deceased, the people recalled Marcellus, that they might put him into his place; and, in spite of the magistrates, succeeded in postponing the election till his arrival, when he was by all the suffrages created consul. But because it happened to thunder, the augurs accounting that he was not legitimately created, and yet not daring, for fear of the people, to declare their sentence openly, Marcellus voluntarily resigned the consulate, retaining however his command.

Being created proconsul, and returning to the camp at Nola, he proceeded to harass those that followed the party of the Carthaginians; on whose coming with speed to succour them, Marcellus declined a challenge to a set battle, but when Hannibal had sent out a party to plunder, and now expected no fight, he broke out upon him with his army. He had distributed to the foot long lances, such as are commonly used in naval fights; and instructed them to throw them with great force at convenient distances against the enemies, who were inexperienced in that way of darting, and used to fight with short darts hand to hand. This seems to have been the cause of the total rout and open flight of all the Carthaginians who were then engaged; there fell of them five thousand; four elephants were killed, and two taken; but what was of the greatest moment, on the third day after, more than three hundred horse, Spaniards and Numidians mixed, deserted to him, a disaster that had never to that day happened to Hannibal, who had long kept together in harmony an army of barbarians, collected out of many various and discordant nations. Marcellus and his successors in all this war made good use of the faithful service of these horsemen.

He now was a third time created consul, and sailed over into Sicily. For the success of Hannibal had excited the Carthaginians to lay claim to that whole island; chiefly because, after the murder of the tyrant, Hieronymus, all things had been in tumult and confusion at Syracuse. For which reason the Romans also had sent before to that city a force under the conduct of Appius, as prætor.

While Marcellus was receiving that army, a number of Roman soldiers cast themselves at his feet, upon occasion of the following calamity. Of those that survived the battle at Cannæ, some had escaped by flight, and some were taken alive by the enemy; so great a multitude, that it was thought there were not remaining Romans enough to defend the walls of the city. And yet the magnanimity and constancy of the city was such that it would not redeem the captives from Hannibal, though it might have done so for a small ransom; a decree of the senate forbade it, and chose rather to leave them to be killed by the enemy, or sold out of Italy; and commanded that all who had saved themselves by flight should be transported into Sicily, and not permitted to return into Italy, until the war with Hannibal should be ended.

These, therefore, when Marcellus was arrived in Sicily, addressed themselves to him in great numbers; and casting themselves at his feet, with much lamentation and tears humbly besought him to admit them to honourable service; and promised to make it appear by their future fidelity and exertions that that defeat had been received rather by misfortune than by cowardice.

Marcellus, pitying them, petitioned the senate by letters that he might have leave at all times to recruit his legions out of them. After much debate about the thing, the senate decreed they were of opinion that the commonwealth did not require the service of cowardly soldiers; if Marcellus perhaps thought otherwise, he might make use of them, provided no one of them be honoured on any occasion with a crown or military gift, as a reward of his virtue or courage. This decree stung Marcellus; and on his return to Rome, after the Sicilian war was ended, he upbraided the senate that they had denied to him, who had so highly deserved of the republic, liberty to relieve so great a number of citizens in great calamity.

At this time Marcellus, first incensed by injuries done him by Hippocrates, commander of the Syracusans (who, to give proof of his good affection to the Carthaginians, and to acquire the tyranny to himself, had killed a number of Romans at Leontini), besieged and took by force the city of Leontini; yet violated none of the townsmen; only deserters, as many as he took, he subjected to the punishment of the rods and axe. But Hippocrates, sending a report to Syracuse that Marcellus had put all the adult population to the sword, and then coming upon the Syracusans, who had risen in tumult upon that false report, made himself master of the city.

Upon this Marcellus moved with his whole army to Syracuse, and encamping near the wall, sent ambassadors into the city to relate to the Syracusans the truth of what had been done in Leontini. When these could not prevail by treaty, the whole power being now in the hands of Hippocrates, he proceeded to attack the city both by land and by sea. The land forces were conducted by Appius: Marcellus, with sixty galleys, each with five rows of oars, furnished with all sorts of arms and missiles, and a huge bridge of planks laid upon eight ships chained together, upon which was carried the engine to cast stones and darts, assaulted the walls, relying on the abundance and magnificence of his preparations, and on his own previous glory; all which, however, were, it would seem, but trifles for Archimedes and his machines.

These machines he had designed and contrived, not as matters of any importance, but as mere amusements in geometry; in compliance with King Hiero's desire and request, some little time before, that he should reduce to practice some part of his admirable speculation in science, and by accommodating the theoretic truth to sensation and ordinary use, bring it more within the appreciation of the people in general.

Eudoxus and Archytas had been the first originators of this far-famed and highly-prized art of mechanics, which they employed as an elegant illustration of geometrical truths, and as means of sustaining experimentally, to the satisfaction of the senses, conclusions too intricate for proof by words and diagrams. As, for example, to solve the problem, so often required in constructing geometrical figures, given the two extremes, to find the two mean lines of a proportion, both these mathematicians had recourse to the aid of instruments, adapting to their purpose certain curves and sections of lines.

But because of Plato's indignation at it, and his invectives against it as the mere corruption and annihilation of the one good of geometry, which was thus shamefully turning its back upon the unembodied objects of pure intelligence to recur to sensation, and to ask help (not to be obtained without base supervisions and depravation) from matter; so it was that mechanics came to be separated from geometry, and, repudiated and neglected by philosophers, took its place as a military art.

Archimedes, however, in writing to King Hiero, whose friend and near relation he was, had stated that given the force, any given weight might be moved, and even boasted, we are told, relying on the strength of demonstration, that if there were another earth, by going into it he could remove this. Hiero being struck with amazement at this, and entreating him to make good this problem by actual experiment, and show some great weight moved by a small engine, he fixed accordingly upon a ship of burden out of the king's arsenal, which could not be drawn out of the dock without great labour and many men; and, loading her with many passengers and a full freight, sitting himself the while far off, with no great endeavour, but only holding the head of the pulley in his hand and drawing the cords by degrees, he drew the ship in a straight line, as smoothly and evenly as if she had been in the sea. The king, astonished at this, and convinced of the power of the art, prevailed upon Archimedes to make him engines accommodated to all the purposes, offensive and defensive, of a siege. These the king himself never made use of, because he spent almost all his life in a profound quiet and the highest affluence. But the apparatus was, in most opportune time, ready at hand for the Syracusans, and with it also the engineer himself.

When, therefore, the Romans assaulted the walls in two places at once, fear and consternation stupefied the Syracusans, believing that nothing was able to resist that violence and those forces. But when Archimedes began to ply his engines, he at once shot against the land forces all sorts of missile weapons, and immense masses of stone that came down with incredible noise and violence; against which no man could stand, for they knocked down those upon whom they fell in heaps, breaking all their ranks and files.

In the meantime huge poles thrust out from the walls over the ships sunk some by the great weights which they let down from on high upon them; others they lifted up into the air by an iron hand or beak like a crane's beak, and, when they had drawn them up by the prow, and set them on end upon the poop, they plunged them to the bottom of the sea; or else the ships, drawn by engines within, and whirled about, were dashed against steep rocks that stood jutting out under the walls, with great destruction of the soldiers that were aboard them.

A ship was frequently lifted up to a great height in the air (a dreadful thing to behold), and was rolled to and fro, and kept swinging, until the mariners were all thrown out, when at length it was dashed against the rocks, or let fall. At the engine that Marcellus brought upon the bridge of ships, which was called *Sambuca,* from some resemblance it had to an instrument of music, while it was as yet approaching the wall, there was discharged a piece of a rock of ten talents weight, then a second and a third, which, striking upon it with immense force and a noise like thunder, broke all its foundation to pieces, shook out all its fastenings, and completely dislodged it from the bridge. So Marcellus, doubtful what counsel to pursue, drew off his ships to a safer distance, and sounded a retreat to his forces on land.

They then took a resolution of coming up under the walls, if it were possible, in the night; thinking that as Archimedes used ropes stretched at length in playing his engines, the soldiers would now be under the shot, and the darts would, for want of sufficient distance to throw them, fly over their heads without effect.

But he, it appeared, had long before framed for such occasions engines accommodated to any distance, and shorter weapons; and had made numerous small openings in the walls, through which, with engines of a shorter range, unexpected blows were inflicted on the assailants. Thus, when they who thought to deceive the defenders came close up to the walls, instantly a shower of darts and other missile weapons was again cast upon them. And when stones came tumbling down perpendicularly upon their heads, and, as it were,

the whole wall shot out arrows at them, they retired.

And now, again, as they were going off, arrows and darts of a longer range inflicted a great slaughter among them, and their ships were driven one against another; while they themselves were not able to retaliate in any way. For Archimedes had provided and fixed most of his engines immediately under the wall; whence the Romans, seeing that indefinite mischief overwhelmed them from no visible means, began to think they were fighting with the gods.

Yet Marcellus escaped unhurt, and deriding his own artificers and engineers, "What," said he, "must we give up fighting with this geometrical Briareus, who plays pitch-and-toss with our ships, and, with the multitude of darts which he showers at a single moment upon us, really outdoes the hundred-handed giants of mythology?" And, doubtless, the rest of the Syracusans were but the body of Archimedes's designs, one soul moving and governing all; for, laying aside all other arms, with this alone they infested the Romans and protected themselves. In fine, when such terror had seized upon the Romans, that, if they did but see a little rope or a piece of wood from the wall, instantly crying out, that there it was again, Archimedes was about to let fly some engine at them, they turned their backs and fled, Marcellus desisted from conflicts and assaults, putting all his hope in a long siege.

Yet Archimedes possessed so high a spirit, so profound a soul, and such treasures of scientific knowledge, that though these inventions had now obtained him the renown of more than human sagacity, he yet would not deign to leave behind him any commentary or writing on such subjects; but, repudiating as sordid and ignoble the whole trade of engineering, and every sort of art that lends itself to mere use and profit, he placed his whole affection and ambition in those purer speculations where there can be no reference to the vulgar needs of life: studies, the superiority of which to all others is unquestioned, and in which the only doubt can be whether the beauty and grandeur of the subjects examined, or the precision and cogency of the methods and means of proof, most deserve our admiration. It is not possible to find in all geometry more difficult and intricate questions, or more simple and lucid explanations. Some ascribe this to his natural genius; while others think that incredible effort and toil produced these, to all appearances, easy and unlaboured results. No amount of investigation of yours would succeed in attaining the proof, and yet, once seen, you immediately believe you would have discovered it; by so smooth and so rapid a path he leads you to the conclusion required. And thus it ceases to be incredible that (as is commonly told of him) the charm of his familiar and domestic Siren made him forget his food and neglect his person, to that degree that when he was occasionally carried by absolute violence to bathe or have his body anointed, he used to trace geometrical figures in the ashes of the fire, and diagrams in the oil on his body, being in a state of entire preoccupation, and, in the truest sense, divine possession with his love and delight in science. His discoveries were numerous and admirable; but he is said to have requested his friends and relations that, when he was dead, they would place over his tomb a sphere containing a cylinder, inscribing it with the ratio which the containing solid bears to the contained. Such was Archimedes, who now showed himself, and so far as lay in him the city also, invincible.

While the siege continued, Marcellus took Megara, one of the earliest founded of the Greek cities in Sicily, and capturing also the camp of Hippocrates at Acilæ, killed above eight thousand men, having attacked them whilst they were engaged in forming their fortifications. He overran a great part of Sicily; gained over many towns from the Carthaginians, and overcame all that dared to encounter him.

As the siege went on, one Damippus, a Lacedæmonian, putting to sea in a ship from Syracuse, was taken. When the Syracusans much desired to redeem this man, and there were many meetings and treaties about the matter betwixt them and Marcellus, he had opportunity to notice a tower into which a body of men might be secretly introduced, as the wall near to it was not difficult to surmount, and it was itself carelessly guarded. Coming often thither, and entertaining conferences about the release of Damippus, he had pretty well calculated the height of the tower, and got ladders prepared. The Syracusans celebrated a feast to Diana; this juncture of time, when they were given up entirely to wine and sport, Marcellus laid hold of, and before the citizens perceived it, not only possessed himself of the tower, but, be-

fore the break of day, filled the wall around with soldiers, and made his way into the Hexapylum.

The Syracusans now beginning to stir, and to be alarmed at the tumult, he ordered the trumpets everywhere to sound, and thus frightened them all into flight, as if all parts of the city were already won, though the most fortified, and the fairest, and most ample quarter was still ungained. It is called Acradina, and was divided by a wall from the outer city, one part of which they call Neapolis, the other Tycha. Possessing himself of these, Marcellus, about break of day, entered through the Hexapylum, all his officers congratulating him.

But looking down from the higher places upon the beautiful and spacious city below, he is said to have wept much, commiserating the calamity that hung over it, when his thoughts represented to him how dismal and foul the face of the city would be in a few hours, when plundered and sacked by the soldiers. For among the officers of his army there was not one man that durst deny the plunder of the city to the soldiers' demands; nay, many were instant that it should be set on fire and laid level to the ground; but this Marcellus would not listen to.

Yet he granted, but with great unwillingness and reluctance, that the money and slaves should be made prey; giving orders, at the same time, that none should violate any free person, nor kill, misuse, or make a slave of any of the Syracusans. Though he had used this moderation, he still esteemed the condition of that city to be pitiable, and, even amidst the congratulations and joy, showed his strong feelings of sympathy and commiseration at seeing all the riches accumulated during a long felicity now dissipated in an hour. For it is related that no less prey and plunder was taken here than afterward in Carthage. For not long after they obtained also the plunder of the other parts of the city, which were taken by treachery; leaving nothing untouched but the king's money, which was brought into the public treasury.

But nothing afflicted Marcellus so much as the death of Archimedes, who was then, as fate would have it, intent upon working out some problem by a diagram, and having fixed his mind alike and his eyes upon the subject of his speculation, he never noticed the incursion of the Romans, nor that the city was taken. In this transport of study and contemplation, a soldier, unexpectedly coming up to him, commanded him to follow to Marcellus; which he declining to do before he had worked out his problem to a demonstration, the soldier, enraged, drew his sword and ran him through. Others write that a Roman soldier, running upon him with a drawn sword, offered to kill him; and that Archimedes, looking back, earnestly besought him to hold his hand a little while, that he might not leave what he was then at work upon inconclusive and imperfect; but the soldier, nothing moved by his entreaty, instantly killed him. Others again relate that, as Archimedes was carrying to Marcellus mathematical instruments, dials, spheres, and angles, by which the magnitude of the sun might be measured to the sight, some soldiers seeing him, and thinking that he carried gold in a vessel, slew him. Certain it is that his death was very afflicting to Marcellus; and that Marcellus ever after regarded him that killed him as a murderer; and that he sought for his kindred and honoured them with signal favours.

Indeed, foreign nations had held the Romans to be excellent soldiers and formidable in battle; but they had hitherto given no memorable example of gentleness, or humanity, or civil virtue; and Marcellus seems first to have shown to the Greeks that his countrymen were most illustrious for their justice. For such was his moderation to all with whom he had anything to do, and such his benignity also to many cities and private men, that, if anything hard or severe was decreed concerning the people of Enna, Megara, or Syracuse, the blame was thought to belong rather to those upon whom the storm fell, than to those who brought it upon them.

One example of many I will commemorate. In Sicily there is a town called Engyum, not indeed great, but very ancient and ennobled by the presence of the goddesses, called the Mothers. The temple, they say, was built by the Cretans; and they show some spears and brazen helmets, inscribed with the names of Meriones, and (with the same spelling as in Latin) of Ulysses, who consecrated them to the goddesses.

This city highly favouring the party of the Carthaginians, Nicias, the most eminent of the citizens, counselled them to go over to the Romans, to that end acting freely and openly in harangues to their assemblies, arguing the imprudence and madness of the opposite course. They, fearing his power and authority, resolved to deliver him in bonds to the Carthaginians.

Nicias, detecting the design, and seeing that his person was secretly kept in watch, proceeded to speak irreligiously to the vulgar of the Mothers, and showed many signs of disrespect, as if he denied and contemned the received opinion of the presence of those goddesses; his enemies the while rejoicing that he, of his own accord, sought the destruction hanging over his head.

When they were just now about to lay hands upon him, as assembly was held, and here Nicias, making a speech to the people concerning some affair then under deliberation, in the midst of his address, cast himself upon the ground; and soon after, while amazement (as usually happens on such surprising occasions) held the assembly immovable, raising and turning his head round, he began in a trembling and deep tone, but by degrees raised and sharpened his voice. When he saw the whole theatre struck with horror and silence, throwing off his mantle and rending his tunic he leaps up half naked, and runs towards the door, crying out aloud that he was driven by the wrath of the Mothers. When no man durst, out of religious fear, lay hands upon him or stop him, but all gave way before him, he ran out of the gate, not omitting any shriek or gesture of men possessed and mad.

His wife, conscious of his counterfeiting, and privy to his design, taking her children with her, first cast herself as a suppliant before the temple of the goddesses; then, pretending to seek her wandering husband, no man hindering her, went out of the town in safety; and by this means they all escaped to Marcellus at Syracuse. After many other such affronts offered him by the men of Engyum, Marcellus, having taken them all prisoners and cast them into bonds, was preparing to inflict upon them the last punishment, when Nicias, with tears in his eyes, addressed himself to him. In fine, casting himself at Marcellus's feet, and deprecating for his citizens, he begged most earnestly their lives, chiefly those of his enemies. Marcellus, relenting, set them all at liberty, and rewarded Nicias with ample lands and rich presents. This history is recorded by Posidonius, the philosopher.

Marcellus, at length recalled by the people of Rome to the immediate war at home to illustrate his triumph, and adorn the city, carried away with him a great number of the most beautiful ornaments of Syracuse. For, before that, Rome neither had, nor had seen, any of those fine and exquisite rarities; nor was any pleasure taken in graceful and elegant pieces of workmanship. Stuffed with barbarous arms and spoils stained with blood, and everywhere crowned with triumphal memorials and trophies, she was no pleasant or delightful spectacle for the eyes of peaceful or refined spectators; but, as Epaminondas named the fields of Bœotia the stage of Mars; and Xenophon called Ephesus the workhouse of war; so, in my judgment, may you call Rome, at that time (to use the words of Pindar), "the precinct of the peaceless Mars."

Whence Marcellus was more popular with the people in general, because he had adorned the city with beautiful objects that had all the charms of Grecian grace and symmetry; but Fabius Maximus, who neither touched nor brought away anything of this kind from Tarentum, when he had taken it, was more approved of by the elder men. He carried off the money and valuables, but forbade the statues to be moved, adding, as it is commonly related, "Let us leave to the Tarentines these offended gods."

They blamed Marcellus, first for placing the city in an invidious position, as it seemed now to celebrate victories and lead processions of triumph, not only over men, but also over the gods as captives; then, that he had diverted to idleness, and vain talk about curious arts and artificers, the common people, which, bred up in wars and agriculture, had never tasted of luxury and sloth, and, as Euripides said of Hercules, had been—

Rude, unrefined, only for great things good,
so that now they misspent much of their time in examining and criticising trifles. And yet, notwithstanding this reprimand, Marcellus made it his glory to the Greeks themselves, that he had taught his ignorant countrymen to esteem and admire the elegant and wonderful productions of Greece.

But when the envious opposed his being brought triumphant into the city, because there were some relics of the war in Sicily, and a third triumph would be looked upon with jealousy, he gave way. He triumphed upon the Alban mount, and thence entered the city in *ovation,* as it is called in Latin, in Greek *eua;* but in this *ovation* he was neither carried in a chariot, nor crowned with laurel, nor ushered by trumpets sounding; but went afoot with shoes on, many flutes or pipes

sounding in concert, while he passed along, wearing a garland of myrtle, in a peaceable aspect, exciting rather love and respect than fear.

Whence I am, by conjecture, led to think that, originally, the difference observed betwixt *ovation* and triumph did not depend upon the greatness of the achievements, but the manner of performing them. For they who, having fought a set battle, and slain the enemy, returned victors, led that martial, terrible triumph, and, as the ordinary custom then was in lustrating the army, adorned the arms and the soldiers with a great deal of laurel. But they who without force, by colloquy, persuasion, and reasoning, had done the business,—to these captains custom gave the honour of the unmilitary and festive *ovation.* For the pipe is the badge of peace, and myrtle the plant of Venus, who more than the rest of the gods and goddesses abhors force and war.

It is called *ovation,* not as most think, from the Greek *euasmus,* because they act it with shouting and cries of *eua:* for so do they also the proper triumphs. The Greeks have wrested the word to their own language, thinking that this honour, also, must have some connection with Bacchus, who in Greek has the titles of Euius and Thriambus. But the thing is otherwise. For it was the custom for commanders, in their triumph, to immolate an ox, but in their *ovation,* a sheep: hence they named it *ovation,* from the Latin *ovis.*

It is worth observing, how exactly opposite the sacrifices appointed by the Spartan legislator are to those of the Romans. For at Lacedæmon, a captain, who had performed the work he had undertook by cunning, or courteous treaty, on laying down his command, immolated an ox; he that did the business by battle, offered a cock; the Lacedæmonians, though most war-like, thinking an exploit performed by reason and wisdom to be more excellent and more congruous to man, than one effected by mere force and courage. Which of the two is to be preferred I leave to the determination of others.

Marcellus being the fourth time consul, his enemies suborned the Syracusans to come to Rome to accuse him, and to complain that they had suffered indignities and wrongs, contrary to the conditions granted them. It happened that Marcellus was in the capitol offering sacrifice when the Syracusans petitioned the senate, yet sitting, that they might have

leave to accuse him and present their grievances. Marcellus's colleague, eager to protect
him in his absence, put them out of the court.

But Marcellus himself came as soon as he
heard of it. And first, in his curule chair as
consul, he referred to the senate the cogni-
zance of other matters: but when these were
transacted, rising from his seat, he passed as
a private man into the place where the accused were wont to make their defence, and
gave free liberty to the Syracusans to impeach
him. But they, struck with consternation by
his majesty and confidence, stood astonished;
and the power of his presence now, in his
robe of state, appeared far more terrible and
severe than it had done when he was arrayed
in armour.

Yet, reanimated at length by Marcellus's
rivals, they began their impeachment, and
made an oration in which pleas of justice mingled with lamentation and complaint; the sum
of which was, that being allies and friends of
the people of Rome, they had, notwithstanding, suffered things which other commanders
had abstained from inflicting upon enemies.

To this Marcellus answered that they had
committed many acts of hostility against the
people of Rome, and had suffered nothing but
what enemies conquered and captured in war
cannot possibly be protected from suffering;
that it was their own fault they had been
made captives, because they refused to give
ear to his frequent attempts to persuade them
by gentle means; neither were they forced into war by the power of tyrants, but had rather
chosen the tyrants themselves for the express
object that they might make war. The orations ended, and the Syracusans, according to
the custom, having retired, Marcellus left his
colleague to ask the sentences, and, withdrawing with the Syracusans, stayed expecting at
the doors of the senate-house; not in the least
discomposed in spirit, either with alarm at the
accusation, or by anger against the Syracusans, but with perfect calmness and serenity
attending the issue of the cause.

The sentences at length being all asked,
and a decree of the senate made in vindication of Marcellus, the Syracusans, with tears
flowing from their eyes, cast themselves at his
knees, beseeching him to forgive themselves
there present, and to be moved by the misery
of the rest of their city, which would ever be
mindful of, and grateful for, his benefits.
Thus Marcellus, softened by their tears and
distress, was not only reconciled to the depu-

ties, but ever afterwards continued to find
opportunity of doing kindness to the Syracusans. The liberty which he had restored
to them, and their rights, laws, and goods
that were left, the senate confirmed. Upon
which account the Syracusans, besides other
signal honours, made a law, that if Marcellus
should at any time come into Sicily, or any
of his posterity, the Syracusans should wear
garlands and offer public sacrifice to the gods.

After this he moved against Hannibal. And
whereas the other consuls and commanders,
since the defeat received at Cannæ, had all
made use of the same policy against Hannibal, namely, to decline coming to a battle with
him; and none had had the courage to encounter him in the field and put themselves
to the decision by the sword; Marcellus entered upon the opposite course, thinking that
Italy would be destroyed by the very delay by
which they looked to wear out Hannibal; and
that Fabius, who, adhering to his cautious
policy, waited to see the war extinguished,
while Rome itself meantime wasted away
(like timid physicians, who, dreading to administer remedies, stay waiting, and believe
that what is the decay of the patient's strength
is the decline of the disease), was not taking
a right course to heal the sickness of his country.

And first, the great cities of the Samnites,
which had revolted, came into his power; in
which he found a large quantity of corn and
money, and three thousand of Hannibal's soldiers, that were left for the defence.

After this, the proconsul Cnæus Fulvius
with eleven tribunes of the soldiers being slain
in Apulia, and the greatest part of the army
also at the same time cut off, he despatched
letters to Rome, and bade the people be of
good courage, for that he was now upon the
march against Hannibal, to turn his triumph
into sadness. On these letters being read, Livy
writes that the people were not only not encouraged, but more discouraged than before.
For danger, they thought, was but the greater
in proportion as Marcellus was of more value
than Fulvius.

He, as he had written, advancing into the
territories of the Lucanians, came up to him
at Numistro, and, the enemy keeping himself
upon the hills, pitched his camp in a level
plain, and the next day drew forth his army
in order for fight. Nor did Hannibal refuse
the challenge. They fought long and obstinately on both sides, victory yet seeming unde-

cided, when, after three hours' conflict, night hardly parted them. The next day, as soon as the sun was risen, Marcellus again brought forth his troops, and ranged them among the dead bodies of the slain, challenging Hannibal to solve the question by another trial. When he dislodged and drew off, Marcellus, gathering up the spoils of the enemies, and burying the bodies of his slain soldiers, closely followed him.

And though Hannibal often used stratagems, and laid ambushes to entrap Marcellus, yet he never could circumvent him. By skirmishes, meantime, in all of which he was superior, Marcellus gained himself such high repute, that, when the time of the Comitia at Rome was near at hand, the senate thought fit rather to recall the other consul from Sicily than to withdraw Marcellus from his conflict with Hannibal; and on his arrival they bid him name Quintus Fulvius dictator. For the dictator is created neither by the people nor by the senate, but the consul of the prætor, before the popular assembly, pronounces him to be dictator whom he himself chooses. Hence he is called dictator, *dicere* meaning to name. Others say that he is named dictator because his word is a *law,* and he orders what he pleases, without submitting it to the vote. For the Romans call the orders of magistrates *Edicts.*

And now because Marcellus's colleague, who was recalled from Sicily, had a mind to name another man dictator, and would not be forced to change his opinion, he sailed away by night back to Sicily. So the common people made an order that Quintus Fulvius should be chosen dictator, and the senate, by an express, commanded Marcellus to nominate him. He obeying proclaimed him dictator according to the order of the people; but the office of proconsul was continued to himself for a year.

And having arranged with Fabius Maximus that, while he besieged Tarentum, he himself would, by following Hannibal and drawing him up and down, detain him from coming to the relief of the Tarentines, he overtook him at Canusium; and as Hannibal often shifted his camp, and still declined the combat, he everywhere sought to engage him. At last, pressing upon him while encamping, by light skirmishes he provoked him to a battle; but night again divided them in the very heat of the conflict. The next day Marcellus again showed himself in arms, and brought up his forces in array.

Hannibal, in extreme grief, called his Carthaginians together to an harangue, and vehemently prayed them to fight to-day worthily of all their former successes; "For you see," said he, "how, after such great victories, we have not liberty to respire, nor to repose ourselves, though victors; unless we drive this man back." Then the two armies, joining battle, fought fiercely; when the event of an untimely movement showed Marcellus to have been guilty of an error. The right wing being hard pressed upon, he commanded one of the legions to be brought up to the front. This change, disturbing the array and posture of the legions, gave the victory to the enemies; and there fell two thousand seven hundred Romans.

Marcellus, after he had retreated into his camp, called his soldiers together. "I see," said he, "many Roman arms and bodies, but I see not so much as one Roman." To their entreaties for his pardon, he returned a refusal while they remained beaten, but promised to give it so soon as they should overcome; and he resolved to bring them into the field the next day, that the fame of their victory might arrive at Rome before that of their flight. Dismissing the assembly, he commanded barley instead of wheat to be given to those companies that had turned their backs. These rebukes were so bitter to the soldiers, that though a great number of them were grievously wounded, yet they relate there was not one to whom the general's oration was not more painful and smarting than his wounds.

The day breaking, a scarlet toga, the sign of instant battle, was displayed. The companies marked with ignominy begged they might be posted in the foremost place, and obtained their request. Then the tribunes bring forth the rest of the forces, and draw them up. On news of which, "O strange!" said Hannibal, "What will you do with this man, who can bear neither good nor bad fortune? He is the only man who neither suffers us to rest when he is victor, nor rests himself when he is overcome. We shall have, it seems, perpetually to fight with him; as in good success his confidence, and in ill success his shame, still urges him to some further enterprise." Then the armies engaged.

When the fight was doubtful, Hannibal commanded the elephants to be brought into the first battalion, and to be driven upon the van of the Romans. When the beasts, trampling upon many, soon caused disorder, Flavius, a tribune of soldiers, snatching an ensign, met them, and wounding the first elephant with the spike at the bottom of the ensign staff, put him to flight. The beast turned around upon the next, and drove back both him and the rest that followed. Marcellus, seeing this, poured in his horse with great force upon the elephants, and upon the enemy disordered by their flight. The horse, making a fierce impression, pursued the Carthaginians home to their camp, while the elephants, wounded and running upon their own party, caused a considerable slaughter. It is said more than eight thousand were slain; of the Roman army three thousand, and almost all wounded. This gave Hannibal opportunity to retire in the silence of the night, and to remove to greater distance from Marcellus; who was kept from pursuing by the number of his wounded men, and removed, by gentle marches, into Campania, and spent the summer at Sinuessa, engaged in restoring them.

But as Hannibal, having disentangled himself from Marcellus, ranged with his army round about the country and wasted Italy free from all fear, at Rome Marcellus was evil spoken of. His detractors induced Publicius Bibulus, tribune of the people, an eloquent and violent man, to undertake his accusation. He, by assiduous harangues, prevailed upon the people to withdraw from Marcellus the command of the army; "Seeing that Marcellus," said he, "after brief exercise in the war, has withdrawn as it might be from the wrestling ground to the warm baths to refresh himself." Marcellus, on hearing this, appointed lieutenants over his camp and hasted to Rome to refute the charges against him, and there found ready drawn up an impeachment consisting of these calumnies.

At the day prefixed, in the Flaminian circus, into which place the people had assembled themselves, Bibulus rose and accused him. Marcellus himself answered, briefly and simply, but the first and most approved men of the city spoke largely and in high terms, very freely advising the people not to show themselves worse judges than the enemy, condemning Marcellus of timidity, from whom alone of all their captains the enemy fled, and as perpetually endeavoured to avoid fighting with him as to fight with others. When they made an end of speaking, the accuser's hope to obtain judgment so far deceived him that Marcellus was not only absolved, but the fifth time created consul.

No sooner had he entered upon this consulate, but he suppressed a great commotion in Etruria that had proceeded near to revolt, and visited and quieted the cities. Then, when the dedication of the temple, which he had vowed out of his Sicilian spoils to Honour and Virtue, was objected to by the priests, because they denied that one temple could be lawfully dedicated to two gods, he began to adjoin another to it, resenting the priests' opposition, and almost converting the thing into an omen.

And, truly, many other prodigies also affrighted him; some temples had been struck with lightning, and in Jupiter's temple mice had gnawed the gold; it was reported, also, that an ox had spoken, and that a boy had been born with a head like an elephant's. All which prodigies had indeed been attended to, but due reconciliation had not been obtained from the gods. The aruspices therefore detained him at Rome, glowing and burning with desire to return to the war. For no man was ever inflamed with so great desire of anything as was he to fight a battle with Hannibal. It was the subject of his dreams in the night, the topic of all his consultations with his friends and familiars, nor did he present to the gods any other wish, but that he might meet Hannibal in the field. And I think that he would most gladly have set upon him, with both armies environed within a single camp. Had he not been even loaded with honours, and had he not given proofs in many ways of his maturity of judgment and of prudence equal to that of any commander, you might have said that he was agitated by a youthful ambition, above what became a man of that age, for he had passed the sixtieth year of his life when he began his fifth consulship.

The sacrifices having been offered, and all that belonged to the propitiation of the gods performed, according to the prescription of the diviners, he at last with his colleague went forth to carry on the war. He tried all possible means to provoke Hannibal, who at that time had a standing camp betwixt Bantia and Venusia. Hannibal declined an engagement, but having obtained intelligence that some troops were on their way to the town of Locri Epizephyrii, placing an ambush under the little hill of Petelia, he slew two thousand five hundred soldiers. This incensed Marcellus to revenge; and he therefore moved nearer Hannibal.

Betwixt the two camps was a little hill, a tolerably secure post, covered with wood; it had steep descents on either side, and there were springs of water seen trickling down. This place was so fit and advantageous that the Romans wondered that Hannibal, who had come thither before them, had not seized upon it, but had left it to the enemies. But to him the place had seemed commodious indeed for a camp, but yet more commodious for an ambuscade; and to that use he chose to put it.

So in the wood and the hollows he hid a number of archers and spearmen, confident that the commodiousness of the place would allure the Romans. Nor was he deceived in his expectation. For presently in the Roman camp they talked and disputed, as if they had all been captains, how the place ought to be seized, and what great advantage they should thereby gain upon the enemies, chiefly if they transferred their camp thither, at any rate, if they strengthened the place with a fort. Marcellus resolved to go, with a few horse, to view it. Having called a diviner he proceeded to sacrifice.

In the first victim the aruspex showed him the liver without a head; in the second the head appeared of unusual size, and all the other indications highly promising. When these seemed sufficient to free them from the dread of the former, the diviners declared that they were all the more terrified by the latter; because entrails too fair and promising when they appear after others that are maimed and monstrous render the change doubtful and suspicious. But—

Nor fire nor brazen wall can keep out fate;

as Pindar observes. Marcellus, therefore, taking with him his colleague Crispinus, and his son, a tribune of soldiers, with two hundred and twenty horse at most (among whom there was not one Roman, but all were Etruscans, except forty Fregellans, of whose courage and fidelity he had on all occasions received full proof), went to view the place.

The hill was covered with woods all over; on the top of it sat a scout concealed from the sight of the enemy, but having the Roman camp exposed to his view. Upon signs received from him, the men that were placed in ambush stirred not till Marcellus came near; and then all starting up in an instant, and encompassing him from all sides, attacked him with darts, struck about and wounded the backs of those that fled, and pressed upon those who

resisted. These were the forty Fregellans. For though the Etruscans fled in the very beginning of the fight, the Fregellans formed themselves into a ring, bravely defending the consuls, till Crispinus, struck with two darts, turned his horse to fly away; and Marcellus's side was run through with a lance with a broad head. Then the Fregellans, also, the few that remained alive, leaving the fallen consul, and rescuing young Marcellus, who also was wounded, got into the camp by flight.

There were slain not much above forty; five lictors and eighteen horsemen came alive into the enemy's hands. Crispinus also died of his wounds a few days after. Such a disaster as the loss of both consuls in a single engagement was one that had never before befallen the Romans.

Hannibal, little valuing the other events, as soon as he was told of Marcellus's death, immediately hasted to the hill. Viewing the body, and continuing for some time to observe its strength and shape, he allowed not a word to fall from him expressive of the least pride or arrogancy, nor did he show in his countenance any sign of gladness, as another perhaps would have done, when his fierce and troublesome enemy had been taken away; but amazed by so sudden and unexpected an end, taking off nothing but his ring, gave order to have the body properly clad and adorned and honourably burned. The relics put into a silver urn, with a crown of gold to cover it, he sent back to his son.

But some of the Numidians, setting upon these that were carrying the urn, took it from them by force, and cast away the bones; which being told to Hannibal, "It is impossible, it seems then," he said, "to do anything against the will of God!" He punished the Numidians; but took no further care of sending or re-collecting the bones; conceiving that Marcellus so fell, and so lay unburied, by a certain fate.

So Cornelius Nepos and Vaerius Maximus have left upon record: but Livy and Augustus Cæsar affirm that the urn was brought to his son, and honoured with a magnificent funeral. Besides the monuments raised for him at Rome, there was dedicated to his memory at Catana, in Sicily, an ample wrestling place called after him; statues and pictures, out of those he took from Syracuse, were set up in Samothrace, in the temple of the gods, named Cabiri, and in that of Minerva at Lindus, where also there was a statue of him, says

Posidonius, with the following inscription:—

This was, O stranger, once Rome's star divine,
Claudius Marcellus of an ancient line;
To fight her wars seven times her consul made,
Low in the dust her enemies he laid.

The writer of the inscription has added to Marcellus's five consulates his two proconsulates. His progeny continued in high honour

even down to Marcellus, son of Octavia, sister of Augustus, whom she bore to her husband Caius Marcellus; and who died a bridegroom, in the year of his ædileship, having not long before married Cæsar's daughter. His mother, Octavia, dedicated the library to his honour and memory, and Cæsar the theatre which bears his name.

MARCELLUS and PELOPIDAS
Compared

THESE are the memorable things I have found in historians concerning Marcellus and Pelopidas. Betwixt which two great men, though in natural character and manners they nearly resembled each other, because both were valiant and diligent, daring and high-spirited, there was yet some diversity in the one point, that Marcellus in many cities which he reduced under his power committed great slaughter; but Epaminondas and Pelopidas never after any victory put men to death, or reduced citizens to slavery. And we are told, too, that the Thebans would not, had these been present, have taken the measures they did against the Orchomenians. Marcellus's exploits against the Gauls are admirable and ample; when, accompanied by a few horse, he defeated and put to flight a vast number of horse and foot together (an action you cannot easily in historians find to have been done by any other captain), and took their king prisoner. To which honour Pelopidas aspired, but did not attain; he was killed by the tyrant in the attempt.

But to these you may perhaps oppose those two most glorious battles at Leuctra and Tegyræ; and we have no statement of any achievement of Marcellus, by stealth or ambuscade, such as were those of Pelopidas, when he returned from exile, and killed the tyrants at Thebes; which, indeed, may claim to be called the first in rank of all achievements ever performed by secrecy and cunning. Hannibal was, indeed, a most formidable enemy for the Romans; but so for that matter were the Lacedæmonians for the Thebans. And that these were, in the fights of Leuctra and Tegyræ, beaten and put to flight by Pelopidas is confessed; whereas Polybius writes that Hannibal was never so much as once vanquished by Marcellus, but remained invincible in all encounters till Scipio came. I myself, indeed, have followed rather Livy,

Cæsar, Cornelius Nepos, and, among the Greeks, king Juba, in stating that the troops of Hannibal were in some encounters routed and put to flight by Marcellus; but certainly these defeats conduced little to the sum of the war. It would seem as if they had been merely feints of some sort on the part of the Carthaginians.

What was indeed truly and really admirable was, that the Romans, after the defeat of so many armies, the slaughter of so many captains, and, in fine, the confusion of almost the whole Roman empire, still showed a courage equal to their losses, and were as willing as their enemies to engage in new battles. And Marcellus was the one man who overcame the great and inveterate fear and dread, and revived, raised, and confirmed the spirits of the soldiers to that degree of emulation and bravery that would not let them easily yield the victory, but made them contend for it to the last. For the same men, whom continual defeats had accustomed to think themselves happy, if they could but save themselves by running from Hannibal, were by him taught to esteem it base and ignominious to return safe but unsuccessful; to be ashamed to confess that they had yielded one step in the terrors of the fight; and to grieve to extremity if they were not victorious.

In short, as Pelopidas was never overcome in any battle, where himself was present and commanded in chief, and as Marcellus gained more victories than any of his contemporaries, truly he that could not be easily overcome, considering his many successes, may fairly be compared with him who was undefeated. Marcellus took Syracuse; whereas Pelopidas was frustrated of his hope of capturing Sparta.

But in my judgment it was more difficult to advance his standard even to the walls of Sparta, and to be the first of mortals that ever passed the river Eurotas in arms, than it was to reduce Sicily; unless, indeed, we say that that adventure is with more of right to be attributed to Epaminondas, as was also the Leuctrian battle; whereas Marcellus's renown, and the glory of his brave actions, came entire and undiminished to him alone. For he alone took Syracuse; and without his colleague's help defeated the Gauls, and, when all others declined, alone, without one companion, ventured to engage with Hannibal; and changing the aspect of the war first showed the example of daring to attack him.

I cannot commend the death of either of these great men; the suddenness and strangeness of their ends gives me a feeling rather of pain and distress. Hannibal has my admiration who, in so many severe conflicts, more than can be reckoned in one day, never received so much as one wound. I honour Chrysantes also (in Xenophon's *Cyropædia*), who, having raised his sword in the act of striking his enemy, so soon as a retreat was sounded, left him, and retired sedately and modestly. Yet the anger which provoked Pelopidas to pursue revenge in the heat of fight may excuse him.

The first thing for a captain is to gain
Safe victory; the next to be with honour slain,

as Euripides says. For then he cannot be said to *suffer* death; it is rather to be called an action. The very object, too, of Pelopidas's victory, which consisted in the slaughter of the tyrant, presenting itself to his eyes, did not wholly carry him away unadvisedly: he could not easily expect again to have another equally glorious occasion for the exercise of his courage in a noble and honourable cause.

But Marcellus, when it made little to his advantage, and when no such violent ardour as present danger naturally calls out transported him to passion, throwing himself into danger, fell into an unexplored ambush; he, namely, who had borne five consulates, led three triumphs, won the spoils and glories of kings and victories, to act the part of a mere scout, or sentinel, and to expose all his achievements to be trod under foot by the mercenary Spaniards and Numidians, who sold themselves and their lives to the Carthaginians; so that even they themselves felt unworthy, and almost grudged themselves the unhoped-for success of having cut off, among a few Fregellan scouts, the most valiant, the most potent, and most renowned of the Romans.

Let no man think that we have thus spoken out of a design to accuse these noble men; it is merely an expression of frank indignation in their own behalf, at seeing them thus wasting all their other virtues upon that of bravery, and throwing away their lives, as if the loss would be only felt by themselves, and not by their country, allies, and friends.

After Pelopidas's death, his friends, for whom he died, made a funeral for him; the enemies, by whom he had been killed, made one for Marcellus. A noble and happy lot indeed the former; yet there is something higher and greater in the admiration rendered by enemies to the virtue that had been their own obstacle, than in the grateful acknowledgments of friends. Since, in the one case, it is virtue alone that challenges itself the honour; while, in the other, it may be rather men's personal profit and advantage that is the real origin of what they do.

ARISTIDES
530?–?468 B.C.

ARISTIDES, the son of Lysimachus, was of the tribe Antiochis, and township of Alopece. As to wealth, statements differ; some say he passed his life in extreme poverty, and left behind him two daughters whose indigence long kept them unmarried; but Demetrius, the Phalerian, in opposition to this general report, professes in his *Socrates* to know a farm at Phalerum going by Aristides's name, where he was interred; and, as

marks of his opulence, adduces first, the office of archon eponymus, which he obtained by the lot of the bean; which was confined to the highest assessed families, called the Pentacosiomedimni; second, the ostracism, which was not usually inflicted on the poorer citizens, but on those of great houses, whose station exposed them to envy; third and last, that he left certain tripods in the temple of Bacchus, offerings for his victory in conduct-

ing the representation of dramatic performances, which were even in our age still to be
seen, retaining this inscription upon them,
"The tribe Antiochis obtained the victory:
Aristides defrayed the charges: Archestratus's
play was acted."

But this argument, though in appearance
the strongest, is of the least moment of any.
For Epaminondas, who all the world knows
was educated, and lived his whole life in
much poverty, and also Plato, the philosopher,
exhibited magnificent shows, the one an entertainment of flute-players, the other of dithyrambic singers; Dion, the Syracusan, supplying the expenses of the latter, and Pelopidas
those of Epaminondas. For good men do not
allow themselves any inveterate and irreconcilable hostility to receiving presents from
their friends, but while looking upon those
that are accepted to be hoarded up and with
avaricious intentions as sordid and mean, they
do not refuse such as, apart from all profit,
gratify the pure love of honour and magnificence.

Panætius, again, shows that Demetrius was
deceived concerning the tripod by an identity
of name. For, from the Persian war to the
end of the Peloponnesian, there are upon record only two of the name of Aristides who
defrayed the expense of representing plays
and gained the prize, neither of which was the
same with the son of Lysimachus; but the
father of the one was Xenophilus, and the
other lived at a much later time, as the way
of writing, which is that in use since the time
of Euclides, and the addition of the name
of Archestratus prove, a name which, in the
time of the Persian war, no writer mentions,
but which several, during the Peloponnesian
war, record as that of a dramatic poet.

The argument of Panætius requires to be
more closely considered. But as for the ostracism, every one was liable to it, whom his
reputation, birth, or eloquence raised above
the common level; insomuch that even Damon,
preceptor to Pericles, was thus banished, because he seemed a man of more than ordinary
sense. And, moreover, Idomeneus says that
Aristides was not made archon by the lot of
the bean, but the free election of the people.
And if he held the office after the battle of
Platæa, as Demetrius himself has written, it
is very probable that his great reputation and
success in the war made him be preferred for
his virtue to an office which others received
in consideration of their wealth. But Deme-

trius manifestly is eager not only to exempt
Aristides, but Socrates likewise, from poverty,
as from a great evil; telling us that the latter
had not only a house of his own, but also
seventy minæ put out at interest with Crito.

Aristides being the friend and supporter of
that Clisthenes, who settled the government
after the expulsion of the tyrants, and emulating and admiring Lycurgus, the Lacedæmonian, above all politicians, adhered to the aristocratical principles of government; and had
Themistocles, son to Neocles, his adversary
on the side of the populace.

Some say that, being boys and bred up together from their infancy, they were always
at variance with each other in all their words
and actions, as well serious as playful, and
that in this their early contention they soon
made proof of their natural inclinations; the
one being ready, adventurous, and subtle, engaging readily and eagerly in everything; the
other of a staid and settled temper, intent on
the exercise of justice, not admitting any degree of falsity, indecorum, or trickery, no, not
so much as at his play.

Ariston of Chios says the first origin of the
enmity which rose to so great a height was a
love affair; they were rivals for the affection
of the beautiful Stesilaus of Ceos, and were
passionate beyond all moderation, and did not
lay aside their animosity when the beauty that
had excited it passed away; but, as if it had
only exercised them in it, immediately carried
their heats and differences into public business.

Themistocles, therefore, joining an association of partisans, fortified himself with considerable strength; insomuch that when some
one told him that were he impartial he would
make a good magistrate; "I wish," replied he,
"I may never sit on that tribunal where my
friends shall not plead a greater privilege than
strangers."

But Aristides walked, so to say, alone on
his own path in politics, being unwilling, in
the first place, to go along with his associates
in ill-doing, or to cause them vexation by not
gratifying their wishes; and, secondly, observing that many were encouraged by the support they had in their friends to act injuriously, he was cautious; being of opinion that
the integrity of his words and actions was the
only right security for a good citizen.

However, Themistocles making many dangerous alterations, and withstanding and interrupting him in the whole series of his ac-

tions, Aristides also was necessitated to set himself against all Themistocles did, partly in self-defence, and partly to impede his power from still increasing by the favour of the multitude; esteeming it better to let slip some public conveniences, rather than that he by prevailing should become powerful in all things. In fine, when he once had opposed Themistocles in some measures that were expedient, and had got the better of him, he could not refrain from saying, when he left the assembly, that unless they sent Themistocles and himself to the barathrum, there could be no safety for Athens.

Another time, when urging some proposal upon the people, though there were much opposition and stirring against it, he yet was gaining the day; but just as the president of the assembly was about to put it to the vote, perceiving by what had been said in debate the inexpediency of his advice, he let it fall. Also he often brought in his bills by other persons, lest Themistocles, through party spirit against him, should be any hindrance to the good of the public.

In all the vicissitudes of public affairs, the constancy he showed was admirable, not being elated with honours, and demeaning himself tranquilly and sedately in adversity; holding the opinion that he ought to offer himself to the service of his country without mercenary views and irrespectively of any reward, not only of riches, but even of glory itself. Hence it came, probably, that at the recital of these verses of Æschylus in the theatre, relating to Amphiaraus—

> For not at seeming just, but being so
> He aims; and from his depth of soil below
> Harvests of wise and prudent counsels grow,

the eyes of all the spectators turned on Aristides, as if this virtue, in an especial manner, belonged to him.

He was a most determined champion for justice, not only against feelings of friendship and favour, but wrath and malice. Thus it is reported of him that when prosecuting the law against one who was his enemy, on the judges after accusation refusing to hear the criminal, and proceeding immediately to pass sentence upon him, he rose in haste from his seat and joined in petition with him for a hearing, and that he might enjoy the privilege of the law.

Another time, when judging between two private persons, on the one declaring his adversary had very much injured Aristides; "Tell me rather, good friend," he said, "what wrong he has done you; for it is your cause, not my own, which I now sit judge of." Being chosen to the charge of the public revenue, he made it appear that not only those of his time, but the preceding officers, had embezzled much treasure, and especially Themistocles—

> Well known he was an able man to be,
> But with his fingers apt to be too free.

Therefore, Themistocles, associating several persons against Aristides, and impeaching him when he gave in his accounts, caused him to be condemned of robbing the public; so Idomeneus states; but the best and chiefest men of the city much resenting it, he was not only exempted from the fine imposed upon him, but likewise again called to the same employment. Pretending now to repent him of his former practice, and carrying himself with more remissness, he became acceptable to such as pillaged the treasury by not detecting or calling them to an exact account. So that those who had their fill of the public money began highly to applaud Aristides, and sued to the people making interest to have him once more chosen treasurer.

But when they were upon the point of election, he reproved the Athenians. "When I discharged my office well and faithfully," said he, "I was insulted and abused; but now that I have allowed the public thieves in a variety of malpractices, I am considered an admirable patriot. I am more ashamed, therefore, of this present honour than of the former sentence; and I commiserate your condition, with whom it is more praiseworthy to oblige ill men than to conserve the revenue of the public." Saying thus, and proceeding to expose the thefts that had been committed, he stopped the mouths of those who cried him up and vouched for him, but gained real and true commendations from the best men.

When Datis, being sent by Darius under pretence of punishing the Athenians for their burning of Sardis, but in reality to reduce the Greeks under his dominion, landed at Marathon and laid waste the country, among the ten commanders appointed by the Athenians for the war, Miltiades was of the greatest name; but the second place, both for reputation and power, was possessed by Aristides; and when his opinion to join battle was added to that of Miltiades, it did much to incline the balance.

Every leader by his day having the command in chief, when it came to Aristides's turn he delivered it into the hands of Milti-ades, showing his fellow-officers that it is not dishonourable to obey and follow wise and able men, but, on the contrary, noble and prudent. So appeasing their rivalry, and bring-ing them to acquiesce in one and the best ad-vice, he confirmed Miltiades in the strength of an undivided and unmolested authority. For now every one, yielding his day of com-mand, looked for orders only to him.

During the fight the main body of the Athe-nians being the hardest put to it, the bar-barians, for a long time, making opposition there against the tribes Leontis and Antiochis, Themistocles and Aristides being ranged to-gether fought valiantly; the one being of the tribe Leontis, the other of the Antiochis. But after they had beaten the barbarians back to their ships, and perceived that they sailed not for the isles, but were driven in by the force of sea and wind towards the country of Attica, fearing lest they should take the city, unpro-vided of defence, they hurried away thither with nine tribes, and reached it the same day. Aristides, being left with his tribe at Marathon to guard the plunder and prisoners, did not disappoint the opinion they had of him.

Amidst the profusion of gold and silver, all sorts of apparel, and other property, more than can be mentioned, that were in the tents and the vessels which they had taken, he neither felt the desire to meddle with any-thing himself, nor suffered others to do it; unless it might be some who took away any-thing unknown to him; as Callias, the torch-bearer, did. One of the barbarians, it seems, prostrated himself before this man, supposing him to be a king by his hair and fillet; and, when he had so done, taking him by the hand, showed him a great quantity of gold hid in a ditch. But Callias, most cruel and impious of men, took away the treasure, but slew the man, lest he should tell of him.

Hence, they say, the comic poets gave his family the name of *Laccopluti*, or enriched by the ditch, alluding to the place where Callias found the gold. Aristides, immediately after this, was archon; although Demetrius, the Phalerian, says he held the office a little be-fore he died after the battle of Platæa. But in the records of the successors of Xanthippides, in whose year Mardonius was overthrown at Platæa, amongst very many there mentioned, there is not so much as one of the same name as Aristides; while immediately after Phænip-pus, during whose term of office they obtained the victory of Marathon, Aristides is regis-tered.

Of all his virtues, the common people were most affected with his justice, because of its continual and common use; and thus, al-though of mean fortune and ordinary birth, he possessed himself of the most kingly and divine appellation of Just: which kings how-ever and tyrants have never sought after; but have taken delight to be surnamed besiegers of cities, thunderers, conquerors, or eagles again, and hawks; affecting, it seems, the rep-utation which proceeds from power and vio-lence, rather than that of virtue.

Although the divinity, to whom they desire to compare and assimilate themselves, excels, it is supposed, in three things, immortality, power, and virtue; of which three the noblest and divinest is virtue. For the elements and vacuum have an everlasting existence; earth-quakes, thunders, storms, and torrents have great power; but in justice and equity nothing participates except by means of reason and the knowledge of that which is divine. And thus, taking the three varieties of feeling com-monly entertained towards the deity, the sense of his happiness, fear, and honour of him, people would seem to think him blest and happy for his exemption from death and cor-ruption, to fear and dread him for his power and dominion, but to love, honour, and adore him for his justice. Yet though thus disposed, they covet that immortality which our nature is not capable of, and that power the greatest part of which is at the disposal of fortune; but give virtue, the only divine good really in our reach, the last place, most unwisely; since justice makes the life of such as are in pros-perity, power, and authority the life of a god, and injustice turns it to that of a beast.

Aristides, therefore, had at first the fortune to be beloved for this surname, but at length envied. Especially when Themistocles spread a rumour amongst the people that, by deter-mining and judging all matters privately, he had destroyed the courts of judicature, and was secretly making way for a monarchy in his own person, without the assistance of guards.

Moreover, the spirit of the people, now grown high, and confident with their late vic-tory, naturally entertained feelings of dislike to all of more than common fame and repu-tation. Coming together, therefore, from all parts into the city, they banished Aristides by the ostracism, giving their jealousy of his reputation the name of fear of tyranny. For ostracism was not the punishment of any criminal act, but was speciously said to be the mere depression and humiliation of excessive greatness and power; and was in fact a gentle relief and mitigation of envious feeling, which was thus allowed to vent itself in inflicting no intolerable injury, only a ten years' banishment. But after it came to be exercised upon base and villainous fellows, they desisted from it, Hyperbolus being the last whom they banished by the ostracism.

The cause of Hyperbolus's banishment is said to have been this. Alcibiades and Nicias, men that bore the greatest sway in the city, were of different factions. As the people, therefore, were about to vote the ostracism, and obviously to decree it against one of them, consulting together and uniting their parties they contrived the banishment of Hyperbolus. Upon which the people, being offended, as if some contempt or affront was put upon the thing, left off and quite abolished it.

It was performed, to be short, in this manner. Every one taking an *ostracon,* a sherd, that is, or piece of earthenware, wrote upon it the citizen's name he would have banished, and carried it to a certain part of the market-place surrounded with wooden rails. First, the magistrates numbered all the sherds in gross (for if there were less than six thousand, the ostracism was imperfect); then, laying every name by itself, they pronounced him whose name was written by the larger number banished for ten years, with the enjoyment of his estate.

As, therefore, they were writing the names on the sherds, it is reported that an illiterate clownish fellow, giving Aristides his sherd, supposing him a common citizen, begged him to write *Aristides* upon it; and he being surprised and asking if Aristides had ever done him any injury, "None at all," said he, "neither know I the man; but I am tired of hearing him everywhere called the Just." Aristides, hearing this, is said to have made no reply, but returned the sherd with his own name inscribed. At his departure from the city, lifting up his hands to heaven, he made a prayer (the reverse, it would seem, of that of Achilles), that the Athenians might never have any occasion which should constrain them to remember Aristides.

Nevertheless, three years after, when Xerxes marched through Thessaly and Bœotia into the country of Attica, repealing the law, they decreed the return of the banished, chiefly fearing Aristides, lest, joining himself to the enemy, he should corrupt and bring over many of his fellow-citizens to the party of the barbarians; much mistaking the man, who, already before the decree, was exerting himself to excite and encourage the Greeks to the defence of their liberty.

And afterwards, when Themistocles was general with absolute power, he assisted him in all ways both in action and counsel; rendering, in consideration of the common security, the greatest enemy he had the most glorious of men. For when Eurybiades was deliberating to desert the isle of Salamis, and the galleys of the barbarians putting out by night to sea surrounded and beset the narrow passage and islands, and nobody was aware how they were environed, Aristides, with great hazard, sailed from Ægina through the enemy's fleet; and coming by night to Themistocles's tent, and calling him out by himself; "If we have any discretion," said he, "Themistocles, laying aside at this time our vain and childish contention, let us enter upon a safe and honourable dispute, vying with each other for the preservation of Greece; you in the ruling and commanding, I in the subservient and advising part; even indeed, as I now understand you alone to be adhering to the best advice, in counselling without any delay to engage in the straits.

"And in this, though our own party oppose, the enemy seems to assist you. For the sea behind, and all around us, is covered with their fleet; so that we are under a necessity of approving ourselves men of courage, and fighting, whether we will or no; for there is no room left us for flight."

To which Themistocles answered, "I would not willingly, Aristides, be overcome by you on this occasion; and shall endeavour, in emulation of this good beginning, to outdo it in my actions." Also relating to him the stratagem he had framed against the barbarians, he entreated him to persuade Eurybiades and show him how it was impossible they should save themselves without an engagement; as he was the more likely to be believed.

Whence, in the council of war, Cleocritus, the Corinthian, telling Themistocles that Aristides did not like his advice, as he was present and said nothing, Aristides answered that he should not have held his peace if Themistocles had not been giving the best advice; and that he was now silent, not out of any good-will to the person, but in approbation of his counsel.

Thus the Greek captains were employed. But Aristides perceiving Psyttalea, a small island that lies within the straits over against Salamis, to be filled by a body of the enemy, put aboard his small boats the most forward and courageous of his countrymen, and went ashore upon it; and, joining battle with the barbarians, slew them all, except such more remarkable persons as were taken alive.

Amongst these were three children of Sandauce, the king's sister, whom he immediately sent away to Themistocles, and it is stated that, in accordance with a certain oracle, they were, by the command of Euphrantides, the seer, sacrificed to Bacchus, called Omestes, or the devourer. But Aristides, placing armed men all around the island, lay in wait for such as were cast upon it, to the intent that none of his friends should perish, nor any of his enemies escape. For the closest engagement of the ships, and the main fury of the whole battle, seems to have been about this place; for which reason a trophy was erected in Psyttalea.

After the fight, Themistocles, to sound Aristides, told him they had performed a good piece of service, but there was a better yet to be done, the keeping Asia in Europe, by sailing forthwith to the Hellespont and cutting in sunder the bridge. But Aristides, with an exclamation, bid him think no more of it, but deliberate and find out means for removing the Mede, as quickly as possible, out of Greece; lest being enclosed, through want of means to escape, necessity should compel him to force his way with so great an army. So Themistocles once more despatched Arnaces, the eunuch, his prisoner, giving him in command privately to advertise the king that he had diverted the Greeks from their intention of setting sail for the bridges, out of the desire he felt to preserve him.

Xerxes, being much terrified with this, immediately hasted to the Hellespont. But Mardonius was left with the most serviceable part of the army, about three hundred thousand men, and was a formidable enemy, confident in his infantry, and writing messages of defiance to the Greeks: "You have overcome by sea men accustomed to fight on land, and unskilled at the oar; but there lies now the open country of Thessaly; and the plains of Bœotia offer a broad and worthy field for brave men, either horse or foot, to contend in."

But he sent privately to the Athenians, both by letter and word of mouth from the king, promising to rebuild their city, to give them a vast sum of money, and constitute them lords of all Greece, on condition they were not engaged in the war. The Lacedæmonians, receiving news of this, and fearing, despatched an embassy to the Athenians, entreating that they would send their wives and children to Sparta, and receive support from them for their superannuated. For, being despoiled both of their city and country, the people were suffering extreme distress. Having given audience to the ambassadors, they returned an answer, upon the motion of Aristides, worthy of the highest admiration; declaring that they forgave their enemies if they thought all things purchasable by wealth, than which they knew nothing of greater value; but that they felt offended at the Lacedæmonians for looking only to their present poverty and exigence, without any remembrance of their valour and magnanimity, offering them their victuals to fight in the cause of Greece.

Aristides, making this proposal and bringing back the ambassadors into the assembly, charged them to tell the Lacedæmonians that all the treasure on the earth or under it was of less value with the people of Athens than the liberty of Greece. And, showing the sun to those who came from Mardonius, "As long as that retains the same course, so long," said he, "shall the citizens of Athens wage war with the Persians for the country which has been wasted, and the temples that have been profaned and burnt by them." Moreover, he proposed a decree that the priests should anathematise him who sent any herald to the Medes, or deserted the alliance of Greece.

When Mardonius made a second incursion into the country of Attica, the people passed over again into the isle of Salamis. Aristides, being sent to Lacedæmon, reproved them for their delay and neglect in abandoning Athens once more to the barbarians; and demanded their assistance for that part of Greece which was not yet lost. The Ephori, hearing this, made show of sporting all day, and of carelessly keeping holy day (for they were then celebrating the Hyacinthian festival), but in the night, selecting five thousand Spartans, each of whom was attended by seven Helots, they sent them forth unknown to those from Athens. And when Aristides again reprehended them, they told him in derision that he either doted or dreamed, for the army was already at Oresteum, in their march towards the *strangers;* as they called the Persians. Aristides answered that they jested unseasonably, deluding their friends instead of their enemies. Thus says Idomeneus. But in the decree of Aristides, not himself, but Cimon, Xanthippus, and Myronides are appointed ambassadors.

Being chosen general for the war, he repaired to Platæa with eight thousand Athenians, where Pausanias, generalissimo of all Greece, joined him with the Spartans; and the forces of the other Greeks came into them. The whole encampment of the barbarians extended all along the bank of the river Asopus, their numbers being so great there was no enclosing them all, but their baggage and most valuable things were surrounded with a square bulwark, each side of which was the length of ten furlongs.

Tisamenus, the Elean, had prophesied to Pausanias and all the Greeks, and foretold them victory if they made no attempt upon the enemy, but stood on their defence. But Aristides sending to Delphi, the god answered that the Athenians should overcome their enemies in case they made supplication to Jupiter and Juno of Cithæron, Pan, and the nymphs Sphragitides, and sacrificed to the heroes Androcrates, Leucon, Pisander, Damocrates, Hypsion, Actæon, and Polyidus; and if they fought within their own territories in the plain of Ceres Eleusinia and Proserpine.

Aristides was perplexed upon the tidings of this oracle; since the heroes to whom it commanded him to sacrifice had been chieftains of the Platæans, and the cave of the nymphs Sphragitides was on the top of Mount Cithæron, on the side facing the setting sun of summer time; in which place, as the story goes, there was formerly an oracle, and many that lived in the district were inspired with it, whom they called *Nympholepti,* possessed with the nymphs.

But the plain of Ceres Eleusinia, and the offer of victory to the Athenians, if they fought in their own territories, recalled them again, and transferred the war into the country of Attica. In this juncture, Arimnestus, who commanded the Platæans, dreamed that Jupiter, the Saviour, asked him what the Greeks had resolved upon; and that he answered, "To-morrow, my Lord, we march our army to Eleusis, and there give the barbarians battle according to the directions of the oracle of Apollo."

And that the god replied they were utterly mistaken, for that the places spoken of by the oracle were within the bounds of Platæa, and if they sought there they should find them. This manifest vision having appeared to Arimnestus, when he awoke he sent for the most aged and experienced of his countrymen, with whom, communicating and examining the matter, he found that near Hysiæ, at the foot of Mount Cithæron, there was a very ancient temple called the temple of Ceres Eleusinia and Proserpine. He therefore forthwith took Aristides to the place, which was very convenient for drawing up an army on foot, because the slopes at the bottom of the mountain Cithæron rendered the plain, where it comes up to the temple, unfit for the movements of cavalry.

Also, in the same place, there was the fane of Androcrates, environed with a thick shady grove. And that the oracle might be accomplished in all particulars for the hope of victory, Arimnestus proposed, and the Platæans decreed, that the frontiers of their country towards Attica should be removed, and the land given to the Athenians, that they might fight in defence of Greece in their own proper territory. This zeal and liberality of the Platæans became so famous that Alexander, many years after, when he had obtained the dominion of all Asia, upon erecting the walls of Platæa, caused proclamation to be made, by the herald at the Olympic games, that the king did the Platæans this favour in consideration of their nobleness and magnanimity, because, in the war with the Medes, they freely gave up their land and zealously fought with the Greeks.

The Tegeatans, contesting the post of honour with the Athenians, demanded that, according to custom, the Lacedæmonians being ranged on the right wing of the battle, they might have the left, alleging several matters in commendation of their ancestors. The Athenians being indignant at the claim, Aristides came forward: "To contend with the Tegeatans," said he, "for noble descent and valour, the present time permits not; but this we say to you, O you Spartans, and you the rest of the Greeks, that place neither takes away nor contributes courage; we shall endeavour by crediting and maintaining the post you assign us to reflect no dishonour on our former performances. For we are come, not to differ with our friends, but to fight our enemies; not to extol our ancestors, but ourselves to behave as valiant men. This battle will manifest how much each city, captain, and private soldier is worth to Greece." The council of war, upon this address, decided for the Athenians, and gave them the other wing of the battle.

All Greece being in suspense, and especially the affairs of the Athenians unsettled, certain persons of great families and possessions having been impoverished by the war, and seeing all their authority and reputation in the city vanished with their wealth, and others in possession of their honours and places, convened privately at a house in Platæa, and conspired for the dissolution of the democratic government; and, if the plot should not succeed, to ruin the cause and betray all to the barbarians.

These matters being in agitation in the camp, and many persons already corrupted, Aristides, perceiving the design, and dreading the present juncture of time, determined neither to let the business pass unanimadverted upon, nor yet altogether to expose it; not knowing how many the accusation might reach, and willing to set bounds to his justice with a view to the public convenience. Therefore, of many that were concerned, he apprehended eight only, two of whom, who were first proceeded against and most guilty, Æschines of Lampra and Agesias of Acharnæ, made their escape out of the camp. The rest he dismissed; giving opportunity to such as thought themselves concealed to take courage and repent; intimating that they had in the war a great tribunal, where they might clear their guilt by manifesting their sincere and good intentions towards their country.

After this, Mardonius made trial of the Grecian courage, by sending his whole number of horse, in which he thought himself much the stronger, against them, while they were all pitched at the foot of Mount Cithæron, in strong and rocky places, except the Megarians. They, being three thousand in number, were encamped on the plain, where they were damaged by the horse charging and making inroads upon them on all hands.

They sent, therefore, in haste to Pausanias, demanding relief, as not being able alone to sustain the great numbers of the barbarians. Pausanias, hearing this, and perceiving the tents of the Megarians already hid by the multitude of darts and arrows, and themselves driven together into a narrow space, was at a loss himself how to aid them with his battalion of heavy-armed Lacedæmonians. He proposed it, therefore, as a point of emulation in valour and love of distinction, to the commanders and captains who were around him, if any would voluntarily take upon them the defence and succour of the Megarians.

The rest being backward, Aristides undertook the enterprise for the Athenians, and sent Olympiodorus, the most valiant of his inferior officers, with three hundred chosen men and some archers under his command. These being soon in readiness, and running upon the enemy, as soon as Masistius, who commanded the barbarians' horse, a man of wonderful courage and of extraordinary bulk and comeliness of person, perceived it, turning his steed he made towards them. And they sustaining the shock and joining battle with him, there was a sharp conflict, as though by this encounter they were to try the success of the whole war.

But after Masistius's horse received a wound and flung him, and he falling could hardly raise himself through the weight of his armour, the Athenians, pressing upon him with blows, could not easily get at his person, armed as he was, his breast, his head, and his limbs all over, with gold and brass and iron; but one of them at last, running him in at the visor of his helmet, slew him; and the rest of the Persians, leaving the body, fled.

The greatness of the Greek success was known, not by the multitude of the slain (for an inconsiderable number were killed), but by the sorrow the barbarians expressed. For they shaved themselves, their horses, and mules for the death of Masistius, and filled the plain with howling and lamentation; having lost a person, who, next to Mardonius himself, was by many degrees the chief among them, both for valour and authority.

After this skirmish of the horse, they kept from fighting a long time; for the soothsayers, by the sacrifices, foretold the victory both to Greeks and Persians, if they stood upon the defensive part only, but if they became aggressors, the contrary. At length Mardonius, when he had but a few days' provision, and the Greek forces increased continually by some or other that came in to them, impatient of delay, determined to lie still no longer, but passing Asopus by daybreak, to fall unexpectedly upon the Greeks; and signified the same over night to the captains of his host.

But about midnight, a certain horseman stole into the Greek camp, and coming to the watch, desired them to call Aristides, the Athenian, to him. He coming speedily, "I am," said the stranger, "Alexander, king of the Macedonians, and am arrived here through the greatest danger in the world for the good-will I bear you, lest a sudden onset should dismay you, so as to behave in the fight worse than usual. For to-morrow Mardonius will give you battle, urged, not by any hope of success or courage, but by want of victuals; since, indeed, the prophets prohibit him the battle, the sacrifices and oracles being un-favourable; and the army is in despondency and consternation; but necessity forces him to try his fortune, or sit still and endure the last extremity of want."

Alexander, thus saying, entreated Aristides to take notice and remember him, but not to tell any other. But he told him it was not convenient to conceal the matter from Pausa-nias (because he was general); as for any other, he would keep it secret from them till the battle was fought; but if the Greeks ob-tained the victory, that then no one should be ignorant of Alexander's good-will and kindness towards them. After this, the king of the Macedonians rode back again, and Aris-tides went to Pausanias's tent and told him; and they sent for the rest of the captains and gave orders that the army should be in battle array.

Here, according to Herodotus, Pausanias spoke to Aristides, desiring him to transfer the Athenians to the right wing of the army opposite to the Persians (as they would do better service against them, having been ex-perienced in their way of combat, and em-boldened with former victories), and to give him the left, where the Medizing Greeks were to make their assault. The rest of the Athe-nian captains regarded this as an arrogant and interfering act on the part of Pausanias; be-cause, while permitting the rest of the army to keep their stations, he removed them only from place to place, like so many Helots, op-posing them to the greatest strength of the enemy.

But Aristides said they were altogether in the wrong. If so short a time ago they con-tested the left wing with the Tegeatans, and gloried in being preferred before them, now, when the Lacedæmonians gave them place in the right, and yielded them in a manner the leading of the army, how was it they were dis-contented with the honour that was done them, and did not look upon it as an advantage to have to fight, not against their countrymen and kindred, but barbarians, and such as were by nature their enemies? After this, the Athe-nians very readily changed places with the Lacedæmonians, and there went words amongst them as they were encouraging each other that the enemy approached with no better arms or stouter hearts than those who fought the battle of Marathon; but had the same bows and arrows, and the same embroidered coats and gold, and the same delicate bodies and effeminate minds within; "While we have the same weapons and bodies, and our courage augmented by our victories; and fight not like others in defence of our country only, but for the trophies of Salamis and Mara-thon; that they may not be looked upon as due to Miltiades or fortune, but to the peo-ple of Athens." Thus, therefore, were they making haste to change the order of their battle.

But the Thebans, understanding it by some deserters, forthwith acquainted Mardonius; and he, either for fear of the Athenians, or a desire to engage the Lacedæmonians, marched over his Persians to the other wing, and com-manded the Greeks of his party to be posted opposite to the Athenians. But this change was observed on the other side, and Pausa-nias, wheeling about again, ranged himself on the right, and Mardonius, also, as at first, took the left wing over against the Lacedæ-monians. So the day passed without action.

After this the Greeks determined in coun-cil to remove their camp some distance, to possess themselves of a place convenient for watering, because the springs near them were polluted and destroyed by the barbarian cav-alry. But night being come, and the captains setting out towards the place designed for their camping, the soldiers were not very ready to follow, and keep in a body, but, as soon as they had quitted their first entrench-ments, made towards the city of Platæa; and there was much tumult and disorder as they dispersed to various quarters and proceeded to pitch their tents.

The Lacedæmonians, against their will, had the fortune to be left by the rest. For Amom-pharetus, a brave and daring man, who had long been burning with desire of the fight, and resented their many lingerings and de-lays, calling the removal of the camp a mere running away and flight, protested he would not desert his post, but would there remain with his company and sustain the charge of Mardonius. And when Pausanias came to him and told him he did do these things by the common vote and determination of the Greeks, Amompharetus taking up a great stone flung it at Pausanias's feet, and "By this token," said he, "do I give my suffrage for the battle, nor have I any concern with the cowardly consultations and decrees of other men."

Pausanias, not knowing what to do in the present juncture, sent to the Athenians, who were drawing off, to stay to accompany him; and so he himself set off with the rest of the army for Platæa, hoping thus to make Amompharetus move.

Meantime, day came upon them; and Mardonius (for he was not ignorant of their deserting their camp), having his army in array, fell upon the Lacedæmonians with great shouting and noise of barbarous people, as if they were not about to join battle, but crush the Greeks in their flight. Which within a very little came to pass. For Pausanias, perceiving what was done, made a halt, and commanded every one to put themselves in order for the battle; but either through his anger with Amompharetus, or the disturbance he was in by reason of the sudden approach of the enemy, he forgot to give the signal to the Greeks in general. Whence it was that they did not come in immediately or in a body to their assistance, but by small companies and straggling, when the fight was already begun.

Pausanias, offering sacrifice, could not procure favourable omens, and so commanded the Lacedæmonians, setting down their shields at their feet, to abide quietly and attend his directions, making no resistance to any of their enemies. And he sacrificing again a second time, the horse charged, and some of the Lacedæmonians were wounded.

At this time, also, Callicrates, who, we are told, was the most comely man in the army, being shot with an arrow and upon the point of expiring, said that he lamented not his death (for he came from home to lay down his life in the defence of Greece), but that he died without action. The case was indeed hard, and the forbearance of the men wonderful; for they let the enemy charge without repelling them; and, expecting their proper opportunity from the gods and their general, suffered themselves to be wounded and slain in their ranks.

And some say, that while Pausanias was at sacrifice and prayers, some space out of the battle array, certain Lydians, falling suddenly upon him, plundered and scattered the sacrifice: and that Pausanias and his company, having no arms, beat them with staves and whips; and that, in imitation of this attack, the whipping the boys about the altar, and after it the Lydian procession, are to this day practised in Sparta.

Pausanias, therefore, being troubled at these things, while the priests went on offering one sacrifice after another, turned himself towards the temple with tears in his eyes, and lifting up his hands to heaven besought Juno of Cithæron, and the other tutelar gods of the Platæans, if it were not in the fates for the Greeks to obtain the victory, that they might not perish without performing some remarkable thing, and by their actions demonstrating to their enemies that they waged war with men of courage and soldiers.

While Pausanias was thus in the act of supplication, the sacrifices appeared propitious, and the soothsayers foretold victory. The word being given, the Lacedæmonian battalion of foot seemed, on the sudden, like some one fierce animal, setting up his bristles, and betaking himself to the combat; and the barbarians perceived that they encountered with men who would fight it to the death. Therefore, holding their wicker-shields before them, they shot their arrows amongst the Lacedæmonians.

But they, keeping together in the order of a phalanx, and falling upon the enemies, forced their shields out of their hands, and, striking with their pikes at the breasts and faces of the Persians, overthrew many of them, who, however, fell not either unrevenged or without courage. For taking hold of the spears with their bare hands, they broke many of them, and betook themselves not without effect to the sword; and making use of their falchions and scimitars, and wresting the Lacedæmonians' shields from them, and grappling with them, it was a long time that they made resistance.

Meanwhile, for some time, the Athenians stood still, waiting for the Lacedæmonians to come up. But when they heard much noise as of men engaged in fight, and a messenger, they say, came from Pausanias, to advertise them of what was going on, they soon hasted to their assistance. And as they passed through the plain to the place where the noise was, the Greeks, who took part with the enemy, came upon them. Aristides, as soon as he saw them, going a considerable space before the rest, cried out to them, conjuring them by the guardian gods of Greece to forbear the fight, and be no impediment or stop to those who were going to succour the defenders of Greece.

But when he perceived they gave no attention to him, and had prepared themselves for the battle, then turning from the present relief of the Lacedæmonians, he engaged them, being five thousand in number. But the greatest part soon gave way and retreated, as the barbarians also were put to flight. The sharpest conflict is said to have been against the Thebans, the chiefest and most powerful persons among them at that time siding zealously with the Medes, and leading the multitude not according to their own inclinations, but as being subjects of an oligarchy.

The battle being thus divided, the Lacedæmonians first beat off the Persians; and a Spartan, named Arimnestus, slew Mardonius by a blow on the head with a stone, as the oracle in the temple of Amphiaraus had foretold to him. For Mardonius sent a Lydian thither, and another person, a Carian, to the cave of Trophonius. This latter the priest of the oracle answered in his own language. But the Lydian sleeping in the temple of Amphiaraus, it seemed to him that a minister of the divinity stood before him and commanded him to be gone; and on his refusing to do it, flung a great stone at his head, so that he thought himself slain with the blow.

Such is the story.—They drove the fliers within their walls of wood; and, a little time after, the Athenians put the Thebans to flight, killing three hundred of the chiefest and of greatest note among them in the actual fight itself. For when they began to flee, news came that the army of the barbarians was besieged within their palisade; and so giving the Greeks opportunity to save themselves, they marched to assist at the fortifications; and coming in to the Lacedæmonians, who were altogether unhandy and inexperienced in storming, they took the camp with great slaughter of the enemy.

For of three hundred thousand, forty thousand only are said to have escaped with Artabazus; while on the Greeks' side there perished in all thirteen hundred and sixty; of which fifty-two were Athenians, all of the tribe Æantis, that fought, says Clidemus, with the greatest courage of any; and for this reason the men of this tribe used to offer sacrifice for the victory, as enjoined by the oracle, to the nymphs Sphragitides at the expense of the public; ninety-one were Lacedæmonians, and sixteen Tegeatans.

It is strange, therefore, upon what grounds Herodotus can say, that they only, and none other, encountered the enemy, for the number of the slain and their monuments testify that the victory was obtained by all in general; and if the rest had been standing still, while the inhabitants of three cities only had been engaged in the fight, they would not have set on the altar the inscription—

The Greeks, when, by their courage and their might,
They had repelled the Persian in the fight,
The common altar of freed Greece to be,
Reared this to Jupiter who guards the free.

They fought this battle on the fourth day of the month Boëdromion, according to the Athenians, but according to the Bœotians, on the twenty-seventh of Panemus;—on which day there is still a convention of the Greeks at Platæa, and the Platæans still offer sacrifice for the victory to Jupiter of freedom.

As for the difference of days, it is not to be wondered at, since even at the present time, when there is a far more accurate knowledge of astronomy, some begin the month at one time, and some at another.

After this, the Athenians not yielding the honour of the day to the Lacedæmonians, nor consenting they should erect a trophy, things were not far from being ruined by dissension among the armed Greeks; had not Aristides, by much soothing and counselling the commanders, especially Leocrates and Myronides, pacified and persuaded them to leave the thing to the decision of the Greeks.

And on their proceeding to discuss the matter, Theogiton, the Megarian, declared the honour of the victory was to be given some other city, if they would prevent a civil war; after him Cleocritus of Corinth rising up, made people think he would ask the palm for the Corinthians (for next to Sparta and Athens, Corinth was in greatest estimation); but he delivered his opinion, to the general admiration, in favour of the Platæans; and counselled to take away all contention by giving them the reward and glory of the victory, whose being honoured could be distasteful to neither party. This being said, first Aristides gave consent in the name of the Athenians, and Pausanias, then, for the Lacedæmonians. So, being reconciled, they set apart eighty talents for the Platæans, with which they built the temple and dedicated the image to Minerva, and adorned the temple with pictures, which even to this very day retain their lustre.

But the Lacedæmonians and Athenians each erected a trophy apart by themselves. On their consulting the oracle about offering sacrifice, Apollo answered that they should dedicate an altar to Jupiter of freedom, but should not sacrifice till they had extinguished the fires throughout the country, as having been defiled by the barbarians, and had kindled unpolluted fire at the common altar at Delphi.

The magistrates of Greece, therefore, went forthwith and compelled such as had fire to put it out; and Euchidas, a Platæan, promising to fetch fire, with all possible speed, from the altar of the god, went to Delphi, and having sprinkled and purified his body crowned himself with laurel; and taking the fire from the altar ran back to Platæa, and got back there before sunset, performing in one day a journey of a thousand furlongs; and saluting his fellow-citizens and delivering them the fire, he immediately fell down, and in a short time after expired. But the Platæans, taking him up, interred him in the temple of Diana Euclia, setting this inscription over him: "Euchidas ran to Delphi and back again in one day."

Most people believe that Euclia is Diana, and call her by that name. But some say she was the daughter of Hercules, by Myrto, the daughter of Menœtius, and sister of Patroclus, and dying a virgin, was worshipped by the Bœotians and Locrians. Her altar and image are set up in all their market-places, and those of both sexes that are about marrying sacrifice to her before the nuptials.

A general assembly of all the Greeks being called, Aristides proposed a decree that the deputies and religious representatives of the Greek states should assemble annually at Platæa, and every fifth year celebrate the Eleutheria or games of freedom. And that there should be a levy upon all Greece for the war against the barbarians of ten thousand spearmen, one thousand horse, and a hundred sail of ships; but the Platæans to be exempt, and sacred to the service of the gods, offering sacrifice for the welfare of Greece.

These things being ratified, the Platæans undertook the performance of annual sacrifice to such as were slain and buried in that place; which they still perform in the following manner. On the sixteenth day of Mæmacterion (which with the Bœotians is Alalcomenus) they make their procession, which, beginning by break of day, is led by a trumpeter sounding for onset; then follow certain char-

iots loaded with myrrh and garlands; and then a black bull; then come the young men of free birth carrying libations of wine and milk in large two-handed vessels, and jars of oil and precious ointments, none of servile condition being permitted to have any hand in this ministration, because the men died in defence of freedom; after all comes the chief magistrate of Platæa (for whom it is unlawful at other times either to touch iron or wear any other coloured garment but white), at that time apparelled in a purple robe; and, taking a water-pot out of the city record-office, he proceeds, bearing a sword in his hand, through the middle of the town to the sepulchres. Then drawing water out of a spring, he washes and anoints the monuments, and sacrificing the bull upon a pile of wood, and making supplication to Jupiter and Mercury of the earth, invites those valiant men who perished in the defence of Greece to the banquet and the libations of blood. After this, mixing a bowl of wine, and pouring out for himself, he says, "I drink to those who lost their lives for the liberty of Greece." These solemnities the Platæans observe to this day.

Aristides perceived that the Athenians, after their return into the city, were eager for a democracy; and deeming the people to deserve consideration on account of their valiant behaviour, as also that it was a matter of difficulty, they being well armed, powerful, and full of spirit with their victories, to oppose them by force, he brought forward a decree that every one might share in the government and the archons be chosen out of the whole body of the Athenians.

And on Themistocles telling the people in assembly that he had some advice for them, which could not be given in public, but was most important for the advantage and security of the city, they appointed Aristides alone to hear and consider it with him. And on his acquainting Aristides that his intent was to set fire to the arsenal of the Greeks, for by that means should the Athenians become supreme masters of all Greece, Aristides, returning to the assembly, told them that nothing was more advantageous than what Themistocles designed, and nothing more unjust. The Athenians, hearing this, gave Themistocles order to desist; such was the love of justice felt by the people, and such the credit and confidence they reposed in Aristides.

Being sent in joint commission with Cimon to the war, he took notice that Pausanias and the other Spartan captains made themselves offensive by imperiousness and harshness to the confederates; and by being himself gentle and considerate with them, and by the courtesy and disinterested temper which Cimon, after his example, manifested in the expeditions, he stole away the chief command from the Lacedæmonians, neither by weapons, ships, or horses, but by equity and wise policy. For the Athenians being endeared to the Greeks by the justice of Aristides and by Cimon's moderation, the tyranny and selfishness of Pausanias rendered them yet more desirable.

He on all occasions treated the commanders of the confederates haughtily and roughly; and the common soldiers he punished with stripes, or standing under the iron anchor for a whole day together; neither was it permitted for any to provide straw for themselves to lie on, or forage for their horses, or to come near the springs to water before the Spartans were furnished, but servants with whips drove away such as approached. And when Aristides once was about to complain and expostulate with Pausanias, he told him with an angry look that he was not at leisure, and gave no attention to him.

The consequence was that the sea captains and generals of the Greeks, in particular, the Chians, Samians, and Lesbians, came to Aristides and requested him to be their general, and to receive the confederates into his command, who had long desired to relinquish the Spartans and come over to the Athenians. But he answered that he saw both equity and necessity in what they said, but their fidelity required the test of some action, the commission of which would make it impossible for the multitude to change their minds again. Upon which Uliades, the Samian, and Antagoras of Chios, conspiring together, ran in near Byzantium on Pausanias's galley, getting her between them as she was sailing before the rest.

But when Pausanias, beholding them, arose up and furiously threatened soon to make them know that they had been endangering not his galley, but their own countries, they bid him go his way, and thank Fortune that fought for him at Platæa; for hitherto, in reverence to that, the Greeks had forborne from inflicting on him the punishment he deserved. In fine, they all went off and joined the Athenians.

And here the magnanimity of the Lacedæmonians was wonderful. For when they perceived that their generals were becoming corrupted by the greatness of their authority, they voluntarily laid down the chief command, and left off sending any more of them to the wars, choosing rather to have citizens of moderation and consistent in the observance of their customs, than to possess the dominion of all Greece.

Even during the command of the Lacedæmonians, the Greeks paid a certain contribution towards the maintenance of the war; and being desirous to be rated city by city in their due proportion, they desired Aristides of the Athenians, and gave him command, surveying the country and revenue, to assess every one according to their ability and what they were worth. But he, being so largely empowered, Greece, as it were, submitting all her affairs to his sole management, went out poor and returned poorer, laying the tax not only without corruption and injustice, but to the satisfaction and convenience of all. For as the ancients celebrated the age of Saturn, so did the confederates of Athens Aristides's taxation, terming it the happy time of Greece; and that more especially, as the sum was in a short time doubled, and afterwards trebled. For the assessment which Aristides made was four hundred and sixty talents. But to this Pericles added very near one third part more; for Thucydides says that in the beginning of the Peloponnesian war the Athenians had coming in from their confederates six hundred talents.

But after Pericles's death, the demagogues, increasing by little and little, raised it to the sum of thirteen hundred talents; not so much through the war's being so expensive and changeable either by its length or ill success, as by their alluring the people to spend upon largesses and playhouse allowances, and in erecting statues and temples. Aristides, therefore, having acquired a wonderful and great reputation by this levy of the tribute, Themistocles is said to have derided him, as if this had been not the commendation of a man, but a money-bag; a retaliation, though not in the same kind, for some free words which Aristides had used. For he, when Themistocles once was saying that he thought the highest virtue of a general was to understand and foreknow the measures the enemy would take, replied, "This, indeed, Themistocles, is simply necessary, but the excellent thing in a general is to keep his hands from taking money."

Aristides, moreover, made all the people of Greece swear to keep the league, and himself took the oath in the name of the Athenians, flinging wedges of red-hot iron into the sea, after curses against such as should make breach of their vow. But afterwards, it would seem, when things were in such a state as constrained them to govern with a stronger hand, he bade the Athenians to throw the perjury upon him, and manage affairs as convenience required. And, in general, Theophrastus tells us, that Aristides was, in his own private affairs, and those of his fellow-citizens, rigorously just, but that in public matters he acted often in accordance with his country's policy, which demanded, sometimes, not a little injustice. It is reported of him that he said in a debate, upon the motion of the Samians for removing the treasure from Delos to Athens, contrary to the league, that the thing indeed was not just but was expedient.

In fine, having established the dominion of his city over so many people, he himself remained indigent; and always delighted as much in the glory of being poor, as in that of his trophies; as is evident from the following story. Callias, the torch-bearer, was related to him; and was prosecuted by his enemies in a capital cause, in which, after they had slightly argued the matters on which they indicted him, they proceeded, besides the point, to address the judges: "You know," said they, "Aristides, the son of Lysimachus, who is the admiration of all Greece. In what a condition do you think his family is in at his house, when you see him appear in public in such a threadbare cloak? Is it not probable that one who, out of doors, goes thus exposed to the cold, must want food and other necessaries at home? Callias, the wealthiest of the Athenians, does nothing to relieve either him or his wife and children in their poverty, though he is his own cousin, and has made use of him in many cases, and often reaped advantage by his interest with you."

But Callias, perceiving the judges were moved more particularly by this, and were exasperated against him, called in Aristides, requiring him to testify that when he frequently offered him divers presents, and entreated him to accept them, he had refused, answering that it became him better to be proud of his poverty than Callias of his wealth; since there are many to be seen that make a good or a bad use of riches, but it is difficult, comparatively, to meet with one who supports poverty in a noble spirit; those only should be ashamed of it who incurred it against their

wills. On Aristides deposing these facts in favour of Callias, there was none who heard them that went not away desirous rather to be poor like Aristides than rich as Callias. Thus Æschines, the scholar of Socrates, writes.

But Plato declares that, of all the great renowned men in the city of Athens, he was the only one worthy of consideration; for Themistocles, Cimon, and Pericles filled the city with porticoes, treasure, and many other vain things, but Aristides guided his public life by the rule of justice. He showed his moderation very plainly in his conduct towards Themistocles himself. For though Themistocles had been his adversary in all his undertakings, and was the cause of his banishment, yet when he afforded a similar opportunity of revenge, being accused to the city, Aristides bore him no malice; but while Alcmæon, Cimon, and many others were prosecuting and impeaching him, Aristides alone neither did nor said any ill against him, and no more triumphed over his enemy in his adversity than he had envied him his prosperity.

Some say Aristides died in Pontus, during a voyage upon the affairs of the public. Others that he died of old age at Athens being in great honour and veneration amongst his fellow-citizens.

But Craterus, the Macedonian, relates his death as follows. After the banishment of Themistocles, he says, the people growing insolent, there sprung up a number of false and frivolous accusers, impeaching the best and most influential men and exposing them to the envy of the multitude, whom their good fortune and power had filled with self-conceit. Amongst these, Aristides was condemned of bribery upon the accusation of Diophantus of Amphitrope, for taking money from the Ionians when he was collector of the tribute; and being unable to pay the fine, which was fifty minæ, sailed to Ionia, and died there.

But of this Craterus brings no written proof, neither the sentence of his condemnation, nor the decree of the people; though in general it is tolerably usual with him to set down such things and to cite his authors. Almost all others who have spoken of the misdeeds of the people towards their generals collect them all together, and tell us of the banishment of Themistocles, Miltiades's bonds, Pericles's fine, and the death of Paches in the judgment-hall, who, upon receiving sentence, killed himself on the hustings, with many things of the like nature. They add the banishment of Aristides;

but of this his condemnation they make no mention.

Moreover, his monument is to be seen at Phalerum, which they say was built him by the city, he not having left enough even to defray funeral charges. And it is stated that his two daughters were publicly married out of the *prytaneum,* or state-house, by the city, which decreed each of them three thousand drachmas for her portion; and that upon his son Lysimachus the people bestowed a hundred minæ of money, and as many acres of planted land, and ordered him besides, upon the motion of Alcibiades, four drachmas a day. Furthermore, Lysimachus leaving a daughter, named Polycrite, as Callisthenes says, the people voted her, also, the same allowance for food with those that obtained the victory in the Olympic Games.

But Demetrius the Phalerian, Hieronymus the Rhodian, Aristoxenus, the musician, and Aristotle (if the *Treatise of Nobility* is to be reckoned among the genuine pieces of Aristotle) say that Myrto, Aristides's granddaughter, lived with Socrates, the philosopher, who indeed had another wife, but took her into his house, being a widow, by reason of her in-

digence and want of the necessaries of life. But Panætius sufficiently confutes this in his book concerning Socrates.

Demetrius the Phalerian, in his *Socrates,* says he knew one Lysimachus, son of the daughter of Aristides, extremely poor, who used to sit near what is called the *Iaccheum,* and sustained himself by a table for interpreting dreams; and that, upon his proposal and representations, a decree was passed by the people to give the mother and aunt of this man half a drachma a day. The same Demetrius, when he was legislating himself, decreed each of these women a drachma *per diem.*

And it is not to be wondered at, that the people of Athens should take such care of people living in the city, since, hearing the granddaughter of Aristogiton was in a low condition in the isle of Lemnos, and so poor nobody would marry her, they brought her back to Athens, and marrying her to a man of good birth, gave a farm at Potamus as her marriage-portion; and of similar humanity and bounty the city of Athens, even in our age, has given numerous proofs, and is justly admired and respected in consequence.

MARCUS CATO

234–149 B.C.

MARCUS CATO, we are told, was born at Tusculum, though (till he betook himself to civil and military affairs) he lived and was bred up in the country of the Sabines, where his father's estate lay. His ancestors seeming almost entirely unknown, he himself praises his father Marcus, as a worthy man and a brave soldier, and Cato, his great-grandfather, too, as one who had often obtained military prizes, and who, having lost five horses under him, received, on the account of his valour, the worth of them out of the public exchequer.

Now it being the custom among the Romans to call those who, having no repute by birth, made themselves eminent by their own exertions, new men or upstarts, they called even Cato himself so, and so he confessed himself to be as to any public distinction or employment, but yet asserted that in the ex-

ploits and virtues of his ancestors he was very ancient.

His third name originally was not Cato, but Priscus, though afterwards he had the surname of Cato, by reason of his abilities; for the Romans call a skilful or experienced man *Catus.* He was of a ruddy complexion and grey-eyed; as the writer, who, with no good-will, made the following epigram upon him lets us see:—

Porcius, who snarls at all in every place,
With his grey eyes, and with his fiery face,
Even after death will scarce admitted be
Into the infernal realms by Hecate.

He gained, in early life, a good habit of body by working with his own hands, and living temperately, and serving in war; and seemed to have an equal proportion both of health and strength. And he exerted and practised his eloquence through all the neighbourhood and little villages; thinking it as requisite as a second body, and an all but necessary organ to one who looks forward to something above a mere humble and inactive life. He would never refuse to be counsel for those who needed him, and was, indeed, early reckoned a good lawyer, and, ere long, a capable orator.

Hence his solidity and depth of character showed itself gradually more and more to those with whom he was concerned, and claimed, as it were, employment in great affairs and places of public command. Nor did he merely abstain from taking fees for his counsel and pleading, but did not even seem to put any high price on the honour which proceeded from such kind of combats, seeming much more desirous to signalise himself in the camp and in real fights; and while yet but a youth, had his breast covered with scars he had received from the enemy: being (as he himself says) but seventeen years old when he made his first campaign; in the time when Hannibal, in the height of his success, was burning and pillaging all Italy.

In engagements he would strike boldly, without flinching, stand firm to his ground, fix a bold countenance upon his enemies, and with a harsh threatening voice accost them, justly thinking himself and telling others that such a rugged kind of behaviour sometimes terrifies the enemy more than the sword itself. In his marches he bore his own arms on foot, whilst one servant only followed, to carry the provision for his table, with whom he is said never to have been angry or hasty whilst he made ready his dinner or supper, but would, for the most part, when he was free from military duty, assist and help him himself to dress it. When he was with the army, he used to drink only water; unless, perhaps, when extremely thirsty, he might mingle it with a little vinegar, or if he found his strength fail him, take a little wine.

The little country house of Manius Curius, who had been thrice carried in triumph, happened to be near his farm; so that often going thither, and contemplating the small compass of the place, and plainness of the dwelling, he formed an idea of the mind of the person, who being one of the greatest of the Romans, and having subdued the most warlike nations, nay, had driven Pyrrhus out of Italy, now, after three triumphs, was contented to dig in so small a piece of ground, and live in such a cottage. Here it was that the ambassadors of the Samnites, finding him boiling turnips in the chimney corner, offered him a present of gold; but he sent them away with this saying; that he, who was content with such a supper, had no need of gold; and that he thought it more honourable to conquer those who possessed the gold, than to possess the gold itself. Cato, after reflecting upon these things, used to return and, reviewing his own farm, his servants, and housekeeping, increase his labour and retrench all superfluous expenses.

When Fabius Maximus took Tarentum, Cato, being then but a youth, was a soldier under him; and being lodged with one Nearchus, a Pythagorean, desired to understand some of his doctrine, and hearing from him the language, which Plato also uses—that pleasure is evil's chief bait; the body the principal calamity of the soul; and that those thoughts which most separate and take it off from the affections of the body most enfranchise and purify it—he fell in love the more with frugality and temperance. With this exception, he is said not to have studied Greek until when he was pretty old; and in rhetoric, to have then profited a little by Thucydides, but more by Demosthenes. His writings, however, are considerably embellished with Greek sayings and stories; nay, many of these, translated word for word, are placed with his own apophthegms and sentences.

There was a man of the highest rank, and very influential among the Romans, called Valerius Flaccus, who was singularly skilful in discerning excellence yet in the bud, and also much disposed to nourish and advance it. He, it seems, had lands bordering upon Cato's: nor could he but admire when he understood from his servants the manner of his living, how he laboured with his own hands, went on foot betimes in the morning to the courts to assist those who wanted his counsel: how, returning home again, when it was winter, he would throw a loose frock over his shoulders, and in the summer time would work without anything on among his domestics, sit down with them, eat of the same bread, and drink of the same wine. When they spoke, also, of other good qualities, his fair dealing and moderation, mentioning also some of his wise sayings, he ordered that he should be invited to supper; and thus becoming personally assured of his fine temper and his superior character, which, like a plant, seemed only to require culture and a better situation, he urged and persuaded him to apply himself to state affairs at Rome.

Thither, therefore, he went, and by his pleading soon gained many friends and admirers; but, Valerius chiefly assisting his promotion, he first of all got appointed tribune in the army, and afterwards was made quæstor, or treasurer. And now becoming eminent and noted, he passed, with Valerius himself, through the greatest commands, being first his colleague as consul, and then censor.

But among all the ancient senators, he most attached himself to Fabius Maximus; not so much for the honour of his person, and the greatness of his power, as that he might have before him his habit and manner of life, as the best examples to follow; and so he did not hesitate to oppose Scipio the Great, who, being then but a young man, seemed to set himself against the power of Fabius, and to be envied by him.

For being sent together with him as treasurer, when he saw him, according to his natural custom, make great expenses, and distribute among the soldiers without sparing, he freely told him that the expense in itself was not the greatest thing to be considered, but that he was corrupting the frugality of the soldiers by giving them the means to abandon themselves to unnecessary pleasures and luxuries. Scipio answered that he had no need for so accurate a treasurer (bearing on as he was, so to say, full sail to the war), and that he owed the people an account of his actions, and not of the money he spent.

Hereupon Cato returned from Sicily and, together with Fabius, made loud complaints in the open senate of Scipio's lavishing unspeakable sums, and childishly loitering away his time in wrestling matches and comedies, as if he were not to make war, but holiday; and thus succeeded in getting some of the tribunes of the people sent to call him back to Rome, in case the accusations should prove true. But Scipio demonstrating, as it were, to them, by his preparations, the coming victory, and, being found merely to be living pleasantly with his friends, when there was nothing else to do, but in no respect because of that easiness and liberality at all the more negligent in things of consequence and moment, without impediment, set sail toward the war.

Cato grew more and more powerful by his eloquence, so that he was commonly called the Roman Demosthenes; but his manner of life was yet more famous and talked of. For oratorical skill was, as an accomplishment, commonly studied and sought after by all young men; but he was very rare who would cultivate the old habits of bodily labour, or prefer a light supper, and a breakfast which never saw the fire, or be in love with poor clothes and a homely lodging, or could set his ambition rather on doing without luxuries than on possessing them. For now the state, unable to keep its purity by reason of its greatness, and having so many affairs, and people from all parts under its government, was fain to admit many mixed customs and new examples of living.

With reason, therefore, everybody admired Cato, when they saw others sink under labours and grow effeminate by pleasures; and yet beheld him unconquered by either, and that not only when he was young and desirous of honour, but also when old and greyheaded, after a consulship and triumph; like some famous victor in the games, persevering in his exercise and maintaining his character to the very last. He himself says that he never wore a suit of clothes which cost more than a hundred drachmas; and that, when he was general and consul, he drank the same wine which his workmen did; and that the meat or fish which was bought in the meat-market for his dinner did not cost above thirty asses. All which was for the sake of the commonwealth, that so his body might be the hardier for the war.

Having a piece of embroidered Babylonian tapestry left him, he sold it; because none of his farmhouses were so much as plastered. Nor did he ever buy a slave for above fifteen hundred drachmas; as he did not seek for effeminate and handsome ones, but able sturdy workmen, horse-keepers and cow-herds; and these he thought ought to be sold again, when they grew old, and no useless servants fed in the house. In short, he reckoned nothing a good bargain which was superfluous; but whatever it was, though sold for a farthing, he would think it a great price, if you had no need of it, and was for the purchase of lands for sowing and feeding, rather than grounds for sweeping and watering.

Some imputed these things to petty avarice, but others approved of him, as if he had only the more strictly denied himself for the rectifying and amending of others. Yet certainly, in my judgment, it marks an over-rigid temper for a man to take the work out of his servants as out of brute beasts, turning them off and selling them in their old age, and thinking there ought to be no further commerce between man and man than whilst there arises some profit by it. We see that kindness or humanity has a larger field than bare justice to exercise itself in; law and justice we cannot, in the nature of things, employ on others than men; but we may extend our goodness and charity even to irrational creatures; and such acts flow from a gentle nature, as water from an abundant spring. It is doubtless the part of a kind-natured man to keep even worn-out horses and dogs, and not only take care of them when they are foals and whelps, but also when they are grown old.

The Athenians, when they built their Hecatompedon, turned those mules loose to feed freely which they had observed to have done the hardest labour. One of these (they say) came once of itself to offer its service, and ran along with, nay, and went before, the teams which drew the waggons up to the Acropolis, as if it would incite and encourage them to draw more stoutly; upon which there passed a vote that the creature should be kept at the public charge even till it died.

The graves of Cimon's horses, which thrice won the Olympian races, are yet to be seen close by his own monument. Old Xanthippus, too (amongst many others who buried the dogs they had bred up), entombed his which swam after his galley to Salamis, when the people fled from Athens, on the top of a cliff, which they call the Dog's Tomb to this day. Nor are we to use living creatures like old shoes or dishes, and throw them away when they are worn out or broken with service; but if it were for nothing else, but by way of study and practice in humanity, a man ought always to prehabituate himself in these things to be of a kind and sweet disposition.

As to myself, I would not so much as sell my draught ox on the account of his age, much less for a small piece of money sell a poor old man, and so chase him, as it were, from his own country, by turning him not only out of the place where he has lived a long while, but also out of the manner of living he has been accustomed to, and that more especially when he would be as useless to the buyer as to the seller. Yet Cato, for all this, glories that he left that very horse in Spain which he used in the wars when he was consul, only because he would not put the public to the charge of his freight. Whether

these acts are to be ascribed to the greatness or pettiness of his spirit, let every one argue as they please.

For his general temperance, however, and self-control he really deserves the highest admiration. For when he commanded the army, he never took for himself, and those that belonged to him, above three bushels of wheat for a month, and somewhat less than a bushel and a half a day of barley for his baggage-cattle. And when he entered upon the government of Sardinia, where his predecessors had been used to require tents, bedding, and clothes upon the public account, and to charge the state heavily with the cost of provisions and entertainments for a great train of servants and friends, the difference he showed in his economy was something incredible. There was nothing of any sort for which he put the public to expense; he would walk without a carriage to visit the cities, with one only of the common town officers, who carried his dress, and a cup to offer libation with.

Yet though he seemed thus easy and sparing to all who were under his power, he, on the other hand, showed most inflexible severity and strictness in what related to public justice, and was rigorous and precise in what concerned the ordinances of the commonwealth; so that the Roman government never seemed more terrible, nor yet more mild than under his administration.

His very manner of speaking seemed to have such a kind of idea with it; for it was courteous, and yet forcible; pleasant, yet overwhelming; facetious, yet austere; sententious, and yet vehement; like Socrates, in the description of Plato, who seemed outwardly to those about him to be but a simple, talkative, blunt fellow; whilst at the bottom he was full of such gravity and matter, as would even move tears and touch the very hearts of his auditors. And, therefore, I know not what has persuaded some to say that Cato's style was chiefly like that of Lysias. However, let us leave those to judge of these things who profess most to distinguish between the several kinds of oratorical style in Latin; whilst we write down some of his memorable sayings, being of the opinion that a man's character appears much more by his words than, as some think it does, by his looks.

Being once desirous to dissuade the common people of Rome from their unseasonable and impetuous clamour for largesses and distributions of corn, he began thus to harangue them: "It is a difficult task, O citizens, to make speeches to the belly, which has no ears."

Reproving, also, their sumptuous habits, he said it was hard to preserve a city where a fish sold for more than an ox.

He had a saying, also, that the Roman people were like sheep; for they, when single, do not obey, but when altogether in a flock, they follow their leaders: "So you," said he, "when you have got together in a body, let yourselves be guided by those whom singly you would never think of being advised by."

Discoursing of the power of women: "Men," said he, "usually command women; but we command all men, and the women command us." But this, indeed, is borrowed from the sayings of Themistocles, who, when his son was making many demands of him by means of his mother, said, "O woman, the Athenians govern the Greeks; I govern the Athenians, but you govern me, and your son governs you; so let him use his power sparingly, since, simple as he is, he can do more than all the Greeks together."

Another saying of Cato's was, that the Roman people did not only fix the value of such and such purple dyes, but also of such and such habits of life: "For," said he, "as dyers most of all dye such colours as they see to be most agreeable, so the young men learn, and zealously affect, what is most popular with you."

He also exhorted them that if they were grown great by their virtue and temperance, they should not change for the worse; but if intemperance and vice had made them great, they should change for the better; for by that means they were grown indeed quite great enough. He would say, likewise, of men who wanted to be continually in office, that apparently they did not know their road, since they could not do without beadles to guide them on it.

He also reproved the citizens for choosing still the same men as their magistrates: "For you will seem," said he, "either not to esteem government worth much, or to think few worthy to hold it."

Speaking, too, of a certain enemy of his, who lived a very base and discreditable life: "It is considered," he said, "rather as a curse than a blessing on him, that this fellow's mother prays that she may leave him behind her."

Pointing at one who had sold the land which his father had left him, and which lay near the seaside, he pretended to express his wonder at his being stronger even than the sea itself; for what it washed away with a great deal of labour, he with a great deal of ease drank away.

When the senate, with a great deal of splendour, received King Eumenes on his visit to Rome, and the chief citizens strove who should be most about him, Cato appeared to regard him with suspicion and apprehension; and when one that stood by, too, took occasion to say that he was a very good prince and a great lover of the Romans, "It may be so," said Cato, "but by nature this same animal of a king is a kind of man-eater," nor, indeed, were there ever kings who deserved to be compared with Epaminondas, Pericles, Themistocles, Manius Curius, or Hamilcar, surnamed Barcas.

He used to say, too, that his enemies envied him because he had to get up every day before light and neglect his own business to follow that of the public.

He would also tell you that he had rather be deprived of the reward for doing well than not to suffer the punishment for doing ill; and that he could pardon all offenders but himself.

The Romans having sent three ambassadors to Bithynia, of whom one was gouty, another had his skull trepanned, and the other seemed little better than a fool, Cato, laughing, gave out that the Romans had sent an embassy which had neither feet, head, nor heart.

His interest being entreated by Scipio, on account of Polybius, for the Achæan exiles, and there happening to be a great discussion in the senate about it, some being for, and some against their return, Cato, standing up, thus delivered himself: "Here do we sit all day long, as if we had nothing to do but beat our brains whether these old Greeks should be carried to their graves by the bearers here or by those in Achæa."

The senate voting their return, it seems that a few days after Polybius's friends further wished that it should be further moved in the senate that the said banished persons should receive again the honours which they first had in Achæa; and to this purpose they sounded Cato for his opinion; but he, smiling, answered, that Polybius, Ulysses like, having escaped out of the Cyclops' den, wanted, it would seem, to go back again because he had left his cap and belt behind him.

He used to assert, also, that wise men profited more by fools, than fools by wise men; for that wise men avoided the faults of fools, but that fools would not imitate the good examples of wise men.

He would profess, too, that he was more taken with young men that blushed than with those who looked pale; and that he never desired to have a soldier that moved his hands too much in marching, and his feet too much in fighting, or snored louder than he shouted.

Ridiculing a fat, overgrown man: "What use," said he, "can the state turn a man's body to, when all between the throat and groin is taken up by the belly?"

When one who was much given to pleasures desired his acquaintance, begging his pardon, he said he could not live with a man whose palate was of a quicker sense than his heart.

He would likewise say that the soul of a lover lived in the body of another: and that in his whole life he most repented of three things; one was, that he had trusted a secret to a woman; another that he went by water when he might have gone by land; the third, that he had remained one whole day without doing any business of moment.

Applying himself to an old man who was committing some vice: "Friend," said he, "old age has of itself blemishes enough; do not you add to it the deformity of vice."

Speaking to a tribune, who was reputed a poisoner, and was very violent for the bringing in of a bill, in order to make a certain law: "Young man," cried he, "I know not which would be better, to drink what you mix, or confirm what you would put up for a law."

Being reviled by a fellow who lived a profligate and wicked life: "A contest," replied he, "is unequal between you and me: for you can hear ill words easily, and can as easily give them; but it is unpleasant to me to give such, and unusual to hear them." Such was his manner of expressing himself in his memorable sayings.

Being chosen consul, with his friend and familiar, Valerius Flaccus, the government of that part of Spain which the Romans called the Hither Spain fell to his lot. Here, as he was engaged in reducing some of the tribes by force, and bringing over others by good words, a large army of barbarians fell upon him, so that there was danger of being disgracefully forced out again. He therefore called upon his neighbours, the Celtiberians, for help; and on their demanding two hundred talents for their assistance, everybody else thought it intolerable that even the Romans should promise barbarians a reward for their aid; but Cato said there was no discredit or harm in it; for, if they overcame, they would pay them out of the enemy's purse, and not out of their own; but if they were overcome, there would be nobody left either to demand the reward or to pay it. However, he won that battle completely, and, after that, all his other affairs succeeded splendidly.

Polybius says that, by his command, the walls of all the cities on this side the river Bætis were in one day's time demolished, and yet there were a great many of them full of brave and warlike men. Cato himself says that he took more cities than he stayed days in Spain. Neither is this a mere rhodomontade, if it be true that the number was four hundred.

And though the soldiers themselves had got much in the fights, yet he distributed a pound of silver to every man of them, saying, it was better that many of the Romans should return home with silver, rather than a few with gold.

For himself, he affirms, that of all the things that were taken, nothing came to him beyond what he ate and drank. "Neither do I find fault," continued he, "with those that seek to profit by these spoils, but I had rather compete in valour with the best, than in wealth with the richest, or with the most covetous in love of money." Nor did he merely keep himself clear from taking anything, but even all those who more immediately belonged to him. He had five servants with him in the army; one of whom called Paccus, bought three boys out of those who were taken captive; which Cato coming to understand, the man, rather than venture into his presence, hanged himself. Cato sold the boys, and carried the price he got for them into the public exchequer.

Scipio the Great, being his enemy, and desiring, whilst he was carrying all things so successfully, to obstruct him, and take the affairs of Spain into his own hands, succeeded in getting himself appointed his successor in the government, and, making all possible haste, put a term to Cato's authority. But he, taking with him a convoy of five cohorts of foot and five hundred horse to attend him home, overthrew by the way the Lacetanians, and taking from them six hundred deserters, caused them all to be beheaded; upon which

Scipio seemed to be in indignation, but Cato, in mock disparagement of himself, said, "Rome would become great indeed, if the most honourable and great men would not yield up the first place of valour to those who were more obscure, and when they who were of the commonalty (as he himself was) would contend in valour with those who were most eminent in birth and honour."

The senate having voted to change nothing of what had been established by Cato, the government passed away under Scipio to no manner of purpose, in idleness and doing nothing; and so diminished his credit much more than Cato's. Nor did Cato, who now received a triumph, remit after this and slacken the reins of virtue, as many do, who strive not so much for virtue's sake, as for vainglory, and having attained the highest honours, as the consulship and triumphs, pass the rest of their life in pleasure and idleness, and quit all public affairs. But he, like those who are just entered upon public life for the first time, and thirst after gaining honour and glory in some new office, strained himself, as if he were but just setting out; and offering still publicly his service to his friends and citizens, would give up neither his pleadings nor his soldiery.

He accompanied and assisted Tiberius Sempronius, as his lieutenant, when he went into Thrace and to the Danube; and, in the quality of tribune, went with Manius Acilius into Greece, against Antiochus the Great, who, after Hannibal, more than any one struck terror into the Romans. For having reduced once more under a single command almost the whole of Asia, all, namely, that Seleucus Nicator had possessed, and having brought into obedience many warlike nations of the barbarians, he longed to fall upon the Romans, as if they only were now worthy to fight with him.

So across he came with his forces, pretending, as a specious cause of the war, that it was to free the Greeks, who had indeed no need of it, they having been but newly delivered from the power of king Philip and the Macedonians, and made independent, with the free use of their own laws, by the goodness of the Romans themselves: so that all Greece was in commotion and excitement, having been corrupted by the hopes of royal aid which the popular leaders in their cities put them into.

Manius, therefore, sent ambassadors to the different cities; and Titus Flamininus (as is written in the account of him) suppressed and quieted most of the attempts of the innovators, without any trouble. Cato brought over the Corinthians, those of Patræ and Ægium, and spent a good deal of time at Athens. There is also an oration of his said to be extant which he spoke in Greek to the people, in which he expressed his admiration of the virtue of the ancient Athenians, and signified that he came with a great deal of pleasure to be a spectator of the beauty and greatness of their city.

But this is a fiction; for he spoke to the Athenians by an interpreter, though he was able to have spoken himself; but he wished to observe the usage of his own country, and laughed at those who admired nothing but what was in Greek. Jesting upon Postumius Albinus, who had written an historical work in Greek, and requested that allowances might be made for his attempt, he said that allowance indeed might be made if he had done it under the express compulsion of an Amphictyonic decree. The Athenians, he says, admired the quickness and vehemence of his speech; for an interpreter would be very long in repeating what he expressed with a great deal of brevity; but on the whole he professed to believe that the words of the Greeks came only from their lips, whilst those of the Romans came from their hearts.

Now Antiochus, having occupied with his army the narrow passages about Thermopylæ, and added palisades and walls to the natural fortifications of the place, sat down there, thinking he had done enough to divert the war; and the Romans, indeed, seemed wholly to despair of forcing the passage; but Cato, calling to mind the compass and circuit which the Persians had formerly made to come at this place, went forth in the night, taking along with him part of the army.

Whilst they were climbing up, the guide, who was a prisoner, missed the way, and wandering up and down by impracticable and precipitous paths, filled the soldiers with fear and despondency. Cato perceiving the danger, commanded all the rest to halt, and stay where they were, whilst he himself, taking along with him one Lucius Manlius, a most expert man at climbing mountains, went forward with a great deal of labour and danger, in the dark night, and without the least moonlight, among the wild olive-trees and steep craggy rocks, there being nothing but precipices and darkness before their eyes, till they struck into a little pass which they thought might lead down into the enemy's camp. There they put up marks upon some conspicuous peaks which surmount the hill called Callidromon, and, returning again, they led the army along with them to the said marks, till they got into their little path again, and there once made a halt; but when they began to go further, the path deserted them at a precipice, where they were in another strait and fear; nor did they perceive that they were all this while near the enemy.

And now the day began to give some light, when they seemed to hear a noise, and presently after to see the Greek trenches and the guard at the foot of the rock. Here, therefore, Cato halted his forces, and commanded the troops from Firmum only, without the rest, to stick by him, as he had always found them faithful and ready. And when they came up and formed around him in close order, he thus spoke to them: "I desire," he said, "to take one of the enemy alive, that so I may understand what men these are who guard the passage; their number; and with what discipline, order, and preparation they expect us; but this feat," continued he, "must be an act of a great deal of quickness and boldness, such as that of lions, when they dart upon some timorous animal."

Cato had no sooner thus expressed himself, but the Firmans forthwith rushed down the mountain, just as they were, upon the guard, and, falling unexpectedly upon them, affrighted and dispersed them all. One armed man they took, and brought to Cato, who quickly learned from him that the rest of the forces lay in the narrow passage about the king; that those who kept the tops of the rocks were six hundred choice Ætolians. Cato, therefore, despising the smallness of their number and carelessness, forthwith drawing his sword, fell upon them with a great noise of trumpets and shouting. The enemy, perceiving them thus tumbling, as it were, upon them from the precipices, flew to the main body, and put all things into disorder there.

In the meantime, whilst Manius was forcing the works below, and pouring the thickest of his forces into the narrow passages, Antiochus was hit in the mouth with a stone, so that his teeth being beaten out by it, he felt such excessive pain, that he was fain to turn away with his horse; nor did any part of his army stand the shock of the Romans. Yet, though there seemed no reasonable hope of flight, where all paths were so difficult, and

where there were deep marshes and steep rocks, which looked as if they were ready to receive those who should stumble, the fugitives, nevertheless, crowding and pressing together in the narrow passages, destroyed even one another in their terror of the swords and blows of the enemy.

Cato (as it plainly appears) was never oversparing of his own praises, and seldom shunned boasting of any exploit; which quality, indeed, he seems to have thought the natural accompaniment of great actions; and with these particular exploits he was highly puffed up; he says that those who saw him that day pursuing and slaying the enemies were ready to assert that Cato owed not so much to the public as the public did to Cato; nay, he adds, that Manius the consul, coming hot from the fight, embraced him for a great while, when both were all in a sweat; and then cried out with joy that neither he himself, no, nor all the people together, could make him a recompense equal to his actions.

After the fight he was sent to Rome, that he himself might be the messenger of it: and so, with a favourable wind, he sailed to Brundusium, and in one day got from thence to Tarentum; and having travelled four days more, upon the fifth, counting from the time of his landing, he arrived at Rome, and so brought the first news of the victory himself; and filled the whole city with joy and sacrifices, and the people with the belief that they were able to conquer every sea and every land.

These are pretty nearly all the eminent actions of Cato relating to military affairs: in civil policy, he was of opinion that one chief duty consisted in accusing and indicting criminals. He himself prosecuted many, and he would also assist others who prosecuted them, nay, would even procure such, as he did the Petilii against Scipio; but not being able to destroy him, by reason of the nobleness of his family, and the real greatness of his mind, which enabled him to trample all calumnies under foot, Cato at last would meddle no more with him; yet joining with the accusers against Scipio's brother Lucius, he succeeded in obtaining a sentence against him, which condemned him to the payment of a large sum of money to the state; and being insolvent, and in danger of being thrown into jail, he was, by the interposition of the tribunes of the people, with much ado dismissed.

It is also said of Cato, that when he met a

certain youth, who had effected the disgrace of one of his father's enemies, walking in the market-place, he shook him by the hand, telling him, that this was what we ought to sacrifice to our dead parents—not lambs and goats, but the tears and condemnations of their adversaries.

But neither did he himself escape with impunity in his management of affairs; for if he gave his enemies but the least hold, he was still in danger, and exposed to be brought to justice. He is reported to have escaped at least fifty indictments; and one above the rest, which was the last, when he was eighty-six years old, about which time he uttered the well-known saying, that it was hard for him who had lived with one generation of men, to plead now before another. Neither did he make this the least of his lawsuits; for, four years after, when he was fourscore and ten, he accused Servilius Galba: so that his life and actions extended, we may say, as Nestor's did, over three ordinary ages of man. For, having had many contests, as we have related, with Scipio the Great, about affairs of state, he continued them down to Scipio the younger, who was the adopted grandson of the former, and the son of that Paulus who overthrew Perseus and the Macedonians.

Ten years after his consulship, Cato stood for the office of censor, which was indeed the summit of all honour, and in a manner the highest step in civil affairs; for besides all other power, it had also that of an inquisition into every one's life and manners.

For the Romans thought that no marriage, or rearing of children, nay, no feast or drinking-bout, ought to be permitted according to every one's appetite or fancy, without being examined and inquired into; being indeed of opinion that a man's character was much sooner perceived in things of this sort than in what is done publicly and in open day.

They chose, therefore, two persons, one out of the patricians, the other out of the commons, who were to watch, correct, and punish, if any one ran too much into voluptuousness, or transgressed the usual manner of life of his country; and these they called Censors. They had power to take away a horse, or expel out of the senate any one who lived intemperately and out of order. It was also their business to take an estimate of what every one was worth, and to put down in registers everybody's birth and quality; besides many other prerogatives.

And therefore the chief nobility opposed his pretensions to it. Jealousy prompted the patricians, who thought that it would be a stain to everybody's nobility, if men of no original honour should rise to the highest dignity and power; while others, conscious of their own evil practices, and of the violation of the laws and customs of their country, were afraid of the austerity of the man; which, in an office of such great power, was likely to prove most uncompromising and severe. And so, consulting among themselves, they brought forward seven candidates in opposition to him, who sedulously set themselves to court the people's favour by fair promises, as though what they wished for was indulgent and easy government.

Cato, on the contrary, promising no such mildness, but plainly threatening evil livers, from the very hustings openly declared himself, and exclaiming that the city needed a great and thorough purgation, called upon the people, if they were wise, not to choose the gentlest, but the roughest of physicians; such a one, he said, he was, and Valerius Flaccus, one of the patricians, another; together with him, he doubted not but he should do something worth the while, and that by cutting to pieces and burning like a hydra all luxury and voluptuousness. He added, too, that he saw all the rest endeavouring after the office with ill intent, because they were afraid of those who would exercise it justly, as they ought. And so truly great and so worthy of great men to be its leaders were, it would seem, the Roman people, that they did not fear the severity and grim countenance of Cato, but rejecting those smooth promisers who were ready to do all things to ingratiate themselves, they took him, together with Flaccus; obeying his recommendations not as though he were a candidate, but as if he had had the actual power of commanding and governing already.

Cato named, as chief of the senate, his friend and colleague Lucius Valerius Flaccus, and expelled, among many others, Lucius Quintius, who had been consul seven years before, and (which was greater honour to him than the consulship) brother to that Titus Flamininus who overthrew King Philip. The reason he had for his expulsion was this. Lucius, it seems, took along with him in all his commands a youth whom he had kept as his companion from the flower of his age, and to whom he gave as much power and respect as to the chiefest of his friends and relations.

Now it happened that Lucius being consular governor of one of the provinces, the youth setting himself down by him, as he used to do, among other flatteries with which he played upon him, when he was in his cups, told him he loved him so dearly that, "though there was a show of gladiators to be seen at Rome, and I," he said, "had never beheld one in my life; and though I, as it were, longed to see a man killed, yet I made all possible haste to come to you." Upon this Lucius, returning his fondness, replied, "Do not be melancholy on that account; I can remedy that." Ordering therefore, forthwith, one of those condemned to die to be brought to the feast, together with the headsman and axe, he asked the youth if he wished to see him executed. The boy answering that he did, Lucius commanded the executioner to cut off his neck; and this several historians mention; and Cicero, indeed, in his dialogue de Senectute, introduces Cato relating it himself. But Livy says that he that was killed was a Gaulish deserter, and that Lucius did not execute him by the stroke of the executioner, but with his own hand; and that it is so stated in Cato's speech.

Lucius being thus expelled out of the senate by Cato, his brother took it very ill, and appealing to the people, desired that Cato should declare his reasons; and when he began to relate this transaction of the feast, Lucius endeavoured to deny it; but Cato challenging him to a formal investigation, he fell off and refused it, so that he was then acknowledged to suffer deservedly. Afterwards, however, when there was some show at the theatre, he passed by the seats where those who had been consuls used to be placed, and taking his seat a great way off, excited the compassion of the common people, who presently with a great noise made him go forward, and as much as they could tried to set right and salve over what had happened. Manilius, also, who, according to the public expectation, would have been next consul, he threw out of the senate, because, in the presence of his daughter, and in open day, he had kissed his wife. He said that, as for himself, his wife never came into his arms except when there was great thunder; (so that it was a jest with him that it was a pleasure for him when Jupiter thundered).

His treatment of Lucius, likewise the brother of Scipio, and one who had been honoured with a triumph, occasioned some odium against Cato; for he took his horse from him, and was thought to do it with a design of putting an affront on Scipio Africanus, now dead. But he gave most general annoyance by retrenching people's luxury; for though (most of the youth being thereby already corrupted) it seemed almost impossible to take it away with an open hand and directly, yet going, as it were, obliquely around, he caused all dress carriages, women's ornaments, household furniture, whose price exceeded one thousand five hundred drachmas, to be rated at ten times as much as they were worth; intending by thus making the assessments greater, to increase the taxes paid upon them. He also ordained that upon every thousand asses of property of this kind, three should be paid, so that people, burdened with these extra charges, and seeing others of as good estates, but more frugal and sparing, paying less into the public exchequer, might be tired out of their prodigality.

And thus, on the one side, not only those were disgusted at Cato who bore the taxes for the sake of their luxury, but those, too, who on the other side laid by their luxury for fear of the taxes. For people in general reckon that an order not to display their riches is equivalent to the taking away of their riches, because riches are seen much more in superfluous than in necessary things. Indeed this was what excited the wonder of Ariston, the philosopher; that we account those who possess superfluous things more happy than those who abound with what is necessary and useful. But when one of his friends asked Scopas, the rich Thessalian, to give him some article of no great utility, saying that it was not a thing that he had any great need or use for himself, "In truth," replied he, "it is just these useless and unnecessary things that make my wealth and happiness." Thus the desire of riches does not proceed from a natural passion within us, but arises rather from vulgar out-of-doors opinion of other people.

Cato, notwithstanding, being little solicitous as to those who exclaimed against him, increased his austerity. He caused the pipes, through which some persons brought the public water into their houses and gardens, to be cut, and threw down all buildings which jutted out into the common streets. He beat down also the price in contracts for public works to the lowest, and raised it in contracts for farming the taxes to the highest sum; by which proceedings he drew a great deal of hatred upon himself.

Those who were of Titus Flamininus's party cancelled in the senate all the bargains and contracts made by him for the repairing and carrying on of the sacred and public buildings as unadvantageous to the commonwealth. They incited also the boldest of the tribunes of the people to accuse him and to fine him two talents. They likewise much opposed him in building the court or basilica, which he caused to be erected at the common charge, just by the senate-house, in the market-place, and called by his own name, the Porcian.

However, the people, it seems, liked his censorship wondrously well; for, setting up a statue for him in the temple of the goddess of Health, they put an inscription under it, not recording his commands in war or his triumph, but to the effect that this was Cato the Censor, who, by his good discipline and wise and temperate ordinances, reclaimed the Roman commonwealth when it was declining and sinking down into vice. Before this honour was done to himself, he used to laugh at those who loved such kind of things, saying that they did not see that they were taking pride in the workmanship of brass-founders and painters; whereas the citizens bore about his best likeness in their breasts. And when any seemed to wonder that he should have never a statue, while many ordinary persons had one, "I would," said he, "much rather be asked, why I have not one, than why I have one." In short, he would not have any honest citizen endure to be praised, except it might prove advantageous to the commonwealth.

Yet still he had passed the highest commendation on himself; for he tells us that those who did anything wrong, and were found fault with, used to say it was not worth while to blame them, for they were not Catos. He also adds, that they who awkwardly mimicked some of his actions were called "left-handed Catos"; and that the senate in perilous times would cast their eyes on him, as upon a pilot in a ship, and that often when he was not present they put off affairs of greatest consequence. These things are indeed also testified of him by others; for he had a great authority in the city, alike for his life, his eloquence, and his age.

He was also a good father, an excellent husband to his wife, and an extraordinary economist; and as he did not manage his affairs of this kind carelessly, and as things of little moment, I think I ought to record a little further whatever was commendable in him in these points. He married a wife more noble than rich; being of opinion that the rich and the high-born are equally haughty and proud; but that those of noble blood would be more ashamed of base things, and consequently more obedient to their husbands in all that was fit and right. A man who beat his wife or child laid violent hands, he said, on what was most sacred; and a good husband he reckoned worthy of more praise than a great senator; and he admired the ancient Socrates for nothing so much as for having lived a temperate and contented life with a wife who was a scold, and children who were half-witted.

As soon as he had a son born, though he had never such urgent business upon his hands, unless it were some public matter, he would be by when his wife washed it and dressed it in its swaddling clothes. For she herself suckled it; nay, she often, too, gave her breast to her servants' children, to produce, by suckling the same milk, a kind of natural love in them to her son. When he began to come to years of discretion, Cato himself would teach him to read, although he had a servant, a very good grammarian, called Chilo, who taught many others; but he thought not fit, as he himself said, to have his son reprimanded by a slave, or pulled, it may be, by the ears when found tardy in his lesson: nor would he have him owe to a servant the obligation of so great a thing as his learning; he himself, therefore (as we were saying), taught him his grammar, law, and his gymnastic exercises. Nor did he only show him, too, how to throw a dart, to fight in armour, and to ride, but to box also and to endure both heat and cold, and to swim over the most rapid and rough rivers. He says, likewise, that he wrote histories, in large characters, with his own hand, that so his son, without stirring out of the house, might learn to know about his countrymen and forefathers; nor did he less abstain from speaking anything obscene before his son, than if it had been in the presence of the sacred virgins, called vestals. Nor would he ever go into the bath with him; which seems indeed to have been the common custom of the Romans. Sons-in-law used to avoid bathing with fathers-in-law, disliking to see one another naked; but having, in time, learned of the Greeks to strip before men, they have since taught the Greeks to do it even with the women themselves.

Thus, like an excellent work, Cato formed and fashioned his son to virtue; nor had he any occasion to find fault with his readiness and docility; but as he proved to be of too weak a constitution for hardships, he did not insist on requiring of him any very austere way of living. However, though delicate in health, he proved a stout man in the field, and behaved himself valiantly when Paulus Æmilius fought against Perseus; where when his sword was struck from him by a blow, or rather slipped out of his hand by reason of its moistness, he so keenly resented it, that he turned to some of his friends about him, and taking them along with him again, fell upon the enemy; and having by a long fight and much force cleared the place, at length found it among great heaps of arms, and the dead bodies of friends as well as enemies piled one upon another. Upon which Paulus, his general, much commended the youth; and there is a letter of Cato's to his son, which highly praises his honourable eagerness for the recovery of his sword. Afterwards he married Tertie, Æmilius Paulus's daughter, and sister to Scipio; nor was he admitted into this family less for his own worth than his father's. So that Cato's care in his son's education came to a very fitting result.

He purchased a great many slaves out of the captives taken in war, but chiefly bought up the young ones, who were capable to be, as it were, broken and taught like whelps and colts. None of these ever entered another man's house, except sent either by Cato himself or his wife. If any one of them were asked what Cato did, they answered merely that they did not know.

When a servant was at home, he was obliged either to do some work or sleep, for indeed Cato loved those most who used to lie down often to sleep, accounting them more docile than those who were wakeful, and more fit for anything when they were refreshed with a little slumber. Being also of opinion that the great cause of the laziness and misbehaviour of slaves was their running after their pleasures, he fixed a certain price for them to pay for permission amongst themselves, but would suffer no connections out of the house.

At first, when he was but a poor soldier, he would not be difficult in anything which related to his eating, but looked upon it as a pitiful thing to quarrel with a servant for the belly's sake; but afterwards, when he grew richer, and made any feasts for his friends and colleagues in office, as soon as supper was over he used to go with a leathern thong and scourge those who had waited or dressed the meat carelessly.

He always contrived, too, that his servants should have some difference one among another, always suspecting and fearing a good understanding between them. Those who had committed anything worthy of death, he punished if they were found guilty by the verdict of their fellow-servants.

But being after all much given to the desire of gain, he looked upon agriculture rather as a pleasure than profit; resolving, therefore, to lay out his money in safe and solid things, he purchased ponds, hot baths, grounds full of fuller's earth, remunerative lands, pastures, and woods; from all which he drew large returns, nor could Jupiter himself, he used to say, do him much damage.

He was also given to the form of usury, which is considered most odious, in traffic by sea; and that thus:—he desired that those whom he put out his money to should have many partners; when the number of them and their ships came to be fifty, he himself took one share through Quintio his freedman, who therefore was to sail with the adventurers, and take a part in all their proceedings, so that thus there was no danger of losing his whole stock, but only a little part, and that with a prospect of great profit.

He likewise lent money to those of his slaves who wished to borrow, with which they bought also other young ones, whom, when they had taught and bred up at his charges, they would sell again at the year's end; but some of them Cato would keep for himself, giving just as much for them as another had offered.

To incline his son to be of his kind or temper, he used to tell him that it was not like a man, but rather like a widow woman, to lessen an estate. But the strongest indication of Cato's avaricious humour was when he took the boldness to affirm that he was a most wonderful, nay, a godlike man, who left more behind him than he had received.

He was now grown old, when Carneades the Academic, and Diogenes the Stoic, came as deputies from Athens to Rome, praying for release from a penalty of five hundred talents laid on the Athenians, in a suit, to which they did not appear, in which the Oropians were plaintiffs and Sicyonians judges. All the most studious youth immediately waited on these philosophers, and frequently, with admiration, heard them speak. But the gracefulness of Carneades's oratory, whose ability was really greatest, and his reputation equal to it, gathered large and favourable audiences, and ere long filled, like a wind, all the city with the sound of it. So that it soon began to be told that a Greek, famous even to admiration, winning and carrying all before him, had impressed so strange a love upon the young men, that quitting all their pleasures and pastimes, they ran mad, as it were, after philosophy; which indeed much pleased the Romans in general; nor could they but with much pleasure see the youth receive so welcomely the Greek literature, and frequent the company of learned men.

But Cato, on the other side, seeing the passion for words flowing into the city, from the beginning took it ill, fearing lest the youth should be diverted that way, and so should prefer the glory of speaking well before that of arms and doing well. And when the fame of the Philosophers increased in the city, and Caius Acilius, a person of distinction, at his own request, became their interpreter to the senate at their first audience, Cato resolved, under some specious pretence, to have all philosophers cleared out of the city; and, coming into the senate, blamed the magistrates for letting these deputies stay so long a time without being despatched, though they were persons that could easily persuade the people to what they pleased; that therefore in all haste something should be determined about their petition, that so they might go home again in their own schools, and declaim to the Greek children, and leave the Roman youth to be obedient, as hitherto, to their own laws and governors.

Yet he did this not out of any anger, as some think, to Carneades; but because he wholly despised philosophy, and out of a kind of pride scoffed at the Greek studies and literature; as, for example, he would say, that Socrates was a prating, seditious fellow, who did his best to tyrannise over his country, to undermine the ancient customs, and to entice and withdraw the citizens to opinions contrary to the laws. Ridiculing the school of Isocrates, he would add, that his scholars grew old men before they had done learning with him, as if they were to use their art and plead

causes in the court of Minos in the next world. And to frighten his son from anything that was Greek, in a more vehement tone than became one of his age, he pronounced, as it were, with the voice of an oracle, that the Romans would certainly be destroyed when they began once to be infected with Greek literature; though time indeed has shown the vanity of this his prophecy; as, in truth, the city of Rome has risen to its highest fortune while entertaining Grecian learning.

Nor had he an aversion only against the Greek philosophers, but the physicians also; for having, it seems, heard how Hippocrates, when the king of Persia sent for him with offers of a fee of several talents, said that he would never assist barbarians who were enemies to the Greeks; he affirmed that this was now become a common oath taken by all physicians, and enjoined his son to have a care and avoid them; for that he himself had written a little book of prescriptions for curing those who were sick in his family; he never enjoined fasting to any one, but ordered them either vegetables, or the meat of a duck, pigeon, or leveret; such kind of diet being of light digestion and fit for sick folks, only it made those who ate it dream a little too much; and by the use of this kind of physic, he said, he not only made himself and those about him well, but kept them so.

However, for this his presumption he seemed not to have escaped unpunished; for he lost both his wife and his son; though he himself, being of a strong, robust constitution, held out longer; so that he would often, even in his old days, address himself to women, and when he was past a lover's age, married a young woman, upon the following pretence: Having lost his own wife, he married his son to the daughter of Paulus Æmilius, who was sister to Scipio; so that being now a widower himself, he had a young girl who came privately to visit him, but the house being very small, and a daughter-in-law also in it, this practice was quickly discovered; for the young woman seeming once to pass through it a little too boldly, the youth, his son, though he said nothing, seemed to look somewhat indignantly upon her.

The old man perceiving and understanding that what he did was disliked, without finding any fault or saying a word, went away, as his custom was, with his usual companions to the market: and among the rest, he called aloud to one Salonius, who had been a clerk under him, and asked him whether he had married his daughter. He answered no, nor would he, till he had consulted him. Said Cato, "Then I have found out a fit son-in-law for you, if he should not displease by reason of his age; for in all other points there is no fault to be found in him; but he is indeed, as I said, extremely old." However, Salonius desired him to undertake the business, and to give the young girl to whom he pleased, she being a humble servant of his, who stood in need of his care and patronage. Upon this Cato, without any more ado, told him he desired to have the damsel himself. These words, as may well be imagined, at first astonished the man, conceiving that Cato was as far off from marrying, as he from a likelihood of being allied to the family of one who had been consul and had triumphed; but perceiving him in earnest, he consented willingly; and going onwards to the forum, they quickly completed the bargain.

Whilst the marriage was in hand, Cato's son, taking some of his friends along with him, went and asked his father if it were for any offence he brought in a stepmother upon him. But Cato cried out, "Far from it, my son, I have no fault to find with you or anything of yours; only I desire to have many children, and to leave the commonwealth more such citizens as you are." Pisistratus, the tyrant of Athens, made, they say, this answer to his sons, when they were grown men, when he married his second wife, Timonassa of Argos, by whom he had, it is said, Iophon and Thessalus. Cato had a son by his second wife, to whom, from his mother, he gave the surname of Salonius.

In the meantime, his eldest died in his prætorship; of whom Cato often makes mention in his books, as having been a good man. He is said, however, to have borne the loss moderately and like a philosopher, and was nothing the more remiss in attending to affairs of state; so that he did not, as Lucius Lucullus and Metellus Pius did, grow languid in his old age, as though public business were a duty once to be discharged, and then quitted; nor did he, like Scipio Africanus, because envy had struck at his glory, turn from the public, and change and pass away the rest of his life without doing anything; but as one persuaded Dionysius, that the most honourable tomb he could have would be to die in the exercise of his dominion; so Cato thought that old age to be the most honourable which was busied

in public affairs; though he would, now and then, when he had leisure, recreate himself with husbandry and writing.

And, indeed, he composed various books and histories; and in his youth he addicted himself to agriculture for profit's sake; for he used to say he had but two ways of getting—agriculture and parsimony; and now, in his old age, the first of these gave him both occupation and a subject of study. He wrote one book on country matters, in which he treated particularly even of making cakes and preserving fruit, it being his ambition to be curious and singular in all things.

His suppers, at his country-house, used also to be plentiful; he daily invited his friends and neighbours about him, and passed the time merrily with them; so that his company was not only agreeable to those of the same age, but even to younger men; for he had had experience in many things, and had been concerned in much, both by word and deed, that was worth the hearing. He looked upon a good table as the best place for making friends; where the commendations of brave and good citizens were usually introduced, and little said of base and unworthy ones; as Cato would not give leave in his company to have anything, either good or ill, said about them.

Some will have the overthrow of Carthage to have been one of his last acts of state; when, indeed, Scipio the younger did by his valour give it the last blow, but the war, chiefly by the counsel and advice of Cato, was undertaken on the following occasion. Cato was sent to the Carthaginians and Masinissa, King of Numidia, who were at war with one another, to know the cause of their difference. He, it seems, had been a friend of the Romans from the beginning; and they, too, since they were conquered by Scipio, were of the Roman confederacy, having been shorn of their power by loss of territory and a heavy tax.

Finding Carthage, not (as the Romans thought) low and in an ill condition, but well manned, full of riches and all sorts of arms and ammunition, and perceiving the Carthaginians carry it high, he conceived that it was not a time for the Romans to adjust affairs between them and Masinissa; but rather that they themselves would fall into danger, unless they should find means to check this rapid new growth of Rome's ancient irreconcilable enemy. Therefore, returning quickly to Rome, he acquainted the senate that the former defeats and blows given to the Carthaginians had not so much diminished their strength, as it had abated their imprudence and folly; that they were not become weaker, but more experienced in war, and did only skirmish with the Numidians to exercise themselves the better to cope with the Romans; that the peace and league they had made was but a kind of suspension of war which awaited a fairer opportunity to break out again.

Moreover, they say that, shaking his gown, he took occasion to let drop some African figs before the senate. And on their admiring the size and beauty of them, he presently added that the place that bore them was but three days' sail from Rome. Nay, he never after this gave his opinion, but at the end he would be sure to come out with this sentence, "ALSO, CARTHAGE, METHINKS, OUGHT UTTERLY TO BE DESTROYED." But Publius Scipio Nasica would always declare his opinion to the contrary, in these words, "It seems requisite to me that Carthage should still stand."

For seeing his countrymen to be grown wanton and insolent, and the people made, by their prosperity, obstinate and disobedient to the senate, and drawing the whole city, whither they would, after them, he would have had the fear of Carthage to serve as a bit to hold the contumacy of the multitude; and he looked upon the Carthaginians as too weak to overcome the Romans, and too great to be despised by them. On the other side, it seemed a perilous thing to Cato that a city which had been always great, and was now grown sober and wise, by reason of its former calamities, should still lie, as it were, in wait for the follies and dangerous excesses of the over-powerful Roman people; so that he thought it the wisest course to have all outward dangers removed, when they had so many inward ones among themselves.

Thus Cato, they say, stirred up the third and last war against the Carthaginians: but no sooner was the said war begun, than he died, prophesying of the person that should put an end to it who was then only a young man; but, being tribune in the army, he in several fights gave proof of his courage and conduct. The news of which being brought to Cato's ears at Rome, he thus expressed himself:—

The only wise man of them all is he,
The others e'en as shadows flit and flee.

This prophecy Scipio soon confirmed by his actions.

Cato left no posterity, except one son by his second wife, who was named, as we said, Cato Salonius; and a grandson by his eldest son, who died. Cato Salonius died when he was prætor, but his son Marcus was afterwards consul, and he was grandfather of Cato, the philosopher, who for virtue and renown was one of the most eminent personages of his time.

ARISTIDES and MARCUS CATO
Compared

HAVING mentioned the most memorable actions of these great men, if we now compare the whole life of the one with that of the other, it will not be easy to discern the difference between them, lost as it is amongst such a number of circumstances in which they resemble each other. If, however, we examine them in detail, as we might some piece of poetry, or some picture, we shall find this common to them both, that they advanced themselves to great honour and dignity in the commonwealth by no other means than their own virtue and industry.

But it seems when Aristides appeared, Athens was not at its height of grandeur and plenty, the chief magistrates and officers of his time being men only of moderate and equal fortunes among themselves. The estimate of the greatest estates then was five hundred medimns; that of the second, or knights, three hundred; of the third and last called Zeugitæ, two hundred.

But Cato, out of a petty village from a country life, leaped into the commonwealth, as it were, into a vast ocean; at a time when there were no such governors as the Curii, Fabricii, and Hostilii. Poor labouring men were not then advanced from the plough and spade to be governors and magistrates; but greatness of family, riches, profuse gifts, distributions, and personal application were what the city looked to; keeping a high hand, and, in a manner, insulting over those that courted preferment. It was not as great a matter to have Themistocles for an adversary, a person of mean extraction and small fortune (for he was not worth, it is said, more than four or five talents when he first applied himself to public affairs), as to contest with a Scipio Africanus, a Servius Galba, and a Quintius Flamininus, having no other aid but a tongue free to assert right.

Besides, Aristides at Marathon, and again at Platæa, was but one commander out of ten; whereas Cato was chosen consul with a single colleague, having many competitors, and with a single colleague, also, was preferred before seven most noble and eminent pretenders to be censor. But Aristides was never principal in any action; for Miltiades carried the day at Marathon, at Salamis, Themistocles, and at Platæa, Herodotus tells us, Pausanias got the glory of that noble victory: and men like Sophanes, and Aminias, Callimachus, and Cynægyrus, behaved themselves so well in all those engagements as to contest it with Aristides even for the second place.

But Cato not only in his consulship was esteemed the chief in courage and conduct in the Spanish war, but even whilst he was only serving as tribune at Thermopylæ, under another's command, he gained the glory of the victory, for having, as it were, opened a wide gate for the Romans to rush in upon Antiochus, and for having brought the war on his back, whilst he only minded what was before his face. For that victory, which was beyond dispute all Cato's own work, cleared Asia out of Greece, and by that means made way afterwards for Scipio into Asia.

Both of them, indeed, were always victorious in war; but at home Aristides stumbled, being banished and oppressed by the faction of Themistocles; yet Cato, notwithstanding he had almost all the chief and most powerful of Rome for his adversaries, and wrestled with them even to his old age, kept still his footing. Engaging also in many public suits, sometimes plaintiff, sometimes defendant, he cast the most, and came off clear with all; thanks to his eloquence, that bulwark and powerful instrument to which more truly, than to chance or his fortune, he owed it, that he sustained himself unhurt to the last. Antipater justly gives it as a high commendation to Aristotle, the philosopher, writing of him after his death, that among his other virtues, he was endowed with a faculty of persuading people which way he pleased.

Questionless, there is no perfecter endowment in man than political virtue, and of this Economics is commonly esteemed not the least part; for a city, which is a collection of private households, grows into a stable commonwealth by the private means of prosperous citizens that compose it. Lycurgus by prohibiting gold and silver in Sparta, and making iron, spoiled by the fire, the only currency, did not by these measures discharge them from minding their household affairs, but cutting off luxury, the corruption and tumour of riches, he provided there should be an abundant supply of all necessary and useful things for all persons, as much as any other lawmaker ever did; being more apprehensive of a poor, needy, and indigent member of a community, than of the rich and haughty. And in this management of domestic concerns, Cato was as great as in the government of public affairs; for he increased his estate, and became a master to others in economy and husbandry; upon which subjects he collected in his writings many useful observations.

On the contrary Aristides, by his poverty, made justice odious, as if it were the pest and impoverisher of a family, and beneficial to all, rather than to those that were endowed with it. Yet Hesiod urges us alike to just dealing and to care of our households, and inveighs against idleness as the origin of injustice; and Homer admirably says:—

Work was not dear, nor household cares to me,
Whose increase rears the thriving family;
But well-rigged ships were always my delight,
And wars, and darts, and arrows of the fight:

as if the same characters carelessly neglected their own estates, and lived by injustice and rapine from others.

For it is not as the physicians say of oil, that, outwardly applied, it is very wholesome, but taken inwardly detrimental, that thus a just man provides carefully for others, and is heedless of himself and his own affairs; but in this Aristides's political virtues seem to be defective; since, according to most authors, he took no care to leave his daughters a portion, or himself enough to defray his funeral charges: whereas Cato's family produced senators and generals to the fourth generation; his grandchildren, and their children, came to the highest preferments. But Aristides, who was the principal man of Greece, through extreme poverty reduced some of his to get their living by jugglers' tricks, others, for want, to hold out their hands for public alms; leaving none means to perform any noble action, or worthy his dignity.

Yet why should this needs follow? Since poverty is dishonourable not in itself, but when it is a proof of laziness, intemperance, luxury, and carelessness; whereas in a person that is temperate, industrious, just, and valiant, and who uses all his virtues for the public good, it shows a great and lofty mind. For he has no time for great matters who concerns himself with petty ones; nor can he relieve many needs of others, who himself has many needs of his own. What most of all enables a man to serve the public is not wealth, but content and independence; which, requiring no superfluity at home, distracts not the mind from the common good. God alone is entirely exempt from all want: of human virtues, that which needs least is the most absolute and most divine. For as a body bred to a good habit requires nothing exquisite either in clothes or food, so a sound man and a sound household keep themselves up with a small matter. Riches ought to be proportioned to the use we have of them; for he that scrapes together a great deal, making use of but little, is not independent; for if he wants them not, it is folly in him to make provision for things which he does not desire; or if he does desire them, and restrains his enjoyment out of sordidness, he is miserable.

I would fain know of Cato himself, if we seek riches that we may enjoy them, why is he proud of having a great deal, and being contented with little? But if it be noble, as it is, to feed on coarse bread, and drink the same wine with our hinds, and not to covet purple, and plastered houses, neither Aristides, nor Epaminondas, nor Manius Curius, nor Caius Fabricius wanted necessaries, who took no pains to get those things whose use they approved not. For it was not worth the while of a man who esteemed turnips a most delicate food, and who boiled them himself, whilst his wife made bread, to brag so often of a half-penny, and write a book to show how a man may soonest grow rich; the very good of being contented with little is because it cuts off at once the desire and the anxiety for superfluities. Hence Aristides, it is told, said, on the trial of Callias, that it was for them to blush at poverty who were poor against their wills; they who like him were willingly so might glory in it. For it is ridiculous to think Aristides's neediness imputable to his sloth, who might fairly enough by the spoil of one barbarian, or seizing one tent, have become wealthy. But enough of this.

Cato's expeditions added no great matter to the Roman empire, which already was so great, as that in a manner it could receive no addition; but those of Aristides are the noblest, most splendid, and distinguished actions the Grecians ever did, the battles at Marathon, Salamis, and Platæa. Nor indeed is Antiochus, nor the destruction of the walls of the Spanish towns, to be compared with Xerxes, and the destruction by sea and land of so many myriads of enemies; in all of which noble exploits Aristides yielded to none, though he left the glory and the laurels, like the wealth and money, to those who needed and thirsted more greedily after them, because he was superior to those also.

I do not blame Cato for perpetually boasting and preferring himself before all others, though in one of his orations he says that it is equally absurd to praise and dispraise one's self: yet he who does not so much as desire others' praises, seems to me more perfectly virtuous than he who is always extolling himself. A mind free from ambition is a main help to political gentleness; ambition, on the contrary, is hard-hearted, and the greatest fomenter of envy; from which Aristides was wholly exempt; Cato very subject to it.

Aristides assisted Themistocles in matters of highest importance, and, as his subordinate officer, in a manner raised Athens: Cato, by opposing Scipio, almost broke and defeated his expedition against the Carthaginians, in which he overthrew Hannibal, who till then was even invincible; and, at last, by continually raising suspicions and calumnies against him, he chased him from the city, and inflicted a disgraceful sentence on his brother for robbing the state.

Finally, that temperance which Cato always highly cried up, Aristides preserved truly pure and untainted. But Cato's marriage, unbecoming his dignity and age, is a considerable disparagement, in this respect, to his character. For it was not decent for him at that age to bring home to his son and his wife a young woman, the daughter of a common paid clerk in the public service: but whether it were for his own gratification or out of anger at his son, both the fact and the pretence were unworthy. For the reason he pretended to his son was false; for if he desired to get more children as worthy, he ought to have married a well-born wife; not to have contented himself, so long as it was unnoticed, with a woman to whom he was not married; and, when it was discovered, he ought not to have chosen such a father-in-law as was easiest to be got, instead of one whose affinity might be honourable to him.

PHILOPŒMEN

253?–183 B.C.

CLEANDER was a man of high birth and great power in the city of Mantinea, but by the chances of the time happened to be driven from thence. There being an intimate friendship betwixt him and Craugis, the father of Philopœmen, who was a person of great distinction, he settled at Megalopolis, where, while his friend lived, he had all he could desire. When Craugis died, he repaid the father's hospitable kindness in the care of the orphan son; by which means Philopœmen was educated by him, as Homer says Achilles was by Phœnix, and from his infancy moulded to lofty and noble inclinations.

But Ecdemus and Demophanes had the principal tuition of him, after he was past the years of childhood. They were both Megalopolitans; they had been scholars in the academic philosophy, and friends to Arcesilaus, and had, more than any of their contemporaries, brought philosophy to bear upon action and state affairs. They had freed their country from tyranny by the death of Aristodemus, whom they caused to be killed; they had assisted Aratus in driving out the tyrant Nicocles from Sicyon; and, at the request of the Cyreneans, whose city was in a state of extreme disorder and confusion, went thither by sea, and succeeded in establishing good government and happily settling their commonwealth. And among their best actions they themselves counted the education of Philopœmen, thinking they had done a general good to Greece by giving him the nurture of philosophy. And indeed all Greece (which looked upon him as a kind of latter birth brought forth, after so many noble leaders, in her decrepit age) loved him wonderfully; and, as his glory grew, increased his power. And one of the Romans, to praise him, calls him the last of the Greeks; as if after him Greece had produced no great man, nor one deserving the name of Greek.

His person was not, as some fancy, deformed; for his likeness is yet to be seen at Delphi. The mistake of the hostess of Megara was occasioned, it would seem, merely by his easiness of temper and his plain manners. This hostess having word brought her that the general of the Achæans was coming to her house in the absence of her husband, was all in a hurry about providing his supper. Philopœmen, in an ordinary cloak, arriving in this point of time, she took him for one of his own train who had been sent on before, and bid him lend her his hand in her household work. He forthwith threw off his cloak, and fell to cutting up the firewood. The husband returning, and seeing him at it, "What," says he, "may this mean, O Philopœmen?" "I am," replied he in his Doric dialect, "paying the penalty of my ugly looks." Titus Flamininus, jesting with him upon his figure, told him one day he had well-shaped hands and feet, but no belly, and he was indeed slender in the waist. But this raillery was meant to the poverty of his fortune; for he had good horse and foot, but often wanted money to entertain and pay them. These are common anecdotes told of Philopœmen.

The love of honor and distinction was, in his character, not unalloyed with feelings of personal rivalry and resentment. He made Epaminondas his great example, and came not far behind him in activity, sagacity, and incorruptible integrity; but his hot contentious temper continually carried him out of the bounds of that gentleness, composure, and humanity which had marked Epaminondas, and this made thim thought a pattern rather of military than of civil virtue.

He was strongly inclined to the life of a soldier even from his childhood, and he studied and practised all that belonged to it, taking great delight in managing of horses and handling of weapons. Because he was naturally fitted to excel in wrestling, some of his friends and tutors recommended his attention to athletic exercises. But he would first be satisfied whether it would not interfere with his becoming a good soldier. They told him, as was the truth, that the one life was directly opposite to the other; the requisite state of body, the ways of living, and the exercises all different; the professed athlete sleeping much and feeding plentifully, punctually regular in his set times of exercise and rest, and apt to spoil all by every little excess or breach of his usual method; whereas the soldier ought to train himself in every variety of change and irregularity, and, above all, to bring himself to endure hunger and loss of sleep without difficulty. Philopœmen, hearing this, not only laid by all thoughts of wrestling and contemned it then, but when he came to be general, discouraged it by all marks of reproach and dishonour he could imagine, as a thing which made men, otherwise excellently fit for war, to be utterly useless and unable to fight on necessary occasions.

When he left off his masters and teachers, and began to bear arms in the incursions which his citizens used to make upon the Lacedæmonians for pillage and plunder, he would always march out the first and return the last. When there was nothing to do, he sought to harden his body, and make it strong and active by hunting, or labouring in his ground. He had a good estate about twenty furlongs from the town, and thither he would go every day after dinner and supper; and when night came, throw himself upon the first mattress in his way, and there sleep as one of the labourers. At break of day he would rise with the rest, and work either in the vineyard or at the plough; from thence return again to the town, and employ his time with his friends or the magistrates in public business. What he got in the wars he laid out on horses, or arms, or in ransoming captives; but endeavoured to improve his own property the justest way, by tillage; and this not slightly, by way of diversion, but thinking it his strict duty so to manage his own fortune as to be out of the temptation of wronging others.

He spent much time on eloquence and philosophy, but selected his authors, and cared only for those by whom he might profit in virtue. In Homer's fictions his attention was given to whatever he thought apt to raise the courage. Of all other books he was most devoted to the commentaries of Evangelus on military tactics, and also took delight, at leisure hours, in the histories of Alexander; thinking that such reading, unless undertaken for mere amusement and idle conversation, was to the purpose for action. Even in speculations on military subjects it was his habit to neglect maps and diagrams, and to put the theorems to practical proof on the ground itself. He would be exer-

cising his thoughts and considering as he travelled, and arguing with those about him of the difficulties of steep or broken ground, what might happen at rivers, ditches, or mountain-passes, in marching in close or in open, in this or in that particular form of battle. The truth is, he indeed took an immoderate pleasure in military operations and in warfare, to which he devoted himself, as the special means for exercising all sorts of virtue, and utterly contemned those who were not soldiers, as drones and useless in the commonwealth.

When he was thirty years of age, Cleomenes, King of Lacedæmonians, surprised Megalopolis by night, forced the guards, broke in, and seized the market-place. Philopœmen came out upon the alarm, and fought with desperate courage, but could not beat the enemy out again; yet he succeeded in effecting the escape of the citizens, who got away while he made head against the pursuers, and amused Cleomenes, till, after losing his horse and receiving several wounds, with much ado he came off himself, being the last man in the retreat. The Megalopolitans escaped to Messene, whither Cleomenes sent to offer them their town and goods again. Philopœmen perceiving them to be only too glad at the news, and eager to return, checked them with a speech, in which he made them sensible that what Cleomenes called restoring the city was, rather, possessing himself of the citizens; and through their means securing also the city for the future. The mere solitude would, of itself, ere long force him away, since there was no staying to guard empty houses and naked walls. These reasons withheld the Megalopolitans, but gave Cleomenes a pretext to pillage and destroy a great part of the city, and carry away a great booty.

Awhile after, King Antigonus coming down to succour the Achæans, they marched with their united forces against Cleomenes; who, having seized the avenues, lay advantageously posted on the hills of Sellasia. Antigonus drew up close by him, with a resolution to force him in his strength. Philopœmen, with his citizens, was that day placed among the horse, next to the Illyrian foot, a numerous body of bold fighters, who completed the line of battle, forming, together with the Achæans, the reserve. Their orders were to keep their ground, and not engage till from the other wing, where the king fought in person, they should see a red coat lifted up on the point of a spear. The Achæans obeyed their order and stood fast, but the Illyrians were led on by their commanders to the attack.

Euclides, the brother of Cleomenes, seeing the foot thus severed from the horse, detached the best of his light-armed men, commanding them to wheel about, and charge the unprotected Illyrians in the rear. This charge putting things in confusion, Philopœmen, considering those light-armed men would be easily repelled, went first to the king's officers to make them sensible what the occasion required. But they not minding what he said, but slighting him as a hare-brained fellow (as indeed he was not yet of any repute sufficient to give credit to a proposal of such importance), he charged with his own citizens, at the first encounter disordered, and soon after put the troops to flight with great slaughter.

Then, to encourage the king's army further, to bring them all upon the enemy while he was in confusion, he quitted his horse, and fighting with extreme difficulty in his heavy horseman's dress, in rough uneven ground, full of watercourses and hollows, had both his thighs struck through with a thonged javelin. It was thrown with great force, so that the head came out on the other side, and made a severe, though not a mortal, wound. There he stood awhile, as if he had been shackled, unable to move. The fastening which joined the thong to the javelin made it difficult to get it drawn out, nor would any about him venture to do it. But the fight being now at the hottest, and likely to be quickly decided, he was transported with the desire of partaking in it, and struggled and strained so violently, setting one leg forward, the other back, that at last he broke the shaft in two; and thus got the pieces pulled out. Being in this manner set at liberty, he caught up his sword, and running through the midst of those who were fighting in the first ranks, animated his men, and set them afire with emulation.

Antigonus after the victory asked the Macedonians, to try them, how it happened the horse had charged without orders before the signal. They answering, that they were against their wills forced to it by a young man of Megalopolis, who had fallen in before his time: "That young man," replied Antigonus, smiling, "did like an experienced commander."

This, as was natural, brought Philopœmen into great reputation. Antigonus was earnest to have him in his service, and offered him very advantageous conditions, both as to command and pay. But Philopœmen, who knew that his nature brooked not to be under another, would not accept them; yet not enduring to live idle, and hearing of wars in Crete, for practice' sake he passed over thither. He spent some time among those very warlike, and, at the same time, sober and temperate men, improving much by experience in all sorts of service; and then returned with so much fame that the Achæans presently chose him commander of the horse.

These horsemen at that time had neither experience nor bravery, it being the custom to take any common horses, the first and cheapest they could procure, when they were to march; and on almost all occasions they did not go themselves, but hired others in their places, and stayed at home. Their former commanders winked at this, because, it being an honour among the Achæans to serve on horseback, these men had great power in the commonwealth, and were able to gratify or molest whom they pleased. Philopœmen, finding them in this condition, yielded not to any such considerations, nor would pass it over as formerly; but went himself from town to town, where, speaking with the young men, one by one, he endeavoured to excite a spirit of ambition and love of honour among them, using punishment also, where it was necessary. And then by public exercises, reviews, and contests in the presence of numerous spectators, in a little time he made them wonderfully strong and bold, and, which is reckoned of greatest consequence in military service, light and agile. With use and industry they grew so perfect, to such a command of their horses, such a ready exactness in wheeling round in their troops, that in any change of posture the whole body seemed to move with all the facility and promptitude, and, as it were, with the single will of one man.

In the great battle which they fought with the Ætolians and Eleans by the river Larissus, he set them an example himself. Damophantus, general of the Elean horse, singled out Philopœmen, and rode with full speed at him. Philopœmen awaited his charge, and, before receiving the stroke, with a violent blow of his spear threw him dead to the ground: upon whose fall the enemy fled immediately. And now Philopœmen was in everybody's mouth, as a man who in actual fighting with his own hand yielded not to the youngest, nor in good conduct to the oldest, and there came not into the field any better soldier or commander.

Aratus, indeed, was the first who raised the Achæans, inconsiderable till then, into reputation and power, by uniting their divided cities into one commonwealth, and establishing amongst them a humane and truly Grecian form of government; and hence it happened, as in running waters, where, when a few little particles of matter once stop, others stick to them, and one part strengthening another, the whole becomes firm and solid; so in a general weakness, when every city relying only on itself, all Greece was giving way to an easy dissolution, the Achæans, first forming themselves into a body, and then drawing in their neighbours round about, some by protection, delivering them from their tyrants, others by peaceful consent and by naturalization, designed at last to bring all Peloponnesus into one community.

Yet while Aratus lived, they depended much on the Macedonians, courting first Ptolemy, then Antigonus and Philip, who all took part continually in whatever concerned the affairs of Greece. But when Philopœmen came to a command, the Achæans, feeling themselves a match for the most powerful of their enemies, declined foreign support. The truth is, Aratus, as we have written in his life, was not of so warlike a temper, but did most by policy and gentleness, and friendships with foreign princes; but Philopœmen being a man both of execution and command, a great soldier, and fortunate in his first attempts, wonderfully heightened both the power and courage of the Achæans, accustomed to victory under his conduct.

But first he altered what he found amiss in their arms and form of battle. Hitherto they had used light, thin bucklers, too narrow to cover the body, and javelins much shorter than pikes. By which means they were skilful in skirmishing at a distance, but in a close fight had much the disadvantage. Then in drawing their forces up for battle, they were never accustomed to form in regular divisions; and their line being unprotected either by the thick array of projecting spears or by their shields, as in the Macedonian phalanx, where the soldiers close and their shields touch, they were easily opened and broken. Philopœmen reformed all this, persuading them to change the narrow target and short javelin into a large shield and long pike; to arm their heads, bodies, thighs, and legs, and instead of loose skirmishing, fight firmly and foot to foot.

After he had brought them all to wear full armour, and by that means into the confidence of thinking themselves now invincible, he turned what before had been idle profusion and luxury into an honourable expense. For being long used to vie with each other in their dress, the furniture of their houses, and service of their tables, and to glory in outdoing one another, the disease by custom was grown incurable, and there was no possibility of removing it altogether. But he diverted the passion, and brought them, instead of these superfluities, to love useful and more manly display, and reducing their other expenses, to take delight in appearing magnificent in their equipage of war.

Nothing then was to be seen in the shops but plate breaking up, or melting down, gilding of breastplate, and studding bucklers and bits with silver; nothing in the places of exercise, but breaking colts, and young men exercising their arms; nothing in the hands of the women, but helmets and crests of feathers to be dyed, and military cloaks and riding-frocks to be embroidered; the very sight of all which, quickening and raising their spirits, made them contemn dangers, and feel ready to venture on any honourable dangers. Other kinds of sumptuousness give us pleasure, but make us effeminate, the tickling of the sense slackening the vigour of the mind; but magnificence of this kind strengthens and heightens the courage; as Homer makes Achilles at the sight of his new arms exulting with joy, and on fire to use them.

When Philopœmen had obtained of them to arm, and set themselves out in this manner, he proceeded to train them, mustering and exercising them perpetually; in which they obeyed him with great zeal and eagerness. For they were wonderfully pleased with their new form of battle, which being so knit and cemented together, seemed almost incapable of being broken. And then their arms, which for their riches and beauty they wore with pleasure, becoming light and easy to them with constant use, they longed for nothing more than to try them with an enemy, and fight in earnest.

The Achæans at that time were at war with Machanidas, the tyrant of Lacedæmon, who, having a strong army, watched all opportunities of becoming entire master of Peloponnesus. When intelligence came that he was fallen upon the Mantineans, Philopœmen forthwith took the field, and marched towards him.

They met near Mantinea, and drew up in sight of the city. Both, besides the whole strength of their several cities, had a good number of mercenaries in pay. When they came to fall on, Machanidas, with his hired soldiers, beat the spearmen and the Tarentines whom Philopœmen had placed in the front. But when he should have charged immediately into the main battle, which stood close and firm, he hotly followed the chase; and instead of attacking the Achæans, passed on beyond them, while they remained drawn up in their place.

With so untoward a beginning the rest of the confederates gave themselves up for lost; but Philopœmen, professing to make it a matter of small consequence, and observing the enemy's oversight, who had thus left an opening in their main body, and exposed their own phalanx, made no sort of motion to oppose them, but let them pursue the chase freely, till they had placed themselves at a great distance from him. Then seeing the Lacedæmonians before him deserted by their horse, with their flanks quite bare, he charged suddenly, and surprised them without a commander, and not so much as expecting an encounter, as, when they saw Machanidas driving the beaten enemy before him, they thought the victory already gained. He overthrew them with great slaughter (they report above four thousand killed in the place), and then faced about against Machanidas, who was returning with his mercenaries from the pursuit.

There happened to be a broad deep ditch between them, alongside of which both rode their horses for a while, the one trying to get over and flee, the other to hinder him. It looked less like the contest between two generals than like the last defence of some wild beast brought to bay by the keen huntsman Philopœmen, and forced to fight for his life. The tyrant's horse was mettled and strong; and feeling the bloody spurs in his sides, ventured to take the ditch. He had already so far reached the other side, as to have planted his fore-feet upon it, and was struggling to raise himself with these, when Simmias and Polyænus, who used to fight by the side of Philopœmen, came up on horseback to his assistance. But Philopœmen, before either of them, himself met Machanidas; and perceiving that the horse with his head high reared covered his master's body, turned his own a little, and holding his javelin by the middle, drove it against the tyrant with all his force, and tumbled him dead into the ditch. Such is the precise posture in which he

stands at Delphi in the brazen statue which the Achæans set up of him, in admiration of his valour in this single combat, and conduct during the whole day.

We are told that at the Nemean games, a little after this victory, Philopœmen being then general the second time, and at leisure on the occasion of the solemnity, first showed the Greeks his army drawn up in full array as if they were to fight, and executed with it all the manœuvres of a battle with wonderful order, strength, and clerity. After which he went into the theatre, while the musicians were singing for the prize, followed by the young soldiers in their military cloaks and their scarlet frocks under their armour, all in the very height of bodily vigour, and much alike in age, showing a high respect to their general; yet breathing at the same time a noble confidence in themselves, raised by success in many glorious encounters. Just at their coming in, it so happened that the musician Pylades, with a voice well suited to the lofty style of poetry, was in the act of commencing *The Persians* of Timotheus—

Under his conduct Greece was glorious and was free.

The whole theatre at once turned to look at Philopœmen, and clapped with delight; their hopes venturing once more to return to their country's former reputation; and their feelings almost rising to the height of their ancient spirit.

It was with the Achæans as with young horses, which go quietly with their usual riders, but grow unruly and restive under strangers. The soldiers, when any service was in hand, and Philopœmen not at their head, grew dejected and looked about for him; but if he once appeared, came presently to themselves, and recovered their confidence and courage, being sensible that this was the only one of their commanders whom the enemy could not endure to face; but, as appeared on several occasions, were frighted with his very name.

Thus we find that Philip, King of Macedon, thinking to terrify the Achæans into subjection again, if he could rid his hands of Philopœmen, employed some persons privately to assassinate him. But the treachery coming to light, he became infamous, and lost his character through Greece. The Bœotians besieging Megara, and ready to carry the town by storm, upon a groundless rumour that Philopœmen was at hand with succour, ran away, and left their scaling ladders at the wall behind them.

Nabis (who was tyrant of Lacedæmon after Machanidas) had surprised Messene at a time when Philopœmen was out of command. He tried to persuade Lysippus, then general of the Achæans, to succour Messene: but not prevailing with him, because, he said, the enemy being now within it, the place was irrecoverably lost, he resolved to go himself, without order or commission, followed merely by his own immediate fellow-citizens, who went with him as their general by commission from nature, which had made him fittest to command. Nabis, hearing of his coming, though his army quartered within the town, thought it not convenient to stay; but stealing out of the furthest gate with his men, marched away with all the speed he could, thinking himself a happy man if he could get off with safety. And he did escape; but Messene was rescued.

All hitherto makes for the praise and honour of Philopœmen. But when at the request of the Gortynians he went away into Crete to command for them, at a time when his own country was distressed by Nabis, he exposed himself to the charge of either cowardice, or unseasonable ambition of honour amongst foreigners. For the Megalopolitans were then so pressed, that, the enemy being master of the field and encamping almost at their gates, they were forced to keep themselves within their walls, and sow their very streets. And he in the meantime, across the seas, waging war and commanding in chief in a foreign nation, furnished his ill-wishers with matter enough for their reproaches.

Some said he took the offer of the Gortynians, because the Achæans chose other generals, and left him but a private man. For he could not endure to sit still, but looking upon war and command in it as his great business, always coveted to be employed. And this agrees with what he once aptly said of King Ptolemy. Somebody was praising him for keeping his army and himself in an admirable state of discipline and exercise: "And what praise," replied Philopœmen, "for a king of his years, to be always preparing, and never performing?"

However, the Megalopolitans, thinking themselves betrayed, took it so ill that they were about to banish him. But the Achæans put an end to that design by sending their general, Aristæus, to Megalopolis, who, though he were at difference with Philopœmen about affairs of the commonwealth, yet would not suffer him

to be banished. Philopœmen finding himself upon this account out of favour with his citizens, induced divers of the little neighbouring places to renounce obedience to them, suggesting to them to urge that from the beginning they were not subject to their taxes or laws, or any way under their command. In these pretences he openly took their part, and fomented seditious movements amongst the Achæans in general against Megalopolis. But these things happened a while after.

While he stayed in Crete, in the service of the Gortynians, he made war not like a Peloponnesian and Arcanian, fairly in the open field, but fought with them at their own weapon, and turning their stratagems and tricks against themselves, showed them they played craft against skill, and were but children to an experienced soldier.

Having acted here with great bravery, and great reputation to himself, he returned into Peloponnesus, where he found Philip beaten by Titus Quintius, and Nabis at war both with the Romans and Achæans. He was at once chosen general against Nabis, but venturing to fight by sea, met, like Epaminondas, with a result very contrary to the general expectation and his own former reputation. Epaminondas, however, according to some statements, was backward by design, unwilling to give his countrymen an appetite for the advantages of the sea, lest from good soldiers they should by little and little turn, as Plato says, to ill mariners. And therefore he returned from Asia and the Islands without doing anything, on purpose. Whereas Philopœmen, thinking his skill in land-service would equally avail at sea, learned how great a part of valour experience is, and how much it imports in the management of things to be accustomed to them. For he was not only put to the worst in the fight for want of skill, but having rigged up an old ship, which had been a famous vessel forty years before, and shipped his citizens in her, she foundering, he was in danger of losing them all. But finding the enemy, as if he had been driving out of the sea, had, in contempt of him, besieged Gythium, he presently set sail again, and taking them unexpectedly, dispersed and careless after their victory, landed in the night, burnt their camp, and killed a great number.

A few days after, as he was marching through a rough country, Nabis came suddenly upon him. The Achæans were dismayed, and in such difficult ground where the enemy had secured the advantage, despaired to get off with safety. Philopœmen made a little halt, and, viewing the ground, soon made it appear that the one important thing in war is skill in drawing up an army. For by advancing only a few paces, and, without any confusion or trouble, altering his order according to the nature of the place, he immediately relieved himself from every difficulty, and then charging, put the enemy to flight. But when he saw they fled, not towards the city, but dispersed every man a different way all over the field, which for wood and hills, brooks and hollows, was not passable by horse, he sounded a retreat, and encamped by broad daylight. Then foreseeing the enemy would endeavour to steal scatteringly into the city in the dark, he posted strong parties of the Achæans all along the watercourses and sloping ground near the walls. Many of Nabis's men fell into their hands. For returning not in a body, but as the chance of flight had disposed of every one, they were caught like birds ere they could enter into the town.

These actions obtained him distinguished marks of affection and honour in all the theatres of Greece, but not without the secret ill-will of Titus Flamininus, who was naturally eager for glory, and thought it but reasonable a consul if Rome should be otherwise esteemed by the Achæans than a common Arcadian; especially as there was no comparison between what he and what Philopœmen had done for them, he having by one proclamation restored all Greece, as much as had been subject to Philip and the Macedonians, to liberty. After this, Titus made peace with Nabis, and Nabis was circumvented and slain by the Ætolians.

Things being then in confusion at Sparta, Philopœmen laid hold of the occasion, and coming upon them with an army, prevailed with some by persuasion, with others by fear, till he brought the whole city over to the Achæans. As it was no small matter for Sparta to become a member of Achæa, this action gained him infinite praise from the Achæans, for having strengthened their confederacy by the addition of so great and powerful a city, and not a little good-will from the nobility of Sparta itself, who hoped they had now procured an ally who would defend their freedom. Accordingly, having raised a sum of one hundred and twenty silver talents by the sale of the house and goods of Nabis,

they decreed him the money, and sent a deputation in the name of the city to present it.

But here the honesty of Philopœmen showed itself clearly to be a real, uncounterfeited virtue. For, first of all, there was not a man among them who would undertake to make him this offer of a present, but every one excusing himself, and shifting it off upon his fellow, they laid the office at last on Timolaus, with whom he had lodged at Sparta. Then Timolaus came to Megalopolis, and was entertained by Philopœmen; but struck into admiration with the dignity of his life and manners, and the simplicity of his habits, judging him to be utterly inaccessible to any such considerations, he said nothing, but pretending other business, returned without a word mentioned of the present. He was sent again, and did just as formerly. But the third time with much ado, and faltering in his words, he acquainted Philopœmen with the good-will of the city of Sparta to him.

Philopœmen listened obligingly and gladly; and then went himself to Sparta, where he advised them not to bribe good men and their friends, of whose virtue they might be sure without charge to themselves; but to buy off and silence ill citizens, who disquited the city with their seditious speeches in the public assemblies; for it was better to bar liberty of speech in enemies than friends. Thus it appeared how much Philopœmen was above bribery.

Diophanes being afterwards general of the Achæans, and hearing the Lacedæmonians were bent on new commotions, resolved to chastise them; they, on the other side, being set upon war, were embroiling all Peloponnesus. Philopœmen on this occasion did all he could to keep Diophanes quiet and to make him sensible that as the times went, while Antiochus and the Romans were disputing their pretensions with vast armies in the heart of Greece, it concerned a man in his position to keep a watchful eye over them, and dissembling, and putting up with any less important grievances, to preserve all quiet at home. Diophanes would not be ruled, but joined with Titus, and both together falling into Daconia, marched directly to Sparta. Philopœmen, upon this, took, in his indignation, a step which certainly was not lawful, nor in the strictest sense just, but boldly and loftily conceived. Entering into the town himself, he, a private man as he was, refused admission to both the consul of Rome and the general of the Achæans, quieted the disorders in the city, and reunited it on the same terms as before to the Achæan confederacy.

Yet afterwards, when he was general himself, upon some new misdemeanour of the Lacedæmonians, he brought back those who had been banished, put, as Polybius writes, eighty, according to Aristocrates three hundred and fifty, Spartans to death, razed the walls, took away a good part of their territory and transferred it to the Megalopolitans, forced out of the country and carried into Achæa all who had been made citizens of Sparta by tyrants, except three thousand who would not submit to banishment. These he sold for slaves, and with the money, as if to exult over them, built a colonnade at Megalopolis. Lastly, unworthily trampling upon the Lacedæmonians in their calamities, and gratifying his hostility by a most oppressive and arbitrary action, he abolished the laws of Lycurgus, and forced them to educate their children and live after the manner of the Achæans; as though, while they kept to the discipline of Lycurgus, there was no humbling their haughty spirits. In their present distress and adversity they allowed Philopœmen thus to cut the sinews of their commonwealth asunder, and behaved themselves humbly and submissively. But afterwards, in no long time, obtaining the support of the Romans, they abandoned their new Achæan citizenship; and as much as in so miserable and ruined a condition they could, re-established their ancient discipline.

When the war betwixt Antiochus and the Romans broke out in Greece, Philopœmen was a private man. He repined grievously when he saw Antiochus lay idle at Chalcis, spending his time in unreasonable courtship and weddings, while his men lay dispersed in several towns, without order, or commanders, and minding nothing but their pleasures. He complained much that he was not himself in office and said he envied the Romans their victory; and that if he had had the fortune to be then in command, he would have surprised and killed the whole army in the taverns.

When Antiochus was overcome, the Romans pressed harder upon Greece, and encompassed the Achæans with their power; the popular leaders in the several cities yielded before them; and their power speedily, under the divine guidance, advanced to the consummation due to it in the revolutions of fortune. Philopœmen, in this conjuncture, carried himself like a good pilot in a high sea, sometimes shifting sail, and sometimes yielding, but still steering steady; and omitting no opportunity nor effort to keep all who were considerable, whether for eloquence or riches, fast to the defence of their common liberty.

Aristænus, a Megalopolitan of great credit among the Achæans, but always a favourer of the Romans, saying one day in the senate that the Romans should not be opposed, or displeased in any way, Philopœmen heard him with an impatient silence; but at last, not able to hold longer, said angrily to him, "And why be in such haste, wretched man, to behold the end of Greece?" Manius, the Roman consul, after the defeat of Antiochus, requested the Achæans to restore the banished Lacedæmonians to their country, which motion was seconded and supported by all the interest of Titus. But Philopœmen crossed it, not from illwill to the men, but that they might be beholden to him and the Achæans, not to Titus and the Romans. For when he came to be general himself, he restored them. So impatient was his spirit of any subjection and so prone his nature to contest everything with men in power.

Being now three score and ten, and the eighth time general, he was in hope to pass in quiet, not only the year of his magistracy, but his remaining life. For as our diseases decline, as it is supposed with our declining bodily strength, so that quarreling humour of the Greeks abated much with their failing political greatness. But fortune or some divine retributive power threw him down in the close of his life, like a successful runner who stumbles at the goal. It is reported, that being in company where one was praised for a great commander, he replied, there was no great account to be made of a man who had suffered himself to be taken alive by his enemies.

A few days after, news came that Dinocrates the Messenian, a particular enemy to Philopœmen, and for his wickedness and villainies generally hated, had induced Messene to revolt from the Achæans, and was about to seize upon a little place called Colonis. Philopœmen lay then sick of a fever at Argos. Upon the news he hasted away, and reached Megalopolis, which was distant above four hundred furlongs, in a day. From thence he immediately led out the horse, the noblest of the city, young men in the vigour of their age, and eager to proffer their service, both from attachment to Philopœmen and zeal for the cause. As they marched towards Messene, they met with Dinocrates, near the hill of Evander, charged and routed him. But five hundred fresh men, who, being left for a guard to the country, came in late, happening to appear, the fleeing enemy rallied again about the hills.

Philopœmen, fearing to be enclosed, and solicitous for his men, retreated over ground extremely disadvantageous, bringing up the rear himself. As he often faced, and made charges upon the enemy, he drew them upon himself; though they merely made movements at a distance, and shouted about him, nobody daring to approach him. In his care to save every single man, he left his main body so often, that at last he found himself alone among the thickest of his enemies. Yet even then none durst come up to him, but being pelted at a distance, and driven to stony steep places, he had great difficulty, with much spurring, to guide his horse aright. His age was no hindrance to him, for with perpetual exercise he was both strong and active; but being weakened with sickness, and tired with his long journey, his horse stumbling, he fell encumbered with his arms, and faint, upon a hard and rugged piece of ground. His head received such a shock with the fall that he lay awhile speechless, so that the enemy, thinking him dead, began to turn and strip him. But when they saw him lift his head and open his eyes, they threw themselves all together upon him, bound his hands behind him, and carried him off, every kind of insult and contumely being lavished on him who truly had never so much as dreamed of being led in triumph by Dinocrates.

The Messenians, wonderfully elated with the news, thronged in swarms to the city gates. But when they saw Philopœmen in a posture so unsuitable to the glory of his great actions and famous victories, most of them, struck with grief and cursing the deceitful vanity of human fortune, even shed tears of compassion at the spectacle. Such tears by little and little turned to kind words, and it was almost in everybody's mouth that they ought to remember what he had done for them, and how he had preserved the common liberty, by driving away Nabis. Some few, to make their court to Dinocrates, were for torturing and then putting him to death as a dangerous and irreconcilable enemy; all the more formidable to Dinocrates, who had taken him a prisoner, should he after this misfortune regain his liberty. They put him at last into a dungeon underground, which they called the treasury, a place into which there came no air nor light from

abroad; and which, having no doors, was closed with a great stone. This they rolled into the entrance and fixed, and placing a guard about it, left him.

In the meantime Philopœmen's soldiers, recovering themselves after their flight, and fearing he was dead when he appeared nowhere, made a stand, calling him with loud cries, and reproaching one another with their unworthy and shameful escape, having betrayed their general, who, to preserve their lives, had lost his own. Then returning after much inquiry and search, hearing at last that he was taken, they sent away messengers round about with the news. The Achæans resented the misfortune deeply, and decreed to send and demand him; and in the meantime drew their army together for his rescue.

While these things passed in Achæa, Dinocrates, fearing that any delay would save Philopœmen, and resolving to be beforehand with the Achæans, as soon as night had dispersed the multitude, sent in the executioner with poison, with orders not to stir from him till he had taken it. Philopœmen had then laid down, wrapt up in his cloak, not sleeping, but oppressed with grief and trouble; but seeing light, and a man with poison by him, struggled to sit up; and taking the cup, asked the man if he heard anything of the horsemen, particularly Lycortas? The fellow answering, that the most part had got off safe, he nodded, and looking cheerfully upon him, "It is well," he said, "that we have not been every way unfortunate"; and without a word more, drank it off, and laid him down again. His weakness offering but little resistance to the poison, it despatched him presently.

The news of his death filled all Achæa with grief and lamentation. The youth, with some of the chief of the several cities, met at Magalopolis with a resolution to take revenge without delay. They chose Lycortas general, and falling upon the Messenians, put all to fire and sword, till they all with one consent made their submission. Dinocrates, with as many as had voted for Philopœmen's death, anticipated their vengeance and killed themselves. Those who would have had him tortured, Lycortas put in chains and reserved for severer punishment. They burnt his body, and put the ashes into an urn, and then marched homeward, not as in an ordinary march, but with a kind of solemn pomp, half triumph, half funeral, crowns of victory on their heads, and tears in their eyes, and their captive enemies in fetters by them. Polybius the general's son, carried the urn, so covered with garlands and ribbons as scarcely to be visible; and the noblest of the Achæans accompanied him. The soldiers followed fully armed and mounted, with looks neither altogether sad as in mourning, nor lofty as in victory. The people from all towns and villages in their way flocked out to meet him, as at his return from conquest, and, saluting the urn, fell in with the company and followed on to Megalopolis; where, when the old men, the women and children were mingled with the rest, the whole city was filled with sighs, complaints and cries, the loss of Philopœmen seeming to them the loss of their own greatness, and of their rank among the Achæans. Thus he was honourably buried according to his worth, and the prisoners were stoned about his tomb.

Many statues were set up, and many honours decreed to him by the several cities. One of the Romans in the time of Greece's afflictions, after the destruction of Corinth, publicly accusing Philopœmen, as if he had been still alive, of having been the enemy of Rome, proposed that these memorials should be all removed. A discussion ensued, speeches were made, and Polybius answered the sycophant at large. And neither Mummius nor the lieutenants would suffer the honourable monuments of so great a man to be defaced, though he had often crossed both Titus and Manius. They justly distinguished, and as became honest men, betwixt usefulness and virtue—what is good in itself, and what is profitable to particular parties—judging thanks and reward due to him who does a benefit from him who receives it, and honour never to be denied by the good to the good. And so much concerning Philopœmen.

FLAMININUS

230?–174 B.C.

WHAT Titus Quintius Flamininus, whom we select as a parallel to Philopœmen, was in personal appearance, those who are curious may see by the brazen statue of him, which stands in Rome near that of the great Apollo, brought from Carthage, opposite to the Circus Maximus, with a Greek inscription upon it. The temper of his mind is said to have been of the warmest both in anger and in kindness, not indeed equally so in both respects; as in punishing he was ever moderate, never inflexible; but whatever courtesy or good turn he set about, he went through with it, and was as perpetually kind and obliging to those on whom he had poured his favours, as if they, not he, had been the benefactors: exerting himself for the security and preservation of what he seemed to consider his noblest possessions, those to whom he had done good. But being ever thirsty after honour, and passionate for glory, if anything of a greater and more extraordinary nature were to be done, he was eager to be the doer of it himself; and took more pleasure in those that needed, than in those that were capable of conferring favours; looking on the former as objects for his virtue, and on the latter as competitors in glory.

Rome had then many sharp contests going on, and her youth betaking themselves early to the wars, learned betimes the art of commanding; and Flamininus, having passed through the rudiments of soldiery, received his first charge in the war against Hannibal, as tribune under Marcellus, then consul. Marcellus, indeed, falling into an ambuscade, was cut off. But Titus, receiving the appointment of governor, as well of Tarentum, then retaken, as of the country about it, grew no less famous for his administration of justice, than for his military skill. This obtained him the office of leader and founder of two colonies which were sent into the cities of Narnia and Cossa; which filled him with loftier hopes, and made him aspire to step over those previous honours which it was usual first to pass through, the offices of tribune of the people, prætor and ædile, and to level his aim immediately at the consulship. Having these colonies, and all their interest ready at his service, he offered himself as candidate; but the tribunes of the people, Fulvius and Manius [Curius], and their party, strongly opposed him; alleging how unbecoming a thing it was that a man of such raw years, one who was yet, as it were, untrained, uninitiated in the first sacred rites and mysteries of government, should, in contempt of the laws, intrude and force himself into the sovereignty. However, the senate remitted it to the people's choice and suffrage; who elected him (though not then arrived at his thirtieth year) consul with Sextus Ælius.

The war against Philip and the Macedonians fell to Titus by lot, and some kind fortune, propitious at that time to the Romans, seems to have so determined it; as neither the people nor the state of things which were now to be dealt with were such as to require a general who would always be upon the point of force and mere blows, but rather were accessible to persuasion and gentle usage. It is true that the kingdom of Macedon furnished supplies enough to Philip for actual battle with the Romans; but to maintain a long and lingering war he must call in aid from Greece; must thence procure his supplies; there find his means of retreat. Greece, in a word, would be his resource for all the requisites of his army. Unless, therefore, the Greeks could be withdrawn from siding with Philip, this war with him must not expect its decision from a single battle. Now Greece (which had not hitherto held much correspondence with the Romans, but first began an intercourse on this occasion) would not so soon have embraced a foreign authority, instead of the commanders she had been inured to, had not the general of these strangers been of a kind, gentle nature, one who worked rather by fair means than force; of a persuasive address in all applications to others, and no less courteous and open to all addresses of others to him; and above all bent and determined on justice. But the story of his actions will best illustrate these particulars.

Titus observed that both Sulpicius and Publius, who had been his predecessors in that command, had not taken the field against the Macedonians till late in the year; and then, too, had not set their hands properly to the war, but had kept skirmishing and scouting here and there for passes and provisions, and never came to close fighting with Philip. He resolved not to trifle away a year, as they had done, at home in ostentation of the honour, and in domestic administration, and only then to join the army, with the pitiful hope of protracting the term of office through a second year, acting as consul in the first, and as general in the latter. He was, moreover, infinitely desirous to employ his authority with effect upon the war,

which made him slight those home honours and prerogatives.

Requesting, therefore, of the senate, that his brother Lucius might act with him as admiral of the navy, and taking with him to be the edge, as it were, of the expedition three thousand still young and vigorous soldiers, of those who, under Scipio, had defeated Hasdrubal in Spain, and Hannibal in Africa, he got safe into Epirus; and found Publius encamped with his army, over against Philip, who had long made good the pass over the river Apsus, and the straits there; Publius not having been able, for the natural strength of the place, to effect anything against him. Titus therefore took upon himself the conduct of the army, and, having dismissed Publius, examined the ground. The place is in strength not inferior to Tempe, though it lacks the trees and green woods, and the pleasant meadows and walks that adorn Tempe. The Apsus, making its way between vast and lofty mountains which all but meet above a single deep ravine in the midst, is not unlike the river Peneus in the rapidity of its current and in its general appearance. It covers the foot of those hills, and leaves only a craggy, narrow path cut out beside the stream, not easily passable at any time for an army, but not at all when guarded by an enemy.

There were some, therefore, who would have had Titus make a circuit through Dassaretis, and take an easy and safe road by the district of Lyncus. But he, fearing that if he should engage himself too far from the sea in barren and untilled countries, and Philip should decline fighting, he might, through want of provisions, be constrained to march back again to the seaside without effecting anything, as his predecessor had done before him, embraced the resolution of forcing his way over the mountains. But Philip, having possessed himself of them with his army, showered down his darts and arrows from all parts upon the Romans.

Sharp encounters took place, and many fell wounded and slain on both sides, and there seemed but little likelihood of thus ending the war; when some of the men, who fed their cattle thereabouts, came to Titus with a discovery that there was a round-about way which the enemy neglected to guard: through which they undertook to conduct his army, and to bring it, within three days at furthest, to the top of the hills. To gain the surer credit with him, they said that Charops, son of Machatas, a leading man in Epirus, who was friendly to the Romans, and aided them (though, for fear of Philip, secretly), was privy to the design. Titus gave their information belief, and sent a captain with four thousand foot and three hundred horse, these herdsmen being their guides, but kept in bonds. In the daytime they lay still under the covert of the hollow and woody places, but in the night they marched by moonlight, the moon being then at the full.

Titus, having detached this party, lay quiet with his main body, merely keeping up the attention of the enemy by some slight skirmishing. But when the day arrived that those who stole round were expected upon the top of the hill, he drew up his forces early in the morning, as well the light-armed as the heavy, and, dividing them into three parts, himself led the van, marching his men up the narrow passage along the bank, darted at by the Macedonians and engaging, in this difficult ground, hand to hand with his assailants; whilst the other two divisions on either side of him threw themselves with great alacrity among the rocks. Whilst they were struggling forward, the sun rose, and a thin smoke, like a mist, hanging on the hills, was seen rising at a distance, unperceived by the enemy, being behind them, as they stood on the heights; and the Romans, also, as yet under suspense, in the toil and difficulty they were in, could only doubtfully construe the sight according to their desires. But as it grew thicker and thicker, blackening the air, and mounting to a greater height, they no longer doubted but it was the fire-signal of their companions; and, raising a triumphant shout, forcing their way onwards, they drove the enemy back into the roughest ground; while the other party echoed back their acclamations from the top of the mountain.

The Macedonians fled with all the speed they could make; there fell, indeed, not more than two thousand of them; for the difficulties of the place rescued them from pursuit. But the Romans pillaged their camp, seized upon their money and slaves, and, becoming absolute masters of the pass, traversed all Epirus; but with such order and discipline, with such temperance and moderation, that, though they were far from the sea, at a great distance from their vessels, and stinted of their monthly allowance of corn, and though they had much difficulty in buying, they nevertheless abstained altogether from plundering the country,

which had provisions enough of all sorts in it.

For intelligence being received that Philip, making a flight, rather than a march, through Thessaly, forced the inhabitants from the towns to take shelter in the mountains, burnt down the towns themselves, and gave up as spoil to his soldiers all the property which it had been found impossible to remove, abandoning, as it would seem, the whole country to the Romans. Titus was, therefore, very desirous, and entreated his soldiers, that they would pass through it as if it were their own, or as if a place trusted into their hands; and, indeed, they quickly perceived, by the event, what benefit they derived from this moderate and orderly conduct. For they no sooner set foot in Thessaly, but the cities opened their gates, and the Greeks within Thermopylæ, were all eagerness and excitement to ally themselves with them. The Achæans abandoned their alliance with Philip, and voted to join with the Romans in actual arms against him; and the Opuntians, though the Ætolians, who were zealous allies of the Romans, were willing and desirous to undertake the protection of the city, would not listen to proposals from them; but sending for Titus, intrusted and committed themselves to his charge.

It is told of Pyrrhus, that when first, from an adjacent hill or watch-tower which gave him a prospect of the Roman army, he descried them drawn up in order, he observed that he saw nothing barbarian-like in this barbarian line of battle. And all who came near Titus could not choose but say as much of him, at their first view. For they had been told by the Macedonians of an invader, at the head of a barbarian army, carrying everywhere slavery and destruction on his sword's point; when, in lieu of such an one, they met a man, in the flower of his age, of a gentle and humane aspect, a Greek in his voice and language, and a lover of honour, they were wonderfully pleased and attracted; and when they left him, they filled the cities, wherever they went, with favourable feelings for him, and with the belief that in him they might find the protector and assertor of their liberties. And when afterwards, on Philip's professing a desire for peace, Titus made a tender to him of peace and friendship, upon the condition that the Greeks be left to their own laws, and that he should withdraw his garrisons, which he refused to comply with. Now after these proposals the universal belief even of the favourers and partisans of Philip was, that the Romans came not to fight against the Greeks, but for the Greeks against the Macedonians.

Accordingly, all the rest of Greece came to peaceable terms with him. But as he marched into Bœotia, without committing the least act of hostility, the nobility and chief men of Thebes came out of their city to meet him, devoted under the influence of Brachylles to the Macedonian alliance, but desirous at the same time to show honour and deference to Titus; as they were, they conceived, in amity with both parties. Titus received them in the most obliging and courteous manner, but kept going gently on, questioning and inquiring of them, and sometimes entertaining them with narratives of his own, till his soldiers might a little recover from the weariness of their journey. Thus passing on, he and the Thebans came together into their city, not much to their satisfaction; but yet they could not well deny him entrance, as a good number of his men attended him in. Titus, however, now he was within, as if he had not had the city at his mercy, came forward and addressed them, urging them to join the Roman interest. King Attalus followed to the same effect. And he, indeed, trying to play the advocate, beyond what it seems his age could bear, was seized, in the midst of his speech, with a sudden flux or dizziness, and swooned away; and, not long after, was conveyed by ship into Asia, and died there. The Bœotians joined the Roman alliance.

But now, when Philip sent an embassy to Rome, Titus despatched away agents on his part, too, to solicit the senate, if they should continue the war, to continue him in his command, or if they determined an end to that, that he might have the honour of concluding the peace. Having a great passion for distinction, his fear was, that if another general were commissioned to carry on the war, the honour even of what was passed would be lost to him; and his friends transacted matters so well on his behalf, that Philip was unsuccessful in his proposals, and the management of the war was confirmed in his hands.

He no sooner received the senate's determination, but, big with hopes, he marched directly into Thessaly to engage Philip; his army consisting of twenty-six thousand men, out of which the Ætolians furnished six thousand foot and four hundred horse. The forces of Philip were much about the same number. In this eagerness to encounter, they advanced against each other, till both were near Sco-tussa, where they resolved to hazard a battle. Nor had the approach of these two formidable armies the effect that might have been supposed, to strike into the generals a mutual terror of each other; it rather inspired them with ardour and ambition; on the Romans' part, to be the conquerors of Macedon, a name which Alexander had made famous amongst them for strength and valour; whilst the Macedonians, on the other hand, esteeming the Romans as an enemy very different from the Persians, hoped, if victory stood on their side, to make the name of Philip more glorious than that of Alexander.

Titus, therefore, called upon his soldiers to play the part of valiant men, because they were now to act their parts upon the most illustrious theatre of the world, Greece, and to contend with the bravest antagonists. And Philip, on the other side, commenced a harangue to his men, as usual before an engagement, and to be the better heard (whether it were merely a mischance, or the result of unseasonable haste, not observing what he did), mounted an eminence outside their camp, which proved to be a burying-place; and much disturbed by the despondency that seized his army at the unluckiness of the omen, all that day kept in his camp, and declined fighting.

But on the morrow, as day came on, after a soft and rainy night, the clouds changing into a mist filled all the plain with thick darkness; and a dense foggy air descending, by the time it was full day, from the adjacent mountains into the ground betwixt the two camps, concealed them from each other's view. The parties sent out on either side, some for ambuscade, some for discovery, falling in upon one another quickly after they were thus detached, began the fight at what are called the Cynos Cephalæ, a number of sharp tops of hills that stand close to one another, and have the name from some resemblance in their shape. Now many vicissitudes and changes happening, as may well be expected, in such an uneven field of battle, sometimes hot pursuit, and sometimes as rapid a flight, the generals on both sides kept sending in succours from the main bodies, as they saw their men pressed or giving ground, till at length the heavens clearing up, let them see what was going on, upon which the whole armies engaged.

Philip, who was in the right wing, from the advantage of the higher ground which he had, threw on the Romans the whole weight of his phalanx, with a force which they were unable to sustain; the dense array of spears, and the pressure of the compact mass overpowering them. But the king's left wing being broken up by the hilliness of the place, Titus observing it, and cherishing little or no hopes on that side where his own gave ground, made in all haste to the other, and there charged in upon the Macedonians; who, in consequence of the inequality and roughness of the ground, could not keep their phalanx entire, nor line their ranks to any great depth (which is the great point of their strength), but were forced to fight man for man under heavy and unwieldy armour. For the Macedonian phalanx is like some single powerful animal, irresistible so long as it is embodied into one, and keeps its order, shield touching shield, all as in a piece; but if it be once broken, not only is the joint force lost, but the individual soldiers also who composed it lose each one his own single strength, because of the nature of their armour; and because each of them is strong, rather, as he makes a part of the whole, than in himself.

When these were routed, some gave chase to the fleeing, others charged the flanks of those Macedonians who were still fighting, so that the conquering wing, also, was quickly disordered, took to flight, and threw down its arms. There were then slain no less than eight thousand, and about five thousand were taken prisoners; and the Ætolians were blamed as having been the main occasion that Philip himself got safe off. For whilst the Romans were in pursuit, they fell to ravaging and plundering the camp, and did it so completely, that when the others returned, they found no booty in it.

This bred at first hard words, quarrels, and misunderstandings betwixt them. But, afterwards, they galled Titus more by ascribing the victory to themselves, and prepossessing the Greeks with reports to that effect; insomuch that poets, and people in general in the songs that were sung or written in honour of the action, still ranked the Ætolians foremost. One of the pieces most current was the following epigram:—

Naked and tombless see, O passer-by
The thirty thousand men of Thessaly,
Slain by the Ætolians and the Latin band,
That came with Titus from Italia's land;
Alas for mighty Macedon! that day,
Swift as a roe, King Philip fled away.

This was composed by Alcæus in mockery of Philip, exaggerating the number of the slain. However, being everywhere repeated, and by almost everybody, Titus was more nettled at it than Philip. The latter merely retorted upon Alcæus with some elegiac verses of his own:—

Naked and leafless see, O passer-by,
The cross that shall Alcæus crucify.

But such little matters extremely fretted Titus, who was ambitious of a reputation among the Greeks; and he therefore acted in all after-occurrences by himself, paying but very slight regard to the Ætolians. This offended them in their turn; and when Titus listened to terms of accommodation, and admitted an embassy upon the proffers of the Macedonian king, the Ætolians made it their business to publish through all the cities of Greece that this was the conclusion of all; that he was selling Philip a peace at a time when it was in his hand to destroy the very roots of the war, and to overthrow the power which had first inflicted servitude upon Greece.

But whilst with these and the like rumours the Ætolians laboured to shake the Roman confederates, Philip, making overtures of submission of himself and his kingdom to the discretion of Titus and the Romans, put an end to those jealousies, as Titus, by accepting them, did to the war. For he reinstated Philip in his kingdom of Macedon, but made it a condition that he should quit Greece, and that he should pay one thousand talents; he took from him also all his shipping, save ten vessels; and sent away Demetrius, one of his sons, hostage to Rome; improving his opportunity to the best advantage, and taking wise precautions for the future.

For Hannibal the African, a professed enemy to the Roman name, an exile from his own country, and not long since arrived at King Antiochus's court, was already stimulating that prince, not to be wanting to the good fortune that had been hitherto so propitious to his affairs; the magnitude of his successes having gained him the surname of the Great. He had begun to level his aim at universal monarchy, but above all he was eager to measure himself with the Romans. Had not, therefore, Titus, upon a principle of prudence and foresight, lent an ear to peace, and had Antiochus found the Romans still at war in Greece with Philip, and had these two, the most powerful and warlike princes of that age, confederated for their common interests against the Roman state, Rome might once more have run no less a risk, and been reduced to no less extremities, than she had experienced under Hannibal. But now, Titus opportunely introducing this peace between the wars, despatching the present danger before the new one had arrived, at once disappointed Antiochus of his first hopes and Philip of his last.

When the ten commissioners, delegated to Titus from the senate, advised him to restore the rest of Greece to their liberty, but that Corinth, Chalcis, and Demetrias should be kept garrisoned for security against Antiochus; the Ætolians on this, breaking out into loud accusations, agitated all the cities, calling upon Titus to strike off the shackles of Greece (so Philip used to term those three cities), and asking the Greeks whether it were not matter of much consolation to them that, though their chains weighed heavier, yet they were now smoother and better polished than formerly, and whether Titus were not deservedly admired by them as their benefactor, who had unshackled the feet of Greece, and tied her up by the neck; Titus, vexed and angry at this, made it his request to the senate, and at last prevailed in it, that the garrisons in these cities should be dismissed, that so the Greeks might be no longer debtors to him for a partial, but for an entire favour.

It was now the time of the celebration of the Isthmian games; and the seats around the racecourse were crowded with an unusual multitude of spectators; Greece, after long wars, having regained not only peace, but hopes of liberty, and being able once more to keep holiday in safety. A trumpet sounded to command silence; and the crier, stepping forth amidst the spectators, made proclamation that the Roman senate and Titus Quintius, the proconsular general, having vanquished King Philip and the Macedonians, restored the Corinthians, Locrians, Phocians, Eubœans, Achæans of Phthiotis, Magnetians, Thessalians, and Perrhæbians to their own lands, laws, and liberties; remitting all impositions upon them, and withdrawing all garrisons from their cities. At first, many heard not at all, and others not distinctly, what was said; but there was a confused and uncertain stir among the assembled people, some wondering, some asking, some calling out to have it proclaimed again.

When, therefore, fresh silence was made, the crier raising his voice, succeeded in making himself generally heard and recited the decree again. A shout of joy followed it, so loud that it was heard as far as the sea. The whole assembly rose and stood up; there was no further thought of the entertainment; all were only eager to leap up and salute and address their thanks to the deliverer and champion of Greece. What we often hear alleged, in proof of the force of human voices, was actually verified upon this occasion. Crows that were accidentally flying over the course fell down dead into it. The disruption of the air must be the cause of it; for the voices being numerous, and the acclamation violent, the air breaks with it and can no longer give support to the birds, but lets them tumble, like one that should attempt to walk upon a vacuum; unless we should rather imagine them to fall and die, shot with the noise as a dart. It is possible, too, that there may be a circular agitation of the air, which, like marine whirlpools, may have a violent direction of this sort given to it from the excess of its fluctuation.

But for Titus; the sports being now quite at an end, so beset was he on every side, and by such multitudes, that had he not, foreseeing the probable throng and concourse of the people, timely withdrawn, he would scarce, it is thought, have ever got clear of them. When they had tired themselves with acclamations all about his pavilion, and night was now come, wherever friends or fellow-citizens met, they joyfully saluted and embraced each other, and went home to feast and carouse together.

And there, no doubt, redoubling their joy, they began to recollect and talk of the state of Greece, what wars she had incurred in defence of her liberty, and yet was never perhaps mistress of a more settled or grateful one than this which other men's labours had won for her; almost without one drop of blood, or one citizen's loss to be mourned for, she had this day had put into her hands the most glorious of rewards, and best worth the contending for. Courage and wisdom are, indeed, rarities amongst men, but of all that is good, a just man it would seem is the most scarce. Such as Agesilaus, Lysander, Nicias, and Alcibiades, knew how to play the general's part, how to manage a war, how to bring off their men victorious by land and sea; but how to employ that success to generous and honest purposes they had not known. For should a man except the achievement at Marathon, the sea-fight at Salamis, the engagements at Platæa and Thermopylæ, Cimon's exploits at Eurymedon, and on the coast of Cyprus, Greece fought all her battles against, and to enslave, herself; she erected all her trophies to her own shame and misery, and was brought to ruin and desolation almost wholly by the guilt and ambition of her great men. A foreign people, appearing just to retain some embers, as it were, some faint remainders of a common character derived to them from their ancient sires, a nation from whom it was a mere wonder that Greece should reap any benefit by word or thought, these are they who have retrieved Greece from her severest dangers and distresses, have rescued her out of the hands of insulting lords and tyrants, and reinstated her in her former liberties.

Thus they entertained their tongues and thoughts: whilst Titus by his actions made good what had been proclaimed. For he immediately despatched away Lentulus to Asia, to set the Bargylians free, Titillius to Thrace, to see the garrisons of Philip removed out of the towns and islands there, while Publius Villius set sail, in order to treat with Antiochus about the freedom of the Greeks under him. Titus himself passed on to Chalcis, and sailing thence to Magnesia, dismantled the garrisons there, and surrendered the government into the people's hands. Shortly after, he was appointed at Argos to preside in the Nemean games, and did his part in the management of that solemnity singularly well; and made a second publication there by the crier of liberty to the Greeks; and, visiting all the cities, he exhorted them to the practice of obedience to law, of constant justice, and unity, and friendship one towards another. He suppressed their factions, brought home their political exiles; and, in short, his conquest over the Macedonians did not seem to give him a more lively pleasure, than to find himself prevalent in reconciling Greeks with Greeks; so that their liberty seemed now the least part of the kindness he conferred upon them.

The story goes, that when Lycurgus the orator had rescued Xenocrates, the philosopher, from the collectors who were hurrying him away to prison for non-payment of the alien tax, and had them punished for the licence they had been guilty of, Xenocrates afterwards meeting the children of Lycurgus, "My sons," said he, "I am nobly repaying your father for his kindness; he has the praises of the whole people in return for it." But the returns which attended Titus Quintius and the Romans, for their beneficence to the Greeks, terminated not in empty praises only; for these proceedings gained them, deservedly, credit and confidence, and thereby power, among all nations, for many not only admitted the Roman commanders, but even sent and entreated to be under their protection; neither was this done by popular governments alone, or by single cities; but kings oppressed by kings cast themselves into these protecting hands. Insomuch that in a very short time (though perchance not without divine influence in it) all the world did homage to them. Titus himself thought more highly of his liberation of Greece than of any other of his actions, as appears by the inscription with which he dedicated some silver targets, together with his own shields, to Apollo at Delphi:

Ye Spartan Tyndarids, twin sons of Jove,
Who in swift horsemanship have placed your
love,
Titus, of great Æneas's race, leaves this
In honour of the liberty of Greece.

He offered also to Apollo a golden crown, with this inscription:—

This golden crown upon thy locks divine,
O blest Latona's son, was set to shine
By the great captain of the Ænean name.
O Phœbus, grant the noble Titus fame!

The same event has twice occurred to the Greeks in the city of Corinth. Titus, then, and Nero again in our days, both at Corinth, and both alike at the celebration of the Isthmian games, permitted the Greeks to enjoy their own laws and liberty. The former (as has been said) proclaimed it by the crier; but Nero did it in the public meeting-place from the tribunal, in a speech which he himself made to the people. This, however, was long after.

Titus now engaged in a most gallant and just war upon Nabis, that most profligate and lawless tyrant of the Lacedæmonians, but in the end disappointed the expectations of the Greeks. For when he had an opportunity of taking him, he purposely let it slip, and struck up a peace with him, leaving Sparta to bewail an unworthy slavery; whether it were that he feared, if the war should be protracted, Rome would send a new general who might rob him of the glory of it; or that emulation and envy of Philopœmen (who had signalised himself among the Greeks upon all other occasions, but in that war especially had done wonders both for matter of courage and counsel, and whom the Achæans magnified in their theatres, and put into the same balance of glory with Titus), touched him to the quick; and that he scorned that an ordinary Arcadian, who had commanded in a few rencounters upon the confines of his native district, should be spoken of in terms of equality with a Roman consul, waging war as the protector of Greece in general. But, besides, Titus was not without an apology, too, for what he did, namely, that he put an end to the war only when he foresaw that the tyrant's destruction must have been attended with the ruin of the other Spartans.

The Achæans, by various decrees, did much to show Titus honour: none of these returns, however, seemed to come up to the height of the actions that merited them, unless it were one present they made him, which affected and pleased him beyond all the rest, which was this. The Romans, who in the war with Hannibal had the misfortune to be taken captives, were sold about here and there, and dispersed into slavery; twelve hundred in number were at that time in Greece. The reverse of their fortune always rendered them objects of compassion; but more particularly, as well might be, when they now met, some with their sons, some with their brothers, others with their acquaintance; slaves with their free, and captives with their victorious countrymen. Titus, though deeply concerned on their behalf, yet took none of them from their masters by constraint. But the Achæans, redeeming them at five pounds a man, brought them altogether into one place, and made a present of them to him, as he was just going on shipboard, so that he now sailed away with the fullest satisfaction; his generous actions having procured him as generous returns, worthy a brave man and a lover of his country.

This seemed the most glorious part of all his succeeding triumph; for these redeemed Romans (as it is the custom for slaves, upon their manumission, to shave their heads and wear felt hats) followed in that habit in the procession. To add to the glory of this show, there were the Grecian helmets, the Macedonian targets and long spears, borne with the rest of the spoils in public view, besides vast sums of money; Tuditanus says 3,713 pounds weight of massy gold, 43,270 of silver, 14,514 pieces of coined gold, called philippics, which was all over and above the thousand talents which Philip owed, and which the Romans were afterwards prevailed upon, chiefly by the mediation of Titus, to remit to Philip, declaring him their ally and confederate and sending him home his hostage son.

Shortly after, Antiochus entered Greece with a numerous fleet and a powerful army, soliciting the cities there to sedition and revolt; abetted in all and seconded by the Ætolians, who for this long time had borne a grudge and secret enmity to the Romans, and now suggested to him, by the way of a cause and pretext of war, that he came to bring the Greeks liberty. When, indeed, they never wanted it less, as they were free already, but, in lack of really honourable grounds, he was instructed to employ these lofty professions.

The Romans, in the interim, in the great apprehension of revolutions and revolt in Greece, and of his great reputation for military strength, despatched the consul Manius Acilius to take the charge of the war, and Titus, as his lieutenant, out of regard to the Greeks, some of whom he no sooner saw, but he confirmed them in the Roman interests; others, who began to falter, like a timely physician, by the use of the strong remedy of their own affection for himself, he was able to arrest in the first stage of the disease, before they had committed themselves to any great error. Some few there were whom the Ætolians were beforehand with, and had so wholly perverted that he could do no good with them; yet these, however angry and exasperated before, he saved and protected when the engagement was over.

For Antiochus, receiving a defeat at Thermopylæ, not only fled the field, but hoisted sail instantly for Asia. Manius, the consul, himself invaded and besieged a part of the Ætolians, while King Philip had permission to reduce the rest. Thus while, for instance, the Dolopes and Magnetians on the one hand, the Athamanes and Aperantians on the other, were ransacked by the Macedonians, and while Manius laid Heraclea waste, and besieged Naupactus, then in the Ætolians' hands, Titus, still with a compassionate care for Greece, sailed across from Peloponnesus to the consul: and began first of all to chide him, that the victory should be owing alone to his arms, and yet he should suffer Philip to bear away the prize and profit of the war, and set wreaking his anger upon a single town, whilst the Macedonians overran several nations and kingdoms. But as he happened to stand then in view of the besieged, they no sooner spied him out, but they called to him from their wall; they stretched forth their hands; they supplicated and entreated him.

At the time, he said not a word more, but turning about with tears in his eyes, went his way. Some little while after he discussed the matter so effectually with Manius, that he won him over from his passion, and prevailed with him to give a truce and time to the Ætolians to send deputies to Rome to petition the senate for terms of moderation.

But the hardest task, and that which put Titus to the greatest difficulty, was to entreat with Manius for the Chalcidians, who had incensed him on account of a marriage which Antiochus had made in their city, even whilst the war was on foot; a match noways suitable in point of age, he an elderly man being enamoured with a mere girl, and as little proper for the time, in the midst of a war. She was the daughter of one Cleoptolemus, and is said to have been wonderfully beautiful. The Chalcidians, in consequence, embraced the king's interests with zeal and alacrity, and let him make their city the basis of his operations during the war. Thither, therefore, he made with all speed, when he was routed and fled; and reaching Chalcis, without making any stay, taking this young lady, and his money and friends with him, away he sailed to Asia. And now Manius's indignation carrying him in all haste against the Chalcidians, Titus hurried after him, endeavouring to pacify and to entreat him; and at length succeeded both with him and the chief men among the Romans.

The Chalcidians, thus owing their lives to Titus, dedicated to him all the best and most magnificent of their sacred buildings, inscriptions upon which may be seen to run thus to this day: THE PEOPLE DEDICATE THIS GYMNASIUM TO TITUS AND TO HERCULES; so again: THE PEOPLE CONSECRATE THE DELPHINIUM TO TITUS AND TO HERCULES; and what is yet more, even in our time, a priest of Titus was formally elected and declared; and after sacrifice and libation, they sang a set song, much of which for the length of it we omit, but shall transcribe the closing verses—

The Roman, Faith, whose aid of yore
Our vows were offered to implore,
We worship now and evermore.
To Rome, to Titus, and to Jove,
O maidens, in the dances move.
Dances and Io-Pæans too
Unto the Roman Faith are due,
O Saviour Titus, and to you.

Other parts of Greece also heaped honours upon him suitable to his merits, and what made all those honours true and real, was the surprising good-will and affection which his moderation and equity of character had won for him. For if he were at any time at variance with anybody in matters of business, or out of emulation and rivalry (as with Philopœmen, and again with Diophanes, when in office as general of the Achæans), his resentment never went far, nor did it ever break out into acts; but when it had vented itself in some citizen-like freedom of speech, there was an end of it. In fine, nobody charged malice or bitterness upon his nature, though many imputed hastiness and levity to it.

In general, he was the most attractive and agreeable of companions, and could speak, too, both with grace and forcibly. For instance, to divert the Achæans from the conquest of the isle of Zacynthus, "If," said he, "they put their head too far out of Peloponnesus, they may hazard themselves as much as a tortoise out of its shell." Again, when he and Philip first met to treat of a cessation and peace, the latter complaining that Titus came with a mighty train, while he himself came alone and unattended, "Yes," replied Titus, "you have left yourself alone by killing your friends." At another time, Dinocrates, the Messenian, having drunk too much at a merrymeeting in Rome, danced there in woman's clothes, and the next day addressed himself to Titus for assistance in his design to get Messene out of the hands of the Achæans. "This," replied Titus, "will be matter for consideration; my only surprise is that a man with such purposes on his hands should be able to dance and sing at drinking parties." When, again, the ambassadors of Antiochus were recounting to those of Achæa the various multitudes composing their royal master's forces, and ran over a long catalogue of hard names, "I supped once," said Titus, "with a friend, and could not forbear expostulating with him at the number of dishes he had provided, and said I wondered where he had furnished himself with such a variety; 'Sir,' replied he, 'to confess the truth, it is all hog's flesh differently cooked.' And so, men of Achæa, when you are told of Antiochus's lancers, and pikemen, and foot-guards, I advise you not to be surprised; since in fact they are all Syrians, differently armed."

After his achievements in Greece, and when the war with Antiochus was at an end, Titus was created censor; the most eminent office, and, in a manner, the highest preferment, in the commonwealth. The son of Marcellus, who had been five times consul, was his colleague. These, by virtue of their office, cashiered four senators of no great distinction, and admitted to the roll of citizens all free-born residents. But this was more by constraint than their own choice; for Terentius Culeo, then tribune of the people, to spite the nobility, spurred on the populace to order it to be done.

At this time, the two greatest and most eminent persons in the city, Africanus Scipio and Marcus Cato, were at variance. Titus named Scipio first member of the senate; and involved himself in a quarrel with Cato, on the following unhappy occasion. Titus had a brother, Lucius Flamininus, very unlike him in all points of character, and, in particular, low and dissolute in his pleasures, and flagrantly regardless of all decency. He kept as a companion a boy whom he used to carry about with him, not only when he had troops under his charge, but even when the care of a province was committed to him. One day at a drinking-bout, when the youngster was wantoning with Lucius, "I love you, sir, so dearly," said he, "that preferring your satisfaction to my own, I came away without seeing the gladiators, though I have never seen a man killed in my life." Lucius, delighted with what the boy said, answered, "Let not that trouble you; I can satisfy that longing," and with that ordered a condemned man to be fetched out of the prison, and the executioner to be sent for, and commanded him to strike off the man's head before they rose from table. Valerius Antias only so far varies the story as to make it a woman for whom he did it. But Livy says that in Cato's own speech the statement is that a Gaulish deserter coming with his wife and children to the door, Lucius took him into the banqueting-room, and killed him with his own hand, to gratify his paramour. Cato, it is probable, might say this by way of aggravation of the crime; but that the slain was no such fugitive, but a prisoner, and one condemned to die, not to mention other authorities, Cicero tells us in his treatise *On Old Age,* where he brings in Cato, himself giving that account of the matter.

However, this is certain; Cato, during his censorship, made a severe scrutiny into the senators' lives in order to the purging and reforming the house, and expelled Lucius, though he had been once consul before, and though the punishment seemed to reflect dishonour on his brother also. Both of them presented themsleves to the assembly of the people in a suppliant manner, not without tears in their eyes, requesting that Cato might show the reason and cause of his fixing such a stain upon so honourable a family. The citizens thought it a modest and moderate request. Cato, however, without any retraction or reserve, at once came forward, and standing up with his colleague interrogated Titus as to whether he knew the story of the supper. Titus answered in the negative. Cato related it, and challenged Lucius to a formal denial of it. Lucius made no reply, whereupon the people adjudged the disgrace just and suitable, and waited upon Cato home from the tribunal in great state.

But Titus still so deeply resented his brother's degradation, that he allied himself with those who had long borne a grudge against Cato; and winning over a major part of the senate, he revoked and made void all the contracts, leases, and bargains made by Cato, relating to public revenues, and also got numerous actions and accusations brought against him; carrying on against a lawful magistrate and excellent citizens for the sake of one who was indeed his relation, but was unworthy to be so, and had but gotten his deserts, a course of bitter and violent attacks, which it would be hard to say were either right or patriotic. Afterwards, however, at a public spectacle in the theatre, at which the senators appeared as usual, sitting, as became their rank, in the first seats, when Lucius was spied at the lower end, seated in a mean, dishonourable place, it made a great impression upon the people, nor could they endure the sight, but kept calling out to him to move, until he did move, and went in among those of consular dignity, who received him into their seats.

This natural ambition of Titus was well enough looked upon by the world whilst the wars we have given a relation of afforded competent fuel to feed it; as, for instance, when after the expiration of his consulship, he had a command as military tribune, which nobody pressed upon him. But being now out of all employ in the government, and advanced in years, he showed his defects more plainly; allowing himself in this inactive remainder of life to be carried away with the passion for reputation, as uncontrollably as any youth.

Some such transport, it is thought, betrayed him into a proceeding against Hannibal, which lost him the regard of many. For Hannibal, having fled his country, first took sanctuary with Antiochus; but he, having been glad to obtain a peace, after the battle in Phrygia, Hannibal was put to shift for himself, by a second flight, and, after wandering through many countries, fixed at length in Bithynia, proffering his service to King Prusias. Every one at Rome knew where he was, but looked upon him, now in his weakness and old age, with no sort of apprehension, as one whom fortune had quite cast off. Titus, however, coming thither as ambassador, though he was sent from the senate to Prusias upon another errand, yet seeing Hannibal resident there, it stirred up resentment in him to find that he was yet alive. And though Prusias used much intercession and entreaties in favour of him, as his suppliant and familiar friend, Titus was not to be entreated.

There was an ancient oracle, it seems, which prophesied thus of Hannibal's end:—

Libyssan earth shall Hannibal inclose.

He interpreted this to be meant of the African Libya, and that he should be buried in Carthage; as if he might yet expect to return and end his life there. But there is a sandy place in Bithynia, bordering on the sea, and near it a little village called Libyssa. It was Hannibal's chance to be staying here, and, having ever from the beginning had a distrust of the easiness and cowardice of Prusias, and a fear of the Romans, he had, long before, ordered seven underground passages to be dug from his house, leading from his lodging and running a considerable distance in various opposite directions, all undiscernible from without. As soon, therefore, as he heard what Titus had ordered, he attempted to make his escape through these mines; but finding them beset with the king's guards, he resolved upon making away with himself. Some say that, wrapping his upper garment about his neck, he commanded his servant to set his knee against his back, and not to cease twisting and pulling it till he had completely strangled him. Others say he drank bull's blood, after the example of Themistocles and Midas. Livy writes that he had poison in readiness, which he mixed for the purpose, and that, taking the cup in his hand, "Let us ease," said he, "the Romans of their continual dread and care, who think it long and tedious to await the death of a hated old man. Yet Titus will not bear away a glorious victory, nor one worthy of those ancestors who sent to caution Pyrrhus, an enemy, and a conqueror too, against the poison prepared for him by traitors."

Thus various are the reports of Hannibal's death; but when the news of it came to the senators' ears, some felt indignation against Titus for it, blaming as well his officiousness as his cruelty; who, when there was nothing to urge it, out of mere appetite for distinction to have it said that he had caused Hannibal's death, sent him to his grave when he was now like a bird that in its old age has lost its feathers, and incapable of flying, is let alone to live tamely without molestation.

They began also now to regard with increased admiration the clemency and magnanimity of Scipio Africanus, and called to mind how he, when he had vanquished in Africa the till then invincible and terrible Hannibal, neither banished him his country, nor exacted of his countrymen that they should give him up. At a parley just before they joined battle, Scipio gave him his hand, and in the peace made after it, he put no hard article upon him, nor insulted over his fallen fortune. It is told, too, that they had another meeting afterwards, at Ephesus, and that when Hannibal, as they were walking together, took the upper hand, Africanus let it pass, and walked on without the least notice of it; and that then they began to talk of generals, and Hannibal affirmed that Alexander was the greatest commander the world had seen, next to him Pyrrhus, and the third was himself; Africanus, with a smile asked, "What would you have said, if I had not defeated you?" "I would not then, Scipio," he replied, "have made myself the third, but the first commander."

Such conduct was much admired in Scipio, and that of Titus, who had, as it were, insulted the dead whom another had slain, was no less generally found fault with. Not but that there were some who applauded the action, looking upon a living Hannibal as a fire, which only wanted blowing to become a flame. For when he was in the prime and flower of his age, it was not his body nor his hand that had been so formidable, but his consummate skill and experience, together with his innate malice and rancour against the Roman name, things which do not impair with age. For the temper and bent of the soul remains constant, while fortune continually varies; and some new hope might easily rouse to a fresh attempt those whose hatred made them enemies to the last.

And what really happened afterwards does to a certain extent tend yet further to the exculpation of Titus. Aristonicus, of the family of a common musician, upon the reputation of being the son of Eumenes, filled all Asia with tumults and rebellion. Then again, Mithridates, after his defeats by Sulla and Fimbria, and vast slaughter as well among his prime officers as common soldiers, made head again, and proved a most dangerous enemy, against Lucullus, both by sea and land. Hannibal was never reduced to so contemptible a state as Caius Marius; he had the friendship of a king, and the free exercise of his faculties, employment and charge in the navy, and over the horse and foot, of Prusias; whereas those who but now were laughing to hear of Marius wandering about Africa, destitute and begging, in no long time after were seen entreating his mercy in Rome, with his rods at their backs, and his axes at their necks. So true it is, that looking to the possible future, we can call nothing that

we see either great or small; as nothing puts an end to the mutability and vicissitude of things but what puts an end to their very being. Some authors accordingly tell us that Titus did not do this of his own head, but that he was joined in commission with Lucius Scipio, and that the whole object of the embassy was to effect Hannibal's death.

And now, as we find no further mention in history of anything done by Titus, either in war or in the administration of the government, but simply that he died in peace, it is time to look upon him as he stands in comparison with Philopœmen.

FLAMININUS and PHILOPŒMEN
Compared

FIRST then, as for the greatness of the benefits which Titus conferred on Greece, neither Philopœmen, nor many braver men than he, can make good the parallel. They were Greeks fighting against Greeks, but Titus, a stranger to Greece, fought for her. And at the very time when Philopœmen went over into Crete, destitute of means to succor his besieged countrymen, Titus, by a defeat given to Philip in the heart of Greece, set them and their cities free. Again, if we examine the battles they fought, Philopœmen, whilst he was the Achæans' general, slew more Greeks than Titus, in aiding the Greeks, slew Macedonians. As to their failings, ambition was Titus's weak side, and obstinacy Philopœmen's; in the former, anger was easily kindled; in the latter, it was as hardly quenched. Titus reserved to Philip the royal dignity; he pardoned the Ætolians, and stood their friend; but Philopœmen, exasperated against his country, deprived it of its supremacy over the adjacent villages. Titus was ever constant to those he had once befriended; the other, upon any offence, as prone to cancel kindnesses. He who had once been a benefactor to the Lacedæmonians, afterwards laid their walls level with the ground, wasted their country, and in the end changed and destroyed the whole frame of their government. He seems, in truth, to have prodigalled away his own life, through passion and perverseness; for he fell upon the Messenians, not with that conduct and caution that characterised the movements of Titus, but with unnecessary and unreasonable haste.

The many battles he fought, and the many trophies he won, may make us ascribe to Philo-

pœmen the more thorough knowledge of war. Titus decided the matter betwixt Philip and himself in two engagements; but Philopœmen came off victorious in ten thousand encounters, to all which fortune had scarcely any pretence, so much were they owing to his skill. Besides, Titus got his renown, assisted by the power of a flourishing Rome; the other flourished under a declined Greece, so that his successes may be accounted his own; in Titus's glory Rome claims a share. The one had brave men under him, the other made his brave, by being over them.

And though Philopœmen was unfortunate, certainly, in always being opposed to his countrymen, yet this misfortune is at the same time a proof of his merit. Where the circumstances are the same, superior success can only be ascribed to superior merit. And he had, indeed, to do with the two most warlike nations of all Greece, the Cretans on the one hand, and the Lacedæmonians on the other, and he mastered the craftiest of them by art and the bravest of them by valour.

It may also be said that Titus, having his men armed and disciplined to his hand, had in a manner his victories made for him; whereas Philopœmen was forced to introduce a discipline and tactics of his own, and to new-mould and model his soldiers; so that what is of greatest import towards insuring a victory was in his case his own creation, while the other had it ready provided for his benefit. Philopœmen effected many gallant things with his own hand, but Titus none; so much so that one Archedemus, an Ætolian, made it a jest against him that while he, the Ætolian, was running with his drawn sword, where he saw the Macedonians drawn up closest and fighting hardest, Titus was standing still, and with hands stretched out to heaven, praying to the gods for aid.

It is true Titus acquitted himself admirably, both as a governor and as an ambassador; but Philopœmen was no less serviceable and useful to the Achæans in the capacity of a private man than in that of a commander. He was a private citizen when he restored the Messenians to their liberty, and delivered their city from Nabis; he was also a private citizen when he rescued the Lacedæmonians, and shut the gates of Sparta against the general, Diophanes, and Titus. He had a nature so truly formed for command that he could govern even the laws themselves for the public good; he did not need to wait for the formality of being elected into command by the governed, but employed their service, if occasion required, at his own discretion; judging that he who understood their real interests was more truly their supreme magistrate, than he whom they had elected to the office. The equity, clemency, and humanity of Titus towards the Greeks display a great and generous nature; but the actions of Philopœmen, full of courage, and forward to assert his country's liberty against the Romans, have something yet greater and nobler in them. For it is not as hard a task to gratify the indigent and distressed, as to bear up against and to dare to incur the anger of the powerful. To conclude, since it does not appear to be easy, by any review or discussion, to establish the true difference of their merits and decide to which a preference is due, will it be an unfair award in the case, if we let the Greek bear away the crown for military conduct and warlike skill, and the Roman for justice and clemency?

PYRRHUS

365?–272 B.C.

O F THE Thesprotians and Molossians after the great inundation, the first king, according to some historians, was Phæthon, one of those who came into Epirus with Pelasgus. Others tell us that Deucalion and Pyrrha, having set up the worship of Jupiter at Dodona, settled there among the Molossians. In after time, Neoptolemus, Achilles's son, planting a colony, possessed these parts himself, and left a succession of kings, who, after him, were named Pyrrhidæ, as he in his youth was called Pyrrhus, and of his legitimate children, one born of Lanassa, daughter of Cleodæus, Hyllus's son, had also that name. From him Achilles came to have divine honours in Epirus, under the name of Aspetus, in the language of the country.

After these first kings, those of the following intervening times becoming barbarous, and insignificant both in their power and their lives, Tharrhypas is said to have been the first who, by introducing Greek manners and learning, and humane laws into his cities, left any fame of himself. Alcetas was the son of Tharrhypas, Arybas of Alcetas, and of Arybas and Troas, his queen, Æacides; he married Phthia, the daughter of Menon, the Thessalian, a man of note at the time of the Lamiac war, and of highest command in the confederate army next to Leosthenes. To Æacides were born of Phthia, Deidamia and Troas, daughters, and Pyrrhus, a son.

The Molossians, afterwards falling into factions and expelling Æacides, brought in the sons of Neoptolemus, and such friends of Æacides as they could take were all cut off; Pyrrhus, yet an infant, and searched for by the enemy, had been stolen away and carried off by Androclides and Angelus; who, however, being obliged to take with them a few servants, and women to nurse the child, were much impeded and retarded in their flight, and when they were now overtaken, they delivered the infant to Androcleon, Hippias, and Neander, faithful and able young fellows, giving them in charge to make for Megara, a town of Macedon, with all their might, while they themselves, partly by entreaty, and partly by force, stopped the course of the pursuers till late in the evening.

At last, having hardly forced them back, they joined those who had the care of Pyrrhus; but the sun being already set, at the point of attaining their object they suddenly found themselves cut off from it. For on reaching the river that runs by the city they found it looking formidable and rough, and endeavouring to pass over, they discovered it was not fordable; late rains having heightened the water and made the current violent. The darkness of the night added to the horror of all, so that they durst not venture of themselves to carry over the child and the women that attended it; but, perceiving some of the country people on the other side, they desired them to assist their passage, and showed them Pyrrhus, calling out aloud, and importuning them. They, however, could not hear for the noise and roaring of the water.

Thus time was spent while those called out, and the others did not understand what was said, till one recollecting himself, stripped off a piece of bark from an oak, and wrote on it with the tongue of a buckle, stating the necessities and the fortunes of the child, and then rolling it about a stone, which was made use of to give force to the motion, threw it over to the other side, or, as some say, fastened it to the end of a javelin, and darted it over. When the men on the other shore read what was on the bark, and saw how time pressed, without delay they cut down some trees, and lashing them together, came over to them. And it so fell out, that he who first got ashore, and took Pyrrhus in his arms, was named Achilles, the rest being helped over by others as they came to hand.

Thus being safe, and out of the reach of pursuit, they addressed themselves to Glaucias, then King of the Illyrians, and finding him sitting at home with his wife, they laid down the child before them. The king began to weigh the matter, fearing Cassander, who was a mortal enemy of Æacides, and, being in deep consideration, said nothing for a long time; while Pyrrhus, crawling about on the ground, gradually got near and laid hold with his hand upon the king's robe, and so helping himself upon his feet against the knees of Glaucias first moved laughter, and then pity, as a little, humble, crying petitioner. Some say he did not throw himself before Glaucias, but catching hold of an altar of the gods, and spreading his hands about it, raised himself up by that; and that Glaucias took the act as an omen. At present, therefore, he gave Pyrrhus into the charge of his wife, commanding he should be brought up with his own children; and a little after, the enemies sending to demand him, and Cassander himself offering two hundred talents, he would not deliver him up; but when he was twelve years old, bringing him with an army into Epirus, made him king.

Pyrrhus in the air of his face had something more of the terrors than of the augustness of kingly power; he had not a regular set of upper teeth, but in the place of them one continued bone, with small lines marked on it, resembling the divisions of a row of teeth. It was a general belief he could cure the spleen by sacrificing a white cock and gently pressing with his right foot on the spleen of the persons as they lay down on their backs, nor was any one so poor or inconsiderable as not to be welcome, if he desired it, to the benefit of his touch. He accepted the cock for the sacrifice as a reward, and was always much pleased with the present. The large toe of that foot was said to have a divine virtue; for after his death, the rest of the body being consumed, this was found unhurt, and untouched by the fire. But of these things hereafter.

Being now about seventeen years old, and the government in appearance well settled, he took a journey out of the kingdom to attend the marriage of one of Glaucias's sons, with whom he was brought up; upon which opportunity the Molossians again rebelling; turned out all of his party, plundered his property, and gave themselves up to Neoptolemus. Pyrrhus having thus lost the kingdom, and being in want of all things, applied to Demetrius, the son of Antigonus, the husband of his sister, Deidamia, who, while she was but a child, had been in name the wife of Alexander, son of Roxana, but their affairs afterwards proving unfortunate, when she came to age, Demetrius married her.

At the great battle of Ipsus, where so many kings were engaged, Pyrrhus, taking part with Demetrius, though yet but a youth, routed those that encountered him, and highly signalised himself among all the soldiery, and afterwards, when Demetrius's fortunes were low, he did not forsake him then, but secured for him the cities of Greece with which he was intrusted; and upon articles of agreement being made between Demetrius and Ptolemy, he went over as an hostage for him into Egypt, where both in hunting and other exercises he gave Ptolemy an ample proof of his courage and strength. Here observing Berenice in greatest power, and of all Ptolemy's wives highest in esteem for virtue and understanding, he made his court principally to her. He had a particular art of gaining over the great to his own interest, as on the other hand he readily overlooked such as were below him; and being also well-behaved and temperate in his life, among all the young princes then at court he was thought most fit to have Antigone for his wife, one of the daughters of Berenice by Philip, before she married Ptolemy.

After this match, advancing in honour, and Antigone being a very good wife to him, having procured a sum of money, and raised an army, he so ordered matters as to be sent into his kingdom of Epirus, and arrived there to the great satisfaction of many, from their hate to Neoptolemus, who was governing in a violent and arbitrary way. But fearing lest Neoptolemus should enter into alliance with some neighbouring princes, he came to terms and friendship with him, agreeing that they should share the government between them. There were people, however, who, as time went on, secretly exasperated them, and fomented jealousies between them.

The cause chiefly moving Pyrrhus is said to have had this beginning. It was customary for the kings to offer sacrifice to Mars at Passaro, a place in the Molossian country, and that done to enter into a solemn covenant with the Epirots; they to govern according to law, these to preserve the government as by law established. This was performed in the presence of both kings, who were there with their immediate friends, giving and receiving many presents; here Gelo, one of the friends of Neoptolemus, taking Pyrrhus by the hand, presented him with two pair of draught oxen. Myrtilus, his cup-bearer, being then by, begged these of Pyrrhus, who not giving them to him, but to another, Myrtilus extremely resented it, which Gelo took notice of, and, inviting him to a banquet (amidst drinking and other excesses, as some relate, Myrtilus being then in the flower of his youth), he entered into discourse, persuading him to adhere to Neoptolemus, and destroy Pyrrhus by poison. Myrtilus received the design, appearing to approve and consent to it, but privately discovered it to Pyrrhus, by whose command he recommended Alexicrates, his chief cup-bearer, to Gelo, as a fit instrument for their design, Pyrrhus being very desirous to have proof of the plot by several evidences.

So Gelo, being deceived, Neoptolemus, who was no less deceived, imagining the design went prosperously on, could not forbear, but in his joy spoke of it among his friends, and once at an entertainment at his sister Cadmea's talked openly of it, thinking none heard but themselves. Nor was any one there but Phæ-narete, the wife of Samon, who had the care of Neoptolemus's flocks and herds. She, turning her face towards the wall upon a couch, seemed fast asleep, and having heard all that passed, unsuspected, next day came to Antigone, Pyrrhus's wife, and told her what she had heard Neoptolemus say to his sister. On understanding which Pyrrhus for the present said little, but on a sacrifice day, making an invitation for Neoptolemus, killed him; being satisfied before that the great men of the Epirots were his friends and that they were eager for him to rid himself of Neoptolemus and not to content himself with a mere petty share of the government, but to follow his own natural vocation to great designs, and now when a just ground of suspicion appeared, to anticipate Neoptolemus by taking him off first.

In memory of Berenice and Ptolemy he named his son by Antigone, Ptolemy, and having built a city in the peninsula of Epirus, called it Berenicis. From this time he began to revolve many and vast projects in his thoughts; but his first special hope and design lay near home, and he found means to engage himself in the Macedonian affairs under the following pretext. Of Cassander's sons, Antipater, the eldest, killed Thessalonica, his mother, and expelled his brother, Alexander, who sent to Demetrius entreating his assistance, and also called in Pyrrhus; but Demetrius being retarded by multitude of business, Pyrrhus, coming first, demanded in reward of his service the districts called Tymphæa and Parauæa in Macedon itself, and of their new conquests, Ambracia, Acarnania, and Amphilochia. The young prince giving way, he took possession of these countries, and secured them with good garrisons, and proceeded to reduce for Alexander himself other parts of the kingdom which he gained from Antipater.

Lysimachus, designing to send aid to Antipater, was involved in much other business, but knowing Pyrrhus would not disoblige Ptolemy, or deny him anything, sent pretended letters to him as from Ptolemy, desiring him to give up his expedition, upon the payment of three hundred talents to him by Antipater. Pyrrhus, opening the letter, quickly discovered the fraud of Lysimachus; for it had not the accustomed style of salutation, "The father to the son, health," but "King Ptolemy to Pyrrhus, the king, health"; and reproaching Lysimachus, he notwithstanding made a peace, and they all met to confirm it by a solemn oath upon sacrifice. A goat, a bull, and a ram being brought out, the ram on a sudden fell dead. The others laughed, but Theodotus, the prophet, forbade Pyrrhus to swear, declaring that Heaven by that portended the death of one of the three kings, upon which he refused to ratify the peace.

The affairs of Alexander being now in some kind of settlement, Demetrius arrived, contrary, as soon appeared, to the desire and indeed not without the alarm of Alexander. After they had been a few days together, their mutual jealousy led them to conspire against each other; and Demetrius, taking advantage of the first occasion, was beforehand with the young king, and slew him, and proclaimed himself King of Macedon.

There had been formerly no very good understanding between him and Pyrrhus; for besides the inroads he made into Thessaly, the innate disease of princes, ambition of greater empire, had rendered them formidable and suspected neighbours to each other, especially since Deidamia's death; and both having seized Macedon, they came into conflict for the same object, and the difference between them had the stronger motives.

Demetrius having first attacked the Ætolians and subdued them, left Pantauchus there with a considerable army, and marched direct against Pyrrhus, and Pyrrhus, as he thought, against him; but by mistake of the ways they passed by one another, and Demetrius falling into Epirus wasted the country, and Pyrrhus, meeting with Pantauchus, prepared for an engagement. The soldiers fell to, and there was a sharp and terrible conflict, especially where the generals were.

Pantauchus, in courage, dexterity, and strength of body, being confessedly the best of all Demetrius's captains, and having both resolution and high spirit, challenged Pyrrhus to fight hand to hand; on the other side Pyrrhus, professing not to yield to any king in valour and glory, and esteeming the fame of Achilles more truly to belong to him for his courage than for his blood, advanced against Pantauchus through the front of the army. First they used their lances, then came to a close fight, and managed their swords both with art and force; Pyrrhus receiving one wound, but returning two for it, one in the thigh and the other near the neck, repulsed and overthrew Pantauchus, but did not kill him outright, as he was rescued by his friends. But the Epirots exulting in the victory of their king, and admiring his courage, forced through and cut in pieces the phalanx of the Macedonians, and pursuing those that fled, killed many, and took five thousand prisoners.

This fight did not so much exasperate the Macedonians with anger for their loss, or with hatred to Pyrrhus, as it caused esteem and admiration of his valour, and great discourse of him among those that saw what he did, and were engaged against him in the action. They thought his countenance, his swiftness, and his motions expressed those of the great Alexander, and that they beheld here an image and resemblance of his rapidity and strength in fight; other kings merely by their purple and their guards, by the formal bending of their necks and lofty tone of their speech, Pyrrhus only by arms and in action, represented Alexander.

Of his knowledge of military tactics and the art of a general, and his great ability that way, we have the best information from the commentaries he left behind him. Antigonus, also, we are told, being asked who was the greatest soldier, said, "Pyrrhus, if he lives to be old," referring only to those of his own time; but Hannibal of all great commanders esteemed Pyrrhus for skill and conduct the first, Scipio the second, and himself the third, as is related in the life of Scipio. In a word, he seemed ever to make this all his thought and philosophy, as the most kingly part of learning; other curiosities he held in no account. He is reported, when asked at a feast whether he thought Python or Caphisias the best musician, to have said, Polysperchon was the best soldier, as though it became a king to examine and understand only such things.

Towards his familiars he was mild and not easily incensed; zealous and even vehement in returning kindnesses. Thus when Aeropus was dead, he could not bear it with moderation, saying, he indeed had suffered what was common to human nature, but condemning and blaming himself, that by puttings off and delays he had not returned his kindness in time. For our debts may be satisfied to the creditor's heirs, but not to have made the acknowledgment of received favours, while they to whom it is due can be sensible of it, afflicts a good and worthy nature. Some thinking it fit that Pyrrhus should banish a certain ill-tongued fellow in Ambracio, who had spoken very indecently of him, "Let him rather," said he, "speak against us here to a few, than rambling about to a great many." And others who in their wine had made reflections upon him, being afterward questioned for it, and asked by him whether they had said such words, on one of the young fellows answering, "Yes, all that, king; and should have said more if we had had more wine," he laughed and discharged them.

After Antigone's death, he married several wives to enlarge his interest and power. He had the daughter of Autoleon, King of the Pæonians, Bircenna, Bardyllis the Illyrian's daughter, Lanassa, daughter of Agathocles the Syracusan, who brought with her in dower the city of Corcyra, which had been taken by Agathocles. By Antigone he had Ptolemy, Alexander by Lanassa, and Helenus, his youngest son, by Bircenna: he brought them up all in arms, hot and eager youths, and by him sharpened and whetted to war from their very infancy. It is said when one of them, while yet a child, asked him to which he would leave the kingdom, he replied, to him that had the sharpest sword, which indeed was much like that tragical curse of Œdipus to his sons:—

Not by the lot decide,
But within the sword the heritage divide.

So unsocial and wild-beast-like is the nature of ambition and cupidity.

After this battle Pyrrhus, returning gloriously home, enjoyed his fame and reputation, and being called "Eagle" by the Epirots, "By you," said he, "I am an eagle; for how should I not be such, while I have your arms as wings to sustain me?"

A little after, having intelligence that Demetrius was dangerously sick, he entered on a sudden into Macedonia, intending only an incursion, and to harass the country; but was very near seizing upon all, and taking the kingdom without a blow. He marched as far as Edessa unresisted, great numbers deserting and coming in to him. This danger excited Demetrius beyond his strength, and his friends and commanders in a short time got a considerable army together, and with all their forces briskly attacked Pyrrhus, who, coming only to pillage, would not stand a fight, but retreating, lost part of his army, as he went off, by the close pursuit of the Macedonians.

Demetrius, however, although he had easily and quickly forced Pyrrhus out of the country, yet did not slight him, but having resolved upon great designs, and to recover his father's kingdom with an army of one hundred thousand men, and a fleet of five hundred ships, would neither embroil himself with Pyrrhus, nor leave the Macedonians so active and troublesome a neighbour; and since he had no leisure to continue the war with him, he was willing to treat and conclude a peace, and to turn his forces upon the other kings.

Articles being agreed upon, the designs of Demetrius quickly discovered themselves by the greatness of his preparation. And the other kings, being alarmed, sent to Pyrrhus ambassadors and letters, expressing their wonder that he should choose to let his own opportunity pass by, and wait till Demetrius could use his; and whereas he was now able to chase him out of Macedon, involved in designs and disturbed, he should wait till Demetrius at leisure, and grown great, should bring the war home to his own door, and make him fight for his temples and sepulchres in Molossia; especially having so lately, by his means, lost Corcyra and his wife together. For Lanassa had taken offence at Pyrrhus for too great an inclination to those wives of his that were barbarians, and so withdrew to Corcyra, and desiring to marry some king, invited Demetrius, knowing of all the kings he was most ready to entertain offers of marriage; so he sailed thither, married Lanassa, and placed a garrison in the city.

The kings having written thus to Pyrrhus, themselves likewise contrived to find Demetrius work, while he was delaying and making his preparations. Ptolemy, setting out with a great fleet, drew off many of the Greek cities. Lysimachus out of Thrace wasted the upper Macedon; and Pyrrhus, also taking arms at the same time, marched to Berœa, expecting, as it fell out, that Demetrius, collecting his forces against Lysimachus, would leave the lower country undefended. That very night he seemed in his sleep to be called by Alexander the Great, and approaching, saw him sick abed, but was received with very kind words, and much respect, and promised zealous assistance. He making bold to reply, "How, sir, can you, being sick, assist me?" "With my name," said he, and mounting a Nisæan horse, seemed to lead the way. At the sight of this vision he was much assured, and with swift marches overrunning all the interjacent places, took Berœa, and making his headquarters there, reduced the rest of the country by his commanders.

When Demetrius received intelligence of this, and perceived likewise the Macedonians ready to mutiny in the army, he was afraid to advance further, lest, coming near Lysimachus, a Macedonian king, and of great fame, they should revolt to him. So returning, he marched directly against Pyrrhus, as a stranger, and hated by the Macedonians. But while he lay encamped there near him, many who came out of Berœa infinitely praised Pyrrhus as invincible in arms, a glorious warrior, who treated those he had taken kindly and humanely. Several of these Pyrrhus himself sent privately, pretending to be Macedonians, and saying, now was the time to be delivered from the severe government of Demetrius by coming over to Pyrrhus, a gracious prince and a lover of soldiers.

By this artifice a great part of the army was in a state of excitement, and the soldiers began to look every way about inquiring for Pyrrhus. It happened he was without his helmet, till understanding they did not know him, he put it on again, and so was quickly recognised by his lofty crest and the goat's horns he wore upon it. Then the Macedonians, running to him, desired to be told his password, and some put oaken boughs upon their heads, because they saw them worn by the soldiers about him. Some persons even took the confidence to say to Demetrius himself, that he would be well advised to withdraw and lay down the government. And he, indeed, seeing the mutinous movements of the army to be only too consistent with what they said, privately got away, disguised in a broad hat and a common soldier's coat. So Pyrrhus became master of the army without fighting, and was declared King of the Macedonians.

But Lysimachus now arriving, and claiming the defeat of Demetrius as the joint exploit of them both, and that therefore the kingdom should be shared between them, Pyrrhus, not as yet quite assured of the Macedonians, and in doubt of their faith, consented to the proposition of Lysimachus, and divided the country and cities between them accordingly.

This was for the present useful, and prevented a war; but shortly after they found the partition not so much a peaceful settlement as an occasion of further complaint and difference. For men whose ambition neither seas, nor mountains, nor unpeopled deserts can limit, nor the bounds dividing Europe from Asia confine their vast desires, it would be hard to expect to forbear from injuring one another when they touch and are close together. These are ever naturally at war, envying and seeking advantages of one another, and merely make use of those two words, peace and war, like current coin, to serve their occasions, not as justice but as expediency suggests, and are really better men when they openly enter on a war, than when they give to the mere forbearance from doing wrong, for want of opportunity, the sacred names of justice and friendship.

Pyrrhus was an instance of this; for setting himself against the rise of Demetrius again, and endeavouring to hinder the recovery of his power, as it were from a kind of sickness, he assisted the Greeks, and came to Athens, where having ascended the Acropolis, he offered sacrifice to the goddess, and the same day came down again, and told the Athenians he was much gratified by the good-will and the confidence they had shown to him; but if they were wise he advised them never to let any king come thither again, or open their city gates to him. He concluded also a peace with Demetrius, but shortly after he was gone into Asia, at the persuasion of Lysimachus, he tampered with the Thessalians to revolt, and besieged his cities in Greece; finding he could better preserve the attachment of the Macedonians in war than in peace, and being of his own inclination not much given to rest.

At last, after Demetrius had been overthrown in Syria, Lysimachus, who had secured his affairs, and had nothing to do, immediately turned his whole forces upon Pyrrhus, who was in quarters at Edessa, and falling upon and seizing his convoy of provisions, brought first a great scarcity into the army; then partly by letters, partly by spreading rumours abroad, he corrupted the principal officers of the Macedonians, reproaching them that they had made one their master who was both a stranger and descended from those who had ever been servants to the Macedonians, and that they had thrust the old friends and familiars of Alexander out of the country. The Macedonian soldiers being much prevailed upon, Pyrrhus withdrew himself with his Epirots and auxiliary forces, relinquishing Macedon, just after the same manner he took it. So little reason have kings to condemn popular governments for changing sides as suits their interests, as in this they do but imitate them who are the great instructors of unfaithfulness and treachery; holding him the wisest that makes the least account of being an honest man.

Pyrrhus having thus retired into Epirus, and left Macedon, fortune gave him a fair occasion of enjoying himself in quiet, and peaceably governing his own subjects, but he who thought it a nauseous course of life not to be doing mischief to others, or receiving some from them, like Achilles, could not endure repose—

——But sad and languished far,
Desiring battle and the shout of war,

and gratified his inclination by the following pretext for new troubles. The Romans were at war with the Tarentines, who, not being able to go on with the war, nor yet, through the foolhardiness and the viciousness of their popular speakers, to come to terms and give it up, proposed now to make Pyrrhus their general, and engage him in it, as of all the neighbouring kings the most at leisure, and the most skilful as a commander. The more grave and discreet citizens opposing these counsels, were partly overborne by the noise and violence of the multitude; while others, seeing this, absented themselves from the assemblies; only one Meton, a very sober man, on the day this public decree was to be ratified, when the people were now seating themselves, came dancing into the assembly like one quite drunk, with a withered garland and a small lamp in his hand, and a woman playing on a flute before him. And as in great multitudes met at such popular assemblies no decorum can be well observed, some clapped him, others laughed, none forbade him, but called to the woman to play, and to him to sing to the company, and when they thought he was going to do so, " 'Tis right of you, O men of Tarentum," he said, "not to hinder any from making themselves merry that have a mind to it, while it is yet in their power; and if you are wise, you will take out your pleasure of your freedom while you can, for you must change your course of life, and follow other diet when Pyrrhus comes to town."

These words made a great impression upon many of the Tarentines, and a confused murmur went about that he had spoken much to the purpose; but some who feared they should be sacrificed if a peace were made with the Romans, reviled the whole assembly for so tamely suffering themselves to be abused by a drunken sot, and crowding together upon Meton, thrust him out. So the public order was passed and ambassadors sent into Epirus, not only in their own names, but in those of all the Italian Greeks, carrying presents to

Pyrrhus, and letting him know they wanted a general of reputation and experience; and that they could furnish him with large forces of Lucanians, Messapians, Samnites, and Tarentines, amounting to twenty thousand horse, and three hundred and fifty thousand foot. This did not only quicken Pyrrhus, but raised an eager desire for the expedition in the Epirots.

There was one Cineas, a Thessalian, considered to be a man of very good sense, a disciple of the great orator, Demosthenes, who, of all that were famous at that time for speaking well, most seemed, as in a picture, to revive in the minds of the audience the memory of his force and vigour of eloquence; and being always about Pyrrhus, and sent about in his service to several cities, verified the saying of Euripides, that—

——the force of words
Can do whate'er is done by conquering swords.

And Pyrrhus was used to say, that Cineas had taken more towns with his words than he with his arms, and always did him the honour to employ him in his most important occasions.

This person, seeing Pyrrhus eagerly preparing for Italy, led him one day when he was at leisure into the following reasonings: "The Romans, sir, are reported to be great warriors and conquerors of many warlike nations; if God permit us to overcome them, how should we use our victory?" "You ask," said Pyrrhus, "a thing evident of itself. The Romans once conquered, there is neither Greek nor barbarian city that will resist us, but we shall presently be masters of all Italy, the extent and resources and strength of which any one should rather profess to be ignorant of than yourself."

Cineas after a little pause, "And having subdued Italy, what shall we do next?" Pyrrhus not yet discovering his intention, "Sicily," he replied, "next holds out her arms to receive us, a wealthy and populous island, and easy to be gained; for since Agathocles left it, only faction and anarchy, and the licentious violence of the demagogues prevail."

"You speak," said Cineas, "what is perfectly probable, but will the possession of Sicily put an end to the war?" "God grant us," answered Pyrrhus, "victory and success in that, and we will use these as forerunners of greater things; who could forbear from Libya and Carthage then within reach, which Agathocles, even when forced to flee from

Syracuse, and passing the sea only with a few ships, had all but surprised? These conquests once perfected, will any assert that of the enemies who now pretend to despise us, any one will dare to make further resistance?"

"None," replied Cineas, "for then it is manifest we may with such mighty forces regain Macedon, and make an absolute conquest of Greece; and when all these are in our power what shall we do then?" Said Pyrrhus, smiling, "We will live at our ease, my dear friend, and drink all day, and divert ourselves with pleasant conversation."

When Cineas had led Pyrrhus with his argument to this point: "And what hinders us now, sir, if we have a mind to be merry, and entertain one another, since we have at hand without trouble all those necessary things, to which through much blood and great labour, and infinite hazards and mischief done to ourselves and to others, we design at last to arrive?" Such reasonings rather troubled Pyrrhus with the thought of the happiness he was quitting, than any way altered his purpose, he being unable to abandon the hopes of what he so much desired.

And first, he sent away Cineas to the Tarentines with three thousand men; presently after, many vessels for transport of horse, and galleys, and flat-bottomed boats of all sorts arriving from Tarentum, he shipped upon them twenty elephants, three thousand horse, twenty thousand foot, two thousand archers, and five hundred slingers.

All being thus in readiness, he set sail, and being half-way over, was driven by the wind, blowing, contrary to the season of the year, violently from the north, and carried from his course, but by the great skill and resolution of his pilots and seamen, he made the land with infinite labour, and beyond expectation. The rest of the fleet could not get up, and some of the dispersed ships, losing the coast of Italy, were driven into the Libyan and Sicilian Sea; others, not able to double the cape of Japygium, were overtaken by the night; and, with a boisterous and heavy sea, throwing them upon a dangerous and rocky shore, they were all very much disabled except the royal galley. She, while the sea bore upon her sides, resisted with her bulk and strength, and avoided the force of it, till the wind coming about, blew directly in their teeth from the shore, and the vessel keeping up with her head against it, was in danger of going to pieces; yet on the other hand, to

suffer themselves to be driven off to sea again, which was thus raging and tempestuous, with the wind shifting about every way, seemed to them the most dreadful of all their present evils. Pyrrhus, rising up, threw himself overboard.

His friends and guards strove eagerly who should be most ready to help him, but night and the sea, with its noise and violent surge, made it extremely difficult to do this; so that hardly, when with the morning the wind began to subside, he got ashore, breathless and weakened in body, but with high courage and strength of mind resisting his hard fortune. The Messapians, upon whose shore they were thrown by the tempest, came up eagerly to help them in the best manner they could; and some of the straggling vessels that had escaped the storm arrived; in which were a very few horse, and not quite two thousand foot, and two elephants.

With these Pyrrhus marched straight to Tarentum, where Cineas, being informed of his arrival, led out the troops to meet him. Entering the town, he did nothing unpleasing to the Tarentines, nor put any force upon them, till the ships were all in harbour, and the greatest part of the army got together; but then perceiving that the people, unless some strong compulsion was used to them, were not capable either of saving others or being saved themselves, and were rather intending, while he engaged for them in the field, to remain at home bathing and feasting themselves, he first shut up the places of public exercise, and the walks, where, in their idle way, they fought their country's battles and conducted her campaigns in their talk; he prohibited likewise all festivals, revels, and drinking-parties as unseasonable, and summoning them to arms, showed himself vigorous and inflexible in carrying out the conscription for service in the war. So that many, not understanding what it was to be commanded, left the town, calling it mere slavery not to do as they pleased.

He now received intelligence that Lævinus, the Roman consul, was upon his march with a great army, and plundering Lucania as he went. The confederate forces were not come up to him, yet he thought it impossible to suffer so near an approach of an enemy, and drew out with his army, but first sent an herald to the Romans to know if before the war they would decide the differences between them and the Italian Greeks by his arbitrament and mediation. But Lævinus returning answer that the Romans neither accepted him as arbitrator nor feared him as an enemy, Pyrrhus advanced, and encamped in the plain between the cities of Pandosia and Heraclea, and having notice the Romans were near, and lay on the other side of the river Siris, he rode up to take a view of them, and seeing their order, the appointment of the watches, their method and the general form of their encampment, he was amazed, and addressing one of his friends next to him: "This order," said he, "Megacles, of the barbarians, is not at all barbarian in character; we shall see presently what they can do"; and growing a little more thoughtful of the event, resolved to expect the arriving of the confederate troops.

And to hinder the Romans, if in the meantime they should endeavour to pass the river, he planted men all along the bank to oppose them. But they, hastening to anticipate the coming up of the same forces which he had determined to wait for, attempted the passage with their infantry, where it was fordable, and with the horse in several places, so that the Greeks, fearing to be surrounded, were obliged to retreat, and Pyrrhus, perceiving this, and being much surprised, bade his foot officers draw their men up in line of battle, and continue in arms, while he himself with three thousand horse advanced, hoping to attack the Romans as they were coming over, scattered and disordered.

But when he saw a vast number of shields appearing above the water, and the horse following them in good order, gathering his men in a closer body, himself at the head of them, he began the charge, conspicuous by his rich and beautiful armour, and letting it be seen that his reputation had not outgone what he was able effectually to perform. While exposing his hands and body in the fight, and bravely repelling all that engaged him, he still guided the battle with a steady and undisturbed reason, and such presence of mind, as if he had been out of the action and watching it from a distance, passing still from point to point, and assisting those whom he thought most pressed by the enemy.

Here Leonnatus the Macedonian, observing one of the Italians very intent upon Pyrrhus, riding up towards him, and changing places as he did, and moving as he moved: "Do you see, sir," said he, "that barbarian on the black horse with white feet? He seems to be one that designs some great and dangerous thing, for he looks constantly at you, and fixes his whole attention, full of vehement purpose, on you alone, taking no notice of others. Be on your guard, sir, against him." "Leonnatus," said Pyrrhus, "it is impossible for any man to avoid his fate; but neither he nor any other Italian shall have much satisfaction in engaging with me."

While they were in this discourse, the Italian, lowering his spear and quickening his horse, rode furiously at Pyrrhus, and ran his horse through with his lance; at the same instant Leonnatus ran his through. Both horses falling, Pyrrhus's friends surrounded him and brought him off safe, and killed the Italian, bravely defending himself. He was by birth a Frentanian, captain of a troop, and named Oplacus.

This made Pyrrhus use greater caution, and now seeing his horse give ground, he brought up the infantry against the enemy, and changing his scarf and his arms with Megacles, one of his friends, and obscuring himself, as it were, in his, charged upon the Romans, who received and engaged him, and a great while the success of the battle remained undetermined; and it is said there were seven turns of fortune both of pursuing and being pursued. And the change of his arms was very opportune for the safety of his person, but had like to have overthrown his cause and lost him the victory; for several falling upon Megacles, the first that gave him his mortal wound was one Dexous, who, snatching away his helmet and his robe, rode at once to Lævinus, holding them up, and saying aloud he had killed Pyrrhus.

These spoils being carried about and shown among the ranks, the Romans were transported with joy, and shouted aloud; while equal discouragement and terror prevailed among the Greeks, until Pyrrhus, understanding what had happened, rode about the army with his face bare, stretching out his hand to his soldiers, and telling them aloud it was he.

At last, the elephants more particularly began to distress the Romans, whose horses, before they came near, nor enduring them, went back with their riders; and upon this, he commanded the Thessalian cavalry to charge them in their disorder, and routed them with great loss. Dionysius affirms near fifteen thousand of the Romans fell; Hieronymus, no more than seven thousand. On Pyrrhus's side, the same Dionysius makes thirteen thousand slain, the other under four thousand; but they were the flower of his men, and amongst them his particular friends as well as officers whom he most trusted and made use of. However, he possessed himself of the Romans' camp which they deserted, and gained over several confederate cities, and wasted the country round about, and advanced so far that he was within about thirty-seven miles of Rome itself. After the fight many of the Lucanians and Samnites came in and joined him, whom he chid for their delay, but yet he was evidently well pleased and raised in his thoughts, that he had defeated so great an army of the Romans with the assistance of the Tarentines alone.

The Romans did not remove Lævinus from the consulship; though it is told that Caius Fabricius said, that the Epirots had not beaten the Romans, but only Pyrrhus, Lævinus; insinuating that their loss was not through want of valour but of conduct; but filled up their legions, and enlisted fresh men with all speed, talking high and boldly of war, which struck Pyrrhus with amazement. He thought it advisable by sending first to make an experiment whether they had any inclination to treat, thinking that to take the city and make an absolute conquest was no work for such an army as his was at that time, but to settle a friendship, and bring them to terms, would be highly honourable after his victory.

Cineas was despatched away, and applied himself to several of the great ones, with presents for themselves and their ladies from the king; but not a person would receive any, and answered, as well men as women, that if an agreement were publicly concluded, they also should be ready, for their parts, to express their regard to the king. And Cineas, discoursing with the senate in the most persuasive and obliging manner in the world, yet was not heard with kindness or inclination, although Pyrrhus offered also to return all the prisoners he had taken in the fight without ransom, and promised his assistance for the entire conquest of all Italy, asking only their friendship for himself, and security for the Tarentines, and nothing further. Nevertheless, most were well inclined to a peace, having already received one great defeat, and fearing another from an additional force of the native Italians, now joining with Pyrrhus.

At this point Appius Claudius, a man of great distinction, but who, because of his great age and loss of sight, had declined the fatigue of public business, after these proposi-

tions had been made by the king, hearing a report that the senate was ready to vote the conditions of peace, could not forbear, but commanding his servants to take him up, was carried in his chair through the Forum to the senate-house. When he was set down at the door, his sons and sons-in-law took him up in their arms, and, walking close round about him, brought him into the senate. Out of reverence for so worthy a man, the whole assembly was respectfully silent.

And a little after raising up himself: "I bore," said he, "until this time, the misfortune of my eyes with some impatience, but now while I hear of these dishonourable motions and resolves of yours, destructive to the glory of Rome, it is my affliction, that being already blind, I am not deaf, too. Where is now that discourse of yours that became famous in all the world, that if he, the great Alexander, had come into Italy, and dared to attack us when we were young men, and our fathers, who were then in their prime, he had not now been celebrated as invincible, but either fleeing hence, or falling here, had left Rome more glorious? You demonstrate now that all that was but foolish arrogance and vanity, by fearing Molossians and Chaonians, ever the Macedonian's prey, and by trembling at Pyrrhus who was himself but an humble servant to one of Alexander's life-guard, and comes here, not so much to assist the Greeks that inhabit among us, as to escape from his enemies at home, a wanderer about Italy, and yet dares to promise you the conquest of it all by that army which has not been able to preserve for him a little part of Macedon. Do not persuade yourselves that making him your friend is the way to send him back; it is the way rather to bring over other invaders from thence, contemning you as easy to be reduced, if Pyrrhus goes off without punishment for his outrages on you, but, on the contrary, with the reward of having enabled the Tarentines and Samnites to laugh at the Romans."

When Appius had done, eagerness for the war seized on every man, and Cineas was dismissed with this answer, that when Pyrrhus had withdrawn his forces out of Italy, then, if he pleased, they would treat with him about friendship and alliance, but while he stayed there in arms, they were resolved to prosecute the war against him with all their force, though he should have defeated a thousand Lævinuses.

It is said that Cineas, while he was managing this affair, made it his business carefully to inspect the manners of the Romans, and to understand their methods of government, and having conversed with their noblest citizens, he afterwards told Pyrrhus, among other things, that the senate seemed to him an assembly of kings, and as for the people, he feared lest it might prove that they were fighting with a Lernæan hydra, for the consul had already raised twice as large an army as the former, and there were many times over the some number of Romans able to bear arms.

Then Caius Fabricius came in embassy from the Romans to treat about the prisoners that were taken, one whom Cineas had reported to be a man of highest consideration among them as an honest man and a good soldier, but extremely poor. Pyrrhus received him with much kindness, and privately would have persuaded him to accept of his gold, not for any evil purpose, but calling it a mark of respect and hospitable kindness.

Upon Fabricius's refusal, he pressed him no further, but the next day, having a mind to discompose him, as he had never seen an elephant before, he commanded one of the largest, completely armed, to be placed behind the hangings, as they were talking together. Which being done, upon a sign given, the hanging was drawn aside, and the elephant, raising his trunk over the head of Fabricius, made an horrid and ugly noise. He, gently turning about and smiling, said to Pyrrhus, "Neither your money yesterday, nor this beast to-day, makes any impression upon me."

At supper, amongst all sorts of things that were discoursed of, but more particularly Greece and the philosophers there, Cineas, by accident, had occasion to speak of Epicurus, and explained the opinions his followers hold about the gods and the commonwealth, and the objects of life, placing the chief happiness of man in pleasure, and declining public affairs as an injury and disturbance of a happy life, removing the gods afar off both from kindness or anger, or any concern for us at all, to a life wholly without business and flowing in pleasures. Before he had done speaking, "O Hercules!" Fabricius cried out to Pyrrhus, "may Pyrrhus and the Samnites entertain themselves with this sort of opinions as long as they are in war with us."

Pyrrhus, admiring the wisdom and gravity of the man, was the more transported with desire of making friendship instead of war with the city, and entreated him, personally, after the peace should be concluded, to accept of living with him as the chief of his ministers and generals. Fabricius answered quietly, "Sir, this will not be for your advantage, for they who now honour and admire you, when they have had experience of me, will rather choose to be governed by me than by you."

Such was Fabricius. And Pyrrhus received his answer without any resentment or tyrannic passion; nay, among his friends he highly commended the great mind of Fabricius, and intrusted the prisoners to him alone, on condition that if the senate should not vote a peace, after they had conversed with their friends and celebrated the festival of Saturn, they should be remanded. And, accordingly, they were sent back after the holidays, it being decreed pain of death for any that stayed behind.

After this Fabricius taking the consulate, a person came with a letter to the camp written by the king's principal physician, offering to take off Pyrrhus by poison, and so end the war without further hazard to the Romans, if he might have a reward proportionable to his services. Fabricius, hating the villainy of the man, and disposing the other consul to the same opinion, sent dispatches immediately to Pyrrhus to caution him against the treason.

His letter was to this effect: "Caius Fabricius and Quintus Æmilius, consuls of the Romans, to Pyrrhus, the king, health. You seem to have made an ill-judgment both of your friends and enemies; you will understand by reading this letter sent to us, that you are at war with honest men, and trust villains and knaves. Nor do we disclose this to you out of any favour to you, but lest your ruin might bring a reproach upon us, as if we had ended the war, by treachery, as not able to do it by force."

When Pyrrhus had read the letter and made inquiry into the treason, he punished the physician, and as an acknowledgment to the Romans sent to Rome the prisoners without ransom, and again employed Cineas to negotiate a peace for him. But they, regarding it as at once too great a kindness from an enemy, and too great a reward for not doing an ill thing to accept their prisoners so, released in return an equal number of the Tarentines and Samnites, but would admit of no debate of alliance or peace until he had removed his arms and forces out of Italy, and sailed back to Epirus with the same ships that brought him over.

Afterwards, his affairs demanding a second fight, when he had refreshed his men, he decamped, and met the Romans about the city Asculum, where, however, he was much incommoded by a woody country unfit for his horse, and a swift river, so that the elephants, for want of sure treading, could not get up with the infantry. After many wounded and many killed, night put an end to the engagement.

Next day, designing to make the fight on even ground, and have the elephants among the thickest of the enemy, he caused a detachment to possess themselves of those incommodious grounds, and, mixing slingers and archers among the elephants, with full strength and courage, he advanced in a close and well-ordered body. The Romans, not having those advantages of retreating and falling on as they pleased, which they had before, were obliged to fight man to man upon plain ground, and, being anxious to drive back the infantry before the elephants could get up, they fought fiercely with their swords among the Macedonian spears, not sparing themselves, thinking only to wound and kill, without regard to what they suffered.

After a long and obstinate fight, the first giving ground is reported to have been where Pyrrhus himself engaged with extraordinary courage; but they were most carried away by the overwhelming force of the elephants, not being able to make use of their valour, but overthrown as it were by the irruption of a sea or an earthquake, before which it seemed better to give way than to die without doing anything, and not gain the least advantage by suffering the utmost extremity, the retreat to their camp not being far. Hieronymus says there fell six thousand of the Romans, and of Pyrrhus's men, the king's own commentaries reported three thousand five hundred and fifty lost in this action. Dionysius, however, neither gives any account of two engagements at Asculum, nor allows the Romans to have been certainly beaten, stating that once only after they had fought till sunset, both armies were unwillingly separated by the night, Pyrrhus being wounded by a javelin in the arm, and his baggage plundered by the Samnites, that in all there died of Pyrrhus's men and the Romans above fifteen thousand.

The armies separated; and, it is said, Pyrrhus replied to one that gave him joy of his victory that one other such would utterly undo him. For he had lost a great part of the forces he brought with him, and almost all his particular friends and principal commanders; there were no others there to make recruits, and he found the confederates in Italy backward. On the other hand, as from a fountain continually flowing out of the city, the Roman camp was quickly and plentifully filled up with fresh men, not at all abating in courage for the losses they sustained, but even from their very anger gaining new force and resolution to go on with the war.

Among these difficulties he fell again into new hopes and projects distracting his purposes. For at the same time some persons arrived from Sicily, offering into his hands the cities of Agrigentum, Syracuse, and Leontini, and begging his assistance to drive out the Carthaginians and rid the island of tyrants; and others brought him news out of Greece that Ptolemy, called Ceranus, was slain in a fight, and his army cut in pieces by the Gauls, and that now, above all others, was his time to offer himself to the Macedonians, in great need of a king. Complaining much of fortune for bringing him so many occasions of great things all together at a time, and thinking that to have both offered to him was to lose one of them, he was doubtful, balancing in his thoughts. But the affairs of Sicily seeming to hold out the greater prospects, Africa lying so near, he turned himself to them, and presently despatched away Cineas, as he used to do, to make terms beforehand with the cities.

Then he placed a garrison in Tarentum, much to the Tarentines' discontent, who required him either to perform what he came for, and continue with them in a war against the Romans, or leave the city as he found it. He returned no pleasing answer, but commanded them to be quiet and attend his time, and so sailed away.

Being arrived in Sicily, what he had designed in his hopes was confirmed effectually, and the cities frankly surrendered to him; and wherever his arms and force were necessary, nothing at first made any considerable resistance. For advancing with thirty thousand foot, and twenty-five hundred horse, and two hundred ships, he totally routed the Phœnicians, and overran their whole province, and Eryx being the strongest town they held, and having a great garrison in it, he resolved to take it by storm. The army being in readiness to give the assault, he put on his arms, and

coming to the head of his men made a vow
of plays and sacrifices in honour to Hercules,
if he signalised himself in that day's action
before the Greeks that dwelt in Sicily, as became his great descent and his fortunes.

The sign being given by sound of trumpet,
he first scattered the barbarians with his
shot, and then brought his ladders to the wall,
and was the first that mounted upon it himself, and, the enemy appearing in great numbers, he beat them back; some he threw down
from the walls on each side, others he laid
dead in a heap round about him with his
sword, nor did he receive the least wound,
but by his very aspect inspired terror in the
enemy; and gave a clear demonstration that
Homer was in the right, and pronounced according to the truth of fact, that fortitude
alone, of all the virtues, is wont to display
itself in divine transports and frenzies. The
city being taken, he offered to Hercules most
magnificently, and exhibited all varieties of
shows and plays.

A sort of barbarous people about Messena,
called Mamertines, gave much trouble to the
Greeks, and put several of them under contribution. These being numerous and valiant
(from whence they had their name, equivalent in the Latin tongue to *warlike*,[1]) he first
intercepted the collectors of the contribution
money, and cut them off, then beat them in
open fight, and destroyed many of their places
of strength.

The Carthaginians being now inclined to
composition, and offering him a round sum
of money, and to furnish him with shipping,
if a peace were concluded, he told them
plainly, aspiring still to greater things, there
was but one way for a friendship and right
understanding between them, if they, wholly
abandoning Sicily, would consent to make
the African sea the limit between them and
the Greeks. And being elevated with his good
fortune, and the strength of his forces, and
pursuing those hopes in prospect of which he
first sailed thither, his immediate aim was at
Africa; and as he had abundance of shipping,
but very ill equipped, he collected seamen,
not by fair and gentle dealing with the cities,
but by force in a haughty and insolent way,
and menacing them with punishments. And
as at first he had not acted thus, but had been
unusually indulgent and kind, ready to believe, and uneasy to none; now of a popular
leader becoming a tyrant by these severe pro-

[1] *Mamers* being another and older form for *Mars*.

ceedings, he got the name of an ungrateful
and a faithless man.

However, they gave way to these things as
necessary, although they took them very ill
from him; and especially when he began to
show suspicion of Thœnon and Sosistratus,
men of the first position in Syracuse, who invited him over into Sicily, and when he was
come, put the cities into his power, and were
most instrumental in all he had done there
since his arrival, whom he now would neither
suffer to be about his person, nor leave at
home; and when Sosistratus out of fear withdrew himself, and then he charged Thœnon,
as in a conspiracy with the other, and put him
to death, with this all his prospects changed,
not by little and little, nor in a single place
only, but a mortal hatred being raised in the
cities against him, some fell off to the Carthaginians, others called in the Mamertines.

And seeing revolts in all places, and desires
of alteration, and a potent faction against him,
at the same time he received letters from the
Samnites and Tarentines, who were beaten
quite out of the field, and scarce able to secure
their towns against the war, earnestly begging
his help. This served as a colour to make his
relinquishing Sicily no flight, nor a despair of
good success; but in truth not being able to
manage Sicily, which was as a ship labouring
in a storm, and willing to be out of her, he
suddenly threw himself over into Italy. It is
reported that at his going off he looked back
upon the island, and said to those about him,
"How brave a field of war do we leave, my
friends, for the Romans and Carthaginians to
fight in," which, as he then conjectured, fell
out indeed not long after.

When he was sailing off, the barbarians
having conspired together, he was forced to a
fight with the Carthaginians in the very road,
and lost many of his ships; with the rest he
fled into Italy. There, about one thousand
Mamertines, who had crossed the sea a little
before, though afraid to engage him in open
field, setting upon him where the passages
were difficult, put the whole army in confusion. Two elephants fell, and a great part of
his rear was cut off. He, therefore, coming
up in person, repulsed the enemy, but ran
into great danger among men long trained
and bold in war.

His being wounded in the head with a
sword, and retiring a little out of the fight,
much increased their confidence, and one of
them advancing a good way before the rest,

large of body and in bright armour, with an haughty voice challenged him to come forth if he were alive. Pyrrhus, in great anger, broke away violently from his guards, and, in his fury, besmeared with blood, terrible to look upon, made his way through his own men, and struck the barbarian on the head with his sword such a blow, as with the strength of his arm, and the excellent temper of the weapon, passed downward so far that his body being cut asunder fell in two pieces.

This stopped the course of the barbarians, amazed and confounded at Pyrrhus, as one more than man; so that continuing his march all the rest of the way undisturbed, he arrived at Tarentum with twenty thousand foot and three thousand horse, where, reinforcing himself with the choicest troops of the Tarentines, he advanced immediately against the Romans, who then lay encamped in the territories of the Samnites, whose affairs were extremely shattered, and their counsels broken, having been in many fights beaten by the Romans. There was also a discontent amongst them at Pyrrhus for his expedition into Sicily, so that not many came in to join him.

He divided his army into two parts, and despatched the first into Lucania to oppose one of the consuls there, so that he should not come in to assist the other; the rest he led against Manius Curius, who had posted himself very advantageously near Beneventum, and expected the other consul's forces, and partly because the priests had dissuaded him by unfavourable omens, was resolved to remain inactive. Pyrrhus, hastening to attack these before the other could arrive, with his best men, and the most serviceable elephants, marched in the night toward their camp. But being forced to go round about, and through a very woody country, their lights failed them, and the soldiers lost their way.

A council of war being called, while they were in debate, the night was spent, and, at the break of day, his approach, as he came down the hills, was discovered by the enemy, and put the whole camp into disorder and tumult. But the sacrifices being auspicious, and the time absolutely obliging them to fight, Manius drew his troops out of the trenches, and attacked the vanguard, and, having routed them all, put the whole army into consternation, so that many were cut off and some of the elephants taken.

This success drew on Manius into the level plain, and here, in open battle, he defeated part of the enemy; but, in other quarters, finding himself overpowered by the elephants and forced back to his trenches, he commanded out those who were left to guard them, a numerous body, standing thick at the ramparts, all in arms and fresh. These coming down from their strong position, and charging the elephants, forced them to retire; and they in the flight turning back upon their own men, caused great disorder and confusion, and gave into the hands of the Romans the victory and the future supremacy. Having obtained from these efforts, and these contests, the feeling as well as the fame of invincible strength, they at once reduced Italy under their power, and not long after Sicily, too.

Thus fell Pyrrhus from his Italian and Sicilian hopes, after he had consumed six years in these wars, and though unsuccessful in his affairs, yet preserved his courage unconquerable among all these misfortunes, and was held, for military experience, and personal valour and enterprise, much the bravest of all the princes of his time, only what he got by great actions he lost again by vain hopes, and by new desires of what he had not, kept nothing of what he had. So that Antigonus used to compare him to a player with dice, who had excellent throws, but knew not how to use them.

He returned into Epirus with eight thousand foot and five hundred horse, and for want of money to pay them, was fain to look out for a new war to maintain the army. Some of the Gauls joining him, he invaded Macedonia, where Antigonus, son of Demetrius, governed, designing merely to plunder and waste the country. But after he had made himself master of several towns, and two thousand men came over to him, he began to hope for something greater, and adventured upon Antigonus himself, and meeting him at a narrow passage, put the whole army in disorder.

The Gauls, who brought up Antigonus's rear, were very numerous and stood firm, but after a sharp encounter, the greatest part of them were cut off, and they who had the charge of the elephants being surrounded every way, delivered up both themselves and the beasts, Pyrrhus, taking this advantage, and advising more with his good fortune than his reason, boldly set upon the main body of the Macedonian foot, already surprised with fear, and troubled at the former loss. They declined any action or engagement with him; and he, holding out his hand and calling aloud both to the superior and under officers by name, brought over the foot from Antigonus, who, flying away secretly, was only able to retain some of the seaport towns.

Pyrrhus, among all these kindnesses of fortune, thinking what he had effected against the Gauls the most advantageous for his glory, hung up their richest and goodliest spoils in the temple of Minerva Itonis, with this inscription:—

Pyrrhus, descendant of Molossian kings,
These shields to thee, Itonian goddess, brings,
Won from the valiant Gaul when in the fight
Antigonus and all his host took flight;
'Tis not today or yesterday alone
That for brave deeds the Æacidæ are known.

After this victory in the field, he proceeded to secure the cities, and having possessed himself of Ægæ, besides other hardships put upon the people there, he left in the town a garrison of Gauls, some of those in his own army, who being insatiably desirous of wealth, instantly dug up the tombs of the kings that lay buried there, and took away the riches, and insolently scattered about their bones. Pyrrhus, in appearance, made no great matter of it, either deferring it on account of the pressure of other business, or wholly passing it by, out of fear of punishing those barbarians; but this made him very ill spoken of among the Macedonians, and his affairs being yet unsettled and brought to no firm consistence, he began to entertain new hopes and projects, and in raillery called Antigonus a shameless man, for still wearing his purple and not changing it for an ordinary dress; but upon Cleonymus, the Spartan, arriving and inviting him to Lacedæmon, he frankly embraced the overture. Cleonymus was of royal descent, but seeming too arbitrary and absolute, had no great respect nor credit at home; and Areus was king there.

This was the occasion of an old and public grudge between him and the citizens; but, beside that, Cleonymus, in his old age, had married a young lady of great beauty and royal blood, Chilonis, daughter of Leotychides, who, falling desperately in love with Acrotatus, Areus's son, a youth in the flower of manhood, rendered this match both uneasy and dishonourable to Cleonymus, as there was none of the Spartans who did not very well know how much his wife slighted him; so these domestic troubles added to his public discontent. He brought Pyrrhus to Sparta with an army of twenty-five thousand foot, two thousand horse, and twenty-four elephants.

So great a preparation made it evident to the whole world that he came, not so much to gain Sparta for Cleonymus, as to take all Peloponnesus for himself, although he expressly denied this to the Lacedæmonian ambassadors that came to him at Megalopolis, affirming he came to deliver the cities from the slavery of Antigonus, and declaring he would send his younger sons to Sparta, if he might, to be brought up in Spartan habits, that so they might be better bred than all other kings.

With these pretensions amusing those who came to meet him in his march, as soon as ever he entered Laconia he began to plunder and waste the country, and on the ambassadors complaining that he began the war upon them before it was proclaimed: "We know," said he, "very well that neither do you Spartans, when you design anything, talk of it beforehand." One Mandroclidas, then present, told him, in the broad Spartan dialect: "If you are a god, you will do us no harm, we are wronging no man; but if you are a man, there may be another stronger than you."

He now marched away directly for Lacedæmon, and being advised by Cleonymus to give the assault as soon as he arrived, fearing, as it is said, lest the soldiers, entering by night, should plunder the city, he answered, they might do it as well next morning, because there were but few soldiers in town, and those unprovided against his sudden approach, as Areus was not there in person, but gone to aid the Gortynians in Crete. And it was this alone that saved the town, because he despised it as not tenable, and so imagining no defense would be made, he sat down before it that night.

Cleonymus's friends, and the Helots, his domestic servants, had made great preparation at his house, as expecting Pyrrhus there at supper. In the night the Lacedæmonians held a consultation to ship over all the women into Crete, but they unanimously refused, and Archidamia came into the senate with a sword in her hand, in the name of them all, asking if the men expected the women to survive the ruins of Sparta.

It was next resolved to draw a trench in a line directly over against the enemy's camp, and, here and there in it, to sink waggons in the ground, as deep as the naves of the wheels, that, so being firmly fixed, they might obstruct the passage of the elephants. When they had just begun the work, both maids and women came to them, the married women with their robes tied like girdles round their under-frocks, and the unmarried girls in their single frocks only, to assist the elder men at the work. As for the youth that were next day to engage, they left them to their rest, and undertaking their proportion, they themselves finished a third part of the trench, which was in breadth six cubits, four in depth, and eight hundred feet long, as Phylarchus says; Hieronymus makes it somewhat less.

The enemy beginning to move by break of day, they brought their arms to the young men, and giving them also in charge the trench, exhorted them to defend and keep it bravely, as it would be happy for them to con-quer in the view of their whole country, and glorious to die in the arms of their mothers and wives, falling as became Spartans. As for Chilonis, she retired with a halter about her neck, resolving to die so rather than fall into the hands of Cleonymus, if the city were taken.

Pyrrhus himself, in person, advanced with his foot to force through the shields of the Spartans ranged against him, and to get over the trench, which was scarce passable, because the looseness of the fresh earth afforded no firm footing for the soldiers.

Ptolemy, his son, with two thousand Gauls, and some choice men of the Chaonians, went around the trench, and endeavoured to get over where the waggons were. But they, being so deep in the ground, and placed close to-gether, not only made his passage, but also the defence of the Lacedæmonians, very trou-blesome. Yet now the Gauls had got the wheels out of the ground, and were drawing off the waggons toward the river, when young Acrotatus, seeing the danger, passing through the town with three hundred men, surround-ed Ptolemy undiscerned, taking the advantage of some slopes of the ground, until he fell upon his rear, and forced him to wheel about. And thrusting one another into the ditch, and falling among the waggons, at last with much loss, not without difficulty, they with-drew.

The elderly men and all the women saw this brave action of Acrotatus, and when he returned back into the town to his first post, all covered with blood and fierce and elate with victory, he seemed to the Spartan women to have become taller and more beautiful than be-fore, and they envied Chilonis so worthy a lov-er. And some of the old men followed him, crying aloud, "Go on, Acrotatus, be happy

with Chilonis, and beget brave sons for Sparta."

Where Pyrrhus himself fought was the hottest of the action and many of the Spartans did gallantly, but in particular one Phyllius signalised himself, made the best resistance, and killed most assailants; and when he found himself ready to sink with the many wounds he had received, retiring a little out of his place behind another, he fell down among his fellow-soldiers, that the enemy might not carry off his body.

The fight ended with the day, and Pyrrhus, in his sleep, dreamed that he drew thunder-bolts upon Lacedæmon, and set it all on fire, and rejoiced at the sight; and waking, in this transport of joy, he commanded his officers to get all things ready for a second assault, and relating his dream among his friends, suppos-ing it to mean that he should take the town by storm, the rest assented to it with admira-tion, but Lysimachus was not pleased with the dream, and told him he feared lest as places struck with lightning are held sacred, and not to be trodden upon, so the gods might by this let him know the city should not be taken. Pyrrhus replied, that all these things were but idle talk, full of uncertainty, and only fit to amuse the vulgar; their thought, with their swords in their hands, should always be—

The one good omen is King Pyrrhus's cause,

and so got up, and drew out his army to the walls by break of day.

The Lacedæmonians, in resolution and courage, made a defence even beyond their power; the women were all by, helping them to arms, and bringing bread and drink to those that desired it, and taking care of the wounded. The Macedonians attempted to fill up the trench, bringing huge quantities of materials and throwing them upon the arms and dead bodies, that lay there and were cov-ered over. While the Lacedæmonians opposed this with all their force, Pyrrhus, in person, appeared on their side of the trench and the waggons, pressing on horseback toward the city, at which the men who had that post calling out, and the women shrieking and run-ning about, while Pyrrhus violently pushed on, and beat down all that disputed his way, his horse received a shot in the belly from a Cretan arrow, and, in his convulsions as he died, threw off Pyrrhus on slippery and steep ground. And all about him being in confu-sion at this, the Spartans came boldly up, and making good use of their missiles, forced them off again.

After this Pyrrhus, in other quarters also, put an end to the combat, imagining the Lacedæmonians would be inclined to yield, as almost all of them were wounded, and very great numbers killed outright; but the good fortune of the city, either satisfied with the experiment upon the bravery of the citizens, or willing to prove how much even in the last extremities such interposition may effect, brought, when the Lacedæmonians had now but very slender hopes left, Aminias, the Phocian, one of Antigonus's commanders, from Corinth to their assistance, with a force of mercenaries; and they were no sooner received into the town, but Areus, their king, arrived there himself, too, from Crete, with two thousand men more. The women upon this went all home to their houses, finding it no longer necessary for them to meddle with the business of the war; and they also were sent back, who, though not of military age, were by necessity forced to take arms, while the rest prepared to fight Pyrrhus.

He, upon the coming of these additional forces, was indeed possessed with a more eager desire and ambition than before to make himself master of the town; but his designs not succeeding, and receiving fresh losses every day, he gave over the siege, and fell to plundering the country, determining to winter thereabouts.

But fate is unavoidable, and a great feud happening at Argos between Aristeas and Aristippus, two principal citizens, after Aristippus had resolved to make use of the friendship of Antigonus, Aristeas to anticipate him invited Pyrrhus thither. And he always revolving hopes upon hopes, and treating all his successes as occasions of more, and his reverses as defects to be amended by new enterprises, allowed neither losses nor victories to limit him in his receiving or giving trouble, and so presently went for Argos. Areus, by frequent ambushes, and seizing positions where the ways were most unpracticable, harassed the Gauls and Molossians that brought up the rear.

It had been told Pyrrhus by one of the priests that found the liver of the sacrificed beast imperfect that some of his near relations would be lost; in this tumult and disorder of his rear, forgetting the prediction, he commanded out his son, Ptolemy, with some of his guards to their assistance, while he

himself led on the main body rapidly out of the pass. And the fight being very warm where Ptolemy was (for the most select men of the Lacedæmonians, commanded by Evalcus, were there engaged), one Oryssus of Aptera in Crete, a stout man and swift of foot, running on one side of the young prince, as he was fighting bravely, gave him a mortal wound and slew him. On his fall those about him turned their backs, and the Lacedæmonian horse, pursuing and cutting off many, got into the open plain, and found themselves engaged with the enemy before they were aware, without their infantry.

Pyrrhus, who had received the ill news of his son, and was in great affliction, drew out his Molossian horse against them, and charging at the head of his men, satiated himself with the blood and slaughter of the Lacedæmonians, as indeed he always showed himself a terrible and invincible hero in actual fight, but now he exceeded all he had ever done before in courage and force. On his riding his horse up to Evalcus, he, by declining a little to one side, had almost cut off Pyrrhus's hand in which he held the reins, but lighting on the reins, only cut them; at the same instant Pyrrhus, running him through with his spear, fell from his horse, and there on foot as he was proceeded to slaughter all those choice men that fought about the body of Evalcus; a severe additional loss to Sparta, incurred after the war itself was now at an end, by the mere animosity of the commanders.

Pyrrhus having thus offered, as it were, a sacrifice to the ghost of his son, and fought a glorious battle in honour of his obsequies, and having vented much of his pain in action against the enemy, marched away to Argos. And having intelligence that Antigonus was already in possession of the high grounds, he encamped about Nauplia, and the next day despatched a herald to Antigonus calling him a villain, and challenging him to descend into the plain field and fight with him for the kingdom. He answered, that his conduct should be measured by times as well as by arms, and that if Pyrrhus had no leisure to live, there were ways enough open to death. To both the kings, also, came ambassadors from Argos, desiring each party to retreat, and to allow the city to remain in friendship with both, without falling into the hands of either. Antigonus was persuaded, and sent his son as a hostage to the Argives; but Pyrrhus, although he consented to retire, yet, as he sent no hostage, was suspected.

A remarkable portent happened at this time to Pyrrhus; the heads of the sacrificed oxen, lying apart from the bodies, were seen to thrust out their tongues and lick up their own gore. And in the city of Argos, the priestess of Apollo Lycius rushed out of the temple, crying she saw the city full of carcases and slaughter, and an eagle coming out to fight, and presently vanishing again.

In the dead of the night, Pyrrhus, approaching the walls, and finding the gate called Diamperes set open for them by Aristeas, was undiscovered long enough to allow all his Gauls to enter and take possession of the market-place. But the gate being too low to let in the elephants, they were obliged to take down the towers which they carried on their backs, and put them on again in the dark and in disorder, so that time being lost, the city took the alarm, and the people ran, some to Apis, the chief citadel, and others to other places of defence, and sent away to Antigonus to assist them. He, advancing within a short distance, made an halt, but sent in some of his principal commanders, and his son with a considerable force: Areus came thither, too, with one thousand Cretans, and some of the most active men among the Spartans, and all falling on at once upon the Gauls, put them in great disorder.

Pyrrhus, entering in with noise and shouting near the Cylarabis, when the Gauls returned the cry, noticed that it did not express courage and assurance, but was the voice of men distressed, and that had their hands full. He, therefore, pushed forward in haste the van of his horse that marched but slowly and dangerously, by reason of the drains and sinks of which the city is full. In this night engagement there was infinite uncertainty as to what was being done, or what orders were given; there was much mistaking and struggling in the narrow streets; all generalship was useless in that darkness and noise and pressure; so both sides continued without doing anything, expecting daylight.

At the first dawn, Pyrrhus, seeing the great citadel, Aspis, full of enemies, was disturbed, and remarking, among a variety of figures dedicated in the market-place, a wolf and bull of brass, as it were ready to attack one another, he was struck with alarm, recollecting an oracle that formerly predicted fate had determined his death when he should see a wolf

fighting with a bull. The Argives say these figures were set up in record of a thing that long ago had happened there. For Danaus, at his first landing in the country, near the Pyramia in Thyreatis, as he was on his way towards Argos, espied a wolf fighting with a bull, and conceiving the wolf to represent him (for this stranger fell upon a native as he designed to do), stayed to see the issue of the fight, and the wolf prevailing, he offered vows to Apollo Lycius, and thus made his attempt upon the town, and succeeded; Gelanor, who was then king, being displaced by a faction. And this was the cause of dedicating those figures.

Pyrrhus, quite out of heart at this sight, and seeing none of his designs succeed, thought best to retreat, but fearing the narrow passage at the gate, sent to his son, Helenus, who was left without the town with a great part of his forces, commanding him to break down part of the wall, and assist the retreat if the enemy pressed hard upon them. But what with haste and confusion, the person that was sent delivered nothing clearly; so that quite mistaking, the young prince with the best of his men and the remaining elephants marched straight through the gates into the town to assist his father.

Pyrrhus was now making good his retreat, and while the market-place afforded them ground enough both to retreat and fight, frequently repulsed the enemy that bore upon him. But when he was forced out of that broad place into the narrow street leading to the gate, and fell in with those who came the other way to his assistance, some did not hear him call out to them to give back, and those who did, however eager to obey him, were pushed forward by others behind, who poured in at the gate. Besides, the largest of his elephants falling down on his side in the very gate, and lying roaring on the ground, was in the way of those that would have got out.

Another of the elephants already in the town, called Nicon, striving to take up his rider, who, after many wounds received, was fallen off his back, bore forward upon those that were retreating, and, thrusting upon friends as well as enemies, tumbled them all confusedly upon one another, till having found the body, and taken it up with his trunk, he carried it on his tusks, and, returning in a fury, trod down all before him. Being thus pressed and crowded together, not a man could do anything for himself, but being wedged, as it were, together into one mass, the whole multitude rolled and swayed this way and that altogether, and did very little execution either upon the enemy in their rear, or on any of them who were intercepted in the mass, but very much harm to one another. For he who had either drawn his sword or directed his lance could neither restore it again, nor put his sword up; with these weapons they wounded their own men, as they happened to come in the way, and they were dying by mere contact with each other.

Pyrrhus, seeing this storm and confusion of things, took off the crown he wore upon his helmet, by which he was distinguished, and gave it to one nearest his person, and trusting to the goodness of his horse, rode in among the thickest of the enemy, and being wounded with a lance through his breastplate, but not dangerously, nor indeed very much, he turned about upon the man who struck him, who was an Argive, not of any illustrious birth, but the son of a poor old woman; she was looking upon the fight among other women from the top of a house, and perceiving her son engaged with Pyrrhus, and affrighted at the danger he was in, took up a tile with both hands and threw it at Pyrrhus. This falling on his head below the helmet, and bruising the vertebræ of the lower part of the neck, stunned and blinded him; his hands let go the reins, and sinking down from his horse he fell just by the tomb of Licymnius.

The common soldiers knew not who it was; but one Zopyrus, who served under Antigonus, and two or three others running thither, and knowing it was Pyrrhus, dragged him to a doorway hard by, just as he was recovering a little from the blow. But when Zopyrus drew out an Illyrian sword, ready to cut off his head, Pyrrhus gave him so fierce a look that, confounded with terror, and sometimes his hands trembling and then again endeavouring to do it, full of fear and confusion, he could not strike him right, but cutting over his mouth and chin, it was a long time before he got off the head.

By this time what had happened was known to a great many, and Alcyoneus hastening to the place, desired to look upon the head, and see whether he knew it, and taking it in his hand rode away to his father, and threw it at his feet, while he was sitting with some of his particular favourites. Antigonus, looking upon it, and knowing it, thrust his son from him, and struck him with his staff, calling him wicked and barbarous, and covering his eyes with his robe shed tears, thinking of his own father and grandfather, instances in his own family of the changefulness of fortune, and caused the head and body of Pyrrhus to be burned with all due solemnity.

After this, Alcyoneus, discovering Helenus under a mean disguise in a threadbare coat, used him very respectfully, and brought him to his father. When Antigonus saw him, "This, my son," said he, "is better; and yet even now you have not done wholly well in allowing these clothes to remain, to the disgrace of those who it seems now are the victors." And treating Helenus with great kindness, and as became a prince, restored him to his kingdom of Epirus, and gave the same obliging reception to all Pyrrhus's principal commanders, his camp and whole army having fallen into his hands.

CAIUS MARIUS

155?–86 B.C.

W E ARE altogether ignorant of any third name of Caius Marius; as also of Quintus Sertorius, that possessed himself of Spain; or of Lucius Mummius that destroyed Corinth, though this last was surnamed Achaicus from his conquests, as Scipio was called Africanus, and Metellus, Macedonicus. Hence Posidonius draws his chief argument to confute those that hold the third to be the Roman proper name, as Camillus, Marcellus, Cato; as in this case, those that had but two names would have no proper name at all. He did not, however, observe that by his own reasoning he must rob the women absolutely of their names; for none of them have the first, which Posidonius imagines the proper name with the Romans. Of the other two, one was common to the whole family, Pompeii, Manlii, Cornelii (as with us Greeks, the Heraclidæ, and Pelopidæ), the other titular, and personal, taken either from their natures, or actions, or bodily characteristics, as Macrinus, Torquatus, Sulla; such as are Mnemon, Grypus, or Callinicus among the Greeks. On the subject of names, however, the irregularity of custom, would we insist upon it, might furnish us with discourse enough.

There is a likeness of Marius in stone at Ravenna, in Gaul, which I myself saw, quite corresponding with that roughness and harshness of character that is ascribed to him. Being naturally valiant and warlike, and more acquainted also with the discipline of the camp than of the city, he could not moderate his passion when in authority. He is said never to have either studied Greek, or to have use of that language in any matter of consequence; thinking it ridiculous to bestow time in that learning, the teachers of which were little better than slaves. So after his second triumph, when at the dedication of a temple he presented some shows after the Greek fashion, coming into the theatre, he only sat down and immediately departed. And, accordingly, as Plato used to say to Xenocrates, the philosopher, who was thought to show more than ordinary harshness of disposition, "I pray you, good Xenocrates, sacrifice to the Graces"; so if any could have persuaded Marius to pay his devotions to the Greek Muses and Graces, he had never brought his incomparable actions, both in war and peace, to so unworthy a conclusion, or wrecked himself, so to say, upon an old age of cruelty and vindictiveness, through passion, ill-timed ambition, and insatiable cupidity. But this will further appear by and by from the facts.

He was born of parents altogether obscure and indigent, who supported themselves by their daily labour; his father of the same name with himself, his mother called Fulcinia. He had spent a considerable part of his life before he saw and tasted the pleasures of the city; having passed previously in Cirrhæaton, a village of the territory of Arpinum, a life, compared with city delicacies, rude and unrefined, yet temperate, and conformable to the ancient Roman severity.

He first served as a soldier in the war against the Celtiberians, when Scipio Africanus besieged Numantia; where he signalised himself to his general by courage far above his comrades, and particularly by his cheerfully complying with Scipio's reformation of his army, being almost ruined by pleasures and luxury. It is stated, too, that he encountered and vanquished an enemy in single combat, in his general's sight. In consequence of all this he had several honours conferred upon him; and once when at an entertainment a question arose about commanders, and one of the company (whether really desirous to know, or only in complaisance) asked Scipio where the Romans, after him, should obtain such another general, Scipio, gently clapping Marius on the shoulder as he sat next him, replied, "Here, perhaps." So promising was his early youth of his future greatness, and so discerning was Scipio to detect the distant future in the present first beginnings.

It was this speech of Scipio, we are told, which, like a divine admonition, chiefly emboldened Marius to aspire to a political career. He sought, and by the assistance of Cæcilius Metellus, of whose family he as well as his father were dependants, obtained the office of tribune of the people. In which place, when he brought forward a bill for the regulation of voting, which seemed likely to lessen the authority of the great men in the courts of justice, the consul Cotta opposed him, and persuaded the senate to declare against the law, and called Marius to account for it. He, however, when this decree was prepared, coming into the senate, did not behave like a young man newly and undeservedly advanced to authority, but, assuming all the courage that his future actions would have warranted, threatened Cotta, unless he recalled the decree, to throw him into prison. And on his returning to Metellus, and asking his vote, and Metellus, rising up to concur with the consul, Marius, calling for the officer outside, commanded him to take Metellus into custody. He appealed to the other tribunes, but not one of them assisted him; so that the senate, immediately complying, withdrew the decree.

Marius came forth with glory to the people and confirmed his law, and was henceforth esteemed a man of undaunted courage and assurance, as well as a vigorous opposer of the senate in favour of the commons. But he immediately lost their opinion of him by a contrary action; for when a law for the distribution of corn was proposed, he vigorously and successfully resisted it, making himself equally honoured by both parties, in gratifying neither, contrary to the public interest.

After his tribuneship, he was candidate for the office of chief ædile; there being two orders of them, one the curules, from the stool with crooked feet on which they sat when they performed their duty, the other and inferior, called ædiles of the people. As soon as they have chosen the former, they give their voices again for the latter. Marius, finding he was likely to be put by for the greater, immediately changed and stood for the less; but because he seemed too forward and hot, he was disappointed of that also. And yet though he was in one day twice frustrated of his desired preferment (which never happened to any before), yet he was not at all discouraged, but a little while after sought for the prætorship and was nearly suffering a repulse, and then, too, though he was returned last of all, was nevertheless accused of bribery.

Cassius Sabaco's servant, who was observed within the rails among those who voted, chiefly occasioned the suspicion, as Sabaco was an intimate friend of Marius; but on being called to appear before the judges, he alleged, that being thirsty by reason of the heat, he called for cold water, and that his servant brought him a cup, and as soon as he had drunk, departed; he was, however, excluded from the senate by the succeeding censors, and not undeservedly either, as was thought, whether it might be for his false evidence, or his want of temperance.

Caius Herennius was also cited to appear as evidence, but pleaded that it was not customary for a patron (the Roman word for protector) to witness against his clients, and that the law excused them from that harsh duty; and both Marius and his parents had always been clients to the family of Herennii. And when the judges would have accepted of this plea, Marius himself opposed it, and told Herennius, that when he was first created magistrate he ceased to be his client; which was not altogether true. For it is not every office that frees clients and their posterity from the observance due to their patrons, but only those to which the law has assigned a curule chair. Notwithstanding, though at the beginning of the suit it went somewhat hard with Marius, and he found the judges no way favourable to him, yet at last, their voices being equal, contrary to all expectation, he was acquitted.

In his prætorship he did not get much honour, yet after it he obtained the further Spain; which province he is said to have cleared of robbers, with which it was much infested, the old barbarous habits still prevailing, and the Spaniards, in those days, still regarding robbery as a piece of valour. In the city he had neither riches nor eloquence to trust to, with which the leading men of the time obtained power with the people, but his vehement disposition, his indefatigable labours, and his plain way of living, of themselves gained him esteem and influence; so that he made an honourable match with Julia, of the distinguished family of the Cæsars, to whom that Cæsar was nephew who was afterwards so great among the Romans, and, in some degree, from his relationship, made Marius his example, as in his life we have observed.

Marius is praised for both temperance and endurance, of which latter he gave a decided instance in an operation of surgery. For having, as it seems, both his legs full of great tumours, and disliking the deformity, he determined to put himself into the hands of an operator; when, without being tied, he stretched out one of his legs, and silently, without changing countenance, endured most excessive torments in the cutting, never either flinching or complaining; but when the surgeon went to the other, he declined to have it done, saying, "I see the cure is not worth the pain."

The consul Cæcilius Metellus, being declared general in the war against Jugurtha in Africa, took with him Marius for lieutenant; where, eager himself to do great deeds and services that would get him distinction, he did not, like others, consult Metellus's glory and the serving his interest, and attributing his honour of lieutenancy not to Metellus, but to fortune, which had presented him with a proper opportunity and theatre of great actions, he exerted his utmost courage.

That war, too, affording several difficulties, he neither declined the greatest, nor disdained undertaking the least of them, but surpassing his equals in counsel and conduct, and matching the very common soldiers in labour and abstemiousness, he gained great popularity with them; as indeed any voluntary partaking with people in their labour is felt as an easing of that labour, as it seems to take away the constraint and necessity of it. It is the most obliging sight in the world to the Roman soldier to see a commander eat the same bread as himself, or lie upon an ordinary bed, or assist the work in the drawing a trench and raising a bulwark. For they do not so much admire those that confer honours and riches upon them, as those that partake of the same labour and danger with themselves; but love them better that will vouchsafe to join in their work, than those that encourage their idleness.

Marius thus employed, and thus winning the affections of the soldiers, before long filled both Africa and Rome with his fame, and some, too, wrote home from the army that the war with Africa would never be brought to a conclusion unless they chose Caius Marius consul. All which was evidently unpleasing to Metellus; but what more especially grieved him was the calamity of Turpillius.

This Turpillius had, from his ancestors, been a friend of Metellus, and kept up a constant hospitality with him, and was now serving in the war in command of the smiths and carpenters of the army. Having the charge of a garrison in Vaga, a considerable city, and trusting too much to the inhabitants, because he treated them civilly and kindly, he unawares fell into the enemy's hands. They received Jugurtha into the city; yet nevertheless, at their request, Turpillius was dismissed safe and without receiving any injury; whereupon he was accused of betraying it to the enemy. Marius, being one of the council of war, was not only violent against him himself, but also incensed most of the others, so that Metellus was forced, much against his will, to put him to death. Not long after the accusation proved false, and when others were comforting Metellus, who took heavily the loss of his friend, Marius, rather insulting and arrogating it to himself, boasted in all companies that he had involved Metellus in the guilt of putting his friend to death.

Henceforward they were at open variance; and it is reported that Metellus once, when Marius was present, said insultingly, "You, sir, design to leave us to go home and stand for the consulship, and will not be content to wait and be consul with this boy of mine?" Metellus's son being a mere boy at the time.

Yet for all this Marius being very importunate to be gone, after several delays, he was dismissed about twelve days before the election of consuls; and performed that long journey from the camp to the seaport of Utica in two days and a night, and there doing sacrifice before he went on shipboard, it is said the augur told him that heaven promised him some incredible good fortune, and such as was beyond all expectation. Marius, not a little elated with this good omen, began his voyage, and in four days, with a favourable wind, passed the sea; he was welcomed with great joy by the people, and being brought into the assembly by one of the tribunes, sued for the consulship, inveighing in all ways against Metellus, and promising either to slay Jugurtha or take him alive.

He was elected triumphantly, and at once proceeded to levy soldiers contrary both to law and custom, enlisting slaves and poor people; whereas former commanders never accepted of such, but bestowed arms, like other favours, as a matter of distinction, on persons who had the proper qualification, a man's property being thus a sort of security for his good behaviour.

These were not the only occasions of illwill against Marius; some haughty speeches, uttered with great arrogance and contempt, gave great offence to the nobility; as, for example, his saying that he had carried off the consulship as a spoil from the effeminacy of the wealthy and high-born citizens, and telling the people that he gloried in wounds he had himself received for them, as much as others did in the monuments of dead men, and images of their ancestors. Often speaking of the commanders that had been unfortunate in Africa, naming Bestia, for example, and Albinus, men of very good families, but unfit for war, and who had miscarried through want of experience, he asked the people about him if they did not think that the ancestors of these nobles had much rather have left a descendant like him, since they themselves grew famous not by nobility, but by their valour and great actions.

This he did not say merely out of vanity and arrogance, or that he were willing, without any advantage, to offend the nobility; but the people delighting in affronts and scurrilous contumelies against the senate, making boldness of speech their measure of greatness of spirit, continually encouraged him in it, and strengthened his inclination not to spare persons of repute, so he might gratify the multitude.

As soon as he arrived again in Africa, Metellus, no longer able to control his feelings of jealousy, and his indignation that now when he had really finished the war, and nothing was left but to secure the person of Jugurtha, Marius, grown great merely through his ingratitude to him, should come to bereave him both of his victory and triumph, could not bear to have any interview with him; but retired himself, whilst Rutilius, his lieutenant, surrendered up the army to Marius, whose conduct, however, in the end of the war, met with some sort of retribution, as Sulla deprived him of the glory of the action as he had done Metellus.

I shall state the circumstances briefly here as they are given at large in the life of Sulla. Bocchus was king of the more distant bar-barians and was father-in-law to Jugurtha, yet sent him little or no assistance in his war, professing fears of his unfaithfulness, and really jealous of his growing power; but after Jugurtha fled, and in his distress came to him as his last hope, he received him as a sup-pliant, rather because ashamed to do other-wise than out of real kindness; and when he had him in his power, he openly entreated Marius on his behalf, and interceded for him with bold words, giving out that he would by no means deliver him. Yet privately de-signing to betray him, he sent for Lucius Sulla, quæstor to Marius, and who had on a previous occasion befriended Bocchus in the war. When Sulla, relying on his word, came to him, the African began to doubt and re-pent of his purpose, and for several days was unresolved with himself, whether he should deliver Jugurtha or retain Sulla; at length he fixed upon his former treachery, and put Jugurtha alive into Sulla's possession.

Thus was the first occasion given of that fierce and implacable hostility which so nearly ruined the whole Roman empire. For many that envied Marius attributed the success wholly to Sulla, and Sulla himself got a seal made, on which was engraved Bocchus be-traying Jugurtha to him, and constantly used it, irritating the hot and jealous temper of Marius, who was naturally greedy of distinc-tion, and quick to resent any claim to share in his glory, and whose enemies took care to promote the quarrel, ascribing the beginning and chief business of the war to Metellus and its conclusion to Sulla; that so the people might give over admiring and esteeming Marius as the worthiest person.

But these envyings and calumnies were soon dispersed and cleared away from Marius by the danger that threatened Italy from the west; when the city, in great need of a good com-mander, sought about whom she might set at the helm to meet the tempest of so great a war, no one would have anything to say to any members of noble or potent families who offered themselves for the consulship, and Marius, though then absent, was elected.

Jugurtha's apprehension was only just

known, when the news of the invasion of the Teutones and Cimbri began. The accounts at first exceeded all credit, as to the number and strength of the approaching army, but in the end report proved much inferior to truth, as they were three hundred thousand effective fighting men, besides a far greater number of women and children. They professed to be seeking new countries to sustain these great multitudes, and cities where they might settle and inhabit, in the same way as they had heard the Celti before them had driven out the Tyrrhenians, and possessed themselves of the best part of Italy. Having had no com-merce with the southern nations, and travel-ling over a wide extent of country, no man knew what people they were, or whence they came, that thus like a cloud burst over Gaul and Italy; yet by their grey eyes and the large-ness of their stature they were conjectured to be some of the German races dwelling by the northern sea; besides that, the Germans call plunderers Cimbri.

There are some that say that the country of the Celti, in its vast size and extent, reaches from the furthest sea and the arctic regions to the lake Mæotis eastward, and to that part of Scythia which is near Pontus, and that there the nations mingle together; that they did not swarm out of their country all at once, or on a sudden, but advancing by force of arms, in the summer season, every year, in the course of time they crossed the whole continent. And thus, though each party had several ap-pellations, yet the whole army was called by the common name of Celto-Scythians.

Others say that the Cimmerii, anciently known to the Greeks, were only a small part of the nation, who were driven out upon some quarrel among the Scythians, and passed all along from the lake Mæotis to Asia, under the conduct of one Lygdamis; and that the greater and more warlike part of them still inhabit the remotest regions lying upon the outer ocean. These, they say, live in a dark and woody country hardly penetrable by the sunbeams, the trees are so close and thick, ex-tending into the interior as far as the Her-cynian forest; and their position on the earth is under that part of heaven where the pole is so elevated that, by the declination of the parallels, the zenith of the inhabitants seems to be but little distant from it; and that their days and nights being almost of an equal length, they divide their year into one of each. This was Homer's occasion for the story of

Ulysses calling up the dead, and from this region the people, anciently called Cimmerii, and afterwards, by an easy change, Cimbri, came into Italy. All this, however, is rather conjecture than an authentic history.

Their numbers, most writers agree, were not less, but rather greater than was reported. They were of invincible strength and fierceness in their wars, and hurried into battle with the violence of a devouring flame; none could withstand them; all they assaulted became their prey. Several of the greatest Roman commanders with their whole armies, that advanced for the defence of Transalpine Gaul, were ingloriously overthrown, and, indeed, by their faint resistance, chiefly gave them the impulse of marching towards Rome. Having vanquished all they had met, and found abundance of plunder, they resolved to settle themselves nowhere till they should have razed the city and wasted all Italy.

The Romans, being from all parts alarmed with this news, sent for Marius to undertake the war, and nominated him the second time consul, though the law did not permit any one that was absent, or that had not waited a certain time after his first consulship, to be again created. But the people rejected all opposers, for they considered this was not the first time that the law gave place to the common interest; nor the present occasion less urgent than that when, contrary to law, they made Scipio consul, not in fear for the destruction of their own city, but desiring the ruin of that of the Carthaginians.

Thus it was decided; and Marius, bringing over his legions out of Africa on the very first day of January, which the Romans count the beginning of the year, received the consulship, and then, also, entered in triumph, showing Jugurtha a prisoner to the people, a sight they had despaired of ever beholding, nor could any, so long as he lived, have hoped to reduce the enemy in Africa; so fertile in expedients was he to adapt himself to every turn of fortune, and so bold as well as subtle. When, however, he was led in triumph, it is said that he fell distracted, and when he was afterwards thrown into prison, where some tore off his clothes by force, and others, whilst they struggled for his golden earring, with it pulled off the tip of his ear, and when he was, after this, cast naked into the dungeon, in his amazement and confusion, with a ghastly laugh, he cried out, "O Hercules! how cold your bath is!" Here for six days struggling with hunger, and to the very last minute desirous of life, he was overtaken by the just reward of his villainies.

In this triumph was brought, as is stated, of gold three thousand and seven pounds' weight, of silver bullion five thousand seven hundred and seventy-five, of money in gold and silver coin two hundred and eighty-seven thousand drachmas. After the solemnity, Marius called together the senate in the capitol, and entered, whether through inadvertency or unbecoming exultation with his good fortune, in his triumphal habit; but presently observing the senate offended at it, went out, and returned in his ordinary purple-bordered robe.

On the expedition he carefully disciplined and trained his army whilst they were on their way, giving them practice in long marches, and running of every sort, and compelling every man to carry his own baggage and prepare his own victuals; insomuch that thenceforward laborious soldiers, who did their work silently without grumbling, had the name of "Marius's mules." Some, however, think the proverb had a different occasion; that when Scipio besieged Numantia, and was careful to inspect not only their horses and arms, but their mules and carriages too, and see how well equipped and in what readiness each one's was, Marius brought forth his horse which he had fed extremely well, and a mule in better case, stronger and gentler than those of others; that the general was very well pleased, and often afterwards mentioned Marius's beasts; and that hence the soldiers, when speaking jestingly in the praise of a drudging laborious fellow, called him Marius's mule.

But to proceed; very great fortune seemed to attend Marius, for by the enemy in manner changing their course, and falling first upon Spain, he had time to exercise his soldiers, and confirm their courage, and, which was most important, to show them what he himself was. For that fierce manner of his in command, and inexorableness in punishing, when his men became used not to do amiss or disobey, was felt to be wholesome and advantageous, as well as just, and his violent spirit, stern voice, and harsh aspect, which in a little while grew familiar to them, they esteemed terrible not to themselves, but only to their enemies.

But his uprightness in judging more especially pleased the soldiers, one remarkable instance of which is as follows. One Caius Lusius, his own nephew, had a command under him in the army, a man not in other respects of bad character, but shamefully licentious with young men. He had one young man under his command called Trebonius, with whom notwithstanding many solicitations he could never prevail. At length one night he sent a messenger for him and Trebonius came, as it was not lawful for him to refuse when he was sent for, and being brought into his tent, when Lusius began to use violence with him, he drew his sword and ran him through. This was done whilst Marius was absent. When he returned, he appointed Trebonius a time for his trial, where, whilst many accused him, and not any one appeared in his defence, he himself boldly related the whole matter, and brought witness of his previous conduct to Lusius, who had frequently offered him considerable presents. Marius, admiring his conduct and much pleased, commanded the garland, the usual Roman reward for valour, to be brought, and himself crowned Trebonius with it, as having performed an excellent action, at a time that very much wanted such good examples.

This being told at Rome, proved no small help to Marius towards his third consulship; to which also conduced the expectation of the barbarians at the summer season, the people being unwilling to trust their fortunes with any other general but him. However, their arrival was not so early as was imagined, and the time of Marius's consulship was again expired. The election coming on, and his colleague being dead, he left the command of the army to Manius Aquilius, and hastened to Rome, where, several eminent persons being candidates for the consulship, Lucius Saturninus, who more than any of the other tribunes swayed the populace, and of whom Marius himself was very observant, exerted his eloquence with the people, advising them to choose Marius consul. He playing the modest part, and professing to decline the office, Saturninus called him traitor to his country if, in such apparent danger, he would avoid command. And though it was not difficult to discover that he was merely helping Marius in putting this pretence upon the people, yet, considering that the present juncture much required his skill, and his good fortunes too, they voted him the fourth time consul, and made Catulus Lutatius his colleague, a man very much esteemed by the nobility and not unagreeable to the commons.

Marius, having notice of the enemy's approach, with all expedition passed the Alps, and pitching his camp by the river Rhone, took care first for plentiful supplies of victuals: lest at any time he should be forced to fight at a disadvantage for want of necessaries. The carriage of provision for the army from the sea, which was formerly long and expensive, he made speedy and easy. For the mouth of the Rhone, by the influx of the sea, being barred and almost filled up with sand and mud mixed with clay, the passage there became narrow, difficult, and dangerous for the ships that brought their provisions. Hither, therefore, bringing his army, then at leisure, he drew a great trench; and by turning the course of a great part of the river, brought it to a convenient point on the shore where the water was deep enough to receive ships of considerable burden, and where there was a calm and easy opening to the sea. And this still retains the name it took from him.

The enemy dividing themselves into two parts, the Cimbri arranged to go against Catulus higher up through the country of the Norici, and to force that passage; the Teutones and Ambrones to march against Marius by the seaside through Liguria. The Cimbri were a considerable time in doing their part. But the Teutones and Ambrones with all expedition passing over the interjacent country, soon came in sight, in numbers beyond belief, of a terrible aspect, and uttering strange cries and shouts. Taking up a great part of the plain with their camp, they challenged Marius to battle; he seemed to take no notice of them, but kept his soldiers within their fortification, and sharply reprehended those that were too forward and eager to show their courage, and who, out of passion, would needs be fighting, calling them traitors to their country, and telling them they were not now to think of the glory of triumphs and trophies, but rather how they might repel such an impetuous tempest of war and save Italy.

Thus he discoursed privately with his officers and equals, but placed the soldiers by turns upon the bulwarks to survey the enemy, and so made them familiar with their shape and voice, which were indeed altogether extravagant and barbarous, and he caused them to observe their arms, and the way of using them, so that in a little time what at first appeared terrible to their apprehensions, by often viewing became familiar. For he very rationally supposed that the strangeness of things often makes them seem formidable when they are not so; and that by our better acquaintance, even things which are really terrible lose much of their frightfulness. This daily converse not only diminished some of the soldiers' fears, but their indignation warmed and inflamed their courage when they heard the threats and insupportable insolence of their enemies; who not only plundered and depopulated all the country round, but would even contemptuously and confidently attack the ramparts.

Complaints of the soldiers now began to come to Marius's ears. "What effeminacy does Marius see in us, that he should thus like women lock us up from encountering our enemies? Come on, let us show ourselves men, and ask him if he expects others to fight for Italy; and means merely to employ us in servile offices, when he would dig trenches, cleanse places of mud and dirt, and turn the course of the rivers. It was to do such works as these, it seems, that he gave us all our long training; he will return home, and boast of these great performances of his consulships to the people. Does the defeat of Carbo and Cæpio, who were vanquished by the enemy, affright him? Surely they were much inferior to Marius both in glory and valour, and commanded a much weaker army; at the worst, it is better to be in action, though we suffer for it like them, than to sit idle spectators of the destruction of our allies and companions." Marius, not a little pleased to hear this, gently appeased them, pretending that he did not distrust their valour, but that he took his measures as to the time and place of victory from some certain oracles.

And, in fact, he used solemnly to carry about in a litter a Syrian woman, called Martha, a supposed prophetess, and to do sacrifice by her directions. She had formerly been driven away by the senate, to whom she addressed herself, offering to inform them about these affairs, and to foretell future events; and after this betook herself to the women, and gave them proofs of her skill, especially Marius's wife, at whose feet she sat when she was viewing a contest of gladiators, and correctly foretold which of them should overcome. She was for this and the like predictings sent by her to Marius and the army, where she was very much looked up to, and, for the most part, carried about in a litter. When she went to sacrifice, she wore a purple robe lined and buckled up, and had in her hand a little spear

trimmed with ribbons and garlands. This theatrical show made many question whether Marius really gave any credit to her himself, or only played the counterfeit, when he showed her publicly, to impose upon the soldiers.

What, however, Alexander the Myndian relates about the vultures does really deserve admiration; that always before Marius's victories there appeared two of them, and accompanied the army, which were known by their brazen collars (the soldiers having caught them and put these about their necks, and so let them go, from which time they in a manner knew and saluted the soldiers), and whenever these appeared in their marches, they used to rejoice at it, and thought themselves sure of some success.

Of the many other prodigies that then were taken notice of, the greater part were but of the ordinary stamp; it was, however, reported that at Ameria and Tuder, two cities in Italy, there were seen at nights in the sky flaming darts and shields, now waved about, and then again clashing against one another, all in accordance with the postures and motions soldiers use in fighting; that at length one party retreating, and the other pursuing, they all disappeared westward.

Much about the same time came Bataces, one of Cybele's priests, from Pessinus, and reported how the goddess had declared to him out of her oracle that the Romans should obtain the victory. The senate giving credit to him, and voting the goddess a temple to be built in hopes of the victory, Aulus Pompeius, a tribune, prevented Bataces, when he would have gone and told the people this same story, calling him impostor, and ignominiously pulling him off the hustings; which action in the end was the main thing that gained credit for the man's story, for Aulus had scarce dissolved the assembly, and returned home, when a violent fever seized him, and it was matter of universal remark, and in everybody's mouth, that he died within a week after.

Now the Teutones, whilst Marius lay quiet, ventured to attack his camp; from whence, however, being encountered with showers of darts, and losing several of their men, they determined to march forward, hoping to reach the other side of the Alps without opposition, and, packing up their baggage, passed securely by the Roman camp, where the greatness of their number was especially made evident by the long time they took in their march, for they were said to be six days continually going on in passing Marius's fortifications; they marched pretty near, and revilingly asked the Romans if they would send any commands by them to their wives, for they would shortly be with them.

As soon as they were passed and had gone on a little distance ahead, Marius began to move, and follow them at his leisure, always encamping at some small distance from them; choosing also strong positions, and carefully fortifying them, that he might quarter with safety. Thus they marched till they came to the place called Sextilius's Waters, from whence it was but a short way before being amidst the Alps, and here Marius put himself in readiness for the encounter.

He chose a place for his camp of considerable strength, but where there was a scarcity of water; designing, it is said, by this means, also to put an edge on his soldiers' courage; and when several were not a little distressed, and complained of thirst, pointing to a river that ran near the enemy's camp, "There," said he, "you may have drink, if you will buy it with your blood." "Why, then," replied they, "do you not lead us to them, before our blood is dried up in us?" He answered, in a softer tone, "Let us first fortify our camp," and the soldiers, though not without repining, proceeded to obey.

Now a great company of their boys and camp followers, having neither drink for themselves nor for their horses, went down to that river; some taking axes and hatchets, and some, too, swords and darts with their pitchers, resolving to have water though they fought for it. These were first encountered by a small party of the enemies; for most of them had just finished bathing, and were eating and drinking, and several were still bathing, the country thereabouts abounding in hot springs; so that the Romans partly fell upon them whilst they were enjoying themselves and occupied with the novel sights and pleasantness of the place.

Upon hearing the shouts, great numbers still joining in the fight, it was not a little difficult for Marius to contain his soldiers, who were afraid of losing the camp servants; and the more warlike part of the enemies, who had overthrown Manlius and Cæpio (they were called Ambrones, and were in number, one with another, above thirty thousand), taking the alarm, leaped up and hurried to arms.

These, though they had just been gorging themselves with food, and were excited and disordered with drink, nevertheless did not advance with an unruly step, or in mere senseless fury, nor were their shouts mere inarticulate cries; but clashing their arms in concert and keeping time as they leapt and bounded onward, they continually repeated their own name, "Ambrones!" either to encourage one another, or to strike the greater terror into their enemies.

Of all the Italians in Marius's army, the Ligurians were the first that charged; and when they caught the word of the enemy's confused shout, they, too, returned the same, as it was an ancient name also in their country, the Ligurians always using it when speaking of their descent. This acclamation, bandied from one army to the other before they joined, served to rouse and heighten their fury, while the men on either side strove, with all possible vehemence, the one to overshout the other.

The river disordered the Ambrones; before they could draw up all their army on the other side of it, the Ligurians presently fell upon the van, and began to charge them hand to hand. The Romans, too, coming to their assistance, and from the higher ground pouring upon the enemy, forcibly repelled them, and the most of them (one thrusting another into the river) were there slain, and filled it with their blood and dead bodies.

Those that got safe over, not daring to make head, were slain by the Romans, as they fled to their camp and waggons; where the women meeting them with swords and hatchets, and making a hideous outcry, set upon those that fled as well as those that pursued, the one as traitors, the other as enemies, and mixing themselves with the combatants, with their bare arms pulling away the Romans' shields, and laying hold on their swords, endured the wounds and slashing of their bodies to the very last with undaunted resolution. Thus the battle seems to have happened at that river rather by accident than by the design of the general.

After the Romans were retired from the great slaughter of the Ambrones, night came on; but the army was not indulged, as was the usual custom, with songs of victory, drinking in their tents, and mutual entertainments and (what is most welcome to soldiers after successful fighting) quiet sleep, but they passed that night, above all others, in fears and alarm.

For their camp was without either rampart or palisade, and there remained thousands upon thousands of their enemies yet unconquered; to whom were joined as many of the Ambrones as escaped. There were heard from these all through the night wild bewailings, nothing like the sighs and groans of men, but a sort of wild-beast-like howling and cursing joined with threats and lamentations rising from the vast multitude, and echoed among the neighbouring hills and hollow banks of the river.

The whole plain was filled with hideous noise, insomuch that the Romans were not a little afraid, and Marius himself was apprehensive of a confused tumultuous night engagement. But the enemy did not stir either this night or the next day, but were employed in disposing and drawing themselves up to the greatest advantage.

Of this occasion Marius made good use; for there were beyond the enemies some wooded ascents and deep valleys thickly set with trees, whither he sent Claudius Marcellus, secretly, with three thousand regular soldiers, giving him orders to post them in ambush there, and show themselves at the rear of the enemies when the fight was begun.

The others, refreshed with victuals and sleep, as soon as it was day he drew up before the camp, and commanded the horse to sally out into the plain, at the sight of which the Teutones could not contain themselves till the Romans should come down and fight them on equal terms, but hastily arming themselves, charged in their fury up the hillside.

Marius, sending officers to all parts, commanded his men to stand still and keep their ground; when they came within reach, to throw their javelins, then use their swords, and joining their shields, force them back; pointing out to them that the steepness of the ground would render the enemy's blows inefficient, nor could their shields be kept close together, the inequality of the ground hindering the stability of their footing.

This counsel he gave them, and was the first that followed it; for he was inferior to none in the use of his body, and far excelled all in resolution. The Romans accordingly stood for their approach, and, checking them in their advance upwards, forced them little by little to give way and yield down the hill, and here, on level ground, no sooner had the Ambrones begun to restore their van into a posture of resistance, but they found their rear disordered.

For Marcellus had not let slip the opportunity; but as soon as the shout was raised among the Romans on the hills, he, setting his men in motion, fell in upon the enemy behind, at full speed, and with loud cries, and routed those nearest him, and they, breaking the ranks of those that were before them, filled the whole army with confusion. They made no long resistance after they were thus broke in upon, but having lost all order, fled.

The Romans, pursuing them, slew and took prisoners above one hundred thousand, and possessing themselves of their spoil, tents, and carriages, voted all that was not purloined to Marius's share, which, though so magnificent a present, yet was generally thought less than his conduct deserved in so great a danger.

Other authors give a different account, both about the division of the plunder and the number of the slain. They say, however, that the inhabitants of Massilia made fences round their vineyards with the bones, and that the ground, enriched by the moisture of the putrefied bodies (soaked with the rain of the following winter), yielded at the season a prodigious crop, and fully justified Archilochus, who said, that the fallows thus are fattened.

It is an observation, also, that extraordinary rains pretty generally fall after great battles; whether it be that some divine power thus washes and cleanses the polluted earth with showers from above, or that moist and heavy evaporations, steaming forth from the blood and corruption, thicken the air, which naturally is subject to alteration from the smallest causes.

After the battle, Marius chose out from amongst the barbarians' spoils and arms those that were whole and handsome, and that would make the greatest show in his triumph; the rest he heaped upon a large pile, and offered a very splendid sacrifice. Whilst the army stood round about with their arms and garlands, himself attired (as the fashion is on such occasions) in the purple-bordered robe, and taking a lighted torch, and with both hands lifting it up towards heaven, he was then going to put it to the pile, when some friends were espied with all haste coming towards him on horseback. Upon which every one remained in silence and expectation.

They, upon their coming up, leapt off and saluted Marius, bringing him the news of his fifth consulship, and delivered him letters to that effect. This gave the addition of no small joy to the solemnity; and while the soldiers clashed their arms and shouted, the officers again crowned Marius with a laurel wreath, and he thus set fire to the pile, and finished his sacrifice.

But whatever it be which interferes to prevent the enjoyment of prosperity ever being pure and sincere, and still diversifies human affairs with the mixture of good and bad, whether fortune or divine displeasure, or the necessity of the nature of things, within a few days Marius received an account of his colleague, Catulus, which, as a cloud in serenity and calm, terrified Rome with the apprehension of another imminent storm.

Catulus, who marched against the Cimbri, despairing of being able to defend the passes of the Alps, lest, being compelled to divide his forces into several parties, he should weaken himself, descended again into Italy, and posted his army behind the river Adige; where he occupied the passages with strong fortifications on both sides the river, and made a bridge that so he might cross to the assistance of his men on the other side, if so be the enemy, having forced their way through the mountain passes, should storm the fortresses.

The barbarians, however, came on with such insolence and contempt of their enemies, that to show their strength and courage, rather than out of any necessity, they went naked in the showers of snow, and through the ice and deep snow climbed up to the tops of the hills, and from thence, placing their broad shields under their bodies, let themselves slide from the precipices along their vast slippery descents.

When they had pitched their camp at a little distance from the river, and surveyed the passage, they began to pile it up, giant-like, tearing down the neighbouring hills; and brought trees pulled up by the roots, and heaps of earth to the river, damming up its course; and with great heavy materials which they rolled down the stream and dashed against the bridge, they forced away the beams which supported it; in consequence of which the greatest part of the Roman soldiers, much affrighted, left the large camp and fled.

Here Catulus showed himself a generous and noble general, in preferring the glory of his people before his own; for when he could not prevail with his soldiers to stand to their colours, but saw how they all deserted them, he commanded his own standard to be taken up, and running to the foremost of those that fled, he led them forward, choosing rather that the disgrace should fall upon himself than upon his country, and that they should not seem to fly, but, following their captain, to make a retreat.

The barbarians assaulted and took the fortress on the other side the Adige; where much admiring the few Romans there left, who had shown extreme courage, and had fought worthily of their country, they dismissed them upon terms, swearing them upon their brazen bull, which was afterwards taken in the battle, and carried, they say, to Catulus's house, as the chief trophy of victory.

Thus falling in upon the country destitute of defence, they wasted it on all sides. Marius was presently sent for to the city; where, when he arrived, every one supposing he would triumph, the senate, too, unanimously voting it, he himself did not think it convenient; whether that he were not willing to deprive his soldiers and officers of their share of the glory or that, to encourage the people in this juncture, he would leave the honour due to his past victory on trust, as it were, in the hands of the city and its future fortune, deferring it now to receive it afterwards with the greater splendour.

Having left such orders as the occasion required, he hastened to Catulus, whose drooping spirits he much raised, and sent for his own army from Gaul; and as soon as it came, passing the river Po, he endeavoured to keep the barbarians out of that part of Italy which lies south of it.

They professed they were in expectation of the Teutones, and, saying they wondered they were so long in coming, deferred the battle; either that they were really ignorant of their defeat or were willing to seem so. For they certainly much maltreated those that brought them such news, and, sending to Marius, required some part of the country for themselves and their brethren, and cities fit for them to inhabit.

When Marius inquired of the ambassadors who their brethren were, upon their saying the Teutones, all that were present began to laugh; and Marius scoffingly answered them, "Do not trouble yourself for your brethren, for we have already provided lands for them, which they shall possess forever."

The ambassadors, understanding the mockery, broke into insults, and threatened that the Cimbri would make him pay for this, and the Teutones, too, when they came. "They are not far off," replied Marius, "and it will be unkindly done of you to go away before greeting your brethren."

Saying so, he commanded the kings of the Teutones to be brought out, as they were, in chains; for they were taken by the Sequani among the Alps, before they could make their escape. This was no sooner made known to the Cimbri, but they with all expedition came against Marius, who then lay still and guarded his camp.

It is said that, against this battle, Marius first altered the construction of the Roman javelins. For before, at the place where the wood was joined to the iron, it was made fast with two iron pins; but now Marius let one of them alone as it was, and pulling out the other, put a weak wooden peg in its place, thus contriving that when it was driven into the enemy's shield, it should not stand right out, but the wooden peg breaking, the iron should bend, and so the javelin should hold fast by its crooked point and drag.

Bœorix, King of the Cimbri, came with a small party of horse to the Roman camp, and challenged Marius to appoint the time and place where they might meet and fight for the country. Marius answered that the Romans never consulted their enemies when to fight; however, he would gratify the Cimbri so far; and so they fixed upon the third day after, and for the place, the plain near Vercellæ, which was convenient enough for the Roman horse, and afforded room for the enemy to display their numbers.

They observed the time appointed, and drew out their forces against each other. Catulus commanded twenty thousand three hundred, and Marius thirty-two thousand, who were placed in the two wings, leaving Catulus the centre. Sulla, who was present at the fight, gives this account; saying, also, that Marius drew up his army in this order, because he expected that the armies would meet on the wings, since it generally happens that in such extensive fronts the centre falls back, and thus he would have the whole victory to himself and his soldiers, and Catulus would not be even engaged. They tell us, also, that Catulus himself alleged this in vindication of his honour, accusing, in various ways, the enviousness of Marius.

The infantry of the Cimbri marched quietly out of their fortifications, having their flanks equal to their front, every side of the army taking up thirty furlongs. Their horse, that were in number fifteen thousand, made a very splendid appearance. They wore helmets, made to resemble the heads and jaws of wild beasts, and other strange shapes, and heightening these with plumes of feathers, they made themselves appear taller than they were. They had breastplates of iron and white glittering shields; and for their offensive arms every one had two darts, and when they came hand to hand, they used large and heavy swords.

The cavalry did not fall directly upon the front of the Romans, but, turning to the right, they endeavoured to draw them on in that direction by little and little, so as to get them between themselves and their infantry, who were placed in the left wing. The Roman commanders soon perceived the design, but could not contain the soldiers; for one happening to shout out that the enemy fled, they all rushed to pursue them, while the whole barbarian foot came on, moving like a great ocean.

Here Marius, having washed his hands, and lifting them up towards heaven, vowed an hecatomb to the gods; and Catulus, too, in the same posture, solemnly promised to consecrate a temple to the "Fortune of that day." They say, too, that Marius, having the victim shown to him as he was sacrificing, cried out with a loud voice, "The victory is mine."

However, in the engagement, according to the accounts of Sulla and his friends, Marius met with what might be called a mark of divine displeasure. For a great dust being raised, which (as it might very probably happen) almost covered both the armies, he, leading on his forces to the pursuit, missed the enemy, and having passed by their array, moved, for a good space, up and down the field; meanwhile the enemy, by chance, engaged with Catulus, and the heat of the battle was chiefly with him and his men, among whom Sulla says he was; adding, that the Romans had great advantage of the heat and sun that shone in the faces of the Cimbri.

For they, well able to endure cold, and having been bred up (as we observed before) in cold and shady countries, were overcome with the excessive heat; they sweated extremely, and were much out of breath, being forced to hold their shields before their faces; for the battle was fought not long after the summer solstice, or, as the Romans reckon, upon the third day before the new moon of the month now called August, and then Sextilis.

The dust, too, gave the Romans no small addition to their courage, inasmuch as it hid the enemy. For afar off they could not discover their number; but every one advancing to encounter those that were nearest to them, they came to fight hand to hand before the sight of so vast a multitude had struck terror into them. They were so much used to labour, and so well exercised, that in all the heat and toil of the encounter, not one of them was observed either to sweat or to be out of breath; so much so, that Catulus himself, they say, recorded it in commendation of his soldiers.

Here the greatest part and most valiant of the enemy were cut to pieces; for those that fought in the front, that they might not break their ranks, were fast tied to one another, with long chains put through their belts. But as they pursued those that fled to their camp, they witnessed a most fearful tragedy; the women, standing in black clothes on their waggons, slew all that fled, some their husbands, some their brethren, others their fathers; and strangling their little children with their own hands, threw them under the wheels and the feet of the cattle, and then killed themselves.

They tell of one who hung herself from the end of the pole of a waggon, with her children tied dangling at her heels. The men, for want of trees, tied themselves, some to the horns of the oxen, others by the neck to their legs, that so pricking them on, by the starting and springing of the beasts, they might be torn and trodden to pieces. Yet for all they thus massacred themselves, above sixty thousand were taken prisoners, and those that were slain were said to be twice as many.

The ordinary plunder was taken by Marius's soldiers, but the other spoils, as ensigns, trumpets, and the like, they say, were brought to Catulus's camp; which he used for the best argument that the victory was obtained by himself and his army. Some dissensions arising, as was natural, among the soldiers, the deputies from Parma, being then present, were made judges of the controversy; whom Catulus's men carried about among their slain enemies, and manifestly showed them that they were slain by their javelins, which were known by the inscriptions, having Catulus's name cut in the wood.

Nevertheless the whole glory of the action was ascribed to Marius, on account of his former victory, and under colour of his present authority; the populace more especially styling him the third founder of their city, as having diverted a danger no less threatening than was that when the Gauls sacked Rome; and every one, in their feasts and rejoicings at home with their wives and children, made offerings and libations in honour of "The Gods and Marius"; and would have had him solely have the honour of both the triumphs. However, he did not do so, but triumphed together with Catulus, being desirous to show his moderation even in such great circumstances of good fortune; besides he was not a little afraid of the soldiers in Catulus's army, lest, if he should wholly bereave their general of the honour, they should endeavour to hinder him of his triumph.

Marius was now in his fifth consulship, and he sued for his sixth in such a manner as never any man before him had done, even for his first; he courted the people's favour and ingratiated himself with the multitude by every sort of complaisance; not only derogating from the state and dignity of his office, but also belying his own character, by attempting to seem popular and obliging, for which nature had never designed him. His passion for distinction did, indeed, they say, make him exceedingly timorous in any political matters, or in confronting public assemblies; and that undaunted presence of mind he always showed in battle against the enemy forsook him when he was to address the people; he was easily upset by the most ordinary commendation or dispraise.

It is told of him, that having at one time given the freedom of the city to one thousand men of Camerinum who had behaved valiantly in this war, and this seeming to be illegally done, upon some one or other calling him to an account for it, he answered, that the law spoke too softly to be heard in such a noise of war; yet he himself appeared to be more disconcerted and overcome by the clamour made in the assemblies. The need they had of him in time of war procured him power and dignity; but in civil affairs, when he despaired of getting the first place, he was forced to betake himself to the favour of the people, never caring to be a good man so that he were but a great one.

He thus became very odious to all the nobility; and above all, he feared Metellus, who had been so ungratefully used by him, and whose true virtue made him naturally an enemy to those that sought influence with the people, not by the honourable course, but by subservience and complaisance. Marius, therefore, endeavoured to banish him from the city, and for this purpose he contracted a close alliance with Glaucia and Saturninus, a couple of daring fellows, who had the great mass of the indigent and seditious multitude at their control; and by their assistance he enacted various laws, and bringing the soldiers, also, to attend the assembly, he was enabled to overpower Metellus. And as Rutilius relates (in all other respects a fair and faithful authority, but, indeed, privately an enemy to Marius), he obtained his sixth consulship by distributing vast sums of money among the tribes, and by this bribery kept out Metellus, and had Valerius Flaccus given him as his instrument, rather than his colleague, in the consulship. The people had never before bestowed so many consulships on any one man, except on Valerius Corvinus only, and he, too, they say, was forty-five years between his first and last; but Marius, from his first, ran through five more, with one current of good fortune.

In the last, especially, he contracted a great deal of hatred, by committing several gross misdemeanours in compliance with the desires of Saturninus; among which was the murder of Nonius, whom Saturninus slew because he stood in competition with him for the tribuneship. And when, afterwards, Saturninus, on becoming tribune, brought forward his law for the division of lands, with a clause enacting that the senate should publicly swear to confirm whatever the people should vote, and not to oppose them in anything, Marius, in the senate, cunningly feigned to be against this provision, and said that he would not take any such oath, nor would any man, he thought, who was wise; for if there were no ill design in the law, still it would be an affront to the senate to be compelled to give their approbation, and not to do it willingly and upon persuasion.

This, he said, not that it was agreeable to his own sentiments, but that he might entrap Metellus beyond any possibility of escape. For Marius, in whose ideas virtue and capacity consisted largely in deceit, made very little account of what he had openly professed to the senate; and knowing that Metellus was one of a fixed resolution, and, as Pindar has it, esteemed "truth the first principle of heroic virtue," he hoped to ensnare him into a declaration before the senate, and on his refusing, as he was sure to do, afterwards to take the oath, he expected to bring him into such odium with the people as should never be wiped off. The design succeeded to his wish. As soon as Metellus had declared that he would not swear to it, the senate adjourned.

A few days after, on Saturninus citing the senators to make their appearance, and take the oath before the people, Marius stepped forth, amidst a profound silence, every one being intent to hear him, and bidding farewell to those fine speeches he had before made in the senate, said, that his back was not so broad that he should think himself bound, once for all, by any opinion once given on so important a matter; he would willingly swear and submit to the law, if so be it were one, a proviso which he added as a mere cover for his effrontery.

The people, in great joy at his taking the oath, loudly clapped and applauded him, while the nobility stood by ashamed and vexed at his inconstancy; but they submitted out of fear of the people, and all in order took the oath, till it came to Metellus's turn. But he, though his friends begged and entreated him to take it, and not to plunge himself irrecoverably into the penalties which Saturninus had provided for those that should refuse it, would not flinch from his resolution, nor swear; but, according to his fixed custom, being ready to suffer anything rather than do a base, unworthy action, he left the Forum, telling those that were with him that to do a wrong thing is base, and to do well where there is no danger, common; the good man's characteristic is to do so where there is danger.

Hereupon Saturninus put it to the vote, that the consuls should place Metellus under their interdict, and forbid him fire, water, and lodging. There were enough, too, of the basest of people ready to kill him. Nevertheless, when many of the better sort were extremely concerned, and gathered about Metellus, he would not suffer them to raise a sedition upon his account, but with this calm reflection left the city, "Either when the posture of affairs is mended and the people repent, I shall be recalled, or if things remain in their present condition, it will be best to be absent." But what great favour and honour Metellus received in his banishment, and in what manner he spent his time at Rhodes, in philosophy, will be more fitly our subject when we write his life.

Marius, in return for this piece of service, was forced to connive with Saturninus, now proceeding to the very height of insolence and violence, and was, without knowing it, the instrument of mischief beyond endurance, the only course of which was through outrages and massacres to tyranny and the subversion of the government. Standing in some awe of the nobility, and, at the same time, eager to court the commonalty, he was guilty of a most mean and dishonest action.

When some of the great men came to him at night to stir him up against Saturninus, at the other door, unknown to them, he let him in; then making the same pretence of some disorder of body to both, he ran from one party to the other, and staying at one time with them and another with him, he instigated and exasperated them one against another.

At length when the senate and equestrian order concerted measures together, and openly manifested their resentment, he did bring his soldiers into the Forum, and driving the insurgents into the capitol, and then cutting off the conduits, forced them to surrender by want of water. They, in this distress, addressing themselves to him, surrendered, as it is termed, on the public faith. He did his utmost to save their lives, but so wholly in vain, that when they came down into the Forum they were all basely murdered.

Thus he had made himself equally odious both to the nobility and commons, and when the time was come to create censors, though he was the most obvious man, yet he did not petition for it; but fearing the disgrace of being repulsed, permitted others, his inferiors, to be elected, though he pleased himself by giving out that he was not willing to disoblige too many by undertaking a severe inspection into their lives and conduct.

There was now an edict preferred to recall Metellus from banishment; this he vigorously, but in vain, opposed both by word and deed, and was at length obliged to desist. The people unanimously voted for it; and he, not able to endure the sight of Metellus's return, made a voyage to Cappadocia and Galatia, giving out that he had to perform the sacrifices which he had vowed to Cybele, but actuated really by other less apparent reasons.

For, in fact, being a man altogether ignorant of civil life and ordinary politics, he received all his advancement from war; and supposing his power and glory would by little and little decrease by his lying quietly out of action, he was eager by every means to excite some new commotions, and hoped that by setting at variance some of the kings, and by exasperating Mithridates, especially, who was then apparently making preparations for war, he himself should be chosen general against him, and so furnish the city with new matter of triumph, and his own house with the plunder of Pontus and the riches of its king.

Therefore, though Mithridates entertained him with all imaginable attention and respect, yet he was not at all wrought upon or softened by it; but said, "O king, either endeavour to be stronger than the Romans, or else quietly submit to their commands." With which he left Mithridates, who indeed had often heard the fame of the bold speaking of the Romans, but now for the first time experienced it.

When Marius returned again to Rome, he built a house close by the Forum, either, as he himself gave out, that he was not willing his clients should be tired with going far, or that he imagined distance was the reason why more did not come. This, however, was not so; the real reason was, that, being inferior to others in agreeableness of conversation and the arts of political life, like a mere tool and implement of war, he was thrown aside in time of peace.

Amongst all those whose brightness eclipsed his glory, he was most incensed against Sulla, who had owed his rise to the hatred which the nobility bore Marius; and had made his disagreement with him the one principle of his political life. When Bocchus, King of Numidia, who was styled the associate of the Romans, dedicated some figures of Victory in the capitol, and with them a representation in gold of himself delivering Jugurtha to Sulla, Marius upon this was almost distracted with rage and ambition, as though Sulla had arrogated this honour to himself, and endeavoured forcibly to pull down these presents; Sulla, on the other side, as vigorously resisted him; but the Social War, then on a sudden threatening the city, put a stop to this sedition when just ready to break out.

For the most warlike and best-peopled

countries of all Italy formed a confederacy together against Rome, and were within a little of subverting the empire; as they were indeed strong, not only in their weapons and the valour of their soldiers, but stood nearly upon equal terms with the Romans as to the skill and daring of their commanders.

As much glory and power as this war, so various in its events and so uncertain as to its success, conferred upon Sulla, so much it took away from Marius, who was thought tardy, unenterprising and timid, whether it were that his age was now quenching his former heat and vigour (for he was above sixty-five years old), or that having, as he himself said, some distemper that affected his muscles, and his body being unfit for action, he did service above his strength. Yet, for all this, he came off victor in a considerable battle, wherein he slew six thousand of the enemies, and never once gave them any advantage over him; and when he was surrounded by the works of the enemy, he contained himself, and though insulted over, and challenged, did not yield to the provocation.

The story is told that when Publius Silo, a man of the greatest repute and authority among the enemies, said to him, "If you are indeed a great general, Marius, leave your camp and fight a battle," he replied, "If you are one, make me do so." And another time, when the enemy gave them a good opportunity of a battle, and the Romans through fear durst not charge, so that both parties retreated, he called an assembly of his soldiers, and said, "It is no small question whether I should call the enemies or you the greater cowards, for neither did they dare to face your backs, nor you to confront theirs." At length, professing to be worn out with the infirmity of his body, he laid down his command.

Afterwards when the Italians were worsted, there were several candidates suing with the aid of the popular leaders for the chief command in the war with Mithridates. Sulpicius, tribune of the people, a bold and confident man, contrary to everybody's expectation, brought forward Marius, and proposed him as proconsul and general in that war.

The people were divided; some were on Marius's side, others voted for Sulla, and jeeringly bade Marius go to the baths at Baiæ, to cure his body, worn out, as himself confessed, with age and catarrhs. Marius had indeed, there, about Misenum, a villa more effeminately and luxuriously furnished than seemed to become

one that had seen service in so many and great wars and expeditions. This same house Cornelia bought for seventy-five thousand drachmas, and not long after Lucius Lucullus, for two million five hundred thousand; so rapid and so great was the growth of Roman sumptuousness.

Yet, in spite of all this, out of a mere boyish passion for distinction, affecting to shake off his age and weakness, he went down daily to the Campus Martius, and exercising himself with the youth, showed himself still nimble in his armour, and expert in riding; though he was undoubtedly grown bulky in his old age, and inclining to excessive faintness and corpulency.

Some people were pleased with this, and went continually to see him competing and displaying himself in these exercises; but the better sort that saw him pitied the cupidity and ambition that made one who had risen from utter poverty to extreme wealth, and out of nothing into greatness, unwilling to admit any limit to his high fortune, or to be content with being admired, and quietly enjoying what he had already got. Why, as if he still were indigent, should he at so great an age leave his glory and his triumphs to go into Cappadocia and the Euxine Sea, to fight Archelaus and Neoptolemus, Mithridates's generals? Marius's pretences for this action of his seemed very ridiculous, for he said he wanted to go and teach his son to be a general.

The condition of the city, which had long been unsound and diseased, became hopeless now that Marius found so opportune an instrument for the public destruction as Sulpicius's insolence. This man professed, in all other respects, to admire and imitate Saturninus; only he found fault with him for backwardness and want of spirit in his designs. He, therefore, to avoid this fault, got six hundred of the equestrian order about him as his guard, whom he named anti-senators; and with these confederates he set upon the consuls, whilst they were at the assembly, and took the son of one of them who fled from the Forum and slew him.

Sulla, being hotly pursued, took refuge in Marius's house, which none could suspect, by that means escaping those that sought him, who hastily passed by there, and, it is said, was safely conveyed by Marius himself out at the other door, and came to the camp. Yet Sulla, in his memoirs, positively denies that he fled to Marius, saying he was carried thither to consult upon the matters to which Sulpicius would have forced him, against his will, to consent; that he, surrounding him with drawn swords, hurried him to Marius, and constrained him thus, till he went thence to the Forum and removed, as they required him to do, the interdict on business.

Sulpicius, having thus obtained the mastery, decreed the command of the army to Marius, who proceeded to make preparations for his march, and sent two tribunes to receive the charge of the army from Sulla. Sulla hereupon exasperating his soldiers, who were about thirty-five thousand full-armed men, led them towards Rome. First falling upon the tribunes Marius had sent, they slew them; Marius having done as much for several of Sulla's friends in Rome, and now offering their freedom to the slaves on condition of their assistance in the war; of whom, however, they say, there were but three who accepted his proposal.

For some small time he made head against Sulla's assault, but was soon overpowered and fled; those that were with him, as soon as he had escaped out of the city, were dispersed, and night coming on, he hastened to a country-house of his, called Solonium. Hence he sent his son to some neighbouring farms of his father-in-law, Mucius, to provide necessaries; he went himself to Ostia, where his friend, Numerius, had prepared him a ship, and hence, not staying for his son, he took with him his son-in-law, Granius, and weighed anchor.

Young Marius, coming to Mucius's farms, made his preparations; and the day breaking, was almost discovered by the enemy. For there came thither a party of horse that suspected some such matter; but the farm steward, foreseeing their approach, hid Marius in a cart full of beans, then yoking in his team and driving toward the city, met those that were in search of him. Marius, thus conveyed home to his wife, took with him some necessaries, and came at night to the seaside; where, going on board a ship that was bound for Africa, he went away thither.

Marius, the father, when he had put to sea, with a strong gale passing along the coast of Italy, was in no small apprehension of one Geminius, a great man at Terracina, and his enemy; and therefore bade the seamen hold off from that place. They were indeed willing to gratify him, but the wind now blowing in from the sea and making the waves swell to a great height, they were afraid the ship would not be able to weather out the storm, and Marius, too, being indisposed and sea-sick, they made for land, and not without some difficulty reached the shore near Circeium.

The storm now increasing and their victuals failing, they left their ship, and wandered up and down without any certain purpose, simply as in great distresses people shun the present as the greatest evil, and rely upon the hopes of uncertainties. For the land and sea were both equally unsafe for them; it was dangerous to meet with people, and it was no less so to meet with none, on account of their want of necessaries.

At length, though late, they lighted upon a few poor shepherds, that had not anything to relieve them; but knowing Marius, advised him to depart as soon as might be, for they had seen a little beyond that place a party of horse that were gone in search of him. Finding himself in a great strait, especially because those that attended him were not able to go further, being spent with their long fasting, for the present he turned aside out of the road, and hid himself in a thick wood, where he passed the night in great wretchedness. The next day, pinched with hunger, and willing to make use of the little strength he had, before it were all exhausted, he travelled by the seaside, encouraging his companions not to fall away from him before the fulfillment of his final hopes, for which, in reliance on some old predictions, he professed to be sustaining himself.

For when he was yet but very young, and lived in the country, he caught in the skirt of his garment an eagle's nest, as it was falling, in which were seven young ones, which his parents seeing and much admiring, consulted the augurs about it, who told them he should become the greatest man in the world, and that the fates had decreed he should seven times be possessed of the supreme power and authority.

Some are of opinion that this really happened to Marius, as we have related it; others say, that those who then and through the rest of his exile heard him tell these stories, and believed him, have merely repeated a story that is altogether fabulous; for an eagle never hatches more than two; and even Musæus was deceived, who, speaking of the eagle, says that—

She lays three eggs, hatches two, and rears one.

However this be, it is certain Marius, in his

exile and greatest extremities, would often say that he should attain a seventh consulship.

When Marius and his company were now about twenty furlongs distant from Minturnæ, a city in Italy, they espied a troop of horse making up toward them with all speed, and by chance, also, at the same time, two ships under sail. Accordingly, they ran every one with what speed and strength they could to the sea, and plunging into it swam to the ships. Those that were with Granius, reaching one of them, passed over to an island opposite, called Ænaria; Marius himself, whose body was heavy and unwieldy, was with great pains and difficulty kept above the water by two servants, and put into the other ship.

The soldiers were by this time come to the seaside, and from thence called out to the seamen to put to shore, or else to throw out Marius, and then they might go whither they would. Marius besought them with tears to the contrary, and the masters of the ship, after frequent changes, in a short space of time, of their purpose, inclining first to one, then to the other side, resolved at length to answer the soldiers that they would not give up Marius.

As soon as they had ridden off in a rage, the seamen, again changing their resolution, came to land, and casting anchor at the mouth of the river Liris, where it overflows and makes a marsh, they advised him to land, refresh himself on shore, and take some care of his discomposed body, till the wind came fairer; which, said they, will happen at such an hour, when the wind from the sea will calm, and that from the marshes rise.

Marius, following their advice, did so, and when the seamen had set him on shore, he laid him down in an adjacent field, suspecting nothing less than what was to befall him. They, as soon as they had got into the ship, weighed anchor and departed, as thinking it neither honourable to deliver Marius into the hands of those that sought him, nor safe to protect him.

He thus, deserted by all, lay a good while silently on the shore; at length collecting himself, he advanced with pain and difficulty, without any path, till, wading through deep bogs and ditches full of water and mud, he came upon the hut of an old man that worked in the fens, and falling at his feet besought him to assist and preserve one who, if he escaped the present danger, would make him returns beyond his expectation. The poor man, whether he had formerly known him, or was

then moved with his superior aspect, told him that if he wanted only rest his cottage would be convenient; but if he were fleeing from anybody's search, he would hide him in a more retired place. Marius desiring him to do so, he carried him into the fens and bade him hide himself in an hollow place by the riverside, where he laid upon him a great many reeds, and other things that were light, and would cover, but not oppress him.

But within a very short time he was disturbed with a noise and tumult from the cottage, for Geminius had sent several from Terracina in pursuit of him; some of whom happening to come that way, frightened and threatened the old man for having entertained and hid an enemy of the Romans. Whereupon Marius, arising and stripping himself, plunged into a puddle full of thick muddy water; and even there he could not escape their search, but was pulled out covered with mire, and carried away naked to Minturnæ and delivered to the magistrates. For there had been orders sent through all the towns to make public search for Marius, and if they found him to kill him; however, the magistrates thought convenient to consider a little better of it first, and sent him prisoner to the house of one Fannia.

This woman was supposed not very well affected towards him upon an old account. One Tinnius had formerly married this Fannia; from whom she afterwards, being divorced, demanded her portion, which was considerable, but her husband accused her of adultery; so the controversy was brought before Marius in his sixth consulship. When the case was examined thoroughly, it appeared both that Fannia had been incontinent, and that her husband, knowing her to be so, had married and lived a considerable time with her. So that Marius was severe enough with both, commanding him to restore her portion, and laying a fine of four copper coins upon her by way of disgrace.

But Fannia did not then behave like a woman that had been injured, but as soon as she saw Marius, remembered nothing less than old affronts; took care of him according to her ability, and comforted him. He made her his returns and told her he did not despair, for he had met with a lucky omen, which was thus. When he was brought to Fannia's house, as soon as the gate was opened, an ass came running out to drink at a spring hard by, and giving a bold and encouraging look, first stood still before him, then brayed aloud and pranced by him. From which Marius drew his conclusion, and said, that the fates designed his safety, rather by sea than land, because the ass neglected his dry fodder, and turned from it to the water. Having told Fannia this story, he bade the chamber door to be shut and went to rest.

Meanwhile, the magistrates and councillors of Minturnæ consulted together, and determined not to delay any longer, but immediately to kill Marius; and when none of their citizens durst undertake the business, a certain soldier, a Gaulish or Cimbrian horseman (the story is told both ways), went in with his sword drawn to him. The room itself was not very light, that part of it especially where he then lay was dark, from whence Marius's eyes, they say, seemed to the fellow to dart out flames at him, and a loud voice to say, out of the dark, "Fellow, darest thou kill Caius Marius?"

The barbarian hereupon immediately fled, and leaving his sword in the place, rushed out of doors, crying only this, "I cannot kill Caius Marius." At which they were all at first astonished, and presently began to feel pity, and remorse, and anger at themselves for making so unjust and ungrateful a decree against one who had preserved Italy, and whom it was bad enough not to assist. "Let him go," said they, "where he please to banishment, and find his fate somewhere else; we only entreat pardon of the gods for thrusting Marius distressed and deserted out of our city."

Impelled by thoughts of this kind, they went in a body into the room, and taking him amongst them, conducted him towards the seaside; on his way to which, though every one was very officious to him, and all made what haste they could, yet a considerable time was likely to be lost. For the grove of Marica (as she is called), which the people hold sacred and make it a point of religion not to let anything that is once carried into it be taken out, lay just in their road to the sea, and if they should go round about, they must needs come very late thither. At length one of the old men cried out and said, there was no place so sacred but they might pass through it for Marius's preservation; and thereupon, first of all, he himself, taking up some of the baggage that was carried for his accommodation to the ship, passed through the grove, all the rest immediately, with the same readiness, accompanying him.

And one Belæus (who afterwards had a picture of these things drawn, and put it in a temple at the place of embarkation), having by this time provided him a ship, Marius went on board, and hoisting sail, was by fortune thrown upon the island Ænaria, where meeting with Granius, and his other friends, he sailed with them for Africa. But their water failing them in the way, they were forced to put in near Eryx, in Sicily, where was a Roman quæstor on the watch, who all but captured Marius himself on his landing, and did kill sixteen of his retinue that went to fetch water. Marius, with all expedition loosing thence, crossed the sea to the isle of Meninx, where he first heard the news of his son's escape with Cethegus, and of his going to implore the assistance of Hiempsal, King of Numidia.

With this news, being somewhat comforted, he ventured to pass from that isle towards Carthage. Sextilius, a Roman, was then governor in Africa; one that had never received either any injury or any kindness from Marius; but who from compassion, it was hoped, might lend him some help. But he was scarce got ashore with a small retinue when an officer met him, and said, "Sextilius, the governor, forbids you, Marius, to set foot in Africa; if you do, he says he will put the decree of the senate in execution, and treat you as an enemy to the Romans."

When Marius heard this, he wanted words to express his grief and resentment, and for a good while held his peace, looking sternly upon the messenger, who asked him what he should say, or what answer he should return to the governor. Marius answered him with a deep sigh: "Go tell him that you have seen Caius Marius sitting in exile among the ruins of Carthage"; appositely applying the example of the fortune of that city to the change of his own condition.

In the interim, Hiempsal, King of Numidia, dubious of what he should determine to do, treated young Marius and those that were with him very honourably; but when they had a mind to depart, he still had some pretence or other to detain them, and it was manifest he made these delays upon no good design. However, there happened an accident that made well for their preservation.

The hard fortune which attended young Marius, who was of a comely aspect, touched one of the king's concubines, and this pity of hers was the beginning and occasion of love for him. At first he declined the woman's solicitations, but when he perceived that there was no other way of escaping, and that her offers were more serious than for the gratification of intemperate passion, he accepted her kindness, and she finding means to convey them away, he escaped with his friends and fled to his father.

As soon as they had saluted each other, and were going by the seaside, they saw some scorpions fighting, which Marius took for an ill omen, whereupon they immediately went on board a little fishing-boat, and made towards Cercinas, an island not far distant from the continent. They had scarce put off from shore when they espied some horse, sent after them by the king, with all speed making towards that very place from which they were just retired. And Marius thus escaped a danger, it might be said, as great as any he ever incurred.

At Rome news came that Sulla was engaged with Mithridates' generals in Bœotia; the consuls, from factious opposition, were fallen to downright fighting, wherein Octavius prevailing, drove Cinna out of the city for attempting despotic government, and made Cornelius Merula consul in his stead; while Cinna, raising forces in other parts of Italy, carried the war against them.

As soon as Marius heard of this he resolved, with all expedition, to put to sea again, and taking with him from Africa some Mauritanian horse, and a few of the refugees out of Italy, all together not above one thousand, he, with this handful, began his voyage. Arriving at Telamon, in Etruria, and coming ashore, he proclaimed freedom for the slaves; and many of the countrymen, also, and shepherds thereabouts, who were already freemen, at hearing his name, flocked to him to the seaside. He persuaded the youngest and strongest to join him, and in a small time got together a competent force with which he filled forty ships.

Knowing Octavius to be a good man and willing to execute his office with the greatest justice imaginable, and Cinna to be suspected by Sulla, and in actual warfare against the established government, he determined to join himself and his forces with the latter. He therefore sent a message to him, to let him know that he was ready to obey him as consul.

When Cinna had joyfully received his offer, naming him proconsul, and sending him the fasces and other ensigns of authority, he said that grandeur did not become his present fortune; but wearing an ordinary habit, and still letting his hair grow as it had done, from that very day he first went into banishment, and being now above threescore and ten years old, he came slowly on foot, designing to move people's compassion; which did not prevent, however, his natural fierceness of expression from still predominating, and his humiliation still let it appear that he was not so much dejected as exasperated by the change of his condition.

Having saluted Cinna and the soldiers, he immediately prepared for action, and soon made a considerable alteration in the posture of affairs. He first cut off the provision ships, and plundering all the merchants, made himself master of the supplies of corn; then bringing his navy to the seaport towns, he took them, and at last, becoming master of Ostia by treachery, he pillaged that town, and slew a multitude of the inhabitants, and, blocking up the river, took from the enemy all hopes of supply by the sea; then marched with his army toward the city, and posted himself upon the hill called Janiculum.

The public interest did not receive so great damage from Octavius's unskilfulness in his management of affairs as from his omitting needful measures through too strict observance of the law. As when several advised him to make the slaves free, he said that he would not give slaves the privilege of the country from which he then, in defence of the laws, was driving away Marius.

When Metellus, son to that Metellus who was general in the war in Africa, and afterwards banished through Marius's means, came to Rome, being thought a much better commander than Octavius, the soldiers, deserting the consul, came to him and desired him to take the command of them and preserve the city; that they, when they had got an experienced valiant commander, should fight courageously, and come off conquerors. But when Metellus, offended at it, commanded them angrily to return to the consul, they revolted to the enemy.

Metellus, too, seeing the city in a desperate condition, left it; but a company of Chaldæans, sacrificers, and interpreters of the Sibyl's books persuaded Octavius that things could turn out happily, and kept him at Rome. He was, indeed, of all the Romans the most upright and just, and maintained the honour of the consulate, without cringing or compliance, as strictly in accordance with ancient laws and usages as though they had been immutable mathematical truths; and yet fell, I know not how, into some weaknesses, giving more observance to fortune-tellers and diviners, than to men skilled in civil and military affairs.

He therefore, before Marius entered the city, was pulled down from the rostra and murdered by those that were sent before by Marius; and it is reported there was a Chaldæan writing found in his gown when he was slain. And it seemed a thing very unaccountable, that of two famous generals, Marius should be often successful by the observing of divinations, and Octavius ruined by the same means.

When affairs were in this posture, the senate assembled, and sent a deputation to Cinna and Marius, desiring them to come into the city peaceably and spare the citizens. Cinna, as consul, received the embassy, sitting in the curule chair, and returned a kind answer to the messengers; Marius stood by him and said nothing, but gave sufficient testimony, by the gloominess of his countenance and the sternness of his looks, that he would in a short time fill the city with blood.

As soon as the council arose, they went toward the city, where Cinna entered with his guards, but Marius stayed at the gates, and, dissembling his rage, professed that he was then an exile and banished his country by course of law; that if his presence were necessary, they must, by a new decree, repeal the former act by which he was banished; as though he were, indeed, a religious observer of the laws, and as if he were returning to a city free from fear or oppression.

Hereupon the people were assembled, but before three or four tribes had given their votes, throwing up his pretences and his legal scruples about his banishment, he came into the city with a select guard of the slaves who had joined him, whom he called Bardyæi. These proceeded to murder a number of citizens, as he gave command, partly by word of mouth, partly by the signal of his nod.

At length Ancharius, a senator, and one that had been prætor, coming to Marius, and not being re-saluted by him, they with their drawn swords slew him before Marius's face; and henceforth this was their token, immediately to kill all those who met Marius and saluting him were taken no notice of, nor answered with the like courtesy; so that his very friends were not without dreadful apprehensions and horror, whensoever they came to speak with him.

When they had now butchered a great number, Cinna grew more remiss and cloyed with murders; but Marius's rage continued still fresh and unsatisfied, and he daily sought for all that were any way suspected by him. Now was every road and every town filled with those that pursued and hunted them that fled and hid themselves; and it was remarkable that there was no more confidence to be placed, as things stood, either in hospitality or friendship; for there were found but a very few that did not betray those that fled to them for shelter.

And thus the servants of Cornutus deserve the greater praise and admiration, who, having concealed their master in the house, took the body of one of the slain, cut off the head, put a gold ring on the finger, and showed it to Marius's guards, and buried it with the same solemnity as if it had been their own master. This trick was perceived by nobody, and so Cornutus escaped, and was conveyed by his domestics into Gaul.

Marcus Antonius, the orator, though he, too, found a true friend, had ill-fortune. The man was but poor and a plebeian, and as he was entertaining a man of the greatest rank in Rome, trying to provide for him with the best he could, he sent his servant to get some wine of a neighbouring vintner. The servant carefully tasting it and bidding him draw better, the fellow asked him what was the matter, that he did not buy new and ordinary wine as he used to do, but richer and of a greater price; he without any designs told him, as his old friend and acquaintance, that his master entertained Marcus Antonius, who was concealed with him.

The villainous vintner, as soon as the servant was gone, went himself to Marius, then at supper, and being brought into his presence, told him he would deliver Antonius into his hands. As soon as he heard it, it is said he gave a great shout, and clapped his hands for joy, and had very nearly risen up and gone to the place himself; but being detained by his friends, he sent Annius, and some soldiers with him, and commanded him to bring Antonius's head to him with all speed.

When they came to the house, Annius stayed at the door, and the soldiers went upstairs into the chamber; where, seeing Antonius, they endeavoured to shuffle off the murder from one another; for so great it seems were the graces and charms of his oratory, that as soon as he began to speak and beg his life, none of them durst touch or so much as look upon him; but hanging down their heads, every one fell a-weeping. When their stay seemed something tedious, Annius came up himself and found Antonius discoursing, and the soldiers astonished and quite softened by it, and calling them cowards, went himself and cut off his head.

Catulus Lutatius, who was colleague with Marius, and his partner in the triumph over the Cimbri, when Marius replied to those that interceded for him and begged his life, merely with the words, "He must die," shut himself up in a room, and making a great fire, smothered himself. When maimed and headless carcasses were now frequently thrown about and trampled upon in the streets, people were not so much moved with compassion at the sight, as struck into a kind of horror and consternation.

The outrages of those that were called Bardyæi was the greatest grievance. These murdered the masters of families in their own houses, abused their children, and ravished their wives, and were uncontrollable in their rapine and murders, till those of Cinna's and Sertorius's party, taking counsel together, fell upon them in the camp and killed them every man.

In the interim, as if a change of wind was coming on, there came news from all parts that Sulla, having put an end to the war with Mithridates, and taken possession of the provinces, was returning into Italy with a great army. This gave some small respite and intermission to these unspeakable calamities. Marius and his friends believing war to be close at hand, Marius was chosen consul the seventh time, and appearing on the very calends of January, the beginning of the year, threw one Sextus Lucinus from the Tarpeian precipice; an omen, as it seemed, portending the renewed misfortunes both of their party and of the city.

Marius, himself now worn out with labour and sinking under the burden of anxieties, could not sustain his spirits, which shook within him with the apprehension of a new war and fresh encounters and dangers, the formidable character of which he knew by his own experience. He was not now to hazard the war with Octavius or Merula, commanding an inexperienced multitude or seditious rabble; but Sulla himself was approaching, the same who had formerly banished him, and since that, had driven Mithridates as far as the Euxine Sea.

Perplexed with such thoughts as these, and calling to mind his banishment, and the tedious wanderings and dangers he underwent, both by sea and land, he fell into despondency, nocturnal frights, and unquiet sleep, still fancying that he heard some one telling him, that—

> ——the lion's lair
> *Is dangerous, though the lion be not there.*

Above all things fearing to lie awake, he gave himself up to drinking deep and besotting himself at night in a way most unsuitable to his age; by all means provoking sleep, as a diversion to his thoughts.

At length, on the arrival of a messenger from the sea, he was seized with new alarms, and so what with his fear for the future, and what with the burden and satiety of the present, on some slight predisposing cause, he fell into a pleurisy, as Posidonius, the philosopher, relates, who says he visited and conversed with him when he was sick, about some business relating to his embassy.

Caius Piso, an historian, tells us that Marius, walking after supper with his friends, fell into a conversation with them about his past life, and after reckoning up the several changes of his condition that from the beginning had happened to him, said, that it did not become a prudent man to trust himself any longer with fortune; and, thereupon taking leave of those that were with him, he kept his bed seven days, and then died.

Some say his ambition betrayed itself openly in his sickness, and that he ran into an extravagant frenzy, fancying himself to be general in the war against Mithridates, throwing himself into such postures and motions of his body as he had formerly used when he was in battle, with frequent shouts and loud cries, with so strong and invincible a desire of being employed in that business had he been possessed through his pride and emulation. Though he had now lived seventy years, and was the first man that ever was chosen seven times consul, and had an establishment and riches sufficient for many kings, he yet complained of his ill fortune, that he must now die before he had attained what he desired.

Plato, when he saw his death approaching, thanked the guiding providence and fortune of his life, first, that he was born a man and a

Grecian, not a barbarian or a brute, and next, that he happened to live in Socrates's age. And so, indeed, they say Antipater of Tarsus, in like manner, at his death, calling to mind the happiness that he had enjoyed, did not so much as omit his prosperous voyage to Athens; thus recognising every favour of his indulgent fortune with the greatest acknowledgments, and carefully saving all to the last in that safest of human treasure-chambers, the memory.

Unmindful and thoughtless persons, on the contrary, let all that occurs to them slip away from them as time passes on. Retaining and preserving nothing, they lose the enjoyment of their present prosperity by fancying something better to come; whereas by fortune we may be prevented to this, but that cannot be taken from us. Yet they reject their present success, as though it did not concern them, and do nothing but dream of future uncertainties; not indeed unnaturally; as till men have by reason and education laid a good foundation for external superstructures, in the seeking after and gathering them they can never satisfy the unlimited desires of their mind.

Thus died Marius on the seventeenth day of his seventh consulship, to the great joy and content of Rome, which thereby was in good hopes to be delivered from the calamity of a cruel tyranny; but in a small time they found that they had only changed their old and worn-out master for another, young and vigorous; so much cruelty and savageness did his son, Marius, show in murdering the noblest and most approved citizens. At first, being esteemed resolute and daring against his enemies, he was named the son of Mars, but afterwards, his actions betraying his contrary disposition, he was called the son of Venus. At last, besieged by Sulla in Præneste, where he endeavoured in many ways, but in vain, to save his life, when on the capture of the city there was no hope of escape, he killed himself with his own hand.

LYSANDER
445?–395 B.C.

THE treasure-chamber of the Acanthians at Delphi has this inscription: "The spoils which Brasidas and the Acanthians took from the Athenians." And, accordingly, many take the marble statue, which stands within the building by the gates, to be Brasidas's; but, indeed, it is Lysander's, representing him with his hair at full length, after the old fashion, and with an ample beard.

Neither is it true, as some give out, that because the Argives, after their great defeat, shaved themselves for sorrow, that the Spartans contrarywise triumphing in their achievements, suffered their hair to grow; neither did the Spartans come to be ambitious of wearing long hair, because the Bacchiadæ, who fled from Corinth to Lacedæmon, looked mean and unsightly, having their heads all close cut. But this, also, is indeed one of the ordinances of Lycurgus, who, as it is reported, was used to say, that long hair made good-looking men more beautiful, and ill-looking men more terrible.

Lysander's father is said to have been Aristoclitus, who was not indeed of the royal family but yet of the stock of the Heraclidæ. He was brought up in poverty, and showed himself obedient and conformable, as ever any one did, to the customs of his country; of a manly spirit, also, and superior to all pleasures, excepting only that which their good actions bring to those who are honoured and successful; and it is accounted no base thing in Sparta for their young men to be overcome with this kind of pleasure. For they are desirous, from the very first, to have their youth susceptible to good and bad repute, to feel pain at disgrace, and exultation at being commended; and any one who is insensible and unaffected in these respects is thought poor-spirited and of no capacity for virtue.

Ambition and the passion for distinction were thus implanted in his character by his Laconian education, nor, if they continued there, must we blame his natural disposition much for this. But he was submissive to great men, beyond what seems agreeable to the Spartan temper, and could easily bear the haughtiness of those who were in power, when it was any way for his advantage, which some are of opinion is no small part of political discretion.

Aristotle, who says all great characters are more or less atrabilious, as Socrates and Plato and Hercules were, writes that Lysander, not indeed early in life, but when he was old, became thus affected. What is singular in his character is that he endured poverty very well, and that he was not at all enslaved or corrupted by wealth, and yet he filled his country with riches and the love of them, and took away from them the glory of not admiring money; importing amongst them an abundance of gold and silver after the Athenian war, though keeping not one drachma for himself.

When Dionysius, the tyrant, sent his daughters some costly gowns of Sicilian manufacture, he would not receive them, saying he was afraid they would make them look more unhandsome. But a while after, being sent ambassador from the same city to the same tyrant, when he had sent him a couple of robes, and bade him choose which of them he would, and carry to his daughter: "She," said he, "will be able to choose best for herself," and taking both of them, went his way.

The Peloponnesian war having now been carried on a long time, and it being expected, after the disaster of the Athenians in Sicily, that they would at once lose the mastery of the sea, and ere long be routed everywhere, Alcibiades, returning from banishment, and taking the command, produced a great change, and made the Athenians again a match for their opponents by sea; and the Lacedæmonians, in great alarm at this, and calling up fresh courage and zeal for the conflict, feeling the want of an able commander and of a powerful armament, sent out Lysander to be admiral of the seas.

Being at Ephesus, and finding the city well affected towards him, and favourable to the Lacedæmonian party, but in ill condition, and in danger to become barbarised by adopting the manners of the Persians, who were much mingled among them, the country of Lydia bordering upon them, and the king's generals being quartered there for a long time, he pitched his camp there, and commanded the merchant ships all about to put in thither, and proceeded to build ships of war there; and thus restored their ports by the traffic he created, and their market by the employment he gave, and filled their private houses and their workshops with wealth, so that from that time the city began, first of all by Lysander's means, to have some hopes of growing to that stateliness and grandeur which now it is at.

Understanding that Cyrus, the king's son, was come to Sardis, he went up to talk with him, and to accuse Tisaphernes, who, receiving a command to help the Lacedæmonians, and to drive the Athenians from the sea, was thought, on account of Alcibiades, to have become remiss and unwilling, and by paying the seamen slenderly to be ruining the fleet. Now Cyrus was willing that Tisaphernes might be found in blame, and be ill reported of, as being, indeed, a dishonest man, and privately at feud with himself.

By these means, and by their daily intercourse together, Lysander, especially by the submissiveness of his conversation, won the affection of the young prince, and greatly roused him to carry on the war; and when he would depart, Cyrus gave him a banquet, and desired him not to refuse his goodwill, but to speak and ask whatever he had a mind to, and that he should not be refused anything whatsoever: "Since you are so very kind," replied Lysander, "I earnestly request you to add one penny to the seamen's pay, that instead of three pence, they may now receive four pence."

Cyrus, delighted with his public spirit, gave him ten thousand darics, out of which he added the penny to the seamen's pay, and by the renown of this in a short time emptied the ships of the enemies, as many would come over to that side which gave the most pay, and those who remained, being disheartened and mutinous, daily created trouble to the captains. Yet for all Lysander had so distracted and weakened his enemies, he was afraid to engage by sea, Alcibiades being an energetic commander, and having the superior number of ships, and having been hitherto, in all battles, unconquered both by sea and land.

But afterwards, when Alcibiades sailed from Samos to Phocæa, leaving Antiochus, the pilot, in command of all his forces, this Antiochus, to insult Lysander, sailed with two galleys into the port of the Ephesians, and with mocking and laughter proudly rowed along before the place where the ships lay drawn up. Lysander, in indignation, launched at first a few ships only and pursued him, but as soon as he saw the Athenians come to his help, he added some other ships, and, at last, they fell to a set battle together; and Lysander won the victory, and taking fifteen of their ships, erected a trophy. For this, the people in the city being angry, put Alcibiades out of command, and finding himself despised by the soldiers in Samos, and ill spoken of, he sailed from the army into the Chersonese. And this battle, although not important in itself, was made remarkable by its consequences to Alcibiades.

Lysander, meanwhile, invited to Ephesus such persons in the various cities as he saw to be bolder and haughtier-spirited than the rest, proceeded to lay the foundations of that government by bodies of ten, and those revolutions which afterwards came to pass, stirring up and urging them to unite in clubs and apply themselves to public affairs, since as soon as ever the Athenians should be put down, the popular government, he said, should be suppressed and they should become supreme in their several countries. And he made them believe these things by present deeds, promoting those who were his friends already to great employments, honours, and offices, and, to gratify their covetousness, making himself a partner in injustice and wickedness. So much so, that all flocked to him, and courted and desired him, hoping, if he remained in power, that the highest wishes they could form would all be gratified.

And therefore, from the very beginning, they could not look pleasantly upon Callicratidas, when he came to succeed Lysander as admiral; nor, afterwards, when he had given them experience that he was a most noble and just person, were they pleased with the manner of his government, and its straightforward, Dorian, honest character. They did, indeed, admire his virtue, as they might the beauty of some hero's image; but their wishes were for Lysander's zealous and profitable support of the interests of his friends and partisans, and they shed tears, and were much disheartened when he sailed from them.

He himself made them yet more disaffected to Callicratidas; for what remained of the money which had been given him to pay the navy, he sent back again to Sardis, bidding them, if they would, apply to Callicratidas himself, and see how he was able to maintain the soldiers. And, at the last, sailing away, he declared to him that he delivered up the fleet in possession and command of the sea. But Callicratidas, to expose the emptiness of these high pretensions, said, "In that case, leave Samos on the left hand, and sailing to Miletus, there deliver up the ships to me; for if we are masters of the sea, we need not fear sailing by our enemies in Samos." To which Lysander answering, that not himself but he commanded the ships, sailed to Peloponnesus, leaving Callicratidas in great perplexity. For neither had he brought any money from home with him, nor could he endure to tax the towns or force them, being in hardship enough.

Therefore, the only course that was to be taken was to go and beg at the doors of the king's commanders, as Lysander had done; for which he was most unfit of any man, being of a generous and great spirit, and one who thought it more becoming for the Greeks to suffer any damage from one another, than to flatter and wait at the gates of barbarians, who, indeed, had gold enough, but nothing else that was commendable. But being compelled by necessity, he proceeded to Lydia, and went at once to Cyrus's house, and sent in word that Callicratidas, the admiral, was there to speak with him; one of those who kept the gates replied, "Cyrus, O stranger, is not now at leisure, for he is drinking." To which Callicratidas answered, most innocently, "Very well, I will wait till he has done his draught."

This time, therefore, they took him for some clownish fellow, and he withdrew, merely laughed at by the barbarians; but when, afterwards, he came a second time to the gate, and was not admitted, he took it hardly and set off for Ephesus, wishing a great many evils to those who first let themselves be insulted over by these barbarians, and taught them to be insolent because of their riches; and added vows to those who were present, that as soon as ever he came back to Sparta, he would do all he could to reconcile the Greeks, that they might be formidable to barbarians, and that they should cease henceforth to need their aid against one another. But Callicratidas, who entertained purposes worthy a Lacedæmonian, and showed himself worthy to compete with the very best of Greece, for his justice, his greatness of mind and courage, not long after, having been beaten in a sea fight at Arginusæ, died.

And now, affairs going backwards, the associates in the war sent an embassy to Sparta, requiring Lysander to be their admiral, professing themselves ready to undertake the business much more zealously if he was commander; and Cyrus also sent to request the same thing. But because they had a law which would not suffer any one to be admiral twice, and wished, nevertheless, to gratify their allies, they gave the title of admiral to one Aracus, and sent Lysander nominally as vice-admiral, but, indeed, with full powers. So he came out, long wished for by the greatest part of the chief persons and leaders in the towns, who hoped to grow to greater power still by his means, when the popular governments should be everywhere destroyed.

But to those who loved honest and noble behaviour in their commanders, Lysander, compared with Callicratidas, seemed cunning and subtle, managing most things in the war by deceit, extolling what was just when it was profitable, and when it was not, using that which was convenient, instead of that which was good; and not judging truth to be in nature better than falsehood, but setting a value upon both according to interest. He would laugh at those who thought Hercules's posterity ought not to use deceit in war: "For where the lion's skin will not reach, you must patch it out with the fox's."

Such is the conduct recorded of him in the business about Miletus; for when his friends and connections, whom he had promised to assist in suppressing popular government, and expelling their political opponents, had altered their minds, and were reconciled to their enemies, he pretended openly as if he was pleased with it, and was desirous to further the reconciliation, but privately he railed at and abused them, and provoked them to set upon the multitude. And as soon as ever he perceived a new attempt to be commencing, he at once came up and entered into the city, and the first of the conspirators he lit upon, he pretended to rebuke, and spoke roughly, as if he would punish them; but the others, meantime, he bade be courageous, and to fear nothing, now he was with them. And all this acting and dissembling was with the object that the most considerable men of the popular party might not fly away, but might stay in the city and be killed; which so fell out, for all who believed him were put to death.

There is a saying also, recorded by Androclides, which makes him guilty of great indifference to the obligations of an oath. His recommendation, according to this account, was to "cheat boys with dice, and men with oaths," an imitation of Polycrates of Samos, not very honourable to a lawful commander, to take example, namely, from a tyrant; nor in character with Laconian usages, to treat gods as ill as enemies, or, indeed, even more injuriously; since he who overreaches by an oath admits that he fears his enemy, while he despises his God.

Cyrus now sent for Lysander to Sardis, and gave him some money, and promised him some more, youthfully protesting in favour to him, that if his father gave him nothing, he would supply him of his own; and if he himself should be destitute of all, he would cut up, he said, to make money, the very throne upon which he sat to do justice, it being made of gold and silver; and, at last, on going up into Media to his father, he ordered that he should receive the tribute of the towns, and committed his government to him, and so taking his leave, and desiring him not to fight by sea before he returned, for he would come back with a great many ships out of Phœnicia and Cilicia, departed to visit the king.

Lysander's ships were too few for him to venture to fight, and yet too many to allow of his remaining idle; he set out, therefore, and reduced some of the islands, and wasted Ægina and Salamis; and from thence landing in Attica, and saluting Agis, who came from Decelea to meet him, he made a display to the land-forces of the strength of the fleet as though he could sail where he pleased, and were absolute master by sea. But hearing the Athenians pursued him, he fled another way through the island into Asia. And finding the Hellespont without any defence, he attacked Lampsacus with his ships by sea; while Thorax, acting in concert with him with the land army, made an assault on the walls; and so having taken the city by storm, he gave it up to his soldiers to plunder.

The fleet of the Athenians, a hundred and eighty ships, had just arrived at Elæus in the Chersonese; and hearing the news, that Lampsacus was destroyed, they presently sailed to Sestos; where, taking in victuals, they advanced to Ægos Potami, over against their enemies, who were still stationed about Lampsacus. Amongst other Athenian captains who were now in command was Philocles, he who persuaded the people to pass a decree to cut off the right thumb of the captives in the war, that they should not be able to hold the spear, though they might the oar.

Then they all rested themselves, hoping they should have battle the next morning. But Lysander had other things in his head; he commanded the mariners and pilots to go on board at dawn, as if there should be a battle as soon as it was day, and to sit there in order, and without any noise, excepting what should be commanded, and in like manner that the land army should remain quietly in their ranks by the sea. But the sun rising, and the Athenians sailing up with their whole fleet in line, and challenging them to battle, though he had had his ships all drawn up and manned before daybreak, nevertheless did not stir. He merely sent some small boats to those who lay foremost, and bade them keep still and stay in their order; not to be disturbed, and none of them to sail out and offer battle. So about evening, the Athenians sailing back, he would not let the seamen go out of the ships before two or three, which he had sent to espy, were returned, after seeing the enemies disembark. And thus they did the next day, and the third, and so to the fourth. So that the Athenians grew extremely confident, and disdained their enemies as if they had been afraid and daunted.

At this time, Alcibiades, who was in his castle in the Chersonese, came on horseback to the Athenian army, and found fault with their captains; first of all that they had pitched their camp neither well nor safely on an exposed and open beach, a very bad landing for the ships; and secondly, that where they were they had to fetch all they wanted from Sestos, some considerable way off; whereas if they sailed round a little way to the town and harbour of Sestos, they would be at a safer distance from an enemy who lay watching their movements, at the command of a single general, terror of whom made every order rapidly executed. This advice, however, they would not listen to; and Tydeus answered disdainfully, that not he, but others, were in office now. So Alcibiades, who even suspected there must be treachery, departed.

But on the fifth day, the Athenians having sailed towards them, and gone back again as they were used to do, very proudly and full of contempt, Lysander sending some ships, as usual, to look out, commanded the masters of them that when they saw the Athenians go to land, they should row back again with all their speed, and that when they were about half-way across, they should lift up a brazen shield from the foredeck, as the sign of battle. And he himself sailing round, encouraged the pilots and masters of the ships, and exhorted them to keep all their men to their places, seamen and soldiers alike, and as soon as ever the sign should be given, to row up boldly to their enemies. Accordingly, when the shield had been lifted up from the ships, and the trumpet from the admiral's vessel had sounded for the battle, the ships rowed up, and the foot soldiers strove to get along by the shore to the promontory.

The distance there between the two continents is fifteen furlongs, which, by the zeal and eagerness of the rowers, was quickly traversed.

Conon, one of the Athenian commanders, was the first who saw from the land the fleet advancing, and shouted out to embark, and in the greatest distress bade some and entreated others, and some he forced to man the ships. But all his diligence signified nothing, because the men were scattered about; for as soon as they came out of the ships, expecting no such matter, some went to market, others walked about the country, or went to sleep in their tents, or got their dinners ready, being, through their commanders' want of skill, as far as possible from any thought of what was to happen; and the enemy now coming up with shouts and noise, Conon, with eight ships, sailed out, and making his escape, passed from thence to Cyprus, to Evagoras.

The Peloponnesians falling upon the rest, some they took quite empty, and some they destroyed while they were filling; the men, meantime, coming unarmed and scattered to help, died at their ships, or fleeing by land, were slain, their enemies disembarking and pursuing them. Lysander took three thousand prisoners, with the generals, and the whole fleet, excepting the sacred ship, Paralus, and those which fled with Conon.

So taking their ships in tow, and having plundered their tents, with pipe and songs of victory, he sailed back to Lampsacus, having accomplished a great work with small pains, and having finished in one hour a war which had been protracted in its continuance, and diversified in its incidents and in its fortunes, to a degree exceeding belief, compared with all before it. After altering its shape and character a thousand times, and after having been the destruction of more commanders than all the previous wars of Greece put together, it was now put an end to by the good counsel and ready conduct of one man.

Some, therefore, looked upon the result as a divine intervention, and there were certain who affirmed that the stars of Castor and Pollux were seen on each side of Lysander's ship, when he first set sail from the haven toward his enemies, shining about the helm; and some say the stone which fell down was a sign of this slaughter. For a stone of a great size did fall, according to the common belief, from heaven, at Ægos Potami, which is shown to this day, and held in great esteem by the Chersonites.

And it is said that Anaxagoras foretold that the occurrence of a slip or shake among the bodies fixed in the heavens, dislodging any one of them, would be followed by the fall of the whole of them. For no one of the stars is now in the same place in which it was at first; for they, being, according to him, like stones and heavy, shine by the refraction of the upper air round about them, and are carried along forcibly by the violence of the circular motion by which they were originally withheld from falling, when cold and heavy bodies were first separated from the general universe. But there is a more probable opinion than this maintained by some, who say that falling stars are no effluxes, nor discharges of ethereal fire, extinguished almost at the instant of its igniting by the lower air; neither are they the sudden combustion and blazing up of a quantity of the lower air let loose in great abundance into the upper region; but the heavenly bodies, by a relaxation of the force of their circular movement, are carried by an irregular course, not in general into the inhabited part of the earth, but for the most part into the wide sea; which is the cause of their not being observed.

Daimachus, in his treatise *On Religion,* supports the view of Anaxagoras. He says, that before this stone fell, for seventy-five days continually, there was seen in the heavens a vast fiery body, as if it had been a flaming cloud, not resting, but carried about with several intricate and broken movements, so that the flaming pieces, which were broken off by this commotion and running about, were carried in all directions, shining as falling stars do. But when it afterwards came down to the ground in this district, and the people of the place recovering from their fear and astonishment came together, there was no fire to be seen, neither any sign of it; there was only a stone lying, big indeed, but which bore no proportion, to speak of, to that fiery compass.

It is manifest that Daimachus needs to have indulgent hearers; but if what he says be true, he altogether proves those to be wrong who say that a rock broken off from the top of some mountain, by winds and tempests, and caught and whirled about like a top, as soon as this impetus began to slacken and cease, was precipitated and fell to the ground. Unless, indeed, we choose to say that the phenomenon which was observed for so many days was really fire, and that the change in

the atmosphere ensuing on its extinction was attended with violent winds and agitations, which might be the cause of this stone being carried off. The exacter treatment of this subject belongs, however, to a different kind of writing.

Lysander, after the three thousand Athenians whom he had taken prisoners were condemned by the commissioners to die, called Philocles, the general, and asked him what punishment he considered himself to deserve, for having advised the citizens, as he had done, against the Greeks; but he, being nothing cast down at his calamity, bade him not to accuse him of matters of which nobody was a judge, but to do to him, now he was a conqueror, as he would have suffered, had he been overcome. Then washing himself, and putting on a fine cloak, he led the citizens the way to the slaughter, as Theophrastus writes in his history.

After this Lysander, sailing about to the various cities, bade all the Athenians he met go into Athens, declaring that he would spare none, but kill every man whom he found out of the city, intending thus to cause immediate famine and scarcity there, that they might not make the siege laborious to him, having provisions sufficient to endure it. And suppressing the popular governments and all other constitutions, he left one Lacedæmonian chief officer in every city, with ten rulers to act with him, selected out of the societies which he had previously formed in the different towns. And doing thus as well in the cities of his enemies as of his associates, he sailed leisurely on, establishing, in a manner, for himself supremacy over the whole of Greece.

Neither did he make choice of rulers by birth or by wealth, but bestowed the offices on his own friends and partisans, doing everything to please them, and putting absolute power of reward and punishment into their hands. And thus, personally appearing on many occasions of bloodshed and massacre, and aiding his friends to expel their opponents, he did not give the Greeks a favourable specimen of the Lacedæmonian government; and the expression of Theopompus, the comic poet, seemed but poor, when he compared the Lacedæmonians to tavern women, because when the Greeks had first tasted the sweet wine of liberty, they then poured vinegar into the cup; for from the very first it had a rough and bitter taste, all government by the people being suppressed by Lysander, and the boldest and least scrupulous of the oligarchical party selected to rule the cities.

Having spent some little time about these things, and sent some before to Lacedæmon to tell them he was arriving with two hundred ships, he united his forces in Attica with those of the two kings, Agis and Pausanias, hoping to take the city without delay. But when the Athenians defended themselves, he with his fleet passed again to Asia, and in like manner destroyed the forms of government in all the other cities, and placed them under the rule of ten chief persons, many in every one being killed, and many driven into exile; and in Samos he expelled the whole people, and gave their cities to the exiles whom he brought back. And the Athenians still possessing Sestos, he took it from them, and suffered not the Sestians themselves to dwell in it, but gave the city and country to be divided out among the pilots and masters of the ships under him; which was his first act that was disallowed by the Lacedæmonians, who brought the Sestians back again into their country. All Greece, however, rejoiced to see the Æginetans, by Lysander's aid, now again, after a long time, receiving back their cities, and the Melians and Scionæans restored, while the Athenians were driven out, and delivered up the cities.

But when he now understood they were in a bad case in the city because of the famine, he sailed to Piræus, and reduced the city, which was compelled to surrender on what conditions he demanded. One hears it said by Lacedæmonians that Lysander wrote to the Ephors thus: "Athens is taken"; and that these magistrates wrote back to Lysander, " 'Taken' were enough."

But this saying was invented for its neatness' sake; for the true decree of the magistrates was in this manner: "The government of the Lacedæmonians has made these orders; pull down the Piræus and the long walls; quit all the towns, and keep to your own land; if you do these things, you shall have peace, if you wish it, restoring also your exiles. As concerning the number of the ships, whatsoever there be judged necessary to appoint, that do."

This scroll of conditions the Athenians accepted. Theramenes, son of Hagnon, supporting it. At which time, too, they say that when Cleomenes, one of the young orators, asked him how he durst act and speak contrary to Themistocles, delivering up the walls to the Lacedæmonians, which he had built against the will of the Lacedæmonians, he said, "O young man, I do nothing contrary to Themistocles, for he raised these walls for the safety of the citizens, and we pull them down for their safety; and if walls make a city happy, then Sparta must be the most wretched of all, as it has none."

Lysander, as soon as he had taken all the ships except twelve, and the walls of the Athenians, on the sixteenth day of the month Munychion, the same on which they had overcome the barbarians at Salamis, then proceeded to take measures for altering the government. But the Athenians taking that very unwillingly, and resisting, he sent to the people and informed them that he found that the city had broken the terms, for the walls were standing when the days were past within which they should have been pulled down. He should, therefore, consider their case anew, they having broken their first articles. And some state, in fact, the proposal was made in the congress of the allies, that the Athenians should all be sold as slaves; on which occasion, Erianthus, the Theban, gave his vote to pull down the city, and turn the country into sheep-pasture; yet afterwards, when there was a meeting of the captains together, a man of Phocis, singing the first chorus in Euripides's *Electra*, which begins—

Electra, Agamemnon's child, I came unto thy desert home,

they were all melted with compassion, and it seemed to be a cruel deed to destroy and pull down a city which had been so famous, and produced such men.

Accordingly Lysander, the Athenians yielding up everything, sent for a number of flute-women out of the city, and collected together all that were in the camp, and pulled down the walls, and burnt the ships to the sound of the flute, the allies being crowned with garlands, and making merry together, as counting that day the beginning of their liberty. He proceeded also at once to alter the government, placing thirty rulers in the city and ten in the Piræus: he put, also, a garrison into the Acropolis, and made Callibius, a Spartan, the governor of it; who afterwards taking up his staff to strike Autolycus, the athlete, about whom Xenophon wrote his *Banquet*, on his tripping up his heels and throwing him to the ground, Lysander was not vexed at it, but chid Callibius, telling him he did not know how to govern freemen. The thirty rulers, however, to gain Callibius's favour, a little after killed Autolycus.

Lysander, after this, sailed out to Thrace, and what remained of the public money, and the gifts and crowns which he had himself received, numbers of people, as might be expected, being anxious to make presents to a man of such great power, who was, in a manner, the lord of Greece, he sent to Lacedæmon by Gylippus, who had commanded formerly in Sicily. But he, it is reported, unsewed the sacks at the bottom, took a considerable amount of silver out of every one of them, and sewed them up again, not knowing there was a writing in every one stating how much there was. And coming into Sparta, what he had thus stolen away he hid under the tiles of his house, and delivered up the sacks to the magistrates, and showed the seals were upon them. But afterwards, on their opening the sacks and counting it, the quantity of the silver differed from what the writing expressed; and the matter causing some perplexity to the magistrates, Gylippus's servant told them in a riddle, that under the tiles lay many owls; for, as it seems, the greatest part of the money then current bore the Athenian stamp of the owl. Gylippus having committed so foul and base a deed, after such great and distinguished exploits before, removed himself from Lacedæmon.

But the wisest of the Spartans, very much on account of this occurrence, dreading the influence of money, as being what had corrupted the greatest citizens, exclaimed against Lysander's conduct, and declared to the ephors that all the silver and gold should be sent away, as mere "alien mischiefs."

These consulted about it; and Theopompus says it was Sciraphidas, but Ephorus that it was Phlogidas, who declared they ought not to receive any gold or silver into the city; but to use their own country coin, which was iron, and was first of all dipped in vinegar when it was red-hot, that it might not be worked up anew, but because of the dipping might be hard and unpliable. It was also, of course, very heavy and troublesome to carry, and a great deal of it in quantity and weight was but a little in value. And perhaps all the old money was so, coin consisting of iron, or, in some countries, copper skewers, whence it comes that we still find a great number of small pieces of money retain the name of obol, and the drachma is six of these, because so much may be grasped in one's hand.

But Lysander's friends being against it, and endeavouring to keep the money in the city, it was resolved to bring in this sort of money to be used publicly, enacting, at the same time, that if any one was found in possession of any privately, he should be put to death, as if Lycurgus had feared the coin, and not the covetousness resulting from it, which they did not repress by letting no private man keep any, so much as they encouraged it, by allowing the state to possess it; attaching thereby a sort of dignity to it, over and above its ordinary utility.

Neither was it possible, that what they saw was so much esteemed publicly should be privately despised as unprofitable; and that every one should think that thing could be worth nothing for his own personal use, which was so extremely valued and desired for the use of the state. And moral habits, induced by public practices, are far quicker in making their way into men's private lives, than the failings and faults of individuals are in infecting the city at large. For it is probable that the parts will be rather corrupted by the whole if that grows bad; while the vices which flow from a part into the whole find many correctives and remedies from that which remains sound. Terror and the law were now to keep guard over the citizens' houses, to prevent any money entering into them; but their minds could no longer be expected to remain superior to the desire of it when wealth in general was thus set up to be striven after, as a high and noble object. On this point, however, we have given our censure of the Lacedæmonians in one of our other writings.

Lysander erected out of the spoils brazen statues at Delphi of himself, and of every one of the masters of the ships, as also figures of the golden stars of Castor and Pollux, which vanished before the battle at Leuctra. In the treasury of Brasidas and the Acanthians there was a trireme made of gold and ivory, of two cubits, which Cyrus sent Lysander in honour of his victory. But Alexandrides of Delphi writes, in his history, that there was also a deposit of Lysander's, a talent of silver, and fifty-two minæ, besides eleven staters; a statement not consistent with the generally received account of his poverty. And at that time, Lysander, being in fact of greater power than any Greek before, was yet thought to show a pride, and to affect a superiority greater even than his power warranted. He was the first, as Duris

says in his history, among the Greeks to whom
the cities reared altars as to a god, and sacrificed; to him were songs of triumph first sung,
the beginning of one of which still remains
recorded:—

*Great Greece's general from spacious Sparta we
Will celebrate with songs of victory.*

And the Samians decreed that their solemnities of Juno should be called the Lysandria;
and out of the poets he had Chœrilus always
with him, to extol his achievements in verse;
and to Antilochus, who had made some verses
in his commendation, being pleased with them,
he gave a hat full of silver; and when Antimachus of Colophon, and one Niceratus of Heraclea, competed with each other in a poem on
the deeds of Lysander, he gave the garland to
Niceratus; at which Antimachus, in vexation,
suppressed his poem; but Plato, being then a
young man and admiring Antimachus for his
poetry, consoled him for his defeat by telling
him that it is the ignorant who are the sufferers
by ignorance, as truly as the blind by want of
sight. Afterwards, when Aristonus, the musician, who had been a conqueror six times at the
Pythian games, told him as a piece of flattery,
that if he were successful again, he would proclaim himself in the name of Lysander, "That
is," he answered, "as his slave?"

This ambitious temper was indeed only
burdensome to the highest personages and to
his equals, but through having so many people devoted to serve him, an extreme haughtiness and contemptuousness grew up, together
with ambition, in his character. He observed
no sort of moderation, such as befitted a
private man, either in rewarding or in punishing; the recompense of his friends and
guests was absolute power over cities, and
irresponsible authority, and the only satisfaction of his wrath was the destruction of his
enemy; banishment would not suffice. As for
example, at a later period, fearing lest the
popular leaders of the Milesians should fly,
and desiring also to discover those who lay
hid, he swore he would do them no harm,
and on their believing him and coming forth,
he delivered them up to the oligarchical leaders to be slain, being in all no less than eight
hundred.

And, indeed, the slaughter in general of
those of the popular party in the towns exceeded all computation; as he did not kill
only for offences against himself, but granted
those favours without sparing, and joined in
the execution of them, to gratify the many

hatreds and the great cupidity of his friends
everywhere round about him. From whence
the saying of Eteocles, the Lacedæmonian,
came to be famous, that "Greece could not
have borne two Lysanders." Theophrastus
says, that Archestratus said the same thing
concerning Alcibiades. But in his case what
had given most offence was a certain licentious and wanton self-will; Lysander's power
was feared and hated because of his unmerci-
ful disposition.

The Lacedæmonians did not at all concern
themselves for any other accusers; but afterwards, when Pharnabazus, having been injured by him, he having pillaged and wasted
his country, sent some to Sparta to inform
against him, the ephors taking it very ill, put
one of his friends and fellow-captains, Thorax,
to death, taking him with some silver privately in his possession; and they sent him a
scroll, commanding him to return home.

This scroll is made up thus: When the
ephors send an admiral or general on his
way, they take two round pieces of wood,
both exactly of a length and thickness, and
cut even to one another; they keep one themselves, and the other they give to the person
they send forth; and these pieces of wood
they call *scytales*. When, therefore, they have
occasion to communicate any secret or important matter, making a scroll of parchment
long and narrow like a leathern thong, they
roll it about their own staff of wood, leaving no
space void between, but covering the surface
of the staff with the scroll all over. When they
have done this, they write what they please
on the scroll, as it is wrapped about the staff;
and when they have written, they take off
the scroll, and send it to the general without
the wood. He, when he has received it, can
read nothing of the writing, because the
words and letters are not connected, but all
broken up; but taking his own staff, he
winds the slip of the scroll about it, so that
this folding, restoring all the parts into the
same order that they were in before, and putting what comes first into connection with
what follows, brings the whole consecutive
contents to view round the outside. And this
scroll is called a *staff*, after the name of the
wood, as a thing measured is by the name of
the measure.

But Lysander, when the staff came to him
to the Hellespont, was troubled, and fearing
Pharnabazus's accusations most, made haste
to confer with him, hoping to end the differ-

ence by a meeting together. When they met, he desired him to write another letter to the magistrates, stating that he had not been wronged, and had no complaint to prefer. But he was ignorant that Pharnabazus, as it is in the proverb, played Cretan against Cretan; for pretending to do all that was desired, openly he wrote such a letter as Lysander wanted, but kept by him another, written privately; and when they came to put on the seals, changed the tablets, which differed not at all to look upon, and gave him the letter which had been written privately.

Lysander, accordingly, coming to Lacedæmon, and going, as the custom is, to the magistrates' office, gave Pharnabazus's letter to the ephors, being persuaded that the greatest accusation against him was now withdrawn; for Pharnabazus was beloved by the Lacedæmonians, having been the most zealous on their side in the war of all the king's captains. But after the magistrates had read the letter they showed it him, and he understanding now that—

> Others beside Ulysses deep can be,
> Not the one wise man of the world is he,

in extreme confusion, left them at the time. But a few days after, meeting the ephors, he said he must go to the temple of Ammon, and offer the god the sacrifices which he had vowed in war.

For some state it as a truth, that when he was besieging the city of Aphytæ in Thrace, Ammon stood by him in his sleep; whereupon raising the siege, supposing the god had commanded it, he bade the Aphytæans sacrifice to Ammon, and resolved to make a journey into Libya to propitiate the god. But most were of opinion that the god was but the pretence, and that in reality he was afraid of the ephors, and that impatience of the yoke at home, and dislike of living under authority, made him long for some travel and wandering, like a horse just brought in from open feeding and pasture to the stable, and put again to his ordinary work. For that which Ephorus states to have been the cause of this travelling about, I shall relate by and by.

And having hardly and with difficulty obtained leave of the magistrates to depart, he set sail. But the kings, while he was on his voyage, considering that keeping, as he did, the cities in possession by his own friends and partisans, he was in fact their sovereign and the lord of Greece, took measures for restoring the power to the people, and for throwing his friends out.

Disturbances commencing again about these things, and, first of all, the Athenians from Phyle setting upon their thirty rulers and overpowering them, Lysander, coming home in haste, persuaded the Lacedæmonians to support the oligarchies and to put down the popular governments, and to the thirty in Athens, first of all, they sent a hundred talents for the war, and Lysander himself, as general, to assist them. But the kings envying him, and fearing lest he should take Athens again, resolved that one of themselves should take the command. Accordingly, Pausanias went, and in words, indeed, professed as if he had been for the tyrant against the people, but in reality exerted himself for peace, that Lysander might not by the means of his friends become lord of Athens again.

This he brought easily to pass; for, reconciling the Athenians, and quieting the tumults, he defeated the ambitious hope of Lysander, though shortly after, on the Athenians rebelling again, he was censured for having thus taken, as it were, the bit out of the mouth of the people, which, being freed from the oligarchy, would now break out again into affronts and insolence; and Lysander regained the reputation of a person who employed his command not in gratification of others, not for applause, but strictly for the good of Sparta.

His speech, also, was bold and daunting to such as opposed him. The Argives, for example, contended about the bounds of their land, and thought they brought juster pleas than the Lacedæmonians; holding out his sword, "He," said Lysander, "that is master of this, brings the best argument about the bounds of territory." A man of Megara, at some conference, taking freedom with him, "This language, my friend," said he, "should come from a city." To the Bœotians, who were acting a doubtful part, he put the question, whether he should pass through their country with spears upright or levelled. After the revolt of the Corinthians, when, on coming to their walls, he perceived the Lacedæmonians hesitating to make the assault, and a hare was seen to leap through the ditch: "Are you not ashamed," he said, "to fear an enemy, for whose laziness the very hares sleep upon their walls?"

When King Agis died, leaving a brother, Agesilaus, and Leontychides, who was supposed his son, Lysander, being attached to

Agesilaus, persuaded him to lay claim to the kingdom, as being a true descendant of Hercules; Leontychides lying under the suspicion of being the son of Alcibiades, who lived privately in familiarity with Timæa, the wife of Agis, at the time he was a fugitive in Sparta. Agis, they say, computing the time, satisfied himself that she could not have conceived by him, and had hitherto always neglected and manifestly disowned Leontychides; but now when he was carried sick to Heræa, being ready to die, what by importunities of the young man himself, and of his friends, in the presence of many he declared Leontychides to be his; and desiring those who were present to bear witness to this to the Lacedæmonians, died. They accordingly did so testify in favour of Leontychides.

And Agesilaus, being otherwise highly reputed of, and strong in the support of Lysander, was, on the other hand, prejudiced by Diopithes, a man famous for his knowledge of oracles, who adduced this prophecy in reference to Agesilaus's lameness:—

Beware, great Sparta, lest there come of thee,
Though sound thyself, an halting sovereignty;
Troubles, both long and unexpected too,
And storms of deadly warfare shall ensue.

When many, therefore, yielded to the oracle, and inclined to Leontychides, Lysander said that Diopithes did not take the prophecy rightly; for it was not that the god would be offended if any lame person ruled over the Lacedæmonians, but that the kingdom would be a lame one if bastards and false-born should govern with the posterity of Hercules. By this argument, and by his great influence among them, he prevailed, and Agesilaus was made king.

Immediately, therefore, Lysander spurred him on to make an expedition into Asia, putting him in hopes that he might destroy the Persians, and attain the height of greatness. And he wrote to his friends in Asia, bidding them request to have Agesilaus appointed to command them in the war against the barbarians; which they were persuaded to, and sent ambassadors to Lacedæmon to entreat it. And this would seem to be a second favour done Agesilaus by Lysander, not inferior to his first in obtaining him the kingdom.

But with ambitious natures, otherwise not ill qualified for command, the feeling of jealousy of those near them in reputation continually stands in the way of the performance of noble actions; they make those their rivals

in virtue, whom they ought to use as their helpers to it. Agesilaus took Lysander, among the thirty counsellors that accompanied him, with intentions of using him as his especial friend; but when they were come into Asia, the inhabitants there, to whom he was but little known, addressed themselves to him but little and seldom; whereas Lysander, because of their frequent previous intercourse, was visited and attended by large numbers, by his friends out of observance, and by others out of fear; and just as in tragedies it not uncommonly is the case with the actors, the person who represents a messenger or servant is much taken notice of, and plays the chief part, while he who wears the crown and sceptre is hardly heard to speak, even so was it about the counsellor, he had all the real honours of the government, and to the king was left the empty name of power.

This disproportionate ambition ought very likely to have been in some way softened down, and Lysander should have been reduced to his proper second place, but wholly to cast off and to insult and affront for glory's sake one who was his benefactor and friend was not worthy of Agesilaus to allow in himself. For, first of all, he gave him no opportunity for any action, and never set him in any place of command; then, for whomsoever he perceived him exerting his interest, these persons he always sent away with a refusal, and with less attention than any ordinary suitors, thus silently undoing and weakening his influence.

Lysander, miscarrying in everything, and perceiving that his diligence for his friends was but a hindrance to them, forbore to help them, entreating them that they would not address themselves to, nor observe him, but that they would speak to the king, and to those who could be of more service to friends than at present he could; most, on hearing this, forbore to trouble him about their concerns, but continued their observances to him, waiting upon him in the walks and places of exercise; at which Agesilaus was more annoyed than ever, envying him the honour; and, finally, when he gave many of the officers places of command and the governments of cities, he appointed Lysander carver at his table, adding, by way of insult to the Ionians, "Let them go now, and pay their court to my carver."

Upon this, Lysander thought fit to come and speak with him; and a brief laconic dialogue passed between them as follows: "Truly, you know very well, O Agesilaus, how to depress your friends"; "Those friends," replied he, "who would be greater than myself; but those who increase my power, it is just should share in it." "Possibly, O Agesilaus," answered Lysander, "in all this there may be more said on your part than done on mine, but I request you, for the sake of observers from without, to place me in any command under you where you may judge I shall be the least offensive, and most useful."

Upon this he was sent ambassador to the Hellespont; and though angry with Agesilaus, yet did not neglect to perform his duty, and having induced Spithridates the Persian, being offended with Pharnabazus, a gallant man, and in command of some forces, to revolt, he brought him to Agesilaus. He was not, however, employed in any other service, but having completed his time returned to Sparta, without honour, angry with Agesilaus, and hating more than ever the whole Spartan government, and resolved to delay no longer, but while there was yet time, to put into execution the plans which he appears some time before to have concerted for a revolution and change in the constitution.

These were as follows. The Heraclidæ who joined with the Dorians, and came into Peloponnesus, became a numerous and glorious race in Sparta, but not every family belonging to it had the right of succession in the kingdom, but the kings were chosen out of two only, called the Eurypontidæ and the Agiadæ; the rest had no privilege in the government by their nobility of birth, and the honours which followed from merit lay open to all who could obtain them.

Lysander, who was born of one of these families, when he had risen into great renown for his exploits, and had gained great friends and power, was vexed to see the city, which had increased to what it was by him, ruled by others not at all better descended than himself, and formed a design to remove the government from the two families, and to give it in common to all the Heraclidæ; or, as some say, not to the Heraclidæ only, but to all the Spartans; that the reward might not belong to the posterity of Hercules, but to those who were like Hercules, judging by that personal merit which raised even him to the honour of the Godhead; and he hoped that when the kingdom was thus to be competed for, no Spartan would be chosen before himself.

Accordingly he first attempted and prepared to persuade the citizens privately, and studied an oration composed for this purpose by Cleon, the Halicarnassian. Afterwards, perceiving so unexpected and great an innovation required bolder means of support, he proceeded, as it might be on the stage, to avail himself of machinery, and to try the effects of divine agency upon his countrymen. He collected and arranged for his purpose answers and oracles from Apollo, not expecting to get any benefit from Cleon's rhetoric, unless he should first alarm and overpower the minds of his fellow-citizens by religious and superstitious terrors, before bringing them to the consideration of his arguments.

Ephorus relates, after he had endeavoured to corrupt the oracle of Apollo, and had again failed to persuade the priestess of Dodona by means of Pherecles, that he went to Ammon, and discoursed with the guardians of the oracle there, proffering them a great deal of gold, and that they, taking this ill, sent some to Sparta to accuse Lysander; and on his acquittal the Libyans, going away, said, "You will find us, O Spartans, better judges, when you come to dwell with us in Libya," there being a certain ancient oracle that the Lacedæmonians should dwell in Libya. But as the whole intrigue and the course of the contrivance was no ordinary one, nor lightly undertaken, but depended as it went on, like some mathematical proposition, on a variety of important admissions, and proceeded through a series of intricate and difficult steps to its conclusion, we will go into it at length, following the account of one who was at once an historian and a philosopher.

There was a woman in Pontus who professed to be pregnant by Apollo, which many, as was natural, disbelieved, and many also gave credit to, and when she had brought forth a man-child, several, not unimportant persons, took an interest in its rearing and bringing up. The name given the boy was Silenus, for some reason or other. Lysander, taking this for the groundwork, framed and devised the rest himself, making use of not a few, nor these insignificant champions of his story, who brought the report of the child's birth into credit without any suspicion.

Another report, also, was procured from Delphi and circulated in Sparta, that there were some very old oracles which were kept by the priests in private writings; and they were not to be meddled with, neither was it lawful to read them, till one in aftertimes should come, descended from Apollo, and, on giving some known token to the keepers, should take the books in which the oracles were. Things being thus ordered beforehand, Silenus, it was intended, should come and ask for the oracles, as being the child of Apollo, and those priests who were privy to the design were to profess to search narrowly into all particulars, and to question him concerning his birth; and, finally, were to be convinced, and, as to Apollo's son, to deliver up to him the writings. Then he, in the presence of many witnesses, should read, amongst other prophecies, that which was the object of the whole contrivance, relating to the office of the kings, that it would be better and more desirable to the Spartans to choose their kings out of the best citizens. And now, Silenus being grown up to a youth, and being ready for the action, Lysander miscarried in his drama through the timidity of one of his actors, or assistants, who just as he came to the point, lost heart and drew back. Yet nothing was found out while Lysander lived, but only after his death.

He died before Agesilaus came back from Asia, being involved, or perhaps more truly having himself involved Greece, in the Bœotian war. For it is stated both ways; and the cause of it some make to be himself, others the Thebans, and some both together; the Thebans, on the one hand, being charged with casting away the sacrifices at Aulis, and that being bribed with the king's money brought by Androclides and Amphitheus, they had, with the object of entangling the Lacedæmonians in a Grecian war, set upon the Phocians, and wasted their country; it being said, on the other hand, that Lysander was angry that the Thebans had preferred a claim to the tenth part of the spoils of the war, while the rest of the confederates submitted without complaint; and because they expressed indignation about the money which Lysander sent to Sparta, but more especially, because from them the Athenians had obtained the first opportunity of freeing themselves from the thirty tyrants, whom Lysander had made, and to support whom the Lacedæmonians issued a decree that political refugees from Athens might be arrested in whatever country they were found, and that those who impeded their arrest should be excluded from the confederacy.

In reply to this the Thebans issued counter decrees of their own, truly in the spirit and temper of the actions of Hercules and Bacchus, that every house and city in Bœotia should be opened to the Athenians who required it, and that he who did not help a fugitive who was seized should be fined a talent for damages, and if any one should bear arms through Bœotia to Attica against the tyrants, that none of the Thebans should either see or hear of it. Nor did they pass these human and truly Greek decrees without at the same time making their acts conformable to their words. For Thrasybulus, and those who with him occupied Phyle, set out upon that enterprise from Thebes, with arms and money, and secrecy and a point to start from, provided for them by the Thebans. Such were the causes of complaint Lysander had against Thebes.

And being now grown violent in his temper through the atrabilious tendency which increased upon him in his old age, he urged the ephors and persuaded them to place a garrison in Thebes, and taking the commander's place, he marched forth with a body of troops. Pausanias, also, the king, was sent shortly after with an army.

Now Pausanias, going round by Cithæron, was to invade Bœotia; Lysander, meantime, advanced through Phocis to meet him, with a numerous body of soldiers. He took the city of the Orchomenians, who came over to him of their own accord, and plundered Lebadea. He despatched also letters to Pausanias, ordering him to move from Platæa to meet him at Haliartus, and that himself would be at the walls of Haliartus by break of day. These letters were brought to the Thebans, the carrier of them falling into the hands of some Theban scouts. They, having received aid from Athens, committed their city to the charge of the Athenian troops, and sallying out about the first sleep, succeeded in reaching Haliartus a little before Lysander, and part of them entered into the city.

He upon this first of all resolved, posting his army upon a hill, to stay for Pausanias; then as the day advanced, not being able to rest, he bade his men take up their arms, and encouraging the allies, led them in a column along the road to the walls. But those Thebans who had remained outside, taking the city on the left hand, advanced against the rear of their enemies, by the fountain which is called Cissusa; here they tell the story that the nurses washed the infant Bacchus after his birth; the water of it is of a bright wine-colour, clear, and most pleasant to drink; and not far off the Cretan storax grows all about, which the Haliartians adduce in token of Rhadamanthus having dwelt there, and they show his sepulchre, calling it Alea. And the monument also of Alcmena is hard by; for there, as they say, she was buried, having married Rhadamanthus after Amphitryon's death.

But the Thebans inside the city, forming in order of battle with the Haliartians, stood still for some time, but on seeing Lysander with a party of those who were foremost approaching, on a sudden opening the gates and falling on, they killed him with the soothsayer at his side, and a few others; for the greater part immediately fled back to the main force. But the Thebans not slackening, but closely pursuing them, the whole body turned to fly towards the hills. There were one thousand of them slain; there died, also, of the Thebans three hundred, who were killed with their enemies; while chasing them into craggy and difficult places. These had been under suspicion of favouring the Lacedæmonians, and in their eagerness to clear themselves in the eyes of their fellow-citizens, exposed themselves in the pursuit, and so met their death.

News of the disaster reached Pausanias as he was on the way from Platæa to Thespiæ, and having set his army in order he came to Haliartus; Thrasybulus, also, came from Thebes, leading the Athenians.

Pausanias proposing to request the bodies of the dead under truce, the elders of the Spartans took it ill, and were angry among themselves, and coming to the king, declared that Lysander should not be taken away upon any conditions; if they fought it out by arms about his body, and conquered, then they might bury him; if they were overcome, it was glorious to die upon the spot with their commander.

When the elders had spoken these things, Pausanias saw it would be a difficult business to vanquish the Thebans, who had but just been conquerors; that Lysander's body also lay near the walls, so that it would be hard for them, though they overcame, to take it away without a truce; he therefore sent a herald, obtained a truce, and withdrew his forces, and carrying away the body of Lysander, they buried it in the first friendly soil they reached on crossing the Bœotian frontier, in the country of the Panopæans; where the monument still stands as you go on the road from Delphi to Chæronea.

Now the army quartering there, it is said that a person of Phocis, relating the battle to one who was not in it, said, the enemies fell upon them just after Lysander had passed over the Hoplites; surprised at which a Spartan, a friend of Lysander, asked what Hoplites he meant, for he did not know the name. "It was there," answered the Phocian, "that the enemy killed the first of us; the rivulet by the city is called Hoplites." On hearing which the Spartan shed tears and observed how impossible it is for any man to avoid his appointed lot; Lysander, it appears, having received an oracle as follows:—

Sounding Hoplites see thou bear in mind,
And the earthborn dragon following behind.

Some, however, say that Hoplites does not run by Haliartus, but is a watercourse near Coronea, falling into the river Philarus, not far from the town in former times called Hoplias, and now Isomantus.

The man of Haliartus who killed Lysander, by name Neochorus, bore on his shield the device of a dragon; and this, it was supposed, the oracle signified. It is said also that at the time of the Peloponnesian war, the Thebans received an oracle from the sanctuary of Ismenus, referring at once to the battle at Delium, and to this which thirty years after took place at Haliartus. It ran thus:—

Hunting the wolf, observe the utmost bound,
And the hill Orchalides where foxes most are
found.

By the words, "the utmost bound," Delium being intended, where Bœotia touches Attica, and by Orchalides, the hill now called Alopecus, which lies in the parts of Haliartus towards Helicon.

But such a death befalling Lysander, the Spartans took it so grievously at the time, that they put the king to a trial for his life, which he not daring to await, fled to Tegea, and there lived out his life in the sanctuary of Minerva. The poverty also of Lysander being discovered by his death made his merit more manifest, since from so much wealth and power, from all the homage of the cities, and of the Persian kingdom, he had not in the least degree, so far as money goes, sought any private aggrandisement, as Theopompus in his history relates, whom any one may rather give credit to when he commends than when he finds fault, as it is more agreeable to him to blame than to praise.

But subsequently, Ephorus says, some controversy arising among the allies at Sparta, which made it necessary to consult the writings which Lysander had kept by him, Agesilaus came to his house, and finding the book in which the oration on the Spartan constitution was written at length, to the effect that the kingdom ought to be taken from the Eurypontidæ and Agiadæ, and to be offered in common, and a choice made out of the best citizens, at first he was eager to make it public, and to show his countrymen the real character of Lysander. But Lacratidas, a wise man, and at that time chief of the ephors, hindered Agesilaus, and said they ought not to dig up Lysander again, but rather to bury with him a discourse, composed so plausibly and subtly.

Other honours, also, were paid him, after his death; and amongst these they imposed a fine upon those who had engaged themselves to marry his daughters, and then when Lysander was found to be poor, after his decease, refused them; because when they thought him rich they had been observant of him, but now his poverty had proved him just and good, they forsook him. For there was, it seems, in Sparta, a punishment for not marrying, for a late, and for a bad marriage; and to the last penalty those were most especially liable who sought alliances with the rich instead of with the good and with their friends. Such is the account we have found given of Lysander.

SULLA

138–78 B.C.

Lucius Cornelius Sulla was descended of a patrician or noble family. Of his ancestors, Rufinus, it is said, had been consul, and incurred a disgrace more signal than his distinction. For being found possessed of more than ten pounds of silver plate, contrary to the law, he was for this reason put out of the senate.

His posterity continued ever after in obscurity, nor had Sulla himself any opulent parentage. In his younger days he lived in hired lodgings, at a low rate, which in aftertimes was adduced against him as proof that he had been fortunate above his quality. When he was boasting and magnifying himself for his exploits in Libya, a person of noble station made answer, "And how can you be an honest man, who, since the death of a father who left you nothing, have become so rich?" The time in which he lived was no longer an age of pure and upright manners, but had already declined, and yielded to the appetite for riches and luxury; yet still, in the general opinion, they who deserted the hereditary poverty of their family were as much blamed as those who had run out a fair patrimonial estate. And afterwards, when he had seized the power into his hands, and was putting many to death, a freedman, suspected of having concealed one of the proscribed, and for that reason sentenced to be thrown down the Tarpeian rock, in a reproachful way recounted how

they had lived long together under the same roof, himself for the upper rooms paying two thousand sesterces, and Sulla for the lower three thousand; so that the difference between their fortunes then was no more than one thousand sesterces, equivalent in Attic coin to two hundred and fifty drachmas. And thus much concerning his early fortune.

His general personal appearance may be known by his statues; only his blue eyes, of themselves extremely keen and glaring, were rendered all the more forbidding and terrible by the complexion of his face, in which white was mixed with rough blotches of fiery red. Hence, it is said, he was surnamed Sulla, and in allusion to it one of the scurrilous jesters at Athens made the verse upon him—

Sulla is a mulberry sprinkled o'er with meal.

Nor is it out of place to make use of marks of character like these, in the case of one who was by nature so addicted to raillery, that in his youthful obscure years he would converse freely with players and professed jesters, and join them in all their low pleasures. And when supreme master of all, he was often wont to muster together the most impudent players and stage-followers of the town, and to drink and bandy jests with them without regard to his age or the dignity of his place, and to the prejudice of important affairs that required his attention. When he was once at table, it was not in Sulla's nature to admit of anything that was serious, and whereas at other times he was a man of business and austere of countenance, he underwent all of a sudden, at his first entrance upon wine and goodfellowship, a total revolution, and was gentle and tractable with common singers and dancers, and ready to oblige any one that spoke with him.

It seems to have been a sort of diseased result of this laxity that he was so prone to amorous pleasures, and yielded without resistance to any temptation of voluptuousness, from which even in his old age he could not refrain. He had a long attachment for Metrobius, a player. In his first amours, it happened that he made court to a common but rich lady, Nicopolis by name, and what by the air of his youth, and what by long intimacy, won so far on her affections, that she rather than he was the lover, and at her death she bequeathed him her whole property. He likewise inherited the estate of a stepmother who loved him as her own son. By these means he had pretty well advanced his fortunes.

He was chosen quæstor to Marius in his first consulship, and set sail with him for Libya, to war upon Jugurtha. Here, in general, he gained approbation; and more especially, by closing in dexterously with an accidental occasion, made a friend of Bocchus, King of Numidia. He hospitably entertained the king's ambassadors on their escape from some Numidian robbers, and after showing them much kindness, sent them on their journey with presents, and an escort to protect them.

Bocchus had long hated and dreaded his son-in-law, Jugurtha, who had now been worsted in the field and had fled to him for shelter; and it so happened he was at this time entertaining a design to betray him. He accordingly invited Sulla to come to him, wishing the seizure and surrender of Jugurtha to be effected rather through him, than directly by himself. Sulla, when he had communicated the business to Marius, and received from him a small detachment, voluntarily put himself into this imminent danger; and confiding in a barbarian, who had been unfaithful to his own relations, to apprehend another man's person, made surrender of his own. Bocchus, having both of them now in his power, was necessitated to betray one or other, and after long debate with himself, at last resolved on his first design, and gave up Jugurtha into the hands of Sulla.

For this Marius triumphed, but the glory of the enterprise, which through people's envy of Marius was ascribed to Sulla, secretly grieved him. And the truth is, Sulla himself was by nature vainglorious, and this being the first time that from a low and private condition he had risen to esteem amongst the citizens and tasted of honour, his appetite for distinction carried him to such a pitch of ostentation, that he had a representation of this action engraved on a signet ring, which he carried about with him, and made use of ever after. The impress was Bocchus delivering, and Sulla receiving, Jugurtha. This touched Marius to the quick; however, judging Sulla to be beneath his rivalry, he made use of him as lieutenant, in his second consulship, and in his third as tribune; and many considerable services were effected by his means. When acting as lieutenant he took Copillus, chief of the Tectosages, prisoner, and compelled the Marsians, a great and populous nation, to become friends and confederates of the Romans.

Henceforward, however, Sulla, perceiving that Marius bore a jealous eye over him, and would no longer afford him opportunities of action, but rather opposed his advance, attached himself to Catulus, Marius's colleague, a worthy man, but not energetic enough as a general. And under this commander, who intrusted him with the highest and most important commissions, he rose at once to reputation and to power. He subdued by arms most part of the Alpine barbarians; and when there was a scarcity in the armies, he took that care upon himself and brought in such a store of provisions as not only to furnish the soldiers of Catulus with abundance, but likewise to supply Marius. This, as he writes himself, wounded Marius to the very heart. So slight and childish were the first occasions and motives of that enmity between them, which, passing afterwards through a long course of civil bloodshed and incurable divisions to find its end in tyranny, and the confusion of the whole state, proved Euripides to have been truly wise and thoroughly acquainted with the causes of disorders in the body politic, when he forewarned all men to beware of Ambition, as of all the higher Powers the most destructive and pernicious to her votaries.

Sulla, by this time thinking that the reputation of his arms abroad was sufficient to entitle him to a part in the civil administration, betook himself immediately from the camp to the assembly, and offered himself as a candidate for a prætorship, but failed. The fault of this disappointment he wholly ascribes to the populace, who, knowing his intimacy with King Bocchus, and for that reason expecting, that if he was made ædile before his prætorship, he would then show them magnificent hunting-shows and combats between Libyan wild beasts, chose other prætors, on purpose to force him into the ædileship.

The vanity of this pretext is sufficiently disproved by matter-of-fact. For the year following, partly by flatteries to the people, and partly by money, he got himself elected prætor. Accordingly, once while he was in office, on his angrily telling Cæsar that he should make use of his authority against him, Cæsar answered him with a smile, "You do well to call it your own, as you bought it."

At the end of his prætorship he was sent over into Cappadocia, under the pretence of re-establishing Ariobarzanes in his kingdom, but in reality to keep in check the restless movements of Mithridates, who was gradually procuring himself as vast a new acquired power and dominion as was that of his ancient inheritance. He carried over with him no great forces of his own, but making use of the cheerful aid of the confederates, succeeded, with considerable slaughter of the Cappadocians, and yet greater of the Armenian succours, in expelling Gordius and establishing Ariobarzanes as king.

During his stay on the banks of the Euphrates, there came to him Orobazus, a Parthian, ambassador from King Arsaces, as yet there having been no correspondence between the two nations. And this also we may lay to the account of Sulla's felicity, that he should be the first Roman to whom the Parthians made address for alliance and friendship. At the time of which reception, the story is, that, having ordered three chairs of state to be set, one for Ariobarzanes, one for Orobazus, and a third for himself, he placed himself in the middle, and so gave audience. For this the King of Parthia afterwards put Orobazus to death.

Some people commended Sulla for his lofty carriage towards the barbarians; others again accused him of arrogance and unseasonable display. It is reported that a certain Chaldæan, of Orobazus's retinue, looking Sulla wistfully in the face, and observing carefully the motions of his mind and body, and forming a judgment of his nature, according to the rules of his art, said that it was impossible for him not to become the greatest of men; it was rather a wonder how he could even then abstain from being head of all.

At his return, Censorinus impeached him of extortion, for having exacted a vast sum of money from a well-affected and associate kingdom. However, Censorinus did not appear at the trial, but dropped his accusation. His quarrel, meantime, with Marius began to break out afresh, receiving new material from the ambition of Bocchus, who, to please the people of Rome, and gratify Sulla, set up in the temple of Jupiter Capitolinus images bearing trophies, and a representation in gold of the surrender of Jugurtha to Sulla. When Marius, in great anger, attempted to pull them down, and others aided Sulla, the whole city would have been in tumult and commotion with this dispute, had not the Social War, which had long lain smouldering, blazed forth at last, and for the present put an end to the quarrel.

In the course of this war, which had many great changes of fortune, and which, more than any, afflicted the Romans, and, indeed, endangered the very being of the Commonwealth, Marius was not able to signalise his valour in any action, but left behind him a clear proof, that warlike excellence requires a strong and still vigorous body. Sulla, on the other hand, by his many achievements, gained himself, with his fellow-citizens, the name of a great commander, while his friends thought him the greatest of all commanders, and his enemies called him the most fortunate.

Nor did this make the same sort of impression on him as it made on Timotheus, the son of Conon, the Athenian; who, when his adversaries ascribed his successes to his good luck, and had a painting made, representing him asleep, and Fortune by his side, casting her nets over the cities, was rough and violent in his indignation at those who did it, as if, by attributing all to Fortune, they had robbed him of his just honours; and said to the people on one occasion at his return from war, "In this, ye men of Athens, Fortune had no part." A piece of boyish petulance, which the deity, we are told, played back upon Timotheus; who from that time was never able to achieve anything that was great, but proving altogether unfortunate in his attempts, and falling into discredit with the people, was at last banished the city.

Sulla, on the contrary, not only accepted with pleasure the credit of such divine felicities and favours, but joining himself and extolling and glorifying what was done, gave the honour of all to Fortune, whether it were out of boastfulness, or a real feeling of divine agency. He remarks, in his Memoirs, that of all his well-advised actions, none proved so lucky in the execution as what he had boldly enterprised, not by calculation, but upon the moment. And, in the character which he gives of himself, that he was born for fortune rather than war, he seems to give Fortune a higher place than merit, and, in short, makes himself entirely the creature of a superior power, accounting even his concord with Metellus, his equal in office, and his connection by marriage, a piece of preternatural felicity. For expecting to have met in him a most troublesome, he found him a most accommodating, colleague.

Moreover, in the Memoirs which he dedicated to Lucullus, he admonished him to esteem nothing more trustworthy than what the divine powers advise him by night. And when he was leaving the city with an army, to fight in the Social War, he relates that the earth near the Laverna opened, and a quantity of fire came rushing out of it, shooting up with a bright flame into the heavens. The soothsayers upon this foretold that a person of great qualities, and of a rare and singular aspect, should take the government in hand, and quiet the present troubles of the city. Sulla affirms he was the man, for his golden head of hair made him an extraordinary-looking man, nor had he any shame, after the great actions he had done, in testifying to his own great qualities. And thus much of his opinion as to divine agency.

In general he would seem to have been of a very irregular character, full of inconsistencies with himself; much given to rapine, to prodigality yet more; in promoting or disgracing whom he pleased, alike unaccountable; cringing to those he stood in need of, and domineering over others who stood in need of him, so that it was hard to tell whether his nature had more in it of pride or of servility.

As to his unequal distribution of punishments, as, for example, that upon slight grounds he would put to the torture, and again would bear patiently with the greatest wrongs; would readily forgive and be reconciled after the most heinous acts of enmity, and yet would visit small and inconsiderable offences with death and confiscation of goods; one might judge that in himself he was really of a violent and revengeful nature, which, however, he could qualify, upon reflection, for his interest. In this very Social War, when the soldiers with stones and clubs had killed an officer of prætorian rank, his own lieutenant, Albinus by name, he passed by this flagrant crime without any inquiry, giving it out moreover in a boast, that the soldiers would behave all the better now, to make amends, by some special bravery, for their breach of discipline. He took no notice of the clamours of those that cried for justice, but designing already to supplant Marius, now that he saw the Social War near its end, he made much of his army, in hopes to get himself declared general of the forces against Mithridates.

At his return to Rome he was chosen consul with Quintus Pompeius, in the fiftieth year of his age, and made a most distinguished marriage with Cæcilia, daughter of Metellus, the chief priest. The common people made a variety of verses in ridicule of the marriage, and many of the nobility also were disgusted at it, esteeming him, as Livy writes, unworthy of this connection, whom before they thought worthy of a consulship.

This was not his only wife, for first, in his younger days, he was married to Ilia, by whom he had a daughter; after her to Ælia; and thirdly to Clœlia, whom he dismissed as barren, but honourably, and with professions of respect, adding, moreover, presents. But the match between him and Metella, falling out a few days after, occasioned suspicions that he had complained of Clœlia without due cause.

To Metella he always showed great deference, so much so that the people, when anxious for the recall of the exiles of Marius's party, upon his refusal, entreated the intercession of Metella. And the Athenians, it is thought, had harder measure, at the capture of their town, because they used insulting language to Metella in their jests from the walls during the siege. But of this hereafter.

At present esteeming the consulship but a small matter in comparison of things to come, he was impatiently carried away in thought to the Mithridatic War. Here he was withstood by Marius; who out of mad affectation of glory and thirst for distinction, those never dying passions, though he were now unwieldy in body, and had given up service, on account of his age, during the late campaigns, still coveted after command in a distant war beyond the seas.

And whilst Sulla was departed for the

camp, to order the rest of his affairs there, he sat brooding at home, and at last hatched that execrable sedition, which wrought Rome more mischief than all her enemies together had done, as was indeed foreshown by the gods. For a flame broke forth of its own accord, from under the staves of the ensigns, and was with difficulty extinguished. Three ravens brought their young into the open road, and ate them, carrying the relics into the nest again. Mice having gnawed the consecrated gold in one of the temples, the keepers caught one of them, a female, in a trap; and she bringing forth five young ones in the very trap, devoured three of them. But what was greatest of all, in a calm and clear sky there was heard the sound of a trumpet, with such a loud and dismal blast as struck terror and amazements into the hearts of the people.

The Etruscan sages affirmed that this prodigy betokened the mutation of the age, and a general revolution in the world. For according to them there are in all eight ages, differing one from another in the lives and the characters of men, and to each of these God has allotted a certain measure of time, determined by the circuit of the great year. And when one age is run out, at the approach of another, there appears some wonderful sign from earth or heaven, such as makes it manifest at once to those who have made it their business to study such things, that there has succeeded in the world a new race of men, differing in customs and institutes of life, and more or less regarded by the gods than the preceding. Among other great changes that happen, as they say, at the turn of ages, the art of divination, also, at one time rises in esteem, and is more successful in its predictions, clearer and surer tokens being sent from God, and then, again, in another generation declines as low, becoming mere guesswork for the most part, and discerning future events by dim and uncertain intimations. This was the mythology of the wisest of the Tuscan sages, who were thought to possess a knowledge beyond other men.

Whilst the senate sat in consultation with the soothsayers, concerning these prodigies, in the temple of Bellona, a sparrow came flying in, before them all, with a grasshopper in its mouth, and letting fall one part of it, flew away with the remainder. The diviners foreboded commotions and dissensions between the great landed proprietors and the common city populace; the latter, like the grasshopper, being loud and talkative; while the sparrow might represent the "dwellers in the field."

Marius had taken into alliance Sulpicius, the tribune, a man second to none in any villainies, so that it was less the question what others he surpassed, but rather in what respects he most surpassed himself in wickedness. He was cruel, bold, rapacious, and in all these points utterly shameless and unscrupulous; not hesitating to offer Roman citizenship by public sale to freed slaves and aliens, and to count out the price on public moneytables in the Forum. He maintained three thousand swordmen, and had always about him a company of young men of the equestrian class ready for all occasions, whom he styled his Anti-senate. Having had a law enacted, that no senator should contract a debt of above two thousand drachmas, he himself, after death, was found indebted three millions.

This was the man whom Marius let in upon the Commonwealth, and who, confounding all things by force and the sword, made several ordinances of dangerous consequence, and amongst the rest one giving Marius the conduct of the Mithridatic war. Upon this the consuls proclaimed a public cessation of business, but as they were holding an assembly near the temple of Castor and Pollux, he let loose the rabble upon them, and amongst many others slew the consul Pompeius's young son in the Forum, Pompeius himself hardly escaping in the crowd. Sulla, being closely pursued into the house of Marius, was forced to come forth and dissolve the cessation; and for his doing this, Sulpicius, having deposed Pompeius, allowed Sulla to continue his consulship, only transferring the Mithridatic expedition to Marius.

There were immediately despatched to Nola tribunes to receive the army, and bring it to Marius; but Sulla, having got first to the camp, and the soldiers, upon hearing the news, having stoned the tribunes, Marius, in requital, proceeded to put the friends of Sulla in the city to the sword, and rifled their goods. Every kind of removal and flight went on, some hastening from the camp to the city, others from the city to the camp.

The senate, no more in its own power, but wholly governed by the dictates of Marius and Sulpicius, alarmed at the report of Sulla's advancing with his troops towards the city, sent forth two of the prætors, Brutus and Servilius, to forbid his nearer approach. The soldiers would have slain these prætors in a fury, for their bold language to Sulla; contenting themselves, however, with breaking their rods, and tearing off their purple-edged robes, after much contumelious usage they sent them back, to the sad dejection of the citizens, who beheld their magistrates despoiled of their badges of office, and announcing to them that things were now manifestly come to a rupture past all cure.

Marius put himself in readiness, and Sulla with his colleague moved from Nola, at the head of six complete legions, all of them willing to march up directly against the city, though he himself as yet was doubtful in thought, and apprehensive of the danger. As he was sacrificing, Postumius, the soothsayer, having inspected the entrails, stretching forth both hands to Sulla, required to be bound and kept in custody till the battle was over, as willing, if they had not speedy and complete success, to suffer the utmost punishment. It is said, also, that there appeared to Sulla himself, in a dream, a certain goddess, whom the Romans learnt to worship from the Cappadocians, whether it be the Moon, or Pallas, or Bellona. This same goddess, to his thinking, stood by him, and put into his hand thunder and lightning, then naming his enemies one by one, bade him strike them, who, all of them, fell on the discharge and disappeared. Encouraged by this vision, and relating it to his colleague, next day he led on towards Rome.

About Picinæ being met by a deputation, beseeching him not to attack at once, in the heat of a march, for that the senate had decreed to do him all the right imaginable, he consented to halt on the spot, and sent his officers to measure out the ground, as is usual, for a camp; so that the deputation, believing it, returned. They were no sooner gone, but he sent a party on under the command of Lucius Basillus and Caius Mummius, to secure the city gate, and the walls on the side of the Esquiline hill, and then close at their heels followed himself with all speed.

Basillus made his way successfully into the city, but the unarmed multitude, pelting him with stones and tiles from off the houses, stopped his further progress, and beat him back to the wall. Sulla by this time was come up, and seeing what was going on, called aloud to his men to set fire to the houses, and taking a flaming torch, he himself led the way, and commanded the archers to make use of their fire-darts, letting fly at the tops of houses; all which he did, not upon any plan, but simply in his fury, yielding the conduct of that day's work to passion, and as if all he saw were enemies, without respect or pity either to friends, relations, or acquaintance, made his entry by fire, which knows no distinction betwixt friend or foe.

In this conflict, Marius, being driven into the temple of Mother-Earth, thence invited the slaves by proclamation of freedom, but the enemy coming on, he was overpowered and fled the city.

Sulla, having called a senate, had sentence of death passed on Marius, and some few others, amongst whom was Sulpicius, tribune of the people. Sulpicius was killed, being betrayed by his servant, whom Sulla first made free, and then threw him headlong down the Tarpeian rock. As for Marius, he set a price on his life, by proclamation, neither gratefully nor politically, if we consider into whose house, not long before, he put himself at mercy, and was safely dismissed. Had Marius at that time not let Sulla go, but suffered him to be slain by the hands of Sulpicius, he might have been lord of all; nevertheless, he spared his life, and a few days after, when in a similar position himself, received a different measure.

By these proceedings Sulla excited the secret distaste of the senate; but the displeasure and free indignation of the commonalty showed itself plainly by their actions. For they ignominiously rejected Nonius, his nephew, and Servius, who stood for offices of state by his interest, and elected others as magistrates, by honouring whom they thought they should most annoy him. He made semblance of extreme satisfaction at all this, as if the people by his means had again enjoyed the liberty of doing what seemed best to them.

And to pacify the public hostility, he created Lucius Cinna consul, one of the adverse party, having first bound him under oaths and imprecations to be favourable to his interest. For Cinna, ascending the capitol with a stone in his hand, swore solemnly, and prayed with direful curses, that he himself, if he were not true to his friendship with Sulla, might be cast out of the city, as that stone out of his hand; and thereupon cast the stone to the ground, in the presence of many people. Nevertheless, Cinna had no sooner entered on his charge, but he took measures to disturb the present settlement, having prepared an impeachment against Sulla, got Virginius, one of the tribunes of the people, to be his accuser; but Sulla, leaving him and the court of judicature to themselves, set forth against Mithridates.

About the time that Sulla was making ready to put off with his force from Italy, besides many other omens which befell Mithridates, then staying at Pergamus, there goes a story that a figure of Victory, with a crown in her hand, which the Pergamenians by machinery from above let down on him, when it had almost reached his head, fell to pieces, and the crown tumbling down into the midst of the theatre, there broke against the ground, occasioning a general alarm among the populace, and considerably disquieting Mithridates himself, although his affairs at that time were succeeding beyond expectation.

For having wrested Asia from the Romans, and Bithynia and Cappadocia from their kings, he made Pergamus his royal seat, distributing among his friends riches, principalities, and kingdoms. Of his sons, one residing in Pontus and Bosporus held his ancient realm as far as the deserts beyond the lake Mæotis, without molestation; while Ariarathes, another, was reducing Thrace and Macedon, with a great army, to obedience. His generals, with forces under them, were establishing his supremacy in other quarters. Archelaus, in particular, with his fleet, held absolute mastery of the sea, and was bringing into subjection the Cyclades, and all the other islands as far as Malea, and had taken Eubœa itself.

Making Athens his headquarters, from thence as far as Thessaly he was withdrawing the states of Greece from the Roman allegiance, without the least ill-success, except at Chæronea. For here Bruttius Sura, lieutenant to Sentius, governor of Macedon, a man of singular valour and prudence, met him, and, though he came like a torrent pouring over Bœotia, made stout resistance, and thrice giving him battle near Chæronea, repulsed and forced him back to the sea. But being commanded by Lucius Lucullus to give place to his successor, Sulla, and resign the war to whom it was decreed, he presently left Bœotia, and retired back to Sentius, although his success had outgone all hopes, and Greece was well disposed to a new revolution, upon account of his gallant behaviour. These were the glorious actions of Bruttius.

Sulla, on his arrival, received by their deputations the compliments of all the cities of Greece, except Athens, against which, as it was compelled by the tyrant Aristion to hold for the king, he advanced with all his forces, and investing the Piræus, laid formal siege to it, employing every variety of engines, and trying every manner of assault; whereas, had he forborne but a little while, he might without hazard have taken the Upper City by famine, it being already reduced to the last extremity, through want of necessaries. But eager to return to Rome, and fearing innovation there, at great risk, with continual fighting and vast expense, he pushed on the war.

Besides other equipage, the very work about the engines of battery was supplied with no less than ten thousand yoke of mules, employed daily in that service. And when timber grew scarce, for many of the works failed, some crushed to pieces by their own weight, others taking fire by the continual play of the enemy, he had recourse to the sacred groves, and cut down the trees of the Academy, the shadiest of all the suburbs, and the Lyceum.

And a vast sum of money being wanted to carry on the war, he broke into the sanctuaries of Greece, that of Epidaurus and that of Olympia, sending for the most beautiful and precious offerings deposited there. He wrote, likewise, to the Amphictyons at Delphi, that it were better to remit the wealth of the god to him, for that he would keep it more securely, or in case he made use of it, restore as much. He sent Caphis, the Phocian, one of his friends, with this message, commanding him to receive each item by weight.

Caphis came to Delphi, but was loth to touch the holy things, and with many tears, in the presence of the Amphictyons, bewailed the necessity. And on some of them declaring they heard the sound of a harp from the inner shrine, he, whether he himself believed it, or was willing to try the effect of religious fear upon Sulla, sent back an express. To which Sulla replied in a scoffing way, that it was surprising to him that Caphis did not know that music was a sign of joy, not anger; he should, therefore, go on boldly, and accept what a gracious and bountiful god offered.

Other things were sent away without much notice on the part of the Greeks in general, but in the case of the silver tun, that only relic of the regal donations, which its weight and bulk made it impossible for any carriage to receive, the Amphictyons were forced to cut it into pieces, and called to mind in so doing, how Titus Flamininus, and Manius Acilius, and again Paulus Æmilius, one of whom drove Antiochus out of Greece, and the others subdued the Macedonian kings, had not only abstained from violating the Greek temples, but had even given them new gifts and honours, and increased the general veneration for them. They, indeed, the lawful commanders of temperate and obedient soldiers, and themselves great in soul, and simple in expenses, lived within the bounds of the ordinary established charges, accounting it a greater disgrace to seek popularity with their men, than to feel fear of their enemy.

Whereas the commanders of these times, attaining to superiority by force, not worth, and having need of arms one against another, rather than against the public enemy, were constrained to temporise in authority, and in order to pay for the gratifications with which they purchased the labour of their soldiers, were driven, before they knew it, to sell the commonwealth itself, and, to gain the mastery over men better than themselves, were content to become slaves to the vilest of wretches. These practices drove Marius into exile, and again brought him in against Sulla. These made Cinna the assassin of Octavius, and Fimbria of Flaccus. To which courses Sulla contributed not the least; for to corrupt and win over those who were under the command of others, he would be munificent and profuse towards those who were under his own; and so, while tempting the soldiers of other generals to treachery, and his own to dissolute living, he was naturally in want of a large treasury, and especially during that siege.

Sulla had a vehement and an implacable desire to conquer Athens, whether out of emulation, fighting as it were against the shadow of the once famous city, or out of anger, at the foul words and scurrilous jests with which the tyrant Aristion, showing himself daily, with unseemly gesticulations, upon the walls, had provoked him and Metella.

The tyrant Aristion had his very being compounded of wantonness and cruelty, having gathered into himself all the worst of Mithridates's diseased and vicious qualities, like some fatal malady which the city, after its deliverance from innumerable wars, many tyrannies and seditions, was in its last days destined to endure. At the time when a medimnus of wheat was sold in the city for one thousand drachmas and men were forced to live on the feverfew growing round the citadel, and to boil down shoes and oil-bags for their food, he, carousing and feasting in the open face of day, then dancing in armour, and making jokes at the enemy, suffered the holy lamp of the goddess to expire for want of oil, and to the chief priestess, who demanded of him the twelfth part of a medimnus of wheat, he sent the like quantity of pepper.

The senators and priests who came as suppliants to beg of him to take compassion on the city, and treat for peace with Sulla, he drove away and dispersed with a flight of arrows. At last, with much ado, he sent forth two or three of his revelling companions to parley, to whom Sulla, perceiving that they made no serious overtures towards an accommodation, but went on haranguing in praise of Theseus, Eumolpus, and the Median trophies, replied, "My good friends, you may put up your speeches and be gone. I was sent by the Romans to Athens, not to take lessons, but to reduce rebels to obedience."

In the meantime news came to Sulla that some old men, talking in the Ceramicus, had been overheard to blame the tyrant for not securing the passages and approaches near the Heptachalcum, the one point where the enemy might easily get over. Sulla neglected not the report, but going in the night, and discovering the place to be assailable, set instantly to work. Sulla himself makes mention in his Memoirs that Marcus Teius, the first man who scaled the wall, meeting with an adversary, and striking him on the headpiece a home-stroke, broke his own sword, but, notwithstanding, did not give ground, but stood and held him fast. The city was certainly taken from that quarter, according to the tradition of the oldest of the Athenians.

When they had thrown down the wall, and made all level betwixt the Piraic and Sacred Gate, about midnight Sulla entered the breach, with all the terrors of trumpets and cornets sounding, with the triumphant shout and cry of an army let loose to spoil and slaughter, and scouring through the streets with swords drawn.

There was no numbering the slain; the amount is to this day conjectured only from the space of ground overflowed with blood. For without mentioning the execution done in other quarters of the city, the blood that was shed about the market-place spread over the whole Ceramicus within the Double-gate, and, according to most writers, passed through the gate and overflowed the suburb. Nor did the multitudes which fell thus exceed the number of those who, out of pity and love for their country which they believed was now finally to perish, slew themselves; the best of them, through despair of their country's surviving, dreading themselves to survive, expecting neither humanity nor moderation in Sulla.

At length, partly at the instance of Midias and Calliphon, two exiled men, beseeching and casting themselves at his feet, partly by the intercession of those senators who followed the camp, having had his fill of revenge, and making some honourable mention of the ancient Athenians, "I forgive," said he, "the many for the sake of the few, the living for the dead." He took Athens, according to his own Memoirs, on the Calends of March, coinciding pretty nearly with the new moon of Anthesterion, on which day it is the Athenian usage to perform various acts in commemoration of the ruins and devastations occasioned by the deluge, that being supposed to be the time of its occurrence.

At the taking of the town, the tyrant fled into the citadel, and was there besieged by Curio, who had that charge given him. He held out a considerable time, but at last yielded himself up for want of water, and divine power immediately intimated its agency in the matter. For on the same day and hour that Curio conducted him down, the clouds gathered in a clear sky, and there came down a great quantity of rain and filled the citadel with water.

Not long after, Sulla won the Piræus, and burnt most of it; amongst the rest, Philo's arsenal, a work very greatly admired.

In the meantime Taxiles, Mithridates's general, coming down from Thrace and Macedon, with an army of one hundred thousand foot, ten thousand horse, and ninety chariots, armed with scythes at the wheels, would have joined Archelaus, who lay with a navy on the coast near Munychia, reluctant to quit the sea, and yet unwilling to engage the Romans in battle, but desiring to protract the war and cut off the enemy's supplies.

Which Sulla perceiving much better than himself, passed with his forces into Bœotia, quitting a barren district which was inadequate to maintain an army even in time of peace. He was thought by some to have taken false measures in thus leaving Attica, a rugged country, and ill suited for cavalry to move in, and entering the plain and open fields of Bœotia, knowing as he did the barbarian strength to consist most in horses and chari-

ots. But as was said before, to avoid famine and scarcity, he was forced to run the risk of a battle. Moreover, he was in anxiety for Hortensius, a bold and active officer, whom on his way to Sulla with forces from Thessaly, the barbarians awaited in the straits. For these reasons Sulla drew off into Bœotia.

Hortensius, meantime, was conducted by Caphis, our countryman, another way unknown to the barbarians, by Parnassus, just under Tithora, which was then not so large a town as it is now, but a mere fort, surrounded by steep precipices whither the Phocians also, in old times, when flying from the invasion of Xerxes, carried themselves and their goods and were saved. Hortensius, encamping here, kept off the enemy by day, and at night descending by difficult passages to Patronis, joined the forces of Sulla, who came to meet him. Thus united they posted themselves on a fertile hill in the middle of the plain of Elatea, shaded with trees and watered at the foot. It is called Philobœotus, and its situation and natural advantages are spoken of with great admiration by Sulla.

As they lay thus encamped, they seemed to the enemy a contemptible number, for there were not above fifteen hundred horse, and less than fifteen thousand foot. Therefore, the rest of the commanders, over-persuading Archelaus and drawing up the army, covered the plain with horses, chariots, bucklers, targets. The clamour and cries of so many nations forming for battle rent the air, nor was the pomp and ostentation of their costly array altogether idle and unserviceable for terror; for the brightness of their armour, embellished magnificently with gold and silver, and the rich colours of their Median and Scythian coats, intermixed with brass and shining steel, presented a flaming and terrible sight as they swayed about and moved in their ranks, so much so that the Romans shrunk within their trenches, and Sulla, unable by any arguments to remove their fear, and unwilling to force them to fight against their wills, was fain to sit down in quiet, ill-brooking to become the subject of barbarian insolence and laughter.

This, however, above all advantaged him, for the enemy, from contemning of him, fell into disorder amongst themselves, being already less thoroughly under command, on account of the number of their leaders. Some few of them remained within the encampment, but others, the major part, lured out with hopes of prey and rapine, strayed about the country many days' journey from the camp, and are related to have destroyed the city of Panope, to have plundered Lebadea, and robbed the oracle without any orders from their commanders.

Sulla, all this while, chafing and fretting to see the cities all around destroyed, suffered not the soldiery to remain idle, but leading them out, compelled them to divert the Cephisus from its ancient channel by casting up ditches, and giving respite to none, showed himself rigorous in punishing the remiss, that growing weary of labour, they might be induced by hardship to embrace danger. Which fell out accordingly, for on the third day, being hard at work as Sulla passed by, they begged and clamoured to be led against the enemy.

Sulla replied, that this demand of war proceeded rather from a backwardness to labour than any forwardness to fight, but if they were in good earnest martially inclined, he bade them take their arms and get up thither, pointing to the ancient citadel of the Parapotamians, of which at present, the city being laid waste, there remained only the rocky hill itself, steep and craggy on all sides, and severed from Mount Hedylium by the breadth of the river Assus, which, running between, and at the bottom of the same hill falling into the Cephisus with an impetuous confluence, makes this eminence a strong position for soldiers to occupy.

Observing that the enemy's division, called the Brazen Shields, were making their way up thither, Sulla was willing to take first possession, and by the vigorous efforts of the soldiers, succeeded. Archelaus, driven from hence, bent his forces upon Chæronea. The Chæroneans who bore arms in the Roman camp beseeching Sulla not to abandon the city, he despatched Gabinius, a tribune, with one legion, and sent out also the Chæroneans, who endeavoured, but were not able to get in before Gabinius; so active was he, and more zealous to bring relief than those who had entreated it. Juba writes that Ericius was the man sent, not Gabinius. Thus narrowly did our native city escape.

From Lebadea and the cave of Trophonius there came favourable rumours and prophecies of victory to the Romans, of which the inhabitants of those places gave a fuller account, but as Sulla himself affirms in the tenth book of his Memoirs, Quintus Titius, a man of some repute among the Romans who were engaged in mercantile business in Greece, came to him after the battle won at Chæronea, and declared that Trophonius had foretold another fight and victory on the place, within a short time. After

him a soldier, by name Salvenius, brought an account from the god of the future issue of affairs in Italy. As to the vision, they both agreed in this, that they had seen one who in stature and in majesty was similar to Jupiter Olympius.

Sulla, when he had passed over the Assus, marching under the Mount Hedylium, encamped close to Archelaus, who had intrenched himself strongly between the mountains Acontium and Hedylium, close to what are called the Assia. The place of his intrenchment is to this day named from him, Archelaus. Sulla, after one day's respite, having left Murena behind him with one legion and two cohorts to amuse the enemy with continual alarms, himself went and sacrificed on the banks of Cephisus, and the holy rites ended, held on towards Chæronea to receive the forces there and view Mount Thurium, where a party of the enemy had posted themselves.

This is a craggy height running up in a conical form to a point called by us Orthopagus; at the foot of it is the river Morius and the temple of Apollo Thurius. The god had his surname from Thuro, mother of Chæron, whom ancient record makes founder of Chæronea. Others assert that the cow, which Apollo gave to Cadmus for a guide, appeared there, and that the place took its name from the beast, *thor* being the Phœnician word for cow.

At Sulla's approach to Chæronea, the tribune who had been appointed to guard the city led out his men in arms, and met him with a garland of laurel in his hand, which Sulla accepting, and at the same time saluting the soldiers and animating them to the encounter, two men of Chæronea, Homoloichus and Anaxidamus, presented themselves before him, and offered, with a small party, to dislodge those who were posted on Thurium. For there lay a path out of sight of the barbarians, from what is called Petrochus along by the Museum, leading right down from above upon Thurium. By this way it was easy to fall upon them and either stone them from above or force them down into the plain.

Sulla, assured of their faith and courage by Gabinius, bade them proceed with the enterprise, and meantime drew up the army, and disposing the cavalry on both wings, himself took command of the right; the left being committed to the direction of Murena. In the rear of all, Galba and Hortensius, his lieutenants, planted themselves on the upper grounds with the cohorts of reserve, to watch the motions of the enemy, who, with numbers of horse and swift-footed, light-armed infantry, were noticed to have so formed their wing as to allow it readily to change about and alter its position, and thus gave reason for suspecting that they intended to carry it far out and so to inclose the Romans.

In the meanwhile, the Chæroneans, who had Ericius for commander by appointment of Sulla, covertly making their way around Thurium, and then discovering themselves, occasioned a great confusion and rout among the barbarians, and slaughter, for the most part by their own hands. For they kept not their place, but making down the steep descent, ran themselves on their own spears, and violently sent each other over the cliffs, the enemy from above pressing on and wounding them where they exposed their bodies; insomuch that there fell three thousand about Thurium. Some of those who escaped, being met by Murena as he stood in array, were cut off and destroyed. Others breaking through to their friends and falling pell-mell into the ranks, filled most part of the army with fear and tumult, and caused a hesitation and delay among the generals, which was no small disadvantage.

For immediately upon the discomposure, Sulla coming full speed to the charge, and quickly crossing the interval between the armies, lost them the service of their armed chariots, which require a considerable space of ground to gather strength and impetuosity in their career, a short course being weak and ineffectual, like that of missiles without a full swing. Thus it fared with the barbarians at present, whose first chariots came feebly on and made but a faint impression; the Romans, repulsing them with shouts and laughter, called out, as they do at the races in the circus, for more to come.

By this time the mass of both armies met; the barbarians on one side fixed their long pikes, and with their shields locked close together, strove so far as in them lay to preserve their line of battle entire. The Romans, on the other side, having discharged their javelins, rushed on with their drawn swords, and struggled to put by the pikes to get at them the sooner, in the fury that possessed them at seeing in the front of the enemy fifteen thousand slaves, whom the royal commanders had set free by proclamation, and ranged amongst the men of arms. And a Roman centurion is reported to have said at this sight, that he never knew servants allowed to play the masters, unless at the Saturnalia.

These men, by their deep and solid array, as well as by their daring courage, yielded but slowly to the legions, till at last by slinging engines, and darts, which the Romans poured in upon them behind, they were forced to give way and scatter.

As Archelaus was extending the right wing to encompass the enemy, Hortensius with his cohorts came down in force, with intention to charge him in the flank. But Archelaus wheeling about suddenly with two thousand horse, Hortensius, out-numbered and hard pressed, fell back towards the higher grounds, and found himself gradually getting separated from the main body and likely to be surrounded by the enemy. When Sulla heard this, he came rapidly up to his succour from the right wing, which as yet had not engaged. But Archelaus, guessing the matter by the dust of his troops, turned to the right wing, from whence Sulla came, in hopes to surprise it without a commander. At the same instant, likewise, Taxiles, with his Brazen Shields, assailed Murena, so that a cry coming from both places, and the hills repeating it around, Sulla stood in suspense which way to move.

Deciding to resume his own station, he sent in aid to Murena four cohorts under Hortensius, and commanding the fifth to follow him, returned hastily to the right wing, which of itself held its ground on equal terms against Archelaus; and, at his appearance, with one bold effort forced them back, and, obtaining the mastery, followed them, flying in disorder to the river and Mount Acontium. Sulla, however, did not forget the danger Murena was in; but hasting thither and finding him victorious also, then joined in the pursuit.

Many barbarians were slain in the field, many more were cut in pieces as they were making into the camp. Of all the vast multitude, ten thousand only got safe into Chalcis. Sulla writes that there were but fourteen of his soldiers missing, and that two of these returned towards evening; he, therefore, inscribed on the trophies the names of Mars, Victory, and Venus, as having won the day no less by good fortune than by management and force of arms. This trophy of the battle in the plain stands on the place where Archelaus first gave way, near the stream of the Molus; another is erected high on the top of Thurium, where the barbarians were environed, with an inscription in Greek, recording that the glory of the day belonged to Homoloichus and Anaxidamus.

Sulla celebrated his victory at Thebes with spectacles, for which he erected a stage, near Œdipus's well. The judges of the performances were Greeks chosen out of other cities; his hostility to the Thebans being implacable, half of their territory he took away and consecrated to Apollo and Jupiter, ordering that out of the revenue compensation should be made to the gods for the riches he had taken from them.

After this, hearing that Flaccus, a man of the contrary faction, had been chosen consul, and was crossing the Ionian Sea with an army, professedly to act against Mithridates, but in reality against himself, he hastened towards Thessaly, designing to meet him, but in his march, when near Melitea, received advices from all parts that the countries behind him were overrun and ravaged by no less a royal army than the former. For Dorylaus, arriving at Chalcis with a large fleet, on board of which he brought over with him eighty thousand of the best appointed and best disciplined soldiers of Mithridates's army, at once invaded Bœotia, and occupied the country in hopes to bring Sulla to a battle, making no account of the dissuasions of Archelaus, but giving it out as to the last fight, that without treachery so many thousand men could never have perished.

Sulla, however, facing about expeditiously, made it clear to him that Archelaus was a wise man, and had good skill in the Roman valour; insomuch that he himself, after some small skirmishes with Sulla near Tilphossium, was the first of those who thought it not advisable to put things to the decision of the sword, but rather to wear out the war by expense of time and treasure. The ground, however, near Orchomenus, where they then lay encamped, gave some encouragement to Archelaus, being a battlefield admirably suited for an army superior in cavalry.

Of all the plains in Bœotia that are renowned for their beauty and extent, this alone, which commences from the city of Orchomenus, spreads out unbroken and clear of trees to the edge of the fens in which the Melas, rising close under Orchomenus, loses itself, the only Greek river which is a deep and navigable water from the very head, increasing also about the summer solstice like the Nile, and producing plants similar to those that grow there, only small and without fruit. It does not run far before the main stream disappears among the blind and woody marsh-grounds; a small branch, however, joins the Cephisus, about the place where the lake is thought to produce the best flute-reeds.

Now that both armies were posted near each other, Archelaus lay still, but Sulla employed himself in cutting ditches from either side; that if possible, by driving the enemies from the firm and open champaign, he might force them into the fens. They, on the other hand, not enduring this, as soon as their leaders allowed them the word of command, issued out furiously in large bodies; when not only the men at work were dispersed, but most part of those who stood in arms to protect the work fled in disorder.

Upon this, Sulla leaped from his horse, and snatching hold of an ensign, rushed through the midst of the rout upon the enemy, crying out aloud, "To me, O Romans, it will be glorious to fall here. As for you, when they ask you where you betrayed your general, remember and say, at Orchomenus." His men rallying again at these words, and two cohorts coming to his succour from the right wing, he led them to the charge and turned the day.

Then retiring some short distance and refreshing his men, he proceeded again with his works to block up the enemy's camp. They again sallied out in better order than before. Here Diogenes, stepson to Archelaus, fighting on the right wing with much gallantry, made an honourable end. And the archers, being hard pressed by the Romans, and wanting space for a retreat, took their arrows by handfuls, and striking with these as with swords, beat them back. In the end, however, they were all driven into the intrenchment and had a sorrowful night of it with their slain and wounded.

The next day again, Sulla, leading forth his men up to their quarters, went on finishing the lines of intrenchment, and when they issued out again with larger numbers to give him battle, fell on them and put them to the rout, and in the consternation ensuing, none daring to abide, he took the camp by storm. The marshes were filled with blood, and the lake with dead bodies, insomuch that to this day many bows, helmets, fragments of iron, breastplates, and swords of barbarian make continue to be found buried deep in mud, two hundred years after the fight. Thus much of the actions of Chæronea and Orchomenus.

At Rome, Cinna and Carbo were now using injustice and violence towards persons of the greatest eminence, and many of them to avoid this tyranny repaired, as to a safe harbour, to Sulla's camp, where, in a short space, he had about him the aspect of a senate. Metella, likewise, having with difficulty conveyed herself and children away by stealth, brought him word that his houses, both in town and country, had been burnt by his enemies, and entreated his help at home.

Whilst he was in doubt what to do, being impatient to hear of his country being thus outraged, and yet not knowing how to leave so great a work as the Mithridatic war unfinished, there came to him Archelaus, a merchant of Delos, with hopes of an accommodation, and private instructions from Archelaus, the king's general. Sulla liked the business so well as to desire a speedy conference with Archelaus in person, and a meeting took place on the seacoast near Delium, where the temple of Apollo stands.

When Archelaus opened the conversation, and began to urge Sulla to abandon his pretensions to Asia and Pontus, and to set sail for the war in Rome, receiving money and shipping, and such forces as he should think fitting from the king, Sulla, interposing, bade Archelaus take no further care for Mithridates, but assume the crown to himself, and become a confederate of Rome, delivering up the navy. Archelaus professing his abhorrence of such treason, Sulla proceeded: "So you, Archelaus, a Cappadocian, and slave, or if it so please you friend, to a barbarian king, would not, upon such vast considerations, be guilty of what is dishonourable, and yet dare to talk to me, Roman general and Sulla, of treason? As if you were not the self-same Archelaus who ran away at Chæronea, with few remaining out of one hundred and twenty thousand men; who lay for two days in the fens of Orchomenus, and left Bœotia impassable for heaps of dead carcasses!" Archelaus, changing his tone at this, humbly besought him to lay aside the thoughts of war, and make peace with Mithridates.

Sulla consenting to this request, articles of agreement were concluded on. That Mithridates should quit Asia and Paphlagonia, restore Bithynia to Nicomedes, Cappadocia to Ariobarzanes, and pay the Romans two thousand talents, and give him seventy ships of war with all their furniture. On the other hand, that Sulla should confirm to him his other dominions, and declare him a Roman confederate.

On these terms he proceeded by the way of Thessaly and Macedon towards the Hellespont, having Archelaus with him, and treating him with great attention. For Archelaus being taken dangerously ill at Larissa, he stopped the march of the army, and took care of him, as if he had been one of his own captains, or his colleague in command. This gave suspicion of foul play in the battle of Chæronea; as it was also observed that Sulla had released all the friends of Mithridates taken prisoners in war, except only Aristion the tyrant, who was at enmity with Archelaus, and was put to death by poison; and, above all, ten thousand acres of land in Eubœa had been given to the Cappadocian, and he had received from Sulla the style of friend and ally of the Romans. On all which points Sulla defends himself in his Memoirs.

The ambassadors of Mithridates arriving and declaring that they accepted of the conditions, only Paphlagonia they could not part with; and as for the ships, professing not to know of any such capitulation, Sulla in a rage exclaimed, "What say you? Does Mithridates then withhold Paphlagonia, and as to the ships, deny that article? I thought to have seen him prostrate at my feet to thank me for leaving him so much as that right hand of his, which has cut off so many Romans. He will shortly, at my coming over into Asia, speak another language; in the meantime, let him at his ease in Pergamus sit managing a war which he never saw."

The ambassadors in terror stood silent by, but Archelaus endeavoured with humble supplications to assuage his wrath, laying hold on his right hand and weeping. In confusion he obtained permission to go himself in person to Mithridates; for that he would either mediate a peace to the satisfaction of Sulla, or if not, slay himself.

Sulla having thus despatched him away, made an inroad into Mædica, and after wide depopulations returned back again into Macedon, where he received Archelaus about Philippi, bringing word that all was well, and that Mithridates earnestly requested an interview. The chief cause of this meeting was Fimbria; for he, having assassinated Flaccus, the consul of the contrary faction, and worsted the Mithridatic commanders, was advancing against Mithridates himself, who, fearing this, chose rather to seek the friendship of Sulla.

And so met at Dardanus in the Troad, on one side Mithridates, attended with two hundred ships, and land-forces consisting of twenty thousand men at arms, six thousand horse, and a large train of scythed chariots; on the other, Sulla with only four cohorts and two hundred horse.

As Mithridates drew near and put out his hand, Sulla demanded whether he was willing or no to end the war on the terms Archelaus had agreed to, but seeing the king made no answer, "How is this?" he continued. "Ought not the petitioner to speak first, and the conqueror to listen in silence?" And when Mithridates, entering upon his plea, began to shift off the war, partly on the gods, and partly to blame the Romans themselves, he took him up, saying that he had heard, indeed, long since from others, and now he knew it himself for truth, that Mithridates was a powerful speaker, who in defence of the most foul and unjust proceedings, had not wanted for specious pretences. Then charging him with and inveighing bitterly against the outrages he had committed, he asked again whether he was willing or no to ratify the treaty of Archelaus? Mithridates answering in the affirmative, Sulla came forward, embraced and kissed him. Not long after he introduced Ariobarzanes and Nicomedes, the two kings, and made them friends. Mithridates, when he had handed over to Sulla seventy ships and five hundred archers, set sail for Pontus.

Sulla, perceiving the soldiers to be dissatisfied with the peace (as it seemed indeed a monstrous thing that they should see the king who was their bitterest enemy, and who had caused one hundred and fifty thousand Romans to be massacred in one day in Asia, now sailing off with the riches and spoils of Asia, which he had pillaged, and put under contribution for the space of four years), in his defence to them alleged that he could not have made head against Fimbria and Mithridates, had they both withstood him in conjunction. Thence he set out and went in search of Fimbria, who lay with the army about Thyatira, and pitching his camp not far off, proceeded to fortify it with a trench. The soldiers of Fimbria came out in their single coats, and saluting his men, lent ready assistance to the work; which change Fimbria beholding, and apprehending Sulla as irreconcilable, laid violent hands on himself in the camp.

Sulla imposed on Asia in general a tax of twenty thousand talents, and despoiled individually each family by the licentious behaviour and long residence of the soldiery in private quarters. For he ordained that every host should allow his guest four tetradrachmas each day, and moreover entertain him, and as many friends as he should invite, with a supper; that a centurion should receive fifty drachmas a day, together with one suit of clothes to wear within doors, and another when he went abroad.

Having set out from Ephesus with the whole navy, he came the third day to anchor in the Piraeus. Here he was initiated in the mysteries, and seized for his use the library of Apellicon the Teian, in which were most of the works of Theophrastus and Aristotle, then not in general circulation. When the whole was afterwards conveyed to Rome, there, it is said, the greater part of the collection passed through the hands of Tyrannion, the grammarian, and that Andronicus, the Rhodian, having through his means the command of numerous copies, made the treatises public, and drew up the catalogues that are now current. The elder Peripatetics appear themselves, indeed, to have been accomplished and learned men, but of the writings of Aristotle and Theophrastus they had no large or exact knowledge, because Theophrastus bequeathing his books to the heir of Neleus of Scepsis, they came into careless and illiterate hands.

During Sulla's stay about Athens, his feet were attacked by a heavy benumbing pain, which Strabo calls the first inarticulate sounds of the gout. Taking, therefore, a voyage to Aedepsus, he made use of the hot waters there, allowing himself at the same time to forget all anxieties, and passing away his time with actors. As he was walking along the seashore, certain fishermen brought him some magnificent fish. Being much delighted with the gift, and understanding, on inquiry, that they were men of Halae, "What," said he, "are there any men of Halae surviving?" For after his victory at Orchomenus, in the heat of pursuit, he had destroyed three cities of Boeotia, Anthedon, Larymna, and Halae. The men not knowing what to say for fear, Sulla, with a smile, bade them cheer up and return in peace, as they had brought with them no insignificant intercessors. The Halaeans say that this first gave them courage to re-unite and return to their city.

Sulla, having marched through Thessaly and Macedon to the sea coast, prepared, with twelve hundred vessels, to cross over from Dyrrhachium to Brundisium. Not far from hence is Apollonia, and near it the Nymphaeum, a spot of ground where, from among green trees and meadows, there are found at various points springs of fire continually streaming out. Here, they say, a satyr, such as statuaries and painters represent, was caught asleep, and brought before Sulla, where he was asked by several interpreters who he was, and, after much trouble, at last uttered nothing intelligible, but a harsh noise, something between the neighing of a horse and crying of a goat. Sulla, in dismay, and deprecating such an omen, bade it be removed.

At the point of transportation, Sulla being in alarm lest at their first setting foot upon Italy the soldiers should disband and disperse one by one among the cities, they of their own accord first took an oath to stand firm by him, and not of their good-will to injure Italy; then seeing him in distress for money, they made, so they say, a free-will offering, and contributed each man according to his ability. However, Sulla would not accept of their offering, but praising their good-will, and arousing up their courage, went over (as he himself writes) against fifteen hostile generals in command of four hundred and fifty cohorts; but not without the most unmistakable divine intimations of his approaching happy successes.

For when he was sacrificing at his first landing near Tarentum, the victim's liver showed the figure of a crown of laurel with two fillets hanging from it. And a little while before his arrival in Campania, near the mountain Hephæus, two stately goats were seen in the daytime, fighting together, and performing all the motions of men in battle. It proved to be an apparition, and rising up gradually from the ground, dispersed in the air, like fancied representations in the clouds, and so vanished out of sight.

Not long after, in the selfsame place, when Marius the younger and Norbanus the consul attacked him with two great armies, without prescribing the order of battle, or arranging his men according to their divisions, by the sway only of one common alacrity and transport of courage, he overthrew the enemy, and shut up Norbanus into the city of Capua, with the loss of seven thousand of his men. And this was the reason, he says, that the soldiers did not leave him and disperse into the different towns, but held fast to him, and despised the enemy, though infinitely more in number.

At Silvium (as he himself relates it), there met him a servant of Pontius, in a state of divine possession, saying that he brought him the power of the sword and victory from Bel-

lona, the goddess of war, and if he did not make haste, that the capitol would be burnt, which fell out on the same day the man foretold it, namely, on the sixth day of the month Quintilis, which we now call July.

At Fidentia, also, Marcus Lucullus, one of Sulla's commanders, reposed such confidence in the forwardness of the soldiers as to dare to face fifty cohorts of the enemy with only sixteen of his own; but because many of them were unarmed delayed the onset. As he stood thus waiting, and considering with himself, a gentle gale of wind, bearing along with it from the neighbouring meadows a quantity of flowers, scattered them down upon the army, on whose shields and helmets they settled, and arranged themselves spontaneously so as to give the soldiers, in the eyes of the enemy, the appearance of being crowned with chaplets. Upon this, being yet further animated, they joined battle, and victoriously slaying eight thousand men, took the camp. This Lucullus was brother to that Lucullus who in aftertimes conquered Mithridates and Tigranes.

Sulla, seeing himself still surrounded by so many armies, and such mighty hostile powers, had recourse to art, inviting Scipio, the other consul, to a treaty of peace. The motion was willingly embraced, and several meetings and consultations ensued, in all which Sulla, still interposing matter of delay and new pretences, in the meanwhile debauched Scipio's men by means of his own, who were as well practised as the general himself in all the artifices of inveigling. For entering into the enemy's quarters and joining in conversation, they gained some by present money, some by promises, others by fair words and persuasions; so that in the end, when Sulla with twenty cohorts drew near, on his men saluting Scipio's soldiers, they returned the greeting and came over, leaving Scipio behind them in his tent, where he was found all alone and dismissed. And having used his twenty cohorts as decoys to ensnare the forty of the enemy, he led them all back into camp. On this occasion, Carbo was heard to say that he had both a fox and a lion in the breast of Sulla to deal with, and was most troubled with the fox.

Some time after, at Signa, Marius the younger with eighty-five cohorts, offered battle to Sulla, who was extremely desirous to have it decided on that very day; for the night before he had seen a vision in his sleep, of Marius the elder, who had been some time dead, advising his son to beware of the following day, as of fatal consequence to him. For this reason, Sulla, longing to come to a battle, sent off for Dolabella, who lay encamped at some distance. But because the enemy had beset and blocked up the passes, his soldiers got tired with skirmishing and marching at once. To these difficulties was added, moreover, tempestuous rainy weather, which distressed them most of all. The principal officers, therefore, came to Sulla, and besought him to defer the battle that day, showing him how the soldiers lay stretched on the ground, where they had thrown themselves down in their weariness, resting their heads upon their shields to gain some repose.

When, with much reluctance, he had yielded, and given orders for pitching the camp, they had no sooner begun to cast up the rampart and draw the ditch, but Marius came riding up furiously at the head of his troops, in hopes to scatter them in that disorder and confusion. Here the gods fulfilled Sulla's dream. For the soldiers, stirred up with anger, left off their work, and sticking their javelins into the bank, with drawn swords and a courageous shout, came to blows with the enemy, who made but small resistance, and lost great numbers in the flight. Marius fled to Præneste, but finding the gates shut, tied himself round by a rope that was thrown down to him, and was taken up on the walls. Some there are (as Fenestella for one) who affirm that Marius knew nothing of the fight, but, overwatched and spent with hard duty, had reposed himself, when the signal was given, beneath some shade, and was hardly to be awakened at the flight of his men. Sulla, according to his own account, lost only twenty-three men in this fight, having killed of the enemy twenty thousand, and taken alive eight thousand.

The like success attended his lieutenants, Pompey, Crassus, Metellus, Servilius, who with little or no loss cut off vast numbers of the enemy, insomuch that Carbo, the prime supporter of the cause, fled by night from his charge of the army, and sailed over into Libya.

In the last struggle, however, the Samnite, Telesinus, like some champion, whose lot it is to enter last of all into the lists and take up the wearied conqueror, came nigh to have foiled and overthrown Sulla before the gates of Rome. For Telesinus with his second, Lamponius, the Lucanian, having collected a large force, had been hastening towards Præneste, to relieve Marius from the siege; but perceiving Sulla ahead of him, and Pompey behind, both hurrying up against him, straitened thus before and behind, as a valiant and experienced soldier, he arose by night, and marching directly with his whole army, was within a little of making his way unexpectedly into Rome itself.

He lay that night before the city, at ten furlongs distance from the Colline gate, elated and full of hope at having thus out-generalled so many eminent commanders. At break of day, being charged by the noble youth of the city, among many others he overthrew Appius Claudius, renowned for high birth and character. The city, as is easy to imagine, was all in an uproar, the women shrieking and running about, as if it had already been entered forcibly by assault, till at last Balbus, sent forward by Sulla, was seen riding up with seven hundred horse at full speed. Halting only long enough to wipe the sweat from the horses, and then hastily bridling again, he at once attacked the enemy.

Presently Sulla himself appeared, and commanding those who were foremost to take immediate refreshment, proceeded to form in order for battle. Dolabella and Torquatus were extremely earnest with him to desist awhile, and not with spent forces to hazard the last hope, having before them in the field, not Carbo or Marius, but two warlike nations bearing immortal hatred to Rome, the Samnites and Lucanians, to grapple with. But he put them by, and commanded the trumpets to sound a charge, when it was now about four o'clock in the afternoon.

In the conflict which followed, as sharp a one as ever was, the right wing where Crassus was posted had clearly the advantage; the left suffered and was in distress, when Sulla came to its succour, mounted on a white courser, full of mettle and exceedingly swift, which two of the enemy knowing him by, had their lances ready to throw at him; he himself observed nothing, but his attendant behind him giving the horse a touch, he was, unknown to himself, just so far carried forward that the points, falling beside the horse's tail, stuck in the ground.

There is a story that he had a small golden image of Apollo from Delphi, which he was always wont in battle to carry about him in his bosom, and that he then kissed it with these words, "O Apollo Pythius, who in so many battles hast raised to honour and greatness the fortunate Cornelius Sulla, wilt thou now cast him down, bringing him before the gate of his country, to perish shamefully with his fellow-citizens?"

Thus, they say, addressing himself to the god, he entreated some of his men, threatened some, and seized others with his hand, till at length the left wing being wholly shattered, he was forced, in the general rout, to betake himself to the camp, having lost many of his friends and acquaintances. Many, likewise, of the city spectators, who had come out, were killed or trodden under foot. So that it was generally believed in the city that all was lost, and the siege of Præneste was all but raised; many fugitives from the battle making their way thither, and urging Lucretius Ofella, who was appointed to keep on the siege, to rise in all haste, for that Sulla had perished, and Rome fallen into the hands of the enemy.

About midnight there came into Sulla's camp messengers from Crassus, to fetch provision for him and his soldiers; for having vanquished the enemy, they had pursued him to the walls of Antemna, and had sat down there. Sulla, hearing this, and that most of the enemy were destroyed, came to Antemna by break of day, where three thousand of the besieged having sent forth a herald, he promised to receive them to mercy, on condition they did the enemy some mischief in their coming over. Trusting to his word, they fell foul on the rest of their companions, and made a great slaughter one of another.

Nevertheless, Sulla gathered together in the circus, as well these as other survivors of the party, to the number of six thousand, and just as he commenced speaking to the senate, in the temple of Bellona, proceeded to cut them down, by men appointed for that service. The cry of so vast a multitude put to the sword, in so narrow a space, was naturally heard some distance, and startled the senators. He, however, continuing his speech with a calm and unconcerned countenance, bade them listen to what he had to say, and not busy themselves with what was doing out of doors; he had given directions for the chastisement of some offenders. This gave the most stupid of the Romans to understand that they had merely exchanged, not escaped, tyranny.

And Marius, being of a naturally harsh temper, had not altered, but merely continued what he had been, in authority; whereas Sulla, using his fortune moderately and unambitiously at first, and giving good hopes of a true patriot, firm to the interests both of the nobility and commonalty, being, moreover, of a gay and cheerful temper from his youth, and so easily moved to pity as to shed tears readily, has, perhaps deservedly, cast a blemish upon offices of great authority, as if they deranged men's former habits and character, and gave rise to violence, pride, and inhumanity. Whether this be a real change and revolution in the mind, caused by fortune, or rather a lurking viciousness of nature, discovering itself in authority, it were matter of another sort of disquisition to decide.

Sulla being thus wholly bent upon slaughter, and filling the city with executions without number or limit, many wholly uninterested persons falling a sacrifice to private enmity, through his permission and indulgence to his friends, Caius Metellus, one of the younger men, made bold in the senate to ask him what end there was of these evils, and at what point he might be expected to stop? "We do not ask you," said he, "to pardon any whom you have resolved to destroy, but to free from doubt those whom you are pleased to save." Sulla answering that he knew not as yet whom to spare, "Why, then," said he, "tell us whom you will punish." This Sulla said he would do. These last words, some authors say, were spoken not by Metellus, but by Afidius, one of Sulla's fawning companions.

Immediately upon this, without communicating with any of the magistrates, Sulla proscribed eighty persons, and notwithstanding the general indignation, after one day's respite, he posted two hundred and twenty more, and on the third again, as many. In an address to the people on this occasion, he told them he had put up as many names as he could think of; those which had escaped his memory, he would publish at a future time. He issued an edict likewise, making death the punishment of humanity, proscribing any who should dare to receive and cherish a proscribed person without exception to brother, son, or parents. And to him who should slay any one proscribed person, he ordained two talents reward, even were it a slave who had killed his master, or a son his father. And what was thought most unjust of all, he caused the attainder to pass upon their sons, and sons' sons, and made open sale of all their property.

Nor did the proscription prevail only at Rome, but throughout all the cities of Italy the effusion of blood was such, that neither sanctuary of the gods, nor hearth of hospitality, nor ancestral home escaped. Men were butchered in the embraces of their wives, children in the arms of their mothers. Those who perished through public animosity or private enmity were nothing in comparison of the numbers of those who suffered for their riches. Even the murderers began to say, that "his fine house killed this man, a garden that, a third, his hot baths." Quintus Aurelius, a quiet, peaceable man, and one who thought all his part in the common calamity consisted in condoling with the misfortunes of others, coming into the Forum to read the list, and finding himself among the proscribed, cried out, "Woe is me, my Alban farm has informed against me." He had not gone far before he was despatched by a ruffian, sent on that errand.

In the meantime, Marius, on the point of being taken, killed himself; and Sulla, coming to Præneste, at first proceeded judicially against each particular person, till at last, finding it a work of too much time, he cooped them up together in one place, to the number of twelve thousand men, and gave order for the execution of them all, his own host alone excepted. But he, brave man, telling him he could not accept the obligation of life from the hands of one who had been the ruin of his country, went in among the rest, and submitted willingly to the stroke. What Lucius Catilina did was thought to exceed all other acts. For having, before matters came to an issue, made away with his brother, he besought Sulla to place him on the list of proscription, as though he had been alive, which was done; and Catilina, to return the kind office, assassinated a certain Marcus Marius, one of the adverse party, and brought the head to Sulla, as he was sitting in the Forum, and then going to the holy water of Apollo, which was nigh, washed his hands.

There were other things, besides this bloodshed, which gave offence. For Sulla had declared himself dictator, an office which had then been laid aside for the space of one hundred and twenty years. There was, likewise, an act of grace passed on his behalf, granting indemnity for what was passed, and for the future intrusting him with the power of life and death, confiscation, division of lands, erecting and demolishing of cities, taking away of kingdoms, and bestowing them at pleasure. He conducted the sale of confiscated property after such an arbitrary, imperious way, from the tribunal, that his gifts excited greater odium even than his usurpations; women mimes, and musicians, and the lowest of the freed slaves had presents made them of the territories of nations and the revenues of cities: and women of rank were married against their will to some of them. Wishing to insure the fidelity of Pompey the Great by a nearer tie of blood, he bade him divorce his present wife, and forcing Æmilia, the daughter of Scaurus and Metella, his own wife, to leave her husband, Manius Glabrio, he bestowed her, though then with child, on Pompey, and she died in childbirth at his house.

When Lucretius Ofella, the same who reduced Marius by siege, offered himself for the consulship, he first forbade him; then, seeing he could not restrain him, on his coming down into the Forum with a numerous train of followers, he sent one of the centurions who were immediately about him, and slew him, himself sitting on the tribunal in the temple of Castor, and beholding the murder from above. The citizens apprehending the centurion, and dragging him to the tribunal, he bade them cease their clamouring and let the centurion go, for he had commanded it.

His triumph was, in itself, exceedingly splendid, and distinguished by the rarity and magnificence of the royal spoils; but its yet greatest glory was the noble spectacle of the exiles. For in the rear followed the most eminent and most potent of the citizens, crowned with garlands, and calling Sulla saviour and father, by whose means they were restored to their own country, and again enjoyed their wives and children. When the solemnity was over, and the time come to render an account of his actions, addressing the public assembly, he was as profuse in enumerating the lucky chances of war as any of his own military merits. And, finally, from this felicity he requested to receive the surname of Felix.

In writing and transacting business with the Greeks, he styled himself Epaphroditus, and on his trophies which are still extant with us the name is given Lucius Cornelius Sulla Epaphroditus. Moreover, when his wife had brought him forth twins, he named the male Faustus and the female Fausta, the Roman words for what is auspicious and of happy omen. The confidence which he reposed in his good genius, rather than in any abilities of his own, emboldened him, though deeply involved in bloodshed, and though he had been the author of such great changes and revolutions of state, to lay down his authority, and place the right of consular elections once more in the hands of the people.

And when they were held, he not only declined to seek that office, but in the Forum exposed his person publicly to the people, walking up and down as a private man. And contrary to his will, a certain bold man and his enemy, Marcus Lepidus, was expected to become consul, not so much by his own interest, as by the power and solicitation of Pompey, whom the people were willing to oblige. When the business was over, seeing Pompey going home overjoyed with the success, he called him to him and said, "What a polite act, young man, to pass by Catulus, the best of men, and choose Lepidus, the worst! It will be well for you to be vigilant, now that you have strengthened your opponent against yourself." Sulla spoke this, it may seem, by a prophetic instinct, for, not long after, Lepidus grew insolent and broke into open hostility to Pompey and his friends.

Sulla, consecrating the tenth of his whole substance to Hercules, entertained the people with sumptuous feastings. The provision was so much above what was necessary, that they were forced daily to throw great quantities of meat into the river, and they drank wine forty years old and upwards. In the midst of the banqueting, which lasted many days, Metella died of a disease. And because that the priest forbade him to visit the sick, or suffer his house to be polluted with mourning, he drew up an act of divorce and caused her to be removed into another house whilst alive. Thus far, out of religious apprehension, he observed the strict rule to the very letter, but in the funeral expenses he transgressed the law he himself had made, limiting the amount, and spared no cost. He transgressed, likewise, his own sumptuary laws respecting expenditure in banquets, thinking to allay his grief by luxurious drinking parties and revellings with common buffoons.

Some few months after, at a show of gladiators, when men and women sat promiscuously in the theatre, no distinct places being as yet appointed, there sat down by Sulla a beautiful woman of high birth, by name Valeria, daughter of Messala, and sister to Hortensius, the orator. Now it happened that she had been lately divorced from her husband. Passing along behind Sulla, she leaned on him with her hand, and plucking a bit of wool from his garment, so proceeded to her seat. And on Sulla looking up and wondering what it meant, "What harm, mighty sir," said she, "if I also was desirous to partake a little in your felicity?"

It appeared at once that Sulla was not displeased, but even tickled in his fancy, for he sent out to inquire her name, her birth, and past life. From this time there passed between them many side glances, each continually turning round to look at the other, and frequently interchanging smiles. In the end, overtures were made, and a marriage concluded on. All which was innocent, perhaps, on the lady's side, but, though she had been never so modest and virtuous, it was scarcely a temperate and worthy occasion of marriage on the part of Sulla, to take fire, as a boy might, at a face and a bold look, incentives not seldom to the most disorderly and shameless passions.

Notwithstanding this marriage, he kept company with actresses, musicians, and dancers, drinking with them on couches night and day. His chief favourites were Roscius, the comedian, Sorex, the arch mime, and Metrobius, the player, for whom, though past his prime, he still professed a passionate fondness. By these courses he encouraged a disease which had begun from unimportant cause; and for a long time he failed to observe that his bowels were ulcerated, till at length the corrupted flesh broke out into lice. Many were employed day and night in destroying them, but the work so multiplied under their hands, that not only his clothes, baths, basins, but his very meat was polluted with that flux and contagion, they came swarming out in such numbers. He went frequently by day into the bath to scour and cleanse his body, but all in vain; the evil generated too rapidly and too abundantly for any ablutions to overcome it. There died of this disease, amongst those of the most ancient times, Acastus, the son of Pelias; of later date, Alcman, the poet, Pherecydes, the theologian, Callisthenes, the Olynthian, in the time of his imprisonment, as also Mucius, the lawyer; and if we may mention ignoble, but notorious names, Eunus, the fugitive, who stirred up the slaves of Sicily to rebel against their masters, after he was brought captive to Rome, died of this creeping sickness.

Sulla not only foresaw his end, but may be also said to have written of it. For in the two-and-twentieth book of his Memoirs, which he finished two days before his death, he writes that the Chaldeans foretold him that after he had led a life of honour, he should conclude it in fulness of prosperity. He declares, moreover, that in a vision he had seen his son, who had died not long before Metella, stand by in mourning attire, and beseech his father to cast off further care, and come along with him to his mother, Metella, there to live at ease and quietness with her. However, he could not refrain from intermeddling in public affairs. For, ten days before his decease, he composed the differences of the people of Dicæarchia, and prescribed laws for their better government. And the very day before his end, it being told him that the magistrate Granius deferred the payment of a public debt, in expectation of his death, he sent for him to his house, and placing his attendants about him, caused him to be strangled; but through the straining of his voice and body, the imposthume breaking, he lost a great quantity of blood. Upon this, his strength failing him, after spending a troublesome night, he died, leaving behind him two young children by Metella. Valeria was afterwards delivered of a daughter, named Posthuma; for so the Romans call those who are born after the father's death.

Many ran tumultuously together, and joined with Lepidus to deprive the corpse of the accustomed solemnities; but Pompey, though offended at Sulla (for he alone of all his friends was not mentioned in his will), having kept off some by his interest and entreaty, others by menaces, conveyed the body to Rome, and gave it a secure and honourable burial. It is said that the Roman ladies contributed such vast heaps of spices, that besides what was carried on two hundred and ten litters, there was sufficient to form a large figure of Sulla himself, and another representing a lictor, out of the costly frankincense and cinnamon. The day being cloudy in the morning, they deferred carrying forth the corpse till about three in the afternoon, expecting it would rain. But a strong wind blowing full upon the funeral pile, and setting it all in a bright flame, the body was consumed so exactly in good time, that the pyre had begun to smoulder, and the fire was upon the point of expiring, when a violent rain came down, which continued till night. So that his good fortune was firm even to the last, and did as it were officiate at his funeral. His monument stands in the Campus Martius, with an epitaph of his own writing; the substance of it being, that he had not been outdone by any of his friends in doing good turns, nor by any of his foes in doing bad.

LYSANDER and SULLA
Compared

Having completed this Life also, come we now to the comparison. That which was common to them both was that they were founders of their own greatness, with this difference, that Lysander had the consent of his fellow-citizens, in times of sober judgment, for the honours he received; nor did he force anything from them against their good-will, nor hold any power contrary to the laws.

In civil strife e'en villains rise to fame.

And so then at Rome, when the people were distempered, and the government out of order, one or other was still raised to despotic power; no wonder, then, if Sulla reigned, when the Glauciæ and Saturnini drove out the Metelli, when sons of consuls were slain in the assemblies, when silver and gold purchased men and arms, and fire and sword enacted new laws and put down lawful opposition. Nor do I blame any one, in such circumstances, for working himself into supreme power, only I would not have it thought a sign of great goodness to be head of a state so wretchedly discomposed.

Lysander, being employed in the greatest commands and affairs of state, by a sober and well-governed city, may be said to have had repute as the best and most virtuous man, in the best and most virtuous commonwealth. And thus, often returning the government into the hands of the citizens, he received it again as often, the superiority of his merit still awarding him the first place. Sulla, on the other hand, when he had once made himself general of an army, kept his command for ten years together, creating himself sometimes consul, sometimes proconsul, and sometimes dictator, but always remaining a tyrant.

It is true Lysander, as was said, designed to introduce a new form of government; by milder methods, however, and more agreeably to law than Sulla, not by force of arms, but persuasion, nor by subverting the whole state at once, but simply by amending the succession of the kings; in a way, moreover, which seemed the naturally just one, that the most deserving should rule, especially in a city which itself exercised command in Greece, upon account of virtue, not nobility. For as the hunter considers the whelp itself, not the bitch, and the horse-dealer the foal, not the mare (for what if the foal should prove a mule?), so likewise were that politician extremely out, who, in the choice of a chief magistrate, should inquire, not what the man is, but how descended. The very Spartans themselves have deposed several of their kings for want of kingly virtues, as degenerated and good for nothing. As a vicious nature, though of an ancient stock, is dishonourable, it must be virtue itself, and not birth, that makes virtue honourable.

Furthermore, the one committed his acts of injustice for the sake of his friends; the other extended his to his friends themselves. It is confessed on all hands that Lysander offended most commonly for the sake of his companions, committing several slaughters to uphold their power and dominion; but as for Sulla, he, out of envy, reduced Pompey's command by land and Dolabella's by sea, although he himself had given them those places; and ordered Lucretius Ofella, who sued for the consulship as the reward of many great services, to be slain before his eyes, exciting horror and alarm in the minds of all men, by his cruelty to his dearest friends.

As regards the pursuit of riches and pleasures, we yet further discover in one a princely, in the other a tyrannical, disposition. Lysander did nothing that was intemperate or licentious, in that full command of means and opportunity, but kept clear, as much as ever man did, of that trite saying—

Lions at home, but foxes out of doors;
and ever maintained a sober, truly Spartan, and well-disciplined course of conduct. Whereas Sulla could never moderate his unruly affections, either by poverty when young, or by years when grown old, but would be still prescribing laws to the citizens concerning chastity and sobriety, himself living all that time, as Sallust affirms, in lewdness and adultery. By these ways he so impoverished and drained the city of her treasures, as to be forced to sell privileges and immunities to allied and friendly cities for money, although he daily gave up the wealthiest and the greatest families to public sale and confiscation.

There was no end of his favours vainly spent and thrown away on flatterers; for what hope could there be, or what likelihood of forethought or economy, in his more private moments over wine, when, in the open face of the people, upon the auction of a large estate, which he would have passed over to one of his friends at a small price, because another bid

higher, and the officer announced the advance, he broke out into a passion, saying: "What a strange and unjust thing is this, O citizens, that I cannot dispose of my own booty as I please!" But Lysander, on the contrary, with the rest of the spoil, sent home for public use even the presents which were made him. Nor do I commend him for it, for he, perhaps, by excessive liberality, did Sparta more harm than ever the other did Rome by rapine; I only use it as an argument of his indifference to riches.

They exercised a strange influence on their respective cities. Sulla, a profuse debauchee, endeavoured to restore sober living amongst the citizens; Lysander, temperate himself, filled Sparta with the luxury he disregarded. So that both were blameworthy, the one for raising himself above his own laws, the other for causing his fellow-citizens to fall beneath his own example. He taught Sparta to want the very things which he himself had learned to do without. And thus much concerning their civil administration.

As for feats of arms, wise conduct in war, innumerable victories, perilous adventures, Sulla was beyond compare. Lysander, indeed, came off twice victorious in two battles by sea; I shall add to that the siege of Athens, a work of greater fame than difficulty. What occurred in Bœotia, and at Haliartus, was the result, perhaps, of ill fortune; yet it certainly looks like ill counsel, not to wait for the king's forces, which had all but arrived from Platæa, but out of ambition and eagerness to fight, to approach the walls at disadvantage, and so to be cut off by a sally of inconsiderable men. He received his death-wound, not as Cleombrotus, at Leuctra, resisting manfully the assault of an enemy in the field; not as Cyrus or Epaminondas, sustaining the declining battle, or making sure the victory; all these died the death of kings and generals; but he, as it had been some common skirmisher or scout, cast away his life ingloriously, giving testimony to the wisdom of the ancient Spartan maxim, to avoid attacks on walled cities, in which the stoutest warrior may chance to fall by the hand, not only of a man utterly his inferior, but by that of a boy or woman, as Achilles, they say, was slain by Paris in the gates. As for Sulla, it were hard to reckon up how many set battles he won, or how many thousand he slew; he took Rome itself twice, as also the Athenian Piræus, not by famine, as Lysander did, but by a series of great battles, driving Archelaus into the sea.

And what is most important, there was a

vast difference between the commanders they had to deal with. For I look upon it as an easy task, or rather sport, to beat Antiochus, Alcibiades's pilot, or to circumvent Philocles, the Athenian demagogue—

Sharp only at the inglorious point of tongue,

whom Mithridates would have scorned to compare with his groom, or Marius with his lictor. But of the potentates, consuls, commanders, and demagogues, to pass by all the rest who opposed themselves to Sulla, who amongst the Romans so formidable as Marius, what king more powerful than Mithridates? Who of the Italians more warlike than Lamponious and Telesinus? Yet of these, one he drove into banishment, one he quelled, and the others he slew.

And what is more important, in my judgment, than anything yet adduced, is that Lysander had the assistance of the state in all his achievements; whereas Sulla decided that he was a banished person, and overpowered by a faction, at a time when his wife was driven from home, his houses demolished, adherents slain, himself then in Bœotia, stood embattled against countless numbers of the public enemy, and, endangering himself for the sake of his country, raised a trophy of victory; and not even when Mithridates came with proposals of alliance and aid against his enemies would he show any sort of compliance, or even clemency;

did not so much as address him, or vouchsafe him his hand, until he had it from the king's own mouth that he was willing to quit Asia, surrender the navy, and restore Bithynia and Cappadocia to the two kings. Than which action Sulla never performed a braver, or with a nobler spirit, when preferring the public good to the private, and like good hounds, where he had once fixed, never letting go his hold, till the enemy yielded, then, and not until then, he set himself to revenge his own private quarrels.

We may perhaps let ourselves be influenced, moreover, in our comparison of their characters, by considering their treatment of Athens. Sulla, when he had made himself master of the city, which then upheld the dominion and power of Mithridates in opposition to him, restored her to liberty and the free exercise of her own laws; Lysander, on the contrary, when she had fallen from a vast height of dignity and rule, showed her no compassion, but abolishing her democratic government, imposed on her the most cruel and lawless tyrants. We are now qualified to consider whether we should go far from the truth or no in pronouncing that Sulla performed the more glorious deeds, but Lysander committed the fewer faults, as, likewise, by giving to one the pre-eminence for moderation and self-control, to the other for conduct and valour.

CIMON

507?–449 B.C.

PERIPOLTAS, the prophet, having brought the King Opheltas, and those under his command, from Thessaly into Bœotia, left there a family, which flourished a long time after; the greater part of them inhabiting Chæronea, the first city out of which they expelled the barbarians. The descendants of this race, being men of bold attempts and warlike habits, exposed themselves to so many dangers in the invasions of the Medes, and in battles against the Gauls, that at last they were almost wholly consumed.

There was left one orphan of this house, called Damon, surnamed Peripoltas, in beauty and greatness of spirit surpassing all of his age, but rude and undisciplined in temper. A Roman captain of a company that wintered in

Chæronea became passionately fond of this youth, who was now pretty nearly grown a man. And finding all his approaches, his gifts, his entreaties, alike repulsed, he showed violent inclinations to assault Damon.

Our native Chæronea was then in a distressed condition, too small and too poor to meet with anything but neglect. Damon, being sensible of this, and looking upon himself as injured already, resolved to inflict punishment. Accordingly, he and sixteen of his companions conspired against the captain; but that the design might be managed without any danger of being discovered, they all daubed their faces at night with soot. Thus disguised and inflamed with wine, they set upon him by break of day, as he was sacrificing in the market-place; and having killed him, and several others that were with him, they fled out of the city, which was extremely alarmed and troubled at the murder.

The council assembled immediately, and pronounced sentence of death against Damon and his accomplices. This they did to justify the city to the Romans. But that evening, as the magistrates were at supper together, according to the custom, Damon and his confederates, breaking into the hall, killed them, and then again fled out of the town. About this time, Lucius Lucullus chanced to be passing that way with a body of troops, upon some expedition, and this disaster having but recently happened, he stayed to examine the matter. Upon inquiry, he found the city was in no wise faulty, but rather that they themselves had suffered; therefore he drew out the soldiers, and carried them away with him. Yet Damon continuing to ravage the country all about, the citizens, by messages and decrees, in appearance favourable, enticed him into the city, and upon his return, made him Gymnasiarch; but afterwards as he was anointing himself in the vapour baths, they set upon him and killed him.

For a long while after apparitions continuing to be seen, and groans to be heard in that place, so our fathers have told us, they ordered the gates of the baths to be built up; and even to this day those who live in the neighbourhood believe that they sometimes see spectres and hear alarming sounds. The posterity of Damon, of whom some still remain, mostly in Phocis, near the town of Stiris, are called Asbolomeni, that is, in the Æolian idiom, men daubed with soot, because Damon was thus besmeared when he committed this murder.

But there being a quarrel between the people of Chæronea and the Orchomenians, their neighbours, these latter hired an informer, a Roman, to accuse the community of Chæronea as if it had been a single person of the murder of the Romans, of which only Damon and his companions were guilty; accordingly, the process was commenced, and the cause pleaded before the Prætor of Macedon, since the Romans as yet had not sent governors into Greece.

The advocates who defended the inhabitants appealed to the testimony of Lucullus, who, in answer to a letter the prætor wrote to him, returned a true account of the matter-of-fact. By this means the town obtained its acquittal, and escaped a most serious danger. The citizens, thus preserved, erected a statue to Lucullus in the market-place, near that of the god Bacchus.

We also have the same impressions of gratitude; and though removed from the events by the distance of several generations, we yet feel the obligation to extend to ourselves; and as we think an image of the character and habits to be a greater honour than one merely representing the face and the person, we will put Lucullus's life amongst our parallels of illustrious men, and without swerving from the truth, will record his actions. The commemoration will be itself a sufficient proof of our grateful feeling, and he himself would not thank us, if in recompense for a service which consisted in speaking the truth, we should abuse his memory with a false and counterfeit narration.

For as we would wish that a painter who is to draw a beautiful face, in which there is yet some imperfection, should neither wholly leave out, nor yet too pointedly express what is defective, because this would deform it, and that spoil the resemblance; so since it is hard, or indeed perhaps impossible, to show the life of a man wholly free from blemish, in all that is excellent we must follow truth exactly, and give it fully; any lapses or faults that occur, through human passions or political necessities, we may regard rather as the shortcomings of some particular virtue, than as the natural effects of vice; and may be content without introducing them, curiously and officiously, into our narrative, if it be but out of tenderness to the weakness of nature, which has never succeeded in producing any human character so perfect in virtue as to be pure from all admixture and open to no criticism. On considering with myself to whom I should compare Lucullus I find none so exactly his parallel as Cimon.

They were both valiant in war, and successful against the barbarians; both gentle in political life, and more than any others gave their countrymen a respite from civil troubles at home, while abroad each of them raised trophies and gained famous victories. No Greek before Cimon, nor Roman before Lucullus, ever carried the scene of war so far from their own country; putting out of the question the acts of Bacchus and Hercules, and any exploit of Perseus against the Ethiopians, Medes, and Armenians, or again of Jason, of which any record that deserves credit can be said to have come down to our days.

Moreover in this they were alike, that they did not finish the enterprises they undertook. They brought their enemies near their ruin, but never entirely conquered them. There was yet a great conformity in the free good-will and lavish abundance of their entertainments and general hospitalities, and in the youthful laxity of their habits. Other points of resemblance, which we have failed to notice, may be easily collected from our narrative itself.

Cimon was the son of Miltiades and Hegesipyle, who was by birth a Thracian, and daughter to the King Olorus, as appears from the poem of Melanthius and Archelaus, written in praise of Cimon. By this means the historian Thucydides was his kinsman by the mother's side; for his father's name also, in remembrance of this common ancestor, was Olorus, and he was the owner of the gold mines in Thrace, and met his death, it is said, by violence, in Scapte Hyle, a district of Thrace; and his remains having afterwards been brought into Attica, a monument is shown as his among those of the family of Cimon, near the tomb of Elpinice, Cimon's sister. But Thucydides was of the township of Halimus, and Miltiades and his family were Laciadæ. Miltiades, being condemned in a fine of fifty talents of the state, and unable to pay it, was cast into prison, and there died.

Thus Cimon was left an orphan very young, with his sister Elpinice, who was also young and unmarried. And at first he had but an indifferent reputation, being looked upon as disorderly in his habits, fond of drinking, and resembling his grandfather, also called Cimon, in character, whose simplicity got him the surname of Coalemus. Stesimbrotus of Thasos, who lived near about the same time with Cimon, reports of him that he had little acquaintance either with music, or any of the other liberal studies and accomplishments, then common among the Greeks; that he had nothing whatever of the quickness and the ready speech of his countrymen in Attica; that he had great nobleness and candour in his disposition, and in his character in general resembled rather a native of Peloponnesus than of Athens; as Euripides describes Hercules—

————Rude

And unrefined, for great things well endued:
for this may fairly be added to the character which Stesimbrotus has given of him.

They accused him, in his younger years, of cohabiting with his own sister Elpinice, who, indeed, otherwise had no very clear reputation, but was reported to have been over-intimate with Polygnotus, the painter; and hence, when he painted the Trojan women in the porch, then called the Plesianactium, and now the Pœcile, he made Laodice a portrait of her. Polygnotus was not an ordinary mechanic, nor was he paid for this work, but out of a desire to please the Athenians painted the portico for nothing. So it is stated by the historians, and in the following verses by the poet Melanthius:—

Wrought by his hand the deeds of heroes grace
At his own charge our temples and our place.

Some affirm that Elpinice lived with her brother, not secretly, but as his married wife, her poverty excluding her from any suitable match. But afterwards, when Callias, one of the richest men of Athens, fell in love with her, and proffered to pay the fine the father was condemned in, if he could obtain the daughter in marriage, with Elpinice's own consent, Cimon betrothed her to Callias.

There is no doubt but that Cimon was, in general, of an amorous temper. For Melanthius, in his elegies, rallies him on his attachment for Asteria of Salamis, and again for a certain Mnestra. And there can be no doubt of his unusually passionate affection for his lawful wife Isodice, the daughter of Euryptolemus, the son of Megacles; nor of his regret, even to impatience, at her death, if any conclusion may be drawn from those elegies of condolence, addressed to him upon his loss of her. The philosopher Panætius is of opinion that Archelaus, the writer on physics, was the author of them, and indeed the time seems to favour that conjecture.

All the other points of Cimon's character were noble and good. He was as daring as Miltiades, and not inferior to Themistocles in judgment, and was incomparably more just and honest than either of them. Fully their equal in all military virtues, in the ordinary duties of a citizen at home he was immeasurably their superior. And this, too, when he was very young, his years not yet strengthened by any experience.

For when Themistocles, upon the Median invasion, advised the Athenians to forsake their city and their country, and to carry all their arms on shipboard and fight the enemy by sea, in the straits of Salamis; when all the people stood amazed at the confidence and rashness of this advice, Cimon was seen, the first of all men, passing with a cheerful countenance through the Ceramicus, on his way with his companions to the citadel, carrying a bridle in his hand to offer to the goddess, intimating that there was no more need of horsemen now, but of mariners. There, after he had paid his devotions to the goddess, and offered up the bridle, he took down one of the bucklers that hung upon the walls of the temple, and went down to the port; by this example giving confidence to many of the citizens.

He was also of a fairly handsome person, according to the poet Ion, tall and large, and let his thick and curly hair grow long. After he had acquitted himself gallantly in this battle of Salamis, he obtained great repute among the Athenians, and was regarded with affection, as well as admiration. He had many who followed after him, and bade him aspire to actions not less famous than his father's battle of Marathon. And when he came forward in political life, the people welcomed him gladly, being now weary of Themistocles; in opposition to whom, and because of the frankness and easiness of his temper, which was agreeable to every one, they advanced Cimon to the highest employments in the government. The man that contributed most to his promotion was Aristides, who early discerned in his character his natural capacity, and purposely raised him, that he might be a counterpoise to the craft and boldness of Themistocles.

After the Medes had been driven out of Greece, Cimon was sent out as an admiral, when the Athenians had not yet attained their dominion by sea, but still followed Pausanias and the Lacedæmonians; and his fellow-citizens under his command were highly distinguished, both for the excellence of their discipline, and for their extraordinary zeal and readiness. And further, perceiving that Pausanias was carrying on secret communications with the barbarians, and writing letters to the King of Persia to betray Greece, and puffed up with authority and success, was treating the allies haughtily, and committing many wanton injustices, Cimon, taking this advantage, by acts of kindness to those who were suffering wrong, and by his general humane bearing, robbed him of the command of the Greeks, before he was aware, not by arms, but by his mere language and character.

The greatest part of the allies, no longer able to endure the harshness and pride of Pausanias, revolted from him to Cimon and Aristides, who accepted the duty, and wrote to the Ephors of Sparta, desiring them to recall a man who was causing dishonour to Sparta and trouble to Greece.

They tell of Pausanias, that when he was in Byzantium, he solicited a young lady of a noble family in the city, whose name was Cleonice, to debauch her. Her parents, dreading his cruelty, were forced to consent, and so abandoned their daughter to his wishes. The daughter asked the servants outside the chamber to put out all the lights; so that approaching silently and in the dark towards his bed, she stumbled upon the lamp, which she overturned. Pausanias, who was fallen asleep, awakened and, startled with the noise, thought an assassin had taken that dead time of night to murder him, so that hastily snatching up his poniard that lay by him, he struck the girl, who fell with the blow, and died. After this, he never had rest, but was continually haunted by her, and saw an apparition visiting him in his sleep, and addressing him with these angry words:—

> Go on thy way, unto the evil end,
> That doth on lust and violence attend.

This was one of the chief occasions of indignation against him among the confederates, who now, joining their resentments and forces with Cimon's, besieged him in Byzantium. He escaped out of their hands, and, continuing, as it is said, to be disturbed by the apparition, fled to the oracle of the dead at Heraclea, raised the ghost of Cleonice, and entreated her to be reconciled. Accordingly she appeared to him, and answered that, as soon as he came to Sparta, he should speedily be freed from all evils; obscurely foretelling, it would seem, his imminent death. This story is related by many authors.

Cimon, strengthened with the accession of the allies, went as general into Thrace. For he was told that some great men among the Persians, of the king's kindred, being in possession of Eion, a city situated upon the river Strymon, infested the neighbouring Greeks. First he defeated these Persians in battle, and shut them up within the walls of their town. Then he fell upon the Thracians of the country beyond the Strymon, because they supplied Eion with victuals, and driving them entirely out of the country, took possession of it as conqueror, by which means he reduced the besieged to such straits, that Butes, who commanded there for the king, in desperation set fire to the town, and burned himself, his goods, and all his relations, in one common flame.

By this means, Cimon got the town, but no great booty; as the barbarians had not only consumed themselves in the fire, but the richest of their effects. However, he put the country about into the hands of the Athenians, a most advantageous and desirable situation for a settlement. For this action, the people permitted him to erect the stone Mercuries, upon the first of which was this inscription:—

Of bold and patient spirit, too, were those,
Who, where the Strymon under Eion flows,
With famine and the sword, to utmost need,
Reduced at last the children of the Mede.

Upon the second stood this:—

The Athenians to their leaders this reward
For great and useful service did accord;
Others hereafter shall, from their applause,
Learn to be valiant in their country's cause.

And upon the third the following:—

With Atreus' sons, this city sent of yore
Divine Menestheus to the Trojan shore;
Of all the Greeks, so Homer's verses say,
The ablest man an army to array:
So old the title of her sons the name
Of chiefs and champions in the field to claim.

Though the name of Cimon is not mentioned in these inscriptions, yet his contemporaries considered them to be the very highest honours to him; as neither Miltiades nor Themistocles ever received the like. When Miltiades claimed a garland, Sochares of Decelea stood up in the midst of the assembly and opposed it, using words which, though ungracious, were received with applause by the people: "When you have gained a victory by yourself, Miltiades, then you may ask to triumph so, too."

What then induced them so particularly to honour Cimon? Was it that under other commanders they stood upon the defensive? But by his conduct, they not only attacked their enemies, but invaded them in their own country, and acquired new territory, becoming masters of Eion and Amphipolis, where they planted colonies, as also they did in the isle of Scyros, which Cimon had taken on the following occasion.

The Dolopians were the inhabitants of this isle, a people who neglected all husbandry, and had, for many generations, been devoted to piracy; this they practised to that degree, that at last they began to plunder foreigners that brought merchandise into their ports. Some merchants of Thessaly, who had come to shore near to Ctesium, were not only spoiled of their goods, but themselves put into confinement. These men afterwards escaping from their prison, went and obtained sentence against the Scyrians in a court of Amphictyons, and when the Scyrian people declined to make public restitution, and called upon the individuals who had got the plunder to give it up, these persons, in alarm, wrote to Cimon to succour them, with his fleet, and declared themselves ready to deliver the town into his hands.

Cimon, by these means, got the town, expelled the Dolopian pirates, and so opened the traffic of the Ægean sea. And, understanding that the ancient Theseus, the son of Ægeus, when he fled from Athens and took refuge in this isle, was here treacherously slain by King Lycomedes, who feared him, Cimon endeavoured to find out where he was buried. For an oracle had commanded the Athenians to bring home his ashes, and pay him all due honours as a hero; but hitherto they had not been able to learn where he was interred, as the people of Scyros dissembled the knowledge of it, and were not willing to allow a search. But now, great inquiry being made, with some difficulty he found out the tomb and carried the relics into his own galley, and with great pomp and show brought them to Athens, four hundred years, or thereabouts, after his expulsion.

This act got Cimon great favour with the people, one mark of which was the judgment, afterwards so famous, upon the tragic poets. Sophocles, still a young man, had just brought forward his first plays; opinions were much divided, and the spectators had taken sides with some heat. So, to determine the case, Apsephion, who was at that time archon, would not cast lots who should be judges; but when Cimon and his brother commanders with him came into the theatre, after they had performed the usual rites to the god of the festival, he would not allow them to retire, but came forward and made them swear (being ten in all, one from each tribe) the usual oath; and so being sworn judges, he made them sit down to give sentence. The eagerness for victory grew all the warmer from the ambition to get the suffrages of such honourable judges. And the victory was at last adjudged to Sophocles, which Æschylus is said to have taken so ill, that he left Athens shortly after, and went in anger to Sicily, where he died, and was buried near the city of Gela.

Ion relates that when he was a young man, and recently come from Chios to Athens, he chanced to sup with Cimon at Laomedon's house. After supper, when they had, according to custom, poured out wine to the honour of the gods, Cimon was desired by the company to give them a song, which he did with sufficient success, and received the commendations of the company, who remarked on his superiority to Themistocles, who, on a like occasion, had declared he had never learnt to sing, nor to play, and only knew how to make a city rich and powerful.

After talking of things incident to such entertainments, they entered upon the particulars of the several actions for which Cimon had been famous. And when they were mentioning the most signal, he told them they had omitted one, upon which he valued himself most for address and good contrivance. He gave this account of it. When the allies had taken a great number of the barbarians prisoners in Sestos and Byzantium, they gave him the preference to divide the booty; he accordingly put the prisoners in one lot, and the spoils of their rich attire and jewels in the other. This the allies complained of as an unequal division; but he gave them their choice to take which lot they would, for that the Athenians should be content with that which they refused.

Herophytus of Samos advised them to take the ornaments for their share, and leave the slaves to the Athenians; and Cimon went away, and was much laughed at for his ridiculous division. For the allies carried away the golden bracelets, and armlets, and collars, and purple robes, and the Athenians had only the naked bodies of the captives, which they could make no advantage of, being unused to labour. But a little while after, the friends and kinsmen of the prisoners coming from Lydia and Phrygia, redeemed everyone his relations at a high ransom; so that by this means Cimon got so much treasure that he maintained his whole fleet of galleys with the money for four months; and yet there was some left to lay up in the treasury at Athens.

Cimon now grew rich, and what he gained from the barbarians with honour, he spent yet more honourably upon the citizens. For he pulled down all the enclosures of his gardens and grounds, that strangers, and the needy of his fellow-citizens, might gather of his fruits freely. At home he kept a table, plain, but sufficient for a considerable number; to which any poor townsman had free access, and so might support himself without labour, with his whole time left free for public duties. Aristotle states, however, that this reception did not extend to all the Athenians, but only to his own fellow-townsmen, the Laciadæ.

Besides this, he always went attended by two or three young companions, very well clad; and if he met with an elderly citizen in a poor habit, one of these would change clothes with the decayed citizen, which was looked upon as very nobly done. He enjoined them, likewise, to carry a considerable quantity of coin about them, which they were to convey silently into the hands of the better class of poor men, as they stood by them in the market-place. This, Cratinus, the poet, speaks of in one of his comedies, the Archilochi—

> For I, Metrobius, too, the scrivener poor,
> Of ease and comfort in my age secure
> By Greece's noblest son in life's decline,
> Cimon, the generous-hearted, the divine,
> Well-fed and feasted hoped till death to be,
> Death which, alas! has taken him ere me.

Gorgias, the Leontine, gives him this character, that he got riches that he might use them, and used them that he might get honour by them. And Critias, one of the thirty tyrants, makes it, in his elegies, his wish to have—

> The Scopads' wealth, and Cimon's nobleness,
> And King Agesilaus's success.

Lichas, we know, became famous in Greece, only because on the days of the sports, when the young boys run naked, he used to entertain the strangers that came to see these diversions. But Cimon's generosity outdid all the old Athenian hospitality and good-nature. For though it is the city's just boast that their forefathers taught the rest of Greece to sow corn, and how to use springs of water, and to kindle fire, yet Cimon, by keeping open house for his fellow-citizens, and giving travellers liberty to eat the fruits which the several seasons produced in his land, seemed to restore to the world that community of goods which mythology says existed in the reign of Saturn.

Those who object to him, that he did this to be popular and gain the applause of the vulgar, are confuted by the constant tenor of the rest of his actions, which all tended to uphold the interests of the nobility and the Spartan policy, of which he gave instances, when together with Aristides he opposed Themistocles, who was advancing the authority of the people beyond its just limits, and resisted Ephialtes, who, to please the multitude, was for abolishing the jurisdiction of the court of Areopagus.

And when all of his time, except Aristides and Ephialtes, enriched themselves out of the public money, he still kept his hands clean and untainted, and to his last day never acted or spoke for his own private gain or emolument. They tell us that Rhœsaces, a Persian, who had traitorously revolted from the king his master, fled to Athens, and there, being harassed by sycophants, who were still accusing him to the people, he applied himself to Cimon for redress, and, to gain his favour, laid down in his doorway two cups, the one full of gold and the other of silver Darics. Cimon smiled and asked him whether he wished to have Cimon's hired service or his friendship. He replied, his friendship. "If so," said he, "take away these pieces, for, being your friend, when I shall have occasion for them, I will send and ask for them."

The allies of the Athenians began now to be weary of war and military service, willing to have repose, and to look after their husbandry and traffic. For they saw their enemies driven out of the country, and did not fear any new vexations from them. They still paid the tax they were assessed at, but did not send men and galleys, as they had done before. This the other Athenian generals wished to constrain them to, and by judicial proceedings against defaulters, and penalties which they inflicted on them, made the government uneasy, and even odious.

But Cimon practised a contrary method; he forced no man to go that was not willing, but of those that desired to be excused from service he took money and vessels unmanned, and let them yield to the temptation of staying at home, to attend to their private business. Thus they lost their military habits and luxury, and their own folly quickly changed them into unwarlike husbandmen and traders; while Cimon, continually embarking large numbers of Athenians on board his galleys, thoroughly disciplined them in his expeditions, and ere long made them the lords of their own paymasters. The allies, whose indolence maintained them, while they thus went sailing about everywhere, and incessantly bearing arms and acquiring skill, began to fear and flatter them, and found themselves after a while allies no longer, but unwittingly become tributaries and slaves.

Nor did any man ever do more than Cimon did to humble the pride of the Persian king. He was not content with getting rid of him out of Greece; but following close at his heels, before the barbarians could take breath and recover themselves, he was already at work, and what with his devastations, and his forcible reduction of some places, and the revolts and voluntary accession of others in the end from Ionia to Pamphylia, all Asia was clear of Persian soldiers.

Word being brought him that the royal commanders were lying in wait upon the coast of Pamphylia with a numerous land army and a large fleet, he determined to make the whole sea on his side the Chelidonian islands so formidable to them that they should never dare to show themselves in it; and setting off from Cnidos and the Triopian headland with two hundred galleys, which had been originally built with particular care by Themistocles, for speed and rapid evolutions, and to which he now gave greater width and roomier decks along the sides to move to and fro upon, so as to allow a great number of full-armed soldiers to take part in the engagements and fight from them, he shaped his course first of all against the town of Phaselis, which though inhabited by Greeks, yet would not quit the interests of Persia, but denied his galleys entrance into their port.

Upon this he wasted the country, and drew up his army to their very walls; but the soldiers of Chios, who were then serving under him, being ancient friends to the Phaselites, endeavouring to propitiate the general in their behalf, at the same time shot arrows into the town, to which were fastened letters conveying intelligence. At length he concluded peace with them, upon the conditions that they should pay down ten talents, and follow him against the barbarians.

Ephorus says the admiral of the Persian fleet was Tithraustes, and the general of the land army Pherendates; but Callisthenes is positive that Ariomandes, the son of Gobryas, had the supreme command of all the forces. He lay waiting with the whole fleet at the mouth of the river Eurymedon, with no design to fight, but expecting a reinforcement of eighty Phœnician ships on their way from Cyprus.

Cimon, aware of this, put out to sea, resolved, if they would not fight a battle willingly, to force them to it. The barbarians, seeing this, retired within the mouth of the river to avoid being attacked; but when they saw the Athenians come upon them, notwithstanding their retreat, they met them with six hundred ships, as Phanodemus relates, but, according to Ephorus, only with three hundred and fifty. However, they did nothing worthy such mighty forces, but immediately turned the prows of their galleys toward the shore, where those that came first threw themselves upon the land, and fled to their army drawn up thereabout, while the rest perished with their vessels or were taken. By this, one may guess at their number, for though a great many escaped out of the fight, and a great many others were sunk, yet two hundred galleys were taken by the Athenians.

When their land army drew toward the seaside, Cimon was in suspense whether he should venture to try and force his way on shore; as he should thus expose his Greeks, wearied with slaughter in the first engagement, to the swords of the barbarians, who were all fresh men, and many times their number. But seeing his men resolute, and flushed with victory, he bade them land, though they were not yet cool from their first battle. As soon as they touched ground, they set up a shout and ran upon the enemy, who stood firm and sustained the first shock with great courage, so that the fight was a hard one, and some principal men of the Athenians in rank and courage were slain. At length, though with much ado, they routed the barbarians, and killing some, took others prisoners, and plundered all their tents and pavilions, which were full of rich spoil.

Cimon, like a skilled athlete at the games, having in one day carried off two victories wherein he surpassed that of Salamis by sea and that of Platæa by land, was encouraged to try for yet another success. News being brought that the Phœnician succours, in number eighty sail, had come in sight at Hydrum, he set off with all speed to find them, while they as yet had not received any certain account of the larger fleet, and were in doubt what to think; so that, thus surprised, they lost all their vessels and most of their men with them.

This success of Cimon so daunted the King of Persia that he presently made that celebrated peace, by which he engaged that his armies should come no nearer the Grecian sea than the length of a horse's course, and that none of his galleys or vessels of war should appear between the Cyanean and Chelidonian isles. Callisthenes, however, says that he did not agree to any such articles, but that, upon the fear this victory gave him, he did in reality thus act, and kept off so far from Greece, that when Pericles with fifty and Ephialtes with thirty galleys cruised beyond the Chelidonian isles, they did not discover one Persian vessel. But in the collection which Craterus made of the public acts of the people, there is a draft of this treaty given. And it is told, also, that at Athens they erected the altar of Peace upon this occasion, and decreed particular honours to Callias, who was employed as ambassador to procure the treaty.

The people of Athens raised so much money from the spoils of this war, which were publicly sold, that besides other expenses, and raising the south wall of the citadel, they laid the foundation of the long walls, not, indeed, finished till at a later time, which were called the Legs. And the place where they built them being soft and marshy ground, they were forced to sink great weights of stone and rubble to secure the foundation, and did all this out of the money Cimon supplied them with. It was he, likewise, who first embellished the upper city with those fine and ornamental places of exercise and resort, which they afterwards so much frequented and delighted in. He set the market-place with plane-trees; and the Academy, which was before a bare, dry, and dirty spot, he converted into a well-watered grove, with shady alleys to walk in, and open courses for races.

When the Persians who had made themselves masters of the Chersonese, so far from quitting it, called in the people of the interior of Thrace to help them against Cimon, whom they despised for the smallness of his forces, he set upon them with only four galleys, and took thirteen of theirs; and having driven out the Persians, and subdued the Thracians, he made the whole Chersonese the property of Athens.

Next he attacked the people of Thasos, who had revolted from the Athenians; and, having defeated them in a fight at sea, where he took thirty-three of their vessels, he took their town by siege, and acquired for the Athenians all the mines of gold on the opposite coast, and the territory dependent on Thasos. This opened him a fair passage into Macedon, so that he might, it was thought, have acquired a good portion of that country; and because he neglected the opportunity, he was suspected of corruption, and of having been bribed off by King Alexander.

So, by the combination of his adversaries, he was accused of being false to his country. In his defence he told the judges that he had always shown himself in his public life the friend, not, like other men, of rich Ionians and Thessalians, to be courted, and to receive presents, but of the Lacedæmonians; for as he admired, so he wished to imitate, the plainness of their habits, their temperance, and simplicity of living, which he preferred to any sort of riches; but that he always had been, and still was, proud to enrich his country with the spoils of her enemies. Stesimbrotus, making mention of this trial, states that Elpinice, in behalf of her brother, addressed herself to Pericles, the most vehement of his accusers, to whom Pericles answered, with a smile, "You are old, Elpinice, to meddle with affairs of this nature." However, he proved the mildest of his prosecutors, and rose up but once all the while, almost as a matter of form, to plead against him. Cimon was acquitted.

In his public life after this he continued,

whilst at home, to control and restrain the common people, who would have trampled upon the nobility, and drawn all the power and sovereignty to themselves. But when he afterwards was sent out to war, the multitude broke loose, as it were, and overthrew all the ancient laws and customs they had hitherto observed, and, chiefly at the instigation of Ephialtes, withdrew the cognisance of almost all causes from the Areopagus; so that all jurisdiction now being transferred to them, the government was reduced to a perfect democracy, and this by the help of Pericles, who was already powerful, and had pronounced in favour of the common people.

Cimon, when he returned, seeing the authority of this great council so upset, was exceedingly troubled, and endeavoured to remedy these disorders by bringing the courts of law to their former state, and restoring the old aristocracy of the time of Clisthenes. This the others declaimed against with all the vehemence possible, and began to revive those stories concerning him and his sister, and cried out against him as the partisan of the Lacedæmonians. To these calumnies the famous verses of Eupolis, the poet, upon Cimon refer:—

He was as good as others that one sees,
But he was fond of drinking and of ease;
And would at nights to Sparta often roam,
Leaving his sister desolate at home.

But if, though slothful and a drunkard, he could capture so many towns and gain so many victories, certainly if he had been sober and minded his business, there had been no Grecian commander, either before or after him, that could have surpassed him for exploits of war.

He was, indeed, a favourer of the Lacedæmonians, even from his youth, and he gave the names of Lacedæmonius and Eleus to two sons, twins, whom he had, as Stesimbrotus says, by a woman of Clitorium, whence Pericles often upbraided them with their mother's blood. But Diodorus, the geographer, asserts that both these, and another son of Cimon's, whose name was Thessalus, were born of Isodice, the daughter of Euryptolemus, the son of Megacles.

However, this is certain, that Cimon was countenanced by the Lacedæmonians in opposition to Themistocles, whom they disliked; and while he was yet very young, they endeavoured to raise and increase his credit in Athens. This the Athenians perceived at first with pleasure, and the favour the Lacedæmonians

showed him was in various ways advantageous to them and their affairs; as at that time they were just rising to power, and were occupied in winning the allies to their side. So they seemed not at all offended with the honour and kindness shown to Cimon, who then had the chief management of all the affairs of Greece, and was acceptable to the Lacedæmonians, and courteous to the allies.

But afterwards the Athenians, grown more powerful, when they saw Cimon so entirely devoted to the Lacedæmonians, began to be angry, for he would always in his speeches prefer them to the Athenians, and upon every occasion, when he would reprimand them for a fault, or incite them to emulation, he would exclaim, "The Lacedæmonians would not do thus." This raised the discontent, and got him in some degree the hatred of the citizens; but that which ministered chiefly to the accusation against him fell out upon the following occasion.

In the fourth year of the reign of Archidamus, the son of Zeuxidamus, King of Sparta, there happened in the country of Lacedæmon the greatest earthquake that was known in the memory of man; the earth opened into chasms, and the mountain Taygetus was so shaken, that some of the rocky points of it fell down, and except five houses, all the town of Sparta was shattered to pieces.

They say that a little before any motion was perceived, as the young men and the boys just grown up were exercising themselves together in the middle of the portico, a hare, of a sudden, started out just by them, which the young men, though all naked and daubed with oil, ran after for sport. No sooner were they gone from the place, than the gymnasium fell down upon the boys who had stayed behind, and killed them all. Their tomb is to this day called Sismatias.

Archidamus, by the present danger made apprehensive of what might follow, and seeing the citizens intent upon removing the most valuable of their goods out of their houses, commanded an alarm to be sounded, as if an enemy were coming upon them, in order that they should collect about him in a body, with arms. It was this alone that saved Sparta at that time, for the Helots were got together from the country about, with design to surprise the Spartans, and overpower those whom the earthquake had spared. But finding them armed and well prepared, they retired into the towns and openly made war with them, gaining over a number of the Laconians of the country districts; while at the same time the Messenians, also, made an attack upon the Spartans, who therefore despatched Periclidas to Athens to solicit succours, of whom Aristophanes says in mockery that he came and—

In a red jacket, at the altars seated,
With a white face, for men and arms entreated.

This Ephialtes opposed, protesting that they ought not to raise up or assist a city that was a rival to Athens; but that being down, it were best to keep her so, and let the pride and arrogance of Sparta be trodden under. But Cimon, as Critias says, preferring the safety of Lacedæmon to the aggrandisement of his own country, so persuaded the people, that he soon marched out with a large army to their relief. Ion records, also, the most successful expression which he used to move the Athenians: "They ought not to suffer Greece to be lamed, nor their own city to be deprived of her yoke-fellow."

In his return from aiding the Lacedæmonians, he passed with his army through the territory of Corinth; whereupon Lachartus reproached him for bringing his army into the country without first asking leave of the people. For he that knocks at another man's door ought not to enter the house till the master gives him leave. "But you Corinthians, O Lachartus," said Cimon, "did not knock at the gates of the Cleonæans and Megarians, but broke them down, and entered by force, thinking that all places should be open to the stronger." And having thus rallied the Corinthian, he passed on with his army.

Some time after this, the Lacedæmonians sent a second time to desire succours of the Athenians against the Messenians and Helots, who had seized upon Ithome. But when they came, fearing their boldness and gallantry, of all that came to their assistance, they sent them only back, alleging they were designing innovations. The Athenians returned home, enraged at this usage, and vented their anger upon all those who were favourers of the Lacedæmonians, and seizing some slight occasion, they banished Cimon for ten years, which is the time prescribed to those that are banished by the ostracism.

In the meantime, the Lacedæmonians, on their return after freeing Delphi from the Phocians, encamped their army at Tanagra, whither the Athenians presently marched with design to fight them. Cimon, also, came thither

armed, and ranged himself among those of his own tribe, which was the Œneis, desirous of fighting with the rest against the Spartans; but the council of five hundred being informed of this, and frighted at it, his adversaries crying out he would disorder the army, and bring the Lacedæmonians to Athens, commanded the officers not to receive him.

Wherefore Cimon left the army, conjuring Euthippus, the Anaphlystian, and the rest of his companions, who were most suspected as favouring the Lacedæmonians, to behave themselves bravely against their enemies, and by their actions make their innocence evident to their countrymen. These, being in all a hundred, took the arms of Cimon, and followed his advice; and making a body by themselves, fought so desperately with the enemy, that they were all cut off, leaving the Athenians deep regret for the loss of such brave men, and repentance for having so unjustly suspected them.

Accordingly, they did not long retain their severity toward Cimon, partly upon remembrance of his former services, and partly, perhaps, induced by the juncture of the times. For being defeated at Tanagra in a great battle, and fearing the Peloponnesians would come upon them at the opening of the spring, they recalled Cimon by a decree, of which Pericles himself was author. So reasonable were men's resentments in those times, and so moderate their anger, that it always gave way to the public good. Even ambition, the least governable of all human passions, could then yield to the necessities of the state.

Cimon, as soon as he returned, put an end to the war, and reconciled the two cities. Peace thus established, seeing the Athenians impatient of being idle, and eager after the honour and aggrandisement of war, lest they should set upon the Greeks themselves, or with so many ships cruising about the isles and Peloponnesus they should give occasions to intestine wars, or complaints of their allies against them, he equipped two hundred galleys, with design to make an attempt upon Egypt and Cyprus; purposing, by this means, to accustom the Athenians to fight against the barbarians, and enrich themselves honestly by spoiling those who were the natural enemies of Greece.

But when all things were prepared, and the army ready to embark, Cimon had this dream. It seemed to him that there was a furious bitch barking at him, and mixed with the barking a kind of human voice uttered these words:—

Come on, for thou shalt shortly be,
A pleasure to my whelps and me.

This dream was hard to interpret, yet Astyphilus of Posidonia, a man skilled in divinations, and intimate with Cimon, told him that his death was presaged by this vision, which he thus explained. A dog is enemy to him he barks at; and one is always most a pleasure to one's enemies when one is dead; the mixture of human voice with barking signifies the Medes, for the army of the Medes is mixed up of Greeks and barbarians. After this dream, as he was sacrificing to Bacchus, and the priest cutting up the victim, a number of ants, taking up the congealed particles of the blood, laid them about Cimon's great toe. This was not observed for a good while, but at the very time when Cimon spied it, the priest came and showed him the liver of the sacrifice imperfect, wanting that part of it called the head.

But he could not then recede from the enterprise, so he set sail. Sixty of his ships he sent toward Egypt; with the rest he went and fought the King of Persia's fleet, composed of Phœnician and Cilician galleys, recovered all the cities thereabout, and threatened Egypt; designing no less than the entire ruin of the Persian empire. And all the more for that he was informed Themistocles was in great repute among the barbarians, having promised the king to lead his army, whenever he should make war upon Greece. But Themistocles, it is said, abandoning all hopes of compassing his designs, very much out of the despair of overcoming the valour and good fortune of Cimon, died a voluntary death.

Cimon, intent on great designs, which he was now to enter upon, keeping his navy about the isle of Cyprus, sent messengers to consult the oracle of Jupiter Ammon upon some secret matter. For it is not known about what they were sent, and the god would give them no answer, but commanded them to return again, for that Cimon was already with him. Hearing this, they returned to sea, and as soon as they came to the Grecian army, which was then about Egypt, they understood that Cimon was dead; and computing the time of the oracle, they found that his death had been signified, he being then already with the gods.

He died, some say, of sickness, while besieging Citium, in Cyprus; according to others, of a wound he received in a skirmish with the barbarians. When he perceived he should die, he commanded those under his charge to return, and by no means to let the news of his death be known by the way; this they did with such secrecy that they all came home safe, and neither their enemies nor the allies knew what had happened. Thus, as Phanodemus relates, the Grecian army was, as it were, conducted by Cimon thirty days after he was dead.

But after his death there was not one commander among the Greeks that did anything considerable against the barbarians, and instead of uniting against their common enemies, the popular leaders and partisans of war animated them against one another to that degree, that none could interpose their good offices to reconcile them. And while, by their mutual discord, they ruined the power of Greece, they gave the Persians time to recover breath, and repair all their losses.

It is true, indeed, Agesilaus carried the arms of Greece into Asia, but it was a long time after; there were, indeed, some brief appearances of a war against the king's lieutenants in the maritime provinces, but they all quickly vanished; before he could perform anything of moment, he was recalled by fresh civil dissensions and disturbances at home. So that he was forced to leave the Persian king's officers to impose what tribute they pleased on the Greek cities in Asia, the confederates and allies of the Lacedæmonians. Whereas, in the time of Cimon, not so much as a letter-carrier, or a single horseman, was ever seen to come within four hundred furlongs of the sea.

The monuments, called Cimonian to this day, in Athens, show that his remains were conveyed home, yet the inhabitants of the city Citium pay particular honour to a certain tomb which they call the tomb of Cimon, according to Nausicrates, the rhetorician, who states that in a time of famine, when the crops of their land all failed, they sent to the oracle, which commanded them not to forget Cimon, but give him the honours of a superior being. Such was the Greek commander.

LUCULLUS

110?-56 B.C.

THE grandfather of Lucullus had been consul; his uncle by the mother's side was Metellus, surnamed Numidicus. As for his parents, his father was convicted of extortion, and his mother Cæcilia's reputation was bad.

The first thing that Lucullus did before ever he stood for any office, or meddled with the affairs of state, being then but a youth, was to accuse the accuser of his father, Servilius, the augur, having caught him in offence against the state. This thing was much taken notice of among the Romans, who commended it as an act of high merit. Even without the provocation the accusation was esteemed no unbecoming action, for they delighted to see young men as eagerly attacking injustice as good dogs do wild beasts. But when great animosities ensued, insomuch that some were wounded and killed in the fray, Servilius escaped.

Lucullus followed his studies and became a competent speaker, in both Greek and Latin, insomuch that Sulla, when composing the commentaries of his own life and actions, dedicated them to him, as one who could have performed the task better himself. His speech was not only elegant and ready for purposes of mere business, like the ordinary oratory which will in the public market-place—

> Lash as a wounded tunny does the sea,

but on every other occasion shows itself—

> Dried up and perished with the want of wit;

but even in his younger days he addicted himself to the study, simply for its own sake, of the liberal arts; and when advanced in years, after a life of conflicts, he gave his mind, as it were, its liberty, to enjoy in full leisure the refreshment of philosophy; and summoning up his contemplative faculties, administered a timely check, after his difference with Pompey, to his feelings of emulation and ambition.

Besides what has been said of his love of learning already, one instance more was, that in his youth, upon a suggestion of writing the Marsian war in Greek and Latin verse and prose, arising out of some pleasantry that passed into a serious proposal, he agreed with Hortensius, the lawyer, and Sisenna, the historian, that he would take his lot; and it seems that the lot directed him to the Greek tongue, for a Greek history of that war is still extant.

Among the many signs of the great love which he bore to his brother Marcus, one in particular is commemorated by the Romans. Though he was elder brother, he would not step into authority without him, but deferred his own advance until his brother was qualified to bear a share with him, and so won upon the people as, when absent, to be chosen ædile with him.

He gave many and early proofs of his valour and conduct in the Marsian war, and was admired by Sulla for his constancy and mildness, and always employed in affairs of importance, especially in the mint; most of the money for carrying on the Mithridatic war being coined by him in Peloponnesus, which, by the soldiers' wants, was brought into rapid circulation and long continued current under the name of Lucullean coin.

After this, when Sulla conquered Athens, and was victorious by land, but found the supplies for his army cut off, the enemy being master at sea, Lucullus was the man whom he sent into Libya and Egypt to procure him shipping. It was the depth of winter when he ventured with but three small Greek vessels, and as many Rhodian galleys, not only into the main sea, but also among multitudes of vessels belonging to the enemies who were cruising about as absolute masters. Arriving at Crete he gained it, and finding the Cyrenians harassed by long tyrannies and wars, he composed their troubles, and settled their government; putting the city in mind of that saying which Plato once had oracularly uttered of them, who, being requested to prescribe laws to them, and mould them into some sound form of government, made answer that it was a hard thing to give laws to the Cyrenians, abounding, as they did, in wealth and plenty. For nothing is more intractable than man when in felicity, nor anything more docile, when he has been reduced and humbled by fortune. This made the Cyrenians so willingly submit to the laws which Lucullus imposed upon them.

From thence sailing into Egypt, and pressed by pirates, he lost most of his vessels; but he himself narrowly escaping, made a magnificent entry into Alexandria. The whole fleet, a compliment due only to royalty, met him in full array, and the young Ptolemy showed wonderful kindness to him, appointing him lodging and diet in the palace, where no foreign commander before him had been received. Besides, he gave him gratuities and presents, not such as were usually given to men of his condition, but four times as much; of which, however, he took nothing more than served his necessity and accepted of no gift, though what was worth eighty talents was offered him. It is reported he neither went to see Memphis, nor any of the celebrated wonders of Egypt. It was for a man of no business and much curiosity to see such things, not for him who had left his commander in the field lodging under the ramparts of his enemies.

Ptolemy, fearing the issue of that war, deserted the confederacy, but nevertheless sent a convoy with him as far as Cyprus, and at parting, with much ceremony, wishing him a good voyage, gave him a very precious emerald set in gold. Lucullus at first refused it, but when the king showed him his own likeness cut upon it, he thought he could not persist in a denial, for had he parted with such open offence, it might have endangered his passage.

Drawing a considerable squadron together, which he summoned as he sailed by out of all the maritime towns except those suspected of piracy, he sailed for Cyprus, and there understanding that the enemy lay in wait under the promontories for him, he laid up his fleet, and sent to the cities to send in provisions for his wintering among them. But when time served, he launched his ships suddenly, and went off, and hoisting all his sails in the night, while he kept them down in the day, thus came safe to Rhodes. Being furnished with ships at Rhodes, he also prevailed upon the inhabitants of Cos and Cnidus to leave the king's side, and join in an expedition against the Samians. Out of Chios he himself drove the king's party, and set the Colophonians at liberty, having seized Epigonus, the tyrant, who oppressed them.

About this time Mithridates left Pergamus, and retired to Pitane, where being closely besieged by Fimbria on the land, and not daring to engage with so bold and victorious a commander, he was concerting means for escape by sea, and sent for all his fleets from every quarter to attend him. Which when Fimbria perceived, having no ships of his own, he sent to Lucullus, entreating him to assist him with his, in subduing the most odious and warlike of kings, lest the opportunity of humbling Mithridates, the prize which the Romans had pursued with so much blood and trouble, should now at last be lost, when he was within the net and easily to be taken. And were he caught, no one would be more highly commended than Lucullus, who stopped his passage and seized him in his flight. Being driven from the land by the one, and met in the sea by the other, he would give matter of renown and glory to them both, and the much applauded actions of Sulla at Orchomenus and about Chæronea would no longer be thought of by the Romans.

The proposal was no unreasonable thing; it being obvious to all men, that if Lucullus had hearkened to Fimbria, and with his navy, which was then near at hand, had blocked up the haven, the war soon had been brought to an end, and infinite numbers of mischiefs prevented thereby. But he, whether from the sacredness of friendship between himself and Sulla, reckoning all other considerations of public or of private advantage inferior to it, or out of detestation of the wickedness of Fimbria, whom he abhorred for advancing himself by the late death of his friend and the general of the army, or by a divine fortune sparing Mithridates then, that he might have him an adversary for a time to come, for whatever reason, refused to comply, and suffered Mithridates to escape and laugh at the attempts of Fimbria.

He himself alone first, near Lectum, in Troas, in a sea-fight, overcame the king's ships; and afterwards, discovering Neoptolemus lying in wait for him near Tenedos, with a greater fleet, he went aboard a Rhodian quinquereme galley, commanded by Damagoras, a man of great experience at sea, and friendly to the Romans, and sailed before the rest. Neoptolemus made up furiously at him, and commanded the master, with all imaginable might, to charge; but Damagoras, fearing the bulk and massy stem of the admiral, thought it dangerous to meet him prow to prow, and, rapidly wheeling round, bid his men back water, and so received him astern; in which place, though violently borne upon, he received no manner of harm, the blow being defeated by falling on those parts of the ship which lay under water. By which time, the rest of the fleet coming up to him, Lucullus gave order to turn again, and vigorously falling upon the enemy, put them to flight, and pursued Neoptolemus. After this he came to Sulla, in Chersonesus, as he was preparing to pass the strait, and brought timely assistance for the safe transportation of the army.

Peace being presently made, Mithridates sailed off to the Euxine sea, but Sulla taxed the inhabitants of Asia twenty thousand talents, and ordered Lucullus to gather and coin the money. And it was no small comfort to the cities under Sulla's severity, that a man of not only incorrupt and just behaviour, but also of moderation, should be employed in so heavy and odious an office. The Mitylenæans, who absolutely revolted, he was willing should return to their duty, and submit to a moderate penalty for the offence they had given in the case of Marius. But finding them bent upon their own destruction, he came up to them, defeated them at sea, blocked them up in their city and besieged them; then sailing off from them openly in the day to Elæa, he returned privately, and posting an ambush near the city, lay quiet himself. And on the Mitylenæans coming out eagerly and in disorder to plunder the deserted camp, he fell upon them, took many of them, and slew five hundred, who stood upon their defence. He gained six thousand slaves and a very rich booty.

He was no way engaged in the great and general troubles of Italy which Sulla and Marius created, a happy providence at that time detaining him in Asia upon business. He was as much in Sulla's favour, however, as any of his other friends; Sulla, as was said before, dedicated his Memoirs to him as a token of kindness, and at his death, passing by Pompey, made him guardian to his son; which seems, indeed, to have been the rise of the quarrel and jealousy between them two, being both young men, and passionate for honour.

A little after Sulla's death, he was made consul with Marcus Cotta, about the one hundred and seventy-sixth Olympiad. The Mithridatic war being then under debate, Marcus declared that it was not finished, but only respited for a time, and therefore, upon choice of provinces, the lot falling to Lucullus to have Gaul within the Alps, a province where no great action was to be done, he was ill-pleased.

But chiefly, the success of Pompey in Spain fretted him, as, with the renown he got there, if the Spanish war were finished in time, he was likely to be chosen general before any one else against Mithridates. So that when Pompey sent for money, and signified by letter that, unless it were sent him, he would leave the country and Sertorius, and bring his forces home to Italy, Lucullus most zealously supported his request, to prevent any pretence of his returning home during his own consulship; for all things would have been at his disposal, at the head of so great an army.

For Cethegus, the most influential popular leader at that time, owing to his always both acting and speaking to please the people, had, as it happened, a hatred to Lucullus, who had not concealed his disgust at his debauched, insolent, and lawless life. Lucullus, therefore, was at open warfare with him. And Lucius Quintius, also, another demagogue, who was taking steps against Sulla's constitution, and endeavouring to put things out of order, by private exhortations and public admonitions he checked in his designs, and repressed his ambition, wisely and safely remedying a great evil at the very outset.

At this time news came that Octavius, the governor of Cilicia, was dead, and many were eager for the place, courting Cethegus, as the man best able to serve them. Lucullus set little value upon Cilicia itself, no otherwise than as he thought, by his acceptance of it, no other man besides himself might be employed in the war against Mithridates, by reason of its nearness to Cappadocia. This made him strain every effort that that province might be allotted to himself, and to none other; which led him at last into an expedient not so honest or commendable, as it was serviceable for compassing his design, submitting to necessity against his own inclination.

There was one Præcia, a celebrated wit and beauty, but in other respects nothing better than an ordinary harlot; who, however, to the charms of her person adding the reputation of one that loved and served her friends, by making use of those who visited her to assist their designs and promote their interests, had thus gained great power. She had seduced Cethegus, the first man at that time in reputation and authority of all the city, and enticed him to her love, and so had made all authority follow her. For nothing of moment was done in which Cethegus was not concerned, and nothing by Cethegus without Præcia. This woman Lucullus gained to his side by gifts and flattery (and a great price it was in itself to so stately and magnificent a dame, to be seen engaged in the same cause with Lucullus), and thus he presently found Cethegus his friend, using his utmost interest to procure Cilicia for him; which when once obtained, there was no more need of applying himself either to Præcia or Cethegus; for all unanimously voted him to the Mithridatic war, by no hands likely to be so successfully managed as his. Pompey was still contending with Sertorius, and Metellus by age unfit for service; which two alone were the competitors who could prefer any claim with Lucullus for that command. Cotta, his colleague, after much ado in the senate, was sent away with a fleet to guard the Propontis, and defend Bithynia.

Lucullus carried with him a legion under his own orders, and crossed over into Asia and took the command of the forces there, composed of men who were all thoroughly disabled by dissoluteness and rapine, and the Fimbrians, as they were called, utterly unmanageable by long want of any sort of discipline. For these were they who under Fimbria had slain Flaccus, the consul and general, and afterwards betrayed Fimbria to Sulla; a wilful and lawless set of men, but warlike, expert and hardy in the field. Lucullus in a short time took down the courage of these, and disciplined the others, who then first, in all probability, knew what a true commander and governor was; whereas in former times they had been courted to service, and took up arms at nobody's command, but their own wills.

The enemy's provisions for war stood thus: Mithridates, like the Sophists, boastful and haughty at first, set upon the Romans, with a very inefficient army, such, indeed, as made a good show, but was nothing for use; but being shamefully routed, and taught a lesson for a second engagement, he reduced his forces to a proper, serviceable shape. Dispensing with the mixed multitudes, and the noisy menaces of barbarous tribes of various languages, and with the ornaments of gold and precious stones, a greater temptation to the victors than security to the bearers, he gave his men broad swords like the Romans', and massy shields; chose horses better for service than show, drew up an hundred and twenty thousand foot in the figure of the Roman phalanx, and had sixteen thousand horse, besides chariots armed with scythes, no less than a hundred. Besides which, he set out a fleet not at all cumbered with gilded cabins, luxurious baths, and women's furniture, but stored with weapons and darts, and other necessaries, and thus made a descent upon Bithynia. Not only did these parts willingly receive him again, but almost all Asia regarded him as their salvation from the intolerable miseries which they were suffering from the Roman money-lenders and revenue farmers. These, afterwards, who like harpies stole away their very nourishment, Lucullus drove away, and at this time, by reproving them, did what he could to make them more moderate, and to prevent a general secession, then breaking out in all parts.

While Lucullus was detained in rectifying these matters, Cotta, finding affairs ripe for action, prepared for battle with Mithridates; and news coming from all hands that Lucullus had already entered Phrygia, on his march against the enemy, he, thinking he had a triumph all but actually in his hands, lest his colleague should share in the glory of it, hasted to battle without him. But being routed, both by sea and land, he lost sixty ships with their men, and four thousand foot, and himself was forced into and besieged in Chalcedon, there waiting for relief from Lucullus. There were those about Lucullus who would have had him leave Cotta, and go forward, in hope of surprising the defenceless kingdom of Mithridates. And this was the feeling of the soldiers in general, who were indignant that Cotta should by his ill-counsel not only lose his own army, but hinder them also from conquest, which at that time, without the hazard of a battle, they might have obtained. But Lucullus, in a public address, declared to them that he would rather save one citizen from the enemy, than be master of all that they had.

Archelaus, the former commander in Bœotia under Mithridates, who afterwards deserted him and accompanied the Romans, protested to Lucullus that, upon his bare coming, he would possess himself of all Pontus. But he answered, that it did not become him to be more cowardly than huntsmen, to leave the wild beasts abroad and seek after sport in their deserted dens. Having so said, he made towards Mithridates with thirty thousand foot and two thousand five hundred horse. But on being come in sight of his enemies, he was astonished at their numbers, and thought to forbear fighting, and wear out time.

But Marius, whom Sertorius had sent out of Spain to Mithridates with forces under him, stepping out and challenging him, he prepared for battle. In the very instant before joining battle, without any perceptible alteration preceding, on a sudden the sky opened, and a large luminous body fell down in the midst between the armies, in shape like a hogshead, but in colour like melted silver, insomuch that both armies in alarm withdrew. This wonderful prodigy happened in Phrygia, near Otryæ.

Lucullus after this began to think with himself that no human power and wealth could suffice to sustain such great numbers as Mithridates had for any long time in the face of an enemy, and commanded one of the captives to be brought before him, and first of all asked him how many companions had been quartered with him and how much provision he had left behind him, and when he had answered him, commanded him to stand aside; then asked a second and a third the same question; after which, comparing the quantity of provision with the men, he found that in three or four days' time his enemies would be brought to want. This all the more determined him to trust to time, and he took measures to store his camp with all sorts of provision, and thus living in plenty, trusted to watch the necessities of his hungry enemy.

This made Mithridates set out against the Cyzicenians, miserably shattered in the fight at Chalcedon, where they lost no less than three thousand citizens and ten ships. And that he might the safer steal away unobserved by Lucullus, immediately after supper, by the help of a dark and wet night, he went off, and by the morning gained the neighbourhood of the city, and sat down with his forces upon the Adrastean mount. Lucullus, on finding him gone, pursued, but was well pleased not to overtake him with his own forces in disorder; and he sat down near what is called the Thracian village, an admirable position for commanding all the roads and the places whence, and through which, the provisions for Mithridates's camp must of necessity come. And judging now of the event, he no longer kept his mind from his soldiers, but when the camp was fortified and their work finished, called them together, and with great assurance told them that in a few days, without the expense of blood, he would give them victory.

Mithridates besieged the Cyzicenians with ten camps by land, and with his ships occupied the strait that was betwixt their city and the mainland, and so blocked them up on all sides; they, however, were fully prepared stoutly to receive him, and resolved to endure the utmost extremity, rather than forsake the Romans. That which troubled them most was, that they knew not where Lucullus was, and heard nothing of him, though at that time his army was visible before them. But they were imposed upon by the Mithridatians, who, showing them the Romans encamped on the hills, said, "Do ye see those? Those are the auxiliary Armenians and Medes, whom Tigranes has sent to Mithridates."

They were thus overwhelmed with thinking of the vast numbers round them, and could not believe any way of relief was left them, even if Lucullus should come up to their assistance. Demonax, a messenger sent in by Archelaus, was the first who told them of Lucullus's arrival; but they disbelieved his report, and thought he came with a story invented merely to encourage them. At which time it happened that a boy, a prisoner who had run away from the enemy, was brought before them; who, being asked where Lucullus was, laughed at their jesting, as he thought, but, finding them in earnest, with his finger pointed to the Roman camp; upon which they took courage. The lake Dascylitis was navigated with vessels of some little size; one, the biggest of them, Lucullus drew ashore, and carrying her across in a waggon to the sea, filled her with soldiers, who, sailing along unseen in the dead of the night, came safe into the city.

The gods themselves, too, in admiration of the constancy of the Cyzicenians, seem to have animated them with manifest signs, more especially now in the festival of Proserpine, where a black heifer being wanting for sacrifice, they supplied it by a figure made of dough, which they set before the altar. But the holy heifer set apart for the goddess, and at that time grazing with the other herds of the Cyzicenians, on the other side of the strait, left the herd and swam over to the city alone, and offered herself for sacrifice. By night, also, the goddess appearing to Aristagoras, the town clerk, "I am come," said she, "and have brought the Libyan piper against the Pontic trumpeter; bid the citizens, therefore, be of good courage."

While the Cyzicenians were wondering what the words could mean, a sudden wind sprung up and caused a considerable motion on the sea. The king's battering engines, the wonderful contrivance of Niconides of Thessaly, then under the walls, by their cracking and rattling soon demonstrated what would follow; after which an extraordinarily tempestuous south wind succeeding shattered, in a short space of time, all the rest of the works, and, by a violent concussion, threw down the wooden tower a hundred cibits high. It is said that in Ilium Minerva appeared to many that night in their sleep, with the sweat running down her person, and showed them her robe torn in one place, telling them that she had just arrived from relieving the Cyzicenians; and the inhabitants to this day show a monument, with an inscription, including a public decree, referring to the fact.

Mithridates, through the knavery of his officers, not knowing for some time the want of provision in his camp, was troubled in mind that the Cyzicenians should hold out against him. But his ambition and anger fell, when he saw his soldiers in the extremity of want, and feeding on men's flesh; as, in truth, Lucullus was not carrying on the war as mere matter of show and stage-play, but, according to the proverb, made the seat of war in the belly, and did everything to cut off their supplies of food. Mithridates, therefore, took advantage of the time while Lucullus was storming a fort, and sent away almost all his horse to Bithynia, with the sumpter cattle, and as many of the foot as were unfit for service.

On intelligence of which, Lucullus, while it was yet night, came to his camp, and in the morning, though it was stormy weather, took with him ten cohorts of foot, and the horse, and pursued them under falling snow and in cold so severe that many of his soldiers were unable to proceed; and with the rest coming upon the enemy, near the river Rhyndacus, he overthrew them with so great a slaughter that the very women of Apollonia came out to seize on the booty and strip the slain. Great numbers, as we may suppose, were slain; six thousand horses were taken, with an infinite number of beasts of burden, and no less than fifteen thousand men. All which he led along by the enemy's camp.

I cannot but wonder on this occasion at Sallust, who says that this was the first time camels were seen by the Romans, as if he thought those who, long before, under Scipio defeated Antiochus, or those who lately had fought against Archelaus near Orchomenus and Chæronea, had not known what a camel was.

Mithridates himself, fully determined upon flight, as mere delays and diversions for Lucullus, sent his admiral, Aristonicus, to the Greek sea; who, however, was betrayed in the very instant of going off, and Lucullus became master of him, and ten thousand pieces of gold which he was carrying with him to corrupt some of the Roman army. After which, Mith-

ridates himself made for the sea, leaving the foot officers to conduct the army, upon whom Lucullus fell, near the river Granicus, where he took a vast number alive, and slew twenty thousand. It is reported that the total number killed, of fighting men and of others who followed the camp, amounted to something not far short of three hundred thousand.

Lucullus first went to Cyzicus, where he was received with all the joy and gratitude suiting the occasion, and then collected a navy, visiting the shores of the Hellespont. And arriving at Troas, he lodged in the temple of Venus, where, in the night, he thought he saw the goddess coming to him, and saying—

Sleep'st thou, great lion, when the fawns are nigh?

Rising up hereupon, he called his friends to him, it being yet night, and told them his vision; at which instant some Ilians came up and acquainted him that thirteen of the king's quinqueremes were seen off the Achæan harbour, sailing for Lemnos. He at once put to sea, took these, and slew their admiral, Isidorus.

And then he made after another squadron, who were just come into port, and were hauling their vessels ashore, but fought from the decks, and sorely galled Lucullus's men; there being neither room to sail round them, nor to bear upon them for any damage, his ships being afloat, while theirs stood secure and fixed on the sand. After much ado, at the only landing-place of the island, he disembarked the choicest of his men, who, falling upon the enemy behind, killed some, and forced others to cut their cables, and thus making from the shore, they fell foul upon one another, or came within the reach of Lucullus's fleet. Many were killed in the action. Among the captives was Marius, the commander sent by Sertorius, who had but one eye. And it was Lucullus's strict command to his men before the engagement, that they should kill no man who had but one eye, that he might rather die under disgrace and reproach.

This being over, he hastened his pursuit after Mithridates, whom he hoped to find still in Bithynia, intercepted by Voconius, whom he sent out before to Nicomedia with part of the fleet to stop his flight. But Voconius, loitering in Samothrace to get initiated and celebrate a feast, let slip his opportunity, Mithridates being passed by with all his fleet. He, hastening into Pontus before Lucullus should come up to him, was caught in a storm, which dispersed his fleet and sank several ships. The wrecks floated on all the neighbouring shore for many days after. The merchant ship, in which he himself was, could not well in that heavy swell be brought ashore by the masters for its bigness, and it being heavy with water and ready to sink, he left it and went aboard a pirate vessel, delivering himself into the hands of pirates, and thus unexpectedly and wonderfully came safe to Heraclea, in Pontus.

Thus the proud language Lucullus had used to the senate ended without any mischance. For they having decreed him three thousand talents to furnish out a navy, he himself was against it, and sent them word that without any such great and costly supplies, by the confederate shipping alone, he did not in the least doubt but to rout Mithridates from the sea. And so he did, by divine assistance, for it is said that the wrath of Diana of Priapus brought the great tempest upon the men of Pontus, because they had robbed her temple and removed her image.

Many were persuading Lucullus to defer the war, but he rejected their counsel, and marched through Bithynia and Galatia into the king's country, in such great scarcity of provision at first, that thirty thousand Galatians followed, every man carrying a bushel of wheat on his back. But subduing all in his progress before him, he at last found himself in such great plenty that an ox was sold in the camp for a single drachma, and a slave for four. The other booty they made no account of, but left it behind or destroyed it; there being no disposing of it, where all had such abundance.

But when they had made frequent incursions with their cavalry, and had advanced as far as Themiscyra, and the plains of the Thermodon, merely laying waste the country before them, they began to find fault with Lucullus, asking why he took so many towns by surrender, and never one by storm, which might enrich them with the plunder; and now, forsooth, leaving Amisus behind, a rich and wealthy city of easy conquest if closely besieged, he would carry them into the Tibarenian and Chaldean wilderness to fight with Mithridates.

Lucullus, little thinking this would be of such dangerous consequence as it afterwards proved, took no notice and slighted it; and was rather anxious to excuse himself to those who blamed his tardiness, in losing time about small, pitiful places not worth the while, and allowing Mithridates opportunity to recruit.

"That is what I design," said he, "and sit here contriving by my delay, that he may grow great again, and gather a considerable army, which may induce him to stand, and not fly away before us. For do you not see the wide and unknown wilderness behind? Caucasus is not far off, and a multitude of vast mountains, enough to conceal ten thousand kings that wished to avoid a battle. Besides this, a journey but of few days leads from Cabira to Armenia, where Tigranes reigns, king of kings, and holds in his hands a power that has enabled him to keep the Parthians in narrow bounds, to remove Greek cities bodily into Media, to conquer Syria and Palestine, to put to death the kings of the royal line of Seleucus, and carry away their wives and daughters by violence. This same is relation and son-in-law to Mithridates, and cannot but receive him upon entreaty, and enter into war with us to defend him; so that, while we endeavour to dispose Mithridates, we shall endanger the bringing in of Tigranes against us, who already has sought occasion to fall out with us, but can never find one so justifiable as the succour of a friend and prince in his necessity. Why, therefore, should we put Mithridates upon this resource, who as yet does not see how he may best fight with us, and disdains to stoop to Tigranes, and not rather allow him time to gather a new army and grow confident again, that we may thus fight with Colchians and Tibarenians, whom we have often defeated already, and not with Medes and Armenians?"

Upon these motives, Lucullus sat down before Amisus, and slowly carried on the siege. But the winter being well spent, he left Murena in charge of it, and went himself against Mithridates, then rendezvousing at Cabira, and resolving to await the Romans, with forty thousand foot about him, and fourteen thousand horse, on whom he chiefly confided. Passing the river Lycus, he challenged the Romans into the plains, where the cavalry engaged, and the Romans were beaten.

Pomponius, a man of some note, was taken wounded; and sore, and in pain as he was, was carried before Mithridates, and asked by the king if he would become his friend, if he saved his life. He answered, "Yes, if you become reconciled to the Romans; if not, your enemy." Mithridates wondered at him, and did him no hurt.

The enemy being with their cavalry master of the plains, Lucullus was something afraid, and hesitated to enter the mountains, being very large, woody, and almost inaccessible, when, by good luck, some Greeks who had fled into a cave were taken, the eldest of whom, Artemidorus by name, promised to bring Lucullus, and seat him in a place of safety for his army, where there was a fort that overlooked Cabira. Lucullus, believing him, lighted his fires, and marched in the night; and safely passing the defile, gained the place, and in the morning was seen above the enemy, pitching his camp in a place advantageous to descend upon them if he desired to fight, and secure from being forced if he preferred to lie still.

Neither side was willing to engage at present. But it is related that some of the king's party were hunting a stag, and some Romans wanting to cut them off, came out and met them. Whereupon they skirmished, more still drawing together to each side, and at last the king's party prevailed, on which the Romans, from their camp seeing their companions fly, were enraged, and ran to Lucullus with entreaties to lead them out, demanding that the sign might be given for battle. But he, that they might know of what consequence the presence and appearance of a wise commander is in time of conflict and danger, ordered them to stand still.

But he went down himself into the plains, and meeting with the foremost that fled, commanded them to stand and turn back with him. These obeying, the rest also turned and formed again in a body, and thus, with no great difficulty, drove back the enemies, and pursued them to their camp. After his return, Lucullus inflicted the customary punishment upon the fugitives, and made them dig a trench of twelve foot, working in their frocks unfastened, while the rest stood by and looked on.

There was in Mithridates's camp one Olthacus, a chief of the Dandarians, a barbarous people living near the lake Mæotis, a man remarkable for strength and courage in fight, wise in council, and pleasant and ingratiating in conversation. He, out of emulation, and a constant eagerness which possessed him to outdo one of the other chiefs of his country, promised a great piece of service to Mithridates, no less than the death of Lucullus. The king commended his resolution, and, according to agreement, counterfeited anger, and put some disgrace upon him; whereupon he took horse, and fled to Lucullus, who kindly received him, being a man of great name in the army.

After some short trial of his sagacity and perseverance, he found way to Lucullus's board and council. The Dandarian, thinking he had a fair opportunity, commanded his servants to lead his horse out of the camp, while he himself, as the soldiers were refreshing and resting themselves, it being then high noon, went to the general's tent, not at all expecting that entrance would be denied to one who was so familiar with him, and came under pretence of extraordinary business with him.

He had certainly been admitted had not sleep, which has destroyed many captains, saved Lucullus. For so it was, and Menedemus, one of the bedchamber, was standing at the door, who told Olthacus that it was altogether unseasonable to see the general, since, after long watching and hard labour, he was but just before laid down to repose himself. Olthacus would not go away upon this denial, but still persisted, saying that he must go in to speak of some necessary affairs, whereupon Menedemus grew angry, and replied that nothing was more necessary than the safety of Lucullus, and forced him away with both hands. Upon which, out of fear, he straightway left the camp, took horse, and without effect returned to Mithridates. Thus in action as in physic, it is the critical moment that gives both the fortunate and the fatal effect.

After this, Sornatius being sent out with ten companies for forage, and pursued by Menander, one of Mithridates's captains, stood his ground, and after a sharp engagement, routed and slew a considerable number of the enemy. Adrianus being sent afterward, with some forces, to procure food enough and to spare for the camp, Mithridates did not let the opportunity slip, but despatched Menemachus and Myro, with a great force, both horse and foot, against him, all which except two men, it is stated, were cut off by the Romans.

Mithridates concealed the loss, giving it out that it was a small defeat, nothing near so great as reported, and occasioned by the unskilfulness of the leaders. But Adrianus in great pomp passed by his camp, having many waggons full of corn and other booty, filling Mithridates with distress, and the army with confusion and consternation.

It was resolved, therefore, to stay no longer. But when the king's servants sent away their own goods quietly, and hindered others from doing so too, the soldiers in great fury thronged and crowded to the gates, seized on the king's servants and killed them, and plundered the baggage. Dorylaus, the general, in this confusion, having nothing else besides his purple cloak, lost his life for that, and Hermæus, the priest, was trod underfoot in the gate.

Mithridates, having not one of his guards, nor even a groom remaining with him, got out of the camp in the throng, but had none of his horses with him; until Ptolemy, the eunuch, some little time after, seeing him in the press making his way among the others, dismounted and gave his horse to the king. The Romans were already close upon him in their pursuit, nor was it through want of speed that they failed to catch him, but they were as near as possible doing so.

But greediness and a petty military avarice hindered them from acquiring that booty which in so many fights and hazards they had sought after, and lost Lucullus the prize of his victory. For the horse which carried the king was within reach, but one of the mules that carried the treasure either by accident stepping in, or by order of the king so appointed to go between him and the pursuers, they seized and pilfered the gold; and falling out among themselves about the prey, let slip the great prize. Neither was their greediness prejudicial to Lucullus in this only, but also they slew Callistratus, the king's confidential attendant, under suspicion of having five hundred pieces of gold in his girdle; whereas Lucullus had specially ordered that he should be conveyed safe into the camp. Notwithstanding all which, he gave them leave to plunder the camp.

After this, in Cabira, and other strongholds which he took, he found great treasures, and private prisons, in which many Greeks and many of the king's relations had been confined, who, having long since counted themselves no other than dead men, by the favour of Lucullus met not with relief so truly as with a new life and second birth.

Nyssa, also, sister of Mithridates, enjoyed the like fortunate captivity; while those who seemed to be most out of danger, his wives and sisters at Phernacia, placed in safety as they thought, miserably perished, Mithridates in his flight sending Bacchides, the eunuch, to them. Among others there were two sisters of the king, Roxana and Statira, unmarried women forty years old, and two Ionian wives, Berenice of Chios and Monime of Miletus.

This latter was the most celebrated among the Greeks, because she so long withstood the king in his courtship to her, though he presented her with fifteen thousand pieces of gold, until a covenant of marriage was made, and a

crown was sent her, and she was saluted queen. She had been a sorrowful woman before, and often bewailed her beauty, that had procured her a keeper, instead of a husband, and a watch of barbarians, instead of the home and attendance of a wife; and, removed far from Greece, she enjoyed the pleasure which she proposed to herself only in a dream, being in the meantime robbed of that which is real. And when Bacchides came and bade them prepare for death, as every one thought most easy and painless, she took the diadem from her head, and fastening the string to her neck, suspended herself with it; which soon breaking, "O wretched headband!" said she, "not able to help me even in this small thing!" And throwing it away she spat on it, and offered her throat to Bacchides.

Berenice had prepared a potion for herself, but at her mother's entreaty, who stood by, she gave her part of it. Both drank of the potion, which prevailed over the weaker body. But Berenice, having drunk too little, was not released by it, but lingering on unable to die, was strangled by Bacchides for haste.

It is said that one of the unmarried sisters drank the poison, with bitter execrations and curses; but Statira uttered nothing ungentle or reproachful, but, on the contrary, commended her brother, who in his own danger neglected not theirs, but carefully provided that they might go out of the world without shame or disgrace.

Lucullus, being a good and humane man, was concerned at these things. However, going on, he came to Talaura, from whence four days before his arrival Mithridates had fled, and was got to Tigranes in Armenia. He turned off, therefore, and subdued the Chaldeans and Tibarenians, with the lesser Armenia, and having reduced all their forts and cities, he sent Appius to Tigranes to demand Mithridates.

He himself went to Amisus, which still held out under the command of Callimachus, who, by his great engineering skill, and his dexterity at all the shifts and subtleties of a siege, had greatly incommoded the Romans. For which afterward he paid dear enough, and was now outmanœuvred by Lucullus, who, unexpectedly coming upon him at the time of the day when the soldiers used to withdraw and rest themselves, gained part of the wall, and forced him to leave the city, in doing which he fired it; either envying the Romans the booty, or to secure his own escape the better.

No man looked after those who went off in

the ships, but as soon as the fire had seized on most part of the wall, the soldiers prepared themselves for plunder; while Lucullus, pitying the ruin of the city, brought assistance from without, and encouraged his men to extinguish the flames. But all, being intent upon the prey, and giving no heed to him, with loud outcries, beat and clashed their arms together, until he was compelled to let them plunder, that by that means he might at least save the city from fire.

But they did quite the contrary, for in searching the houses with lights and torches everywhere, they were themselves the cause of the destruction of most of the buildings, inasmuch that when Lucullus the next day went in, he shed tears, and said to his friends that he had often before blessed the fortune of Sulla, but never so much admired it as then, because when he was willing he was also able to save Athens, "but my infelicity is such, that while I endeavour to imitate him, I become like Mummius." Nevertheless, he endeavoured to save as much of the city as he could, and at the same time, also, by a happy providence a fall of rain concurred to extinguish the fire. He himself while present repaired the ruins as much as he could, receiving back the inhabitants who had fled, and settling as many other Greeks as were willing to live there, adding a hundred furlongs of ground to the place.

This city was a colony of Athens, built at that time when she flourished and was powerful at sea, upon which account many who fled from Aristion's tyranny settled here, and were admitted as citizens, but had the ill-luck to fly from evils at home into greater abroad. As many of these as survived Lucullus furnished every one with clothes, and two hundred drachmas, and sent them away into their own country.

On this occasion Tyrannion, the grammarian, was taken. Murena begged him of Lucullus, and took him and made him a freedman; but in this he abused Lucullus's favor, who by no means liked that a man of high repute for learning should be first made a slave and then freed; for freedom thus speciously granted again was a real deprivation of what he had before. But not in this case alone Murena showed himself far inferior in generosity to the general.

Lucullus was now busy in looking after the cities of Asia, and having no war to divert his time, spent it in the administration of law and justice, the want of which had for a long time left the province a prey to unspeakable and incredible miseries; so plundered and enslaved by tax-farmers and usurers that private people were compelled to sell their sons in the flower of their youth, and their daughters in their virginity, and the states publicly to sell their consecrated gifts, pictures, and statutes. In the end their lot was to yield themselves up slaves to their creditors, but before this worse troubles befell them, tortures, inflicted with ropes and by horses, standing abroad to be scorched when the sun was hot, and being driven into ice and clay in the cold; insomuch that slavery was no less than redemption and joy to them.

Lucullus in a short time freed the cities from all these evils and oppressions; for, first of all, he ordered there should be no more taken than one per cent. Secondly, where the interest exceeded the principal, he struck it off. The third and most considerable order was, that the creditor should receive the fourth part of the debtor's income; but if any lender had added the interest to the principal, it was utterly disallowed. Insomuch, that in the space of four years all debts were paid and lands returned to their right owners.

The public debt was contracted when Asia was fined twenty thousand talents by Sulla, but twice as much was paid to the collectors, who by their usury had by this time advanced it to a hundred and twenty thousand talents. And accordingly they inveighed against Lucullus at Rome, as grossly injured by him, and by their money's help (as, indeed, they were very powerful, and had many of the statesmen in their debt), they stirred up several leading senators against him. But Lucullus was not only beloved by the cities which he obliged, but was also wished for by other provinces, who blessed the good-luck of those who had such a governor over them.

Appius Clodius, who was sent to Tigranes (the same Clodius was brother to Lucullus's wife), being led by the king's guides a roundabout way, unnecessarily long and tedious, through the upper country, being informed by his freedman, a Syrian by nation, of the direct road, left that lengthy and fallacious one; and bidding the barbarians, his guides, adieu, in a few days passed over Euphrates, and came to Antioch upon Daphne.

There being commanded to wait for Tigranes, who at that time was reducing some towns in Phœnicia, he won over many chiefs to his side, who unwillingly submitted to the King of Armenia, among whom was Zarbienus, King of the Gordyenians; also many of the conquered cities corresponded privately with him, whom he assured of relief from Lucullus, but ordered them to lie still at present.

The Armenian government was an oppressive one, and intolerable to the Greeks, especially that of the present king, who, growing insolent and overbearing with his success, imagined all things valuable and esteemed among men not only were his in fact, but had been purposely created for him alone. From a small and inconsiderable beginning, he had gone on to be the conqueror of many nations, had humbled the Parthian power more than any before him, and filled Mesopotamia with Greeks, whom he carried in numbers out of Cilicia and Cappadocia. He transplanted also the Arabs, who lived in tents, from their country and home, and settled them near him, that by their means he might carry on the trade.

He had many kings waiting on him, but four he always carried with him as servants and guards, who, when he rode, ran by his horse's side in ordinary under-frocks, and attended him, when sitting on his throne, and publishing his decrees to the people, with their hands folded together; which posture of all others was that which most expressed slavery, it being that of men who had bidden adieu to liberty, and had prepared their bodies more for chastisement than the service of their masters.

Appius, nothing dismayed or surprised at this theatrical display, as soon as audience was granted him, said he came to demand Mithridates for Lucullus's triumph, otherwise to denounce war against Tigranes: insomuch that though Tigranes endeavoured to receive him with a smooth countenance and a forced smile, he could not dissemble his discomposure to those who stood about him at the bold language of the young man; for it was the first time, perhaps in twenty-five years, the length of his reign, or, more truly, of his tyranny, that any free speech had been uttered to him.

However, he made answer to Appius, that he would not desert Mithridates, and would defend himself, if the Romans attacked him. He was angry, also, with Lucullus for calling him only King in his letter, and not King of Kings, and, in his answer, would not give him his title of Imperator. Great gifts were sent to Appius, which he refused; but on their being sent again, and augmented, that he might not seem to refuse in anger, he took one goblet and sent the rest back, and without delay went off to the general.

Tigranes before this neither vouchsafed to see nor speak with Mithridates, though a near kinsman, and forced out of so considerable a kingdom, but proudly and scornfully kept him at a distance, as a sort of prisoner, in a marshy and unhealthy district; but now, with much profession of respect and kindness, he sent for him, and at a private conference between them in the palace, they healed up all private jealousies between them, punishing their favourites, who bore all the blame; among whom Metrodorus of Scepsis was one, an eloquent and learned man, and so close an intimate as commonly to be called the king's father.

This man, as it happened, being employed in an embassy by Mithridates to solicit help against the Romans, Tigranes asked him, "What would you, Metrodorus, advise me to in this affair?" In return to which, either out of good-will to Tigranes, or a want of solicitude for Mithridates, he made answer, that as ambassador he counselled him to it, but as a friend dissuaded him from it. This Tigranes reported and affirmed to Mithridates, thinking that no irreparable harm would come of it to Metrodorus. But upon this he was presently taken off, and Tigranes was sorry for what he had done, though he had not, indeed, been absolutely the cause of his death; yet he had given the fatal turn to the anger of Mithridates, who had privately hated him before, as appeared from his cabinet papers when taken, among which there was an order that Metrodorus should die. Tigranes buried him splendidly, sparing no cost to his dead body, whom he betrayed when alive.

In Tigranes's court died, also, Amphicrates, the orator, (if, for the sake of Athens, we may also mention him), of whom it is told that he left his country and fled to Seleucia, upon the river Tigris, and, being desired to teach logic among them, arrogantly replied, that the dish was too little to hold a dolphin. He, therefore, came to Cleopatra, daughter of Mithridates, and queen to Tigranes, but, being accused of misdemeanours, prohibited all commerce with his countrymen, ended his days by starving himself. He, in like manner, received from Cleopatra an honourable burial, near Sapha, a place so called in that country.

Lucullus, when he had re-established law and a lasting peace in Asia, did not altogether forget pleasure and mirth, but, during his residence at Ephesus, gratified the cities with sports, festival triumphs, wrestling games, and single combats of gladiators. And they, in requital, instituted others, called Lucullean games, in honour to him, thus manifesting their love to him, which was of more value to him than all the honour.

But when Appius came to him and told him he must prepare for war with Tigranes, he went again into Pontus, and, gathering together his army, besieged Sinope, or rather the Cilicians of the king's side who held it; who thereupon killed a number of the Sinopians, and set the city on fire, and by night endeavoured to escape. Which when Lucullus perceived, he entered the city, and killed eight thousand of them who were still left behind; but restored to the inhabitants what was their own, and took special care for the welfare of the city.

To which he was chiefly prompted by this vision. One seemed to come to him in his sleep, and say, "Go on a little further, Lucullus, for Autolycus is coming to see thee." When he arose he could not imagine what the vision meant. The same day he took the city, and as he was pursuing the Cilicians, who were flying by sea, he saw a statue lying on the shore, which the Cilicians carried so far, but had not time to carry aboard. It was one of the masterpieces of Sthenis. And one told him that it was the statue of Autolycus, the founder of the city.

This Autolycus is reported to have been son to Deimachus, and one of those who, under Hercules, went on the expedition out of Thessaly against the Amazons; from whence in his return with Demoleon and Phlogius, he lost his vessel on a point of the Chersonesus, called Pedalium. He himself, with his companions and their weapons, being saved, came to Sinope, and dispossessed the Syrians there. The Syrians who held it were descended from Syrus, as is the story, the son of Apollo and Sinope, the daughter of Asopus. Which as soon as Lucullus heard, he remembered the admonition of Sulla, whose advice it is in his Memoirs to treat nothing as so certain and so worthy of reliance as an intimation given in dreams.

When it was now told him that Mithridates and Tigranes were just ready to transport their forces into Lycaonia and Cilicia, with the object of entering Asia before him, he wondered much why the Armenian, supposing him to entertain any real intentions to fight with the Romans, did not assist Mithridates in his flourishing condition, and join forces when he was fit for service, instead of suffering him to be vanquished and broken in pieces, and now at last beginning the war, when its hopes were grown cold, and throwing himself down headlong with them, who were irrevocably fallen already. But when Machares, the son of Mithridates, and governor of Bosporus, sent him a crown, valued at a thousand pieces of gold, and desired to be enrolled as a friend and confederate of the Romans, he fairly reputed that war at an end, and left Sornatius, his deputy, with six thousand soldiers, to take care of Pontus.

He himself, with twelve thousand foot and a little less than three thousand horse, went forth to the second war, advancing, it seemed very plain, with too great and ill-advised speed, into the midst of warlike nations and many thousands upon thousands of horse, into an unknown extent of country, every way inclosed with deep rivers and mountains, never free from snow; which made the soldiers, already far from orderly, follow him with great unwillingness and opposition. For the same reason, also, the popular leaders at home publicly inveighed and declaimed against him, as one that raised up war after war, not so much for the interest of the republic, as that he himself, being still in commission, might not lay down arms, but go on enriching himself by the public dangers. These men, in the end, effected their purpose.

But Lucullus, by long journeys, came to the Euphrates, where, finding the waters high and rough from the winter, he was much troubled for fear of delay and difficulty while he should procure boats and make a bridge of them. But in the evening the flood beginning to retire, and decreasing all through the night, the next day they saw the river far down within his banks, so much so that the inhabitants, discovering the little islands in the river, and the water stagnating among them, a thing which had rarely happened before, made obeisance to Lucullus, before whom the very river was humble and submissive, and yielded an easy and swift passage.

Making use of the opportunity, he carried over his army, and met with a lucky sign at landing. Holy heifers are pastured on purpose for Diana Persia, whom, of all the gods, the barbarians beyond Euphrates chiefly adore. They use these heifers only for her sacrifices. At other times they wander up and down undisturbed, with the mark of the goddess, a torch, branded on them; and it is no such light or easy thing, when occasion requires, to seize one of them. But one of these, when the army had passed the Euphrates, coming to a rock consecrated to the goddess, stood upon it, and then, laying down her neck, like others that are forced down with a rope, offered herself to Lucullus for sacrifice. Besides which, he offered also a bull to Euphrates, for his safe passage.

That day he tarried there, but on the next, and those that followed, he travelled through Sophene, using no manner of violence to the people who came to him and willingly received his army. And when the soldiers were desirous to plunder a castle that seemed to be well stored within, "That is the castle," said he, "that we must storm," showing them Taurus at a distance; "the rest is reserved for those who conquer there." Wherefore hastening his march, and passing the Tigris, he came over into Armenia.

The first messenger that gave notice of Lucullus's coming was so far from pleasing Tigranes that he had his head cut off for his pains; and no man daring to bring further information, without any intelligence at all, Tigranes sat while war was already blazing around him, giving ear only to those who flattered him, by saying that Lucullus would show himself a great commander if he ventured to wait for Tigranes at Ephesus, and did not at once fly out of Asia at the mere sight of the many thousands that were come against him. He is a man of a strong body that can carry off a great quantity of wine, and of a powerful constitution of mind that can sustain felicity.

Mithrobarzanes, one of his chief favourites, first dared to tell him the truth, but had no more thanks for his freedom of speech than to be immediately sent out against Lucullus with three thousand horse, and a great number of foot, with peremptory demands to bring him alive and trample down his army. Some of Lucullus's men were then pitching their camp, and the rest were coming up to them, when the scouts gave notice that the enemy was approaching, whereupon he was in fear lest they should fall upon him, while his men were divided and unarranged; which made him stay to pitch the camp himself, and send out Sextilius, the legate, with sixteen hundred horse, and about as many heavy and light arms, with orders to advance towards the enemy, and wait until intelligence came to him that the camp was finished. Sextilius designed to have kept this order; but Mithrobarzanes coming furiously upon him, he was forced to fight. In the engagement, Mithrobarzanes himself was slain, fighting, and all his men, except a few who ran away, were destroyed. After this, Tigranes left Tigranocerta, a great city built by himself, and

retired to Taurus, and called all his forces about him.

But Lucullus, giving him no time to rendezvous, sent out Murena to harass and cut off those who marched to Tigranes, and Sextilius, also, to disperse a great company of Arabians then on the way to the king. Sextilius fell upon the Arabians in their camp, and destroyed most of them, and also Murena, in his pursuit after Tigranes through a craggy and narrow pass, opportunely fell upon him. Upon which Tigranes, abandoning all his baggage, fled; many of the Armenians were killed and more taken.

After this success, Lucullus went to Tigranocerta, and sitting down before the city, besieged it. In it were many Greeks carried away out of Cilicia, and many barbarians in like circumstances with the Greeks, Adiabenians, Assyrians, Gordyenians, and Cappadocians, whose native cities he had destroyed, and forced away the inhabitants to settle here. It was a rich and beautiful city; every common man, and every man of rank, in imitation of the king, studied to enlarge and adorn it. This made Lucullus more vigorously press the siege, in the belief that Tigranes would not patiently endure it, but even against his own judgment would come down in anger to force him away; in which he was not mistaken.

Mithridates earnestly dissuaded him from it, sending messengers and letters to him not to engage, but rather with his horse to try and cut off the supplies. Taxiles, also, who came from Mithridates, and who stayed with his army, very much entreated the king to forbear, and to avoid the Roman arms, things it was not safe to meddle with.

To this he hearkened at first, but when the Armenians and Gordyenians in a full body, and the whole forces of Medes and Adiabenians, under their respective kings, joined him; when many Arabians came up from the sea beyond Babylon; and from the Caspian sea, the Albanians and the Iberians, their neighbours, and not a few of the free people, without kings, living about the Araxes, by entreaty and hire also came together to him; and all the king's feasts and councils rang of nothing but expectations, boastings, and barbaric threatenings, Taxiles went in danger of his life for giving council against fighting, and it was imputed to envy in Mithridates thus to discourage him from so glorious an enterprise. Therefore, Tigranes would by no means tarry for him, for fear he should share in the glory, but marched on with all his army, lamenting to his friends, as it is said, that he should fight with Lucullus alone and not with all the Roman generals together.

Neither was his boldness to be accounted wholly frantic or unreasonable, when he had so many nations and kings attending him, and so many tens of thousands of well-armed foot and horse about him. He had twenty thousand archers and slingers, fifty-five thousand horse, of which seventeen thousand were in complete armour, as Lucullus wrote to the senate, a hundred and fifty thousand heavy-armed men, drawn up partly into cohorts, partly into phalanxes, besides various divisions of men appointed to make roads and lay bridges, to drain off waters and cut wood, and to perform other necessary services, to the number of thirty-five thousand, who, being quartered behind the army, added to its strength, and made it the more formidable to behold.

As soon as he had passed Taurus, and appeared with his forces, and saw the Romans beleaguering Tigranocerta, the barbarous people within, with shoutings and acclamations, received the sight, and threatening the Romans from the wall, pointed to the Armenians.

In a council of war, some advised Lucullus to leave the siege, and march up to Tigranes, others that it would not be safe to leave the siege, and so many enemies behind. He answered that neither side by itself was right, but together both gave sound advice; and accordingly he divided his army, and left Murena with six thousand foot in charge of the siege, and himself went out with twenty-four cohorts, in which were no more than ten thousand men-at-arms, and with all the horse and slingers and archers and about a thousand sitting down by the river in a large plain, he appeared, indeed, very inconsiderable to Tigranes, and a fit subject for the flattering wits about him. Some of whom jeered, others cast lots for the spoil, and every one of the kings and commanders came and desired to undertake the engagement alone, and that he would be pleased to sit still and behold. Tigranes himself, wishing to be witty and pleasant upon the occasion, made use of the well-known saying, that they were too many for ambassadors, and too few for soldiers. Thus they continued sneering and scoffing.

As soon as day came, Lucullus brought out his forces under arms. The barbarian army stood on the eastern side of the river, and there being a bend of the river westward in that part of it, where it was easiest forded, Lucullus,

while he led his army on in haste, seemed to Tigranes to be flying; who thereupon called Taxiles, and in derision said, "Do you not see these invincible Romans flying?" But Taxiles replied, "Would, indeed, O king, that some such unlikely piece of fortune might be destined you; but the Romans do not, when going on a march, put on their best clothes, nor use bright shields, and naked headpieces, as now you see them, with the leathern coverings all taken off, but this is a preparation for war of men just ready to engage with their enemies."

While Taxiles was thus speaking, as Lucullus wheeled about, the first eagle appeared, and the cohorts, according to their divisions and companies, formed in order to pass over, when with much ado, and like a man that is just recovering from a drunken fit, Tigranes cried out twice or thrice, "What, are they upon us?" In great confusion, therefore, the army got in array, the king keeping the main body to himself, while the left wing given in charge to the Adiabenian, and the right to the Mede, in front of which latter were posted most of the heavy-armed cavalry. Some officers advised Lucullus, just as he was going to cross the river, to lie still, that day being one of the unfortunate ones which they call black days, for on it the army under Cæpio, engaging with the Cimbrians, was destroyed. But he returned the famous answer, "I will make it a happy day to the Romans." It was the day before the Nones of October.

Having so said, he bade them take courage, passed over the river, and himself first of all led them against the enemy, clad in a coat of mail, with shining steel scales and a fringed mantle; and his sword might already be seen out of the scabbard, as if to signify that they must without delay come to a hand-to-hand combat with an enemy whose skill was in distant fighting, and by the speed of their advance curtail the space that exposed them to the archery.

But when he saw the heavy-armed horse, the flower of the army, drawn up under a hill, on the top of which was a broad and open plain about four furlongs distant, and of no very difficult or troublesome access, he commanded his Thracian and Galatian horse to fall upon their flank, and beat down their lances with their swords. The only defence of these horsemen-at-arms are their lances; they have nothing else that they can use to protect themselves or annoy their enemy, on account of the weight and stiffness of their armour, with which they are, as it were, built up.

He himself, with two cohorts, made to the mountain, the soldiers briskly following, when they saw him in arms afoot first toiling and climbing up. Being on the top and standing in an open place, with a loud voice he cried out, "We have overcome, we have overcome, fellow-soldiers!" And having so said, he marched against the armed horsemen, commanding his men not to throw their javelins, but coming up hand to hand with the enemy, to hack their shins and thighs, which parts alone were unguarded in these heavy-armed horsemen.

But there was no need of this way of fighting, for they stood not to receive the Romans, but with great clamour and worse flight they and their heavy horses threw themselves upon the ranks of the foot, before ever these could so much as begin to fight, insomuch that without a wound or bloodshed, so many thousands were overthrown. The greatest slaughter was made in the flight, or rather in the endeavouring to fly away, which they could not well do by reason of the depth and closeness of their own ranks, which hindered them.

Tigranes at first fled with a few, but seeing his son in the same misfortune, he took the diadem from his head, and with tears gave it him, bidding him save himself by some other road if he could. But the young man, not daring to put it on, gave it to one of his trustiest servants to keep for him. This man, as it happened, being taken, was brought to Lucullus, and so, among the captives, the crown of Tigranes was also taken.

It is stated that above a hundred thousand foot were lost, and that of the horse but very few escaped at all. Of the Romans, a hundred were wounded and five killed.

Antiochus, the philosopher, making mention of this fight in his book about the gods, says that the sun never saw the like. Strabo, a second philosopher, in his historical collection, says that the Romans could not but blush and deride themselves for putting on armour against such pitiful slaves. Livy also says that the Romans never fought an enemy with such unequal forces, for the conquerors were not so much as one-twentieth part of the number of the conquered.

The most sagacious and experienced Roman commanders made it a chief commendation of Lucullus that he had conquered two great and potent kings by two most opposite ways, haste and delay. For he wore out the flourishing power of Mithridates by delay and time, and crushed that of Tigranes by haste; being one of the rare examples of generals who made use of delay for active achievement and speed for security.

On this account it was that Mithridates had made no haste to come up to fight, imagining Lucullus would, as he had done before, use caution and delay, which made him march at his leisure to join Tigranes. And first, as he began to meet some straggling Armenians in the way, making off in great fear and consternation, he suspected the worst, and when greater numbers of stripped and wounded men met him and assured him of the defeat, he set out to seek for Tigranes. And finding him destitute and humiliated, he by no means requited him with insolence, but alighting from his horse, and condoling with him on their common loss, he gave him his own royal guard to attend him, and animated him for the future. And they together gathered fresh forces about them.

In the city Tigranocerta, the Greeks meantime, dividing from the barbarians, sought to deliver it up to Lucullus, and he attacked and took it. He seized on the treasure himself, but gave the city to be plundered by the soldiers, in which were found, amongst other property, eight thousand talents of coined money. Besides this, also, he distributed eight hundred drachmas to each man out of the spoils. When he understood that many players were taken in the city, whom Tigranes had invited from all parts for opening the theatre which he had built, he made use of them for celebrating his triumphal games and spectacles. The Greeks he sent home, allowing them money for their journey, and the barbarians also, as many as had been forced away from their own dwellings. So that by this one city being dissolved, many, by the restitution of their former inhabitants, were restored. By all of which Lucullus was beloved as a benefactor and founder.

Other successes, also, attended him, such as he well deserved, desirous as he was far more of praise for acts of justice and clemency, than for feats in war, these being due partly to the soldiers, and very greatly to fortune, while those are the sure proofs of a gentle and liberal soul; and by such aids Lucullus, at that time, even without the help of arms, succeeded in reducing the barbarians. For the kings of the Arabians came to him, tendering what they had, and with them the Sophenians also submitted. And he so dealt with the Gordyenians, that they were willing to leave their own habitations, and to follow him with their wives and children.

Which was for this cause. Zarbienus, King of the Gordyenians, as has been told, being impatient under the tyranny of Tigranes, had by Appius secretly made overtures of confederacy with Lucullus, but, being discovered, was executed, and his wife and children with him, before the Romans entered Armenia. Lucullus forgot not this, but coming to the Gordyenians made a solemn interment in honour of Zarbienus, and adorning the funeral pile with royal robes, and gold, and the spoils of Tigranes, he himself in person kindled the fire, and poured in perfumes with the friends and relations of the deceased, calling him his companion and the confederate of the Romans. He ordered, also, a costly monument to be built for him. There was a large treasure of gold and silver found in Zarbienus's palace, and no less than three million measures of corn, so that the soldiers were provided for, and Lucullus had the high commendation of maintaining the war at its own charge, without receiving one drachma from the public treasury.

After this came an embassy from the King of Parthia to him, desiring amity and confederacy; which being readily embraced by Lucullus, another was sent by him in return to the Parthian, the members of which discovered him to be a double-minded man, and to be dealing privately at the same time with Tigranes, offering to take part with him, upon condition Mesopotamia were delivered up to him. Which as soon as Lucullus understood, he resolved to pass by Tigranes and Mithridates as antagonists already overcome, and to try the power of Parthia, by leading his army against them, thinking it would be a glorious result, thus in one current of war, like an athlete in the games, to throw down three kings one after another, and successively to deal as a conqueror with three of the greatest powers under heaven.

He sent, therefore, into Pontus to Sornatius and his colleagues, bidding them bring the army thence, and join with him in his expedition out of Gordyene. The soldiers there, however, who had been restive and unruly before, now openly displayed their mutinous temper. No manner of entreaty or force availed with them, but they protested and cried out that they would stay no longer even there, but would go away and desert Pontus. The news of which, when reported to Lucullus, did no small harm to the soldiers about him, who were already corrupted with wealth and plenty, and desirous of ease. And on hearing the boldness of the others, they called them men, and declared they themselves ought to follow their example, for the actions which they had done did now well deserve release from service and repose.

Upon these and worse words, Lucullus gave up the thoughts of invading Parthia, and in the height of summer-time went against Tigranes. Passing over Taurus, he was filled with apprehension at the greenness of the fields before him, so long is the season deferred in this region by the coldness of the air. But nevertheless, he went down, and twice or thrice putting to flight the Armenians who dared to come out against him, he plundered and burnt their villages, and seizing on the provision designed for Tigranes, reduced his enemies to the necessity which he had feared for himself.

But when, after doing all he could to provoke the enemy to fight, by drawing entrenchments round their camp and by burning the country before them, he could by no means bring them to venture out, after their frequent defeats before, he rose up and marched to Artaxata, the royal city of Tigranes, where his wives and young children were kept, judging that Tigranes would never suffer that to go without the hazard of a battle. It is related that Hannibal the Carthaginian, after the defeat of Antiochus by the Romans, coming to Artaxas, King of Armenia, pointed out to him many other matters to his advantage, and observing the great natural capacities and the pleasantness of the site, then lying unoccupied and neglected, drew a model of a city for it, and bringing Artaxas thither, showed it to him and encouraged him to build. At which the king being pleased, and desiring him to oversee the work, erected a large and stately city which was called after his own name, and made metropolis of Armenia.

And in fact, when Lucullus proceeded against it, Tigranes no longer suffered it but came with his army, and on the fourth day sat down by the Romans, the river Arsanias lying between them, which of necessity Lucullus must pass in his march to Artaxata. Lucullus, after sacrifice to the gods, as if victory were already obtained, carried over his army, having twelve cohorts in the first division in front, the rest being disposed in the rear to prevent the enemy's inclosing them. For there were many choice horse drawn up against him; in the front stood the Mardian horse-archers, and Iberians with long spears, in whom, being the most warlike, Tigranes more confided than in any other of his foreign troops. But nothing of moment was done by them, for though they skirmished with the Roman horse at a distance, they were not able to stand when the foot came up to them; but being broken, and flying on both sides, drew the horse in pursuit after them.

Though these were routed, yet Lucullus was not without alarm when he saw the cavalry about Tigranes with great bravery and in large numbers coming upon him; he recalled his horse from pursuing, and he himself, first of all, with the best of his men, engaged the Satrapenians who were opposite him, and before ever they came to close fight routed them with the mere terror. Of three kings in battle against him, Mithridates of Pontus fled away the most shamefully, being not so much as able to endure the shout of the Romans. The pursuit reached a long way, and all through the night the Romans slew and took prisoners, and carried off spoils and treasure, till they were weary. Livy says there were more taken and destroyed in the first battle, but in the second, men of greater distinction.

Lucullus, flushed and animated by this victory, determined to march on into the interior and there complete his conquests over the barbarians, but winter weather came on, contrary to expectation, as early as the autumnal equinox, with storms and frequent snows, and, even in the most clear days, hoar frost and ice, which made the waters scarcely drinkable for the horses by their exceeding coldness, and scarcely passable through the ice breaking and cutting the horses' sinews. The country for the most part being quite uncleared, with difficult passes, and much wood, kept them continually wet, the snow falling thickly on them as they marched in the day, and the ground that they lay upon at night being damp and watery. After the battle they followed not Lucullus many days before they began to be refractory, first of all entreating and sending the tribunes to him, but presently they tumultuously gathered together, and made a shouting all night long in their tents, a plain sign of a mutinous army. But Lucullus as earnestly entreated them, desiring them to have patience, till they took the Armenian Carthage, and overturned the work of their great enemy, meaning Hannibal.

But when he could not prevail, he led them back, and crossing Taurus by another road, came into the fruitful and sunny country of Mygdonia, where was a great and populous city, by the barbarians called Nisibis, by the Greeks Antioch of Mygdonia. This was defended by Guras, brother of Tigranes, with the dignity of governor, and by the engineering skill and dexterity of Callimachus, the same who so much annoyed the Romans at Amisus. Lucullus, however, brought his army up to it, and laying close siege, in a short time took it by storm. He used Guras, who surrendered himself, kindly, but gave no attention to Callimachus, though he offered to make discovery of hidden treasures, commanding him to be kept in chains, to be punished for firing the city of Amisus, which had disappointed his ambition of showing favour and kindness to the Greeks.

Hitherto, one would imagine fortune had attended and fought with Lucullus, but afterwards, as if the wind had failed of a sudden, he did all things by force, and as it were against the grain; and showed certainly the conduct and patience of a wise captain, but in the results met with no fresh honour or reputation; and indeed, by bad success and vain embarrassments with his soldiers, he came within a little of losing even what he had before. He himself was not the least cause of all this, being far from inclined to seek popularity with the mass of the soldiers, and more ready to think any indulgence shown to them an invasion of his own authority. But what was worst of all, he was naturally unsociable to his great officers in commission with him, despising others and thinking them worthy of nothing in comparison with himself. These faults, we are told, he had with all his many excellences; he was of a large and noble person, an eloquent speaker, and a wise counsellor, both in the Forum and the camp.

Sallust says the soldiers were ill-affected to him from the beginning of the war, because they were forced to keep the field two winters at Cyzicus and afterwards at Amisus. Their other winters, also, vexed them, for they either spent them in an enemy's country, or else were confined to their tents in the open field among their confederates; for Lucullus not so much as once went into a Greek confederate town with his army. To this ill-affection abroad, the tribunes yet more contributed at home, invidiously accusing Lucullus as one who for empire and riches prolonged the war, holding, it might almost be said, under his sole power Cilicia, Asia, Bithynia, Paphlagonia, Pontus, Armenia, all as far as the river Phasis; and now of late had plundered the royal city of Tigranes, as if he had been commissioned not so much to subdue as to strip kings. This is what we are told was said by Lucius Quintius, one of the prætors, at whose instance, in particular, the people determined to send one who should succeed Lucullus in his province, and voted, also, to relieve many of the soldiers under him from further service.

Besides these evils, that which most of all prejudiced Lucullus was Publius Clodius, an insolent man, very vicious and bold, brother to Lucullus's wife, a woman of bad conduct, with whom Clodius was himself suspected of criminal intercourse. Being then in the army under Lucullus, but not in as great authority as he expected (for he would fain have been the chief of all, but on account of his character was placed after many), he ingratiated himself secretly with the Fimbrian troops, and stirred them up against Lucullus, using fair speeches to them, who of old had been used to be flattered in such a manner. These were those whom Fimbria before had persuaded to kill the consul Flaccus, and choose him their leader.

And so they listened not unwillingly to Clodius, and called him the soldiers' friend, for the concern he professed for them, and the indignation he expressed at the prospect that "there must be no end of wars and toils, but in fighting with all nations, and wandering throughout all the world they must wear out their lives receiving no other reward for their service than to guard the carriages and camels of Lucullus, laden with gold and precious goblets; while as for Pompey's soldiers, they were all citizens, living safe at home with their wives and children, on fertile lands, or in towns, and that, not after driving Mithridates and Tigranes into wild deserts, and overturning the royal cities of Asia, but after having merely reduced exiles in Spain, or fugitive slaves in Italy. Nay, if indeed we must never have an end of fighting, should we not rather reserve the remainder of our bodies and souls for a general who will reckon his chiefest glory to be the wealth of his soldiers."

By such practices the army of Lucullus, being corrupted, neither followed him against Tigranes, nor against Mithridates, when he now at once returned into Pontus out of Armenia, and was recovering his kingdom, but under pretence of the winter, sat idle in Gordyene, every minute expecting either Pompey, or some other general, to succeed Lucullus. But when news came that Mithridates had defeated Fabius, and was marching against Sornatius and Triarius, out of shame they followed Lucullus.

Triarius, ambitiously aiming at victory before ever Lucullus came to him, though he was then very near, was defeated in a great battle, in which it is said that above seven thousand Romans fell, among whom were a hundred and fifty centurions and four-and-twenty tribunes, and that the camp itself was taken. Lucullus, coming up a few days after, concealed Triarius from the search of the angry soldiers.

But when Mithridates declined battle, and waited for the coming of Tigranes, who was then on his march with great forces, he resolved before they joined their forces to turn once more and engage with Tigranes. But in the way the mutinous Fimbrians deserted their ranks, professing themselves released from service by a decree, and that Lucullus, the provinces being allotted to others, had no longer any right to command them. There was nothing beneath the dignity of Lucullus which he did not now submit to bear, entreating them one by one, from tent to tent, going up and down humbly and in tears, and even taking some like a suppliant by the hand. But they turned away from his salutes, and threw down their empty purses, bidding him engage alone with the enemy, as he alone made advantage of it.

At length by the entreaty of the other soldiers, the Fimbrians, being prevailed upon, consented to tarry that summer under him, but if during that time no enemy came to fight them, to be free. Lucullus of necessity was forced to comply with this, or else to abandon the country to the barbarians. He kept them, indeed, with him, but without urging his authority upon them; nor did he lead them out to battle, being contented if they should but stay with him, though he then saw Cappadocia wasted by Tigranes, and Mithridates again triumphing, whom not long before he reported to the senate to be wholly subdued; and commissioners were now arrived to settle the affairs of Pontus, as if all had been quietly in his possession.

But when they came, they found him not so much as master of himself, but contemned and derided by the common soldiers, who arrived at that height of insolence against their general, that at the end of summer they put on their armour and drew their swords, and defied their enemies then absent and gone off a long while before, and with great outcries and waving their swords in the air they quitted the camp, proclaiming that the time was expired which they promised to stay with Lucullus. The rest were summoned by letters from Pompey to come and join him; he by the favour of the people and by flattery of their leaders having been chosen general of the army against Mithridates and Tigranes, though the senate and the nobility all thought that Lucullus was injured, having those put over his head who succeeded rather to his triumph than to his commission, and that he was not so truly deprived of his command, as of the glory he had deserved in his command, which he was forced to yield to another.

It was yet more of just matter of pity and indignation to those who were present; for Lucullus remained no longer master of rewards or punishments for any actions done in the war; neither would Pompey suffer any man to go to him, or pay any respect to the orders and arrangements he made with advice of his ten commissioners, but expressly issued edicts to the contrary, and could not but be obeyed by reason of his greater power.

Friends, however, on both sides, thought it desirable to bring them together, and they met in a village of Galatia, and saluted each other in a friendly manner, with congratulations on each other's successes. Lucullus was the elder, but Pompey the more distinguished by his more numerous commands and his two triumphs. Both had rods dressed with laurel carried before them for their victories, and as Pompey's laurels were withered with passing through hot and droughty countries, Lucullus's lictors courteously gave Pompey's some of the fresh and green ones which they had, which Pompey's friends counted a good omen, as indeed, of a truth, Lucullus's actions furnished the honours of Pompey's command. The interview, however, did not bring them to any amicable agreement; they parted even less friends than they met. Pompey repealed all the acts of Lucullus, drew off his soldiers, and left him no more than sixteen hundred for his triumph, and even those unwilling to go with him.

So wanting was Lucullus, either through natural constitution or adverse circumstances, in that one first and most important requisite of a general, which had he but added to his other many and remarkable virtues, his fortitude, vigilance, wisdom, justice, the Roman empire had not had Euphrates for its boundary, but the utmost ends of Asia and the Hyrcanian sea; as other nations were then disabled by the late conquests of Tigranes, and the pow-

er of Parthia had not in Lucullus's time shown itself so formidable as Crassus afterwards found it, nor had as yet gained that consistency, being crippled by wars at home and on its frontiers, and unable even to make head against the encroachments of the Armenians. And Lucullus, as it was, seems to me through others' agency to have done Rome greater harm than he did her advantage by his own. For the trophies in Armenia, near the Parthian frontier, and Tigranocerta, and Nisibis, and the great wealth brought from thence to Rome, with the captive crown of Tigranes carried in triumph, all helped to puff up Crassus, as if the barbarians had been nothing else but spoil and booty, and he, falling among the Parthian archers, soon demonstrated that Lucullus's triumphs were not beholden to the inadvertency and effeminacy of his enemies, but to his own courage and conduct. But of this afterwards.

Lucullus, upon his return to Rome, found his brother Marcus accused by Caius Memmius for his acts as quæstor, done by Sulla's orders; and on his acquittal, Memmius changed the scene, and animated the people against Lucullus himself, urging them to deny him a triumph for appropriating the spoils and prolonging the war. In this great struggle, the nobility and chief men went down, and mingling in person among the tribes, with much entreaty and labour, scarce at length prevailed upon them to consent to his triumph.

The pomp of which proved not so wonderful or so wearisome with the length of the procession and the number of things carried in it, but consisted chiefly in vast quantities of arms and machines of the king's with which he adorned the Flaminian circus, a spectacle by no means despicable. In his progress there passed by a few horsemen in heavy armour, ten chariots armed with scythes, sixty friends and officers of the king's, and a hundred and ten brazen beaked ships of war, which were conveyed along with them, a golden image of Mithridates six feet high, a shield set with precious stones, twenty loads of silver vessels, and thirty-two of golden cups, armour, and money, all carried by men. Besides which, eight mules were laden with golden couches, fifty-six with bullion, and a hundred and seven with coined silver, little less than two million seven hundred thousand pieces. There were tablets, also, with inscriptions, stating what moneys he gave Pompey for prosecuting the piratic war, what he delivered into the treasury, and what he gave to every soldier, which was nine hundred

and fifty drachmas each. After all which he nobly feasted the city and adjoining villages or
vici.

Being divorced from Clodia, a dissolute and
wicked woman, he married Servilia, sister to
Cato. This also proved an unfortunate match,
for she only wanted one of all of Clodia's vices,
the criminality she was accused of with her
brothers. Out of reverence to Cato, he for a
while connived her impurity and immodesty,
but at length dismissed her.

When the senate expected great things from
him, hoping to find in him a check to the
usurpations of Pompey, and that with the
greatness of his station and credit he would
come forward as the champion of the nobility,
he retired from business and abandoned public life; either because he saw the state to be in
a difficult and diseased condition, or, as others
say, because he was as great as he could well
be, and inclined to a quiet and easy life, after
those many labours and toils which had ended
with him so far from fortunately.

There are those who highly commend his
change of life, saying that he thus avoided the
rock on which Marius split. For he, after the
great and glorious deeds of his Cimbrian victories, was not contented to retire upon his
honours, but out of an insatiable desire of glory
and power, even in his old age, headed a political party against young men, and let himself
fall into miserable actions, and yet more miserable sufferings.

Better in like manner, they say, had it been
for Cicero, after Catiline's conspiracy, to have
retired and grown old, and for Scipio, after his
Numantine and Carthaginian conquests, to
have sat down contented. For the administration of public affairs has, like other things, its
proper term, and statesmen, as well as wrestlers, will break down when strength and youth
fail. But Crassus and Pompey, on the other
hand, laughed to see Lucullus abandoning himself to pleasure and expense, as if luxurious
living were not a thing that as little became his
years as government of affairs at home or of an
army abroad.

And, indeed, Lucullus's life, like the Old
Comedy, presents us at the commencement
with acts of policy and of war, at the end offering nothing but good eating and drinking,
feastings, and revellings, and mere play. For I
give no higher name to his sumptuous buildings, porticos, and baths, still less to his paintings and sculptures, and all his industry about
these curiosities, which he collected with vast

expense, lavishly bestowing all the wealth and
treasure which he got in the war upon them,
insomuch that even now, with all the advance
of luxury, the Lucullean gardens are counted
the noblest the emperor has.

Tubero, the stoic, when he saw his buildings
at Naples, where he suspended the hills upon
vast tunnels, brought in the sea for moats and
fish-ponds round his house, and built pleasure-
houses in the waters, called him Xerxes in a
gown. He had also fine seats in Tusculum, bel-
vederes, and large open balconies for men's
apartments, and porticos to walk in, where
Pompey coming to see him, blamed him for
making a house which would be pleasant in
summer, but uninhabitable in winter; whom
he answered with a smile, "You think me,
then, less provident than cranes and storks, not
to change my home with the season." When a
prætor, with great expense and pains, was preparing a spectacle for the people, and asked
him to lend him some purple robes for the performers in a chorus, he told him he would go
home and see, and if he had got any, would let
him have them; and the next day asking how
many he wanted, and being told that a hundred would suffice, bade him to take twice as
many; on which the poet Horace observes that
a house is but a poor one where the valuables
unseen and unthought of do not exceed all
those that meet the eye.

Lucullus's daily entertainments were osten-
tatiously extravagant, not only with purple coverlets, and plate adorned with precious stones,
and dancings, and interludes, but with the
greatest diversity of dishes and the most elaborate cookery, for the vulgar to admire and envy.
It was a happy thought of Pompey in his sickness, when his physician prescribed a thrush
for his dinner, and his servants told him that
in summer-time thrushes were not to be found
anywhere but in Lucullus's fattening coops,
that he would not suffer them to fetch one
thence, but observing to his physician, "So if
Lucullus had not been an epicure, Pompey had
not lived," ordered something else that could
easily be got to be prepared for him. Cato was
his friend and connection, but, nevertheless, so
hated his life and habits, that when a young
man in the senate made a long and tedious
speech in praise of frugality and temperance,
Cato got up and said, "How long do you mean
to go on making money like Crassus, living
like Lucullus, and talking like Cato?" There
are some, however, who say the words were
said, but not by Cato.

It is plain from the anecdotes on record of him that Lucullus was not only pleased with, but even gloried in his way of living. For he is said to have feasted several Greeks upon their coming to Rome day after day, who of a true Grecian principle, being ashamed, and declining the invitations, where so great an expense was every day incurred for them, he with a smile told them, "Some of this, indeed, my Grecian friends, is for your sakes, but more for that of Lucullus."

Once when he supped alone, there being only one course, and that but moderately furnished, he called his steward and reproved him, who professing to have supposed that there would be no need of any great entertainment, when nobody was invited, was answered, "What, did not you know, then, that to-day Lucullus dines with Lucullus?"

Which being much spoken of about the city, Cicero and Pompey one day met him loitering in the Forum, the former his intimate friend and familiar, and, though there had been some ill-will between Pompey and him about the command in the war, still they used to see each other and converse on easy terms together. Cicero accordingly saluted him, and asked him whether to-day were a good time for asking a favour of him, and on his answering, "Very much so," and begging to hear what it was, "Then," said Cicero, "we should like to dine with you to-day, just on the dinner that is prepared for yourself." Lucullus being surprised, and requesting a day's time, they refused to grant it, neither suffered him to talk with his servants, for fear he should give order for more than was appointed before. But thus much they consented to, that before their faces he might tell his servants, that to-day he would sup in the Apollo (for so one of his best dining-rooms was called), and by this evasion he outwitted his guests.

For every room, as it seems, had its own assessment of expenditure, dinner at such a price, and all else in accordance; so that the servants, on knowing where he would dine, knew also how much was to be expended, and in what style and form dinner was to be served. The expense for the Apollo was fifty thousand drachmas, and thus much being that day laid out, the greatness of the cost did not so much amaze Pompey and Cicero, as the rapidity of the outlay. One might believe Lucullus thought his money really captive and barbarian, so wantonly and contumeliously did he treat it.

His furnishing a library, however, deserves praise and record, for he collected very many choice manuscripts; and the use they were put to was even more magnificent than the purchase, the library being always open, and the walks and reading-rooms about it free to all Greeks, whose delight it was to leave their other occupations and hasten thither as to the habitation of the Muses, there walking about, and diverting one another. He himself often passed his hours there, disputing with the learned in the walks, and giving his advice to statesmen who required it, insomuch that his house was altogether a home, and in a manner a Greek prytaneum for those that visited Rome.

He was fond of all sorts of philosophy, and was well read and expert in them all. But he always from the first specially favoured and valued the Academy; not the New one, which at that time under Philo flourished with the precepts of Carneades, but the Old one, then sustained and represented by Antiochus of Ascalon, a learned and eloquent man. Lucullus with great labour made him his friend and champion, and set him up against Philo's auditors, among whom Cicero was one, who wrote an admirable treatise in defence of his sect, in which he puts the argument in favour of *comprehension* in the mouth of Lucullus, and the opposite argument in his own. The book is called *Lucullus*.

For, as has been said, they were great friends, and took the same side in politics. For Lucullus did not wholly retire from the republic, but only from the ambition, and from the dangerous and often lawless struggle for political preeminence, which he left to Crassus and Cato, whom the senators, jealous of Pompey's greatness, put forward as their champions, when Lucullus refused to head them. For his friends' sake he came into the Forum and into the senate, when occasion offered to humble the ambition and pride of Pompey, whose settlement, after his conquests over the kings, he got cancelled, and, by the assistance of Cato, hindered a division of lands to his soldiers, which he proposed.

So Pompey went over to Crassus and Cæsar's alliance, or rather conspiracy, and filling the city with armed men, procured the ratification of his decrees by force, and drove Cato and Lucullus out of the Forum. Which being resented by the nobility, Pompey's party produced one Vettius, pretending they apprehended him in a design against Pompey's life. Vettius in the senate-house accused others, but before the people named Lucullus, as if he had been suborned by him to kill Pompey. Nobody gave heed to what he said, and it soon appeared that they had put him forward to make false charges and accusations.

And after a few days the whole intrigue became yet more obvious, when the dead body of Vettius was thrown out of prison, he being reported, indeed, to have died a natural death, but carrying marks of a halter and blows about him, and seeming rather to have been taken off by those who suborned him. These things kept Lucullus at a greater distance from the republic.

But when Cicero was banished the city, and Cato sent to Cyprus, he quitted public affairs altogether. It is said, too, that before his death his intellects failed him by degrees. But Cornelius Nepos denies that either age or sickness impaired his mind, which was rather affected by a potion, given him by Callisthenes, his freedman. The potion was meant by Callis-

thenes to strengthen his affection for him, and was supposed to have that tendency, but it stood quite otherwise, and so disabled and unsettled his mind, that while he was yet alive, his brother took charge of his affairs.

At his death, as though it had been the death of one taken off in the very height of military and civil glory, the people were much concerned, and flocked together, and would have forcibly taken his corpse, as it was carried into the market-place by young men of the highest rank, and have buried it in the field of Mars, where they buried Sulla. Which being altogether unexpected, and necessaries not easily to be procured on a sudden, his brother, after much entreaty and solicitation, prevailed upon them to suffer him to be buried on his Tusculan estate as had been appointed. He himself survived him but a short time, coming not far behind in death, as he did in age and renown, in all respects, a most loving brother.

CIMON and LUCULLUS
Compared

ONE might bless the end of Lucullus, which was so timid as to let him die before the great revolution, which fate, by intestine wars, was already effecting against the established government, and to close his life in a free though troubled commonwealth. And in this, above all other things, Cimon and he are alike. For he died also when Greece was as yet undisordered, in its highest felicity; though in the field at the head of his army, not recalled, nor out of his mind, nor sullying the glory of his wars, engagements, and conquests, by making feastings and debauches seem the apparent end and aim of them all; as Plato says scornfully of Orpheus, that he makes an eternal debauch hereafter the reward of those who lived well here.

Indeed, ease and quiet, and the study of pleasant and speculative learning, to an old man retiring from command and office, is a most suitable and becoming solace; but to misguide virtuous actions to pleasure as their utmost end, and as the conclusion of campaigns and commands, to keep the feast of Venus, did not become the noble Academy, and the follower of Xenocrates, but rather one that inclined to Epicurus. And this is one surprising point of contrast between them; Cimon's youth was ill reputed and intemperate, Lucullus's well disciplined and sober. Undoubtedly we

must give the preference to the change for good, for it argues the better nature, where vice declines and virtue grows.

Both had great wealth, but employed it in different ways; and there is no comparison between the south wall of the Acropolis built by Cimon, and the chambers and galleries, with their sea-views, built at Naples by Lucullus, out of the spoils of the barbarians. Neither can we compare Cimon's popular and liberal table with the sumptuous oriental one of Lucullus, the former receiving a great many guests every day at small cost, the latter expensively spread for a few men of pleasure, unless you will say that different times made the alteration. For who can tell but that Cimon, if he had retired in his old age from business and war to quiet and solitude, might have lived a more luxurious and self-indulgent life, as he was fond of wine and company, and accused, as has been said, of laxity with women? The better pleasures gained in successful action and effort leave the baser appetites no time or place, and make active and heroic men forget them. Had but Lucullus ended his days in the field, and in command, envy and detraction itself could never have accused him. So much for their manner of life.

In war, it is plain they were both soldiers of excellent conduct, both at land and sea. But as in the games they honour those champions who on the same day gain the garland, both in wrestling and in the pancratium, with the name of "victors and more," so Cimon, honouring Greece with a sea and land victory on the same day, may claim a certain pre-eminence among commanders.

Lucullus received command from his country, whereas Cimon brought it to his.

He annexed the territories of enemies to her, who ruled over confederates before, but Cimon made his country, which when he began was a mere follower of others, both rule over confederates, and conquer enemies too, forcing the Persians to relinquish the sea, and inducing the Lacedæmonians to surrender their command.

If it be the chiefest thing in a general to obtain the obedience of his soldiers by good-will, Lucullus was despised by his own army, but Cimon highly prized even by others. His soldiers deserted the one, the confederates came over to the other. Lucullus came home without the forces which he led out; Cimon, sent out at first to serve as one confederate among others, returned home with authority even over these also, having successfully effected for his city three most difficult services, establishing peace with the enemy, dominion over confederates, and concord with Lacedæmon. Both aiming to destroy great kingdoms, and subdue all Asia, failed in their enterprise, Cimon by a simple piece of ill-fortune, for he died when general, in the height of success; but Lucullus no man can wholly acquit of being in fault with his soldiers, whether it were he did not know, or would not comply with, the distastes and complaints of his army, which brought him at last into such extreme unpopularity among them. But did not Cimon also suffer like him in this? For the citizens arraigned him, and did not leave off till they had banished him, that, as Plato says, they might not hear him for the space of ten years. For high and noble minds seldom please the vulgar, or are acceptable to them; for the force they use to straighten their distorted actions gives the same pain as surgeons' bandages do in bringing dislocated bones to their natural position. Both of them, perhaps, come off pretty much with an equal acquittal on this count.

Lucullus very much outwent him in war, being the first Roman who carried an army over

Taurus, passed the Tigris, took and burned the royal palaces of Asia in the sight of the kings, Tigranocerta, Cabira, Sinope, and Nisibis, seizing and overwhelming the northern parts as far as the Phasis, the east as far as Media, and making the South and Red Sea his own through the kings of the Arabians. He shattered the power of the kings, and narrowly missed their persons, while like wild beasts they fled away into deserts and thick and impassable woods.

In demonstration of this superiority, we see that the Persians, as if no great harm had befallen them under Cimon, soon after appeared in arms against the Greeks, and overcame and destroyed their numerous forces in Egypt. But after Lucullus, Tigranes and Mithridates were able to do nothing; the latter, being disabled and broken in the former wars, never dared to show his army to Pompey outside the camp, but fled away to Bosporus, and there died. Tigranes threw himself, naked and unarmed, down before Pompey, and taking his crown from his head laid it at his feet, complimenting Pompey with what was not his own, but, in real truth, the conquest already effected by Lucullus. And when he received the ensigns of majesty again, he was well pleased, evidently because he had forfeited them before. And the commander, as the wrestler, is to be accounted to have done most who leaves an adversary almost conquered for his successor.

Cimon, moreover, when he took the command, found the power of the king broken, and the spirits of the Persians humbled by their great defeats and incessant routs under Themistocles, Pausanias, and Leontychides, and thus easily overcame the bodies of men whose souls were quelled and defeated beforehand. But Tigranes had never yet in many combats been beaten, and was flushed with success when he engaged with Lucullus. There is no comparison between the numbers which came against Lucullus and those subdued by Cimon.

All which things being rightly considered, it is a hard matter to give judgment. For supernatural favour also appears to have attended both of them, directing the one what to do, the other what to avoid, and thus they have, both of them, so to say, the vote of the gods, to declare them noble and divine characters.

NICIAS

D. 413 B.C.

CRASSUS, in my opinion, may most properly be set against Nicias, and the Parthian disaster compared with that in Sicily. But here it will be well for me to entreat the reader, in all courtesy, not to think that I contend with Thucydides in matters so pathetically, vividly, and eloquently, beyond all imitation, and even beyond himself, expressed by him; nor to believe me guilty of the like folly with Timæus, who, hoping in his history to surpass Thucydides in art, and to make Philistus appear a trifler and a novice, pushes on in his descriptions, through all the battles, sea-fights, and public speeches, in recording which they have been most successful, without meriting so much as to be compared, in Pindar's phrase, to—

One that on his feet
Would with the Lydian cars compete.

He simply shows himself all along a half-lettered, childish writer; in the words of Diphilus—

—— of wit obese,
O'erlarded with Sicilian grease.

Often he sinks to the very level of Xenarchus, telling us that he thinks it ominous to the Athenians that their general, who had victory in his name, was unwilling to take command in the expedition; and that the defacing of the Hermæ was a divine intimation that they should suffer much in the war by Hermocrates, the son of Hermon; and, moreover, how it was likely that Hercules should aid the Syracusans for the sake of Proserpine, by whose means he took Cerberus, and should be angry with the Athenians for protecting the Egesteans, descended from Trojan ancestors, whose city he, for an injury of their king Laomedon, had overthrown. However, all these may be merely other instances of the same happy taste that makes him correct the diction of Philistus, and abuse Plato and Aristotle.

This sort of contention and rivalry with others in matter of style, to my mind, in any case, seems petty and pedantic, but when its objects are works of inimitable excellence, it is absolutely senseless. Such actions in Nicias's life as Thucydides and Philistus have related, since they cannot be passed by, illustrating as they do most especially his character and temper, under his many and great troubles, that I may not seem altogether negligent, I shall briefly run over. And such things as are not commonly known, and lie scattered here and there in other men's writings, or are found amongst the old monuments and archives, I shall endeavour to bring together; not collecting mere useless pieces of learning, but adducing what may make his disposition and habit of mind understood.

First of all, I would mention what Aristotle has said of Nicias, that there had been three good citizens eminent above the rest for their hereditary affection and love to the people, Nicias, the son of Niceratus, Thucydides, the son of Melesias, and Theramenes, the son of Hagnon, but the last less than the others; for he had his dubious extraction cast in his teeth, as a foreigner from Ceos, and his inconstancy, which made him side sometimes with one party, sometimes with another, in public life, and which obtained him the nickname of the Buskin.

Thucydides came earlier, and, on the behalf of the nobility, was a great opponent of the measures by which Pericles courted the favour of the people.

Nicias was a younger man, yet was in some reputation even whilst Pericles lived; so much so as to have been his colleague in the office of general, and to have held command by himself more than once. But on the death of Pericles, he presently rose to the highest place, chiefly by the favour of the rich and eminent citizens, who set him up for their bulwark against the presumption and insolence of Cleon; nevertheless, he did not forfeit the good-will of the commonalty, who, likewise, contributed to his advancement. For though Cleon got great influence by his exertions—

—— to please
The old men, who trusted him to find them fees,
yet even those, for whose interest and to gain

whose favour he acted, nevertheless observing the avarice, the arrogance, and the presumption of the man, many of them supported Nicias.

For his was not that sort of gravity which is harsh and offensive, but he tempered it with a certain caution and deference, winning upon the people, by seeming afraid of them. And being naturally diffident and unhopeful in war, his good fortune supplied his want of courage, and kept it from being detected, as in all his commands he was constantly successful. And his timorousness in civil life, and his extreme dread of accusers, was thought very suitable in a citizen of a free state; and from the people's good-will towards him, got him no small power over them, they being fearful of all that despised them, but willing to promote one who seemed to be afraid of them; the greatest compliment their betters could pay them being not to contemn them.

Pericles, who by solid virtue and the pure force of argument ruled the commonwealth, had stood in need of no disguises nor persuasions with the people. Nicias, inferior in these respects, used his riches, of which he had abundance, to gain popularity. Neither had he the nimble wit of Cleon to win the Athenians to his purposes by amusing them with bold jests; unprovided with such qualities, he courted them with dramatic exhibitions, gymnastic games, and other public shows, more sumptuous and more splendid than had been ever known in his or in former ages.

Amongst his religious offerings, there was extant, even in our days, the small figure of Minerva in the citadel, having lost the gold that covered it; and a shrine in the temple of Bacchus, under the tripods, that were presented by those who won the prize in the shows or plays. For at these he had often carried off the prize, and never once failed.

We are told that on one of these occasions, a slave of his appeared in the character of Bacchus, of a beautiful person and noble stature, and with as yet no beard upon his chin; and on the Athenians being pleased with the sight, and applauding a long time, Nicias stood up, and said he could not in piety keep as a slave one whose person had been consecrated to represent a god. And forthwith he set the young man free.

His performances at Delos are, also, on record, as noble and magnificent works of devotion. For whereas the choruses which the cities sent to sing hymns to the god were wont to arrive in no order, as it might happen, and, being there met by a crowd of people crying out to them to sing, in their hurry to begin, used to disembark confusedly, putting on their garlands, and changing their dresses as they left the ships, he, when he had to convoy the sacred company, disembarked the chorus at Rhenea, together with the sacrifice, and other holy appurtenances. And having brought along with him from Athens a bridge fitted by measurement for the purpose, and magnificently adorned with gilding and colouring, and with garlands and tapestries, this he laid in the night over the channel betwixt Rhenea and Delos, being no great distance.

And at break of day he marched forth with all the procession to the god, and led the chorus, sumptuously ornamented, and singing their hymns, along over the bridge. The sacrifices, the games, and the feast being over, he set up a palm-tree of brass for a present to the god, and bought a parcel of land with ten thousand drachmas which he consecrated; with the revenue the inhabitants of Delos were to sacrifice and to feast, and to pray the gods for many good things to Nicias. This he engraved on a pillar, which he left in Delos to be a record of his bequest. This same palm-tree, afterwards broken down by the wind, fell on the great statue which the men of Naxos presented, and struck it to the ground.

It is plain that much of this might be vainglory, and the mere desire of popularity and applause; yet from other qualities and carriages of the man one might believe all this cost and public display to be the effect of devotion. For he was one of those who dreaded the divine powers extremely, and, as Thucydides tells us, was much given to arts of divination. In one of Pasiphon's dialogues, it is stated that he daily sacrificed to the gods, and keeping a diviner at his house, professed to be consulting always about the commonwealth, but for the most part inquired about his own private affairs, more especially concerning his silver mines; for he owned many works at Laurium, of great value, but somewhat hazardous to carry on. He maintained there a multitude of slaves, and his wealth consisted chiefly in silver. Hence he had many hangers-on about him, begging and obtaining. For he gave to those who could do him mischief no less than to those who deserved well. In short, his timidity was a revenue to rogues, and his humanity to honest men.

We find testimony in the comic writers, as

when Teleclides, speaking of one of the professed informers, says:—

Charicles gave the man a pound, the matter
   not to name,
That from inside a money-bag into the
   world he came;
And Nicias, also, paid him four; I know
   the reason well,
But Nicias is a worthy man, and so I will
   not tell.

So, also, the informer whom Eupolis introduces in his *Maricas*, attacking a good, simple, poor man:—

How long ago did you and Nicias meet?

I did but see him just now in the street.

The man has seen him and denies it not,
'Tis evident that they are in a plot.

See you, O citizens! 'tis fact,
Nicias is taken in the act.

Taken, Fools! take so good a man
In aught that's wrong none will or can.

Cleon, in Aristophanes, makes it one of his threats:—

I'll outscream all the speakers, and make Nicias
   stand aghast.

Phrynichus also implies his want of spirit and his easiness to be intimidated in the verses—

A noble man he was, I well can say,
Nor walked like Nicias, cowering on his way.

So cautious was he of informers, and so reserved, that he never would dine out with any citizen, nor allow himself to indulge in talk and conversation with his friends, nor give himself any leisure for such amusements; but when he was general he used to stay at the office till night, and was the first that came to the council-house, and the last that left it. And if no public business engaged him, it was very hard to have access, or to speak with him, he being retired at home and locked up. And when any came to the door, some friend of his gave them good words, and begged them to excuse him, Nicias was very busy; as if affairs of state and public duties still kept him occupied.

He who principally acted this part for him, and contributed most to this state and show, was Hiero, a man educated in Nicias's family, and instructed by him in letters and music. He professed to be the son of Dionysius, surnamed Chalcus, whose poems are yet extant, and had led out the colony to Italy and founded Thurii.

This Hiero transacted all his secrets for Nicias with the diviners; and gave out to the people what a toilsome and miserable life he led for the sake of the commonwealth.

"He," said Hiero, "can never be either at the bath or at his meat but some public business interferes. Careless of his own and zealous for the public good, he scarcely ever goes to bed till after others have had their first sleep. So that his health is impaired and his body out of order, nor is he cheerful or affable with his friends, but loses them as well as his money in the service of the state, while other men gain friends by public speaking, enrich themselves, fare delicately and make government their amusement." And in fact this was Nicias's manner of life, so that he well might apply to himself the words of Agamemnon:—

Vain pomp's the ruler of the life we live,
And a slave's service to the crowd we give.

He observed that the people, in the case of men of eloquence, or of eminent parts, make use of their talents upon occasion, but were always jealous of their abilities, and held a watchful eye upon them, taking all opportunities to humble their pride and abate their reputation; as was manifest in their condemnation of Pericles, their banishment of Damon, their distrust of Antiphon the Rhamnusian, but especially in the case of Paches who took Lesbos, who, having to give an account of his conduct, in the very court of justice unsheathed his sword and slew himself. Upon such considerations, Nicias declined all difficult and lengthy enterprises; if he took a command, he was for doing what was safe; and if, as thus was likely, he had for the most part success, he did not attribute it to any wisdom, conduct, or courage of his own, but, to avoid envy, he thanked fortune for all, and gave the glory to the divine powers.

And the actions themselves bore testimony in his favour; the city met at that time with several considerable reverses, but he had not a hand in any of them. The Athenians were routed in Thrace by the Chalcidians, Calliades and Xenophon commanding in chief. Demosthenes was the general when they were unfortunate in Ætolia. At Delium they lost a thousand citizens under the conduct of Hippocrates; the plague was principally laid to the charge of Pericles, he, to carry on the war, having shut up close together in the town the crowd of people from the country who, by the change of place, and of their usual course of living, bred the pestilence.

Nicias stood clear of all this; under his conduct was taken Cythera, an island most commodious against Laconia, and occupied by the Lacedæmonian settlers; many places, likewise, in Thrace, which had revolted, were taken or won over by him; he shutting up the Megarians within their town, seized upon the isle of Minoa; and soon after, advancing from thence to Nisæa, made himself master there, and then making a descent upon the Corinthian territory, fought a successful battle, and slew a great number of the Corinthians with their captain, Lycophron.

There it happened that two of his men were left by an oversight, when they carried off the dead, which when he understood, he stopped the fleet, and sent a herald to the enemy for leave to carry off the dead; though by law and custom, he that by a truce craved leave to carry off the dead was hereby supposed to give up all claim to the victory. Nor was it lawful for him that did this to erect a trophy, for his is the victory who is master of the field, and he is not master who asks leave, as wanting power to take. But he chose rather to renounce his victory and his glory than to let two citizens lie unburied.

He scoured the coast of Laconia all along, and beat the Lacedæmonians that made head against him. He took Thyrea, occupied by the Æginetans, and carried the prisoners to Athens.

When Demosthenes had fortified Pylos, and the Peloponnesians brought together both their sea and land forces before it, after the fight, about the number of four hundred native Spartans were left ashore in the isle, Sphacteria. The Athenians thought it a great prize, as indeed it was, to take these men prisoners. But the siege, in places that wanted water, being very difficult and untoward, and to convey necessaries about by sea in summer tedious and expensive, in winter doubtful, or plainly impossible, they began to be annoyed, and to repent their having rejected the embassy of the Lacedæmonians, that had been sent to propose a treaty of peace, which had been done at the importunity of Cleon, who opposed it chiefly out of a pique to Nicias; for, being his enemy, and observing him to be extremely solicitous to support the offers of the Lacedæmonians, he persuaded the people to refuse them.

Now, therefore, that the siege was protracted, and they heard of the difficulties that pressed their army, they grew enraged against Cleon. But he turned all the blame upon Nicias, charging it on his softness and cowardice, that

the besieged were not yet taken. "Were I general," said he, "they should not hold out so long." The Athenians not unnaturally asked the question, "Why, then, as it is, do not you go with a squadron against them?" And Nicias standing up resigned his command at Pylos to him, and bade him take what forces he pleased along with him, and not be bold in words, out of harm's way, but go forth and perform some real service for the commonwealth.

Cleon, at the first, tired to draw back, disconcerted at the proposal, which he had never expected; but the Athenians insisting, and Nicias loudly upbraiding him, he thus provoked, and fired with ambition, took upon him the charge, and said further, that within twenty days after he embarked, he would either kill the enemy upon the place, or bring them alive to Athens. This the Athenians were readier to laugh at than to believe, as on other occasions, also, his bold assertions and extravagances used to make them sport, and were pleasant enough.

As, for instance, it is reported that once when the people were assembled, and had waited his coming a long time, at last he appeared with a garland on his head, and prayed them to adjourn to the next day. "For," said he, "I am not at leisure to-day; I have sacrificed to the gods, and am to entertain some strangers." Whereupon the Athenians, laughing, rose up, and dissolved the assembly.

However, at this time he had good fortune, and in conjunction with Demosthenes, conducted the enterprise so well that, within the time he had limited, he carried captive to Athens all the Spartans that had not fallen in battle.

This brought great disgrace on Nicias; for this was not to throw away his shield, but something yet more shameful and ignominious, to quit his charge voluntarily out of cowardice, and voting himself, as it were, out of his command of his own accord, to put into his enemy's hand the opportunity of achieving so brave an action. Aristophanes has a jest against him on this occasion in *The Birds:*—

Indeed, not now the word that must be said
Is, do like Nicias, or retire to bed.

And, again, in his *Husbandmen:*—

I wish to stay at home and farm,
What then?
Who should prevent you?
    You, my countrymen;
Whom I would pay a thousand drachmas down,
To let me give up office and leave town.

Enough; content; the sum two thousand is,
With those that Nicias paid to give up his.

Besides all this, he did great mischief to the city by suffering the accession of so much reputation and power to Cleon, who now assumed such lofty airs, and allowed himself in such intolerable audacity, as led to many unfortunate results, a sufficient part of which fell to his own share. Amongst other things, he destroyed all the decorum of public speaking; he was the first who ever broke out into exclamations, flung open his dress, smote his thigh, and ran up and down whilst he was speaking, things which soon after introduced, amongst those who managed the affairs of state, such licence and contempt of decency as brought all into confusion.

Already, too, Alcibiades was beginning to show his strength at Athens, a popular leader, not, indeed, as utterly violent as Cleon, but as the land of Egypt, through the richness of its soil, is said—

——great plenty to produce,
Both wholesome herbs, and drugs of deadly juice,
so the nature of Alcibiades was strong and luxuriant in both kinds, and made way for many serious innovations.

Thus it fell out that after Nicias had got his hands clear of Cleon, he had not opportunity to settle the city perfectly into quietness. For having brought matters to a pretty hopeful condition, he found everything carried away and plunged again into confusion by Alcibiades, through the wildness and vehemence of his ambition, and all embroiled again in war worse than ever.

Which fell out thus. The persons who had principally hindered the peace were Cleon and Brasidas. War setting off the virtue of the one and hiding the villainy of the other, gave to the one occasions of achieving brave actions, to the other opportunity of committing equal dishonesties. Now when these two were in one battle both slain near Amphipolis, Nicias was aware that the Spartans had long been desirous of a peace, and that the Athenians had no longer the same confidence in the war.

Both being alike tired, and, as it were by consent, letting fall their hands, he, therefore, in this nick of time, employed his efforts to make a friendship betwixt the two cities, and to deliver the other states of Greece from the evils and calamities they laboured under, and so establish his own good name for success as a statesman for all future time. He found the men of substance, the elder men, and the landowners and farmers pretty generally all inclined to peace.

And when, in addition to these, by conversing and reasoning, he had cooled the wishes of a good many others for war, he now encouraged the hopes of the Lacedæmonians, and counselled them to seek peace. They confided in him, as on account of his general character for moderation and equity, so, also, because of the kindness and care he had shown to the prisoners taken at Pylos and kept in confinement, making their misfortune the more easy to them.

The Athenians and the Spartans had before this concluded a truce for a year, and during this, by associating with one another, they had tasted again the sweets of peace and security and unimpeded intercourse with friends and connections, and thus longed for an end of that fighting and bloodshed, and heard with delight the chorus sing such verses as—

——my lance I'll leave
Laid by, for spiders to o'erweave,
and remembered with joy the saying, "In peace, they who sleep are awaked by the cockcrow, not by the trumpet."

So shutting their ears, with loud reproaches, to the forebodings of those who said that the Fates decreed this to be a war of thrice nine years, the whole question having been debated, they made a peace. And most people thought, now, indeed, they had got an end of all their evils. And Nicias was in every man's mouth, as one especially beloved of the gods, who, for his piety and devotion, had been appointed to give a name to the fairest and greatest of all blessings. For in fact they considered the peace Nicias's work, as the war the work of Pericles; because he, on light occasions, seemed to have plunged the Greeks into great calamities, while Nicias had induced them to forget all the evils they had done each other and to be friends again; and so to this day it is called the Peace of Nicias.

The articles were that the garrisons and towns taken on either side and the prisoners should be restored, and they to restore the first to whom it should fall by lot. Nicias, as Theophrastus tells us, by a sum of money procured that the lot should fall for the Lacedæmonians to deliver the first. Afterwards, when the Corinthians and the Bœotians showed their dislike of what was done, and by their complaints and accusations were well nigh bringing the war back again, Nicias persuaded the Athenians and the Lacedæmonians, besides the peace, to make a treaty of alliance, offensive and defensive, as a tie and confirmation of the peace, which would make them more terrible to those that held out, and the firmer to each other.

Whilst these matters were on foot, Alcibiades, who was no lover of tranquillity, and who was offended with the Lacedæmonians because of their applications and attentions to Nicias, while they overlooked and despised himself, from first to last, indeed, had opposed the peace, though all in vain, but now finding that the Lacedæmonians did not altogether continue to please the Athenians, but were thought to have acted unfairly in having made a league with the Bœotians, and had not given up Panactum, as they should have done, with its fortifications unrazed, nor yet Amphipolis, he laid hold on these occasions for his purpose, and availed himself of every one of them to irritate the people. And, at length, sending for ambassadors from the Argives, he exerted himself to effect a confederacy between the Athenians and them.

And now, when Lacedæmonian ambassadors were come with full powers, and at their preliminary audience by the council seemed to come in all points with just proposals, he, fearing that the general assembly, also, would be won over to their offers, overreached them with false professions and oaths of assistance, on the condition that they would not avow that they came with full powers; this, he said, being the only way for them to attain their desires. They being overpersuaded and decoyed from Nicias to follow him, he introduced them to the assembly, and asked them presently whether or no they came in all points with full powers, which, when they denied, he, contrary to their expectation, changing his countenance, called the council to witness their words, and now bade the people beware how they trust or transact anything with such manifest liars, who say at one time one thing, and at another the very opposite upon the same subject.

These plenipotentiaries were, as well they might be, confounded at this, and Nicias, also being at a loss what to say, and struck with amazement and wonder, the assembly resolved to send immediately for the Argives, to enter into a league with them. An earthquake, which interrupted the assembly, made for Nicias's advantage; and the next day the people being again assembled, after much speaking and soliciting, with great ado he brought it about that the treaty with the Argives should

be deferred, and he be sent to the Lacedæmonians, in full expectation that so all would go well.

When he arrived at Sparta, they received him there as a good man, and one well inclined towards them; yet he effected nothing, but, baffled by the party that favoured the Bœotians, he returned home, not only dishonoured and hardly spoken of, but likewise in fear of the Athenians, who were vexed and enraged that through his persuasions they had released so many and such considerable persons, their prisoners, for the men who had been brought from Pylos were of the chiefest families of Sparta, and had those who were highest there in place and power for their friends and kindred. Yet did they not in their heat proceed against him, otherwise than that they chose Alcibiades general, and took the Mantineans and Eleans, who had thrown up their alliance with the Lacedæmonians, into the league, together with the Argives, and sent to Pylos freebooters to infest Laconia, whereby the war began to break out afresh.

But the enmity betwixt Nicias and Alcibiades running higher and higher, and the time being at hand for decreeing the ostracism or banishment, for ten years, which the people, putting the name on a sherd, were wont to inflict at certain times on some person suspected or regarded with jealousy for his popularity or wealth, both were now in alarm and apprehension, one of them, in all likelihood, having to undergo this ostracism; as the people abominated the life of Alcibiades, and stood in fear of his boldness and resolution, as is shown particularly in the history of him; while as for Nicias, his riches made him envied, and his habits of living, in particular his unsociable and exclusive ways, not like those of a fellow-citizen, or even a fellow-man, went against him, and having many times opposed their inclinations, forcing them against their feelings to do what was their interest, he had got himself disliked.

To speak plainly, it was a contest of the young men who were eager for war, against the men of years and lovers of peace, they turning the ostracism upon the one, these upon the other. But—

In civil strife e'en villains rise to fame.

And so now it happened that the city, distracted into two factions, allowed free course to the most impudent and profligate persons, among whom was Hyperbolus of the Perithœdæ, one who could not, indeed, be said to be presuming upon any power, but rather by his presumption arose into power, and by the honour he found in the city, became the scandal of it. He, at this time, thought himself far enough from the ostracism, as more properly deserving the slave's gallows, and made account, that one of these men being despatched out of the way he might be able to play a part against the other that should be left, and openly showed his pleasure at the dissension, and his desire to inflame the people against both of them.

Nicias and Alcibiades, perceiving his malice, secretly combined together, and setting both their interests jointly at work, succeeded in fixing the ostracism not on either of them, but even on Hyperbolus. This, indeed, at the first made sport, and raised laughter among the people; but afterwards it was felt as an affront, that the thing should be dishonoured by being employed upon so unworthy a subject; punishment, also, having its proper dignity, and ostracism being one that was appropriate rather for Thucydides, Aristides, and such like persons; whereas for Hyperbolus it was a glory, and a fair ground for boasting on his part, when for his villainy he suffered the same with the best men. As Plato, the comic poet, said of him:—

The man deserved the fate, deny who can;
Yes, but the fate did not deserve the man;
Not for the like of him and his slave-brands,
Did Athens put the sherd into our hands.

And, in fact, none ever afterwards suffered this sort of punishment, but Hyperbolus was the last, as Hipparchus the Cholargian, who was kin to the tyrant, was the first.

There is no judgment to be made of fortune; nor can any reasoning bring us to a certainty about it. If Nicias had run the risk with Alcibiades, whether of the two should undergo the ostracism, he had either prevailed, and, his rival being expelled the city, he had remained secure; or, being overcome, he had avoided the utmost disasters, and preserved the reputation of a most excellent commander. Meantime I am not ignorant that Theophrastus says, that when Hyperbolus was banished, Phæax, not Nicias, contested it with Alcibiades; but most authors differ from him.

It was Alcibiades, at any rate, whom, when the Ægestean and Leontine ambassadors arrived and urged the Athenians to make an expedition against Sicily, Nicias opposed, and by whose persuasions and ambition he found himself overborne, who, even before the peo-

ple could be assembled, had preoccupied and corrupted their judgment with hopes and with speeches; insomuch that the young men at their sports, and the old men in their workshops, and sitting together on the benches, would be drawing maps of Sicily, and making charts showing the seas, the harbours, and general character of the coast of the island opposite Africa. For they made not Sicily the end of the war but rather its starting-point and headquarters from whence they might carry it to the Carthaginians, and possess themselves of Africa, and of the seas as far as the pillars of Hercules.

The bulk of the people, therefore, pressing this way, Nicias, who opposed them, found but few supporters, nor those of much influence; for the men of substance, fearing lest they should seem to shun the public charges and ship-money, were quiet against their inclination; nevertheless he did not tire nor give it up, but even after the Athenians decreed a war and chose him in the first place general, together with Alcibiades and Lamachus, when they were again assembled, he stood up, dissuaded them, and protested against the decision, and laid the blame on Alcibiades, charging him with going about to involve the city in foreign dangers and difficulties, merely with a view to his own private lucre and ambition.

Yet it came to nothing. Nicias, because of his experience, was looked upon as the fitter for the employment, and his wariness with the bravery of Alcibiades, and the easy temper of Lamachus, all compounded together, promised such security, that he did but confirm the resolution. Demostratus, who, of the popular leaders, was the one who chiefly pressed the Athenians to the expedition, stood up and said he would stop the mouth of Nicias from urging any more excuses, and moved that the generals should have absolute power, both at home and abroad, to order and to act as they thought best; and this vote the people passed.

The priests, however, are said to have very earnestly opposed the enterprise. But Alcibiades had his diviners of another sort, who from some old prophecies announced that "there shall be great fame of the Athenians in Sicily," and messengers came back to him from Jupiter Ammon with oracles importing that "the Athenians shall take all the Syracusans." Those, meanwhile, who knew anything that boded ill, concealed it lest they might seem to fore-speak ill-luck.

For even prodigies that were obvious and

plain would not deter them; not the defacing of the Hermæ, all maimed in one night except one, called the Hermes of Andocides, erected by the tribe of Ægeus, placed directly before the house then occupied by Andocides; nor what was perpetrated on the altar of the twelve gods, upon which a certain man leaped suddenly up, and then turning round mutilated himself with a stone. Likewise at Delphi there stood a golden image of Minerva, set on a palm-tree of brass, erected by the city of Athens from the spoils they won from the Medes; this was pecked at several days together by crows flying upon it, who also plucked off and knocked down the fruit, made of gold, upon the palm-tree. But the Athenians said these were all but inventions of the Delphians, corrupted by the men of Syracuse.

A certain oracle bade them bring from Clazomenæ the priestess of Minerva there; they sent for the woman and found her named *Hesychia*, Quietness, this being, it would seem, what the divine powers advised the city at this time, to be quiet. Whether, therefore, the astrologer Meton feared these presages, or that from human reason he doubted its success (for he was appointed to a command in it), feigning himself mad, he set his house on fire. Others say he did not counterfeit madness, but set his house on fire in the night, and the next morning came before the assembly in great distress, and besought the people, in consideration of the sad disaster, to release his son from the service, who was about to go captain of a galley for Sicily.

The genius, also, of the philosopher Socrates, on this occasion, too, gave him intimation by the usual tokens, that the expedition would prove the ruin of the commonwealth; this he imparted to his friends and familiars, and by them it was mentioned to a number of people. Not a few were troubled because the days on which the fleet set sail happened to be the time when the women celebrated the death of Adonis; there being everywhere then exposed to view images of dead men, carried about with mourning and lamentation, and women beating their breasts. So that such as laid any stress on these matters were extremely troubled, and feared lest that all this warlike preparation, so splendid and so glorious, should suddenly, in a little time, be blasted in its very prime of magnificence, and come to nothing.

Nicias, in opposing the voting of this expedition, and neither being puffed up with hopes, nor transported with the honour of his high command so as to modify his judgment, showed himself a man of virtue and constancy.

But when his endeavours could not diverge the people from the war, nor get leave for himself to be discharged of the command, but the people, as it were, violently took him up and carried him, and against his will put him in the office of general, this was no longer now a time for his excessive caution and his delays, nor was it for him, like a child, to look back from the ship, often repeating and reconsidering over and over again how that his advice had not been over-ruled by fair arguments, thus blunting the courage of his fellow-commanders and spoiling the season of action. Whereas, he ought speedily to have closed with the enemy and brought the matter to an issue, and put fortune immediately to the test in battle.

But, on the contrary, when Lamachus counselled to sail directly to Syracuse, and fight the enemy under their city walls, and Alcibiades advised to secure the friendship of the other towns, and then to march against them, Nicias dissented from them both, and insisted that they should cruise quietly around the island and display their armament, and having landed a small supply of men for the Ægesteans, return to Athens, weakening at once the resolution and casting down the spirits of the men. And when, a little while after, the Athenians called Alcibiades home in order to stand trial, he being, though joined nominally with another in commission, in effect the only general, made now no end of loitering, of cruising, and considering, till their hopes were grown stale, and all the disorder and consternation which the first approach and view of their forces had cast amongst the enemy was worn off and had left them.

Whilst yet Alcibiades was with the fleet, they went before Syracuse with a squadron of sixty galleys, fifty of them lying in array without the harbour, while the other ten rowed in to reconnoitre, and by a herald called upon the citizens of Leontini to return to their own country. These scouts took a galley of the enemy's, in which they found certain tablets, on which was set down a list of all the Syracusans, according to their tribes. These were wont to be laid up at a distance from the city, in the temple of Jupiter Olympius, but were now brought forth for examination to furnish a muster-roll of young men for the war. These being so taken by the Athenians, and carried to the officers, and the multitude of names appearing, the diviners thought it unpropitious, and were in apprehension lest this should be the only destined fulfilment of the prophecy, that "the Athenians shall take all the Syracusans." Yet, indeed, this was said to be accomplished by the Athenians at another time, when Callippus the Athenian, having slain Dion, became master of Syracuse.

But when Alcibiades shortly after sailed away from Sicily, the command fell wholly to Nicias. Lamachus was, indeed, a brave and honest man, and ready to fight fearlessly with his own hand in battle, but so poor and ill-off that, whenever he was appointed general, he used always, in accounting for his outlay of public money, to bring some little reckoning or other of money for his very clothes and shoes.

On the contrary, Nicias, as on other accounts, so, also, because of his wealth and station, was very much thought of. The story is told that once upon a time the commission of generals being in consultation together in their public office, he bade Sophocles, the poet, give his opinion first, as the senior of the board. "I," replied Sophocles, "am the older, but you are the senior."

And so now, also, Lamachus, who better understood military affairs, being quite his subordinate, he himself, evermore delaying and avoiding risk, and faintly employing his forces, first by his sailing about Sicily at the greatest distance aloof from the enemy, gave them confidence, then by afterwards attacking Hybla, a petty fortress, and drawing off before he could take it, made himself utterly despised. At the last he retreated to Catana without having achieved anything, save that he demolished Hyccara, an humble town of the barbarians, out of which, the story goes, that Lais, the courtesan, yet a mere girl, was sold amongst the other prisoners, and carried thence away to Peloponnesus.

But when the summer was spent, after reports began to reach him that the Syracusans were grown so confident that they would come first to attack him, and troopers skirmishing to the very camp twitted his soldiers, asking whether they came to settle with the Catanians, or to put the Leontines in possession of their city, at last, with much ado, Nicias resolved to sail against Syracuse. And wishing to form his camp safely and without molestation, he procured a man to carry from Catana intelligence to the Syracusans that they might seize the camp of the Athenians unprotected, and all their arms, if on such a day they should march with all their forces to Catana; and that, the Athenians living mostly in the town, the friends of the Syracusans had concerted, as soon as they should perceive them coming, to possess themselves of one of the gates, and to fire the arsenal; that many now were in the conspiracy and waited their arrival.

This was the ablest thing Nicias did in the whole of his conduct of the expedition. For having drawn out all the strength of the enemy, and made the city destitute of men, he set out from Catana, entered the harbour, and chose a fit place for his camp, where the enemy could least incommode him with the means in which they were superior to him, while with the means in which he was superior to them he might expect to carry on the war without impediment.

When the Syracusans returned from Catana, and stood in battle array before the city gates, he rapidly led up the Athenians and fell on them and defeated them, but did not kill many, their horse hindering the pursuit. And his cutting and breaking down the bridges that lay over the river gave Hermocrates, when cheering up the Syracusans, occasion to say that Nicias was ridiculous, whose great aim seemed to be to avoid fighting, as if fighting were not the thing he came for. However, he put the Syracusans into a very great alarm and consternation, so that instead of fifteen generals then in service, they chose three others, to whom the people engaged by oath to allow absolute authority.

There stood near them the temple of Jupiter Olympius, which the Athenians (there being in it many consecrated things of gold and silver) were eager to take, but were purposely withheld from it by Nicias, who let the opportunity slip, and allowed a garrison of the Syracusans to enter it, judging that if the soldiers should make booty of that wealth it would be no advantage to the public, and he should bear the guilt of the impiety.

Not improving in the least this success, which was everywhere famous, after a few days' stay, away he went to Naxos, and there wintered, spending largely for the maintenance of so great an army, and not doing anything except some matters of little consequence with some native Sicilians that revolted to him. Insomuch that the Syracusans took heart again, made excursions to Catana, wasted the country, and fired the camp of the Athenians. For which everybody blamed Nicias, who, with his long reflection, his deliberateness, and his caution, had let slip the time for action. None ever found fault with the man when once at work, for in the brunt he showed vigour and activity enough, but was slow and wanted assurance to engage.

When, therefore, he brought again the army to Syracuse, such was his conduct, and with such celerity, and at the same time security, he came upon them, that nobody knew of his approach, when already he had come to shore with his galleys at Thapsus, and had landed his men; and before any could help it, he had surprised Epipolæ, had defeated the body of picked men that came to its succour, took three hundred prisoners, and routed the cavalry of the enemy, which had been thought invincible.

But what chiefly astonished the Syracusans, and seemed incredible to the Greeks, was in so short a space of time the walling about of Syracuse, a town not less than Athens, and far more difficult, by the unevenness of the ground, and the nearness of the sea and the marshes adjacent, to have such a wall drawn in a circle round it; yet this, all within a very little, finished by a man that had not even his health for such weighty cares, but lay ill of the stone, which may justly bear the blame for what was left undone. I admire the industry of the general, and the bravery of the soldiers for what they succeeded in. Euripides, after their ruin and disaster, writing their funeral elegy, said that—

Eight victories over Syracuse they gained,
While equal yet to both the gods remained

And in truth one shall not find eight, but many more victories, won by these men against the Syracusans, till the gods, in real truth, or fortune intervened to check the Athenians in this advance to the height of power and greatness.

Nicias, therefore, doing violence to his body, was present in most actions. But once, when his disease was the sharpest upon him, he lay in the camp with some few servants to attend him. And Lamachus, having the command, fought the Syracusans, who were bringing a cross-wall from the city along to that of the Athenians, to hinder them from carrying it round; and in the victory, the Athenians hurrying in some disorder the pursuit, Lamachus getting separated from his men, had to resist the Syracusan horse that came upon him. Before the rest advanced Callicrates, a man of good courage and skill in war. Lamachus, upon a challenge, engaged with him in single combat, and receiving the first wound, re-

turned it so home to Callicrates, that they both fell and died together.

The Syracusans took away his body and arms, and at full speed advanced to the wall of the Athenians, where Nicias lay without any troops to oppose to them, yet roused by this necessity, and seeing the danger, he bade those about him go and set on fire all the wood and materials that lay provided before the wall for the engines, and the engines themselves; this put a stop to the Syracusans, saved Nicias, saved the walls and all the money of the Athenians. For when the Syracusans saw such a fire blazing up between them and the wall, they retired.

Nicias now remained sole general, and with great prospects; for cities began to come over to alliance with him, and ships laden with corn from every coast came to the camp, every one favouring when matters went well. And some proposals from among the Syracusans despairing to defend the city, about a capitulation, were already conveyed to him. And in fact Gylippus, who was on his way with a squadron to their aid from Lacedæmon, hearing on his voyage of the wall surrounding them, and of their distress, only continued his enterprise thenceforth, that, giving Sicily up for lost, he might, if even that should be possible, secure the Italians their cities. For a strong report was everywhere spread about that the Athenians carried all before them, and had a general alike for conduct and for fortune invincible.

And Nicias himself, too, now against his nature grown bold in his present strength and success, especially from the intelligence he received underhand of the Syracusans, believing they would almost immediately surrender the town upon terms, paid no manner of regard to Gylippus coming to their assistance, nor kept any watch of his approach, so that, neglected altogether and despised, Gylippus went in a long-boat ashore without the knowledge of Nicias, and, having landed in the remotest parts from Syracuse, mustered up a considerable force, the Syracusans not so much as knowing of his arrival nor expecting him; so that an assembly was summoned to consider the terms to be arranged with Nicias, and some were actually on the way, thinking it essential to have all despatched before the town should be quite walled round, for now there remained very little to be done, and the materials for the building lay all ready along the line.

In this very nick of time and danger arrived Gongylus in one galley from Corinth, and every one, as may be imagined, flocking about him, he told them that Gylippus would be with them speedily, and that other ships were coming to relieve them. And, ere yet they could perfectly believe Gongylus, an express was brought from Gylippus, to bid them go forth to meet him. So now taking good heart, they armed themselves; and Gylippus at once led on his men from their march in battle array against the Athenians, as Nicias also embattled these. And Gylippus, piling his arms in view of the Athenians, sent a herald to tell them he would give them leave to depart from Sicily without molestation. To this Nicias would not vouchsafe any answer, but some of his soldiers laughing, asked if with the sight of one coarse coat and Laconian staff the Syracusan prospects had become so brilliant that they could despise the Athenians who had released to the Lacedæmonians three hundred, whom they held in chains, bigger men than Gylippus, and longer-haired?

Timæus, also, writes that even the Syracusans made no account of Gylippus, at the first sight mocking at his staff and long hair, as afterwards they found reason to blame his covetousness and meanness. The same author, however, adds that on Gylippus's first appearance, as it might have been at the sight of an owl abroad in the air, there was a general flocking together of men to serve in the war. And this is the truer saying of the two; for in the staff and the cloak they saw the badge and authority of Sparta, and crowded to him accordingly. And not only Thucydides affirms that the whole thing was done by him alone, but so, also, does Philistus, who was a Syracusan and an actual witness of what happened.

However, the Athenians had the better in the first encounter, and slew some few of the Syracusans, and amongst them Gongylus of Corinth. But on the next day Gylippus showed what it is to be a man of experience; for with the same arms, the same horses, and on the same spot of ground, only employing them otherwise, he overcame the Athenians; and they fleeing to their camp, he set the Syracusans to work, and with the stone and materials that had been brought together for finishing the wall of the Athenians, he built a cross-wall to intercept theirs and break it off, so that even if they were successful in the field, they would not be able to do anything.

And after this the Syracusans taking courage manned their galleys, and with their horse and followers ranging about took a good many prisoners; and Gylippus going himself to the cities, called upon them to join with him, and was listened to and supported vigorously by them. So that Nicias fell back again to his old views, and, seeing the face of affairs change, desponded, and wrote to Athens, bidding them either send another army, or recall this out of Sicily, and that he might, in any case, be wholly relieved of the command, because of his disease.

Before this the Athenians had been intending to send another army to Sicily, but envy of Nicias's early achievements and high fortune had occasioned, up to this time, many delays; but now they were all eager to send off succours. Eurymedon went before, in midwinter, with money, and to announce that Euthydemus and Menander were chosen out of those that served there under Nicias to be joint commanders with him. Demosthenes was to go after in the spring with a great armament.

In the meantime Nicias was briskly attacked, both by sea and land; in the beginning he had the disadvantage on the water, but in the end repulsed and sunk many galleys of the enemy. But by land he could not provide succour in time, so Gylippus surprised and captured Plemmyrium, in which the stores for the navy, and a great sum of money being there kept, all fell into his hands, and many were slain, and many taken prisoners. And what was of greatest importance, he now cut off Nicias's supplies, which had been safely and readily conveyed to him under Plemmyrium, while the Athenians still held it, but now that they were beaten out, he could only procure them with great difficulty, and with opposition from the enemy, who lay in wait with their ships under that fort. Moreover, it seemed manifest to the Syracusans that their navy had not been beaten by strength, but by their disorder in the pursuit. Now, therefore, all hands went to work to prepare for a new attempt that should succeed better than the former.

Nicias had no wish for a sea-fight, but said it was mere folly for them, when Demosthenes was coming in all haste with so great a fleet and fresh forces to their succour, to engage the enemy with a less number of ships and ill provided. But, on the other hand, Menander and Euthydemus, who were just commencing their new command, prompted by a feeling of rivalry and emulation of both the generals, were eager to gain some great success before Demosthenes came, and to prove themselves superior to Nicias. They urged the honour of the city, which, said they, would be blemished and utterly lost if they should decline a challenge from the Syracusans. Thus they forced Nicias to a sea-fight; and by the stratagem of Ariston, the Corinthian pilot (his trick, described by Thucydides, about the men's dinners), they were worsted, and lost many of their men, causing the greatest dejection to Nicias, who had suffered so much from having the sole command, and now again miscarried through his colleagues.

But now by this time Demosthenes with his splendid fleet came in sight outside the harbour, a terror to the enemy. He brought along, in seventy-three galleys, five thousand men-at-arms; of darters, archers, and slingers, not less than three thousand; with the glittering of their armour, the flags waving from the galleys, the multitude of coxswains and flute-players giving time to the rowers, setting off the whole with all possible warlike pomp and ostentation to dismay the enemy. Now one may believe the Syracusans were again in extreme alarm, seeing no end or prospect of release before them, toiling, as it seemed, in vain, and perishing to no purpose.

Nicias, however, was not long overjoyed with the reinforcement, for the first time he conferred with Demosthenes, who advised forthwith to attack the Syracusans, and to put all to the speediest hazard, to win Syracuse, or else return home, afraid, and wondering at his promptness and audacity, he besought him to do nothing rashly and desperately, since delay would be the ruin of the enemy, whose money would not hold out, nor their confederates be long kept together; that when once they came to be pinched with want, they would presently come again to him for terms, as formerly. For, indeed, many in Syracuse held secret correspondence with him, and urged him to stay, declaring that even now the people were quite worn out with the war and weary of Gylippus. And if their necessities should the least sharpen upon them they would give up all.

Nicias glancing darkly at these matters, and unwilling to speak out plainly, made his colleagues imagine that it was cowardice which made him talk in this manner. And saying that this was the old story over again, the well-known procrastinations and delays and refinements with which at first he let slip the opportunity in not immediately falling on the enemy, but suffering the armament to become a thing of yesterday, that nobody was alarmed with, they took the side of Demosthenes, and

with much ado forced Nicias to comply. And so Demosthenes, taking the land-forces, by night made an assault upon Epipolæ; part of the enemy he slew ere they took the alarm, the rest defending themselves he put to flight. Nor was he content with this victory there, but pushed on further, till he met the Bœotians. For these were the first that made head against the Athenians, and charged them with a shout, spear against spear, and killed many on the place. And now at once there ensued a panic and confusion throughout the whole army; the victorious portion got infected with the fears of the flying part, and those who were still disembarking and coming forward, falling foul of the retreaters, came into conflict with their own party, taking the fugitives for pursuers, and treating their friends as if they were the enemy.

Thus huddled together in disorder, distracted with fear and uncertainties, and unable to be sure of seeing anything, the night not being absolutely dark, nor yielding any steady light, the moon then towards setting, shadowed with the many weapons and bodies that moved to and fro, and glimmering so as not to show an object plain, but to make friends through fear suspected for foes, the Athenians fell into utter perplexity and desperation. For, moreover, they had the moon at their backs, and consequently their own shadows fell upon them, and both hid the number and the glittering of their arms; while the reflection of the moon from the shields of the enemy made them show more numerous and better appointed than, indeed, they were. At last, being pressed on every side, when once they had given way, they took to rout, and in their flight were destroyed, some by the enemy, some by the hand of their friends, and some tumbling down the rocks, while those that were dispersed and straggled about were picked off in the morning by the horsemen and put to the sword. The slain were two thousand; and of the rest few came off safe with their arms.

Upon this disaster which to him was not wholly an unexpected one, Nicias accused the rashness of Demosthenes; but he, making his excuses for the past, now advised to be gone in all haste, for neither were other forces to come, nor could the enemy be beaten with the present. And, indeed, even supposing they were yet too hard for the enemy in any case, they ought to remove and quit a situation which they understood to be always accounted a sickly one, and dangerous for an army, and was more particularly unwholesome now, as they could see themselves, because of the time of year. It was the beginning of autumn, and many now lay sick, and all were out of heart.

It grieved Nicias to hear of flight and departing home, not that he did not fear the Syracusans, but he was worse afraid of the Athenians, their impeachments and sentences; he professed that he apprehended no further harm there, or if it must be, he would rather die by the hand of an enemy than by his fellow-citizens. He was not of the opinion which Leo of Byzantium declared to his fellow-citizens: "I had rather," said he, "perish by you, than with you." As to the matter of place and quarter whither to remove their camp, that, he said, might be debated at leisure. And Demosthenes, his former counsel having succeeded so ill, ceased to press him further; others thought Nicias had reasons for expectation, and relied on some assurance from people within the city, and that this made him so strongly oppose their retreat, so they acquiesced. But fresh forces now coming to the Syracusans and the sickness growing worse in his camp, he, also, now approved of their retreat, and commanded the soldiers to make ready to go abroad.

And when all were in readiness, and none of the enemy had observed them, not expecting such a thing, the moon was eclipsed in the night, to the great fright of Nicias and others, who, for want of experience, or out of superstition, felt alarm at such appearances. That the sun might be darkened about the close of the month, this even ordinary people now understood pretty well to be the effect of the moon; but the moon itself to be darkened, how that could come about, and how, on the sudden, a broad full moon should lose her light, and show such various colours, was not easy to be comprehended; they concluded it to be ominous, and a divine intimation of some heavy calamities.

For he who the first, and the most plainly of any, and with the greatest assurance committed to writing how the moon is enlightened and overshadowed, was Anaxagoras; and he was as yet but recent, nor was his argument much known, but was rather kept secret, passing only amongst a few, under some kind of caution and confidence. People would not then tolerate natural philosophers, and theorists, as they then called them, about things above; as lessening the divine power, by explaining away its agency into the operation of irrational causes and senseless forces acting by necessity, without anything of Providence or a free agent. Hence it was that Protagoras was banished, and Anaxagoras cast in prison, so that Pericles had much difficulty to procure his liberty; and Socrates, though he had no concern whatever with this sort of learning, yet was put to death for philosophy.

It was only afterwards that the reputation of Plato, shining forth by his life, and because he subjected natural necessity to divine and more excellent principles, took away the obloquy and scandal that had attached to such contemplations, and obtained these studies currency among all people. So his friend, Dion, when the moon, at the time he was to embark from Zacynthus to go against Dionysius, was eclipsed, was not in the least disturbed, but went on, and arriving at Syracuse, expelled the tyrant.

But it so fell out with Nicias, that he had not at this time a skilful diviner with him; his former habitual adviser who used to moderate much of his superstition, Stilbides, had died a little before. For, in fact, this prodigy, as Philochorus observes, was not unlucky for men wishing to flee, but on the contrary very favourable; for things done in fear require to be hidden, and the light is their foe. Nor was it usual to observe signs in the sun or moon more than three days, as Autoclides states in his *Commentaries*. But Nicias persuaded them to wait another full course of the moon, as if he had not seen it clear again as soon as ever it had passed the region of shadow where the light was obstructed by the earth.

In a manner abandoning all other cares, he betook himself wholly to his sacrifices, till the enemy came upon them with their infantry, besieging the forts and camp, and placing their ships in a circle about the harbour. Nor did the men in the galleys only, but the little boys everywhere got into the fishing-boats and rowed up and challenged the Athenians, and insulted over them. Amongst these a youth of noble parentage, Heraclides by name, having ventured out beyond the rest, an Athenian ship pursued and well-nigh took him. His uncle, Pollichus, in fear for him, put out with ten galleys which he commanded, and the rest, to relieve Pollichus, in like manner drew forth; the result of it being a very sharp engagement, in which the Syracusans had the victory, and slew Eurymedon, with many others.

After this the Athenian soldiers had no patience to stay longer, but raised an outcry against their officers, requiring them to depart by land; for the Syracusans, upon their victory, immediately shut and blocked up the entrance of the harbour; but Nicias would not consent to this, as it was a shameful thing to leave behind so many ships of burden, and galleys little less than two hundred. Putting, therefore, on board the best of the foot, and the most serviceable darters, they filled one hundred and ten galleys; the rest wanted oars. The remainder of his army Nicias posted along by the seaside, abandoning the great camp and the fortifications adjoining the temple of Hercules; so the Syracusans, not having for a long time performed their usual sacrifice to Hercules, went up now, both priests and captains, to sacrifice.

And their galleys being manned, the diviners predicted from their sacrifices victory and glory to the Syracusans, provided they would not be the aggressors, but fight upon the defensive; for so Hercules overcame all, by only defending himself when set upon. In this confidence they set out; and this proved the hottest and fiercest of all their sea-fights, raising no less concern and passion in the beholders than in the actors; as they could oversee the whole action with all the various and unexpected turns of fortune which, in a short space, occurred in it; the Athenians suffering no less from their own preparations, than from the enemy; for they fought against light and nimble ships, that could attack from any quarter, with theirs laden and heavy. And they were thrown at with stones that fly indifferently any way, for which they could only return darts and arrows, the direct aim of which the motion of the water disturbed, preventing their coming true, point foremost to their mark. This the Syracusans had learned from Ariston, the Corinthian pilot, who, fighting stoutly, fell himself in this very engagement, when the victory had already been declared for the Syracusans.

The Athenians, their loss and slaughter being very great, their flight by sea cut off, their safety by land so difficult, did not attempt to hinder the enemy towing away their ships, under their eyes, nor demanded their dead, as, indeed, their want of burial seemed a less calamity than the leaving behind the sick and wounded which they now had before them. Yet more miserable still than those did they reckon themselves, who were to work on yet, through more such sufferings, after all to reach the same end.

They prepared to dislodge that night. And Gylippus and his friends seeing the Syracusans engaged in their sacrifices and at their cups, for their victories, and it being also a holiday, did not expect either by persuasion or by force to rouse them up and carry them against the Athenians as they decamped. But Hermocrates, of his own head, put a trick upon Nicias, and sent some of his companions to him, who pretended they came from those that were wont to hold secret intelligence with him, and advised him not to stir that night, the Syracusans having laid ambushes and beset the ways.

Nicias, caught with this stratagem, remained, to encounter presently in reality what he had feared when there was no occasion. For they, the next morning, marching before, seized the defiles, fortified the passes where the rivers were fordable, cut down the bridges, and ordered their horsemen to range the plains and ground that lay open, so as to leave no part of the country where the Athenians could move without fighting. They stayed both that day and another night, and then went along as if they were leaving their own, not an enemy's country, lamenting and bewailing for want of necessaries, and for their parting from friends and companions that were not able to help themselves; and, nevertheless, judging the present evils lighter than those they expected to come.

But among the many miserable spectacles that appeared up and down in the camp, the saddest sight of all was Nicias himself, labouring under his malady, and unworthily reduced to the scantiest supply of all the accommodations necessary for human wants, of which he in his condition required more than ordinary, because of his sickness, yet bearing up under all this illness, and doing and undergoing more than many in perfect health.

And it was plainly evident that all this toil was not for himself, or from any regard to his own life, but that purely for the sake of those under his command he would not abandon hope. And, indeed, the rest were given over to weeping and lamentation through fear or sorrow, but he, whenever he yielded to anything of the kind, did so, it was evident, from reflection upon the shame and dishonour of the enterprise, contrasted with the greatness and glory of the success he had anticipated, and not only the sight of his person, but, also, the recollection of the arguments and the dissuasions he used to prevent this expedition enhanced their sense of the undeservedness of his sufferings, nor had they any heart to put their trust in the gods, considering that a man so religious, who had performed to the divine powers so many and so great acts of devotion, should have no more favourable treatment than the wickedest and meanest of the army.

Nicias, however, endeavoured all the while by his voice, his countenance, and his carriage, to show himself undefeated by these misfortunes. And all along the way shot at, and receiving wounds eight days continually from the enemy, he yet preserved the forces with him in a body entire, till that Demosthenes was taken prisoner with the party that he led, whilst they fought and made a resistance, and so got behind and were surrounded near the country house of Polyzelus. Demosthenes thereupon drew his sword, and wounded but did not kill himself, the enemy speedily running in and seizing upon him. So soon as the Syracusans had gone and informed Nicias of this, and he had sent some horsemen, and by them knew the certainty of the defeat of that division, he then vouchsafed to sue to Gylippus for a truce for the Athenians to depart out of Sicily, leaving hostages for payment of money that the Syracusans had expended in the war.

But now they would not hear of these proposals, but threatening and reviling them, angrily and insultingly continued to ply their missiles at them, now destitute of every necessary. Yet Nicias still made good his retreat all that night, and the next day, through all their darts, made his way to the river Asinarus. There, however, the enemy encountering them, drove some into the stream, while others, ready to die for thirst, plunged in headlong, while they drank at the same time, and were cut down by their enemies. And here was the cruellest and the most immoderate slaughter. Till at last Nicias falling down to Gylippus, "Let pity, O Gylippus," said he, "move you in your victory; not for me, who was destined, it seems, to bring the glory I once had to this end, but for the other Athenians; as you well know that the chances of war are common to all, and the Athenians used them moderately and mildly towards you in their prosperity."

At these words, and at the sight of Nicias, Gylippus was somewhat troubled, for he was sensible that the Lacedæmonians had received good offices from Nicias in the late treaty, and he thought it would be a great and glorious thing for him to carry off the chief commanders of the Athenians alive. He therefore raised Nicias with respect, and bade him be of good cheer, and commanded his men to spare the lives of the rest. But the word of command being communicated slowly, the slain were a far greater number than the prisoners. Many, however, were privately conveyed away by particular soldiers. Those taken openly were hurried together in a mass; their arms and spoils hung up on the finest and largest trees along the river. The conquerors, with garlands on their heads, with their own horses splendidly adorned, and cropping short the manes and tails of those of their enemies, entered the city, having, in the most signal conflict ever waged by Greeks against Greeks, and with the greatest strength and the utmost effort of valour and manhood won a most entire victory.

And a general assembly of the people of Syracuse and their confederates sitting, Eurycles, the popular leader, moved, first, that the day on which they took Nicias should from thenceforward be kept holiday by sacrificing and forbearing all manner of work, and from the river be called the Asinarian Feast. This was the twenty-sixth day of the month Carneus, the Athenian Metagitnion. And that the servants of the Athenians with the other confederates be sold for slaves, and they themselves and the Sicilian auxiliaries be kept and employed in the quarries, except the generals, who should be put to death.

The Syracusans favoured the proposals, and when Hermocrates said, that to use well a victory was better than to gain a victory, he was met with great clamour and outcry. When Gylippus, also, demanded the Athenian generals to be delivered to him, that he might carry them to the Lacedæmonians, the Syracusans, now insolent with their good-fortune, gave him ill words. Indeed, before this, even in the war, they had been impatient at his rough behaviour and Lacedæmonian haughtiness, and had, as Timæus tells us, discovered sordidness and avarice in his character, vices which may have descended to him from his father, Cleandrides, who was convicted of bribery and banished. And the very man himself, of the one thousand talents which Lysander sent to Sparta, embezzled thirty, and hid them under the tiles of his house, and was detected and shamefully fled his country. But this is related more at large in the life of Lysander.

Timæus says that Demosthenes and Nicias did not die, as Thucydides and Philistus have written, by the order of the Syracusans, but that upon a message sent them from Hermocrates, whilst yet the assembly were sitting, by the connivance of some of their guards, they were enabled to put an end to themselves. Their bodies, however, were thrown out before the gates and offered for a public spectacle. And I have heard that to this day in a temple at Syracuse is shown a shield, said to have been Nicias's, curiously wrought and embroidered with gold and purple intermixed.

Most of the Athenians perished in the quarries by diseases and ill diet, being allowed only one pint of barley every day, and one half pint of water. Many of them, however, were carried off by stealth, or, from the first, were supposed to be servants, and were sold as slaves. These latter were branded on their foreheads with the figure of a horse. There were, however, Athenians who, in addition to slavery, had to endure even this. But their discreet and orderly conduct was an advantage to them; they were either soon set free, or won the respect of their masters with whom they continued to live.

Several were saved for the sake of Euripides, whose poetry, it appears, was in request among the Sicilians more than among any of the settlers out of Greece. And when any travellers arrived that could tell them some passage, or give them any specimen of his verses, they were delighted to be able to communicate them to one another. Many of the captives who got safe back to Athens are said, after they reached home, to have gone and made their acknowledgments to Euripides, relating how that some of them had been released from their slavery by teaching what they could remember of his poems, and others, when straggling after the fight, been relieved with meat and drink for repeating some of his lyrics. Nor need this be any wonder, for it is told that a ship of Caunus fleeing into one of their harbours for protection, pursued by pirates, was not received, but forced back, till one asked if they knew any of Euripides's verses, and on their saying they did, they were admitted, and their ship brought into harbour.

It is said that the Athenians would not believe their loss, in a great degree because of the person who first brought them news of it. For a certain stranger, it seems, coming to Piræus, and there sitting in a barber's shop, began to talk of what had happened, as if the Athenians already knew all that had passed; which the barber hearing, before he acquainted anybody else, ran as fast as he could up into the city, addressed himself to the Archons, and presently spread it about in the public place. On which, there being everywhere, as may be imagined, terror and consternation, the Archons summoned a general assembly, and there brought in the man and questioned him how he came to know. And he, giving no satisfactory account, was taken for a spreader of false intelligence and a disturber of the city, and was, therefore, fastened to the wheel and racked a long time, till other messengers arrived that related the whole disaster particularly. So hardly was Nicias believed to have suffered the calamity which he had often predicted.

CRASSUS

115?–53 B.C.

MARCUS CRASSUS, whose father had borne the office of a censor, and received the honour of a triumph, was educated in a little house together with his two brothers, who both married in their parents' lifetime; they kept but one table amongst them; all which, perhaps, was not the least reason of his own temperance and moderation in diet. One of his brothers dying, he married his widow, by whom he had his children; neither was there in these respects any of the Romans who lived a more orderly life than he did, though later in life he was suspected to have been too familiar with one of the vestal virgins, named Licinia, who was, nevertheless, acquitted, upon an impeachment brought against her by one Plotinus. Licinia stood possessed of a beautiful property in the suburbs, which Crassus desiring to purchase at a low price, for this reason was frequent in his attentions to her, which gave occasion to the scandal, and his avarice, so to say, serving to clear him of the crime, he was acquitted. Nor did he leave the lady till he had got the estate.

People were wont to say that the many virtues of Crassus were darkened by the one vice of avarice, and indeed he seemed to have no other but that; for it being the most predominant, obscured others to which he was inclined. The arguments in proof of his avarice were the vastness of his estate, and the manner of raising it; for whereas at first he was not worth above three hundred talents, yet, though in the course of his political life he dedicated the tenth of all he had to Hercules, and feasted the people, and gave to every citizen corn enough to serve him three months, upon casting up his accounts, before he went upon his Parthian expedition, he found his possessions to amount to seven thousand one hundred talents; most of which, if we may scandal him with a truth, he got by fire and rapine, making his advantages of the public calamities.

For when Sulla seized the city, and exposed to sale the goods of those that he had caused to be slain, accounting them booty and spoils, and, indeed, calling them so too, and was desirous of making as many, and as eminent men as he could, partakers in the crime, Crassus never was the man that refused to accept, or give money for them. Moreover, observing how extremely subject the city was to fire and falling down of houses, by reason of their height and their standing so near together, he bought slaves that were builders and architects, and when he had collected these to the number of more than five hundred, he made it his practice to buy houses that were on fire, and those in the neighbourhood, which, in the immediate danger and uncertainty the proprietors were willing to part with for little or nothing, so that the greatest part of Rome, at one time or other, came into his hands. Yet for all he had so many workmen, he never built anything but his own house, and used to say that those that were addicted to building would undo themselves soon enough without the help of other enemies.

And though he had many silver mines, and much valuable land, and labourers to work in it, yet all this was nothing in comparison of his slaves, such a number and variety did he possess of excellent readers, amanuenses, silversmiths, stewards and table-waiters, whose instruction he always attended to himself, superintending in person while they learned, and teaching them himself, accounting it the main duty of a master to look over the servants that are, indeed, the living tools of housekeeping; and in this, indeed, he was in the right, in thinking, that is, as he used to say, that servants ought to look after all other things, and the master after them. For economy, which in things inanimate is but money-making, when exercised over men becomes policy.

But it was surely a mistaken judgment, when he said no man was to be accounted rich that could not maintain an army at his own cost and charges, for war, as Archidamus well observed, is not fed at a fixed allowance, so that there is no saying what wealth suffices for it, and certainly it was one very far removed from that of Marius; for when he had distributed fourteen acres of land a man, and understood that some desired more, "God forbid," said he, "that any Roman should think that too little which is enough to keep him alive and well."

Crassus, however, was very eager to be hospitable to strangers; he kept open house, and to his friends he would lend money without interest, but called it in precisely at the time; so that his kindness was often thought worse than the paying the interest would have been. His entertainments were, for the most part, plain and citizenlike, the company general and popular; good taste and kindness made them pleasanter than sumptuosity would have done.

As for learning he chiefly cared for rhetoric, and what would be serviceable with large numbers; he became one of the best speakers at Rome, and by his pains and industry outdid the best natural orators. For there was no trial how soever mean and contemptible that he came to unprepared; nay, several times he undertook and concluded a cause when Pompey and Cæsar and Cicero refused to stand up, upon which account particularly he got the love of the people, who looked upon him as a diligent and careful man, ready to help and succour his fellow citizens. Besides, the people were pleased with his courteous and unpretending salutations and greetings, for he never met any citizen however humble and low, but he returned him his salute by name.

He was looked upon as a man well-read in history, and pretty well versed in Aristotle's philosophy, in which one Alexander instructed him, a man whose intercourse with Crassus gave a sufficient proof of his good nature and gentle disposition; for it is hard to say whether he was poorer when he entered into his service, or while he continued in it; for being his only friend that used to accompany him when travelling, he used to receive from him a cloak for the journey, and when he came home had it demanded from him again; poor, patient sufferer, when even the philosophy he professed did not look upon poverty as a thing indifferent. But of this hereafter.

When Cinna and Marius got the power in their hands it was soon perceived that they had not come back for any good they intended to their country, but to effect the ruin and utter destruction of the nobility. And as many as they could lay their hands on they slew, amongst whom were Crassus's father and brother; he himself, being very young, for the moment escaped the danger; but understanding that he was every way beset and hunted after by the tyrants, taking with him three friends and ten servants, with all possible speed he fled into Spain, having formerly been there and secured a great number of friends, while his father was prætor of that country.

But finding all people in a consternation, and trembling at the cruelty of Marius, as if he was already standing over them in person, he durst not discover himself to anybody, but hid himself in a large cave which was by the seashore, and belonged to Vibius Pacianus, to whom he sent one of his servants to sound him, his provisions, also, beginning to fail. Vibius was well pleased at his escape, and inquiring the place of his abode and the number of his companions, he went not to him himself, but commanded his steward to provide every day a good meal's meat, and carry it and leave it near such a rock, and to return without taking any further notice or being inquisitive, promising him his liberty if he did as he commanded and that he would kill him if he intermeddled.

The cave is not far from the sea; a small and insignificant looking opening in the cliffs conducts you in; when you are entered, a wonderfully high roof spreads above you, and large chambers open out one beyond another, nor does it lack either water or light, for a very pleasant and wholesome spring runs at the foot of the cliffs, and natural chinks, in the most advantageous place, let in the light all day long, and the thickness of the rock makes the air within pure and clear, all the wet and moisture being carried off into the spring.

While Crassus remained here, the steward brought them what was necessary, but never saw them, nor knew anything of the matter, though they within saw, and expected him at the customary times. Neither was their enter-

tainment such as just to keep them alive, but given them in abundance and for their enjoyment; for Pacianus resolved to treat him with all imaginable kindness, and considering that he was a young man, thought it well to gratify a little his youthful inclinations; for to give just what is needful seems rather to come from necessity than from a hearty friendship. Once taking with him two female servants, he showed them the place and bade them go in boldly. whom when Crassus and his friends saw, they were afraid of being betrayed and demanded what they were, and what they would have. They, according as they were instructed, answered, they came to wait upon their master, who was hid in that cave. And so Crassus perceiving it was a piece of pleasantry and of good-will on the part of Vibius, took them in and kept them there with him as long as he stayed, and employed them to give information to Vibius of what they wanted, and how they were. Fenestella says he saw one of them, then very old, and often heard her speak of the time and repeat the story with pleasure.

After Crassus had lain concealed there eight months, on hearing that Cinna was dead, he appeared abroad, and a great number of people flocking to him, out of whom he selected a body of two thousand five hundred, he visited many cities, and, as some write, sacked Malaca, which he himself, however, always denied, and contradicted all who said so.

Afterwards, getting together some ships, he passed into Africa, and joined with Metellus Pius, an eminent person that had raised a very considerable force; but upon some difference between him and Metellus, he stayed not long there, but went over to Sulla, by whom he was very much esteemed. When Sulla passed over into Italy, he was anxious to put all the young men that were with him in employment; and as he despatched some one way, and some another, Crassus, on its falling to his share to raise men among the Marsians, demanded a guard, having to pass through the enemy's country, upon which Sulla replied sharply, "I give you for guard your father, your brother, your friends and kindred, whose unjust and cruel murder I am now going to revenge"; and Crassus, being nettled, went his way, broke boldly through the enemy, collected a considerable force, and in all Sulla's wars acted with great zeal and courage.

And in these times and occasions, they say, began the emulation and rivalry for glory between him and Pompey; for though Pompey was the younger man, and had the disadvantage to be descended of a father that was disesteemed by the citizens, and hated as much as ever man was, yet in these actions he shone out and was proved so great that Sulla always used, when he came in, to stand up and uncover his head, an honour which he seldom showed to older men and his own equals, and always saluted him Imperator. This fired and stung Crassus, though, indeed, he could not with any fairness claim to be preferred; for he both wanted experience, and his two innate vices, sordidness and avarice, tarnished all the lustre of his actions.

For when he had taken Tudertia, a town of the Umbrians, he converted, it was said, all the spoils to his own use, for which he was complained of to Sulla. But in the last and greatest battle before Rome itself, when Sulla was worsted, some of his battalions giving ground, and others being quite broken, Crassus got the victory on the right wing, which he commanded, and pursued the enemy till night, and then sent to Sulla to acquaint him with his success, and demand provision for his soldiers. In the time, however, of the proscriptions and sequestrations, he lost his repute again, by making great purchases for little or nothing, and asking for grants. Nay, they say he proscribed one of the Bruttians without Sulla's order, only for his own profit, and that, on discovering this, Sulla never after trusted him in any public affairs.

As no man was more cunning than Crassus to ensnare others by flattery, so no man lay more open to it, or swallowed it more greedily than himself. And this particularly was observed of him, that though he was the most covetous man in the world, yet he habitually disliked and cried out against others who were so.

It troubled him to see Pompey so successful in all his undertakings; that he had had a triumph before he was capable to sit in the senate, and that the people had surnamed him Magnus, or the great. When somebody was saying Pompey the Great was coming, he smiled, and asked him, "How big is he?" Despairing to equal him by feats of arms, he betook himself to civil life, where by doing kindnesses, pleading, lending money, by speaking and canvassing among the people for those who had objects to obtain from them, he gradually gained as great honour and power as Pompey had from his many famous expeditions.

And it was a curious thing in their rivalry, that Pompey's name and interests in the city were greatest when he was absent, for his renown in war, but when present he was often less successful than Crassus, by reason of his superciliousness and haughty way of living, shunning crowds of people, and appearing rarely in the Forum, and assisting only some few, and that not readily, that his influence might be the stronger when he came to use it for himself. Whereas Crassus, being a friend always at hand, ready to be had and easy of access, and always with his hands full of other people's business, with his freedom and courtesy, got the better of Pompey's formality. In point of dignity of person, eloquence of language, and attractiveness of countenance, they were pretty equally excellent.

But, however, this emulation never transported Crassus so far as to make him bear enmity or any ill-will; for though he was vexed to see Pompey and Cæsar preferred to him, yet he never mingled any hostility or malice with his jealousy; though Cæsar, when he was taken captive by the corsairs in Asia, cried out, "O Crassus, how glad you will be at the news of my captivity!" Afterwards they lived together on friendly terms, for when Cæsar was going prætor into Spain, and his creditors, he being then in want of money, came upon him and seized his equipage, Crassus then stood by him and relieved him, and was his security for eight hundred and thirty talents.

And in general, Rome being divided into three great interests, those of Pompey, Cæsar, and Crassus (for as for Cato, his fame was greater than his power, and he was rather admired than followed), the sober and quiet part were for Pompey, the restless and hot-headed followed Cæsar's ambition, but Crassus trimmed between them, making advantages of both, and changed sides continually, being neither a trusty friend nor an implacable enemy, and easily abandoned both his attachments and his animosities, as he found it for his advantage, so that in short spaces of time the same men and the same measures had him both as their supporter and as their opponent.

He was much liked, but was feared as much or even more. At any rate, when Sicinius, who was the greatest troubler of the magistrates and ministers of his time, was asked how it was he let Crassus alone, "Oh," said he, "he carries hay on his horns," alluding to the custom of tying hay to the horns of the bull that used to butt, that people might keep out of his way.

The insurrection of the gladiators and the devastation of Italy, commonly called the war of Spartacus, began upon this occasion. One Lentulus Batiates trained up a great many gladiators in Capua, most of them Gauls and Thracians, who, not for any fault by them committed, but simply through the cruelty of their master, were kept in confinement for this object of fighting one with another. Two hundred of these formed a plan to escape, but being discovered, those of them who became aware of it in time to anticipate their master, being seventy-eight, got out of a cook's shop chopping-knives and spits, and made their way through the city, and lighting by the way on several waggons that were carrying gladiators' arms to another city, they seized upon them and armed themselves.

And seizing upon a defensible place, they chose three captains, of whom Spartacus was chief, a Thracian of one of the nomad tribes, and a man not only of high spirit and valiant, but in understanding, also, and in gentleness superior to his condition, and more of a Grecian than the people of his country usually are. When he first came to be sold at Rome, they say a snake coiled itself upon his face as he lay asleep, and his wife, who at this latter time also accompanied him in his flight, his country-woman, a kind of prophetess, and one of those possessed with the bacchanal frenzy, declared that it was a sign portending great and formidable power to him with no happy event.

First, then, routing those that came out of Capua against them, and thus procuring a quantity of proper soldiers' arms, they gladly threw away their own as barbarous and dishonourable. Afterwards Clodius, the prætor, took the command against them with a body of three thousand men from Rome, and besieged them within a mountain, accessible only by one narrow and difficult passage, which Clodius kept guarded, encompassed on all other sides with steep and slippery precipices. Upon the top, however, grew a great many wild vines, and cutting down as many of their boughs as they had need of, they twisted them into strong ladders long enough to reach from thence to the bottom, by which, without any danger, they got down all but one, who stayed there to throw them down their arms, and after this succeeded in saving himself. The Romans were ignorant of all this, and, therefore, coming upon them in the rear, they assaulted them unawares and took their camp. Several, also, of the shepherds and herdsmen that were

there, stout and nimble fellows, revolted over to them, to some of whom they gave complete arms, and made use of others as scouts and light-armed soldiers.

Publius Varinus, the prætor, was now sent against them, whose lieutenant, Furius, with two thousand men, they fought and routed. Then Cossinius was sent with considerable forces, to give his assistance and advice, and him Spartacus missed but very little of capturing in person, as he was bathing at Salinæ; for he with great difficulty made his escape, while Spartacus possessed himself of his baggage, and following the chase with a great slaughter, stormed his camp and took it, where Cossinius himself was slain.

After many successful skirmishes with the prætor himself, in one of which he took his lictors and his own horse, he began to be great and terrible; but wisely considering that he was not to expect to match the force of the empire, he marched his army towards the Alps, intending, when he had passed them, that every man should go to his own home, some to Thrace, some to Gaul. But they, grown confident in their numbers, and puffed up with their success, would give no obedience to him, but went about and ravaged Italy; so that now the senate was not only moved at the indignity and baseness, both of the enemy and of the insurrection, but, looking upon it as a matter of alarm and of dangerous consequence, sent out both the consuls to it, as to a great and difficult enterprise.

The consul Gellius, falling suddenly upon a party of Germans, who through contempt and confidence had straggled from Spartacus, cut them all to pieces. But when Lentulus with a large army besieged Spartacus, he sallied out upon him, and, joining battle, defeated his chief officers, and captured all his baggage. As he made toward the Alps, Cassius, who was prætor of that part of Gaul that lies about the Po, met him with ten thousand men, but being overcome in battle, he had much ado to escape himself, with the loss of a great many of his men.

When the senate understood this, they were displeased at the consuls, and ordering them to meddle no further, they appointed Crassus general of the war, and a great many of the nobility went volunteers with him, partly out of friendship, and partly to get honour. He stayed himself on the borders of Picenum, expecting Spartacus would come that way, and sent his lieutenant, Mummius, with two legions, to wheel about and observe the enemy's motions, but upon no account to engage or skirmish. But he, upon the first opportunity, joined battle, and was routed, having a great many of his men slain, and a great many only saving their lives with the loss of their arms.

Crassus rebuked Mummius severely, and arming the soldiers again, he made them find sureties for their arms, that they would part with them no more, and five hundred that were the beginners of the flight he divided into fifty tens, and one of each was to die by lot, thus reviving the ancient Roman punishment of decimation, where ignominy is added to the penalty of death, with a variety of appalling and terrible circumstances, presented before the eyes of the whole army, assembled as spectators.

When he had thus reclaimed his men, he led them against the enemy; but Spartacus retreated through Lucania toward the sea, and in the straights meeting with some Cilician pirate ships, he had thoughts of attempting Sicily, where, by landing two thousand men, he hoped to new kindle the war of the slaves, which was but lately extinguished, and seemed to need but little fuel to set it burning again. But after the pirates had struck a bargain with him, and received his gifts, they deceived him and sailed away. He thereupon retired again from the sea, and established his army in the peninsula of Rhegium; there Crassus came upon him, and considering the nature of the place, which of itself suggested the undertaking, he set to work to build a wall across the isthmus; thus keeping his soldiers at once from idleness and his foes from forage.

This great and difficult work he perfected in a space of time short beyond all expectation, making a ditch from one sea to the other, over the neck of land, three hundred furlongs long, fifteen feet broad, and as much in depth, and above it built a wonderfully high and strong wall. All which Spartacus at first slighted and despised, but when provisions began to fail, and on his proposing to pass further, he found he was walled in, and no more was to be had in the peninsula, taking the opportunity of a snowy, stormy night, he filled up part of the ditch with earth and boughs of trees, and so passed the third part of his army over.

Crassus was afraid lest he should march directly to Rome, but was soon eased of that fear when he saw many of his men break out in a mutiny and quit him, and encamp by themselves upon the Lucanian lake. This lake they say changes at intervals of time, and is sometimes sweet, and sometimes so salt that it cannot be drunk. Crassus falling upon these beat them from the lake, but he could not pursue the slaughter, because of Spartacus suddenly coming up and checking the flight.

Now he began to repent that he had previously written to the senate to call Lucullus out of Thrace, and Pompey out of Spain; so that he did all he could to finish the war before they came, knowing that the honour of the action would redound to him that came to his assistance. Resolving, therefore, first to set upon those that had mutinied and encamped apart, whom Caius Cannicius and Castus commanded, he sent six thousand men before to secure a little eminence, and to do it as privately as possible, which that they might do they covered their helmets, but being discovered by two women that were sacrificing for the enemy, they had been in great hazard, had not Crassus immediately appeared, and engaged in a battle which proved a most bloody one. Of twelve thousand three hundred whom he killed, two only were found wounded in their backs, the rest all having died standing in their ranks and fighting bravely.

Spartacus, after this discomfiture, retired to the mountains of Petelia, but Quintius, one of Crassus's officers, and Scrofa, the quæstor, pursued and overtook him. But when Spartacus rallied and faced them, they were utterly routed and fled, and had much ado to carry off their quæstor, who was wounded. This success, however, ruined Spartacus, because it encouraged the slaves, who now disdained any longer to avoid fighting, or to obey their officers, but as they were upon the march, they came to them with their swords in their hands, and compelled them to lead them back again through Lucania, against the Romans, the very thing which Crassus was eager for.

For news was already brought that Pompey was at hand; and people began to talk openly that the honour of this war was reserved to him, who would come and at once oblige the enemy to fight and put an end to the war. Crassus, therefore, eager to fight a decisive battle, encamped very near the enemy, and began to make lines of circumvallation; but the slaves made a sally and attacked the pioneers. As fresh supplies came in on either side, Spartacus, seeing there was no avoiding it, set all his army in array, and when his horse was brought him, he drew out his sword and killed him, saying, if he got the day he should have a great many better horses of the enemies', and if he lost it he should have no need of this. And so making directly towards Crassus himself, through the midst of arms and wounds, he missed him, but slew two centurions that fell upon him together. At last being deserted by those that were about him, he himself stood his ground, and, surrounded by the enemy, bravely defending himself, was cut in pieces.

But though Crassus had good fortune, and not only did the part of a good general, but gallantly exposed his person, yet Pompey had much of the credit of the action. For he met with many of the fugitives, and slew them, and wrote to the senate that Crassus indeed had vanquished the slaves in a pitched battle, but that he had put an end to the war. Pompey was honoured with a magnificent triumph for his conquest over Sertorius and Spain, while Crassus could not himself so much as desire a triumph in its full form, and indeed it was thought to look but meanly in him to accept of the lesser honour, called the ovation, for a servile war, and perform a procession on foot. The difference between this and the other, and the origin of the name, are explained in the life of Marcellus.

And Pompey being immediately invited to the consulship, Crassus, who had hoped to be joined with him, did not scruple to request his assistance. Pompey most readily seized the opportunity, as he desired by all means to lay some obligation upon Crassus, and zealously promoted his interest; and at last he declared in one of his speeches to the people that he should be not less beholden to them for his colleague than for the honour of his own appointment.

But once entered upon the employment, this amity continued not long; but differing almost in everything, disagreeing, quarrelling, and contending, they spent the time of their consulship without effecting any measure of consequence, except that Crassus made a great sacrifice to Hercules, and feasted the people at ten thousand tables, and measured them out corn for three months.

When their command was now ready to expire, and they were, as it happened, addressing the people, a Roman knight, one Onatius Aurelius, an ordinary private person, living in the country, mounted the hustings, and declared a vision he had in his sleep. "Jupiter," said he, "appeared to me, and commanded me to tell you, that you should not suffer your consuls to lay down their charge before they are made friends."

When he had spoken, the people cried out that they should be reconciled. Pompey stood still and said nothing, but Crassus, first offering him his hand, said, "I cannot think, my countrymen, that I do anything humiliating or unworthy of myself, if I make the first offers of accommodation and friendship with Pompey, whom you yourselves styled the Great before he was of man's estate, and decreed him a triumph before he was capable of sitting in the senate."

This is what was memorable in Crassus's consulship, but as for his censorship, that was altogether idle and inactive, for he neither made a scrutiny of the senate, nor took a review of the horsemen, nor a census of the people, though he had as mild a man as could be desired for his colleague, Lutatius Catulus. It is said, indeed, that when Crassus intended a violent and unjust measure, which was the reducing Egypt to be tributary to Rome, Catulus strongly opposed it, and falling out about it, they laid down their office by consent.

In the great conspiracy of Cataline, which was very near subverting the government, Crassus was not without some suspicion of being concerned, and one man came forward and declared him to be in the plot; but nobody credited him. Yet Cicero, in one of his orations, clearly charges both Crassus and Cæsar with the guilt of it, though that speech was not published till they were both dead. But in his speech upon his consulship, he declares that Crassus came to him by night, and brought a letter concerning Cataline, stating the details of the conspiracy. Crassus hated him ever after, but was hindered by his son from doing him any injury; for Publius was a great lover of learning and eloquence, and a constant follower of Cicero, insomuch that he put himself into mourning when he was accused, and induced the other young men to do the same. And at last he reconciled him to his father.

Cæsar now returning from his command, and designing to get the consulship, and seeing that Crassus and Pompey were again at variance, was unwilling to disoblige one by making application to the other, and despaired of success without the help of one of them; he therefore made it his business to reconcile them, making it appear that by weakening each other's influence they were promoting the interest of the Ciceros, the Catuli, and the Catos, who would really be of no account if they would join their interests and their factions, and act together in public with one policy and one united power.

And so reconciling them by his persuasions, out of the three parties he set up one irresistible power, which utterly subverted the government both of senate and people. Not that he made either Pompey or Crassus greater than they were before, but by their means made himself greatest of all; for by the help of the adherents of both, he was at once gloriously declared consul, which office when he administered with credit, they decreed him the command of an army, and allotted him Gaul for his province, and so placed him as it were in the citadel, not doubting but they should divide the rest at their pleasure between themselves, when they had confirmed him in his allotted command. Pompey was actuated in all this by an immoderate desire of ruling, but Crassus, adding to his old disease of covetousness, a new passion after trophies and triumphs, emulous of Cæsar's exploits, not content to be beneath him in these points, though above him in all others, could not be at rest, till it ended in an ignominious overthrow and a public calamity.

When Cæsar came out of Gaul to Lucca, a great many went thither from Rome to meet him. Pompey and Crassus had various conferences with him in secret, in which they came to the resolution to proceed to still more decisive steps, and to get the whole management of affairs into their hands, Cæsar to keep his army, and Pompey and Crassus to obtain new ones and new provinces. To effect all which there was but one way, the getting the consulate a second time, which they were to stand for, and Cæsar to assist them by writing to his friends and sending many of his soldiers to vote.

But when they returned to Rome, their design was presently suspected, and a report was soon spread that this interview had been for no good. When Marcellinus and Domitius asked Pompey in the senate if he intended to stand for the consulship, he answered, perhaps he would, perhaps not; and being urged again, replied, he would ask it of the honest citizens, but not of the dishonest. Which answer appearing too haughty and arrogant, Crassus said, more modestly, that he would desire it if it might be for the advantage of the public, otherwise he would decline it.

Upon this some others took confidence and came forward as candidates, among them Domitius. But when Pompey and Crassus now

openly appeared for it, the rest were afraid and drew back; only Cato encouraged Domitius, who was his friend and relation, to proceed, exciting him to persist, as though he was now defending the public liberty, as these men, he said, did not so much aim at the consulate as at arbitrary government, and it was not a petition for office, but a seizure of provinces and armies. Thus spoke and thought Cato, and almost forcibly compelled Domitius to appear in the Forum, where many sided with them. For there was, indeed, much wonder and question among the people, "Why should Pompey and Crassus want another consulship? And why they two together, and not with some third person? We have a great many men not unworthy to be fellow-consuls with either the one or the other."

Pompey's party, being apprehensive of this, committed all manner of indecencies and violences, and amongst other things lay in wait for Domitius, as he was coming thither before daybreak with his friends; his torch-bearer they killed, and wounded several others, of whom Cato was one. And these being beaten back and driven into a house, Pompey and Crassus were proclaimed consuls. Not long after, they surrounded the house with armed men, thrust Cato out of the Forum, killed some that made resistance, and decreed Cæsar his command for five years longer, and provinces for themselves, Syria and both the Spains, which being divided by lots, Syria fell to Crassus, and the Spains to Pompey.

All were well pleased with the change, for the people were desirous that Pompey should not go far from the city, and he, being extremely fond of his wife, was very glad to continue there; but Crassus was so transported with his fortune, that it was manifest he thought he had never had such good luck befall him as now, so that he had much to do to contain himself before company and strangers; but amongst his private friends he let fall many vain and childish words, which were unworthy of his age, and contrary to his usual character, for he had been very little given to boasting hitherto.

But then being strangely puffed up, and his head heated, he would not limit his fortune with Parthia and Syria; but looking on the actions of Lucullus against Tigranes and the exploits of Pompey against Mithridates as but child's play, he proposed to himself in his hopes to pass as far as Bactria and India, and the utmost ocean. Not that he was called upon by the decree which appointed him to his office to undertake any expedition against the Parthians, but it was well known that he was eager for it, and Cæsar wrote to him out of Gaul commending his resolution, and inciting him to the war.

And when Ateius, the tribune of the people, designed to stop his journey, and many others murmured that one man should undertake a war against a people that had done them no injury, and were at amity with them, he desired Pompey to stand by him and accompany him out of the town, as he had a great name amongst the common people. And when several were ready prepared to interfere and raise an outcry, Pompey appeared with a pleasing countenance, and so mollified the people that they let Crassus pass quietly. Ateius, however, met him, and first by word of mouth warned and conjured him not to proceed, and then commanded his attendant officer to seize him and detain him; but the other tribunes not permitting it, the officer released Crassus.

Ateius, therefore, running to the gate, when Crassus was come thither, set down a chafing-dish with lighted fire in it, and burning incense and pouring libations on it, cursed him with dreadful imprecations, calling upon and naming several strange and horrible deities. In the Roman belief there is so much virtue in these sacred and ancient rites, that no man can escape the effects of them, and that the utterer himself seldom prospers; so that they are not often made use of, and but upon a great occasion. And Ateius was blamed at the time for resorting to them, as the city itself, in whose cause he used them, would be the first to feel the ill effects of these curses and supernatural terrors.

Crassus arrived at Brundusium, and though the sea was very rough, he had not patience to wait, but went on board, and lost many of his ships. With the remnant of his army he marched rapidly through Galatia, where meeting with King Deiotarus, who, though he was very old, was about building a new city, Crassus scoffingly told him, "Your majesty begins to build at the twelfth hour." "Neither do you," said he, "O general, undertake your Parthian expedition very early." For Crasssus was then sixty years old, and he seemed older than he was.

At his first coming, things went as he would have them, for he made a bridge over the Euphrates without much difficulty, and passed over his army in safety, and occupied many cities of Mesopotamia, which yielded voluntarily. But a hundred of his men were killed in one, in which Apollonius was tyrant; therefore, bringing his forces against it, he took it by storm, plundered the goods, and sold the inhabitants. The Greeks call this city Zenodotia, upon the taking of which he permitted the army to salute him Imperator, but this was very ill thought of, and it looked as if he despaired a nobler achievement, that he made so much of this little success.

Putting garrisons of seven thousand foot and one thousand horse in the new conquests, he returned to take up his winter quarters in Syria, where his son was to meet him coming from Cæsar out of Gaul, decorated with rewards for his valour, and bringing with him one thousand select horse. Here Crassus seemed to commit his first error, and except, indeed, the whole expedition, his greatest; for whereas he ought to have gone forward and seized Babylon and Seleucia, cities that were ever at enmity with the Parthians, he gave the enemy time to provide against him.

Besides, he spent his time in Syria more like an usurer than a general, not in taking an account of the arms, and in improving the skill and discipline of his soldiers, but in computing the revenue of the cities, wasting many days in weighing by scale and balance the treasure that was in the temple of Hierapolis, issuing requisitions for levies of soldiers upon particular towns and kingdoms, and then again withdrawing them on payment of sums of money, by which he lost his credit and became despised.

Here, too, he met with the first ill-omen from that goddess, whom some call Venus, others Juno, others Nature, or the Cause that produces out of moisture the first principles and seeds of all things, and gives mankind their earliest knowledge of all that is good for them. For as they were going out of the temple young Crassus stumbled and his father fell upon him.

When he drew his army out of winter quarters, ambassadors came to him from Arsaces, with this short speech: If the army was sent by the people of Rome, this meant mortal war, but if, as he understood was the case, against the consent of his country, Crassus for his own private profit had invaded his territory, then their king would be more merciful, and taking pity upon Crassus's dotage, would send those soldiers back who had been left not so truly to keep guard on him as to be his prisoners. Crassus boastfully told them he would return his answer at Seleucia, upon which Vagises, the eldest of them, laughed and showed the palm of his hand, saying, "Hair will grow here before you will see Seleucia"; so they returned to their king, Hyrodes, telling him it was war.

Several of the Romans that were in garrison in Mesopotamia with great hazard made their escape, and brought word that the danger was worth consideration, urging their own eye-witness of the numbers of the enemy, and the manner of their fighting, when they assaulted their towns; and, as men's manner is, made all seem greater than really it was. By flight it was impossible to escape them, and as impossible to overtake them when they fled, and they had a new and strange sort of darts, as swift as sight, for they pierced whatever they met with, before you could see who threw them; their men-at-arms were so provided that their weapons would cut through anything, and their armour give way to nothing.

All which when the soldiers heard their hearts failed them; for till now they thought there was no difference between the Parthians and the Armenians or Cappadocians, whom Lucullus grew weary with plundering, and had been persuaded that the main difficulty of the war consisted only in the tediousness of the march and the trouble of chasing men that durst not come to blows, so that the danger of a battle was beyond their expectation; accordingly, some of the officers advised Crassus to proceed no further at present, but reconsider the whole enterprise, amongst whom in particular was Cassius, the quæstor. The soothsayers, also, told him privately the signs found in the sacrifices were continually adverse and unfavourable. But he paid no heed to them, or to anybody who gave any other advice than to proceed.

Nor did Artavasdes, King of Armenia, confirm him a little, who came to his aid with six thousand horse; who, however, were said to be only the king's life-guard and suit, for he promised ten thousand cuirassiers more, and thirty thousand foot, at his own charge. He urged Crassus to invade Parthia by the way of Armenia, for not only would he be able there to supply his army with abundant provision, which he would give him, but his passage would be more secure in the mountains and hills, with which the whole country was covered, making it almost impassable to horse, in which the main strength of the Parthians consisted. Crassus returned him but cold thanks for his readiness to serve him, and for the splendour of his assistance, and told him he was resolved to pass through Mesopotamia, where he had left a great many brave Roman soldiers; whereupon the Armenian went his way.

As Crassus was taking the army over the river at Zeugma, he encountered preternaturally violent thunder, and the lightning flashed in the faces of the troops, and during the storm a hurricane broke upon the bridge, and carried part of it away; two thunderbolts fell upon the very place where the army was going to encamp; and one of the general's horses, magnificently caparisoned, dragged away the groom into the river and was drowned. It is said, too, that when they went to take up the first standard, the eagle of itself turned its head backward; and after he had passed over his army, as they were distributing provisions, the first thing they gave was lentils and salt, which with the Romans are the food proper to funerals, and are offered to the dead. And as Crassus was haranguing his soldiers, he let fall a word which was thought very ominous in the army; for "I am going," he said, "to break down the bridge, that none of you may return"; and whereas he ought, when he had perceived his blunder, to have corrected himself, and explained his meaning, seeing the men alarmed at the expression, he would not do it out of mere stubbornness. And when at the last general sacrifice the priest gave him the entrails, they slipt out of his hand, and when he saw the standers-by concerned at it, he laughed and said, "See what it is to be an old man; but I shall hold my sword fast enough."

So he marched his army along the river with seven legions, little less than four thousand horse, and as many light-armed soldiers, and the scouts returning declared that not one man appeared, but that they saw the footing of a great many horses which seemed to be retiring in flight, whereupon Crassus conceived great hopes, and the Romans began to despise the Parthians, as men that would not come to combat, hand to hand. But Cassius spoke with him again, and advised him to refresh his army in some of the garrison towns, and remain there till they could get some certain intelligence of the enemy, or at least to make toward Seleucia, and keep by the river, that so they might have the convenience of having provision constantly supplied by the boats, which might always accompany the army, and the river would secure them from being environed, and, if they should fight, it might be upon equal terms.

While Crassus was still considering, and as yet undetermined, there came to the camp an Arab chief named Ariamnes, a cunning and wily fellow, who, of all the evil chances which combined to lead them on to destruction, was the chief and the most fatal. Some of Pompey's old soldiers knew him, and remembered him to have received some kindnesses of Pompey, and to have been looked upon as a friend to the Romans, but he was now suborned by the king's generals, and sent to Crassus to entice him if possible from the river and hills into the wide open plain, where he might be surrounded. For the Parthians desired anything rather than to be obliged to meet the Romans face to face.

He, therefore, coming to Crassus (and he had a persuasive tongue), highly commended Pompey as his benefactor, and admired the forces that Crassus had with him, but seemed to wonder why he delayed and made preparations, as if he should not use his feet more than any arms, against men that, taking with them their best goods and chattels, had designed long ago to fly for refuge to the Scythians or Hyrcanians. "If you meant to fight, you should have made all possible haste, before the king should recover courage, and collect his forces together; at present you see Surena and Sillaces opposed to you, to draw you off in pursuit of them, while the king himself keeps out of the way."

But this was all a lie, for Hyrodes had divided his army in two parts; with one he in person wasted Armenia, revenging himself upon Artavasdes, and sent Surena against the Romans, not out of contempt, as some pretend, for there is no likelihood that he should despise Crassus, one of the chiefest men of Rome, to go and fight with Artavasdes, and invade Armenia; but much more probably he really apprehended the danger, and therefore waited to see the event, intending that Surena should first run the hazard of a battle, and draw the enemy on.

Nor was this Surena an ordinary person, but in wealth, family, and reputation, the second man in the kingdom, and in courage and prowess the first, and for bodily stature and beauty no man like him. Whenever he travelled privately, he had one thousand camels to carry his baggage, two hundred chariots for his concubines, one thousand completely armed men for life-guards, and a great many more light-armed; and he had at least ten thousand horsemen altogether, of his servants and retinue. The honour had long belonged to his family, that at the king's coronation he put the crown upon his head, and when this very king Hyrodes had been exiled, he brought him in. It was he, also, that took the great city of Seleucia; he was the first man that scaled the walls, and with his own hand beat off the defenders. And though at this time he was not above thirty years old, he had a great name for wisdom and sagacity, and, indeed, by these qualities chiefly, he overthrew Crassus, who first through his overweening confidence, and afterwards because he was cowed by his calamities, fell a ready victim to his subtlety.

When Ariamnes had thus worked upon him, he drew him from the river into vast plains, by a way that at first was pleasant and easy but afterwards very troublesome by reason of the depth of the sand; no tree, nor any water, and no end of this to be seen; so that they were not only spent with thirst, and the difficulty of the passage, but were dismayed with the uncomfortable prospect of not a bough, not a stream, not a hillock, not a green herb, but in fact a sea of sand, which encompassed the army with its waves. They began to suspect some treachery, and at the same time came messengers from Artavasdes, that he was fiercely attacked by Hyrodes, who had invaded his country, so that now it was impossible for him to send any succours, and that he therefore advised Crassus to turn back, and with joint forces to give Hyrodes battle, or at least that he should march and encamp where horses could not easily come, and keep to the mountains. Crassus, out of anger and perverseness, wrote him no answer, but told them, at present he was not at leisure to mind the Armenians, but he would call upon them another time, and revenge himself upon Artavasdes for his treachery.

Cassius and his friends began again to complain, but when they perceived that it merely displeased Crassus, they gave over, but privately railed at the barbarian, "What evil genius, O thou worst of men, brought thee to our camp, and with what charms and potions hast thou bewitched Crassus, that he should march his army through a vast and deep desert, through ways which are rather fit for a captain of Arabian robbers, than for the general of a Roman army?" But the barbarian, being a wily fellow, very submissively exhorted them, and encouraged them to sustain it a little further, and ran about the camp, and, professing to cheer up the soldiers, asked them, jokingly, "What, do you think you march through Campania, expecting everywhere to find springs, and shady trees, and baths, and inns of entertainment? Consider you now travel through the confines of Arabia and Assyria." Thus he managed them like children, and before the cheat was discovered, he rode away; not but that Crassus was aware of his going, but he had persuaded him that he would go and contrive how to disorder the affairs of the enemy.

It is related that Crassus came abroad that day not in his scarlet robe, which Roman generals usually wear, but in a black one, which, as soon as he perceived, he changed. And the standard-bearers had much ado to take up their eagles, which seemed to be fixed to the place. Crassus laughed at it, and hastened their march, and compelled his infantry to keep pace with his cavalry, till some few of the scouts returned and told them that their fellows were slain and they hardly escaped, that the enemy was at hand in full force, and resolved to give them battle.

On this all was in an uproar; Crassus was struck with amazement, and for haste could scarcely put his army in good order. First, as Cassius advised, he opened their ranks and files that they might take up as much space as could be, to prevent their being surrounded, and distributed the horse upon the wings, but afterwards changing his mind, he drew up his army in a square, and made a front every way, each of which consisted of twelve cohorts, to every one of which he allotted a troop of horse, that no part might be destitute of the assistance that the horse might give, and that they might be ready to assist everywhere, as need should require. Cassius commanded one of the wings, young Crassus the other, and he himself was in the middle.

Thus they marched on till they came to a little river named Balissus, a very inconsiderable one in itself, but very grateful to the soldiers, who had suffered so much by drouth and heat all along their march. Most of the commanders were of the opinion that they ought to remain there that night, and to inform themselves as much as possible of the number of the enemies, and their order, and so march against them at break of day; but Crassus was so carried away by the eagerness of his son, and the horsemen that were with him, who desired and urged him to lead them on

and engage, that he commanded those that had a mind to it to eat and drink as they stood in their ranks, and before they had all well done, he led them on, not leisurely and with halts to take breath, as if he was going to battle, but kept on his pace as if he had been in haste, till they saw the enemy, contrary to their expectation, neither so many nor so magnificently armed as the Romans expected.

For Surena had hid his main force behind the first ranks, and ordered them to hide the glittering of their armour with coats and skins. But when they approached and the general gave the signal, immediately all the field rung with a hideous noise and terrible clamour. For the Parthians do not encourage themselves to war with cornets and trumpets, but with a kind of kettle-drum, which they strike all at once in various quarters. With these they make a dead, hollow noise, like the bellowing of beasts, mixed with sounds resembling thunder, having, it would seem, very correctly observed that of all our senses hearing most confounds and disorders us, and that the feelings excited through it most quickly disturb and most entirely overpower the understanding.

When they had sufficiently terrified the Romans with their noise, they threw off the covering of their armour, and shone like lightning in their breastplates and helmets of polished Margianian steel, and with their horses covered with brass and steel trappings. Surena was the tallest and finest looking man himself, but the delicacy of his looks and effeminacy of his dress did not promise so much manhood as he really was master of; for his face was painted, and his hair parted after the fashion of the Medes, whereas the other Parthians made a more terrible appearance, with their shaggy hair gathered in a mass upon their foreheads after the Scythian mode. Their first design was with their lances to beat down and force back the first ranks of the Romans, but when they perceived the depth of their battle, and that the soldiers firmly kept their ground, they made a retreat, and pretending to break their order and disperse, they encompassed the Roman square before they were aware of it.

Crassus commanded his light-armed soldiers to charge, but they had not gone far before they were received with such a shower of arrows that they were glad to retire amongst the heavy-armed, with whom this was the first occasion of disorder and terror, when they perceived the strength and force of their darts, which pierced their arms, and passed through every kind of covering, hard and soft alike. The Parthians now placing themselves at distances began to shoot from all sides, not aiming at any particular mark (for, indeed, the order of the Romans was so close, that they could not miss if they would), but simply sent their arrows with great force out of strong bent bows, the strokes from which came with extreme violence. The position of the Romans was a very bad one from the first; for if they kept their ranks, they were wounded, and if they tried to charge, they hurt the enemy none the more, and themselves suffered none the less. For the Parthians threw their darts as they fled, an art in which none but the Scythians excel them, and it is, indeed, a cunning practice, for while they thus fight to make their escape, they avoid the dishonour of a flight.

However, the Romans had some comfort to think that when they had spent all their arrows, they would either give over or come to blows; but when they presently understood that there were numerous camels loaded with arrows, and that when the first ranks had discharged those they had, they wheeled off and took more, Crassus seeing no end of it, was out of all heart, and sent to his son that he should endeavour to fall in upon them before he was quite surrounded; for the enemy advanced most upon that quarter, and seemed to be trying to ride round and come upon the rear.

Therefore, the young man, taking with him thirteen hundred horse, one thousand of which he had from Cæsar, five hundred archers, and eight cohorts of the full-armed soldiers that stood next him, led them up with design to charge the Parthians. Whether it was that they found themselves in a piece of marshy ground, as some think, or else designing to entice young Crassus as far as they could from his father, they turned and began to fly; whereupon he crying out that they durst not stand, pursued them, and with him Censorinus and Megabacchus, both famous, the latter for his courage and prowess, the other for being of a senator's family, and an excellent orator, both intimates of Crassus, and of about the same age. The horse thus pushing on, the infantry stayed a little behind, being exalted with hopes and joy, for they supposed they had already conquered, and now were only pursuing; till when they were gone too far, they perceived the deceit, for they that seemed to fly now turned again, and a great many fresh ones came on.

Upon this they made a halt, for they doubt-ed not but now the enemy would attack them, because they were so few. But they merely placed their cuirassiers to face the Romans, and with the rest of their horse rode about scouring the field, and thus stirring up the sand, they raised such a dust that the Romans could neither see nor speak to one another, and being driven in upon one another in one close body, they were thus hit and killed, dying, not by a quick and easy death, but with miserable pains and convulsions; for writhing upon the darts in their bodies, they broke them in their wounds, and when they would by force pluck out the barbed points, they caught the nerves and veins, so that they tore and tortured themselves. Many of them died thus, and those that survived were disabled for any service, and when Publius exhorted them to charge the cuirassiers, they showed him their hands nailed to their shields, and their feet stuck to the ground, so that they could neither fly nor fight.

He charged in himself boldly, however, with his horse, and came to close quarters with them, but was very unequal, whether as to the offensive or defensive part; for with his weak and little javelins, he struck against targets that were of tough raw hides and iron, whereas, the lightly-clad bodies of his Gaulish horsemen were exposed to the strong spears of the enemy. For upon these he mostly depended, and with them he wrought wonders; for they would catch hold of the great spears, and close upon the enemy, and so pull them off from their horses, where they could scarce stir by reason of the heaviness of their armour, and many of the Gauls quitting their own horses, would creep under those of the enemy, and stick them in the belly; which, growing unruly with the pain, trampled upon their riders and upon the enemies promiscuously.

The Gauls were chiefly tormented by the heat and drouth, being not accustomed to either, and most of their horses were slain by being spurred on against the spears, so that they were forced to retire among the foot, bearing off Publius grievously wounded. Observing a sandy hillock not far off, they made to it, and tying their horses to one another, and placing them in the midst, and joining all their shields together before them, they thought they might make some defence against the barbarians. But it fell out quite contrary, for when they were drawn up in a plain, the front in some measure secured those that were behind; but when they were upon the hill, one being of necessity higher up than another, none were in shelter, but all alike stood equally exposed, bewailing their inglorious and useless fate.

There were with Publius two Greeks that lived near there at Carrhæ, Hieronymus and Nicomachus; these men urged him to retire with them and fly to Ichnæ, a town not far from thence, and friendly to the Romans. "No," said he, "there is no death so terrible, for the fear of which Publius would leave his friends that die upon his account"; and bidding them to take care of themselves, he embraced them and sent them away, and, because he could not use his arm, for he was run through with a dart, he opened his side to his armour-bearer, and commanded him to run him through. It is said Sensorimus fell in the same manner. Megabacchus slew himself, as did also the rest of best note. The Parthians coming upon the rest with their lances, killed them fighting, nor were there above five hundred taken prisoners. Cutting off the head of Publius, they rode off directly towards Crassus.

His condition was thus. When he had commanded his son to fall upon the enemy, and word was brought him that they fled and that there was a distant pursuit, and perceiving also that the enemy did not press upon him so hard as formerly, for they were mostly gone to fall upon Publius, he began to take heart a little; and drawing his army towards some sloping ground, expected when his son would return from the pursuit. Of the messengers whom Publius sent to him (as soon as he saw his danger), the first were intercepted by the enemy, and slain; the last, hardly escaping, came and declared that Publius was lost, unless he had speedy succours.

Crassus was terribly distracted, not knowing what counsel to take, and indeed no longer capable of taking any; overpowered now by fear for the whole army, now by desire to help his son. At last he resolved to move with his forces. Just upon this, up came the enemy with their shouts and noises more terrible than before, their drums sounding again in the ears of the Romans, who now feared a fresh engagement.

And they who brought Publius's head upon the point of a spear, riding up near enough that it could be known, scoffingly inquired where were his parents, and what family he was of, for it was impossible that so brave and gallant a warrior should be the son of so pitiful a coward as Crassus. This sight above all the rest dismayed the Romans, for it did not in-cite them to anger as it might have done, but to horror and trembling, though they say Crassus outdid himself in this calamity, for he passed through the ranks and cried out to them, "This, O my countrymen, is my own peculiar loss, but the fortune and the glory of Rome is safe and untainted so long as you are safe. But if any one be concerned for my loss of the best of sons, let him show it in revenging him upon the enemy. Take away their joy, revenge their cruelty, nor be dismayed at what is past; for whoever tries for great objects must suffer something. Neither did Lucullus overthrow Tigranes without bloodshed, nor Scipio Antiochus; our ancestors lost one thousand ships about Sicily, and how many generals and captains in Italy? No one of which losses hindered them from overthrowing their conquerors; for the State of Rome did not arrive to this height by fortune, but by perseverance and virtue in confronting danger."

While Crassus thus spoke exhorting them, he saw but few that gave much heed to him, and when he ordered them to shout for battle, he could no longer mistake the despondency of his army, which made but a faint and unsteady noise, while the shout of the enemy was clear and bold. And when they came to the business, the Parthian servants and dependants riding about shot their arrows, and the horsemen in the foremost ranks with their spears drove the Romans close together, except those who rushed upon them for fear of being killed by their arrows. Neither did these do much execution, being quickly despatched; for the strong, thick spear made large and mortal wounds, and often ran through two men at once.

As they were thus fighting, the night coming on parted them, the Parthians boasting that they would indulge Crassus with one night to mourn his son, unless upon better consideration he would rather go to Arsaces than be carried to him. These, therefore, took up their quarters near them, being flushed with their victory. But the Romans had a sad night of it; for neither taking care for the burial of their dead, nor the cure of the wounded, nor the groans of the expiring, every one bewailed his own fate. For there was no means of escaping, whether they should stay for the light, or venture to retreat into the vast desert in the dark. And now the wounded men gave them new trouble, since to take them with them would retard their flight, and if they should leave them, they might serve as guides to the enemy by their cries.

However, they were all desirous to see and hear Crassus, though they were sensible that he was the cause of all their mischief. But he wrapped his cloak around him, and hid himself, where he lay as an example, to ordinary minds, of the caprice of fortune, but to the wise, of inconsiderateness and ambition; who, not content to be superior to so many millions of men, being inferior to two, esteemed himself as the lowest of all. Then came Octavius, his lieutenant, and Cassius, to comfort him, but he being altogether past helping, they themselves called together the centurions and tribunes, and agreeing that the best way was to flee, they ordered the army out, without sound of trumpet, and at first with silence.

But before long, when the disabled men found they were left behind, strange confusion and disorder, with an outcry and lamentation, seized the camp, and a trembling and dread presently fell upon them, as if the enemy were at their heels. By which means, now and then turning out of their way, now and then standing to their ranks, sometimes taking up the wounded that followed, sometimes laying them down, they wasted the time, except three hundred horse, whom Egnatius brought safe to Carrhæ about midnight; where calling, in the Roman tongue, to the watch, as soon as they heard him, he bade them tell Coponius, the governor, that Crassus had fought a very great battle with the Parthians; and having said but this, and not so much as telling his name, he rode away at full speed to Zeugma. And by this means he saved himself and his men, but lost his reputation by deserting his general.

However, his message to Coponius was for the advantage of Crassus; for he, suspecting by this hasty and confused delivery of the message that all was not well, immediately ordered the garrison to be in arms; and as soon as he understood that Crassus was upon the way towards him, he went out to meet him, and received him with his army into the town.

The Parthians, although they perceived their dislodgment in the night, yet did not pursue them, but as soon as it was day, they came upon those that were left in the camp, and put no less than four thousand to the sword, and with their light horse picked up a great many stragglers. Varguntinus, the lieutenant, while it was yet dark, had broken off from the main body with four cohorts which had strayed out of the way; and the Parthians encompassing these on a small hill, slew every man of them excepting twenty, who with their drawn swords forced their way through the thickest, and they admiring their courage, opened their ranks to the right and left, and let them pass without molestation to Carrhæ.

Soon after a false report was brought to Surena, that Crassus, with his principal officers, had escaped, and that those who were got into Carrhæ were but a confused rout of insignificant people, not worth further pursuit. Supposing, therefore, that he had lost the very crown and glory of his victory, and yet being uncertain whether it were so or not, and anxious to ascertain the fact, that so he should either stay and besiege Carrhæ or follow Crassus, he sent one of his interpreters to the walls, commanding him in Latin to call for Crassus or Cassius, for that the general, Surena, desired a conference.

As soon as Crassus heard this, he embraced the proposal, and soon after there came up a band of Arabians, who very well knew the faces of Crassus and Cassius, as having been frequently in the Roman camp before the battle. They having espied Cassius from the wall, told him that Surena desired a peace, and would give them safe convoy, if they would make a treaty with the king his master, and withdraw all their troops out of Mesopotamia; and this he thought most advisable for them both, before things came to the last extremity; Cassius, embracing the proposal, desired that a time and place might be appointed where Crassus and Surena might have an interview. The Arabians, having charged themselves with the message, went back to Surena, who was not a little rejoiced that Crassus was there to be besieged.

Next day, therefore, he came up with his army, insulting over the Romans, and haughtily demanded of them Crassus and Cassius, bound, if they expected any mercy. The Romans, seeing themselves deluded and mocked, were much troubled at it, but advising Crassus to lay aside his distant and empty hopes of aid from the Armenians, resolved to flee for it; and this design ought to have been kept private, till they were upon their way, and not have been told to any of the people of Carrhæ.

But Crassus let this also be known to Andromachus, the most faithless of men, nay, he was so infatuated as to choose him for his guide. The Parthians then, to be sure, had punctual intelligence of all that passed; but it being contrary to their usage, and also difficult for them to fight by night, and Crassus having chosen that time to set out, Andromachus, lest he should get the start too far of his pursuers, led him hither and thither, and at last conveyed him into the midst of morasses and places full of ditches, so that the Romans had a troublesome and perplexing journey of it, and some there were who, supposing by these windings and turnings of Andromachus that no good was intended, resolved to follow him no further.

And at last Cassius himself returned to Carrhæ, and his guides, the Arabians, advising him to tarry there till the moon was got out of Scorpio, he told them that he was most afraid of Sagittarius, and so with five hundred horse went off to Syria. Others there were who, having got honest guides, took their way by the mountains called Sinnaca, and got into places of security by daybreak; these were five thousand under the command of Octavius, a very gallant man.

But Crassus fared worse; day overtook him still deceived by Andromachus, and entangled in the fens and the difficult country. There were with him four cohorts of legionary soldiers, a very few horsemen, and five lictors, with whom having with great difficulty got into the road, and not being a mile and a half from Octavius, instead of going to join him, although the enemy were already upon him, he retreated to another hill, neither so defensible nor impassable for the horse, but lying under the hills at Sinnaca, and continued so as to join them in a long ridge through the plain.

Octavius could see in what danger the general was, and himself, at first but slenderly followed, hurried to the rescue. Soon after, the rest, upbraiding one another with baseness in forsaking their officers, marched down, and falling upon the Parthians, drove them from the hill, and compassing Crassus about, and fencing him with their shields, declared proudly, that no arrow in Parthia should ever touch their general, so long as there was a man of them left alive to protect him.

Surena, therefore, perceiving his soldiers less inclined to expose themselves, and knowing that if the Romans should prolong the battle till night, they might then gain the mountains and be out of his reach, betook himself to his usual craft. Some of the prisoners were set free, who had, as it was contrived, been in hearing, while some of the barbarians spoke a set purpose in the camp to the effect that the king did not design the war to be pursued to extremity against the Romans, but rather desired, by his general treatment of Crassus, to make a step towards reconciliation. And the barbarians desisted from fighting, and Surena himself, with his chief officers, riding gently to the hill, unbent his bow and held out his hand, inviting Crassus to an agreement, and saying that it was beside the king's intentions, that they had thus had experience of the courage and the strength of his soldiers; that now he desired no other contention but that of kindness and friendship, by making a truce, and permitting them to go away in safety.

These words of Surena the rest received joyfully, and were eager to accept the offer; but Crassus, who had had sufficient experience of their perfidiousness, and was unable to see any reason for the sudden change, would give no ear to them, and only took time to consider. But the soldiers cried out and advised him to treat, and then went on to upbraid and affront him, saying that it was very unreasonable that he should bring them to fight with such men armed, whom himself, without their arms, durst not look in the face. He tried first to prevail with them by entreaties, and told them that if they would have patience till evening, they might get into the mountains and passes, inaccessible for horse, and be out of danger, and withal he pointed out the way with his hand, entreating them not to abandon their preservation, now close before them.

But when they mutinied and clashed their targets in a threatening manner, he was overpowered and forced to go, and only turning about at parting, said, "You, Octavius and Petronius, and the rest of the officers who are present, see the necessity of going which I lie under, and cannot but be sensible of the indignities and violence offered to me. Tell all men when you have escaped, that Crassus perished rather by the subtlety of his enemies than by the disobedience of his countrymen."

Octavius, however, would not stay there, but with Petronius went down from the hill; as for the lictors, Crassus bade them be gone. The first that met him were two half-blood Greeks, who, leaping from their horses, made a profound reverence to Crassus, and desired him, in Greek, to send some before him, who might see that Surena himself was coming towards them, his retinue disarmed, and not having so much as their wearing swords along with them. But Crassus answered, that if he had the least concern for his life, he would never have intrusted himself in their hands, but sent two brothers of the name of Roscius to inquire on what terms and in what numbers they should meet.

These Surena ordered immediately to be seized, and himself with his principal officers came up on horseback, and greeting him, said, "How is this, then? A Roman commander is on foot, whilst I and my train are mounted." But Crassus replied, that there was no error committed on either side, for they both met according to the custom of their own country. Surena told him that from that time there was a league between the king his master and the Romans, but that Crassus must go with him to the river to sign it, "for you Romans," said he, "have not good memories for conditions," and so saying, reached out his hand to him. Crassus, therefore, gave order that one of his horses should be brought; but Surena told him there was no need, "the king, my master, presents you with this"; and immediately a horse with a golden bit was brought up to him, and himself was forcibly put into the saddle by the grooms, who ran by the side and struck the horse to make the more haste.

But Octavius running up, got hold of the bridle, and soon after one of the officers, Petronius, and the rest of the company came up, striving to stop the horse, and pulling back those who on both sides of him forced Crassus forward. Thus from pulling and thrusting one another, they came to a tumult, and soon after to blows. Octavius, drawing his sword, killed a groom of one of the barbarians, and one of them, getting behind Octavius, killed him. Petronius was not armed, but being struck on the breastplate, fell down from his horse, though without hurt. Crassus was killed by a Parthian, called Pomaxathres; others say by a different man, and that Pomaxathres only cut off his head and right hand after he had fallen.

But this is conjecture rather than certain knowledge, for those that were by had not leisure to observe particulars, and were either killed fighting about Crassus, or ran off at once to get to their comrades on the hill. But the Parthians coming up to them, and saying that Crassus had the punishment he justly deserved, and that Surena bade the rest come down from the hill without fear, some of them came down and surrendered themselves, others were scattered up and down in the night, a very few of whom got safe home, and others the Arabians, beating through the country, hunted down and put to death. It is generally said, that in all twenty thousand men were slain and ten thousand taken prisoners.

Surena sent the head and hand of Crassus to Hyrodes, the king, into Armenia, but himself by his messengers scattering a report that he was bringing Crassus alive to Seleucia, made a ridiculous procession, which, by way of scorn, he called a triumph. For one Caius Paccianus, who of all the prisoners was most like Crassus, being put into a woman's dress of the fashion of the barbarians, and instructed to answer to the title of Crassus and Imperator, was brought sitting upon his horse, while before him went a parcel of trumpeters and lictors upon camels. Purses were hung at the end of the bundles of rods, and the heads of the slain fresh bleeding at the end of their axes. After them followed the Seleucian singing women, repeating scurrilous and abusive songs upon the effeminacy and cowardliness of Crassus.

This show was seen by everybody; but Surena, calling together the senate of Seleucia, laid before them certain wanton books, of the writings of Aristides, his *Milesiaca;* neither, indeed, was this any forgery, for they had been found among the baggage of Rustius, and were a good subject to supply Surena with insulting remarks upon the Romans, who were not able even in the time of war to forget such writings and practices.

But the people of Seleucia had reason to commend the wisdom of Æsop's fable of the wallet, seeing their general, Surena, carrying a bag full of loose Melesian stories before him, but keeping behind him a whole Parthian Sybaris in his many waggons full of concubines; like the vipers and asps people talk of, all the foremost and more visible parts fierce and terrible with spears and arrows and horsemen, but the rear terminating in loose women and castanets, music of the lute, and midnight revellings. Rustius, indeed, is not to be excused, but the Parthians had forgot, when they mocked at the Milesian stories, that many of the royal line of their Arsacidæ had been born of Milesian and Ionian mistresses.

Whilst these things were doing, Hyrodes had struck up a peace with the King of Armenia, and made a match between his son, Pacorus, and the King of Armenia's sister. Their feastings and entertainments in consequence were very sumptuous, and various Grecian compositions, suitable to the occasion, were recited before them. For Hyrodes was not ignorant of the Greek language and literature, and Artavasdes was so expert in it, that he wrote tragedies and orations and histories, some of which are still extant.

When the head of Crassus was brought to the door, the tables were just taken away, and one Jason, a tragic actor, of the town of Tralles, was singing the scene in the *Bacchæ* of Euripides concerning Agave. He was receiving much applause, when Sillaces, coming to the room, and having made obeisance to the king, threw down the head of Crassus into the midst of the company. The Parthians receiving it with joy and acclamations, Sillaces, by the king's command, was made to sit down, while Jason handed over the costume of Pentheus to one of the dancers in the chorus, and taking up the head of Crassus, and acting the part of a bacchante in her frenzy, in a rapturous impassioned manner, sang the lyric passages—

We've hunted down a mighty chase to-day,
And from the mountain bring the noble prey,

to the great delight of all the company; but when the verses of the dialogue followed—

What happy hand the glorious victim slew?
I claim that honour to my courage due,

Pomaxathres, who happened to be there at the supper, started up and would have got the head into his own hands, "for it is my due," said he, "and no man's else." The king was greatly pleased, and gave presents, according to the custom of the Parthians, to them, and to Jason, the actor, a talent. Such was the burlesque that was played, they tell us, as the afterpiece to the tragedy of Crassus's expedition.

But divine justice failed not to punish both Hyrodes for his cruelty and Surena for his perjury; for Surena not long after was put to death by Hyrodes, out of mere envy to his glory; and Hyrodes himself, having lost his son, Pacorus, who was beaten in a battle with the Romans, falling into a disease which turned to a dropsy, had aconite given him by his second son, Phraates; but the poison working only upon the disease, and carrying away the dropsical matter with itself, the king began suddenly to recover, so that Phraates at length was forced to take the shortest course, and strangled him.

CRASSUS and NICIAS
Compared

IN THE comparison of these two, first, if we compare the estate of Nicias with that of Crassus, we must acknowledge Nicias's to have been more honestly got. In itself, indeed, one cannot much approve of gaining riches by working mines, the greatest part of which is done by malefactors and barbarians, some of them, too, bound, and perishing in those close and unwholesome places. But if we compare this with the sequestrations of Sulla, and the contracts for houses ruined by fire, we shall then think Nicias came very honestly by his money. For Crassus publicly and avowedly made use of these arts, as other men do of husbandry, and putting out money to interest; while as for other matters which he used to deny, when taxed with them, as, namely, selling his voice in the senate for gain's sake, and injuring allies, and courting women, and conniving at criminals, these are things which Nicias was never so much as falsely accused of; nay, he was rather laughed at for giving money to those who made a trade of impeachments, merely out of timorousness, a course, indeed, that would by no means become Pericles and Aristides, but necessary for him who by nature was wanting in assurance, even as Lycurgus,

the orator, frankly acknowledged to the people; for when he was accused for buying off an evidence, he said that he was very much pleased that, having administered their affairs for so long a time, he was at last accused, rather for giving than receiving.

Again, Nicias, in his expenses, was of a more public spirit than Crassus, priding himself much on the dedication of gifts in temples, on presiding at gymnastic games, and furnishing choruses for the plays, and adorning processions, while the expenses of Crassus, in feasting and afterwards providing food for so many myriads of people, were much greater than all that Nicias possessed as well as spent put together. So that one might wonder at any one's failing to see that vice is a certain inconsistency and incongruity of habit, after such an example of money dishonourably obtained and wastefully lavished away.

Let so much be said of their estates; as for their management of public affairs, I see not that any dishonesty, injustice, or arbitrary action can be objected to Nicias, who was rather the victim of Alcibiades's tricks, and was always careful and scrupulous in his dealings with the people. But Crassus is very generally blamed for his changeableness in his friendships and enmities, for his unfaithfulness, and his mean and underhand proceedings; since he himself could not deny that to compass the consulship he hired men to lay violent hands upon Domitius and Cato. Then at the assembly held for assigning the provinces, many were wounded and four actually killed, and he himself, which I had omitted in the narrative of his life, struck with his fist one Lucius Analius, a senator, for contradicting him, so that he left the place bleeding.

But as Crassus was to be blamed for his violent and arbitrary courses, so is Nicias no less to be blamed for his timorousness and meanness of spirit, which made him submit and give in to the basest people, whereas in this respect Crassus showed himself lofty-spirited and magnanimous, who having to do not with such as Cleon or Hyperbolus, but with the splendid acts of Cæsar and the three triumphs of Pompey, would not stoop, but bravely bore up against their joint interests, and in obtaining the office of censor, surpassed even Pompey himself. For a statesman ought not to regard how invidious the thing is, but how noble, and by his greatness to overpower envy; but if he will be always aiming at security and quiet, and dread Alcibiades upon the hustings, and the Lacedæmonians at Pylos, and Perdiccas in Thrace, there is room and opportunity enough for retirement, and he may sit out of the noise of business, and weave himself, as one of the sophists says, his triumphal garland of inactivity. His desire of peace, indeed, and of finishing the war was a divine and truly Grecian ambition, nor in this respect would Crassus deserve to be compared to him, though he had enlarged the Roman empire to the Caspian Sea or the Indian Ocean.

In a state where there is a sense of virtue, a powerful man ought not to give way to the ill-affected, or expose the government to those that are incapable of it, nor suffer high trusts to be committed to those who want common honesty. Yet Nicias, by his connivance, raised Cleon, a fellow remarkable for nothing but his loud voice and brazen face, to the command of an army. Indeed, I do not commend Crassus, who in the war with Spartacus was more forward to fight than became a discreet general, though he was urged into it by a point of honour, lest Pompey by his coming should rob him of the glory of the action, as Mummius did Metellus at the taking of Corinth, but Nicias's proceedings are inexcusable.

For he did not yield up a mere opportunity of getting honour and advantage to his competitor, but believing that the expedition would be very hazardous, was thankful to take care of himself, and left the commonwealth to shift for itself. And whereas Themistocles, lest a mean and incapable fellow should ruin the state by holding command in the Persian war, bought him off, and Cato, in a most dangerous and critical conjuncture, stood for the tribuneship for the sake of his country, Nicias, reserving himself for trifling expeditions against Minoa and Cythera, and the miserable Melians, if there be occasion to come to blows with the Lacedæmonians, slips off his general's cloak and hands over to the unskilfulness and rashness of Cleon, fleet, men, and arms, and the whole command, where the utmost possible skill was called for. Such conduct, I say, is not to be thought so much carelessness of his own fame, as of the interest and preservation of his country. By this means it came to pass he was compelled to the Sicilian war, men generally believing that he was not so much honestly convinced of the difficulty of the enterprise, as ready out of mere love of ease and cowardice to lose the city the conquest of Sicily.

But yet it is a great sign of his integrity, that though he was always averse from war, and unwilling to command, yet they always continued to appoint him as the best experienced and ablest general they had. On the other hand Crassus, though always ambitious of command, never attained to it, except by mere necessity in the servile war, Pompey and Metellus and the two brothers Lucullus being absent, although at that time he was at his highest pitch of interest and reputation. Even those who thought most of him seem to have thought him, as the comic poet says—

A brave man anywhere but in the field.

There was no help, however, for the Romans, against his passion for command and for distinction. The Athenians sent out Nicias against his will to the war, and Crassus led out the Romans against theirs; Crassus brought misfortune on Rome, as Athens brought it on Nicias.

Still this is rather ground for praising Nicias, than for finding fault with Crassus. His experience and sound judgment as a general saved him from being carried away by the delusive hopes of his fellow-citizens, and made him refuse to entertain any prospect of conquering Sicily. Crassus, on the other hand, mistook, in entering on a Parthian war as an easy matter. He was eager, while Cæsar was subduing the west, Gaul, Germany, and Britain, to advance for his part to the east and the Indian Sea, by the conquest of Asia, to complete the incursions of Pompey and the attempts of Lucullus, men of prudent temper and of unimpeachable worth, who nevertheless entertained the same projects as Crassus, and acted under the same convictions. When Pompey was appointed to the like command, the senate was opposed to it; and after Cæsar had routed three hundred thousand Germans, Cato recommended that he should be surrendered to the defeated enemy, to expiate in his own person the guilt of breach of faith. The people, meantime (their service to Cato!), kept holiday for fifteen days, and were overjoyed. What would have been their feelings, and how many holidays would they have celebrated, if Crassus had sent news from Babylon of victory, and thence marching onward had converted Media and Persia, and Hyrcanians, Susa and Bactra, into Roman provinces?

If wrong we must do, as Euripides says, and cannot be content with peace and present good things, let it not be for such results as destroying Mende or Scandea, or beating up the exiled Æginetans in the coverts to which like hunted birds they had fled, when expelled from their homes, but let it be for some really great remuneration; nor let us part with justice, like a

cheap and common thing, for a small and trifling price. Those who praise Alexander's enterprise and blame that of Crassus, judge of the beginning unfairly by the results.

In actual service, Nicias did much that deserves high praise. He frequently defeated the enemy in battle, and was on the very point of capturing Syracuse; nor should he bear the whole blame of the disaster, which may fairly be ascribed in part to his want of health and to the jealousy entertained of him at home. Crassus, on the other hand, committed so many errors as not to leave fortune room to show him favour. It is no surprise to find such imbecility fall a victim to the power of Parthia; the only wonder is to see it prevailing over the wonted good fortune of Rome. One scrupulously observed, the other entirely slighted the arts of divination; and as both equally perished, it is difficult to see what inference we should draw. Yet the fault of over-caution, supported by old and general opinion, better deserves forgiveness than that of self-willed and lawless transgression.

In his death, however, Crassus had the advantage, as he did not surrender himself, nor submit to bondage, nor let himself be taken in by trickery, but was the victim only of the entreaties of his friends and the perfidy of his enemies; whereas Nicias enhanced the shame of his death by yielding himself up in the hope of disgraceful and inglorious escape.

SERTORIUS

130?–72 B.C.

It is no great wonder if in long process of time, while Fortune takes her course hither and thither, numerous coincidences should spontaneously occur. If the number and variety of subjects to be wrought upon be infinite, it is all the more easy for Fortune, with such an abundance of material, to effect this similarity of results. Or if, on the other hand, events are limited to the combinations of some finite number, then of necessity the same must often recur, and in the same sequence.

There are people who take a pleasure in making collections of all such fortuitous occurrences that they have heard or read of, as look like works of a rational power and design; they observe, for example, that two emi-

nent persons whose names were Attis, the one a Syrian, the other of Arcadia, were both slain by a wild boar; that of two whose names were Actæon, the one was torn in pieces by his dogs, the other by his lovers; that of two famous Scipios, the one overthrew the Carthaginians in war, the other totally ruined and destroyed them; the city of Troy was the first time taken by Hercules for the horses promised him by Laomedon, the second time by Agamemnon, by means of the celebrated great wooden horse, and the third time by Charidemus, by occasion of a horse falling down at the gate, which hindered the Trojans, so that they could not shut them soon enough; and of two cities which take their names from the most agreeable odoriferous plants, Ios and Smyrna, the one from a violet, the other from myrrh, the poet Homer is reported to have been born in the one and to have died in the other.

And so to these instances let us further add, that the most warlike commanders, and most remarkable for exploits of skilful stratagem, have had but one eye; as Philip, Antigonus, Hannibal, and Sertorius, whose life and actions we describe at present; of whom, indeed, we might truly say, that he was more continent than Philip, more faithful to his friends than Antigonus, and more merciful to his enemies than Hannibal; and that for prudence and judgment he gave place to none of them, but in fortune was inferior to them all. Yet though he had continually in her a far more difficult adversary to contend against than his open enemies, he nevertheless maintained his ground, with the military skill of Metellus, the boldness of Pompey, the success of Sulla, and the power of the Roman people, all to be encountered by one who was a banished man and a stranger at the head of a body of barbarians.

Among Greek commanders, Eumenes of Cardia may be best compared with him; they were both of them men born for command, for warfare, and for stratagem; both banished from their countries, and holding command over strangers; both had fortune for their adversary, in their last days so harshly so, that they were both betrayed and murdered by those who served them, and with whom they had formerly overcome their enemies.

Quintus Sertorius was of a noble family, born in the city of Nursia, in the country of the Sabines; his father died when he was young, and he was carefully and decently educated by his mother, whose name was Rhea, and whom he appears to have extremely loved and honoured. He paid some attention to the study of oratory and pleading in his youth, and acquired some reputation and influence in Rome by his eloquence; but the splendour of his actions in arms, and his successful achievements in the wars, drew off his ambition in that direction.

At his first beginning, he served under Cæpio, when the Cimbri and Teutones invaded Gaul; where the Romans fighting unsuccessfully, and being put to flight, he was wounded in many parts of his body, and lost his horse, yet, nevertheless, swam across the river Rhone in his armour, with his breastplate and shield, bearing himself up against the violence of the current; so strong and so well inured to hardship was his body.

The second time that the Cimbri and Teutones came down with some hundreds of thousands, threatening death and destruction to all, when it was no small piece of service for a Roman soldier to keep his ranks and obey his commander, Sertorius undertook, while Marius led the army, to spy out the enemy's camp. Procuring a Celtic dress, and acquainting himself with the ordinary expressions of their language requisite for common intercourse, he threw himself in amongst the barbarians; where having carefully seen with his own eyes, or having been fully informed by persons upon the place of all their most important concerns, he returned to Marius, from whose hands he received the rewards of valour; and afterwards giving frequent proof both of conduct and courage in all the following war, he was advanced to places of honour and trust under his general.

After the wars with the Cimbri and Teutones, he was sent into Spain, having the command of a thousand men under Didius, the Roman general, and wintered in the country of the Celtiberians, in the city of Castulo, where the soldiers enjoying great plenty, and growing insolent and continually drinking, the inhabitants despised them and sent for aid by night to the Gyriscenians, their near neighbours, who fell upon the Romans in their lodgings and slew a great number of them. Sertorius, with a few of his soldiers, made his way out, and rallying together the rest who escaped, he marched round about the walls, and finding the gate open, by which the Gyriscenians had made their secret entrance, he gave not them the same opportunity, but placing a guard at the gate, and seizing upon all quarters of the city, he slew all who were of age to bear arms, and then ordering his soldiers to lay aside their weapons and put off their own clothes, and put on the accoutrements of the barbarians, he commanded them to follow him to the city from whence the men came who had made this night attack upon the Romans. And thus deceiving the Gyriscenians with the sight of their own armour, he found the gates of their city open, and took a great number prisoners, who came out thinking to meet their friends and fellow-citizens come home from a successful expedition. Most of them were thus slain by the Romans at their own gates, and the rest within yielded up themselves and were sold for slaves.

This action made Sertorius highly renowned throughout all Spain, and as soon as he returned to Rome he was appointed quæstor of Cisalpine Gaul, at a very seasonable moment for his country, the Marsian war being on the point of breaking out. Sertorius was ordered to raise soldiers and provide arms, which he performed with a diligence and alacrity, so contrasting with the feebleness and slothfulness of other officers of his age, that he got the repute of a man whose life would be one of action.

Nor did he relinquish the part of a soldier, now that he had arrived at the dignity of a commander, but performed wonders with his own hands, and never sparing himself, but exposing his body freely in all conflicts, he lost one of his eyes. This he always esteemed an honour to him; observing that others do not continually carry about with them the marks and testimonies of their valour, but must often lay aside their chains of gold, their spears and crowns; whereas his ensigns of honour, and the manifestations of his courage, always remained with him, and those who beheld his misfortune must at the same time recognise his merits.

The people also paid him the respect he deserved, and when he came into the theatre, received him with plaudits and joyful acclamations, an honour rarely bestowed even on persons of advanced standing and established reputation. Yet, notwithstanding this popularity, when he stood to be tribune of the people, he was disappointed, and lost the place, being opposed by the party of Sulla, which seems to have been the principal cause of his subsequent enmity to Sulla.

After that Marius was overcome by Sulla and fled into Africa, and Sulla had left Italy to go to the wars against Mithridates, and of the two consuls Octavius and Cinna, Octavius remained steadfast to the policy of Sulla, but Cinna, desirous of a new revolution, attempted to recall the lost interest of Marius, Sertorius joined Cinna's party, more particularly as he saw that Octavius was not very capable, and was also suspicious of any one that was a friend to Marius. When a great battle was fought between the two consuls in the Forum, Octavius overcame, and Cinna and Sertorius, having lost not less than ten thousand men, left the city, and gaining over most part of the troops who were dispersed about and remained still in many parts of Italy, they in a short time mustered up a force against Octavius sufficient to give him battle again, and Marius, also, now coming by sea out of Africa, proffered himself to serve under Cinna, as a private soldier under his consul and commander.

Most were for the immediate reception of Marius, but Sertorius openly declared against it, whether he thought that Cinna would not now pay as much attention to himself, when a man of higher military repute was present, or feared that the violence of Marius would bring all things to confusion, by his boundless wrath and vengeance after victory. He insisted upon it with Cinna that they were already victorious, that there remained little to be done, and that if they admitted Marius, he would deprive them of the glory and advantage of the war, as there was no man less easy to deal with, or less to be trusted in, as a partner in power. Cinna answered, that Sertorius rightly judged the affair, but that he himself was at a loss, and ashamed, and knew not how to reject him, after he had sent for him to share in his fortunes. To which Sertorius immediately replied, that he had thought that Marius came into Italy of his own accord, and therefore had deliberated as to what might be most expedient, but that Cinna ought not so much as to have questioned whether he should accept him whom he had already invited, but should have honourably received and employed him, for his word once passed left no room for debate.

Thus Marius being sent for by Cinna, and their forces being divided into three parts, under Cinna, Marius, and Sertorius, the war was brought to a successful conclusion; but those about Cinna and Marius committing all manner of insolence and cruelty, made the Romans think the evils of war a golden time in comparison. On the contrary, it is reported of Sertorius that he never slew any man in his anger to satisfy his own private revenge, nor ever insulted over any one whom he had overcome, but was much offended with Marius, and often privately entreated Cinna to use his power more moderately. And in the end, when the slaves whom Marius had freed at his landing to increase his army, being made not only his fellow-soldiers in the war, but also now his guard in his usurpation, enriched and powerful by his favour, either by the command or permission of Marius, or by their own lawless violence, committed all sorts of crimes, killed their masters, ravished their masters' wives and abused their children, their conduct appeared so intolerable to Sertorius that he slew the whole body of them, four thousand in number, commanding his soldiers to shoot them down with their javelins, as they lay encamped together.

Afterwards when Marius died, and Cinna shortly after was slain, when the younger Marius made himself consul against Sertorius's wishes and contrary to law, when Carbo, Norbanus, and Scipio fought unsuccessfully against Sulla, now advancing to Rome, when much was lost by the cowardice and remissness of the commanders, but more by the treachery of their party, when with the want of prudence in the chief leaders, all went so ill that Sertorius's presence could do no good; and in the end when Sulla had placed his camp near to Scipio, and by pretending friendship, and putting him in hopes of a peace, corrupted his army, and Scipio could not be made sensible of this, although often forewarned of it by Sertorius—at last he utterly despaired of Rome, and hasted into Spain, that by taking possession there beforehand, he might secure a refuge to his friends from their misfortunes at home.

Having bad weather in his journey, and travelling through mountainous countries, and the inhabitants stopping the way, and demanding a toll and money for passage, those who were with him were out of all patience at the indignity and shame it would be for a proconsul of Rome to pay tribute to a crew of wretched barbarians. But he little regarded their censure, and slighting that which had only the appearance of an indecency, told them he must buy time, the most precious of all things to those who go upon great enterprises; and pacifying the barbarous people with money, he hastened his journey, and took possession of Spain, a country flourishing and populous, abounding with young men fit to bear arms; but on account of the insolence and covetousness of the governors from time to time sent thither from Rome they had generally an aversion to Roman supremacy.

He, however, soon gained the affection of their nobles by intercourse with them, and the good opinion of the people by remitting their taxes. But that which won him most popularity was his exempting them from finding lodgings for the soldiers, when he commanded his army to take up their winter quarters outside the cities, and to pitch their camp in the suburbs; and when he himself, first of all, caused his own tent to be raised without the walls. Yet not being willing to rely totally upon the good inclination of the inhabitants he armed all the Romans who lived in those countries that were of military age, and undertook the building of ships and the making of all sorts of warlike engines, by which means he kept the cities in due obedience, showing himself gentle in all peaceful business, and at the same time formidable to his enemies by his great preparations for war.

As soon as he was informed that Sulla had made himself master of Rome, and that the party which sided with Marius and Carbo was going to destruction, he expected that some commander with a considerable army would speedily come against him, and therefore sent away Julius Salinator immediately, with six thousand men fully armed, to fortify and defend the passes of the Pyrenees.

And Caius Annius not long after being sent out by Sulla, finding Julius unassailable, sat down short at the foot of the mountains in perplexity. But a certain Calpurnius, surnamed Lanarius, having treacherously slain Julius, and his soldiers then forsaking the heights of the Pyrenees, Caius Annius advanced with large numbers and drove before him all who endeavoured to hinder his march. Sertorius, also, not being strong enough to give him battle, retreated with three thousand men into New Carthage, where he took shipping, and crossed the seas into Africa. And coming near the coast of Mauritania, his men went on shore to water, and straggling about negligently, the natives fell upon them and slew a great number.

This new misfortune forced him to sail back again into Spain, whence he was also repulsed, and, some Cilician private ships joining with him, they made for the island of Pityussa, where they landed and overpowered the garrison placed there by Annius, who, however, came not long after with a great fleet of ships and five thousand soldiers. And Sertorius made ready to fight him by sea, although his ships were not built for strength, but for lightness and swift sailing; but a violent west wind raised such a sea that many of them were run aground and shipwrecked, and he himself, with a few vessels, being kept from putting further out to sea by the fury of the weather, and from landing by the power of his enemies, was tossed about painfully for ten days together, amidst the boisterous and adverse waves.

He escaped with difficulty, and after the wind ceased, ran for certain desert islands scattered in those seas, affording no water, and after passing a night there, making out to sea again, he went through the straits of Cadiz, and sailing outward, keeping the Spanish shore on his right hand, he landed a little above the mouth of the river Bætis, where it falls into the Atlantic Sea, and gives the name to that part of Spain.

Here he met with seamen recently arrived from the Atlantic islands, two in number, divided from one another only by a narrow channel, and distant from the coast of Africa ten thousand furlongs. These are called the Islands of the Blest; rain falls there seldom, and in moderate showers, but for the most part they have gentle breezes, bringing along with them soft dews, which render the soil not only rich for ploughing and planting, but so abundantly fruitful that it produces spontaneously an abundance of delicate fruits, sufficient to feed the inhabitants, who may here enjoy all things without trouble or labour. The seasons of the year are temperate, and the transitions from one to another so moderate that the air is almost always serene and pleasant. The rough northerly and easterly winds which blow from the coasts of Europe and Africa, dissipated in the vast open space, utterly lose their force before they reach the islands. The soft western and southerly winds which breathe upon them sometimes produce gentle sprinkling showers, which they convey along with them from the sea, but more usually bring days of moist, bright weather, cooling and gently fertilising the soil, so that the firm belief prevails, even among the barbarians, that this is the seat of the blessed, and that these are the Elysian Fields celebrated by Homer.

When Sertorius heard this account, he was seized with a wonderful passion for these islands, and had an extreme desire to go and live there in peace and quietness, and safe from oppression and unending wars; but his inclinations being perceived by the Cilician pirates, who desired not peace nor quiet, but riches and spoils, they immediately forsook him and sailed away into Africa to assist Ascalis, the son of Iphtha, and to help to restore him to his kingdom of Mauritania. Their sudden departure noways discouraged Sertorius; he presently resolved to assist the enemies of Ascalis, and by this new adventure trusted to keep his soldiers together, who from this might conceive new hopes, and a prospect of a new scene of action. His arrival in Mauritania being very acceptable to the Moors, he lost no time, but immediately giving battle to Ascalis, beat him out of the field and besieged him; and Paccianus being sent by Sulla, with a powerful supply, to

raise the siege, Sertorius slew him in the field, gained over all his forces, and took the city of Tingis, into which Ascalis and his brothers were fled for refuge.

The Africans tell that Antæus was buried in this city, and Sertorius had the grave opened, doubting the story because of the prodigious size, and finding there his body, in effect, it is said, full sixty cubits long, he was infinitely astonished, offered sacrifice, and heaped up the tomb again, gave his confirmation to the story, and added new honours to the memory of Antæus.

The Africans tell that after the death of Antæus, his wife Tinga lived with Hercules, and had a son by him called Sophax, who was king of these countries, and gave his mother's name to this city, whose son, also, was Diodorus, a great conqueror, who brought the greatest part of the Libyan tribes under his subjection, with an army of Greeks, raised out of the colonies of the Olbians and Myceneans placed here by Hercules. Thus much I may mention for the sake of King Juba, of all monarchs the greatest student of history, whose ancestors are said to have sprung from Diodorus and Sophax.

When Sertorius had made himself absolute master of the whole country, he acted with great fairness to those who had confided in him, and who yielded to his mercy; he restored to them their property, cities, and government, accepting only of such acknowledgments as they themselves freely offered. And whilst he considered which way next to turn his arms, the Lusitanians sent ambassadors to desire him to be their general; for being terrified with the Roman power, and finding the necessity of having a commander of great authority and experience in war, being also sufficiently assured of his worth and valour by those who had formerly known him, they were desirous to commit themselves especially to his care.

And in fact Sertorius is said to have been of a temper unassailable either by fear or pleasure, in adversity and dangers undaunted, and noways puffed up with prosperity. In straightforward fighting, no commander in his time was more bold and daring, and in whatever was to be performed in war by stratagem, secrecy, or surprise, if any strong place was to be secured, any pass to be gained speedily, for deceiving and overreaching an enemy, there was no man equal to him in subtlety and skill. In bestowing rewards and conferring honours upon those who had performed good service in the wars, he was bountiful and magnificent, and was no less sparing and moderate in inflicting punishment.

It is true that that piece of harshness and cruelty which he executed in the latter part of his days upon the Spanish hostages seems to argue that his clemency was not natural to him, but only worn as a dress, and employed upon calculation, as his occasion or necessity required. As to my own opinion, I am persuaded that pure virtue, established by reason and judgment, can never be totally perverted or changed into its opposite by any misfortune whatever. Yet I think it at the same time possible that virtuous inclinations and natural good qualities may, when unworthily oppressed by calamities, show, with change of fortune, some change and alteration of their temper; and thus I conceive it happened to Sertorius, who, when prosperity failed him, became exasperated by his disasters against those who had done him wrong.

The Lusitanians having sent for Sertorius, he left Africa, and being made general with absolute authority, he put all in order amongst them, and brought the neighbouring parts of Spain under subjection. Most of the tribes voluntarily submitted themselves, won by the fame of his clemency and of his courage, and, to some extent, also, he availed himself of cunning artifices of his own devising to impose upon them and gain influence over them.

Amongst which, certainly, that of the hind was not the least. Spanus, a countryman who lived in those parts, meeting by chance a hind that had recently calved, flying from the hunters, let the dam go, and pursuing the fawn, took it, being wonderfully pleased with the rarity of the colour, which was all milk-white. As at that time Sertorius was living in the neighbourhood, and accepted gladly any presents of fruit, fowl, or venison that the country afforded, and rewarded liberally those who presented them, the countryman brought him his young hind, which he took and was well pleased with at the first sight; but when in time he had made it so tame and gentle that it would come when he called, and follow him wheresoever he went, and could endure the noise and tumult of the camp, knowing well that uncivilised people are naturally prone to superstition, by little and little he raised it into something preternatural, saying that it was given him by the goddess Diana, and that it revealed to him many secrets.

He added, also, further contrivances. If he had received at any time private intelligence that the enemies had made an incursion into any part of the districts under his command, or had solicited any city to revolt, he pretended that the hind had informed him of it in his sleep, and charged him to keep his forces in readiness. Or if again he had noticed that any of the commanders under him had got a victory, he would hide the messengers and bring forth the hind crowned with flowers, for joy of the good news that was to come, and would encourage them to rejoice and sacrifice to the gods for the good account they should soon receive of their prosperous success.

By such practices, he brought them to be more tractable and obedient in all things; for now they thought themselves no longer to be led by a stranger, but rather conducted by a god, and the more so, as the facts themselves seemed to bear witness to it, his power, contrary to all expectation or probability, continually increasing. For with two thousand six hundred men, whom for honour's sake he called Romans, combined with seven hundred Africans, who landed with him when he first entered Lusitania, together with four thousand targeteers and seven hundred horse of the Lusitanians themselves, he made war against four Roman generals, who commanded a hundred and twenty thousand foot, six thousand horse, two thousand archers and slingers, and had cities innumerable in their power; whereas at the first he had not above twenty cities in all.

From this weak and slender beginning, he raised himself to the command of large nations of men, and the possession of numerous cities; and of the Roman commanders who were sent against him, he overthrew Cotta in a sea-fight, in the channel near the town of Mellaria; he routed Fufidius, the governor of Bætica, with the loss of two thousand Romans, near the banks of the river Bætis; Lucius Domitius, proconsul of the other province of Spain, was overthrown by one of his lieutenants; Thoranius, another commander sent against him by Metellus with a great force, was slain, and Metellus, one of the greatest and most approved Roman generals then living, by a series of defeats, was reduced to such extremities, that Lucius Manlius came to his assistance out of Gallia Narbonensis, and Pompey the Great was sent from Rome itself in all haste with considerable forces.

Nor did Metellus know which way to turn himself, in a war with such a bold and ready commander, who was continually molesting him, and yet could not be brought to a set battle, but by the swiftness and dexterity of his Spanish soldiery was enabled to shift and adapt himself to any change of circumstances. Metellus had had experience in battles fought by regular legions of soldiers, fully armed and drawn up in due order into a heavy standing phalanx, admirably trained for encountering and overpowering an enemy who came to close combat, hand to hand, but entirely unfit for climbing among the hills, and competing incessantly with the swift attacks and retreats of a set of fleet mountaineers, or to endure hunger and thirst, and live exposed like them to the wind and weather, without fire or covering.

Besides, being now in years, and having been formerly engaged in many fights and dangerous conflicts, he had grown inclined to a more remiss, easy, and luxurious life, and was the less able to contend with Sertorius, who was in the prime of his strength and vigour, and had a body wonderfully fitted for war, being strong, active, and temperate, continually accustomed to endure hard labour, to take long, tedious journeys, to pass many nights together without sleep, to eat little, and to be satisfied with very coarse fare, and who was never stained with the least excess in wine, even when he was most at leisure. What leisure time he allowed himself he spent in hunting and riding about, and so made himself thoroughly acquainted with every passage for escape when he would flee, and for overtaking and intercepting a pursuit, and gained a perfect knowledge of where he could and where he could not go.

Insomuch that Metellus suffered all the inconveniences of defeat, although he earnestly desired to fight, and Sertorius, though he refused the field, reaped all the advantages of a conqueror. For he hindered them from foraging, and cut them off from water; if they advanced, he was nowhere to be found; if they stayed in any place and encamped, he continually molested and alarmed them; if they besieged any town, he presently appeared and besieged them again, and put them to extremities for want of necessaries. Thus he so wearied out the Roman army that when Sertorius challenged Metellus to fight singly with him, they commended it, and cried out it was a fair offer, a Roman to fight against a Roman, and a general against a general; and when Metellus refused the challenge, they reproached him.

Metellus derided and contemned this, and rightly so; for, as Theophrastus observes, a general should die like a general, and not like a skirmisher. But perceiving that the town of the Langobritæ, which gave great assistance to Sertorius, might easily be taken for want of water, as there was but one well within the walls, and the besieger would be master of the springs and fountains in the suburbs, he advanced against the place, expecting to carry it in two days' time, there being no more water, and gave command to his soldiers to take five days' provision only. Sertorius, however, resolving to send speedy relief, ordered two thousand skins to be filled with water, naming a considerable sum of money for the carriage of every skin; and many Spaniards and Moors undertaking the work, he chose out those who were the strongest and swiftest of foot, and sent them through the mountains, with order that when they had delivered the water, they should convey away privately all those who would be least serviceable in the siege, that there might be water sufficient for the defendants.

As soon as Metellus understood this, he was disturbed, as he had already consumed most part of the necessary provisions for his army, but he sent out Aquinus with six thousand soldiers to fetch in fresh supplies. But Sertorius having notice of it, laid an ambush for him, and having sent out beforehand three thousand men to take post in a thickly wooded watercourse, with these he attacked the rear of Aquinus in his return, while he himself, charging him in the front, destroyed part of his army, and took the rest prisoners, Aquinus only escaping, after the loss of both his horse and his armour. And Metellus, being forced shamefully to raise the siege, withdrew amidst the laughter and contempt of the Spaniards; while Sertorius became yet more the object of their esteem and admiration.

He was also highly honoured for his introducing discipline and good order amongst them, for he altered their furious savage manner of fighting, and brought them to make use of the Roman armour, taught them to keep their ranks, and observe signals and watchwords; and out of a confused number of thieves and robbers he constituted a regular, well-disciplined army. He bestowed silver and gold upon them liberally to gild and adorn their helmets, he had their shields worked with various figures and designs, he brought them into the mode of wearing flowered and embroidered cloaks and coats, and by supplying money for these purposes, and joining with them in all improvements, he won the hearts of all.

That, however, which delighted them most was the care that he took of their children. He sent for all the boys of noblest parentage out of all their tribes, and placed them in the great city of Osca, where he appointed masters to instruct them in the Grecian and Roman learning, that when they came to be men, they might, as he professed, be fitted to share with him in authority, and in conducting the government, although under this pretext he really made them hostages. However, their fathers were wonderfully pleased that their children went daily to the schools in good order, handsomely dressed in gowns edged with purple, and that Sertorius paid for their lessons, examined them often, distributed rewards to the most deserving, and gave them the golden bosses to hang about their necks, which the Romans called *bullæ*.

There being a custom in Spain that when a commander was slain in battle, those who attended his person fought it out till they all died with him, which the inhabitants of those countries called an *offering,* or libation, there were few commanders that had any considerable guard or number of attendants; but Sertorius was followed by many thousands who offered themselves, and vowed to spend their blood with his. And it is told that when his army was defeated near a city in Spain, and the enemy pressed hard upon them, the Spaniards, with no care for themselves, but being totally solicitous to save Sertorius, took him upon their shoulders and passed him from one to another, till they carried him into the city, and only when they had thus placed their general in safety, provided afterwards each man for his own security.

Nor were the Spaniards alone ambitious to serve him, but the Roman soldiers, also, that came out of Italy, were impatient to be under his command; and when Perpenna Vento, who was of the same faction with Sertorius, came into Spain with a quantity of money and a large number of troops, and designed to make war against Metellus on his own account, his own soldiers opposed it, and talked continually of Sertorius, much to the mortification of Perpenna, who was puffed up with the grandeur of his family and his riches. And when they afterwards received tidings that Pompey was passing the Pyrenees, they took up their arms, laid hold on their ensigns, called upon Perpenna to lead them to Sertorius, and threatened him that if he refused they would go without him and place themselves under a commander who was able to defend himself and those that served him. And so Perpenna

was obliged to yield to their desires, and joining Sertorius, added to his army three-and-fifty cohorts.

When now all the cities on this side of the river Ebro also united their forces together under his command, his army grew great, for they flocked together and flowed in upon him from all quarters. But when they continually cried out to attack the enemy, and were impatient of delay, their inexperienced, disorderly rashness caused Sertorius much trouble, who at first strove to restrain them with reason and good counsel; but when he perceived them refractory and unseasonably violent, he gave way to their impetuous desires, and permitted them to engage with the enemy, in such sort that they might, being repulsed, yet not totally routed, become more obedient to his commands for the future. Which happening as he had anticipated, he soon rescued them, and brought them safe into his camp.

After a few days, being willing to encourage them again, when he had called all his army together, he caused two horses to be brought into the field, one old, feeble, lean animal, the other a lusty, strong horse, with a remarkable thick and long tail. Near the lean one he placed a tall, strong man, and near the strong young horse a weak, despicable-looking fellow; and at a sign given, the strong man took hold of the weak horse's tail with both his hands, and drew it to him with his whole force, as if he would pull it off; the other, the weak man, in the meantime, set to work to pluck off hair by hair from the great horse's tail. When the strong man had given trouble enough to himself in vain, and sufficient diversion to the company, and had abandoned his attempt, whilst the weak, pitiful fellow in a short time and with little pains had left not a hair on the great horse's tail, Sertorius rose up and spoke to his army. "You see, fellow-soldiers, that perseverance is more prevailing than violence, and that many things which cannot be overcome when they are together, yield themselves up when taken little by little. Assiduity and persistence are irresistible, and in time overthrow and destroy the greatest powers whatever. Time being the favourable friend and assistant of those who use their judgment to await his occasions, and the destructive enemy of those who are unseasonably urging and pressing forward." With a frequent use of such words and such devices, he soothed the fierceness of the barbarous people, and taught them to attend and watch for their opportunities.

Of all his remarkable exploits, none raised greater admiration than that which he put in practice against the Characitanians. These are a people beyond the river Tagus, who inhabit neither cities nor towns, but live in a vast high hill, within the deep dens and caves of the rocks, the mouths of which open all towards the north. The country below is of a soil resembling a light clay, so loose as easily to break into powder, and is not firm enough to bear any one that treads upon it, and if you touch it in the least it flies about like ashes or unslacked lime. In any danger of war, these people descended into their caves, and carrying in their booty and prey along with them, stayed quietly within, secure from every attack.

And when Sertorius, leaving Metellus some distance off, had placed his camp near this hill, they slighted and despised him, imagining that he retired into these parts, being overthrown by the Romans. And whether out of anger or resentment, or out of his unwillingness to be thought to fly from his enemies, early in the morning he rode up to view the situation of the place. But finding there was no way to come at it, as he rode about, threatening them in vain and disconcerted, he took notice that the wind raised the dust and carried it up towards the caves of the Characitanians, the mouths of which, as I said before, opened towards the north; and the northerly wind, which some call Cæcias, prevailing most in those parts, coming up out of moist plains or mountains covered with snow, at this particular time, in the heat of summer, being further supplied and increased by the melting of the ice in the northern regions, blew a delightful fresh gale, cooling and refreshing the Characitanians and their cattle all the day long. Sertorius, considering well all circumstances in which either the information of the inhabitants or his own experience had instructed him, commanded his soldiers to shovel up a great quantity of this light, dusty earth, to heap it up together, and make a mount of it over against the hill in which those barbarous people resided, who, imagining that all this preparation was for raising a mound to get at them, only mocked and laughed at it. However, he continued the work till the evening, and brought his soldiers back into their camp.

The next morning a gentle breeze at first arose, and moved the lightest parts of the earth and dispersed it about as the chaff before the wind; but when the sun coming to be higher, the strong northerly wind had covered the hills with the dust, the soldiers came and turned this mound of earth over and over, and broke the hard clods in pieces, whilst others on horseback rode through it backward and forward, and raised a cloud of dust into the air; there with the wind the whole of it was carried away and blown into the dwellings of the Characitanians, all lying open to the north. And there being no other vent or breathing-place than that through which the Cæcias rushed in upon them, it quickly blinded their eyes and filled their lungs, and all but choked them, whilst they strove to draw in the rough air mingled with dust and powdered earth. Nor were they able, with all they could do, to hold out above two days, but yielding up themselves on the third, adding, by their defeat, not so much to the power of Sertorius, as to his renown, in proving that he was able to conquer places by art, which were impregnable by the force of arms.

So long as he had to do with Metellus, he was thought to owe his successes to his opponent's age and slow temper, which were ill suited for coping with the daring and activity of one who commanded a light army more like a band of robbers than regular soldiers. But when Pompey also passed over the Pyrenees, and Sertorius pitched his camp near him, and offered and himself accepted every occasion by which military skill could be put to the proof, and in this contest of dexterity was found to have the better, both in baffling his enemy's designs and in counterscheming himself, the fame of him now spread even to Rome itself, as the most expert commander of his time. For the renown of Pompey was not small, who had already won much honour by his achievements in the wars of Sulla, from whom he received the title of Magnus, and was called Pompey the Great; and who had risen to the honour of a triumph before the beard had grown on his face. And many cities which were under Sertorius were on the very eve of revolting and going over to Pompey, when they were deterred from it by that great action, amongst others, which he performed near the city of Lauron, contrary to the expectation of all.

For Sertorius had laid siege to Lauron, and Pompey came with his whole army to relieve it; and there being a hill near this city very advantageously situated, they both made haste to take it. Sertorius was beforehand, and took possession of it first, and Pompey, having drawn down his forces, was not sorry that it had thus happened, imagining that he had hereby enclosed his enemy between his own army and the city, and sent in a messenger to the citizens of Lauron, to bid them be of good courage, and to come upon their walls, where they might see their besieger besieged. Sertorius, perceiving their intentions, smiled, and said he would now teach Sulla's scholar, for so he called Pompey in derision, that it was the part of a general to look as well behind him as before him, and at the same time showed them six thousand soldiers, whom he had left in his former camp, from whence he marched out to take the hill, where, if Pompey should assault him, they might fall upon his rear.

Pompey discovered this too late, and not daring to give battle, for fear of being encompassed, and yet being ashamed to desert his friends and confederates in their extreme danger, was thus forced to sit still, and see them ruined before his face. For the besieged despaired of relief, and delivered up themselves to Sertorius, who spared their lives and granted them their liberty, but burnt their city, not out of anger or cruelty, for of all commanders that ever were Sertorius seemed least of all to have indulged these passions, but only for the greater shame and confusion of the admirers of Pompey, and that it might be reported amongst the Spaniards, that though he had been so close to the fire which burnt down the city of his confederates as actually to feel the heat of it, he still had not dared to make any opposition.

Sertorius, however, sustained many losses; but he always maintained himself and those immediately with him undefeated, and it was by other commanders under him that he suffered; and he was more admired for being able to repair his losses, and for recovering the victory, than the Roman generals against him for gaining these advantages; as at the battle of the Sucro against Pompey, and at the battle near Tuttia, against him and Metellus together.

The battle near the Sucro was fought, it is said, through the impatience of Pompey, lest Metellus should share with him in the victory, Sertorius being also willing to engage Pompey before the arrival of Metellus. Sertorius delayed the time till the evening, considering that the darkness of the night would be a disadvantage to his enemies, whether fleeing or pursuing, being strangers, and having no knowledge of the country.

When the fight began, it happened that Sertorius was not placed directly against Pompey, but against Afranius, who had command of the left wing of the Roman army, as he commanded the right wing of his own; but when he understood that his left wing began to give way, and yield to the assault of Pompey, he committed the care of his right wing to other commanders, and made haste to relieve those in distress; and rallying some that were fleeing, and encouraging others that still kept their ranks, he renewed the fight, and attacked the enemy in their pursuit so effectively as to cause a considerable rout, and brought Pompey into great danger of his life. For after being wounded and losing his horse, he escaped unexpectedly. For the Africans with Sertorius, who took Pompey's horse, set out with gold, and covered with rich trappings, fell out with one another; and upon the dividing of the spoil, gave over the pursuit.

Afranius, in the meantime, as soon as Sertorius had left his right wing, to assist the other part of his army, overthrew all that opposed him; and pursuing them to their camp, fell in together with them, and plundered them till it was dark night; knowing nothing of Pompey's overthrow, nor being able to restrain his soldiers from pillaging; when Sertorius, returning with victory, fell upon him and upon his men, who were all in disorder, and slew many of them. And the next morning he came into the field again well armed, and offered battle, but perceiving that Metellus was near, he drew off, and returned to his camp, saying, "If this old woman had not come up, I would have whipped that boy soundly, and sent him to Rome."

He was much concerned that his white hind could nowhere be found; as he was thus destitute of an admirable contrivance to encourage the barbarous people at a time when he most stood in need of it. Some men, however, wandering in the night, chanced to meet her, and knowing her by her colour, took her; to whom Sertorius promised a good reward, if they would tell no one of it; and immediately shut her up. A few days after, he appeared in public with a very cheerful look, and declared to the chief men of the country that the gods had foretold him in a dream that some great good fortune should shortly attend him; and, taking his seat, proceeded to answer the petitions of those who applied themselves to him. The keepers of the hind, who were not far off, now let her loose, and she no sooner espied Sertorius, but she came leaping with great joy to his feet, laid her head upon his knees, and licked his hands, as she formerly used to do. And Sertorius stroking her, and making much of her again, with that tenderness that the tears stood in his eyes, all that were present were immediately filled with wonder and astonishment, and accompanying him to his house with loud shouts for joy, looked upon him as a person above the rank of mortal men, and highly beloved by the gods; and were in great courage and hope for the future.

When he had reduced his enemies to the last extremity for want of provision, he was forced to give them battle, in the plains near Saguntum, to hinder them from foraging and plundering the country. Both parties fought gloriously. Memmius, the best commander in Pompey's army, was slain in the heat of the battle. Sertorius overthrew all before him, and with great slaughter of his enemies pressed forward towards Metellus.

This old commander, making a resistance beyond what could be expected from one of his years, was wounded with a lance; an occurrence which filled all who either saw it or heard of it with shame, to be thought to have left their general in distress, but at the same time to provoke them to revenge and fury against their enemies; they covered Metellus with their shields, and brought him off in safety, and then valiantly repulsed the Spaniards; and so victory changed sides, and Sertorius, that he might afford a more secure retreat to his army, and that fresh forces might more easily be raised, retired into a strong city in the mountains.

And though it was the least of his intention to sustain a long siege, yet he began to repair the walls, and to fortify the gates, thus deluding his enemies, who came and sat down before the town, hoping to take it without much resistance; and meantime gave over the pursuit of the Spaniards, and allowed opportunity for raising new forces for Sertorius, to which purpose he had sent commanders to all their cities, with orders, when they had sufficiently increased their numbers, to send him word of it. This news he no sooner received, but he sallied out and forced his way through his enemies, and easily joined them with the rest of his army. Having received this considerable reinforcement, he set upon the Romans again, and by rapidly assaulting them, by alarming them on all sides, by ensnaring, circumventing, and laying ambushes for them, he cut off all provisions by land, while with his piratical vessels he kept all the coast in awe, and hindered their supplies by sea.

He thus forced the Roman generals to dislodge and to separate from one another: Metellus departed into Gaul, and Pompey wintered among the Vaccæans, in a wretched condition, where, being in extreme want of money, he wrote a letter to the senate, to let them know that if they did not speedily supply him, he must draw off his army; for he had already spent his own money in the defence of Italy. To these extremities, the chiefest and the most powerful commanders of the age were reduced by the skill of Sertorius; and it was the common opinion in Rome that he would be in Italy before Pompey.

How far Metellus was terrified, and at what rate he esteemed him, he plainly declared, when he offered by proclamation an hundred talents and twenty thousand acres of land to any Roman that should kill him, and leave, if he were banished, to return; attempting villainously to buy his life by treachery, when he despaired of ever being able to overcome him in open war. When once he gained the advantage in a battle against Sertorius, he was so pleased and transported with his good fortune, that he caused himself to be publicly proclaimed Imperator; and all the cities which he visited received him with altars and sacrifices; he allowed himself, it is said, to have garlands placed on his head, and accepted sumptuous entertainments, at which he sat drinking in triumphal robes, while images and figures of victory were introduced by the motion of machines, bringing in with them crowns and trophies of gold to present to him, and companies of young men and women danced before him, and sang to him songs of joy and triumph. By all which he rendered himself deservedly ridiculous, for being so excessively delighted and puffed up with the thoughts of having followed one who was retiring of his own accord, and for having once had the better of him whom he used to call Sulla's runaway slave, and his forces, the remnant of the defeated troops of Carbo.

Sertorius, meantime, showed the loftiness of his temper in calling together all the Roman senators who had fled from Rome, and had come and resided with him, and giving them the name of a senate; and out of these he chose prætors and quæstors, and adorned his government with all the Roman laws and institutions. And though he made use of the arms, riches, and cities of the Spaniards, yet he would never, even in word, remit to them the imperial authority, but set Roman officers and commanders over them, intimating his purpose to restore liberty to the Romans, not to raise up the Spaniard's power against them.

For he was a sincere lover of his country, and had a great desire to return home; but in his adverse fortune he showed undaunted courage, and behaved himself towards his enemies in a manner free from all dejection and mean-spiritedness; and when he was in his prosperity, and in the height of his victories, he sent word to Metellus and Pompey that he was ready to lay down his arms and live a private life if he were allowed to return home, declaring that he had rather live as the meanest citizen in Rome than, exiled from it, be supreme commander of all other cities together.

And it is thought that his great desire for his country was in no small measure promoted by the tenderness he had for his mother, under whom he was brought up after the death of his father, and upon whom he had placed his entire affection. After that his friends had sent for him into Spain to be their general, as soon as he heard of his mother's death he had almost cast away himself and died for grief; for he lay seven days together continually in his tent, without giving the word, or being seen by the nearest of his friends; and when the chief commanders of the army and persons of the greatest note came about his tent, with great difficulty they prevailed with him at last to come abroad, and speak to his soldiers, and to take upon him the management of affairs, which were in a prosperous condition.

And thus, to many men's judgment, he seemed to have been in himself of a mild and compassionate temper, and naturally given to ease and quietness, and to have accepted of the command of military forces contrary to his own inclination, and not being able to live in safety otherwise, to have been driven by his enemies to have recourse to arms, and to espouse the wars as a necessary guard for the defence of his person.

His negotiations with King Mithridates further argue the greatness of his mind. For when Mithridates recovering himself from his overthrow by Sulla, like a strong wrestler that gets up to try another fall, was again endeavouring to re-establish his power in Asia, at this time the great fame of Sertorius was celebrated in all places; and when the merchants who came out of the western parts of Europe, bringing these, as it were, among their other foreign wares, had filled the kingdom of Pontus with their stories of his exploits in war, Mithri-

dates was extremely desirous to send an embassy to him, being also highly encouraged to it by the boastings of his flattering courtiers, who, comparing Mithridates to Pyrrhus, and Sertorius to Hannibal, professed that the Romans would never be able to make any considerable resistance against such great forces, and such admirable commanders, when they should be set upon on both sides at once, on one by the most warlike general, and on the other by the most powerful prince in existence.

Accordingly, Mithridates sent ambassadors into Spain to Sertorius with letters and instructions, and commission to promise ships and money toward the charge of the war, if Sertorius would confirm his pretensions upon Asia, and authorise him to possess all that he had surrendered to the Romans in his treaty with Sulla. Sertorius summoned a full council which he called a senate, where, when others joyfully approved of the conditions, and were desirous immediately to accept of his offer, seeing that he desired nothing of them but a name, and an empty title to places not in their power to dispose of, in recompense of which they should be supplied with what they then stood most in need of, Sertorius would by no means agree to it; declaring that he was willing that King Mithridates should exercise all royal power and authority over Bithynia and Cappadocia, countries accustomed to a monarchical government, and not belonging to Rome, but he could never consent that he should seize or detain a province, which, by the justest right and title, was possessed by the Romans, which Mithridates had formerly taken away from them, and had afterwards lost in open war to Fimbria, and quitted upon a treaty of peace with Sulla. For he looked upon it as his duty to enlarge the Roman possessions by his conquering arms, and not to increase his own power by the diminution of the Roman territories. Since a noble-minded man, though he willingly accepts of victory when it comes with honour, will never so much as endeavour to save his own life upon any dishonourable terms.

When this was related to Mithridates, he was struck with amazement, and said to his intimate friends, "What will Sertorius enjoin us to do when he comes to be seated in the Palatium in Rome, who at present, when he is driven out to the borders of the Atlantic Sea, sets bounds to our kingdoms in the east, and threatens us with war if we attempt the recovery of Asia?"

However, they solemnly, upon oath, concluded a league between them, upon these terms: that Mithridates should enjoy the free possession of Cappadocia and Bithynia, and that Sertorius should send him soldiers and a general for his army, in recompense of which the king was to supply him with three thousand talents and forty ships. Marcus Marius, a Roman senator who had quitted Rome to follow Sertorius, was sent general into Asia, in company with whom, when Mithridates had reduced divers of the Asian cities, Marius made his entrance with rods and axes carried before him, and Mithridates followed in the second place, voluntarily waiting upon him. Some of these cities he set at liberty, and others he freed from taxes, signifying to them that these privileges were granted to them by the favour of Sertorius, and hereby Asia, which had been miserably tormented by the revenue farmers, and oppressed by the insolent pride and covetousness of the soldiers, began to rise again to new hopes and to look forward with joy to the expected change of government.

But in Spain, the senators about Sertorius, and others of the nobility, finding themselves strong enough for their enemies, no sooner laid aside fear, but their minds were possessed by envy and irrational jealousies of Sertorius's power. And chiefly Perpenna, elevated by the thoughts of his noble birth, and carried away with a fond ambition of commanding the army, threw out villainous discourses in private amongst his acquaintance. "What evil genius," he would say, "hurries us perpetually from worse to worse? We who disdained to obey the dictates of Sulla, the ruler of the sea and land, and thus to live at home in peace and quiet, are come hither to our destruction, hoping to enjoy our liberty, and have made ourselves slaves of our own accord; and are become the contemptible guards and attendants of the banished Sertorius, who, that he may expose us the further, gives us a name that renders us ridiculous to all that hear it, and calls us the senate, when at the same time he makes us undergo as much hard labour, and forces us to be as subject to his haughty commands and insolences, as any Spaniards and Lusitanians."

With these mutinous discourses he seduced them; and though the greater number could not be led into open rebellion against Sertorius, fearing his power, they were prevailed with to endeavour to destroy his interest secretly. For by abusing the Lusitanians and Spaniards, by

inflicting severe punishments upon them, by raising exorbitant taxes, and by pretending that all this was done by the strict command of Sertorius, they caused great troubles, and made many cities to revolt; and those who were sent to mitigate and heal these differences did rather exasperate them, and increase the number of his enemies, and left them at their return more obstinate and rebellious than they found them. And Sertorius, incensed with all this, now so far forgot his former clemency and goodness as to lay hands on the sons of the Spaniards educated in the city of Osca; and, contrary to all justice, he cruelly put some of them to death, and sold others.

In the meantime, Perpenna, having increased the number of his conspirators, drew in Manlius, a commander in the army, who, at that time being attached to a youth, to gain his affections the more, discovered the confederacy to him, bidding him neglect others and be constant to him alone, who, in a few days, was to be a person of great power and authority. But the youth having a greater inclination for Aufidius, disclosed all to him, which much surprised and amazed him. For he was also one of the confederacy, but knew not that Manlius was anyways engaged in it; but when the youth began to name Perpenna, Gracinus, and others, whom he knew very well to be sworn conspirators, he was very much terrified and astonished; but made light of it to the youth, and bade him not regard what Manlius said, a vain, boasting fellow.

However, he went presently to Perpenna, and giving him notice of the danger they were in, and of the shortness of their time, desired him immediately to put their designs in execution. When all the confederates had consented to it, they provided a messenger who brought feigned letters to Sertorius, in which he had notice of a victory obtained, it said, by one of his lieutenants, and of the great slaughter of his enemies; and as Sertorius, being extremely well pleased, was sacrificing and giving thanks to the gods for his prosperous success, Perpenna invited him, and those with him, who were also of the conspiracy, to an entertainment, and being very importunate, prevailed with him to come.

At all suppers and entertainments where Sertorius was present, great order and decency was wont to be observed; for he would not endure to hear or see anything that was rude or unhandsome, but made it the habit of all who kept his company to entertain themselves with quiet and inoffensive amusements. But in the middle of this entertainment, those who sought occasion to quarrel fell into dissolute discourse openly, and making as if they were very drunk, committed many insolences on purpose to provoke him.

Sertorius, being offended with their ill-behaviour, or perceiving the state of their minds by their way of speaking and their unusually disrespectful manner, changed the posture of his lying, and leaned backward, as one that neither heard nor regarded them. Perpenna now took a cup full of wine, and, as he was drinking, let it fall out of his hand and made a noise, which was the sign agreed upon amongst them; and Antonius, who was next to Sertorius, immediately wounded him with his sword. And whilst Sertorius, upon receiving the wound, turned himself, and strove to get up, Antonius threw himself upon his breast, and held both his hands, so that he died by a number of blows, without being able even to defend himself.

Upon the first news of his death, most of the Spaniards left the conspirators, and sent ambassadors to Pompey and Metellus, and yielded themselves up to them. Perpenna attempted to do something with those that remained, but he made only so much use of Sertorius's arms and preparations for war as to disgrace himself in them, and to let it be evident to all that he understood no more how to command than he knew how to obey; and when he came against Pompey, he was soon overthrown and taken prisoner. Neither did he bear this last affliction with any bravery, but having Sertorius's papers and writings in his hands, he offered to show Pompey letters from persons of consular dignity, and of the highest quality in Rome, written with their own hands, expressly to call Sertorius into Italy, and to let him know what great numbers there were that earnestly desired to alter the present state of affairs, and to introduce another manner of government. Upon this occasion, Pompey behaved not like a youth, or one of a light inconsiderate mind, but as a man of a confirmed, mature, and solid judgment; and so freed Rome from great fears and dangers of change. For he put all Sertorius's writings and letters together and read not one of them, nor suffered any one else to read them, but burnt them all, and caused Perpenna immediately to be put to death, lest by discovering their names further troubles and revolutions might ensue.

Of the rest of the conspirators with Perpenna, some were taken and slain by the command of Pompey, others fled into Africa, and were set upon by the Moors, and run through with their darts: and in a short time not one of them was left alive, except only Aufidius, the rival of Manlius, who, hiding himself, or not being much inquired after, died an old man, in an obscure village in Spain, in extreme poverty, and hated by all.

EUMENES

REIGNED 197–?160 B.C.

Duris reports that Eumenes, the Cardian, was the son of a poor waggoner in the Thracian Chersonesus, yet liberally educated, both as a scholar and a soldier; and that while he was but young, Philip, passing through Cardia, diverted himself with a sight of the wrestling matches and other exercises of the youth of that place, among whom Eumenes performing with success, and showing signs of intelligence and bravery, Philip was so pleased with him as to take him into his service. But they seem to speak more probably who tell us that Philip advanced Eumenes for the friendship he bore to his father, whose guest he had sometime been.

After the death of Philip, he continued in the service of Alexander, with the title of his principal secretary, but in as great favour as the most intimate of his familiars, being esteemed as wise and faithful as any person about him, so that he went with troops under his immediate command as general in the expedition against India, and succeeded to the post of Perdiccas, when Perdiccas was advanced to that of Hephæstion, then newly deceased.

And therefore, after the death of Alexander, when Neoptolemus, who had been captain of his life-guard, said that he had followed Alexander with shield and spear, but Eumenes only with pen and paper, the Macedonians laughed at him, as knowing very well that, besides other marks of favour, the king had done him the honour to make him a kind of kinsman to himself by marriage. For Alexander's first mistress in Asia, by whom he had his son, Hercules, was Barsine, the daughter of Artabazus; and in the distribution of the Persian ladies amongst his captains, Alexander gave Apame, one of her sisters, to Ptolemy, and another, also called Barsine, to Eumenes.

Notwithstanding, he frequently incurred Alexander's displeasure, and put himself into some danger, through Hephæstion. The quarters that had been taken up for Eumenes, Hephæstion assigned to Euius, the flute-player. Upon which, in great anger, Eumenes and Mentor came to Alexander and loudly complained, saying that the way to be regarded was to throw away their arms and turn fluteplayers or tragedians; so much so that Alexander took their part and chid Hephæstion; but soon after changed his mind again, and was angry with Eumenes, and accounted the freedom he had taken to be rather an affront to the king than a reflection upon Hephæstion.

Afterwards, when Nearchus, with a fleet, was to be sent to the Southern Sea, Alexander borrowed money of his friends, his own treasury being exhausted, and would have had three hundred talents of Eumenes, but he sent a hundred only, pretending that it was not without great difficulty he had raised so much from his stewards. Alexander neither complained nor took the money, but gave private order to set Eumenes's tent on fire, designing to take him in a manifest lie, when his money was carried out. But before that could be done the tent was consumed, and Alexander repented of his orders, all his papers being burnt; the gold and silver, however, which was melted down in the fire, being afterwards collected, was found to be more than one thousand talents; yet Alexander took none of it, and only wrote to the several governors and generals to send new copies of the papers that were burnt, and ordered them to be delivered to Eumenes.

Another difference happened between him and Hephæstion concerning a gift, and a great deal of ill language passed between them, yet Eumenes still continued in favour. But Hephæstion dying soon after, the king, in his grief, presuming all those that differed with Hephæstion in his lifetime were now rejoicing at his death, showed much harshness and severity in his behaviour with them, especially towards Eumenes, whom he often upbraided with his quarrels and ill language to Hephæstion. But he, being a wise and dexterous courtier, made advantage of what had done him prejudice, and struck in with the king's passion for glorifying his friend's memory, suggesting various plans to do him honour, and contributing largely and readily towards erecting his monument.

After Alexander's death, when the quarrel broke out between the troops of the phalanx and the officers, his companions, Eumenes, though in his judgment he inclined to the latter, yet in his professions stood neuter, as if he thought it unbecoming him, who was a stranger, to interpose in the private quarrels of the Macedonians. When the rest of Alexander's friends left Babylon, he stayed behind, and did much to pacify the foot-soldiers, and to dispose them towards an accommodation. And when the officers had agreed among themselves, and, recovering from the first disorder, proceeded to share out the several commands and provinces, they made Eumenes governor of Cappadocia and Paphlagonia, and all the coast upon the Pontic Sea as far as Trebizond, which at that time was not subject to the Macedonians, for Ariarathes kept it as king, but Leonnatus and Antigonus, with a large army, were to put him in possession of it.

Antigonus, already filled with hopes of his own, and despising all men, took no notice of Perdiccas's letters; but Leonnatus with his army came down into Phrygia to the service of Eumenes. But being visited by Hecatæus, the tyrant of the Cardians, and requested rather to relieve Antipater and the Macedonians that were besieged in Lamia, he resolved upon that expedition, inviting Eumenes to a share in it, and endeavouring to reconcile him to Hecatæus. For there was an hereditary feud between them, arising out of political differences, and Eumenes had more than once been known to denounce Hecatæus as a tyrant, and to exhort Alexander to restore the Cardians their liberty. Therefore at this time, also, he declined the expedition proposed, pretending that he feared lest Antipater, who already hated him, should for that reason, and to gratify Hecatæus, kill him.

Leonnatus so far believed as to impart to Eumenes his whole design, which, as he had pretended and given out, was to aid Antipater, but in truth was to seize the kingdom of Macedon; and he showed him letters from Cleopatra, in which, it appeared, she invited him to Pella, with promises to marry him. But Eumenes, whether fearing Antipater, or looking upon Leonnatus as a rash, headstrong, and unsafe man, stole away from him by night, taking with him all his men, namely, three hundred horse, and two hundred of his own servants armed, and all his gold, to the value of five thousand talents of silver, and fled to Perdiccas, discovered to him Leonnatus's design, and thus gained great interest with him, and was made of the council.

Soon after, Perdiccas, with a great army, which he led himself, conducted Eumenes into Cappadocia, and, having taken Ariarathes prisoner, and subdued the whole country, declared him governor of it. He accordingly proceeded to dispose of the chief cities among his own friends, and made captains of garrisons, judges, receivers, and other officers, of such as he thought fit himself, Perdiccas not at all interposing. Eumenes, however, still continued to attend upon Perdiccas, both out of respect to him, and a desire not to be absent from the royal family.

But Perdiccas, believing he was able enough to attain his own further objects without assistance, and that the country he left behind him might stand in need of an active and faithful governor, when he came into Cilicia dismissed Eumenes, under colour of sending him to his command, but in truth to secure Armenia, which was on its frontier, and was unsettled through the practices of Neoptolemus. Him, a proud and vain man, Eumenes exerted himself to gain by personal attentions; but to balance the Macedonian foot, whom he found insolent and self-willed, he contrived to raise an army of horse, excusing from tax and contribution all those of the country that were able to serve on horseback, and buying up a number of horses, which he distributed among such of his own men as he most confided in, stimulating the courage of his new soldiers by gifts and honours, and inuring their bodies to service by frequent marching and exercising; so that the Macedonians were some of them astonished, others overjoyed to see that in so short a time he had got together a body of no less than six thousand three hundred horsemen.

But when Craterus and Antipater, having subdued the Greeks, advanced into Asia, with intentions to quell the power of Perdiccas, and were reported to design an invasion of Cappadocia, Perdiccas, resolving himself to march against Ptolemy, made Eumenes commander-in-chief of all the forces of Armenia and Cappadocia, and to that purpose wrote letters, requiring Alcetas and Neoptolemus to be obedient to Eumenes, and giving full commission to Eumenes to dispose and order all things as he thought fit. Alcetas flatly refused to serve, because his Macedonians, he said, were ashamed to fight against Antipater, and loved Craterus so well, they were ready to receive him for their commander. Neoptolemus designed treachery against Eumenes, but was discovered, and being summoned, refused to obey, and put himself in a posture of defence.

Here Eumenes first found the benefit of his own foresight and contrivance, for his foot being beaten, he routed Neoptolemus with his horse, and took all his baggage; and coming up with his whole force upon the phalanx while broken and disordered in its flight, obliged the men to lay down their arms and take an oath to serve under him. Neoptolemus, with some few stragglers whom he rallied, fled to Craterus and Antipater.

From them had come an embassy to Eumenes, inviting him over to their side, offering to secure him in his present government and to give him additional command, both of men and of territory, with the advantage of gaining his enemy Antipater to become his friend, and keeping Craterus his friend from turning to be his enemy. To which Eumenes replied that he could not so suddenly be reconciled to his old enemy Antipater, especially at a time when he saw him use his friends like enemies, but was ready to reconcile Craterus to Perdiccas, upon any just and equitable terms; but in case of any aggression, he would resist the injustice to his last breath, and would rather lose his life than betray his word.

Antipater, receiving this answer, took time to consider upon the whole matter; when Neoptolemus arrived from his defeat and acquainted them with the ill success of his arms, and urged them to give him assistance, to come, both of them, if possible, but Craterus at any rate, for the Macedonians loved him so excessively, that if they saw but his hat, or heard his voice, they would all pass over in a body with their arms. And in truth Craterus had a mighty name among them, and the soldiers after Alexander's death were extremely fond of him, remembering how he had often for their sakes incurred Alexander's displeasure, doing his best to withhold him when he began to follow the Persian fashions, and always maintaining the customs of his country, when, through pride and luxuriousness, they began to be disregarded.

Craterus, therefore, sent on Antipater into Cilicia, and himself and Neoptolemus marched with a large division of the army against Eumenes; expecting to come upon him unawares, and to find his army disordered with revelling after the late victory. Now that Eumenes should suspect his coming, and be prepared to receive him, is an argument of his vigilance, but not perhaps a proof of any extraordinary sagacity, but that he should contrive both to conceal from his enemies the disadvantages of his position, and from his own men whom they were to fight with, so that he led them on against Craterus himself, without their knowing that he commanded the enemy, this, indeed, seems to show peculiar address and skill in the general. He gave out that Neoptolemus and Pigres were approaching with some Cappadocian and Paphlagonian horse.

And at night, having resolved on marching, he fell asleep, and had an extraordinary dream. For he thought he saw two Alexanders ready to engage, each commanding his several phalanx, the one assisted by Minerva, the other by Ceres; and that after a hot dispute, he on whose side Minerva was, was beaten, and Ceres, gathering ears of corn, wove them into a crown for the victor. This vision Eumenes interpreted at once as boding success to himself, who was to fight for a fruitful country, and at that very time covered with the young ears, the whole being sown with corn, and the fields so thick with it that they made a beautiful show of a long peace.

And he was further emboldened when he understood that the enemy's password was "Minerva and Alexander." Accordingly he also gave out as his "Ceres and Alexander," and gave his men orders to make garlands for themselves, and to dress their arms with wreaths of corn. He found himself under many temptations to discover to his captains and officers whom they were to engage with, and not to conceal a secret of such moment in his own breast alone, yet he kept to his first resolutions, and ventured to run the hazard of his own judgment.

When he came to give battle, he would not trust any Macedonian to engage Craterus, but appointed two troops of foreign horse, commanded by Pharnabazus, son to Artabazus, and Phœnix of Tenedos, with order to charge as soon as ever they saw the enemy, without giving them leisure to speak or retire, or receiving any herald or trumpet from them. For he was exceedingly afraid about his Macedonians, lest, if they found out Craterus to be there, they should go over to his side. He himself, with three hundred of his best horse, led the right wing against Neoptolemus. When having passed a little hill they came in view, and were seen advancing with more than ordinary briskness, Craterus was amazed, and bitterly reproached Neoptolemus for deceiving him with hopes of the Macedonians' revolt, but he encouraged his men to do bravely, and forthwith charged.

The first engagement was very fierce, and the spears being soon broken to pieces, they came to close fighting with their swords; and here Craterus did by no means dishonour Alexander, but slew many of his enemies and repulsed many assaults, but at last received a wound in his side from a Thracian, and fell off his horse. Being down, many not knowing him went past him, but Gorgias, one of Eumenes's captains, knew him, and alighting from his horse, kept guard over him as he lay badly wounded and slowly dying.

In the meantime, Neoptolemus and Eumenes were engaged; who, being inveterate and mortal enemies, sought for one another, but missed for the two first courses, but in the third discovering one another, they drew their swords, and with loud shouts immediately charged. And their horses striking against one another like two galleys, they quitted their reins, and taking mutual hold pulled at one another's helmets, and at the armour from their shoulders. While they were thus struggling, their horses went from under them, and they fell together to the ground, there again still keeping their hold and wrestling. Neoptolemus was getting up first, but Eumenes wounded him in the ham, and got upon his feet before him. Neoptolemus supporting himself upon one knee, the other leg being disabled, and himself undermost, fought courageously, though his blows were not mortal, but receiving a stroke in the neck he fell and ceased to resist. Eumenes, transported with passion and his inveterate hatred to him, fell to reviling and stripping him, and perceived not that his sword was still in his hand. And with this he wounded Eumenes under the bottom of his corslet in the groin, but in truth more frightened than hurt him, his blow being faint for want of strength.

Having stript the dead body, ill as he was with the wounds he had received in his legs and arms, he took horse again, and hurried towards the left wing of his army, which he supposed to be still engaged. Hearing of the death of Craterus, he rode up to him, and finding there was yet some life in him, alighted from his horse and wept, and laying his right hand upon him, inveighed bitterly against Neoptolemus, and lamented both Craterus's misfortune and his own hard fate, that he should be necessitated to engage against an old friend and acquaintance, and either do or suffer so much mischief.

This victory Eumenes obtained about ten days after the former, and got great reputation alike for his conduct and his valour in achieving it. But, on the other hand, it created him great envy both among his own troops and his enemies that he, a stranger and a foreigner, should employ the forces and arms of Macedon to cut off the bravest and most approved man among them. Had the news of this defeat come timely enough to Perdiccas, he had doubtless been the greatest of all the Macedonians; but now, he being slain in a mutiny in Egypt, two days before the news arrived, the Macedonians in a rage decreed Eumenes's death, giving joint commission to Antigonus and Antipater to prosecute the war against him.

Passing by Mount Ida, where there was a royal establishment of horses, Eumenes took as many as he had occasion for, and sent an account of his doing so to the overseers, at which Antipater is said to have laughed, calling it truly laudable in Eumenes thus to hold himself prepared for giving in to them (or would it be taking from them?) strict account of all matters of administration.

Eumenes had designed to engage in the plains of Lydia, near Sardis, both because his chief strength lay in horse, and to let Cleopatra see how powerful he was. But at her particular request, for she was afraid to give any umbrage to Antipater, he marched into the upper Phrygia and wintered in Celænæ. When Alcetas, Polemon, and Docimus disputed with him who should command in chief, "You know," said he, "the old saying: That destruction regards no punctilios."

Having promised his soldiers pay within three days, he sold them all the farms and castles in the country, together with the men and beasts with which they were filled; every captain or officer that bought received from Eumenes the use of his engines to storm the place, and divided the spoils among his company, proportionably to every man's arrears. By this

Eumenes came again to be popular, so that when letters were found thrown about the camp by the enemy promising one hundred talents, besides great honours, to any one that should kill Eumenes, the Macedonians were extremely offended, and made an order that from that time forward one thousand of their best men should continually guard his person, and keep strict watch about him by night in their several turns. This order was cheerfully obeyed, and they gladly received of Eumenes the same honours which the kings used to confer upon their favourites. He now had leave to bestow purple hats and cloaks, which among the Macedonians is one of the greatest honours the king can give.

Good fortune will elevate even petty minds, and give them the appearance of a certain greatness and stateliness, as from their high place they look down upon the world; but the truly noble and resolved spirit raises itself, and becomes more conspicuous in times of disaster and ill fortune, as was now the case with Eumenes.

For having by the treason of one of his own men lost the field to Antigonus at Orcynii, in Cappadocia, in his flight he gave the traitor no opportunity to escape to the enemy, but immediately seized and hanged him. Then in his flight, taking a contrary course to his pursuers, he stole by them unawares, returned to the place where the battle had been fought, and encamped. There he gathered up the dead bodies and burnt them with the doors and windows of the neighbouring villages, and raised heaps of earth upon their graves; insomuch that Antigonus, who came thither soon after, expressed his astonishment at his courage and firm resolution.

Falling afterwards upon the baggage of Antigonus, he might easily have taken many captives, both bond and freemen, and much wealth collected from the spoils of so many wars; but he feared lest his men, overladen with so much booty, might become unfit for rapid retreat, and too fond of their ease to sustain the continual marches and endure the long waiting on which he depended for success, expecting to tire Antigonus into some other course. But then considering it would be extremely difficult to restrain the Macedonians from plunder, when it seemed to offer itself, he gave them order to refresh themselves, and bait their horses, and then attack the enemy.

In the meantime he sent privately to Menander, who had care of all this baggage, professing a concern for him upon the score of old friendship and acquaintance; and therefore advising him to quit the plain and secure himself upon the sides of the neighbouring hills, where the horse might not be able to hem him in. When Menander, sensible of his danger, had speedily packed up his goods and decamped, Eumenes openly sent his scouts to discover the enemy's posture, and commanded his men to arm and bridle their horses, as designing immediately to give battle; but the scouts returning with news that Menander had secured so difficult a post it was impossible to take him, Eumenes, pretending to be grieved with the disappointment, drew off his men another way.

It is said that when Menander reported this afterwards to Antigonus, and the Macedonians commended Eumenes, imputing it to his singular good-nature, that having it in his power to make slaves of their children and outrage their wives he forbore and spared them all, Antigonus replied, "Alas, good friends, he had no regard to us, but to himself, being loath to wear so many shackles when he designed to flee."

From this time Eumenes, daily fleeing and wandering about, persuaded many of his men to disband, whether out of kindness to them, or unwillingness to lead about such a body of men as were too few to engage and too many to flee undiscovered. Taking refuge at Nora, a place on the confines of Lycaonia and Cappadocia, with five hundred horse and two hundred heavy-armed foot, he again dismissed as many of his friends as desired it, through fear of the probable hardships to be encountered there, and embracing them with all demonstrations of kindness gave them licence to depart.

Antigonus, when he came before this fort, desired to have an interview with Eumenes before the siege; but he returned answer that Antigonus had many friends who might command in his room; but they whom Eumenes defended had nobody to substitute if he should miscarry; therefore, if Antigonus thought it worth while to treat with him, he should first send him hostages. And when Antigonus required that Eumenes should first address himself to him as his superior, he replied, "While I am able to wield a sword, I shall think no man greater than myself." At last, when, according to Eumenes's demand, Antigonus sent his own nephew, Ptolemy, to the fort, Eumenes went out to him, and they mutually embraced with great tenderness and friendship, as having formerly been very intimate.

After long conversation, Eumenes making no mention of his own pardon and security, but requiring that he should be confirmed in his several governments, and restitution be made him of the rewards of his service, all that were present were astonished at his courage and gallantry. And many of the Macedonians flocked to see what sort of person Eumenes was, for since the death of Craterus no man had been so much talked of in the army. But Antigonus, being afraid lest he might suffer some violence, first commanded the soldiers to keep off, calling out and throwing stones at those who pressed forwards. At last, taking Eumenes in his arms, and keeping off the crowd with his guards, not without great difficulty, he returned him safe into the fort.

Then Antigonus, having built a wall round Nora, left a force sufficient to carry on the siege, and drew off the rest of his army; and Eumenes was beleaguered and kept garrison, having plenty of corn and water and salt, but no other thing, either for food or delicacy; yet with such as he had, he kept a cheerful table for his friends, inviting them severally in their turns, and seasoning his entertainment with a gentle and affable behaviour. For he had a pleasant countenance, and looked not like an old and practised soldier, but was smooth and florid, and his shape as delicate as if his limbs had been carved by art in the most accurate proportions. He was not a great orator, but winning and persuasive, as may be seen in his letters.

The greatest distress of the besieged was the narrowness of the place they were in, their quarters being very confined, and the whole place but two furlongs in compass; so that both they and their horses fed without exercise. Accordingly, not only to prevent the listlessness of such inactive living, but to have them in condition to flee if occasion required, he assigned a room one-and-twenty feet long, the largest in all the fort, for the men to walk in, directing them to begin their walk gently, and so gradually mend their pace. And for the horses, he tied them to the roof with great halters, fastening which about their necks, with a pulley he gently raised them, till standing upon the ground with their hinder feet, they just touched it with the very ends of their forefeet. In this posture the grooms plied them with whips and shouts, provoking them to curvet and kick out with their hind legs, struggling and stamping at the same time to find support for their forefeet, and thus their whole body was exercised, till they were all in a foam and sweat; excellent exercise, whether for strength or speed; and then he gave them their corn already coarsely ground, that they might sooner despatch and better digest it.

The siege continuing long, Antigonus received advice that Antipater was dead in Macedon, and that affairs were embroiled by the differences of Cassander and Polysperchon, upon which he conceived no mean hopes, purposing to make himself master of all, and, in order to his design, thought to bring over Eumenes, that he might have his advice and assistance. He, therefore, sent Hieronymus to treat with him, proposing a certain oath, which Eumenes first corrected, and then referred himself to the Macedonians themselves that besieged him, to be judged by them, which of the two forms was the most equitable.

Antigonus in the beginning of his had slightly mentioned the kings as by way of ceremony, while all the sequel referred to himself alone; but Eumenes changed the form of it to Olympias and the kings, and proceeded to swear not to be true to Antigonus, only, but to them, and to have the same friends and enemies, not with Antigonus, but with Olympias and the kings. This form the Macedonians thinking the more reasonable, swore Eumenes according to it, and raised the siege, sending also to Antigonus that he should swear in the same form to Eumenes.

Meantime, all the hostages of the Cappadocians whom Eumenes had in Nora he returned, obtaining from their friends warhorses, beasts of carriage, and tents in exchange. And collecting again all the soldiers who had dispersed at the time of his flight, and were now wandering about the country, he got together a body of near a thousand horse, and with them fled from Antigonus, whom he justly feared. For he had sent orders not only to have him blocked up and besieged again, but had given a very sharp answer to the Macedonians for admitting Eumenes's amendment of the oath.

While Eumenes was fleeing, he received letters from those in Macedonia, who were jealous of Antigonus's greatness, from Olympias, inviting him thither to take the charge and protection of Alexander's infant son, whose person was in danger, and other letters from Polysperchon and Philip, the king, requiring him to make war upon Antigonus, as general

of the forces in Cappadocia, and empowering him out of the treasure at Quinda to take five hundred talents' compensation for his own losses, and to levy as much as he thought necessary to carry on the war. They wrote also to the same effect to Antigenes and Teutamus, the chief officers of the Argyraspids; who, on receiving these letters, treated Eumenes with a show of respect and kindness; but it was apparent enough that they were full of envy and emulation, disdaining to give place to him.

Their envy Eumenes moderated by refusing to accept the money, as if he had not needed it; and their ambition and emulation, which they were neither able to govern nor willing to obey, he conquered by help of superstition. For he told them that Alexander had appeared to him in a dream, and showed him a regal pavilion richly furnished, with a throne in it; and told him if they would sit in council there, he himself would be present, and prosper all the consultations and actions upon which they should enter in his name. Antigenes and Teutamus were easily prevailed upon to believe this, being as little willing to come and consult Eumenes as he himself was to be seen waiting at other men's doors. Accordingly, they erected a tent royal, and a throne, called Alexander's, and there they met to consult upon all affairs of moment.

Afterwards they advanced into the interior of Asia, and in their march met with Peucestes, who was friendly to them and with the other satraps, who joined forces with them, and greatly encouraged the Macedonians with the number and appearance of their men. But they themselves, having since Alexander's decease become imperious and ungoverned in their tempers, and luxurious in their daily habits, imagining themselves great princes, and pampered in their conceit by the flattery of the barbarians, when all these conflicting pretensions now came together, were soon found to be exacting and quarrelsome one with another, while all alike unmeasurably flattered the Macedonians, giving them money for revels and sacrifices, till in a short time they brought the camp to a dissolute place of entertainment, and the army a mere multitude of voters, canvassed as in a democracy for the election of this or that commander. Eumenes, perceiving they despised one another, and all of them feared him, and sought an opportunity to kill him, pretended to be in want of money, and borrowed many talents, of those especially who most hated him, to make them at once confide in him and forbear all violence to him for fear of losing their own money. Thus his enemies' estates were the guard of his person, and by receiving money he purchased safety, for which it is more common to give it.

The Macedonians, also, while there was no show of danger, allowed themselves to be corrupted, and made all their court to those who gave them presents, who had their bodyguards, and affected to appear generals-in-chief. But when Antigonus came upon them with a great army, and their affairs themselves seemed to call out for a true general, then not only the common soldiers cast their eyes upon Eumenes, but these men, who had appeared so great in a peaceful time of ease, submitted all of them to him, and quietly posted themselves severally as he appointed them. And when Antigonus attempted to pass the river Pasitigris, all the rest that were appointed to guard the passes were not so much as aware of his march; only Eumenes met and encountered him, slew many of his men, and filled the river with the dead, and took four thousand prisoners.

But it was most particularly when Eumenes was sick that the Macedonians let it be seen how in their judgment, while others could feast them handsomely and make entertainments, he alone knew how to fight and lead an army. For Peucestes, having made a splendid entertainment in Persia, and given each of the soldiers a sheep to sacrifice with, made himself sure of being commander-in-chief.

Some few days after the army was to march, and Eumenes, having been dangerously ill, was carried in a litter apart from the body of the army, that any rest he got might not be disturbed. But when they were a little advanced, unexpectedly they had a view of the enemy, who had passed the hills that lay between them, and was marching down into the plain. At the sight of the golden armour glittering in the sun as they marched down in their order, the elephants with their castles on their backs, and the men in their purple, as their manner was when they were going to give battle, the front stopped their march, and called out for Eumenes, for they would not advance a step but under his conduct; and fixing their arms in the ground gave the word among themselves to stand, requiring their officers also not to stir or engage or hazard themselves without Eumenes. News of this being brought to Eumenes, he hastened those that carried his litter, and drawing back the curtains on both sides, joyfully put forth his right hand. As soon as the soldiers saw him they saluted him in their Macedonian dialect, and took up their shields, and striking them with their pikes, gave a great shout, inviting the enemy to come on, for now they had a leader.

Antigonus understanding by some prisoners he had taken that Eumenes was out of health, to that degree that he was carried in a litter, presumed it would be no hard matter to crush the rest of them, since he was ill. He therefore made the greater haste to come up with them and engage. But being come so near as to discover how the enemy was drawn up and appointed, he was astonished, and paused for some time; at last he saw the litter carrying from one wing of the army to the other, and, as his manner was, laughing aloud, he said to his friends, "That litter there, it seems, is the thing that offers us battle"; and immediately wheeled about, retired with all his army, and pitched his camp.

The men on the other side, finding a little respite, returned to their former habits, and allowing themselves to be flattered, and making the most of the indulgence of their generals, took up for their winter quarters near the whole country of the Gabeni, so that the front was quartered nearly a thousand furlongs from the rear; which Antigonus understanding, marched suddenly towards them, taking the most difficult road through a country that wanted water; but the way was short though uneven; hoping, if he should surprise them thus scattered in their winter quarters, the soldiers would not easily be able to come up in time enough and join with their officers. But having to pass through a country uninhabited, where he met with violent winds and severe frosts, he was much checked in his march, and his men suffered exceedingly. The only possible relief was making numerous fires, by which his enemies got notice of his coming. For the barbarians who dwelt on the mountains overlooking the desert, amazed at the multitude of fires they saw, sent messengers upon dromedaries to acquaint Peucestes.

He being astonished and almost out of his senses with the news, and finding the rest in no less disorder, resolved to flee, and collect what men he could by the way. But Eumenes relieved him from his fear and trouble, undertaking so to stop the enemy's advance that he should arrive three days later than he was expected. Having persuaded them, he immediately despatched expresses to all the officers to draw the men out of their winter quarters and muster them with all speed. He himself, with some of the chief officers, rode out, and chose an elevated tract within view, at a distance, of such as travelled the desert; this he occupied and quartered out, and commanded many fires to be made in it, as the custom is in a camp.

This done, and the enemies seeing the fire upon the mountains, Antigonus was filled with vexation and despondency, supposing that his enemies had been long since advertised of his march, and were prepared to receive him. Therefore, lest his army, now tired and wearied out with their march, should be immediately forced to encounter with fresh men, who had wintered well and were ready for him, quitting the near way, he marched slowly through the towns and villages to refresh his men. But meeting with no such skirmishes as are usual when two armies lie near one another, and being assured by the people of the country that no army had been seen, but only continual fires at that place, he concluded he had been outwitted by a stratagem of Eumenes, and, much troubled, advanced to give open battle.

By this time, the greater part of the forces were come together to Eumenes, and admiring his sagacity, declared him alone commander-in-chief of the whole army; upon which Antigenes and Teutamus, the commanders of the Argyraspids, being very much offended, and envying Eumenes, formed a conspiracy against him; and assembling the greater part of the satraps and officers, consulted when and how to cut him off. When they had unanimously agreed, first to use his service in the next battle, and then to take an occasion to destroy him, Eudamus, the master of the elephants, and Phædimus gave Eumenes private advice of this design, not out of kindness or good-will to him, but lest they should lose the money they had lent him. Eumenes, having commended them, retired to his tent, and telling his friends he lived among a herd of wild beasts, made his will, and tore up all his letters, lest his correspondents after his death should be questioned or punished on account of anything in his secret papers.

Having thus disposed of his affairs, he thought of letting the enemy win the field, or of flying through Media and Armenia and seizing Cappadocia, but came to no resolution while his friends stayed with him. After turning to many expedients in his mind, which his changeable fortune had made versatile, he at last put his men in array, and encouraged the Greeks and barbarians; as for the phalanx and the Argyraspids, they encouraged him, and bade him be of good heart, for the enemy would never be able to stand them. For indeed they were the oldest of Philip's and Alexander's soldiers, tried men, that had long made war their exercise, that had never been beaten or foiled; most of them seventy, none less than sixty years old. And so when they charged Antigonus's men, they cried out, "You fight against your fathers, you rascals," and furiously falling on, routed the whole phalanx at once, nobody being able to stand them, and the greatest part dying by their hands.

So that Antigonus's foot was routed, but his horse got the better, and he became master of the baggage through the cowardice of Peucestes, who behaved himself negligently and basely; while Antigonus used his judgment calmly in the danger, being aided moreover by the ground. For the place where they fought was a large plain, neither deep nor hard under foot, but, like the seashore, covered with a fine soft sand which the treading of so many men and horses in the time of battle reduced to a small white dust, that like a cloud of lime darkened the air, so that one could not see clearly at any distance, and so made it easy for Antigonus to take the baggage unperceived.

After the battle Teutamus sent a message to Antigonus to demand the baggage. He made answer, he would not only restore it to the Argyraspids, but serve them further in the other things if they would but deliver up Eumenes. Upon which the Argyraspids took a villainous resolution to deliver him up alive into the hands of his enemies. So they came to wait upon him, being unsuspected by him, but watching their opportunity, some lamenting the loss of the baggage, some encouraging him as if he had been victor, some accusing the other commanders, till at last they all fell upon him, and seizing his sword, bound his hands behind him with his own girdle.

When Antigonus had sent Nicanor to receive him he begged he might be led through the body of the Macedonians, and have liberty to speak to them, neither to request nor deprecate anything, but only to advise them what would be for their interest. A silence being made, as he stood upon a rising ground, he stretched out his hands bound, and said, "What trophy, O ye basest of all the Macedonians, could Antigonus have wished for so great as you yourselves have erected for him in delivering up your general captive into his hands? You are not ashamed, when you are conquerors, to own yourselves conquered, for the sake only of your baggage, as if it were wealth, not arms, wherein victory consisted; nay, you deliver up your general to redeem your stuff. As for me I am unvanquished, though a captive, conqueror of my enemies, and betrayed by my fellow-soldiers. For you, I adjure you by Jupiter, the protector of arms, and by all the gods that are the avengers of perjury, to kill me here with your own hands; for it is all one; and if I am murdered yonder it will be esteemed your act, nor will Antigonus complain, for he desires not Eumenes alive, but dead. Or if you withhold your own hands, release but one of mine, it shall suffice to do the work; and if you dare not trust me with a sword, throw me bound as I am under the feet of the wild beasts. This if you do I shall freely acquit you from the guilt of my death, as the most just and kind of men to their general."

While Eumenes was thus speaking, the rest of the soldiers wept for grief, but the Argyraspids shouted out to lead him on, and give no attention to his trifling. For it was no such great matter if this Chersonesian pest should meet his death, who in thousands of battles had annoyed and wasted the Macedonians; it would be a much more grievous thing for the choicest of Philip's and Alexander's soldiers to be defrauded of the fruits of so long service, and in their old age to come to beg their bread, and to leave their wives three nights in the power of their enemies. So they hurried him on with violence.

But Antigonus, fearing the multitude, for nobody was left in the camp, sent ten of his strongest elephants with divers of his Mede and Parthian lances to keep off the press. Then he could not endure to have Eumenes brought into his presence, by reason of their former intimacy and friendship; but when they that had taken him inquired how he would have him kept, "As I would," said he, "an elephant, or

a lion." A little after, being moved with compassion, he commanded the heaviest of his irons to be knocked off, one of his servants to be admitted to anoint him, and that any of his friends that were willing should have liberty to visit him, and bring him what he wanted.

Long time he deliberated what to do with him, sometimes inclining to the advice and promises of Nearchus of Crete and Demetrius, his son, who were very earnest to preserve Eumenes, whilst all the rest were unanimously instant and importunate to have him taken off. It is related that Eumenes inquired of Onomarchus, his keeper, why Antigonus, now he had his enemy in his hands, would not forthwith despatch or generously release him? And that Onomarchus contumeliously answered him, that the field had been a more proper place than this to show his contempt of death. To whom Eumenes replied, "And, by heavens, I showed it there; ask the men else that engaged me, but I could never meet a man that was my superior." "Therefore," rejoined Onomarchus, "now you have found such a man, why don't you submit quietly to his pleasure?"

When Antigonus resolved to kill Eumenes, he commanded to keep his food from him, and so with two or three days' fasting he began to draw near his end; but the camp being on a sudden to remove, an executioner was sent to despatch him. Antigonus granted his body to his friends, permitted them to burn it, and having gathered his ashes into a silver urn, to send them to his wife and children.

Eumenes was thus taken off; and Divine Providence assigned to no other man the chastisement of the commanders and soldiers that had betrayed him; but Antigonus himself, abominating the Argyraspids as wicked and inhuman villains, delivered them up to Sibyrtius, the governor of Arachosia, commanding him by all ways and means to destroy and exterminate them, so that not a man of them might ever come to Macedon, or so much as within sight of the Greek Sea.

* * *

EUMENES and SERTORIUS
Compared

THESE are the most remarkable passages that are come to our knowledge concerning Eumenes and Sertorius. In comparing their lives, we may observe that this was common to them both: that being aliens, strangers,

and banished men, they came to be commanders of powerful forces, and had the leading of numerous and warlike armies, made up of divers nations.

This was peculiar to Sertorius, that the chief

command was, by his whole party, freely yielded to him, as to the person of the greatest merit and renown, whereas Eumenes had many who contested the office with him, and only by his actions obtained the superiority. They followed the one honestly, out of desire to be commanded by him; they submitted themselves to the other for their own security, because they could not command themselves.

The one, being a Roman, was the general of the Spaniards and Lusitanians, who for many years had been under the subjection of Rome; and the other, a Chersonesian, who was chief commander of the Macedonians, who were the great conquerors of mankind, and were at that time subduing the world. Sertorius, being already in high esteem for his former services in the wars and his abilities in the senate, was advanced to the dignity of a general; whereas Eumenes obtained this honour from the office of a writer, or secretary, in which he had been despised.

Nor did he only at first rise from inferior opportunities, but afterwards, also, met with greater impediments in the progress of his authority, and that not only from those who publicly resisted him, but from many others that privately conspired against him. It was much otherwise with Sertorius, not one of whose party publicly opposed him, only late in life, and secretly, a few of his acquaintances entered into a conspiracy against him. Sertorius put an end to his dangers as often as he was victorious in the field, whereas the victories of Eumenes were the beginning of his perils, through the malice of those that envied him.

Their deeds in war were equal and parallel, but their general inclinations different. Eumenes naturally loved war and contention, but Sertorius esteemed peace and tranquillity;

when Eumenes might have lived in safety, with honour, if he would have quietly retired out of their way, he persisted in a dangerous contest with the greatest of the Macedonian leaders; but Sertorius, who was unwilling to trouble himself with any public disturbances, was forced, for the safety of his person, to make war against those who would not suffer him to live in peace. If Eumenes could have contented himself with the second place, Antigonus, freed from his competition for the first, would have used him well, and shown him favour, whereas Pompey's friends would never permit Sertorius so much as to live in quiet. The one made war of his own accord, out of a desire for command; and the other was constrained to accept of command to defend himself from war that was made against him. Eumenes was certainly a true lover of war, for he preferred his covetous ambition before his own security; but Sertorius was truly warlike, who procured his own safety by the success of his arms.

As to the manner of their deaths, it happened to one without the least thought or surmise of it; but to the other when he suspected it daily; which in the first argues an equitable temper, and a noble mind, not to distrust his friends; but in the other it shows some infirmity of spirit, for Eumenes intended to flee and was taken. The death of Sertorius dishonoured not his life; he suffered that from his companions which none of his enemies were ever able to perform. The other, not being able to deliver himself before his imprisonment, being willing also to live in captivity, did neither prevent nor expect his fate with honour or bravery; for by meanly supplicating and petitioning, he made his enemy, that pretended only to have power over his body, to be lord and master of his body and mind.

AGESILAUS

485–401 B.C.

Archidamus, the son of Zeuxidamus, having reigned gloriously over the Lacedæmonians, left behind him two sons, Agis the elder, begotten of Lampido, a noble lady, Agesilaus, much the younger, born of Eupolia, the daughter of Melesippidas. Now the succession belonged to Agis by law, Age-

silaus, who in all probability was to be but a private man, was educated according to the usual discipline of the country, hard and severe, and meant to teach young men to obey their superiors. Whence it was that, men say, Simonides called Sparta "the tamer of men," because by early strictness of education, they, more than any nation, trained the citizens to obedience to the laws, and made them tractable and patient of subjection, as horses that are broken in while colts. The law did not impose this harsh rule on the heirs apparent of the kingdom. But Agesilaus, whose good fortune it was to be born a younger brother, was consequently bred to all the arts of obedience, and so the better fitted for the government, when it fell to his share; hence it was that he proved the most popular-tempered of the Spartan kings, his early life having added to his natural kingly and commanding qualities the gentle and humane feelings of a citizen.

While he was yet a boy, bred up in one of what are called the *flocks,* or classes, he attracted the attachment of Lysander, who was particularly struck with the orderly temper that he manifested. For though he was one of the highest spirits, emulous above any of his companions, ambitious of pre-eminence in everything, and showed an impetuosity and fervour of mind which irresistibly carried him through all opposition or difficulty he could meet with; yet on the other side, he was so easy and gentle in his nature, and so apt to yield to authority, that though he would do nothing on compulsion, upon ingenuous motives he would obey any commands, and was more hurt by the least rebuke or disgrace than he was distressed by any toil or hardship.

He had one leg shorter than the other, but this deformity was little observed in the general beauty of his person in youth. And the easy way in which he bore it (he being the first always to pass a jest upon himself) went far to make it disregarded. And indeed his high spirit and eagerness to distinguish himself were all the more conspicuous by it, since he never let his lameness withhold him from any toil or any brave action. Neither his statue nor picture are extant, he never allowing them in his life, and utterly forbidding them to be made after his death. He is said to have been a little man, of a contemptible presence; but the goodness of his humour, and his constant cheerfulness and playfulness of temper, always free from anything of moroseness or haughtiness, made him more attractive, even to his old age, than the most beautiful and youthful men of the nation. Theophrastus writes that the ephors laid a fine upon Archidamus for marrying a little wife, "For," said they, "she will bring us a race of kinglets, instead of kings."

Whilst Agis, the elder brother, reigned, Alcibiades, being then an exile from Athens, came from Sicily to Sparta; nor had he stayed long there before his familiarity with Timæa, the king's wife, grew suspected, insomuch that Agis refused to own a child of hers, which, he said, was Alcibiades's, not his. Nor, if we may believe Duris, the historian, was Timæa much concerned at it, being herself forward enough to whisper among her helot maid-servants that the infants' true name was Alcibiades, not Leotychides. Meanwhile, it was believed that the amour he had with her was not the effect of his love but of his ambition, that he might have Spartan kings of his posterity. This affair being grown public, it became needful for Alcibiades to withdraw from Sparta.

But the child Leotychides had not the honours due to a legitimate son paid him, nor was he ever owned by Agis, till by his prayers and tears he prevailed with him to declare him his son before several witnesses upon his deathbed. But this did not avail to fix him in the throne of Agis, after whose death Lysander, who had lately achieved his conquest of Athens by sea, and was of the greatest power in Sparta, promoted Agesilaus, urging Leotychides's bastardy as a bar to his pretensions. Many of the other citizens, also, were favourable to Agesilaus, and zealously joined his party, induced by the opinion they had of his merits, of which they themselves had been spectators, in the time that he had been bred up among them.

But there was a man, named Diopithes, at Sparta, who had a great knowledge of ancient oracles, and was thought particularly skilful and clever in all points of religion and divination. He alleged, that it was unlawful to make a lame man king of Lacedæmon, citing in the debate the following oracle:—

Beware, great Sparta, lest there come of thee,
Though sound thyself, an haulting sovereignty:
Troubles, both long and unexpected too,
And storms of deadly warfare shall ensue.

But Lysander was not wanting with an evasion, alleging that if the Spartans were really apprehensive of the oracle, they must have a care of Leotychides; for it was not the limping foot of a king that the gods cared about, but the purity of the Herculean family, into whose rights, if a spurious issue were admitted, it would make the kingdom to halt indeed. Agesilaus likewise alleged that the bastardy of Leotychides was witnessed to by Neptune, who threw Agis out of bed by a violent earthquake, after which time he ceased to visit his wife, yet Leotychides was born above ten months after this.

Agesilaus was upon these allegations declared king, and soon possessed himself of the private estate of Agis, as well as his throne, Leotychides being wholly rejected as a bastard. He now turned his attention to his kindred by the mother's side, persons of worth and virtue, but miserably poor. To them he gave half his brother's estate, and by popular act gained general goodwill and reputation, in the place of the envy and ill-feeling which the inheritance might otherwise have procured him.

What Xenophon tells us of him, that by complying with, and, as it were, being ruled by his country, he grew into such great power with them, that he could do what he pleased, is meant to apply to the power he gained in the following manner with the ephors and elders. These were at that time of the greatest authority in the state; the former, officers annually chosen; the elders, holding their places during life; both instituted, as already told in the life of Lycurgus, to restrain the power of the kings. Hence it was that there was always from generation to generation a feud and contention between them and the kings. But Agesilaus took another course. Instead of contending with them, he courted them; in all proceedings he commenced by taking their advice, was always ready to go, nay almost run, when they called him; if he were upon his royal seat, hearing causes, and the ephors came in, he rose to them; whenever any man was elected into the council of elders he presented him with a gown and an ox. Thus, whilst he made a show of deference to them, and of a desire to extend their authority, he secretly advanced his own, and enlarged the prerogatives of the kings by several liberties which their friendship to his person conceded.

To other citizens he so behaved himself as to be less blamable in his enmities than in his friendships; for against his enemy he forbore to take any unjust advantage, but his friends he would assist, even in what was unjust. If an enemy had done anything praiseworthy, he felt it shameful to detract from his due, but his friends he knew not how to reprove when they did ill, nay, he would eagerly join with them, and assist them in their misdeed, and thought all offices of friendship commendable, let the matter in which they were employed be what it would. Again, when any of his adversaries was overtaken in a fault, he would be the first to pity him; and he soon entreated to procure his pardon, by which he won the hearts of all men. Insomuch that his popularity grew at last

suspected by the ephors, who laid a fine on him, professing that he was appropriating the citizens to himself who ought to be the common property of the state.

For as it is the opinion of philosophers, that could you take away strife and opposition out of the universe, all the heavenly bodies would stand still, generation and motion would cease in the mutual concord and agreement of all things, so the Spartan legislator seems to have admitted ambition and emulation among the ingredients of his commonwealth as the incentives of virtue, distinctly wishing that there should be some dispute and competition among his men of worth, and pronouncing the mere idle, uncontested, mutual compliance to unproved deserts to be but a false sort of concord. And some think Homer had an eye to this when he introduced Agamemnon well pleased with the quarrel arising between Ulysses and Achilles, and with the "terrible words" that passed between them, which he would never have done, unless he had thought emulations and dissensions between the noblest men to be of great public benefit. Yet this maxim is not simply to be granted, without restriction, for if animosities go too far they are very dangerous to cities and of most pernicious consequence.

When Agesilaus was newly entered upon the government, there came news from Asia that the Persian king was making great naval preparations, resolving with a high hand to dispossess the Spartans of their maritime supremacy. Lysander was eager for the opportunity of going over and succouring his friends in Asia, whom he had there left governors and masters of the cities, whose maladministration and tyrannical behaviour was causing them to be driven out, and in some cases put to death.

He therefore persuaded Agesilaus to claim the command of the expedition, and by carrying the war far from Greece into Persia, to anticipate the designs of the barbarian. He also wrote to his friends in Asia, that by embassy they should demand Agesilaus for their captain. Agesilaus, therefore, coming into the public assembly, offered his service, upon condition that he might have thirty Spartans for captains and counsellors, two thousand chosen men of the newly enfranchised helots, and allies to the number of six thousand. Lysander's authority and assistance soon obtained his request, so that he was sent away with the thirty Spartans, of whom Lysander was at once the chief, not only because of his power and reputation, but also on account of his friendship with Agesilaus, who esteemed his procuring him this charge a greater obligation than that of preferring him to the kingdom.

Whilst the army was collecting to the rendezvous at Geræstus, Agesilaus went with some of his friends to Aulis, where in a dream he saw a man approach him, and speak to him after this manner: "O King of the Lacedæmonians, you cannot but know that, before yourself, there hath been but one general captain of the whole of the Greeks, namely, Agamemnon; now, since you succeed him in the same office and command the same men, since you war against the same enemies, and begin your expedition from the same place, you ought also to offer such a sacrifice as he offered before he weighed anchor." Agesilaus at the same moment remembered that the sacrifice which Agamemnon offered was his own daughter, he being so directed by the oracle.

Yet was he not at all disturbed by it, but as soon as he arose, he told his dream to his friends, adding that he would propitiate the goddess with the sacrifices a goddess must delight in, and would not follow the ignorant example of his predecessor. He therefore ordered an hind to be crowned with chaplets, and bade his own soothsayer perform the rite, not the usual person whom the Bœotians, in ordinary course, appointed to that office.

When the Bœotian magistrates understood it, they were much offended, and sent officers to Agesilaus to forbid his sacrificing contrary to the laws of the country. These, having delivered their message to him, immediately went to the altar and threw down the quarters of the hind that lay upon it. Agesilaus took this very ill, and without further sacrifice immediately sailed away, highly displeased with the Bœotians, and much discouraged in his mind at the omen, boding to himself an unsuccessful voyage and an imperfect issue of the whole expedition.

When he came to Ephesus, he found the power and interest of Lysander, and the honours paid to him, insufferably great; all applications were made to him, crowds of suitors attended at his door, and followed upon his steps, as if nothing but the mere name of commander belonged, to satisfy the usage, to Agesilaus, the whole power of it being devolved upon Lysander. None of all the commanders that had been sent into Asia was either so powerful or so formidable as he; no one had rewarded his friends better, or had been more

severe against his enemies; which things having been lately done, made the greater impression on men's minds, especially when they compared the simple and popular behaviour of Agesilaus with the harsh and violent and brief-spoken demeanour which Lysander still retained. Universal preference was yielded to this, and little regard shown to Agesilaus.

This first occasioned offence to the other Spartan captains, who resented that they should rather seem the attendants of Lysander, than the councillors of Agesilaus. And at length Agesilaus himself, though not perhaps an envious man in his nature, nor apt to be troubled at the honours redounding upon other men, yet eager for honour and jealous of his glory, began to apprehend that Lysander's greatness would carry away from him the reputation of whatever great action should happen. He therefore went this way to work. He first opposed him in all his counsels; whatever Lysander specially advised was rejected, and other proposals followed. Then whoever made any address to him, if he found him attached to Lysander, certainly lost his suit. So also in judicial cases, any one whom he spoke strongly against was sure to come off with success, and any man whom he was particularly solicitous to procure some benefit for might think it well if he got away without an actual loss.

These things being clearly not done by chance, but constantly and of a set purpose, Lysander was soon sensible of them, and hesitated not to tell his friends that they suffered for his sake, bidding them apply themselves to the king, and such as were more powerful with him than he was. Such sayings of his seeming to be designed purposely to excite ill-feeling, Agesilaus went on to offer himself a more open affront, appointing him his meat-carver, and would in public companies scornfully say, "Let them go now and pay their court to my carver." Lysander, no longer able to brook these indignities, complained at last to Agesilaus himself, telling him that he knew very well how to humble his friends. Agesilaus answered, "I know certainly how to humble those who pretend to more power than myself." "That," replied Lysander, "is perhaps rather said by you, than done by me: I desire only that you will assign me some office and place in which I may serve you without incurring your displeasure."

Upon this Agesilaus sent him to the Hellespont, whence he procured Spithridates, a Persian of the province of Pharnabazus, to come to the assistance of the Greeks with two hundred horse and a great supply of money. Yet his anger did not so come down, but he thenceforward pursued the design of wresting the kingdom out of the hands of the two families which then enjoyed it, and making it wholly elective; and it is thought that he would on account of this quarrel have excited a great commotion in Sparta, if he had not died in the Bœotian war. Thus ambitious spirits in a commonwealth, when they transgress their bounds, are apt to do more harm than good. For though Lysander's pride and assumption was most ill-timed and insufferable in its display, yet Agesilaus surely could have found some other way of setting him right, less offensive to a man of his reputation and ambitious temper. Indeed, they were both blinded with the same passion, so as one not to recognise the authority of his superior, the other not to bear with the imperfections of his friend.

Tisaphernes, being at first afraid of Agesilaus, treated with him about setting the Grecian cities at liberty, which was agreed on. But soon after finding a sufficient force drawn together, he resolved upon war, for which Agesilaus was not sorry. For the expectation of this expedition was great, and he did not think it for his honour that Xenophon with ten thousand men should march through the heart of Asia to the sea, beating the Persian forces when and how he pleased, and that he at the head of the Spartans, then sovereigns both at sea and land, should not achieve some memorable action for Greece. And so to be even with Tisaphernes, he requited his perjury by a fair stratagem. He pretended to march into Caria, whither, when he had drawn Tisaphernes and his army, he suddenly turned back, and fell upon Phrygia, took many of their cities, and carried away great booty, showing his allies that to break a solemn league was a downright contempt of the gods, but the circumvention of an enemy in war was not only just but glorious, at once a gratification and an advantage.

Being weak in horse, and discouraged by ill-omens in the sacrifices, he retired to Ephesus, and there raised cavalry. He obliged the rich men, that were not inclined to serve in person, to find each of them a horseman armed and mounted; and there being many who preferred doing this, the army was quickly reinforced by a body, not of unwilling recruits for the infantry, but of brave and numerous horsemen. For those that were not good at fighting themselves hired such as were more military in their inclinations, and such as loved not horse-service substituted in their places such as did. Agamemnon's example had been a good one, when he took the present of an excellent mare to dismiss a rich coward from the army.

When by Agesilaus's order the prisoners he had taken in Phrygia were exposed to sale, they were first stripped of their garments and then sold naked. The clothes found many customers to buy them, but the bodies being, from the want of all exposure and exercise, white and tender-skinned, were derided and scorned as unserviceable. Agesilaus, who stood by at the auction, told his Greeks, "These are the men against whom ye fight, and these the things you will gain by it."

The season of the year being come, he boldly gave out that he would invade Lydia; and this plain dealing of his was now mistaken for a stratagem by Tisaphernes, who by not believing Agesilaus, having been already deceived by him, overreached himself. He expected that he should have made choice of Caria, as a rough country, not fit for horse, in which he deemed Agesilaus to be weak, and directed his own marches accordingly. But when he found him to be as good as his word, and to have entered into the country of Sardis, he made great haste after him, and by great marches of his horse, overtaking the loose stragglers who were pillaging the country, he cut them off.

Agesilaus, meanwhile, considering that the horse had outridden the foot, but that he himself had the whole body of his own army entire, made haste to engage them. He mingled his light-armed foot, carrying targets, with the horse, commanding them to advance at full speed and begin the battle, whilst he brought up the heavier-armed men in the rear. The success was answerable to the design; the barbarians were put to the rout, the Grecians pursued hard, took their camp, and put many of them to the sword.

The consequence of this victory was very great; for they had not only the liberty of foraging the Persian country, and plundering at pleasure, but also saw Tisaphernes pay dearly for all the cruelty he had showed the Greeks, to whom he was a professed enemy. For the King of Persia sent Tithraustes, who took off his head, and presently dealt with Agesilaus about his return into Greece, sending to him ambassadors to that purpose with commission to offer him great sums of money. Agesilaus's answer was that the making of peace belonged to the Lacedæmonians, not to him; as for wealth, he had rather see it in his soldiers' hands than his own; that the Grecians thought it not honourable to enrich themselves with the bribes of their enemies, but with their spoils only. Yet, that he might gratify Tithraustes for the justice he had done upon Tisaphernes, the common enemy of the Greeks, he removed his quarters into Phrygia, accepting thirty talents for his expenses.

Whilst he was upon his march, he received a *staff* from the government at Sparta, appointing him admiral as well as general. This was an honour which was never done to any but Agesilaus, who being now undoubtedly the greatest and most illustrious man of his time, still, as Theopompus had said, gave himself more occasion of glory in his own virtue and merit than was given him in this authority and power.

Yet he committed a fault in preferring Pisander to the command of the navy, when there were others at hand both older and more experienced; in this not so much consulting the public good as the gratification of his kindred, and especially his wife, whose brother Pisander was.

Having removed his camp into Pharnabazus's province, he not only met with great plenty of provisions, but also raised great sums of money, and marching on to the bounds of Paphlagonia, he soon drew Cotys, the king of it, into a league, to which he of his own accord inclined, out of the opinion he had of Agesilaus's honour and virtue.

Spithridates, from the time of his abandoning Pharnabazus, constantly attended Agesilaus in the camp withersoever he went. This Spithridates had a son, a very handsome boy, called Megabates, of whom Agesilaus was extremely fond, and also a very beautiful daughter that was marriageable.

Her Agesilaus matched to Cotys, and taking of him a thousand horse, with two thousand light-armed foot, he returned into Phrygia, and there pillaged the country of Pharnabazus, who durst not meet him in the field, nor yet trust to his garrisons, but getting his valuables together, got out of the way and moved about up and down with a fleeing army, till Spithridates, joining with Herippidas the Spartan, took his camp and all his property. Herippidas being too severe an inquirer into the plunder with which the barbarian soldiers had enriched themselves, and forcing them to deliver it up with too much strictness, so disobliged Spithridates with his questioning and examining that

he changed sides again, and went off with the Paphlagonians to Sardis.

This was a very great vexation to Agesilaus, not only that he had lost the friendship of a gallant commander, and with him a considerable part of his army, but still more that it had been done with the disrepute of a sordid and petty covetousness, of which he always had made it a point of honour to keep both himself and his country clear.

Besides these public causes, he had a private one, his excessive fondness for the son, which touched him to the quick, though he endeavoured to master it, and, especially in presence of the boy to suppress all appearance of it; so much so that when Megabates, for that was his name, came once to receive a kiss from him, he declined it. At which, when the young boy blushed and drew back, and afterwards saluted him at a more reserved distance, Agesilaus soon repenting his coldness, and changing his mind, pretended to wonder why he did not salute him with the same familiarity as formerly. His friends about him answered, "You are in the fault, who would not accept the kiss of the boy, but turned away in alarm; he would come to you again if you would have the courage to let him do so." Upon this Agesilaus paused a while, and at length answered, "You need not encourage him to it; I think I had rather be master of myself in that refusal, than see all things that are now before my eyes turned into gold." Thus he demeaned himself to Megabates when present, but he had so great a passion for him in his absence that it may be questioned whether, if the boy had returned again, all the courage he had would have sustained him in such another refusal.

After this Pharnabazus sought an opportunity of conferring with Agesilaus, which Apollophanes of Cyzicus, the common host of them both, procured for him. Agesilaus coming first to the appointed place, threw himself down upon the grass under a tree, lying there in expectation of Pharnabazus, who, bringing with him soft skins and wrought carpets to lie down upon, when he saw Agesilaus's posture, grew ashamed of his luxuries, and made no use of them, but laid himself down upon the grass also, without regard for his delicate and richly dyed clothing.

Pharnabazus had matter enough of complaint against Agesilaus, and therefore, after the mutual civilities were over, he put him in mind of the great services he had done the Lacedæmonians in the Attic war, of which he thought it an ill recompense to have his country thus harassed and spoiled by those men who owed so much to him. The Spartans that were present hung down their heads, as conscious of the wrong they had done to their ally.

But Agesilaus said, "We, O Pharnabazus, when we were in amity with your master the king, behaved ourselves like friends, and now that we are at war with him, we behave ourselves as enemies. As for you, we must look upon you as a part of his property, and must do these outrages upon you, not intending the harm to you, but to him whom we wound through you. But whenever you will choose rather to be a friend to the Grecians than a slave of the King of Persia, you may then reckon this army and navy to be all at your command, to defend both you, your country, and your liberties, without which there is nothing honourable or indeed desirable among men."

Upon this Pharnabazus discovered his mind, and answered, "If the king sends another governor in my room, I will certainly come over to you, but as long as he trusts me with the government I shall be just to him, and not fail to do my utmost endeavours in opposing you." Agesilaus was taken with the answer and shook hands with him; and rising, said, "How much rather had I have so brave a man my friend than my enemy."

Pharnabazus being gone off, his son staying behind, ran up to Agesilaus, and smilingly said, "Agesilaus, I make you my guest"; and thereupon presented him with a javelin which he had in his hand. Agesilaus received it, and being much taken with the good mien and courtesy of the youth, looked about to see if there were anything in his train fit to offer him in return; and observing the horse of Idæus, the secretary, to have very fine trappings on, he took them off, and bestowed them upon the young gentleman.

Nor did his kindness rest there, but he continued ever after to be mindful of him, so that when he was driven out of his country by his brothers, and lived an exile in Peloponnesus, he took great care of him and condescended even to assist him in some love matters. He had an attachment for a youth of Athenian birth, who was bred up as an athlete; and when at the Olympic games this boy, on account of his great size and general strong and full-grown appearance, was in some danger of not being admitted into the list, the Persian betook himself to Agesilaus, and made use of his friendship. Agesilaus readily assisted him, and not without a great deal of difficulty effected his desires.

He was in all other things a man of great and exact justice, but when the case concerned a friend, to be strait-laced in point of justice, he said, was only a colourable pretence of denying him. There is an epistle written to Idrieus, Prince of Caria, that is ascribed to Agesilaus; it is this: "If Nicias be innocent, absolve him; if he be guilty, absolve him upon my account; however, be sure to absolve him." That was his usual character in his deportment towards his friends.

Yet his rule was not without exception; for sometimes he considered the necessity of his affairs more than his friend, of which he once gave an example, when upon a sudden and disorderly removal of his camp, he left a sick friend behind him, and when he called loudly after him, and implored his help, turned his back, and said it was hard to be compassionate and wise too. This story is related by Hieronymus, the philosopher.

Another year of the war being spent, Agesilaus's fame still increased, insomuch that the Persian king received daily information concerning his many virtues, and the great esteem the world had of his temperance, his plain living, and his moderation. When he made any journey, he would usually take up his lodging in a temple, and there make the gods witnesses of his most private actions, which others would scarce permit men to be acquainted with. In so great an army you should scarce find a common soldier lie on a coarser mattress than Agesilaus: he was so indifferent to the varieties of heat and cold that all the seasons, as the gods sent them, seemed natural to him.

The Greeks that inhabited Asia were much pleased to see the great lords and governors of Persia, with all the pride, cruelty, and luxury in which they lived, trembling and bowing before a man in a poor threadbare cloak, and, at one laconic word out of his mouth, obsequiously deferring and changing their wishes and purposes. So that it brought to the minds of many the verses of Timotheus—

Mars is the tyrant, gold Greece does not fear.

Many parts of Asia now revolting from the Persians, Agesilaus restored order in the cities, and without bloodshed or banishment of any of their members re-established the proper constitution in the governments, and now resolved to carry away the war from the seaside, and to march further up into the country, and to attack the King of Persia himself in his own home in Susa and Ecbatana; not willing to let the monarch sit idle in his chair, playing umpire in the conflicts of the Greeks, and bribing their popular leaders.

But these great thoughts were interrupted by unhappy news from Sparta; Epicydidas was from thence sent to remand him home, to assist his own country, which was then involved in a great war:—

Greece to herself doth a barbarian grow,
Others could not, she doth herself o'erthrow.

What better can we say of those jealousies, and that league and conspiracy of the Greeks for their own mischief, which arrested fortune in full career, and turned back arms that were already uplifted against the barbarians, to be used upon themselves, and recalled into Greece the war which had been banished out of her? I by no means assent to Demaratus of Corinth, who said that those Greeks lost a great satisfaction that did not live to see Alexander sit in the throne of Darius. That sight should rather have drawn tears from them, when they considered that they had left that glory to Alexander and the Macedonians, whilst they spent all their own great commanders in playing them against each other in the fields of Leuctra, Coronea, Corinth, and Arcadia.

Nothing was greater or nobler than the behaviour of Agesilaus on this occasion, nor can a nobler instance be found in story of a ready obedience and just deference to orders. Hannibal, though in a bad condition himself, and, almost driven out of Italy, could scarcely be induced to obey when he was called home to serve his country. Alexander made a jest of the battle between Agis and Antipater, laughing and saying, "So, whilst we were conquering Darius in Asia, it seems there was a battle of mice in Arcadia." Happy Sparta, meanwhile, in the justice and modesty of Agesilaus, and in the deference he paid to the laws of his country; who, immediately upon receipt of his orders, though in the midst of his high fortune and power, and in full hope of great and glorious success, gave all up and instantly departed, "his object unachieved," leaving many regrets behind him among his allies in Asia, and proving by his example the falseness of that saying of Demostratus, the son of Phæax, "that the Lacedæmonians were better in public life, but the Athenians in private." For while approving himself an excellent king and general, he likewise showed himself in private an excellent friend and a most agreeable companion.

The coin of Persia was stamped with the figure of an archer; Agesilaus said that a thousand Persian archers had driven him out of Asia; meaning the money that had been laid out in bribing the demagogues and the orators in Thebes and Athens, and thus inciting those two states to hostility against Sparta.

Having passed the Hellespont, he marched by land through Thrace, not begging or entreating a passage anywhere, only he sent his messengers to them to demand whether they would have him pass as a friend or as an enemy. All the rest received him as a friend, and assisted him on his journey. But the Trallians, to whom Xerxes is also said to have given money, demanded a price of him, namely, one hundred talents of silver and one hundred women. Agesilaus in scorn asked why they were not ready to receive them. He marched on, and finding the Trallians in arms to oppose him, fought them, and slew great numbers of them. He sent the like embassy to the King of Macedonia, who replied he would take time to deliberate. "Let him deliberate," said Agesilaus, "we will go forward in the meantime." The Macedonian, being surprised and daunted at the resolution of the Spartan, gave orders to let him pass as a friend.

When he came into Thessaly he wasted the country, because they were in league with the enemy. To Larissa, the chief city of Thessaly, he sent Xenocles and Scythes to treat of a peace, whom when the Larissæans had laid hold of, and put into custody, others were enraged, and advised the siege of the town; but he answered that he valued either of those men at more than the whole country of Thessaly. He therefore made terms with them, and received his men again upon composition.

Nor need we wonder at this saying of Agesilaus, since when he had news brought him from Sparta, of several great captains in a battle near Corinth, in which the slaughter fell upon other Greeks, and the Lacedæmonians obtained a great victory with small loss, he did not appear at all satisfied; but with a great sigh cried out, "O Greece, how many brave men hast thou destroyed; who, if they had been preserved to so good an use, had sufficed to have conquered all Persia!"

Yet when the Pharsalians grew troublesome to him, by pressing upon his army and incommoding his passage, he led out five hundred horse, and in person fought and routed them, setting up a trophy under the mount Narthacius. He valued himself very much upon that victory, that with so small a number of his own training, he had vanquished a body of men that thought themselves the best horsemen of Greece.

Here Diphridas, the ephor, met him, and delivered his message from Sparta, which ordered him immediately to make an inroad into Bœotia; and though he thought this fitter to have been done at another time, and with greater force, he yet obeyed the magistrates. He thereupon told his soldiers that the day had come on which they were to enter upon that employment for the performance of which they were brought out of Asia. He sent for two divisions of the army near Corinth to his assistance. The Lacedæmonians at home, in honour to him, made proclamations for volunteers that would serve under the king to come in and be enlisted. Finding all the young men in the city ready to offer themselves, they chose fifty of the strongest, and sent them.

Agesilaus having gained Thermopylæ, and passed quietly through Phocis, as soon as he had entered Bœotia, and pitched his camp near Chæronea, at once met with an eclipse of the sun, and with ill news from the navy, Pisander, the Spartan admiral, being beaten and slain at Cnidos by Pharnabazus and Conon. He was much moved at it, both upon his own and the public account. Yet lest his army, being now near engaging, should meet with any discouragement, he ordered the messengers to give out that the Spartans were the conquerors, and he himself putting on a garland, solemnly sacrificed for the good news, and sent portions of the sacrifices to his friends.

When he came near to Coronea, and was within view of the enemy, he drew up his army, and giving the left wing to the Orchomenians, he himself led the right. The Thebans took the right wing of their army, leaving the left to the Argives.

Xenophon, who was present, and fought on Agesilaus's side, reports it to be the hardest-fought battle that he had seen. The beginning of it was not so, for the Thebans soon put the Orchomenians to rout, as also did Agesilaus the Argives. But both parties having news of the misfortune of their left wings, they betook themselves to their relief. Here Agesilaus might have been sure of his victory had he contented himself not to charge them in the front, but in the flank or rear; but being angry and heated in the fight he would not wait the opportunity, but fell on at once, thinking to bear them down before him. The Thebans were not behind him in courage, so that the battle was fiercely carried on on both sides, especially near Agesilaus's person, whose new guard of fifty volunteers stood him in great stead that day, and saved his life. They fought with great valour, and interposed their bodies frequently between him and danger, yet could they not so preserve him, but that he received many wounds through his armour with lances and swords, and was with much difficulty gotten off alive by their making a ring about him, and so guarding him, with the slaughter of many of the enemy, and the loss of many of their own number.

At length, finding it too hard a task to break the front of the Theban troops, they opened their own files, and let the enemy march through them (an artifice which in the beginning they scorned), watching in the meantime the posture of the enemy, who, having passed through, grew careless, as esteeming themselves past danger, in which position they were immediately set upon by the Spartans. Yet were they not then put to rout, but marched on to Helicon, proud of what they had done, being able to say that they themselves, as to their part of the army, were not worsted.

Agesilaus, sore wounded as he was, would not be borne to his tent till he had been first carried about the field, and had seen the dead conveyed within his encampment. As many of his enemies as had taken sanctuary in the temple he dismissed. For there stood near the battlefield the temple of Minerva the Itonian, and before it a trophy erected by the Bœotians, for the victory which, under the conduct of Sparton, their general, they obtained over the Athenians under Tolmides, who himself fell in the battle.

Next morning early, to make trial of the Theban courage, whether they had any mind to a second encounter, he commanded his soldiers to put on garlands on their heads, and play with their flutes, and raise a trophy before their faces; but when they, instead of fighting, sent for leave to bury their dead, he gave it them; and having so assured himself of the victory, after this he went to Delphi, to the Pythian games, which were then celebrating, at which feast he assisted, and there solemnly offered the tenth part of the spoils he had brought from Asia, which amounted to a hundred talents.

Thence he returned to his own country, where his way and habits of life quickly excited the affection and admiration of the Spartans; for, unlike other generals, he came home from foreign lands the same man that he went out, having not so learned the fashions of other countries, as to forget his own, much less to dislike or despise them. He followed and respected all the Spartan customs, without any change either in the manner of his supping, or bathing, or his wife's apparel, as if he had never travelled over the river Eurotas. So also with his household furniture and his own armour, nay, the very gates of his house were so old that they might well be thought of Aristodemus's setting up. His daughter's canathrum, says Xenophon, was no richer than that of any one else. The canathrum, as they call it, is a chair or chariot made of wood, in the shape of a griffin, or tragelaphus, on which the children and young virgins are carried in processions. Xenophon has not left us the name of this daughter of Agesilaus; and Dicæarchus expresses some indignation, because we do not know, he says, the name of Agesilaus's daughter, nor of Epaminondas's mother. But in the records of Laconia, we ourselves found his wife's name to have been Cleora, and his two daughters to have been called Eupolia and Prolyta. And you may also to this day see Agesilaus's spear kept in Sparta, nothing differing from that of other men.

There was a vanity he observed among the Spartans, about keeping running horses for the Olympic games, upon which he found they much valued themselves. Agesilaus regarded it as a display not of any real virtue, but of wealth and expense; and to make this evident to the Greeks, induced his sister, Cynisca, to send a chariot into the course.

He kept with him Xenophon, the philosopher, and made much of him, and proposed to him to send for his children and educate them at Sparta, where they would be taught the best of all learning; how to obey, and how to command.

Finding on Lysander's death a large faction formed, which he on his return from Asia had established against Agesilaus, he thought it advisable to expose both him and it, by showing what manner of a citizen he had been whilst he lived. To that end, finding among his writings an oration, composed by Cleon the Halicarnassean, but to have been spoken by Lysander in a public assembly, to excite the people to innovations and changes in the government, he resolved to publish it as an evidence of Lysander's practices. But one of the Elders having the perusal of it, and finding it power-

fully written, advised him to have a care of digging up Lysander again, and rather bury that oration in the grave with him; and this advice he wisely hearkened to, and hushed the whole thing up; and ever after forbore publicly to affront any of his adversaries, but took occasions of picking out the ringleaders, and sending them away upon foreign services. He thus had means for exposing the avarice and the injustice of many of them in their employments; and again when they were by others brought into question, he made it his business to bring them off, obliging them, by that means, of enemies to become his friends, and so by degrees left none remaining.

Agesipolis, his fellow-king, was under the disadvantage of being born of an exiled father, and himself young, modest, and inactive, meddled not much in affairs. Agesilaus took a course of gaining him over and making him entirely tractable. According to the custom of Sparta, the kings, if they were in town, always dined together. This was Agesilaus's opportunity of dealing with Agesipolis, whom he found quick, as he himself was, in forming attachments for young men, and accordingly talked with him always on such subjects, joining and aiding him, and acting as his confidant, such attachments in Sparta being entirely honourable, and attended always with lively feelings of modesty, love of virtue, and a noble emulation; of which more is said in Lycurgus's life.

Having thus established his power in the city, he easily obtained that his half-brother Teleutias might be chosen admiral, and thereupon making an expedition against the Corinthians, he made himself master of the long walls by land, through the assistance of his brother at sea. Coming thus upon the Argives, who then held Corinth, in the midst of their Isthmian festival, he made them fly from the sacrifice they had just commenced, and leave all their festive provision behind them. The exiled Corinthians that were in the Spartan army desired him to keep the feast, and to preside in the celebration of it. This he refused, but gave them leave to carry on the solemnity if they pleased, and he in the meantime stayed and guarded them.

When Agesilaus marched off, the Argives returned and celebrated the games over again, when some who were victors before became victors a second time; others lost the prizes which before they had gained. Agesilaus thus made it clear to everybody that the Argives must in their own eyes have been guilty of great cowardice since they set such a value on presiding at the games, and yet had not dared to fight for it.

He himself was of opinion that to keep a mean in such things was best; he assisted at the sports and dances usual in his own country, and was always ready and eager to be present at the exercises either of the young men or of the girls, but things that many men used to be highly taken with he seemed not at all concerned about.

Callippides, the tragic actor, who had a great name in all Greece and was made much of, once met and saluted him; of which when he found no notice taken, he confidently thrust himself into his train, expecting that Agesilaus would pay him some attention. When all that failed, he boldly accosted him, and asked him whether he did not remember him. Agesilaus turned, and looking him in the face, "Are you not," said he, "Callippides the showman?"

Being invited once to hear a man who admirably imitated the nightingale, he declined, saying he had heard the nightingale itself. Menecrates, the physician, having had great success in some desperate diseases, was by way of flattery called Jupiter; he was so vain as to take the name, and having occasion to write a letter to Agesilaus, thus addressed it: "Jupiter Menecrates to King Agesilaus, greeting." The king returned answer: "Agesilaus to Menecrates, health and a sound mind."

Whilst Agesilaus was in the Corinthian territories, having just taken the Heræum, he was looking on while his soldiers were carrying away the prisoners and the plunder, when ambassadors from Thebes came to him to treat of peace. Having a great aversion for that city, and thinking it then advantageous to his affairs publicly to slight them, he took the opportunity, and would not seem either to see them or hear them speak. But as if on purpose to punish him in his pride, before they parted from him, messengers came with news of the complete slaughter of one of the Spartan divisions by Iphicrates, a greater disaster than had befallen them for many years, and that the more grievous because it was a choice regiment of full-armed Lacedæmonians overthrown by a parcel of mere mercenary targeteers.

Agesilaus leapt from his seat, to go at once to their rescue, but found it too late, the business being over. He therefore returned to the Heræum and sent for the Theban ambassadors to give them audience. They now resolved to be even with him for the affront he gave them, and without speaking one word of the peace, only desired leave to go into Corinth. Agesilaus, irritated with this proposal, told them in scorn, that if they were anxious to go and see how proud their friends were of their success they should do it to-morrow with safety. Next morning, taking the ambassadors with him, he ravaged the Corinthian territories, up to the very gates of the city, where, having made a stand, and let the ambassadors see that the Corinthians durst not come out to defend themselves, he dismissed them. Then gathering up the small remainders of the shattered regiment, he marched homewards, always removing his camp before day, and always pitching his tents after night, that he might prevent their enemies among the Arcadians from taking any opportunity of exulting over their loss.

After this, at the request of the Achæans, he marched with them into Acarnania, and there collected great spoils, and defeated the Acarnanians in battle. The Achæans would have persuaded him to keep his winter quarters there, to hinder the Acarnanians from sowing their corn; but he was of the contrary opinion, alleging that they would be more afraid of a war next summer, when their fields were sown, than they would be if they lay fallow. The event justified his opinion; for next summer, when the Achæans began their expedition again, the Acarnanians immediately made peace with them.

When Conon and Pharnabazus with the Persian navy were grown masters of the sea, and had not only infested the coast of Laconia, but also rebuilt the walls of Athens at the cost of Pharnabazus, the Lacedæmonians thought fit to treat of peace with the King of Persia. To that end, they sent Antalcidas to Tiribazus, basely and wickedly betraying the Asiatic Greeks, on whose behalf Agesilaus had made the war. But no part of this dishonour fell upon Agesilaus, the whole being transacted by Antalcidas, who was his bitter enemy, and was urgent for peace upon any terms, because war was sure to increase his power and reputation. Nevertheless, once being told by way of reproach that the Lacedæmonians had gone over to the Medes, he replied, "No, the Medes had come over to the Lacedæmonians."

And when the Greeks were backward to submit to the agreement, he threatened them with war, unless they fulfilled the King of Persia's conditions, his particular end in this being to weaken the Thebans; for it was made one of the articles of peace that the country of Bœotia should be left independent. This feeling of his to Thebes appeared further afterwards, when Phœbidas, in full peace, most unjustifiably seized upon the Cadmea. The thing was much resented by all Greece, and not well liked by the Lacedæmonians themselves; those especially who were enemies to Agesilaus required an account of the action, and by whose authority it was done, laying the suspicion of it at his door. Agesilaus resolutely answered, on the behalf of Phœbidas, that the profitableness of the act was chiefly to be considered; if it were for the advantage of the commonwealth, it was no matter whether it were done with or without authority.

This was the more remarkable in him, because in his ordinary language he was always observed to be a great maintainer of justice, and would commend it as the chief of virtues, saying, that valour without justice was useless, and if all the world were just, there would be no need of valour. When any would say to him, the Great King will have it so, he would reply, "How is he greater than I, unless he be juster?" nobly and rightly taking, as a sort of royal measure of greatness, justice and not force. And thus when, on the conclusion of the peace, the King of Persia wrote to Agesilaus, desiring a private friendship and relations of hospitality, he refused it, saying that the public friendship was enough; whilst that lasted there was no need of private.

Yet in his acts he was not constant to his doctrine, but sometimes out of ambition, and sometimes out of private pique, he let himself be carried away; and particularly in this case of the Thebans, he not only saved Phœbidas, but persuaded the Lacedæmonians to take the fault upon themselves, and to retain the Cadmea, putting a garrison into it, and to put the government of Thebes into the hands of Archias and Leontidas, who had been betrayers of the castle to them.

This excited strong suspicion that what Phœbidas did was by Agesilaus's order, which was corroborated by after-occurrences. For when the Thebans had expelled the garrison, and asserted their liberty, he, accusing them of the murder of Archias and Leontidas, who indeed were tyrants, though in name holding the office of polemarchs, made war upon them. He sent Cleombrotus on that errand, who was now his fellow-king, in the place of Agesipolis, who was dead, excusing himself by reason of his age; for it was forty years since he had first

borne arms, and he was consequently exempt by the law; meanwhile, the true reason was, that he was ashamed, having so lately fought against tyranny in behalf of the Phliasians, to fight now in defence of a tyranny against the Thebans.

One Sphodrias, of Lacedæmon, of the contrary faction to Agesilaus, was governor in Thespiæ, a bold and enterprising man, though he had perhaps more of confidence than wisdom. This action of Phœbidas fired him, and incited his ambition to attempt some great enterprise, which might render him as famous as he perceived the taking of the Cadmea had made Phœbidas. He thought the sudden capture of the Piræus, and the cutting off thereby the Athenians from the sea, would be a matter of far more glory. It is said, too, that Pelopidas and Melon, the chief captains of Bœotia, put him upon it; that they privily sent men to him, pretending to be of the Spartan faction, who, highly commending Sphodrias, filled him with a great opinion of himself, protesting him to be the only man in the world that was fit for so great an enterprise.

Being thus stimulated, he could hold no longer, but hurried into an attempt as dishonourable and treacherous as that of the Cadmea, but executed with less valour and less success; for the day broke whilst he was yet in the Thriasian plain, whereas he designed the whole exploit to have been done in the night. As soon as the soldiers perceived the rays of light reflecting from the temples of Eleusis, upon the first rising of the sun, it is said that their hearts failed them; nay, he himself, when he saw that he could not have the benefit of the night, had not courage enough to go on with his enterprise; but having pillaged the country, he returned with shame to Thespiæ.

An embassy was upon this sent from Athens to Sparta, to complain of the breach of peace; but the ambassadors found their journey needless, Sphodrias being then under process by the magistrates of Sparta. Sphodrias durst not stay to expect judgment, which he found would be capital, the city being highly incensed against him, out of the shame they felt at the business and their desire to appear in the eyes of the Athenians as fellow-sufferers in the wrong, rather than accomplices in its being done.

This Sphodrias had a son of great beauty named Cleonymus, to whom Archidamus, the son of Agesilaus, was extremely attached. Archidamus, as became him, was concerned for the danger of his friend's father, but yet he durst not do anything openly for his assistance, he being one of the professed enemies of Agesilaus. But Cleonymus having solicited him with tears about it, as knowing Agesilaus to be of all his father's enemies the most formidable, the young man for two or three days followed after his father with such fear and confusion that he durst not speak to him. At last, the day of sentence being at hand, he ventured to tell him that Cleonymus had entreated him to intercede for his father. Agesilaus, though well aware of the love between the two young men, yet did not prohibit it, because Cleonymus from his earliest years had been looked upon as a youth of very great promise; yet he gave not his son any kind or hopeful answer in the case, but coldly told him that he would consider what he could honestly and honourably do in it, and so dismissed him.

Archidamus being ashamed of his want of success, forbore the company of Cleonymus, whom he usually saw several times every day. This made the friends of Sphodrias to think his case desperate, till Etymocles, one of Agesilaus's friends, discovered to them the king's mind; namely, that he abhorred the fact, but yet he thought Sphodrias a gallant man such as the commonwealth much wanted at that time. For Agesilaus used to talk thus concerning the cause, out of a desire to gratify his son. And now Cleonymus quickly understood that Archidamus had been true to him, in using all his interests with his father; and Sphodrias's friend ventured to be forward in his defence.

The truth is, that Agesilaus was excessively fond of his children; and it is to him the story belongs, that when they were little ones, he used to make a horse of a stick, and ride with them; and being caught at this sport by a friend, he desired him not to mention it till he himself were the father of children.

Meanwhile, Sphodrias being acquitted, the Athenians betook themselves to arms, and Agesilaus fell into disgrace with the people; since to gratify the whims of a boy he had been willing to pervert justice, and make the city accessory to the crimes of private men, whose most unjustifiable actions had broken the peace of Greece. He also found his colleague, Cleombrotus, little inclined to the Theban war; so that it became necessary for him to waive the privilege of his age, which he before had claimed, and to lead the army himself into Bœotia; which he did with variety of success, sometimes conquering, and sometimes conquered; insomuch that receiving a wound in a battle,

he was reproached by Antalcidas, that the Thebans had paid him well for the lessons he had given them in fighting. And, indeed, they were now grown far better soldiers than ever they had been, being so continually kept in training by the frequency of the Lacedæmonian expeditions against them. Out of the foresight of which it was that anciently Lycurgus, in three several laws, forbade them to make any wars with the same nation, as this would be to instruct their enemies in the art of it.

Meanwhile, the allies of Sparta were not a little discontented at Agesilaus, because this war was commenced not upon any fair public ground of quarrel, but merely out of his private hatred to the Thebans; and they complained with indignation that they, being the majority of the army, should from year to year be thus exposed to danger and hardship here and there, at the will of a few persons. It was at this time, we are told, that Agesilaus, to obviate the objection, devised this expedient, to show the allies were not the greater number. He gave orders that all the allies, of whatever country, should sit down promiscuously on one side, and all the Lacedæmonians on the other: which being done, he commanded a herald to proclaim, that all the potters of both divisions should stand out; then all the blacksmiths; then all the masons; next the carpenters; and so he went through all the handicrafts. By this time almost all the allies were risen, but of the Lacedæmonians not a man, they being by law forbidden to learn any mechanical business; and now Agesilaus laughed and said, "You see, my friends, how many more soldiers we send out than you do."

When he brought back his army from Bœotia through Megara, as he was going up to the magistrate's office in the Acropolis, he was suddenly seized with pain and cramp in his sound leg, and great swelling and inflammation ensued. He was treated by a Syracusan physician, who let him bleed below the ankle; this soon eased his pain, but then the blood could not be stopped, till the loss of it brought on fainting and swooning; at length, with much trouble, he stopped it. Agesilaus was carried home to Sparta in a very weak condition, and did not recover strength enough to appear in the field for a long time after.

Meanwhile, the Spartan fortune was but ill; they received many losses both by sea and land; but the greatest was that at Tegyræ, when for the first time they were beaten by the Thebans in a set battle.

All the Greeks were, accordingly, disposed to a general peace, and to that end ambassadors came to Sparta. Among these was Epaminondas, the Theban, famous at that time for his philosophy and learning, but he had not yet given proof of his capacity as a general. He, seeing all the others crouch to Agesilaus, and court favour with him, alone maintained the dignity of an ambassador, and with that freedom that became his character made a speech in behalf not of Thebes only, from whence he came, but of all Greece, remonstrating that Sparta alone grew great by war, to the distress and suffering of all her neighbours. He urged that a peace should be made upon just and equal terms, such as alone would be a lasting one, which could not otherwise be done than by reducing all to equality.

Agesilaus, perceiving all the other Greeks to give much attention to this discourse, and to be pleased with it, presently asked him whether he thought it a part of this justice and equality that the Bœotian towns should enjoy their independence. Epaminondas instantly and without wavering asked him in return, whether he thought it just and equal that the Laconian towns should enjoy theirs. Agesilaus started from his seat and bade him once for all speak out and say whether or not Bœotia should be independent. And when Epaminondas replied once again with the same inquiry, whether Laconia should be so, Agesilaus was so enraged that, availing himself of the pretext, he immediately struck the name of the Thebans out of the league, and declared war against them. With the rest of the Greeks he made a peace, and dismissed them with this saying, that what could be peaceably adjusted, should; what was otherwise incurable, must be committed to the success of war, it being a thing of too great difficulty to provide for all things by treaty.

The ephors upon this despatched their orders to Cleombrotus, who was at that time in Phocis, to march directly into Bœotia, and at the same time sent to their allies for aid. The confederates were very tardy in their business and unwilling to engage, but as yet they feared the Spartans too much to dare to refuse. And although many portents and prodigies of ill-presage, which I have mentioned in the life of Epaminondas, had appeared, and though Prothous, the Laconian, did all he could to hinder it, yet Agesilaus would needs go forward, and prevailed so that the war was decreed. He thought the present juncture of affairs very ad-vantageous for their revenge, the rest of Greece being wholly free, and the Thebans excluded from the peace. But that this war was undertaken more upon passion than judgment the event may prove; for the treaty was finished but the fourteenth of Scirophorion, and the Lacedæmonians received their great overthrow at Leuctra on the fifth of Hecatombæon, within twenty days. There fell at that time a thousand Spartans, and Cleombrotus their king, and around him the bravest men of the nation; particularly the beautiful youth, Cleonymus, the son of Sphodrias, who was thrice struck down at the feet of the king, and as often rose, but was slain at the last.

This unexpected blow, which fell so heavy upon the Lacedæmonians, brought greater glory to Thebes than ever was acquired by any other of the Grecian republics in their civil wars against each other. The behaviour, notwithstanding, of the Spartans, though beaten, was as great, and as highly to be admired, as that of the Thebans. And indeed, if, as Xenophon says, in conversation good men even in their sports and at their wine let fall many sayings that are worth the preserving, how much more worthy to be recorded is an exemplary constancy of mind, as shown both in the words and in the acts of brave men when they are pressed by adverse fortune!

It happened that the Spartans were celebrating a solemn feast, at which many strangers were present from other countries, and the town full of them, when this news of the overthrow came. It was the gymnopædiæ, and the boys were dancing in the theatre, when the messengers arrived from Leuctra. The ephors, though they were sufficiently aware that this blow had ruined the Spartan power, and that their primacy over the rest of Greece was gone for ever, yet gave orders that the dances should not break off, nor any of the celebration of the festival abate; but privately sending the names of the slain to each family, out of which they were lost, they continued the public spectacles. The next morning when they had full intelligence concerning it, and everybody knew who were slain, and who survived, the fathers, relatives, and friends of the slain came out rejoicing in the market-place, saluting each other with a kind of exultation; on the contrary, the fathers of the survivors hid themselves at home among the women. If necessity drove any of them abroad they went very dejectedly, with downcast looks and sorrowful countenances. The women outdid the men in it; those whose sons were slain openly rejoicing, cheerfully making visits to one another, and meeting triumphantly in the temples; they who expected their children home being very silent and much troubled.

But the people in general, when their allies now began to desert them, and Epaminondas, in all the confidence of victory, was expected with an invading army in Peloponnesus, began to think again of Agesilaus's lameness, and to entertain feelings of religious fear and despondency, as if their having rejected the sound-footed, and having chosen the halting king, which the oracle had specially warned them against, was the occasion of all their distresses.

Yet the regard they had to the merit and reputation of Agesilaus so far stilled this murmuring of the people that, notwithstanding it, they intrusted themselves to him in this distress, as the only man that was fit to heal the public malady, the arbiter of all their difficulties, whether relating to the affairs of war or peace. One great one was then before them concerning the runaways (as their name is for them) that had fled out of the battle, who being many and powerful, it was feared that they might make some commotion in the republic to prevent the execution of the law upon them for their cowardice.

The law in that case was very severe; for they were not only to be debarred from all honours, but also it was a disgrace to intermarry with them; whoever met any one of them in the streets might beat him if he chose, nor was it lawful for him to resist; they, in the meanwhile, were obliged to go about unwashed and meanly dressed, with their clothes patched with divers colours, and to wear their beards half shaved, half unshaven. To execute so rigid a law as this, in a case where the offenders were so many, and many of them of such distinction, and that in a time when the commonwealth wanted soldiers so much as then it did, was of dangerous consequence. Therefore, they chose Agesilaus as a sort of new lawgiver for the occasion.

But he, without adding to or diminishing from or any way changing the law, came out into the public assembly, and said that the law should sleep for to-day, but from this day forth be vigorously executed. By this means he at once preserved the law from abrogation and the citizens from infamy; and that he might alleviate the despondency and self-distrust of the young men, he made an inroad into Arcadia, where, carefully avoiding all fighting, he contented himself with spoiling the territory, and taking a small town belonging to the Mantineans, thus reviving the hearts of the people, letting them see that they were not everywhere unsuccessful.

Epaminondas now invaded Laconia with an army of forty thousand, besides light-armed men and others that followed the camp only for plunder, so that in all they were at least seventy thousand. It was now six hundred years since the Dorians had possessed Laconia, and in all that time the face of an enemy had not been seen within their territories, no man daring to invade them; but now they made their entrance, and burnt and plundered without resistance the hitherto untouched and sacred territory up to Eurotas and the very suburbs of Sparta; for Agesilaus would not permit them to encounter so impetuous a torrent, as Theopompus calls it, of war.

He contented himself with fortifying the chief parts of the city, and with placing guards in convenient places, enduring meanwhile the taunts of the Thebans, who reproached him by name as the kindler of the war, and the author of all that mischief to his country, bidding him defend himself if he could. But this was not all; he was equally disturbed at home with the tumults of the city, the outcries and running about of the old men, who were enraged at their present condition, and the women yet worse, out of their senses with the clamours and the fires of the enemy in the field. He was also himself afflicted by the sense of his lost glory; who, having come to the throne of Sparta when it was in its most flourishing and powerful condition, now lived to see it laid low in esteem, and all its great vaunts cut down, even that which he himself had been accustomed to use, that the women of Sparta had never seen the smoke of the enemy's fire.

As it is said, also, that when Antalcidas, once being in dispute with an Athenian about the valour of the two nations, the Athenian boasted that they had often driven the Spartans from the river Cephisus, "Yes," said Antalcidas, "but we never had occasion to drive you from Eurotas." And a common Spartan of less note, being in company with an Argive, who was bragging how many Spartans lay buried in the fields of Argos, replied, "None of you are buried in the country of Laconia." Yet now the case was so altered that Antalcidas, being one of the ephors, out of fear sent away his children privately to the island of Cythera.

When the enemy essayed to get over the river, and thence to attack the town, Agesilaus, abandoning the rest, betook himself to the high places and strongholds of it. But it happened Eurotas at that time was swollen to a great height with snow that had fallen and made the passage very difficult to the Thebans, not only by its depth, but much more by its extreme coldness. Whilst this was doing, Epaminondas was seen in the front of the phalanx, and was pointed out to Agesilaus, who looked long at him, and said but these words, "O bold man!" But when he came to the city, and would have fain attempted something within the limits of it that might raise him a trophy there, he could not tempt Agesilaus out of his hold, but was forced to march off again, wasting the country as he went.

Meanwhile, a body of long discontented and bad citizens, about two hundred in number, having got into a strong part of the town called the Issorion, where the temple of Diana stands, seized and garrisoned it. The Spartans would have fallen upon them instantly; but Agesilaus, not knowing how far the sedition might reach, bade them forbear, and going himself in his ordinary dress, with but one servant, when he came near the rebels, called out, and told them that they mistook their orders; this was not the right place; they were to go, one part of them thither, showing them another place in the city, and part to another, which he also showed. The conspirators gladly heard this, thinking themselves unsuspected of treason, and readily went off to the places which he showd them. Whereupon Agesilaus placed in their room a guard of his own; and of the conspirators he apprehended fifteen, and put them to death in the night.

But after this a much more dangerous conspiracy was discovered of Spartan citizens, who had privately met in each other's houses, plotting a revolution. These were men whom it was equally dangerous to prosecute publicly according to law and to connive at. Agesilaus took council with the ephors, and put these also to death privately without process; a thing never before known in the case of any born Spartan.

At this time, also, many of the helots and country people, who were in the army, ran away to the enemy, which was a matter of great consternation to the city. He therefore caused some officers of his, every morning before day, to search the quarters of the soldiers, and where any man was gone, to hide his arms, that so the greatness of the number might not appear.

Historians differ about the cause of the Thebans' departure from Sparta. Some say, the winter forced them; as also that the Arcadian soldiers disbanding, made it necessary for the rest to retire. Others say that they stayed there three months, till they had laid the whole country waste. Theopompus is the only author who says that when the Bœotian generals had already resolved upon the retreat, Phrixus, the Spartan, came to them, and offered them from Agesilaus ten talents to be gone, so hiring them to do what they were already doing of their own accord. How he alone should come to be aware of this I know not; only in this all authors agree, that the saving of Sparta from ruin was wholly due to the wisdom of Agesilaus, who in this extremity of affairs quitted all his ambition and his haughtiness, and resolved to play a saving game.

But all his wisdom and courage was not sufficient to recover the glory of it, and to raise it to its ancient greatness. For as we see in human bodies, long used to a very strict and too exquisitely regular diet, any single great disorder is usually fatal; so here one stroke overthrew the whole state's long prosperity. Nor can we be surprised at this. Lycurgus had formed a polity admirably designed for the peace, harmony, and virtuous life of the citizens; and their fall came from their assuming foreign dominion and arbitrary sway, things wholly undesirable, in the judgment of Lycurgus, for a well-conducted and happy state.

Agesilaus being now in years, gave over all military employments; but his son, Archidamus, having received help from Dionysius of Sicily, gave a great defeat to the Arcadians, in the fight known by the name of the Tearless Battle, in which there was a great slaughter of the enemy without the loss of one Spartan.

Yet this victory, more than anything else, discovered the present weakness of Sparta; for heretofore victory was esteemed so usual a thing with them that for their greatest successes they merely sacrificed a cock to the gods. The soldiers never vaunted, nor did the citizens display any great joy at the news; even when the great victory, described by Thucydides, was obtained at Mantinea, the messenger that brought the news had no other reward than a piece of meat, sent by the magistrates from the common table. But at the news of this Arcadian victory they were not able to contain themselves; Agesilaus went out in procession with tears of joy in his eyes to meet and embrace his son, and all the magistrates and public officers attended him. The old men and the women marched out as far as the river Eurotas, lifting up their hands, and thanking the gods that Sparta was now cleared again of the disgrace and indignity that had befallen her, and once more saw the light of day. Since before, they tell us, the Spartan men, out of shame at their disasters, did not dare so much as to look their wives in the face.

When Epaminondas restored Messene, and recalled from all quarters the ancient citizens to inhabit it, they were not able to obstruct the design, being not in condition of appearing in the field against them. But it went greatly against Agesilaus in the minds of his countrymen, when they found so large a territory, equal to their own in compass, and for fertility the richest of all Greece, which they had enjoyed so long, taken from them in his reign. Therefore it was that the king broke off treaty with the Thebans when they offered him peace, rather than set his hand to the passing away of that country, though it was already taken from him. Which point of honour had like to have cost him dear; for not long after he was overreached by a stratagem, which had almost amounted to the loss of Sparta. For when the Mantineans again revolted from Thebes to Sparta, and Epaminondas understood that Agesilaus was come to their assistance with a powerful army, he privately in the night quitted his quarters of Tegea, and, unknown to the Mantineans, passing by Agesilaus, marched toward Sparta, insomuch that he failed very little of taking it empty and unarmed.

Agesilaus had intelligence sent him by Euthynus, the Thespian, as Callisthenes says, but Xenophon says by a Cretan; and immediately despatched a horseman to Lacedæmon to apprise them of it, and to let them know that he was hastening to them. Shortly after his arrival the Thebans crossed the Eurotas. They made an assault upon the town, and were received by Agesilaus with great courage, and with exertions beyond what was to be expected at his years. For he did not now fight with that caution and cunning which he formerly made use of, but put all upon a desperate push; which, though not his usual method, succeeded so well that he rescued the city out of the very hands of Epaminondas, and forced him to retire, and, at the erection of a trophy, was able, in the presence of their wives and children, to declare that the Lacedæmonians had nobly paid their debt to their country, and particularly his son Archidamus, who had that day made himself illustrious, both by his courage and agility of body, rapidly passing about by the short lanes to every endangered point, and everywhere maintaining the town against the enemy with but few to help him.

Isadas, however, the son of Phœbidas, must have been, I think, the admiration of the enemy as well as of his friends. He was a youth of remarkable beauty and stature, in the very flower of the most attractive time of life, when the boy is just rising into the man. He had no arms upon him and scarcely clothes; he had just anointed himself at home, when, upon the alarm, without further awaiting, in that undress, he snatched a spear in one hand a sword in the other, and broke his way through the combatants to the enemies, striking at all he met. He received no wound, whether it were that a special divine care rewarded his valour with an extraordinary protection, or whether his shape being so large and beautiful, and his dress so unusual, they thought him more than a man. The ephors gave him a garland; but as soon as they had done so, they fined him a thousand drachmas for going out to battle unarmed.

A few days after this there was another battle fought near Mantinea, in which Epaminondas, having routed the van of the Lacedæmonians, was eager in the pursuit of them, when Anticrates, the Laconian, wounded him with a spear, says Dioscorides; but the Spartans to this day call the posterity of this Anticrates, swordsmen, because he wounded Epaminondas with a sword. They so dreaded Epaminondas when living, that the slayer of him was embraced and admired by all; they decreed honours and gifts to him, and an exemption from taxes to his posterity, a privilege enjoyed at this day by Callicrates, one of his descendants.

Epaminondas being slain, there was a general peace again concluded, from which Agesilaus's party excluded the Messenians, as men that had no city, and therefore would not let them swear to the league; to which when the rest of the Greeks admitted them, the Lacedæmonians broke off, and continued the war alone, in hopes of subduing the Messenians. In this Agesilaus was esteemed a stubborn and headstrong man, and insatiable of war, who took such pains to undermine the general peace, and to protract the war at a time when he had not money to carry it on with, but was forced to borrow of his friends and raise subscriptions, with much difficulty, while the city, above all things, needed repose. And all this to recover the one poor town of Messene, after he had lost so great an empire both by sea and land, as the Spartans were possessed of, when he began to reign.

But it added still more to his ill-repute when he put himself into the service of Tachos, the Egyptian. They thought it too unworthy of a man of his high station, who was then looked upon as the first commander in all Greece, who had filled all countries with his renown, to let himself out to hire to a barbarian, an Egyptian rebel (for Tachos was no better), and to fight for pay, as captain only of a band of mercenaries. If, they said, at those years of eighty and odd, after his body had been worn out with age, and enfeebled with wounds, he had resumed that noble undertaking, the liberation of the Greeks from Persia, it had been worthy of some reproof. To make an action honourable, it ought to be agreeable to the age and other circumstances of the person; since it is circumstance and proper measure that give an action its character, and make it either good or bad. But Agesilaus valued not other men's discourses; he thought no public employment dishonourable; the ignoblest thing in his esteem was for a man to sit idle and useless at home, waiting for his death to come and take him. The money, therefore, that he received from Tachos, he laid out in raising men, with whom, having filled his ships, he took also thirty Spartan counsellors with him, as formerly he had done in his Asiatic expedition, and set sail for Egypt.

As soon as he arrived in Egypt, all the great officers of the kingdom came to pay their compliments to him at his landing. His reputation, being so great, had raised the expectation of the whole country, and crowds flocked in to see him; but when they found, instead of the splendid prince whom they looked for, a little old man of contemptible appearance, without ceremony lying down upon the grass, in coarse and threadbare clothes, they fell into laughter and scorn of him, crying out that the old proverb was now made good, "The mountain had brought forth a mouse." They were yet more astonished at his stupidity, as they thought it, who, when presents were made

him of all sorts of provisions, took only the meal, the calves, and the geese, but rejected the sweetmeats, the confections, and perfumes; and when they urged him to the acceptance of them, took them and gave them to the helots in his army. Yet he was taken, Theophrastus tells us, with the garlands they made of the papyrus, because of their simplicity, and when he returned home, he demanded one of the king, which he carried with him.

When he joined with Tachos, he found his expectation of being general-in-chief disappointed. Tachos reserved that place for himself, making Agesilaus only captain of the mercenaries, and Chabrias, the Athenian, commander of the fleet. This was the first occasion of his discontent, but there followed others; he was compelled daily to submit to the insolence and vanity of this Egyptian, and was at length forced to attend him into Phœnicia, in a condition much below his character and dignity, which he bore and put up with for a time, till he had opportunity of showing his feelings.

It was afforded him by Nectanabis, the cousin of Tachos, who commanded a large force under him, and shortly after deserted him, and was proclaimed king by the Egyptians. This man invited Agesilaus to join his party, and the like he did to Chabrias, offering great rewards to both. Tachos, suspecting it, immediately applied himself both to Agesilaus and Chabrias, with great humility beseeching their continuance in his friendship. Chabrias consented to it, and did what he could by persuasion and good words to keep Agesilaus with them. But he gave this short reply, "You, O Chabrias, came hither a volunteer, and may go and stay as you see cause; but I am the servant of Sparta, appointed to head the Egyptians, and therefore I cannot fight against those to whom I was sent as a friend, unless I am commanded to do so by my country."

This being said, he despatched messengers to Sparta, who were sufficiently supplied with matter both for dispraise of Tachos and commendation of Nectanabis. The two Egyptians also sent their ambassadors to Lacedæmon, the one to claim continuance of the league already made, the other to make great offers for the breaking of it, and making a new one. The Spartans having heard both sides, gave in their public answer, that they referred the whole matter to Agesilaus; but privately wrote to him to act as he should find it best for the profit of the commonwealth.

Upon receipt of his orders, he at once changed sides, carrying all the mercenaries with him to Nectanabis, covering, with the plausible pretence of acting for the benefit of his country, a most questionable piece of conduct, which, stripped of that disguise, in real truth was no better than downright treachery. But the Lacedæmonians, who make it their first principle of action to serve their country's interest, knew not anything to be just or unjust by any measure but that.

Tachos, being thus deserted by the mercenaries, fled for it; upon which a new king of the Mendesian province was proclaimed his successor, and came against Nectanabis with an army of one hundred thousand men. Nectanabis, in his talk with Agesilaus, professed to despise them as newly raised men, who, though many in number, were of no skill in war, being most of them mechanics and tradesmen, never bred to war. To whom Agesilaus answered, that he did not fear their numbers, but did fear their ignorance, which gave no room for employing stratagem against them. Stratagem only avails with men who are alive to suspicion, and, expecting to be assailed, expose themselves by their attempts at defence; but one who has no thought or expectation of anything, gives as little opportunity to the enemy as he who stands stock-still does to a wrestler.

The Mendesian was not wanting in solicitations of Agesilaus, insomuch that Nectanabis grew jealous. But when Agesilaus advised to fight the enemy at once, saying it was folly to protract the war and rely on time, in a contest with men who had no experience in fighting battles, but with their great numbers might be able to surround them, and cut off their communications by entrenchments, and anticipate them in many matters of advantage, this altogether confirmed him in his fears and suspicions. He took quite the contrary course, and retreated into a large and strongly fortified town. Agesilaus, finding himself mistrusted, took it very ill, and was full of indignation, yet was ashamed to change sides back again, or to go away without effecting anything, so that he was forced to follow Nectanabis into the town.

When the enemy came up, and began to draw lines about the town, and to entrench, the Egyptian now resolved upon a battle out of fear of a siege. And the Greeks were eager for it, provisions growing already scarce in the town. When Agesilaus opposed it, the Egyptians then suspected him much more, publicly calling him the betrayer of the king. But Agesilaus, being now satisfied within himself, bore these reproaches patiently, and followed the design which he had laid, of overreaching the enemy, which was this.

The enemy were forming a deep ditch and high wall, resolving to shut up the garrison and starve it. When the ditch was brought almost quite round and the two ends had all but met, he took the advantage of the night and armed all his Greeks. Then going to the Egyptian, "This, young man, is your opportunity," said he, "of saving yourself, which I all this while durst not announce, lest discovery should prevent it; but now the enemy has, at his own cost, and the pains and labour of his own men, provided for our security. As much of this wall as is built will prevent them from surrounding us with their multitude, the gap yet left will be sufficient for us to sally out by; now play the man, and follow the example the Greeks will give you, and by fighting valiantly save yourself and your army; their front will not be able to stand against us, and their rear we are sufficiently secured from by a wall of their own making."

Nectanabis, admiring the sagacity of Agesilaus, immediately placed himself in the middle of the Greek troops, and fought with them; and upon the first charge soon routed the enemy. Agesilaus having now gained credit with the king, proceeded to use, like a trick in wrestling, the same stratagem over again. He sometimes pretended a retreat, at other times advanced to attack their flanks, and by this means at last drew them into a place enclosed between two ditches that were very deep and full of water. When he had them at this advantage, he soon charged them, drawing up the front of his battle equal to the space between the two ditches, so that they had no way of surrounding him, being enclosed themselves on both sides. They made but little resistance; many fell, others fled and were dispersed.

Nectanabis, being thus settled and fixed in his kingdom, with much kindness and affection invited Agesilaus to spend his winter in Egypt, but he made haste home to assist in wars of his own country, which was, he knew, in want of money, and forced to hire mercenaries, whilst their own men were fighting abroad. The king, therefore, dismissed him very honourably, and among other gifts presented him with two hundred and thirty talents of silver toward the charge of the war.

But the weather being tempestuous, his ships kept inshore, and passing along the coast of Africa he reached an uninhabited spot called the Port of Menelaus, and here, when his ships were just upon landing, he expired, being eighty-four years old, and having reigned in Lacedæmon forty-one. Thirty of which years he passed with the reputation of being the greatest and most powerful man of all Greece, and was looked upon as, in a manner, general and king of it, until the battle of Leuctra. It was the custom of the Spartans to bury their common dead in the place where they died, whatsoever country it was, but their kings they carried home. The followers of Agesilaus, for want of honey, enclosed his body in wax, and so conveyed him to Lacedæmon.

His son, Archidamus, succeeded him on his throne; so did his posterity successively to Agis, the fifth from Agesilaus; who was slain by Leonidas, while attempting to restore the ancient discipline of Sparta.

POMPEY

106–48 B.C.

THE people of Rome seem to have entertained for Pompey from his childhood the same affection that Prometheus, in the tragedy of Æschylus, expresses for Hercules, speaking of him as the author of his deliverance, in these words:—

Ah cruel Sire! how dear thy son to me!
The generous offspring of my enemy!

For on the one hand, never did the Romans give such demonstrations of a vehement and fierce hatred against any of their generals as they did against Strabo, the father of Pompey; during whose lifetime, it is true, they stood in awe of his military power, as indeed he was a formidable warrior, but immediately upon his death, which happened by a stroke of thunder, they treated him with the utmost contumely, dragging his corpse from the bier, as it was carried to his funeral. On the other side, never had any Roman the people's good-will and devotion more zealous throughout all the changes of fortune, more early in its first springing up, or more steadily rising with his prosperity, or more constant in his adversity than Pompey had. In Strabo, there was one great cause of their hatred, his insatiable covetousness; in Pompey, there were many that helped to make him the object of their love; his temperance, his skill and exercise in war, his eloquence of speech, integrity of mind, and affability in conversation and address; insomuch that no man ever asked a favour with less offence, or conferred one with a better grace. When he gave, it was without assumption; when he received, it was with dignity and honour.

In his youth, his countenance pleaded for him, seeming to anticipate his eloquence, and win upon the affections of the people before he spoke. His beauty even in his bloom of youth had something in it at once of gentleness and dignity; and when his prime of manhood came, the majesty and kingliness of his character at once became visible in it. His hair sat somewhat hollow or rising a little; and this, with the languishing motion of his eyes, seemed to form a resemblance in his face, though perhaps more talked of than really apparent, to the statues of the King Alexander. And because many applied that name to him in his youth, Pompey himself did not decline it, insomuch that some called him so in derision. And Lucius Philippus, a man of consular dignity, when he was pleading in favour of him, thought it not unfit to say, that people could not be surprised if Philip was a lover of Alexander.

It is related of Flora, the courtesan, that when she was now pretty old, she took great delight in speaking of her early familiarity with Pompey, and was wont to say that she could never part after being with him without a bite.

She would further tell, that Geminius, a companion of Pompey's, fell in love with her, and made his court with great importunity; and on her refusing, and telling him, however her inclinations were, yet she could not gratify his desires for Pompey's sake, he therefore made his request to Pompey, and Pompey frankly gave his consent, but never afterwards would have any converse with her, notwithstanding that he seemed to have a great passion for her; and Flora, on this occasion, showed none of the levity that might have been expected of her, but languished for some time after under a sickness brought on by grief and desire.

This Flora, we are told, was such a celebrated beauty, that Cæcilius Metellus, when he adorned the temple of Castor and Pollux with paintings and statues, among the rest dedicated hers for her singular beauty.

In his conduct also to the wife of Demetrius, his freed servant (who had great influence with him in his lifetime, and left an estate of four thousand talents), Pompey acted contrary to his usual habits, not quite fairly or generously, fearing lest he should fall under the common censure of being enamoured and charmed with her beauty, which was irresistible, and became famous everywhere. Nevertheless, though he seemed to be so extremely circumspect and cautious, yet even in matters of this nature he could not avoid the calumnies of his enemies, but upon the score of married women, they accused him, as if he had connived at many things, and embezzled the public revenue to gratify their luxury.

Of his easiness of temper and plainness, in what related to eating and drinking, the story is told that, once in a sickness, when his stomach nauseated common meats, his physician prescribed him a thrush to eat; but upon search, there was none to be bought, for they were not then in season, and one telling him they were to be had at Lucullus's, who kept them all the year round, "So then," said he, "if it were not for Lucullus's luxury, Pompey should not live"; and thereupon, not minding the prescription of the physician, he contented himself with such meat as could easily be procured. But this was at a later time.

Being as yet a very young man, and upon an expedition in which his father was commanding against Cinna, he had in his tent with him one Lucius Terentius, as his companion and comrade, who, being corrupted by Cinna, entered into an engagement to kill Pompey, as others had done to set the general's tent on fire. This conspiracy being discovered to Pompey at supper, he showed no discomposure at it, but on the contrary drank more liberally than usual, and expressed great kindness to Terentius; but about bedtime, pretending to go to his repose, he stole away secretly out of the tent, and setting a guard about his father, quietly expected the event. Terentius, when he thought the proper time come, rose with his naked sword, and coming to Pompey's bedside

stabbed several strokes through the bedclothes, as if he were lying there. Immediately after this there was a great uproar throughout all the camp, arising from the hatred they bore to the general, and an universal movement of the soldiers to revolt, all tearing down their tents and betaking themselves to their arms. The general himself all this while durst not venture out because of the tumult; but Pompey, going about in the midst of them, besought them with tears; and at last threw himself prostrate upon his face before the gate of the camp, and lay there in the passage at their feet shedding tears, and bidding those that were marching off, if they would go, trample upon him. Upon which, none could help going back again, and all, except eight hundred, either through shame or compassion, repented, and were reconciled to the general.

Immediately upon the death of Strabo, there was an action commenced against Pompey, as his heir, for that his father had embezzled the public treasure. But Pompey, having traced the principal thefts, charged them upon one Alexander, a freed slave of his father's, and proved before the judges that he had been the appropriator. But he himself was accused of having in his possession some hunting tackle, and books, that were taken at Asculum. To this he confessed thus far, that he received them from his father when he took Asculum, but pleaded further, that he had lost them since, upon Cinna's return to Rome, when his house was broken open and plundered by Cinna's guards.

In this cause he had a great many preparatory pleadings against his accuser, in which he showed an activity and steadfastness beyond his years, and gained great reputation and favour, insomuch that Antistius, the prætor and judge of the cause, took a great liking to him, and offered him his daughter in marriage, having had some communications with his friends about it. Pompey accepted the proposal, and they were privately contracted; however, the secret was not so closely kept as to escape the multitude, but it was discernible enough, from the favour shown him by Antistius in his cause. And at last, when Antistius pronounced the absolutory sentence of the judges, the people, as if it had been upon a signal given, made the acclamation used according to ancient custom at marriages, *Talasio*.

The origin of which custom is related to be this. At the time when the daughters of the

Sabines came to Rome, to see the shows and sports there, and were violently seized upon by the most distinguished and bravest of the Romans for wives, it happened that some goat-swains and herdsmen of the meaner rank were carrying off a beautiful and tall maiden; and lest any of their betters should meet them, and take her away, as they ran, they cried out with one voice, *Talasio,* Talasius being a well-known and popular person among them, insomuch that all that heard the name clapped their hands for joy, and joined with them in the shout, as applauding and congratulating the chance. Now, say they, because this proved a fortunate match to Talasius, hence it is that this acclamation is sportively used as a nuptial cry at all weddings. This is the most credible of the accounts that are given of the Talasio. And some few days after this judgment, Pompey married Antistia.

After this he went to Cinna's camp, where, finding some false suggestions and calumnies prevailing against him, he began to be afraid, and presently withdrew himself secretly; which sudden disappearance occasioned great suspicion. And there went a rumour and speech through all the camp that Cinna had murdered the young man; upon which all that had been anyways disobliged, and bore any malice to him, resolved to make an assault upon him. He, endeavouring to make his escape, was seized by a centurion, who pursued him with his naked sword. Cinna, in this distress, fell upon his knees, and offered him his seal-ring, of great value, for his ransom; but the centurion repulsed him insolently, saying, "I did not come to seal a covenant, but to be revenged upon a lawless and wicked tyrant"; and so despatched him immediately.

Thus Cinna being slain, Carbo, a tyrant yet more senseless than he, took the command and exercised it, while Sulla meantime was approaching, much to the joy and satisfaction of most people, who in their present evils were ready to find some comfort if it were but in the exchange of a master. For the city was brought to that pass by oppression and calamities that, being utterly in despair of liberty, men were only anxious for the mildest and most tolerable bondage.

At that time Pompey was in Picenum in Italy, where he spent some time amusing himself, as he had estates in the country there, though the chief motive of his stay was the liking he felt for the towns of that district, which all regarded him with hereditary feel-

ings of kindness and attachment. But when he now saw that the noblest and best of the city began to forsake their homes and property, and fly from all quarters to Sulla's camp, as to their haven, he likewise was desirous to go; not, however, as a fugitive, alone and with nothing to offer, but as a friend rather than a suppliant, in a way that would gain him honour, bringing help along with him, and at the head of a body of troops. Accordingly he solicited the Picentines for their assistance, who as cordially embraced his motion, and rejected the messengers sent from Carbo; insomuch that a certain Vindius taking upon him to say that Pompey was come from the school-room to put himself at the head of the people, they were so incensed that they fell forthwith upon this Vindius and killed him.

From henceforward, Pompey, finding a spirit of government upon him, though not above twenty-three years of age, nor deriving an authority by commission from any man, took the privilege to grant himself full power, and, causing a tribunal to be erected in the market-place of Auximum, a populous city, expelled two of their principal men, brothers, of the name of Ventidius, who were acting against him in Carbo's interest, commanding them by a public edict to depart the city; and then proceeded to levy soldiers, issuing out commissions to centurions and other officers, according to the form of military discipline. And in this manner he went round all the rest of the cities in the district.

So that those of Carbo's faction flying, and all others cheerfully submitting to his command, in a little time he mustered three entire legions, having supplied himself besides with all manner of provisions, beasts of burden, carriages, and other necessaries of war. And with this equipage he set forward on his march toward Sulla, not as if he were in haste, or desirous of escaping observation, but by small journeys, making several halts upon the road, to distress and annoy the enemy, and exerting himself to detach from Carbo's interest every part of Italy that he passed through.

Three commanders of the enemy encountered him at once, Carinna, Clœlius, and Brutus, and drew up their forces, not all in the front, nor yet together on any one part, but encamping three several armies in a circle about him, they resolved to encompass and overpower him. Pompey was noway alarmed at this, but collecting all his troops into one body, and placing his horse in the front of the battle, where he himself was in person, he singled out and bent all his forces against Brutus, and when the Celtic horsemen from the enemy's side rode out to meet him, Pompey himself encountering hand to hand with the foremost and stoutest among them, killed him with his spear. The rest seeing this turned their backs and fled, and breaking the ranks of their own foot, presently caused a general rout; whereupon the commanders fell out among themselves, and marched off, some one way, some another, as their fortunes led them, and the towns round about came in and surrendered themselves to Pompey, concluding that the enemy was dispersed for fear.

Next after these, Scipio, the consul, came to attack him, and with as little success; for before the armies could join, or be within the throw of their javelins, Scipio's soldiers saluted Pompey's, and came over to them, while Scipio made his escape by flight.

Last of all, Carbo himself sent down several troops of horse against him by the river Arsis, which Pompey assailed with the same courage and success as before; and having routed and put them to flight, he forced them in the pursuit into difficult ground, unpassable for horse, where, seeing no hopes of escape, they yielded themselves with their horses and armour, all to his mercy.

Sulla was hitherto unacquainted with all these actions; and on the first intelligence he received of his movements was in great anxiety about him, fearing lest he should be cut off among so many and such experienced commanders of the enemy, and marched therefore with all speed to his aid. Now Pompey, having advice of his approach, sent out orders to his officers to marshal and draw up all his forces in full array, that they might make the finest and noblest appearance before the commander-in-chief; for he expected indeed great honours from him, but met with even greater.

For as soon as Sulla saw him thus advancing, his army so well appointed, his men so young and strong, and their spirits so high and hopeful with their successes, he alighted from his horse, and being first, as was his due, saluted by them with the title of Imperator, he returned the salutation upon Pompey, in the same term and style of Imperator, which might well cause surprise, as none could have ever anticipated that he would have imparted, to one so young in years and not yet a senator, a title which was the object of contention between him and the Scipios and Marii. And indeed all the rest of his deportment was agreeable to this first compliment; whenever Pompey came into his presence, he paid some sort of respect to him, either in rising and being uncovered, or the like, which he was rarely seen to do with any one else, notwithstanding that there were many about him of great rank and honour.

Yet Pompey was not puffed up at all, or exalted with these favours. And when Sulla would have sent him with all expedition into Gaul, a province in which it was thought Metellus, who commanded in it, had done nothing worthy of the large forces at his disposal, Pompey urged that it could not be fair or honourable for him to take a province out of the hands of his senior in command and his superior in reputation; however, if Metellus were willing, and should request his service, he should be very ready to accompany and assist him in the war, which when Metellus came to understand, he approved of the proposal, and invited him over by letter. On this Pompey fell immediately into Gaul, where he not only achieved wonderful exploits of himself, but also fired up and kindled again that bold and warlike spirit, which old age had in a manner extinguished in Metellus, into a new heat; just as molten copper, they say, when poured upon that which is cold and solid, will dissolve and melt it faster than fire itself.

But as when a famous wrestler has gained the first place among men, and borne away the prizes at all the games, it is not usual to take account of his victories as a boy, or to enter them upon record among the rest; so with the exploits of Pompey in his youth, though they were extraordinary in themselves, yet because they were obscured and buried in the multitude and greatness of his later wars and conquests, I dare not be particular in them, lest, by trifling away time in the lesser moments of his youth, we should be driven to omit those greater actions and fortunes which best illustrate his character.

Now, when Sulla had brought all Italy under his dominion, and was proclaimed dictator, he began to reward the rest of his followers, by giving them wealth, appointing them to offices in the state, and granting them freely and without restriction any favours they asked for. But as for Pompey, admiring his valour and conduct, and thinking that he might prove a great stay and support to him hereafter in his affairs, he sought means to attach him to himself by some personal alliance, and his wife Metella joining in his wishes, they two persuaded Pompey to put away Antistia, and marry Æmilia, the step-daughter of Sulla, born by Metella to Scaurus, her former husband, she being at that very time the wife of another man, living with him, and with child by him.

These were the very tyrannies of marriage, and much more agreeable to the times under Sulla than to the nature and habits of Pompey; that Æmilia great with child should be, as it were, ravished from the embraces of another for him, and that Antistia should be divorced with dishonour and misery by him, for whose sake she had been but just before bereft of her father. For Antistius was murdered in the senate, because he was suspected to be a favourer of Sulla for Pompey's sake; and her mother, likewise, after she had seen all these indignities, made away with herself, a new calamity to be added to the tragic accompaniments of this marriage, and that there might be nothing wanting to complete them, Æmilia herself died, almost immediately after entering Pompey's house, in childbed.

About this time news came to Sulla that Perpenna was fortifying himself in Sicily, that the island was now become a refuge and receptacle for the relics of the adverse party, that Carbo was hovering about those seas with a navy, that Domitius had fallen in upon Africa, and that many of the exiled men of note who had escaped from the proscriptions were daily flocking into those parts. Against these, therefore, Pompey was sent with a large force; and no sooner was he arrived in Sicily, but Perpenna immediately departed, leaving the whole island to him.

Pompey received the distressed cities into favour, and treated all with great humanity, except the Mamertines in Messena; for when they protested against his court and jurisdiction, alleging their privilege and exemption founded upon an ancient charter or grant of the Romans, he replied sharply, "What! will you never cease prating of laws to us that have swords by our sides?"

It was thought, likewise, that he showed some inhumanity to Carbo, seeming rather to insult over his misfortunes than to chastise his crimes. For if there had been a necessity, as perhaps there was, that he should be taken off, that might have been done at first, as soon as he was taken prisoner, for then it would have been the act of him that commanded it. But here Pompey commanded a man that had been thrice consul of Rome to be brought in fetters to stand at the bar, he himself sitting upon the bench in judgment, examining the cause with the formalities of law, to the offence and indignation of all that were present, and afterwards ordered him to be taken away and put to death. It is related, by the way, of Carbo, that as soon as he was brought to the place, and saw the sword drawn for execution, he was suddenly seized with a looseness or pain in his bowels, and desired a little respite of the executioner, and a convenient place to relieve himself.

And yet further, Caius Oppius, the friend of Cæsar, tells us that Pompey dealt cruelly with Quintus Valerius, a man of singular learning and science. For when he was brought to him, he walked aside, and drew him into conversation, and after putting a variety of questions to him, and receiving answers from him, he ordered his officers to take him away and put him to death. But we must not be too credulous in the case of narratives told by Oppius, especially when he undertakes to relate anything touching the friends or foes of Cæsar.

This is certain, that there lay a necessity upon Pompey to be severe upon many of Sulla's enemies, those at least that were eminent persons in themselves, and notoriously known to be taken; but for the rest, he acted with all the clemency possible for him, conniving at the concealment of some, and himself being the instrument in the escape of others.

So in the case of the Himeræans; for when Pompey had determined on severely punishing their city, as they had been abettors of the enemy, Sthenis, the leader of the people there, craving liberty of speech, told him that what he was about to do was not at all consistent with justice, for that he would pass by the guilty and destroy the innocent; and on Pompey demanding who that guilty person was that would assume the offences of them all, Sthenis replied it was himself, who had engaged his friends by persuasion to what they had done, and his enemies by force; whereupon Pompey, being much taken with the frank speech and noble spirit of the man, first forgave his crime, and then pardoned all the rest of the Himeræ-ans.

Hearing, likewise, that his soldiers were very disorderly in their march, doing violence upon the roads, he ordered their swords to be sealed up in their scabbards, and whosoever kept them not so were severely punished.

Whilst Pompey was thus busy in the affairs and government of Sicily, he received a decree of the senate, and a commission from Sulla, commanding him forthwith to sail into Africa, and make war upon Domitius with all his forces: for Domitius had rallied up a far greater army than Marius had had not long since, when he sailed out of Africa into Italy, and caused a revolution in Rome, and himself, from a fugitive outlaw, became a tyrant. Pompey, therefore, having prepared everything with the utmost speed, left Memmius, his sister's husband, governor of Sicily, and set sail with one hundred and twenty galleys, and eight hundred other vessels laden with provisions, money, ammunition, and engines of battery. He arrived with his fleet, part at the port of Utica, part at Carthage; and no sooner was he landed, but seven thousand of the enemy revolted and came over to him, while his own forces that he brought with him consisted of six entire legions. Here they tell us of a pleasant incident that happened to him at his first arrival.

Some of his soldiers having by accident stumbled upon a treasure, by which they got a good sum of money, the rest of the army hearing this, began to fancy that the field was full of gold and silver, which had been hid there of old by the Carthaginians in the time of their calamities, and thereupon fell to work, so that the army was useless to Pompey for many days, being totally engaged in digging for the fancied treasure, he himself all the while walking up and down only, and laughing to see so many thousands together, digging and turning up the earth. Until at last, growing weary and hopeless, they came to themselves and returned to their general, begging him to lead them where he pleased, for that they had already received the punishment of their folly.

By this time Domitius had prepared himself and drawn out his army in array against Pompey; but there was a watercourse betwixt them, craggy, and difficult to pass over; and this, together with a great storm of wind and rain pouring down even from break of day, seemed to leave but little possibility of their coming together; so that Domitius, not expecting any engagement that day, commanded his forces to draw off and retire to the camp. Now Pompey, who was watchful upon every occasion, making use of the opportunity, ordered a march forthwith, and having passed over the torrent, fell in immediately upon their quarters. The enemy was in great disorder and tumult, and in that confusion attempted a resistance; but they neither were all there, nor supported one another; besides, the wind having veered about beat the rain full in their faces.

Neither indeed was the storm less troublesome to the Romans, for that they could not clearly discern one another, insomuch that even Pompey himself, being unknown, escaped narrowly; for when one of his soldiers demanded of him the word of battle, it happened that he was somewhat slow in his answer, which might have cost him his life.

The enemy being routed with a great slaughter (for it is said that of twenty thousand there escaped but three thousand), the army saluted Pompey by the name of Imperator; but he declined it, telling them that he could not by any means accept of that title as long as he saw the camp of the enemy standing; but if they designed to make him worthy of the honour, they must first demolish that. The soldiers on hearing this went at once and made an assault upon the works and trenches, and there Pompey fought without his helmet, in memory of his former danger, and to avoid the like. The camp was thus taken by storm, and among the rest Domitius was slain. After that overthrow, the cities of the country thereabouts were all either secured by surrender, or taken by storm. King Iarbas, likewise, a confederate and auxiliary of Domitius, was taken prisoner, and his kingdom was given to Hiempsal.

Pompey could not rest here, but being ambitious to follow the good fortune and use the valour of his army, entered Numidia; and marching forward many days' journey up into the country, he conquered all wherever he came. And having revived the terror of the Roman power, which was now almost obliterated among the barbarous nations, he said likewise, that the wild beasts of Africa ought not to be left without some experience of the courage and success of the Romans, and therefore he bestowed some few days in hunting lions and elephants. And it is said that it was not above the space of forty days at the utmost in which he gave a total overthrow to the enemy, reduced Africa, and established the affairs of the kings and kingdoms of all that country, being then in the twenty-fourth year of his age.

When Pompey returned back to the city of Utica, there were presented to him letters and orders from Sulla, commanding him to disband the rest of his army, and himself with one legion only to wait there the coming of another general, to succeed him in the government. This, inwardly, was extremely grievous to Pompey, though he made no show of it. But the army resented it openly, and when Pompey besought them to depart and go home before him, they began to revile Sulla, and declared broadly that they were resolved not to forsake him, neither did they think it safe for him to trust the tyrant.

Pompey at first endeavoured to appease and pacify them by fair speeches; but when he saw that his persuasions were vain, he left the bench, and retired to his tent with tears in his eyes. But the soldiers followed him, and seizing upon him, by force brought him again, and placed him in his tribunal; where great part of that day was spent in dispute, they on their part persuading him to stay and command them, he, on the other side, pressing upon them obedience and the danger of mutiny. At last, when they grew yet more importunate and clamorous, he swore that he would kill himself if they attempted to force him; and scarcely even thus appeased them.

Nevertheless, the first tidings brought to Sulla were that Pompey was up in rebellion; on which he remarked to some of his friends, "I see, then, it is my destiny to contend with children in my old age"; alluding at the same time to Marius, who, being but a mere youth, had given him great trouble, and brought him into extreme danger. But being undeceived afterwards by better intelligence, and finding the whole city prepared to meet Pompey, and receive him with every display of kindness and honour, he resolved to exceed them all. And, therefore, going out foremost to meet him and embracing him with great cordiality, he gave him his welcome aloud in the title of Magnus, or the Great, and bade all that were present call him by that name.

Others say that he had this title first given him by a general acclamation of all the army in Africa, but that it was fixed upon him by this ratification of Sulla. It is certain that he himself was the last that owned the title; for it was a long time after, when he was sent proconsul into Spain against Sertorius, that he began to write himself in his letters and commissions by the name of Pompeius Magnus; common and familiar use having then worn off the invidiousness of the title.

And one cannot but accord respect and admiration to the ancient Romans, who did not reward the successes of action and conduct in war alone with such honourable titles, but adorned likewise the virtue and services of eminent men in civil government with the same distinctions and marks of honour. Two persons received from the people the name of Maximus, or the Greatest, Valerius for reconciling the senate and people, and Fabius Rullus, because he put out of the senate certain sons of freed slaves who had been admitted into it because of their wealth.

Pompey now desired the honour of a triumph, which Sulla opposed, alleging that the law allowed that honour to none but consuls and prætors, and therefore Scipio the elder, who subdued the Carthaginians in Spain in far greater and nobler conflicts, never petitioned for a triumph, because he had never been consul or prætor; and if Pompey, who had scarcely yet fully grown a beard, and was not of age to be a senator, should enter the city in triumph, what a weight of envy would it bring, he said, at once upon his government and Pompey's honour. This was his language to Pompey, intimating that he could not by any means yield to his request, but if he would persist in his ambition, that he was resolved to interpose his power to humble him.

Pompey, however, was not daunted; but bade Sulla recollect that more worshipped the rising than the setting sun; as if to tell him that his power was increasing and Sulla's on the wane. Sulla did not perfectly hear the words, but observing a sort of amazement and wonder in the looks and gestures of those that did hear them, he asked what it was that he said.

When it was told him, he seemed astounded at Pompey's boldness, and cried out twice together, "Let him triumph," and when others began to show their disapprobation and offence at it, Pompey, it is said, to gall and vex them the more, designed to have his triumphant chariot drawn with four elephants (having brought over several which belonged to the African kings), but the gates of the city being too narrow, he was forced to desist from that project, and be content with horses.

And when his soldiers, who had not received as large rewards as they had expected, began to clamour, and interrupt the triumph, Pompey regarded these as little as the rest, and plainly told them that he had rather lose the honour of his triumph than flatter them. Upon which Servilius, a man of great distinction, and at first one of the chief opposers of Pompey's triumph, said he now perceived that Pompey was truly great and worthy of a triumph.

It is clear that he might easily have been a senator, also, if he had wished, but he did not sue for that, being ambitious, it seems, only of unusual honours. For what wonder had it been for Pompey to sit in the senate before his time? But to triumph before he was in the senate was really an excess of glory.

And, moreover, it did not a little ingratiate him with the people, who were much pleased to see him after his triumph take his place again among the Roman knights. On the other side, it was no less distasteful to Sulla to see how fast he came on, and to what a height of glory and power he was advancing; yet being ashamed to hinder him, he kept quiet.

But when, against his direct wishes, Pompey got Lepidus made consul, having openly joined in the canvass and, by the good-will the people felt for himself, conciliated their favour for Lepidus, Sulla could forbear no longer; but when he saw him coming away from the election through the Forum with a great train after him, cried out to him, "Well, young man, I see you rejoice in your victory. And, indeed, is it not a most generous and worthy act, that the consulship should be given to Lepidus, the vilest of men, in preference to Catulus, the best and most deserving in the city, and all by your influence with the people? It will be well, however, for you to be wakeful and look to your interests; as you have been making your enemy stronger than yourself."

But that which gave the clearest demonstration of Sulla's ill-will to Pompey was his last will and testament; for whereas he had bequeathed several legacies to all the rest of his friends, and appointed some of them guardians to his son, he passed by Pompey without the least remembrance. However, Pompey bore this with great moderation and temper; and when Lepidus and others were disposed to obstruct his interment in the Campus Martius, and to prevent any public funeral taking place, came forward in support of it, and saw his obsequies performed with all honour and security.

Shortly after the death of Sulla, his prophetic words were fulfilled; and Lepidus proposing to be the successor to all his power and authority, without any ambiguities or pretences, immediately appeared in arms, rousing once more and gathering about him all the long dangerous remains of the old factions, which had escaped the hand of Sulla.

Catulus, his colleague, who was followed by the sounder part of the senate and people, was a man of the greatest esteem among the Romans for wisdom and justice; but his talent lay in the government of the city rather than the camp, whereas the exigency required the skill of Pompey. Pompey, therefore, was not long

in suspense which way to dispose of himself, but joining with the nobility, was presently appointed general of the army against Lepidus, who had already raised up war in great part of Italy, and held Cisalpine Gaul in subjection with an army under Brutus. As for the rest of his garrisons, Pompey subdued them with ease in his march, but Mutina in Gaul resisted in a formal siege, and he lay here a long time encamped against Brutus.

In the meantime Lepidus marched in all haste against Rome, and sitting down before it with a crowd of followers, to the terror of those within, demanded a second consulship. But that fear quickly vanished upon letters sent from Pompey, announcing that he had ended the war without a battle; for Brutus, either betraying his army, or being betrayed by their revolt, surrendered himself to Pompey, and receiving a guard of horse, was conducted to a little town upon the river Po, where he was slain the next day by Geminius, in execution of Pompey's commands. And for this Pompey was much censured; for, having at the beginning of the revolt written to the senate that Brutus had voluntarily surrendered himself, immediately afterward he sent other letters, with matter of accusation against the man after he was taken off. Brutus, who, with Cassius, slew Cæsar, was son to this Brutus; neither in war nor in his death like his father, as appears at large in his life. Lepidus, upon his being driven out of Italy, fled to Sardinia, where he fell sick and died of sorrow, not for his public misfortunes, as they say, but upon the discovery of a letter proving his wife to have been unfaithful to him.

There yet remained Sertorius, a very different general from Lepidus, in possession of Spain, and making himself formidable to Rome; the final disease, as it were, in which the scattered evils of the civil wars had now collected. He had already cut off various inferior commanders, and was at this time coping with Metellus Pius, a man of repute and a good soldier, though perhaps he might now seem too slow, by reason of his age, to second and improve the happier moments of war, and might be sometimes wanting to those advantages which Sertorius, by his quickness and dexterity, would wrest out of his hands. For Sertorius was always hovering about, and coming upon him unawares, like a captain of thieves rather than soldiers, disturbing him perpetually with ambuscades and light skirmishes; whereas Metellus was accustomed to regular conduct, and fighting in battle array with full-armed soldiers.

Pompey, therefore, keeping his army in readiness, made it his object to be sent in aid to Metellus; neither would he be induced to disband his forces, notwithstanding that Catulus called upon him to do so, but by some colourable device or other he still kept them in arms about the city, until the senate at last thought fit, upon the report of Lucius Philippus, to decree him that government. At that time, they say, one of the senators there expressing his wonder and demanding of Philippus whether his meaning was that Pompey should be sent into Spain as pro-consul, "No," replied Philippus, "but as pro-*consuls*," as if both consuls for that year were in his opinion wholly useless.

When Pompey was arrived in Spain, as is usual upon the fame of a new leader, men began to be inspired with new hopes, and those nations that had not entered into a very strict alliance with Sertorius began to waver and revolt; whereupon Sertorius uttered various arrogant and scornful speeches against Pompey, saying, in derision, that he should want no other weapon but a ferula and rod to chastise this boy with, if he were not afraid of that old woman, meaning Metellus. Yet in deed and reality he stood in awe of Pompey, and kept on his guard against him, as appeared by his whole management of the war, which he was observed to conduct much more warily than before: for Metellus, which one would not have imagined, was grown excessively luxurious in his habits, having given himself over to self-indulgence and pleasure, and from a moderate and temperate became suddenly a sumptuous and ostentatious liver, so that this very thing gained Pompey great reputation and good-will, as he made himself somewhat specially an example of frugality, although that virtue was habitual in him, and required no great industry to exercise it, as he was naturally inclined to temperance, and no ways inordinate in his desires.

The fortune of the war was very various; nothing, however, annoyed Pompey so much as the taking of the town of Lauron by Sertorius. For when Pompey thought he had him safe enclosed, and had boasted somewhat largely of raising the siege, he found himself all of a sudden encompassed; insomuch that he durst not move out of his camp; but was forced to sit still whilst the city was taken and burnt before his face. However, afterwards, in a battle near Valentia, he gave a great defeat to Herennius and Perpenna, two commanders among the refugees who had fled to Sertorius and now lieutenants under him, in which he slew above ten thousand men.

Pompey, being elated and filled with confidence by this victory, made all haste to engage Sertorius himself, and the rather lest Metellus should come in for a share in the honour of the victory. Late in the day towards sunset they joined battle near the river Sucro, both being in fear lest Metellus should come: Pompey, that he might engage alone, Sertorius, that he might have one alone to engage with.

The issue of the battle proved doubtful, for a wing of each side had the better, but of the generals Sertorius had the greater honour, for that he maintained his post, having put to flight the entire division that was opposed to him, whereas Pompey was himself almost made a prisoner; for being set upon by a strong man-at-arms that fought on foot (he being on horseback), as they were closely engaged hand to hand the strokes of their swords chanced to light upon their hands, but with a different success; for Pompey's was a slight wound only, whereas he cut off the other's hand. However, it so happened, that many now falling upon Pompey together, and his own forces there being put to the rout, he made his escape beyond expectation, by quitting his horse, and turning him out among the enemy. For the horse being richly adorned with golden trappings, and having a caparison of great value, the soldiers quarrelled among themselves for the booty, so that while they were fighting with one another, and dividing the spoil, Pompey made his escape.

By break of day the next morning each drew out his forces into the field to claim the victory; but Metellus coming up, Sertorius vanished, having broken up and dispersed his army. For this was the way in which he used to raise and disband his armies, so that sometimes he would be wandering up and down all alone, and at other times again he would come pouring into the field at the head of no less than one hundred and fifty thousand fighting men, swelling of a sudden like a winter torrent.

When Pompey was going, after the battle, to meet and welcome Metellus, and when they were near one another, he commanded his attendants to lower their rods in honour of Metellus, as his senior and superior. But Metellus on the other side forbade it, and behaved himself in general very obligingly to him, not claiming any prerogative either in respect of his consular rank or seniority; excepting only that when they encamped together, the watch-word was given to the whole camp by Metellus. But generally they had their camps asunder, being divided and distracted by the enemy, who took all shapes, and being always in motion, would by some skilful artifice appear in a variety of places almost in the same instant, drawing them from one attack to another. And at last keeping them from foraging, wasting the country, and holding the dominion of the sea, Sertorius drove them both out of that part of Spain which was under his control, and forced them, for want of necessaries, to retreat into provinces that did not belong to them.

Pompey, having made use of and expended the greatest part of his own private revenues upon the war, sent and demanded moneys of the senate, adding that, in case they did not furnish him speedily, he should be forced to return into Italy with his army. Lucullus being consul at that time, though at variance with Pompey, yet in consideration that he himself was a candidate for the command against Mithridates, procured and hastened these supplies, fearing lest there should be any pretence or occasion given to Pompey of returning home, who of himself was no less desirous of leaving Sertorius and of undertaking the war against Mithridates, as an enterprise which by all appearance would prove much more honorable and not so dangerous.

In the meantime, Sertorius died, being treacherously murdered by some of his own party; and Perpenna, the chief among them, took the command and attempted to carry on the same enterprises as Sertorius, having indeed the same forces and the same means, only wanting the same skill and conduct in the use of them. Pompey, therefore, marched directly against Perpenna, and finding him acting merely at random in his affairs, had a decoy ready for him, and sent out a detachment of ten cohorts into the level country with orders to range up and down and disperse themselves abroad. The bait took accordingly, and no sooner had Perpenna turned upon the prey and had them in chase, but Pompey appeared suddenly with all his army, and joining battle, gave him a total overthrow. Most of his officers were slain in the field, and he himself being brought prisoner to Pompey, was by his order put to death.

Neither was Pompey guilty in this of ingratitude or unmindfulness of what had occurred in Sicily, which some have laid to his charge, but was guided by a high-minded policy and a deliberate counsel for the security of his country. For Perpenna, having in his custody all Sertorius's papers, offered to produce several letters from the greatest men in Rome, who, desirous of a change and subversion of the government, had invited Sertorius into Italy. And Pompey, fearing that these might be the occasion of worse wars than those which were now ended, thought it advisable to put Perpenna to death, and burnt the letters without reading them.

Pompey continued in Spain after this so long a time as was necessary for the suppression of all the greatest disorders in the province; and after moderating and allaying the more violent heats of affairs there, returned with his army into Italy, where he arrived, as chance would have it, in the height of the servile war. Accordingly, upon his arrival, Crassus, the commander in that war, at some hazard, precipitated a battle, in which he had great success, and slew upon the place twelve thousand three hundred of the insurgents. Nor yet was he so quick, but that fortune reserved to Pompey some share of honour in the success of this war, for five thousand of those that had escaped out of the battle fell into his hands; and when he had totally cut them off, he wrote to the senate that Crassus had overthrown the slaves in battle, but that he had plucked up the whole war by the roots. And it was agreeable in Rome both thus to say, and thus to hear said, because of the general favour of Pompey.

But of the Spanish war and the conquest of Sertorius, no one, even in jest, could have ascribed the honour to any one else. Nevertheless, all this high respect for him, and this desire to see him come home, were not unmixed with apprehensions and suspicions that he might perhaps not disband his army, but take his way by force of arms and a supreme command to the seat of Sulla. And so in the number of all those that ran out to meet him and congratulate his return, as many went out of fear as affection.

But after Pompey had removed this alarm, by declaring beforehand that he would discharge the army after his triumph, those that envied him could now only complain that he affected popularity, courting the common people more than the nobility, and that whereas Sulla had abolished the tribuneship of the people, he designed to gratify the people by restoring that office, which was indeed the fact. For there was not any one thing that the people of Rome were more wildly eager for, or more passionately desired, than the restoration of that office, insomuch that Pompey thought himself extremely fortunate in this opportunity, despairing (if he were anticipated by some one else in this) of ever meeting with any other sufficient means of expressing his gratitude for the favours which he had received from the people.

Though a second triumph was decreed him, and he was declared consul, yet all these honours did not seem so great an evidence of his power and glory as the ascendant which he had over Crassus; for he, the wealthiest among all the statesmen of his time, and the most eloquent and greatest too, who had looked down on Pompey himself and on all others beneath him, durst not appear a candidate for the consulship before he had applied to Pompey. The request was made accordingly, and was eagerly embraced by Pompey, who had long sought an occasion to oblige him in some friendly office; so that he solicited for Crassus, and entreated the people heartily, declaring that their favour would be no less to him in choosing Crassus his colleague, than in making himself consul.

Yet for all this, when they were created consuls, they were always at variance, and opposing one another. Crassus prevailed most in the senate, and Pompey's power was no less with the people, he having restored to them the office of tribune, and having allowed the courts of judicature to be transferred back to the knights by a new law.

He himself in person, too, afforded them a most grateful spectacle, when he appeared and craved his discharge from the military service. For it is an ancient custom among the Romans that the knights, when they had served out their legal time in the wars, should lead their horses into the market-place before the two officers, called censors, and having given an account of the commanders and generals under whom they served, as also of the places and actions of their service, should be discharged, every man with honour or disgrace, according to his deserts.

There were then sitting in state upon the bench two censors, Gellius and Lentulus, inspecting the knights, who were passing by in muster before them, when Pompey was seen coming down into the Forum, with all the ensigns of a consul, but leading his horse in his hand. When he came up, he bade his lictors make way for him, and so he led his horse to the bench; the people being all this while in a sort of a maze, and all in silence, and the censors themselves regarding the sight with a mixture of respect and gratification.

Then the senior censor examined him: "Pompeius Magnus, I demand of you whether you have served the full time in the wars that is prescribed by the law?" "Yes," replied Pompey, with a loud voice, "I have served all, and all under myself as general." The people hearing this gave a great shout, and made such an outcry for delight, that there was no appeasing it; and the censors rising from their judgment-seat accompanied him home to gratify the multitude who followed after, clapping their hands and shouting.

Pompey's consulship was now expiring, and yet his difference with Crassus increasing, when one Caius Aurelius, a knight, a man who had declined public business all his lifetime, mounted the hustings, and addressed himself in an oration to the assembly, declaring that Jupiter had appeared to him in a dream, commanding him to tell the consuls that they should not give up office until they were friends. After this was said, Pompey stood silent, but Crassus took him by the hand, and spoke in this manner: "I do not think, fellow-citizens, that I shall do anything mean or dishonourable in yielding first to Pompey, whom you were pleased to ennoble with the title of Great, when as yet he scarce had a hair on his face; and granted the honour of two triumphs before he had a place in the senate." Hereupon they were reconciled and laid down their office.

Crassus resumed the manner of life which he had always pursued before; but Pompey in the great generality of causes for judgment declined appearing on either side, and by degrees withdrew himself totally from the Forum, showing himself but seldom in public; and, whenever he did, it was with a great train after him. Neither was it easy to meet or visit him without a crowd of people about him; he was most pleased to make his appearance before large numbers at once, as though he wished to maintain in this way his state and majesty, and as if he held himself bound to preserve his dignity from contact with the addresses and conversation of common people.

And life in the robe of peace is only too apt to lower the reputation of men that have grown great by arms, who naturally find difficulty in adapting themselves to the habits of civil equality. They expect to be treated as the first in the city, even as they were in the camp; and on the other hand, men who in war were nobody think it intolerable if in the city at any rate they are not to take the lead. And so when a warrior renowned for victories and triumphs shall turn advocate and appear among them in the Forum, they endeavour their utmost to obscure and depress him; whereas, if he gives up any pretensions here and retires, they will maintain his military honour and authority beyond the reach of envy. Events themselves not long after showed the truth of this.

The power of the pirates first commenced in Cilicia, having in truth but a precarious and obscure beginning, but gained life and boldness afterwards in the wars of Mithridates, where they hired themselves out and took employment in the king's service. Afterwards, whilst the Romans were embroiled in their civil wars, being engaged against one another even before the very gates of Rome, the seas lay waste and unguarded, and by degrees enticed and drew them on not only to seize upon and spoil the merchants and ships upon the seas, but also to lay waste the islands and seaport towns. So that now there embarked with these pirates men of wealth and noble birth and superior abilities, as if it had been a natural occupation to gain distinction in. They had divers arsenals, or piratic harbours, as likewise watch-towers and beacons, all along the sea-coast; and fleets were here received that were well manned with the finest mariners, and well served with the expertest pilots, and composed of swift-sailing and light-built vessels adapted for their special purpose. Nor was it merely their being thus formidable that excited indignation; they were even more odious for their ostentation than they were feared for their force. Their ships had gilded masts at their stems; the sails woven of purple, and the oars plated with silver, as if their delight were to glory in their iniquity. There was nothing but music and dancing, banqueting and revels, all along the shore. Officers in command were taken prisoners, and cities put under contribution, to the reproach and dishonour of the Roman supremacy.

There were of these corsairs above one thousand sail, and they had taken no less than four hundred cities, committing sacrilege upon the temples of the gods, and enriching themselves with the spoils of many never violated before, such as were those of Claros, Didyma, and Samothrace; and the temple of the Earth in Hermione, and that of Æsculapius in Epidau-

rus, those of Neptune at the Isthmus, at Tænarus, and at Calauria; those of Apollo at Actium and Leucas, and those of Juno in Samos, at Argos, and at Lacinium. They themselves offered strange sacrifices upon Mount Olympus, and performed certain secret rites or religious mysteries, among which those of Mithras have been preserved to our own time, having received their previous institution from them.

But besides these insolencies by sea, they were also injurious to the Romans by land; for they would often go inland up the roads, plundering and destroying their villages and country-houses. Once they seized upon two Roman prætors, Sextilius and Bellinus, in their purple-edged robes, and carried them off together with their officers and lictors. The daughter also of Antonius, a man that had had the honour of a triumph, taking a journey into the country, was seized, and redeemed upon payment of a large ransom.

But it was most abusive of all that, when any of the captives declared himself to be a Roman, and told his name, they affected to be surprised, and feigning fear, smote their thighs and fell down at his feet, humbly beseeching him to be gracious and forgive them. The captives, seeing them so humble and suppliant, believed them to be in earnest; and some of them now would proceed to put Roman shoes on his feet, and to dress him in a Roman gown, to prevent, they said, his being mistaken another time. After all this pageantry, when they had thus deluded and mocked him long enough, at last putting out a ship's ladder, when they were in the midst of the sea, they told him he was free to go, and wished him a pleasant journey; and if he resisted they themselves threw him overboard and drowned him.

This piratic power having got the dominion and control of all the Mediterranean, there was left no place for navigation or commerce. And this it was which most of all made the Romans, finding themselves to be extremely straitened in their markets, and considering that if it should continue, there would be a dearth and famine in the land, determine at last to send out Pompey to recover the seas from the pirates.

Gabinius, one of Pompey's friends, preferred a law, whereby there was granted to him, not only the government of the seas as admiral, but, in direct words, sole and irresponsible sovereignty over all men. For the decree gave him absolute power and authority in all the seas within the pillars of Hercules, and in the adjacent mainland for the space of four hundred furlongs from the sea. Now there were but few regions in the Roman empire out of that compass; and the greatest of the nations and most powerful of the kings were included in the limit. Moreover, by this decree he had a power of selecting fifteen lieutenants out of the senate, and of assigning to each his province in charge; then he might take likewise out of the treasury and out of the hands of the revenue-farmers what moneys he pleased; as also two hundred sail of ships, with a power to press and levy what soldiers and seamen he thought fit.

When this law was read, the common people approved of it exceedingly, but the chief men and most important among the senators looked upon it as an exorbitant power, even beyond the reach of envy, but well deserving their fears. Therefore, concluding with themselves that such unlimited authority was dangerous, they agreed unanimously to oppose the bill, and all went against it, except Cæsar, who gave his vote for the law, not to gratify Pompey, but the people, whose favour he had courted underhand from the beginning, and hoped to compass for himself. The rest inveighed bitterly against Pompey, insomuch that one of the consuls told him that, if he was ambitious of the place of Romulus, he would scarce avoid his end, but he was in danger of being torn in pieces by the multitude for his speech.

Yet when Catulus stood up to speak against the law, the people in reverence to him were silent and attentive. And when, after saying much in the most honourable terms in favour of Pompey, he proceeded to advise the people in kindness to spare him, and not to expose a man of his value to such a succession of dangers and wars, "For," said he, "where could you find another Pompey, or whom would you have in case you should chance to lose him?" they all cried out with one voice, "Yourself." And so Catulus, finding all his rhetoric ineffectual, desisted.

Then Roscius attempted to speak, but could obtain no hearing, and made signs with his fingers, intimating, "Not him alone," but that there might be a second Pompey or colleague in authority with him. Upon this, it is said, the multitude, being extremely incensed, made such a loud outcry, that a crow flying over the market-place at that instant was struck, and dropped down among the crowd; whence it would appear that the cause of birds falling down to the ground is not any rupture or division of the air causing a vacuum, but purely the actual stroke of the voice, which, when carried up in a great mass and with violence, raises a sort of tempest and billow, as it were, in the air.

The assembly broke up for that day; and when the day was come on which the bill was to pass by suffrage into a decree, Pompey went privately into the country; but hearing that it was passed and confirmed, he returned again into the city by night, to avoid the envy that might be occasioned by the concourse of people that would meet and congratulate him.

The next morning he came aboard and sacrificed to the gods, and having audience at an open assembly, so handled the matter that they enlarged his power, giving him many things besides what was already granted, and almost doubling the preparation appointed in the former decree. Five hundred ships were manned for him, and an army raised of one hundred and twenty thousand foot and five thousand horse. Twenty-four senators that had been generals of armies were appointed to serve as lieutenants under him, and to these were added two quæstors. Now it happened within this time that the prices of provisions were much reduced, which gave an occasion to the joyful people of saying that the very name of Pompey had ended the war.

However, Pompey, in pursuance of his charge, divided all the seas and the whole Mediterranean into thirteen parts, allotting a squadron to each, under the command of his officers; and having thus dispersed his power into all quarters, and encompassed the pirates everywhere, they began to fall into his hands by whole shoals, which he seized and brought into his harbours. As for those that withdrew themselves betimes, or otherwise escaped his general chase, they all made to Cilicia, where they hid themselves as in their hives; against whom Pompey now proceeded in person with sixty of his best ships, not, however, until he had first scoured and cleared all the seas near Rome, the Tyrrhenian, and the African, and all the waters of Sardinia, Corsica, and Sicily; all which he performed in the space of forty days by his own indefatigable industry and the zeal of his lieutenants.

Pompey met with some interruption in Rome, through the malice and envy of Piso, the consul, who had given some check to his proceedings by withholding his stores and discharging his seamen; whereupon he sent his fleet round to Brundusium, himself going the

nearest way by land through Tuscany to
Rome; which was no sooner known by the
people than they all flocked out to meet him
upon the way as if they had not sent him out
but a few days before. What chiefly excited
their joy was the unexpectedly rapid change in
the markets, which abounded now with the
greatest plenty, so that Piso was in great danger to have been deprived of his consulship,
Gabinius having a law ready prepared for that
purpose; but Pompey forbade it, behaving
himself as in that, so in all things else, with
great moderation, and when he had made sure
of all that he wanted or desired, he departed
for Brundusium, whence he set sail in pursuit
of the pirates.

And though he was straitened in time, and
his hasty voyage forced him to sail by several
cities without touching, yet he would not pass
by the city of Athens unsaluted; but landing
there, after he had sacrificed to the gods, and
made an address to the people, as he was returning out of the city, he read at the gates two
epigrams, each in a single line, written in his
own praise; one within the gates:—

Thy humbler thoughts make thee a god the more;
the other without:—

Adieu we bid, who welcome bade before.

Now because Pompey had shown himself
merciful to some of these pirates that were yet
roving in bodies about the seas, having upon
their supplication ordered a seizure of their
ships and persons only, without any further
process or severity, therefore the rest of their
comrades, in hopes of mercy too, made their
escape from his other commanders, and surrendered themselves with their wives and children into his protection. He continued to pardon all that came in, and the rather because by
them he might make discovery of those who
fled from his justice, as conscious that their
crimes were beyond an act of indemnity.

The most numerous and important part of
these conveyed their families and treasures,
with all their people that were unfit for war,
into castles and strong forts about Mount Taurus; but they themselves, having well manned
their galleys, embarked for Coracesium in Cilicia, where they received Pompey and gave
him battle. Here they had a final overthrow,
and retired to the land, where they were besieged. At last, having despatched their heralds
to him with a submission, they delivered up to
his mercy themselves, their towns, islands, and
strongholds, all which they had so fortified

that they were almost impregnable, and scarcely even accessible.

Thus was this war ended, and the whole
power of the pirates at sea dissolved everywhere in the space of three months, wherein,
besides a great number of other vessels, he took
ninety men-of-war with brazen beaks; and
likewise prisoners of war to the number of no
less than twenty thousand.

As regarded the disposal of these prisoners,
he never so much as entertained the thought
of putting them to death; and yet it might be
no less dangerous on the other hand to disperse
them, as they might reunite and make head
again, being numerous, poor, and warlike.
Therefore, wisely weighing with himself that
man by nature is not a wild or unsocial creature, neither was he born so, but makes himself what he naturally is not by vicious habit;
and that again, on the other side, he is civilised
and grows gentle by a change of place, occupation, and manner of life, as beasts themselves
that are wild by nature become tame and tractable by housing and gentler usage, upon this
consideration he determined to translate these
pirates from sea to land, and give them a taste
of an honest and innocent course of life by
living in towns and tilling the ground. Some
therefore were admitted into the small and
half-peopled towns of the Cilicians, who, for
an enlargement of their territories, were willing to receive them. Others he planted in the
city of the Solians, which had been lately laid
waste by Tigranes, King of Armenia, and
which he now restored. But the largest number
were settled in Dyme, the town of Achæa, at
that time extremely depopulated, and possessing an abundance of good land.

However, these proceedings could not escape
the envy and censure of his enemies; and the
course he took against Metellus in Crete was
disapproved of even by the chiefest of his
friends. For Metellus, a relation of Pompey's
former colleague in Spain, had been sent prætor into Crete, before this province of the seas
was assigned to Pompey. Now Crete was the
second source of pirates next to Cilicia, and
Metellus having shut up a number of them in
their strongholds there was engaged in reducing and extirpating them. Those that were yet
remaining and besieged sent their supplications to Pompey, and invited him into the island as a part of his province, alleging it to
fall, every part of it, within the distance from
the sea specified in his commission, and so
within the precincts of his charge. Pompey re-

ceiving the submission, sent letters to Metellus, commanding him to leave off the war; and others in like manner to the cities, in which he charged them not to yield any obedience to the commands of Metellus.

And after these he sent Lucius Octavius, one of his lieutenants, to act as general, who entering the besieged fortifications, and fighting in defence of the pirates, rendered Pompey not odious only, but even ridiculous too; that he should lend his name as a guard to a nest of thieves that knew neither god nor law, and made his reputation serve as a sanctuary to them, only out of pure envy and emulation to Metellus.

For neither was Achilles thought to act the part of a man, but rather of a mere boy, mad after glory, when by signs he forbade the rest of the Greeks to strike at Hector—

> For fear
> *Some other hand should give the blow, and he*
> *Lose the first honour of the victory.*

Whereas Pompey even sought to preserve the common enemies of the world only that he might deprive a Roman prætor, after all his labours, of the honour of a triumph. Metellus, however, was not daunted, but prosecuted the war against the pirates, expelled them from their strongholds and punished them; and dismissed Octavius with the insults and reproaches of the whole camp.

When the news came to Rome that the war with the pirates was at an end, and that Pompey was unoccupied, diverting himself in visits to the cities for want of employment, one Manlius, a tribune of the people, preferred a law that Pompey should have all the forces of Lucullus, and the provinces under his government, together with Bithynia, which was under the command of Glabrio; and that he should forthwith conduct the war against the two kings, Mithridates and Tigranes, retaining still the same naval forces and the sovereignty of the seas as before.

But this was nothing less than to constitute one absolute monarch of all the Roman empire. For the provinces which seemed to be exempt from his commission by the former decree, such as were Phrygia, Lycaonia, Galatia, Cappadocia, Cilicia, the upper Colchis, and Armenia, were all added in by this latter law, together with all the troops and forces with which Lucullus had defeated Mithridates and Tigranes.

And though Lucullus was thus simply robbed of the glory of his achievements in hav-ing a successor assigned him, rather to the honour of his triumph than the danger of the war; yet this was of less moment in the eyes of the aristocratical party, though they could not but admit the injustice and ingratitude to Lucullus. But their great grievance was that the power of Pompey should be converted into a manifest tyranny; and they therefore exhorted and encouraged one another privately to bend all their forces in opposition to this law, and not tamely to cast away their liberty; yet when the day came on which it was to pass into a decree, their hearts failed them for fear of the people, and all were silent except Catulus, who boldly inveighed against the law and its proposer, and when he found that he could do nothing with the people, turned to the senate, crying out and bidding them seek out some mountain as their forefathers had done, and fly to the rocks where they might preserve their liberty.

The law passed into a decree, as it is said, by the suffrages of all the tribes. And Pompey, in his absence, was made lord of almost all that power which Sulla only obtained by force of arms, after a conquest of the very city itself.

When Pompey had advice by letters of the decree, it is said that in the presence of his friends, who came to give him joy of his honour, he seemed displeased, frowning and smiting his thigh, and exclaimed as one overburdened and weary of government, "Alas, what a series of labours upon labours! If I am never to end my service as a soldier, nor to escape from this invidious greatness, and live at home in the country with my wife, I had better have been an unknown man." But all this was looked upon as mere trifling, neither indeed could the best of his friends call it anything else, well knowing that his enmity with Lucullus, setting a flame just now to his natural passion for glory and empire, made him feel more than usually gratified.

As indeed appeared not long afterwards by his actions, which clearly unmasked him; for, in the first place, he sent out his proclamations into all quarters, commanding the soldiers to join him, and summoned all the tributary kings and princes within his charge; and in short, as soon as he had entered upon his province, he left nothing unaltered that had been done and established by Lucullus. To some he remitted their penalties, and deprived others of their rewards, and acted in all respects as if with the express design that the admirers of Lucullus might know that all his authority was at an end.

Lucullus expostulated by friends, and it was thought fitting that there should be a meeting betwixt them; and accordingly they met in the country of Galatia. As they were both great and successful generals, their officers bore their rods before them all wreathed with branches of laurel; Lucullus came through a country full of green trees and shady woods, but Pompey's march was through a cold and barren district. Therefore the lictors of Lucullus, perceiving that Pompey's laurels were withered and dry, helped him to some of their own, and adorned and crowned his rods with fresh laurels. This was thought ominous, and looked as if Pompey came to take away the reward and honour of Lucullus's victories. Lucullus had the priority in the order of consulships, and also in age; but Pompey's two triumphs made him the greater man.

Their first addresses in this interview were dignified and friendly, each magnifying the other's actions, and offering congratulations upon his success. But when they came to the matter of their conference or treaty, they could agree on no fair or equitable terms of any kind, but even came to harsh words against each other, Pompey upbraiding Lucullus with avarice, and Lucullus retorting ambition upon Pompey, so that their friends could hardly part them.

Lucullus remaining in Galatia, made a distribution of the lands within his conquests, and gave presents to whom he pleased; and Pompey encamping not far distant from him, sent out his prohibitions, forbidding the execution of any of the orders of Lucullus, and commanded away all his soldiers, except sixteen hundred, whom he thought likely to be unserviceable to himself, being disorderly and mutinous, and whom he knew to be hostile to Lucullus; and to these acts he added satirical speeches, detracting openly from the glory of his actions, and giving out that the battles of Lucullus had been but with the mere stageshows and idle pictures of royal pomp, whereas the real war against a genuine army, disciplined by defeat, was reserved to him, Mithridates having now begun to be in earnest, and having betaken himself to his shields, swords, and horses. Lucullus, on the other side, to be even with him, replied, that Pompey came to fight with the mere image and shadow of war, it being his usual practice, like a lazy bird of prey, to come upon the carcass when others had slain the dead, and to tear in pieces the relics of a war.

Thus he had appropriated to himself the victories over Sertorius, over Lepidus, and over the insurgents under Spartacus; whereas this last had been achieved by Crassus, that obtained by Catulus, and the first won by Metellus. And therefore it was no great wonder that the glory of the Pontic and Armenian war should be usurped by a man who had condescended to any artifices to work himself into the honour of a triumph over a few runaway slaves.

After this Lucullus went away, and Pompey having placed his whole navy in guard upon the seas betwixt Phœnicia and Bosphorus, himself marched against Mithridates, who had a phalanx of thirty thousand foot, with two thousand horse, yet durst not bid him battle. He had encamped upon a strong mountain where it would have been hard to attack him, but abandoned it in no long time as destitute of water.

No sooner was he gone but Pompey occupied it, and observing the plants that were thriving there, together with the hollows which he found in several places, conjectured that such a plot could not be without springs, and therefore ordered his men to sink wells in every corner. After which there was, in a little time, great plenty of water throughout all the camp, insomuch that he wondered how it was possible for Mithridates to be ignorant of this during all that time of his encampment there.

After this Pompey followed him to his next camp, and there drawing lines round about him, shut him in. But he, after having endured a siege of forty-five days, made his escape secretly, and fled away with all the best part of his army, having first put to death all the sick and unserviceable. Not long after Pompey overtook him again near the banks of the river Euphrates, and encamped close by him; but fearing lest he should pass over the river and give him the slip there too, he drew up his army to attack him at midnight.

And at that very time Mithridates, it is said, saw a vision in his dream foreshowing what should come to pass. For he seemed to be under sail in the Euxine Sea with a prosperous gale, and just in view of Bosphorus, discoursing pleasantly with the ship's company, as one overjoyed for his past danger and present security, when on a sudden he found himself deserted of all, and floating upon a broken plank of the ship at the mercy of the sea. Whilst he was thus labouring under these passions and phantasms, his friends came and awaked him with the news of Pompey's approach; who was now indeed so near at hand that the fight must be for the camp itself, and the commanders accordingly drew up the forces in battle array.

Pompey perceiving how ready they were and well prepared for defence began to doubt with himself whether he should put it to the hazard of a fight in the dark, judging it more prudent to encompass them only at present, lest they should fly, and to give them battle with the advantage of numbers the next day. But his oldest officers were of another opinion, and by entreaties and encouragements obtained permission that they might charge them immediately. Neither was the night so very dark, but that, though the moon was going down, it yet gave light enough to discern a body.

And indeed this was one especial disadvantage to the king's army. For the Romans coming upon them with the moon on their backs, the moon, being very low and just upon setting, cast the shadows a long way before their bodies, reaching almost to the enemy, whose eyes were thus so much deceived that not exactly discerning the distance, but imagining them to be near at hand, they threw their darts at the shadows without the least execution. The Romans therefore, perceiving this, ran in upon them with a great shout; but the barbarians, all in a panic, unable to endure the charge, turned and fled, and were put to great slaughter, above ten thousand being slain; the camp also was taken.

As for Mithridates himself, he at the beginning of the onset, with a body of eight hundred horse, charged through the Roman army, and made his escape. But before long all the rest dispersed, some one way, some another, and he was left only with three persons, among whom was his concubine, Hypsicratia, a girl always of a manly and daring spirit, and the king called her on that account Hypsicrates. She being attired and mounted like a Persian horseman, accompanied the king in all his flight, never weary even in the longest journey, nor ever failing to attend the king in person, and look after his horse too, until they came to Inora, a castle of the king's, well stored with gold and treasure. From thence Mithridates took his richest apparel, and gave it among those that had resorted to him in their flight; and so to every one of his friends he gave a deadly poison, that they might not fall into the power of the enemy against their wills. From thence he designed to have gone to Tigranes in Armenia, but being prohibited by Tigranes, who put out a proclamation with a reward of one hundred talents to any one that should apprehend him, he passed by the headwaters of the river Euphrates and fled through the country of Colchis.

Pompey in the meantime made an invasion into Armenia upon the invitation of young Tigranes, who was now in rebellion against his father, and gave Pompey a meeting about the river Araxes, which rises near the head of Euphrates, but turning its course and bending towards the east, falls into the Caspian Sea. They two, therefore, marched together through the country, taking in all the cities by the way, and receiving their submission.

But King Tigranes, having lately suffered much in the war with Lucullus, and understanding that Pompey was of a kind and gentle disposition, admitted Roman troops into his royal palaces, and taking along with him his friends and relations, went in person to surrender himself into the hands of Pompey. He came as far as the trenches on horseback, but there he was met by two of Pompey's lictors, who commanded him to alight and walk on foot, for no man ever was seen on horseback within a Roman camp. Tigranes submitted to this immediately, and not only so, but loosing his sword, delivered up that too; and last of all, as soon as he appeared before Pompey, he pulled off his royal turban, and attempted to have laid it at his feet. Nay, worst of all, even he himself had fallen prostrate as an humble suppliant at his knees had not Pompey prevented it, taking him by the hand and placing him near him, Tigranes himself on one side of him and his son upon the other.

Pompey now told him that the rest of his losses were chargeable upon Lucullus, by whom he had been dispossessed of Syria, Phœnicia, Cilicia, Galatia, and Sophene; but all that he had preserved to himself entire till that time he should peaceably enjoy, paying the sum of six thousand talents as a fine or penalty for injuries done to the Romans, and that his son should have the kingdom of Sophene. Tigranes himself was well pleased with these conditions of peace, and when the Romans saluted him king, seemed to be overjoyed, and promised to every common soldier half a mina of silver, to every centurion ten minae, and to every tribune a talent; but the son was displeased, insomuch that when he was invited to supper he replied that he did not stand in need of Pompey for that sort of honour, for he would find out some other Roman to sup with.

Upon this he was put into close arrest, and reserved for the triumph.

Not long after this Phraates, King of Parthia, sent to Pompey, and demanded to have young Tigranes, as his son-in-law, given up to him, and that the river Euphrates should be the boundary of the empires. Pompey replied that as for Tigranes, he belonged more to his own natural father than his father-in-law, and as for the boundaries, he would take care that they should be according to right and justice.

So Pompey, leaving Armenia in the custody of Afranius, went himself in chase of Mithridates; to do which he was forced of necessity to march through several nations inhabiting about Mount Caucasus. Of these the Albanians and Iberians were the two chiefest. The Iberians stretch out as far as the Moschian mountains and the Pontus; the Albanians lie more eastwardly, and towards the Caspian Sea.

These Albanians at first permitted Pompey, upon his request, to pass through the country; but when winter had stolen upon the Romans whilst they were still in the country, and they were busy celebrating the festival of Saturn, they mustered a body of no less than forty thousand fighting men, and set upon them, having passed over the river Cyrnus, which rising from the mountains of Iberia, and receiving the river Araxes in its course from Armenia, discharges itself by twelve mouths into the Caspian. Or, according to others, the Araxes does not fall into it, but they flow near one another, and so discharge themselves as neighbours into the same sea. It was in the power of Pompey to have obstructed the enemy's passage over the river, but he suffered them to pass over quietly; and then leading on his forces and giving battle he routed them and slew great numbers of them in the field. The king sent ambassadors with his submission, and Pompey upon his supplication pardoned the offence, and making a treaty with him, he marched directly against the Iberians, a nation no less in number than the other, but much more warlike, and extremely desirous of gratifying Mithridates and driving out Pompey.

These Iberians were never subject to the Medes or Persians, and they happened likewise to escape the dominion of the Macedonians, because Alexander was so quick in his march through Hyrcania. But these also Pompey subdued in a great battle, where there were slain nine thousand upon the spot, and more than ten thousand taken prisoners. From thence he entered into the country of Colchis, where Servilius met him by the river Phasis, bringing the fleet with which he was guarding the Pontus.

The pursuit of Mithridates, who had thrown himself among the tribes inhabiting Bosphorus and the shores of the Mæotian Sea, presented great difficulties. News was also brought to Pompey that the Albanians had again revolted. This made him turn back, out of anger and determination not to be beaten by them, and with difficulty and great danger passed back over the Cyrnus, which the barbarous people had fortified a great way down the banks with palisadoes. And after this, having a tedious march to make through a waterless and difficult country, he ordered ten thousand skins to be filled with water, and so advanced towards the enemy, whom he found drawn up in order of battle near the river Abas, to the number of sixty thousand horse and twelve thousand foot, ill-armed generally, and most of them covered only with the skins of wild beasts. Their general was Cosis, the king's brother, who, as soon as the battle was begun, singled out Pompey, and rushing in upon him darted his javelin into the joints of his breastplate; while Pompey, in return, struck him through the body with his lance and slew him.

It is related that in this battle there were Amazons fighting as auxiliaries with the barbarians, and that they came down from the mountains by the river Thermodon. For that after the battle, when the Romans were taking the spoils and plunder of the field, they met with several targets and buskins of the Amazons; but no woman's body was found among the dead. They inhabit the parts of Mount Caucasus that reach down to the Hyrcanian Sea, not immediately bordering upon the Albanians, for the Gelæ and the Leges lie betwixt; and they keep company with these people yearly, for two months only, near the river Thermodon; after which they retire to their own habitations, and live alone all the rest of the year.

After this engagement, Pompey was eager to advance with his forces upon the Hyrcanian and Caspian Sea, but was forced to retreat at a distance of three days' march from it by the number of venomous serpents, and so he retreated into Armenia the Less. Whilst he was there, the kings of the Elymæans and Medes sent ambassadors to him, to whom he gave friendly answer by letter; and sent against the King of Parthia, who had made incursions upon Gordyene, and despoiled the subjects of

Tigranes, an army under the command of Afranius, who put him to the rout, and followed him in chase as far as the district of Arbela.

Of the concubines of King Mithridates that were brought before Pompey, he took none to himself, but sent them all away to their parents and relations; most of them being either the daughters or wives of princes and great commanders.

Stratonice, however, who had the greatest power and influence with him, and to whom he had committed the custody of his best and richest fortress, had been, it seems, the daughter of a musician, an old man, and of no great fortune, and happening to sing one night before Mithridates at a banquet, she struck his fancy so that immediately he took her with him, and sent away the old man much dissatisfied, the king having not so much as said one kind word to himself. But when he rose in the morning, and saw tables in his house richly covered with gold and silver plate, a great retinue of servants, eunuchs, and pages bringing him rich garments, and a horse standing before the door richly caparisoned, in all respects as was usual with the king's favourites, he looked upon it all as a piece of mockery, and thinking himself trifled with, attempted to make off and run away. But the servants laying hold upon him, and informing him really that the king had bestowed on him the house and furniture of a rich man lately deceased, and that these were but the firstfruits or earnests of greater riches and possessions that were to come, he was persuaded at last with much difficulty to believe them. And so putting on his purple robes, and mounting his horse, he rode through the city, crying out, "All this is mine"; and to those that laughed at him, he said, there was no such wonder in this, but it was a wonder rather that he did not throw stones at all he met, he was so transported with joy. Such was the parentage and blood of Stratonice.

She now delivered up this castle into the hands of Pompey, and offered him many presents of great value, of which he accepted only such as he thought might serve to adorn the temples of the gods and add to the splendour of his triumph: the rest he left to Stratonice's disposal, bidding her please herself in the enjoyment of them.

And in the same manner he dealt with the presents offered him by the King of Iberia, who sent him a bedstead, table, and a chair of state, all of gold, desiring him to accept of them; but he delivered them all into the custody of the public treasurers, for the use of the commonwealth.

In another castle called Cænum, Pompey found and read with pleasure several secret writings of Mithridates, containing much that threw light on his character. For there were memoirs by which it appeared that, besides others, he had made away with his son Ariarathes by poison, as also with Alcæus the Sardian, for having robbed him of the first honours in a horse-race. There were several judgments upon the interpretation of dreams, which either he himself or some of his mistresses had had; and besides these, there was a series of wanton letters to and from his concubine Monime. Theophanes tells us that there was found also an address by Rutilius, in which he attempted to exasperate him to the slaughter of all the Romans in Asia; though most men justly conjecture this to be a malicious invention of Theophanes, who probably hated Rutilius because he was a man in nothing like himself; or perhaps it might be to gratify Pompey, whose father is described by Rutilius in his history as the vilest man alive.

From thence Pompey came to the city of Amisus, where his passion for glory put him into a position which might be called a punishment on himself. For whereas he had often sharply reproached Lucullus, in that while the enemy was still living he had taken upon him to issue decrees, and distribute rewards and honours, as conquerors usually do only when the war is brought to an end, yet now was he himself, while Mithridates was paramount in the kingdom of Bosphorus, and at the head of a powerful army, as if all were ended, just doing the same thing, regulating the provinces, and distributing rewards, many great commanders and princes having flocked to him, together with no less than twelve barbarian kings; insomuch that to gratify these other kings, when he wrote to the King of Parthia, he would not condescend, as others used to do, in the superscription of his letter, to give him his title of king of kings.

Moreover, he had a great desire and emulation to occupy Syria, and to march through Arabia to the Red Sea, that he might thus extend his conquests every way to the great ocean that encompasses the habitable earth; as in Africa he was the first Roman that advanced his victories to the ocean; and again in Spain he made the Atlantic Sea the limit of the empire; and then thirdly, in his late pursuit of the

Albanians, he had wanted but little of reaching the Hyrcanian Sea. Accordingly he raised his camp, designing to bring the Red Sea within the circuit of his expedition; especially as he saw how difficult it was to hunt after Mithridates with an army, and that he would prove a worse enemy fleeing than fighting. But yet he declared that he would leave a sharper enemy behind him than himself, namely, famine; and therefore he appointed a guard of ships to lie in wait for the merchants that sailed to Bosphorus, death being the penalty for any who should attempt to carry provisions thither.

Then he set forward with the greatest part of his army, and in his march casually fell in with several dead bodies, still uninterred, of those soldiers who were slain with Triarius in his unfortunate engagement with Mithridates: these he buried splendidly and honourably. The neglect of whom, it is thought, caused, as much as anything, the hatred that was felt against Lucullus, and alienated the affections of the soldiers from him.

Pompey having now by his forces under the command of Afranius subdued the Arabians about the mountain Amanus, himself entered Syria, and finding it destitute of any natural and lawful prince, reduced it into the form of a province, as a possession of the people of Rome. He conquered also Judæa, and took its king, Aristobulus, captive. Some cities he built anew, and to others he gave their liberty, chastising their tyrants.

Most part of the time that he spent there was employed in the administration of justice, in deciding controversies of kings and states; and where he himself could not be present in person, he gave commissions to his friends, and sent them. Thus when there arose a difference betwixt the Armenians and Parthians about some territory, and the judgment was referred to him, he gave a power by commission to three judges and arbiters to hear and determine the controversy. For the reputation of his power was great; nor was the fame of his justice and clemency inferior to that of his power, and served indeed as a veil for a multitude of faults committed by his friends and familiars. For although it was not in his nature to check or chastise wrongdoers, yet he himself always treated those that had to do with him in such a manner that they submitted to endure with patience the acts of covetousness and oppression done by others.

Among these friends of his there was one Demetrius, who had the greatest influence

with him of all; he was a freed slave, a youth of good understanding, but somewhat too insolent in his good fortune, of whom there goes this story.

Cato, the philosopher, being as yet a very young man, but of great repute and a noble mind, took a journey of pleasure to Antioch, at a time when Pompey was not there, having a great desire to see the city. He, as his custom was, walked on foot, and his friends accompanied him on horseback; and seeing before the gates of the city a multitude dressed in white, the young men on one side of the road and the boys on the other, he was somewhat offended at it, imagining that it was officiously done in honour of him, which was more than he had any wish for. However, he desired his companions to alight and walk with him; but when they drew near, the master of the ceremonies in this procession came out with a garland and a rod in his hand and met them, inquiring where they had left Demetrius, and when he would come. Upon which Cato's companions burst out into laughter, but Cato said only, "Alas, poor city!" and passed by without any other answer.

However, Pompey rendered Demetrius less odious to others by enduring his presumption and impertinence to himself. For it is reported how that Pompey, when he had invited his friends to an entertainment, would be very ceremonious in waiting till they all came and were placed, while Demetrius would be already stretched upon the couch as if he cared for no one, with his dress over his ears, hanging down from his head.

Before his return into Italy, he had purchased the pleasantest country-seat about Rome, with the finest walks and places for exercise, and there were sumptuous gardens, called by the name of Demetrius, while Pompey his master, up to his third triumph, was contented with an ordinary and simple habitation. Afterwards, it is true, when he had erected his famous and stately theatre for the people of Rome, he built as a sort of appendix to it a house for himself, much more splendid than his former, and yet no object even this to excite men's envy, since he who came to be master of it after Pompey could not but express wonder and inquire where Pompey the Great used to sup. Such is the story told us.

The king of the Arabs near Petra, who had hitherto despised the power of the Romans, now began to be in great alarm at it, and sent letters to him promising to be at his commands, and to do whatever he should see fit to order. However, Pompey having a desire to confirm and keep him in the same mind, marched forwards for Petra, an expedition not altogether irreprehensible in the opinion of many; who thought it a mere running away from their proper duty, the pursuit of Mithridates, Rome's ancient and inveterate enemy, who was now rekindling the war once more, and taking preparations, it was reported, to lead his army through Scythia and Pæonia into Italy. Pompey, on the other side, judging it easier to destroy his forces in battle than to seize his person in flight, resolved not to tire himself out in a vain pursuit, but rather to spend his leisure upon another enemy, as a sort of digression in the meanwhile.

But fortune resolved the doubt, for when he was now not far from Petra, and had pitched his tents and encamped for that day, as he was taking exercise with his horse outside the camp, couriers came riding up from Pontus, bringing good news, as was known at once by the heads of their javelins, which it is the custom to carry crowned with branches of laurel. The soldiers, as soon as they saw them, flocked immediately to Pompey, who, notwithstanding, was minded to finish his exercise; but when they began to be clamorous and importunate, he alighted from his horse, and taking the letters went before them into the camp.

Now there being no tribunal erected there, not even that military substitute for one which they make by cutting up thick turfs of earth, and piling them one upon another, they, through eagerness and impatience, heaped up a pile of pack-saddles, and Pompey standing upon that, told them the news of Mithridates's death, how that he had himself put an end to his life upon the revolt of his son Pharnaces, and that Pharnaces had taken all things there into his hands and possession, which he did, his letters said, in right of himself and the Romans. Upon this news the whole army, expressing their joy, as was to be expected, fell to sacrificing to the gods, and feasting as if in the person of Mithridates alone there had died many thousands of their enemies.

Pompey by this event having brought this war to its completion, with much more ease than was expected, departed forthwith out of Arabia, and passing rapidly through the intermediate provinces, he came at length to the city Amisus. There he received many presents brought from Pharnaces, with several dead bodies of the royal blood, and the corpse of Mithridates himself, which was not easy to be known by the face, for the physicians that embalmed him had not dried up his brain, but those who were curious to see him knew him by the scars there. Pompey himself would not endure to see him, but to deprecate the divine jealousy sent it away to the city of Sinope. He admired the richness of his robes no less than the size and splendour of his armour. His sword-belt, however, which had cost four hundred talents, was stolen by Publius, and sold to Ariarathes; his tiara also, a piece of admirable workmanship, Gaius, the foster-brother of Mithridates, gave secretly to Faustus, the son of Sulla, at his request. All which Pompey was ignorant of, but afterwards, when Pharnaces came to understand it, he severely punished those that embezzled them.

Pompey now having ordered all things, and established that province, took his journey homewards in greater pomp and with more festivity. For when he came to Mitylene, he gave the city their freedom upon the intercession of Theophanes, and was present at the contest, there periodically held, of the poets, who took at that time no other theme or subject than the actions of Pompey. He was extremely pleased with the theatre itself, and had a model of it taken, intending to erect one in Rome on the same design, but larger and more magnificent. When he came to Rhodes, he attended the lectures of all the philosophers there, and gave to every one of them a talent. Posidonius has published the disputation which he held before him against Hermagoras the rhetorician, upon the subject of Invention in General. At Athens, also, he showed similar munificence to the philosophers, and gave fifty talents towards the repairing and beautifying the city.

So that now by all these acts he well hoped to return into Italy in the greatest splendour and glory possible to man, and find his family as desirous to see him as he felt himself to come home to them. But that supernatural agency, whose province and charge it is always to mix some ingredient of evil with the greatest and most glorious goods of fortune, had for some time back been busy in his household, preparing him a sad welcome. For Mucia during his absence had dishonoured his bed. Whilst he was abroad at a distance he had refused all credence to the report; but when he drew nearer to Italy, where his thoughts were more at leisure to give consideration to the charge, he sent her a bill of divorce; but neither then in writing, nor afterwards by word of mouth, did he ever give a reason why he discharged her; the cause of it is mentioned in Cicero's epistles.

Rumours of every kind were scattered abroad about Pompey, and were carried to Rome before him, so that there was a great tumult and stir, as if he designed forthwith to march with his army into the city and establish himself securely as sole ruler. Crassus withdrew himself, together with his children and property, out of the city, either that he was really afraid, or that he counterfeited rather, as is most probable, to give credit to the calumny and exasperate the jealousy of the people. Pompey, therefore, as soon as he entered Italy, called a general muster of the army; and having made a suitable address and exchanged a kind farewell with his soldiers, he commanded them to depart every man to his country and place of habitation, only taking care that they should not fail to meet again at his triumph.

Thus the army being disbanded, and the news commonly reported, a wonderful result ensued. For when the cities saw Pompey the Great passing through the country unarmed, and with a small train of familiar friends only, as if he was returning from a journey of pleasure, not from his conquests, they came pouring out to display their affection for him, attending and conducting him to Rome with far greater forces than he disbanded; insomuch that if he had designed any movement or innovation in the state, he might have done it without his army.

Now, because the law permitted no commander to enter into the city before his triumph, he sent to the senate, entreating them as a favour to him to prorogue the election of consuls, that thus he might be able to attend and give countenance to Piso, one of the candidates. The request was resisted by Cato, and met with a refusal. However, Pompey could not but admire the liberty and boldness of speech which Cato alone had dared to use in the maintenance of law and justice.

He therefore had a great desire to win him over, and purchase his friendship at any rate; and to that end, Cato having two nieces, Pompey asked for one in marriage for himself, the other for his son. But Cato looked unfavourably on the proposal, regarding it as a design for undermining his honesty, and in a manner bribing him by a family alliance; much to the displeasure of his wife and sister, who were indignant that he should reject a connection with Pompey the Great.

About that time Pompey having a design of setting up Afranius for the consulship, gave a sum of money among the tribes for their votes, and people came and received it in his own gardens, a proceeding which, when it came to be generally known, excited great disapprobation, that he should thus, for the sake of men who could not obtain the honour by their own merits, make merchandise of an office which had been given to himself as the highest reward of his services. "Now," said Cato, to his wife and sister, "had we contracted an alliance with Pompey, we had been allied to this dishonour too"; and this they could not but acknowledge, and allow his judgment of what was right and fitting to have been wiser and better than theirs.

The splendour and magnificence of Pompey's triumph was such that though it took up the space of two days, yet they were extremely straitened in time, so that of what was prepared for that pageantry, there was as much withdrawn as would have set out and adorned another triumph. In the first place, there were tables carried, inscribed with the names and titles of the nations over whom he triumphed, Pontus, Armenia, Cappadocia, Paphlagonia, Media, Colchis, the Iberians, the Albanians, Syria, Cilicia, and Mesopotamia, together with Phœnicia and Palestine, Judæa, Arabia, and all the power of the pirates subdued by sea and land. And in these different countries there appeared the capture of no less than one thousand fortified places, nor much less than nine hundred cities, together with eight hundred ships of the pirates, and the foundation of thirty-nine towns.

Besides, there was set forth in these tables an account of all the tributes throughout the empire, and how that before these conquests the revenue amounted but to fifty millions, whereas from his acquisitions they had a revenue of eighty-five millions; and that in present payment he was bringing into the common treasury ready money, and gold and silver plate, and ornaments, to the value of twenty thousand talents, over and above what had been distributed among the soldiers, of whom he that had least had fifteen hundred drachmas for his share.

The prisoners of war that were led in triumph, besides the chief pirates, were the son of Tigranes, King of Armenia, with his wife and daughter; as also Zosime, wife of King Tigranes himself, and Aristobulus, King of Judæa, the sister of King Mithridates, and her five sons, and some Scythian women. There were likewise the hostages of the Albanians and Iberians, and of the King of Commagene, besides a vast number of trophies, one for every battle in which he was conqueror, either himself in person or by his lieutenants.

But that which seemed to be his greatest glory, being one which no other Roman ever attained to, was this, that he made his third triumph over the third division of the world. For others among the Romans had the honour of triumphing thrice, but his first triumph was over Africa, his second over Europe, and this last over Asia; so that he seemed in these three triumphs to have led the whole world captive.

As for his age, those who affect to make the parallel exact in all things betwixt him and Alexander the Great, do not allow him to have been quite thirty-four, whereas in truth at that time he was near forty. And well had it been for him had he terminated his life at this date, while he still enjoyed Alexander's fortune, since all his after-time served only either to bring him prosperity that made him odious, or calamities too great to be retrieved.

For that great authority which he had gained in the city by his merits he made use of only in patronising the iniquities of others, so that by advancing their fortunes he detracted from his own glory, till at last he was overthrown even by the force and greatness of his own power. And as the strongest citadel or fort in a town, when it is taken by an enemy, does then afford the same strength to the foe as it had done to friends before, so Cæsar, after Pompey's aid had made him strong enough to defy his country, ruined and overthrew at last the power which had availed him against the rest.

The course of things was as follows. Lucullus, when he returned out of Asia, where he had been treated with insult by Pompey, was received by the senate with great honour, which was yet increased when Pompey came home; to check whose ambition they encouraged him to assume the administration of the government, whereas he was now grown cold and disinclined to business, having given himself over to the pleasures of ease and the enjoyment of a splendid fortune. However, he began for the time to exert himself against Pompey, attacked him sharply, and succeeded in having his own acts and decrees, which were repealed by Pompey, re-established, and, with the assistance of Cato, gained the superiority in the senate.

Pompey having fallen from his hopes in such an unworthy repulse, was forced to flee to the tribunes of the people for refuge, and to attach himself to the young men, among whom was Clodius, the vilest and most impudent wretch alive, who took him about, and exposed him as a tool to the people, carrying him up and down among the throngs in the market-place, to countenance those laws and speeches which he made to cajole the people and ingratiate himself. And at last, for his reward, he demanded of Pompey, as if he had not disgraced, but done him a great kindness, that he should forsake (as in the end he did forsake) Cicero, his friend, who on many public occasions had done him the greatest service. And so when Cicero was in danger, and implored his aid, he would not admit him into his presence, but shutting up his gates against those that came to mediate for him, slipt out at a back door, whereupon Cicero, fearing the result of his trial, departed privately from Rome.

About that time Cæsar, returning from military service, started a course of policy which brought him great present favour, and much increased his power for the future, and proved extremely destructive both to Pompey and the commonwealth. For now he stood candidate for his first consulship, and well observing the enmity betwixt Pompey and Crassus, and finding that by joining with one he should make the other his enemy, he endeavoured by all means to reconcile them, an object in itself honourable and tending to the public good, but, as he undertook it, a mischievous and subtle intrigue.

For he well knew that opposite parties or factions in a commonwealth, like passengers in a boat, serve to trim and balance the unsteady motions of power there; whereas if they combine and come all over to one side, they cause a shock which will be sure to overset the vessel and carry down everything. And therefore Cato wisely told those who charged all the calamities of Rome upon the disagreement betwixt Pompey and Cæsar that they were in error in charging all the crime upon the last cause; for it was not their discord and enmity, but their unanimity and friendship, that gave the first and greatest blow to the commonwealth.

Cæsar being thus elected consul, began at once to make an interest with the poor and meaner sort, by preferring and establishing laws for planting colonies and dividing lands, lowering the dignity of his office, and turning his consulship into a sort of tribuneship rather. And when Bibulus, his colleague, opposed him, and Cato was prepared to second Bibulus, and assist him vigorously, Cæsar brought Pompey upon the hustings, and addressing him in the sight of the people, demanded his opinion upon the laws that were proposed. Pompey gave his approbation. "Then," said Cæsar, "in case any man should offer violence to these laws, will you be ready to give assistance to the people?" "Yes," replied Pompey, "I shall be ready, and against those that threaten the sword, I will appear with sword and buckler."

Nothing ever was said or done by Pompey up to that day that seemed more insolent or overbearing; so that his friends endeavoured to apologise for it as a word spoken inadvertently; but by his actions afterwards it appeared plainly that he was totally devoted to Cæsar's service. For on a sudden, contrary to all expectation, he married Julia, the daughter of Cæsar, who had been affianced before and was to be married within a few days to Cæpio. And to appease Cæpio's wrath, he gave him his own daughter in marriage, who had been espoused before to Faustus, the son of Sulla. Cæsar himself married Calpurnia, the daughter of Piso.

Upon this Pompey, filling the city with soldiers, carried all things by force as he pleased. As Bibulus, the consul, was going to the Forum, accompanied by Lucullus and Cato, they fell upon him on a sudden and broke his rods; and somebody threw a vessel of ordure upon the head of Bibulus himself; and two tribunes of the people, who escorted him, were desperately wounded in the fray. And thus having cleared the Forum of all their adversaries, they got their bill for the division of lands established and passed into an act; and not only so, but the whole populace, being taken with this bait, became totally at their devotion, inquiring into nothing and without a word giving their suffrages to whatever they propounded. Thus they confirmed all those acts and decrees of Pompey which were questioned and contested by Lucullus; and to Cæsar they granted the provinces of Gaul, both within and without the Alps, together with Illyricum, for five years, and likewise an army of four entire legions; then they created consuls for the year ensuing, Piso, the father-in-law of Cæsar, and Gabinius, the most extravagant of Pompey's flatterers.

During all these transactions, Bibulus kept close within doors, nor did he appear publicly in person for the space of eight months together, notwithstanding he was consul, but sent out proclamations full of bitter invectives and accusations against them both. Cato turned prophet, and as if he had been possessed with a spirit of divination, did nothing else in the senate but foretell what evils should befall the commonwealth and Pompey. Lucullus pleaded old age, and retired to take his ease, as superannuated for affairs of state; which gave occasion to the saying of Pompey, that the fatigues of luxury were not more seasonable for an old man than those of government. Which in truth proved a reflection upon himself; for he not long after let his fondness for his young wife seduce him also into effeminate habits. He gave all his time to her, and passed his days in her company in country-houses and gardens, paying no heed to what was going on in the Forum.

Insomuch that Clodius, who was then tribune of the people, began to despise him, and engage in the most audacious attempts. For when he had banished Cicero, and sent away Cato into Cyprus under pretence of military duty, and when Cæsar was gone upon his expedition to Gaul, finding the populace now looking to him as the leader who did everything according to their pleasure, he attempted forthwith to repeal some of Pompey's decrees; he took Tigranes, the captive, out of prison, and kept him about him as his companion; and commenced actions against several of Pompey's friends, thus designing to try the extent of his power. At last, upon a time when Pompey was present at the hearing of a certain cause, Clodius, accompanied with a crowd of profligate and impudent ruffians, standing up in a place above the rest, put questions to the populace as follows: "Who is the dissolute general? Who is the man that seeks another man? Who scratches his head with one finger?" And the rabble, upon the signal of his shaking his gown, with a great shout to every question, like singers making responses in a chorus, made answer, "Pompey."

This indeed was no small annoyance to Pompey, who was quite unaccustomed to hear anything ill of himself, and unexperienced altogether in such encounters; and he was yet more vexed when he saw that the senate rejoiced at this foul usage, and regarded it as a just punishment upon him for his treachery to Cicero. But when it came even to blows and wounds in the Forum, and that one of Clodius's bond-slaves was apprehended creeping through the crowd towards Pompey with a sword in his hand, Pompey laid hold of this pretence, though perhaps otherwise apprehensive of Clodius's insolence and bad language, and never appeared again in the Forum during all the time he was tribune, but kept close at home, and passed his time in consulting with his friends by what means he might best allay the displeasure of the senate and nobles against him.

Among other expedients, Culleo advised the divorce of Julia, and to abandon Cæsar's friendship to gain that of the senate; this he would not hearken to. Others again advised him to call home Cicero from banishment, a man who was always the great adversary of Clodius, and as great a favourite of the senate; to this he was easily persuaded. And therefore he brought Cicero's brother into the Forum, attended with a strong party, to petition for his return; where, after a warm dispute, in which several were wounded and some slain, he got the victory over Clodius.

No sooner was Cicero returned home upon this decree, but immediately he used his efforts to reconcile the senate to Pompey; and by speaking in favour of the law upon the importations of corn, did again, in effect, make Pompey sovereign lord of all the Roman possessions by sea and land. For by that law there were placed under his control all ports, markets, and storehouses, and, in short, all the concerns both of the merchants and the husbandmen; which gave occasion to the charge brought against it by Clodius, that the law was not made because of the scarcity of corn, but the scarcity of corn was made that they might pass a law, whereby that power of his, which was now grown feeble and consumptive, might be revived again, and Pompey reinstated in a new empire. Others looked upon it as a politic device of Spinther, the consul, whose design it was to secure Pompey in a greater authority, that he himself might be sent in assistance to King Ptolemy. However, it is certain that Canidius, the tribune, preferred a law to despatch Pompey in the character of an ambassador, without an army, attended only with two lictors, as a mediator betwixt the king and his subjects of Alexandria.

Neither did this proposal seem unacceptable to Pompey, though the senate cast it out upon the specious pretence that they were unwilling to hazard his person. However, there were found several writings scattered about the Forum and near the senate-house intimating how grateful it would be to Ptolemy to have Pompey appointed for his general instead of Spinther. And Timagenes even asserts that Ptolemy went away and left Egypt, not out of necessity, but purely upon the persuasion of The-

ophanes, who was anxious to give Pompey the opportunity for holding a new command and gaining further wealth. But Theophanes's want of honesty does not go so far to make this story credible as does Pompey's own nature, which was averse, with all its ambition, to such base and disingenuous acts, to render it improbable.

Thus Pompey, being appointed chief purveyor, and having within his administration and management all the corn trade, sent abroad his factors and agents into all quarters, and he himself sailing into Sicily, Sardinia, and Africa, collected vast stores of corn. He was just ready to set sail upon his voyage home, when a great storm arose upon the sea, and the ships' commanders doubted whether it were safe. Upon which Pompey himself went first aboard, and bid the mariners weigh anchor, declaring with a loud voice that there was a necessity to sail, but no necessity to live. So that with this spirit and courage, and having met with favourable fortune, he made a prosperous return, and filled the markets with corn, and the sea with ships. So much so that this great plenty and abundance of provisions yielded a sufficient supply, not only to the city of Rome, but even to other places too, dispersing itself, like waters from a spring, into all quarters.

Meantime Cæsar grew great and famous with his wars in Gaul, and while in appearance he seemed far distant from Rome, entangled in the affairs of the Belgians, Suevians, and Britons, in truth he was working craftily by secret practices in the midst of the people, and countermining Pompey in all political matters of most importance. He himself, with his army close about him, as if it had been his own body, not with mere views of conquest over the barbarians, but as though his contests with them were but mere sports and exercises of the chase, did his utmost with this training and discipline to make it invincible and alarming.

In the meantime his gold and silver and other spoils and treasure which he took from the enemy in his conquests, he sent to Rome in presents, tempting people with his gifts, and aiding ædiles, prætors, and consuls, as also their wives, in their expenses, and thus purchasing himself numerous friends. Insomuch, that when he passed back again over the Alps, and took up his winter quarters in the city of Lucca, there flocked to him an infinite number of men and women, striving who should get first to him, two hundred senators included, among whom were Pompey and Crassus; so that there were to be seen at once before Cæsar's door no less than six score rods of proconsuls and prætors.

The rest of his addressers he sent all away full fraught with hopes and money; but with Crassus and Pompey he entered into special articles of agreement, that they should stand candidates for the consulship next year; that Cæsar on his part should send a number of his soldiers to give their votes at the election; that as soon as they were elected, they should use their interest to have the command of some provinces and legions assigned to themselves, and that Cæsar should have his present charge confirmed to him for five years more.

When these arrangements came to be generally known, great indignation was excited among the chief men in Rome; and Marcellinus, in an open assembly of the people, demanded of them both, whether they designed to sue for the consulship or no. And being urged by the people for their answer, Pompey spoke first, and told them, perhaps he would sue for it, perhaps he would not. Crassus was more temperate, and said, that he would do what should be judged most agreeable with the interest of the commonwealth; and when Marcellinus persisted in his attack on Pompey, and spoke, as it was thought, with some vehemence, Pompey remarked that Marcellinus was certainly the unfairest of men, to show him no gratitude for having thus made him an orator out of a mute, and converted him from a hungry starveling into a man so well-fed that he could not contain himself.

Most of the candidates nevertheless abandoned their canvass for the consulship; Cato alone persuaded and encouraged Lucius Domitius not to desist, "since," said he, "the contest now is not for office, but for liberty against tyrants and usurpers." Therefore those of Pompey's party, fearing this inflexible constancy in Cato, by which he kept with him the whole senate, lest by this he should likewise pervert and draw after him all the well-affected part of the commonalty, resolved to withstand Domitius at once, and to prevent his entrance into the Forum. To this end, therefore, they sent in a band of armed men, who slew the torchbearer of Domitius, as he was leading the way before him, and put all the rest to flight; last of all, Cato himself retired, having received a wound in his right arm while defending Domitius.

Thus by these means and practices they obtained the consulship; neither did they behave themselves with more decency in their further proceedings; but in the first place, when the people were choosing Cato prætor, and just ready with their votes for the poll, Pompey broke up the assembly, upon a pretext of some inauspicious appearance, and having gained the tribes by money, they publicly proclaimed Vatinius prætor. Then, in pursuance of their covenants with Cæsar, they introduced several laws by Trebonius, the tribune, continuing Cæsar's commission to another five years' charge of his province; to Crassus there were appointed Syria and the Parthian war; and to Pompey himself, all Africa, together with both Spains, and four legions of soldiers, two of which he lent to Cæsar upon his request for the wars in Gaul.

Crassus, upon the expiration of his consulship, departed forthwith into his province; but Pompey spent some time in Rome, upon the opening or dedication of his theatre, where he treated the people with all sorts of games, shows, and exercises, in gymnastics alike and in music. There was likewise the hunting or baiting of wild beasts, and combats with them, in which five hundred lions were slain; but above all, the battle of elephants was a spectacle full of horror and amazement.

These entertainments brought him great honour and popularity; but on the other side he created no less envy to himself, in that he committed the government of his provinces and legions into the hands of friends as his lieutenants, whilst he himself was going about and spending his time with his wife in all the places of amusement in Italy; whether it were he was so fond of her himself, or she so fond of him, and he unable to distress her by going away, for this also is stated. And the love displayed by this young wife for her elderly husband was a matter of general note, to be attributed, it would seem, to his constancy in married life, and to his dignity of manner, which in familiar intercourse was tempered with grace and gentleness, and was particularly attractive to women, as even Flora, the courtesan, may be thought good enough evidence to prove.

It once happened in a public assembly, as they were at an election of the ædiles, that the people came to blows, and several about Pompey were slain, so that he, finding himself all bloody, ordered a change of apparel; but the servants who brought home his clothes, making a great bustle and hurry about the house, it chanced that the young lady, who was then with child, saw his gown all stained with blood; upon which she dropped immediately into a swoon, and was hardly brought to life again; however, what with her fright and suffering, she fell into labour and miscarried; even those who chiefly censured Pompey for his friendship to Cæsar could not reprove him for his affection to so attached a wife. Afterwards she was great again, and brought to bed of a daughter, but died in childbed; neither did the infant outlive her mother many days. Pompey had prepared all things for the interment of her corpse at his house near Alba, but the people seized upon it by force, and performed the solemnities in the field of Mars, rather in compassion for the young lady, than in favour either for Pompey or Cæsar; and yet of these two, the people seemed at that time to pay Cæsar a greater share of honour in his absence, than to Pompey, though he was present.

For the city now at once began to roll and swell, so to say, with the stir of the coming storm. Things everywhere were in a state of agitation, and everybody's discourse tended to division, now that death had put an end to that relation which hitherto had been a disguise rather than restraint to the ambition of these men. Besides, not long after came messengers from Parthia with intelligence of the death of Crassus there, by which another safeguard against civil war was removed, since both Cæsar and Pompey kept their eyes on Crassus, and awe of him held them together more or less within the bounds of fair-dealing all his lifetime.

But when fortune had taken away this second, whose province it might have been to revenge the quarrel of the conquered, you might then say with the comic poet—

The combatants are waiting to begin,
Smearing their hands with dust and oiling
each his skin.

So inconsiderable a thing is fortune in respect of human nature, and so insufficient to give content to a covetous mind, that an empire of that mighty extent and sway could not satisfy the ambition of two men; and though they knew and had read, that—

The gods, when they divided out 'twixt three,
This massive universe, heaven, hell, and sea,
Each one sat down contented on his throne,
And undisturbed each god enjoys his own,

yet they thought the whole Roman empire not sufficient to contain them, though they were but two.

Pompey once in an oration to the people told them that he had always come into office before he expected he should, and that he had al-ways left it sooner than they expected he would; and, indeed, the disbanding of all his armies witnessed as much. Yet when he perceived that Cæsar would not so willingly discharge his forces, he endeavoured to strengthen himself against him by offices and commands in the city; but beyond this he showed no desire for any change, and would not seem to distrust, but rather to disregard and contemn him. And when he saw how they bestowed the places of government quite contrary to his wishes, because the citizens were bribed in their elections, he let things take their course, and allowed the city to be left without any government at all.

Hereupon there was mention straightway made of appointing a dictator. Lucullus, a tribune of the people, was the man who first adventured to propose it, urging the people to make Pompey dictator. But the tribune was in danger of being turned out of his office by the opposition that Cato made against it. And for Pompey, many of his friends appeared and excused him, alleging that he never was desirous of that government, neither would he accept of it. When Cato therefore made a speech in commendation of Pompey and exhorted him to support the cause of good order in the commonwealth, he could not for shame but yield to it, and so for the present Domitius and Messala were elected consuls.

But shortly afterwards, when there was another anarchy, or vacancy in the government, and the talk of a dictator was much louder and more general than before, those of Cato's party, fearing lest they should be forced to appoint Pompey, thought it policy to keep him from that arbitrary and tyrannical power by giving him an office of more legal authority. Bibulus himself, who was Pompey's enemy, first gave his vote in the senate, that Pompey should be created consul alone; alleging, that by these means either the commonwealth would be freed from its present confusion, or that its bondage should be lessened by serving the worthiest.

This was looked upon as a very strange opinion, considering the man that spoke it; and therefore on Cato's standing up, everybody expected that he would have opposed it; but after silence was made, he said that he would never have been the author of that advice himself, but since it was propounded by another, his advice was to follow it, adding, that any form of government was better than none at all; and that in a time so full of distraction, he thought no man fitter to govern than Pompey. This counsel was unanimously approved of, and a decree passed that Pompey should be made sole consul, with this clause, that if he thought it necessary to have a colleague, he might choose whom he pleased, provided it were not till after two months expired.

Thus was Pompey created and declared sole consul by Sulpicius, regent in this vacancy; upon which he made very cordial acknowledgments to Cato, professing himself much his debtor, and requesting his good advice in conducting the government; to this Cato replied, that Pompey had no reason to thank him, for all that he had said was for the service of the commonwealth, not of Pompey; but that he would be always ready to give his advice privately, if he were asked for it; and if not, he should not fail to say what he thought in public. Such was Cato's conduct on all occasions.

On his return into the city Pompey married Cornelia, the daughter of Metellus Scipio, not a maiden, but lately left a widow by Publius, the son of Crassus, her first husband, who had been killed in Parthia. The young lady had other attractions besides those of youth and beauty; for she was highly educated, played well upon the lute, and understood geometry, and had been accustomed to listen with profit to lectures on philosophy; all this, too, without in any degree becoming unamiable or pretentious, as sometimes young women do when they pursue such studies. Nor could any fault be found either with her father's family or reputation. The disparity of their ages was, however, not liked by everybody; Cornelia being in this respect a fitter match for Pompey's son.

And wiser judges thought it rather a slight upon the commonwealth when he, to whom alone they had committed their broken fortunes, and from whom alone, as from their physician, they expected a cure to these distractions, went about crowned with garlands and celebrating his nuptial feasts, never considering that his very consulship was a public calamity, which would never have been given him, contrary to the rules of law, had his country been in a flourishing state.

Afterwards, however, he took cognisance of the cases of those that had obtained offices by gifts and bribery, and enacted laws and ordinances, setting forth the rules of judgment by which they should be arraigned; and regulating all things with gravity and justice, he restored security, order, and silence to their courts of judicature, himself giving his presence there

with a band of soldiers. But when his father-in-law, Scipio, was accused, he summoned the three hundred and sixty judges to his house, and entreated them to be favourable to him; whereupon his accuser, seeing Scipio come into the court, accompanied by the judges themselves, withdrew the prosecution.

Upon this Pompey was very ill spoken of, and much worse in the case of Plancus; for whereas he himself had made a law putting a stop to the practice of making speeches in praise of persons under trial, yet notwithstanding this prohibition, he came into court and spoke openly in commendation of Plancus, insomuch that Cato, who happened to be one of the judges at that time, stopping his ears with his hands, told him he could not in conscience listen to commendations contrary to law. Cato upon this was refused, and set aside from being a judge, before sentence was given, but Plancus was condemned by the rest of the judges, to Pompey's dishonour. Shortly after, Hypsæus, a man of consular dignity, who was under accusation, waited for Pompey's return from his bath to his supper, and falling down at his feet, implored his favour; but he disdainfully passed him by, saying that he did nothing else but spoil his supper.

Such partiality was looked upon as a great fault in Pompey and highly condemned; however, he managed all things else discreetly, and having put the government in very good order, he chose his father-in-law to be his colleague in the consulship for the last five months. His provinces were continued to him for the term of four years longer, with a commission to take one thousand talents yearly out of the treasury for the payment of his army.

This gave occasion to some of Cæsar's friends to think it reasonable that some consideration should be had of him too, who had done such signal services in war and fought so many battles for the empire, alleging, that he deserved at least a second consulship, or to have the government of his province continued, that so he might command and enjoy in peace what he had obtained in war, and no successor come in to reap the fruits of his labour and carry off the glory of his actions. There arising some debate about this, Pompey took it upon himself, as it were out of kindness to Cæsar, to plead his cause, and allay any jealousy that was conceived against him, telling them that he had letters from Cæsar, expressing his desire for a successor, and his own discharge from the command; but it would be only right that they should give him leave to stand for the consulship though in his absence. But those of Cato's party withstood this, saying, that if he expected any favour from the citizens, he ought to leave his army and come in a private capacity to canvass for it. And Pompey's making no rejoinder, but letting it pass as a matter in which he was overruled, increased the suspicion of his real feelings towards Cæsar. Presently, also, under pretence of a war with Parthia, he sent for his two legions which he had lent him. However, Cæsar, though he well knew why they were asked for, sent them home very liberally rewarded.

About that time Pompey recovered of a dangerous fit of sickness which seized him at Naples, where the whole city, upon the suggestion of Praxagoras, made sacrifices of thanksgiving to the gods for his recovery. The neighbouring towns likewise happening to follow their example, the thing then went its course throughout all Italy, so that there was not a city, either great or small, that did not feast and rejoice for many days together. And the company of those that came from all parts to meet him was so numerous that no place was able to contain them, but the villages, seaport towns, and the very highways were all full of people, feasting and sacrificing to the gods. Nay, many went to meet him with garlands on their heads, and flambeaux in their hands, casting flowers and nosegays upon him as he went along; so that this progress of his, and reception, was one of the noblest and most glorious sights imaginable.

And yet it is thought that this very thing was not one of the least causes and occasions of the civil war. For Pompey, yielding to a feeling of exultation, which in the greatness of the present display of joy lost sight of more solid grounds of consideration, and abandoning that prudent temper which had guided him hitherto to a safe use of all his good fortune and his successes, gave himself up to an extravagant confidence in his own and contempt of Cæsar's power; insomuch that he thought neither force of arms nor care necessary against him, but that he could pull him down much easier than he had set him up. Besides this, Appius, under whose command those legions which Pompey lent to Cæsar were returned, coming lately out of Gaul, spoke slightingly of Cæsar's actions there, and spread scandalous reports about him, at the same time telling Pompey that he was unacquainted with his own strength and reputation if he made use of any other forces against Cæsar than Cæsar's own; for such was the soldiers' hatred to Cæsar, and their love to Pompey so great, that they would all come over to him upon his first appearance. By these flatteries Pompey was so puffed up, and led on into such a careless security, that he could not choose but laugh at those who seemed to fear a war; and when some were saying, that if Cæsar should march against the city, they could not see what forces there were to resist him, he replied with a smile, bidding them to be in no concern, "for," said he, "whenever I stamp with my foot in any part of Italy there will rise up forces enough in an instant, both horse and foot."

Cæsar, on the other side, was more and more vigorous in his proceedings, himself always at hand about the frontiers of Italy, and sending his soldiers continually into the city to attend all elections with their votes. Besides, he corrupted several of the magistrates, and kept them in his pay; among others, Paulus, the consul, who was brought over by a bribe of one thousand and five hundred talents; and Curio, tribune of the people, by a discharge of the debts with which he was overwhelmed; together with Mark Antony, who, out of friendship to Curio, had become bound with him in the same obligations for them all. And it was stated as a fact, that a centurion of Cæsar's, waiting at the senate-house, and hearing that the senate refused to give him a longer term of his government, clapped his hand upon his sword, and said, "But this shall give it." And indeed all his practices and preparations seemed to bear this appearance.

Curio's demands, however, and requests in favour of Cæsar, were more popular in appearance; for he desired one of these two things, either that Pompey also should be called upon to resign his army, or that Cæsar's should not be taken away from him; for if both of them became private persons, both would be satisfied with simple justice; or if both retained their present power, each being a match for the other, they would be contented with what they already had; but he that weakens one, does at the same time strengthen the other, and so doubles that very strength and power which he stood in fear of before.

Marcellus, the consul, replied nothing to all this, but that Cæsar was a robber, and should be proclaimed an enemy to the state if he did not disband his army. However, Curio, with the assistance of Antony and Piso, prevailed, that the matter in debate should be put to the question, and decided by vote in the senate. So that it being ordered upon the question for those to withdraw who were of opinion that Cæsar only should lay down his army, and Pompey command, the majority withdrew. But when it was ordered again for those to withdraw whose vote was that both should lay down their arms, and neither command, there were but twenty-two for Pompey, all the rest remained on Curio's side. Whereupon he, as one proud of his conquest, leaped out in triumph among the people, who received him with as great tokens of joy, clapping their hands and crowning him with garlands and flowers. Pompey was not then present in the senate, because it is not lawful for generals in command of an army to come into the city. But Marcellus rising up, said, that he would not sit there hearing speeches, when he saw ten legions already passing the Alps on their march toward the city, but on his own authority would send some one to oppose them in defence of the country.

Upon this the city went into mourning, as in a public calamity, and Marcellus, accompanied by the senate, went solemnly through the Forum to meet Pompey, and made him this address: "I hereby give you orders, O Pompey, to defend your country, to employ the troops you now command, and to levy more." Lentulus, consul elect for the year following, spoke to the same purpose. Antony, however, contrary to the will of the senate, having in a public assembly read a letter of Cæsar's, containing various plausible overtures such as were likely to gain the common people, proposing, namely, that both Pompey and he, quitting their governments and dismissing their armies, should submit to the judgment of the people, and give an account of their actions before them, the consequence was that when Pompey began to make his levies, he found himself disappointed in his expectations. Some few, indeed, came in, but those very unwillingly; others would not answer to their names, and the generality cried out for peace.

Lentulus, notwithstanding he was now entered upon his consulship, would not assemble the senate; but Cicero, who was lately returned from Cilicia, laboured for a reconciliation, proposing that Cæsar should leave his province of Gaul and army, reserving two legions only, together with the government of Illyricum, and should thus be put in nomination for a second consulship. Pompey disliking this motion, Cæsar's friends were contented that he should surrender one of the two; but Lentulus still oppos-

ing, and Cato crying out that Pompey did ill to be deceived again, the reconciliation did not take effect.

In the meantime, news was brought that Cæsar had occupied Ariminum, a great city in Italy, and was marching directly towards Rome with all his forces. But this latter was altogether false, for he had no more with him at that time than three hundred horse and five thousand foot; and he did not mean to tarry for the body of his army, which lay beyond the Alps, choosing rather to fall in on a sudden upon his enemies, while they were in confusion, and did not expect him, than to give them time, and fight them after they had made preparations.

For when he came to the banks of the Rubicon, a river that made the bounds of his province, there he made a halt, pausing a little, and considering, we may suppose, with himself the greatness of the enterprise which he had undertaken; then, at last, like men that are throwing themselves headlong from some precipice into a vast abyss, having shut, as it were, his mind's eye and put away from his sight the idea of danger, he merely uttered to those near him in Greek the words, *"Anerriphtho kubos"* (let the die be cast), and led his army through it.

No sooner was the news arrived, but there was an uproar throughout all the city, and a consternation in the people even to astonishment, such as never was known in Rome before; all the senate ran immediately to Pompey, and the magistrates followed. And when Tullus made inquiry about his legions and forces, Pompey seemed to pause a little, and answered with some hesitation that he had those two legions ready that Cæsar sent back, and that out of the men who had been previously enrolled he believed he could shortly make up a body of thirty thousand men. On which Tullus crying out aloud, "O Pompey, you have deceived us," gave his advice to send off a deputation to Cæsar.

Favonius, a man of fair character, except that he used to suppose his own petulance and abusive talking a copy of Cato's straightforwardness, bade Pompey stamp upon the ground, and call forth the forces he had promised. But Pompey bore patiently with this unseasonable raillery; and on Cato putting him in mind of what he had foretold from the very beginning about Cæsar, made this answer only, that Cato indeed had spoken more like a prophet, but he had acted more like a friend. Cato then advised them to choose Pompey general with absolute power and authority, saying that the same men who do great evils know best how to cure them. He himself went his way forthwith into Sicily, the province that was allotted him, and all the rest of the senators likewise departed every one to his respective government.

Thus all Italy in a manner being up in arms, no one could say what was best to be done. For those that were without came from all parts flocking into the city; and they who were within, seeing the confusion and disorder so great there, all good things impotent, and dis-obedience and insubordination grown too strong to be controlled by the magistrates, were quitting it as fast as the others came in. Nay, it was so far from being possible to allay their fears, that they would not suffer Pompey to follow out his own judgment, but every man pressed and urged him according to his partic-ular fancy, whether it proceeded from doubt, fear, grief, or any meaner passion; so that even in the same day quite contrary counsels were acted upon. Then, again, it was as impossible to have any good intelligence of the enemy; for what each man heard by chance upon a flying rumour he would report for truth, and exclaim against Pompey if he did not believe it.

Pompey, at length, seeing such a confusion in Rome, determined with himself to put an end to their clamours by his departure, and therefore commanding all the senate to follow him, and declaring that whosoever tarried be-hind should be judged a confederate of Cæ-sar's, about the dusk of the evening he went out and left the city. The consuls also followed after in a hurry, without offering the sacrifices to the gods usual before a war. But in all this, Pompey himself had the glory that, in the midst of such calamities, he had so much of men's love and good-will. For though many found fault with the conduct of the war, yet no man hated the general; and there were more to be found of those that went out of Rome, be-cause that they could not forsake Pompey, than of those that fled for love of liberty.

Some few days after Pompey was gone out, Cæsar came into the city, and made himself master of it, treating every one with a great deal of courtesy, and appeasing their fears, ex-cept only Metellus, one of the tribunes; on whose refusing to let him take any money out of the treasury, Cæsar threatened him with death, adding words yet harsher than the threat, that it was far easier for him to do it than say it. By this means removing Metellus, and taking what moneys were of use for his oc-casions, he set forward in pursuit of Pompey,

endeavoring with all speed to drive him out of Italy before his army, that was in Spain, could join him.

But Pompey arriving at Brundusium, and having plenty of ships there, bade the two consuls embark immediately, and with them shipped thirty cohorts of foot, bound before him for Dyrrhachium. He sent likewise his father-in-law, Scipio, and Cnæus, his son, into Syria, to provide and fit out a fleet there; him-self in the meantime having blocked up the gates, placed his lightest soldiers as guards upon the walls; and giving express orders that the citizens should keep within doors, he dug up all the ground inside the city, cutting trenches, and fixing stakes and palisades throughout all the streets of the city, except only two that led down to the seaside. Thus in three days' space having with ease put all the rest of his army on shipboard, he suddenly gave the signal to those that guarded the walls, who nimbly repairing to the ships were received on board and carried off. Cæsar meantime per-ceiving their departure by seeing the walls un-guarded, hastened after, and in the heat of pur-suit was all but entangled himself among the stakes and trenches. But the Brundusians dis-covering the danger to him, and showing him the way, he wheeled about, and taking a cir-cuit round the city, made towards the haven, where he found all the ships on their way ex-cepting only two vessels that had but a few soldiers aboard.

Most are of opinion that this departure of Pompey's is to be counted among the best of his military performances, but Cæsar himself could not but wonder that he, who was thus engarrisoned in a city well fortified, who was in expectation of his forces from Spain, and was master of the sea besides, should leave and abandon Italy. Cicero accuses him of imitating the conduct of Themistocles, rather than of Pericles, when the circumstances were more like those of Pericles than they were like those of Themistocles. However, it appeared plainly, and Cæsar showed it by his actions, that he was in great fear of delay, for when he had taken Numerius, a friend of Pompey's, prisoner, he sent him as an ambassador to Brundusium, with offers of peace and reconciliation upon equal terms; but Numerius sailed away with Pompey.

And now Cæsar having become master of all Italy in sixty days, without a drop of blood-shed, had a great desire forthwith to follow Pompey; but being destitute of shipping, he was forced to divert his course and march into Spain, designing to bring over Pompey's forces there to his own.

In the meantime, Pompey raised a mighty army both by sea and land. As for his navy, it was irresistible. For there were five hundred men-of-war, besides an infinite company of light vessels, Liburnians, and others; and for his land forces, the cavalry made up a body of seven thousand horse, the very flower of Rome and Italy, men of family, wealth, and high spirit; but the infantry was a mixture of inexperienced soldiers drawn from different quarters, and these he exercised and trained near Berœa, where he quartered his army; himself noways slothful, but performing all his exercises as if he had been in the flower of his youth, conduct which raised the spirits of his soldiers extremely. For it was no small encouragement for them to see Pompey the Great, sixty years of age wanting two, at one time handling his arms among the foot, then again mounted among the horse, drawing out his sword with ease in full career, and sheathing it up as easily; and in darting the javelin, showing not only skill and dexterity in hitting the mark, but also strength and activity in throwing it so far that few of the young men went beyond him.

Several kings and princes of nations came thither to him, and there was a concourse of Roman citizens who had held the magistracies, so numerous that they made up a complete senate. Labienus forsook his old friend Cæsar, whom he had served throughout all his wars in Gaul, and came over to Pompey; and Brutus, son to that Brutus that was put to death in Gaul, a man of a high spirit, and one that to that day had never so much as saluted or spoke to Pompey, looking upon him as the murderer of his father, came then and submitted himself to him as the defender of their liberty. Cicero likewise, though he had written and advised otherwise, yet was ashamed not to be accounted in the number of those that would hazard their lives and fortunes for the safeguard of their country. There came to him also into Macedonia, Tidius Sextius, a man extremely old, and lame of one leg; so that others indeed mocked and laughed at the spectacle, but Pompey, as soon as he saw him, rose and ran to meet him, esteeming it no small testimony in his favour, when men of such age and infirmities should rather choose to be with him in danger than in safety at home.

Afterwards in a meeting of their senate they passed a decree, on the motion of Cato, that no Roman citizen should be put to death but in battle, and that they should not sack or plunder any city that was subject to the Roman empire, a resolution which gained Pompey's party still greater reputation, insomuch that those who were noways at all concerned in the war, either because they dwelt afar off, or were thought incapable of giving help, were yet, in their good wishes, upon his side, and in all their words, so far as that went, supported the good or just cause, as they called it; esteeming those as enemies to the gods and men that wished not victory to Pompey.

Neither was Pompey's clemency such but that Cæsar likewise showed himself as merciful a conqueror; for when he had taken and overthrown all Pompey's forces in Spain, he gave them easy terms, leaving the commanders at their liberty, and taking the common soldiers into his own pay. Then repassing the Alps, and making a running march through Italy, he came to Brundusium about the winter solstice, and crossing the sea there, landed at the port of Oricum. And having Jubius, an intimate friend of Pompey's, with him as his prisoner, he despatched him to Pompey with an invitation that they, meeting together in a conference, should disband their armies within three days, and renewing their former friendship with solemn oaths, should return together into Italy.

Pompey looked upon this again as some new stratagem, and therefore marching down in all haste to the sea-coast, possessed himself of all forts and places of strength suitable to encamp in, and to secure his land-forces, as likewise of all ports and harbours commodious to receive any that came by sea, so that what wind soever blew, it must needs, in some way or other, be favourable to him, bringing in either provision, men, or money; while Cæsar, on the contrary, was so hemmed in both by sea and land that he was forced to desire battle, daily provoking the enemy, and assailing them in their very forts, and in these light skirmishes for the most part had the better. Once only he was dangerously overthrown, and was within a little of losing his whole army, Pompey having fought nobly, routing the whole force and killing two thousand on the spot. But either he was not able, or was afraid, to go on and force his way into their camp with them; so that Cæsar made the remark, that "To-day the victory had been the enemy's had there been any one among them to gain it."

Pompey's soldiers were so encouraged by this victory that they were eager now to have all put to the decision of a battle; but Pompey himself, though he wrote to distant kings, generals, and states in confederacy with him as a conqueror, yet was afraid to hazard the success of a battle, choosing rather by delays and distress of provisions to tire out a body of men who had never yet been conquered by force of arms, and had long been used to fight and conquer together; while their time of life, now an advanced one, which made them quickly weary of those other hardships of war, such as were long marches and frequent decampings, making trenches, and building fortifications, made them eager to come to close combat and venture a battle with all speed.

Pompey had all along hitherto by his persuasions pretty well quieted his soldiers; but after this last engagement, when Cæsar, for want of provisions, was forced to raise his camp, and passed through Athamania into Thessaly, it was impossible to curb or allay the heat of their spirits any longer. For all crying out with a general voice that Cæsar was fled, some were for pursuing and pressing upon him, others for returning into Italy; some there were that sent their friends and servants beforehand to Rome to hire houses near the Forum, that they might be in readiness to sue for offices; several of their own motion sailed off at once to Lesbos to carry to Cornelia (whom Pompey had conveyed thither to be in safety) the joyful news that the war was ended.

And a senate being called and the matter being under debate, Afranius was of opinion that Italy should first be regained, for that it was the grand prize and crown of all the war; and they who were masters of that would quickly have at their devotion all the provinces of Sicily, Sardinia, Corsica, Spain, and Gaul; but what was of greatest weight and moment to Pompey, it was his own native country that lay near, reaching out her hand for his help; and certainly it could not be consistent with his honour to leave her thus exposed to all indignities, and in bondage under slaves and the flatterers of a tyrant.

But Pompey himself, on the contrary, thought it neither honourable to fly a second time before Cæsar, and be pursued, when fortune had given him the advantage of a pursuit; nor indeed lawful before the gods to forsake Scipio and divers other men of consular dignity dispersed throughout Greece and Thessaly, who

must necessarily fall into Cæsar's hands, together with large sums of money and numerous forces; and as to his care for the city of Rome, that would most eminently appear by removing the scene of war to a greater distance, and leaving her, without feeling the distress or even hearing the sound of these evils, to await in peace the return of whichever should be the victor.

With this determination, Pompey marched forwards in pursuit of Cæsar, firmly resolved with himself not to give him battle, but rather to besiege and distress him, by keeping close at his heels, and cutting him short. There were other reasons that made him continue this resolution, but especially because a saying that was current among the Romans serving in the cavalry came to his ear, to the effect that they ought to beat Cæsar as soon as possible, and then humble Pompey too. And some report it was for this reason that Pompey never employed Cato in any matter of consequence during the whole war, but now, when he pursued Cæsar, left him to guard his baggage by sea, fearing lest, if Cæsar should be taken off, he himself also by Cato's means not long after should be forced to give up his power.

Whilst he was thus slowly attending the motions of the enemy, he was exposed on all sides to outcries and imputations of using his generalship to defeat, not Cæsar, but his country and the senate, that he might always continue in authority, and never cease to keep those for his guards and servants who themselves claimed to govern the world. Domitius Ænobarbus, continually calling him Agamemnon, the king of kings, excited jealousy against him; and Favonius, by his unseasonable raillery, did him no less injury than those who openly attacked him, as when he cried out, "Good friends, you must not expect to gather any figs in Tusculum this year." But Lucius Afranius, who had lain under an imputation of treachery for the loss of the army in Spain, when he saw Pompey purposely declining an engagement, declared openly that he could not but admire why those who were so ready to accuse him did not go themselves and fight this buyer and seller of their provinces.

With these and many such speeches they wrought upon Pompey, who never could bear reproach, or resist the expectations of his friends; and thus they forced him to break his measures, so that he forsook his own prudent

resolution to follow their vain hopes and desires: weakness that would have been blamable
in the pilot of a ship, how much more in the
sovereign commander of such an army, and so
many nations. But he, though he had often
commended those physicians who did not
comply with the capricious appetites of their
patients, yet himself could not but yield to the
malady and disease of his companions and advisers in the war, rather than use some severity
in their cure. Truly, who could have said that
health was not disordered and a cure not required in the case of men who went up and
down the camp, suing already for the consulship and office of prætor, while Spinther,
Domitius, and Scipio made friends, raised factions, and quarrelled among themselves who
should succeed Cæsar in the dignity of his
high-priesthood, esteeming all as lightly as if
they were to engage only with Tigranes, King
of Armenia, or some petty Nabathæan king,
not with that Cæsar and his army that had
stormed a thousand towns, and subdued more
than three hundred several nations; that had
fought innumerable battles with the Germans
and Gauls, and always carried the victory; that
had taken a million of men prisoners, and slain
as many upon the spot in pitched battles?

But they went on soliciting and clamouring,
and on reaching the plain of Pharsalia, they
forced Pompey by their pressure and importunities to call a council of war, where Labienus, general of the horse, stood up first and
swore that he would not return out of the battle if he did not rout the enemies; and all the
rest took the same oath. That night Pompey
dreamed that, as he went into the theatre, the
people received him with great applause, and
that he himself adorned the temple of Venus
the Victorious with many spoils. This vision
partly encouraged, but partly also disheartened
him, fearing lest that splendour and ornament
to Venus should be made with spoils furnished
by himself to Cæsar, who derived his family
from that goddess. Besides there were some
panic fears and alarms that ran through the
camp, with such a noise that it awaked him
out of his sleep. And about the time of renewing the watch towards morning, there appeared a great light over Cæsar's camp whilst
they were all at rest, and from thence a ball of
flaming fire was carried into Pompey's camp,
which Cæsar himself says he saw as he was
walking his rounds.

Now Cæsar having designed to raise his
camp with the morning and move to Scotussa,
whilst the soldiers were busy in pulling down
their tents, and sending on their cattle and
servants before them with their baggage, there
came in scouts who brought word that they
saw arms carried to and fro in the enemy's
camp, and heard a noise and running up and
down as of men preparing for battle; not long
after there came in other scouts with further
intelligence, that the first ranks were already
set in battle array. Thereupon Cæsar, when he
had told them that the wished-for day was
come at last, when they should fight with men,
not with hunger and famine, instantly gave
orders for the red colours to be set up before
his tent, that being the ordinary signal of battle among the Romans. As soon as the soldiers
saw that, they left their tents, and with great
shouts of joy ran to their arms; the officers
likewise, on their part, drawing up their companies in order of battle, every man fell into
his proper rank without any trouble or noise,
as quietly and orderly as if they had been in a
dance.

Pompey himself led the right wing of his
army against Antony, and placed his father-
in-law, Scipio, in the middle against Lucius
Calvinus. The left wing was commanded by
Lucius Domitius, and supported by the great
mass of the horse. For almost the whole cavalry was posted there in the hope of crushing
Cæsar, and cutting off the tenth legion, which
was spoken of as the stoutest in all the army,
and in which Cæsar himself usually fought in
person.

Cæsar observing the left wing of the enemy
to be lined and fortified with such a mighty
guard of horse, and alarmed at the gallantry
of their appearance, sent for a detachment of
six cohorts out of the reserves, and placed them
in the rear of the tenth legion, commanding
them not to stir, lest they should be discovered
by the enemy; but when the enemy's horse
should begin to charge, and press upon them,
that they should make up with all speed to the
front through the foremost ranks, and not
throw their javelins at a distance, as is usual
with brave soldiers, that they may come to a
close fight with their swords the sooner, but
that they should strike them upwards into the
eyes and faces of the enemy; telling them that
those fine young dancers would never endure
the steel shining in their eyes, but would fly to
save their handsome faces. This was Cæsar's
employment at that time.

But while he was thus instructing his soldiers, Pompey on horseback was viewing the

order of both armies, and when he saw how well the enemy kept their ranks, expecting quietly the signal of battle, and, on the contrary, how impatient and unsteady his own men were, waving up and down in disorder for want of experience, he was very much afraid that their ranks would be broken upon the first onset; and therefore he gave out orders that the van should make a stand, and keeping close in their ranks should receive the enemy's charge.

Cæsar much condemns this command; which, he says, not only took off from the strength of the blows, which would otherwise have been made with a spring, but also lost the men the impetus, which, more than anything, in the moment of their coming upon the enemy, fills soldiers with impulse and inspiration, the very shouts and rapid pace adding to their fury; of which Pompey deprived his men, arresting them in their course and cooling down their heat.

Cæsar's army consisted of twenty-two thousand, and Pompey's of somewhat above twice as many. When the signal of battle was given on both sides, and the trumpets began to sound a charge, most men of course were fully occupied with their own matters; only some few of the noblest Romans, together with certain Greeks there present, standing as spectators without the battle, seeing the armies now ready to join, could not but consider in themselves to what a pass private ambition and emulation had brought the empire. Common arms, and kindred ranks drawn up under the selfsame standards, the whole flower and strength of the same single city here meeting in collision with itself, offered plain proof how blind and how mad a thing human nature is when once possessed with any passion; for if they had been desirous only to rule, and enjoy in peace what they had conquered in war, the greatest and best part of the world was subject to them both by sea and land.

But if there was yet a thirst in their ambition, that must still be fed with new trophies and triumphs, the Parthian and German wars would yield matter enough to satisfy the most covetous of honour. Scythia, moreover, was yet unconquered, and the Indians too, where their ambition might be coloured over with the specious pretext of civilising barbarous nations. And what Scythian horse, Parthian arrows, or Indian riches could be able to resist seventy thousand Roman soldiers, well appointed in arms, under the command of two

such generals as Pompey and Cæsar, whose names they had heard of before that of the Romans, and whose prowess, by their conquests of such wild, remote, savage, and brutish nations, was spread further than the fame of the Romans themselves?

To-day they met in conflict, and could no longer be induced to spare their country, even out of regard for their own glory or the fear of losing the name which till this day both had held, of having never yet been defeated. As for their former private ties, and the charms of Julia, and the marriage that had made them near connections, these could now only be looked upon as tricks of state, the mere securities of a treaty made to serve the needs of an occasion, not the pledges of any real friendship.

Now, therefore, as soon as the plains of Pharsalia were covered with men, horse, and armour, and that the signal of battle was raised on either side, Caius Crassianus, a centurion, who commanded a company of one hundred and twenty men, was the first that advanced out of Cæsar's army to give the charge and acquit himself of a solemn engagement that he had made to Cæsar. He had been the first man that Cæsar had seen going out of the camp in the morning, and Cæsar, after saluting him, had asked him what he thought of the coming battle. To which he, stretching out his right hand, replied aloud, "Thine is the victory, O Cæsar; thou shalt conquer gloriously, and I myself this day will be the subject of thy praise either alive or dead." In pursuance of this promise he hastened forward, and being followed by many more, charged into the midst of the enemy. There they came at once to a close fight with their swords, and made a great slaughter; but as he was still pressing forward, and breaking the ranks of the vanguard, one of Pompey's soldiers ran him in at the mouth, so that the point of the sword came out behind at his neck; and Crassianus being thus slain, the fight became doubtful, and continued equal on that part of the battle.

Pompey had not yet brought on the right wing, but stayed and looked about, waiting to see what execution his cavalry would do on the left. They had already drawn out their squadrons in form, designing to turn Cæsar's flank, and force those few horse, which he had placed in the front, to give back upon the battalion of foot. But Cæsar, on the other side, having given the signal, his horse retreated back a little, and gave way to those six subsidiary cohorts, which had been posted in the rear, as a reserve to cover the flank, and which now came out, three thousand men in number, and met the enemy; and when they came up, standing by the horses, struck their javelins upwards, according to their instructions, and hit the horsemen full in their faces. They, unskilful in any manner of fight, and least of all expecting or understanding such a kind as this, had not courage enough to endure the blows upon their faces, but turning their backs, and covering their eyes with their hands, shamefully took to flight.

Cæsar's men, however, did not follow them, but marched upon the foot, and attacked the wing, which the flight of the cavalry had left unprotected, and liable to be turned and taken in the rear, so that this wing now being attacked in the flank by these, and charged in the front by the tenth legion, was not able to abide the charge, or make any longer resistance, especially when they saw themselves surrounded and circumvented in the very way in which they had designed to invest the enemy.

Thus these being likewise routed and put to flight, when Pompey, by the dust flying in the air, conjectured the fate of his horse, it were very hard to say what his thoughts or intentions were, but looking like one distracted and beside himself, and without any recollection or reflection that he was Pompey the Great, he retired slowly towards his camp, without speaking a word to any man, exactly according to the description in the verses—

But Jove from heaven struck Ajax with a fear;
Ajax the bold then stood astonished there,
Flung o'er his back the mighty sevenfold shield
And trembling gazed and spied about the field.

In this state and condition he went into his own tent and sat down, speechless still, until some of the enemy fell in together with his men that were flying into the camp, and then he let fall only this one word, "What! into the very camp?" and said no more, but rose up, and putting on a dress suitable to his present fortune, made his way secretly out.

By this time the rest of the army was put to flight, and there was a great slaughter in the camp among the servants and those that guarded the tents, but of the soldiers themselves there were not above six thousand slain, as is stated by Asinius Pollio, who himself fought in this battle on Cæsar's side. When Cæsar's soldiers had taken the camp, they saw clearly the folly and vanity of the enemy; for all their tents and pavilions were richly set out

with garlands of myrtle, embroidered carpets and hangings, and tables laid and covered with goblets. There were large bowls of wine ready, and everything prepared and put in array, in the manner rather of people who had offered sacrifice and were going to celebrate a holiday, than of soldiers who had armed themselves to go out to battle, so possessed with the expectation of success and so full of empty confidence had they gone out that morning.

When Pompey had got a little way from the camp, he dismounted and forsook his horse, having but a small retinue with him; and finding that no man pursued him, walked on softly afoot, taken up altogether with thoughts, such as probably might possess a man that for the space of thirty-four years together had been accustomed to conquest and victory, and was then at last, in his old age, learning for the first time what defeat and flight were. And it was no small affliction to consider that he had lost in one hour all that glory and power which he had been getting in so many wars and bloody battles; and that he who but a little before was guarded with such an army of foot, so many squadrons of horse, and such a mighty fleet, was now flying in so mean a condition, and with such a slender retinue, that his very enemies who fought him could not know him.

Thus, when he had passed by the city of Larissa, and came into the pass of Tempe, being very thirsty, he kneeled down and drank out of the river; then rising up again, he passed through Tempe, until he came to the seaside, and there he betook himself to a poor fisherman's cottage, where he rested the remainder of the night. The next morning about break of day he went into one of the river boats, and taking none of those that followed him except such as were free, dismissed his servants, advising them to go boldly to Cæsar and not be afraid. As he was rowing up and down near the shore, he chanced to spy a large merchant ship, lying off, just ready to set sail; the master of which was a Roman citizen, named Peticius, who, though he was not familiarly acquainted with Pompey, yet knew him well by sight. Now it happened that this Peticius dreamed, the night before, that he saw Pompey, not like the man he had often seen him, but in a humble and dejected condition, and in that posture discoursing with him.

He was then telling his dream to the people on board, as men do when at leisure, and especially dreams of that consequence, when of a sudden one of the mariners told him he saw a river boat with oars putting off from shore, and that some of the men there shook their garments, and held out their hands, with signs to take them in; thereupon Peticius, looking attentively, at once recognised Pompey, just as he appeared in his dream, and smiting his hand on his head, ordered the mariners to let down the ship's boat, he himself waving his hand, and calling to him by his name, already assured of his change and the change of his fortune by that of his garb. So that without waiting for any further entreaty or discourse he took him into his ship, together with as many of his company as he thought fit, and hoisted sail. There were with him the two Lentuli and Favonius; and a little after they spied King Deiotarus, making up towards them from the shore; so they stayed and took him in along with them.

At supper time, the master of the ship having made ready such provisions as he had aboard, Pompey, for want of his servants, began to undo his shoes himself, which Favonius noticing, ran to him and undid them, and helped him to anoint himself, and always after continued to wait upon, and attended him in all things, as servants do their masters, even to the washing of his feet and preparing his supper. Insomuch that any one there present, observing the free and unaffected courtesy of these services, might have well exclaimed—

O heavens, in those that noble are,
Whate'er they do is fit and fair.

Pompey, sailing by the city of Amphipolis, crossed over from thence to Mitylene, with a design to take in Cornelia and his son; and as soon as he arrived at the port in that island, he despatched a messenger into the city with news very different from Cornelia's expectation. For she, by all the former messages and letters sent to please her, had been put in hopes that the war was ended at Dyrrhachium, and that there was nothing more remaining for Pompey but the pursuit of Cæsar. The messenger, finding her in the same hopes still, was not able to salute or speak to her, but declaring the greatness of her misfortune by his tears rather than his words, desired her to make haste if she would see Pompey, with one ship only, and that not of his own. The young lady hearing this, fell down in a swoon, and continued a long time senseless and speechless.

And when with some trouble she was brought to her senses again, being conscious to herself that this was no time for lamentation and tears, she started up and ran through the city towards the seaside, where Pompey meeting and embracing her, as she sank down, supported by his arms, "This, sir," she exclaimed, "is the effect of my fortune, not of yours, that I see you thus reduced to one poor vessel, who before your marriage with Cornelia were wont to sail in these seas with a fleet of five hundred ships. Why therefore should you come to see me, or why not rather have left to her evil genius one who has brought upon you her own ill fortune? How happy a woman had I been if I had breathed out my last before the news came from Parthia of the death of Publius, the husband of my youth, and how prudent if I had followed his destiny, as I designed! But I was reserved for a greater mischief, even the ruin of Pompey the Great."

Thus, they say, Cornelia spoke to him, and this was Pompey's reply: "You have had, Cornelia, but one season of a better fortune, which, it may be, gave you unfounded hopes, by attending me a longer time than is usual. It behooves us, who are mortals born, to endure these events, and to try fortune yet again; neither is it any less possible to recover our former state than it was to fall from that into this." Thereupon Cornelia sent for her servants and baggage out of the city.

The citizens also of Mitylene came out to salute and invite Pompey into the city, but he refused, advising them to be obedient to the conqueror and fear not, for that Cæsar was a man of great goodness and clemency. Then turning to Cratippus, the philosopher, who came among the rest out of the city to visit him, he began to find some fault, and briefly argued with him upon Providence, but Cratippus modestly declined the dispute, putting him in better hopes only, lest by opposing he might seem too austere or unseasonable.

For he might have put Pompey a question in his turn in defence of Providence; and might have demonstrated the necessity there was that the commonwealth should be turned into a monarchy, because of their ill government in the state; and could have asked, "How, O Pompey, and by what token or assurance can we ascertain, that if the victory had been yours, you would have used your fortune better than Cæsar?" We must leave the divine power to act as we find it to do.

Pompey having taken his wife and friends aboard, set sail, making no port, or touching anywhere, but when he was necessitated to take in provisions or fresh water. The first city he entered was Attalia, in Pamphylia, and whilst he was there, there came some galleys thither to him out of Cilicia, together with a small body of soldiers, and he had almost sixty senators with him again; then hearing that his navy was safe too, and that Cato had rallied a considerable body of soldiers after their overthrow, and was crossing with them over into Africa, he began to complain and blame himself to his friends that he had allowed himself to be driven into engaging by land, without making use of his other forces, in which he was irresistibly the stronger, and had not kept near enough to his fleet, that failing by land, he might have reinforced himself from the sea, and would have been again at the head of a power quite sufficient to encounter the enemy on equal terms. And, in truth, neither did Pompey during all the war commit a greater oversight, nor Cæsar use a more subtle stratagem, than in drawing the fight so far off from the naval forces.

As it now was, however, since he must come to some decision and try some plan within his present ability, he despatched his agents to the neighbouring cities, and himself sailed about in person to others, requiring their aid in money and men for his ships. But, fearing lest the rapid approach of the enemy might cut off all his preparations, he began to consider what place would yield him the safest refuge and retreat at present. A consultation was held, and it was generally agreed that no province of the Romans was secure enough. As for foreign kingdoms, he himself was of opinion that Parthia would be the fittest to receive and defend them in their present weakness, and best able to furnish them with new means, and send them out again with large forces. Others of the council were for going into Africa, and to King Juba.

But Theophanes the Lesbian thought it madness to leave Egypt, that was but at a distance of three days' sailing, and make no use of Ptolemy, who was still a boy, and was highly indebted to Pompey for the friendship and favour he had shown to his father, only to put himself under the Parthian, and trust the most treacherous nation in the world; and rather than make any trial of the clemency of a Roman, and his own near connection, to whom if he would but yield to be second he might be the first and chief over all the rest, to go and place himself at the mercy of Arsaces, which even Crassus had not submitted to while alive; and, moreover, to expose his young wife, of the family of the Scipios, among a barbarous

people, who govern by their lusts, and measure their greatness by their power to commit affronts and insolencies; from whom, though she suffered no dishonour, yet it might be thought she did, being in the hands of those who had the power to do it. This argument alone, they say, was persuasive enough to divert his course, that was designed towards Euphrates, if it were so indeed that any counsel of Pompey's and not some superior power, made him take this other way.

As soon, therefore, as it was resolved upon that he should fly into Egypt, setting sail from Cyprus in a galley of Seleucia, together with Cornelia, while the rest of his company sailed along near him, some in ships of war, and others in merchant vessels, he passed over sea without danger. But on hearing that King Ptolemy was posted with his army at the city of Pelusium, making war against his sister, he steered his course that way, and sent a messenger before to acquaint the king with his arrival, and to crave his protection.

Ptolemy himself was quite young, and therefore Pothinus, who had the principal administration of affairs, called a council of the chief men, those being the greatest whom he pleased to make so, and commanded them every man to deliver his opinion touching the reception of Pompey. It was, indeed, a miserable thing that the fate of the great Pompey should be left to the determination of Pothinus the eunuch, Theodotus of Chios, the paid rhetoric master, and Achillas the Egyptian. For these, among the chamberlains and menial domestics that made up the rest of the council, were the chief and leading men. Pompey, who thought it dishonourable for him to owe his safety to Cæsar, riding at anchor at a distance from shore, was forced to wait the sentence of this tribunal.

It seems they were so far different in their opinions that some were for sending the man away, and others, again, for inviting and receiving him; but Theodotus, to show his cleverness and the cogency of his rhetoric, undertook to demonstrate that neither the one nor the other was safe in that juncture of affairs. For if they entertained him, they would be sure to make Cæsar their enemy and Pompey their master; or if they dismissed him, they might render themselves hereafter obnoxious to Pompey, for that inhospitable expulsion, and to Cæsar, for the escape; so that the most expedient course would be to send for him and take away his life, for by that means they would ingratiate themselves with the one, and have no reason to fear the other; adding, it is related, with a smile, that "a dead man cannot bite."

This advice being approved of, they committed the execution of it to Achillas. He, therefore, taking with him as his accomplices one Septimius, a man that had formerly held a command under Pompey, and Salvius, another centurion, with three or four attendants, made up towards Pompey's galley. In the meantime, all the chiefest of those who accompanied Pompey in this voyage were come into his ship to learn the event of their embassy. But when they saw the manner of their reception, that in appearance it was neither princely nor honourable, nor indeed in any way answerable to the hopes of Theophanes, or their expectation (for there came but a few men in a fisherman's boat to meet them), they began to suspect the meanness of their entertainment, and gave warning to Pompey that he should row back his galley, whilst he was out of their reach, and make for the sea.

By this time the Egyptian boat drew near, and Septimius standing up first, saluted Pompey, in the Latin tongue, by the title of Imperator. Then Achillas, saluting him in the Greek language, desired him to come aboard his vessel, telling him that the sea was very shallow towards the shore, and that a galley of that burden could not avoid striking upon the sands. At the same time they saw several of the king's galleys getting their men on board, and all the shore covered with soldiers; so that even if they changed their minds, it seemed impossible for them to escape, and besides, their distrust would have given the assassins a pretence for their cruelty.

Pompey, therefore, taking his leave of Cornelia, who was already lamenting his death before it came, bade two centurions, with Philip, one of his freedmen, and a slave called Scythes, go on board the boat before him. And as some of the crew with Achillas were reaching out their hands to help him, he turned about towards his wife and son, and repeated those iambics of Sophocles—

He that once enters at a tyrant's door
Becomes a slave, though he were free before.

These were the last words he spoke to his friends, and so he went aboard.

Observing presently that notwithstanding there was a considerable distance betwixt his galley and the shore, yet none of the company

addressed any words of friendliness or welcome to him all the way, he looked earnestly upon Septimius, and said, "I am not mistaken, surely, in believing you to have been formerly my fellow-soldier." But he only nodded with his head, making no reply at all, nor showing any other courtesy. Since, therefore, they continued silent, Pompey took a little book in his hand, in which was written out an address in Greek, which he intended to make to King Ptolemy, and began to read it.

When they drew near to the shore, Cornelia, together with the rest of his friends in the galley, was very impatient to see the event, and began to take courage at last when she saw several of the royal escort coming to meet him, apparently to give him a more honourable reception; but in the meantime, as Pompey took Philip by the hand to rise up more easily, Septimius first stabbed him from behind with his sword, and after him likewise Salvius and Achillas drew out their swords. He, therefore, taking up his gown with both hands, drew it over his face, and neither saying nor doing anything unworthy of himself, only groaning a little, endured the wounds they gave him, and so ended his life, in the fifty-ninth year of his age, the very next day after the day of his birth.

Cornelia, with her company from the galley, seeing him murdered, gave such a cry that it was heard on the shore, and weighing anchor with all speed, they hoisted sail, and fled. A strong breeze from the shore assisted their flight into the open sea, so that the Egyptians, though desirous to overtake them, desisted from the pursuit.

But they cut off Pompey's head, and threw the rest of his body overboard, leaving it naked upon the shore, to be viewed by any that had the curiosity to see so sad a spectacle. Philip stayed by and watched till they had glutted their eyes in viewing it; and then washing it with sea-water, having nothing else, he wrapped it up in a shirt of his own for a winding-sheet. Then seeking up and down about the sands, at last he found some rotten planks of a little fisher-boat, not much, but yet enough to make up a funeral pile for a naked body, and that not quite entire.

As Philip was busy in gathering and putting these old planks together, an old Roman citizen, who in his youth had served in the wars under Pompey, came up to him and demanded who he was that was preparing the funeral of Pompey the Great. And Philip making answer that he was his freedman, "Nay, then," said he, "you shall not have this honour alone; let even me, too, I pray you, have my share in such a pious office, that I may not altogether repent me of this pilgrimage in a strange land, but in compensation of many misfortunes may obtain this happiness at last, even with mine own hands to touch the body of Pompey, and do the last duties to the greatest general among the Romans." And in this manner were the obsequies of Pompey performed.

The next day Lucius Lentulus, not knowing what had passed, came sailing from Cyprus along the shore of that coast, and seeing a funeral pile, and Philip standing by, exclaimed, before he was yet seen by any one, "Who is this that has found his end here?" adding after a short pause, with a sigh, "Possibly even thou, Pompeius Magnus!" and so going ashore, he was presently apprehended and slain. This was the end of Pompey.

Not long after, Cæsar arrived in the country that was polluted with this foul act, and when one of the Egyptians was sent to present him with Pompey's head, he turned away from him with abhorrence as from a murderer; and on receiving his seal, on which was engraved a lion holding a sword in his paw, he burst into tears. Achillas and Pothinus he put to death; and King Ptolemy himself, being overthrown in battle upon the banks of the Nile, fled away and was never heard of afterwards. Theodotus, the rhetorician, fleeing out of Egypt, escaped the hands of Cæsar's justice, but lived a vagabond in banishment, wandering up and down, despised and hated of all men, till at last Marcus Brutus, after he had killed Cæsar, finding him in his province of Asia, put him to death with every kind of ignominy. The ashes of Pompey were carried to his wife Cornelia, who deposited them at his country-house near Alba.

* * *

AGESILAUS and POMPEY
Compared

THUS having drawn out the history of the lives of Agesilaus and Pompey, the next thing is to compare them; and in order to this, to take a cursory view, and bring together the points in which they chiefly disagree; which are these.

In the first place, Pompey attained to all his greatness and glory by the fairest and justest means, owing his advancement to his own efforts, and to the frequent and important aid which he rendered Sulla, in delivering Italy from its tyrants. But Agesilaus appears to have obtained his kingdom, not without offence both towards gods and towards men, towards these, by procuring judgment of bastardy against Leotychides, whom his brother had declared his lawful son, and towards those, by putting a false gloss upon the oracle, and eluding its sentence against his lameness.

Secondly, Pompey never ceased to display his respect for Sulla during his lifetime, and expressed it also after his death, by enforcing the honourable interment of his corpse, in despite of Lepidus, and by giving his daughter in marriage to his son Faustus. But Agesilaus, upon a slight pretence, cast off Lysander with reproach and dishonour. Yet Sulla in fact had owed to Pompey services as much as Pompey ever received from him, whereas Lysander made Age-

silaus King of Sparta and general of all Greece.

Thirdly, Pompey's transgressions of right and justice in his political life were occasioned chiefly by his relations with other people, and most of his errors had some affinity, as well as himself, to Cæsar and Scipio, his fathers-in-law. But Agesilaus, to gratify the fondness of his son, saved the life of Sphodrias by a sort of violence, when he deserved death for the wrong he had done to the Athenians; and when Phœbidas treacherously broke the peace with Thebes, zealously abetted him for the sake, it was clear, of the unjust act itself. In short, what mischief soever Pompey might be said to have brought on Rome through compliance with the wishes of his friends or through inadvertency, Agesilaus may be said to have brought on Sparta out of obstinacy and malice, by kindling the Bœotian war.

And if, moreover, we are to attribute any part of these disasters to some personal ill-fortune, attaching to the men themselves, in the case of Pompey, certainly the Romans had no reason to anticipate it. Whereas Agesilaus would not suffer the Lacedæmonians to avoid what they foresaw and were forewarned must attend the "lame sovereignty." For had Leotychides been chargeable ten thousand times as foreign and spurious, yet the race of the Eurypontidæ was still in being, and could easily have furnished Sparta with a lawful king that was sound in his limbs, had not Lysander darkened and disguised the true sense of the oracle in favour of Agesilaus.

Such a politic piece of sophistry as was devised by Agesilaus, in that great perplexity of the people as to the treatment to be given to those who had played the coward at the battle of Leuctra, when after that unhappy defeat he decreed that the laws should sleep for that day, it would be hard to find any parallel to; neither have we the fellow of it in all Pompey's story. But, on the contrary, Pompey for a friend thought it no sin to break those very laws which he himself had made, as if to show at once the force of his friendship, and the greatness of his power; whereas Agesilaus, under the necessity, as it seemed, of either rescinding the laws, or not saving the citizens, contrived an expedient by the help of which the laws should not touch these citizens, and yet should not, to avoid it, be overthrown.

Then I must commend it as an incomparable act of civil virtue and obedience in Agesilaus, that immediately upon the receipt of the scytala, he left the wars in Asia and returned into his country. For he did not, like Pompey, merely advance his country's interest by acts that contributed at the same time to promote his own greatness, but looking to his country's good, for its sake laid aside as great authority and honour as ever any man had before or since, except Alexander the Great.

But now to take another point of view, if we sum up Pompey's military expeditions and exploits of war, the number of his trophies, and the greatness of the powers which he subdued, and the multitude of battles in which he triumphed, I am persuaded even Xenophon himself would not put the victories of Agesilaus in balance with his, though Xenophon has this privilege allowed him, as a sort of special reward for his other excellencies, that he may write and speak, in favour of his hero, whatever he pleases.

Methinks, too, there is a great deal of difference betwixt these men in their clemency and moderation towards their enemies. For Agesilaus, while attempting to enslave Thebes and exterminate Messene, the latter, his country's ancient associate, and Thebes, the mother-city of his own royal house, almost lost Sparta itself, and did really lose the government of Greece; whereas Pompey gave cities to those of the pirates who were willing to change their

manner of life; and when it was in his power to lead Tigranes, King of Armenia, in triumph, he chose rather to make him a confederate of the Romans, saying that a single day was worth less than all future time.

But if the preeminence in that which relates to the office and virtues of a general should be determined by the greatest and most important acts and counsels of war, the Lacedæmonian would not a little exceed the Roman. For Agesilaus never deserted his city, though it was besieged by an army of seventy thousand men, when there were very few soldiers within to defend it, and those had been defeated too, but a little before, at the battle of Leuctra. But Pompey, when Cæsar, with a body only of fifty-three hundred men, had taken but one town in Italy, departed in a panic out of Rome, either through cowardice, when there were so few, or at least through a false and mistaken belief that there were more; and having conveyed away his wife and children, he left all the rest of the citizens defenceless, and fled; whereas he ought either to have conquered in fight for the defence of his country, or yielded upon terms to the conqueror, who was, moreover, his fellow-citizen and allied to him; but now to the same man to whom he refused a prolongation of the terms of his government, and thought it intolerable to grant another consulship, to him he gave the power, by letting him take the city, to tell Metellus, together with all the rest, that they were his prisoners.

That which is chiefly the office of a general, to force the enemy into fighting when he finds himself the stronger, and to avoid being driven into it himself when he is the weaker, this excellence Agesilaus always displayed, and by it kept himself invincible; whereas in contending with Pompey, Cæsar, who was the weaker, successfully declined the danger, and his own strength being in his land-forces, drove him into putting the conflict to issue with these, and thus made himself master of the treasure, stores, and the sea too, which were all in his enemy's hands, and by the help of which the victory could have been secured without fighting.

And what is alleged as an apology in vindication of Pompey, is to a general of his age and standing the greatest of disgraces. For, granting that a young commander might by clamour and outcry be deprived of his fortitude and strength of mind, and weakly forsake his better judgment, and the thing be neither strange nor altogether unpardonable, yet for Pompey the Great, whose camp the Romans called their country, and his tent the senate, styling the consuls, prætors, and all other magistrates who were conducting the government at Rome by no better title than that of rebels and traitors, for him, whom they well knew never to have been under the command of any but himself, having served all his campaigns under himself as sole general, for him upon so small a provocation as the scoffs of Favonius and Domitius, and lest he should bear the nickname of Agamemnon, to be wrought upon, and even forced to hazard the whole empire and liberty of Rome upon the cast of a die, was surely indeed intolerable. Who, if he had so much regarded a present infamy, should have guarded the city at first with his arms, and fought the battle in defence of Rome, nor have left it as he did: nor while declaring his flight from Italy an artifice in the manner of Themistocles, nevertheless be ashamed in Thessaly of a prudent delay before engaging.

Heaven had not appointed the Pharsalian fields to be the stage and theatre upon which they should contend for the empire of Rome, neither was he summoned thither by any herald upon challenge, with intimation that he must either undergo the combat or surrender the prize to another. There were many other fields, thousands of cities, and even the whole earth placed at his command, by the advantage of his fleet and his superiority at sea, if he would but have followed the examples of Maximus, Marius, Lucullus, and even Agesilaus himself, who endured no less tumults within the city of Sparta, when the Thebans provoked him to come out and fight in defence of the land, and sustained in Egypt also numerous calumnies, slanders, and suspicions on the part of the king, whom he counselled to abstain from a battle. And thus following always what he had determined in his own judgment upon mature advice, by that means he not only preserved the Egyptians against their wills, not only kept Sparta, in those desperate convulsions, by his sole act, safe from overthrow, but even was able to set up trophies likewise in the city over the Thebans, having given his countrymen an occasion of being victorious afterwards by not at first leading them out, as they tried to force him to do, to their own destruction.

The consequence was that in the end Agesilaus was commended by the very men, when they found themselves saved, upon whom he had put this compulsion, whereas Pompey, whose error had been occasioned by others, found those his accusers whose advice had misled him. Some indeed profess that he was deceived by his father-in-law Scipio, who, designing to conceal and keep to himself the greatest part of that treasure which he had brought out of Asia, pressed Pompey to battle, upon the pretence that there would be a want of money. Yet admitting he was deceived, one in his place ought not to have been so, nor should have allowed so slight an artifice to cause the hazard of such mighty interests. And thus we have taken a view of each, by comparing together their conduct and actions in war.

As to their voyages into Egypt, one steered his course thither out of necessity in flight; the other neither honourably, nor of necessity, but as a mercenary soldier, having enlisted himself into the service of a barbarous nation for pay, that he might be able afterwards to wage war upon the Greeks. And secondly, what we charge upon the Egyptians in the name of Pompey, the Egyptians lay to the charge of Agesilaus. Pompey trusted them and was betrayed and murdered by them; Agesilaus accepted their confidence and deserted them, transferring his aid to the very enemies who were now attacking those whom he had been brought over to assist.

ALEXANDER

356–323 B.C.

IT BEING my purpose to write the lives of Alexander the king, and of Cæsar, by whom Pompey was destroyed, the multitude of their great actions affords so large a field that I were to blame if I should not by way of apology forewarn my reader that I have chosen rather to epitomise the most celebrated parts of their story, than to insist at large on every particular circumstance of it. It must be borne in mind that my design is not to write histories, but lives. And the most glorious exploits do not always furnish us with the clearest discoveries of virtue or vice in men; sometimes a matter of less moment, an expression or a jest, informs us better of their characters and inclinations, than the most famous sieges, the greatest armaments, or the bloodiest battles whatsoever. Therefore, as portrait-painters are more exact in the lines and features of the face, in which the character is seen, than in the other parts of the body, so I must be allowed to give my more particular attention to the marks and indications of the souls of men, and while I endeavour by these to portray their lives, may be free to leave more weighty matters and great battles to be treated of by others.

It is agreed on by all hands, that on the father's side, Alexander descended from Hercules by Caranus, and from Æacus by Neoptolemus on the mother's side. His father Philip, being in Samothrace, when he was quite young, fell in love there with Olympias, in company with whom he was initiated in the religious ceremonies of the country, and her father and mother being both dead, soon after, with the consent of her brother, Arymbas, he married her.

The night before the consummation of their marriage, she dreamed that a thunderbolt fell upon her body, which kindled a great fire, whose divided flames dispersed themselves all about, and then were extinguished. And Philip, some time after he was married, dreamt that he sealed up his wife's body with a seal, whose impression, as he fancied, was the figure of a lion. Some of the diviners interpreted this as a warning to Philip to look narrowly to his wife; but Aristander of Telmessus, considering how unusual it was to seal up anything that was empty, assured him the meaning of his dream was that the queen was with child of a boy, who would one day prove as stout and courageous as a lion.

Once, moreover, a serpent was found lying by Olympias as she slept, which more than anything else, it is said, abated Philip's passion for her; and whether he feared her as an enchantress, or thought she had commerce with some god, and so looked on himself as excluded, he was ever after fond of her conversation. Others say, that the women of this country having always been extremely addicted to the enthusiastic Orphic rites, and the wild worship of Bacchus (upon which account they were called Clodones, and Mimallones), imitated in many things the practices of the Edo-

nian and Thracian women about Mount Hæmus, from whom the word *threskeuein* seems to have been derived, as a special term for superfluous and over-curious forms of adoration; and that Olympias, zealously affecting these fanatical and enthusiastic inspirations, to perform them with more barbaric dread, was wont in the dances proper to these ceremonies to have great tame serpents about her, which sometimes creeping out of the ivy in the mystic fans, sometimes winding themselves about the sacred spears, and the women's chaplets, made a spectacle which men could not look upon without terror.

Philip, after this vision, sent Chæron of Megalopolis to consult the oracle of Apollo at Delphi, by which he was commanded to perform sacrifice, and henceforth pay particular honour, above all other gods, to Ammon; and was told he should one day lose that eye with which he presumed to peep through the chink of the door, when he saw the god, under the form of a serpent, in the company of his wife. Eratosthenes says that Olympias, when she attended Alexander on his way to the army in his first expedition, told him the secret of his birth, and bade him behave himself with courage suitable to his divine extraction. Others again affirm that she wholly disclaimed any pretensions of the kind, and was wont to say, "When will Alexander leave off slandering me to Juno?"

Alexander was born the sixth of Hecatombæon, which month the Macedonians call Lous, the same day that the temple of Diana at Ephesus was burnt; which Hegesias of Magnesia makes the occasion of a conceit, frigid enough to have stopped the conflagration. The temple, he says, took fire and was burnt while its mistress was absent, assisting at the birth of Alexander. And all the Eastern soothsayers who happened to be then at Ephesus, looking upon the ruin of this temple to be the forerunner of some other calamity, ran about the town, beating their faces, and crying that this day had brought forth something that would prove fatal and destructive to all Asia.

Just after Philip had taken Potidæa, he received these three messages at one time, that Parmenio had overthrown the Illyrians in a great battle, that his race-horse had won the course at the Olympic games, and that his wife had given birth to Alexander; with which being naturally well pleased, as an addition to his satisfaction, he was assured by the diviners that a son, whose birth was accompanied with three such successes, could not fail of being invincible.

The statues that gave the best representation of Alexander's person were those of Lysippus (by whom alone he would suffer his image to be made), those peculiarities which many of his successors afterwards and his friends used to affect to imitate, the inclination of his head a little on one side towards his left shoulder, and his melting eye, having been expressed by this artist with great exactness. But Apelles, who drew him with thunderbolts in his hand, made his complexion browner and darker than it was naturally; for he was fair and of a light colour, passing into ruddiness in his face and upon his breast. Aristoxenus in his Memoirs tells us that a most agreeable odour exhaled from his skin, and that his breath and body all over was so fragrant as to perfume the clothes which he wore next him; the cause of which might probably be the hot and adust temperament of his body. For sweet smells, Theophrastus conceives, are produced by the concoction of moist humours by heat, which is the reason that those parts of the world which are driest and most burnt up afford spices of the best kind and in the greatest quantity; for the heat of the sun exhausts all the superfluous moisture which lies in the surface of bodies, ready to generate putrefaction.

And this hot constitution, it may be, rendered Alexander so addicted to drinking, and so choleric. His temperance, as to the pleasures of the body, was apparent in him in his very childhood, as he was with much difficulty incited to them, and always used them with great moderation; though in other things he was extremely eager and vehement, and in his love of glory, and the pursuit of it, he showed a solidity of high spirit and magnanimity far above his age. For he neither sought nor valued it upon every occasion, as his father Philip did (who affected to show his eloquence almost to a degree of pedantry, and took care to have the victories of his racing chariots at the Olympic games engraven on his coin), but when he was asked by some about him, whether he would run a race in the Olympic games, as he was very swift-footed, he answered, he would, if he might have kings to run with him. Indeed, he seems in general to have looked with indifference, if not with dislike, upon the professed athletes. He often appointed prizes, for which not only tragedians and musicians, pipers and harpers, but rhapsodists also, strove to outvie one another; and delighted in all manner of hunting and cudgel-playing, but never gave any encouragement to contests either of boxing or of the pancratium.

While he was yet very young, he entertained the ambassadors from the King of Persia, in the absence of his father, and entering much into conversation with them, gained so much upon them by his affability, and the questions he asked them, which were far from being childish or trifling (for he inquired of them the length of the ways, the nature of the road into inner Asia, the character of their king, how he carried himself to his enemies, and what forces he was able to bring into the field), that they were struck with admiration of him, and looked upon the ability so much famed of Philip to be nothing in comparison with the forwardness and high purpose that appeared thus early in his son.

Whenever he heard Philip had taken any town of importance, or won any signal victory, instead of rejoicing at it altogether, he would tell his companions that his father would anticipate everything, and leave him and them no opportunities of performing great and illustrious actions. For being more bent upon action and glory than either upon pleasure or riches, he esteemed all that he should receive from his father as a diminution and prevention of his own future achievements; and would have chosen rather to succeed to a kingdom involved in troubles and wars, which would have afforded him frequent exercise of his courage, and a large field of honour, than to one already flourishing and settled, where his inheritance would be an inactive life, and the mere enjoyment of wealth and luxury.

The care of his education, as it might be presumed, was committed to a great many attendants, preceptors, and teachers, over the whole of whom Leonidas, a near kinsman of Olympias, a man of an austere temper, presided, who did not indeed himself decline the name of what in reality is a noble and honourable office, but in general his dignity, and his near relationship, obtained him from other people the title of Alexander's foster-father and governor. But he who took upon him the actual place and style of his pedagogue was Lysimachus the Acarnanian, who, though he had nothing specially to recommend him, but his lucky fancy of calling himself Phœnix, Alexander Achilles, and Philip Peleus, was therefore well enough esteemed, and ranked in the next degree after Leonidas.

Philonicus the Thessalian brought the horse

Bucephalus to Philip, offering to sell him for thirteen talents; but when they went into the field to try him, they found him so very vicious and unmanageable, that he reared up when they endeavoured to mount him, and would not so much as endure the voice of any of Philip's attendants. Upon which, as they were leading him away as wholly useless and untractable, Alexander, who stood by, said, "What an excellent horse do they lose for want of address and boldness to manage him!" Philip at first took no notice of what he said; but when he heard him repeat the same thing several times, and saw he was much vexed to see the horse sent away, "Do you reproach," said he to him, "those who are older than yourself, as if you knew more, and were better able to manage him than they?" "I could manage this horse," replied he, "better than others do." "And if you do not," said Philip, "what will you forfeit for your rashness?" "I will pay," answered Alexander, "the whole price of the horse."

At this the whole company fell a-laughing; and as soon as the wager was settled amongst them, he immediately ran to the horse, and taking hold of the bridle, turned him directly towards the sun, having, it seems, observed that he was disturbed at and afraid of the motion of his own shadow; then letting him go forward a little, still keeping the reins in his hands, and stroking him gently when he found him begin to grow eager and fiery, he let fall his upper garment softly, and with one nimble leap securely mounted him, and when he was seated, by little and little drew in the bridle, and curbed him without either striking or spurring him. Presently, when he found him free from all rebelliousness, and only impatient for the course, he let him go at full speed, inciting him now with a commanding voice, and urging him also with his heel. Philip and his friends looked on at first in silence and anxiety for the result, till seeing him turn at the end of his career, and come back rejoicing and triumphing for what he had performed, they all burst out into acclamations of applause; and his father shedding tears, it is said, for joy, kissed him as he came down from his horse, and in his transport said, "O my son, look thee out a kingdom equal to and worthy of thyself, for Macedonia is too little for thee."

After this, considering him to be of a temper easy to be led to his duty by reason, but by no means to be compelled, he always endeavoured to persuade rather than to command or force him to anything; and now looking upon the instruction and tuition of his youth to be of greater difficulty and importance than to be wholly trusted to the ordinary masters in music and poetry, and the common school subjects, and to require, as Sophocles says—

The bridle and the rudder, too,

he sent for Aristotle, the most learned and most celebrated philosopher of his time, and rewarded him with a munificence proportionable to and becoming the care he took to instruct his son. For he repeopled his native city Stagira, which he had caused to be demolished a little before, and restored all the citizens, who were in exile or slavery, to their habitations.

As a place for the pursuit of their studies and exercise, he assigned the temple of the Nymphs, near Mieza, where, to this very day, they show you Aristotle's stone seats, and the shady walks which he was wont to frequent.

It would appear that Alexander received from him not only his doctrines of morals and of politics, but also something of those more abstruse and profound theories which these philosophers, by the very names they gave them, professed to reserve for oral communications to the initiated, and did not allow many to become acquainted with. For when he was in Asia, and heard Aristotle had published some treatises of that kind, he wrote to him, using very plain language to him in behalf of philosophy, the following letter. "Alexander to Aristotle, greeting. You have not done well to publish your books of oral doctrine; for what is there now that we excel others in, if those things which we have been particularly instructed in be laid open to all? For my part, I assure you, I had rather excel others in the knowledge of what is excellent, than in the extent of my power and dominion. Farewell." And Aristotle, soothing this passion for preeminence, spoke, in his excuse for himself, of these doctrines as in fact both published and not published: as indeed, to say the truth, his books on metaphysics are written in a style which makes them useless for ordinary teaching, and instructive only, in the way of memoranda, for those who have been already conversant in that sort of learning.

Doubtless also it was to Aristotle that he owed the inclination he had, not to the theory only, but likewise to the practice of the art of medicine. For when any of his friends were sick, he would often prescribe them their course of diet, and medicines proper to their disease, as we may find in his epistles. He was naturally a great lover of all kinds of learning and reading; and Onesicritus informs us that he constantly laid Homer's *Iliad* according to the copy corrected by Aristotle, called the casket copy, with his dagger under his pillow, declaring that he esteemed it a perfect portable treasure of all military virtue and knowledge. When he was in the upper Asia, being destitute of other books, he ordered Harpalus to send him some; who furnished him with Philistus's *History,* a great many of the plays of Euripides, Sophocles, and Æschylus, and some dithyrambic odes, composed by Telestes and Philoxenus.

For a while he loved and cherished Aristotle no less, as he was wont to say himself, than if he had been his father, giving this reason for it, that as he had received life from the one, so the other had taught him to live well. But afterwards, upon some mistrust of him, yet not so great as to make him do him any hurt, his familiarity and friendly kindness to him abated so much of its former force and affectionateness, as to make it evident he was alienated from him. However, his violent thirst after and passion for learning, which were once implanted, still grew up with him, and never decayed; as appears by his veneration of Anaxarchus, by the present of fifty talents which he sent to Xenocrates, and his particular care and esteem of Dandamis and Calanus.

While Philip went on his expedition against the Byzantines, he left Alexander, then sixteen years old, his lieutenant in Macedonia, committing the charge of his seal to him; who, not to sit idle, reduced the rebellious Mædi, and having taken their chief town by storm, drove out the barbarous inhabitants, and planting a colony of several nations in their room, called the place after his own name, Alexandropolis. At the battle of Chæronea, which his father fought against the Grecians, he is said to have been the first man that charged the Thebans' Sacred Band. And even in my remembrance, there stood an old oak near the river Cephisus, which people called Alexander's oak, because his tent was pitched under it. And not far off are to be seen the graves of the Macedonians who fell in that battle. This early bravery made Philip so fond of him, that nothing pleased him more than to hear his subjects call himself their general and Alexander their king.

But the disorders of his family, chiefly caused by his new marriages and attachments (the troubles that began in the women's chambers spreading, so to say, to the whole kingdom), raised various complaints and differences between them, which the violence of Olympias, a woman of a jealous and implacable temper, made wider, by exasperating Alexander against his father. Among the rest, this accident contributed most to their falling out.

At the wedding of Cleopatra, whom Philip fell in love with and married, she being much too young for him, her uncle Attalus in his drink desired the Macedonians would implore the gods to give them a lawful successor to the kingdom by his niece. This so irritated Alexander, that throwing one of the cups at his head, "You villain," said he, "what, am I then a bastard?" Then Philip, taking Attalus's part, rose up and would have run his son through; but by good fortune for them both, either his over-hasty rage, or the wine he had drunk, made his foot slip, so that he fell down on the floor. At which Alexander reproachfully insulted over him: "See there," said he, "the man who makes preparations to pass out of Europe into Asia, overturned in passing from one seat to another." After this debauch, he and his mother Olympias withdrew from Philip's company, and when he had placed her in Epirus, he himself retired into Illyria.

About this time, Demaratus the Corinthian, an old friend of the family, who had the freedom to say anything among them without offence, coming to visit Philip, after the first compliments and embraces were over, Philip asked him whether the Grecians were at amity with one another. "It ill becomes you," replied Demaratus, "to be so solicitous about Greece, when you have involved your own house in so many dissensions and calamities." He was so convinced by this seasonable reproach, that he immediately sent for his son home, and by Demaratus's mediation prevailed with him to return.

But this reconciliation lasted not long; for when Pixodorus, viceroy of Caria, sent Aristocritus to treat for a match between his eldest daughter and Philip's son, Arrhidæus hoping by this alliance to secure his assistance upon occasion, Alexander's mother, and some who pretended to be his friends, presently filled his head with tales and calumnies, as if Philip, by a splendid marriage and important alliance, were preparing the way for settling the kingdom upon Arrhidæus. In alarm at this, he despatched Thessalus, the tragic actor, into Caria, to dispose Pixodorus to slight Arrhidæus, both as illegitimate and a fool, and rather to accept of himself for his son-in-law. This proposition was much more agreeable to Pixodorus than the former. But Philip, as soon as he was made acquainted with this transaction, went to his son's apartment, taking with him Philotas, the son of Parmenio, one of Alexander's intimate friends and companions, and there reproved him severely, and reproached him bitterly, that he should be so degenerate, and unworthy of the power he was to leave him, as to desire the alliance of a mean Carian, who was at best but the slave of a barbarous prince. Nor did this satisfy his resentment, for he wrote to the Corinthians to send Thessalus to him in chains, and banished Harpalus, Nearchus, Erigyius, and Ptolemy, his son's friends and favourites, whom Alexander afterwards recalled and raised to great honour and preferment.

Not long after this, Pausanias, having had an outrage done to him at the instance of Attalus and Cleopatra, when he found he could get no reparation for his disgrace at Philip's hands, watched his opportunity and murdered him. The guilt of which fact was laid for the most part upon Olympias, who was said to have encouraged and exasperated the enraged youth to revenge; and some sort of suspicion attached even to Alexander himself, who, it was said, when Pausanias came and complained to him of the injury he had received, repeated the verse out of Euripides's *Medea*—
On husband, and on father, and on bride.
However, he took care to find out and punish the accomplices of the conspiracy severely, and was very angry with Olympias for treating Cleopatra inhumanly in his absence.

Alexander was but twenty years old when his father was murdered, and succeeded to a kingdom, beset on all sides with great dangers and rancorous enemies. For not only the barbarous nations that bordered on Macedonia were impatient of being governed by any but their own native princes, but Philip likewise, though he had been victorious over the Grecians, yet, as the time had not been sufficient for him to complete his conquest and accustom them to his sway, had simply left all things in a general disorder and confusion.

It seemed to the Macedonians a very critical time; and some would have persuaded Alexander to give up all thought of retaining the Grecians in subjection by force of arms, and rather to apply himself to win back by gentle means the allegiance of the tribes who were designing revolt, and try the effect of indulgence in arresting the first motions towards revolution. But he rejected this counsel as weak and timorous, and looked upon it to be more prudence to secure himself by resolution and magnanimity, than, by seeming to truckle to any, to encourage all to trample on him.

In pursuit of this opinion, he reduced the barbarians to tranquillity, and put an end to all fear of war from them, by a rapid expedition into their country as far as the river Danube, where he gave Syrmus, King of the Triballians, an entire overthrow. And hearing the Thebans were in revolt, and the Athenians in correspondence with them, he immediately marched through the pass of Thermopylæ, saying that to Demosthenes, who had called him a child while he was in Illyria and in the country of the Triballians, and a youth when he was in Thessaly, he would appear a man before the walls of Athens.

When he came to Thebes, to show how willing he was to accept of their repentance for what was past, he only demanded of them Phœnix and Prothytes, the authors of the rebellion, and proclaimed a general pardon to those who would come over to him. But when the Thebans merely retorted by demanding Philotas and Antipater to be delivered into their hands, and by a proclamation on their part invited all who would assert the liberty of Greece to come over to them, he presently applied himself to make them feel the last extremities of war.

The Thebans indeed defended themselves with a zeal and courage beyond their strength, being much outnumbered by their enemies. But when the Macedonian garrison sallied out upon them from the citadel, they were so hemmed in on all sides that the greater part of them fell in the battle; the city itself being taken by storm, was sacked and razed; Alexander's hope being that so severe an example might terrify the rest of Greece into obedience, and also in order to gratify the hostility of his confederates, the Phocians and Platæans. So that, except the priests, and some few who had heretofore been the friends and connections of the Macedonians, the family of the poet Pindar, and those who were known to have opposed the public vote for the war, all the rest, to the number of thirty thousand, were publicly sold for slaves; and it is computed that upwards of six thousand were put to the sword.

Among the other calamities that befell the city, it happened that some Thracian soldiers, having broken into the house of a matron of high character and repute, named Timoclea, their captain, after he had used violence with her, to satisfy his avarice as well as lust, asked her, if she knew of any money concealed; to which she readily answered she did, and bade him follow her into a garden, where she showed him a well, into which, she told him, upon the taking of the city, she had thrown what she had of most value. The greedy Thracian presently stooping down to view the place where he thought the treasure lay, she came behind him and pushed him into the well, and then flung great stones in upon him, till she had killed him.

After which, when the soldiers led her away bound to Alexander, her very mien and gait showed her to be a woman of dignity, and of a mind no less elevated, not betraying the least sign of fear or astonishment. And when the king asked her who she was, "I am," said she, "the sister of Theagenes, who fought the battle of Chæronea with your father Philip, and fell there in command for the liberty of Greece." Alexander was so surprised, both at what she had done and what she said, that he could not choose but give her and her children their freedom to go whither they pleased.

After this he received the Athenians into favour, although they had shown themselves so much concerned at the calamity of Thebes that out of sorrow they omitted the celebration of the Mysteries, and entertained those who escaped with all possible humanity. Whether it were, like the lion, that his passion was now satisfied, or that, after an example of extreme cruelty, he had a mind to appear merciful, it happened well for the Athenians; for he not only forgave them all past offences, but bade them look to their affairs with vigilance, remembering that if he should miscarry, they were likely to be the arbiters of Greece.

Certain it is, too, that in aftertime he often repented of his severity to the Thebans, and his remorse had such influence on his temper as to make him ever after less rigorous to all others. He imputed also the murder of Clitus, which he committed in his wine, and the unwillingness of the Macedonians to follow him against the Indians, by which his enterprise and glory was left imperfect, to the wrath and vengeance of Bacchus, the protector of Thebes. And it was observed that whatsoever any Theban, who had the good fortune to survive this victory, asked of him, he was sure to grant without the least difficulty.

Soon after, the Grecians, being assembled at the Isthmus, declared their resolution of joining with Alexander in the war against the Persians, and proclaimed him their general. While he stayed here, many public ministers and philosophers came from all parts to visit him and congratulated him on his election, but contrary to his expectation, Diogenes of Sinope, who then was living at Corinth, thought so little of him, that instead of coming to compliment him, he never so much as stirred out of the suburb called the Cranium, where Alexander found him lying alone in the sun. When he saw so much company near him, he raised himself a little, and vouchsafed to look upon Alexander, and when he kindly asked him whether he wanted anything, "Yes," said he, "I would have you stand from between me and the sun." Alexander was so struck at this answer, and surprised at the greatness of the man, who had taken so little notice of him, that as he went away he told his followers, who were laughing at the moroseness of the philosopher, that if he were not Alexander, he would choose to be Diogenes.

Then he went to Delphi, to consult Apollo concerning the success of the war he had undertaken, and happening to come on one of the forbidden days, when it was esteemed improper to give any answer from the oracle, he sent messengers to desire the priestess to do her office; and when she refused, on the plea of a law to the contrary, he went up himself, and began to draw her by force into the temple, until tired and overcome with his importunity, "My son," said she, "thou art invincible." Alexander taking hold of what she spoke, declared he had received such an answer as he wished for, and that it was needless to consult the god any further. Among other prodigies that attended the departure of his army, the image of Orpheus at Libethra, made of cypress-wood, was seen to sweat in great abundance, to the discouragement of many. But Aristander told him that, far from presaging any ill to him, it signified he should perform acts so important and glorious as would make the poets and musicians of future ages labour and sweat to describe and celebrate them.

His army, by their computation who make the smallest amount, consisted of thirty thousand foot and four thousand horse; and those who make the most of it, speak but of forty-three thousand foot and three thousand horse. Aristobulus says he had not a fund of above seventy talents for their pay; nor had he more than thirty days' provision, if we may believe Duris; Onesicritus tells us he was two hundred talents in debt.

However narrow and disproportionable the

beginnings of so vast an undertaking might seem to be, yet he would not embark his army until he had informed himself particularly what means his friends had to enable them to follow him, and supplied what they wanted, by giving good farms to some, a village to one, and the revenue of some hamlet or harbour-town to another. So that at last he had portioned out or engaged almost all the royal property; which giving Perdiccas an occasion to ask him what he would leave himself, he replied, his hopes. "Your soldiers," replied Perdiccas, "will be your partners in those," and refused to accept of the estate he had assigned him. Some others of his friends did the like, but to those who willingly received or desired assistance of him, he liberally granted it, as far as his patrimony in Macedonia would reach, the most part of which was spent in these donations.

With such vigorous resolutions, and his mind thus disposed, he passed the Hellespont, and at Troy sacrificed to Minerva, and honoured the memory of the heroes who were buried there, with solemn libations; especially Achilles, who gravestone he anointed, and with his friends, as the ancient custom is, ran naked about his sepulchre, and crowned it with garlands, declaring how happy he esteemed him, in having while he lived so faithful a friend, and when he was dead, so famous a poet to proclaim his actions. While he was viewing the rest of the antiquities and curiosities of the place, being told he might see Paris's harp, if he pleased, he said he thought it not worth looking on, but he should be glad to see that of Achilles, to which he used to sing the glories and great actions of brave men.

In the meantime, Darius's captains, having collected large forces, were encamped on the further bank of the river Granicus, and it was necessary to fight, as it were, in the gate of Asia for an entrance into it. The depth of the river, with the unevenness and difficult ascent of the opposite bank, which was to be gained by main force, was apprehended by most, and some pronounced it an improper time to engage, because it was unusual for the kings of Macedonia to march with their forces in the month called Dæsius. But Alexander broke through these scruples, telling them they should call it a second Artemisius. And when Parmenio advised him not to attempt anything that day, because it was late, he told him that he should disgrace the Hellespont should he fear the Granicus. And so, without more saying, he

immediately took the river with thirteen troops of horse, and advanced against whole showers of darts thrown from the steep opposite side, which was covered with armed multitudes of the enemy's horse and foot, notwithstanding the disadvantage of the ground and the rapidity of the stream; so that the action seemed to have more frenzy and desperation in it, than of prudent conduct.

However, he persisted obstinately to gain the passage, and at last with much ado making his way up the banks, which were extremely muddy and slippery, he had instantly to join in a mere confused hand-to-hand combat with the enemy, before he could draw up his men, who were still passing over, into any order. For the enemy pressed him with loud and warlike outcries; and charging horse against horse, plied with their lances; after they had broken and spent these, they fell to it with their swords. And Alexander, being easily known by his buckler, and a large plume of white feathers on each side of his helmet, was attacked on all sides, yet escaped wounding, though his cuirass was pierced by a javelin in one of the joinings. And Rhœsaces and Spithridates, two Persian commanders, falling upon him at once, he avoided one of them, and struck at Rhœsaces, who had a good cuirass on, with such force that, his spear breaking in his hand, he was glad to betake himself to his dagger.

While they were thus engaged, Spithridates came up on one side of him, and raising himself upon his horse, gave him such a blow with his battle-axe on the helmet that he cut off the crest of it, with one of his plumes, and the helmet was only just so far strong enough to save him, that the edge of the weapon touched the hair of his head. But as he was about to repeat his stroke, Clitus, called the black Clitus, prevented him, by running him through the body with his spear. At the same time Alexander despatched Rhœsaces with his sword.

While the horse were thus dangerously engaged, the Macedonian phalanx passed the river, and the foot on each side advanced to fight. But the enemy hardly sustaining the first onset, soon gave ground and fled, all but the mercenary Greeks, who making a stand upon a rising ground, desired quarter, which Alexander, guided rather by passion than judgment, refused to grant, and charging them himself first, had his horse (not Bucephalus, but another) killed under him. And this obstinacy of his to cut off these experienced desperate men cost him the lives of more of his own soldiers than all the battle before, besides those who were wounded.

The Persians lost in this battle twenty thousand foot and two thousand five hundred horse. On Alexander's side, Aristobulus says there were not wanting above four-and-thirty, of whom nine were foot-soldiers; and in memory of them he caused so many statues of brass, of Lysippus's making, to be erected.

And that the Grecians might participate in the honor of his victory he sent a portion of the spoils home to them, particularly to the Athenians three hundred bucklers, and upon all the rest he ordered this inscription to be set: "Alexander the son of Philip, and the Grecians, except the Lacedæmonians, won these from the barbarians who inhabit Asia." All the plate and purple garments, and other things of the same kind that he took from the Persians, except a very small quantity which he reserved for himself, he sent as a present to his mother.

The battle presently made a great change of affairs to Alexander's advantage. For Sardis itself, the chief seat of the barbarian's power in the maritime provinces, and many other considerable places, were surrendered to him; only Halicarnassus and Miletus stood out, which he took by force, together with the territory about them.

After which he was a little unsettled in his opinion how to proceed. Sometimes he thought it best to find out Darius as soon as he could, and put all to the hazard of a battle; another while he looked upon it as a more prudent course to make an entire reduction of the seacoast, and not to seek the enemy till he had first exercised his power here and made himself secure of the resources of these provinces.

While he was thus deliberating what to do, it happened that a spring of water near the city of Xanthus in Lycia, of its own accord, swelled over its banks, and threw up a copper plate, upon the margin of which was engraven in ancient characters, that the time would come when the Persian empire should be destroyed by the Grecians. Encouraged by this accident, he proceeded to reduce the maritime parts of Cilicia and Phœnicia, and passed his army along the sea-coasts of Pamphylia with such expedition that many historians have described and extolled it with that height of admiration, as if it were no less than a miracle, and an extraordinary effect of divine favour, that the waves which usually come rolling in violently from the main, and hardly ever leave so much as a narrow beach under the steep, broken cliffs at any time uncovered, should on a sudden retire to afford him passage.

Menander, in one of his comedies, alludes to this marvel when he says—

Was Alexander ever favoured more?
Each man I wish for meets me at my door,
And should I ask for passage through the sea,
The sea I doubt not would retire me.

But Alexander himself in his epistles mentions nothing unusual in this at all, but says he went from Phaselis, and passed through what they call the Ladders. At Phaselis he stayed some time, and finding the statue of Theodectes, who was a native of this town and was now dead, erected in the marketplace, after he had supped, having drunk pretty plentifully, he went and danced about it, and crowned it with garlands, honouring not ungracefully, in his sport, the memory of a philosopher whose conversation he had formerly enjoyed when he was Aristotle's scholar.

Then he subdued the Pisidians who made head against him, and conquered the Phrygians, at whose chief city, Gordium, which is said to be the seat of the ancient Midas, he saw the famous chariot fastened with cords made of the rind of the cornel-tree, which whosoever should untie, the inhabitants had a tradition, that for him was reserved the empire of the world. Most authors tell the story that Alexander finding himself unable to untie the knot, the ends of which were secretly twisted round and folded up within it, cut it asunder with his sword. But Aristobulus tells us it was easy for him to undo it, by only pulling the pin out of the pole, to which the yoke was tied, and afterwards drawing off the yoke itself from below.

From hence he advanced into Paphlagonia and Cappadocia, both which countries he soon reduced to obedience, and then hearing of the death of Memnon, the best commander Darius had upon the sea-coasts, who, if he had lived, might, it was supposed, have put many impediments and difficulties in the way of the progress of his arms, he was the rather encouraged to carry the war into the upper provinces of Asia.

Darius was by this time upon his march from Susa, very confident, not only in the number of his men, which amounted to six hundred thousand, but likewise in a dream, which the Persian soothsayers interpreted rather in flattery to him than according to the natural probability. He dreamed that he saw the Macedonian phalanx all on fire, and Alexander waiting on him, clad in the same dress which he himself had been used to wear when he was courier to the late king; after which, going into the temple of Belus, he vanished out of his sight. The dream would appear to have supernaturally signified to him the illustrious actions the Macedonians were to perform, and that as he, from a courier's place, had risen to the throne, so Alexander should come to be master of Asia, and not long surviving his conquests, conclude his life with glory.

Darius's confidence increased the more, because Alexander spent so much time in Cilicia, which he imputed to his cowardice. But it was sickness that detained him there, which some say he contracted from his fatigues, others from bathing in the river Cydnus, whose waters were exceedingly cold. However, it happened, none of his physicians would venture to give him any remedies, they thought his case so desperate, and were so afraid of the suspicions and ill-will of the Macedonians if they should fail in the cure; till Philip, the Acarnanian, seeing how critical his case was, but relying on his own well-known friendship for him, resolved to try the last efforts of his art, and rather hazard his own credit and life than suffer him to perish for want of physic, which he confidently administered to him, encouraging him to take it boldly, if he desired a speedy recovery, in order to prosecute the war.

At this very time, Parmenio wrote to Alexander from the camp, bidding him have a care of Philip, as one who was bribed by Darius to kill him, with great sums of money, and a promise of his daughter in marriage. When he had perused the letter, he put it under his pillow, without showing it so much as to any of his most intimate friends, and when Philip came in with the potion, he took it with great cheerfulness and assurance, giving him meantime the letter to read. This was a spectacle well worth being present at, to see Alexander take the draught and Philip read the letter at the same time, and then turn and look upon one another, but with different sentiments; for Alexander's looks were cheerful and open, to show his kindness to and confidence in his physician, while the other was full of surprise and alarm at the accusation, appealing to the gods to witness his innocence, sometimes lifting up his hands to heaven, and then throwing himself down by the bedside, and beseeching Alexander to lay aside all fear, and follow his directions without apprehension. For the medicine at first worked so strongly as to drive, so

to say, the vital forces into the interior; he lost his speech, and falling into a swoon, had scarce any sense or pulse left. However, in no long time, by Philip's means, his health and strength returned, and he showed himself in public to the Macedonians, who were in continual fear and dejection until they saw him abroad again.

There was at this time in Darius's army a Macedonian refugee, named Amyntas, one who was pretty well acquainted with Alexander's character. This man, when he saw Darius intended to fall upon the enemy in the passes and defiles, advised him earnestly to keep where he was, in the open and extensive plains, it being the advantage of a numerous army to have field-room enough when it engages with a lesser force. Darius, instead of taking his counsel, told him he was afraid the enemy would endeavor to run away, and so Alexander would escape out of his hands. "That fear," replied Amyntas, "is needless, for assure yourself that far from avoiding you, he will make all the speed he can to meet you, and is now most likely on his march toward you." But Amyntas's counsel was to no purpose, for Darius immediately decamping, marched into Cilicia at the same time that Alexander advanced into Syria to meet him; and missing one another in the night, they both turned back again.

Alexander, greatly pleased with the event, made all the haste he could to fight in the defiles, and Darius to recover his former ground, and draw his army out of so disadvantageous a place. For now he began to perceive his error in engaging himself too far in a country in which the sea, the mountains, and the river Pinarus running through the midst of it, would necessitate him to divide his forces, render his horse almost unserviceable, and only cover and support the weakness of the enemy.

Fortune was not kinder to Alexander in the choice of the ground, than he was careful to improve it to his advantage. For being much inferior in numbers, so far from allowing himself to be outflanked, he stretched his right wing much further out than the left wing of his enemies, and fighting there himself in the very foremost ranks, put the barbarians to flight. In this battle he was wounded in the thigh, Chares says, by Darius, with whom he fought hand to hand. But in the account which he gave Antipater of the battle, though indeed he owns he was wounded in the thigh with a sword, though not dangerously, yet he takes no notice who it was that wounded him.

Nothing was wanting to complete this victory, in which he overthrew above an hundred and ten thousand of his enemies, but the taking of the person of Darius, who escaped very narrowly by flight. However, having taken his chariot and his bow, he returned from pursuing him, and found his own men busy in pillaging the barbarians' camp, which (though to disburden themselves they had left most of their baggage at Damascus) was exceedingly rich.

But Darius's tent, which was full of splendid furniture and quantities of gold and silver, they reserved for Alexander himself, who, after he had put off his arms, went to bathe himself, saying, "Let us now cleanse ourselves from the toils of war in the bath of Darius." "Not so," replied one of his followers, "but in Alexander's rather; for the property of the conquered is and should be called the conqueror's." Here, when he beheld the bathing vessels, the water-pots, the pans, and the ointment boxes, all of gold curiously wrought, and smelt the fragrant odours with which the whole place was exquisitely perfumed, and from thence passed into a pavilion of great size and height, where the couches and tables and preparations for an entertainment were perfectly magnificent, he turned to those about him and said, "This, it seems, is royalty."

But as he was going to supper, word was brought him that Darius's mother and wife and two unmarried daughters, being taken among the rest of the prisoners, upon the sight of his chariot and bow, were all in mourning and sorrow, imagining him to be dead. After a little pause, more lively affected with their affliction than with his own success, he sent Leonnatus to them, to let them know Darius was not dead, and that they need not fear any harm from Alexander, who made war upon him only for dominion; they should themselves be provided with everything they had been used to receive from Darius.

This kind message could not but be very welcome to the captive ladies, especially being made good by actions no less humane and generous. For he gave them leave to bury whom they pleased of the Persians, and to make use for this purpose of what garments and furniture they thought fit out of the booty. He diminished nothing of their equipage, or of the attentions and respect formerly paid them, and allowed larger pensions for their maintenance than they had before. But the noblest and most royal part of their usage was, that he treated these illustrious prisoners according to their virtue and character, not suffering them to hear, or receive, or so much as to apprehend anything that was unbecoming. So that they seemed rather lodged in some temple, or some holy virgin chambers, where they enjoyed their privacy sacred and uninterrupted, than in the camp of an enemy.

Nevertheless, Darius's wife was accounted the most beautiful princess then living, as her husband the tallest and handsomest man of his time, and the daughters were not unworthy of their parents. But Alexander, esteeming it more kingly to govern himself than to conquer his enemies, sought no intimacy with any one of them, nor indeed with any other woman before marriage, except Barsine, Memnon's widow, who was taken prisoner at Damascus. She had been instructed in the Grecian learning, was of a gentle temper, and by her father, Artabazus, royally descended. These good qualities, added to the solicitations and encouragement of Parmenio, as Aristobulus tells us, made him the more willing to attach himself to so agreeable and illustrious a woman.

Of the rest of the female captives, though remarkably handsome and well proportioned, he took no further notice than to say jestingly that Persian women were terrible eyesores. And he himself, retaliating, as it were, by the display of the beauty of his own temperance and self-control, bade them be removed, as he would have done so many lifeless images.

When Philoxenus, his lieutenant on the sea-coast, wrote to him to know if he would buy two young boys of great beauty, whom one Theodorus, a Tarentine, had to sell, he was so offended that he often expostulated with his friends what baseness Philoxenus had ever observed in him that he should presume to make him such a reproachful offer. And he immediately wrote him a very sharp letter, telling him Theodorus and his merchandise might go with his good-will to destruction. Nor was he less severe to Hagnon, who sent him word he would buy a Corinthian youth named Crobylus, as a present for him.

And hearing that Damon and Timotheus, two of Parmenio's Macedonian soldiers, had abused the wives of some strangers who were in his pay, he wrote to Parmenio, charging him strictly, if he found them guilty, to put them to death, as wild beasts that were only made for the mischief of mankind. In the same letter he added, that he had not so much as seen or desired to see the wife of Darius, no, nor suffered anybody to speak of her beauty before him. He

was wont to say that sleep and the act of generation chiefly made him sensible that he was
mortal; as much as to say, that weariness and
pleasure proceed both from the same frailty
and imbecility of human nature.

In his diet, also, he was most temperate, as
appears, omitting many other circumstances,
by what he said to Ada, whom he adopted,
with the title of mother, and afterwards created Queen of Caria. For when she, out of
kindness, sent him every day many curious
dishes and sweetmeats, and would have furnished him with some cooks and pastry-men
who were thought to have great skill, he told
her he wanted none of them, his preceptor,
Leonidas, having already given him the best,
which were a night march to prepare for breakfast, and a moderate breakfast to create an appetite for supper. Leonidas also, he added, used
to open and search the furniture of his chamber
and his wardrobe, to see if his mother had left
him anything that was delicate or superfluous.

He was much less addicted to wine than was
generally believed; that which gave people occasion to think so of him was, that when he
had nothing else to do, he loved to sit long and
talk, rather than drink, and over every cup
hold a long conversation. For when his affairs
called upon him, he would not be detained, as
other generals often were, either by wine, or
sleep, nuptial solemnities, spectacles, or any
other diversion whatsoever; a convincing argument of which is, that in the short time he
lived, he accomplished so many and so great
actions.

When he was free from employment, after
he was up, and had sacrificed to the gods, he
used to sit down to breakfast, and then spend
the rest of the day in hunting, or writing memoirs, giving decisions on some military questions, or reading. In marches that required no
great haste, he would practise shooting as he
went along, or mount a chariot and alight from
it in full speed. Sometimes, for sport's sake, as
his journals tell us, he would hunt foxes and
go fowling.

When he came in for the evening, after he
had bathed and was anointed, he would call
for his bakers and chief cooks, to know if they
had his dinner ready. He never cared to dine
till it was pretty late and beginning to be dark,
and was wonderfully circumspect at meals that
every one who sat with him should be served
alike and with proper attention; and his love
of talking, as was said before, made him delight to sit long at his wine. And then, though

otherwise no prince's conversation was ever so
agreeable, he would fall into a temper of ostentation and soldierly boasting, which gave his
flatterers a great advantage to ride him, and
made his better friends very uneasy. For
though they thought it too base to strive who
should flatter him most, yet they found it hazardous not to do it; so that between the shame
and the danger, they were in a great strait how
to behave themselves. After such an entertainment, he was wont to bathe, and then perhaps
he would sleep till noon, and sometimes all day
long.

He was so very temperate in his eating that
when any rare fish or fruits were sent him, he
would distribute them among his friends, and
often reserve nothing for himself. His table,
however, was always magnificent, the expense
of it still increasing with his good fortune, till
it amounted to ten thousand drachmas a day,
to which sum he limited it, and beyond this he
would suffer none to lay out in any entertainment where he himself was the guest.

After the battle of Issus, he sent to Damascus
to seize upon the money and baggage, the
wives and children of the Persians, of which
spoil the Thessalian horsemen had the greatest share; for he had taken particular notice
of their gallantry in the fight, and sent them
thither on purpose to make their reward suitable to their courage. Not but that the rest of
the army had so considerable a part of the
booty as was sufficient to enrich them all.

This first gave the Macedonians such a taste
of the Persian wealth and women and barbaric
splendour of living, that they were ready to
pursue and follow upon it with all the eagerness of hounds upon a scent. But Alexander,
before he proceeded any further, thought it
necessary to assure himself of the sea-coast.
Those who governed in Cyprus put that island
into his possession, and Phœnicia, Tyre only
excepted, was surrendered to him.

During the siege of this city, which, with
mounds of earth cast up, and battering engines,
and two hundred galleys by sea, was carried
on for seven months together, he dreamt that
he saw Hercules upon the walls, reaching out
his hands, and calling to him. And many of
the Tyrians in their sleep fancied that Apollo
told them he was displeased with their actions,
and was about to leave them to go over to
Alexander. Upon which, as if the god had been
a deserting soldier, they seized him, so to say,
in the act, tied down the statue with ropes, and
nailed it to the pedestal, reproaching him that

he was a favourer of Alexander. Another time Alexander dreamed he saw a satyr mocking him at a distance, and when he endeavoured to catch him, he still escaped from him, till at last with much perseverance, and running about after him, he got him into his power. The soothsayers, making two words of *Satyrus,* assured him that Tyre should be his own. The inhabitants at this time show a spring of water, near which they say Alexander slept when he fancied the satyr appeared to him.

While the body of the army lay before Tyre, he made an excursion against the Arabians who inhabit the Mount Antilibanus, in which he hazarded his life extremely to bring off his master, Lysimachus, who would needs go along with him, declaring he was neither older nor inferior in courage to Phœnix, Achilles's guardian. For when, quitting their horses, they began to march up the hills on foot, the rest of the soldiers outwent them a great deal, so that night drawing on, and the enemy near, Alexander was fain to stay behind so long, to encourage and help up the lagging and tired old man, that before he was aware he was left behind, a great way from his soldiers, with a slender attendance, and forced to pass an extremely cold night in the dark, and in a very inconvenient place; till seeing a great many scattered fires of the enemy at some distance, and trusting to his agility of body, and as he was always wont by undergoing toils and labours himself to cheer and support the Macedonians in any distress, he ran straight to one of the nearest fires, and with his dagger despatching two of the barbarians that sat by it, snatched up a lighted brand, and returned with it to his own men. They immediately made a great fire, which so alarmed the enemy that most of them fled, and those that assaulted them were soon routed, and thus they rested securely the remainer of the night. Thus Chares writes.

But to return to the siege, it had this issue. Alexander, that he might refresh his army, harassed with many former encounters, had led only a small party towards the walls, rather to keep the enemy busy than with any prospect of much advantage. It happened at this time that Aristander, the soothsayer, after he had sacrificed, upon view of the entrails, affirmed confidently to those who stood by that the city should be certainly taken that very month, upon which there was a laugh and some mockery among the soldiers, as this was the last day of it. The king, seeing him in perplexity, and always anxious to support the credit of the predictions, gave order that they should not count it as the thirtieth, but as the twenty-third of the month, and ordering the trumpets to sound, attacked the walls more seriously than he at first intended. The sharpness of the assault so inflamed the rest of his forces who were left in the camp, that they could not hold from advancing to second it, which they performed with so much vigour that the Tyrians retired, and the town was carried that very day.

The next place he sat down before was Gaza, one of the largest cities of Syria, when this accident befell him. A large bird flying over him let a clod of earth fall upon his shoulder, and then settling upon one of the battering engines, was suddenly entangled and caught in the nets, composed of sinews, which protected the ropes with which the machine was managed. This fell out exactly according to Aristander's prediction, which was, that Alexander should be wounded and the city reduced.

From hence he sent great part of the spoils to Olympias, Cleopatra, and the rest of his friends, not omitting his perceptor Leonidas, on whom he bestowed five hundred talents' weight of frankincense and an hundred of myrrh, in remembrance of the hopes he had once expressed of him when he was but a child. For Leonidas, it seems, standing by him one day while he was sacrificing, and seeing him take both his hands full of incense to throw into the fire, told him it became him to be more sparing in his offerings, and not to be so profuse till he was master of the countries which those sweet gums and spices come from. So Alexander now wrote to him, saying, "We have sent you abundance of myrrh and frankincense, that for the future you may not be stingy to the gods."

Among the treasures and other booty that was taken from Darius, there was a very precious casket, which being brought to Alexander for a great rarity, he asked those about him what they thought fittest to be laid up in it; and when they had delivered their various opinions, he told them he should keep Homer's *Iliad* in it. This is attested by many credible authors, and if what those of Alexandria tell us, relying upon the authority of Heraclides, be true, Homer was neither an idle nor an unprofitable companion to him in his expedition.

For when he was master of Egypt, designing to settle a colony of Grecians there, he resolved to build a large and populous city, and give it his own name. In order to which, after he had measured and staked out the ground with the advice of the best architects, he chanced one night in his sleep to see a wonderful vision; a grey-headed old man, of a venerable aspect, appeared to stand by him, and pronounce these verses:—

An island lies, where loud the billows roar,
Pharos they call it, on the Egyptian shore.

Alexander upon this immediately rose up and went to Pharos, which at that time was an island lying a little above the Canobic mouth of the river Nile, though it has now been joined to the mainland by a mole. As soon as he saw the commodious situation of the place, it being a long neck of land, stretching like an isthmus between large lagoons and shallow waters on one side and the sea on the other, the latter at the end of it making a spacious harbour, he said Homer, besides his other excellences, was a very good architect, and ordered the plan of a city to be drawn out answerable to the place. To do which, for want of chalk, the soil being black, they laid out their lines with flour, taking in a pretty large compass of ground in a semi-circular figure, and drawing into the inside of the circumference equal straight lines from each end, thus giving it something of the form of a cloak or cape.

While he was pleasing himself with his design, on a sudden an infinite number of great birds of several kinds, rising like a black cloud out of the river, and the lake, devoured every morsel of the flour that had been used in setting out the lines; at which omen even Alexander himself was troubled, till the augurs restored his confidence again by telling him it was a sign the city he was about to build would not only abound in all things within itself but also be the nurse and feeder of many nations. He commanded the workmen to proceed, while he went to visit the temple of Ammon.

This was a long and painful, and, in two respects, a dangerous journey; first, if they should lose their provision of water, as for several days none could be obtained; and, secondly, if a violent south wind should rise upon them, while they were travelling through the wide extent of deep sands, as it is said to have done when Cambyses led his army that way, blowing the sand together in heaps, and raising, as it were, the whole desert like a sea upon them, till fifty thousand were swallowed up and destroyed by it.

All these difficulties were weighed and represented to him; but Alexander was not easily to be diverted from anything he was bent up-

on. For fortune having hitherto seconded him in his designs, made him resolute and firm in his opinions, and the boldness of his temper raised a sort of passion in him for surmounting difficulties, as if it were not enough to be always victorious in the field, unless places and seasons and nature herself submitted to him.

In this journey, the relief and assistance the gods afforded him in his distresses were more remarkable, and obtained greater belief than the oracles he received afterwards, which, however, were valued and credited the more on account of those occurrences.

For first, plentiful rains that fell preserved them from any fear of perishing by drought, and, allaying the extreme dryness of the sand, which now became moist and firm to travel on, cleared and purified the air. Besides this, when they were out of their way, and were wandering up and down, because the marks which were wont to direct the guides were disordered and lost, they were set right again by some ravens, which flew before them when on their march, and waited for them when they lingered and fell behind; and the greatest miracle, as Callisthenes tells us, was that if any of the company went astray in the night, they never ceased croaking and making a noise till by that means they had brought them into the right way again.

Having passed through the wilderness, they came to the place where the high priest, at the first salutation, bade Alexander welcome from his father Ammon. And being asked by him whether any of his father's murderers had escaped punishment, he charged him to speak with more respect, since his was not a mortal father. Then Alexander, changing his expression, desired to know of him if any of those who murdered Philip were yet unpunished, and further concerning dominion, whether the empire of the world was reserved for him? This, the god answered, he should obtain, and that Philip's death was fully revenged, which gave him so much satisfaction that he made splendid offerings to Jupiter, and gave the priests very rich presents. This is what most authors write concerning the oracles.

But Alexander, in a letter to his mother, tells her there were some secret answers, which at his return he would communicate to her only. Others say that the priest, desirous as a piece of courtesy to address him in Greek, "O *Paidion*," by a slip in pronunciation ended with the *s* instead of the *n,* and said "O *Paidios,*" which mistake Alexander was well enough pleased with, and it went for current that the oracle had called him so.

Among the sayings of one Psammon, a philosopher, whom he heard in Egypt, he most approved of this, that all men are governed by God, because in everything, that which is chief and commands is divine. But what he pronounced himself upon this subject was even more like a philosopher, for he said, God was the common father of us all, but more particularly of the best of us.

To the barbarians he carried himself very haughtily, as if he were fully persuaded of his divine birth and parentage; but to the Grecians more moderately, and with less affectation of divinity, except it were once in writing to the Athenians about Samos, when he told them that he should not himself have bestowed upon them that free and glorious city; "You received it," he said "from the bounty of him who at that time was called my lord and father," meaning Philip. However, afterwards being wounded with an arrow, and feeling much pain, he turned to those about him, and told them, "This, my friends, is real flowing blood, not ichor—

Such as immortal gods are wont to shed."

And another time, when it thundered so much that everybody was afraid, and Anaxarchus, the sophist, asking him if he who was Jupiter's son could do anything like this, "Nay," said Alexander, laughing, "I have no desire to be formidable to my friends, as you would have me, who despised my table for being furnished with fish, and not with the heads of governors of provinces." For in fact it is related as true, that Anaxarchus, seeing a present of small fishes, which the king sent to Hephæstion, had used this expression, in a sort of irony, and disparagement of those who undergo vast labours and encounter great hazards in pursuit of magnificent objects which after all bring them little more pleasure or enjoyment than what others have. From what I have said upon this subject, it is apparent that Alexander in himself was not foolishly affected, or had the vanity to think himself really a god, but merely used his claims to divinity as a means of maintaining among other people the sense of his superiority.

At his return out of Egypt into Phœnicia, he sacrificed and made solemn processions, to which were added shows of lyric dances and tragedies, remarkable not merely for the splendour of the equipage and decorations, but for the competition among those who exhibited them. For the kings of Cyprus were here the exhibitors, just in the same manner as at Athens those who are chosen by lot out of the tribes. And, indeed, they showed the greatest emulation to outvie each other; especially Nicocreon, King of Salamis, and Pasicrates of Soli, who furnished the chorus, and defrayed the expenses of the two most celebrated actors, Athenodorus and Thessalus, the former performing for Pasicrates, and the latter for Nicocrean. Thessalus was most favoured by Alexander, though it did not appear till Athenodorus was declared victor by the plurality of votes. For then at his going away, he said the judges deserved to be commended for what they had done, but that he would willingly have lost part of his kingdom rather than to have seen Thessalus overcome.

However, when he understood Athenodorus was fined by the Athenians for being absent at the festivals of Bacchus, though he refused his request that he would write a letter in his behalf, he gave him a sufficient sum to satisfy the penalty.

Another time, when Lycon of Scarphia happened to act with great applause in the theatre, and in a verse which he introduced into the comic part which he was acting, begged for a present of ten talents, he laughed and gave him the money.

Darius wrote him a letter, and sent friends to intercede with him, requesting him to accept as a ransom of his captives the sum of a thousand talents, and offering him in exchange for his amity and alliance all the countries on this side the river Euphrates, together with one of his daughters in marriage. These propositions he communicated to his friends, and when Parmenio told him that, for his part, if he were Alexander, he should readily embrace them, "So would I," said Alexander, "if I were Parmenio." Accordingly, his answer to Darius was, that if he would come and yield himself up into his power he would treat him with all possible kindness; if not, he was resolved immediately to go himself and seek him. But the death of Darius's wife in childbirth made him soon after regret one part of this answer, and he showed evident marks of grief at being thus deprived of a further opportunity of exercising his clemency and good nature, which he manifested, however, as far as he could, by giving her a most sumptuous funeral.

Among the eunuchs who waited in the

queen's chamber, and were taken prisoners with the women, there was one Tireus, who, getting out of the camp, fled away on horseback to Darius, to inform him of his wife's death. He, when he heard it, beating his head, and bursting into tears and lamentations, said, "Alas! how great is the calamity of the Persians! Was it not enough that their king's consort and sister was a prisoner in her lifetime, but she must, now she is dead, also be but meanly and obscurely buried?" "O king," replied the eunuch, "as to her funeral rites, or any respect or honour that should have been shown in them, you have not the least reason to accuse the ill fortune of your country; for to my knowledge neither your queen Statira when alive, nor your mother, nor children, wanted anything of their former happy condition, unless it were the light of your countenance, which I doubt not but the lord Oromasdes will yet restore to its former glory. And after her decease, I assure you, she had not only all due funeral ornaments, but was honoured also with the tears of your very enemies; for Alexander is as gentle after victory as he is terrible in the field."

At the hearing of these words, such was the grief and emotion of Darius's mind, that they carried him into extravagant suspicions; and taking Tireus aside into a more private part of his tent, "Unless thou likewise," said he to him, "hast deserted me, together with the good fortune of Persia, and art become a Macedonian in thy heart; if thou yet ownest me for thy master Darius, tell me, I charge thee, by the veneration thou payest the light of Mithras, and this right hand of thy king, do I not lament the least of Statira's misfortunes in her captivity and death? Have I not suffered something more injurious and deplorable in her lifetime? And had I not been miserable with less dishonour if I had met with a more severe and inhuman enemy? For how is it possible a young man as he is should treat the wife of his opponent with so much distinction, were it not from some motive that does me disgrace?"

Whilst he was yet speaking, Tireus threw himself at his feet, and besought him neither to wrong Alexander so much, nor his dead wife and sister, as to give utterance to any such thoughts, which deprived him of the greatest consolation left him in his adversity, the belief that he was overcome by a man whose virtues raised him above human nature; that he ought to look upon Alexander with love and admiration, who had given no less proofs of his continence towards the Persian women, than of his valour among the men.

The eunuch confirmed all he said with solemn and dreadful oaths, and was further enlarging upon Alexander's moderation and magnanimity on other occasions, when Darius, breaking away from him into the other division of the tent, where his friends and courtiers were, lifted up his hands to heaven and uttered this prayer, "Ye gods," said he, "of my family, and of my kingdom, if it be possible, I beseech you to restore the declining affairs of Persia, that I may leave them in as flourishing a condition as I found them, and have it in my power to make a grateful return to Alexander for the kindness which in my adversity he has shown to those who are dearest to me. But if, indeed, the fatal time be come, which is to give a period to the Persian monarchy, if our ruin be a debt that must be paid to the divine jealousy and the vicissitude of things, then I beseech you grant that no other man but Alexander may sit upon the throne of Cyrus." Such is the narrative given by the greater number of the historians.

But to return to Alexander. After he had reduced all Asia on this side the Euphrates, he advanced towards Darius, who was coming down against him with a million of men. In his march a very ridiculous passage happened. The servants who followed the camp for sport's sake divided themselves into two parties, and named the commander of one of them Alexander, and the other Darius. At first they only pelted one another with clods of earth, but presently took to their fists, and at last, heated with contention, they fought in good earnest with stones and clubs, so that they had much ado to part them; till Alexander, upon hearing of it, ordered the two captains to decide the quarrel by single combat, and armed him who bore his name himself, while Philotas did the same to him who represented Darius. The whole army were spectators of this encounter, willing from the event of it to derive an omen of their own future success. After they had fought stoutly a pretty long while, at last he who was called Alexander had the better, and for a reward of his prowess had twelve villages given him, with leave to wear the Persian dress. So we are told by Eratosthenes.

But the great battle of all that was fought with Darius was not, as most writers tell us, at Arbela, but at Gaugamela, which, in their language, signifies the camel's house, forasmuch as one of their ancient kings having escaped the pursuit of his enemies on a swift camel, in gratitude to his beast, settled him at this place, with an allowance of certain villages and rents for his maintenance.

It came to pass that in the month Boëdromion, about the beginning of the feast of Mysteries at Athens, there was an eclipse of the moon, the eleventh night after which, the two armies being now in view of one another, Darius kept his men in arms, and by torchlight took a general review of them. But Alexander, while his soldiers slept, spent the night before his tent with his diviner, Aristander, performing certain mysterious ceremonies, and sacrificing to the god Fear.

In the meanwhile the oldest of his commanders, and chiefly Parmenio, when they beheld all the plain between Niphates and the Gordyæan mountains shining with the lights and fires which were made by the barbarians, and heard the uncertain and confused sounds of voices out of their camp, like the distant roaring of a vast ocean, were so amazed at the thoughts of such a multitude, that after some conference among themselves, they concluded it an enterprise too difficult and hazardous for them to engage so numerous an enemy in the day, and therefore meeting the king as he came from sacrificing, besought him to attack Darius by night, that the darkness might conceal the danger of the ensuing battle.

To this he gave them the celebrated answer, "I will not steal a victory," which though some at the time thought a boyish and inconsiderate speech, as if he played with danger, others, however, regarded as an evidence that he confided in his present condition, and acted on a true judgment of the future, not wishing to leave Darius, in case he were worsted, the pretext of trying his fortune again, which he might suppose himself to have, if he could impute his overthrow to the disadvantage of the night, as he did before to the mountains, the narrow passages, and the sea. For while he had such numerous forces and large dominions still remaining, it was not any want of men or arms that could induce him to give up the war, but only the loss of all courage and hope upon the conviction of an undeniable and manifest defeat.

After they were gone from him with this answer, he laid himself down in his tent and slept the rest of the night more soundly than was usual with him, to the astonishment of the commanders, who came to him early in the morning, and were fain themselves to give order that the soldiers should breakfast. But at last, time not giving them leave to wait any longer, Parmenio went to his bedside, and called him twice or thrice by his name, till he waked him, and then asked him how it was possible, when he was to fight the most important battle of all, he could sleep as soundly as if he were already victorious. "And are we not so, indeed," replied Alexander, smiling, "since we are at last relieved from the trouble of wandering in pursuit of Darius through a wide and wasted country, hoping in vain that he would fight us?"

And not only before the battle, but in the height of the danger, he showed himself great, and manifested the self-possession of a just foresight and confidence. For the battle for some time fluctuated and was dubious. The left wing, where Parmenio commanded, was so impetuously charged by the Bactrian horse that it was disordered and forced to give ground, at the same time that Mazæus had sent a detachment round about to fall upon those who guarded the baggage, which so disturbed Parmenio that he sent messengers to acquaint Alexander that the camp and baggage would be all lost unless he immediately relieved the rear by a considerable reinforcement drawn out of the front. This message being brought him just as he was giving the signal to those about him for the onset, he bade them tell Parmenio that he must have surely lost the use of his reason, and had forgotten, in his alarm, that soldiers, if victorious, become masters of their enemies' baggage; and if defeated, instead of taking care of their wealth or their slaves, have nothing more to do but to fight gallantly and die with honour.

When he had said this, he put on his helmet, having the rest of his arms on before he came out of his tent, which were a coat of the Sicilian make, girt close about him, and over that a breastpiece of thickly quilted linen, which was taken among other booty at the battle of Issus. The helmet, which was made by Theophilus, though of iron, was so well wrought and polished that it was as bright as the most refined silver. To this was fitted a gorget of the same metal, set with precious stones. His sword, which was the weapon he most used in fight, was given him by the King of the Citieans, and was of an admirable temper and lightness. The belt which he also wore in all engagements was of much richer workmanship than the rest of his armour. It was a work of the ancient Helicon, and had been presented to him by the Rhodians, as a mark of their respect to him.

So long as he was engaged in drawing up his men, or riding about to give orders or directions, or to view them, he spared Bucephalus, who was now growing old, and made use of another horse; but when he was actually to fight, he sent for him again, and as soon as he was mounted, commenced the attack.

He made the longest address that day to the Thessalians and other Greeks, who answered him with loud shouts, desiring him to lead them on against the barbarians, upon which he shifted his javelin into his left hand, and with his right lifted up towards heaven, besought the gods, as Callisthenes tells us, that if he was of a truth the son of Jupiter, they would be pleased to assist and strengthen the Grecians. At the same time the augur Aristander, who had a white mantle about him, and a crown of gold on his head, rode by and showed them an eagle that soared just over Alexander, and directed his flight towards the enemy; which so animated the beholders, that after mutual encouragements and exhortations, the horse charged at full speed, and were followed in a mass by the whole phalanx of the foot.

But before they could well come to blows with the first ranks, the barbarians shrunk back, and were hotly pursued by Alexander, who drove those that fled before him into the middle of the battle, where Darius himself was in person, whom he saw from a distance over the foremost ranks, conspicuous in the midst of his life-guard, a tall and fine-looking man, drawn in a lofty chariot, defended by an abundance of the best horse, who stood close in order about it ready to receive the enemy. But Alexander's approach was so terrible, forcing those who gave back upon those who yet maintained their ground, that he beat down and dispersed them almost all. Only a few of the bravest and valiantest opposed the pursuit, who were slain in their king's presence, falling in heaps upon one another, and in the very pangs of death striving to catch hold of the horses.

Darius now seeing all was lost, that those who were placed in front to defend him were broken and beat back upon him, that he could not turn or disengage his chariot without great difficulty, the wheels being clogged and entangled among the dead bodies, which lay in such heaps as not only stopped, but almost covered the horses, and made them rear and grow so unruly that the frightened charioteer could govern them no longer, in this extremity was glad to quit his chariot and his arms, and mounting, it is said, upon a mare that had been taken from her foal, betook himself to flight.

But he had not escaped so either, if Parmenio had not sent fresh messengers to Alexander, to desire him to return and assist him against a considerable body of the enemy which yet stood together, and would not give ground. For, indeed, Parmenio is on all hands accused of having been sluggish and unserviceable in this battle, whether age had impaired his courage, or that, as Callisthenes says, he secretly disliked and envied Alexander's growing greatness. Alexander, though he was not a little vexed to be so recalled and hindered from pursuing his victory, yet concealed the true reason from his men, and causing a retreat to be sounded, as if it were too late to continue the execution any longer, marched back towards the place of danger, and by the way met with the news of the enemy's total overthrow and flight.

This battle being thus over, seemed to put a period to the Persian empire; and Alexander, who was now proclaimed King of Asia, returned thanks to the gods in magnificent sacrifices, and rewarded his friends and followers with great sums of money, and places, and governments of provinces. Eager to gain honour with the Grecians, he wrote to them that he would have all tyrannies abolished, that they might live free according to their own laws, and specially to the Platæans, that their city should be rebuilt, because their ancestors had permitted their countrymen of old to make their territory the seat of the war when they fought with the barbarians for their common liberty. He sent also part of the spoils into Italy, to the Crotoniats, to honour the zeal and courage of their citizen Phayllus, the wrestler, who, in the Median war, when the other Grecian colonies in Italy disowned Greece, that he might have a share in the danger, joined the fleet at Salamis, with a vessel set forth at his own charge. So affectionate was Alexander to all kind of virtue, and so desirous to preserve the memory of laudable actions.

From hence he marched through the province of Babylon, which immediately submitted to him, and in Ecbatana was much surprised at the sight of the place where fire issues in a continuous stream, like a spring of water, out of a cleft in the earth, and the stream of naphtha, which, not far from this spot, flows out so abundantly as to form a sort of lake. This naphtha, in other respects resembling bitumen, is so subject to take fire, that before it touches the flame it will kindle at the very light that surrounds it, and often inflame the intermediate air also. The barbarians, to show the power and nature of it, sprinkled the street that led to the king's lodgings with little drops of it, and when it was almost night, stood at the further end with torches, which being applied to the moistened places, the first at once taking fire, instantly, as quick as a man could think of it, it caught from one end to another, in such a manner that the whole street was one continued flame.

Among those who used to wait on the king and find occasion to amuse him when he anointed and washed himself, there was one Athenophanes, an Athenian, who desired him to make an experiment of the naphtha upon Stephanus, who stood by in the bathing place, a youth with a ridiculously ugly face, whose talent was singing well, "For," said he, "if it take hold of him and is not put out, it must undeniably be allowed to be of the most invincible strength." The youth, as it happened, readily consented to undergo the trial, and as soon as he was anointed and rubbed with it, his whole body broke out into such a flame, and was so seized by the fire, that Alexander was in the greatest perplexity and alarm for him, and not without reason; for nothing could have prevented his being consumed by it, if by good chance there had not been people at hand with a great many vessels of water for the service of the bath, with all which they had much ado to extinguish the fire; and his body was so burned all over that he was not cured of it for a good while after.

Thus it is not without some plausibility that they endeavour to reconcile the fable to truth, who say this was the drug in the tragedies with which Medea anointed the crown and veil which she gave to Creon's daughter. For neither the things themselves, nor the fire, could kindle of their own accord, but being prepared for it by the naphtha, they imperceptibly attracted and caught a flame which happened to be brought near them. For the rays and emanations of fire at a distance have no other effect upon some bodies than bare light and heat, but in others, where they meet with airy dryness, and also sufficient rich moisture, they collect themselves and soon kindle and create a transformation. The manner, however, of the production of naphtha admits of a diversity of opinion . . . or whether this liquid substance that feeds the flame does not rather proceed from a soil that is unctuous and productive of fire, as that of the province of Babylon is, where the ground is so very hot that oftentimes the grains of barley leap up and are thrown out, as if the violent inflammation had made the earth throb; and in the extreme heats the inhabitants are wont to sleep upon skins filled with water.

Harpalus, who was left governor of this country, and was desirous to adorn the palace gardens and walks with Grecian plants, succeeded in raising all but ivy, which the earth would not bear, but constantly killed. For being a plant that loves a cold soil, the temper of this hot and fiery earth was improper for it. But such digressions as these the impatient reader will be more willing to pardon if they are kept within a moderate compass.

At the taking of Susa, Alexander found in the palace forty thousand talents in money ready coined, besides an unspeakable quantity of other furniture and treasure; amongst which was five thousand talents' worth of Hermionian purple, that had been laid up there an hundred and ninety years, and yet kept its colour as fresh and lively as at first. The reason of which, they say, is that in dyeing the purple they made use of honey, and of white oil in the white tincture, both which after the like space of time preserve the clearness and brightness of their lustre. Dinon also relates that the Persian kings had water fetched from the Nile and the Danube, which they laid up in their treasuries as a sort of testimony of the greatness of their power and universal empire.

The entrance into Persia was through a most difficult country, and was guarded by the noblest of the Persians, Darius himself having escaped further. Alexander, however, chanced to find a guide in exact correspondence with what the Pythia had foretold when he was a child, that a *lycus* should conduct him into Persia. For by such an one, whose father was a Lycian, and his mother a Persian, and who spoke both languages, he was now led into the country, by a way something about, yet without fetching any considerable compass.

Here a great many of the prisoners were put to the sword, of which he himself gives this account, that he commanded them to be killed in the belief that it would be for his advantage. Nor was the money found here less, he says, than at Susa, besides other movables and treasure, as much as ten thousand pair of mules and five thousand camels could well carry away. Amongst other things he happened to observe a large statue of Xerxes thrown carelessly down to the ground in the confusion made by the multitude of soldiers pressing into the palace. He stood still, and accosting it as if it had been alive, "Shall we," said he, "neglectfully pass thee by, now thou are prostrate on the ground because thou once invadedst Greece, or shall we erect thee again in consideration of the greatness of thy mind and thy other virtues?" But at last, after he had paused some time, and silently considered with himself, he went on without taking any further notice of it.

In this place he took up his winter quarters, and stayed four months to refresh his soldiers. It is related that the first time he sat on the royal throne of Persia under the canopy of gold, Demaratus the Corinthian, who was much attached to him and had been one of his father's friends, wept, in an old man's manner, and deplored the misfortune of those Greeks whom death had deprived of the satisfaction of seeing Alexander seated on the throne of Darius.

From hence designing to march against Darius, before he set out he diverted himself with his officers at an entertainment of drinking and other pastimes, and indulged so far as to let every one's mistress sit by and drink with them.

The most celebrated of them was Thais, an Athenian, mistress of Ptolemy, who was afterwards King of Egypt. She, partly as a sort of well-turned compliment to Alexander, partly out of sport, as the drinking went on, at last was carried so far as to utter a saying, not misbecoming her native country's character, though somewhat too lofty for her own condition. She said it was indeed some recompense for the toils she had undergone in following the camp all over Asia, that she was that day treated in, and could exult over, the stately palace of the Persian monarchs. But, she added, it would please her much better if, while the king looked on, she might in sport, with her own hands, set fire to the court of that Xerxes who reduced the city of Athens to ashes, that it might be recorded to posterity that the women who followed Alexander had taken a severer revenge on the Persians for the sufferings and affronts of Greece, than all the famed commanders had been able to do by sea or land.

What she said was received with such universal liking and murmurs of applause, and so seconded by the encouragement and eagerness of the company, that the king himself, persuaded to be of the party, started from his seat, and with a chaplet of flowers on his head and a lighted torch in his hand, led them the way, while they went after him in a riotous manner,

dancing and making loud cries about the place; which when the rest of the Macedonians perceived, they also in great delight ran thither with torches; for they hoped the burning and destruction of the royal palace was an argument that he looked homeward, and had no design to reside among the barbarians. Thus some writers give their account of this action, while others say it was done deliberately; however, all agree that he soon repented of it, and gave order to put out the fire.

Alexander was naturally most munificent, and grew more so as his fortune increased, accompanying what he gave with that courtesy and freedom which, to speak truth, is necessary to make a benefit really obliging. I will give a few instances of this kind.

Ariston, the captain of the Pæonians, having killed an enemy, brought his head to show him, and told him that in his country such a present was recompensed with a cup of gold. "With an empty one," said Alexander, smiling, "but I drink to you in this, which I give you full of wine."

Another time, as one of the common soldiers was driving a mule laden with some of the king's treasure, the beast grew tired, and the soldier took it upon his own back, and began to march with it, till Alexander seeing the man so overcharged asked what was the matter; and when he was informed, just as he was ready to lay down his burden for weariness, "Do not faint now," said he to him, "but finish the journey, and carry what you have there to your own tent for yourself."

He was always more displeased with those who would not accept of what he gave than with those who begged of him. And therefore he wrote to Phocion, that he would not own him for his friend any longer if he refused his presents.

He had never given anything to Serapion, one of the youths that played at ball with him, because he did not ask of him, till one day, it coming to Serapion's turn to play, he still threw the ball to others, and when the king asked him why he did not direct it to him, "Because you do not ask for it," said he; which answer pleased him so that he was very liberal to him afterwards.

One Proteas, a pleasant, jesting, drinking fellow, having incurred his displeasure, got his friends to intercede for him, and begged his pardon himself with tears, which at last prevailed, and Alexander declared he was friends with him. "I cannot believe it," said Proteas, "unless you first give me some pledge of it." The king understood his meaning, and presently ordered five talents to be given him.

How magnificent he was in enriching his friends, and those who attended on his person, appears by a letter which Olympias wrote to him, where she told him he should reward and honour those about him in a more moderate way. "For now," said she, "you make them all equal to kings, you give them power and opportunity of making many friends of their own, and in the meantime you leave yourself destitute." She often wrote to him to this purpose, and he never communicated her letters to anybody, unless it were one which he opened when Hephæstion was by, whom he permitted, as his custom was, to read it along with him; but then as soon as he had done, he took off his ring, and set the seal upon Hephæstion's lips.

Mazæus, who was the most considerable man in Darius's court, had a son who was already governor of a province. Alexander bestowed another upon him that was better; he, however, modestly refused, and told him, instead of one Darius, he went the way to make many Alexanders.

To Parmenio he gave Bagoas's house, in which he found a wardrobe of apparel worth more than a thousand talents.

He wrote to Antipater, commanding him to keep a life-guard about him for the security of his person against conspiracies.

To his mother he sent many presents, but would never suffer her to meddle with matters of state or war, not indulging her busy temper, and when she fell out with him on this account, he bore her ill-humour very patiently. Nay more, when he read a long letter from Antipater full of accusations against her, "Antipater," he said, "does not know that one tear of a mother effaces a thousand such letters as these."

But when he perceived his favourites grow so luxurious and extravagant in their way of living and expenses that Hagnon, the Teian, wore silver nails in his shoes, that Leonnatus employed several camels only to bring him powder out of Egypt to use when he wrestled, and that Philotas had hunting nets a hundred furlongs in length, that more used precious ointment than plain oil when they went to bathe, and that they carried about servants everywhere with them to rub them and wait upon them in their chambers, he reproved them in gentle and reasonable terms, telling them he wondered that they who had been engaged in so many single battles did not know by experience, that those who labour sleep more sweetly and soundly than those who are laboured for, and could fail to see by comparing the Persians' manner of living with their own that it was the most abject and slavish condition to be voluptuous, but the most noble and royal to undergo pain and labour. He argued with them further, how it was possible for any one who pretended to be a soldier, either to look well after his horse, or to keep his armour bright and in good order, who thought it much to let his hands be serviceable to what was nearest to him, his own body. "Are you still to learn," said he, "that the end and perfection of our victories is to avoid the vices and infirmities of those whom we subdue?"

And to strengthen his precepts by example, he applied himself now more vigorously than ever to hunting and warlike expeditions, embracing all opportunities of hardship and danger, insomuch that a Lacedæmonian, who was there on an embassy to him, and chanced to be by when he encountered with and mastered a huge lion, told him he had fought gallantly with the beast, which of the two should be king. Craterus caused a representation to be made of his adventure, consisting of the lion and the dogs, of the king engaged with the lion, and himself coming in to his assistance, all expressed in figures of brass, some of which were by Lysippus, and the rest by Leochares; and had it dedicated in the temple of Apollo at Delphi. Alexander exposed his person to danger in this manner, with the object both of inuring himself and inciting others to the performance of brave and virtuous actions.

But his followers, who were grown rich, and consequently proud, longed to indulge themselves in pleasure and idleness, and were weary of marches and expeditions, and at last went on so far as to censure and speak ill of him. All which at first he bore very patiently, saying it became a king well to do good to others, and be evil spoken of.

Meantime, on the smallest occasions that called for a show of kindness to his friends, there was every indication on his part of tenderness and respect. Hearing Peucestes was bitten by a bear, he wrote to him that he took it unkindly he should send others notice of it and not make him acquainted with it; "But now," said he, "since it is so, let me know how you do, and whether any of your companions forsook you when you were in danger, that I may punish them." He sent Hephæstion, who was absent about some business, word how, while they were fighting for their diversion with an ichneumon, Craterus was by chance run through both thighs with Perdiccas's javelin. And upon Peucestes's recovery from a fit of sickness, he sent a letter of thanks to his physician Alexippus. When Craterus was ill, he saw a vision in his sleep, after which he offered sacrifices for his health, and bade him do so likewise. He wrote also to Pausanias, the physician, who was about to purge Craterus with hellebore, partly out of an anxious concern for him, and partly to give him a caution how he used that medicine.

He was so tender of his friends' reputation that he imprisoned Ephialtes and Cissus, who brought him the first news of Harpalus's flight and withdrawal from his service, as if they had falsely accused him.

When he sent the old and infirm soldiers home, Eurylochus, a citizen of Ægæ, got his name enrolled among the sick, though he ailed nothing, which being discovered, he confessed he was in love with a young woman named Telesippa, and wanted to go along with her to the seaside. Alexander inquired to whom the woman belonged, and being told she was a free courtesan, "I will assist you," said he to Eurylochus, "in your amour if your mistress be to be gained either by presents or persuasions; but we must use no other means, because she is free-born."

It is surprising to consider upon what slight occasions he would write letters to serve his friends. As when he wrote one in which he gave order to search for a youth that belonged to Seleucus, who was run away into Cilicia; and in another thanked and commended Peucestes for apprehending Nicon, a servant of Craterus; and in one to Megabyzus, concerning a slave that had taken sanctuary in a temple, gave direction that he should not meddle with him while he was there, but if he could entice him out by fair means, then he gave him leave to seize him. It is reported of him that when he first sat in judgment upon capital causes he would lay his hand upon one of his ears while the accuser spoke, to keep it free and unprejudiced in behalf of the party accused. But afterwards such a multitude of accusations were brought before him, and so many proved true, that he lost his tenderness of heart, and gave credit to those also that were false; and especially when anybody spoke ill of him, he would be transported out of his reason, and

show himself cruel and inexorable, valuing his glory and reputation beyond his life or kingdom.

He now, as we said, set forth to seek Darius, expecting he should be put to the hazard of another battle, but heard he was taken and secured by Bessus, upon which news he sent home the Thessalians, and gave them a largess of two thousand talents over and above the pay that was due to them. This long and painful pursuit of Darius—for in eleven days he marched thirty-three hundred furlongs—harassed his soldiers so that most of them were ready to give it up, chiefly for want of water.

While they were in this distress, it happened that some Macedonians who had fetched water in skins upon their mules from a river they had found out came about noon to the place where Alexander was, and seeing him almost choked with thirst, presently filled an helmet and offered it him. He asked them to whom they were carrying the water; they told him to their children, adding, that if his life were but saved, it was no matter for them, they should be able well enough to repair that loss, though they all perished. Then he took the helmet into his hands, and looking round about, when he saw all those who were near him stretching their heads out and looking earnestly after the drink, he returned it again with thanks without tasting a drop of it. "For," said he, "if I alone should drink, the rest will be out of heart." The soldiers no sooner took notice of his temperance and magnanimity upon this occasion, but they one and all cried out to him to lead them forward boldly, and began whipping on their horses. For whilst they had such a king they said they defied both weariness and thirst, and looked upon themselves to be little less than immortal.

But though they were all equally cheerful and willing, yet not above threescore horse were able, it is said, to keep up, and to fall in with Alexander upon the enemy's camp, where they rode over abundance of gold and silver that lay scattered about, and passing by a great many chariots full of women that wandered here and there for want of drivers, they endeavoured to overtake the first of those that fled, in hopes to meet with Darius among them.

And at last, after much trouble, they found him lying in a chariot, wounded all over with darts, just at the point of death. However, he desired they would give him some drink, and when he had drunk a little cold water, he told

Polystratus, who gave it him, that it had become the last extremity of his ill fortune to receive benefits and not be able to return them. "But Alexander," said he, "whose kindness to my mother, my wife, and my children I hope the gods will recompense, will doubtless thank you for your humanity to me. Tell him, therefore, in token of my acknowledgment, I give him this right hand," with which words he took hold of Polystratus's hand and died. When Alexander came up to them, he showed manifest tokens of sorrow, and taking off his own cloak, threw it upon the body to cover it. And some time afterwards, when Bessus was taken, he ordered him to be torn in pieces in this manner. They fastened him to a couple of trees which were bound down so as to meet, and then being let loose, with a great force returned to their places, each of them carrying that part of the body along with it that was tied to it. Darius's body was laid in state, and sent to his mother with pomp suitable to his quality. His brother Exathres, Alexander received into the number of his intimate friends.

And now with the flower of his army he marched into Hyrcania, where he saw a large bay of an open sea, apparently not much less than the Euxine, with water, however, sweeter than that of other seas, but could learn nothing of certainty concerning it, further than that in all probability it seemed to him to be an arm issuing from the lake of Mæotis. However, the naturalists were better informed of the truth, and had given an account of it many years before Alexander's expedition; that of four gulfs which out of the main sea enter into the continent, this, known indifferently as the Caspian and as the Hyrcanian Sea, is the most northern.

Here the barbarians, unexpectedly meeting with those who led Bucephalus, took them prisoners, and carried the horse away with them, at which Alexander was so much vexed that he sent an herald to let them know he would put them all to the sword, men, women, and children, without mercy, if they did not restore him. But on their doing so, and at the same time surrendering their cities into his hands, he not only treated them kindly, but also paid a ransom for his horse to those who took him.

From hence he marched into Parthia, where not having much to do, he first put on the barbaric dress, perhaps with the view of making the work of civilising them the easier, as nothing gains more upon men than a conformity

to their fashions and customs. Or it may have been as a first trial, whether the Macedonians might be brought to *adore* him as the Persians did their kings, by accustoming them by little and little to bear with the alteration of his rule and course of life in other things.

However, he followed not the Median fashion, which was altogether foreign and uncouth, and adopted neither the trousers nor the sleeved vest, nor the tiara for the head, but taking a middle way between the Persian mode and the Macedonian, so contrived his habit that it was not so flaunting as the one, and yet more pompous and magnificent than the other.

At first he wore this habit only when he conversed with the barbarians, or within doors, among his intimate friends and companions, but afterwards he appeared in it abroad, when he rode out, and at public audiences, a sight which the Macedonians beheld with grief; but they so respected his other virtues and good qualities that they felt it reasonable in some things to gratify his fancies and his passion of glory, in pursuit of which he hazarded himself so far, that, besides his other adventures, he had but lately been wounded in the leg by an arrow, which had so shattered the shank-bone that splinters were taken out. And on another occasion he received a violent blow with a stone upon the nape of the neck, which dimmed his sight for a good while afterwards. And yet all this could not hinder him from exposing himself freely to any dangers, insomuch that he passed the river Orexartes, which he took to be the Tanais, and putting the Scythians to flight, followed them above a hundred furlongs, though suffering all the time from a diarrhœa.

Here many affirm that the Amazon came to give him a visit. So Clitarchus, Polyclitus, Onesicritus, Antigenes, and Ister tell us. But Aristobulus and Chares, who held the office of reporter of requests, Ptolemy and Anticlides, Philon the Theban, Philip of Theangela, Hecatæus the Eretrian, Philip the Chalcidian, and Duris the Samian, say it is wholly a fiction. And truly Alexander himself seems to confirm the latter statement, for in a letter in which he gives Antipater an account of all that happened, he tells him that the King of Scythia offered him his daughter in marriage, but makes no mention at all of the Amazon. And many years after, when Onesicritus read this story in his fourth book to Lysimachus, who then reigned, the king laughed quietly and asked,

"Where could I have been at that time?" But it signifies little to Alexander whether this be credited or no.

Certain it is, that apprehending the Macedonians would be weary of pursuing the war, he left the greater part of them in their quarters; and having with him in Hyrcania the choice of his men only, amounting to twenty thousand foot and three thousand horse, he spoke to them to this effect: That hitherto the barbarians had seen them no otherwise than as it were in a dream, and if they should think of returning when they had only alarmed Asia, and not conquered it, their enemies would set upon them as upon so many women. However, he told them he would keep none of them with him against their will, they might go if they pleased; he should merely enter his protest, that when on his way to make the Macedonians the masters of the world, he was left alone with a few friends and volunteers. This is almost word for word, as he wrote in a letter to Antipater, where he added, that when he had thus spoken to them, they all cried out, they would go along with him whithersoever it was his pleasure to lead them. After succeeding with these, it was no hard matter for him to bring over the multitude, which easily followed the example of their betters.

Now, also, he more and more accommodated himself in his way of living to that of the natives, and tried to bring them also as near as he could to the Macedonian customs, wisely considering that whilst he was engaged in an expedition which would carry him far from thence, it would be wiser to depend upon the good-will which might arise from intermixture and association as a means of maintaining tranquillity, than upon force and compulsion. In order to this, he chose out thirty thousand boys, whom he put under masters to teach them the Greek tongue, and to train them up to arms in the Macedonian discipline.

As for his marriage with Roxana, whose youthfulness and beauty had charmed him at a drinking entertainment, where he first happened to see her taking part in a dance, it was, indeed, a love affair, yet it seemed at the same time to be conducive to the object he had in hand. For it gratified the conquered people to see him choose a wife from among themselves, and it made them feel the most lively affection for him, to find that in the only passion which he, the most temperate of men, was overcome by, he yet forebore till he could obtain her in a lawful and honourable way.

Noticing also that among his chief friends and favourites, Hephæstion most approved all that he did, and complied with and imitated him in his change of habits, while Craterus continued strict in the observation of the customs and fashions of his own country, he made it his practice to employ the first in all transactions with the Persians, and the latter when he had to do with the Greeks or Macedonians. And in general he showed more affection for Hephæstion, and more respect for Craterus; Hephæstion, as he used to say, being Alexander's, and Craterus the king's friend.

And so these two friends always bore in secret a grudge to each other, and at times quarrelled openly, so much so that once in India they drew upon one another, and were proceeding in good earnest, with their friends on each side to second them, when Alexander rode up and publicly reproved Hephæstion, calling him fool and madman, not to be sensible that without his favour he was nothing. He rebuked Craterus also in private, severely, and then causing them both to come into his presence, he reconciled them, at the same time swearing by Ammon and the rest of the gods, that he loved them two above all other men, but if ever he perceived them fall out again he would be sure to put both of them to death, or at least the aggressor. After which they neither ever did or said anything, so much as in jest, to offend one another.

There was scarcely any one who had greater repute among the Macedonians than Philotas, the son of Parmenio. For besides that he was valiant and able to endure any fatigue of war, he was also next to Alexander himself the most munificent, and the greatest lover of his friends, one of whom asking him for some money, he commanded his steward to give it him; and when he told him he had not wherewith, "Have you not any plate, then," said he, "or any clothes of mine to sell?" But he carried his arrogance and his pride of wealth and his habits of display and luxury to a degree of assumption unbecoming a private man; and affecting all the loftiness without succeeding in showing any of the grace or gentleness of true greatness, by this mistaken and spurious majesty he gained so much envy and ill-will, that Parmenio would sometimes tell him, "My son, to be not quite so great would be better."

For he had long before been complained of, and accused to Alexander. Particularly when Darius was defeated in Cilicia, and an immense booty was taken at Damascus, among the rest of the prisoners who were brought into the camp, there was one Antigone of Pydna, a very handsome woman, who fell to Philotas's share. The young man one day in his cups, in the vaunting, outspoken, soldier's manner, declared to his mistress, that all the great actions were performed by him and his father, the glory and benefit of which, he said, together with the title of king, the boy Alexander reaped and enjoyed by their means.

She could not hold, but discovered what he had said to one of her acquaintance, and he, as is usual in such cases, to another, till at last the story came to the ears of Craterus, who brought the woman secretly to the king. When Alexander had heard what she had to say, he commanded her to continue her intrigue with Philotas, and give him an account from time to time of all that should fall from him to this purpose. He, thus unwittingly caught in a snare, to gratify sometimes a fit of anger, sometimes a love of vainglory, let himself utter numerous foolish, indiscreet speeches against the king in Antigone's hearing, of which, though Alexander was informed and convinced by strong evidence, yet he would take no notice of it at present, whether it was that he confided in Parmenio's affection and loyalty, or that he apprehended their authority and interest in the army.

But about this time, one Limnus, a Macedonian of Chalastra, conspired against Alexander's life, and communicated his design to a youth whom he was fond of, named Nicomachus, inviting him to be of the party. But he not relishing the thing, revealed it to his brother Balinus, who immediately addressed himself to Philotas, requiring him to introduce them both to Alexander, to whom they had something of great moment to impart which very nearly concerned him. But he, for what reason is uncertain, went not with them, professing that the king was engaged with affairs of more importance.

And when they had urged him a second time, and were still slighted by him, they applied themselves to another, by whose means being admitted into Alexander's presence, they first told about Limnus's conspiracy, and by the way let Philotas's negligence appear who had twice disregarded their application to him. Alexander was greatly incensed, and on finding that Limnus had defended himself, and had been killed by the soldier who was sent to seize him, he was still more discomposed,

thinking he had thus lost the means of detecting the plot.

As soon as his displeasure against Philotas began to appear, presently all his old enemies showed themselves, and said openly, the king was too easily imposed on, to imagine that one so inconsiderable as Limnus, a Chalastrian, should of his own head undertake such an enterprise; that in all likelihood he was but subservient to the design, an instrument that was moved by some greater spring; that those ought to be more strictly examined about the matter whose interest it was so much to conceal it. When they had once gained the king's ear for insinuations of this sort, they went on to show a thousand grounds of suspicion against Philotas, till at last they prevailed to have him seized and put to the torture, which was done in the presence of the principal officers, Alexander himself being placed behind some tapestry to understand what passed. Where, when he heard in what a miserable tone, and with what abject submissions Philotas applied himself to Hephæstion, he broke out, it is said, in this manner: "Are you so mean-spirited and effeminate, Philotas, and yet can engage in so desperate a design?"

After his death, he presently sent into Media, and put also Parmenio, his father, to death, who had done brave service under Philip, and was the only man of his older friends and counsellors who had encouraged Alexander to invade Asia. Of three sons whom he had had in the army, he had already lost two, and now was himself put to death with the third.

These actions rendered Alexander an object of terror to many of his friends, and chiefly to Antipater, who, to strengthen himself, sent messengers privately to treat for an alliance with the Ætolians, who stood in fear of Alexander, because they had destroyed the town of the Œniadæ; on being informed of which, Alexander had said the children of the Œniadæ need not revenge their father's quarrel, for he would himself take care to punish the Ætolians.

Not long after this happened the deplorable end of Clitus, which, to those who barely hear the matter, may seem more inhuman than that of Philotas; but if we consider the story with its circumstance of time, and weigh the cause, we shall find it to have occurred rather through a sort of mischance of the king's, whose anger and over-drinking offered an occasion to the evil genius of Clitus.

The king had a present of Grecian fruit

brought him from the sea-coast, which was so fresh and beautiful, that he was surprised at it, and called Clitus to him to see it, and to give him a share of it. Clitus was then sacrificing, but he immediately left off and came, followed by three sheep, on whom the drink-offering had been already poured preparatory to sacrificing them. Alexander, being informed of this, told his diviners, Aristander and Cleomantis the Lacedæmonian, and asked them what it meant; on whose assuring him it was an ill omen, he commanded them in all haste to offer sacrifices for Clitus's safety, forasmuch as three days before he himself had seen a strange vision in his sleep, of Clitus all in mourning, sitting by Parmenio's sons who were dead.

Clitus, however, stayed not to finish his devotions, but came straight to supper with the king, who had sacrificed to Castor and Pollux. And when they had drunk pretty hard, some of the company fell a-singing the verses of one Pranichus, or as others say of Pierion, which were made upon those captains who had been lately worsted by the barbarians, on purpose to disgrace and turn them to ridicule.

This gave offence to the older men who were there, and they upbraided both the author and the singer of the verses, though Alexander and the younger men about him were much amused to hear them, and encouraged them to go on, till at last Clitus, who had drunk too much, and was besides of a froward and wilful temper, was so nettled that he could hold no longer, saying it was not well done to expose the Macedonians before the barbarians and their enemies, since though it was their unhappiness to be overcome, yet they were much better men than those who laughed at them.

And when Alexander remarked that Clitus was pleading his own cause, giving cowardice the name of misfortune, Clitus started up: "This cowardice, as you are pleased to term it," said he to him, "saved the life of a son of the gods, when in flight from Spithridates's sword; it is by the expense of Macedonian blood, and by these wounds, that you are now raised to such a height as to be able to disown your father Philip, and call yourself the son of Ammon." "Thou base fellow," said Alexander, who was now thoroughly exasperated, "dost thou think to utter these things everywhere of me, and stir up the Macedonians to sedition, and not be punished for it?" "We are sufficiently punished already," answered Clitus, "if this be the recompense of our toils, and we

must esteem theirs a happy lot who have not lived to see their countrymen scourged with Median rods and forced to sue to the Persians to have access to their king."

While he talked thus at random, and those near Alexander got up from their seats and began to revile him in turn, the elder men did what they could to compose the disorder.

Alexander, in the meantime turning about to Xenodochus, the Pardian, and Artemius, the Colophonian, asked them if they were not of opinion that the Greeks, in comparison with the Macedonians, behaved themselves like so many demigods among wild beasts.

But Clitus for all this would not give over, desiring Alexander to speak out if he had anything more to say, or else why did he invite men who were freeborn and accustomed to speak their minds openly without restraint to sup with him. He had better live and converse with barbarians and slaves who would not scruple to bow the knee to his Persian girdle and his white tunic.

Which words so provoked Alexander that, not able to suppress his anger any longer, he threw one of the apples that lay upon the table at him, and hit him, and then looked about for his sword. But Aristophanes, one of his life-guard, had hid that out of the way, and others came about him and besought him, but in vain; for breaking from them, he called out aloud to his guards in the Macedonian language, which was a certain sign of some great disturbance in him, and commanded a trumpeter to sound, giving him a blow with his clenched fist for not instantly obeying him; though afterwards the same man was commended for disobeying an order which would have put the whole army into tumult and confusion.

Clitus still refusing to yield, was with much trouble forced by his friends out of the room. But he came in again immediately at another door, very irreverently and confidently singing the verses out of Euripides's *Andromache,*

In Greece, alas! how ill things ordered are!

Upon this, at last, Alexander, snatching a spear from one of the soldiers, met Clitus as he was coming forward and was putting by the curtain that hung before the door, and ran him through the body. He fell at once with a cry and a groan.

Upon which the king's anger immediately vanishing, he came perfectly to himself, and when he saw his friends about him all in a profound silence, he pulled the spear out of the dead body, and would have thrust it into his own throat, if the guards had not held his hands, and by main force carried him away into his chamber, where all that night and the next day he wept bitterly, till being quite spent with lamenting and exclaiming, he lay, as it were, speechless, only fetching deep sighs. His friends apprehending some harm from his silence, broke into the room, but he took no notice of what any of them said, till Aristander putting him in mind of the vision he had seen concerning Clitus, and the prodigy that followed, as if all had come to pass by an unavoidable fatality, he then seemed to moderate his grief.

They now brought Callisthenes, the philosopher, who was the near friend of Aristotle, and Anaxarchus of Abdera, to him. Callisthenes used moral language, and gentle and soothing means, hoping to find access for words of reason, and get a hold upon the passion. But Anaxarchus, who had always taken a course of his own in philosophy, and had a name for despising and slighting his contemporaries, as soon as he came in, cried aloud, "Is this the Alexander whom the whole world looks to, lying here weeping like a slave, for fear of the censure and reproach of men, to whom he himself ought to be a law and measure of equity, if he would use the right his conquests have given him as supreme lord and governor of all, and not be the victim of a vain and idle opinion? Do not you know," said he, "that Jupiter is represented to have Justice and Law on each hand of him, to signify that all the actions of a conqueror are lawful and just?" With these and the like speeches, Anaxarchus indeed allayed the king's grief, but withal corrupted his character, rendering him more audacious and lawless than he had been. Nor did he fail by these means to insinuate himself into his favour, and to make Callisthenes's company, which at all times, because of his austerity, was not very acceptable, more uneasy and disagreeable to him.

It happened that these two philosophers met at an entertainment where conversation turned on the subject of climate and the temperature of the air. Callisthenes joined with their opinion who held that those countries were colder, and the winter sharper there than in Greece. Anaxarchus would by no means allow this, but argued against it with some heat. "Surely," said Callisthenes, "you cannot but admit this country to be colder than Greece, for there you used to have but one threadbare cloak to keep out the coldest winter, and here you have three good warm mantles one over another."

This piece of raillery irritated Anaxarchus and the other pretenders to learning, and the crowd of flatterers in general could not endure to see Callisthenes so much admired and followed by the youth, and no less esteemed by the older men for his orderly life and his gravity, and for being contented with his condition; and confirming what he had professed about the object he had in his journey to Alexander, that it was only to get his countrymen recalled from banishment, and to rebuild and repeople his native town.

Besides the envy which his great reputation raised, he also, by his own deportment, gave those who wished him ill opportunity to do him mischief. For when he was invited to public entertainments, he would most times refuse to come, or if he were present at any, he put a constraint upon the company by his austerity and silence, which seemed to intimate his disapproval of what he saw. So that Alexander himself said in application to him,—

That vain pretence to wisdom I detest
Where a man's blind to his own interest.

Being with many more invited to sup with the king, he was called upon when the cup came to him, to make an oration extempore in praise of the Macedonians; and he did it with such a flow of eloquence, that all who heard it rose from their seats to clap and applaud him, and threw their garland upon him; only Alexander told him out of Euripides,—

I wonder not that you have spoke so well,
'Tis easy on good subjects to excel.

"Therefore," said he, "if you will show the force of your eloquence, tell my Macedonians their faults, and dispraise them, that by hearing their errors they may learn to be better for the future." Callisthenes presently obeyed him, retracting all he had said before, and, inveighing against the Macedonians with great freedom, added that Philip thrived and grew powerful, chiefly by the discord of the Grecians, applying this verse to him,—

In civil strife e'en villains rise to fame;

which so offended the Macedonians, that he was odious to them ever after.

And Alexander said that instead of his eloquence, he had only made his ill-will appear in what he had spoken. Hermippus assures us that one Strœbus, a servant whom Callisthenes kept to read to him, gave this account of these passages afterwards to Aristotle; and that when he perceived the king grow more and more averse to him, two or three times, as he was going away, he repeated the verses,—

Death seiz'd at last on great Patroclus too,
Though he in virtue far exceeded you.

Not without reason, therefore, did Aristotle give this character of Callisthenes, that he was, indeed, a powerful speaker, but had no judgment. He acted certainly a true philosopher's part in positively refusing, as he did, to pay adoration; and by speaking out openly against that which the best and gravest of the Macedonians only repined at in secret, he delivered the Grecians and Alexander himself from a great disgrace, when the practice was given up. But he ruined himself by it, because he went too roughly to work, as if he would have forced the king to that which he should have effected by reason and persuasion.

Chares of Mitylene writes that at a banquet Alexander, after he had drunk, reached the cup to one of his friends, who, on receiving it, rose up towards the domestic altar, and when he had drunk, first adored and then kissed Alexander, and afterwards laid himself down at the table with the rest. Which they all did one after another, till it came to Callisthenes's turn, who took the cup and drank, while the king, who was engaged in conversation with Hephæstion, was not observing, and then came and offered to kiss him. But Demetrius, surnamed Phidon, interposed, saying, "Sir, by no means let him kiss you, for he only of us all has refused to adore you"; upon which the king declined it, and all the concern Callisthenes showed was, that he said aloud, "Then I go away with a kiss less than the rest." The displeasure he incurred by this action procured credit for Hephæstion's declaration that he had broken his word to him in not paying the king the same veneration that others did, as he had faithfully promised to do.

And to finish his disgrace, a number of such men as Lysimachus and Hagnon now came in with their asseverations that the sophist went about everywhere boasting of his resistance to arbitrary power, and the young men all ran after him, and honoured him as the only man among so many thousands who had the courage to preserve his liberty.

Therefore, when Hermolaus's conspiracy came to be discovered, the charges which his enemies brought against him were the more easily believed, particularly that when the young man asked him what he should do to be the most illustrious person on earth, he told him the readiest way was to kill him who was already so, and that to incite him to commit the deed, he bade him not be awed by the golden couch, but remember Alexander was a man equally infirm and vulnerable as another. However, none of Hermolaus's accomplices, in the utmost extremity, made any mention of Callisthenes's being engaged in the design. Nay, Alexander himself, in the letters which he wrote soon after to Craterus, Attalus, and Alcetas, tells them that the young men who were put to the torture declared they had entered into the conspiracy of themselves, without any others being privy to or guilty of it.

But yet afterwards, in a letter to Antipater, he accuses Callisthenes. "The young men," he says, "were stoned to death by the Macedonians, but for the sophist" (meaning Callisthenes), "I will take care to punish him with them, too, who sent him to me, and who harbour those in their cities who conspire against my life," an unequivocal declaration against Aristotle, in whose house Callisthenes, for his relationship's sake, being his niece Hero's son, had been educated.

His death is variously related. Some say he was hanged by Alexander's orders; others, that he died of sickness in prison; but Chares writes he was kept in chains seven months after he was apprehended, on purpose that he might be proceeded against in full council, when Aristotle should be present; and that growing very fat, and contracting a disease of vermin, he there died, about the time that Alexander was wounded in India, in the country of the Malli Oxydracæ, all which came to pass afterwards.

For to go on in order, Demaratus of Corinth, now quite an old man, had made a great effort, about this time, to pay Alexander a visit; and when he had seen him, said he pitied the misfortune of those Grecians, who were so unhappy as to die before they had beheld Alexander seated on the throne of Darius. But he did not long enjoy the benefit of the king's kindness for him, in any way except that soon after falling sick and dying, he had a magnificent funeral, and the army raised him a monument of earth fourscore cubits high, and of a vast circumference. His ashes were conveyed in a very rich chariot, drawn by four horses, to the seaside.

Alexander, now intent upon his expedition into India, took notice that his soldiers were so charged with booty that it hindered their marching. Therefore, at break of day, as soon as the baggage wagons were laden, first he set fire to his own, and to those of his friends, and then commanded those to be burnt which belonged to the rest of the army: an act which in the deliberation of it had seemed more dangerous and difficult than it proved in the execution, with which few were dissatisfied; for most of the soldiers, as if they had been inspired, uttering loud outcries and warlike shoutings, supplied one another with what was absolutely necessary, and burnt and destroyed all that was superfluous, the sight of which redoubled Alexander's zeal and eagerness for his design.

And, indeed, he was now grown very severe and inexorable in punishing those who committed any fault. For he put Menander, one of his friends, to death for deserting a fortress where he had placed him in garrison, and shot Orsodates, one of the barbarians who revolted from him, with his own hand.

At this time a sheep happened to yean a lamb, with the perfect shape and colour of a tiara upon the head, and testicles on each side; which portent Alexander regarded with such dislike, that he immediately caused his Babylonian priests, whom he usually carried about with him for such purposes, to purify him, and told his friends he was not so much concerned for his own sake as for theirs, out of an apprehension that after his death the divine power might suffer his empire to fall into the hands of some degenerate, impotent person.

But this fear was soon removed by a wonderful thing that happened not long after, and was thought to presage better. For Proxenus, a Macedonian, who was the chief of those who looked to the king's furniture, as he was breaking up the ground near the river Oxus, to set up the royal pavilion, discovered a spring of a fat oily liquor, which, after the top was taken off, ran pure, clear oil, without any difference either of taste or smell, having exactly the same smoothness and brightness, and that, too, in a country where no olives grew. The water, indeed, of the river Oxus, is said to be the smoothest to the feeling of all waters, and to leave a gloss on the skins of those who bathe themselves in it. Whatever might be the cause, certain it is that Alexander was wonderfully pleased with it, as appears by his letters to Antipater, where he speaks of it as one of the most remarkable presages that God had ever favoured him with. The diviners told him it signified his expedition would be glorious in the event, but very painful, and attended with many difficulties; for oil, they said, was bestowed on mankind by God as a refreshment of their labours.

Nor did they judge amiss, for he exposed himself to many hazards in the battles which he fought, and received very severe wounds, but the greatest loss in his army was occasioned through the unwholesomeness of the air and the want of necessary provisions. But he still applied himself to overcome fortune and whatever opposed him, by resolution and virtue, and thought nothing impossible to true intrepidity, and on the other hand nothing secure or strong for cowardice.

It is told of him that when he besieged Sisimithres, who held an inaccessible, impregnable rock against him, and his soldiers began to despair of taking it, he asked Oxyartes whether Sisimithres was a man of courage, who assuring him he was the greatest coward alive, "Then you tell me," said he, "that the place may easily be taken, since what is in command of it is weak." And in a little time he so terrified Sisimithres that he took it without any difficulty.

At an attack which he made upon such another precipitous place with some of his Macedonian soldiers, he called to one whose name was Alexander, and told him he at any rate must fight bravely if it were but for his name's sake. The youth fought gallantly and was killed in the action, at which he was sensibly afflicted.

Another time, seeing his men march slowly and unwillingly to the siege of the place called Nysa, because of a deep river between them and the town, he advanced before them, and standing upon the bank, "What a miserable man," said he, "am I, that I have not learned to swim!" and then was hardly dissuaded from endeavouring to pass it upon his shield. Here, after the assult was over, the ambassadors who from several towns which he had blocked up came to submit to him and make their peace, were surprised to find him still in his armour, without any one in waiting or attendance upon him, and when at last some one brought him a cushion, he made the eldest of them, named Acuphis, take it and sit down upon it. The old man, marvelling at his magnanimity and courtesy, asked him what his countrymen should do to merit his friendship. "I would have them," said Alexander, "choose you to govern them, and send one hundred of the most worthy men among them to remain with me as hostages." Acuphis laughed and answered, "I shall govern them with more ease, sir, if I send you so many of the worst, rather than the best of my subjects."

The extent of King Taxiles's dominions in India was thought to be as large as Egypt, abounding in good pastures, and producing beautiful fruits. The king himself had the reputation of a wise man, and at his first interview with Alexander he spoke to him in these terms: "To what purpose," said he, "should we make war upon one another, if the design of your coming into these parts be not to rob us of our water or our necessary food, which are the only things that wise men are indispensably obliged to fight for? As for other riches and possessions, as they are accounted in the eye of the world, if I am better provided of them than you, I am ready to let you share with me; but if fortune has been more liberal to you than me, I have no objection to be obliged to you." This discourse pleased Alexander so much that, embracing him, "Do you think," said he to him, "your kind words and courteous behaviour will bring you off in this interview without a contest? No, you shall not escape so. I shall contend and do battle with you so far, that how obliging soever you are, you shall not have the better of me." Then receiving some presents from him, he returned him others of greater value, and to complete his bounty gave him in money ready coined one thousand talents; at which his old friends were much displeased, but it gained him the hearts of many of the barbarians.

But the best soldiers of the Indians now entering into the pay of several of the cities, undertook to defend them, and did it so bravely, that they put Alexander to a great deal of trouble, till at last, after a capitulation, upon the surrender of the place, he fell upon them as they were marching away, and put them all to the sword. This one breach of his word remains as a blemish upon his achievements in war, which he otherwise had performed throughout with that justice and honour that became a king. Nor was he less incommoded by the Indian philosophers, who inveighed against those princes who joined his party, and solicited the free nations to oppose him. He took several of these also and caused them to be hanged.

Alexander, in his own letters, has given us an acount of his war with Porus. He says the two armies were separated by the river Hydaspes, on whose opposite bank Porus continually kept his elephants in order of battle, with their heads towards their enemies, to guard the passage; that he, on the other hand, made every day a great noise and clamour in his camp, to dissipate the apprehensions of the barbarians; that one stormy dark night he passed the river, at a

distance from the place where the enemy lay, into a little island, with part of his foot and the best of his horse. Here there fell a most violent storm of rain, accompanied with lightning and whirlwinds, and seeing some of his men burnt and dying with the lightning, he nevertheless quitted the island and made over to the other side. The Hydaspes, he says, now after the storm, was so swollen and grown so rapid as to have made a breach in the bank, and a part of the river was now pouring in here, so that when he came across it was with difficulty he got a footing on the land, which was slippery and unsteady, and exposed to the force of the currents on both sides.

This is the occasion when he is related to have said, "O ye Athenians, will ye believe what dangers I incur to merit your praise?" This, however, is Onesicritus's story. Alexander says, here the men left their boats, and passed the breach in their armour, up to the breast in water, and that then he advanced with his horse about twenty furlongs before his foot; concluding that if the enemy charged him with their cavalry he should be too strong for them; if with their foot, his own would come up time enough to his assistance. Nor did he judge amiss; for being charged by a thousand horse and sixty armed chariots, which advanced before their main body, he took all the chariots, and killed four hundred horse upon the place.

Porus, by this time, guessing that Alexander himself had crossed over, came on with his whole army, except a party which he left behind, to hold the rest of the Macedonians in play, if they should attempt to pass the river. But he, apprehending the multitude of the enemy, and to avoid the shock of their elephants, dividing his forces, attacked their left wing himself, and commanded Cœnus to fall upon the right, which was performed with good success. For by this means both wings being broken, the enemies fell back in their retreat upon the centre, and crowded in upon their elephants. There rallying, they fought a hand-to-hand battle, and it was the eighth hour of the day before they were entirely defeated. This description the conqueror himself has left us in his own epistles.

Almost all the historians agree in relating that Porus was four cubits and a span high, and that when he was upon his elephant, which was of the largest size, his stature and bulk were so answerable, that he appeared to be proportionably mounted, as a horseman on his horse. This elephant, during the whole battle, gave many singular proofs of sagacity and of particular care of the king, whom as long as he was strong and in a condition to fight, he defended with great courage, repelling those who set upon him; and as soon as he perceived him overpowered with his numerous wounds and the multitude of darts that were thrown at him, to prevent his falling off, he softly knelt down and began to draw out the darts with his proboscis.

When Porus was taken prisoner, and Alexander asked him how he expected to be used, he answered, "As a king." For that expression, he said, when the same question was put to him a second time, comprehended everything. And Alexander, accordingly, not only suffered him to govern his own kingdom as satrap under himself, but gave him also the additional territory of various independent tribes whom he subdued, a district which, it is said, contained fifteen several nations, and five thousand considerable towns, besides abundance of villages. To another government, three times as large as this, he appointed Philip, one of his friends.

Some little time after the battle with Porus, Bucephalus died, as most of the authorities state, under cure of his wounds, or, as Onesicritus says, of fatigue and age, being thirty years old. Alexander was no less concerned at his death than if he had lost an old companion or an intimate friend, and built a city, which he named Bucephalia, in memory of him, on the bank of the river Hydaspes. He also, we are told, built another city, and called it after the name of a favourite dog, Peritas, which he had brought up himself. So Sotion assures us he was informed by Potamon of Lesbos.

But this last combat with Porus took off the edge of the Macedonians' courage, and stayed their further progress into India. For having found it hard enough to defeat an enemy who brought but twenty thousand foot and two thousand horse into the field, they thought they had reason to oppose Alexander's design of leading them on to pass the Ganges, too, which they were told was thirty-two furlongs broad and a hundred fathoms deep, and the banks on the further side covered with multitudes of enemies. For they were told the kings of the Gandaritans and Præsians expected them there with eighty thousand horse, two hundred thousand foot, eight thousand armed chariots, and six thousand fighting elephants. Nor was this a mere vain report, spread to discourage them. For Androcottus, who not long after reigned in those parts, made a present of five hundred elephants at once to Seleucus, and with an army of six hundred thousand men subdued all India.

Alexander at first was so grieved and enraged at his men's reluctancy that he shut himself up in his tent and threw himself upon the ground, declaring, if they would not pass the Ganges, he owed them no thanks for anything they had hitherto done, and that to retreat now was plainly to confess himself vanquished. But at last the reasonable persuasions of his friends and the cries and lamentations of his soldiers, who in a suppliant manner crowded about the entrance of his tent, prevailed with him to think of returning.

Yet he could not refrain from leaving behind him various deceptive memorials of his expedition, to impose upon aftertimes, and to exaggerate his glory with posterity, such as arms larger than were really worn, and mangers for horses, with bits and bridles above the usual size, which he set up, and distributed in several places. He erected altars, also, to the gods, which the kings of the Præsians even in our time do honour to when they pass the river, and offer sacrifice upon them after the Grecian manner.

Androcottus, then a boy, saw Alexander there, and is said often afterwards to have been heard to say that he missed but little of making himself master of those countries; their king, who then reigned, was so hated and despised for the viciousness of his life and the meanness of his extraction.

Alexander was now eager to see the ocean. To which purpose he caused a great many tow-boats and rafts to be built, in which he fell gently down the rivers at his leisure, yet so that his navigation was neither unprofitable nor inactive. For by several descents upon the bank, he made himself master of the fortified towns, and consequently of the country on both sides. But at a siege of a town of the Mallians, who have the repute of being the bravest people of India, he ran in great danger of his life. For having beaten off the defendants with showers of arrows, he was the first man that mounted the wall by a scaling-ladder, which, as soon as he was up, broke and left him almost alone, exposed to the darts which the barbarians threw at him in great numbers from below.

In this distress, turning himself as well as he could, he leaped down in the midst of his enemies, and had the good fortune to light upon his feet. The brightness and clattering of his armour when he came to the ground made the barbarians think they saw rays of light, or some bright phantom playing before his body, which frightened them so at first that they ran away and dispersed. Till seeing him seconded but by two of his guards, they fell upon him hand to hand, and some, while he bravely defended himself, tried to wound him through his armour with their swords and spears. And one who stood further off drew a bow with such just strength that the arrow, finding its way through his cuirass, stuck in his ribs under the breast. This stroke was so violent that it made him give back, and set one knee to the ground, upon which the man ran up with his drawn scimitar, thinking to despatch him, and had done it, if Peucestes and Limnæus had not interposed, who were both wounded, Limnæus mortally, but Peucestes stood his ground, while Alexander killed the barbarians.

But this did not free him from danger; for, besides many other wounds, at last he received so weighty a stroke of a club upon his neck that he was forced to lean his body against the wall, still, however, facing the enemy. At this extremity, the Macedonians made their way in and gathered round him. They took him up, just as he was fainting away, having lost all sense of what was done near him, and conveyed him to his tent, upon which it was presently reported all over the camp that he was dead. But when they had with great difficulty and pains sawed off the shaft of the arrow, which was of wood, and so with much trouble got off his cuirass, they came to cut the head of it, which was three fingers broad and four long, and stuck fast in the bone. During the operation he was taken with almost mortal swoonings, but when it was out he came to himself again.

Yet though all danger was past, he continued very weak, and confined himself a great while to a regular diet and the method of his cure, till one day hearing the Macedonians clamouring outside in their eagerness to see him, he took his cloak and went out. And having sacrificed to the gods, without more delay he went on board again, and as he coasted along subdued a great deal of the country on both sides, and several considerable cities.

In this voyage he took ten of the Indian philosophers prisoners who had been most active in persuading Sabbas to revolt, and had caused the Macedonians a great deal of trouble. These men, called gymnosophists, were reputed to be extremely ready and succinct in their answers, which he made trial of, by putting difficult questions to them, letting them know that those whose answers were not pertinent should be put to death, of which he made the eldest of them judge.

The first being asked which he thought the most numerous, the dead or the living, answered, "The living, because those who are dead are not at all." Of the second, he desired to know whether the earth or the sea produced the largest beasts; who told him, "The earth, for the sea is but a part of it." His question to the third was, "Which is the cunningest of beasts?" "That," said he, "which men have not yet found out." He bade the fourth tell him what argument he used to Sabbas to persuade him to revolt. "No other," said he, "than that he should either live or die nobly." Of the fifth he asked, which was the eldest, night or day. The philosopher replied, "Day was eldest, by one day at least." But perceiving Alexander not well satisfied with that account, he added that he ought not to wonder if strange questions had as strange answers made to them. Then he went on and inquired of the next, what a man should do to be exceedingly beloved. "He must be very powerful," said he, "without making himself too much feared." The answer of the seventh to his question, how a man might become a god, was, "By doing that which was impossible for men to do." The eighth told him, "Life is stronger than death, because it supports so many miseries." And the last being asked how long he thought it decent for a man to live, said, "Till death appeared more desirable than life."

Then Alexander turned to him whom he had made judge, and commanded him to give sentence. "All that I can determine," said he, "is, that they have every one answered worse than another." "Nay," said the king, "then you shall die first, for giving such a sentence." "Not so, O king," replied the gymnosophist, "unless you said falsely that he should die first who made the worst answer." In conclusion he gave them presents and dismissed them.

But to those who were in greatest reputation among them, and lived a private quiet life, he sent Onesicritus, one of Diogenes the Cynic's disciples, desiring them to come to him. Calanus, it is said, very arrogantly and roughly commanded him to strip himself and hear what he said naked, otherwise he would not speak a word to him, though he came from Jupiter himself. But Dandamis received him

with more civility, and hearing him discourse
of Socrates, Pythagoras, and Diogenes, told
him he thought them men of great parts and to
have erred in nothing so much as in having too
great respect for the laws and customs of their
country. Others say Dandamis only asked him
the reason why Alexander undertook so long
a journey to come into those parts.

Taxiles, however, persuaded Calanus to wait
upon Alexander. His proper name was Sphines,
but because he was wont to say *Cale,* which in
the Indian tongue is a form of salutation, to
those he met with anywhere, the Greeks called
him Calanus. He is said to have shown Alexander an instructive emblem of government,
which was this. He threw a dry shrivelled hide
upon the ground, and trod upon the edges of
it. The skin when it was pressed in one place
still rose up in another, wheresoever he trod
round about it, till he set his foot in the middle,
which made all the parts lie even and quiet.
The meaning of this similitude being that he
ought to reside most in the middle of his empire, and not spend too much time on the borders of it.

His voyage down the rivers took up seven
months' time, and when he came to the sea, he
sailed to an island which he himself called
Scillustis, others Psiltucis, where going ashore,
he sacrificed, and made what observations he
could as to the nature of the sea and the sea-
coast. Then having besought the gods that no
other man might ever go beyond the bounds
of this expedition, he ordered his fleet, of which
he made Nearchus admiral and Onesicritus
pilot, to sail round about, keeping the Indian
shore on the right hand, and returned himself
by land through the country of the Orites,
where he was reduced to great straits for want
of provisions, and lost a vast number of his
men, so that of an army of one hundred and
twenty thousand foot and fifteen thousand
horse, he scarcely brought back above a fourth
part out of India, they were so diminished by
disease, ill diet, and the scorching heats, but
most by famine. For their march was through
an uncultivated country whose inhabitants
fared hardly, possessing only a few sheep, and
those of a wretched kind, whose flesh was rank
and unsavoury, by their continual feeding upon
sea-fish.

After sixty days' march he came into Gedrosia, where he found great plenty of all things,
which the neighboring kings and governors of
provinces, hearing of his approach, had taken
care to provide.

When he had here refreshed his army, he
continued his march through Carmania, feasting all the way for seven days together. He
with his most intimate friends banqueted and
revelled night and day upon a platform erected
on a lofty, conspicuous scaffold, which was
slowly drawn by eight horses. This was followed by a great many chariots, some covered
with purple and embroidered canopies, and
some with green boughs, which were continually supplied afresh, and in them the rest of
his friends and commanders drinking, and
crowned with garlands of flowers. Here was
now no target or helmet or spear to be seen; instead of armour, the soldiers handled nothing
but cups and goblets and Thericlean drinking
vessels, which, along the whole way, they
dipped into large bowls and jars, and drank
healths to one another, some seating themselves
to it, others as they went along.

All places resounded with music of pipes
and flutes, with harping and singing, and
women dancing as in the rites of Bacchus. For
this disorderly, wandering march, besides the
drinking part of it, was accompanied with all
the sportiveness and insolence of bacchanals,
as much as if the god himself had been there
to countenance and lead the procession.

As soon as he came to the royal palace of
Gedrosia, he again refreshed and feasted his
army; and one day he had drunk pretty hard,
it is said, he went to see a prize of dancing contended for, in which his favourite, Bagoas, having gained the victory, crossed the theatre in
his dancing habit, and sat down close by him,
which so pleased the Macedonians that they
made loud acclamations for him to kiss Bagoas,
and never stopped clapping their hands and
shouting till Alexander put his arms round
him and kissed him.

Here his admiral, Nearchus, came to him,
and delighted him so with the narrative of his
voyage, that he resolved himself to sail out of
the mouth of the Euphrates with a great fleet,
with which he designed to go round by Arabia
and Africa, and so by Hercules's Pillars into
the Mediterranean; in order for which, he directed all sorts of vessels to be built at Thapsa-
cus, and made great provisions everywhere of
seamen and pilots.

But the tidings of the difficulties he had gone
through in his Indian expedition, the danger
of his person among the Mallians, the reported
loss of a considerable part of his forces, and a
general doubt as to his own safety, had begun
to give occasion for revolt among many of the

conquered nations, and for acts of great injustice, avarice, and insolence on the part of the satraps and commanders in the provinces, so that there seemed to be an universal fluctuation and disposition to change.

Even at home, Olympias and Cleopatra had raised a faction against Antipater, and divided his government between them, Olympias seizing upon Epirus, and Cleopatra upon Macedonia. When Alexander was told of it, he said his mother had made the best choice, for the Macedonians would never endure to be ruled by a woman.

Upon this he despatched Nearchus again to his fleet, to carry the war into the maritime provinces, and as he marched that way himself he punished those commanders who had behaved ill, particularly Oxyartes, one of the sons of Abuletes, whom he killed with his own hand, thrusting him through the body with his spear. And when Abuletes, instead of the necessary provisions which he ought to have furnished, brought him three thousand talents in coined money, he ordered it to be thrown to his horses, and when they would not touch it, "What good," he said, "will this provision do us?" and sent him away to prison.

When he came into Persia, he distributed money among the women, as their own kings had been wont to do, who as often as they came thither gave every one of them a piece of gold; on account of which custom, some of them, it is said, had come but seldom, and Ochus was so sordidly covetous that, to avoid this expense, he never visited his native country once in all his reign. Then finding Cyrus's sepulchre opened and rifled, he put Polymachus, who did it, to death, though he was a man of some distinction, a born Macedonian of Pella. And after he had read the inscription, he caused it to be cut again below the old one in Greek characters; the words being these: "O man, whosoever thou art, and from whencesoever thou comest (for I know thou wilt come), I am Cyrus, the founder of the Persian empire; do not grudge me this little earth which covers my body." The reading of this sensibly touched Alexander, filling him with the thought of the uncertainty and mutability of human affairs.

At the same time Calanus, having been a little while troubled with a disease in the bowels, requested that he might have a funeral pile erected, to which he came on horseback, and, after he had said some prayers and sprinkled himself and cut off some of his hair

to throw into the fire, before he ascended it, he embraced and took leave of the Macedonians who stood by, desiring them to pass that day in mirth and good-fellowship with their king, whom in a little time, he said, he doubted not but to see again at Babylon. Having thus said, he lay down, and covering up his face, he stirred not when the fire came near him, but continued still in the same posture as at first, and so sacrificed himself, as it was the ancient custom of the philosophers in those countries to do. The same thing was done long after by another Indian who came with Cæsar to Athens, where they still show you, "the Indian's monument."

At his return from the funeral pile, Alexander invited a great many of his friends and principal officers to supper, and proposed a drinking match, in which the victor should receive a crown. Promachus drank twelve quarts of wine, and won the prize, which was a talent from them all; but he survived his victory but three days, and was followed, as Chares says, by forty-one more, who died of the same debauch, some extremely cold weather having set in shortly after.

At Susa, he married Darius's daughter Statira, and celebrated also the nuptials of his friends, bestowing the noblest of the Persian ladies upon the worthiest of them, at the same time making it an entertainment in honour of the other Macedonians whose marriages had already taken place. At this magnificent festival, it is reported, there were no less than nine thousand guests, to each of whom he gave a golden cup for the libations. Not to mention other instances of his wonderful magnificence, he paid the debts of his army, which amounted to nine thousand eight hundred and seventy talents.

But Antigenes, who had lost one of his eyes, though he owed nothing, got his name set down in the list of those who were in debt, and bringing one who pretended to be his creditor, and to have supplied him from the bank, received the money. But when the cheat was found out, the king was so incensed at it, that he banished him from court, and took away his command, though he was an excellent soldier and a man of great courage. For when he was but a youth, and served under Philip at the siege of Perinthus, where he was wounded in the eye by an arrow shot out of an engine, he would neither let the arrow be taken out nor be persuaded to quit the field till he had bravely repulsed the enemy and forced them to retire into the town. Accordingly he was not able to support such a disgrace with any patience, and it was plain that grief and despair would have made him kill himself, but the king fearing it, not only pardoned him, but let him also enjoy the benefit of his deceit.

The thirty thousand boys whom he left behind him to be taught and disciplined were so improved at his return, both in strength and beauty, and performed their exercises with such dexterity and wonderful agility, that he was extremely pleased with them, which grieved the Macedonians, and made them fear he would have the less value for them. And when he proceeded to send down the infirm and maimed soldiers to the sea, they said they were unjustly and infamously dealt with, after they were worn out in his service upon all occasions, now to be turned away with disgrace and sent home into their country among their friends and relations in a worse condition than when they came out; therefore they desired him to dismiss them one and all, and to account his Macedonians useless, now he was so well furnished with a set of dancing boys, with whom, if he pleased, he might go on and conquer the world. These speeches so incensed Alexander that, after he had given them a great deal of reproachful language in his passion, he drove them away, and committed the watch to Persians, out of whom he chose his guards and attendants.

When the Macedonians saw him escorted by these men, and themselves excluded and shamefully disgraced, their high spirits fell, and conferring with one another, they found that jealousy and rage had almost distracted them. But at last coming to themselves again, they went without their arms, with only their under garments on, crying and weeping to offer themselves at his tent, and desired him to deal with them as their baseness and ingratitude deserved. However, this would not prevail; for though his anger was already something mollified, yet he would not admit them into his presence, nor would they stir from thence, but continued two days and nights before his tent, bewailing themselves, and imploring him as their lord to have compassion on them.

But the third day he came out to them, and seeing them very humble and penitent, he wept himself a great while, after a gentle reproof spoke kindly to them, and dismissed those who were unserviceable with magnificent rewards, and with his recommendation to Antipater, that when they came home, at all public shows and in the theatres, they should sit on the best and foremost seats, crowned with chaplets of flowers. He ordered, also, that the children of those who had lost their lives in his service should have their father's pay continued to them.

When he came to Ecbatana in Media, and had despatched his most urgent affairs, he began to divert himself again with spectacles and public entertainments, to carry on which he had a supply of three thousand actors and artists, newly arrived out of Greece. But they were soon interrupted by Hephæstion's falling sick of a fever, in which, being a young man and a soldier, too, he could not confine himself to so exact a diet as was necessary; for whilst his physician, Glaucus, was gone to the theatre, he ate a fowl for his dinner, and drank a large draught of wine, upon which he became very ill, and shortly after died.

At this misfortune, Alexander was so beyond all reason transported that, to express his sorrow, he immediately ordered the manes and tails of all his horses and mules to be cut, and threw down the battlements of the neighbouring cities. The poor physician he crucified, and forbade playing on the flute or any other musical instrument in the camp a great while, till directions came from the oracle of Ammon, and enjoined him to honour Hephæstion, and sacrifice to him as to a hero.

Then seeking to alleviate his grief in war, he set out, as it were, to a hunt and chase of men, for he fell upon the Cossæans, and put the whole nation to the sword. This was called a sacrifice to Hephæstion's ghost.

In his sepulchre and monument and the adorning of them he intended to bestow ten thousand talents; and designing that the excellence of the workmanship and the singularity of the design might outdo the expense, his wishes turned, above all other artists, to Stasicrates, because he always promised something very bold, unusual, and magnificent in his projects. Once when they had met before, he had told him that, of all the mountains he knew, that of Athos in Thrace was the most capable of being adapted to represent the shape and lineaments of a man; that if he pleased to command him, he would make it the noblest and most durable statue in the world, which in its left hand should hold a city of ten thousand inhabitants, and out of its right should pour a copious river into the sea. Though Alexander declined this proposal, yet now he spent a great deal of time with workmen to invent and contrive others even more extravagant and sumptuous.

As he was upon his way to Babylon, Nearchus, who had sailed back out of the ocean up the mouth of the river Euphrates, came to tell him he had met with some Chaldæan diviners, who had warned him against Alexander's going thither. Alexander, however, took no thought of it, and went on, and when he came near the walls of the place, he saw a great many crows fighting with one another, some of whom fell down just by him. After this, being privately informed that Apollodorus, the governor of Babylon, had sacrificed to know what would become of him, he sent for Pythagoras, the soothsayer, and on his admitting the thing, asked him in what condition he found the victim; and when he told him the liver was defective in its lobe, "A great presage indeed!" said Alexander. However, he offered Pythagoras no injury, but was sorry that he had neglected Nearchus's advice, and stayed for the most part outside the town, removing his tent from place to place, and sailing up and down the Euphrates.

Besides this, he was disturbed by many other prodigies. A tame ass fell upon the biggest and handsomest lion that he kept, and killed him by a kick. And one day after he had undressed himself to be anointed, and was playing at ball, just as they were going to bring his clothes again, the young men who played with him perceived a man clad in the king's robes with a diadem upon his head, sitting silently upon his throne. They asked him who he was, to which he gave no answer a good while, till at last, coming to himself, he told them his name was Dionysius, that he was of Messena, that for some crime of which he was accused he was brought thither from the seaside, and had been kept long in prison, that Serapis appeared to him, had freed him from his chains, conducted him to that place, and commanded him to put on the king's robe and diadem, and to sit where they found him, and to say nothing. Alexander, when he heard this, by the direction of his soothsayers, put the fellow to death, but he lost his spirits, and grew diffident of the protection and assistance of the gods, and suspicious of his friends.

His greatest apprehension was of Antipater and his sons, one of whom, Iolaus, was his chief cupbearer; and Cassander, who had lately arrived, and had been bred up in Greek manners, the first time he saw some of the barbarians adore the king could not forbear laughing at it aloud, which so incensed Alexander that he took him by the hair with both hands and dashed his head against the wall.

Another time, Cassander would have said something in defence of Antipater to those who accused him, but Alexander interrupting him, said, "What is it you say? Do you think people, if they had received no injury, would come such a journey only to calumniate your father?" To which when Cassander replied, that their coming so far from the evidence was a great proof of the falseness of their charges, Alexander smiled, and said those were some of Aristotle's sophisms, which would serve equally on both sides; and added, that both he and his father should be severely punished if they were found guilty of the least injustice towards those who complained.

All which made such a deep impression of terror in Cassander's mind that, long after, when he was King of Macedonia and master of Greece, as he was walking up and down at Delphi, and looking at the statues, at the sight of that of Alexander he was suddenly struck with alarm, and shook all over; his eyes rolled, his head grew dizzy, and it was long before he recovered himself.

When once Alexander had given way to fears of supernatural influence, his mind grew so disturbed and so easily alarmed that, if the least unusual or extraordinary thing happened, he thought it a prodigy or a presage, and his court was thronged with diviners and priests whose business was to sacrifice and purify and foretell the future. So miserable a thing is incredulity and contempt of divine power on the one hand, and so miserable, also, superstition on the other, which like water, where the level has been lowered, flowing in and never stopping, fills the mind with slavish fears and follies, as now in Alexander's case.

But upon some answers which were brought him from the oracle concerning Hephæstion, he laid aside his sorrow, and fell again to sacrificing and drinking; and having given Nearchus a splendid entertainment, after he had bathed, as was his custom, just as he was going to bed, at Medius's request he went to supper with him. Here he drank all the next day, and was attacked with a fever, which seized him, not as some write, after he had drunk of the bowl of Hercules, nor was he taken with any sudden pain in his back, as if he had been struck with a lance, for these are the inventions of some authors who thought it their duty to make the last scene of so great an action as tragical and moving as they could. Aristobulus tells us, that in the rage of his fever and a violent thirst, he took a draught of wine, upon which he fell into delirium, and died on the thirtieth day of the month Dæsius.

But the journals give the following record. On the eighteenth day of the month he slept in the bathing-room on account of his fever. The next day he bathed and removed into his chamber, and spent his time in playing at dice with Medius. In the evening he bathed and sacrificed, and ate freely, and had the fever on him through the night. On the twentieth, after the usual sacrifices and bathing, he lay in the bathing-room and heard Nearchus's narrative of his voyage, and the observations he had made in the great sea. The twenty-first he passed in the same manner, his fever still increasing, and suffered much during the night. The next day the fever was very violent, and he had himself removed and his bed set by the great bath, and discoursed with his principal officers about finding fit men to fill up the vacant places in the army. On the twenty-fourth he was much worse, and was carried out of his bed to assist at the sacrifices, and gave order that the general officers should wait within the court, whilst the inferior officers kept watch without doors. On the twenty-fifth he was removed to his palace on the other side of the river, where he slept a little, but his fever did not abate, and when the generals came into his chamber, he was speechless and continued so the following day.

The Macedonians, therefore, supposing he was dead, came with great clamours to the gates, and menaced his friends so that they were forced to admit them, and let them all pass through unarmed along by his bedside. The same day Python and Seleucus were despatched to the temple of Serapis to inquire if they should bring Alexander thither, and were answered by the god that they should not remove him. On the twenty-eighth, in the evening, he died. This account is most of it word for word as it is written in the diary.

At the time, nobody had any suspicion of his being poisoned, but upon some information given six years after, they say Olympias put many to death, and scattered the ashes of Iolaus, then dead, as if he had given it him. But those who affirm that Aristotle counselled Antipater to do it, and that by his means the poison was brought, adduce one Hagnothemis as their authority, who, they say, heard King Antigonus speak of it, and tell us that the poison was water, deadly cold as ice, distilled from a rock in the district of Nonacris, which they gathered like a thin dew, and kept in an ass's hoof; for it was so very cold and penetrating that no other vessel would hold it. However, most are of opinion that all this is a mere made-up story, no slight evidence of which is, that during the dissensions among the commanders, which lasted several days, the body continued clear and fresh, without any sign of such taint or corruption, though it lay neglected in a close sultry place.

Roxana, who was now with child, and upon that account much honoured by the Macedonians, being jealous of Statira, sent for her by a counterfeit letter, as if Alexander had been still alive; and when she had her in her power, killed her and her sister, and threw their bodies into a well, which they filled up with earth, not without the privity and assistance of Perdiccas, who in the time immediately following the king's death, under cover of the name of Arrhidæus, whom he carried about him as a sort of guard to his person, exercised the chief authority.

Arrhidæus, who was Philip's son by an obscure woman of the name of Philinna, was himself of weak intellect, not that he had been originally deficient either in body or mind; on the contrary, in his childhood, he had showed a happy and promising character enough. But a diseased habit of body, caused by drugs which Olympias gave him, had ruined, not only his health, but his understanding.

CÆSAR

100–44 B.C.

AFTER Sulla became master of Rome, he wished to make Cæsar put away his wife Cornelia, daughter of Cinna, the late sole ruler of the commonwealth, but was unable to effect it either by promises or intimidation, and so contented himself with confiscating her dowry. The ground of Sulla's hostility to Cæsar was the relationship between him and Marius; for Marius, the elder, married Julia, the sister of Cæsar's father, and had by her the younger Marius, who consequently was Cæsar's first cousin.

And though at the beginning, while so many were to be put to death, and there was so much to do, Cæsar was overlooked by Sulla, yet he would not keep quiet, but presented himself to the people as a candidate for the priesthood, though he was yet a mere boy. Sulla, without any open opposition, took measures to have him rejected, and in consultation whether he should be put to death, when it was urged by some that it was not worth his while to contrive the death of a boy, he answered, that they knew little who did not see more than one Marius in that boy.

Cæsar, on being informed of this saying, concealed himself, and for a considerable time kept out of the way in the country of the Sabines, often changing his quarters, till one night, as he was removing from one house to another on account of his health, he fell into the hands of Sulla's soldiers, who were searching those parts in order to apprehend any who had absconded.

Cæsar, by a bribe of two talents, prevailed with Cornelius, their captain, to let him go, and was no sooner dismissed but he put to sea and made for Bithynia. After a short stay there with Nicomedes, the king, in his passage back he was taken near the island of Pharmacusa by some of the pirates, who, at that time, with large fleets of ships and innumerable smaller vessels, infested the seas everywhere.

When these men at first demanded of him twenty talents for his ransom, he laughed at them for not understanding the value of their prisoner, and voluntarily engaged to give them fifty. He presently despatched those about him to several places to raise the money, till at last he was left among a set of the most bloodthirsty people in the world, the Cilicians, only with one friend and two attendants. Yet he made so little of them, that when he had a mind to sleep, he would send to them, and order them to make no noise.

For thirty-eight days, with all the freedom in the world, he amused himself with joining in their exercises and games, as if they had not been his keepers, but his guards. He wrote verses and speeches, and made them his auditors, and those who did not admire them, he called to their faces illiterate and barbarous, and would often, in raillery, threaten to hang them. They were greatly taken with this, and attributed his free talking to a kind of simplicity and boyish playfulness.

As soon as his ransom was come from Miletus, he paid it, and was discharged, and proceeded at once to man some ships at the port of Miletus, and went in pursuit of the pirates, whom he surprised with their ships still stationed at the island, and took most of them. Their money he made his prize, and the men he secured in prison at Pergamus, and·he made application to Junius, who was then governor of Asia, to whose office it belonged, as prætor, to determine their punishment.

Junius, having his eye upon the money, for the sum was considerable, said he would think at his leisure what to do with the prisoners, upon which Cæsar took his leave of him, and went off to Pergamus, where he ordered the pirates to be brought forth and crucified; the punishment he had often threatened them with whilst he was in their hands, and they little dreamt he was in earnest.

In the meantime Sulla's power being now on the decline, Cæsar's friends advised him to return to Rome, but he went to Rhodes, and entered himself in the school of Apollonius, Molon's son, a famous rhetorician, one who had the reputation of a worthy man, and had Cicero for one of his scholars. Cæsar is said to have been admirably fitted by nature to make a great statesman and orator, and to have taken such pains to improve his genius this way that without dispute he might challenge the second place.

More he did not aim at, as choosing to be first rather amongst men of arms and power, and, therefore, never rose to that height of eloquence to which nature would have carried him, his attention being diverted to those expeditions and designs which at length gained him the empire. And he himself, in his answer to Cicero's panegyric on Cato, desires his reader not to compare the plain discourse of a soldier with the harangues of an orator who had not only fine parts, but had employed his life in this study.

When he was returned to Rome, he accused Dolabella of maladministration, and many cities of Greece came in to attest it. Dolabella was acquitted, and Cæsar, in return for the support he had received from the Greeks, assisted them in their prosecution of Publius Antonius for corrupt practices, before Marcus Lucullus, prætor of Macedonia. In this course he so far succeeded, that Antonius was forced to appeal to the tribunes at Rome, alleging that in Greece he could not have fair play against Grecians.

In his pleadings at Rome, his eloquence soon obtained him great credit and favour, and he won no less upon the affections of the people by the affability of his manners and address, in which he showed a tact and consideration beyond what could have been expected at his age; and the open house he kept, the entertainments he gave, and the general splendour of his manner of life contributed little by little to create and increase his political influence.

His enemies slighted the growth of it at first, presuming it would soon fail when his money was gone; whilst in the meantime it was growing up and flourishing among the common people. When his power at last was established and not to be overthrown, and now openly tended to the altering of the whole constitution, they were aware too late that there is no beginning so mean, which continued application will not make considerable, and that despising a danger at first will make it at last irresistible.

Cicero was the first who had any suspicions of his designs upon the government, and as a good pilot is apprehensive of a storm when the sea is most smiling, saw the designing temper of the man through this disguise of good humour and affability, and said that, in general, in all he did and undertook, he detected the ambition for absolute power, "but when I see his hair so carefully arranged, and observe him adjusting it with one finger, I cannot imagine it should enter into such a man's thoughts to subvert the Roman state." But of this more hereafter.

The first proof he had of the people's goodwill to him was when he received by their suffrages a tribuneship in the army, and came out on the list with a higher place than Caius Popilius. A second and clearer instance of their favour appeared upon his making a magnificent oration in praise of his aunt Julia, wife to Marius, publicly in the Forum, at whose funeral he was so bold as to bring forth the images of Marius, which nobody had dared to produce since the government came into Sulla's hands, Marius's party having from that time been declared enemies of the state. When some who were present had begun to raise a cry against Cæsar, the people answered with loud shouts and clapping in his favour, expressing their joyful surprise and satisfaction at his having, as it were, brought up again from the grave those honours of Marius, which for so long a time had been lost to the city.

It had always been the custom at Rome to make funeral orations in praise of elderly matrons, but there was no precedent of any upon young women till Cæsar first made one upon the death of his own wife. This also procured him favour, and by this show of affection he won upon the feelings of the people, who looked upon him as a man of great tenderness and kindness of heart.

After he had buried his wife, he went as quæstor into Spain under one of the prætors, named Vetus, whom he honoured ever after, and made his son his own quæstor, when he himself came to be prætor. After this employment was ended, he married Pompeia, his third wife, having then a daughter by Cornelia, his first wife, whom he afterwards married to Pompey the Great.

He was so profuse in his expenses that, before he had any public employment, he was in debt thirteen hundred talents, and many thought that by incurring such expense to be popular he changed a solid good for what would prove but a short and uncertain return; but in truth he was purchasing what was of the greatest value at an inconsiderable rate. When he was made surveyor of the Appian Way, he disbursed, besides the public money, a great sum out of his private purse; and when he was ædile, he provided such a number of gladiators, that he entertained the people with three hundred and twenty single combats, and by his great liberality and magnificence in theatrical shows, in processions, and public feastings, he threw into the shade all the attempts that had been made before him, and gained so much upon the people, that every one was eager to find out new offices and new honours for him in return for his munificence.

There being two factions in the city, one that of Sulla, which was very powerful, the other that of Marius, which was then broken and in a very low condition, he undertook to revive this and to make it his own. And to this end, whilst he was in the height of his repute with the people for the magnificent shows he gave as ædile, he ordered images of Marius and figures of Victory, with trophies in their hands, to be carried privately in the night and placed in the capitol. Next morning when some saw them bright with gold and beautifully made, with inscriptions upon them, referring them to Marius's exploits over the Cimbri, they were surprised at the boldness of him who had set them up, nor was it difficult to guess who it was.

The fame of this soon spread and brought together a great concourse of people. Some cried out that it was an open attempt against the established government thus to revive those honours which had been buried by the laws and decrees of the senate; that Cæsar had done it to sound the temper of the people whom he had prepared before, and to try whether they were tame enough to bear his humour, and would quietly give way to his innovations. On the other hand, Marius's party took courage, and it was incredible how numerous they were suddenly seen to be, and what a multitude of them appeared and came shouting into the capitol. Many, when they saw Marius's likeness, cried for joy, and Cæsar was highly extolled as the one man, in the place of all others, who was a relation worthy of Marius.

Upon this the senate met, and Catulus Lutatius, one of the most eminent Romans of that time, stood up and inveighed against Cæsar, closing his speech with the remarkable saying that Cæsar was now not working mines, but planting batteries to overthrow the state. But when Cæsar had made an apology for himself, and satisfied the senate, his admirers were very much animated, and advised him not to depart from his own thoughts for any one, since with the people's good favour he would ere long get the better of them all, and be the first man in the commonwealth.

At this time, Metellus, the high priest, died, and Catulus and Isauricus, persons of the highest reputation, and who had great influence in the senate, were competitors for the office, yet Cæsar would not give way to them, but presented himself to the people as a candidate against them. The several parties seeming very equal, Catulus, who, because he had the most honour to lose, was the most apprehensive of the event, sent to Cæsar to buy him off, with offers of a great sum of money. But his answer was, that he was ready to borrow a larger sum than that to carry on the contest.

Upon the day of election, as his mother conducted him out of doors with tears, after embracing her, "My mother," he said, "to-day you will see me either high priest or an exile." When the votes were taken, after a great struggle, he carried it, and excited among the senate and nobility great alarm lest he might now urge on the people to every kind of insolence. And Piso and Catulus found fault with Cicero for having let Cæsar escape, when in the conspiracy of Catiline he had given the government such advantage against him.

For Catiline, who had designed not only to change the present state of affairs, but to subvert the whole empire and confound all, had himself taken to flight, while the evidence was yet incomplete against him, before his ultimate purposes had been properly discovered. But he had left Lentulus and Cethegus in the city to supply his place in the conspiracy, and whether they received any secret encouragement and assistance from Cæsar is uncertain; all that is certain is, that they were fully convicted in the senate, and when Cicero, the consul, asked the several opinions of the senators, how they would have them punished, all who spoke before Cæsar sentenced them to death; but Cæsar stood up and made a set speech, in which he told them that he thought it without precedent and not just to take away the lives of persons of their birth and distinction before they were fairly tried, unless there was an absolute necessity for it; but that if they were kept confined in any towns of Italy, Cicero himself should choose till Catiline was defeated, then the senate might in peace and at their leisure determine what was best to be done.

This sentence of his carried so much appearance of humanity, and he gave it such advantage by the eloquence with which he urged it, that not only those who spoke after him closed with it, but even they who had before given a contrary opinion now came over to his, till it came about to Catulus's and Cato's turn to speak. They warmly opposed it, and Cato intimated in his speech the suspicion of Cæsar himself, and pressed the matter so strongly that the criminals were given up to suffer execution.

As Cæsar was going out of the senate, many of the young men who at that time acted as guards to Cicero ran in with their naked swords to assault him. But Curio, it is said, threw his gown over him, and conveyed him away, and Cicero himself, when the young men looked up to see his wishes, gave a sign not to kill him, either for fear of the people or because he thought the murder unjust and illegal.

If this be true, I wonder how Cicero came to omit all mention of it in his book about his consulship. He was blamed, however, afterwards, for not having made use of so fortunate an opportunity against Cæsar, as if he had let it escape him out of fear of the populace, who, indeed, showed remarkable solicitude about Cæsar, and some time after, when he went into the senate to clear himself of the suspicions he lay under, and found great clamours raised against him, upon the senate in consequence sitting longer than ordinary, they went up to the house in a tumult, and beset it, demanding Cæsar, and requiring them to dismiss him.

Upon this, Cato, much fearing some movement among the poor citizens, who were always the first to kindle the flame among the people, and placed all their hopes in Cæsar, persuaded the senate to give them a monthly allowance of corn, an expedient which put the commonwealth to the extraordinary charge of seven million five hundred thousand drachmas in the year, but quite succeeded in removing the great cause of terror for the present, and very much weakened Cæsar's power, who at that time was just going to be made prætor, and consequently would have been more formidable by his office.

But there was no disturbance during his prætorship, only what misfortune he met with in his own domestic affairs. Publius Clodius was a patrician by descent, eminent both for his riches and eloquence, but in licentiousness of life and audacity exceeded the most noted profligates of the day. He was in love with Pompeia, Cæsar's wife, and she had no aversion to him. But there was strict watch kept on her apartment, and Cæsar's mother, Aurelia, who was a discreet woman, being contin-

ually about her, made any interview very dangerous and difficult.

The Romans have a goddess whom they call Bona, the same whom the Greeks call Gynæcea. The Phrygians, who claim a peculiar title to her, say she was mother to Midas. The Romans profess she was one of the Dryads, and married to Faunus. The Grecians affirm that she is that mother of Bacchus whose name is not to be uttered, and, for this reason, the women who celebrate her festival cover the tents with vine-branches, and, in accordance with the fable, a consecrated serpent is placed by the goddess.

It is not lawful for a man to be by, nor so much as in the house, whilst the rites are celebrated, but the women by themselves perform the sacred offices, which are said to be much the same with those used in the solemnities of Orpheus. When the festival comes, the husband, who is either consul or prætor, and with him every male creature, quits the house. The wife then taking it under her care sets it in order, and the principal ceremonies are performed during the night, the women playing together amongst themselves as they keep watch, and music of various kinds going on.

As Pompeia was at that time celebrating this feast, Clodius, who as yet had no beard, and so thought to pass undiscovered, took upon him the dress and ornaments of a singing woman, and so came thither, having the air of a young girl. Finding the doors open, he was without any stop introduced by the maid, who was in the intrigue. She presently ran to tell Pompeia, but as she was away a long time, he grew uneasy in waiting for her, and left his post and traversed the house from one room to another, still taking care to avoid the lights, till at last Aurelia's woman met him, and invited him to play with her, as the women did among themselves. He refused to comply, and she presently pulled him forward, and asked him who he was and whence he came.

Clodius told her he was waiting for Pompeia's own maid, Abra, being in fact her own name also, and as he said so, betrayed himself by his voice. Upon which the woman, shrieking, ran into the company where there were lights, and cried out she had discovered a man. The women were all in a fright. Aurelia covered up the sacred things and stopped the proceedings, and having ordered the doors to be shut, went about with lights to find Clodius, who was got into the maid's room that he had come in with, and was seized there. The women knew him, and drove him out of doors, and at once, that same night, went home and told their husbands the story.

In the morning, it was all about the town, what an impious attempt Clodius had made, and how he ought to be punished as an offender, not only against those whom he had offended, but also against the public and the gods. Upon which one of the tribunes impeached him for profaning the holy rites, and some of the principal senators combined together and gave evidence against him, that besides many other horrible crimes, he had been guilty of incest with his own sister, who was married to Lucullus. But the people set themselves against this combination of the nobility, and defended Clodius, which was of great service to him with the judges, who took alarm and were afraid to provoke the multitude.

Cæsar at once dismissed Pompeia, but being summoned as a witness against Clodius, said he had nothing to charge him with. This looking like a paradox, the accuser asked him why he parted with his wife. Cæsar replied, "I wished my wife to be not so much as suspected." Some say that Cæsar spoke this as his real thought; others, that he did it to gratify the people, who were very earnest to save Clodius. Clodius, at any rate, escaped; most of the judges giving their opinions so written as to be illegible that they might not be in danger from the people by condemning him, nor in disgrace with the nobility by acquitting him.

Cæsar, in the meantime, being out of his prætorship, had got the province of Spain, but was in great embarrassment with his creditors, who, as he was going off, came upon him, and were very pressing and importunate. This led him to apply himself to Crassus, who was the richest man in Rome, but wanted Cæsar's youthful vigour and heat to sustain the opposition against Pompey. Crassus took upon him to satisfy those creditors who were most uneasy to him, and would not be put off any longer, and engaged himself to the amount of eight hundred and thirty talents, upon which Cæsar was now at liberty to go to his province.

In his journey, as he was crossing the Alps, and passing by a small village of the barbarians with but few inhabitants, and those wretchedly poor, his companions asked the question among themselves by way of mockery, if there were any canvassing for offices there, any contention which should be uppermost, or feuds of great men one against another. To which Cæsar made answer seriously,

"For my part, I had rather be the first man among these fellows, than the second man in Rome."

It is said that another time, when free from business in Spain, after reading some part of the history of Alexander, he sat a great while very thoughtful, and at last burst out into tears. His friends were surprised, and asked him the reason of it. "Do you think," said he, "I have not just cause to weep, when I consider that Alexander at my age had conquered so many nations, and I have all this time done nothing that is memorable?"

As soon as he came into Spain he was very active, and in a few days had got together ten new cohorts of foot in addition to the twenty which were there before. With these he marched against the Calaici and Lusitani and conquered them, and advancing as far as the ocean, subdued the tribes which never before had been subject to the Romans.

Having managed his military affairs with good success, he was equally happy in the course of his civil government. He took pains to establish a good understanding amongst the several states, and no less care to heal the differences between debtors and creditors. He ordered that the creditor should receive two parts of the debtor's yearly income, and that the other part should be managed by the debtor himself, till by this method the whole debt was at last discharged. This conduct made him leave his province with a fair reputation; being rich himself, and having enriched his soldiers, and having received from them the honourable name of Imperator.

There is a law among the Romans, that whoever desires the honour of a triumph must stay without the city and expect his answer. And another, that those who stand for the consulship shall appear personally upon the place. Cæsar was come home at the very time of choosing consuls, and being in a difficulty between these two opposite laws, sent to the senate to desire that, since he was obliged to be absent, he might sue for the consulship by his friends. Cato, being backed by the law, at first opposed his request; afterwards perceiving that Cæsar had prevailed with a great part of the senate to comply with it, he made it his business to gain time, and went on wasting the whole day in speaking. Upon which Cæsar thought fit to let the triumph fall, and pursued the consulship.

Entering the town and coming forward immediately, he had recourse to a piece of state

policy by which everybody was deceived but
Cato. This was the reconciling of Crassus and
Pompey, the two men who then were most
powerful in Rome. There had been a quarrel
between them, which he now succeeded in
making up, and by this means strengthened
himself by the united power of both, and so
under the cover of an action which carried all
the appearance of a piece of kindness and
good-nature, caused what was in effect a revolution in the government.

For it was not the quarrel between Pompey
and Cæsar, as most men imagine, which was
the origin of the civil wars, but their union,
their conspiring together at first to subvert the
aristocracy, and so quarrelling afterwards between themselves. Cato, who often foretold
what the consequence of this alliance would
be, had then the character of a sullen, interfering man, but in the end the reputation of a
wise but unsuccessful counsellor.

Thus Cæsar, being doubly supported by the
interests of Crassus and Pompey, was promoted to the consulship, and triumphantly
proclaimed with Calpurnius Bibulus. When
he entered on his office he brought in bills
which would have been preferred with better
grace by the most audacious of the tribunes
than by a consul, in which he proposed the
plantation of colonies and the division of lands,
simply to please the commonalty. The best and
most honourable of the senators opposed it,
upon which, as he had long wished for nothing more than for such a colourable pretext,
he loudly protested how much it was against
his will to be driven to seek support from the
people, and how the senate's insulting and
harsh conduct left no other course possible for
him than to devote himself henceforth to the
popular cause and interest.

And so he hurried out of the senate, and
presenting himself to the people, and there
placing Crassus and Pompey, one on each side
of him, he asked them whether they consented
to the bills he had proposed. They owned their
assent, upon which he desired them to assist
him against those who had threatened to oppose him with their swords. They engaged
they would, and Pompey added further, that
he would meet their swords with a sword and
buckler too. These words the nobles much
resented, as neither suitable to his own dignity,
nor becoming the reverence due to the senate,
but resembling rather the vehemence of a boy
or the fury of a madman. But the people were
pleased with it.

In order to get a yet firmer hold upon Pompey, Cæsar having a daughter, Julia, who had
been before contracted to Servilius Cæpio, now
betrothed her to Pompey, and told Servilius he
should have Pompey's daughter, who was not
unengaged either, but promised to Sulla's son,
Faustus. A little time after, Cæsar married
Calpurnia, the daughter of Piso, and got Piso
made consul for the year following. Cato exclaimed loudly against this, and protested,
with a great deal of warmth, that it was intolerable the government should be prostituted
by marriages, and that they should advance
one another to the commands of armies, provinces, and other great posts, by means of
women.

Bibulus, Cæsar's colleague, finding it was to
no purpose to oppose his bills, but that he was
in danger of being murdered in the Forum,
as also was Cato, confined himself to his house,
and there let the remaining part of his consulship expire. Pompey, when he was married,
at once filled the Forum with soldiers, and
gave the people his help in passing the new
laws, and secured Cæsar the government of
all Gaul, both on this and the other side of the
Alps, together with Illyricum, and the command of four legions for five years.

Cato made some attempts against these proceedings, but was seized and led off on the
way to prison by Cæsar, who expected that he
would appeal to the tribunes. But when he
saw that Cato went along without speaking a
word, and not only the nobility were indignant, but the people also, out of respect for
Cato's virtue, were following in silence, and
with dejected looks, he himself privately desired one of the tribunes to rescue Cato.

As for the other senators, some few of them
attended the house, the rest, being disgusted,
absented themselves. Hence Considius, a very
old man, took occasion one day to tell Cæsar
that the senators did not meet because they
were afraid of his soldiers. Cæsar asked, "Why
don't you, then, out of the same fear, keep at
home?" To which Considius replied, that age
was his guard against fear, and that the small
remains of his life were not worth much caution.

But the most disgraceful thing that was
done in Cæsar's consulship was his assisting
to gain the tribuneship for the same Clodius
who had made the attempt on his wife's chastity and intruded upon the secret vigils. He
was elected on purpose to effect Cicero's downfall; nor did Cæsar leave the city to join his

army till they two had overpowered Cicero and driven him out of Italy.

Thus far have we followed Cæsar's actions before the wars of Gaul. After this, he seems to begin his course afresh, and to enter upon a new life and scene of action. And the period of those wars which he now fought, and those many expeditions in which he subdued Gaul, showed him to be a soldier and general not in the least inferior to any of the greatest and most admired commanders who had ever appeared at the head of armies. For if we compare him with the Fabii, the Metelli, the Scipios, and with those who were his contemporaries, or not long before him, Sulla, Marius, the two Luculli, or even Pompey himself, whose glory, it may be said, went up at that time to heaven for every excellence in war, we shall find Cæsar's actions to have surpassed them all.

One he may be held to have outdone in consideration of the difficulty of the country in which he fought, another in the extent of territory which he conquered; some, in the number and strength of the enemy whom he defeated; one man, because of the wildness and perfidiousness of the tribes whose good-will he conciliated, another in his humanity and clemency to those he overpowered; others, again, in his gifts and kindnesses to his soldiers; all alike in the number of the battles which he fought and the enemies whom he killed. For he had not pursued the wars in Gaul full ten years when he had taken by storm above eight hundred towns, subdued three hundred states, and of the three millions of men, who made up the gross sum of those with whom at several times he engaged, he had killed one million and taken captive a second.

He was so much master of the good-will and hearty service of his soldiers that those who in other expeditions were but ordinary men displayed a courage past defeating or withstanding when they went upon any danger where Cæsar's glory was concerned. Such a one was Acilius, who, in the sea-fight before Marseilles, had his right hand struck off with a sword, yet did not quit his buckler out of his left, but struck the enemies in the face with it, till he drove them off and made himself master of the vessel. Such another was Cassius Scæva, who, in a battle near Dyrrhachium, had one of his eyes shot out with an arrow, his shoulder pierced with one javelin, and his thigh with another; and having received one hundred and thirty darts upon his target, called to the ene-

my, as though he would surrender himself. But when two of them came up to him, he cut off the shoulder of one with a sword, and by a blow over the face forced the other to retire, and so with the assistance of his friends, who now came up, made his escape.

Again, in Britain, when some of the foremost officers had accidentally got into a morass full of water, and there were assaulted by the enemy, a common soldier, whilst Cæsar stood and looked on, threw himself into the midst of them, and after many signal demonstrations of his valour, rescued the officers and beat off the barbarians. He himself, in the end, took to the water, and with much difficulty, partly by swimming, partly by wading, passed it, but in the passage lost his shield. Cæsar and his officers saw it and admired, and went to meet him with joy and acclamation. But the soldier, much dejected and in tears, threw himself down at Cæsar's feet and begged his pardon for having let go his buckler.

Another time in Africa, Scipio having taken a ship of Cæsar's in which Granius Petro, lately appointed quæstor, was sailing, gave the other passengers as free prize to his soldiers, but thought fit to offer the quæstor his life. But he said it was not usual for Cæsar's soldiers to take but give mercy, and having said so, fell upon his sword and killed himself.

This love of honour and passion for distinction were inspired into them and cherished in them by Cæsar himself, who, by his unsparing distribution of money and honours, showed them that he did not heap up wealth from the wars for his own luxury, or the gratifying his private pleasures, but that all he received was but a public fund laid by for the reward and encouragement of valour, and that he looked upon all he gave to deserving soldiers as so much increase to his own riches. Added to this also, there was no danger to which he did not willingly expose himself, no labour from which he pleaded an exemption.

His contempt of danger was not so much wondered at by his soldiers because they knew how much he coveted honour. But his enduring so much hardship, which he did to all appearance beyond his natural strength, very much astonished them. For he was a spare man, had a soft and white skin, was distempered in the head and subject to an epilepsy, which, it is said, first seized him at Corduba. But he did not make the weakness of his constitution a pretext for his ease, but rather used war as the best physic against his indispositions; whilst, by indefatigable journeys, coarse diet, frequent lodging in the field, and continual laborious exercise, he struggled with his diseases and fortified his body against all attacks.

He slept generally in his chariots or litters, employing even his rest in pursuit of action. In the day he was thus carried to the forts, garrisons, and camps, one servant sitting with him, who used to write down what he dictated as he went, and a soldier attending behind him with his sword drawn. He drove so rapidly that when he first left Rome he arrived at the river Rhone within eight days. He had been an expert rider from his childhood; for it was usual with him to sit with his hands joined together behind his back, and so to put his horse to its full speed. And in this way he disciplined himself so far as to be able to dictate letters from on horseback, and to give directions to two who took notes at the same time, or, as Oppius says, to more.

And it is thought that he was the first who contrived means for communicating with friends by cipher, when either press of business, or the large extent of the city, left him no time for a personal conference about matters that required despatch.

How little nice he was in his diet may be seen in the following instance. When at the table of Valerius Leo, who entertained him at supper at Milan, a dish of asparagus was put before him on which his host instead of oil had poured sweet ointment. Cæsar partook of it without any disgust, and reprimanded his friends for finding fault with it. "For it was enough," said he, "not to eat what you did not like; but he who reflects on another man's want of breeding, shows he wants it as much himself."

Another time upon the road he was driven by a storm into a poor man's cottage, where he found but one room, and that such as would afford but a mean reception to a single person, and therefore told his companions places of honour should be given up to the greater men, and necessary accommodations to the weaker, and accordingly ordered that Oppius, who was in bad health, should lodge within, whilst he and the rest slept under a shed at the door.

His first war in Gaul was against the Helvetians and Tigurini, who having burnt their own towns, twelve in number, and four hundred villages, would have marched forward through that part of Gaul which was included in the Roman province, as the Cimbri and Teutones formerly had done. Nor were they inferior to these in courage; and in numbers they were equal, being in all three hundred thousand, of which one hundred and ninety thousand were fighting men. Cæsar did not engage the Tigurini in person, but Labienus, under his directions, routed them near the river Arar.

The Helvetians surprised Cæsar, and unexpectedly set upon him as he was conducting his army to a confederate town. He succeeded, however, in making his retreat into a strong position, where, when he had mustered and marshalled his men, his horse was brought to him; upon which he said, "When I have won the battle, I will use my horse for the chase, but at present let us go against the enemy," and accordingly charged them on foot.

After a long and severe combat, he drove the main army out of the field, but found the hardest work at their carriages and ramparts, where not only the men stood and fought, but the women also and children defended themselves till they were cut to pieces; insomuch that the fight was scarcely ended till midnight.

This action, glorious in itself, Cæsar crowned with another yet more noble, by gathering in a body all the barbarians that had escaped out of the battle, above one hundred thousand in number, and obliging them to re-occupy the country which they had deserted and the cities which they had burnt. This he did for fear the Germans should pass it and possess themselves of the land whilst it lay uninhabited.

His second war was in defence of the Gauls against the Germans, though some time before he had made Ariovistus, their king, recognised at Rome as an ally. But they were very insufferable neighbours to those under his government; and it was probable, when occasion offered, they would renounce the present arrangements, and march on to occupy Gaul. But finding his officers timorous, and especially those of the young nobility who came along with him in hopes of turning their campaigns with him into a means for their own pleasure or profit, he called them together, and advised them to march off, and not run the hazard of a battle against their inclinations, since they had such weak and unmanly feelings; telling them that he would take only the tenth legion and march against the barbarians, whom he did not expect to find an enemy more formidable than the Cimbri, nor, he added, should they find him a general inferior to Marius. Upon this, the tenth legion deputed some of their body to pay him their acknowledgments and thanks, and the other legions blamed their officers, and all, with great vigour and zeal, followed him many days' journey, till they encamped within two hundred furlongs of the enemy.

Ariovistus's courage to some extent was cooled upon their very approach; for never expecting the Romans would attack the Germans, whom he had thought it more likely they would not venture to withstand even in defence of their own subjects, he was the more surprised at Cæsar's conduct, and saw his army to be in consternation. They were still more discouraged by the prophecies of their holy women, who foretell the future by observing the eddies of rivers, and taking signs from the windings and noise of streams, and who now warned them not to engage before the next new moon appeared.

Cæsar having had intimation of this, and seeing the Germans lie still, thought it expedient to attack them whilst they were under these apprehensions, rather than sit still and wait their time. Accordingly, he made his approaches to the strongholds and hills on which they lay encamped, and so galled and fretted them that at last they came down with great fury to engage. But he gained a signal victory, and pursued them for four hundred furlongs, as far as the Rhine; all which space was covered with spoils and bodies of the slain. Ariovistus made shift to pass the Rhine with the small remains of an army, for it is said the number of the slain amounted to eighty thousand.

After this action, Cæsar left his army at their winter quarters in the country of the Sequani, and, in order to attend to affairs at Rome, went into that part of Gaul which lies on the Po, and was part of his province; for the river Rubicon divides Gaul, which is on this side the Alps, from the rest of Italy. There he sat down and employed himself in courting people's favour; great numbers coming to him continually, and always finding their requests answered; for he never failed to dismiss all with present pledges of his kindness in hand, and further hopes for the future.

And during all this time of the war in Gaul, Pompey never observed how Cæsar was on the one hand using the arms of Rome to effect his conquests, and on the other was gaining over and securing to himself the favour of the Romans with the wealth which those conquests obtained him.

But when he heard that the Belgæ, who were the most powerful of all the Gauls, and inhabited a third part of the country, were revolted, and had got together a great many thousand men in arms, he immediately set out and took his way hither with great expedition, and falling upon the enemy as they were ravaging the Gauls, his allies, he soon defeated and put to flight the largest and least scattered division of them. For though their numbers were great, yet they made but a slender defence, and the marshes and deep rivers were made passable to the Roman foot by the vast quantity of dead bodies.

Of those who revolted, all the tribes that lived near the ocean came over without fighting, and he, therefore, led his army against the Nervii, the fiercest and most warlike people of all in those parts. These live in a country covered with continuous woods, and having lodged their children and property out of the way in the depth of the forest, fell upon Cæsar with a body of sixty thousand men, before he was prepared for them, while he was making his encampment. They soon routed his cavalry, and having surrounded the twelfth and seventh legions, killed all the officers, and had not Cæsar himself snatched up a buckler and forced his way through his own men to come up to the barbarians, or had not the tenth legion, when they saw him in danger, run in from the tops of the hills, where they lay, and broken through the enemy's ranks to rescue him, in all probability not a Roman would have been saved.

But now, under the influence of Cæsar's bold example, they fought a battle, as the phrase is, of more than human courage, and yet with their utmost efforts they were not able to drive the enemy out of the field, but cut them down fighting in their defence. For out of sixty thousand men, it is stated that not above five hundred survived the battle, and of four hundred of their senators not above three.

When the Roman senate had received news of this, they voted sacrifices and festivals to the gods, to be strictly observed for the space of fifteen days, a longer space than ever was observed for any victory before. The danger to which they had been exposed by the joint outbreak of such a number of nations was felt to have been great; and the people's fondness for Cæsar gave additional lustre to successes achieved by him.

He now, after settling everything in Gaul, came back again, and spent the winter by the Po, in order to carry on the designs he had in hand at Rome. All who were candidates for offices used his assistance, and were supplied with money from him to corrupt the people and buy their votes, in return of which, when they were chosen, they did all things to advance his power. But what was more considerable, the most eminent and powerful men in Rome in great numbers came to visit him at Lucca; Pompey, and Crassus, and Appius, the governor of Sardinia, and Nepos, the pro-consul of Spain, so that there were in the place at one time one hundred and twenty lictors and more than two hundred senators.

In deliberation here held, it was determined that Pompey and Crassus should be consuls again for the following year; that Cæsar should have a fresh supply of money, and that his command should be renewed to him for five years more. It seemed very extravagant to all thinking men that those very persons who had received so much money from Cæsar should persuade the senate to grant him more, as if he were in want. Though in truth it was not so much upon persuasion as compulsion that, with sorrow and groans for their own acts, they passed the measure. Cato was not present, for they had sent him seasonably out of the way into Cyprus; but Favonius, who was a zealous imitator of Cato, when he found he could do no good by opposing it, broke out of the house, and loudly declaimed against these proceedings to the people, but none gave him any hearing; some slighting him out of respect to Crassus and Pompey, and the greater part to gratify Cæsar, on whom depended their hopes.

After this, Cæsar returned again to his forces in Gaul, when he found that country involved in a dangerous war, two strong nations of the Germans having lately passed the Rhine to conquer it; one of them called the Usipes, the other the Tenteritæ.

Of the war with the people, Cæsar himself has given this account in his *Commentaries,* that the barbarians, having sent ambassadors to treat with him, did, during the treaty, set upon him in his march, by which means with eight hundred men they routed five thousand of his horse, who did not suspect their coming; that afterwards they sent other ambassadors to renew the same fraudulent practices, whom he kept in custody, and led on his army against the barbarians, as judging it mere simplicity to keep faith with those who had so faithlessly broken the terms they had agreed to.

But Tanusius states that when the senate decreed festivals and sacrifices for this victory, Cato declared it to be his opinion that Cæsar ought to be given into the hands of the barbarians, that so the guilt which this breach of faith might otherwise bring upon the state might be expiated by transferring the curse on him, who was the occasion of it.

Of those who passed the Rhine, there were four hundred thousand cut off; those few who escaped were sheltered by the Sugambri, a people of Germany.

Cæsar took hold of this pretence to invade the Germans, being at the same time ambitious of the honour of being the first man that should pass the Rhine with an army. He carried a bridge across it, though it was very wide, and the current at that particular point very full, strong, and violent, bringing down with its waters trunks of trees, and other lumber, which much shook and weakened the foundations of his bridge. But he drove great piles of wood into the bottom of the river above the passage, to catch and stop these as they floated down, and thus fixing his bridle upon the stream, successfully finished his bridge, which no one who saw could believe to be the work but of ten days.

In the passage of his army over it he met with no opposition; the Suevi themselves, who are the most warlike people of all Germany, flying with their effects into the deepest and most densely wooded valleys. When he had burnt all the enemy's country, and encouraged those who embraced the Roman interest, he went back into Gaul, after eighteen days' stay in Germany.

But his expedition into Britain was the most famous testimony of his courage. For he was the first who brought a navy into the western ocean, or who sailed into the Atlantic with an army to make war; and by invading an island, the reported extent of which had made its existence a matter of controversy among historians, many of whom questioned whether it were not a mere name and fiction, not a real place, he might be said to have carried the Roman empire beyond the limits of the known world. He passed thither twice from that part of Gaul which lies over against it, and in several battles which he fought did more hurt to the enemy than service to himself, for the islanders were so miserably poor that they had nothing worth being plundered of. When he found himself unable to put such an end to the war as he wished, he was content to take hostages from the king, and to impose a tribute, and then quitted the island.

At his arrival in Gaul, he found letters which lay ready to be conveyed over the water to him from his friends at Rome, announcing his daughter's death, who died in labour of a child by Pompey. Cæsar and Pompey both were much afflicted with her death, nor were their friends less disturbed, believing that the alliance was now broken, which had hitherto kept the sickly commonwealth in peace, for the child also died within a few days after the mother. The people took the body of Julia, in spite of the opposition of the tribunes, and carried it into the field of Mars, and there her funeral rites were performed, and there her remains are laid.

Cæsar's army was now grown very numerous, so that he was forced to disperse them into various camps for their winter quarters, and he having gone himself to Italy as he used to do, in his absence a general outbreak throughout the whole of Gaul commenced, and large armies marched about the country, and attacked the Roman quarters, and attempted to make themselves masters of the forts where they lay.

The greatest and strongest party of the rebels, under the command of Abriorix, cut off Cotta and Titurius with all their men, while a force sixty thousand strong besieged the legion under the command of Cicero, and had almost taken it by storm, the Roman soldiers being all wounded, and having quite spent themselves by a defence beyond their natural strength. But Cæsar, who was at a great distance, having received the news, quickly got together seven thousand men, and hastened to relieve Cicero. The besiegers were aware of it, and went to meet him, with great confidence that they should easily overpower such a handful of men.

Cæsar, to increase their presumption, seemed to avoid fighting, and still marched off, till he found a place conveniently situated for a few to engage against many, where he encamped. He kept his soldiers from making any attack upon the enemy, and commanded them to raise the ramparts higher and barricade the gates, that by show of fear they might heighten the enemy's contempt of them. Till at last they came without any order in great security to make an assault, when he issued forth and put them in flight with the loss of many men.

This quieted the greater part of the commotions in these parts of Gaul, and Cæsar, in the course of the winter, visited every part of the country, and with great vigilance took precautions against all innovations. For there were three legions now come to him to supply the place of the men he had lost, of which Pompey furnished him with two out of those under his command; the other was newly raised in the part of Gaul by the Po.

But in a while the seeds of war, which had long since been secretly sown and scattered by the most powerful men in those warlike nations, broke forth into the greatest and most dangerous war that was in those parts, both as regards the number of men in the vigour of their youth who were gathered and armed from all quarters, the vast funds of money collected to maintain it, the strength of the towns, and the difficulty of the country where it was carried on. It being winter, the rivers were frozen, the woods covered with snow, and the level country flooded, so that in some places the ways were lost through the depth of the snow; in others, the overflowing of marshes and streams made every kind of passage uncertain. All which difficulties made it seem impracticable for Cæsar to make any attempt upon the insurgents. Many tribes had revolted together, the chief of them being the Arverni and Carnutini; the general who had the supreme command in war was Vercingetorix, whose father the Gauls had put to death on suspicion of his aiming at absolute government.

He having disposed his army in several bodies, and set officers over them, drew over to him all the country round about as far as those that lie upon the Arar, and having intelligence of the opposition which Cæsar now experienced at Rome, thought to engage all Gaul in the war. Which if he had done a little later, when Cæsar was taken up with the civil wars, Italy had been put into as great a terror as before it was by the Cimbri.

But Cæsar, who above all men was gifted with the faculty of making the right use of everything in war, and most especially of seizing the right moment, as soon as he heard of the revolt, returned immediately the same way he went, and showed the barbarians, by the quickness of his march in such a severe season, that an army was advancing against them which was invincible. For in the time that one would have thought it scarce credible that a courier or express should have come with a message from him, he himself appeared with all his army, ravaging the country, reducing their posts, subduing their towns, receiving into his protection those who declared for him. Till at last the Edui, who hitherto had styled themselves brethren to the Romans, and had been much honoured by them, declared against him, and joined the rebels, to the great discouragement of his army.

Accordingly he removed thence, and passed the country of the Ligones, desiring to reach the territories of the Sequani, who were his friends, and who lay like a bulwark in front of Italy against the other tribes of Gaul. There the enemy came upon him, and surrounded him with many myriads, whom he also was eager to engage; and at last, after some time and with much slaughter, he gained generally a complete victory; though at first he appears to have met with some reverse, and the Aruveni show you a small sword hanging up in a temple, which they say was taken from Cæsar. Cæsar saw this afterwards himself, and smiled, and when his friends advised it should be taken down, would not permit it, because he looked upon it as consecrated.

After the defeat, a great part of those who had escaped fled with their king into a town called Alesia, which Cæsar besieged, though the height of the walls, and number of those who defended them, made it appear impregnable; and meantime, from without the walls, he was assailed by a greater danger than can be expressed. For the choice men of Gaul, picked out of each nation, and well armed, came to relieve Alesia, to the number of three hundred thousand; nor were there in the town less than one hundred and seventy thousand.

So that Cæsar, being shut up betwixt two such forces, was compelled to protect himself by two walls, one towards the town, the other against the relieving army, as knowing if these forces should join, his affairs would be entirely ruined. The danger that he underwent before Alesia justly gained him great honour on many accounts, and gave him an opportunity of showing greater instances of his valour and conduct than any other contest had done.

One wonders much how he should be able to engage and defeat so many thousands of men without the town, and not be perceived by those within, but yet more, that the Romans themselves, who guarded their wall which was next to the town, should be strangers to it. For even they knew nothing of the victory, till they heard the cries of the men and lamentations of the women who were in the town, and had from thence seen the Romans at a distance carrying into their camp a great quantity of bucklers, adorned with gold and silver, many breastplates stained with blood, besides cups and tents made in the Gallic fashion. So soon did so vast an army dissolve and vanish like a ghost or dream, the greatest part of them being killed upon the spot.

Those who were in Alesia, having given themselves and Cæsar much trouble, surrendered at last; and Vercingetorix, who was the chief spring of all the war, putting his best armour on, and adorning his horse, rode out of the gates, and made a turn about Cæsar as he was sitting, then quitting his horse, threw off his armour, and remained quietly sitting at Cæsar's feet until he was led away to be reserved for the triumph.

Cæsar had long ago resolved upon the overthrow of Pompey, as had Pompey, for that matter, upon his. For Crassus, the fear of whom had hitherto kept them in peace, having now been killed in Parthia, if the one of them wished to make himself the greatest man in Rome, he had only to overthrow the other; and if he again wished to prevent his own fall, he had nothing for it but to be beforehand with him whom he feared.

Pompey had not been long under any such apprehensions, having till lately despised Cæsar, as thinking it no difficult matter to put down him whom he himself had advanced. But Cæsar had entertained this design from the beginning against his rivals, and had retired, like an expert wrestler, to prepare himself apart for the combat. Making the Gallic wars his exercise-ground, he had at once improved the strength of his soldiery, and had heightened his own glory by his great actions, so that he was looked on as one who might challenge comparison with Pompey.

Nor did he let go any of those advantages which were now given him both by Pompey himself and the times, and the ill-government of Rome, where all who were candidates for offices publicly gave money, and without any shame bribed the people, who, having received their pay, did not contend for their benefactors with their bare suffrages, but with bows, swords, and slings. So that after having many times stained the place of election with blood of men killed upon the spot, they left the city at last without a government at all, to be carried about like a ship without a pilot to steer her; while all who had any wisdom could only be thankful if a course of such wild and stormy disorder and madness might end no worse than in a monarchy.

Some were so bold as to declare openly that the government was incurable but by a monarchy, and that they ought to take that remedy from the hands of the gentlest physician, meaning Pompey, who, though in words he pretended to decline it, yet in reality made his utmost efforts to be declared dictator. Cato, perceiving his design, prevailed with the senate to make him sole consul, that with the offer of a more legal sort of monarchy he might be withheld from demanding the dictatorship. They over and above voted him the continuance of his provinces, for he had two, Spain and all Africa, which he governed by his lieutenants, and maintained armies under him, at the yearly charge of a thousand talents out of the public treasury.

Upon this Cæsar also sent and petitioned for the consulship and the continuance of his provinces. Pompey at first did not stir in it, but Marcellus and Lentulus opposed it, who had always hated Cæsar, and now did everything, whether fit or unfit, which might disgrace and affront him. For they took away the privilege of Roman citizens from the people of New Comum, who were a colony that Cæsar had lately planted in Gaul, and Marcellus, who was then consul, ordered one of the senators of that town, then at Rome, to be whipped, and told him he laid that mark upon him to signify he was no citizen of Rome, bidding him, when he went back again, to show it to Cæsar.

After Marcellus's consulship, Cæsar began to lavish gifts upon all the public men out of the riches he had taken from the Gauls; discharged Curio, the tribune, from his great debts; gave Paulus, then consul, fifteen hundred talents, with which he built the noble court of justice adjoining the Forum, to supply the place of that called the Fulvian.

Pompey, alarmed at these preparations, now openly took steps, both by himself and his friends, to have a successor appointed in Cæsar's room, and sent to demand back the soldiers whom he had lent him to carry on the wars in Gaul. Cæsar returned them, and made each soldier a present of two hundred and fifty drachmas. The officer who brought them home to Pompey spread amongst the people no very fair or favourable report of Cæsar, and flattered Pompey himself with false suggestions that he was wished for by Cæsar's army; and though his affairs here were in some embarrassment

through the envy of some, and the ill state of the government, yet there the army was at his command, and if they once crossed into Italy would presently declare for him; so weary were they of Cæsar's endless expeditions, and so suspicious of his designs for a monarchy.

Upon this Pompey grew presumptuous, and neglected all warlike preparations, as fearing no danger, and used no other means against him than mere speeches and votes, for which Cæsar cared nothing. And one of his captains, it is said, who was sent by him to Rome, standing before the senate house one day, and being told that the senate would not give Cæsar a longer time in his government, clapped his hand on the hilt of his sword and said, "But this shall."

Yet the demands which Cæsar made had the fairest colours of equity imaginable. For he proposed to lay down his arms, and that Pompey should do the same, and both together should become private men, and each expect a reward of his services from the public. For that those who proposed to disarm him, and at the same time to confirm Pompey in all the power he held, were simply establishing the one in the tyranny which they accused the other of aiming at.

When Curio made these proposals to the people in Cæsar's name, he was loudly applauded, and some threw garlands towards him, and dismissed him as they do successful wrestlers, crowned with flowers. Antony, being tribune, produced a letter sent from Cæsar on this occasion, and read it, though the consuls did what they could to oppose it.

But Scipio, Pompey's father-in-law, proposed in the senate, that if Cæsar did not lay down his arms within such a time he should be voted an enemy; and the consuls putting it to the question, whether Pompey should dismiss his soldiers, and again, whether Cæsar should disband his, very few assented to the first, but almost all to the latter. But Antony proposing again, that both should lay down their commissions, all but a very few agreed to it. Scipio was upon this very violent, and Lentulus, the consul, cried aloud, that they had need of arms, and not of suffrages, against a robber; so that the senators for the present adjourned, and appeared in mourning as a mark of their grief for the dissension.

Afterwards there came other letters from Cæsar, which seemed yet more moderate, for he proposed to quit everything else, and only to retain Gaul within the Alps, Illyricum, and two legions, till he should stand a second time for consul.

Cicero, the orator, who was lately returned from Cilicia, endeavoured to reconcile differences, and softened Pompey, who was willing to comply in other things, but not to allow him the soldiers. At last Cicero used his persuasions with Cæsar's friends to accept of the provinces and six thousand soldiers only, and so to make up the quarrel. And Pompey was inclined to give way to this, but Lentulus, the consul, would not hearken to it, but drove Antony and Curio out of the senate-house with insults, by which he afforded Cæsar the most plausible pretence that could be, and one which he could readily use to inflame the soldiers, by showing them two persons of such repute and authority who were forced to escape in a hired carriage in the dress of slaves. For so they were glad to disguise themselves when they fled out of Rome.

There were not about him at that time above three hundred horse and five thousand foot; for the rest of his army, which was left behind the Alps, was to be brought after him by officers who had received orders for that purpose. But he thought the first motion towards the design which he had on foot did not require large forces at present, and that what was wanted was to make this first step suddenly, and so as to astound his enemies with the boldness of it; as it would be easier, he thought, to throw them into consternation by doing what they never anticipated than fairly to conquer them, if he had alarmed them by his preparations.

And therefore he commanded his captains and other officers to go only with their swords in their hands, without any other arms, and make themselves masters of Ariminum, a large city of Gaul, with as little disturbance and bloodshed as possible. He committed the care of these forces to Hortensius, and himself spent the day in public as a stander-by and spectator of the gladiators, who exercised before him.

A little before night he attended to his person, and then went into the hall, and conversed for some time with those he had invited to supper, till it began to grow dusk, when he rose from table and made his excuses to the company, begging them to stay till he came back, having already given private directions to a few immediate friends that they should follow him, not all the same way, but some one way, some another. He himself got into one of the hired carriages, and drove at first another way, but presently turned towards Ariminum.

When he came to the river Rubicon, which parts Gaul within the Alps from the rest of Italy, his thoughts began to work, now he was just entering upon the danger, and he wavered much in his mind when he considered the greatness of the enterprise into which he was throwing himself. He checked his course and ordered a halt, while he revolved with himself, and often changed his opinion one way and the other, without speaking a word. This was when his purposes fluctuated most; presently he also discussed the matter with his friends who were about him (of which number Asinius Pollio was one), computing how many calamities his passing that river would bring upon mankind, and what a relation of it would be transmitted to posterity. At last, in a sort of passion, casting aside calculation, and abandoning himself to what might come, and using the proverb frequently in their mouths who enter upon dangerous and bold attempts, "The die is cast," with these words he took the river. Once over, he used all expedition possible, and before it was day reached Ariminum and took it. It is said that the night before he passed the river he had an impious dream that he was unnaturally familiar with his own mother.

As soon as Ariminum was taken, wide gates, so to say, were thrown open, to let in war upon every land alike and sea, and with the limits of the province, the boundaries of the laws were transgressed. Nor would one have thought that, as at other times, the mere men and women fled from one town of Italy to another in their consternation, but that the very towns themselves left their sites and fled for succour to each other.

The city of Rome was overrun, as it were, with a deluge, by the conflux of people flying in from all the neighbouring places. Magistrates could no longer govern, nor the eloquence of any orator quiet it; it was all but suffering shipwreck by the violence of its own tempestuous agitation. The most vehement contrary passions and impulses were at work everywhere. Nor did those who rejoiced at the prospect of the change altogether conceal their feelings, but when they met, as in so great a city they frequently must, with the alarmed and dejected of the other party, they provoked quarrels by their bold expressions of confidence in the event.

Pompey, sufficiently disturbed of himself, was yet more perplexed by the clamours of others; some telling him that he justly suffered for having armed Cæsar against himself and the government; others blaming him for permitting Cæsar to be insolently used by Lentulus, when he made such ample concessions, and offered such reasonable proposals towards an accommodation. Favonius bade him now stamp upon the ground; for once talking big in the senate, he desired them not to trouble themselves about making any preparations for the war, for that he himself, with one stamp of his foot, would fill all Italy with soldiers. Yet, still Pompey at that time had more forces than Cæsar; but he was not permitted to pursue his own thoughts, but, being continually disturbed with false reports and alarms, as if the enemy was close upon him and carrying all before him, he gave way, and let himself be borne down by the general cry. He put forth an edict declaring the city to be in a state of anarchy, and left it with orders that the senate should follow him, and that no one should stay behind who did not prefer tyranny to their country and liberty.

The consuls at once fled, without making even the usual sacrifices; so did most of the senators, carrying off their own goods in as much haste as if they had been robbing their neighbours. Some, who had formerly much favoured Cæsar's cause, in the prevailing alarm quitted their own sentiments, and without any prospect of good to themselves, were carried along by the common stream. It was a melancholy thing to see the city tossed in these tumults, like a ship given up by her pilots, and left to run, as chance guides her, upon any rock in her way. Yet, in spite of their sad condition, people still esteemed the place of their exile to be their country for Pompey's sake, and fled from Rome, as if it had been Cæsar's camp. Labienus even, who had been one of Cæsar's nearest friends, and his lieutenant, and who had fought by him zealously in the Gallic wars, now deserted him and went over to Pompey.

Cæsar sent all his money and equipage after him, and then sat down before Corfinium, which was garrisoned with thirty cohorts under the command of Domitius. He, in despair of maintaining the defence, requested a physician, whom he had among his attendants, to give him poison; and taking the dose, drank it, in hopes of being despatched by it. But soon after, when he was told that Cæsar showed the utmost clemency towards those he took prisoners, he lamented his misfortune, and blamed the hastiness of his resolution. His physician consoled him by informing him that he had taken a sleeping draught, not a poison; upon which, much rejoiced, and rising from his bed, he went presently to Cæsar, and gave him the pledge of his hand, yet afterwards again went over to Pompey. The report of these actions at Rome quieted those who were there, and some who had fled thence returned.

Cæsar took into his army Domitius's soldiers, as he did all those whom he found in any town enlisted for Pompey's service. Being now strong and formidable enough, he advanced against Pompey himself, who did not stay to receive him, but fled to Brundusium, having sent the consuls before with a body of troops to Dyrrhachium. Soon after, upon Cæsar's approach, he set to sea, as shall be more particularly related in his Life. Cæsar would have immediately pursued him, but wanted shipping, and therefore went back to Rome, having made himself master of all Italy without bloodshed in the space of sixty days.

When he came thither, he found the city more quiet than he expected, and many senators present, to whom he addressed himself with courtesy and deference, desiring them to send to Pompey about any reasonable accommodations towards a peace. But nobody complied with this proposal; whether out of fear of Pompey, whom they had deserted, or that they thought Cæsar did not mean what he said, but thought it his interest to talk plausibly.

Afterwards, when Metellus, the tribune, would have hindered him from taking money out of the public treasury, and adduced some laws against it, Cæsar replied that arms and laws had each their own time; "If what I do displeases you, leave the place; war allows no free talking. When I have laid down my arms, and made peace, come back and make what speeches you please. And this," he added, "I tell you in diminution of my own just right, as indeed you and all others who have appeared against me and are now in my power may be treated as I please." Having said this to Metellus, he went to the doors of the treasury, and the keys being not to be found, sent for smiths to force them open. Metellus again making resistance and some encouraging him in it, Cæsar, in a louder tone, told him he would put him to death if he gave him any further disturbance. "And this," said he, "you know, young man, is more disagreeable for me to say than to do." These words made Metellus withdraw for fear, and obtained speedy execution henceforth for all orders that Cæsar gave for procuring necessaries for the war.

He was now proceeding to Spain, with the determination of first crushing Afranius and Varro, Pompey's lieutenants, and making himself master of the armies and provinces under them, that he might then more securely advance against Pompey, when he had no enemy left behind him. In this expedition his person was often in danger from ambuscades, and his army by want of provisions, yet he did not desist from pursuing the enemy, provoking them to fight, and hemming them with his fortifications, till by main force he made himself master of their camps and their forces. Only the generals got off, and fled to Pompey.

When Cæsar came back to Rome, Piso, his father-in-law, advised him to send men to Pompey to treat of a peace; but Isauricus, to ingratiate himself with Cæsar, spoke against it.

After this, being created dictator by the senate, he called home the exiles, and gave back their rights as citizens to the children of those who had suffered under Sulla; he relieved the debtors by an act remitting some part of the interest on their debts, and passed some other measures of the same sort, but not many. For within eleven days he resigned his dictatorship, and having declared himself consul, with Servilius Isauricus, hastened again to the war.

He marched so fast that he left all his army behind him, except six hundred chosen horse and five legions, with which he put to sea in the very middle of winter, about the beginning of the month of January (which corresponds pretty nearly with the Athenian month Poseideon), and having passed the Ionian Sea, took Oricum and Apollonia, and then sent back the ships to Brundusium, to bring over the soldiers who were left behind in the march.

They, while yet on the march, their bodies now no longer in the full vigour of youth, and they themselves weary with such a multitude of wars, could not but exclaim against Cæsar, "When at last, and where, will this Cæsar let us be quiet? He carries us from place to place, and uses us as if we were not to be worn out, and had no sense of labour. Even our iron itself is spent by blows, and we ought to have some pity on our bucklers and breastplates, which have been used so long. Our wounds, if nothing else, should make him see that we are mortal men whom he commands, subject to the same pains and sufferings as other human beings. The very gods themselves cannot force the winter season, or hinder the storms in their time; yet he pushes forward, as if he were not pursuing, but flying from an enemy." So they talked as they marched leisurely towards Brundusium.

But when they came thither, and found Cæsar gone off before them, their feelings changed, and they blamed themselves as traitors to their general. They now railed at their officers for marching so slowly, and placing themselves on the heights overlooking the sea towards Epirus, they kept watch to see if they could espy the vessels which were to transport them to Cæsar.

He in the meantime was posted in Apollonia, but had not an army with him able to fight the enemy, the forces from Brundusium being so long in coming, which put him to great suspense and embarrassment what to do. At last he resolved upon a most hazardous experiment, and embarked, without any one's knowledge, in a boat of twelve oars, to cross over to Brundusium, though the sea was at that time covered with a vast fleet of the enemy. He got on board in the night-time, in the dress of a slave, and throwing himself down like a person of no consequence, lay along at the bottom of the vessel. The river Anius was to carry them down to sea, and there used to blow a gentle gale every morning from the land, which made it calm at the mouth of the river, by driving the waves forward; but this night there had blown a strong wind from the sea, which overpowered that from the land, so that where the river met the influx of the sea-water and the opposition of the waves it was extremely rough and angry; and the current was beaten back with such a violent swell that the master of the boat could not make good his passage, but ordered his sailors to tack about and return.

Cæsar, upon this, discovered himself, and taking the man by the hand, who was surprised to see him there, said, "Go on, my friend, and fear nothing; you carry Cæsar and his fortune in your boat." The mariners, when they heard that, forgot the storm, and laying all their strength to their oars, did what they could to force their way down the river. But when it was to no purpose, and the vessel now took in much water, Cæsar finding himself in such danger in the very mouth of the river, much against his will permitted the master to turn back. When he was come to land, his soldiers ran to him in a multitude, reproaching him for what he had done, and indignant that he should think himself not strong enough to get a victory by their sole assistance, but must disturb himself, and expose his life for those who were absent, as if he could not trust those who were with him.

After this, Antony came over with the forces from Brundusium, which encouraged Cæsar to give Pompey battle, though he was encamped very advantageously, and furnished with plenty of provisions both by sea and land, whilst he himself was at the beginning but ill supplied, and before the end was extremely pinched for want of necessaries, so that his soldiers were forced to dig up a kind of root which grew there, and tempering it with milk, to feed on it. Sometimes they made a kind of bread of it, and advancing up to the enemy's outposts, would throw in these loaves, telling them, that as long as the earth produced such roots they would not give up blockading Pompey. But Pompey took what care he could that neither the loaves nor the words should reach his men, who were out of heart and despondent through terror at the fierceness and hardihood of their enemies, whom they looked upon as a sort of wild beasts.

There were continual skirmishes about Pompey's outworks, in all which Cæsar had the better, except one, when his men were forced to fly in such a manner that he had like to have lost his camp. For Pompey made such a vigorous sally on them that not a man stood his ground; the trenches were filled with the slaughter, many fell upon their own ramparts and bulwarks, whither they were driven in flight by the enemy. Cæsar met them and would have turned them back, but could not. When he went to lay hold of the ensigns, those who carried them threw them down, so that the enemy took thirty-two of them. He himself narrowly escaped; for taking hold of one of his soldiers, a big and strong man, that was flying by him, he bade him stand and face about; but the fellow, full of apprehensions from the danger he was in, laid hold of his sword, as if he would strike Cæsar, but Cæsar's armour-bearer cut off his arm.

Cæsar's affairs were so desperate at that time that when Pompey, either through over-cautiousness or his ill fortune, did not give the finishing stroke to that great success, but retreated after he had driven the routed enemy within their camp, Cæsar, upon seeing his withdrawal, said to his friends, "The victory to-day had been on the enemies' side if they had had a general who knew how to gain it."

When he was retired into his tent, he laid himself down to sleep, but spent that night as miserable as ever he did any, in perplexity and consideration with himself, coming to the conclusion that he had conducted the war amiss. For when he had a fertile country before him, and all the wealthy cities of Macedonia and Thessaly, he had neglected to carry the war thither, and had sat down by the seaside, where his enemies had such a powerful fleet, so that he was in fact rather besieged by the want of necessaries, than besieging others with his arms. Being thus distracted in his thoughts with the view of the difficulty and distress he was in, he raised his camp, with the intention of advancing towards Scipio, who lay in Macedonia; hoping either to entice Pompey into a country where he should fight without the advantage he now had of supplies from the sea, or to overpower Scipio if not assisted.

This set all Pompey's army and officers on fire to hasten and pursue Cæsar, whom they concluded to be beaten and flying. But Pompey was afraid to hazard a battle on which so much depended, and being himself provided with all necessaries for any length of time, thought to tire out and waste the vigour of Cæsar's army, which could not last long. For the best part of his men, though they had great experience, and showed an irresistible courage in all engagements, yet by their frequent marches, changing their camps, attacking fortifications, and keeping long night-watches, were getting worn out and broken; they being now old, their bodies less fit for labour, and their courage, also, beginning to give way with the failure of their strength. Besides, it was said that an infectious disease, occasioned by their irregular diet, was prevailing in Cæsar's army, and what was of greatest moment, he was neither furnished with money nor provisions, so that in a little time he must needs fall of himself.

For these reasons Pompey had no mind to fight him, but was thanked for it by none but Cato, who rejoiced at the prospect of sparing his fellow-citizens. For he, when he saw the dead bodies of those who had fallen in the last battle on Cæsar's side, to the number of a thousand, turned away, covered his face, and shed tears. But every one else upbraided Pompey for being reluctant to fight, and tried to goad him on by such nicknames as Agamemnon, and King of Kings, as if he were in no hurry to lay down his sovereign authority, but was pleased to see so many commanders attending on him, and paying their attendance at his tent. Favonius, who affected Cato's free way of speaking his mind, complained bitterly that they should eat no figs even this year at Tusculum, because of Pompey's love of command. Afranius, who was lately returned out of Spain, and, on account of his ill success there, laboured under the suspicion of having been bribed to betray the army, asked why they did not fight this purchaser of provinces. Pompey was driven, against his own will, by this kind of language, into offering battle, and proceeded to follow Cæsar.

Cæsar had found great difficulties in his march, for no country would supply him with provisions, his reputation being very much fallen since his late defeat. But after he took Gomphi, a town of Thessaly, he not only found provisions for his army, but physic too. For there they met with plenty of wine, which they took very freely, and heated with this, sporting and revelling on their march in bacchanalian fashion, they shook off the disease, and their whole constitution was relieved and changed into another habit.

When the two armies were come into Pharsalia, and both encamped there, Pompey's thoughts ran the same way as they had done before, against fighting, and the more because of some unlucky presages, and a vision he had in a dream. But those who were about him were so confident of success, that Domitius, and Spinther, and Scipio, as if they had already conquered, quarrelled which should succeed Cæsar in the pontificate. And many sent to Rome to take houses fit to accommodate consuls and prætors, as being sure of entering upon those offices as soon as the battle was over. The cavalry especially were obstinate for fighting, being splendidly armed and bravely mounted, and valuing themselves upon the fine horses they kept, and upon their own handsome persons; as also upon the advantage of their numbers, for they were five thousand against one thousand of Cæsar's. Nor were the numbers of the infantry less disproportionate, there being forty-five thousand of Pompey's against twenty-two thousand of the enemy.

Cæsar, collecting his soldiers together, told them that Corfinius was coming up to them with two legions, and that fifteen cohorts more under Calenus were posted at Megara and Athens; he then asked them whether they would stay till these joined them, or would hazard the battle by themselves. They all cried out to him not to wait, but on the contrary to do whatever he could to bring about an engagement as soon as possible.

When he sacrificed to the gods for the lustration of his army, upon the death of the first victim the augur told him within three days he should come to a decisive action. Cæsar asked him whether he saw anything in the entrails which promised a happy event. "That," said the priest, "you can best answer yourself; for the gods signify a great alteration from the present posture of affairs. If, therefore, you think yourself well off now, expect worse fortune; if unhappy, hope for better."

The night before the battle, as he walked the rounds about midnight, there was a light seen in the heavens, very bright and flaming, which seemed to pass over Cæsar's camp and fall into Pompey's. And when Cæsar's soldiers came to relieve the watch in the morning, they perceived a panic disorder among the enemies. However, he did not expect to fight that day, but set about raising his camp with the intention of marching towards Scotussa.

But when the tents were now taken down, his scouts rode up to him, and told him the enemy would give him battle. With this news he was extremely pleased, and having performed his devotions to the gods, set his army in battle array, dividing them into three bodies. Over the middlemost he placed Domitius Calvinus; Antony commanded the left wing, and he himself the right, being resolved to fight at the head of the tenth legion. But when he saw the enemy's cavalry taking position against him, being struck with their fine appearance and their number, he gave private orders that six cohorts from the rear of the army should come round and join him, whom he posted behind the right wing, and instructed them what they should do when the enemy's horse came to charge.

On the other side, Pompey commanded the right wing, Domitius the left, and Scipio, Pompey's father-in-law, the centre. The whole weight of the cavalry was collected on the left wing, with the intent that they should outflank the right wing of the enemy, and rout that part where the general himself commanded. For they thought no phalanx of infantry could be solid enough to sustain such a shock, but that they must necessarily be broken and shattered all to pieces upon the onset of so immense a force of cavalry.

When they were ready on both sides to give the signal for battle, Pompey commanded his foot, who were in the front, to stand their ground, and without breaking their order, receive, quietly, the enemy's first attack, till they came within javelin's cast. Cæsar, in this respect, also, blames Pompey's generalship, as if he had not been aware how the first encounter, when made with an impetus and upon the run, gives weight and force to the strokes, and fires the men's spirits into a flame, which the general concurrence fans to full heat.

He himself was just putting the troops into motion and advancing to the action, when he found one of his captains, a trusty and experienced soldier, encouraging his men to exert their utmost. Cæsar called him by his name, and said, "What hopes, Caius Crassinius, and what grounds for encouragement?" Crassinius stretched out his hand, and cried in a loud voice, "We shall conquer nobly, Cæsar; and I this day will deserve your praises, either alive or dead." So he said, and was the first man to run in upon the enemy, followed by the hundred and twenty soldiers about him, and breaking through the first rank, still pressed on forwards with much slaughter of the enemy, till at last he was struck back by the wound of a sword, which went in at his mouth with such force that it came out at his neck behind.

Whilst the foot was thus sharply engaged in the main battle, on the flank Pompey's horse rode up confidently, and opened their ranks very wide, that they might surround the right wing of Cæsar. But before they engaged, Cæsar's cohorts rushed out and attacked them, and did not dart their javelins at a distance, nor strike at the thighs and legs, as they usually did in close battle, but aimed at their faces. For thus Cæsar had instructed them, in hopes that young gentlemen, who had not known much of battles and wounds, but came wearing their hair long, in the flower of their age and height of their beauty, would be more apprehensive of such blows, and not care for hazarding both a danger at present and a blemish for the future. And so it proved, for they were so far from bearing the stroke of the javelins, that they could not stand the sight of them, but turned about, and covered their faces to secure them.

Once in disorder, presently they turned about to fly; and so most shamefully ruined all. For those who had beat them back at once outflanked the infantry, and falling on their rear, cut them to pieces. Pompey, who commanded the other wing of the army, when he saw his cavalry thus broken and flying, was no longer himself, nor did he now remember that he was Pompey the Great, but, like one whom some god had deprived of his senses, retired to his tent without speaking a word, and there sat to expect the event, till the whole army was

routed and the enemy appeared upon the works which were thrown up before the camp, where they closely engaged with his men who were posted there to defend it. Then first he seemed to have recovered his senses, and uttering, it is said, only these words, "What, into the camp too?" he laid aside his general's habit, and putting on such clothes as might best favour his flight, stole off. What fortune he met with afterwards, how to took shelter in Egypt, and was murdered there, we tell you in his Life.

Cæsar, when he came to view Pompey's camp, and saw some of his opponents dead upon the ground, others dying, said, with a groan, "This they would have; they brought me to this necessity. I, Caius Cæsar, after succeeding in so many wars, had been condemned had I dismissed my army." These words, Pollio says, Cæsar spoke in Latin at that time, and that he himself wrote them in Greek; adding, that those who were killed at the taking of the camp were most of them servants; and that not above six thousand soldiers fell. Cæsar incorporated most of the foot whom he took prisoners with his own legions, and gave a free pardon to many of the distinguished persons, and amongst the rest to Brutus, who afterwards killed him. He did not immediately appear after the battle was over, which put Cæsar, it is said, into great anxiety for him; nor was his pleasure less when he saw him present himself alive.

There were many prodigies that foreshowed this victory, but the most remarkable that we are told of was that at Tralles. In the temple of Victory stood Cæsar's statue. The ground on which it stood was naturally hard and solid, and the stone with which it was paved still harder; yet it is said that a palm-tree shot itself up near the pedestal of this statue. In the city of Padua, one Caius Cornelius, who had the character of a good augur, the fellow-citizen and acquaintance of Livy, the historian, happened to be making some augural observations that very day when the battle was fought. And first, as Livy tells us, he pointed out the time of the fight, and said to those who were by him that just then the battle was begun and the men engaged. When he looked a second time, and observed the omens, he leaped up as if he had been inspired, and cried out, "Cæsar, you are victorious." This much surprised the standers-by, but he took the garland which he had on from his head, and swore he would never wear it again till the events should give authority to his art. This Livy positively states for a truth.

Cæsar, as a memorial of his victory, gave the Thessalians their freedom, and then went in pursuit of Pompey. When he was come into Asia, to gratify Theopompus, the author of the collection of fables, he enfranchised the Cnidians, and remitted one-third of their tribute to all the people of the province of Asia. When he came to Alexandria, where Pompey was already murdered, he would not look upon Theodotus, who presented him with his head, but taking only his signet, shed tears. Those of Pompey's friends who had been arrested by the King of Egypt, as they were wandering in those parts, he relieved, and offered them his own friendship. In his letter to his friends at Rome, he told them that the greatest and most signal pleasure his victory had given him was to be able continually to save the lives of fellow-citizens who had fought against him.

As to the war in Egypt, some say it was at once dangerous and dishonourable, and no-ways necessary, but occasioned only by his passion for Cleopatra. Others blame the ministers of the king, and especially the eunuch Pothinus, who was the chief favourite and had lately killed Pompey; he had banished Cleopatra, and was now secretly plotting Cæsar's destruction (to prevent which, Cæsar from that time began to sit up whole nights, under pretence of drinking, for the security of his person), while openly he was intolerable in his affronts to Cæsar, both by his words and actions. For when Cæsar's soldiers had musty and unwholesome corn measured out to them, Pothinus told them they must be content with it, since they were fed at another's cost.

He ordered that his table should be served with wooden and earthen dishes, and said Cæsar had carried off all the gold and silver plate, under pretence of arrears of debt. For the present king's father owed Cæsar one thousand seven hundred and fifty myriads of money. Cæsar had formerly remitted to his children the rest, but thought fit to demand the thousand myriads at that time to maintain his army. Pothinus told him that he had better go now and attend to his other affairs of greater consequence, and that he should receive his money at another time with thanks. Cæsar replied that he did not want Egyptians to be his counsellors, and soon after privately sent for Cleopatra from her retirement.

She took a small boat, and one only of her confidants, Apollodorus, the Sicilian, along with her, and in the dusk of the evening landed near the palace. She was at a loss how to get in undiscovered, till she thought of putting herself into the coverlet of a bed and lying at length, whilst Apollodorus tied up the bedding and carried it on his back through the gates to Cæsar's apartment. Cæsar was first captivated by this proof of Cleopatra's bold wit, and was afterwards so overcome by the charm of her society that he made a reconciliation between her and her brother, on condition that she should rule as his colleague in the kingdom.

A festival was kept to celebrate this reconciliation, where Cæsar's barber, a busy listening fellow, whose excessive timidity made him inquisitive into everything, discovered that there was a plot carrying on against Cæsar by Achillas, general of the king's forces, and Pothinus, the eunuch. Cæsar, upon the first intelligence of it, set a guard upon the hall where the feast was kept and killed Pothinus.

Achillas escaped to the army, and raised a troublesome and embarrassing war against Cæsar, which it was not easy for him to manage with his few soldiers against so powerful a city and so large an army. The first difficulty he met with was want of water, for the enemies had turned the canals. Another was, when the enemy endeavoured to cut off his communication by sea, he was forced to divert that danger by setting fire to his own ships, which, after burning the docks, thence spread on and destroyed the great library. A third was, when in an engagement near Pharos, he leaped from the mole into a small boat to assist his soldiers who were in danger, and when the Egyptians pressed him on every side, he threw himself into the sea, and with much difficulty swam off. This was the time when, according to the story, he had a number of manuscripts in his hand, which, though he was continually darted at, and forced to keep his head often under water, yet he did not let go, but held them up safe from wetting in one hand, whilst he swam with the other. His boat, in the meantime, was quickly sunk. At last, the king having gone off to Achillas and his party, Cæsar engaged and conquered them. Many fell in that battle, and the king himself was never seen after. Upon this, he left Cleopatra Queen of Egypt, who soon after had a son by him, whom the Alexandrians called Cæsarion, and then departed for Syria.

Thence he passed to Asia, where he heard that Domitius was beaten by Pharnaces, son of Mithridates, and had fled out of Pontus with a handful of men; and that Pharnaces pursued the victory so eagerly, that though he was already master of Bithynia and Cappadocia, he had a further design of attempting the Lesser Armenia, and was inviting all the kings and tetrarchs there to rise. Cæsar immediately marched against him with three legions, fought him near Zela, drove him out of Pontus, and totally defeated his army. When he gave Amantius, a friend of his at Rome, an account of this action, to express the promptness and rapidity of it he used three words, "I came, saw, and conquered", which in Latin, having all the same cadence, carry with them a very suitable air of brevity.

Hence he crossed into Italy, and came to Rome at the end of that year, for which he had been a second time chosen dictator, though that office had never before lasted a whole year, and was elected consul for the next. He was ill spoken of, because upon a mutiny of some soldiers, who killed Cosconius and Galba, who had been prætors, he gave them only the slight reprimand of calling them *Citizens* instead of *Fellow-Soldiers,* and afterwards assigned to each man a thousand drachmas, besides a share of lands in Italy. He was also reflected on for Dolabella's extravagance, Amantius's covetousness, Antony's debauchery, and Corfinius's profuseness, who pulled down Pompey's house and rebuilt it, as not magnificent enough; for the Romans were much displeased with all these. But Cæsar, for the prosecution of his own scheme of government, though he knew their characters and disapproved them, was forced to make use of those who would serve him.

After the battle of Pharsalia, Cato and Scipio fled into Africa, and there, with the assistance of King Juba, got together a considerable force, which Cæsar resolved to engage. He accordingly passed into Sicily about the winter solstice, and to remove from his officers' minds all hopes of delay there, encamped by the seashore, and as soon as ever he had a fair wind, put to sea with three thousand foot and a few horse. When he had landed them, he went back secretly, under some apprehensions for the larger part of his army, but met them upon the sea, and brought them all to the same camp.

There he was informed that the enemies relied much upon an ancient oracle, that the family of the Scipios should be always victorious in Africa. There was in his army a man, otherwise mean and contemptible, but of the house of the Africani, and his name Scipio Sallutio. This man Cæsar (whether in raillery to ridicule Scipio, who commanded the enemy, or seriously to bring over the omen to his side, it were hard to say), put at the head of his troops, as if he were general, in all the frequent battles which he was compelled to fight.

For he was in such want both of victualling for his men and forage for his horses, that he was forced to feed the horses with seaweed, which he washed thoroughly to take off its saltness, and mixed with a little grass to give it a more agreeable taste. The Numidians, in great numbers, and well horsed, whenever he went, came up and commanded the country.

Cæsar's cavalry, being one day unemployed, diverted themselves with seeing an African, who entertained them with dancing, and at the same time played upon the pipe to admiration. They were so taken with this, that they alighted, and gave their horses to some boys, when on a sudden the enemy surrounded them, killed some, pursued the rest, and fell in with them into their camp; and had not Cæsar himself and Asinius Pollio come to their assistance, and put a stop to their flight, the war had been then at an end. In another engagement, also, the enemy had again the better, when Cæsar, it is said, seized a standard-bearer, who was running away, by the neck, and forcing him to face about, said, "Look, that is the way to the enemy."

Scipio, flushed with this success at first, had a mind to come to one decisive action. He therefore left Afranius and Juba in two distinct bodies not far distant and marched himself towards Thapsus, where he proceeded to build a fortified camp above a lake, to serve as a centre-point for their operations, and also as a place of refuge. Whilst Scipio was thus employed, Cæsar with incredible despatch made his way through thick woods, and a country supposed to be impassable, cut off one part of the enemy and attacked another in the front. Having routed these, he followed up his opportunity and the current of his good fortune, and on the first onset carried Afranius's camp, and ravaged that of the Numidians, Juba, their king, being glad to save himself by flight; so that in a small part of a single day he made himself master of three camps, and killed fifty thousand of the enemy, with the loss only of fifty of his own men. This is the account some give of that fight.

Others say he was not in the action, but that he was taken with his usual distemper just as he was setting his army in order. He perceived the approaches of it, and before it had too far disordered his senses, when he was already beginning to shake under its influence, withdrew into a neighbouring fort where he reposed himself. Of the men of consular and prætorian dignity that were taken after the fight, several Cæsar put to death, others anticipated him by killing themselves.

Cato had undertaken to defend Utica, and for that reason was not in the battle. The desire which Cæsar had to take him alive made him hasten thither; and upon the intelligence that he had despatched himself, he was much discomposed, for what reason is not so well agreed. He certainly said, "Cato, I must grudge you your death, as you grudged me the honour of saving your life." Yet the discourse he wrote against Cato after his death is no great sign of his kindness, or that he was inclined to be reconciled to him. For how is it probable that he would have been tender of his life when he was so bitter against his memory? But from his clemency to Cicero, Brutus, and many others who fought against him, it may be divined that Cæsar's book was not written so much out of animosity to Cato, as in his own vindication. Cicero had written an encomium upon Cato, and called it by his name. A composition by so great a master upon so excellent a subject was sure to be in every one's hands. This touched Cæsar, who looked upon a panegyric on his enemies as no better than an invective against himself; and therefore he made in his *Anti-Cato* a collection of whatever could be said in his derogation. The two compositions, like Cato and Cæsar themselves, have each of them their several admirers.

Cæsar, upon his return to Rome, did not omit to pronounce before the people a magnificent account of his victory, telling them that he had subdued a country which would supply the public every year with two hundred thousand attic bushels of corn and three million pounds' weight of oil. He then led three triumphs for Egypt, Pontus, and Africa, the last for the victory over, not Scipio, but King Juba, as it was professed, whose little son was then carried in the triumph, the happiest captive that ever was, who, from a barbarian Numidian, came by this means to obtain a place among the most learned historians of Greece. After the triumphs, he distributed rewards to his soldiers, and treated the people with feasting and shows. He entertained the whole people together at one feast, where twenty-two

thousand dining couches were laid out, and he made a display of gladiators, and of battles by sea, in honour, as he said, of his daughter Julia, though she had been long since dead. When these shows were over, an account was taken of the people who, from three hundred and twenty thousand, were now reduced to one hundred and fifty thousand. So great a waste had the civil war made in Rome alone, not to mention what the other parts of Italy and the provinces suffered.

He was now chosen a fourth time consul, and went into Spain against Pompey's sons. They were but young, yet had gathered together a very numerous army, and showed they had courage and conduct to command it, so that Cæsar was in extreme danger. The great battle was near the town of Munda, in which Cæsar, seeing his men hard pressed, and making but a weak resistance, ran through the ranks among the soldiers, and crying out, asked them whether they were not ashamed to deliver him into the hands of boys. At last, with great difficulty, and the best efforts he could make, he forced back the enemy, killing thirty thousand of them, though with the loss of one thousand of his best men. When he came back from the fight, he told his friends that he had often fought for victory, but this was the first time he had ever fought for life. This battle was won on the feast of Bacchus, the very day in which Pompey, four years before, had set out for the war. The younger of Pompey's sons escaped; but Didius, some days after the fight, brought the head of the elder to Cæsar. This was the last war he was engaged in.

The triumph which he celebrated for this victory displeased the Romans beyond anything, for he had not defeated foreign generals or barbarian kings, but had destroyed the children and family of one of the greatest men of Rome, though unfortunate; and it did not look well to lead a procession in celebration of the calamities of his country, and to rejoice in those things for which no other apology could be made either to gods or men than their being absolutely necessary. Besides that, hitherto he had never sent letters or messengers to announce any victory over his fellow-citizens, but had seemed rather to be ashamed of the action than to expect honour from it.

Nevertheless his countrymen, conceding all to his fortune, and accepting the bit, in the hope that the government of a single person would give them time to breathe after so many civil wars and calamities, made him dictator for life. This was indeed a tyranny avowed, since his power now was not only absolute, but perpetual, too. Cicero made the first proposals to the senate for conferring honours upon him, which might in some sort be said not to exceed the limits of ordinary human moderation. But others, striving which should deserve most, carried them so excessively high, that they made Cæsar odious to the most indifferent and moderate sort of men, by the pretensions and extravagance of the titles which they decreed him. His enemies, too, are thought to have had some share in this, as well as his flatterers. It gave them advantage against him, and would be their justification for any attempt they should make upon him; for since the civil wars were ended, he had nothing else that he could be charged with.

And they had good reason to decree a temple to Clemency, in token of their thanks for the mild use he made of his victory. For he not only pardoned many of those who fought against him, but, further, to some gave honours and offices; as particularly to Brutus and Cassius, who both of them were prætors. Pompey's images that were thrown down he set up again, upon which Cicero also said that by raising Pompey's statues he had fixed his own. When his friends advised him to have a guard, and several offered their services, he would not hear of it; but said it was better to suffer death once than always to live in fear of it. He looked upon the affections of the people to be the best and surest guard, and entertained them again with public feasting and general distributions of corn; and to gratify his army, he sent out colonies to several places, of which the most remarkable were Carthage and Corinth; which as before they had been ruined at the same time, so now were restored and repeopled together.

As for the men of high rank, he promised to some of them future consulships and prætorships, some he consoled with other offices and honours, and to all held out hopes of favour by the solicitude he showed to rule with the general good-will, insomuch that upon the death of Maximus one day before his consulship was ended, he made Caninius Revilius consul for that day. And when many went to pay the usual compliments and attentions to the new consul, "Let us make haste," said Cicero, "lest the man be gone out of his office before we come."

Cæsar was born to do great things, and had a passion after honour, and the many noble exploits he had done did not now serve as an inducement to him to sit still and reap the fruit of his past labours, but were incentives and encouragements to go on, and raised in him ideas of still greater actions, and a desire of new glory, as if the present were all spent. It was in fact a sort of emulous struggle with himself, as it had been with another, how he might outdo his past actions by his future.

In pursuit of these thoughts, he resolved to make war upon the Parthians, and when he had subdued them, to pass through Hyrcania; thence to march along by the Caspian Sea to Mount Caucasus, and so on about Pontus, till he came into Scythia; then to overrun all the countries bordering upon Germany, and Germany itself; and so to return through Gaul into Italy, after completing the whole circle of his intended empire, and bounding it on every side by the ocean.

While preparations were making for this expedition, he proposed to dig through the isthmus on which Corinth stands; and appointed Anienus to superintend the work. He had also a design of diverting the Tiber, and carrying it by a deep channel directly from Rome to Circeii, and so into the sea near Tarracina, that there might be a safe and easy passage for all merchants who traded to Rome. Besides this, he intended to drain all the marshes by Pomentium and Setia, and gain ground enough from the water to employ many thousands of men in tillage. He proposed further to make great mounds on the shore nearest Rome, to hinder the sea from breaking in upon the land, to clear the coast at Ostia of all the hidden rocks and shoals that made it unsafe for shipping, and to form ports and harbours fit to receive the large number of vessels that would frequent them.

These things were designed without being carried into effect; but his reformation of the calendar in order to rectify the irregularity of time was not only projected with great scientific ingenuity, but was brought to its completion, and proved of very great use. For it was not only in ancient time that the Romans had wanted a certain rule to make the revolutions of their months fall in with the course of the year, so that their festivals and solemn days for sacrifice were removed by little and little, till at last they came to be kept at seasons quite the contrary to what was at first intended, but even at this time the people had no way of computing the solar year; only the priests could say the time, and they, at their pleasure, without giving any notice, slipped in the intercalary month, which they called Mercedonius. Numa was the first who put in this month, but his expedient was but a poor one and quite inadequate to correct all the errors that arose in the returns of the annual cycles, as we have shown in his Life.

Cæsar called in the best philosophers and mathematicians of his time to settle the point, and out of the systems he had before him formed a new and more exact method of correcting the calendar, which the Romans use to this day, and seem to succeed better than any nation in avoiding the errors occasioned by the inequality of the cycles. Yet even this gave offence to those who looked with an evil eye on his position, and felt oppressed by his power. Cicero the orator, when some one in his company chanced to say the next morning Lyra would rise, replied, "Yes, in accordance with the edict," as if even this were a matter of compulsion.

But that which brought upon him the most apparent and mortal hatred was his desire of being king; which gave the common people the first occasion to quarrel with him, and proved the most specious pretence to those who had been his secret enemies all along. Those who would have procured him that title gave it out that it was foretold in the Sibyls' books that the Romans should conquer the Parthians when they fought against them under the conduct of a king, but not before. And one day, as Cæsar was coming down from Alba to Rome, some were so bold as to salute him by the name of king; but he, finding the people disrelished it, seemed to resent it himself, and said his name was Cæsar, not King. Upon this there was a general silence, and he passed on looking not very well pleased or contented.

Another time, when the senate had conferred on him some extravagant honours, he chanced to receive the message as he was sitting on the rostra, where, though the consuls and prætors themselves waited on him, attended by the whole body of the senate, he did not rise, but behaved himself to them as if they had been private men, and told them his honours wanted rather to be retrenched than increased. This treatment offended not only the senate, but the commonalty too, as if they thought the affront upon the senate equally reflected upon the whole republic; so that all who could decently leave him went off, looking much discomposed.

Cæsar, perceiving the false step he had made, immediately retired home; and laying his throat bare, told his friends that he was ready to offer this to any one who would give the stroke. But afterwards he made the malady from which he suffered the excuse for his sitting, saying that those who are attacked by it lose their presence of mind if they talk much standing; that they presently grow giddy, fall into convulsions, and quite lose their reason. But this was not the reality, for he would willingly have stood up to the senate, had not Cornelius Balbus, one of his friends, or rather flatterers, hindered him. "Will you not remember," said he, "you are Cæsar, and claim the honour which is due to your merit?"

He gave a fresh occasion of resentment by his affront to the tribunes. The Lupercalia were then celebrated, a feast at the first institution belonging, as some writers say, to the shepherds, and having some connection with the Arcadian Lycæa. Many young noblemen and magistrates run up and down the city with their upper garments off, striking all they meet with thongs of hide, by way of sport; and many women, even of the highest rank, place themselves in the way, and hold out their hands to the lash, as boys in a school do to the master, out of a belief that it procures an easy labour to those who are with child, and makes those conceive who are barren. Cæsar, dressed in a triumphal robe, seated himself in a golden chair at the rostra to view this ceremony.

Antony, as consul, was one of those who ran this course, and when he came into the Forum, and the people made way for him, he went up and reached to Cæsar a diadem wreathed with laurel. Upon this there was a shout, but only a slight one, made by the few who were planted there for that purpose; but when Cæsar refused it, there was universal applause. Upon the second offer, very few, and upon the second refusal, all again applauded. Cæsar finding it would not take, rose up, and ordered the crown to be carried into the capitol.

Cæsar's statues were afterwards found with royal diadems on their heads. Flavius and Marullus, two tribunes of the people, went presently and pulled them off, and having apprehended those who first saluted Cæsar as king committed them to prison. The people followed them with acclamations, and called them by the name of Brutus, because Brutus was the first who ended the succession of kings, and transferred the power which before was lodged in one man into the hands of the senate and people. Cæsar so far resented this, that he displaced Marullus and Flavius; and in urging his charges against them, at the same time ridiculed the people, by himself giving the men more than once the names of Bruti and Cumæi.

This made the multitude turn their thoughts to Marcus Brutus, who, by his father's side, was thought to be descended from that first Brutus, and by his mother's side from the Servilii, another noble family, being besides nephew and son-in-law to Cato. But the honours and favours he had received from Cæsar took off the edge from the desires he might himself have felt for overthrowing the new monarchy. For he had not only been pardoned himself after Pompey's defeat at Pharsalia, and had procured the same grace for many of his friends, but was one in whom Cæsar had a particular confidence.

He had at that time the most honourable prætorship for the year, and was named for the consulship four years after, being preferred before Cassius, his competitor. Upon the question as to the choice, Cæsar, it is related, said that Cassius had the fairer pretensions, but that he could not pass by Brutus. Nor would he afterwards listen to some who spoke against Brutus, when the conspiracy against him was already afoot, but laying his hand on his body, said to the informers, "Brutus will wait for this skin of mine," intimating that he was worthy to bear rule on account of his virtue, but would not be base and ungrateful to gain it.

Those who desired a change, and looked on him as the only, or at least the most proper, person to effect it, did not venture to speak with him; but in the night-time laid papers about his chair of state, where he used to sit and determine causes, with such sentences in them as, "You are asleep, Brutus," "You are no longer Brutus." Cassius, when he perceived his ambition a little raised upon this, was more instant than before to work him yet further, having himself a private grudge against Cæsar for most reasons that we have mentioned in the Life of Brutus.

Nor was Cæsar without suspicions of him, and said once to his friends, "What do you think Cassius is aiming at? I don't like him, he looks so pale." And when it was told him that Antony and Dolabella were in a plot against him, he said he did not fear such fat, luxurious men, but rather the pale, lean fellows, meaning Cassius and Brutus.

Fate, however, is to all appearance more unavoidable than unexpected. For many strange prodigies and apparitions are said to have been observed shortly before this event. As to the lights in the heavens, the noises heard in the night, and the wild birds which perched in the Forum, these are not perhaps worth taking notice of in so great a case as this. Strabo, the philosopher, tells us that a number of men were seen, looking as if they were heated through with fire, contending with each other; that a quantity of flame issued from the hand of a soldier's servant, so that they who saw it thought he must be burnt, but that after all he had no hurt. As Cæsar was sacrificing, the victim's heart was missing, a very bad omen, because no living creature can subsist without a heart. One finds it also related by many that a soothsayer bade him prepare for some great danger on the Ides of March. When this day was come, Cæsar, as he went to the senate, met this soothsayer, and said to him by way of raillery, "The Ides of March are come," who answered him calmly, "Yes, they are come, but they are not past." The day before his assassination he supped with Marcus Lepidus; and as he was signing some letters according to his custom, as he reclined at table, there arose a question what sort of death was the best. At which he immediately, before any one could speak, said, "A sudden one."

After this, as he was in bed with his wife, all the doors and windows of the house flew open together; he was startled at the noise and the light which broke into the room, and sat up in his bed, where by the moonshine he perceived Calpurnia fast asleep, but heard her utter in her dream some indistinct words and inarticulate groans. She fancied at that time she was weeping over Cæsar, and holding him butchered in her arms. Others say this was not her dream, but that she dreamed that a pinnacle, which the senate, as Livy relates, had ordered to be raised on Cæsar's house by way of ornament and grandeur, was tumbling down, which was the occasion of her tears and ejaculations. When it was day, she begged of Cæsar, if it were possible, not to stir out, but to adjourn the senate to another time; and if he slighted her dreams, that she would be pleased to consult his fate by sacrifices and other kinds of divination. Nor was he himself without some suspicion and fears; for he never before discovered any womanish superstition in Calpurnia, whom he now saw in such great alarm. Upon the report which the priests made to him, that they had killed several sacrifices, and still found them inauspicious, he resolved to send Antony to dismiss the senate.

In this juncture, Decimus Brutus, surnamed Albinus, one whom Cæsar had such confidence in that he made him his second heir, who nevertheless was engaged in the conspiracy with the other Brutus and Cassius, fearing lest if Cæsar should put off the senate to another day the business might get wind, spoke scoffingly and in mockery of the diviners, and blamed Cæsar for giving the senate so fair an occasion of saying he had put a slight upon them, for that they were met upon his summons, and were ready to vote unanimously that he should be declared king of all the provinces out of Italy, and might wear a diadem in any other place but Italy, by sea or land. If any one should be sent to tell them they might break up for the present, and meet again when Calpurnia should chance to have better dreams, what would his enemies say? Or who would with any patience hear his friends, if they should presume to defend his government as not arbitrary and tyrannical? But if he was possessed so far as to think this day unfortunate, yet it were more decent to go himself to the senate, and to adjourn it in his own person.

Brutus, as he spoke these words, took Cæsar by the hand, and conducted him forth. He was not gone far from the door, when a servant of some other person's made towards him, but not being able to come up to him, on account of the crowd of those who pressed about him, he made his way into the house, and committed himself to Calpurnia, begging of her to secure him till Cæsar returned, because he had matters of great importance to communicate to him.

Artemidorus, a Cnidian, a teacher of Greek logic, and by that means so far acquainted with Brutus and his friends as to have got into the secret, brought Cæsar in a small written memorial the heads of what he had to depose. He had observed that Cæsar, as he received any papers, presently gave them to the servants who attended on him; and therefore came as near to him as he could, and said, "Read this, Cæsar, alone, and quickly, for it contains matter of great importance which nearly concerns you." Cæsar received it, and tried several times to read it, but was still hindered by the crowd of those who came to speak to him. However, he kept it in his hand by itself till he came into the senate. Some say it

was another who gave Cæsar this note, and that Artemidorus could not get to him, being all along kept off by the crowd.

All these things might happen by chance. But the place which was destined for the scene of this murder, in which the senate met that day, was the same in which Pompey's statue stood, and was one of the edifices which Pompey had raised and dedicated with his theatre to the use of the public, plainly showing that there was something of a supernatural influence which guided the action and ordered it to that particular place. Cassius, just before the act, is said to have looked towards Pompey's statue, and silently implored his assistance, though he had been inclined to the doctrines of Epicurus. But this occasion, and the instant danger, carried him away out of all his reasonings, and filled him for the time with a sort of inspiration. As for Antony, who was firm to Cæsar, and a strong man, Brutus Albinus kept him outside the house, and delayed him with a long conversation contrived on purpose.

When Cæsar entered, the senate stood up to show their respect to him, and of Brutus's confederates, some came about his chair and stood behind it, others met him, pretending to add their petitions to those of Tillius Cimber, in behalf of his brother who was in exile; and they followed him with their joint applications till he came to his seat. When he was sat down, he refused to comply with their requests, and upon their urging him further began to reproach them severely for their importunities, when Tillius, laying hold of his robe with both his hands, pulled it down from his neck, which was the signal for the assault.

Casca gave him the first cut in the neck, which was not mortal nor dangerous, as coming from one who at the beginning of such a bold action was probably very much disturbed; Cæsar immediately turned about, and laid his hand upon the dagger and kept hold of it. And both of them at the same time cried out, he that received the blow, in Latin, "Vile Casca, what does this mean?" and he that gave it, in Greek, to his brother, "Brother, help!"

Upon this first onset, those who were not privy to the design were astonished, and their horror and amazement at what they saw were so great that they durst not flee, nor assist Cæsar, nor so much as speak a word. But those who came prepared for the business enclosed him on every side, with their naked daggers in their hands. Which way soever he turned he met with blows, and saw their swords levelled at his face and eyes, and was encompassed, like a wild beast in the toils, on every side.

For it had been agreed they should each of them make a thrust at him, and flesh themselves with his blood; for which reason Brutus also gave him one stab in the groin. Some say that he fought and resisted all the rest, shifting his body to avoid the blows, and calling out for help, but that when he saw Brutus's sword drawn, he covered his face with his robe and submitted, letting himself fall, whether it were by chance, or that he was pushed in that direction by his murderers, at the foot of the pedestal on which Pompey's statue stood, and which was thus wetted with his blood. So that Pompey himself seemed to have presided, as it were, over the revenge done upon his adversary, who lay here at his feet, and breathed out his soul through his multitude of wounds, for they say he received three-and-twenty. And the conspirators themselves were many of them wounded by each other, whilst they all levelled their blows at the same person.

When Cæsar was despatched, Brutus stood forth to give a reason for what they had done, but the senate would not hear him, but flew out of doors in all haste, and filled the people with so much alarm and distraction, that some shut up their houses, others left their counters and shops. All ran one way or the other, some to the place to see the sad spectacle, others back again after they had seen it. Antony and Lepidus, Cæsar's most faithful friends, got off privately, and hid themselves in some friends' houses.

Brutus and his followers, being yet hot from the deed, marched in a body from the senatehouse to the capitol with their drawn swords, not like persons who thought of escaping, but with an air of confidence and assurance, and as they went along, called to the people to resume their liberty, and invited the company of any more distinguished people whom they met. And some of these joined the procession and went up along with them, as if they also had been of the conspiracy, and could claim a share in the honour of what had been done. As, for example, Caius Octavius and Lentulus Spinther, who suffered afterwards for their vanity, being taken off by Antony and the young Cæsar, and lost the honour they desired, as well as their lives, which it cost them, since no one believed they had any share in the action. For neither did those who punished them profess to revenge the fact, but the ill-will.

The day after, Brutus with the rest came down from the capitol and made a speech to the people, who listened without expressing either any pleasure or resentment, but showed by their silence that they pitied Cæsar and respected Brutus. The senate passed acts of oblivion for what was past, and took measures to reconcile all parties. They ordered that Cæsar should be worshipped as a divinity, and nothing, even of the slightest consequence, should be revoked which he had enacted during his government. At the same time they gave Brutus and his followers the command of provinces, and other considerable posts. So that all the people now thought things were well settled, and brought to the happiest adjustment.

But when Cæsar's will was opened, and it was found that he had left a considerable legacy to each one of the Roman citizens, and when his body was seen carried through the market-place all mangled with wounds, the multitude could no longer contain themselves within the bounds of tranquillity and order, but heaped together a pile of benches, bars, and tables, which they placed the corpse on, and setting fire to it, burnt it on them. Then they took brands from the pile and ran, some to fire the houses of the conspirators, others up and down the city to find out the men and tear them to pieces, but met, however, with none of them, they having taken effectual care to secure themselves.

One Cinna, a friend of Cæsar's, chanced the night before to have an odd dream. He fancied that Cæsar invited him to supper, and that upon his refusal to go with him, Cæsar took him by the hand and forced him, though he hung back. Upon hearing the report that Cæsar's body was burning in the market-place, he got up and went thither, out of respect to his memory, though his dream gave him some ill apprehensions, and though he was suffering from a fever. One of the crowd who saw him there asked another who that was, and having learned his name, told it to his next neighbour. It presently passed for a certainty that he was one of Cæsar's murderers, as, indeed, there was another Cinna, a conspirator, and they, taking this to be the man, immediately seized him and tore him limb from limb upon the spot.

Brutus and Cassius, frightened at this, within a few days retired out of the city. What they afterwards did and suffered, and how they died, is written in the Life of Brutus. Cæsar died in his fifty-sixth year, not having survived Pompey above four years. That empire and power which he had pursued through the whole course of his life with so much hazard, he did at last with much difficulty compass, but reaped no other fruits from it than the empty name and invidious glory. But the great genius which attended him through his lifetime even after his death remained as the avenger of his murder, pursuing through every sea and land all those who were concerned in it, and suffering none to escape, but reaching all who in any sort or kind were either actually engaged in the fact, or by their counsels any way promoted it.

The most remarkable of mere human coincidences was that which befell Cassius, who, when he was defeated at Philippi, killed himself with the same dagger which he had made use of against Cæsar. The most signal preternatural appearances were the great comet, which shone very bright for seven nights after Cæsar's death, and then disappeared, and the dimness of the sun, whose orb continued pale and dull for the whole of that year, never showing its ordinary radiance at its rising, and giving but a weak and feeble heat. The air consequently was damp and gross for want of stronger rays to open and rarify it. The fruits, for that reason, never properly ripened, and began to wither and fall off for want of heat before they were fully formed. But above all, the phantom which appeared to Brutus showed the murder was not pleasing to the gods. The story of it is this.

Brutus, having to pass his army from Abydos to the continent on the other side, laid himself down one night, as he used to do, in his tent, and was not asleep, but thinking of his affairs, and what events he might expect. For he is related to have been the least inclined to sleep of all men who have commanded armies, and to have had the greatest natural capacity for continuing awake, and employing himself without need of rest. He thought he heard a noise at the door of his tent, and looking that way, by the light of his lamp, which was almost out, saw a terrible figure, like that of a man, but of unusual stature and severe countenance. He was somewhat frightened at first, but seeing it neither did nor spoke anything to him, only stood silently by his bedside, he asked who it was. The spectre answered him, "Thy evil genius, Brutus, and thou shalt see me at Philippi." Brutus answered courageously, "Well, I shall see you," and immediately the appearance vanished.

When the time was come, he drew up his army near Philippi against Antony and Cæsar, and in the first battle won the day, routed the enemy, and plundered Cæsar's camp. The night before the second battle, the same phantom appeared to him again, but spoke not a word. He presently understood his destiny was at hand, and exposed himself to all the danger of the battle. Yet he did not die in the fight, but seeing his men defeated, got up to the top of a rock, and there presenting his sword to his naked breast, and assisted, as they say, by a friend, who helped him to give the thrust, met his death.

PHOCION

402?–317 B.C.

DEMADES, the orator, when in the height of the power which he obtained at Athens, by advising the state in the interest of Antipater and the Macedonians, being necessitated to write and speak many things below the dignity, and contrary to the character, of the city, was wont to excuse himself by saying he steered only the shipwrecks of the commonwealth. This hardy saying of his might have some appearance of truth, if applied to Phocion's government. For Demades, indeed, was himself the mere wreck of his country, living and ruling so dissolutely, that Antipater took occasion to say of him, when he was now grown old, that he was like a sacrificed beast, all consumed except the tongue and the belly. But Phocion's was a real virtue, only overmatched in the unequal contest with an adverse time, and rendered, by the ill fortunes of Greece, inglorious and obscure.

We must not, indeed, allow ourselves to concur with Sophocles in so far diminishing the force of virtue as to say that—

When fortune fails, the sense we had before
Deserts us also, and is ours no more.

Yet thus much, indeed, must be allowed to

happen in the conflicts between good men and ill fortune, that instead of due returns of honour and gratitude, obloquy and unjust surmises may often prevail, to weaken, in a considerable degree, the credit of their virtue.

It is commonly said that public bodies are most insulting and contumelious to a good man, when they are puffed up with prosperity and success. But the contrary often happens; afflictions and public calamities naturally embittering and souring the minds and tempers of men, and disposing them to such peevishness and irritability that hardly any word or sentiment of common vigour can be addressed to them, but they will be apt to take offence. He that remonstrates with them on their errors is presumed to be insulting over their misfortunes, and any free-spoken expostulation is construed into contempt. Honey itself is searching in sore and ulcerated parts; and the wisest and most judicious counsels prove provoking to distempered minds, unless offered with those soothing and compliant approaches which made the poet, for instance, characterise agreeable things in general by a word expressive of a grateful and easy touch, exciting nothing of offence or resistance. Inflamed eyes require a retreat into dusky places, amongst colours of the deepest shades, and are unable to endure the brilliancy of light.

So fares it in the body politic, in times of distress and humiliation; a certain sensitiveness and soreness of humour prevail, with a weak incapacity of enduring any free and open advice, even when the necessity of affairs most requires such plain dealing, and when the consequences of any single error may be beyond retrieving. At such times the conduct of public affairs is on all hands most hazardous. Those who humour the people are swallowed up in the common ruin; those who endeavour to lead them aright perish the first in their attempt.

Astronomers tell us, the sun's motion is neither exactly parallel with that of the heavens in general, nor yet directly and diametrically opposite, but describing an oblique line, with insensible declination he steers his course in such a gentle, easy curve, as to dispense his light and influence, in his annual revolution, at several seasons in just proportions to the whole creation. So it happens in political affairs; if the motions of rulers be constantly opposite and cross to the tempers and inclinations of the people, they will be resented as arbitrary and harsh; as, on the other side, too much deference, or encouragement, as too often it has been, to popular faults and errors, is full of danger and ruinous consequences.

But where concession is the response to willing obedience, and a statesman gratifies his people, that he may the more imperatively recall them to a sense of the common interest, then, indeed, human beings, who are ready enough to serve well and submit to much, if they are not always ordered about and roughly handled, like slaves, may be said to be guided and governed upon the method that leads to safety. Though it must be confessed it is a nice point, and extremely difficult, so to temper this lenity as to preserve the authority of the government. But if such a blessed mixture and temperament may be obtained, it seems to be of all concords and harmonies the most concordant and most harmonious. For thus we are taught even God governs the world, not by irresistible force, but persuasive argument and reason, controlling it into compliance with his eternal purposes.

Cato the younger is a similar instance. His manners were little agreeable or acceptable to the people, and he received very slender marks of their favour; witness his repulse when he sued for the counsulship, which he lost, as Cicero says, for acting rather like a citizen in Plato's commonwealth, than among the dregs of Romulus's posterity, the same thing happening to him, in my opinion, as we observe in fruits ripe before their season, which we rather take pleasure in looking at and admiring than actually use; so much was his old-fashioned virtue out of the present mode, among the depraved customs which time and luxury had introduced, that it appeared, indeed, remarkable and wonderful, but was too great and too good to suit the present exigencies, being so out of all proportion to the times. Yet his circumstances were not altogether like Phocion's, who came to the helm when the ship of the state was just upon sinking. Cato's time was, indeed, stormy and tempestuous; yet so, as he was able to assist in managing the sails, and lend his helping hand to those who commanded at the helm, which he was not allowed to do, others were to blame for the result; yet his courage and virtue made it in spite of all a hard task for fortune to ruin the commonwealth, and it was only with long time and effort and by slow degrees, when he himself had all but succeeded in averting it, that the catastrophe was at last effected.

Phocion and he may be well compared together, not for any mere general resemblances, as though we should say both were good men and great statesmen. For, assuredly, there is difference enough among virtues of the same denomination, as between the bravery of Alcibiades and that of Epaminondas, the prudence of Themistocles and that of Aristides, the justice of Numa and that of Agesilaus. But these men's virtue, even looking to the most minute points of difference, bear the same colour, stamp, and character impressed upon them, so as not to be distinguishable. The mixture is still made in the same exact proportions whether we look at the combination to be found in them, both of lenity on the one hand, with austerity on the other; their boldness upon some occasions, and caution on others; their extreme solicitude for the public, and perfect neglect of themselves; their fixed and immovable bent to all virtuous and honest actions, accompanied with an extreme tenderness and scrupulosity as to doing anything which might appear mean or unworthy; so that we should need a very nice and subtle logic of discrimination to detect and establish the distinctions between them.

As to Cato's extraction, it is confessed by all to have been illustrious, as will be said hereafter, nor was Phocion's, I feel assured, obscure or ignoble. For had he been the son of a turner, as Idomeneus reports, it had certainly not been forgotten to his disparagement by Glaucippus, the son of Hyperides, when heaping up a thousand spiteful things to say against him. Nor, indeed, had it been possible for him, in such circumstances, to have had such a liberal breeding and education in his youth, as to be first Plato's and afterwards Xenocrates's scholar in the Academy, and to have devoted himself from the first to the pursuit of the noblest studies and practices. His countenance was so composed that scarcely was he ever seen by any Athenian either laughing or in tears. He was rarely known, so Duris has recorded, to appear in the public baths, or was observed with his hand exposed outside his cloak,–when he wore one. Abroad, and in the camp, he was so hardy in going always thin clad and barefoot, except in a time of excessive and intolerable cold, that the soldiers used to say in merriment, that it was like to be a hard winter when Phocion wore his coat.

Although he was most gentle and humane in his disposition, his aspect was stern and forbidding, so that he was seldom accosted alone by any who were not intimate with him. When Chares once made some remark on his frowning looks, and the Athenians laughed at the jest, "My sullenness," said Phocion, "never yet made any of you sad, but these men's jollities have given you sorrow enough." In like manner Phocion's language, also, was full of instruction, abounding in happy maxims and wise thoughts, but admitted no embellishment to its austere and commanding brevity. Zeno said a philosopher should never speak till his words had been steeped in meaning; and such, it may be said, were Phocion's, crowding the greatest amount of significance into the smallest allowance of space.

And to this, probably, Polyeuctus, the Sphettian, referred, when he said that Demosthenes was, indeed, the best orator of his time, but Phocion the most powerful speaker. His oratory, like small coin of great value, was to be estimated, not by its bulk, but its intrinsic worth. He was once observed, it is said, when the theatre was filling with the audience, to walk musing alone behind the scenes, which one of his friends taking notice of said, "Phocion, you seem to be thoughtful." "Yes," replied he, "I am considering how I may shorten what I am going to say to the Athenians." Even Demosthenes himself, who used to despise the rest of the haranguers, when Phocion stood up, was wont to say quietly to those about him, "Here is the pruning-knife of my periods." This, however, might refer, perhaps, not so much to his eloquence as to the influence of his character, since not only a word, but even a nod from a person who is esteemed, is of more force than a thousand arguments or studied sentences from others.

In his youth he followed Chabrias, the general, from whom he gained many lessons in military knowledge, and in return did something to correct his unequal and capricious humour. For whereas at other times Chabrias was heavy and phlegmatic, in the heat of battle he used to be so fired and transported that he threw himself headlong into danger beyond the forwardest, which indeed, in the end, cost him his life in the island of Chios, he having pressed his own ship foremost to force a landing. But Phocion, being a man of temper as well as courage, had the dexterity at some times to rouse the general, when in his procrastinating mood, to action, and at others to moderate and cool the impetuousness of his unseasonable fury. Upon which account Chabrias, who was a good-natured, kindly-tempered man, loved him much, and procured him commands and opportunities for action, giving himself means to make himself known in Greece, and using his assistance in all his affairs of moment. Particularly the sea-fight of Naxos added not a little to Phocion's reputation, when he had the left squadron committed to him by Chabrias, as in this quarter the battle was sharply contested, and was decided by a speedy victory. And this being the first prosperous sea-battle the city had engaged in with its own force since its captivity, Chabrias won great popularity by it, and Phocion, also, got the reputation of a good commander. The victory was gained at the time of the Great Mysteries, and Chabrias used to keep the commemoration of it by distributing wine among the Athenians, yearly, on the sixteenth day of Boëdromion.

After this, Chabrias sent Phocion to demand their quota of the charges of the war from the islanders, and offered him a guard of twenty ships. Phocion told him, if he intended him to go against them as enemies, that force was insignificant; if as to friends and allies, one vessel was sufficient. So he took his own single galley, and having visited the cities, and treated with the magistrates in an equitable and open manner, he brought back a number of ships, sent by the confederates to Athens, to convey the supplies. Neither did his friendship and attention close with Chabrias's life, but after his decease he carefully maintained it to all that were related to him, and chiefly to his son, Ctesippus, whom he laboured to bring to some good, and although he was a stupid and intractable young fellow, always endeavoured, so far as in him lay, to correct and cover his faults and follies. Once, however, when the youngster was very impertinent and troublesome to him in the camp, interrupting him with idle questions, and putting forward his opinions and suggestions of how the war should be conducted, he could not forbear exclaiming, "O Chabrias, Chabrias, how grateful I show myself for your friendship, in submitting to endure your son!"

Upon looking into public matters, and the way in which they were now conducted, he observed that the administration of affairs was cut and parcelled out, like so much land by allotment, between the military men and the public speakers, so that neither these nor those should interfere with the claims of the others. As the one were to address the assemblies, to draw up votes and prepare motions, men, for example, like Eubulus, Aristophon, Demosthenes, Lycurgus, and Hyperides, and were to push their interests here; so, in the meantime, Diopithes, Menestheus, Leosthenes, and Chares were to make their profit by war and in military commands.

Phocion, on the other hand, was desirous to restore and carry out the old system, more complete in itself, and more harmonious and uniform, which prevailed in the times of Pericles, Aristides, and Solon; when statesmen showed themselves, to use Archilochus's words—

Mars' and the Muses' friends alike designed,
To arts and arms indifferently inclined.

and the presiding goddess of his country was, he did not fail to see, the patroness and protectress of both civil and military wisdom. With these views, while his advice at home was always for peace and quietness, he nevertheless held the office of general more frequently than any of the statesmen, not only of his own times, but of those preceding, never, indeed, promoting or encouraging military expeditions, yet never, on the other hand, shunning or declining, when he was called upon by the public voice. Thus much is well known, that he was no less than forty-five several times chosen general, he being never on any one of those occasions present at the election, but having the command, in his absence, by common suffrage, conferred on him, and he sent for on purpose to undertake it. Insomuch that it amazed those who did not well consider to see the people always prefer Phocion, who was so far from humouring them or courting their favour, that he always thwarted and opposed them.

But so it was, as great men and princes are said to call in their flatterers when dinner has been served, so the Athenians, upon slight occasions, entertained and diverted themselves with their spruce speakers and trim orators, but when it came to action, they were sober and considerate enough to single out the austerest and wisest for public employment, however much he might be opposed to their wishes and sentiments. This, indeed, he made no scruple to admit, when the oracle from Delphi was read, which informed them that the Athenians were all of one mind, a single dissentient only excepted, frankly coming forward and declaring that they need look no further; he was the man; there was no one but he who was dissatisfied with everything they did. And when once he gave his opinion to the people, and was met with the general approbation and applause of the assembly, turning to some of his friends, he asked them, "Have I inadvertently said something foolish?"

Upon occasion of a public festivity, being solicited for his contribution by the example of others, and the people pressing him much, he bade them apply themselves to the wealthy; for his part he should blush to make a present here, rather than a repayment *there,* turning and pointing to Callicles, the money-lender. Being still clamoured upon and importuned, he told them this tale. A certain cowardly fellow setting out for the wars, hearing the ravens croak in his passage, threw down his arms, resolving to wait. Presently he took them and ventured out again, but hearing the same music, once more made a stop. "For," said he, "you may croak till you are tired, but you shall make no dinner upon me."

The Athenians urging him at an unseasonable time to lead them out against the enemy, he peremptorily refused, and being upbraided by them with cowardice and pusillanimity, he told them, "Just now, do what you will, I shall not be brave; and do what I will, you will not be cowards. Nevertheless, we know well enough what we are." And when again, in a time of great danger, the people were very harsh upon him, demanding a strict account how the public money had been employed, and the like, he bade them, "First, good friends, make sure you are safe." After a war, during which they had been very tractable and timorous, when, upon peace being made, they began again to be confident and overbearing, and to cry out upon Phocion, as having lost them the honour of victory, to all their clamour he made only this answer, "My friends, you are fortunate in having a leader who knows you; otherwise, you had long since been undone."

Having a controversy with the Bœotians about boundaries, which he counselled them to decide by negotiation, they inclined to blows. "You had better," said he, "carry on the contest with the weapons in which you excel (your tongues), and not by war, in which you are inferior." Once when he was addressing them, and they would not hear him or let him go on, said he, "You may compel me to act against my wishes, but you shall never force me to speak against my judgment." Among the many public speakers who opposed him, Demosthenes, for example, once told him, "The Athenians, Phocion, will kill you some day when they once are in a rage." "And you," said he, "if they once are in their senses."

Polyeuctus, the Sphettian, once on a hot day was urging war with Philip, and being a corpulent man, and out of breath and in a great heat with speaking, took numerous draughts of water as he went on. "Here, indeed," said Phocion, "is a fit man to lead us into a war! What think you he will do when he is carrying his corselet and his shield to meet the enemy, if even here, delivering a prepared speech to you has almost killed him with exhaustion?" When Lycurgus in the assembly made many reflections on his past conduct, upbraiding him above all for having advised them to deliver up the ten citizens whom Alexander had demanded, he replied that he had been the author of much safe and wholesome counsel, which had not been followed.

There was a man called Archibiades, nicknamed the Lacedæmonian, who used to go about with a huge, over-grown beard, wearing an old threadbare cloak, and affecting a very stern countenance. Phocion once, when attacked in council by the rest, appealed to this man for his support and testimony. And when he got up and began to speak on the popular side, putting his hand to his beard, "O Archibiades," said he, "it is time you should shave." Aristogiton, a common accuser, was a terrible man of war within the assembly, always inflaming the people to battle, but when the muster-roll came to be produced, he appeared limping on a crutch, with a bandage on his leg; Phocion descried him afar off, coming in, and cried out to the clerk, "Put down Aristogiton, too, as lame and worthless."

So that it is a little wonderful, how a man so severe and harsh upon all occasions should, notwithstanding, obtain the name of the Good. Yet, though difficult, it is not, I suppose, impossible for men's tempers, any more than for wines, to be at the same time harsh and agreeable to the taste; just as on the other hand many that are sweet at the first taste are found, on further use, extremely disagreeable and unwholesome. Hyperides, we are told, once said to the people, "Do not ask yourselves, men of Athens, whether or not I am bitter, but whether or not I am paid for being so," as though a covetous purpose were the only thing that should make a harsh temper insupportable, and as if men might not even more justly render themselves obnoxious to popular dislike and censure, by using their power and influence in the indulgence of their own private passions of pride and jealousy, anger and animosity.

Phocion never allowed himself from any feeling of personal hostility to do hurt to any fellow-citizen, nor, indeed, reputed any man his enemy, except so far as he could not but contend sharply with such as opposed the measures he urged for the public good; in which argument he was, indeed, a rude, obstinate, and uncompromising adversary. For his general conversation, it was easy, courteous, and obliging to all, to that point that he would befriend his very opponents in their distress, and espouse the cause of those who differed most from him, when they needed his patronage. His friends reproaching him for pleading in behalf of a man of indifferent character, he told them the innocent had no need of an advocate. Aristogiton, the sycophant, whom we mentioned before, having, after sentence passed upon him, sent earnestly to Phocion to speak with him in the prison, his friends dissuaded him from going; "Nay, by your favour," said he, "where should I rather choose to pay Aristogiton a visit?"

As for the allies of the Athenians, and the islanders, whenever any admiral besides Phocion was sent, they treated him as an enemy suspect, barricaded their gates, blocked up their havens, brought in from the country their cattle, slaves, wives, and children, and put them in garrison; but upon Phocion's arrival, they went out to welcome him in their private boats and barges, with streamers and garlands, and received him at landing with every demonstration of joy and pleasure.

When King Philip was effecting his entry into Eubœa, and was bringing over troops from Macedonia, and making himself master of the cities, by means of the tyrants who ruled in them, Plutarch of Eretria sent to request aid of the Athenians for the relief of the island, which was in imminent danger of falling wholly into the hands of the Macedonians. Phocion was sent thither with a handful of men in comparison, in expectation that the Eubœans themselves would flock in and join him. But when he came, he found all things in confusion, the country all betrayed, the whole ground, as it were, undermined under his feet, by the secret pensioners of King Philip, so that he was in the greatest risk imaginable. To secure himself as far as he could, he seized a small rising ground, which was divided from the level plains about Tamynæ by a deep watercourse, and here he enclosed and

fortified the choicest of his army. As for the idle talkers and disorderly bad citizens who ran off from his camp and made their way back, he bade his officers not to regard them, since here they would have been not only useless and ungovernable themselves, but an actual hindrance to the rest: and further, being conscious to themselves of the neglect of their duty, they would be less ready to misrepresent the action, or raise a cry against them at their return home.

When the enemy drew nigh, he bade his men stand to their arms, until he had finished the sacrifice, in which he spent a considerable time, either by some difficulty of the thing itself, or on purpose to invite the enemy nearer. Plutarch, interpreting this tardiness as a failure in his courage, fell on alone with the mercenaries, which the cavalry perceiving, could not be contained, but issuing also out of the camp, confusedly and in disorder, spurred up to the enemy. The first who came up were defeated, the rest were put to the rout. Plutarch himself took to flight, and a body of the enemy advanced in the hope of carrying the camp, supposing themselves to have secured the victory.

But by this time, the sacrifice being over, the Athenians within the camp came forward, and falling upon them put them to flight, and killed the greater number as they fled among the intrenchments, while Phocion, ordering his infantry to keep on the watch and rally those who came in from the previous flight, himself, with a body of his best men, engaged the enemy in a sharp and bloody fight, in which all of them behaved with signal courage and gallantry. Thallus, the son of Cineas, and Glaucus of Polymedes, who fought near the general, gained the honours of the day. Cleophanes, also, did good service in the battle. Recovering the cavalry from its defeat, and with his shouts and encouragement bringing them up to succour the general, who was in danger, he confirmed the victory obtained by the infantry.

Phocion now expelled Plutarch from Eretria, and possessed himself of the very important fort of Zaretra, situated where the island is pinched in, as it were, by the seas on each side, and its breadth most reduced to a narrow girth. He released all the Greeks whom he took, out of fear of the public speakers at Athens, thinking they might very likely persuade the people in their anger into committing some act of cruelty.

This affair thus despatched and settled, Phocion set sail homewards, and the allies had soon as good reason to regret the loss of his just and humane dealing as the Athenians that of his experience and courage. Molossus, the commander who took his place, had no better success than to fall alive into the enemy's hands.

Philip, full of great thoughts and designs, now advanced with all his forces into the Hellespont, to seize the Chersonesus and Perinthus, and after them Byzantium. The Athenians raised a force to relieve them, but the popular leaders made it their business to prefer Chares to be general, who, sailing thither, effected nothing worthy of the means placed in his hands. The cities were afraid, and would not receive his ships into their harbours, so that he did nothing but wander about, raising money from their friends, and despised by their enemies. When the people, chafed by the orators, were extremely indignant, and repented having ever sent any help to the Byzantines, Phocion rose and told them they ought not to be angry with the allies for distrusting, but with their generals for being distrusted. "They make you suspected," he said, "even by those who cannot possibly subsist without your succour." The assembly being moved with this speech of his, changed their minds on the sudden, and commanded him immediately to raise another force, and go himself to assist their confederates in the Hellespont: an appointment which, in effect, contributed more than anything to the relief of Byzantium.

For Phocion's name was already honourably known; and an old acquaintance of his, who had been his fellow-student in the Academy, Leon, a man of high renown for virtue among the Byzantines, having vouched for Phocion to the city, they opened their gates to receive him, not permitting him, though he desired it, to encamp without the walls, but entertained him and all the Athenians with perfect reliance, while they, to requite their confidence, behaved among their new hosts soberly and inoffensively, and exerted themselves on all occasions with the greatest zeal and resolution for their defence. Thus King Philip was driven out of the Hellespont, and was despised to boot, whom, till now, it had been thought impossible to match, or even to oppose. Phocion also took some of his ships, and recaptured some of the places he had garrisoned, making besides several inroads into the country, which he plundered and overran, until he received a wound from some of the enemy who came

to the defence, and, thereupon, sailed away home.

The Megarians at this time privately praying aid of the Athenians, Phocion, fearing lest the Bœotians should hear of it, and anticipate them, called an assembly at sunrise, and brought forward the petition of the Megarians, and immediately after the vote had been put, and carried in their favour, he sounded the trumpet, and led the Athenians straight from the assembly, to arm and put themselves in posture. The Megarians received them joyfully, and he proceeded to fortify Nisæa, and built two new long walls from the city to the arsenal, and so joined it to the sea, so that having now little reason to regard the enemies on the land side, it placed its dependence entirely on the Athenians.

When final hostilities with Philip were now certain, and in Phocion's absence other generals had been nominated, he, on his arrival from the islands, dealt earnestly with the Athenians, that since Philip showed peaceable inclinations towards them, and greatly apprehended the danger, they would consent to a treaty. Being contradicted in this by one of the ordinary frequenters of the courts of justice, a common accuser, who asked him if he durst presume to persuade the Athenians to peace, now their arms were in their hands, "Yes," said he, "though I know that if there be war, I shall be in office over you, and if peace, you over me." But when he could not prevail, and Demosthenes's opinion carried it, advising them to make war as far off from home as possible, and fight the battle out of Attica, "Good friends," said Phocion, "let us not ask where we shall fight, but how we may conquer in the war. That will be the way to keep it at a distance. If we are beaten, it will be quickly at our doors."

After the defeat, when the clamourers and incendiaries in the town would have brought up Charidemus to the hustings, to be nominated to the command, the best of the citizens were in a panic, and supporting themselves with the aid of the council of the Areopagus, with entreaties and tears, hardly prevailed upon the people to have Phocion entrusted with the care of the city. He was of opinion, in general, that the fair terms to be expected from Philip should be accepted, yet after Demades had made a motion that the city should receive the common conditions of peace in concurrence with the rest of the states of Greece, he opposed it, till it were known what the particulars were which Philip demanded. He was overborne in this advice, under the pressure of the time, but almost immediately after the Athenians repented it, when they understood that by these articles they were obliged to furnish Philip both with horse and shipping.

"It was the fear of this," said Phocion, "that occasioned my opposition. But since the thing is done, let us make the best of it, and not be discouraged. Our forefathers were sometimes in command, and sometimes under it; and by doing their duty, whether as rulers or as subjects, saved their own country and the rest of Greece."

Upon the news of Philip's death, he opposed himself to any public demonstrations of joy and jubilee, saying it would be ignoble to show malice upon such an occasion, and that the army that had fought them at Chæronea was only diminished by a single man.

When Demosthenes made his invectives against Alexander, now on his way to attack Thebes, he repeated those verses of Homer:—

Unwise one, wherefore to a second stroke
His anger be foolhardy to provoke?

and asked, "Why stimulate his already eager passion for glory? Why take pains to expose the city to the terrible conflagration now so near? We, who accepted office to save our fellow-citizens, will not, however they desire it, be consenting to their destruction."

After Thebes was lost, and Alexander had demanded Demosthenes, Lycurgus, Hyperides, and Charidemus to be delivered up, the whole assembly turning their eyes to him, and calling on him by name to deliver his opinion, at last he rose up, and showing them one of his most intimate friends, whom he loved and confided in above all others, told them, "You have brought things amongst you to that pass, that for my part, should he demand this my friend Nicocles, I would not refuse to give him up. For as for myself, to have it in my power to sacrifice my own life and fortune for the common safety, I should think the greatest of good fortune. Truly," he added, "it pierces my heart to see those who are fled hither for succour from the desolation of Thebes. Yet it is enough for Greece to have Thebes to deplore. It will be more for the interest of all that we should deprecate the conqueror's anger, and intercede for both, than run the hazard of another battle."

When this was decreed by the people, Alexander is said to have rejected their first address when it was presented, throwing it from him scornfully, and turning his back upon the deputation, who left him in affright. But the second, which was presented by Phocion, he received, understanding from the older Macedonians how much Philip had admired and esteemed him. And he not only gave him audience and listened to his memorial and petition, but also permitted him to advise him, which he did to this effect, that if his designs were for quietness, he should make peace at once; if glory were his aim, he should make war, not upon Greece, but on the barbarians.

With various counsels and suggestions, happily designed to meet the genius and feelings of Alexander, he so won upon him, and softened his temper, that he bade the Athenians not forget their position, as if anything went wrong with him, the supremacy belonged to them. And to Phocion himself, whom he adopted as his friend and guest, he showed a respect, and admitted him to distinctions which few of those who were continually near his person ever received. Duris, at any rate, tells us, that when he became great, and had conquered Darius, in the heading of all his letters he left off the word *Greeting,* except in those he wrote to Phocion. To him, and to Antipater alone, he condescended to use it. This also is stated by Chares.

As for his munificence to him, it is well known he sent him a present at one time of one hundred talents; and this being brought to Athens, Phocion asked of the bearers how it came to pass that among all the Athenians he alone should be the object of this bounty. Being told that Alexander esteemed him alone a person of honour and worth, "Let him, then," said he, "permit me to continue so and be still so reputed." Following him to his house, and observing his simple and plain way of living, his wife employed in kneading bread with her own hands, himself drawing water to wash his feet, they pressed him to accept it, with some indignation, being ashamed, as they said, that Alexander's friend should live so poorly and pitifully. So Phocion, pointing out to them a poor old fellow, in a dirty worn-out coat, passing by, asked them if they thought him in worse condition than this man. They bade him not mention such a comparison. "Yet," said Phocion, "he, with less to live upon than I, finds it sufficient, and, in brief," he continued, "if I do not use this money, what good is there in my having it; and if I do use it, I shall procure an ill name, both for myself and for Alexander, among my countrymen."

So the treasure went back again from Athens, to prove to Greece, by a signal example, that he who could afford to give so magnificent a present, was yet not so rich as he who could afford to refuse it. And when Alexander was displeased, and wrote back to him to say that he could not esteem those his friends who would not be obliged by him, not even would this induce Phocion to accept the money, but he begged leave to intercede with him in behalf of Echecratides, the sophist, and Athenodorus, the Imbrian, as also for Demaratus and Sparton, two Rhodians, who had been arrested upon some charges, and were in custody at Sardis. This was instantly granted by Alexander, and they were set at liberty.

Afterwards, when sending Craterus into Macedonia, he commanded him to make him an offer of four cities in Asia, Cius, Gergithus, Mylasa, and Elæa, any one of which, at his choice, should be delivered to him; insisting yet more positively with him, and declaring he should resent it, should he continue obstinate in his refusal. But Phocion was not to be prevailed with at all, and, shortly after, Alexander died.

Phocion's house is shown to this day in Melita, ornamented with small plates of copper, but otherwise plain and homely. Concerning his wives, of the first of them there is little said, except that she was sister of Cephisodotus, the statuary. The other was a matron of no less reputation for her virtues and simple living among the Athenians than Phocion was for his probity.

It happened once when the people were entertained with a new tragedy, that the actor, just as he was to enter the stage to perform the part of a queen, demanded to have a number of attendants sumptuously dressed, to follow in his train, and on their not being provided, was sullen and refused to act, keeping the audience waiting, till at last Melanthius, who had to furnish the chorus, pushed him on the stage, crying out, "What, don't you know that Phocion's wife is never attended by more than a single waiting-woman, but you must needs be grand, and fill our women's heads with vanity?" This speech of his, spoken loud enough to be heard, was received with great applause, and clapped all round the theatre. She herself, when once entertaining a visitor out of Ionia, who showed her all her rich ornaments, made of gold and set with jewels, her wreaths, necklaces, and the like, "For my part," said she, "all my ornament is my husband, Phocion, now for the twentieth year in office as general at Athens."

He had a son named Phocus, who wished to take part in the games at the great feast of Minerva. He permitted him so to do, in the contest of leaping, not with any view to the victory, but in the hope that the training and discipline for it would make him a better man, the youth being in a general way a lover of drinking, and ill-regulated in his habits. On his having succeeded in the sports, many were eager for the honour of his company at banquets in celebration of the victory. Phocion declined all these invitations but one, and when he came to this entertainment and saw the costly preparations, even the water brought to wash the guests' feet being mingled with wine and spices, he reprimanded his son, asking him why he would so far permit his friend to sully the honour of his victory. And in the hope of wholly weaning the young man from such habits and company, he sent him to Lacedæmon, and placed him among the youths then under the course of the Spartan discipline.

This the Athenians took offence at, as though he slighted and contemned the education at home; and Demades twitted him with it publicly. "Suppose, Phocion, you and I advise the Athenians to adopt the Spartan constitution. If you like, I am ready to introduce a bill to that effect, and to speak in its favour." "Indeed," said Phocion, "you, with that strong scent of perfumes about you, and with that mantle on your shoulders, are just the very man to speak in honour of Lycurgus, and recommend the Spartan table."

When Alexander wrote to demand a supply of galleys, and the public speakers objected to sending them, Phocion, on the council requesting his opinion, told them freely, "Sirs, I would either have you victorious yourselves, or friends of those who are so." He took up Pytheas, who about this time first began to address the assembly, and already showed himself a confident, talking fellow, by saying that a young slave whom the people had but bought yesterday ought to have the manners to hold his tongue.

And when Harpalus, who had fled from Alexander out of Asia, carrying off a large sum of money, came to Attica, and there was a perfect race among the ordinary public men of the assembly who should be the first to take his pay, he distributed amongst these some trifling sums by way of a bait and provocative, but to Phocion he made an offer of no less than seven hundred talents and all manner of other advantages he pleased to demand; with the compliment that he would entirely commit himself and all his affairs to his disposal. Phocion answered sharply, Harpalus should repent of it, if he did not quickly leave off corrupting and debauching the city, which for the time silenced him, and checked his proceedings.

But afterwards, when the Athenians were deliberating in council about him, he found those that had received money from him to be his greatest enemies, urging and aggravating matters against him, to prevent themselves being discovered, whereas Phocion, who had never touched his pay, now, so far as the public interest would admit of it, showed some regard to his particular security. This encouraged him once more to try his inclinations, and upon further survey finding that he himself was a fortress, inaccessible on every quarter to the approaches of corruption, he professed a particular friendship to Phocion's son-in-law, Charicles. And admitting him into his confidence in all his affairs, and continually requesting his assistance, he brought him under some suspicion.

Upon the occasion, for example, of the death of Pythonice, who was Harpalus's mistress, for whom he had a great fondness, and had a child by her, he resolved to build her a sumptuous monument, and committed the care of it to his friend Charicles. This commission, disreputable enough in itself, was yet further disparaged by the figure the piece of workmanship made after it was finished. It is yet to be seen in the Hermeum, as you go from Athens to Eleusis, with nothing in its appearance answerable to the sum of thirty talents, with which Charicles is said to have charged Harpalus for its erection. After Harpalus's own decease, his daughter was educated by Phocion and Charicles with great care.

But when Charicles was called to account for his dealings with Harpalus, and entreated his father-in-law's protection, begging that he would appear for him in the court, Phocion refused, telling him, "I did not choose you for my son-in-law for any but honourable purposes."

Asclepiades, the son of Hipparchus, brought the first tidings of Alexander's death to Athens, which Demades told them was not to be credited; for were it true, the whole world would ere this have stunk with the dead body. But Phocion, seeing the people eager for an instant revolution, did his best to quiet and repress them. And when numbers of them rushed up to the hustings to speak, and cried out that the news was true, and Alexander was dead, "If he is dead to-day," said he, "he will be so to-morrow and the day after to-morrow equally. So that there is no need to take counsel hastily or before it is safe."

When Leosthenes now had embarked the city in the Lamian war, greatly against Phocion's wishes, to raise a laugh against Phocion, he asked him scoffingly, what the state had been benefited by his having now so many years been general. "It is not a little," said Phocion, "that the citizens have been buried in their own sepulchres." And when Leosthenes continued to speak boldly and boastfully in the assembly, "Young man," he said, "your speeches are like cypress-trees, stately and tall, and no fruit to come of them." When he was then attacked by Hyperides, who asked him when the time would come that he would advise the Athenians to make war, "As soon," said he, "as I find the young men keep their ranks, the rich men contribute their money, and the orators leave off robbing the treasury." Afterwards, when many admired the forces raised, and the preparations for war that were made by Leosthenes, they asked Phocion how he approved of the new levies. "Very well," said he, "for the short course; but what I fear is the long race. Since, however late the war may last, the city has neither money, ships, nor soldiers, but these."

The event justified his prognostics. At first all things appeared fair and promising. Leosthenes gained great reputation by worsting the Bœotians in battle, and driving Antipater within the walls of Lamia, and the citizens were so transported with the first successes, that they kept solemn festivities for them, and offered public sacrifices to the gods. So that some, thinking Phocion must now be convinced of his error, asked him whether he would not willingly have been author of these successful actions. "Yes," said he, "most gladly, but also of the former counsel." And when one express after another came from the camp, confirming and magnifying the victories, "When," said he, "will the end of them come?"

Leosthenes, soon after, was killed, and now those who feared lest if Phocion obtained the command he would put an end to the war, arranged with an obscure person in the assembly, who should stand up and profess himself to be a friend and old confidant of Phocion's, and persuade the people to spare him at this time, and reserve him (with whom none could compare) for a more pressing occasion, and now to give Antiphilus the command of the army. This pleased the generality, but Phocion made it appear he was so far from having any friendship with him of old standing, that he had not so much as the least familiarity with him; "Yet now, sir," says he, "give me leave to put you down among the number of my friends and well-wishers, as you have given a piece of advice so much to my advantage."

When the people were eager to make an expedition against the Bœotians, he at first opposed it; and on his friends telling him the people would kill him for always running counter to them, "That will be unjust of them," he said, "if I give them honest advice; if not, it will be just of them." But when he found them persisting and shouting to him to lead them out, he commanded the crier to make proclamation that all the Athenians under sixty should instantly provide themselves with five days' provision, and follow him from the assembly. This caused a great tumult. Those in years were startled, and clamoured against the order; he demanded wherein he injured them, "For I," says he, "am now fourscore, and am ready to lead you." This succeeded in pacifying them for the present.

But when Micion, with a large force of Macedonians and mercenaries, began to pillage the sea-coast, having made a descent upon Rhamnus, and overrun the neighbouring country, Phocion led out the Athenians to attack him. And when sundry private persons came, intermeddling with his dispositions, and telling him that he ought to occupy such or such a hill, detach the cavalry in this or that direction, engage the enemy on this point or that, "O Hercules," said he, "how many generals have we here, and how few soldiers!" Afterwards, having formed the battle, one who wished to show his bravery advanced out of his post before the rest, but on the enemy's approaching, lost heart, and retired back into his rank. "Young man," said Phocion, "are you not ashamed twice in one day to desert your station, first that on which I had placed you, and secondly that on which you had placed yourself?"

However, he entirely routed the enemy, killing Micion and many more on the spot. The Grecian army, also, in Thessaly, after Leonnatus and the Macedonians who came with him out of Asia had arrived and joined Antipater, fought and beat them in a battle. Leonnatus was killed in the fight, Antiphilus commanding the foot, and Menon, the Thessalian, the horse.

But not long after, Craterus crossed from Asia with numerous forces; a pitched battle was fought at Cranon; the Greeks were beaten; though not, indeed, in a signal defeat, nor with any great loss of men. But what with their want of obedience to their commanders, who were young and over-indulgent with them, and what with Antipater's tampering and treating with their separate cities, one by one, the end of it was that the army was dissolved, and the Greeks shamefully surrendered the liberty of their country.

Upon the news of Antipater's now advancing at once against Athens, with all his force, Demosthenes and Hyperides deserted the city, and Demades, who was altogether insolvent for any part of the fines that had been laid upon him by the city, for he had been condemned no less than seven times for introducing bills contrary to the laws, and who had been disfranchised, and was no longer competent to vote in the assembly, laid hold of this season of impunity to bring in a bill for sending ambassadors with plenipotentiary power to Antipater, to treat about a peace. But the people distrusted him, and called upon Phocion to give his opinion, as the person they only and entirely confided in. He told them, "If my former counsels had been prevalent with you, we had not been reduced to deliberate on the question at all." However, the vote passed; and a decree was made, and he with others deputed to go to Antipater, who lay now encamped in the Theban territories, but intended to dislodge immediately, and pass into Attica.

Phocion's first request was that he would make the treaty without moving his camp. And when Craterus declared that it was not fair to ask them to be burdensome to the country of their friends and allies by their stay, when they might rather use that of their enemies for provisions and the support of their army, Antipater, taking him by the hand said, "We must grant this favour to Phocion." For the rest he bade them return to their principals, and acquaint them that he could only offer them the same terms, namely, to surrender at discretion, which Leosthenes had offered to him when he was shut up in Lamia.

When Phocion had returned to the city and acquainted them with this answer, they made a virtue of necessity and complied, since it would be no better. So Phocion returned to Thebes with the other ambassadors, and among the rest Xenocrates, the philosopher, the reputation of whose virtue and wisdom was so great and famous everywhere, that they conceived there could not be any pride, cruelty, or anger arising in the heart of man, which would not at the mere sight of him be subdued into something of reverence and admiration. But the result, as it happened, was the very opposite, Antipater showed such a want of feeling, and such a dislike of goodness. He saluted every one else, but would not so much as notice Xenocrates. Xenocrates, they tell us, observed upon it that Antipater, when meditating such cruelty to Athens, did well to be ashamed of seeing him. When he began to speak, he would not hear him, but broke in and rudely interrupted him, until at last he was obliged to be silent.

But when Phocion had declared the purport of their embassy, he replied shortly, that he would make peace with the Athenians on these conditions, and no others: that Demosthenes and Hyperides should be delivered up to him; that they should retain their ancient form of government, the franchise being determined by a property qualification; that they should receive a garrison into Munychia, and pay a certain sum for the cost of the war. As things stood, these terms were judged tolerable by the rest of the ambassadors; Xenocrates only said, that if Antipater considered the Athenians slaves, he was treating them fairly; but if free, severely. Phocion pressed him only to spare them the garrison, and used many arguments and entreaties. Antipater replied, "Phocion, we are ready to do you any favour which will not bring ruin both on ourselves and on you."

Others report it differently: that Antipater asked Phocion, supposing he remitted the garrison to the Athenians, would he, Phocion, stand surety for the city's observing the terms and attempting no revolution. And when he hesitated, and did not at once reply, Callimedon, the Carabus, a hot partisan and professed enemy of free states, cried out, "And if he should talk so idly, Antipater, will you be so much abused as to believe him and not carry out your own purpose?" So the Athenians received the garrison, and Menyllus for the governor, a fair-dealing man, and one of Phocion's acquaintance.

But the proceeding seemed sufficiently im-perious and arbitrary, indeed rather a spiteful and insulting ostentation of power than that the possession of the fortress would be of any great importance. The resentment felt upon it was heightened by the time it happened in, for the garrison was brought in on the twentieth of the month of Boëdromion, just at the time of the great festival, when they carry forth Iacchus with solemn pomp from the city to Eleusis; so that the solemnity being disturbed, many began to call to mind instances, both ancient and modern, of divine interventions and intimations. For in old time, upon the occasions of their happiest successes, the presence of the shapes and voices of the mystic ceremonies had been vouchsafed to them, striking terror and amazement into their enemies; but now, at the very season of their celebration, the gods themselves stood witnesses of the saddest oppressions of Greece, the most holy time being profaned, and their greatest jubilee made the unlucky date of their most extreme calamity.

Not many years before, they had a warning from the oracle at Dodona that they should carefully guard the summits of Diana, lest haply strangers should seize them. And about this very time, when they dyed the ribbons and garlands with which they adorn the couches and cars of the procession, instead of a purple, they received only a faint yellow colour; and to make the omen yet greater, all the things that were dyed for common use, took the natural colour. While a candidate for initiation was washing a young pig in the haven of Cantharus, a shark seized him, bit off all his lower parts up to the belly, and devoured them, by which the god gave them manifestly to understand, that having lost the lower town and seacoast, they should keep only the upper city.

Menyllus was sufficient security that the garrison should behave itself inoffensively. But those who were now excluded from the franchise by poverty amounted to more than twelve thousand; so that both those that remained in the city thought themselves oppressed and shamefully used, and those who on this account left their homes and went away into Thrace, where Antipater offered them a town and some territory to inhabit, regarded themselves only as a colony of slaves and exiles. And when to this was added the deaths of Demosthenes at Calauria, and of Hyperides at Cleonæ, as we have elsewhere related, the citizens began to think with regret of Philip and Alexander, and almost to wish the return of those times.

And as, after Antigonus was slain, when those that had taken him off were afflicting and oppressing the people, a countryman in Phrygia, digging in the fields, was asked what he was doing, "I am," said he, fetching a deep sigh, "searching for Antigonus"; so said many that remembered those days, and the contests they had with those kings, whose anger, however great, was yet generous and placable; whereas Antipater, with the counterfeit humility of appearing like a private man, in the meanness of his dress and his homely fare, merely belied his real love of that arbitrary power, which he exercised, as a cruel master and despot, to distress those under his command.

Yet Phocion had interest with him to recall many from banishment by his intercession, and prevailed also for those who were driven out, that they might not, like others, be hurried beyond Tænarus, and the mountains of Ceraunia, but remain in Greece, and plant themselves in Peloponnesus, of which number was Agnonides, the sycophant. He was no less studious to manage the affairs within the city with equity and moderation, preferring constantly those that were men of worth and good education to the magistracies, and recommending the busy and turbulent talkers, to whom it was a mortal blow to be excluded from office and public debating, to learn to stay at home, and be content to till their land. And observing that Xenocrates paid his alien-tax as a foreigner, he offered him the freedom of the city, which he refused, saying he could not accept a franchise which he had been sent as an ambassador to deprecate.

Menyllus wished to give Phocion a considerable present of money, who, thanking him, said neither was Menyllus greater than Alexander, nor his own occasions more urgent to receive it now than when he refused it from him. And on his pressing him to permit his son Phocus to receive it, he replied, "If my son returns to a right mind, his patrimony is sufficient; if not, all supplies will be insufficient." But to Antipater he answered more sharply, who would have him engaged in something dishonourable. "Antipater," said he, "cannot have me both as his friend and his flatterer." And, indeed, Antipater was wont to say he had two friends at Athens, Phocion and Demades; the one would never suffer him to gratify him at all, the other would never be satisfied. Phocion might well think that poverty a virtue, in which, after having so often been general of the Athenians, and admitted to the friendship of potentates and princes, he had now grown old.

Demades, meantime, delighted in lavishing his wealth even in positive transgressions of the law. For there having been an order that no foreigner should be hired to dance in any chorus on the penalty of a fine of one thousand drachmas on the exhibitor, he had the vanity to exhibit an entire chorus of a hundred foreigners, and paid down the penalty of a thousand drachmas a head upon the stage itself. Marrying his son Demeas, he told him with the like vanity, "My son, when I married your mother, it was done so privately it was not known to the next neighbours, but kings and princes give presents at your nuptials."

The garrison in Munychia continued to be felt as a great grievance, and the Athenians did not cease to be importunate upon Phocion, to prevail with Antipater for its removal; but whether he despaired of effecting it, or perhaps observed the people to be more orderly, and public matters more reasonably conducted by the awe that was thus created, he constantly declined the office, and contented himself with obtaining from Antipater the postponement for the present of the payment of the sum of money in which the city was fined.

So the people, leaving him off, applied themselves to Demades, who readily undertook the employment, and took along with him his son also into Macedonia; and some superior power, as it seems, so ordering it, he came just at that nick of time when Antipater was already seized with his sickness, and Cassander, taking upon himself the command, had found a letter of Demades's, formerly written by him to Antigonus in Asia, recommending him to come and possess himself of the empire of Greece and Macedon, now hanging, he said (a scoff at Antipater), "by an old and rotten thread." So when Cassander saw him come, he seized him; and first brought out the son, and killed him so close before his face that the blood ran all over his clothes and person, and then, after bitterly taunting and upbraiding him with his ingratitude and treachery, despatched him himself.

Antipater being dead, after nominating Polysperchon general-in-chief and Cassander commander of the cavalry, Cassander at once set up for himself, and immediately despatched Nicanor to Menyllus, to succeed him in the command of the garrison, commanding him to possess himself of Munychia before the news of Antipater's death should be heard; which being done, and some days after the Athenians hearing the report of it, Phocion was taxed as privy to it before and censured heavily for dissembling it, out of friendship for Nicanor. But he slighted their talk, and making it his duty to visit and confer continually with Nicanor, he succeeded in procuring his good-will and kindness for the Athenians, and induced him even to put himself to trouble and expense to seek popularity with them, by undertaking the office of presiding at the games.

In the meantime Polysperchon, who was intrusted with the charge of the king, to countermine Cassander, sent a letter to the city, declaring, in the name of the king, that he restored them their democracy, and that the whole Athenian people were at liberty to conduct their commonwealth according to their ancient customs and constitutions. The object of these pretences was merely the overthrow of Phocion's influence, as the event manifested. For Polysperchon's design being to possess himself of the city, he despaired altogether of bringing it to pass whilst Phocion retained his credit; and the most certain way to ruin him would be again to fill the city with a crowd of disfranchised citizens, and let loose the tongues of the demagogues and common accusers.

With this prospect the Athenians were all in excitement, and Nicanor, wishing to confer with them on the subject, at a meeting of the council in Piræus, came himself, trusting for the safety of his person to Phocion. And when Dercyllus, who commanded the guard there, made an attempt to seize him, upon notice of it beforehand, he made his escape, and there was little doubt he would now lose no time in righting himself upon the city for the affront; and when Phocion was found fault with for letting him get off and not securing him, he defended himself by saying that he had no mistrust of Nicanor, nor the least reason to expect any mischief from him, but should it prove otherwise, for his part he would have them all know, he would rather receive than do the wrong.

And so far as he spoke for himself alone, the answer was honourable and high-minded enough, but he who hazards his country's safety, and that, too, when he is her magistrate and chief commander, can scarcely be acquitted, I fear, of transgressing a higher and more sacred obligation of justice, which he owed to his fellow-citizens. For it will not even do to say that he dreaded involving the city in war, by seizing Nicanor, and hoped by professions of confidence and just-dealing to retain him in the observance of the like; but it was, indeed, his credulity and confidence in him, and an overweening opinion of his sincerity, that imposed upon him.

Thus, notwithstanding the sundry intimations he had of his making preparations to attack Piræus, sending soldiers over into Salamis, and tampering with and endeavouring to corrupt various residents in Piræus, he would, notwithstanding all this evidence, never be persuaded to believe it. And even when Philomedes of Lampra had got a decree passed, that all the Athenians should stand to their arms, and be ready to follow Phocion their general, he yet sat still and did nothing, until Nicanor actually led his troops out from Munychia, and drew trenches about Piræus; upon which, when Phocion at last would have let out the Athenians, they cried out against him, and slighted his orders.

Alexander, the son of Polysperchon, was at hand with a considerable force, and professed to come to give them succour against Nicanor, but intended nothing less, if possible, than to surprise the city, whilst they were in tumult and divided among themselves. For all that had previously been expelled from the city, now coming back with him, made their way into it, and were joined by a mixed multitude of foreigners and disfranchised persons, and of these a motley and irregular public assembly came together, in which they presently divested Phocion of all power, and chose other generals; and if by chance Alexander had not been spied from the walls, alone in close conference with Nicanor, and had not this, which was often repeated, given the Athenians cause of suspicion, the city had not escaped the snare.

The orator Agnonides, however, at once fell foul upon Phocion, and impeached him of treason; Callimedon and Charicles, fearing the worst, consulted their own security by fleeing from the city. Phocion, with a few of his friends that stayed with him, went over to Polysperchon, and out of respect for him, Solon of Platæa, and Dinarchus of Corinth, who were reputed friends and confidants of Polysperchon, accompanied him. But on account of Dinarchus falling ill, they remained several days in Elatea, during which time, upon the persuasion of Agnonides and on the motion of Archestratus, a decree passed that the people should send delegates thither to accuse Phocion. So both parties reached Polysperchon at the same time, who was going through the country with the king, and was then at a small village of Phocis, Pharygæ, under the mountain now called Galate, but then Acrurium.

There Polysperchon, having set up the golden canopy, and seated the king and his company under it, ordered Dinarchus at once to be taken, and tortured, and put to death; and that done, gave audience to the Athenians, who filled the place with noise and tumult, accusing and recriminating on one another, till at last Agnonides came forward, and requested they might all be shut up together in one cage, and conveyed to Athens, there to decide the controversy. At that the king could not forbear smiling, but the company that attended, for their own amusement, Macedonians and strangers, were eager to hear the altercation, and made signs to the delegates to go on with their case at once. But it was no sort of fair hearing. Polysperchon frequently interrupted Phocion, till at last Phocion struck his staff on the grounds and declined to speak further. And when Hegemon said, Polysperchon himself could bear witness to his affection for the people, Polysperchon called out fiercely, "Give over slandering me to the king," and the king starting up was about to have run him through with his javelin, but Polysperchon interposed and hindered him; so that the assembly dissolved.

Phocion, then, and those about him, were seized; those of his friends that were not immediately by him, on seeing this, hid their faces, and saved themselves by flight. The rest Clitus took and brought to Athens, to be submitted to trial, but, in truth, as men already sentenced to die. The manner of conveying them was indeed extremely moving; they were carried in chariots through the Ceramicus, straight to the place of judicature, where Clitus secured them till they had convoked an assembly of the people, which was open to all comers, neither foreigners, nor slaves, nor those who had been punished with disfranchisement being refused admittance, but all alike, both men and women, being allowed to come into the court, and even upon the place of speaking. So having read the king's letters, in which he declared he was satisfied himself that these men were traitors, however, they being a free city, he willingly accorded them the grace of trying and judging them according to their own laws, Clitus brought in his prisoners.

Every respectable citizen, at the sight of Phocion, covered up his face, and stooped down to conceal his tears. And one of them had the courage to say, that since the king had committed so important a cause to the judgment of the people, it would be well that the strangers, and those of servile condition, should withdraw. But the populace would not endure it, crying out they were oligarchs, and enemies to the liberty of the people, and deserved to be stoned; after which no man durst offer anything further in Phocion's behalf. He was himself with difficulty heard at all, when he put the question, "Do you wish to put us to death lawfully or unlawfully?" Some answered, "According to law." He replied, "How can you, except we have a fair hearing?" But when they were deaf to all he said, approaching nearer, "As to myself," said he, "I admit my guilt, and pronounce my public conduct to have deserved sentence of death. But why, O men of Athens, kill others who have offended in nothing?" The rabble cried out that they were his friends; that was enough. Phocion therefore drew back, and said no more.

Then Agnonides read the bill, in accordance with which the people should decide by show of hands whether they judged them guilty, and if so it should be found, the penalty should be death. When this had been read out, some desired it might be added to the sentence, that Phocion should be tortured also, and the rack should be produced with the executioners. But Agnonides perceiving even Clitus to dislike this, and himself thinking it horrid and barbarous, said, "When we catch that slave, Callimedon, men of Athens, we will put him to the rack, but I shall make no motion of the kind in Phocion's case." Upon which one of the better citizens remarked, he was quite right; "If he should torture Phocion, what could we do to you?" So the form of the bill was approved of, and the show of hands called for; upon which, not one man retaining his seat, but all rising up, and some with garlands on their heads, they condemned them all to death.

There were present with Phocion, Nicocles, Thudippus, Hegemon, and Pythocles. Demetrius the Phalerian, Callimedon, Charicles, and some others, were included in the condemnation, being absent.

After the assembly was dismissed, they were carried to the prison; the rest with cries and lamentations, their friends and relatives following and clinging about them, but Phocion looking (as men observed with astonishment at his calmness and magnanimity), just the same as when he had been used to return to his home attended, as general, from the assembly. His enemies ran along by his side, reviling and abusing him. And one of them coming up to him, spat in his face; at which Phocion, turning to the officers, only said, "You should stop this indecency."

Thudippus, on their reaching the prison, when he observed the executioner tempering the poison and preparing it for them, gave away to his passion, and began to bemoan his condition and the hard measure he received, thus unjustly to suffer with Phocion. "You cannot be contented," said he, "to die with Phocion?" One of his friends that stood by, asked him if he wished to have anything said to his son. "Yes, by all means," said he, "bid him bear no grudge against the Athenians." Then Nicocles, the dearest and most faithful of his friends, begged to be allowed to drink the poison first. "My friend," said he, "you ask what I am loath and sorrowful to give, but as I never yet in all my life was so thankless as to refuse you, I must gratify you in this also." After they had all drunk of it, the poison ran short; and the executioner refused to prepare more, except they would pay him twelve drachmas, to defray the cost of the quantity required. Some delay was made, and time spent, when Phocion called one of his friends, and observing that a man could not even die at Athens without paying for it, requested him to give the sum.

It was the nineteenth day of the month Munychion, on which it was the usage to have a solemn procession in the city, in honour of Jupiter. The horsemen, as they passed by, some of them threw away their garlands, others stopped, weeping, and casting sorrowful looks towards the prison doors, and all the citizens whose minds were not absolutely debauched by spite and passion, or who had any humanity left, acknowledged it to have been most impiously done, not, at least, to let that day pass, and the city so be kept pure from death and a public execution at the solemn festival. But as if this triumph had been insufficient, the mal-

ice of Phocion's enemies went yet further; his dead body was excluded from burial within the boundaries of the country, and none of the Athenians could light a funeral pile to burn the corpse; neither durst any of his friends venture to concern themselves about it.

A certain Conopion, a man who used to do these offices for hire, took the body and carried it beyond Eleusis, and procuring fire from over the frontier of Megara, burned it. Phocion's wife, with her servant-maids, being present and assisting at the solemnity, raised there an empty tomb, and performed the customary libations, and gathering up the bones in her lap, and bringing them home by night, dug a place for them by the fireside in her house, saying, "Blessed hearth, to your custody I commit the remains of a good and brave man, and, I beseech you, protect and restore them to the sepulchre of his fathers, when the Athenians return to their right minds."

And, indeed, a very little time and their own sad experience soon informed them what an excellent governor, and how great an example and guardian of justice and of temperance they had bereft themselves of. And now they decreed him a statue of brass, and his bones to be buried honourably at the public charge; and for his accusers, Agnonides they took themselves, and caused him to be put to death. Epicurus and Demophilus, who fled from the city for fear, his son met with, and took his revenge upon them. This son of his, we are told, was in general of an indifferent character, and once when enamoured of a slave girl kept by a common harlot merchant, happened to hear Theodorus, the atheist, arguing in the Lyceum, that if it were a good and honourable thing to buy the freedom of a friend in the masculine, why not also of a friend in the feminine; if, for example, a master, why not also a mistress? So putting the good argument and his passion together, he went off and purchased the girl's freedom.

The death which was thus suffered by Phocion revived among the Greeks the memory of that of Socrates, the two cases being so similar, and both equally the sad fault and misfortune of the city.

CATO THE YOUNGER

95–46 B.C.

THE family of Cato derived its first lustre from his great-grandfather Cato, whose virtue gained him such great reputation and authority among the Romans, as we have written in his life.

This Cato was, by the loss of both his parents, left an orphan, together with his brother Cæpio, and his sister Porcia. He had also a half-sister, Servilia, by the mother's side. All these lived together, and were bred up in the house of Livius Drusus, their uncle by the mother, who, at that time, had a great share in the government, being a very eloquent speaker, a man of the greatest temperance, and yielding in dignity to none of the Romans.

It is said of Cato that even from his infancy, in his speech, his countenance, and all his childish pastimes, he discovered an inflexible temper, unmoved by any passion, and firm in everything. He was resolute in his purposes, much beyond the strength of his age, to go through with whatever he undertook. He was rough and ungentle toward those that flattered him, and still more unyielding to those who threatened him. It was difficult to excite him to laughter,—his countenance seldom relaxed even into a smile; he was not quickly or easily provoked to anger, but if once incensed, he was no less difficult to pacify.

When he began to learn, he proved dull, and slow to apprehend, but of what he once received, his memory was remarkably tenacious. And such, in fact, we find generally to be the course of nature; men of fine genius are readily reminded of things, but those who receive with most pains and difficulty, remember best; every new thing they learn, being, as it were, burnt and branded in on their minds. Cato's natural stubbornness and slowness to be persuaded may also have made it more difficult for him to be taught. For to learn is to submit to having something done to one; and persuasion comes soonest to those who have least strength to resist it. Hence young men are sooner persuaded than those that are more in years, and sick men, than those that are well in health. In fine, where there is least previous doubt and difficulty, the new impression is most easily accepted. Yet Cato, they say, was very obedient to his preceptor, and would do whatever he was commanded; but he would also ask the reason, and inquire the cause of everything. And, indeed, his teacher was a very well-bred man, more ready to instruct than to beat his scholars. His name was Sarpedon.

When Cato was a child, the allies of the Romans sued to be made free citizens of Rome. Pompædius Silo, one of their deputies, a brave soldier and a man of great repute, who had contracted a friendship with Drusus, lodged at his house for several days, in which time being grown familiar with the children, "Well," said he to them, "will you entreat your uncle to befriend us in our business?" Cæpio, smiling, assented, but Cato made no answer, only he looked steadfastly and fiercely on the strangers. Then said Pompædius, "And you, young sir, what say you to us? Will not you, as well as your brother, intercede with your uncle in our behalf?" And when Cato continued to give no answer, by his silence and his countenance seeming to deny their petition, Pompædius snatched him up to the window as if he would throw him out, and told him to consent, or he would fling him down, and, speaking in a harsher tone, held his body out of the window, and shook him several times. When Cato had suffered this a good while, unmoved and unalarmed, Pompædius, setting him down, said in an undervoice to his friend, "What a blessing for Italy that he is but a child! If he were a man, I believe we should not gain one voice among the people."

Another time, one of his relations, on his birthday, invited Cato and some other children to supper, and some of the company diverted themselves in a separate part of the house, and were at play, the elder and the younger together, their sport being to act the pleadings before the judges, accusing one another, and carrying away the condemned to prison. Among these a very beautiful young child, being bound and carried by a bigger into prison, cried out to Cato, who seeing what was going on presently

620

ran to the door, and thrusting away those who stood there as a guard, took out the child, and went home in anger, followed by some of his companions.

Cato at length grew so famous among them, that when Sulla designed to exhibit the sacred game of young men riding courses on horseback, which they called "Troy," having gotten together the youth of good birth, he appointed two for their leaders. One of them they accepted for his mother's sake, being the son of Metella, the wife of Sulla; but as for the other, Sextus, the nephew of Pompey, they would not be led by him, nor exercise under him. Then Sulla asking whom they would have, they all cried out, "Cato"; and Sextus willingly yielded the honour to him, as the more worthy.

Sulla, who was a friend of their family, sent at times for Cato and his brother to see them and talk with them; a favour which he showed to very few, after gaining his great power and authority. Sarpedon, full of the advantage it would be, as well for the honour as the safety of his scholars, would often bring Cato to wait upon Sulla at his house, which, for the multitude of those that were being carried off in custody, and tormented there, looked like a place of execution. Cato was then in his fourteenth year, and seeing the heads of men said to be of great distinction brought thither, and observing the secret sighs of those that were present, he asked his preceptor, "Why does nobody kill this man?" "Because," said he, "they fear him, child, more than they hate him." "Why, then," replied Cato, "did you not give me a sword, that I might stab him, and free my country from this slavery?" Sarpedon hearing this, and at the same time seeing his countenance swelling with anger and determination, took care thenceforward to watch him strictly, lest he should hazard any desperate attempt.

While he was yet very young, to some that asked him whom he loved best, he answered, his brother. And being asked, whom next, he replied, his brother, again. So likewise the third time, and still the same, till they left off to ask any further. As he grew in age, this love to his brother grew yet the stronger. When he was about twenty years old, he never supped, never went out of town, nor into the Forum, without Cæpio. But when his brother made use of precious ointments and perfumes, Cato declined them; and he was, in all his habits, very strict and austere, so that when Cæpio was admired for his moderation and temper-

ance, he would acknowledge that indeed he might be accounted such, in comparison with some other men, "but," said he, "when I compare myself with Cato, I find myself scarcely different from Sippius," one at that time notorious for his luxurious and effeminate living.

Cato being made priest of Apollo, went to another house, took his portion of their paternal inheritance, amounting to a hundred and twenty talents, and began to live yet more strictly than before. Having gained the intimate acquaintance of Antipater the Tyrian, the Stoic philosopher, he devoted himself to the study, above everything, of moral and political doctrine. And though possessed, as it were, by a kind of inspiration for the pursuit of every virtue, yet what most of all virtue and excellence fixed his affection was that steady and inflexible justice which is not to be wrought upon by favour or compassion. He learned also the art of speaking and debating in public, thinking that political philosophy, like a great city, should maintain for its security the military and warlike element. But he would never recite his exercises before company, nor was he ever heard to declaim. And to one that told him men blamed his silence, "But I hope not my life," he replied. "I will begin to speak, when I have that to say which had not better be unsaid."

The great Porcian Hall, as it was called, had been built and dedicated to the public use by the old Cato, when ædile. Here the tribunes of the people used to transact their business, and because one of the pillars was thought to interfere with the convenience of their seats, they deliberated whether it were best to remove it to another place, or to take it away. This occasion first drew Cato, much against his will, into the Forum; for he opposed the demand of the tribunes, and in so doing gave a specimen both of his courage and his powers of speaking, which gained him great admiration. His speech had nothing youthful or refined in it, but was straightforward, full of matter, and rough, at the same time that there was a certain grace about his rough statements which won the attention; and the speaker's character, showing itself in all he said, added to his severe language something that excited feelings of natural pleasure and interest. His voice was full and sounding, and sufficient to be heard by so great a multitude, and its vigour and capacity of endurance quite indefatigable, for he often would speak a whole day and never stop.

When he had carried this cause, he betook himself again to study and retirement. He employed himself in inuring his body to labour and violent exercise; and habituated himself to go bareheaded in the hottest and the coldest weather, and to walk on foot at all seasons. When he went on a journey with any of his friends, though they were on horseback and he on foot, yet he would often join now one, then another, and converse with them on the way. In sickness the patience he showed in supporting, and the abstinence he used for curing, his distempers were admirable. When he had an ague, he would remain alone, and suffer nobody to see him, till he began to recover, and found the fit was over. At supper, when he threw dice for the choice of dishes, and lost, and the company offered him nevertheless his choice, he declined to dispute, as he said, the decision of Venus. At first, he was wont to drink only once after supper, and then go away; but in process of time he grew to drink more, insomuch that oftentimes he would continue till morning. This his friends explained by saying that state affairs and public business took him up all day, and being desirous of knowledge, he liked to pass the night at wine in the conversation of philosophers. Hence, upon one Memmius saying in public, that Cato spent whole nights in drinking, "You should add," replied Cicero, "that he spends whole days in gambling."

And in general Cato esteemed the customs and manners of men at that time so corrupt, and a reformation in them so necessary, that he thought it requisite, in many things, to go contrary to the ordinary way of the world. Seeing the lightest and gayest purple was then most in fashion, he would always wear that which was the nearest black; and he would often go out of doors, after his morning meal, without either shoes or tunic; not that he sought vain-glory from such novelties, but he would accustom himself to be ashamed only of what deserves shame, and to despise all other sorts of disgrace.

The estate of one Cato, his cousin, which was worth one hundred talents, falling to him, he turned it all into ready money, which he kept by him for any of his friends that should happen to want, to whom he would lend it without interest. And for some of them, he suffered his own land and his slaves to be mortgaged to the public treasury.

When he thought himself of an age to marry, having never before known any woman, he was contracted to Lepida, who had before been contracted to Metellus Scipio, but on Scipio's own withdrawal from it, the contract had been dissolved, and she left at liberty. Yet Scipio afterwards repenting himself, did all he could to regain her, before the marriage with Cato was completed, and succeeded in so doing. At which Cato was violently incensed, and resolved at first to go to law about it; but his friends persuaded him to the contrary. However, he was so moved by the heat of youth and passion that he wrote a quantity of iambic verses against Scipio, in the bitter, sarcastic style of Archilochus, without, however, his licence and scurrility. After this, he married Atilia, the daughter of Soranus, the first but not the only woman he ever knew, less happy thus far than Lælius, the friend of Scipio, who in the whole course of so long a life never knew but the one woman, to whom he was united in his first and only marriage.

In the war of the slaves, which took its name from Spartacus, their ringleader, Gellius was general, and Cato went a volunteer, for the sake of his brother Cæpio, who was a tribune in the army. Cato could find here no opportunity to show his zeal or exercise his valour, on account of the ill conduct of the general. However, amidst the corruption and disorders of that army, he showed such a love of discipline, so much bravery upon occasion, and so much courage and wisdom in everything, that it appeared he was in no way inferior to the old Cato. Gellius offered him great rewards, and would have decreed him the first honours; which, however, he refused, saying he had done nothing that deserved them. This made him to be thought a man of strange and eccentric temper.

There was a law passed, moreover, that the candidates who stood for any office should not have prompters in their canvass, to tell them the names of the citizens; and Cato, when he sued to be elected tribune, was the only man that obeyed this law. He took great pains to learn by his own knowledge to salute those he had to speak with, and to call them by their names; yet even those who praised him for this, did not do so without some envy and jealousy, for the more they considered the excellence of what he did, the more they were grieved at the difficulty they found to do the like.

Being chosen tribune, he was sent into Macedon to join Rubrius, who was general there. It is said that his wife showing much concern, and weeping at his departure, Munatius, one of Cato's friends, said to her, "Do not trouble yourself, Atilia, I will engage to watch over him for you." "By all means," replied Cato; and when they had gone one day's journey together, "Now," said he to Munatius, after they had supped, "that you may be sure to keep your promise to Atilia, you must not leave me day nor night," and from that time, he ordered two beds to be made in his own chamber, that Munatius might lie there. And so he continued to do, Cato making it his jest to see that he was always there. There went with him fifteen slaves, two freedmen, and four of his friends; these rode on horseback, but Cato always went on foot, yet would he keep by them, and talk with each of them in turn as they went.

When he came to the army, which consisted of several legions, the general gave him the command of one; and as he looked upon it as a small matter, and not worthy a commander, to give evidence of his own signal valour, he resolved to make his soldiers, as far as he could, like himself, not, however, in this relaxing the terrors of his office, but associating reason with his authority. He persuaded and instructed every one in particular, and bestowed rewards or punishments according to desert; and at length his men were so well disciplined, that it was hard to say whether they were more peaceable or more warlike, more valiant or more just; they were alike formidable to their enemies and courteous to their allies, fearful to do wrong, and forward to gain honour.

And Cato himself acquired in the fullest measure what it had been his least desire to seek, glory and good repute; he was highly esteemed by all men, and entirely beloved by the soldiers. Whatever he commanded to be done, he himself took part in the performing; in his apparel, his diet, and mode of travelling, he was more like a common soldier than an officer; but in character, high purpose, and wisdom, he far exceeded all that had the names and titles of commanders, and he made himself, without knowing it, the object of general affection. For the true love of virtue is in all men produced by the love and respect they bear to him that teaches it; and those who praise good men, yet do not love them, may respect their reputation, but do not really admire, and will never imitate their virtue.

There dwelt at that time in Pergamus, Athenodorus, surnamed Cordylio, a man of high repute for his knowledge of the Stoic philosophy, who was now grown old, and had always steadily refused the friendship and acquaintance of princes and great men. Cato understood this; so that imagining he should not be able to prevail with him by sending or writing, and being by the laws allowed two months' absence from the army, he resolved to go into Asia to see him in person, trusting to his own good qualities not to lose his labour. And when he had conversed with him, and succeeded in persuading him out of his former resolutions, he returned and brought him to the camp as joyful and as proud of this victory as if he had done some heroic exploit, greater than any of those of Pompey or Lucullus, who with their armies at that time were subduing so many nations and kingdoms.

While Cato was yet in the service, his brother, on a journey towards Asia, fell sick at Ænus in Thrace, letters with intelligence of which were immediately despatched to him. The sea was very rough, and no convenient ship of any size to be had; so Cato getting into a small trading-vessel, with only two of his friends, and three servants, set sail from Thessalonica, and having very narrowly escaped drowning, he arrived at Ænus just as Cæpio expired. Upon this occasion, he was thought to have showed himself more a fond brother than a philosopher, not only in the excess of his grief, bewailing and embracing the dead body, but also in the extravagant expenses of the funeral, the vast quantity of rich perfumes and costly garments which were burnt with the corpse, and the monument of Thasian marble, which he erected, at the cost of eight talents, in the public place of the town of Ænus.

For there were some who took upon them to cavil at all this as not consistent with his usual calmness and moderation, not discerning that though he were steadfast, firm, and inflexible to pleasure, fear or foolish entreaties, yet he was full of natural tenderness and brotherly affection. Divers of the cities and princes of the country sent him many presents, to honour the funeral of his brother; but he took none of their money, only the perfumes and ornaments he received, and paid for them also. And afterwards, when the inheritance was divided between him and Cæpio's daughter, he did not require any portion of the funeral expenses to be discharged out of it. Notwithstanding this, it has been affirmed that he made his brother's ashes be passed through a sieve, to find the gold that was melted down when burnt with the body. But he who made this statement appears to have anticipated an exemption for his pen, as much as for his sword, from all question and criticism.

The time of Cato's service in the army being expired, he received, at his departure, not only the prayers and praises, but the tears and embraces of the soldiers, who spread their clothes at his feet and kissed his hand as he passed, an honour which the Romans at that time scarcely paid even to a very few of their generals and commanders-in-chief. Having left the army, he resolved, before he would return home and apply himself to state affairs, to travel in Asia, and observe the manners, the customs, and the strength of every province. He was also unwilling to refuse the kindness of Deiotarus, King of Galatia, who having had great familiarity and friendship with his father, was very desirous to receive a visit from him.

Cato's arrangements in his journey were as follows. Early in the morning he sent out his baker and his cook towards the place where he designed to stay the next night; these went soberly and quietly into the town, in which, if there happened to be no friend or acquaintance of Cato or his family, they provided for him in an inn, and gave no disturbance to anybody; but if there were no inn, then, and in this case only, they went to the magistrates, and desiring them to help them to lodgings, took without complaint whatever was allotted to them. His servants thus behaving themselves towards the magistrates, without noise and threatening, were often discredited, or neglected by them, so that Cato many times arrived and found nothing provided for him. And it was all the worse when he appeared himself; still less account was taken of him. When they saw him sitting, without saying anything, on his baggage, they set him down at once as a person of no consequence, who did not venture to make any demand.

Sometimes, on such occasions, he would call them to him and tell them, "Foolish people, lay aside this inhospitality. All your visitors will not be Catos. Use your courtesy, to take off the sharp edge of power. There are men enough who desire but a pretence, to take from you by force, what you give with such reluctance."

While he travelled in this manner, a diverting accident befell him in Syria. As he was going into Antioch, he saw a great multitude of people outside the gates, ranged in order on either side the way; here the young men with long cloaks, there the children decently dressed;

others wore garlands and white garments who were the priests and magistrates. Cato, imagining all this could mean nothing but a display in honour of his reception, began to be angry with his servants, who had been sent before, for suffering it to be done; then making his friends alight, he walked along with them on foot.

As soon as he came near the gate, an elderly man, who seemed to be master of these ceremonies, with a wand and a garland in his hand, came up to Cato, and without saluting him, asked him where he had left Demetrius, and how soon he thought he would be there. This Demetrius was Pompey's servant, and as at this time the whole world, so to say, had its eyes fixed upon Pompey, this man also was highly honoured, on account of his influence with his master. Upon this Cato's friends fell into such violent laughter, that they could not restrain themselves while they passed through the crowd; and he himself, ashamed and distressed, uttered the words, "Unfortunate city!" and said no more. Afterwards, however, it always made him laugh, when he either told the story or was otherwise reminded of it.

Pompey himself shortly after made the people ashamed of their ignorance and folly in thus neglecting him, for Cato, coming in his journey to Ephesus, went to pay his respects to him, who was the elder man, had gained much honour, and was then general of a great army. Yet Pompey would not receive him sitting, but as soon as he saw him, rose up, and going to meet him, as the more honourable person, gave him his hand, and embraced him with great show of kindness. He said much in commendation of his virtue both at that time when receiving him, and also yet more after he had withdrawn. So that now all men began at once to display their respect for Cato, and discovered in him the very same things for which they despised him before, an admirable mildness of temper and greatness of spirit.

And indeed the civility that Pompey himself showed him appeared to come from one that rather respected than loved him; and the general opinion was, that while Cato was there he paid him admiration, but was not sorry when he was gone. For when other young men came to see him he usually urged and entreated them to continue with him. Now he did not at all invite Cato to stay, but as if his own power were lessened by the other's presence, he very willingly allowed him to take his leave. Yet to Cato alone, of all those who went for Rome, he recommended his children and his wife, who was indeed connected by relationship with Cato.

After this, all the cities through which he passed strove and emulated each other in showing him respect and honour. Feasts and entertainments were made for his reception, so that he bade his friends keep strict watch and take care of him, lest he should end by making good what was said by Curio, who though he were his familiar friend, yet disliking the austerity of his temper, asked him one day if, when he left the army, he designed to see Asia, and Cato answering, "Yes, by all means." "You do well," replied Curio, "you will bring back with you a better temper and pleasanter manners"; pretty nearly the very words he used.

Deiotarus, being now an old man, had sent for Cato, to recommend his children and family to his protection; and as soon as he came, brought him presents of all sorts of things, which he begged and entreated him to accept. And his importunities displeased Cato so much, that though he came but in the evening, he stayed only that night, and went away early the next morning. After he was gone one day's journey, he found at Pessinus a yet greater quantity of presents provided for him there, and also letters from Deiotarus entreating him to receive them, or at least to permit his friends to take them, who for his sake deserved some gratification, and could not have much done for them out of Cato's own means. Yet he would not suffer it, though he saw some of them very willing to receive such gifts, and ready to complain of his severity; but he answered that corruption would never want pretence, and his friends should share with him in whatever he should justly and honestly obtain, and so returned the presents to Deiotarus.

When he took ship for Brundusium, his friends would have persuaded him to put his brother's ashes into another vessel; but he said he would sooner part with his life than leave them, and so set sail. And as it chanced, he, we are told, had a very dangerous passage, though others at the same time went over safely enough.

After he was returned to Rome, he spent his time for the most part either at home, in conversation with Athenodorus, or at the Forum, in the service of his friends. Though it was now the time that he should become quæstor, he would not stand for the place till he had studied the laws relating to it, and by inquiry

from persons of experience, had attained a distinct understanding of the duty and authority belonging to it.

With this knowledge, as soon as he came into the office, he made a great reformation among the clerks and under-officers of the treasury, people who had long practice and familiarity in all the public records and the laws, and, when new magistrates came in year by year so ignorant and unskilful as to be in absolute need of others to teach them what to do, did not submit and give way, but kept the power in their own hands, and were in effect the treasurers themselves. Till Cato, applying himself roundly to the work, showed that he possessed not only the title and honour of a quæstor, but the knowledge and understanding and full authority of his office.

Thus, he used the clerks and under-officers like servants as they were, exposing their corrupt practices, and instructing their ignorance. Being bold, impudent fellows, they flattered the other quæstors, his colleagues, and by their means endeavoured to maintain an opposition against him. But he convicted the chiefest of them of a breach of trust in the charge of an inheritance, and turned him out of his place. A second he brought to trial for dishonesty, who was defended by Lutatius Catulus, at that time censor, a man very considerable for his office, but yet more for his character, as he was eminent above all the Romans of that age for his reputed wisdom and integrity. He was also intimate with Cato, and much commended his way of living. So perceiving he could not bring off his client, if he stood a fair trial, he openly began to beg him off. Cato objected to his doing this. And when he continued still to be importunate, "It would be shameful, Catulus," he said, "that the censor, the judge of all our lives, should incur the dishonour of removal by our officers."

At this expression, Catulus looked as if he would have made some answer; but he said nothing, and either through anger or shame went away silent, and out of countenance. Nevertheless, the man was not found guilty, for the voices that acquitted him were but one in number less than those that condemned him, and Marcus Lollius, one of Cato's colleagues, who was absent by reason of sickness, was sent for by Catulus, and entreated to come and save the man. So Lollius was brought into court in a chair, and gave his voice also for acquitting him. Yet Cato never after made use of that clerk, and never paid him his salary, nor would he make any account of the vote given by Lollius.

Having thus humbled the clerks, and brought them to be at command, he made use of the books and registers as he thought fit, and in a little while gained the treasury a higher name than the senate house itself; and all men said, Cato had made the office of a quæstor equal to the dignity of a consul. When he found many indebted to the state upon old accounts, and the state also in debt to many private persons, he took care that the public might no longer either do or suffer wrong; he strictly and punctually exacted what was due to the treasury, and as freely and speedily paid all those to whom it was indebted. So that the people were filled with sentiments of awe and respect, on seeing those made to pay, who thought to have escaped with their plunder, and others receiving all their due, who despaired of getting anything.

And whereas usually those who brought false bills and pretended orders of the senate could through favour get them accepted, Cato would never be so imposed upon; and in the case of one particular order, on the question arising whether it had passed the senate, he would not believe a great many witnesses that attested it, nor would admit of it, till the consuls came and affirmed it upon oath.

There were at that time a great many whom Sulla had made use of as his agents in the proscription, and to whom he had for their service in putting men to death, given twelve thousand drachmas apiece. These men everybody hated as wicked and polluted wretches, but nobody durst be revenged upon them. Cato called every one to account, as wrongfully possessed of the public money, and exacted it of them, and at the same time sharply reproved them for their unlawful and impious actions. After these proceedings they were presently accused of murder, and being already in a manner prejudged as guilty, they were easily found so, and accordingly suffered; at which the whole people rejoiced and thought themselves now to see the old tyranny finally abolished, and Sulla himself, so to say, brought to punishment.

Cato's assiduity also, and indefatigable diligence, won very much upon the people. He always came first of any of his colleagues to the treasury, and went away the last. He never missed any assembly of the people, or sitting of the senate; being always anxious and on the watch for those who lightly, or as a matter of interest, passed votes in favour of this or that person, for remitting debts or granting away customs that were owing to the state. And at length, having kept the exchequer pure and clear from base informers, and yet having filled it with treasure, he made it appear that the state might be rich without oppressing the people. At first he excited feelings of dislike and irritation in some of his colleagues, but after a while they were well contented with him, since he was perfectly willing that they should cast all the odium on him, when they declined to gratify their friends with the public money, or to give dishonest judgments in passing their accounts; and when hard-pressed by suitors, they could readily answer it was impossible to do anything unless Cato would consent.

On the last day of his office, he was honourably attended to his house by almost all the people; but on the way he was informed that several powerful friends were in the treasury with Marcellus, using all their interest with him to pass a certain debt to the public revenue, as if it had been a gift. Marcellus had been one of Cato's friends from his childhood, and so long as Cato was with him, was one of the best of his colleagues in this office, but when alone, was unable to resist the importunity of suitors, and prone to do anybody a kindness. So Cato immediately turned back, and finding that Marcellus had yielded to pass the thing, he took the book, and while Marcellus silently stood by and looked on, struck it out. This done, he brought Marcellus out of the treasury, and took him home with him; who for all this, neither then, nor ever after, complained of him, but always continued his friendship and familiarity with him.

Cato, after he had laid down his office, yet did not cease to keep a watch upon the treasury. He had his servants who continually wrote out the details of the expenditure, and he himself kept always by him certain books, which contained the accounts of the revenue from Sulla's time to his own quæstorship, which he had bought for five talents.

He was always first at the senate, and went out last; and often, while the others were slowly collecting, he would sit and read by himself, holding his gown before his book. He was never once out of town when the senate was to meet. And when afterwards Pompey and his party, finding that he could never be either persuaded or compelled to favour their unjust designs, endeavoured to keep him from the senate, by engaging him in business for his friends, to plead their causes, or arbitrate in their differences, or the like, he quickly discovered the trick, and to defeat it, fairly told all his acquaintance that he would never meddle in any private business when the senate was assembled.

Since it was not in the hope of gaining honour or riches, nor out of mere impulse, or by chance that he engaged himself in politics, but he undertook the service of the state as the proper business of an honest man, and therefore he thought himself obliged to be as constant to his public duty as the bee to the honeycomb. To this end, he took care to have his friends and correspondents everywhere, to send him reports of the edicts, decrees, judgments, and all the important proceedings that passed in any of the provinces.

Once when Clodius, the seditious orator, to promote his violent and revolutionary projects, traduced to the people some of the priests and priestesses (among whom Fabia, sister to Cicero's wife, Terentia, ran great danger), Cato having boldly interfered, and having made Clodius appear so infamous that he was forced to leave the town, was addressed, when it was over, by Cicero, who came to thank him for what he had done. "You must thank the commonwealth," said he, for whose sake alone he professed to do everything.

Thus he gained a great and wonderful reputation; so that an advocate in a cause, where there was only one witness against him, told the judges they ought not to rely upon a single witness, though it were Cato himself. And it was a sort of proverb with many people, if any very unlikely and incredible thing were asserted, to say they would not believe it, though Cato himself should affirm it. One day a debauched and sumptuous liver talking in the senate about frugality and temperance, Anæus standing up, cried, "Who can endure this, sir, to have you feast like Crassus, build like Lucullus, and talk like Cato." So likewise those who were vicious and dissolute in their manners, yet affected to be grave and severe in their language, were in derision called Catos.

At first, when his friends would have persuaded him to stand to be tribune of the people, he thought it undesirable; for that the power of so great an office ought to be reserved, as the strongest medicines, for occasions of the last necessity. But afterwards in a vacation time, as he was going, accompanied with his books and philosophers, to Lucania, where he had lands with a pleasant residence, they met by the way a great many horses, carriages, and attendants, of whom they understood that Metellus Nepos was going to Rome, to stand to be tribune of the people. Hereupon Cato stopped, and after a little pause, gave orders to return back immediately; at which the company seeming to wonder, "Don't you know," said he, "how dangerous of itself the madness of Metellus is? And now that he comes armed with the support of Pompey, he will fall like lightning on the state, and bring it to utter disorder; therefore this is no time for idleness and diversion, but we must go and prevent this man in his designs, or bravely die in defence of our liberty." Nevertheless, by the persuasion of his friends, he went first to his countryhouse, where he stayed but a very little time, and then returned to town.

He arrived in the evening, and went straight the next morning to the Forum, where he began to solicit for the tribuneship, in opposition to Metellus. The power of this office consists rather in controlling than performing any business; for though all the rest except any one tribune should be agreed, yet his denial or intercession could put a stop to the whole matter. Cato, at first, had not many that appeared for him; but as soon as his design was known, all the good and distinguished persons of the city quickly came forward to encourage and support him, looking upon him, not as one that desired a favour of them, but one that proposed to do a great favour to his country and all honest men; who had many times refused the same office, when he might have had it without trouble, but now sought it with danger, that he might defend their liberty and their government. It is reported that so great a number flocked about him that he was like to be stifled amidst the press, and could scarce get through the crowd. He was declared tribune, with several others, among whom was Metellus.

When Cato was chosen into this office, observing that the election of consuls was become a matter of purchase, he sharply rebuked the people for this corruption, and in the conclusion of his speech protested he would bring to trial whomever he should find giving money, making an exception only in the case of Silanus, on account of their near connection, he having married Servilia, Cato's sister. He therefore did not prosecute him, but accused Lucius Murena, who had been chosen consul by corrupt means with Silanus. There was a law that the party accused might appoint a person to keep watch upon his accuser, that he might know fairly what means he took in preparing the accusation. He that was set upon Cato by Murena, at first followed and observed him strictly, yet never found him dealing any way unfairly or insidiously, but always generously and candidly going on in the just and open methods of proceeding. And he so admired Cato's great spirit, and so entirely trusted to his integrity, that meeting him in the Forum, or going to his house, he would ask him if he designed to do anything that day in order to the accusation, and if Cato said no, he went away, relying on his word.

When the cause was pleaded, Cicero, who was then consul and defended Murena, took occasion to be extremely witty and jocose, in reference to Cato, upon the Stoic philosophers, and their paradoxes, as they call them, and so excited great laughter among the judges; upon which Cato, smiling, said to the standersby, "What a pleasant consul we have, my friends." Murena was acquitted, and afterwards showed himself a man of no ill-feeling or want of sense; for when he was consul, he always took Cato's advice in the most weighty affairs and, during all the time of his office, paid him much honour and respect. Of which not only Murena's prudence, but also Cato's own behaviour, was the cause; for though he were terrible and severe as to matters of justice, in the senate, and at the bar, yet after the thing was over his manner to all men was perfectly friendly and humane.

Before he entered on the office of tribune, he assisted Cicero, at that time consul, in many contests that concerned his office, but most especially in his great and noble acts at the time of Catiline's conspiracy; which owed their last successful issue to Cato. Catiline had plotted a dreadful and entire subversion of the Roman state by sedition and open war, but being convicted by Cicero, was forced to fly the city. Yet Lentulus and Cethegus remained, with several others, to carry on the same plot; and blaming Catiline, as one that wanted courage, and had been timid and petty in his designs, they themselves resolved to set the whole town on fire, and utterly to overthrow the empire, rousing whole nations to revolt and exciting foreign wars. But the design was discovered by Cicero (as we have written in his life), and the matter brought before the senate.

Silanus, who spoke first, delivered his opinion, that the conspirators ought to suffer the last of punishments, and was therein followed by all who spoke after him; till it came to Cæsar, who being an excellent speaker, and looking upon all changes and commotions in the state as materials useful for his own purposes, desired rather to increase than extinguish them; and standing up, he made a very merciful and persuasive speech, that they ought not to suffer death without fair trial according to law, and moved that they might be kept in prison. Thus was the house almost wholly turned by Cæsar, apprehending also the anger of the people; insomuch that even Silanus retracted, and said he did not mean to propose death, but imprisonment, for that was the utmost a Roman could suffer.

Upon this they were all inclined to the milder and more merciful opinion, when Cato, standing up, began at once with great passion and vehemence to reproach Silanus for his change of opinion, and to attack Cæsar, who would, he said, ruin the commonwealth by soft words and popular speeches, and was endeavouring to frighten the senate, when he himself ought to fear, and be thankful, if he escaped unpunished or unsuspected, who thus openly and boldly dared to protect the enemies of the state, and while finding no compassion for his own native country, brought, with all its glories, so near to utter ruin, could yet be full of pity for those men who had better never have been born, and whose death must deliver the commonwealth from bloodshed and destruction.

This only of all Cato's speeches, it is said, was preserved; for Cicero, the consul, had disposed in various parts of the senate-house, several of the most expert and rapid writers, whom he had taught to make figures comprising numerous words in a few short strokes; as up to that time they had not used those we call shorthand writers, who then, as it is said, established the first example of the art.

Thus Cato carried it, and so turned the house again, that it was decreed the conspirators should be put to death.

Not to omit any small matters that may serve to show Cato's temper, and add something to the portraiture of his mind, it is reported, that while Cæsar and he were in the very heat, and the whole senate regarding them both, a little note was brought in to Cæsar which Cato declared to be suspicious, and urging that some seditious act was going on, bade the letter be read. Upon which Cæsar handed the paper to Cato; who, discovering it to be a love-letter from his sister Servilia to Cæsar, by whom she had been corrupted, threw it to him again, saying, "Take it, drunkard," and so went on with his discourse.

And, indeed, it seems Cato had but ill-fortune in women; for this lady was ill-spoken of for her familiarity with Cæsar, and the other Servilla, Cato's sister also, was yet more ill-conducted; for being married to Lucullus, one of the greatest men in Rome, and having brought him a son, she was afterwards divorced for incontinency. But what was worst of all, Cato's own wife Atilia was not free from the same fault; and after she had borne him two children, he was forced to put her away for her misconduct. After that, he married Marcia, the daughter of Philippus, a woman of good reputation, who yet has occasioned much discourse; and the life of Cato, like a dramatic piece, has this one scene or passage full of perplexity and doubtful meaning.

It is thus related by Thrasea, who refers to the authority of Munatius, Cato's friend and constant companion. Among many that loved and admired Cato, some were more remarkable and conspicuous than others. Of these was Quintus Hortensius, a man of high repute and approved virtue, who desired not only to live in friendship and familiarity with Cato, but also to unite his whole house and family with him by some sort or other of alliance in marriage. Therefore he set himself to persuade Cato that his daughter Porcia, who was already married to Bibulus, and had borne him two children, might nevertheless be given to him as a fair plot of land, to bear fruit also for him.

"For," said he, "though this in the opinion of men may seem strange, yet in nature it is honest and profitable for the public that a woman in the prime of her youth should not lie useless, and lose the fruit of her womb, nor, on the other side, should burden and impoverish one man, by bringing him too many children. Also by this communication of families among worthy men, virtue would increase, and be diffused through their posterity; and the commonwealth would be united and cemented by their alliances."

Yet if Bibulus would not part with his wife altogether, he would restore her as soon as she had brought him a child, whereby he might be united to both their families. Cato answered, that he loved Hortensius very well, and much approved of uniting their houses, but he thought it strange to speak of marrying his daughter, when she was already given to another. Then Hortensius, turning the discourse, did not hesitate to speak openly and ask for Cato's own wife, for she was young and fruitful, and he had already children enough. Neither can it be thought that Hortensius did this, as imagining Cato did not care for Marcia; for, it is said, she was then with child. Cato, perceiving his earnest desire, did not deny his request, but said that Philippus, the father of Marcia, ought also to be consulted. Philippus, therefore, being sent for, came; and finding they were well agreed, gave his daughter Marcia to Hortensius in the presence of Cato, who himself also assisted at the marriage. This was done at a later time, but since I was speaking of women, I thought it well to mention it now.

Lentulus and the rest of the conspirators were put to death; but Cæsar, finding so much insinuated and charged against him in the senate, betook himself to the people, and proceeded to stir up the most corrupt and dissolute elements of the state to form a party in his support. Cato, apprehensive of what might ensue, persuaded the senate to win over the poor and unprovided-for multitude by a distribution of corn, the annual charge of which amounted to twelve hundred and fifty talents. This act of humanity and kindness unquestionably dissipated the present danger. But Metellus, coming into his office of tribune, began to hold tumultuous assemblies, and had prepared a decree that Pompey the Great should presently be called into Italy, with all his forces, to preserve the city from the danger of Catiline's conspiracy. This was the fair pretence; but the true design was to deliver all into the hands of Pompey, and to give him an absolute power.

Upon this the senate was assembled, and Cato did not fall sharply upon Metellus, as he often did, but urged his advice in the most reasonable and moderate tone. At last he descended even to entreaty, and extolled the house of Metellus as having always taken part with the nobility. At this Metellus grew the more insolent, and despising Cato, as if he yielded and were afraid, let himself proceed to the most audacious menaces, openly threatening to do whatever he pleased in spite of the senate. Upon this Cato changed his countenance, his voice, and his language; and after many sharp expressions, boldly concluded that, while he lived, Pompey should never come armed into the city. The senate thought them both extravagant, and not well in their safe senses; for the design of Metellus seemed to be mere rage and frenzy, out of excess of mischief bringing all things to ruin and confusion, and Cato's virtue looked like a kind of ecstasy of contention in the cause of what was good and just.

But when the day came for the people to give their voices for the passing this decree, and Metellus beforehand occupied the Forum with armed men, strangers, gladiators, and slaves, those that in hopes of change followed Pompey were known to be no small part of the people, and besides, they had great assistance from Cæsar, who was then prætor; and though the best and chiefest men of the city were no less offended at these proceedings than Cato, they seemed rather likely to suffer with him than able to assist him. In the meantime Cato's whole family were in extreme fear and apprehension for him; some of his friends neither ate nor slept all the night, passing the whole time in debating the perplexity; his wife and sisters also bewailed and lamented him. But he himself, void of all fear, and full of assurance, comforted and encouraged them by his own words and conversation with them. After supper he went to rest at his usual hour, and was the next day waked out of a profound sleep by Minucius Thermus, one of his colleagues.

So soon as he was up, they two went together into the Forum, accompanied by very few, but met by a great many, who bade them have a care of themselves. Cato, therefore, when he saw the temple of Castor and Pollux encompassed with armed men, and the steps guarded by gladiators, and at the top Metellus and Cæsar seated together, turning to his friends, "Behold," said he, "this audacious coward, who has levied a regiment of soldiers against one unarmed naked man"; and so he went on with Thermus. Those who kept the passages gave way to these two only, and would not let anybody else pass. Yet Cato taking Munatius by the hand, with much difficulty pulled him through along with him. Then going directly to Metellus and Cæsar, he sat himself down between them, to prevent their talking to one another, at which they were both amazed and confounded. And those of the honest party, observing the countenance, and admiring the high spirit and boldness of Cato, went nearer, and cried out to him to have courage, exhorting also one another to stand together, and not betray their liberty nor the defender of it.

Then the clerk took out the bill, but Cato forbade him to read it, whereupon Metellus took it, and would have read it himself, but Cato snatched the book away. Yet Metellus, having the decree by heart, began to recite it without book; but Thermus put his hand to his mouth, and stopped his speech. Metellus seeing them fully bent to withstand him, and the people cowed, and inclining to the better side, sent to his house for armed men. And on their rushing in with great noise and terror, all the rest dispersed and ran away, except Cato, who alone stood still, while the other party threw sticks and stones at him from above, until Murena, whom he had formerly accused, came up to protect him, and holding his gown before him, cried out to them to leave off throwing; and, in fine, persuading and pulling him along, he forced him into the temple of Castor and Pollux.

Metellus, now seeing the place clear, and all the adverse party fled out of the Forum, thought he might easily carry his point; so he commanded the soldiers to retire, and recommencing in an orderly manner, began to proceed to passing the decree. But the other side having recovered themselves, returned very boldly, and with loud shouting, insomuch that Metellus's adherents were seized with a panic, supposing them to be coming with a reinforcement of armed men, fled every one out of the place. They being thus dispersed, Cato came in again, and confirmed the courage, and commended the resolution of the people; so that now the majority were, by all means, for deposing Metellus from his office. The senate also being assembled, gave orders once more for supporting Cato, and resisting the motion as of a nature to excite sedition and perhaps civil war in the city.

But Metellus continued still very bold and resolute; and seeing his party stood greatly in fear of Cato, whom they looked upon as invincible, he hurried out of the senate into the Forum, and assembled the people, to whom he made a bitter and invidious speech against Cato, crying out, he was forced to fly from his tyranny, and this conspiracy against Pompey; that the city would soon repent their having dishonoured so great a man. And from hence he started to go to Asia, with the intention, as would be supposed, of laying before Pompey all the injuries that were done him. Cato was highly extolled for having delivered the state from this dangerous tribuneship, and having in some measure defeated, in the person of Metellus, the power of Pompey; but he was yet more commended when, upon the senate proceeding to disgrace Metellus and depose him from his office, he altogether opposed and at length diverted the design. The common people admired his moderation and humanity, in not trampling wantonly on an enemy whom he had overthrown, and wiser men acknowledged his prudence and policy in not exasperating Pompey.

Lucullus soon after returned from the war in Asia, the finishing of which, and thereby the glory of the whole, was thus, in all appearance, taken out of his hands by Pompey. And he was also not far from losing his triumph, for Caius Memmius traduced him to the people, and threatened to accuse him; rather, however, out of love to Pompey, than for any particular enmity to him. But Cato, being allied to Lucullus, who had married his sister Servilia, and also thinking it a great injustice, opposed Memmius, thereby exposing himself to much slander and misrepresentation, insomuch that they would have turned him out of his office, pretending that he used his power tyrannically. Yet at length Cato so far prevailed against Memmius that he was forced to let fall the accusations, and abandon the contest. And Lucullus having thus obtained his triumph, yet more sedulously cultivated Cato's friendship, which he looked upon as a great guard and defence for him against Pompey's power.

And now Pompey also returning with glory from the war, and confiding in the good-will of the people, shown in their splendid reception of him, thought he should be denied nothing, and sent therefore to the senate to put off the assembly for the election of consuls, till he could be present to assist Piso, who stood for that office. To this most of the senators were disposed to yield; Cato only, not so much thinking that this delay would be of great importance, but desiring to cut down at once Pompey's high expectations and designs, withstood his request, and so overruled the senate that it was carried against him.

This not a little disturbed Pompey, who found he should very often fail in his projects unless he could bring over Cato to his interest. He sent, therefore, for Munatius, his friend; and Cato having two nieces that were marriageable, he offered to marry the eldest himself, and take the youngest for his son. Some say they were not his nieces, but his daughters. Munatius proposed the matter to Cato, in presence of his wife and sisters; the women were full of joy at the prospect of an alliance with so great and important a person. But Cato, without delay or balancing, forming his decision at once, answered, "Go, Munatius, go and tell Pompey that Cato is not assailable on the side of the women's chamber; I am grateful indeed for the intended kindness, and so long as his actions are upright, I promise him a friendship more sure than any marriage alliance, but I will not give hostages to Pompey's glory against my country's safety."

This answer was very much against the wishes of the women, and to all his friends it seemed somewhat harsh and haughty. But afterwards, when Pompey, endeavouring to get the consulship for one of his friends, gave pay to the people for their votes, and the bribery was notorious, the money being counted out in Pompey's own gardens, Cato then said to the women, they must necessarily have been concerned in the contamination of these misdeeds of Pompey, if they had been allied to his family; and they acknowledged that he did best in refusing it.

Yet if we may judge by the event, Cato was much to blame in rejecting that alliance, which thereby fell to Cæsar. And then that match was made, which, uniting his and Pompey's power, had well-nigh ruined the Roman empire, and did destroy the commonwealth. Nothing of which, perhaps, had come to pass, but that Cato was too apprehensive of Pompey's least faults, and did not consider how he forced him into conferring on another man the opportunity of committing the greatest.

These things, however, were yet to come. Lucullus and Pompey, meantime, had a great dispute concerning their orders and arrangements in Pontus, each endeavouring that his own ordinances might stand. Cato took part with Lucullus, who was manifestly suffering wrong; and Pompey, finding himself the weaker in the senate, had recourse to the people, and to gain votes he proposed a law for dividing the lands among the soldiers. Cato opposing him in this also made the bill be rejected. Upon this he joined himself with Clodius, at that time the most violent of all the demagogues, and entered also into friendship with Cæsar, upon an occasion of which also Cato was the cause.

For Cæsar, returning from his government in Spain, at the same time sued to be chosen consul, and yet desired not to lose his triumph. Now the law requiring that those who stood for any office should be present, and yet that whoever expected a triumph should continue without the walls, Cæsar requested the senate that his friends might be permitted to canvass for him in his absence. Many of the senators were willing to consent to it, but Cato opposed it, and perceiving them inclined to favour Cæsar, spent the whole day in speaking, and so prevented the senate from coming to any conclusion. Cæsar, therefore, resolving to let fall his pretensions to the triumph, came into the town, and immediately made a friendship with Pompey, and stood for the consulship. As soon as he was declared consul elect, he married his daughter Julia to Pompey.

And having thus combined themselves together against the commonwealth, the one proposed laws for dividing the lands among the poor people, and the other was present to support the proposals. Lucullus, Cicero, and their friends, joined with Bibulus, the other consul, to hinder their passing, and, foremost of them all, Cato, who already looked upon the friendship and alliance of Pompey and Cæsar as very dangerous, declared he did not so much dislike the advantage the people should get by this division of the lands, as he feared the reward these men would gain, by thus courting and cozening the people. And in this he gained over the senate to his opinion, as likewise many who were not senators, who were offended at Cæsar's ill conduct, that he, in the office of consul, should thus basely and dishonourably flatter the people; practising, to win their favour, the same means that were wont to be used only by the most rash and rebellious tribunes.

Cæsar, therefore, and his party, fearing they should not carry it by fair dealing, fell to open force. First a basket of dung was thrown upon Bibulus as he was going to the Forum; then they set upon his lictors and broke their rods; at length several darts were thrown, and many men wounded; so that all that were against those laws fled out of the Forum, the rest with what haste they could, and Cato, last of all, walking out slowly, often turning back and calling down vengeance upon them.

Thus the other party not only carried their point of dividing the lands, but also ordained that all the senate should swear to confirm this law, and to defend it against whoever should attempt to alter it, inflicting great penalties on those that should refuse the oath. All these senators, seeing the necessity they were in, took the oath, remembering the example of Metellus in old time, who, refusing to swear upon the like occasion, was forced to leave Italy.

As for Cato, his wife and children with tears besought him, his friends and familiars persuaded and entreated him, to yield and take the oath; but he that principally prevailed with him was Cicero, the orator, who urged upon him that it was perhaps not even right in itself, that a private man should oppose what the public had decreed; that the thing being already past altering, it were folly and madness to throw himself into danger without the chance of doing his country any good; it would be the greatest of all evils to embrace, as it were, the opportunity to abandon the commonwealth, for whose sake he did everything, and to let it fall into the hands of those who designed nothing but its ruin, as if he were glad to be saved from the trouble of defending it. "For," said he, "though Cato have no need of Rome, yet Rome has need of Cato, and so likewise have all his friends." Of whom Cicero professed he himself was the chief, being at that time aimed at by Clodius, who openly threatened to fall upon him, as soon as ever he should get to be tribune.

Thus Cato, they say, moved by the entreaties and the arguments of his friends, went unwillingly to take the oath, which he did the last of all, except only Favonius, one of his intimate acquaintance.

Cæsar, exalted with this success, proposed another law, for dividing almost all the country of Campania among the poor and needy citizens. Nobody durst speak against it but Cato, whom Cæsar therefore pulled from the rostra and dragged to prison: yet Cato did not even thus remit his freedom of speech, but as he went along continued to speak against the law, and advised the people to put down all legislators who proposed the like. The senate and the best of the citizens followed him with sad and dejected looks, showing their grief and indignation by their silence, so that Cæsar could not be ignorant how much they were offended; but for contention's sake he still persisted, expecting Cato should either supplicate him, or make an appeal. But when he saw that he did not so much as think of doing either, ashamed of what he was doing and of what people thought of it, he himself privately bade one of the tribunes interpose and procure his release.

However, having won the multitude by these laws and gratifications, they decreed that Cæsar should have the government of Illyricum, and all Gaul, with an army of four legions, for the space of five years, though Cato still cried out they were, by their own vote, placing a tyrant in their citadel. Publius Clodius, a patrician, who illegally became a plebeian, was declared tribune of the people, as he had promised to do all things according to their pleasure, on condition he might banish Cicero. And for consuls, they set up Calpurnius Piso, the father of Cæsar's wife, and Aulus Gabinius, one of Pompey's creatures, as they tell us, who best knew his life and manners.

Yet when they had thus firmly established all things, having mastered one part of the city by favour, and the other by fear, they themselves were still afraid of Cato, and remembered with vexation what pains and trouble their success over him had cost them, and indeed what shame and disgrace, when at last they were driven to use violence to him. This made Clodius despair of driving Cicero out of Italy while Cato stayed at home. Therefore, having first laid his design, as soon as he came into his office, he sent for Cato, and told him that he looked upon him as the most incorrupt of all the Romans, and was ready to show he did so. "For whereas," said he, "many have applied to be sent to Cyprus on the commission in the case of Ptolemy and have solicited to have the appointment, I think you alone are deserving of it, and I desire to give you the favour of the appointment."

Cato at once cried out it was a mere design upon him, and no favour, but an injury. Then Clodius proudly and fiercely answered, "If you will not take it as a kindness, you shall go, though never so unwillingly"; and immediately going into the assembly of the people he made them pass a decree, that Cato should be sent to Cyprus. But they ordered him neither ship, nor soldier, nor any attendant, except two secretaries, one of whom was a thief and a rascal, and the other a retainer to Clodius. Besides, as if Cyprus and Ptolemy were not work sufficient, he was ordered also to restore the refugees of Byzantium. For Clodius was resolved to keep him far enough off whilst he himself continued tribune.

Cato, being in this necessity of going away, advised Cicero, who was next to be set upon, to make no resistance, lest he should throw the state into civil war and confusion, but to give way to the times, and thus become once more the preserver of his country. He himself sent forward Canidius, one of his friends, to Cyprus, to persuade Ptolemy to yield, without being forced; which if he did, he should want neither riches nor honour, for the Romans would give him the priesthood of the goddess at Paphos. He himself stayed at Rhodes,

making some preparations, and expecting an answer from Cyprus.

In the meantime, Ptolemy, King of Egypt, who had left Alexandria, upon some quarrel between him and his subjects, and was sailing for Rome, in hopes that Pompey and Cæsar would send troops to restore him, in his way thither desired to see Cato, to whom he sent, supposing he would come to him. Cato had taken purging medicine at the time when the messenger came, and made answer that Ptolemy had better come to him, if he thought fit. And when he came, he neither went forward to meet him, nor so much as rose up to him, but saluting him as an ordinary person, bade him sit down.

This at once threw Ptolemy into some confusion, who was surprised to see such stern and haughty manners in one who made so plain and unpretending an appearance; but afterwards, when he began to talk about his affairs, he was no less astonished at the wisdom and freedom of his discourse. For Cato blamed his conduct, and pointed out to him what honour and happiness he was abandoning, and what humiliations and troubles he would run himself into; what bribery he must resort to, and what cupidity he would have to satisfy when he came to the leading men at Rome, whom all Egypt turned into silver would scarcely content. He therefore advised him to return home, and be reconciled to his subjects, offering to go along with him, and assist him in composing the differences.

And by this language Ptolemy being brought to himself, as it might be out of a fit of madness or delirium, and discerning the truth and wisdom of what Cato said, resolved to follow his advice; but he was again over-persuaded by his friends to the contrary, and so, according to his first design, went to Rome. When he came there, and was forced to wait at the gate of one of the magistrates, he began to lament his folly in having rejected, rather, as it seemed to him, the oracle of a god than the advice merely of a good and wise man.

In the meantime, the other Ptolemy, in Cyprus, very luckily for Cato, poisoned himself. It was reported he had left great riches; therefore, Cato designing to go first to Byzantium, sent his nephew Brutus to Cyprus, as he would not wholly trust Canidius. Then, having reconciled the refugees and the people of Byzantium, he left the city in peace and quietness; and so sailed to Cyprus, where he found a royal treasure of plate, tables, precious stones and purple, all which was to be turned into ready money. And being determined to do everything with the greatest exactness, and to raise the price of everything to the utmost, to this end he was always present at selling the things, and went carefully into all the accounts. Nor would he trust to the usual customs of the market, but looked doubtfully upon all alike, the officers, criers, purchasers, and even his own friends; and so in fine he himself talked with the buyers, and urged them to bid high, and conducted in this manner the greatest part of the sales.

This mistrustfulness offended most of his friends, and in particular, Munatius, the most intimate of them all, became almost irreconcilable. And this afforded Cæsar the subject of his severest censures in the book he wrote against Cato. Yet Munatius himself relates, that the quarrel was not so much occasioned by Cato's mistrust, as by his neglect of him, and by his own jealousy of Canidius. For Munatius also wrote a book concerning Cato, which is the chief authority followed by Thrasea. Munatius says, that coming to Cyprus after the other, and having a very poor lodging provided for him, he went to Cato's house, but was not admitted, because he was engaged in private with Canidius; of which he afterwards complained in very gentle terms to Cato, but received a very harsh answer, that too much love, according to Theophrastus, often causes hatred; "and you," he said, "because you bear me much love, think you receive too little honour, and presently grow angry. I employ Canidius on account of his industry and his fidelity; he has been with me from the first, and I have found him to be trusted."

These things were said in private between those two; but Cato afterwards told Canidius what had passed, on being informed of which, Munatius would no more go to sup with him, and when he was invited to give his counsel, refused to come. Then Cato threatened to seize his goods, as was the custom in the case of those who were disobedient; but Munatius not regarding his threats, returned to Rome, and continued a long time thus discontented. But afterwards, when Cato was come back also, Marcia, who as yet lived with him, contrived to have them both invited to sup together at the house of one Barca; Cato came in last of all, when the rest were laid down, and asked where he should be. Barca answered him, where he pleased; then looking about, he said he would be near Munatius, and went and placed himself next to him; yet he showed him no other mark of kindness all the time they were at table together. But another time, at the entreaty of Marcia, Cato wrote to Munatius that he desired to speak with him. Munatius went to his house in the morning, and was kept by Marcia till all the company was gone; then Cato came, threw both his arms about him, and embraced him very kindly, and they were reconciled.

I have the more fully related this passage, for that I think the manners and tempers of men are more clearly discovered by things of this nature, than by great and conspicuous actions.

Cato got together little less than seven thousand talents of silver; but apprehensive of what might happen in so long a voyage by sea, he provided a great many coffers that held two talents and five hundred drachmas apiece; to each of these he fastened a long rope, and to the other end of the rope a piece of cork, so that if the ship should miscarry, it might be discovered whereabout the chests lay under water. Thus all the money, except a very little, was safely transported.

But he had made two books, in which all the accounts of his commission were carefully written out, and neither of these was preserved. For his freedman Philargyrus, who had the charge of one of them, setting sail from Cenchreæ, was lost, together with the ship and all her freight. And the other Cato himself kept safe till he came to Corcyra, but there he set up his tent in the market-place, and the sailors, being very cold in the night, made a great many fires, some of which caught the tents, so that they were burnt, and the book lost. And though he had brought with him several of Ptolemy's stewards, who could testify to his integrity, and stop the mouths of enemies and false accusers, yet the loss annoyed him, and he was vexed with himself about the matter, as he had designed them not so much for a proof of his own fidelity, as for a pattern of exactness to others.

The news did not fail to reach Rome that he was coming up the river. All the magistrates, the priests, and the whole senate, with great part of the people, went out to meet him; both the banks of the Tiber were covered with people; so that his entrance was in solemnity and honour not inferior to a triumph. But it was thought somewhat strange, and looked like wilfulness and pride, that when the consuls and prætors appeared, he did not disembark, nor stay to salute them, but rowed up the stream in a royal galley of six banks of oars, and stopped not till he brought his vessels to the dock. However, when the money was carried through the streets, the people much wondered at the vast quantity of it, and the senate being assembled, decreed him in honourable terms an extraordinary prætorship, and also the privilege of appearing at the public spectacles in a robe faced with purple. Cato declined all these honours, but declaring what diligence and fidelity he had found in Nicias, the steward of Ptolemy, he requested the senate to give him his freedom.

Philippus, the father of Marcia, was that year consul, and the authority and power of the office rested in a manner in Cato; for the other consul paid him no less regard for his virtue's sake than Philippus did on account of the connection between them. And Cicero, now being returned from his banishment, into which he was driven by Clodius, and having again obtained great credit among the people, went, in the absence of Clodius, and by force took away the records of his tribuneship, which had been laid up in the capitol. Hereupon the senate was assembled and Clodius complained of Cicero, who answered that Clodius was never legally tribune, and therefore whatever he had done was void, and of no authority.

But Cato interrupted him while he spoke, and at last standing up said that indeed he in no way justified or approved of Clodius's proceedings; but if they questioned the validity of what had been done in his tribuneship, they might also question what himself had done at Cyprus, for the expedition was unlawful, if he that sent him had no lawful authority: for himself, he thought Clodius was legally made tribune, who, by permission of the law, was from a patrician adopted into a plebeian family; if he had done ill in his office, he ought to be called to account for it, but the authority of the magistracy ought not to suffer for the faults of the magistrate. Cicero took this ill, and for a long time discontinued his friendship with Cato; but they were afterwards reconciled.

Pompey and Crassus, by agreement with Cæsar, who crossed the Alps to see them, had formed a design, that they two should stand to be chosen consuls a second time, and when they should be in their office, they would continue to Cæsar his government for five years more, and take to themselves the greatest provinces, with armies and money to maintain them. This seemed a plain conspiracy to sub-

vert the constitution and parcel out the empire. Several men of high character had intended to stand to be consuls that year, but upon the appearance of these great competitors, they all desisted, except only Lucius Domitius, who had married Porcia, the sister of Cato, and was by him persuaded to stand it out, and not abandon such an undertaking, which, he said, was not merely to gain the consulship, but to save the liberty of Rome.

In the meantime, it was the common topic among the more prudent part of the citizens, that they ought not to suffer the power of Pompey and Crassus to be united, which would then be carried beyond all bounds, and become dangerous to the state; that therefore one of them must be denied. For these reasons they took part with Domitius, whom they exhorted and encouraged to go on, assuring him that many who feared openly to appear for him, would privately assist him. Pompey's party fearing this, laid wait for Domitius, and set upon him as he was going before daylight, with torches, into the field. First, he that bore the light next before Domitius was knocked down and killed; then several others being wounded, all the rest fled, except Cato and Domitius, whom Cato held, though himself were wounded in the arm, and crying out, conjured the others to stay, and not, while they had any breath, forsake the defence of their liberty against those tyrants, who plainly showed with what moderation they were likely to use the power which they endeavoured to gain by such violence. But at length Domitius, also, no longer willing to face the danger, fled to his own house, and so Pompey and Crassus were declared elected.

Nevertheless, Cato would not give over, but resolved to stand himself to be prætor that year, which he thought would be some help to him in his design of opposing them; that he might not act as a private man, when he was to contend with public magistrates. Pompey and Crassus apprehended this; and fearing that the office of prætor in the person of Cato might be equal in authority to that of consul, they assembled the senate unexpectedly, without giving notice to a great many of the senators, and made an order, that those who were chosen prætors should immediately enter upon their office, without attending the usual time, in which, according to law, they might be accused, if they had corrupted the people with gifts. When by this order they had got leave to bribe freely, without being called to account, they set up their own friends and dependents to stand for the prætorship, giving money, and watching the people as they voted. Yet the virtue and reputation of Cato was like to triumph over all these stratagems; for the people generally felt it to be shameful that a price should be paid for the rejection of Cato, who ought rather to be paid himself to take upon him the office. So he carried it by the voices of the first tribe.

Hereupon Pompey immediately framed a lie, crying out it thundered; and straight broke up the assembly, for the Romans religiously observed this as a bad omen, and never concluded any matter after it had thundered. Before the next time, they had distributed larger bribes, and driving also the best men out of the field, by these foul means they procured Vatinius to be chosen prætor, instead of Cato. It is said, that those who had thus corruptly and dishonestly given their voices hurried, as if it were in flight, out of the field. The others staying together, and exclaiming at the event, one of the tribunes continued the assembly, and Cato standing up, as it were by inspiration, foretold all the miseries that afterwards befell the state, exhorted them to beware of Pompey and Crassus, who were guilty of such things, and had laid such designs, that they might well fear to have Cato prætor. When he had ended this speech, he was followed to his house by a greater number of people than all the new prætors elect put together.

Caius Trebonius now proposed the law for alloting provinces to the consuls, one of whom was to have Spain and Africa, the other Egypt and Syria, with full power of making war, and carrying it on both by sea and land, as they should think fit. When this was proposed, all others despaired of putting any stop to it, and neither did nor said anything against it. But Cato, before the voting began, went up into the place of speaking, and desiring to be heard, was with much difficulty allowed two hours to speak. Having spent that time in informing them and reasoning with them, and in foretelling to them much that was to come, he was not suffered to speak any longer; but as he was going on, a serjeant came and pulled him down; yet when he was down, he still continued speaking in a loud voice, and finding many to listen to him, and join in his indignation. Then the serjeant took him, and forced him out of the Forum; but as soon as he got loose, he returned again to the place of speaking, crying out to the people to stand by him.

When he had done thus several times, Trebonius grew very angry, and commanded him to be carried to prison; but the multitude followed him, and listened to the speech which he made to them as he went along; so that Trebonius began to be afraid again, and ordered him to be released.

Thus that day was expended, and the business staved off by Cato. But in the days succeeding, many of the citizens being overawed by fears and threats, and others won by gifts and favours, Aquillius, one of the tribunes, they kept by an armed force within the senate-house; Cato, who cried it thundered, they drove out of the Forum; many were wounded, and some slain; and at length by open force they passed the law. At this many were so incensed that they got together and were going to throw down the statues of Pompey; but Cato went and diverted them from that design.

Again, another law was proposed, concerning the provinces and legions of Cæsar. Upon this occasion Cato did not apply himself to the people, but appealed to Pompey himself; and told him, he did not consider now that he was setting Cæsar upon his own shoulders, who would shortly grow too weighty for him; and at length, not able to lay down the burden, nor yet to bear it any longer, he would precipitate both it and himself with it upon the commonwealth; and then he would remember Cato's advice, which was no less advantageous to him than just and honest in itself. Thus was Pompey often warned, but still disregarded and slighted it, never mistrusting Cæsar's change, and always confiding in his own power and good fortune.

Cato was made prætor the following year; but, it seems, he did not do more honour and credit to the office by his signal integrity than he disgraced and diminished it by his strange behaviour. For he would often come to the court without his shoes, and sit upon the bench without any undergarment, and in this attire would give judgment in capital causes, and upon persons of the highest rank. It is said, also, he used to drink wine after his morning meal, and then transact the business of his office; but this was wrongfully reported of him. The people were at that time extremely corrupted by the gifts of those who sought offices, and most made a constant trade of selling their voices.

Cato was eager utterly to root this corruption out of the commonwealth; he therefore persuaded the senate to make an order, that those who were chosen into any office, though nobody should accuse them, should be obliged to come into the court, and give account upon oath of their proceedings in their election. This was extremely obnoxious to those who stood for the offices, and yet more to those vast numbers who took the bribes. Insomuch that one morning, as Cato was going to the tribunal, a great multitude of people flocked together, and with loud cries and maledictions reviled him, and threw stones at him. Those that were about the tribunal presently fled, and Cato himself being forced thence, and jostled about in the throng, very narrowly escaped the stones that were thrown at him, and with much difficulty got hold of the rostra; where, standing up with a bold and undaunted countenance, he at once mastered the tumult, and silenced the clamour; and addressing them in fit terms for the occasion, was heard with great attention, and perfectly quelled the sedition. Afterwards, on the senate commending him for this, "But I," said he, "do not commend you for abandoning your prætor in danger, and bringing him no assistance."

In the meantime, the candidates were in great perplexity; for every one dreaded to give money himself, and yet feared lest his competitors should. At length they agreed to lay down one hundred and twenty-five thousand drachmas apiece, and then all of them to canvass fairly and honestly, on condition, that if any one was found to make use of bribery he should forfeit the money. Being thus agreed, they chose Cato to keep the stakes, and arbitrate the matter; to him they brought the sum concluded on, and before him subscribed the agreement. The money he did not choose to have paid for them, but took their securities who stood bound for them. Upon the day of election, he placed himself by the tribune who took the votes, and very watchfully observing all that passed, he discovered one who had broken the agreement, and immediately ordered him to pay his money to the rest. They, however, commending his justice highly, remitted the penalty, as thinking the discovery a sufficient punishment.

This raised, however, as much envy against Cato as it gained him reputation, and many were offended at his thus taking upon himself the whole authority of the senate, the courts of judicature, and the magistracies. For there is no virtue, the honour and credit for which procures a man more odium than that of justice; and this, because more than any other, it

acquires a man power and authority among the common people. For they only honour the valiant and admire the wise, while in addition they also love just men, and put entire trust and confidence in them. They fear the bold man, and mistrust the clever man, and moreover think them rather beholding to their natural complexion, than to any goodness of their will, for these excellences; they look upon valour as a certain natural strength of the mind, and wisdom as a constitutional acuteness; whereas a man has it in his power to be just, if he have but the will to be so, and therefore injustice is thought the most dishonourable, because it is least excusable.

Cato upon this account was opposed by all the great men, who thought themselves reproved by his virtue. Pompey especially looked upon the increase of Cato's credit as the ruin of his own power, and therefore continually set up men to rail against him. Among these was the seditious Clodius, now again united to Pompey, who declared openly, that Cato had conveyed away a great deal of the treasure that was found in Cyprus; and that he hated Pompey only because he refused to marry his daughter. Cato answered, that although they had allowed him neither horse nor man, he had brought more treasure from Cyprus alone, than Pompey had, after so many wars and triumphs, from the ransacked world; that he never sought the alliance of Pompey; not that he thought him unworthy of being related to him, but because he differed so much from him in things that concerned the commonwealth.

"For," said he, "I laid down the province that was given me, when I went out of my prætorship; Pompey, on the contrary, retains many provinces for himself, and he bestows many on others; and but now he sent Cæsar a force of six thousand men into Gaul, which Cæsar never asked the people for, nor had Pompey obtained their consent to give. Men, and horse, and arms, in any number, are become the mutual gifts of private men to one another; and Pompey, keeping the titles of commander and general, hands over the armies and provinces to others to govern, while he himself stays at home to preside at the contests of the canvass, and to stir up tumults at elections; out of the anarchy he thus creates amongst us, seeking, we see well enough, a monarchy for himself." Thus he retorted on Pompey.

He had an intimate friend and admirer of

the name of Marcus Favonius, much the same to Cato as we are told Apollodorus, the Phalerian, was in old time to Socrates, whose words used to throw him into perfect transports and ecstasies, getting into his head, like strong wine, and intoxicating him to a sort of frenzy. This Favonius stood to be chosen ædile, and was like to lose it; but Cato, who was there to assist him, observed that all the votes were written in one hand, and discovering the cheat, appealed to the tribunes, who stopped the election. Favonius was afterwards chosen ædile, and Cato, who assisted him in all things that belonged to his office, also undertook the care of the spectacles that were exhibited in the theatre; giving the actors crowns, not of gold, but of wild olive, such as used to be given at the Olympic games; and instead of the magnificent presents that were usually made, he offered to the Greeks beet root, lettuces, radishes, and pears; and to the Romans earthen pots of wine, pork, figs, cucumbers, and little faggots of wood. Some ridiculed Cato for his economy, others looked with respect on this gentle relaxation of his usual rigour and austerity. In fine, Favonius himself mingled with the crowd, and sitting among the spectators, clapped and applauded Cato, bade him bestow rewards on those who did well, and called on the people to pay their honours to him, as for himself he had placed his whole authority in Cato's hands.

At the same time, Curio, the colleague of Favonius, gave very magnificent entertainments in another theatre; but the people left his, and went to those of Favonius, which they much applauded, and joined heartily in the diversion, seeing him act the private man, and Cato the master of the shows, who, in fact, did all this in derision of the great expenses that others incurred, and to teach them, that in amusements men ought to seek amusement only, and the display of a decent cheerfulness, not great preparations and costly magnificence, demanding the expenditure of endless care and trouble about things of little concern.

After this, Scipio, Hypsæus, and Milo, stood to be consuls, and that not only with the usual and now recognised disorders of bribery and corruption, but with arms and slaughter, and every appearance of carrying their audacity and desperation to the length of actual civil war. Whereupon it was proposed that Pompey might be empowered to preside over that election. This Cato at first opposed, saying that the laws ought not to seek protection from Pompey, but Pompey from the laws. Yet the confusion lasting a long time, the Forum continually, as it were, besieged with three armies, and no possibility appearing of a stop being put to these disorders, Cato at length agreed that, rather than fall into the last extremity, the senate should freely confer all on Pompey; since it was necessary to make use of a lesser illegality as a remedy against the greatest of all, and better to set up a monarchy themselves than to suffer a sedition to continue that must certainly end in one.

Bibulus, therefore, a friend of Cato's, moved the senate to create Pompey sole consul; for that either he would re-establish the lawful government, or they should serve under the best master. Cato stood up, and, contrary to all expectation, seconded this motion, concluding that any government was better than mere confusion, and that he did not question but Pompey would deal honourably, and take care of the commonwealth thus committed to his charge. Pompey being hereupon declared consul, invited Cato to see him in the suburbs. When he came, he saluted and embraced him very kindly, acknowledged the favour he had done him, and desired his counsel and assistance in the management of this office. Cato made answer, that what he had spoken on any former occasion was not out of hate to Pompey, nor what he had now done out of love to him, but all for the good of the commonwealth; that in private, if he asked him, he would freely give his advice; and in public, though he asked him not, he would always speak his opinion.

And he did accordingly. For first, when Pompey made severe laws, for punishing and laying great fines on those who had corrupted the people with gifts, Cato advised him to let alone what was already passed, and to provide for the future; for if he should look up past misdemeanours, it would be difficult to know where to stop; and if he would ordain new penalties, it would be unreasonable to punish men by a law, which at that time they had not the opportunity of breaking. Afterwards, when many considerable men, and some of Pompey's own relations, were accused, and he grew remiss, and disinclined to the prosecution, Cato sharply reproved him, and urged him to proceed. Pompey had made a law, also, to forbid the custom of making commendatory orations in behalf of those that were accused; yet he himself wrote one for Munatius

Plancus, and sent it while the cause was pleading; upon which Cato, who was sitting as one of the judges, stopped his ears with his hands, and would not hear it read. Whereupon Plancus, before sentence was given, excepted against him, but was condemned notwithstanding.

And indeed Cato was a great trouble and perplexity to almost all that were accused of anything, as they feared to have him one of their judges, yet did not dare to demand his exclusion. And many had been condemned because, by refusing him, they seemed to show that they could not trust to their own innocence; and it was a reproach thrown in the teeth of some by their enemies, that they had not accepted Cato for their judge.

In the meanwhile, Cæsar kept close with his forces in Gaul, and continued in arms; and at the same time employed his gifts, his riches, and his friends above all things, to increase his power in the city. And now Cato's old admonitions began to rouse Pompey out of the negligent security in which he lay, into a sort of imagination of danger at hand; but seeing him slow and unwilling, and timorous to undertake any measures of prevention against Cæsar, Cato resolved himself to stand for the consulship, and presently force Cæsar either to lay down his arms or discover his intentions. Both Cato's competitors were persons of good position; Sulpicius, who was one, owed much to Cato's credit and authority in the city, and it was thought unhandsome and ungratefully done, to stand against him; not that Cato himself took it ill, "For it is no wonder," said he, "if a man will not yield to another, in that which he esteems the greatest good."

He had persuaded the senate to make an order, that those who stood for offices should themselves ask the people for their votes, and not solicit by others, nor take others about with them to speak for them, in their canvass. And this made the common people very hostile to him, if they were to lose not only the means of receiving money, but also the opportunity of obliging several persons, and so to become by his means both poor and less regarded. Besides this, Cato himself was by nature altogether unfit for the business of canvassing, as he was more anxious to sustain the dignity of his life and character than to obtain the office. Thus by following his own way of soliciting, and not suffering his friends to do those things which take away the multitude, he was rejected and lost the consulship.

But whereas, upon such occasions, not only those who missed the office, but even their friends and relations, used to feel themselves disgraced and humiliated, and observed a sort of mourning for several days after, Cato took it so unconcernedly that he anointed himself, and played at ball in the field, and after breakfasting, went into the Forum, as he used to do, without his shoes or his tunic, and there walked about with his acquaintance. Cicero blames him, for that when affairs required such a consul, he would not take more pains, nor condescend to pay some court to the people, as also because that he afterwards neglected to try again; whereas he had stood a second time to be chosen prætor. Cato answered that he lost the prætorship the first time, not by the voice of the people, but by the violence and corrupt dealing of his adversaries; whereas in the election of consuls there had been no foul play. So that he plainly saw the people did not like his manners, which an honest man ought not to alter for their sake; nor yet would a wise man attempt the same thing again, while liable to the same prejudices.

Cæsar was at this time engaged with many warlike nations, and was subduing them at great hazards. Among the rest, it was believed he had set upon the Germans, in a time of truce, and had thus slain three hundred thousand of them. Upon which, some of his friends moved the senate for a public thanksgiving; but Cato declared they ought to deliver Cæsar into the hands of those who had been thus unjustly treated, and so expiate the offence and not bring a curse upon the city; "Yet we have reason," said he, "to thank the gods, for that they spared the commonwealth, and did not take vengeance upon the army, for the madness and folly of the general."

Hereupon Cæsar wrote a letter to the senate which was read openly, and was full of reproachful language and accusations against Cato; who, standing up, seemed not at all concerned, and without any heat or passion, but in a calm and, as it were, premeditated discourse, made all Cæsar's charges against him show like mere common scolding and abuse, and in fact a sort of pleasantry and play on Cæsar's part; and proceeding then to go into all Cæsar's political courses, and to explain and reveal (as though he had been not his constant opponent, but his fellow-conspirator) his whole conduct and purpose from its commencement, he concluded by telling the senate, it was not the sons of the Britons or the Gauls they need fear, but Cæsar himself, if they were wise. And this discourse so moved and awakened the senate, that Cæsar's friends repented they had had a letter read, which had given Cato an opportunity of saying so many reasonable things, and such severe truths against him.

However, nothing was then decided upon; it was merely said, that it would be well to send him a successor. Upon that, Cæsar's friends required that Pompey also should lay down his arms, and resign his provinces, or else that Cæsar might not be obliged to either. Then Cato cried out, what he had foretold was come to pass; now it was manifest he was using his forces to compel their judgment, and was turning against the state those armies he had got from it by imposture and trickery. But out of the senate-house Cato could do but little, as the people were ever ready to magnify Cæsar; and the senate, though convinced by Cato, were afraid of the people.

But when the news was brought that Cæsar had seized Ariminum, and was marching with his army toward Rome, then all men, even Pompey, and the common people too, cast their eyes on Cato, who had alone foreseen and first clearly declared Cæsar's intentions. He therefore told them, "If you had believed me, or regarded my advice, you would not now have been reduced to stand in fear of one man, or to put all your hopes in one alone." Pompey acknowledged that Cato indeed had spoken most like a prophet, while he himself had acted too much like a friend. And Cato advised the senate to put all into the hands of Pompey; "For those who can raise up great evils," said he, "can best allay them."

Pompey, finding he had not sufficient forces, and that those he could raise were not very resolute, forsook the city. Cato, resolving to follow Pompey into exile, sent his younger son to Munatius, who was then in the country of Brutium, and took his eldest son with him; but wanting somebody to keep his house and take care of his daughters, he took Marcia again, who was now a rich widow, Hortensius being dead, and having left her all his estate. Cæsar afterward made use of this action also, to reproach him with covetousness, and a mercenary design in his marriage. "For," said he, "if he had need of a wife why did he part with her? And if he had not, why did he take her again? Unless he gave her

only as a bait to Hortensius; and lent her when she was young, to have her again when she was rich."

But in answer to this, we might fairly apply the saying of Euripides—

To speak of mysteries—the chief of these
Surely were cowardice in Hercules.

For it is much the same thing to reproach Hercules for cowardice, and to accuse Cato of covetousness; though otherwise, whether he did altogether right in this marriage, might be disputed. As soon, however, as he had again taken Marcia, he committed his house and his daughters to her, and himself followed Pompey. And it is said, that from that day he never cut his hair, nor shaved his beard, nor wore a garland, but was always full of sadness, grief, and dejectedness for the calamities of his country, and continually showed the same feeling to the last, whatever party had misfortune or success.

The government of Sicily being allotted to him, he passed over to Syracuse; where, understanding that Asinius Pollio was arrived at Messena, with forces from the enemy, Cato sent to him, to know the reason of his coming thither: Pollio, on the other side, called upon him to show reason for the present convulsions. And being at the same time informed how Pompey had quite abandoned Italy, and lay encamped at Dyrrhachium, he spoke of the strangeness and incomprehensibility of the divine government of things; "Pompey, when he did nothing wisely nor honestly, was always successful; and now that he would preserve his country, and defend her liberty, he is altogether unfortunate." As for Asinius, he said, he could drive him out of Sicily, but as there were larger forces coming to his assistance, he would not engage the island in a war. He therefore advised the Syracusans to join the conquering party and provide for their own safety; and so set sail from thence.

When he came to Pompey, he uniformly gave advice to protract the war; as he always hoped to compose matters, and was by no means desirous that they should come to action; for the commonwealth would suffer extremely, and be the certain cause of its own ruin, whoever were conqueror by the sword. In like manner, he persuaded Pompey and the council to ordain that no city should be sacked that was subject to the people of Rome; and that no Roman should be killed but in the heat of battle; and hereby he got himself great honour, and brought over many to Pompey's party, whom his moderation and humanity attracted. Afterwards being sent into Asia, to assist those who were raising men and preparing ships in those parts, he took with him his sister Servilia, and a little boy whom she had by Lucullus. For since her widowhood, she had lived with her brother, and much recovered her reputation, having put herself under his care, followed him in his voyages, and complied with his severe way of living. Yet Cæsar did not fail to asperse him upon her account also.

Pompey's officers in Asia, it seems, had no great need of Cato; but he brought over the people of Rhodes by his persuasions, and leaving his sister Servilia and her child there, he returned to Pompey, who had now collected very great forces both by sea and land. And here Pompey, more than in any other act, betrayed his intentions. For at first he designed to give Cato the command of the navy, which consisted of no less than five hundred ships of war, besides a vast number of light galleys, scouts, and open boats. But presently bethinking himself, or put in mind by his friends, that Cato's principal and only aim being to free his country from all usurpation, if he were master of such great forces, as soon as ever Cæsar should be conquered, he would certainly call upon Pompey, also, to lay down his arms, and be subject to the laws, he changed his mind, and though he had already mentioned it to Cato, nevertheless made Bibulus admiral.

Notwithstanding this, he had no reason to suppose that Cato's zeal in the cause was in any way diminished. For before one of the battles at Dyrrhachium, when Pompey himself, we are told, made an address to the soldiers and bade the officers do the like, the men listened to them but coldly and with silence, until Cato, last of all, came forward, and in the language of philosophy, spoke to them, as the occasion required, concerning liberty, manly virtue, death, and a good name; upon all which he delivered himself with strong natural passion, and concluded with calling in the aid of the gods, to whom he directed his speech, as if they were present to behold them fight for their country. And at this the army gave such a shout and showed such excitement that their officers led them on full of hope and confidence to the danger. Cæsar's party were routed and put to flight; but his presiding fortune used the advantage of Pompey's cautiousness and diffidence to render the victory incomplete. But of this we have spoken in the life of Pompey. While, however, all the rest rejoiced, and magnified their success, Cato alone bewailed his country, and cursed that fatal ambition which made so many brave Romans murder one another.

After this Pompey, following Cæsar into Thessaly, left at Dyrrhachium a quantity of munitions, money, and stores, and many of his domestics and relations; the charge of all which he gave to Cato, with the command only of fifteen cohorts. For though he trusted him much, yet he was afraid of him too, knowing full well, that if he had bad success, Cato would be the last to forsake him, but if he conquered, would never let him use his victory at his pleasure. There were, likewise, many persons of high rank that stayed with Cato at Dyrrhachium.

When they heard of the overthrow at Pharsalia, Cato resolved with himself, that if Pompey were slain, he would conduct those that were with him into Italy, and then retire as far from the tyranny of Cæsar as he could, and live in exile; but if Pompey were safe, he would keep the army together for him. With this resolution he passed over to Corcyra, where the navy lay; there he would have resigned his command to Cicero, because he had been consul, and himself only a prætor, but Cicero refused it, and was going for Italy. At which Pompey's son being incensed, would rashly and in heat have punished all those who were going away, and in the first place have laid hands on Cicero; but Cato spoke with him in private, and diverted him from that design. And thus he clearly saved the life of Cicero, and rescued several others also from ill-treatment.

Conjecturing that Pompey the Great was fled toward Egypt or Africa, Cato resolved to hasten after him; and having taken all his men aboard, he set sail; but first to those who were not zealous to continue the contest, he gave free liberty to depart. When they came to the coast of Africa they met with Sextus, Pompey's younger son, who told them of the death of his father in Egypt; at which they were all exceedingly grieved, and declared that after Pompey they would follow no other leader but Cato. Out of compassion, therefore, to so many worthy persons, who had given such testimonies of their fidelity, and whom he could not for shame leave in a desert country, amidst so many difficulties, he took upon himself the command, and marched against the city of Cyrene, which presently received him, though not long before they had shut their gates against Labienus. Here he was informed that Scipio, Pompey's father-in-law, was received by King Juba, and that Attius Varus, whom Pompey had made governor of Africa, had joined them with his forces. Cato therefore resolved to march toward them by land, it being now winter; and got together a number of asses to carry water, and furnished himself likewise with plenty of all other provision, and a number of carriages. He took also with him some of those they call Psylli, who cure the biting of serpents, by sucking out the poison with their mouths, and have likewise certain charms by which they stupefy and lay asleep the serpents.

Thus they marched seven days together, Cato all the time going on foot at the head of his men, and never making use of any horse or chariot. Ever since the battle of Pharsalia, he used to sit at table, and added this to his other ways of mourning, that he never lay down but to sleep.

Having passed the winter in Africa, Cato drew out his army, which amounted to little less than ten thousand. The affairs of Scipio and Varus went very ill, by reason of their dissensions and quarrels among themselves, and their submissions and flatteries to King Juba, who was insupportable for his vanity, and the pride he took in his strength and riches. The first time be came to a conference with Cato, he had ordered his own seat to be placed in the middle, between Scipio and Cato; which Cato observing, took up his chair and set himself on the other side of Scipio, to whom he thus gave the honour of sitting in the middle, though he were his enemy, and had formerly published some scandalous writing against him. There are people who speak as if this were quite an insignificant matter, and who, nevertheless, find fault with Cato, because in Sicily, walking one day with Philostratus, he gave him the middle place, to show his respect for philosophy.

However, he now succeeded both in humbling the pride of Juba, who was treating Scipio and Varus much like a pair of satraps under his orders, and also in reconciling them to each other. All the troops desired him to be their leader; Scipio, likewise, and Varus gave way to it, and offered him the command; but he said he would not break those laws which he sought to defend, and he, being but pro-

prietor, ought not to command in the presence of a proconsul (for Scipio had been created proconsul), besides that people took it as a good omen to see a Scipio command in Africa, and the very name inspired the soldiers with hopes of success.

Scipio, having taken upon himself the command, presently resolved, at the instigation of Juba, to put all the inhabitants of Utica to the sword, and to raze the city, for having, as they professed, taken part with Cæsar. Cato would by no means suffer this; but invoking the gods, exclaiming and protesting against it in the council of war, he with much difficulty delivered the poor people from this cruelty. And afterwards, upon the entreaty of the inhabitants, and at the instance of Scipio, Cato took upon himself the government of Utica, lest, one way or the other, it should fall into Cæsar's hands; for it was a strong place, and very advantageous for either party. And it was yet better provided and more strongly fortified by Cato, who brought in great store of corn, repaired the walls, erected towers, and made deep trenches and palisades around the town. The young men of Utica he lodged among these works, having first taken their arms from them; the rest of the inhabitants he kept within the town, and took the greatest care that no injury should be done nor affront offered them by the Romans. From hence he sent great quantity of arms, money, and provision to the camp, and made this city their chief magazine.

He advised Scipio, as he had before done Pompey, by no means to hazard a battle against a man experienced in war, and formidable in the field, but to use delay; for time would gradually abate the violence of the crisis, which is the strength of usurpation. But Scipio out of pride rejected this counsel, and wrote a letter to Cato, in which he reproached him with cowardice; and that he could not be content to lie secure himself within walls and trenches, but he must hinder others from boldly using their own good sense to seize the right opportunity. In answer to this, Cato wrote word again, that he would take the horse and foot which he had brought into Africa, and go over into Italy, to make a diversion there, and draw Cæsar off from them. But Scipio derided this proposition also.

Then Cato openly let it be seen that he was sorry he had yielded the command to Scipio, who he saw would not carry on the war with any wisdom, and if, contrary to all appearance, he should succeed, he would use his success as unjustly at home. For Cato had then made up his mind, and so he told his friends, that he could have but slender hopes in those generals that had so much boldness and so little conduct; yet if anything should happen beyond expectation, and Cæsar should be overthrown, for his part he would not stay at Rome, but would retire from the cruelty and inhumanity of Scipio, who had already uttered fierce and proud threats against many.

But what Cato had looked for fell out sooner than he expected. Late in the evening came one from the army, whence he had been three days coming, who brought word there had been a great battle near Thapsus; that all was utterly lost; Cæsar had taken the camps, Scipio and Juba were fled with a few only, and all the rest of the army was lost. This news arriving in time of war, and in the night, so alarmed the people, that they were almost out of their wits, and could scarce keep themselves within the walls of the city. But Cato came forward, and meeting the people in this hurry and clamour, did all he could to comfort and encourage them, and somewhat appeased the fear and amazement they were in, telling them that very likely things were not so bad in truth, but much exaggerated in the report. And so he pacified the tumult for the present.

The next morning he sent for the three hundred, whom he used as his council; these were Romans, who were in Africa upon business, in commerce and money-lending; they were also several senators and their sons. They were summoned to meet in the temple of Jupiter. While they were coming together, Cato walked about very quietly and unconcerned, as if nothing new had happened. He had a book in his hand, which he was reading; in this book was an account of what provision he had for war, armour, corn, ammunition, and soldiers.

When they were assembled, he began his discourse; first, as regarded the three hundred themselves, and very much commended the courage and fidelity they had shown, and their having very well served their country with their persons, money, and counsel. Then he entreated them by no means to separate, as if each single man could hope for any safety in forsaking his companions; on the contrary, while they kept together, Cæsar would have less reason to despise them, if they fought against him, and be more forward to pardon them, if they submitted to him. Therefore he advised them to consult among themselves, nor should he find fault whichever course they adopted. If they thought fit to submit to fortune, he would impute their change to necessity; but if they resolved to stand firm, and undertake the danger for the sake of liberty, he should not only commend, but admire their courage, and would himself be their leader and companion too, till they had put to the proof the utmost fortune of their country; which was not Utica or Adrumetum but Rome, and she had often, by her own greatness, raised herself after worse disasters.

Besides, as there were many things that would conduce to their safety, so chiefly this, that they were to fight against one whose affairs urgently claimed his presence in various quarters. Spain was already revolted to the younger Pompey; Rome was unaccustomed to the bridle, and impatient of it, and would therefore be ready to rise in insurrection upon any turn of affairs. As for themselves, they ought not to shrink from the danger; and in this might take example from their enemy, who so freely exposed his life to effect the most unrighteous designs, yet never could hope for so happy a conclusion as they might promise themselves; for notwithstanding the uncertainty of war, they would be sure of a most happy life if they succeeded, or a most glorious death if they miscarried. However, he said, they ought to deliberate among themselves; and he joined with them in praying the gods that in recompense of their former courage and goodwill, they would prosper their present determinations.

When Cato had thus spoken, many were moved and encouraged by his arguments, but the greatest part were so animated by the sense of his intrepidity, generosity, and goodness, that they forgot the present danger, and as if he were the only invincible leader, and above all fortune, they entreated him to employ their persons, arms, and estates, as he thought fit; for they esteemed it far better to meet death in following his counsel, than to find their safety in betraying one of so great virtue. One of the assembly proposed the making a decree to set the slaves at liberty; and most of the rest approved the motion. Cato said that it ought not to be done, for it was neither just nor lawful; but if any of their masters would willingly set them free, those that were fit for service should be received.

Many promised so to do, whose names he ordered to be enrolled, and then withdrew.

Presently after this he received letters from Juba and Scipio. Juba, with some few of his men, was retired to a mountain, where he waited to hear what Cato would resolve upon; and intended to stay there for him, if he thought fit to leave Utica, or to come to his aid with his troops, if he were besieged. Scipio was on shipboard, near a certain promontory, not far from Utica, expecting an answer upon the same account. But Cato thought fit to retain the messengers till the three hundred should come to some resolution.

As for the senators that were there, they showed great forwardness, and at once set free their slaves, and furnished them with arms. But the three hundred being men occupied in merchandise and money-lending, much of their substance also consisting in slaves, the enthusiasm that Cato's speech had raised in them did not long continue. As there are substances that easily admit heat, and as suddenly lose it, when the fire is removed, so these men were heated and inflamed while Cato was present; but when they began to reason among themselves, the fear they had of Cæsar soon overcame their reverence for Cato and for virtue.

"For who are we," said they, "and who is it we refuse to obey? Is it not that Cæsar who is now invested with all the power of Rome? and which of us is a Scipio, a Pompey, or a Cato? But now that all men make their honour give way to their fear, shall we alone engage for the liberty of Rome, and in Utica declare war against him, before whom Cato and Pompey the Great fled out of Italy? Shall we set free our slaves against Cæsar, who have ourselves no more liberty than he is pleased to allow? No, let us, poor creatures, know ourselves, submit to the victor, and send deputies to implore his mercy."

Thus said the most moderate of them; but the greatest part were for seizing the senators, that by securing them they might appease Cæsar's anger. Cato, though he perceived the change, took no notice of it; but wrote to Juba and Scipio to keep away from Utica, because he mistrusted the three hundred.

A considerable body of horse, which had escaped from the late fight, riding up towards Utica, sent three men before to Cato, who yet did not all bring the same message; for one party was for going to Juba, another for joining with Cato, and some again were afraid to go into Utica. When Cato heard this, he ordered Marcus Rubrius to attend upon the three hundred, and quietly take the names of those who, of their own accord, set their slaves at liberty, but by no means to force anybody. Then taking with him the senators, he went out of the town, and met the principal officers of these horsemen, whom he entreated not to abandon so many Roman senators, not to prefer Juba for their commander before Cato, but consult the common safety, and to come into the city, which was impregnable, and well furnished with corn and other provision, sufficient for many years. The senators likewise with tears besought them to stay. Hereupon the officers went to consult their soldiers, and Cato with the senators sat down upon an embankment, expecting their resolution. In the meantime came Rubrius in great disorder, crying out the three hundred were all in commotion and exciting revolt and tumult in the city. At this all the rest fell into despair, lamenting and bewailing their condition. Cato endeavoured to comfort them, and sent to the three hundred, desiring them to have patience.

Then the officers of the horse returned with no very reasonable demands. They said they did not desire to serve Juba for his pay, nor should they fear Cæsar, while they followed Cato, but they dreaded to be shut up with the Uticans, men of traitorous temper, and Carthaginian blood; for though they were quiet at present, yet as soon as Cæsar should appear, without doubt they would conspire together, and betray the Romans. Therefore, if he expected they should join with him, he must drive out of the town or destroy all the Uticans, that he might receive them into a place clear both of enemies and barbarians. This Cato thought utterly cruel and barbarous; but he mildly answered, he would consult the three hundred.

Then he returned to the city, where he found the men, not framing excuses, or dissembling out of reverence to him, but openly declaring that no one should compel them to make war against Cæsar; which, they said, they were neither able nor willing to do. And some there were who muttered words about retaining the senators till Cæsar's coming; but Cato seemed not to hear this, as indeed he had the excuse of being a little deaf. At the same time came one to him and told him the horse were going away. And now, fearing lest the three hundred should take some desperate resolution concerning the senators, he presently went out with some of his friends, and seeing they were gone some way, he took horse, and rode after them. They, when they saw him coming, were very glad, and received him very kindly, entreating him to save himself with them.

At this time, it is said, Cato shed tears, while entreating them on behalf of the senators, and stretching out his hands in supplication. He turned some of their horses' heads, and laid hold of the men by their armour, till in fine he prevailed with them out of compassion to stay only that one day, to procure a safe retreat for the senators. Having thus persuaded them to go along with him, some he placed at the gates of the town, and to others gave the charge of the citadel. The three hundred began to fear they should suffer for their inconstancy, and sent to Cato, entreating him by all means to come to them; but the senators flocking about him would not suffer him to go, and said they would not trust their guardian and saviour to the hands of perfidious traitors.

For there had never, perhaps, been a time when Cato's virtue appeared more manifestly; and every class of men in Utica could clearly see, with sorrow and admiration, how entirely free was everything that he was doing from any secret motives or any mixture of self-regard; he, namely, who had long before resolved on his own death, was taking such extreme pains, toil, and care, only for the sake of others, that when he had secured their lives, he might put an end to his own. For it was easily perceived that he had determined to die, though he did not let it appear.

Therefore, having pacified the senators, he complied with the request of the three hundred, and went to them alone without any attendance. They gave him many thanks, and entreated him to employ and trust them for the future; and if they were not Catos, and could not aspire to his greatness of mind, they begged he would pity their weakness; and told him they had determined to send to Cæsar and entreat him, chiefly and in the first place, for Cato, and if they could not prevail for him, they would not accept of pardon for themselves, but as long as they had breath, would fight in his defence. Cato commended their good intentions, and advised them to send speedily, for their own safety, but by no means to ask anything in his behalf; for those who are conquered, entreat, and those who

have done wrong, beg pardon; for himself, he did not confess to any defeat in all his life, but rather, so far as he had thought fit, he had got the victory, and had conquered Cæsar in all points of justice and honesty. It was Cæsar that ought to be looked upon as one surprised and vanquished; for he was now convicted and found guilty of those designs against his country, which he had so long practised and so constantly denied.

When he had thus spoken, he went out of the assembly, and being informed that Cæsar was coming with his whole army, "Ah," said he, "he expects to find us brave men." Then he went to the senators, and urged them to make no delay, but hasten to be gone, while the horsemen were yet in the city. So ordering all the gates to be shut, except one towards the sea, he assigned their several ships to those that were to depart, and gave money and provision to those that wanted; all which he did with great order and exactness, taking care to suppress all tumults, and that no wrong should be done to the people.

Marcus Octavius, coming with two legions, now encamped near Utica, sent to Cato to arrange about the chief command. Cato returned him no answer; but said to his friends, "Can we wonder all has gone ill with us, when our love of office survives even in our very ruin?" In the meantime, word was brought him, that the horse were going away, and were beginning to spoil and plunder the citizens. Cato ran to them, and from the first he met, snatched what they had taken; the rest threw down all they had gotten, and went away silent and ashamed of what they had done. Then he called together all the people of Utica, and requested them, upon the behalf of the three hundred, not to exasperate Cæsar against them, but all to seek their common safety together with them.

After that, he went again to the port to see those who were about to embark; and there he embraced and dismissed those of his friends and acquaintance whom he had persuaded to go. As for his son, he did not counsel him to be gone, nor did he think fit to persuade him to forsake his father. But there was one Statyllius, a young man, in the flower of his age, of a brave spirit, and very desirous to imitate the constancy of Cato. Cato entreated him to go away, as he was a noted enemy to Cæsar, but without success. Then Cato looked at Apollonides, the stoic philosopher, and Demetrius, the peripatetic; "It belongs to you to cool the fever of this young man's spirit, and to make him know what is good for him." And thus, in setting his friends upon their way, and in despatching the business of any that applied to him, he spent that night and the greatest part of the next day.

Lucius Cæsar, a kinsman of Cæsar's, being appointed to go deputy for the three hundred, came to Cato, and desired he would assist him to prepare a persuasive speech for them; "And as to you yourself," said he, "it will be an honour for me to kiss the hands and fall at the knees of Cæsar, in your behalf." But Cato would by no means permit him to do any such thing; "For as to myself," said he, "if I would be preserved by Cæsar's favour, I should myself go to him; but I would not be beholden to a tyrant for his acts of tyranny. For it is but usurpation in him to save, as their rightful lord, the lives of men over whom he has no title to reign. But if you please, let us consider what you had best say for the three hundred." And when they had continued some time together, as Lucius was going away, Cato recommended to him his son and the rest of his friends; and taking him by the hand bade him farewell.

Then he retired to his house again, and called together his son and his friends, to whom he conversed on various subjects; among the rest he forbade his son to engage himself in the affairs of state. For to act therein as became him was now impossible; and to do otherwise, would be dishonourable. Toward evening he went into his bath. As he was bathing, he remembered Statyllius and called out aloud, "Apollonides, have you tamed the high spirit of Statyllius, and is he gone without bidding us farewell?" "No," said Apollonides, "I have said much to him, but to little purpose; he is still resolute and unalterable, and declares he is determined to follow your example." At this, it is said, Cato smiled, and answered, "That will soon be tried."

After he had bathed, he went to supper, with a great deal of company; at which he sat up, as he had always used to do ever since the battle of Pharsalia; for since that time he never lay down but when he went to sleep. There supped with him all his own friends and the magistrates of Utica.

After supper, the wine produced a great deal of lively and agreeable discourse, and a whole series of philosophical questions was discussed. At length they came to the strange dogmas of the stoics, called their Paradoxes;

and to this in particular, That the good man only is free, and that all wicked men are slaves. The peripatetic, as was to be expected, opposing this, Cato fell upon him very warmly; and somewhat raising his voice, he argued the matter at great length, and urged the point with such vehemence, that it was apparent to everybody he was resolved to put an end to his life, and set himself at liberty. And so, when he had done speaking, there was a great silence and evident dejection. Cato, therefore, to divert them from any suspicion of his design, turned the conversation, and began again to talk of matters of present interest and expectation, showing great concern for those that were at sea, as also for the others, who, travelling by land, were to pass through a dry and barbarous desert.

When the company was broke up, he walked with his friends, as he used to do after supper, gave the necessary orders to the officers of the watch, and going into his chamber, he embraced his son and every one of his friends with more than usual warmth, which again renewed their suspicion of his design. Then laying himself down, he took into his hand Plato's dialogue concerning the soul. Having read more than half the book, he looked up, and missing his sword, which his son had taken away while he was at supper, he called his servant, and asked who had taken away his sword. The servant making no answer, he fell to reading again; and a little after, not seeming importunate, or hasty for it, but as if he would only know what had become of it, he bade it be brought. But having waited some time, when he had read through the book, and still nobody brought the sword, he called up all his servants, and in a louder tone demanded his sword. To one of them he gave such a blow in the mouth, that he hurt his own hand; and now grew more angry, exclaiming that he was betrayed and delivered naked to the enemy by his son and his servants.

Then his son, with the rest of his friends, came running into the room, and falling at his feet, began to lament and beseech him. But Cato, raising himself and looking fiercely: "When," said he, "and how did I become deranged, and out of my senses, that thus no one tries to persuade me by reason, or show me what is better, if I am supposed to be ill-advised? Must I be disarmed, and hindered from using my own reason? And you, young man, why do you not bind your father's hands behind him that, when Cæsar comes, he may find me unable to defend myself? To despatch myself I want no sword; I need but hold my breath awhile, or strike my head against the wall."

When he had thus spoken, his son went weeping out of the chamber, and with him all the rest, except Demetrius and Apollonides, to whom, being left alone with him, he began to speak more calmly. "And you," said he," do you also think to keep a man of my age alive by force, and to sit here and silently watch me? Or do you bring me some reasons to prove that it will not be base and unworthy for Cato, when he can find his safety no other way, to seek it from his enemy? If so, adduce your arguments, and show cause why we should now unlearn what we formerly were taught, in order that rejecting all the convictions in which we lived, we may now by Cæsar's help grow wiser, and be yet more obliged to him than for life only. Not that I have determined aught concerning myself, but I would have it in my power to perform what I shall think fit to resolve; and I shall not fail to take you as my advisers, in holding counsel, as I shall do, with the doctrines which your philosophy teaches; in the meantime, do not trouble yourselves, but go tell my son that he should not compel his father to what he cannot persuade him to."

They made him no answer, but went weeping out of the chamber. Then the sword being brought in by a little boy, Cato took it, drew it out, and looked at it; and when he saw the point was good, "Now," said he, "I am master of myself"; and laying down the sword, he took his book again, which, it is related, he read twice over. After this he slept so soundly that he was heard to snore by those that were without.

About midnight, he called up two of his freedmen, Cleanthes, his physician, and Butas, whom he chiefly employed in public business. Him he sent to the port, to see if all his friends had sailed; to the physician he gave his hand to be dressed, as it was swollen with the blow he had struck one of his servants. At this they all rejoiced, hoping that now he designed to live.

Butas, after a while, returned, and brought word they were all gone except Crassus, who had stayed about some business, but was just ready to depart; he said, also, that the wind was high, and the sea very rough. Cato, on hearing this, sighed, out of compassion to those who were at sea, and sent Butas again

to see if any of them should happen to return for anything they wanted, and to acquaint him therewith.

Now the birds began to sing, and he again fell into a little slumber. At length Butas came back, and told him all was quiet in the port. Then Cato, laying himself down, as if he would sleep out the rest of the night, bade him shut the door after him. But as soon as Butas was gone out, he took his sword, and stabbed it into his breast; yet not being able to use his hand so well, on account of the swelling, he did not immediately die of the wound; but struggling, fell off the bed, and throwing down a little mathematical table that stood by, made such a noise that the servants, hearing it, cried out. And immediately his son and all his friends came into the chamber, where, seeing him lie weltering in his blood, a great part of his bowels out of his body, but himself still alive and able to look at them, they all stood in horror. The physician went to him, and would have put in his bowels, which were not pierced, and sewed up the wound; but Cato, recovering himself, and understanding the intention, thrust away the physician, plucked out his own bowels, and tearing open the wound, immediately expired.

In less time than one would think his own family could have known this accident, all the three hundred were at the door. And a little after, the people of Utica flocked thither, crying out with one voice he was their benefactor and their saviour, the only free and only undefeated man. At the very same time, they had news that Cæsar was coming; yet neither fear of the present danger, nor desire to flatter the conqueror, nor the commotions and discord among themselves, could divert them from doing honour to Cato. For they sumptuously set out his body, made him a magnificent funeral, and buried him by the seaside, where now stands his statue, holding a sword. And only when this had been done, they returned to consider of preserving themselves and their city.

Cæsar had been informed that Cato stayed at Utica, and did not seek to fly; that he had sent away the rest of the Romans, but himself, with his son and a few of his friends, continued there very unconcernedly, so that he could not imagine what might be his design. But having a great consideration for the man, he hastened thither with his army. When he heard of his death, it is related he said these words, "Cato, I grudge you your death, as you have grudged me the preservation of your life." And, indeed, if Cato would have suffered himself to owe his life to Cæsar, he would not so much have impaired his own honour, as augmented the other's glory. What would have been done, of course, we cannot know, but from Cæsar's usual clemency, we may guess what was most likely.

Cato was forty-eight years old when he died. His son suffered no injury from Cæsar; but, it is said, he grew idle, and was thought to be dissipated among women. In Cappadocia, he stayed at the house of Marphadates, one of the royal family there, who had a very handsome wife; and continuing his visit longer than was suitable, he made himself the subject of various epigrams; such as, for example—

> To-morrow (being the thirtieth day)
> Cato, 'tis thought, will go away;

> Porcius and Marphadates, friends so true,
> One Soul, they say, suffices for the two,

that being the name of the woman, and so again,—

> To Cato's greatness every one confesses,
> A royal Soul he certainly possesses.

But all these stains were entirely wiped off by the bravery of his death. For in the battle of Philippi, where he fought for his country's liberty against Cæsar and Antony, when the ranks were breaking, he, scorning to fly, or to escape unknown, called out to the enemy, showed himself to them in front, and encouraged those of his party who stayed; and at length fell, and left his enemies full of admiration of his valour.

Nor was the daughter of Cato inferior to the rest of her family for sober-living and greatness of spirit. She was married to Brutus, who killed Cæsar; was acquainted with the conspiracy, and ended her life as became one of her birth and virtue. All which is related in the life of Brutus.

Statyllius, who said he would imitate Cato, was at that time hindered by the philosophers, when he would have put an end to his life. He afterwards followed Brutus, to whom he was very faithful and very serviceable, and died in the field of Philippi.

AGIS

264-241 B.C

THE fable of Ixion, who, embracing a cloud instead of Juno, begot the Centaurs, has been ingeniously enough supposed to have been invented to represent to us ambitious men, whose minds, doting on glory, which is a mere image of virtue, produce nothing that is genuine or uniform, but only, as might be expected of such a conjunction, misshapen and unnatural actions. Running after their emulations and passions, and carried away by the impulses of the moment, they may say with the herdsmen in the tragedy of Sophocles—

> We follow these, though born their rightful lords,
> And they command us, though they speak no words.

For this is indeed the true condition of men in public life, who, to gain the vain title of being the people's leaders and governors, are content to make themselves the slaves and followers of all the people's humours and caprices. For as the lookout men at the ship's prow, though they see what is ahead before the men at the helm, yet constantly look back to the pilots there, and obey the orders they give; so these men, steered, as I may say, by popular applause, though they bear the name of governors, are in reality the mere underlings of the multitude. The man who is completely wise and virtuous has no need at all of glory, except so far as it disposes and eases his way to action by the greater trust that it procures him. A young man, I grant, may be permitted, while yet eager for distinction, to pride himself a little in his good deeds; for (as Theophrastus says) his virtues, which are yet tender and, as it were, in the blade, cherished and supported by praises, grow stronger, and take the deeper root. But when this passion is exorbitant, it is dangerous in all men, and in those who govern a commonwealth, utterly destructive. For in the possession of large power and authority, it transports men to a degree of madness; so that now they no more think what is good, glorious, but will have those actions only esteemed good that are glorious. As Phocion, therefore, answered King Antipater, who sought his approbation of some unworthy action, "I cannot be your flatterer, and your friend," so these men should answer the people, "I cannot govern and obey you."

For it may happen to the commonwealth, as to the serpent in the fable, whose tail, rising in rebellion against the head, complained, as of a great grievance, that it was always forced to follow, and required that it should be permitted by turns to lead the way. And taking the command accordingly, it soon inflicted, by its senseless courses, mischiefs in abundance upon itself, while the head was torn and lacerated with following, contrary to nature, a guide that was deaf and blind. And such we see to have been the lot of many, who, submitting to be guided by the inclinations of an uninformed and unreasoning multitude, could neither stop, nor recover themselves out of the confusion.

This is what has occurred to us to say of that glory which depends on the voice of large numbers, considering the sad effects of it in the misfortunes of Caius and Tiberius Gracchus, men of noble nature, and whose generous natural dispositions were improved by the best of educations, and who came to the administration of affairs with the most laudable intentions; yet they were ruined, I cannot say by an immoderate desire of glory, but by a more excusable fear of disgrace. For being excessively beloved and favoured by the people, they thought it a discredit to them not to make full repayment, endeavouring by new public acts to outdo the honours they had received, and again, because of these new kindnesses, incurring yet further distinctions; till the people and they, mutually inflamed, and vying thus with each other in honours and benefits, brought things at last to such a pass that they might say that to engage so far was indeed a folly, but to retreat would now be a shame.

This the reader will easily gather from the story. I will now compare with them two Lacedæmonian popular leaders, the kings Agis and Cleomenes. For they, being desirous also to raise the people, and to restore the noble and just form of government, now long fallen into disuse, incurred the hatred of the rich and powerful, who could not endure to be deprived of the selfish enjoyment to which they were accustomed. These were not indeed brothers by nature, as the two Romans, but they had a kind of brotherly resemblance in their actions and designs, which took a rise from such beginnings and occasions as I am now about to relate.

When the love of gold and silver had once gained admittance into the Lacedæmonian commonwealth, it was quickly followed by avarice and baseness of spirit in the pursuit of it, and by luxury, effeminacy, and prodigality in the use. Then Sparta fell from almost all her former virtue and repute, and so continued till the days of Agis and Leonidas, who both together were kings of the Lacedæmonians.

Agis was of the royal family of Eurypon, son of Eudamidas, and the sixth in descent from Agesilaus, who made the expedition into Asia, and was the greatest man of his time in Greece. Agesilaus left behind him a son called Archidamus, the same who was slain at Mandonium, in Italy, by the Messapians, and who was then succeeded by his eldest son Agis. He being killed by Antipater near Megalopolis, and leaving no issue, was succeeded by his brother Eudamidas; he by a son called Archidamus; and Archidamus by another Eudamidas, the father of this Agis of whom we now treat.

Leonidas, son of Cleonymus, was of the other royal house of the Agiadæ, and the eighth in descent from Pausanias, who defeated Mardonius in the battle of Platæa. Pausanias was succeeded by a son called Plistoanax; and he by another Pausanias who was banished, and lived as a private man at Tegea, while his eldest son, Agesipolis, reigned in his place. He, dying without issue, was succeeded by a younger brother, called Cleombrotus, who left two sons; the elder was Agesipolis, who reigned but a short time, and died without issue; the younger, who then became king, was called Cleomenes, and had also two sons, Acrotatus and Cleonymus. The first died before his father, but left a son called Areus, who succeeded, and being slain at Corinth, left the kingdom to his son Acrotatus. This Acrotatus was defeated, and slain near Megalopolis, in a battle against the tyrant Aristodemus; he left his wife big with child, and on her being delivered of a son, Leonidas, son of the above-named Cleonymus, was made his guardian, and as the young king died before becoming a man, he succeeded in the kingdom.

Leonidas was a king not particularly suitable to his people. For though there were at that time at Sparta a general decline in manners, yet a greater revolt from the old habits appeared in him than in others. For having lived a long time among the great lords of Persia, and been a follower of King Seleucus, he unadvisedly thought to imitate, among Greek institutions and in a lawful government, the pride and assumption usual in those courts. Agis, on the contrary, in fineness of nature and elevation of mind, not only far excelled Leonidas, but in a manner all the kings that had reigned since the great Agesilaus. For though he had been bred very tenderly, in abundance and even in luxury, by his mother Agesistrata and his grandmother Archidamia, who were the wealthiest of the Lacedæmonians, yet, before the age of twenty, he renounced all indulgence in pleasures. Withdrawing himself as far as possible from the gaiety and ornament which seemed becoming to the grace of his person, he made it his pride to appear in the coarse Spartan coat. In his meals, his bathings, and in all his exercises, he followed the old Laconian usage, and was often heard to say he had no desire for the place of king, if he did not hope by means of that authority to restore their ancient laws and discipline.

The Lacedæmonians might date the beginning of their corruption from their conquest of Athens, and the influx of gold and silver among them that thence ensued. Yet, nevertheless, the number of houses which Lycurgus appointed being still maintained, and the law remaining in force by which every one was obliged to leave his lot or portion of land entirely to his son, a kind of order and equality was thereby preserved, which still in some degree sustained the state amidst its errors in other respects. But one Epitadeus happening to be ephor, a man of great influence, and of a wilful, violent spirit, on some occasion of a quarrel with his son, proposed a decree that all men should have liberty to dispose of their land by gift in their lifetime, or by their last will and testament.

This being promoted by him to satisfy a passion of revenge, and through covetousness consented to by others, and thus enacted for a law, was the ruin of the best state of the commonwealth. For the rich men without scruple drew the estate into their own hands, excluding the rightful heirs from their succession; and all the wealth being centred upon the few, the generality were poor and miserable. Honourable pursuits, for which there was no

longer leisure, were neglected; the state was filled with sordid business, and with hatred and envy of the rich. There did not remain above seven hundred of the old Spartan families, of which, perhaps, one hundred might have estates in land; the rest were destitute alike of wealth and of honour, were tardy and unperforming in the defence of their country against its enemies abroad, and eagerly watched the opportunity for change and revolution at home.

Agis, therefore, believing it a glorious action, as in truth it was, to equalise and repeople the state, began to sound the inclinations of the citizens. He found the young men disposed beyond his expectation; they were eager to enter with him upon the contest in the cause of virtue, and to fling aside, for freedom's sake, their old manner of life, as readily as the wrestler does his garment. But the old men, habituated and more confirmed in their vices, were most of them as alarmed at the very name of Lycurgus, as a fugitive slave to be brought back before his offended master. These men could not endure to hear Agis continually deploring the present state of Sparta, and wishing she might be restored to her ancient glory.

But on the other side, Lysander, the son of Libys, Mandroclidas, the son of Ecphanes, together with Agesilaus, not only approved his design, but assisted and confirmed him in it. Lysander had a great authority and credit with the people; Mandroclidas was esteemed the ablest Greek of his time to manage an affair and put it in train, and, joined with skill and cunning, had a great degree of boldness. Agesilaus was the king's uncle, by the mother's side; an eloquent man, but covetous and voluptuous, who was not moved by considerations of public good, but rather seemed to be persuaded in it by his son Hippomedon, whose courage and signal actions in war had gained him a high esteem and great influence among the young men of Sparta, though indeed the true motive was, that he had many debts, and hoped by this means to be freed from them.

As soon as Agis had prevailed with his uncle, he endeavoured by his mediation to gain his mother also, who had many friends and followers, and a number of persons in her debt in the city, and took a considerable part in public affairs. At the first proposal she was very averse, and strongly advised her son not to engage in so difficult and so unprofitable an enterprise. But Agesilaus endeavoured to persuade her that the thing was not so difficult as she imagined, and that it might, in all likelihood, redound to the advantage of her family; while the king, her son, besought her not for money's sake to decline assisting his hopes of glory. He told her he could not pretend to equal other kings in riches, the very followers and menials of the satraps and stewards of Seleucus or Ptolemy abounding more in wealth than all the Spartan kings put together; but if by contempt of wealth and pleasure, by simplicity and magnanimity, he could surpass their luxury and abundance; if he could restore their former equality to the Spartans, then he should be a great king indeed.

In conclusion, the mother and the grandmother also were so taken, so carried away with the inspiration, as it were, of the young man's noble and generous ambition, that they not only consented, but were ready on all occasions to spur him on to a perseverance, and not only sent to speak on his behalf with the men with whom they had an interest, but addressed the other women also, knowing well that the Lacedæmonian wives had always a great power with their husbands, who used to impart to them their state affairs with greater freedom than the women would communicate with the men in the private business of their families. Which was indeed one of the greatest obstacles to this design; for the money of Sparta being most of it in the women's hands, it was their interest to oppose it, not only as depriving them of those superfluous trifles, in which, through want of better knowledge and experience, they placed their chief felicity, but also because they knew their riches were the main support of their power and credit.

Those, therefore, who were of this faction had recourse to Leonidas, representing to him how it was his part, as the elder and more experienced, to put a stop to the ill-advised projects of a rash young man. Leonidas, though of himself sufficiently inclined to oppose Agis, durst not openly, for fear of the people, who were manifestly desirous of this change; but underhand he did all he could to discredit and thwart the project, and to prejudice the chief magistrates against him, and on all occasions craftily insinuated that it was at the price of letting him usurp arbitrary power that Agis thus proposed to divide the property of the rich among the poor, and that the

object of these measures for cancelling debts and dividing the lands, was not to furnish Sparta with citizens, but purchase him a tyrant's body guard.

Agis, nevertheless, little regarding these rumours, procured Lysander's election as ephor; and then took the first occasion of proposing through him his *rhetra* to the council, the chief articles of which were these: That every one should be free from their debts: all the lands to be divided into equal portions, those that lay betwixt the watercourse near Pellene and Mount Taygetus, and as far as the cities of Malea and Sellasia, into four thousand five hundred lots, the remainder into fifteen thousand; these last to be shared out among those of the country people who were fit for service as heavy-armed soldiers, the first among the natural-born Spartans, and their number also should be supplied from any among the country people or strangers who had received the proper breeding of freemen, and were of vigorous body and of age for military service. All these were to be divided into fifteen companies, some of four hundred, and some of two, with a diet and discipline agreeable to the laws of Lycurgus.

This decree being proposed in the council of Elders met there with opposition; so that Lysander immediately convoked the great assembly of the people, to whom he, Mandroclidas, and Agesilaus made orations exhorting them that they would not suffer the majesty of Sparta to remain abandoned to contempt, to gratify a few rich men, who lorded it over them; but that they should call to mind the oracles in old times which had forewarned them to beware of the love of money, as the great danger and probable ruin of Sparta, and, moreover, those recently brought from the temple of Pasiphae. This was a famous temple and oracle at Thalamæ; and this Pasiphae some say, was one of the daughters of Atlas, who had by Jupiter a son called Ammon; others are of opinion it was Cassandra, the daughter of King Priam, who dying in this place, was called Pasiphae, as the *revealer* of oracles to *all* men. Phylarchus says, that this was Daphne, the daughter of Amyclas, who, flying from Apollo, was transformed into a laurel, and honoured by that god with the gift of prophecy.

But be it as it will, it is certain the people were made to apprehend that this oracle had commanded them to return to their former state of equality settled by Lycurgus. As soon as these had done speaking, Agis stood up, and after a few words, told them he would make the best contribution in his power to the new legislation, which was proposed for their advantage. In the first place, he would divide among them all his patrimony, which was of large extent in tillage and pasture; he would also give six hundred talents in ready money, and his mother, grandmother, and his other friends and relations, who were the richest of the Lacedæmonians, were ready to follow his example.

The people were transported with admiration of the young man's generosity, and with joy that, after three hundred years' interval, at last there had appeared a king worthy of Sparta. But, on the other side, Leonidas was now more than ever averse, being sensible that he and his friends would be obliged to contribute with their riches, and yet all the honour and obligation would redound to Agis. He asked him then before them all, whether Lycurgus were not in his opinion a wise man, and a lover of his country. Agis answering he was, "And when did Lycurgus," replied Leonidas, "cancel debts, or admit strangers to citizenship,—he who thought the commonwealth not secure unless from time to time the city was cleared of all strangers?"

To this Agis replied, "It is no wonder that Leonidas, who was brought up and married abroad, and has children by a wife taken out of a Persian court, should know little of Lycurgus or his laws. Lycurgus took away both debts and loans, by taking away money; and objected indeed to the presence of men who were foreign to the manners and customs of the country, not in any case from an ill-will to their persons, but lest the example of their lives and conduct should infect the city with the love of riches, and of delicate and luxurious habits. For it is well known that he himself gladly kept Terpander, Thales, and Pherecydes though they were strangers, because he perceived they were in their poems and in their philosophy of the same mind with him. And you that are wont to praise Ecprepes, who, being ephor, cut with his hatchet two of the nine strings from the instrument of Phrynis the musician, and to commend those who afterwards imitated him, in cutting the strings of Timotheus's harp, with what face can you blame us for designing to cut off superfluity and luxury and display from the commonwealth? Do you think those men

were so concerned only about a lute-string, or intended anything else than to check in music that same excess and extravagance which rule in our present lives and manners, and have disturbed and destroyed all the harmony and order of our city?"

From this time forward, as the common people followed Agis, so the rich men adhered to Leonidas. They besought him not to forsake their cause; and with persuasions and entreaties so far prevailed with the council of elders, whose power consisted in preparing all laws before they were proposed to the people, that the designed *rhetra* was rejected, though but by only one vote. Whereupon Lysander, who was still ephor, resolving to be revenged on Leonidas, drew up an information against him, grounded on two old laws: the one forbids any of the blood of Hercules to raise up children by a foreign woman, and the other makes it capital for a Lacedæmonian to leave his country to settle among foreigners.

Whilst he set others on to manage this accusation, he with his colleagues went *to observe the sign,* which was a custom they had, and performed in this manner. Every ninth year, the ephors, choosing a starlight night, when there is neither cloud nor moon, sit down together in quiet and silence, and watch the sky. And if they chance to see the shooting of a star, they presently pronounce their king guilty of some offence against the gods, and thereupon he is immediately suspended from all exercise of regal power, till he is relieved by an oracle from Delphi or Olympia.

Lysander, therefore, assured the people he had seen a star shoot, and at the same time Leonidas was cited to answer for himself. Witnesses were produced to testify he had married an Asian woman, bestowed on him by one of King Seleucus's lieutenants: that he had two children by her, but she so disliked and hated him, that against his wishes, flying from her, he was in a manner forced to return to Sparta, where his predecessor dying without issue, he took upon him the government. Lysander, not content with this, persuaded also Cleombrotus to lay claim to the kingdom. He was of the royal family, and son-in-law to Leonidas; who, fearing now the event of this process, fled as a suppliant to the temple of Minerva of the Brazen House, together with his daughter, the wife of Cleombrotus; for she in this occasion resolved to leave her husband, and to follow her father. Leonidas being again cited, and not appearing, they pronounced a sentence of deposition against him, and made Cleombrotus king in his place.

Soon after this revolution, Lysander, his year expiring, went out of his office, and new ephors were chosen, who gave Leonidas assurance of safety, and cited Lysander and Mandroclidas to answer for having, contrary to law, cancelled debts, and designed a new division of lands. They, seeing themselves in danger, had recourse to the two kings, and represented to them how necessary it was for their interest and safety to act with united authority, and bid defiance to the ephors. For, indeed, the power of the ephors, they said, was only grounded on the dissensions of the kings, it being their privilege, when the kings differed in opinion, to add their suffrage to whichever they judged to have given the best advice; but when the two kings were unanimous, none ought or durst resist their authority, the magistrate, whose office it was to stand as umpire when they were at variance, had no call to interfere when they were of one mind.

Agis and Cleombrotus, thus persuaded, went together with their friends into the market-place, where removing the ephors from their seats, they placed others in their room, of whom Agesilaus was one; proceeding then to arm a company of young men, and releasing many out of prison; so that those of the contrary faction began to be in great fear of their lives; but there was no blood spilt. On the contrary, Agis, having notice that Agesilaus had ordered a company of soldiers to lie in wait for Leonidas, to kill him as he fled to Tegea, immediately sent some of his followers to defend him, and to convey him safely into that city.

Thus far all things proceeded prosperously, none daring to oppose; but through the sordid weakness of one man, these promising beginnings were blasted, and a most noble and truly Spartan purpose overthrown and ruined by the love of money. Agesilaus, as we said, was much in debt, though in possession of one of the largest and best estates in land; and while he gladly joined in this design to be quit of his debts, he was not at all willing to part with his land. Therefore, he persuaded Agis that if both these things should be put in execution at the same time, so great and so sudden an alteration might cause some dangerous commotion; but if debts were in the first place cancelled, the rich men would

afterwards more easily be prevailed with to part with their land.

Lysander, also, was of the same opinion, being deceived in like manner by the craft of Agesilaus; so that all men were presently commanded to bring in their bonds, or deeds of obligation, by the Lacedæmonians called *claria,* into the market-place, where being laid together in a heap, they set fire to them. The wealthy, money-lending people, one may easily imagine, beheld it with a heavy heart; but Agesilaus told them scoffingly, his eyes had never seen so bright and so pure a flame.

And now the people pressed earnestly for an immediate division of lands; the kings also had ordered it should be done; but Agesilaus, sometimes pretending one difficulty, and sometimes another, delayed the execution, till an occasion happened to call Agis to the wars. The Achæans, in virtue of a defensive treaty of alliance, sent to demand succours, as they expected every day that the Ætolians would attempt to enter Peloponnesus, from the territory of Megara. They had sent Aratus, their general, to collect forces to hinder this incursion. Aratus wrote to the ephors, who immediately gave order that Agis should hasten to their assistance with the Lacedæmonian auxiliaries.

Agis was extremely pleased to see the zeal and bravery of those who went with him upon this expedition. They were for the most part young men, and poor; and being just released from their debts and set at liberty, and hoping on their return to receive each man his lot of land, they followed their king with wonderful alacrity. The cities through which they passed were in admiration to see how they marched from one end of Peloponnesus to the other, without the least disorder, and, in a manner, without being heard. It gave the Greeks occasion to discourse with one another, how great might be the temperance and modesty of a Laconian army in old time, under their famous captains Agesilaus, Lysander, or Leonidas, since they saw such discipline and exact obedience under a leader who perhaps was the youngest man in all the army. They saw also how he was himself content to fare hardly, ready to undergo any labours, and not to be distinguished by pomp or richness of habit or arms from the meanest of his soldiers; and to people in general it was an object of regard and admiration. But rich men viewed the innovation with dislike and alarm, lest haply the example might spread, and work changes to their prejudice in their own countries as well.

Agis joined Aratus near the city of Corinth, where it was still a matter of debate whether or no it were expedient to give the enemy battle. Agis, on this occasion, showed great forwardness and resolution, yet without temerity or presumption. He declared it was his opinion they ought to fight, thereby to hinder the enemy from passing the gates of Peloponnesus, but nevertheless he would submit to the judgment of Aratus, not only as the elder and more experienced captain, but as he was general of the Achæans, whose forces he would not pretend to command, but was only come thither to assist them.

I am not ignorant that Baton of Sinope relates it in another manner; he says Aratus would have fought, and that Agis was against it; but it is certain he was mistaken, not having read what Aratus himself wrote in his own justification, that knowing the people had well-nigh got in their harvest, he thought it much better to let the enemy pass than put all to the hazard of a battle. And, therefore, giving thanks to the confederates for their readiness, he dismissed them. And Agis, not without having gained a great deal of honour, returned to Sparta, where he found the people in disorder, and a new revolution imminent, owing to the ill-government of Agesilaus.

For he, being now one of the ephors, and freed from the fear which formerly kept him in some restraint, forbore no kind of oppression which might bring in gain. Among other things, he exacted a thirteenth month's tax, whereas the usual cycle required at this time no such addition to the year. For these and other reasons fearing those whom he injured, and knowing how he was hated by the people, he thought it necessary to maintain a guard, which always accompanied him to the magistrate's office. And presuming now on his power, he was grown so insolent, that of the two kings, the one he openly contemned, and if he showed any respect towards Agis, would have it thought rather an effect of his near relationship, than any duty or submission to the royal authority. He gave it out also that he was to continue ephor the ensuing year.

His enemies, therefore, alarmed by this report, lost no time in risking an attempt against him; and openly bringing back Leonidas from Tegea, re-established him in the kingdom, to which even the people, highly incensed for having been defrauded in the promised division of lands, willingly consented. Agesilaus himself would hardly have escaped their fury, if his son, Hippomedon, whose manly virtues made him dear to all, had not saved him out of their hands, and then privately conveyed him from the city.

During the commotion, the two kings fled, Agis to the temple of the Brazen House, and Cleombrotus to that of Neptune. For Leonidas was more incensed against his son-in-law; and leaving Agis alone, went with his soldiers to Cleombrotus's sanctuary, and there with great passion reproached him for having, though he was son-in-law, conspired with his enemies, usurped his throne, and forced him from his country. Cleombrotus, having little to say for himself, sat silent. His wife, Chilonis, the daughter of Leonidas, had chosen to follow her father in his sufferings; for when Cleombrotus usurped the kingdom, she forsook him, and wholly devoted herself to comfort her father in his affliction; whilst he still remained in Sparta, she remained also, as a suppliant, with him, and when he fled, she fled with him, bewailing his misfortune, and extremely displeased with Cleombrotus.

But now, upon this turn of fortune, she changed in like manner, and was seen sitting now, as a suppliant, with her husband, embracing him with her arms, and having her two little children beside her. All men were full of wonder at the piety and tender affection of the young woman, who pointing to her robes and her hair, both alike neglected and unattended to, said to Leonidas, "I am not brought, my father, to this condition you see me in, on account of the present misfortunes of Cleombrotus; my mourning habit is long since familiar to me. It was put on to condole with you in your banishment; and now you are restored to your country, and to your kingdom, must I still remain in grief and misery? Or would you have me attired in my royal ornaments, that I may rejoice with you, when you have killed, within my arms, the man to whom you gave me for a wife?

"Either Cleombrotus must appease you by mine and my children's tears, or he must suffer a punishment greater than you propose for his faults, and shall see me, whom he loves so well, die before him. To what end should I live, or how shall I appear among the Spartan women, when it shall so manifestly be seen, that I have not been able to move to compassion either a husband or a father? I was born, it seems, to participate in the ill-fortune and in the disgrace, both as a wife and a daughter, of those nearest and dearest to me. As for Cleombrotus, I sufficiently surrendered any honourable plea on his behalf, when I forsook him to follow you; but you yourself offer the fairest excuse for his proceedings, by showing to the world that for the sake of a kingdom, it is just to kill a son-in-law, and be regardless of a daughter."

Chilonis, having ended this lamentation, rested her face on her husband's head, and looked round with her weeping and woe-begone eyes upon those who stood before her.

Leonidas, touched with compassion, withdrew a while to advise with his friends; then returning, bade Cleombrotus leave the sanctuary and go into banishment; Chilonis, he said, ought to stay with him, it not being just she should forsake a father whose affection had granted to her intercession the life of her husband. But all he could say would not prevail. She rose up immediately, and taking one of her children in her arms, gave the other to her husband; and making her reverence to the altar of the goddess, went out and followed him. So that, in a word, if Cleombrotus were not utterly blinded by ambition, he must surely choose to be banished with so excellent a woman rather than without her to possess a kingdom.

Cleombrotus thus removed, Leonidas proceeded also to displace the ephors, and to choose others in their room; then he began to consider how he might entrap Agis. At first, he endeavoured by fair means to persuade him to leave the sanctuary, and partake with him in the kingdom. The people, he said, would easily pardon the errors of a young man, ambitious of glory, and deceived by the craft of Agesilaus. But finding Agis was suspicious, and not to be prevailed with to quit his sanctuary, he gave up that design; yet what could not then be effected by the dissimulation of an enemy, was soon after brought to pass by the treachery of friends.

Amphares, Damochares, and Arcesilaus often visited Agis, and he was so confident of their fidelity that after a while he was prevailed on to accompany them to the baths, which were not far distant, they constantly returning to see him safe again in the temple. They were all three his familiars; and Amphares had borrowed a great deal of plate and rich household stuff from Agesistrata, and hoped if he could destroy her and the whole family, he might peaceably enjoy those goods. And he, it

is said, was the readiest of all to serve the purposes of Leonidas, and being one of the ephors, did all he could to incense the rest of his colleagues against Agis.

These men, therefore, finding that Agis would not quit his sanctuary, but on occasion would venture from it to go to the bath, resolved to seize him on the opportunity thus given them. And one day as he was returning, they met and saluted him as formerly, conversing pleasantly by the way, and jesting, as youthful friends might, till coming to the turning of a street which led to the prison, Amphares, by virtue of his office, laid his hand on Agis, and told him, "You must go with me, Agis, before the other ephors, to answer for your misdemeanours." At the same time Damochares, who was a tall, strong man, drew his cloak tight round his neck, and dragged him after by it, whilst the others went behind to thrust him on.

None of Agis's friends being near to assist him, nor any one by, they therefore easily got him into the prison, where Leonidas was already arrived, with a company of soldiers, who strongly guarded all the avenues; the ephors also came in, with as many of the elders as they knew to be true to their party, being desirous to proceed with some semblance of justice. And thus they bade him give an account of his actions.

Agis, smiling at their dissimulation, answered not a word. Amphares told him it was more seasonable to weep, for now the time was come in which he should be punished for his presumption. Another of the ephors, as though he would be more favourable, and offering as it were an excuse, asked him whether he was not forced to what he did by Agesilaus and Lysander. But Agis answered he had not been constrained by any man, nor had any other intent in what he did but only to follow the example of Lycurgus, and to govern conformably to his laws. The same ephor asked him whether now at least he did not repent his rashness. To which the young man answered that though he were to suffer the extremest penalty for it, yet he could never repent of so just and so glorious a design. Upon this they passed sentence of death on him, and bade the officers carry him to the Dechas, as it is called, a place in the prison where they strangle malefactors. And when the officers would not venture to lay hands on him, and the very mercenary soldiers declined it, believing it an illegal and a wicked act to lay violent hands on a king, Demochares, threatening and reviling them for it, himself thrust him into the room.

For by this time the news of his being seized had reached many parts of the city, and there was a concourse of people with lights and torches about the prison gates, and in the midst of them the mother and the grandmother of Agis, crying out with a loud voice that their king ought to appear, and to be heard and judged by the people. But this clamour, instead of preventing, hastened his death; his enemies fearing, if the tumult should increase, he might be rescued during the night out of their hands.

Agis, being now at the point to die, perceived one of the officers bitterly bewailing his misfortune; "Weep not, friend," said he, "for me, who die innocent, by the lawless act of wicked men. My condition is much better than theirs." As soon as he had spoken these words, not showing the least sign of fear, he offered his neck to the noose.

Immediately after he was dead, Amphares went out of the prison gate, where he found Agesistrata, who, believing him still the same friend as before, threw herself at his feet. He gently raised her up, and assured her, she need not fear any further violence or danger of death for her son, and that if she pleased she might go in and see him. She begged her mother might also have the favour to be admitted, and he replied, nobody should hinder it. When they were entered, he commanded the gate should again be locked, and Archidamia, the grandmother, to be first introduced. She was now grown very old, and had lived all her days in the highest repute among her fellows.

As soon as Amphares thought she was despatched, he told Agesistrata she might now go in if she pleased. She entered, and beholding her son's body stretched on the ground, and her mother hanging by the neck, the first thing she did was, with her own hands, to assist the officers in taking down the body;

then covering it decently, she laid it out by her son's, whom then embracing and kissing his cheeks, "O my son," said she, "it was thy too great mercy and goodness which brought thee and us to ruin." Amphares, who stood watching behind the door, on hearing this, broke in, and said angrily to her, "Since you approve so well of your son's actions, it is fit you should partake in his reward." She, rising up to offer herself to the noose, said only, "I pray that it may redound to the good of Sparta."

The three bodies being now exposed to view, and the fact divulged, no fear was strong enough to hinder the people from expressing their abhorrence of what was done, and their detestation of Leonidas and Amphares, the contrivers of it. So wicked and barbarous an act had never been committed in Sparta since first the Dorians inhabited Peloponnesus; the very enemies in war, they said, were always cautious in spilling the blood of a Lacedæmonian king, insomuch that in any combat they would decline, and endeavour to avoid them, from feelings of respect and reverence for their station. And certainly we see that in the many battles fought betwixt the Lacedæmonians and the other Greeks, up to the time of Philip of Macedon, not one of their kings was ever killed, except Cleombrotus by a javelin-wound at the battle of Leuctra. I am not ignorant that the Messenians affirm, Theopompus was also slain by their Aristomenes; but the Lacedæmonians deny it, and say he was only wounded.

Be it as it will, it is certain at least that Agis was the first king put to death in Lacedæmon by the ephors, for having undertaken a design noble in itself and worthy of his country, at a time of life when men's errors usually meet with an easy pardon. And if errors he did commit, his enemies certainly had less reason to blame him than had his friends for that gentle and compassionate temper which made him save the life of Leonidas and believe in other men's professions.

CLEOMENES

263–219 B.C.

THUS fell Agis. His brother Archidamus was too quick for Leonidas, and saved himself by a timely retreat. But his wife, then mother of a young child, he forced from her own house, and compelled Agiatis, for that was her name, to marry his son Cleomenes, though at that time too young for a wife, because he was unwilling that any one else should have her, being heiress to her father Gylippus's great estate; in person the most youthful and beautiful woman in all Greece and well-conducted in her habits of life. And therefore, they say, she did all she could that she might not be compelled to this new marriage. But being thus united to Cleomenes, she indeed hated Leonidas, but to the youth showed herself a kind and obliging wife. He, as soon as they came together, began to love her very much, and the constant kindness that she still retained for the memory of Agis brought somewhat of the like feeling in the young man for him, so that he would often inquire of her concerning what had passed, and attentively listen to the story of Agis's purpose and design.

Now Cleomenes had a generous and great soul; he was as temperate and moderate in his pleasures as Agis, but not so scrupulous, circumspect, and gentle. There was something of heat and passion always goading him on, and an impetuosity and violence in his eagerness to pursue anything which he thought good and just. To have men obey him of their own free-will, he conceived to be the best discipline; but likewise, to subdue resistance, and force them to the better course was, in his opinion, commendable and brave.

This disposition made him dislike the management of the city. The citizens lay dissolved in supine idleness and pleasures, the king let everything take its own way, thankful if nobody gave him any disturbance, nor called him away from the enjoyment of his wealth and luxury. The public interest was neglected, and each man intent upon his private gain. It was dangerous, now Agis was killed, so much as to name such a thing as the exercis-

ing and training of their youth; and to speak of the ancient temperance, endurance, and equality, was a sort of treason against the state.

It is said also that Cleomenes, whilst a boy, studied philosophy under Sphærus, the Borystenite, who crossed over to Sparta, and spent some time and trouble in instructing the youth. Sphærus was one of the first of Zeno the Citiean's scholars, and it is likely enough that he admired the manly temper of Cleomenes and inflamed his generous ambition. The ancient Leonidas, as story tells, being asked what manner of poet he thought Tyrtæus, replied, "Good to whet young men's courage;" for being filled with a divine fury by his poems, they rushed into any danger. And so the Stoic philosophy is a dangerous incentive to strong and fiery dispositions, but where it combines with a grave and gentle temper, is most successful in leading it to its proper good.

Upon the death of his father Leonidas, he succeeded, and observing the citizens of all sorts to be debauched, the rich neglecting the public good, and intent on their private gain and pleasure, and the poor distressed in their own homes, and therefore without either spirit for war or ambition to be trained up as Spartans, that he had only the name of king, and the ephors all the power, he was resolved to change the posture of affairs. He had a friend whose name was Xenares, his lover (such an affection the Spartans express by the term, being *inspired,* or *imbreathed* with); him he sounded, and of him he would commonly inquire what manner of king Agis was, by what means and by what assistance he began and pursued his designs. Xenares, at first, willingly complied with his request, and told him the whole story, with all the particular circumstances of the actions. But when he observed Cleomenes to be extremely affected at the relation, and more than ordinarily taken with Agis's new model of the government, and begging a repetition of the story, he at first severely chid him, told him he was frantic, and at last left off all sort of familiarity and intercourse, yet he never told any man the cause of their disagreement, but would only say, Cleomenes knew very well.

Cleomenes, finding Xenares averse to his designs, and thinking all others to be of the same disposition, consulted with none, but contrived the whole business by himself. And considering that it would be easier to bring about an alteration when the city was at war than when in peace, he engaged the common-wealth in a quarrel with the Achæans, who had given them fair occasions to complain. For Aratus, a man of the greatest power amongst all the Achæans, designed from the very beginning to bring all the Peloponnesians into one common body. And to effect this was the one object of all his many commander-ships and his long political course; as he thought this the only means to make them a match for their foreign enemies. Pretty nearly all the rest agreed to his proposals, only the Lacedæmonians, the Eleans, and as many of the Arcadians as inclined to the Spartan inter-est, remained unpersuaded.

And so, as soon as Leonidas was dead, he began to attack the Arcadians, and wasted those especially that bordered on Achæa; by this means designing to try the inclinations of the Spartans, and despising Cleomenes as a youth, and of no experience in affairs of state or war. Upon this, the ephors sent Cleomenes to surprise the Athenæum, near Belbina, which is a pass commanding an entrance into La-conia, and was then the subject of litigation with the Megalopolitans. Cleomenes possessed himself of the place, and fortified it, at which action Aratus showed no public resentment, but marched by night to surprise Tegea and Orchomenus.

The design failed, for those that were to be-tray the cities into his hands turned afraid; so Aratus retreated, imagining that his design had been undiscovered. But Cleomenes wrote a sarcastic letter to him, and desired to know, as from a friend, whither he intended to march at night; and Aratus answering, that having heard of his design to fortify Belbina, he meant to march thither to oppose him, Cleomenes rejoined that he did not dispute it, but begged to be informed, if he might be allowed to ask the question, why he carried those torches and ladders with him. Aratus laughing at the jest, and asking what manner of youth this was, Damocrates, a Spartan ex-ile, replied, "If you have any designs upon the Lacedæmonians, begin before this young eagle's talons are grown."

Presently after this, Cleomenes, encamping in Arcadia with a few horse and three hun-dred foot, received orders from the ephors, who feared to engage in the war, command-ing him to return home; but when upon his retreat Aratus took Caphyæ, they commis-sioned him again. In this expedition he took Methydrium, and overran the country of the Argives; and the Achæans, to oppose him, came out with an army of twenty thousand foot and one thousand horse, under the com-mand of Aristomachus. Cleomenes faced them at Pallantium, and offered battle, but Aratus, being cowed by his bravery, would not suffer the general to engage, but retreated, amidst the reproaches of the Achæans and the deri-sion and scorn of the Spartans, who were not above five thousand.

Cleomenes, encouraged by this success, be-gan to speak boldly among the citizens, and reminding them of a sentence of one of their ancient kings, said, it was in vain now that the Spartans asked not how many their ene-mies were, but where they were. After this, marching to the assistance of the Eleans, whom the Achæans were attacking, falling upon the enemy in their retreat near the Lycæum, he put their whole army to flight, taking a great number of captives, and leaving many dead upon the place; so that it was commonly re-ported amongst the Greeks that Aratus was slain. But Aratus, making the best advantage of the opportunity, immediately after the de-feat marched to Mantinea, and before any-body suspected it, took the city, and put a garrison into it.

Upon this, the Lacedæmonians being quite discouraged, and opposing Cleomenes's de-signs of carrying on the war, he now exerted himself to have Archidamus, the brother of Agis, sent for from Messene, as he, of the other family, had a right to the kingdom; and besides, Cleomenes thought that the power of the ephors would be reduced, when the kingly state was thus filled up, and raised to its proper position. But those that were con-cerned in the murder of Agis, perceiving the design, and fearing that upon Archidamus's return that they should be called to an ac-count, received him on his coming privately into town, and joined in bringing him home, and presently after murdered him. Whether Cleomenes was against it, as Phylarchus thinks, or whether he was persuaded by his friends, or let him fall into their hands, is uncertain; however, they were most blamed, as having forced his consent.

He, still resolving to remodel the state, bribed the ephors to send him out to war; and won the affections of many others by means of his mother Cratesiclea, who spared no cost and was very zealous to promote her son's ambition; and though of herself she had no inclination to marry, yet for his sake she accepted, as her husband, one of the chiefest citizens for wealth and power. Cleomenes, marching forth with the army now under his command, took Leuctra, a place belonging to Megalopolis; and the Achæans quickly coming up to resist him with a good body of men commanded by Aratus, in a battle under the very walls of the city, some part of his army was routed. But whereas Aratus had commanded the Achæans not to pass a deep watercourse, and thus put a stop to the pursuit, Lydiadas, the Megalopolitan, fretting at the orders, and encouraging the horse which he led, and following the routed enemy, got into a place full of vines, hedges, and ditches; and being forced to break his ranks, began to retire in disorder.

Cleomenes, observing the advantage, commanded the Tarentines and Cretans to engage him, by whom, after a brave defence, he was routed and slain. The Lacedæmonians, thus encouraged, fell with a great shout upon the Achæans, and routed their whole army. Of the slain, who were very many, the rest Cleomenes delivered up, when the enemy petitioned for them; but the body of Lydiadas he commanded to be brought to him; and then putting on it a purple robe, and a crown upon its head, sent a convoy with it to the gates of Megalopolis. This is that Lydiadas who resigned his power as tyrant, restored liberty to the citizens, and joined the city to the Achæan interest.

Cleomenes, being very much elated by this success, and persuaded that if matters were wholly at his disposal he should soon be too hard for the Achæans, persuaded Magistonus, his mother's husband, that it was expedient for the state to shake off the power of the ephors, and to put all their wealth into one common stock for the whole body; thus Sparta, being restored to its old equality, might aspire again to the command of all Greece. Megistonus liked the design, and engaged two or three more of his friends. About that time, one of the ephors, sleeping in Pasiphæ's tem-

ple, dreamed a very surprising dream; for he thought he saw the four chairs removed out of the place where the ephors used to sit and do the business of their office, and one only set there; and whilst he wondered, he heard a voice out of the temple, saying, "This is best for Sparta."

The person telling Cleomenes this dream, he was a little troubled at first, fearing that he used this as a trick to sift him, upon some suspicion of his design, but when he was satisfied that the relator spoke truth, he took heart again. And carrying with him those whom he thought would be most against his project, he took Heræa and Alsæa, two towns in league with the Achæans, furnished Orchomenus with provisions, encamped before Mantinea, and with long marches up and down so harassed the Lacedæmonians that many of them at their own request were left behind in Arcadia, while he with the mercenaries went on toward Sparta, and by the way communicated his design to those whom he thought fitted for his purpose, and marched slowly, that he might catch the ephors at supper.

When he was come near the city, he sent Euryclidas to the public table, where the ephors supped, under pretence of carrying some message from him from the army; Therycion, Phœbis, and two of those who had been bred up with Cleomenes, whom they call *mothaces,* followed with a few soldiers; and whilst Euryclidas was delivering his message to the ephors, they ran upon them with their drawn swords, and slew them. The first of them, Agylæus, on receiving the blow, fell, and lay as dead; but in a little time quietly raising himself, and drawing himself out of the room, he crept, without being discovered, into a little building which was dedicated to Fear, and which always used to be shut, but then by chance was open; and being got in, he shut the door, and lay close. The other four were killed, and above ten more that came to their assistance; to those that were quiet they did no harm, stopped none that fled from the city, and spared Agylæus when he came out of the temple the next day.

The Lacedæmonians have not only sacred places dedicated to Fear, but also to Death, Laughter, and the like passions. Now they worship Fear, not as they do supernatural powers which they dread, esteeming it hurtful, but thinking their polity is chiefly kept up by fear. Therefore the ephors, Aristotle is my author, when they entered upon their government, made proclamation to the people, that they should shave their mustaches and be obedient to the laws, that the laws might not be hard upon them, making, I suppose, this trivial injunction to accustom their youth to obedience even in the smallest matters. And the ancients, I think, did not imagine bravery to be plain fearlessness, but a cautious fear of blame and disgrace. For those that show most timidity towards the laws are most bold against their enemies; and those are least afraid of any danger who are most afraid of a just reproach. Therefore, it was well said that—

A reverence still attends on fear;

and by Homer,—

Feared you shall be, dear father, and revered;

and again,—

In silence fearing those that bore the sway;

for the generality of men are most ready to reverence those whom they fear. And, therefore, the Lacedæmonians placed the temple of Fear by the Syssitium of the ephors, having raised that magistracy to almost royal authority.

The next day, Cleomenes proscribed eighty of the citizens whom he thought necessary to banish, and removed all the seats of the ephors, except one, in which he himself designed to sit and give audience; and calling the citizens together he made an apology for his proceedings, saying, that by Lycurgus the counsel of elders was joined to the kings, and that that model of government had continued a long time, and no other sort of magistrates had been wanted. But afterwards, in the long war with the Messenians, when the kings, having to command the army, found no time to administer justice, they chose some of their friends, and left them to determine the suits of the citizens in their stead. These were called ephors, and at first behaved themselves as servants to the kings; but afterwards, by degrees, they appropriated the power to themselves, and erected a distinct magistracy.

An evidence of the truth of this was the custom still observed by the kings, who, when the ephors send for them, refuse, upon the first and second summons, to go, but upon the third rise up and attend them. And Asteropus, the first that raised the ephors to that height of power, lived a great many years after their institution. So long, therefore, he continued, as they contained themselves within their own proper sphere, it had been better

to bear with them than to make a disturbance. But that an upstart introduced power should so far subvert the ancient form of government as to banish some kings, murder others, without hearing their defence, and threaten those who desired to see the best and most divine constitution restored in Sparta, was not to be borne.

Therefore, if it had been possible for him without bloodshed to free Lacedæmon from those foreign plagues, luxury, sumptuosity, debts, and usury, and from those yet more ancient evils, poverty and riches, he should have thought himself the happiest king in the world, to have succeeded, like an expert physician, in curing the diseases of his country without pain. But now, in this necessity, Lycurgus's example favoured his proceedings, who being neither king nor magistrate, but a private man, and aiming at the kingdom, came armed into the market-place, so that King Charillus fled in alarm to the altar. He, being a good man, and a lover of his country, readily concurred in Lycurgus's designs, and admitted the revolution in the state. But, by his own actions, Lycurgus had nevertheless borne witness that it was difficult to change the government without force and fear, in the use of which he himself, he said, had been so moderate as to do no more than put out of the way those who opposed themselves to Sparta's happiness and safety.

For the rest of the nation, he told them, the whole land was now their common property; debtors should be cleared of their debts, and examination made of those who were not citizens, that the bravest men might thus be made free Spartans, and give aid in arms to save the city, and "we," he said, "may no longer see Laconia, for want of men to defend it, wasted by the Ætolians and Illyrians."

Then he himself first, with his step-father, Megistonus, and his friends, gave up all their wealth into one public stock, and all the other citizens followed the example. The land was divided, and every one that he had banished had a share assigned him; for he promised to restore all as soon as things were settled and in quiet. And completing the number of citizens out of the best and most promising of the country people, he raised a body of four thousand men; and instead of a spear, taught them to use a *sarissa,* with both hands, and to carry their shields by a band, and not by a handle, as before. After this he began to consult about the education of the youth, and the discipline, as they call it; most of the particulars of which Sphærus, being then at Sparta, assisted in arranging; and in a short time the schools of exercise and the common tables recovered their ancient decency and order, a few out of necessity, but the most voluntarily, returning to that generous and Laconic way of living. And, that the name of monarch might give them no jealousy, he made Euclidas, his brother, partner in the throne; and that was the only time that Sparta had two kings of the same family.

Then, understanding that the Achæans and Aratus imagined that this change had disturbed and shaken his affairs, and that he would not venture out of Sparta and leave the city now unsettled in the midst of so great an alteration, he thought it great and serviceable to his designs to show his enemies the zeal and forwardness of his troops. And, therefore, making an incursion into the territories of Megalopolis, he wasted the country far and wide, and collected considerable booty. And at last, taking a company of actors as they were travelling from Messene, and building a theatre in the enemy's country, and offering a prize of forty minæ in value, he sat spectator a whole day; not that he either desired or needed such amusement, but wishing to show his disregard for his enemies, and by a display of his contempt, to prove the extent of his superiority to them. For his alone, of all the Greek or royal armies, had no stage-players, no jugglers, no dancing or singing women attending it, but was free from all sorts of looseness, wantonness, and festivity; the young men being for the most part at their exercises, and the old men giving them lessons, or, at leisure times, diverting themselves with their native jests, and quick Laconian answers; the good results of which we have noticed in the life of Lycurgus.

He himself instructed all by his example; he was a living pattern of temperance before every man's eyes; and his course of living was neither more stately, nor more expensive, nor in any way more pretentious, than that of his people. And this was a considerable advantage to him in his designs on Greece. For men when they waited upon other kings did not so much admire their wealth, costly furniture, and numerous attendance, as they hated their pride and state, their difficulty of access, and imperious answers to their addresses.

But when they came to Cleomenes, who was both really a king and bore that title, and saw no purple, no robes of state upon him, no

couches and litters about him for his ease, and that he did not receive requests and return answers after a long delay and difficulty, through a number of messengers and door-keepers, or by memorials, but that he rose and came forward in any dress he might happen to be wearing, to meet those that came to wait upon him, stayed, talked freely and affably with all that had business, they were extremely taken, and won to his service, and professed that he alone was the true son of Hercules. His common every-day's meal was in an ordinary room, very sparing, and after the Laconic manner; and when he entertained ambassadors, or strangers, two more couches were added, and a little better dinner provided by his servants, but no savouring sauces or sweetmeats; only the dishes were larger, and the wine more plentiful. For he reproved one of his friends for entertaining some strangers with nothing but barley bread and black broth, such diet as they usually had in their *phiditia;* saying that upon such occasions, and when they entertained strangers, it was not well to be too exact Laconians. After the table was removed, a stand was brought in with a brass vessel full of wine, two silver bowls, which held about a pint apiece, a few silver cups, of which he that pleased might drink, but wine was not urged on any of the guests.

There was no music, nor was any required; for he entertained the company himself, sometimes asking questions, sometimes telling stories; and his conversation was neither too grave or disagreeably serious, nor yet in any way rude or ungraceful in its pleasantry. For he thought those ways of entrapping men by gifts and presents, which other kings use, dishonest and artificial; and it seemed to him to be the most noble method, and most suitable to a king, to win the affections of those that came near him, by personal intercourse and agreeable conversation, since between a friend and a mercenary the only distinction is, that the one is gained by one's character and conversation, the other by one's money.

The Mantineans were the first that requested his aid; and when he entered their city by night, they aided him to expel the Achæan garrison, and put themselves under his protection. He restored them their polity and laws, and the same day marched to Tegea; and a little while after, fetching a compass through Arcadia, he made a descent upon Pheræ, in Achæa, intending to force Aratus to a battle, or bring him into disrepute for refusing to engage, and suffering him to waste the country. Hyperbatas at that time was general, but Aratus had all the power amongst the Achæans, marching forth with their whole strength, and encamping in Dymæ, near the Hecatombæum. Cleomenes came up, and thinking it not advisable to pitch between Dymæ, a city of the enemies, and the camp of the Achæans, he boldly dared the Achæans, and forced them to a battle, and routing their phalanx, slew a great many in the fight, and took many prisoners, and thence marching to Langon, and driving out the Achæan garrison, he restored the city to the Eleans.

The affair of the Achæans being in this unfortunate condition, Aratus, who was wont to take the office every other year, refused the command, though they entreated and urged him to accept it. And this was ill-done, when the storm was high, to put the power out of his own hands, and set another to the helm. Cleomenes at first proposed fair and easy conditions by his ambassadors to the Achæans, but afterwards he sent others, and required the chief command to be settled upon him; in other matters offering to agree to reasonable terms, and to restore their captives and their country. The Achæans were willing to come to an agreement upon those terms, and invited Cleomenes to Lerna, where an assembly was to be held; but it happened that Cleomenes, hastily marching on, and drinking water at a wrong time, brought up a quantity of blood and lost his voice; therefore being unable to continue his journey, he sent the chiefest of the captives to the Achæans, and, putting off the meeting for some time, retired to Lacedæmon.

This ruined the affairs of Greece, which was just beginning in some sort to recover from its disasters, and to show some capability of delivering itself from the insolence and rapacity of the Macedonians. For Aratus (whether fearing or distrusting Cleomenes, or envying his unlooked-for success, or thinking it a disgrace for him who had commanded thirty-three years to have a young man succeed to all his glory and his power, and be head of that government which he had been raising and settling so many years), first endeavoured to keep the Achæans from closing with Cleomenes; but when they would not hearken to him, fearing Cleomenes' daring spirit, and thinking the Lacedæmonians' proposals to be very reasonable, who designed only to reduce Peloponnesus to its own model, upon this he took his last refuge in an action which was unbecoming

any of the Greeks, most dishonourable to him, and most unworthy his former bravery and exploits.

For he called Antigonus into Greece and filled Peloponnesus with Macedonians, whom he himself, when a youth, having beaten their garrison out of the castle of Corinth, had driven from the same country. And there had been constant suspicion and variance between him and all the kings; and of Antigonus, in particular, he has said a thousand dishonourable things in the commentaries he has left behind him. And though he declares himself how he suffered considerable losses, and underwent great dangers, that he might free Athens from the garrison of the Macedonians, yet, afterwards, he brought the very same men armed into his own country, and his own house, even to the women's apartment.

He would not endure that one of the family of Hercules, and king of Sparta, and one that reformed the polity of his country, as it were, from a disordered harmony, and returned it to the plain Doric measure and rule of life of Lycurgus, should be styled head of the Tritæans and Sicyonians; and whilst he fled the barley-cake and coarse coat, and, which were his chief accusations against Cleomenes, the extirpation of wealth and reformation of poverty, he basely subjected himself, together with Achæa, to the diadem and purple, to the imperious commands of the Macedonians and their satraps. That he might not seem to be under Cleomenes, he offered sacrifices, called Antigonea, in honour of Antigonus, and sang pæans himself, with a garland on his head, to the praise of a wasted, consumptive Macedonian.

I write this not out of any design to disgrace Aratus, for in many things he showed himself a true lover of Greece, and a great man, but out of pity to the weakness of human nature, which, in characters like this, so worthy and in so many ways disposed to virtue, cannot maintain its honours unblemished by some envious fault.

The Achæans meeting again in assembly at Argos, and Cleomenes having come from Tegea, there were great hopes that all differences would be composed. But Aratus, Antigonus and he having already agreed upon the chief articles of their league, fearing that Cleomenes would carry all before him, and either win or force the multitude to comply with his demands, proposed that, having three hundred hostages put into his hands, he should come alone into the town, or bring his army to the place of exercise, called the Cyllarabium, outside the city, and treat there.

Cleomenes, hearing this, said that he was unjustly dealt with; for they ought to have told him so plainly at first, and not now he was come even to their doors, show their jealousy and deny him admission. And writing a letter to the Achæans about the same subject, the greatest part of which was an accusation of Aratus, while Aratus, on the other side, spoke violently against him to the assembly, he hastily dislodged, and sent a trumpeter to denounce war against the Achæans, not to Argos, but to Ægium, as Aratus writes, that he might not give them notice enough to make provision for their defence. There had also been a movement among the Achæans themselves, and the cities were eager for revolt; the common people expecting a division of the land, and a release from their debts, and the chief men being in many places ill-disposed to Aratus, and some of them angry and indignant with him for having brought the Macedonians into Peloponnesus.

Encouraged by these misunderstandings, Cleomenes invaded Achæa, and first took Pellene by surprise, and beat out the Achæan garrison, and afterwards brought over Pheneus and Pentelleum to his side. Now the Achæans, suspecting some treacherous designs at Corinth and Sicyon, sent their horse and mercenaries out of Argos, to have an eye upon those cities, and they themselves went to Argos to celebrate the Nemean games. Cleomenes, advertised of this march, and hoping, as it afterwards fell out, that upon an unexpected advance to the city, now busied in the solemnity of the games, and thronged with numerous spectators, he should raise a considerable terror and confusion amongst them by night, marched with his army to the walls, and taking the quarter of the town called Aspis, which lies above the theatre, well fortified, and hard to be approached, he so terrified them that none offered to resist, but they agreed to accept a garrison, to give twenty citizens for hostages, and to assist the Lacedæmonians, and that he should have the chief command.

This action considerably increased his reputation and his power; for the ancient Spartan kings, though they in many ways endeavoured to effect it, could never bring Argos to be permanently theirs. And Pyrrhus, the most experienced captain, though he entered the city by force, could not keep possession, but was slain himself, with a considerable part of his army.

Therefore they admired the despatch and contrivance of Cleomenes; and those that before derided him, for imitating, as they said, Solon and Lycurgus, in releasing the people from their debts, and in equalising the property of the citizens, were now fain to admit that this was the cause of the change in the Spartans. For before they were very low in the world, and so unable to secure their own, that the Ætolians, invading Laconia, brought away fifty thousand slaves; so that one of the elder Spartans is reported to have said, that they had done Laconia a kindness by unburdening it; and yet a little while after, by merely recurring once again to their native customs, and reentering the track of the ancient discipline, they were able to give, as though it had been under the eyes and conduct of Lycurgus himself, the most signal instances of courage and obedience, raising Sparta to her ancient place as the commanding state of Greece, and recovering all Peloponnesus.

When Argos was captured, and Cleonæ and Phlius came over, as they did at once, to Cleomenes, Aratus was at Corinth, searching after some who were reported to favour the Spartan interest. The news, being brought to him, disturbed him very much; for he perceived the city inclining to Cleomenes, and willing to be rid of the Achæans. Therefore he summoned the citizens to meet in the council hall, and slipping away without being observed to the gate, he mounted his horse that had been brought for him thither, and fled to Sicyon. And the Corinthians made such haste to Cleomenes at Argos, that, as Aratus says, striving who should be first there, they spoiled all their horses; he adds that Cleomenes was very angry with the Corinthians for letting him escape; and that Megistonus came from Cleomenes to him, desiring him to deliver up the castle at Corinth, which was then garrisoned by the Achæans, and offered him a considerable sum of money, and that he answered that matters were not now in his power, but he in theirs. Thus Aratus himself writes.

But Cleomenes, marching from Argos, and taking in the Trœzenians, Epidaurians, and Hermioneans, came to Corinth, and blocked up the castle, which the Achæans would not surrender; and sending for Aratus's friends and stewards, committed his house and estate to their care and management; and sent Tritymallus, the Messenian, to him a second time, desiring that the castle might be equally garrisoned by the Spartans and Achæans, and promising to Aratus himself double the pension that he received from King Ptolemy. But Aratus, refusing the conditions, and sending his own son with the other hostages to Antigonus, and persuading the Achæans to make a decree for delivering the castle into Antigonus's hands, upon this Cleomenes invaded the territory of the Sicyonians, and by a decree of the Corinthians, accepted Aratus's estate as a gift.

In the meantime Antigonus, with a great army, was passing Geranea; and Cleomenes, thinking it more advisable to fortify and garrison, not the isthmus, but the mountains called Onea, and by a war of posts and positions to weary the Macedonians, rather than to venture a set battle with the highly disciplined phalanx, put his design into execution, and very much distressed Antigonus. For he had not brought victuals sufficient for his army; nor was it easy to force a way through whilst Cleomenes guarded the pass. He attempted by night to pass through Lechæum, but failed and lost some men; so that Cleomenes and his army were mightily encouraged, and so flushed with the victory that they went merrily to supper; and Antigonus was very much dejected, being driven, by the necessity he was in, to most unpromising attempts. He was proposing to march to the promontory of Heræum, and thence transport his army in boats to Sicyon, which would take up a great deal of time, and require much preparation and means. But when it was now evening, some of Aratus's friends came from Argos by sea, and invited him to return, for the Argives would revolt from Cleomenes. Aristoteles was the man that wrought the revolt, and he had no hard task to persuade the common people; for they were all angry with Cleomenes for not releasing them from their debts as they expected.

Accordingly, obtaining fifteen hundred of Antigonus's soldiers, Aratus sailed to Epidaurus; but Aristoteles, not staying for his coming, drew out the citizens, and fought against the garrison of the castle; and Timoxenus, with the Achæans from Sicyon, came to his assistance.

Cleomenes heard the news about the second watch of the night, and sending for Megistonus, angrily commanded him to go and set things right at Argos. Megistonus had passed his word for the Argives' loyalty, and had persuaded him not to banish the suspected. Therefore, despatching him with two thousand soldiers, he himself kept watch upon Antigonus,

and encouraged the Corinthians, pretending that there was no great matter in the commotions at Argos, but only a little disturbance raised by a few inconsiderable persons. But when Megistonus, entering Argos, was slain, and the garrison could scarce hold out, and frequent messengers came to Cleomenes for succours, he fearing lest the enemy, having taken Argos, should shut up the passes and securely waste Laconia, and besiege Sparta itself, which he had left without forces, dislodged from Corinth, and immediately lost that city; for Antigonus entered it, and garrisoned the town. He turned aside from his direct march, and assaulting the walls of Argos, endeavoured to carry it by a sudden attack; and then, having collected his forces from their march, breaking into the Aspis, he joined the garrison, which still held out against the Achæans; some parts of the city he scaled and took, and his Cretan archers cleared the streets.

But when he saw Antigonus with his phalanx descending from the mountains into the plain, and the horse on all sides entering the city, he thought it impossible to maintain his post, and, gathering together all his men, came safely down and made his retreat under the walls, having in so short a time possessed himself of great power, and in one journey, so to say, having made himself master of all Peloponnesus, and now lost all again in as short a time. For some of his allies at once withdrew and forsook him, and others not long after put their cities under Antigonus's protection. His hopes thus defeated, as he was leading back the relics of his forces, messengers from Lacedæmon met him in the evening at Tegea, and brought him news of as great a misfortune as that which he had lately suffered, and this was the death of his wife, to whom he was so attached, and thought so much of her that even in his most successful expeditions, when he was most prosperous, he could not refrain, but would every now and then come home to Sparta, to visit Agiatis.

The news afflicted him extremely, and he grieved, as a young man would do, for the loss of a very beautiful and excellent wife; yet he did not let his passion disgrace him or impair the greatness of his mind, but keeping his usual voice, his countenance, and his habit, he gave necessary orders to his captains, and took the precautions required for the safety of Tegea. Next morning he came to Sparta, and having at home, with his mother and children, bewailed the loss, and finished his mourning, he at once devoted himself to the public affairs of the state.

Now Ptolemy, the king of Egypt, promised him assistance, but demanded his mother and children for hostages. This, for some considerable time, he was ashamed to discover to his mother; and though he often went to her on purpose, and was just upon the discourse, yet he still refrained, and kept it to himself; so that she began to suspect, and asked his friends, whether Cleomenes had something to say to her, which he was afraid to speak. At last, Cleomenes venturing to tell her, she laughed aloud, and said, "Was this the thing that you had so often a mind to tell me, and were afraid? Make haste and put me on ship-board, and send this carcase where it may be most serviceable to Sparta, before age destroys it unprofitably here." Therefore, all things being provided for the voyage, they went by land to Tænarus, and the army waited on them. Cratesiclea, when she was ready to go on board, took Cleomenes aside into Neptune's temple, and embracing him, who was much dejected and extremely discomposed, she said, "Go to, King of Sparta; when we come forth at the door, let none see us weep, or show any passion that is unworthy of Sparta, for that alone is in our own power; as for success or disappointment, those wait on us as the deity decrees."

Having thus said, and composed her countenance, she went to the ship with her little grandson, and bade the pilot put at once out to sea. When she came to Egypt, and understood that Ptolemy entertained proposals and overtures of peace from Antigonus, and that Cleomenes, though the Achæans invited and urged him to an agreement, was afraid, for her sake, to come to any, without Ptolemy's consent, she wrote to him, advising him to do that which was most becoming and most profitable for Sparta, and not, for the sake of an old woman and a little child, stand always in fear of Ptolemy. This character she maintained in her misfortunes.

Antigonus, having taken Tegea, and plundered Orchomenus and Mantinea, Cleomenes was shut up within the narrow bounds of Laconia; and making such of the helots as could pay five Attic pounds free of Sparta; and, by that means, getting together five hundred talents, and arming two thousand after the Macedonian fashion, that he might make a body fit to oppose Antigonus's Leucaspides, he undertook a great and unexpected enterprise. Me-

galopolis was at that time a city of itself as great and as powerful as Sparta, and had the forces of the Achæans and of Antigonus encamping beside it; and it was chiefly the Megalopolitans' doing, that Antigonus had been called in to assist the Achæans.

Cleomenes, resolving to snatch the city (no other word so well suits so rapid and so surprising an action), ordered his men to take five days' provision, and marched to Sellasia, as if he intended to ravage the country of the Argives; but from thence making a descent into the territories of Megalopolis, and refreshing his army about Rhœteum, he suddenly took the road by Helicus, and advanced directly upon the city. When he was not far off the town, he sent Panteus, with two regiments, to surprise a portion of the wall between two towers, which he learnt to be the most unguarded quarter of the Megalopolitans' fortifications, and with the rest of his forces he followed leisurely. Panteus not only succeeded at that point, but finding a great part of the wall without guards, he at once proceeded to pull it down in some places, and make openings through it in others, and killed all the defenders that he found.

Whilst he was thus busied, Cleomenes came up to him, and was got with his army within the city, before the Megalopolitans knew of the surprise. When, after some time, they learned their misfortune, some left the town immediately, taking with them what property they could; others armed and engaged the enemy; and though they were not able to beat them out, yet they gave their citizens time and opportunity safely to retire, so that there were not above one thousand persons taken in the town, all the rest flying, with their wives and children, and escaping to Messene. The greater number, also, of those that armed and fought the enemy were saved, and very few taken, amongst whom were Lysandridas and Thearidas, two men of great power and reputation amongst the Megalopolitans; and therefore the soldiers, as soon as they were taken, brought them to Cleomenes. And Lysandridas, as soon as he saw Cleomenes afar off, cried out, "Now, King of Sparta, it is in your power, by doing a most kingly and a nobler action than you have already performed, to purchase the greatest glory."

Cleomenes, guessing at his meaning, replied, "What, Lysandridas, you will not surely advise me to restore your city to you again?" "It is that which I mean," Lysandridas replied; "and

I advise you not to ruin so brave a city, but to fill it with faithful and steadfast friends and allies, by restoring their country to the Megalopolitans, and being the saviour of so considerable a people." Cleomenes paused a while, and then said: "It is very hard to trust so far in these matters; but with us let profit always yield to glory." Having said this, he sent the two men to Messene with a herald from himself, offering the Megalopolitans their city again, if they would forsake the Achæan interest, and be on his side. But though Cleomenes made these generous and humane proposals, Philopœmen would not suffer them to break their league with the Achæans; and accusing Cleomenes to the people, as if his design was not to restore the city, but to take the citizens too, he forced Thearidas and Lysandridas to leave Messene.

This was that Philopœmen who was afterwards chief of the Achæans and a man of the greatest reputation amongst the Greeks, as I have related it in his own life.

This news coming to Cleomenes, though he had before taken strict care that the city should not be plundered, yet then, being in anger, and out of all patience, he despoiled the place of all the valuables, and sent the statues and pictures to Sparta; and demolishing a great part of the city, he marched away for fear of Antigonus and the Achæans; but they never stirred, for they were at Ægium, at a council of war. There Aratus mounted the speaker's place, and wept a long while, holding his mantle before his face; and at last, the company being amazed, and commanding him to speak, he said, "Megalopolis is destroyed by Cleomenes." The assembly instantly dissolved, the Achæans being astounded at the suddenness and greatness of the loss; and Antigonus, intending to send speedy succours, when he found his forces gather very slowly out of their winter-quarters, sent them orders to continue there still; and he himself marched to Argos with a small body of men.

And now the second enterprise of Cleomenes, though it had the look of a desperate and frantic adventure, yet in Polybius's opinion, was done with mature deliberation and great foresight. For knowing very well that the Macedonians were dispersed into their winter-quarters, and that Antigonus with his friends and a few mercenaries about him wintered in Argos, upon these considerations he invaded the country of the Argives, hoping to shame Antigonus to a battle upon unequal terms; or

else if he did not dare to fight, to bring him into disrepute with the Achæans. And this accordingly happened. For Cleomenes wasting, plundering, and spoiling the whole country, the Argives, in grief and anger at the loss, gathered in crowds at the king's gates, crying out that he should either fight, or surrender his command to better and braver men. But Antigonus, as became an experienced captain, accounting it rather dishonourable foolishly to hazard his army and quit his security, than merely to be railed at by other people, would not march out against Cleomenes, but stood firm to his convictions. Cleomenes, in the meantime, brought his army up to the very walls, and having without opposition spoiled the country, and insulted over his enemies, drew off again.

A little while after, being informed that Antigonus designed a new advance to Tegea, and thence to invade Laconia, he rapidly took his soldiers, and marching by a side-road, appeared early in the morning before Argos, and wasted the fields about it. The corn he did not cut down, as is usual, with reaping hooks and knives, but beat it down with great wooden staves made like broadswords, as if, in mere contempt and wanton scorn, while travelling on this way, without any effort or trouble, he spoiled and destroyed their harvest. Yet when his soldiers would have set Cyllabaris, the exercise ground, on fire, he stopped the attempt, as if he felt that the mischief he had done at Megalopolis had been the effects of his passion rather than his wisdom. And when Antigonus, first of all, came hastily back to Argos, and then occupied the mountains and passes with his posts, he professed to disregard and despise it all; and sent heralds to ask for the keys of the temple of Juno, as though he proposed to offer sacrifice there and then return. And with this scornful pleasantry upon Antigonus, having sacrificed to the goddess under the walls of the temple, which was shut, he went to Phlius; and from thence driving out those that garrisoned Oligyrtus, he marched down to Orchomenus.

These enterprises not only encouraged the citizens, but made him appear to the very enemies to be a man worthy of high command, and capable of great things. For with the strength of one city, not only to fight the power of the Macedonians and all the Peloponnesians, supported by all the royal treasures, not only to preserve Laconia from being spoiled, but to waste the enemy's country, and to take so many and such considerable cities, was an argument of no common skill and genius for command.

But he that first said that money was the sinews of affairs, seems especially in that saying to refer to war. Demades, when the Athenians had voted that their galleys should be launched and equipped for action, but could produce no money, told them, "The baker was wanted first, and the pilot after." And the old Archidamus, in the beginning of the Peloponnesian war, when the allies desired that the amount of their contributions should be determined, is reported to have answered, that war cannot be fed upon so much a day. For as wrestlers, who have thoroughly trained and disciplined their bodies, in time tire down and exhaust the most agile and most skilful combatant, so Antigonus, coming to the war with great resources to spend from, wore out Cleomenes, whose poverty made it difficult for him to provide the merest sufficiency of pay for the mercenaries, or of provisions for the citizens. For, in all other respects, time favoured Cleomenes; for Antigonus's affairs at home began to be disturbed. For the barbarians wasted and overran Macedonia whilst he was absent, and at that particular time a vast army of Illyrians had entered the country; to be freed from whose devastations, the Macedonians sent for Antigonus, and the letters had almost been brought to him before the battle was fought; upon the receipt of which he would at once have marched away home, and left the Achæans to look to themselves.

But Fortune, that loves to determine the greatest affairs by a minute, in this conjuncture showed such an exact niceness of time, that immediately after the battle in Sellasia was over, and Cleomenes had lost his army and his city, the messengers came up and called for Antigonus. And this above everything made Cleomenes's misfortune to be pitied; for if he had gone on retreating and had forborne fighting two days longer, there had been no need of hazarding a battle; since upon the departure of the Macedonians, he might have had what conditions he pleased from the Achæans. But now, as was said before, for want of money, being necessitated to trust everything to arms, he was forced with twenty thousand (such is Polybius's account), to engage thirty thousand. And approving himself an admirable commander in this difficulty, his citizens showing an extraordinary courage, and his mercenaries bravery enough, he was overborne by the different way of fighting, and the weight of the heavy-armed phalanx. Phylarchus also affirms that the treachery of some about him was the chief cause of Cleomenes's ruin.

For Antigonus gave orders that the Illyrians and Acarnanians should march round by a secret way, and encompass the other wing, which Euclidas, Cleomenes's brother, commanded; and then drew out the rest of his forces to the battle. And Cleomenes, from a convenient rising, viewing his order, and not seeing any of the Illyrians and Acarnanians, began to suspect that Antigonus had sent them upon some such design; and calling for Damoteles, who was at the head of those specially appointed to such ambush duty, he bade him carefully to look after and discover the enemy's designs upon his rear. But Damoteles, for some say Antigonus had bribed him, telling him that he should not be solicitous about that matter, for all was well enough, but mind and fight those that met him in the front, he was satisfied, and advanced against Antigonus.

By the vigorous charge of his Spartans, he made the Macedonian phalanx give ground, and pressed upon them with great advantage about half a mile; but then making a stand, and seeing the danger which the surrounding wing, commanded by his brother Euclidas, was in, he cried out, "Thou art lost, dear brother, thou art lost, thou brave example to our Spartan youth and theme of our matrons' songs." And Euclidas's wing being cut in pieces, and the conquerors from that part falling upon him, he perceived his soldiers to be disordered, and unable to maintain the fight, and therefore provided for his own safety. There fell, we are told, in the battle, besides many of the mercenary soldiers, all the Spartans, six thousand in number, except two hundred.

When Cleomenes came into the city, he advised those citizens that he met to receive Antigonus; and as for himself, he said, which should appear most advantageous to Sparta, whether his life or death, that he would choose. Seeing the women running out to those that had fled with him, taking their arms, and bringing drink to them, he entered into his own house, and his servant, who was a free-born woman, taken from Megalopolis after his wife's death, offering, as usual, to do the service he needed on returning from war, though he was very thirsty, he refused to drink, and though very weary to sit down; but in his corselet as he was, he laid his arm sideway against a pillar, and leaning his forehead upon his elbow, he rested his body a little while, and ran over in his thoughts all the courses he could take; and then with his friends set out at once for Gythium; where, finding ships which had been got ready for this very purpose, they embarked.

Antigonus, taking the city, treated the Lacedæmonians courteously, and in no way offering any insult or offence to the dignity of Sparta, but permitting them to enjoy their own laws and polity, and sacrificing to the gods, dislodged the third day. For he heard that there was a great war in Macedonia, and that the country was devastated by the barbarians. Besides, his malady had now thoroughly settled into a consumption and continual catarrh. Yet he still kept up, and managed to return and deliver his country, and meet there a most glorious death, in a great defeat and vast slaughter of the barbarians. As Phylarchus says, and as is probable in itself, he broke a blood-vessel by shouting in the battle itself. In the schools we used to be told that, after the victory was won, he cried out for joy, "O glorious day!" and presently bringing up a quantity of blood, fell into a fever, which never left him till his death. And thus much concerning Antigonus.

Cleomenes, sailing from Cythera, touched at another island called Ægialia, whence as he was about to depart for Cyrene, one of his friends, Therycion by name, a man of a noble spirit in all enterprises, and bold and lofty in his talk, came privately to him, and said thus: "Sir, death in battle, which is the most glorious, we have let go; though all heard us say that Antigonus should never tread over the King of Sparta, unless dead. And now that course which is next in honour and virtue is presented to us. Whither do we madly sail, flying the evil which is near, to seek that which is at a distance? For if it is not dishonourable for the race of Hercules to serve the successors of Philip and Alexander, we shall save a long voyage by delivering ourselves up to Antigonus, who, probably, is as much better than Ptolemy, as the Macedonians are better than the Egyptians; but if we think it mean to submit to those whose arms have conquered us, why should we choose him for our master, by whom we have not yet been beaten? Is it to acknowledge two superiors instead of one, whilst we run away from Antigonus, and flatter Ptolemy? Or, is it for your mother's sake that you retreat to Egypt? It will indeed

be a very fine and very desirable sight for her to show her son to Ptolemy's women, now changed from a prince into an exile and a slave. Are we not still masters of our own swords? And whilst we have Laconia in view, shall we not here free ourselves from this disgraceful misery, and clear ourselves to those who at Sellasia died for the honour and defence of Sparta? Or, shall we sit lazily in Egypt, inquiring what news from Sparta, and whom Antigonus hath been pleased to make governor of Lacedæmon?"

Thus spoke Therycion; and this was Cleomenes's reply: "By seeking death, you coward, the most easy and most ready refuge, you fancy that you shall appear courageous and brave, though this flight is baser than the former. Better men than we have given way to their enemies, having been betrayed by fortune, or oppressed by multitude; but he that gives way under labour or distresses, under the ill-opinions or reports of men, yields the victory of his own effeminacy. For a voluntary death ought not to be chosen as a relief from action, but as an exemplary action itself; and it is base either to live or to die only to ourselves. That death to which you now invite us, is proposed only as a release from our present miseries, but carries nothing of nobleness or profit in it. And I think it becomes both me and you not to despair of our country; but when there are no hopes of that left, those that have an inclination may quickly die."

To this Therycion returned no answer; but as soon as he had an opportunity of leaving Cleomenes's company, went aside on the seashore, and ran himself through.

But Cleomenes sailed from Ægialia, landed in Libya, and, being honourably conducted through the king's country, came to Alexandria. When he was first brought to Ptolemy, no more than common civilities and usual attentions were paid him; but when, upon trial, he found him a man of deep sense and great reason, and that his plain Laconic way of conversation carried with it a noble and becoming grace, that he did nothing unbecoming his birth, nor bent under fortune, and was evidently a more faithful counsellor than those who made it their business to please and flatter, he was ashamed, and repented that he had neglected so great a man, and suffered Antigonus to get so much power and reputation by ruining him. He now offered him many marks of respect and kindness, and gave him hopes that he would furnish him with ships and money to return to Greece, and would reinstate him in his kingdom. He granted him a yearly pension of four-and-twenty talents; a little part of which sum supplied his and his friends' thrifty temperance, and the rest was employed in doing good offices to, and in relieving the necessities of, the refugees that had fled from Greece, and retired into Egypt.

But the elder Ptolemy dying before Cleomenes's affairs had received a full dispatch, and the successor being a loose, voluptuous, and effeminate prince, under the power of his pleasures and his women, his business was neglected. For the king was so besotted with his women and his wine, that the employments of his most busy and serious hours consisted at the utmost in celebrating religious feasts in his palace, carrying a timbrel, and taking part in the show; while the greatest affairs of state were managed by Agathoclea, the king's mistress, her mother, and the pimp Œnanthes. At the first, indeed, they seemed to stand in need of Cleomenes; for Ptolemy, being afraid of his brother Magas, who by his mother's means had a great interest among the soldiers, gave Cleomenes a place in his secret councils, and acquainted him with the design of taking off his brother. He, though all were for it, declared his opinion to the contrary, saying, "The king, if it were possible, should have more brothers for the better security and stability of his affairs."

And Sosibius, the greatest favourite, replying that they were not secure of the mercenaries whilst Magas was alive, Cleomenes returned, that he need not trouble himself about that matter; for amongst the mercenaries there were above three thousand Peloponnesians, who were his fast friends, and whom he could command at any time with a nod. This discourse made Cleomenes for the present to be looked upon as a man of great influence and assured fidelity; but afterwards, Ptolemy's weakness increasing his fear, and he, as it usually happens, where there is no judgment and wisdom, placing his security in general distrust and suspicion, it rendered Cleomenes suspected to the courtiers, as having too much interest with the mercenaries; and many had this saying in their mouths, that he was a lion amidst a flock of sheep. For, in fact, such he seemed to be in the court, quietly watching and keeping his eye upon all that went on.

He therefore gave up all thought of asking for ships and soldiers from the king. But receiving news that Antigonus was dead, that the Achæans were engaged in a war with the Ætolians, and that the affairs of Peloponnesus, being now in very great distraction and disorder, required and invited his assistance, he desired leave to depart only with his friends, but could not obtain that, the king not so much as hearing his petition, being shut up amongst his women, and wasting his hours in bacchanalian rites and drinking parties. But Sosibius, the chief minister and counsellor of state, thought that Cleomenes, being detained against his will, would grow ungovernable and dangerous, and yet that it was not safe to let him go, being an aspiring, daring man, and well acquainted with the diseases and weakness of the kingdom. For neither could presents and gifts conciliate or content him; but even as Apis, while living in all possible plenty and apparent delight, yet desires to live as nature would provide for him, to range at liberty, and bound about the fields, and can scarce endure to be under the priests' keeping, so he could not brook their courtship and soft entertainment, but sat like Achilles—

and languished far,
Desiring battle and the shout of war.

His affairs standing in this condition, Nicagoras, the Messenian, came to Alexandria, a man that deeply hated Cleomenes, yet pretended to be his friend; for he had formerly sold Cleomenes a fair estate, but never received the money because Cleomenes was either unable, as it may be, or else, by reason of his engagement in the wars and other distractions, had no opportunity to pay him. Cleomenes, seeing him landing, for he was then walking upon the quay, kindly saluted him, and asked what business brought him to Egypt. Nicagoras returned his compliment, and told him that he came to bring some excellent war-horses to the king. And Cleomenes, with a smile, subjoined, "I could wish you had rather brought young boys and music-girls; for those now are the king's chief occupation."

Nicagoras at the moment smiled at the conceit, but a few days after, he put Cleomenes in mind of the estate that he had bought of him, and desired his money, protesting that he would not have troubled him, if his merchandise had turned out as profitable as he had thought it would. Cleomenes replied, that he had nothing left of all that had been given him. At which answer, Nicagoras, being nettled, told Sosibius Cleomenes's scoff upon the king. He was delighted to receive the information; but desiring to have some greater reason to excite the king against Cleomenes, persuaded Nicagoras to leave a letter written against Cleomenes, importing that he had a design, if he could have gotten ships and soldiers, to surprise Cyrene. Nicagoras wrote such a letter, and left Egypt. Four days after, Sosibius brought the letter to Ptolemy, pretending it was just then delivered him, and excited the young man's fear and anger; upon which it was agreed that Cleomenes should be invited into a large house, and treated as formerly, but not suffered to go out again.

This usage was grievous to Cleomenes, and another incident that occurred made him feel his hopes to be yet more entirely overcast. Ptolemy, the son of Chrysermas, a favourite of the king's, had always shown civility to Cleomenes; there was a considerable intimacy between them, and they had been used to talk freely together about the state. He, upon Cleomenes's desire, came to him, and spoke to him in fair terms, softening down his suspicions and excusing the king's conduct. But as he went out again, not knowing that Cleomenes followed him to the door, he severely reprimanded the keepers for their carelessness in looking after "so great and so furious a wild beast." This Cleomenes himself heard, and retiring before Ptolemy perceived it, told his friends what had been said. Upon this they cast off all former hopes and determined for violent proceedings, resolving to be revenged on Ptolemy for his base and unjust dealing, to have satisfaction for the affronts, to die as it became Spartans, and not stay till, like fatted sacrifices, they were butchered. For it was both grievous and dishonourable for Cleomenes, who had scorned to come to terms with Antigonus, a brave warrior, and a man of action, to wait an effeminate king's leisure, till he should lay aside his timbrel and end his dance, and then kill him.

These courses being resolved on, and Ptolemy happening at the same time to make a progress to Canopus, they first spread abroad a report that his freedom was ordered by the king, and, it being the custom for the king to send presents and an entertainment to those whom he would free, Cleomenes's friends made that provision, and sent it into the prison, thus imposing upon the keepers, who thought it had been sent by the king. For he sacrificed, and gave them large portions, and with a garland upon his head, feasted and made merry with his friends.

It is said that he began the action sooner than he designed, having understood that a servant who was privy to the plot had gone out to visit a mistress that he loved. This made him afraid of a discovery; and therefore, as soon as it was full moon, and all the keepers sleeping off their wine, he put on his coat, and opening his seam to bare his right shoulder, with his drawn sword in his hand, he issued forth, together with his friends provided in the same manner, making thirteen in all. One of them, by name Hippitas, was lame, and followed the first onset very well, but when he presently perceived that they were more slow in their advances for his sake, he desired them to run him through, and not ruin their enterprise by staying for a useless, unprofitable man. By chance an Alexandrian was then riding by the door; him they threw off, and setting Hippitas on horseback, ran through the streets and proclaimed liberty to the people.

But they, it seems, had courage enough to praise and admire Cleomenes's daring, but not one had the heart to follow and assist him. Three of them fell on Ptolemy, the son of Chrysermas, as he was coming out of the palace, and killed him. Another Ptolemy, the officer in charge of the city, advancing against them in a chariot, they set upon, dispersed his guards and attendants, and pulling him out of the chariot, killed him upon the place. Then they made toward the castle, designing to break open the prison, release those who were confined, and avail themselves of their numbers; but the keepers were too quick for them, and secured the passages. Being baffled in this attempt, Cleomenes with his company roamed about the city, none joining with him, but all retreating from and flying his approach. Therefore, despairing of success, and saying to his friends, that it was no wonder that women ruled over men that were afraid of liberty, he bade them all die as bravely as became his followers and their own past actions.

This said, Hippitas was first, as he desired, run through by one of the younger men, and then each of them readily and resolutely fell upon his own sword, except Panteus, the same who first surprised Megalopolis. This man, being of a very handsome person, and a great lover of the Spartan discipline, the king had made his dearest friend; and he now bade him, when he had seen him and the rest fallen, die by their example. Panteus walked over them as they lay, and pricked every one with his dagger, to try whether any was alive; when he pricked Cleomenes in the ankle, and saw him turn upon his back, he kissed him, sat down by him, and when he was quite dead, covered up the body, and then killed himself over it.

Thus fell Cleomenes, after the life which we have narrated, having been King of Sparta sixteen years. The news of their fall being noised through the city, Cratesiclea, though a woman of a great spirit, could not bear up against the weight of this affliction; but embracing Cleomenes's children, broke out into lamentations. But the eldest boy, none suspecting such a spirit in a child, threw himself headlong from the top of the house. He was bruised very much, but not killed by the fall, and was taken up crying, and expressing his resentment for not being permitted to destroy himself. Ptolemy, as soon as an account of the action was brought him, gave order that Cleomenes's body should be flayed and hung up, and that his children, mother, and the women that were with her, should be killed.

Amongst these was Panteus's wife, a beautiful and noble-looking woman, who had been but lately married, and suffered these disasters in the height of her love. Her parents would not have her embark with Panteus so shortly after they were married, though she eagerly desired it, but shut her up, and kept her forcibly at home. But a few days after she procured a horse and a little money, and escaping by night, made speed to Tænarus, where she embarked for Egypt, came to her husband, and with him cheerfully endured to live in a foreign country. She gave her hand to Cratesiclea, as she was going with the soldiers to execution, held up her robe, and begged her to be courageous; who of herself was not in the least afraid of death, and desired nothing else but only to be killed before the children. When they were come to the place of execution, the children were first killed before Cratesiclea's eyes, and afterwards she, herself, with only these words in her mouth, "O children, whither are you gone?"

But Panteus's wife, fastening her dress close about her, and being a strong woman, in silence and perfect composure, looked after every one that was slain, and laid them decently out as far as circumstances would permit; and after all were killed, rearraying her dress, and drawing her clothes close about her, suffering none to come near or be an eye-witness of her fall, besides the executioner, she courageously submitted to the stroke, and wanted nobody to look after her or wind her up after she was dead. Thus in her death the modesty of her mind appeared, and set that guard upon her body which she always kept when alive. And she, in the declining age of the Spartans, showed that women were no unequal rivals of the men, and was an instance of a courage superior to the affronts of fortune.

A few days after, those that watched the hanging body of Cleomenes, saw a large snake winding about his head, and covering his face, so that no bird of prey would fly at it. This made the king superstitiously afraid, and set the women upon several expiations, as if he had been some extraordinary being, and one beloved by the gods, that had been slain. And the Alexandrians made processions to the place, and gave Cleomenes the title of hero, and son of the gods, till the philosophers satisfied them by saying, that as oxen breed bees, putrifying horses breed wasps, and beetles rise from the carcasses of dead asses, so the humours and juices of the marrow of a man's body, coagulating, produce serpents. And this the ancients observing, appropriate a serpent, rather than any other creature, to heroes.

TIBERIUS GRACCHUS

163–133 B.C.

HAVING completed the first two narratives, we now may proceed to take a view of misfortunes, not less remarkable, in the Roman couple, and with the lives of Agis and Cleomenes, compare these of Tiberius and Caius. They were the sons of Tiberius Gracchus, who though he had been once censor, twice consul, and twice had triumphed, yet was more renowned and esteemed for his virtue than his honours. Upon this account, after the death of Scipio who overthrew Hannibal, he was thought worthy to match with his daughter Cornelia, though there had been no friendship or familiarity between Scipio and him, but rather the contrary. There is a story told that he once found in his bed-chamber a couple of snakes, and that the soothsayers, being consulted concerning the prodigy, advised that he should neither kill them both nor let them both escape; adding, that if the male serpent was killed, Tiberius should die, and if the female, Cornelia. And that therefore Tiberius, who extremely loved his wife, and thought, besides, that it was much more his part, who was an old man, to die, than it was hers, who as yet was but a young woman, killed the male serpent, and let the female escape; and soon after himself died, leaving behind him twelve children borne to him by Cornelia.

Cornelia, taking upon herself all the care of the household and the education of her children, approved herself so discreet a matron, so affectionate a mother, and so constant and noble-spirited a widow, that Tiberius seemed to all men to have done nothing unreasonable in choosing to die for such a woman; who, when King Ptolemy himself proffered her his crown, and would have married her, refused it, and chose rather to live a widow. In this state she continued, and lost all her children, except one daughter, who was married to Scipio the younger, and two sons Tiberius and Caius, whose lives we are now writing.

These she brought up with such care, that though they were without dispute in natural endowments and dispositions the first among the Romans of their time, yet they seemed to owe their virtues even more to their education than to their birth. And as in the statues and pictures made of Castor and Pollux, though the brothers resemble one another, yet there is a difference to be perceived in their countenances, between the one, who delighted in the cestus, and the other, that was famous in the course, so between these two noble youths, though there was a strong general likeness in their common love of fortitude and temperance, in their liberality, their eloquence, and their greatness of mind, yet in their actions and administrations of public affairs, a considerable variation showed itself. It will not be amiss before we proceed to mark the difference between them.

Tiberius, in the form and expression of his countenance, and in his gesture and motion, was gentle and composed; but Caius, earnest and vehement. And so in their public speeches

to the people, the one spoke in a quiet, orderly manner, standing throughout on the same spot; the other would walk about on the hustings, and in the heat of his orations pull his gown off his shoulders, and was the first of all the Romans that used such gestures; as Cleon is said to have been the first orator among the Athenians that pulled off his cloak and smote his thigh, when addressing the people. Caius's oratory was impetuous and passionate, making everything tell to the utmost, whereas Tiberius was gentle and persuasive, awakening emotions of pity. His diction was pure and carefully correct, while that of Caius was vehement and rich. So likewise in their way of living and at their tables, Tiberius was frugal and plain, Caius, compared with other men, temperate and even austere, but contrasting with his brother in a fondness for new fashions and rarities, as appears in Drusus's charge against him, that he had bought some silver dolphins, to the value of twelve hundred and fifty drachmas for every pound weight.

The same difference that appeared in their diction was observable also in their tempers. The one was mild and reasonable, the other rough and passionate, and to that degree, that often, in the midst of speaking, he was so hurried away by his passion against his judgment, that his voice lost its tone, and he began to pass into mere abusive talking, spoiling his whole speech. As a remedy to this excess, he made use of an ingenious servant of his, one Licinius, who stood constantly behind him with a sort of pitchpipe, or instrument to regulate the voice by, and whenever he perceived his master's tone alter and break with anger, he struck a soft note with his pipe, on hearing which Caius immediately checked the vehemence of his passion and his voice, grew quieter, and allowed himself to be recalled to temper. Such are the differences between the two brothers; but their valour in war against their country's enemies, their justice in the government of its subjects, their care and industry in office, and their self-command in all that regarded their pleasures, were equally remarkable in both.

Tiberius was the elder by nine years; owing to which their actions as public men were divided by the difference of the times in which those of the one and those of the other were performed. And one of the principal causes of the failure of their enterprises was this interval between their careers, and the want of combination of their efforts. The power they would have exercised, had they flourished both together, could scarcely have failed to overcome all resistance. We must therefore give an account of each of them singly, and first of the eldest.

Tiberius, immediately on his attaining manhood, had such a reputation that he was admitted into the college of the augurs, and that in consideration more of his early virtue than of his noble birth. This appeared by what Appius Claudius did, who, though he had been consul and censor, and was now the head of the Roman senate, and had the highest sense of his own place and merit, at a public feast of the augurs, addressed himself openly to Tiberius, and with great expressions of kindness, offered him his daughter in marriage. And when Tiberius gladly accepted, and the agreement had thus been completed, Appius returning home, no sooner had reached his door, but he called to his wife and cried out in a loud voice, "O Antistia, I have contracted our daughter Claudia to a husband." She, being amazed, answered, "But why so suddenly, or what means this haste? Unless you have provided Tiberius Gracchus for her husband." I am not ignorant that some apply this story to Tiberius, the father of the Gracchi, and Scipio Africanus; but most relate it as we have done. And Polybius writes, that after the death of Scipio Africanus, the nearest relations of Cornelia, preferring Tiberius to all other competitors, gave her to him in marriage, not having been engaged or promised to any one by her father.

This young Tiberius, accordingly, serving in Africa under the younger Scipio, who had married his sister, and living there under the same tent with him, soon learned to estimate the noble spirit of his commander, which was so fit to inspire strong feelings of emulation in virtue and desire to prove merit in action, and in a short time he excelled all the young men of the army in obedience and courage; and he was the first that mounted the enemy's wall, as Fannius says, who writes that he himself climbed up with him, and was partaker in the achievement. He was regarded, while he continued with the army, with great affection and left behind him on his departure a strong desire for his return.

After that expedition, being chosen paymaster, it was his fortune to serve in the war against the Numantines, under the command of Caius Mancinus, the consul, a person of no

bad character, but the most unfortunate of all the Roman generals. Notwithstanding, amidst the greatest misfortunes, and in the most unsuccessful enterprises, not only the discretion and valour of Tiberius, but also, which was still more to be admired, the great respect and honour which he showed for his general, were most eminently remarkable; though the general himself, when reduced to straits, forgot his own dignity and office. For being beaten in various great battles, he endeavoured to dislodge by night and leave his camp; which the Numantines perceiving, immediately possessed themselves of his camp, and pursuing that part of the forces which was in flight, slew those that were in the rear, hedged the whole army in on every side, and forced them into difficult ground, whence there could be no possibility of an escape.

Mancinus, despairing to make his way through by force, sent a messenger to desire a truce and conditions of peace. But they refused to give their confidence to any one except Tiberius, and required that he should be sent to treat with them. This was not only in regard to the young man's own character, for he had a great reputation amongst the soldiers, but also in remembrance of his father Tiberius, who, in his command against the Spaniards, had reduced great numbers of them to subjection, but granted a peace to the Numantines, and prevailed upon the Romans to keep it punctually and inviolably.

Tiberius was accordingly despatched to the enemy, whom he persuaded to accept of several conditions, and he himself complied with others and by this means, it is beyond a question, that he saved twenty thousand of the Roman citizens, besides attendants and camp followers. However, the Numantines retained possession of all the property they had found and plundered in the encampment; and amongst other things were Tiberius's books of accounts, containing the whole transactions of his quæstorship, which he was extremely anxious to recover. And therefore, when the army were already upon their march, he returned to Numantia, accompanied with only three or four of his friends; and making his application to the officers of the Numantines, he entreated that they would return him his books, lest his enemies should have it in their power to reproach him with not being able to give an account of the moneys intrusted to him.

The Numantines joyfully embraced this opportunity of obliging him, and invited him into the city; as he stood hesitating, they came up and took him by the hands, and begged that he would no longer look upon them as enemies, but believe them to be his friends, and treat them as such. Tiberius thought it well to consent, desirous as he was to have his books returned, and was afraid lest he should disoblige them by showing any distrust. As soon as he entered into the city, they first offered him food, and made every kind of entreaty that he would sit down and eat something in their company. Afterwards they returned his books, and gave him the liberty to take whatever he wished for in the remaining spoils. He, on the other hand, would accept of nothing but some frankincense, which he used in his public sacrifices, and bidding them farewell with every expression of kindness, departed.

When he returned to Rome, he found the whole transaction censured and reproached, as a proceeding that was base and scandalous to the Romans. But the relations and friends of the soldiers, forming a large body among the people, came flocking to Tiberius, whom they acknowledged as the preserver of so many citizens, imputing to the general all the miscarriages which had happened. Those who cried out against what had been done, urged for imitation the example of their ancestors, who stripped and handed over to the Samnites not only the generals who had consented to the terms of release, but also all the quæstors, for example, and tribunes, who had in any way implicated themselves in the agreement, laying the guilt of perjury and breach of conditions on their heads. But, in this affair, the populace, showing an extraordinary kindness and affection for Tiberius, indeed voted that the consul should be stripped and put in irons, and so delivered to the Numantines; but, for the sake of Tiberius, spared all the other officers.

It may be probable, also, that Scipio, who at that time was the greatest and most powerful man among the Romans, contributed to save him, though indeed he was also censured for not protecting Mancinus, too, and that he did not exert himself to maintain the observance of the articles of peace which had been agreed upon by his kinsman and friend Tiberius. But it may be presumed that the difference between them was for the most part due to ambitious feelings, and to the friends and reasoners who urged on Tiberius, and, as it was, it never amounted to anything that might

not have been remedied, or that was really bad. Nor can I think that Tiberius would ever have met with his misfortunes, if Scipio had been concerned in dealing with his measures; but he was away fighting at Numantia when Tiberius, upon the following occasion, first came forward as a legislator.

Of the land which the Romans gained by conquest from their neighbours, part they sold publicly, and turned the remainder into common; this common land they assigned to such of the citizens as were poor and indigent, for which they were to pay only a small acknowledgment into the public treasury. But when the wealthy men began to offer larger rents, and drive the poorer people out, it was enacted by law that no person whatever should enjoy more than five hundred acres of ground. This act for some time checked the avarice of the richer, and was of great assistance to the poorer people, who retained under it their respective proportions of ground which had been formerly rented by them. Afterwards the rich men of the neighbourhood contrived to get these lands again into their possession, under other people's names, and at last would not stick to claim most of them publicly in their own. The poor, who were thus deprived of their farms, were no longer either ready, as they had formerly been, to serve in war or careful in the education of their children; insomuch that in a short time there were comparatively few freemen remaining in all Italy, which swarmed with workhouses full of foreign-born slaves. These the rich men employed in cultivating their ground of which they dispossessed the citizens.

Caius Lælius, the intimate friend of Scipio, undertook to reform this abuse; but meeting with opposition from men of authority, and fearing a disturbance, he soon desisted, and received the name of the Wise or the Prudent, both which meanings belong to the Latin word *Sapiens*. But Tiberius, being elected tribune of the people, entered upon that design without delay, at the instigation, as is most commonly stated, of Diophanes, the rhetorician, and Blossius, the philosopher. Diophanes was a refugee from Mitylene, the other was an Italian, of the city of Cuma, and was educated there under Antipater of Tarsus, who afterwards did him the honour to dedicate some of his philosophical lectures to him.

Some have also charged Cornelia, the mother of Tiberius, with contributing towards it, because she frequently upbraided her sons, that the Romans as yet rather called her the daughter of Scipio, than the mother of the Gracchi. Others again say that Spurius Postumius was the chief occasion. He was a man of the same age with Tiberius, and his rival for reputation as a public speaker, and when Tiberius, at his return from the campaign, found him to have got far beyond him in fame and influence, and to be much looked up to, he thought to outdo him by attempting a popular enterprise of this difficulty and of such great consequence. But his brother Caius has left it us in writing, that when Tiberius went through Tuscany to Numantia, and found the country almost depopulated, there being hardly any free husbandmen or shepherds, but for the most part only barbarian, imported slaves, he then first conceived the course of policy which in the sequel proved so fatal to his family. Though it is also most certain that the people themselves chiefly excited his zeal and determination in the prosecution of it, by setting up writings upon the porches, walls, and monuments, calling upon him to reinstate the poor citizens in their former possessions.

However, he did not draw up his law without the advice and assistance of those citizens that were then most eminent for their virtue and authority; amongst whom were Crassus, the high-priest, Mucius Scævola, the lawyer, who at that time was consul, and Claudius Appius, his father-in-law. Never did any law appear more moderate and gentle, especially being enacted against such great oppression and avarice. For they who ought to have been severely punished for transgressing the former laws, and should at least have lost all their titles to such lands which they had unjustly usurped, were notwithstanding to receive a price for quitting their unlawful claims, and giving up their lands to those fit owners who stood in need of help. But though this reformation was managed with so much tenderness that, all the former transactions being passed over, the people were only thankful to prevent abuses of the like nature for the future, yet, on the other hand, the moneyed men, and those of great estates, were exasperated, through their covetous feelings against the law itself, and against the lawgiver, through anger and party-spirit. They therefore endeavoured to seduce the people, declaring that Tiberius was designing a general redivision of lands, to overthrow the government, and put all things into confusion.

But they had no success. For Tiberius, maintaining an honourable and just cause, and possessed of eloquence sufficient to have made a less creditable action appear plausible, was no safe or easy antagonist, when, with the people crowding around the hustings, he took his place, and spoke in behalf of the poor. "The savage beasts," said he, "in Italy, have their particular dens, they have their places of repose and refuge; but the men who bear arms, and expose their lives for the safety of their country, enjoy in the meantime nothing more in it but the air and light; and, having no houses or settlements of their own, are constrained to wander from place to place with their wives and children." He told them that the commanders were guilty of a ridiculous error, when, at the head of their armies, they exhorted the common soldiers to fight for their sepulchres and altars; when not any amongst so many Romans is possessed of either altar or monument, neither have they any houses of their own, or hearths of their ancestors to defend. They fought indeed and were slain, but it was to maintain the luxury and the wealth of other men. They were styled the masters of the world, but in the meantime had not one foot of ground which they could call their own.

An harangue of this nature, spoken to an enthusiastic and sympathising audience, by a person of commanding spirit and genuine feelings, no adversaries at that time were competent to oppose. Forbearing, therefore, all discussion and debate, they addressed themselves to Marcus Octavius, his fellow-tribune, who being a young man of a steady, orderly character, and an intimate friend of Tiberius, upon this account declined at first the task of opposing him; but at length, over-persuaded with the repeated importunities of numerous considerable persons, he was prevailed upon to do so, and hindered the passing of the law; it being the rule that any tribune has a power to hinder an act, and that all the rest can effect nothing, if only one of them dissents.

Tiberius, irritated at these proceedings, presently laid aside this milder bill, but at the same time preferred another; which, as it was more grateful to the common people, so it was much more severe against the wrongdoers, commanding them to make an immediate surrender of all lands which, contrary to former laws, had come into their possession. Hence there arose daily contentions between him and Octavius in their orations. However, though they expressed themselves with the utmost heat and determination, they yet were never known to descend to any personal reproaches, or in their passion to let slip any indecent expressions, so as to derogate from one another.

For not alone—

In revellings and Bacchic play,

but also in contentions and political animosities, a noble nature and a temperate education stay and compose the mind. Observing that Octavius himself was an offender against this law, and detained a great quantity of ground from the commonalty, Tiberius desired him to forbear opposing him any further, and proffered, for the public good, though he himself had but an indifferent estate, to pay a price for Octavius's share at his own cost and charges. But upon the refusal of this proffer by Octavius, he then interposed an edict, prohibiting all magistrates to exercise their respective functions, till such time as the law was either ratified or rejected by public votes. He further sealed up the gates of Saturn's temple, so that the treasurers could neither take any money out from thence, nor put any in. He threatened to impose a severe fine upon those of the prætors who presumed to disobey his commands, insomuch that all the officers, for fear of this penalty, intermitted the exercise of their several jurisdictions. Upon this the rich proprietors put themselves into mourning, and went up and down melancholy and dejected; they entered also into a conspiracy against Tiberius, and procured men to murder him; so that he also, with all men's knowledge, whenever he went abroad, took with him a sword-staff, such as robbers use, called in Latin a *dolo*.

When the day appointed was come, and the people summoned to give their votes, the rich men seized upon the voting urns and carried them away by force; thus all things were in confusion. But when Tiberius's party appeared strong enough to oppose the contrary faction, and drew together in a body, with the resolution to do so, Manlius and Fulvius, two of the consular quality, threw themselves before Tiberius, took him by the hand, and, with tears in their eyes, begged of him to desist. Tiberius, considering the mischiefs that were all but now occurring, and having a great respect for two such eminent persons, demanded of them what they would advise him to do. They acknowledged themselves unfit to advise in a matter of so great importance, but earnestly entreated him to leave it to the determination of the senate. But when the senate assembled, and could not bring the business to any result, through the prevalence of the rich faction, he then was driven to a course neither legal nor fair, and proposed to deprive Octavius of his tribuneship, it being impossible for him in any other way to get the law brought to the vote.

At first he addressed Octavius publicly, with entreaties couched in the kindest terms, and taking him by his hands, besought him, that now, in the presence of all the people, he would take this opportunity to oblige them, in granting only that request which was in itself so just and reasonable, being but a small recompense in regard of those many dangers and hardships which they had undergone for the public safety. Octavius, however, would by no means be persuaded to compliance; upon which Tiberius declared openly, that, seeing they two were united in the same office, and of equal authority, it would be a difficult matter to compose their difference on so weighty a matter without a civil war; and that the only remedy which he knew must be the deposing one of them from his office. He desired, therefore, that Octavius would summon the people to pass their verdict upon him first, averring that he would willingly relinquish his authority if the citizens desired it. Octavius refused; and Tiberius then said he would himself put to the people the question of Octavius's deposition, if upon mature deliberation he did not alter his mind, and after this declaration he adjourned the assembly till the next day.

When the people were met together again, Tiberius placed himself in the rostra, and endeavoured a second time to persuade Octavius. But all being to no purpose, he referred the whole matter to the people, calling on them to vote at once, whether Octavius should be deposed or not; and when seventeen of the thirty-five tribes had already voted against him, and there wanted only the votes of one tribe more for his final deprivation, Tiberius put a short stop to the proceedings, and once more renewed his importunities; he embraced and kissed him before all the assembly, begging with all the earnestness imaginable, that he would neither suffer himself to incur the dishonour, nor him to be reputed the author and promoter of so odious a measure. Octavius, we are told, did seem a little softened and moved with these entreaties; his eyes filled with tears, and he continued silent for a considerable time. But presently looking towards the rich men and proprietors of estates, who stood gathered in a body together, partly for shame, and partly for fear of disgracing himself with them, he boldly bade Tiberius use any severity he pleased.

The law for his deprivation being thus voted, Tiberius ordered one of his servants, whom he had made a freeman, to remove Octavius from the rostra, employing his own domestic freed servants in the stead of the public officers. And it made the action seem all the sadder, that Octavius was dragged out in such an ignominious manner. The people immediately assaulted him, whilst the rich men ran in to his assistance. Octavius, with some difficulty, was snatched away and safely conveyed out of the crowd; though a trusty servant of his, who had placed himself in front of his master that he might assist his escape, in keeping off the multitude, had his eyes struck out, much to the displeasure of Tiberius, who ran with all haste, when he perceived the disturbance, to appease the rioters.

This being done, the law concerning the lands was ratified and confirmed, and three commissioners were appointed, to make a survey of the grounds, and see the same equally divided. These were Tiberius himself, Claudius Appius, his father-in-law, and his brother, Caius Gracchus, who at this time was not at Rome, but in the army under the command of Scipio Africanus before Numantia. These things were transacted by Tiberius without any disturbance, none daring to offer any resistance to him; besides which, he gave the appointment as tribune in Octavius's place, not to any person of distinction, but to a certain Mucius, one of his own clients.

The great men of the city were therefore utterly offended, and, fearing lest he grew yet more popular, they took all opportunities of affronting him publicly in the senate house. For when he requested, as was usual, to have a tent provided at the public charge for his use, while dividing the lands, though it was a favour commonly granted to persons employed in business of much less importance, it was peremptorily refused to him; and the allowance made him for his daily expenses was fixed to nine obols only. The chief promoter of these affronts was Publius Nasica, who openly abandoned himself to his feelings of hatred against Tiberius, being a large holder of the public lands, and not a little resenting now to be turned out of them by force.

The people, on the other hand, were still more and more excited, insomuch that a little after this, it happening that one of Tiberius's friends died suddenly, and his body being marked with malignant-looking spots, they ran, in a tumultuous manner, to his funeral, crying aloud that the man was poisoned. They took the bier upon their shoulders, and stood over it, while it was placed on the pile, and really seemed to have fair grounds for their suspicion of foul play. For the body burst open, and such a quantity of corrupt humours issued out, that the funeral fire was extinguished, and when it was again kindled, the wood still would not burn; insomuch that they were constrained to carry the corpse to another place, where with much difficulty it took fire. Besides this, Tiberius, that he might incense the people yet more, put himself into mourning, brought his children amongst the crowd, and entreated the people to provide for them and their mother, as if he now despaired of his own security.

About this time king Attalus, surnamed Philometor died, and Eudemus, a Pergamenian, brought his last will to Rome, by which he had made the Roman people his heirs. Tiberius, to please the people, immediately proposed making a law, that all the money which Attalus left should be distributed amongst such poor citizens as were to be sharers of the public lands, for the better enabling them to proceed in stocking and cultivating their ground; and as for the cities that were in the territories of Attalus, he declared that the disposal of them did not at all belong to the senate, but to the people, and that he himself would ask their pleasure herein.

By this he offended the senate more than ever he had done before, and Pompeius stood up and acquainted them that he was the next neighbour to Tiberius, and so had the opportunity of knowing that Eudemus, the Pergamenian, had presented Tiberius with a royal diadem and a purple robe, as before long he was to be king of Rome. Quintus Metellus also upbraided him, saying, that when his father was censor, the Romans, whenever he happened to be going home from a supper, used to put out all their lights, lest they should be seen to have indulged themselves in feasting and drinking at unseasonable hours, whereas now the most indigent and audacious of the people were found with their torches at night, following Tiberius home.

Titus Annius, a man of no great repute for

either justice or temperance, but famous for his skill in putting and answering questions, challenged Tiberius to the proof by wager, declaring him to have deposed a magistrate who by law was sacred and inviolable. Loud clamour ensued, and Tiberius, quitting the senate hastily, called together the people, and summoning Annius to appear, was proceeding to accuse him. But Annius, being no great speaker, nor of any repute compared to him, sheltered himself in his own particular art, and desired that he might propose one or two questions to Tiberius before he entered upon the chief argument. This liberty being granted, and silence proclaimed, Annius proposed his question. "If you," said he, "had a design to disgrace and defame me, and I should apply myself to one of your colleagues for redress, and he should come forward to my assistance, would you for that reason fall into a passion, and depose him?" Tiberius, they say, was so much disconcerted at this question, that, though at other times his assurance as his readiness of speech was always remarkable, yet now he was silent and made no reply.

For the present he dismissed the assembly. But beginning to understand that the course he had taken with Octavius had created offence even among the populace as well as the nobility, because the dignity of the tribunes seemed to be violated, which had always continued till that day sacred and honourable, he made a speech to the people in justification of himself; out of which it may not be improper to collect some particulars, to give an impression of his force and persuasiveness in speaking.

"A tribune," he said, "of the people, is sacred indeed, and ought to be inviolable, because in a manner consecrated to be the guardian and protector of them; but if he degenerate so far as to oppress the people, abridge their powers, and take away their liberty of voting, he stands deprived by his own act of honours and immunities, by the neglect of the duty for which the honour was bestowed upon him. Otherwise we should be under the obligation to let a tribune do this pleasure, though he should proceed to destroy the capitol or set fire to the arsenal. He who should make these attempts would be a bad tribune. He who assails the power of the people is no longer a tribune at all. Is it not inconceivable that a tribune should have power to imprison a consul, and the people have no authority to degrade him when he uses that honour which he received from them, to their detriment? For

the tribunes, as well as the consuls, hold office by the people's votes.

"The kingly government, which comprehends all sorts of authority in itself alone, is moreover elevated by the greatest and most religious solemnity imaginable into a condition of sanctity. But the citizens, notwithstanding this, deposed Tarquin, when he acted wrongfully; and for the crime of one single man, the ancient government under which Rome was built was abolished for ever. What is there in all Rome so sacred and venerable as the vestal virgins, to whose care alone the preservation of the eternal fire is committed? Yet if one of these transgress she is buried alive; the sanctity which for the gods' sakes is allowed them, is forfeited when they offend against the gods. So likewise a tribune retains not his inviolability, which for the people's sake was accorded to him, when he offends against the people, and attacks the foundations of that authority from whence he derived his own. We esteem him to be legally chosen tribune who is elected only by the majority of votes; and is not therefore the same person much more lawfully degraded when, by a general consent of them all, they agree to depose him?

"Nothing is so sacred as religious offerings; yet the people were never prohibited to make use of them, but suffered to remove and carry them wherever they pleased; so likewise, as it were some sacred present, they have lawful power to transfer the tribuneship from one man's hands to another's. Nor can that authority be thought inviolable and irremovable which many of those who have held have of their own act surrendered and desired to be discharged from."

These were the principal heads of Tiberius's apology. But his friends, apprehending the dangers which seemed to threaten him, and the conspiracy that was gathering head against him, were of opinion that the safest way would be for him to petition that he might be continued tribune for the year ensuing. Upon this consideration he again endeavoured to secure the people's good-will with fresh laws, making the years of serving in the war fewer than formerly, granting liberty of appeal from the judges to the people, and joining to the senators, who were judges at that time, an equal number of citizens of the horsemen's degree, endeavouring as much as in him to lessen the power of the senate, rather from passion and partisanship than from any rational regard to equity and the public good. And when it came to the question whether these laws should be passed, and they perceived that the opposite party were strongest, the people as yet being not got together in a full body, they began first of all to gain time by speeches in accusation of some of their fellow-magistrates, and at length adjourned the assembly till the day following.

Tiberius then went down into the market-place amongst the people, and made his addresses to them humbly and with tears in his eyes; and told them he had just reason to suspect that his adversaries would attempt in the night-time to break open his house and murder him. This worked so strongly with the multitude, that several of them pitched tents round about his house, and kept guard all night for the security of his person. By break of day came one of the soothsayers, who prognosticate good or bad success by the pecking of fowls, and threw them something to eat. The soothsayer used his utmost endeavours to fright the fowls out of their coop; but none of them except one would venture out, which fluttered with his left wing, and stretched out his leg, and ran back again into the coop, without eating anything. This put Tiberius in mind of another ill-omen which had formerly happened to him. He had a very costly head-piece, which he made use of when he engaged in any battle, and into this piece of armour two serpents crawled, laid eggs, and brought forth young ones.

The remembrance of which made Tiberius more concerned now than otherwise he would have been. However, he went towards the capitol as soon as he understood that the people were assembled there; but before he got out of the house he stumbled upon the threshold with such violence, that he broke the nail of his great toe, insomuch that blood gushed out of his shoes. He was not gone very far before he saw two ravens fighting on the top of a house which stood on his left hand as he passed along; and though he was surrounded with a number of people, a stone struck from its place by one of the ravens, fell just at his foot. This even the boldest men about him felt as check. But Blossius of Cuma, who was present, told him that it would be a shame and an ignominious thing for Tiberius, who was a son of Gracchus, the grandson of Scipio Africanus, and the protector of the Roman people to refuse, for fear of a silly bird, to answer when his countrymen called to him; and that his adversaries would represent it not as a mere matter for their ridi-

cule, but would declaim about it to the people as the mark of a tyrannical temper, which felt a pride in taking liberties with the people.

At the same time several messengers came also from his friends, to desire his presence at the capitol, saying that all things went there according to expectation. And indeed Tiberius's first entrance there was in every way successful; as soon as ever he appeared, the people welcomed him with loud acclamations, and as he went up to his place, they repeated their expressions of joy, and gathered in a body around him, so that no one who was not well known to be his friend might approach. Mucius then began to put the business again to the vote; but nothing could be performed in the usual course and order, because of the disturbance caused by those who were on the outside of the crowd, where there was a struggle going on with those of the opposite party, who were pushing on and trying to force their way in and establish themselves among them.

Whilst things were in this confusion, Flavius Flaccus, a senator, standing in a place where he could be seen, but at such a distance from Tiberius that he could not make him hear, signified to him by motions of his hand, that he wished to impart something of consequence to him in private. Tiberius ordered the multitude to make way for him, by which means, though not without some difficulty, Flavius got to him, and informed him that the rich men, in a sitting of the senate, seeing they could not prevail upon the consul to espouse their quarrel, had come to a final determination amongst themselves that he should be assassinated, and to that purpose had a great number of their friends and servants ready armed to accomplish it. Tiberius no sooner communicated this confederacy to those about him, but they immediately tucked up their gowns, broke the halberts which the officers used to keep the crowd off into pieces, and distributed them among themselves, resolving to resist the attack with these. Those who stood at a distance wondered, and asked what was the occasion; Tiberius, knowing that they could not hear him at that distance, lifted his hand to his head wishing to intimate the great danger which he apprehended himself to be in.

His adversaries, taking notice of that action, ran off at once to the senate house, and declared that Tiberius desired the people to bestow a crown upon him, as if this were the meaning of his touching his head. This news created general confusion in the senators, and

Nasica at once called upon the consul to punish this tyrant, and defend the government. The consul mildly replied, that he would not be the first to do any violence; and as he would not suffer any freeman to be put to death, before sentence had lawfully passed upon him, so neither would he allow any measure to be carried into effect, if by persuasion or compulsion on the part of Tiberius the people had been induced to pass an unlawful vote. But Nasica, rising from his seat, "Since the consul," said he, "regards not the safety of the commonwealth, let every one who will defend the laws, follow me." He then, casting the skirt of his gown over his head, hastened to the capitol; those who bore him company, wrapped their gowns also about their arms, and forced their way after him.

As they were persons of the greatest authority in the city, the common people did not venture to obstruct their passing, but were rather so eager to clear the way for them, that they tumbled over one another in haste. The attendants they brought with them had furnished themselves with clubs and staves from their houses, and they themselves picked up the feet and other fragments of stools and chairs, which were broken by the hasty flight of the common people. Thus armed, they made towards Tiberius, knocking down those whom they found in front of him, and those were soon wholly dispersed and many of them slain. Tiberius tried to save himself by flight. As he was running, he was stopped by one who caught hold of him by the gown; but he threw it off, and fled in his under-garment only. And stumbling over those who before had been knocked down, as he was endeavouring to get up again, Publius Satureius, a tribune, one of his colleagues, was observed to give him the first fatal stroke, by hitting him upon the head with the foot of a stool. The second blow was claimed, as though it had been a deed to be proud of, by Lucius Rufus. And of the rest there fell above three hundred killed by clubs and staves only, none by an iron weapon.

This, we are told, was the first sedition amongst the Romans, since the abrogation of kingly government, that ended in the effusion of blood. All former quarrels which were neither small nor about trivial matters, were always amicably composed, by mutual concessions on either side, the senate yielding for fear of the commons, and the commons out of respect to the senate. And it is probable indeed that Tiberius himself might then have been easily induced, by mere persuasion, to give way, and certainly, if attacked at all, must have yielded without any recourse to violence and bloodshed, as he had not at that time above three thousand men to support him. But it is evident, that this conspiracy was fomented against him, more out of the hatred and malice which the rich men had to his person, than for the reasons which they commonly pretended against him.

In testimony of this, we may adduce the cruelty and unnatural insults which they used to his dead body. For they would not suffer his own brother, though he earnestly begged the favour, to bury him in the night, but threw him, together with the other corpses, into the river. Neither did their animosity stop here; for they banished some of his friends without legal process, and slew as many of the others as they could lay their hands on; amongst whom Diophanes, the orator, was slain, and one Caius Villius cruelly murdered by being shut up in a large tun with vipers and serpents. Blossius of Cuma, indeed, was carried before the consuls, and examined touching what had happened, and freely confessed that he had done, without scruple, whatever Tiberius bade him. "What," cried Nasica, "then if Tiberius had bidden you burn the capitol, would you have burnt it?" His answer was, that Tiberius never would have ordered any such thing; but being pressed with the same question by several, he declared, "If Tiberius had commanded it, it would have been right for me to do it; for he never would have commanded it, if it had not been for the people's good." Blossius at this time was pardoned, and afterwards went away to Aristonicus in Asia, and when Aristonicus was overthrown and ruined, killed himself.

The senate, to soothe the people after these transactions, did not oppose the division of the public lands, and permitted them to choose another commissioner in the room of Tiberius. So they elected Publius Crassus, who was Gracchus's near connection, as his daughter Licinia was married to Caius Gracchus; although Cornelius Nepos says that it was not Crassus's daughter whom Caius married, but Brutus's, who triumphed for his victories over the Lusitanians; but most writers state it as we have done. The people, however, showed evident marks of their anger at Tiberius's death; and were clearly waiting only for the opportunity to be revenged, and Nasica was already threatened with an impeachment. The senate, therefore, fearing lest some mischief should befall him, sent him ambassador into Asia, though there was no occasion for his going thither. For the people did not conceal their indignation, even in the open streets, but railed at him whenever they met him abroad, calling him a murderer and a tyrant, one who had polluted the most holy and religious spot in Rome with the blood of a sacred and inviolable magistrate. And so Nasica left Italy, although he was bound, being the chief priest, to officiate in all principal sacrifices. Thus wandering wretchedly and ignominiously from one place to another, he died in a short time after, not far from Pergamus.

It is no wonder that the people had such an aversion to Nasica, when even Scipio Africanus, though so much and so deservedly beloved by the Romans, was in danger of quite losing the good opinion which the people had of him, only for repeating, when the news of Tiberius's death was first brought to Numantia, the verse out of Homer—

Even so perish all who do the same.

And afterwards, being asked by Caius and Fulvius, in a great assembly, what he thought of Tiberius's death, he gave an answer adverse to Tiberius's public actions. Upon which account, the people thenceforth used to interrupt him when he spoke, which, until that time, they had never done, and he, on the other hand, was induced to speak ill of the people. But of this the particulars are given in the life of Scipio.

CAIUS GRACCHUS

153–121 B.C.

CAIUS GRACCHUS at first, either for fear of his brother's enemies, or designing to render them more odious to the people, absented himself from the public assemblies, and lived quietly in his own house, as if he were not only reduced for the present to live unambitiously, but was disposed in general to pass his life in inaction. And some, indeed, went so far as to say that he disliked his brother's measures, and had wholly abandoned the defence of them. However, he was not but very young, being not so old as Tiberius by nine years; and he was not yet thirty when he was slain.

In some little time, however, he quietly let his temper appear, which was one of an utter antipathy to a lazy retirement and effeminacy, and not the least likely to be contented with a life of eating, drinking, and money-getting. He gave great pains to the study of eloquence, as wings upon which he might aspire to public business; and it was very apparent that he did not intend to pass his days in obscurity. When Vettius, a friend of his, was on his trial, he defended his cause, and the people were in an ecstasy, and transported with joy, finding him master of such eloquence that the other orators seemed like children in comparison, and jealousies and fears on the other hand began to be felt by the powerful citizens, and it was generally spoken of amongst them that they must hinder Caius from being made tribune.

But soon after, it happened that he was elected quæstor, and obliged to attend Orestes, the consul, into Sardinia. This, as it pleased his enemies, so it was not ungrateful to him, being naturally of a warlike character, and as well trained in the art of war as in that of pleading. And, besides, as yet he very much dreaded meddling with state affairs, and appearing publicly in the rostra, which, because of the importunity of the people and his friends, he could not otherwise avoid than by taking this journey. He was therefore most thankful for the opportunity of absenting himself. Notwithstanding which, it is the prevailing opinion that Caius was a far more thorough demagogue, and more ambitious than ever Tiberius had been, of popular applause; yet it is certain that he was borne rather by a sort of necessity than by any purpose of his own into public business. And Cicero, the orator, relates, that when he declined all such concerns, and would have lived privately, his brother appeared to him in a dream, and calling him by his name, said, "Why do you tarry, Caius? There is no escape; one life and one death is appointed for us both, to spend the one and to meet the other in the service of the people."

Caius was no sooner arrived in Sardinia, but he gave exemplary proofs of his high merit; he not only excelled all the young men of his age in his actions against his enemies, in doing justice to his inferiors, and in showing all obedience and respect to his superior officer; but likewise in temperance, frugality, and industry, he surpassed even those who were much older than himself. It happened to be a sharp and sickly winter in Sardinia, insomuch that the general was forced to lay an imposition upon several towns to supply the soldiers with necessary clothes. The cities sent to Rome, petitioning to be excused from that burden; the senate found their request reasonable, and ordered the general to find some other way of new clothing the army.

While he was at a loss what course to take in this affair, the soldiers were reduced to great distress; but Caius went from one city to another, and by his mere representations he prevailed with them, that of their own accord they clothed the Roman army. This again being reported to Rome, and seeming to be only an intimation of what was to be expected of him as a popular leader hereafter, raised new jealousies amongst the senators. And, besides, there came ambassadors out of Africa from King Micipsa, to acquaint the senate that their master, out of respect to Caius Gracchus, had sent a considerable quantity of corn to the general in Sardinia; at which the senators were so much offended, that they turned the ambassadors out of the senate house, and made an order that the soldiers should be relieved by sending others in their room; but that Orestes should continue at his post, with whom Caius, also, as they presumed, being his quæstor, would remain.

But he, finding how things were carried, immediately in anger took ship for Rome, where his unexpected appearance obtained him the censure not only of his enemies, but also of the people; who thought it strange that a quæstor should leave before his commander. Nevertheless, when some accusation upon this ground was made against him to the censors, he desired leave to defend himself, and did it so effectually, that, when he ended, he was regarded as one who had been very much injured. He made it then appear that he had served twelve years in the army, whereas others are obliged to serve only ten; that he had continued quæstor to the general three years, whereas he might by law have returned at the end of one year; and alone of all who went on the ex-

pedition, he had carried out a full and had brought home an empty purse, while others, after drinking up the wine they had carried out with them, brought back the wine-jars filled again with gold and silver from the war.

After this they brought other accusations and writs against him, for exciting insurrection amongst the allies, and being engaged in the conspiracy that was discovered about Fregellæ. But having cleared himself of every suspicion, and proved his entire innocence, he now at once came forward to ask for the tribuneship; in which, though he was universally opposed by all persons of distinction, yet there came such infinite numbers of people from all parts of Italy to vote for Caius, that lodgings for them could not be supplied in the city; and the Field being not large enough to contain the assembly, there were numbers who climbed upon the roofs and the tilings of the houses to use their voices in his favour. However, the nobility so far forced the people to their pleasure and disappointed Caius's hope, that he was not returned the first, as was expected, but the fourth tribune.

But when he came to the execution of his office, it was seen presently who was really first tribune, as he was a better orator than any of his contemporaries, and the passion with which he still lamented his brother's death made him the bolder in speaking. He used on all occasions to remind the people of what had happened in that tumult, and laid before them the examples of their ancestors, how they declared war against the Faliscans, only for giving scurrilous language to one Genucius, a tribune of the people; and sentenced Caius Veturius to death, for refusing to give way in the forum to a tribune; "Whereas," said he, "these men did, in the presence of you all, murder Tiberius with clubs, and dragged the slaughtered body through the middle of the city, to be cast into the river. Even his friends, as many as could be taken, were put to death immediately, without any trial, notwithstanding that just and ancient custom, which has always been observed in our city, that whenever any one is accused of a capital crime, and does not make his personal appearance in court, a trumpeter is sent in the morning to his lodging, to summon him by sound of trumpet to appear; and before this ceremony is performed, the judges do not proceed to the vote; so cautious and reserved were our ancestors about business of life and death."

Having moved the people's passion with

such addresses (and his voice was of the loudest and strongest), he proposed two laws. The first was, that whoever was turned out of any public office by the people, should be thereby rendered incapable of bearing any office afterwards; the second, that if any magistrate condemn a Roman to be banished without a legal trial, the people be authorised to take cognisance thereof.

One of these laws was manifestly levelled at Marcus Octavius, who, at the instigation of Tiberius, had been deprived of his tribuneship. The other touched Popilius, who, in his prætorship, had banished all Tiberius's friends; whereupon Popilius, being unwilling to stand the hazard of a trial, fled out of Italy. As for the former law, it was withdrawn by Caius himself, who said he yielded in the case of Octavius, at the request of his mother Cornelia.

This was very acceptable and pleasing to the people, who had a great veneration for Cornelia, not more for the sake of her father than for that of her children; and they afterwards erected a statue of brass in honour of her, with this inscription, *Cornelia, the mother of the Gracchi.* There are several expressions recorded, in which he used her name perhaps with too much rhetoric, and too little self-respect, in his attacks upon his adversaries. "How," said he, "dare you presume to reflect upon Cornelia, the mother of Tiberius?" And because the person who made the reflections had been suspected of effeminate courses, "With what face," said he, "can you compare Cornelia with yourself? Have you brought forth children as she has done? And yet all Rome knows that she has refrained from the conversation of men longer than you yourself have done." Such was the bitterness he used in his language; and numerous similar expressions might be adduced from his written remains.

Of the laws which he now proposed, with the object of gratifying the people and abridging the power of the senate, the first was concerning the public lands, which were to be divided amongst the poor citizens; another was concerning the common soldiers, that they should be clothed at the public charge, without any diminution of their pay, and that none should be obliged to serve in the army who was not full seventeen years old; another gave the same right to all the Italians in general, of voting at elections, as was enjoyed by the citizens of Rome; a fourth related to the price of corn, which was to be sold at a lower rate than formerly to the poor; and a fifth regulated the

courts of justice, greatly reducing the power of the senators. For hitherto, in all causes, senators only sat as judges, and were therefore much dreaded by the Roman knights and the people. But Caius joined three hundred ordinary citizens of equestrian rank with the senators, who were three hundred likewise in number, and ordained that the judicial authority should be equally invested in the six hundred.

While he was arguing for the ratification of this law, his behaviour was observed to show in many respects unusual earnestness, and whereas other popular leaders had always hitherto, when speaking, turned their faces towards the senate house, and the place called the comitium, he, on the contrary, was the first man that in his harangue to the people turned himself the other way, towards them, and continued after that time to do so. An insignificant movement and change of posture, yet it marked no small revolution in state affairs, the conversion, in a manner, of the whole government from an aristocracy to a democracy, his action intimating that public speakers should address themselves to the people, not the senate.

When the commonalty ratified this law, and gave him power to select those of the knights whom he approved of, to be judges, he was invested with a sort of a kingly power, and the senate itself submitted to receive his advice in matters of difficulty; nor did he advise anything that might derogate from the honour of that body. As, for example, his resolution about the corn which Fabius the proprietor sent from Spain was very just and honourable; for he persuaded the senate to sell the corn, and return the money to the same provinces which had furnished them with it; and also that Fabius should be censured for rendering the Roman government odious and insupportable. This got him extraordinary respect and favour among the provinces. Besides all this, he proposed measures for the colonisation of several cities, for making roads, and for building public granaries; of all which works he himself undertook the management and superintendence, and was never wanting to give necessary orders for the despatch of all these different and great undertakings; and that with such wonderful expedition and diligence, as if he had been but engaged upon one of them; insomuch that all persons, even those who hated or feared him, stood amazed to see what a capacity he had for effecting and completing all he undertook.

As for the people themselves, they were transported at the very sight, when they saw him surrounded with a crowd of contractors, artificers, public deputies, military officers, soldiers, and scholars. All these he treated with an easy familiarity, yet without abandoning his dignity in his gentleness; and so accommodated his nature to the wants and occasions of every one who addressed him, that those were looked upon as no better than envious detractors, who had represented him as a terrible, assuming, and violent character. He was even a greater master of the popular leader's art in his common talk and his actions, than he was in his public addresses.

His most especial exertions were given to constructing the roads, which he was careful to make beautiful and pleasant, as well as convenient. They were drawn by his directions through the fields, exactly in a straight line, partly paved with hewn stone, and partly laid with solid masses of gravel. When he met with any valleys or deep watercourses crossing the line, he either caused them to be filled up with rubbish, or bridges to be built over them, so well levelled, that all being of an equal height on both sides, the work presented one uniform and beautiful prospect. Besides this, he caused the roads to be all divided into miles (each mile containing little less than eight furlongs), and erected pillars of stone to signify the distance from one place to another. He likewise placed other stones at small distances from one another, on both sides of the way, by the help of which travellers might get easily on horseback without wanting a groom.

For these reasons, the people highly extolled him, and were ready upon all occasions to express their affection towards him. One day, in an oration to them, he declared that he had only one favour to request, which, if they granted, he should think the greatest obligation in the world; yet if it were denied, he would never blame them for the refusal. This expression made the world believe that his ambition was to be consul; and it was generally expected that he wished to be both consul and tribune at the same time. When the day for election of consuls was at hand, and all in great expectation, he appeared in the Field with Caius Fannius, canvassing together with his friends for his election. This was of great effect in Fannius's favour. He was chosen consul, and Caius elected tribune the second time, without his own seeking or petitioning for it, but at the voluntary motion of the people. But

when he understood that the senators were his declared enemies, and that Fannius himself was none of the most zealous of friends, he began again to rouse the people with other new laws. He proposed that a colony of Roman citizens might be sent to re-people Tarentum and Capua, and that the Latins should enjoy the same privileges with the citizens of Rome.

But the senate, apprehending that he would at last grow too powerful and dangerous, took a new and unusual course to alienate the people's affections from him, by playing the demagogue in opposition to him, and offering favours contrary to all good policy. Livius Drusus was fellow-tribune with Caius, a person of as good a family and as well educated as any amongst the Romans, and noways inferior to those who for their eloquence and riches were the most honoured and most powerful men of that time. To him, therefore, the chief senators made their application, exhorting him to attack Caius, and join in their confederacy against him; which they designed to carry on, not by using any force, or opposing the common people, but by gratifying and obliging them with such unreasonable things as otherwise they would have felt it honourable for them to incur the greatest unpopularity in resisting.

Livius offered to serve the senate with his authority in this business; and proceeded accordingly to bring forward such laws as were in reality neither honourable nor advantageous for the public; his whole design being to outdo Caius in pleasing and cajoling the populace (as if it had been in some comedy), with obsequious flattery and every kind of gratifications; the senate thus letting it be seen plainly that they were not angry with Caius's public measures, but only desirous to ruin him utterly, or at least to lessen his reputation. For when Caius proposed the settlement of only two colonies, and mentioned the better class of citizens for that purpose, they accused him of abusing the people; and yet, on the contrary, were pleased with Drusus, when he proposed the sending out of twelve colonies, each to consist of three thousand persons, and those, too, the most needy that he could find. When Caius divided the public land amongst the poor citizens, and charged them with a small rent, annually to be paid into the exchequer, they were angry at him, as one who sought to gratify the people only for his own interest; yet afterwards they commended Livius, though he exempted them from paying even that little acknowledgment. They were displeased with Caius for offering the Latins an equal right with the Romans of voting at the election of magistrates; but when Livius proposed that it might not be lawful for a Roman captain to scourge a Latin soldier, they promoted the passing of that law.

For Livius, in all his speeches to the people, always told them that he proposed no laws but such as were agreeable to the senate, who had a particular regard to the people's advantage. And this truly was the only point in all his proceedings which was of any real service, as it created more kindly feelings towards the senate in the people; and whereas they formerly suspected and hated the principal senators, Livius appeased and mitigated this perverseness and animosity, by his profession that he had done nothing in favour and for the benefit of the commons without their advice and approbation.

But the greatest credit which Drusus got for kindness and justice towards the people was, that he never seemed to propose any law for his own sake, or his own advantage; he committed the charge of seeing the colonies rightly settled to other commissioners; neither did he ever concern himself with the distribution of the moneys; whereas Caius always took the principal part in any important transactions of this kind. Rubrius, another tribune of the people, had proposed to have Carthage again inhabited, which had been demolished by Scipio, and it fell to Caius's lot to see this performed, and for that purpose he sailed to Africa.

Drusus took this opportunity of his absence to insinuate himself still more into the people's affections, which he did chiefly by accusing Fulvius, who was a particular friend to Caius, and was appointed a commissioner with him for the division of the lands. Fulvius was a man of a turbulent spirit, and notoriously hated by the senate; and besides, he was suspected by others to have fomented the difference between the citizens and their confederates, and underhand to be inciting the Italians to rebel; though there was little other evidence of the truth of these accusations than his being an unsettled character and of a well-known seditious temper. This was one principal cause of Caius's ruin; for part of the envy which fell upon Fulvius was extended to him.

And when Scipio Africanus died suddenly, and no cause of such an unexpected death could be assigned, only some marks of blows upon his body seemed to intimate that he had suffered violence, as is related in the history of his life, the greatest part of the odium attached to Fulvius, because he was his enemy, and that very day had reflected upon Scipio in a public address to the people. Nor was Caius himself clear from suspicion. However, this great outrage, committed too upon the person of the greatest and most considerable man in Rome, was never either punished or inquired into thoroughly, for the populace opposed and hindered any judicial investigation, for fear that Caius should be implicated in the charge if proceedings were carried on. This, however, had happened some time before.

But in Africa, where at present Caius was engaged in the re-peopling of Carthage, which he named Junonia, many ominous appearances, which presaged mischief, are reported to have been sent from the gods. For a sudden gust of wind falling upon the first standard, and the standard-bearer holding it fast, the staff broke; another sudden storm blew away the sacrifices, which were laid upon the altars, and carried them beyond the bounds laid out for the city, and the wolves came and carried away the very marks that were set up to show the boundary.

Caius, notwithstanding all this, ordered and despatched the whole business in the space of seventy days, and then returned to Rome, understanding how Fulvius was prosecuted by Drusus, and that the present juncture of affairs would not suffer him to be absent. For Lucius Opimius, one who sided with the nobility, and was of no small authority in the senate, who had formerly sued to be consul, but was repulsed by Caius's interest, at the time when Fannius was elected, was in a fair way now of being chosen consul, having a numerous company of supporters. And it was generally believed, if he did obtain it, that he would wholly ruin Caius, whose power was already in a declining condition; and the people were not so apt to admire his actions as formerly, because there were so many others who every day contrived new ways to please them, with which the senate readily complied.

After his return to Rome, he quitted his house on the Palatine Mount, and went to live near the market-place, endeavouring to make himself more popular in those parts, where most of the humble and poorer citizens lived. He then brought forward the remainder of his proposed laws, as intending to have them ratified by the popular vote; to support which a vast number of people collected from all quarters. But the senate persuaded Fannius, the consul, to command all persons who were not born Romans to depart the city. A new and unusual proclamation was thereupon made, prohibiting any of the allies or Confederates to appear at Rome during that time. Caius, on the contrary, published an edict, accusing the consul for what he had done, and setting forth to the Confederates, that if they would continue upon the place, they might be assured of his assistance and protection. However, he was not so good as his word; for though he saw one of his own familiar friends and companions dragged to prison by Fannius's officers, he, notwithstanding, passed by without assisting him; either because he was afraid to stand the test of his power, which was already decreased, or because as he himself reported, he was unwilling to give his enemies an opportunity, which they very much desired, of coming to actual violence and fighting.

About that time there happened likewise a difference between him and his fellow-officers upon this occasion. A show of gladiators was to be exhibited before the people in the market-place, and most of the magistrates erected scaffolds round about, with an intention of letting them for advantage. Caius commanded them to take down their scaffolds, that the poor people might see the sport without paying anything. But nobody obeying these orders of his, he gathered together a body of labourers, who worked for him, and overthrew all the scaffolds the very night before the contest was to take place. So that by the next morning the market-place was cleared, and the common people had an opportunity of seeing the pastime. In this, the populace thought he had acted the part of a man; but he much disobliged the tribunes, his colleagues, who regarded it as a piece of violent and presumptuous interference.

This was thought to be the chief reason that he failed of being the third time elected tribune; not but that he had the most votes, but because his colleagues out of revenge caused false returns to be made. But as to this matter there was a controversy. Certain it is, he very much resented this repulse, and behaved with unusual arrogance towards some of his adversaries who were joyful at his defeat, telling them that all this was but a false, sardonic mirth, as they little knew how much his actions threw them into obscurity.

As soon as Opimius also was chosen consul, they presently cancelled several of Caius's laws, and especially called in question his proceedings at Carthage, omitting nothing that was likely to irritate him, that from some effect of his passion they might find out a tolerable pretence to put him to death. Caius at first bore these things very patiently; but afterwards, at the instigation of his friends, especially Fulvius, he resolved to put himself at the head of a body of supporters, to oppose the consul by force. They say also that on this occasion his mother, Cornelia, joined in the sedition, and assisted him by sending privately several strangers into Rome, under pretence as if they came to be hired there for harvest-men; for that intimations of this are given in her letters to him. However, it is confidently affirmed by others that Cornelia did not in the least approve of these actions.

When the day came in which Opimius designed to abrogate the laws of Caius, both parties met very early at the capitol; and the consul having performed all the rites usual in their sacrifices, one Quintus Antyllius, an attendant on the consul, carrying out the entrails of the victim, spoke to Fulvius and his friends who stood about him, "Ye factious citizens, make way for honest men." Some report that, besides this provoking language, he extended his naked arm towards them, as a piece of scorn and contempt. Upon this he was presently killed with the strong styles which are commonly used in writing, though some say that on this occasion they had been manufactured for this purpose only. This murder caused a sudden consternation in the whole assembly, and the heads of each faction had their different sentiments about it. As for Caius, he was much grieved, and severely reprimanded his own party, because they had given their adversaries a reasonable pretence to proceed against them, which they had so long hoped for. Opimius, immediately seizing the occasion thus offered, was in great delight, and urged the people to revenge; but there happening a great shower of rain on a sudden, it put an end to the business of that day.

Early the next morning, the consul summoned the senate, and whilst he advised with the senators in the senate-house, the corpse of Antyllius was laid upon a bier, and brought through the market-place, being there exposed to open view, just before the senate-house, with a great deal of crying and lamentation. Opimius was not at all ignorant that this was designed to be done; however, he seemed to be surprised, and wondered what the meaning of it should be; the senators, therefore, presently went out to know the occasion of it, and, standing about the corpse, uttered exclamations against the inhuman and barbarous act. The people, meantime, could not but feel resentment and hatred for the senators, remembering how they themselves had not only assassinated Tiberius Gracchus, as he was executing his office in the very capitol, but had also thrown his mangled body into the river; yet now they could honour with their presence and their public lamentations in the Forum the corpse of an ordinary hired attendant (who, though he might perhaps die wrongfully, was, however, in a great measure the occasion of it himself), by these means hoping to undermine him who was the only remaining defender and safeguard of the people.

The senators, after some time, withdrew, and presently ordered that Opimius, the consul, should be invested with extraordinary power to protect the commonwealth and suppress all tyrants. This being decreed, he presently commanded the senators to arm themselves, and the Roman knights to be in readiness very early the next morning, and every one of them to be attended with two servants well armed. Fulvius, on the other side, made his preparations and collected the populace. Caius at that time returning from the market-place, made a stop just before his father's statue, and fixing his eyes for some time upon it, remained in a deep contemplation; at length he sighed, shed tears, and departed. This made no small impression upon those who saw it, and they began to upbraid themselves that they should desert and betray so worthy a man as Caius. They therefore went directly to his house, remaining there as a guard about it all night, though in a different manner from those who were a guard to Fulvius; for they passed away the night with shouting and drinking, and Fulvius himself, being the first to get drunk, spoke and acted many things very unbecoming a man of his age and character.

On the other side, the party which guarded Caius, were quiet and diligent, relieving one another by turns, and forecasting, as in a public calamity, what the issue of things might be. As soon as daylight appeared, they roused Fulvius, who had not yet slept off the effects of his drinking; and having armed themselves with the weapons hung up in his house, that were formerly taken from the Gauls, whom he conquered in the time of his consulship, they presently, with threats and loud acclamations, made their way towards the Aventine Mount.

Caius could not be persuaded to arm himself, but put on his gown, as if he had been going to the assembly of the people, only with this difference, that under it he had then a short dagger by his side. As he was going out, his wife came running to him at the gate, holding him with one hand, and with the other a young child of his. She bespoke him: "Alas, Caius, I do not now part with you to let you address the people either as a tribune or a lawgiver, nor as if you were going to some honourable war, when, though you might perhaps have encountered that fate which all must some time or other submit to, yet you had left me this mitigation of my sorrow, that my mourning was respected and honoured. You go now to expose your person to the murderers of Tiberius, unarmed indeed, and rightly so, choosing rather to suffer the worst of injuries than do the least yourself. But even your very death at this time will not be serviceable to the public good. Faction prevails; power and arms are now the only measures of justice. Had your brother fallen before Numantia, the enemy would have given back what then had remained of Tiberius; but such is my hard fate, that I probably must be an humble suppliant to the floods or the waves, that they would somewhere restore to me your relics; for since Tiberius was not spared, what trust can we place either on the laws, or in the gods?"

Licinia, thus bewailing, Caius, by degrees getting loose from her embraces, silently withdrew himself, being accompanied by his friends; she, endeavouring to catch him by the gown, fell prostrate upon the earth, lying there for some time speechless. Her servants took her up for dead, and conveyed her to her brother Crassus.

Fulvius, when the people were gathered together in a full body, by the advice of Caius sent his youngest son into the market-place, with a herald's rod in his hand. He, being a very handsome youth, and modestly addressing himself, with tears in his eyes and a becoming bashfulness, offered proposals of agreement to the consul and the whole senate. The greatest part of the assembly were inclinable to accept of the proposals; but Opimius said that it did not become them to send messengers and capitulate with the senate, but to surrender at discretion to the laws, like loyal citizens, and endeavour to merit their pardon by submission. He commanded the youth not to return, unless they would comply with these conditions.

Caius, as it is reported, was very forward to go and clear himself before the senate; but none of his friends consenting to it, Fulvius sent his son a second time to intercede for them, as before. But Opimius, who was resolved that a battle should ensue, caused the youth to be apprehended and committed into custody; and then with a company of his foot-soldiers and some Cretan archers set upon the party under Fulvius. These archers did such execution, and inflicted so many wounds, that a rout and flight quickly ensued. Fulvius fled into an obscure bathing-house; but shortly after being discovered, he and his eldest son were slain together. Caius was not observed to use any violence against any one; but, extremely disliking all these outrages, retired to Diana's temple. There he attempted to kill himself, but was hindered by his faithful friends, Pomponius and Licinius; they took his sword away from him, and were very urgent that he would endeavour to make his escape. It is reported that, falling upon his knee and lifting up his hands, he prayed the goddess that the Roman people, as a punishment for their ingratitude and treachery, might always remain in slavery. For as soon as a proclamation was made of a pardon, the greater part openly deserted him.

Caius, therefore, endeavoured now to make his escape, but was pursued so close by his enemies, as far as the wooden bridge, that from thence he narrowly escaped. There his two trusty friends begged of him to preserve his own person by flight, whilst they in the meantime would keep their post, and maintain the passage; neither could their enemies, until they were both slain, pass the bridge. Caius had no other companion in his flight but one Philocrates, a servant of his. As he ran along, everybody encouraged him, and wished him success, as standers-by may do to those who are engaged in a race, but nobody either lent him any assistance, or would furnish him with a horse, though he asked for one; for his enemies had gained ground, and got very near him. However, he had still time enough to hide himself in a little grove, consecrated to the Furies. In that place, his servant Philocrates having first slain him, presently afterwards killed himself also, and fell dead upon his master. Though some affirm it for a truth, that they were both taken alive by their enemies, and that Philocrates embraced his master so close, that they could not wound Caius until his servant was slain.

They say that when Caius's head was cut off, and carried away by one of his murderers, Septimuleius, Opimius's friend, met him, and forced it from him; because, before the battle began, they had made proclamation, that whoever should bring the head either of Caius or Fulvius, should, as a reward, receive its weight in gold. Septimuleius, therefore, having fixed Caius's head upon the top of his spear, came and presented it to Opimius. They presently brought the scales, and it was found to weigh above seventeen pounds. But in this affair, Septimuleius gave as great signs of his knavery as he had done before of his cruelty; for having taken out the brains, he had filled the skull with lead. There were others who brought the head of Fulvius, too, but, being mean, inconsiderable persons, were turned away without the promised reward.

The bodies of these two persons, as well as of the rest who were slain, to the number of three thousand men, were all thrown into the river; their goods were confiscated, and their widows forbidden to put themselves into mourning. They dealt even more severely with Licinia, Caius's wife, and deprived her even of her jointure; and as in addition still to all their inhumanity, they barbarously murdered Fulvius's youngest son; his only crime being, not that he took up arms against them, or that he was present in the battle, but merely that he had come with articles of agreement; for this he was first imprisoned, then slain.

But that which angered the common people most was, that at this time, in memory of his success, Opimius built the Temple of Concord, as if he gloried and triumphed in the slaughter of so many citizens. Somebody in the night time, under the inscription of the temple added this verse:—

Folly and Discord Concord's temple built.

Yet this Opimius, the first who, being consul, presumed to usurp the power of a dictator, condemning, without any trial, with three thousand other citizens, Caius Gracchus and Fulvius Flaccus, one of whom had triumphed and been consul, the other far excelled all his contemporaries in virtue and honour, afterwards was found incapable of keeping his hands from thieving: and when he was sent ambassador to Jugurtha, King of Numidia, he was there corrupted by presents, and at his return, being shamefully convicted of it, lost all his honours, and grew old amidst the hatred and the insults of the people; who, though humble, and affrighted at the time, did not fail before long to let everybody see what respect and veneration they had for the memory of the Gracchi. They ordered their statues to be made and set up in public view; they consecrated the places where they were slain, and thither brought the first-fruits of everything, according to the season of the year, to make their offerings. Many came likewise thither to their devotions, and daily worshipped there, as at the temple of the gods.

It is reported that as Cornelia, their mother, bore the loss of her two sons with a noble and undaunted spirit, so, in reference to the holy places in which they were slain, she said their dead bodies were well worthy of such sepulchres. She removed afterwards, and dwelt near the place called Misenum, not at all altering her former way of living. She had many friends, and hospitably received many strangers at her house; many Greeks and learned men were continually about her; nor was there any foreign prince but received gifts from her and presented her again.

Those who were conversant with her, were much interested, when she pleased to entertain them with her recollections of her father Scipio Africanus, and of his habits and way of living. But it was most admirable to hear her make mention of her sons, without any tears or sign of grief, and give the full account of all their deeds and misfortunes, as if she had been relating the history of some ancient heroes. This made some imagine, that age, or the greatness of her afflictions, had made her senseless and devoid of natural feelings. But they who so thought were themselves more truly insensible not to see how much a noble nature and education avail to conquer any affliction; and though fortune may often be more successful, and may defeat the efforts of virtue to avert misfortunes, it cannot, when we incur them, prevent our bearing them reasonably.

CAIUS and TIBERIUS GRACCHUS
and
AGIS and CLEOMENES
Compared

Having given an account severally of these persons, it remains only that we should take a view of them in comparison with one another.

As for the Gracchi, the greatest detractors and their worst enemies could not but allow that they had a genius to virtue beyond all other Romans, which was improved also by a generous education. Agis and Cleomenes may be supposed to have had stronger natural gifts, since, though they wanted all the advantages of good education, and were bred up in those very customs, manners, and habits of living which had for a long time corrupted others, yet they were public examples of temperance and frugality. Besides, the Gracchi, happening to live when Rome had her greatest repute for honour and virtuous actions, might justly have been ashamed, if they had not also left to the next generation the noble inheritance of the virtues of their ancestors. Whereas the other two had parents of different morals, and though they found their country in a sinking condition, and debauched, yet that did not quench their forward zeal to what was just and honourable.

The integrity of the two Romans, and their superiority to money, was chiefly remarkable in this: that in office and the administration of public affairs, they kept themselves from the imputation of unjust gain; whereas Agis might justly be offended if he had only that mean commendation given him, that he took nothing wrongfully from any man, seeing he distributed his own fortunes which, in ready money only, amounted to the value of six hundred talents, amongst his fellow-citizens. Extortion would have appeared a crime of a strange nature to him, who esteemed it a piece of covetousness to possess, though never so justly gotten, greater riches than his neighbours.

Their political actions, also, and the state revolutions they attempted, were very difficult in magnitude. The chief things in general that the two Romans commonly aimed at, were the settlement of cities and mending of highways; and, in particular, the boldest design which

Tiberius is famed for, was the recovery of the public lands; and Caius gained his greatest reputation by the addition, for the exercise of judiciary powers, of three hundred of the order of knights to the same number of senators. Whereas the alteration which Agis and Cleomenes made was in a quite different kind. They did not set about removing partial evils and curing petty incidents of disease, which would have been (as Plato says) like cutting off one of the Hydra's heads, the very means to increase the number; but they instituted a thorough reformation, such as would free the country from all its grievances, or rather, to speak more truly, they reversed that former change which had been the cause of all their calamities, and so restored their city to its ancient state.

However, this must be confessed in the behalf of the Gracchi, that their undertakings were always opposed by men of the greatest influence. On the other side, those things which were first attempted by Agis, and afterwards consummated by Cleomenes, were supported by the great and glorious precedent of those ancient laws concerning frugality and levelling which they had themselves received upon the authority of Lycurgus, and he had instituted on that of Apollo. It is also further observable, that from the actions of the Gracchi, Rome received no additions to her former greatness; whereas, under the conduct of Cleomenes, Greece presently saw Sparta exert her sovereign power over all Peloponnesus, and contest the supreme command with the most powerful princes of the time; success in which would have freed Greece from Illyrian and Gaulish violence, and placed her once again under the orderly rule of the sons of Hercules.

From the circumstances of their deaths, also, we may infer some difference in the quality of their courage. The Gracchi, fighting with their fellow-citizens, were both slain as they endeavoured to make their escape: Agis willingly submitted to his fate, rather than any citizen should be in danger of his life. Cleomenes, being shamefully and unjustly treated, made an effort toward revenge, but failing of that, generously fell by his own hand.

On the other side it must be said, that Agis never did a great action worthy a commander, being prevented by an untimely death. And as for those heroic actions of Cleomenes, we may justly compare with them that of Tiberius, when he was the first who attempted to scale the walls of Carthage, which was no mean exploit. We may add the peace which he concluded with the Numantines, by which he saved the lives of twenty thousand Romans, who otherwise had certainly been cut off. And Caius, not only at home, but in war in Sardinia, displayed distinguished courage. So that their early actions were no small argument that afterwards they might have rivalled the best of the Roman commanders, if they had not died so young.

In civil life, Agis showed a lack of determination; he let himself be baffled by the craft of Agesilaus, disappointed the expectations of the citizens as to the division of the lands, and generally left all the designs, which he had deliberately formed and publicly announced, unperformed and unfulfilled through a young man's want of resolution. Cleomenes, on the other hand, proceeded to effect the revolution with only too much boldness and violence, and unjustly slew the ephors whom he might, by superiority in arms, have gained over to his party, or else might easily have banished, as he did several others of the city. For to use the knife, unless in the extremest necessity, is neither good surgery nor wise policy, but in both cases mere unskilfulness; and in the latter, unjust as well as unfeeling.

Of the Gracchi, neither the one nor the other was the first to shed the blood of his fellow-citizens; and Caius is reported to have avoided all manner of resistance, even when his life was aimed at, showing himself always valiant against a foreign enemy, but wholly inactive in a sedition. This was the reason that he went from his own house unarmed, and withdrew when the battle began, and in all respects showed himself anxious rather not to do any harm to others, than not to suffer any himself. Even the very flight of the Gracchi must not be looked upon as an argument of their mean spirit, but an honourable retreat from endangering of others. For if they had stayed, they must either have yielded to those who assailed them, or else have fought them in their own defence.

The greatest crime that can be laid to Tiberius's charge was the deposing of his fellow tribune, and seeking afterwards a second tribuneship for himself. As for the death of Antyllius, it is falsely and unjustly attributed to Caius, for he was slain unknown to him, and much to his grief.

On the contrary, Cleomenes (not to mention the murder of the ephors) set all the slaves at liberty, and governed by himself alone in reality, having a partner only for show; having made choice of his brother Euclidas, who was one of the same family. He prevailed upon Archidamus, who was the right heir to the kingdom of the other line, to venture to return home from Messene; but after his being slain, by not doing anything to revenge his death, confirmed the suspicion that he was privy to it himself. Lycurgus, whose example he professed to imitate, after he had voluntarily settled his kingdom upon Charillus, his brother's son, fearing lest, if the youth should chance to die by accident, he might be suspected for it, travelled a long time, and would not return again to Sparta until Charillus had a son, and an heir to his kingdom. But we have indeed no other Grecian who is worthy to be compared with Lycurgus, and it is clear enough that in the public measures of Cleomenes various acts of considerable audacity and lawlessness may be found.

Those, therefore, who incline to blame their characters may observe that the two Grecians were disturbers even from their youth, lovers of contest, and aspirants to despotic power;

that Tiberius and Caius by nature had an excessive desire after glory and honours. Beyond this, their enemies could find nothing to bring against them; but as soon as the contention began with their adversaries, their heat and passions would so far prevail beyond their natural temper, that by them, as by ill winds, they were driven afterwards to all their rash undertakings. What could be more just and honourable than their first design, had not the power and the faction of the rich, by endeavouring to abrogate that law, engaged them both in those fatal quarrels, the one, for his own preservation, the other, to revenge his brother's death, who was murdered without any law or justice?

From the account, therefore, which has been given, you yourself may perceive the difference; which if it were to be pronounced of every one singly, I should affirm Tiberius to have excelled them all in virtue; that young Agis had been guilty of the fewest misdeeds; and that in action and boldness Caius came far short of Cleomenes.

DEMOSTHENES

385?–322 B.C.

WHOEVER it was, Sosius, that wrote the poem in honour of Alcibiades, upon his winning the chariot-race at the Olympian Games, whether it were Euripides, as is most commonly thought, or some other person, he tells us that to a man's being happy it is in the first place requisite he should be born in "some famous city." But for him that would attain to true happiness, which for the most part is placed in the qualities and disposition of the mind, it is, in my opinion, of no other disadvantage to be of a mean, obscure country, than to be born of a small or plain-looking woman. For it were ridiculous to think that Iulis, a little part of Ceos, which itself is no great island, and Ægina, which an Athenian once said ought to be removed, like a small eyesore, from the port of Piræus, should breed good actors and poets, and yet should never be able to produce a just, temperate, wise, and high-minded man. Other arts, whose end it is to acquire riches or honour, are likely enough to wither and decay in poor and

undistinguished towns; but virtue, like a strong and durable plant, may take root and thrive in any place where it can lay hold of an ingenuous nature, and a mind that is industrious.

I, for my part, shall desire that for any deficiency of mine in right judgment or action, I myself may be, as in fairness, held accountable, and shall not attribute it to the obscurity of my birthplace.

But if any man undertake to write a history that has to be collected from materials gathered by observation and the reading of works not easy to be got in all places, nor written always in his own language, but many of them foreign and dispersed in other hands, for him, undoubtedly, it is in the first place and above all things most necessary to reside in some city of good note, addicted to liberal arts, and populous; where he may have plenty of all sorts of books, and upon inquiry may hear and inform himself of such particulars as, having escaped the pens of writers, are more faithfully preserved in the memories of men, lest his work be deficient in many things, even those which it can least dispense with.

But for me, I live in a little town, where I am willing to continue, lest it should grow less; and having had no leisure, while I was in Rome and other parts of Italy, to exercise myself in the Roman language, on account of public business and of those who came to be instructed by me in philosophy, it was very late, and in the decline of my age, before I applied myself to the reading of Latin authors. Upon which that which happened to me may seem strange, though it be true; for it was not so much by the knowledge of words that I came to the understanding of things, as by my experience of things I was enabled to follow the meaning of words. But to appreciate the graceful and ready pronunciation of the Roman tongue, to understand the various figures and connection of words, and such other ornaments, in which the beauty of speaking consists, is, I doubt not, an admirable and delightful accomplishment; but it requires a degree of practice and study which is not easy, and will better suit those who have more leisure, and time enough yet before them for the occupation.

And so in this fifth book of my Parallel Lives, in giving an account of Demosthenes and Cicero, my comparison of their natural dispositions and their characters will be formed upon their actions and their lives as statesmen, and I shall not pretend to criticise their orations one against the other, to show which of the two was the more charming or the more powerful speaker. For there, as Ion says—

We are but like a fish upon dry land;

a proverb which Cæcilius perhaps forgot, when he employed his always adventurous talents in so ambitious an attempt as a comparison of Demosthenes and Cicero; and, possibly, if it were a thing obvious and easy for every man to *know himself,* the precept had not passed for an oracle.

The divine power seems originally to have designed Demosthenes and Cicero upon the same plan, giving them many similarities in their natural characters, as their passion for distinction and their love of liberty in civil life, and their want of courage in dangers and war, and at the same time also to have added many accidental resemblances. I think there can hardly be found two other orators, who, from small and obscure beginnings, became

so great and mighty; who both contested with kings and tyrants, both lost their daughters, were driven out of their country, and returned with honour; who, flying from thence again, were both seized upon by their enemies, and at last ended their lives with the liberty of their countrymen. So that if we were to suppose there had been a trial of skill between nature and fortune, as there is sometimes between artists, it would be hard to judge whether that succeeded best in making them alike in their dispositions and manners, or this in the coincidences of their lives. We will speak of the eldest first.

Demosthenes, the father of Demosthenes, was a citizen of good rank and quality, as Theopompus informs us, surnamed the Sword-maker, because he had a large workhouse, and kept servants skilful in that art at work. But of that which Æschines the orator said of his mother, that she was descended of one Gylon, who fled his country upon an accusation of treason, and of a barbarian woman, I can affirm nothing, whether he spoke true, or slandered and maligned her. This is certain, that Demosthenes, being as yet but seven years old, was left by his father in affluent circumstances, the whole value of his estate being little short of fifteen talents, and that he was wronged by his guardians, part of his fortune being embezzled by them, and the rest neglected; insomuch that even his teachers were defrauded of their salaries. This was the reason that he did not obtain the liberal education that he should have had; besides that, on account of weakness and delicate health, his mother would not let him exert himself, and his teachers forbore to urge him.

He was meagre and sickly from the first, and hence had his nickname of Batalus given him, it is said, by the boys, in derision of his appearance; Batalus being, as some tell us, a certain enervated flute-player, in ridicule of whom Antiphanes wrote a play. Others speak of Batalus as a writer of wanton verses and drinking songs. And it would seem that some part of the body, not decent to be named, was at that time called *batalus* by the Athenians. But the name of Argas, which also they say was a nickname of Demosthenes, was given him for his behaviour, as being savage and spiteful, *argas* being one of the poetical words for a snake; or for his disagreeable way of speaking, Argas being the name of a poet who composed very harshly and disagreeably. So much, as Plato says, for such matters.

The first occasion of his eager inclination to oratory, they say, was this. Callistratus, the orator, going to plead in open court for Oropus, the expectation of the issue of that cause was very great, as well for the ability of the orator, who was then at the height of his reputation, as also for the fame of the action itself. Therefore, Demosthenes, having heard the tutors and schoolmasters agreeing among themselves to be present at this trial, with much importunity persuaded his tutor to take him along with him to the hearing; who, having some acquaintance with the doorkeepers, procured a place where the boy might sit unseen, and hear what was said. Callistratus having got the day, and being much admired, the boy began to look upon his glory with a kind of emulation, observing how he was courted on all hands, and attended on his way by the multitude; but his wonder was more than all excited by the power of his eloquence, which seemed able to subdue and win over anything.

From this time, therefore, bidding farewell to other sorts of learning and study, he now began to exercise himself, and to take pains in declaiming, as one that meant to be himself also an orator. He made use of Isæus as his guide to the art of speaking, though Isocrates at that time was giving lessons; whether, as some say, because he was an orphan, and was not able to pay Isocrates his appointed fee of ten minæ, or because he preferred Isæus's speaking, as being more business-like and effective in actual use. Hermippus says that he met with certain memoirs without any author's name, in which it was written that Demosthenes was a scholar to Plato, and learnt much of his eloquence from him; and he also mentions Ctesibius, as reporting from Callias of Syracuse and some others, that Demosthenes secretly obtained a knowledge of the systems of Isocrates and Alcidamas, and mastered them thoroughly.

As soon, therefore, as he was grown up to man's estate, he began to go to law with his guardians, and to write orations against them; who, in the meantime, had recourse to various subterfuges and pleas for new trials, and Demosthenes, though he was thus, as Thucydides says, taught his business in dangers, and by his own exertions was successful in his suit, was yet unable for all this to recover so much as a small fraction of his patrimony. He only attained some degree of confidence in speaking, and some competent experience in it. And having got a taste of the honour and power which are acquired by pleadings, he now ventured to come forth, and to undertake public business.

And, as it is said of Laomedon, the Orchomenian, that, by advice of his physician, he used to run long distances to keep off some disease of his spleen, and by that means having, through labour and exercise, framed the habit of his body, he betook himself to the great garland games, and became one of the best runners at the long race; so it happened to Demosthenes, who, first venturing upon oratory for the recovery of his own private property, by this acquired ability in speaking, and at length, in public business, as it were in the great games, came to have the pre-eminence of all competitors in the assembly. But when he first addressed himself to the people, he met with great discouragements, and was derided for his strange and uncouth style, which was cumbered with long sentences and tortured with formal arguments to a most harsh and disagreeable excess. Besides, he had, it seems, a weakness in his voice, a perplexed and indistinct utterance and a shortness of breath, which, by breaking and disjointing his sentences, much obscured the sense and meaning of what he spoke.

Thus in the end being quite disheartened, he forsook the assembly; and as he was walking carelessly and sauntering about the Piræus, Eunomus, the Thriasian, then a very old man, seeing him, upbraided him, saying that his diction was very much like that of Pericles, and that he was wanting to himself through cowardice and meanness of spirit, neither bearing up with courage against popular outcry, nor fitting his body for action, but suffering it to languish through mere sloth and negligence.

Another time, when the assembly had refused to hear him, and he was going home with his head muffled up, taking it very heavily, they relate that Satyrus, the actor, followed him, and being his familiar acquaintance, entered into conversation with him. To whom, when Demosthenes bemoaned himself, that having been the most industrious of all the pleaders, and having almost spent the whole strength and vigour of his body in that employment, he could not yet find any acceptance with the people, that drunken sots, mariners, and illiterate fellows were heard, and had the hustings for their own, while he himself was despised, "You say true, Demosthenes," replied Satyrus, "but I will quickly remedy the cause of all this, if you will repeat to me some passage out of Euripides or Sophocles." Which when Demosthenes had pronounced, Satyrus presently taking it up after him, gave the same passage, in his rendering of it, such a new form, by accompanying it with the proper mien and gesture, that to Demosthenes it seemed quite another thing.

By this, being convinced how much grace and ornament language acquires from action, he began to esteem it a small matter, and as good as nothing for a man to exercise himself in declaiming, if he neglected enunciation and delivery. Hereupon he built himself a place to study in under ground (which was still remaining in our time), and hither he would come constantly every day to form his action and to exercise his voice; and here he would continue, oftentimes without intermission, two or three months together, shaving one half of his head, that so for shame he might not go abroad, though he desired it ever so much.

Nor was this all, but he also made his conversation with people abroad, his common speech, and his business, subservient to his studies, taking from hence occasions and arguments as matter to work upon. For as soon as he was parted from his company, down he would go at once into his study, and run over everything in order that had passed, and the reasons that might be alleged for and against it. Any speeches, also, that he was present at, he would go over again with himself, and reduce into periods; and whatever others spoke to him, or he to them, he would correct, transform, and vary several ways. Hence it was that he was looked upon as a person of no great natural genius, but one who owed all the power and ability he had in speaking to labour and industry. Of the truth of which it was thought to be no small sign that he was very rarely heard to speak upon the occasion, but though he were by name frequently called upon by the people, as he sat in the assembly, yet he would not rise unless he had previously considered the subject, and came prepared for it.

Thus it was that many of the popular pleaders used to make it a jest against him; and Pytheas once, scoffing at him, said that his arguments smelt of the lamp. To which Demosthenes gave the sharp answer, "It is true, indeed, Pytheas, that your lamp and mine are not conscious of the same things." To others, however, he would not much deny it, but would admit frankly enough, that he neither entirely wrote his speeches beforehand, nor yet spoke wholly extempore. And he would affirm

that it was the more truly popular act to use premeditation, such preparation being a kind of respect to the people; whereas, to slight and take no care how what is said is likely to be received by the audience, shows something of an oligarchical temper, and is the course of one that intends force rather than persuasion. Of his want of courage and assurance to speak offhand, they make it also another argument that, when he was at a loss and discomposed, Demades would often rise up on the sudden to support him, but he was never observed to do the same for Demades.

Whence then, may some say, was it, that Æschines speaks of him as a person so much to be wondered at for his boldness in speaking? Or, how could it be, when Python, the Byzantine, with so much confidence and such a torrent of words inveighed against the Athenians, that Demosthenes alone stood up to oppose him? Or when Lamarchus, the Myrinæan, had written a panegyric upon King Philip and Alexander, in which he uttered many things in reproach of the Thebans and Olynthians, and at the Olympic Games recited it publicly, how was it that he, rising up, and recounting historically and demonstratively what benefits and advantages all Greece had received from the Thebans and Chalcidians, and, on the contrary, what mischiefs the flatterers of the Macedonians had brought upon it, so turned the minds of all that were present that the sophist, in alarm at the outcry against him, secretly made his way out of the assembly?

But Demosthenes, it should seem, regarded other points in the character of Pericles to be unsuited to him; but his reserve and his sustained manner, and his forbearing to speak on the sudden, or upon every occasion, as being the things to which principally he owed his greatness, these he followed, and endeavoured to imitate, neither wholly neglecting the glory which present occasion offered, nor yet willing too often to expose his faculty to the mercy of chance. For, in fact, the orations which were spoken by him had much more of boldness and confidence in them than those that he wrote, if we may believe Eratosthenes, Demetrius the Phalerian, and the Comedians. Eratosthenes says that often in his speaking he would be transported into a kind of ecstasy, and Demetrius, that he uttered the famous metrical adjuration to the people—

By the earth, the springs, the rivers, and the streams,

as a man inspired and beside himself. One of the comedians calls him a *rhopoperperethras*, and another scoffs at him for his use of antithesis:—

And what he took, took back; a phrase to please,
The very fancy of Demosthenes.

Unless, indeed, this also is meant by Antiphanes for a jest upon the speech on Halonesus, which Demosthenes advised the Athenians not to *take* at Philip's hands, but to *take back.*

All, however, used to consider Demades, in the mere use of his natural gifts, an orator impossible to surpass, and that in what he spoke on the sudden, he excelled all the study and preparation of Demosthenes. And Ariston, the Chian, has recorded a judgment which Theophrastus passed upon the orators; for being asked what kind of orator he accounted Demosthenes, he answered, "Worthy of the city of Athens"; and then what he thought of Demades, he answered, "Above it." And the same philosopher reports that Polyeuctus, the Sphettian, one of the Athenian politicians about that time, was wont to say that Demosthenes was the greatest orator, but Phocion the ablest, as he expressed the most sense in the fewest words. And, indeed, it is related that Demosthenes himself, as often as Phocion stood up to plead against him, would say to his acquaintance, "Here comes the knife to my speech." Yet it does not appear whether he had this feeling for his powers of speaking, or for his life and character, and meant to say that one word or nod from a man who was really trusted would go further than a thousand lengthy periods from others.

Demetrius, the Phalerian, tells us that he was informed by Demosthenes himself, now grown old, that the ways he made use of to remedy his natural bodily infirmities and defects were such as these; his inarticulate and stammering pronunciation he overcame and rendered more distinct by speaking with pebbles in his mouth; his voice he disciplined by declaiming and reciting speeches or verses when he was out of breath, while running or going up steep places; and that in his house he had a large looking-glass, before which he would stand and go through his exercises. It is told that some one once came to request his assistance as a pleader, and related how he had been assaulted and beaten. "Certainly," said Demosthenes, "nothing of the kind can have happened to you." Upon which the other, raising his voice, exclaimed loudly, "What, De-

mosthenes, nothing has been done to me?" "Ah," replied Demosthenes, "now I hear the voice of one that has been injured and beaten." Of so great consequence towards the gaining of belief did he esteem the tone and action of the speaker.

The action which he used himself was wonderfully pleasing to the common people, but by well-educated people, as, for example, by Demetrius, the Phalerian, it was looked upon as mean, humiliating, and unmanly. And Hermippus says of Æsion, that, being asked his opinion concerning the ancient orators, and those of his own time, he answered that it was admirable to see with what composure and in what high style they addressed themselves to the people; but that the orations of Demosthenes, when they are read, certainly appear to be superior in point of construction, and more effective. His written speeches, beyond all question, are characterised by austere tone and by their severity. In his extempore retorts and rejoinders, he allowed himself the use of jest and mockery. When Demades said, "Demosthenes teach me! So might the sow teach Minerva!" he replied, "Was it this Minerva, that was lately found playing the harlot in Collytus?" When a thief, who had the nickname of the Brazen, was attempting to upbraid him for sitting up late, and writing by candle-light, "I know very well," said he, "that you had rather have all lights out; and wonder not, O ye men of Athens, at the many robberies which are committed, since we have thieves of brass and walls of clay."

But on these points, though we have much more to mention, we will add nothing at present. We will proceed to take an estimate of his character from his actions and his life as a statesman.

His first entering into public business was much about the time of the Phocian war, as himself affirms, and may be collected from his Philippic orations. For of these, some were made after that action was over, and the earliest of them refer to its concluding events. It is certain that he engaged in the accusation of Midias when he was but two-and-thirty years old, having as yet no interest or reputation as a politician. And this it was, I consider, that induced him to withdraw the action, and accept a sum of money as a compromise. For of himself—

He was no easy or good-natured man,
but of a determined disposition, and resolute to see himself righted; however, finding it a

hard matter and above his strength to deal with Midias, a man so well secured on all sides with money, eloquence, and friends, he yielded to the entreaties of those who interceded for him. But had he seen any hopes or possibility of prevailing, I cannot believe that three thousand drachmas could have taken off the edge of his revenge.

The object which he chose for himself in the commonwealth was noble and just, the defence of the Grecians against Philip; and in this he behaved himself so worthily that he soon grew famous, and excited attention everywhere for his eloquence and courage in speaking. He was admired through all Greece; the King of Persia courted him, and by Philip himself he was more esteemed than all the other orators. His very enemies were forced to confess that they had to do with a man of mark; for such a character even Æschines and Hyperides give him, where they accuse and speak against him.

So that I cannot imagine what ground Theopompus had to say that Demosthenes was of a fickle, unsettled disposition, and could not long continue firm either to the same men or the same affairs; whereas the contrary is most apparent, for the same party and post in politics which he held from the beginning, to these he kept constant to the end; and was so far from leaving them while he lived that he chose rather to forsake his life than his purpose. He was never heard to apologise for shifting sides like Demades, who would say he often spoke against himself, but never against the city; nor as Melanopus, who, being generally against Callistratus, but being often bribed off with money, was wont to tell the people, "The man indeed is my enemy, but we must submit for the good of our country"; nor again as Nicodemus, the Messenian, who having first appeared on Cassander's side, and afterwards taken part with Demetrius, said the two things were not in themselves contrary, it being always most advisable to obey the conqueror. We have nothing of this kind to say against Demosthenes, as one who would turn aside or prevaricate, either in word or deed. There could not have been less variation in his public acts if they had all been played, so to say, from first to last, from the same score.

Panætius, the philosopher, said that most of his orations are so written as if they were to prove this one conclusion, that what is honest and virtuous is for itself only to be chosen; as that of the Crown, that against Aristocrates, that for the Immunities, and the Philippics; in all which he persuades his fellow-citizens to pursue not that which seems most pleasant, easy, or profitable, but declares, over and over again, that they ought in the first place to prefer that which is just and honourable before their own safety and preservation. So that if he had kept his hands clean, if his courage for the wars had been answerable to the generosity of his principles, and the dignity of his orations, he might deservedly have his name placed, not in the number of such orators as Mœrocles, Polyeuctus, and Hyperides, but in the highest rank with Cimon, Thucydides, and Pericles.

Certainly amongst those who were contemporary with him, Phocion, though he appeared on the less commendable side in the commonwealth, and was counted as one of the Macedonian party, nevertheless, by his courage and his honesty, procured himself a name not inferior to those of Ephialtes, Aristides, and Cimon. But Demosthenes, being neither fit to be relied on for courage in arms, as Demetrius says, nor on all sides inaccessible to bribery (for how invincible soever he was against the gifts of Philip and the Macedonians, yet elsewhere he lay open to assault, and was overpowered by the gold which came down from Susa and Ecbatana), was therefore esteemed better able to recommend than to imitate the virtues of past times.

And yet (excepting only Phocion), even in his life and manners, he far surpassed the other orators of his time. None of them addressed the people so boldly. He attacked the faults, and opposed himself to the unreasonable desires of the multitude, as may be seen in his orations. Theopompus writes that the Athenians having by name selected Demosthenes, and called upon him to accuse a certain person, he refused to do it; upon which the assembly being all in an uproar, he rose up and said, "Your counsellor, whether you will or no, O ye men of Athens, you shall always have me; but a sycophant or false accuser, though you would have me, I shall never be." And his conduct in the case of Antiphon was perfectly aristocratical; whom, after he had been acquitted in the assembly, he took and brought before the court of Areopagus, and, setting at naught the displeasure of the people, convicted him there of having promised Philip to burn the arsenal; whereupon the man was condemned by that court, and suffered for it. He accused, also, Theoris, the priestess, amongst other misdemeanours, of having instructed and taught the slaves to deceive and cheat their masters, for which the sentence of death was passed upon her, and she was executed.

The oration which Apollodorus made use of, and by it carried the cause against Timotheus, the general, in an action of debt, it is said was written for him by Demosthenes; as also those against Phormion and Stephanus, in which latter case he was thought to have acted dishonourably, for the speech which Phormion used against Apollodorus was also of his making; he, as it were, having simply furnished two adversaries out of the same shop with weapons to wound one another. Of his orations addressed to the public assemblies, that against Androtion, and those against Timocrates and Aristocrates, were written for others, before he had come forward himself as a politician. They were composed, it seems, when he was but seven or eight-and-twenty years old. That against Aristogiton, and that for the Immunities, he spoke himself, at the request, as he says, of Ctesippus, the son of Chabrias, but, as some say, out of courtship to the young man's mother. Though, in fact, he did not marry her, for his wife was a woman of Samos, as Demetrius, the Magnesian, writes, in his book *On Persons of the Same Name*.

It is not certain whether his oration against Æschines, for misconduct as ambassador, was ever spoken; although Idomeneus says that Æschines wanted only thirty voices to condemn him. But this seems not to be correct, at least so far as may be conjectured from both their orations concerning the crown; for in these, neither of them speaks clearly or directly of it, as a cause that ever came to trial. But let others decide this controversy.

It was evident, even in time of peace, what course Demosthenes would steer in the commonwealth; for whatever was done by the Macedonian, he criticised and found fault with, and upon all occasions was stirring up the people of Athens, and inflaming them against him. Therefore, in the court of Philip, no man was so much talked of, or of so great account as he; and when he came thither, one of the ten ambassadors who were sent into Macedonia, though all had audience given them, yet his speech was answered with most care and exactness. But in other respects, Philip entertained him not so honourably as the rest, neither did he show him the same kindness and civility with which he applied himself to the party of Æschines and Philocrates. So that, when the others commended Philip for his able speaking, his beautiful person, nay, and also for his good companionship in drinking, Demosthenes could not refrain from cavilling at these praises; the first, he said, was a quality which might well enough become a rhetorician, the second a woman, and the last was only the property of a sponge; no one of them was the proper commendation of a prince.

But when things came at last to war, Philip on the one side being not able to live in peace, and the Athenians, on the other side, being stirred up by Demosthenes, the first action he put them upon was the reducing of Eubœa, which, by the treachery of the tyrants, was brought under subjection to Philip. And on his proposition, the decree was voted, and they crossed over thither and chased the Macedonians out of the island. The next was the relief of the Byzantines and Perinthians, whom the Macedonians at that time were attacking. He persuaded the people to lay aside their enmity against these cities, to forget the offences committed by them in the Confederate War, and to send them such succours as eventually saved and secured them. Not long after, he undertook an embassy through the states of Greece, which he solicited and so far incensed against Philip that, a few only excepted, he brought them all into a general league. So that, besides the forces composed of the citizens themselves, there was an army consisting of fifteen thousand foot and two thousand horse, and the money to pay these strangers was levied and brought in with great cheerfulness. On which occasion it was, says Theophrastus, on the allies requesting that their contributions for the war might be ascertained and stated, Crobylus, the orator, made use of the saying, "War can't be fed at so much a day."

Now was all Greece up in arms, and in great expectation what would be the event. The Euboeans, the Achaeans, the Corinthians, the Megarians, the Leucadians, and Corcyræans, their people and their cities, were all joined together in a league. But the hardest task was yet behind, left for Demosthenes, to draw the Thebans into this confederacy with the rest. Their country bordered next upon Attica, they had great forces for the war, and at that time they were accounted the best soldiers of all Greece, but it was no easy matter to make them break with Philip, who, by many good offices, had so lately obliged them in the Phocian war; especially considering how the subjects of dispute and variance between the two cities were continually renewed and exasperated by petty quarrels, arising out of the proximity of their frontiers.

But after Philip, being now grown high and puffed up with his good success at Amphissa, on a sudden surprised Elatea and possessed himself of Phocis, and the Athenians were in a great consternation, none durst venture to rise up to speak, no one knew what to say, all were at a loss, and the whole assembly in silence and perplexity; in this extremity of affairs Demosthenes was the only man who appeared, his counsel to them being alliance with the Thebans. And having in other ways encouraged the people, and, as his manner was, raised their spirits up with hopes, he, with some others, was sent ambassador to Thebes. To oppose him, as Marsyas says, Philip also sent thither his envoys, Amyntas and Clearchus, two Macedonians, besides Daochus, a Thessalian, and Thrasydæus. Now, the Thebans, in their consultations, were well enough aware what suited best with their own interest, but every one had before his eyes the terrors of war, and their losses in the Phocian troubles were still recent: but such was the force and power of the orator, fanning up, as Theopompus says, their courage, and firing their emulation, that, casting away every thought of prudence, fear, or obligation, in a sort of divine possession they chose the path of honour, to which his words invited them.

And this success, thus accomplished by an orator, was thought to be so glorious and of such consequence, that Philip immediately sent heralds to treat and petition for a peace: all Greece was aroused, and up in arms to help. And the commanders-in-chief, not only of Attica, but of Bœotia, applied themselves to Demosthenes, and observed his directions. He managed all the assemblies of the Thebans, no less than those of the Athenians; he was beloved both by the one and by the other, and exercised the same supreme authority with both; and that not by unfair means, or without just cause, as Theopompus professes, but indeed it was no more than was due to his merit.

But there was, it would seem, some divinely ordered fortune, commissioned, in the revolution of things, to put a period at this time to the liberty of Greece, which opposed and thwarted all their actions, and by many signs foretold what should happen. Such were the sad predictions uttered by the Pythian priestess, and this old oracle cited out of the Sibyl's verses:—

The battle on Thermodon that shall be
Safe at a distance I desire to see,
Far, like an eagle, watching in the air,
Conquered shall weep, and conqueror perish
there.

This Thermodon, they say, is a little rivulet here in our country in Chæronea, running into the Cephisus. But we know of none that is so called at the present time; and can only conjecture that the streamlet which is now called Hæmon, and runs by the temple of Hercules, where the Grecians were encamped, might perhaps in those days be called Thermodon, and after the fight, being filled with blood and dead bodies, upon this occasion, as we guess, might change its old name for that which it now bears. Yet Duris says that this Thermodon was no river, but that some of the soldiers, as they were pitching their tents and digging trenches about them, found a small stone statue, which, by the inscription, appeared to be the figure of Thermodon, carrying a wounded Amazon in his arms; and that there was another oracle current about it, as follows:—

The battle on Thermodon that shall be,
Fail not, black raven, to attend and see;
The flesh of men shall there abound for thee.

In fine, it is not easy to determine what is the truth. But of Demosthenes it is said that he had such great confidence in the Grecian forces, and was so excited by the sight of the courage and resolution of so many brave men ready to engage the enemy, that he would by no means endure they should give any heed to oracles, or hearken to prophecies, but gave out that he suspected even the prophetess herself, as if she had been tampered with to speak in favour of Philip. The Thebans he put in mind of Epaminondas, the Athenians of Pericles, who always took their own measures and governed their actions by reason, looking upon things of this kind as mere pretexts for cowardice. Thus far, therefore, Demosthenes acquitted himself like a brave man. But in the fight he did nothing honourable, nor was his performance answerable to his speeches. For he fled, deserting his place disgracefully, and throwing away his arms, not ashamed, as Pytheas observed, to belie the inscription written on his shield, in letters of gold, "With good fortune."

In the meantime, Philip, in the first moment of victory, was so transported with joy that he grew extravagant, and going out after he had drunk largely to visit the dead bodies, he chanted the first words of the decree that had been passed on the motion of Demosthenes—

The motion of Demosthenes, Demosthenes's son,

dividing it metrically into feet, and marking the beats.

But when he came to himself, and had well considered the danger he was lately under, he could not forbear from shuddering at the wonderful ability and power of an orator who had made him hazard his life and empire on the issue of a few brief hours. The fame of it also reached even to the court of Persia, and the king sent letters to his lieutenants commanding them to supply Demosthenes with money, and to pay every attention to him, as the only man of all the Grecians who was able to give Philip occupation and find employment for his forces near home, in the troubles of Greece. This afterwards came to the knowledge of Alexander, by certain letters of Demosthenes which he found at Sardis, and by other papers of the Persian officers, stating the large sums which had been given him.

At this time, however, upon the ill-success which now happened to the Grecians, those of the contrary faction in the commonwealth fell foul upon Demosthenes and took the opportunity to frame several informations and indictments against him. But the people not only acquitted him of these accusations, but continued towards him their former respect, and still invited him, as a man that meant well, to take a part in public affairs. Insomuch that when the bones of those who had been slain at Chæronea were brought home to be solemnly interred, Demosthenes was the man they chose to make the funeral oration. They did not show, under the misfortunes which befell them, a base or ignoble mind, as Theopompus writes in his exaggerated style, but on the contrary, by the honour and respect paid to their counsellor, they made it appear that they were noway dissatisfied with the counsels he had given them. The speech, therefore, was spoken by Demosthenes. But the subsequent decrees he would not allow to be passed in his own name, but made use of those of his friends, one after another, looking upon his own as unfortunate and inauspicious; till at length he took courage again after the death of Philip, who did not long outlive his victory at Chæronea. And this, it seems, was that which was foretold in the last verse of the oracle—

Conquered shall weep, and conqueror perish there.

Demosthenes had secret intelligence of the death of Philip, and laying hold of this opportunity to prepossess the people with courage and better hopes for the future, he came into the assembly with a cheerful countenance, pretending to have had a dream that presaged some great good fortune for Athens; and, not long after, arrived the messengers who brought the news of Philip's death. No sooner had the people received it, but immediately they offered sacrifice to the gods, and decreed that Pausanias should be presented with a crown. Demosthenes appeared publicly in a rich dress, with a chaplet on his head, though it were but the seventh day since the death of his daughter, as is said by Æschines, who upbraids him upon this account, and rails at him as one void of natural affection towards his children. Whereas, indeed, he rather betrays himself to be of a poor, low spirit, and effeminate mind, if he really means to make wailings and lamentation the only signs of a gentle and affectionate nature, and to condemn those who bear such accidents with more temper and less passion.

For my own part, I cannot say that the behaviour of the Athenians on this occasion was wise or honourable, to crown themselves with garlands and to sacrifice to the gods for the death of a prince who, in the midst of his success and victories, when they were a conquered people, had used them with so much clemency and humanity. For besides provoking fortune, it was a base thing, and unworthy in itself, to make him a citizen of Athens, and pay him honours while he lived, and yet as soon as he fell by another's hand, to set no bounds to their jollity, to insult over him dead, and to sing triumphant songs of victory, as if by their own valour they had vanquished him.

I must at the same time commend the behaviour of Demosthenes, who, leaving tears and lamentations and domestic sorrows to the women, made it his business to attend to the interests of the commonwealth. And I think it the duty of him who would be accounted to have a soul truly valiant, and fit for government, that, standing always firm to the common good, and letting private griefs and troubles find their compensation in public blessings, he should maintain the dignity of his character and station, much more than actors who represent the persons of kings and tyrants, who, we see, when they either laugh or weep on the stage, follow, not their own private inclinations, but the course consistent with the subject and with their position. And if, moreover, when our neighbour is in misfortune, it is not our duty to forbear offering any consolation, but rather to say whatever may tend to cheer him, and to invite his attention to any agreeable objects, just as we tell people who are troubled with sore eyes to withdraw their sight from bright and offensive colours to green and those of a softer mixture, from whence can a man seek, in his own case, better arguments of consolation for afflictions in his family, than from the prosperity of his country, by making public and domestic chances count, so to say, together, and the better fortune of the state obscure and conceal the less happy circumstances of the individual?

I have been induced to say so much, because I have known many readers melted by Æschines's language into a soft and unmanly tenderness.

But now to turn to my narrative. The cities of Greece were inspirited once more by the efforts of Demosthenes to form a league together. The Thebans, whom he had provided with arms, set upon their garrison, and slew many of them; the Athenians made preparations to join their forces with them; Demosthenes ruled supreme in the popular assembly, and wrote letters to the Persian officers who commanded under the king in Asia, inciting them to make war upon the Macedonian, calling him child and simpleton. But as soon as Alexander had settled matters in his own country, and came in person with his army into Bœotia, down fell the courage of the Athenians, and Demosthenes was hushed; the Thebans, deserted by them, fought by themselves, and lost their city. After which, the people of Athens, all in distress and great perplexity, resolved to send ambassadors to Alexander, amongst others, made choice of Demosthenes for one; but his heart failing him for fear of the king's anger, he returned back from Cithæron, and left the embassy.

In the meantime, Alexander sent to Athens, requiring ten of their orators to be delivered up to him, as Idomeneus and Duris have reported, but as the most and best historians say, he demanded these eight only,—Demosthenes, Polyeuctus, Ephialtes, Lycurgus, Mœrocles, Demon, Callisthenes, and Charidemus. It was upon this occasion that Demosthenes related to them the fable in which the sheep are said to deliver up their dogs to the wolves; himself and those who with him contended for the people's safety being, in his comparison, the dogs that defended the flock, and Alexander "the Macedonian arch-wolf." He further told them, "As we see corn-masters sell their whole stock by a few grains of wheat which they carry about with them in a dish, as a sample of the rest, so you by delivering up us, who are but a few, do at the same time unawares surrender up yourselves all together with us"; so we find it related in the history of Aristobulus, the Cassandrian.

The Athenians were deliberating, and at a loss what to do, when Demades, having agreed with the persons whom Alexander had demanded, for five talents, undertook to go ambassador, and to intercede with the king for them; and, whether it was that he relied on his friendship and kindness, or that he hoped to find him satiated, as a lion glutted with slaughter, he certainly went, and prevailed with him both to pardon the men, and to be reconciled to the city.

So he and his friends, when Alexander went away, were great men, and Demosthenes was quite put aside. Yet when Agis, the Spartan, made his insurrection, he also for a short time attempted a movement in his favour; but he soon shrunk back again, as the Athenians would not take any part in it, and, Agis being slain, the Lacedæmonians were vanquished. During this time it was that the indictment against Ctesiphon, concerning the crown, was brought to trial. The action was commenced a little before the battle in Chæronea, when Chærondas was archon, but it was not proceeded with till about ten years after, Aristophon being then archon. Never was any public cause more celebrated than this, alike for the fame of the orators, and for the generous courage of the judges, who, though at that time the accusers of Demosthenes were in the height of power, and supported by all the favour of the Macedonians, yet would not give judgment against him, but acquitted him so honourably, that Æschines did not obtain the fifth part of their suffrages on his side, so that, immediately after, he left the city, and spent the rest of his life in teaching rhetoric about the island of Rhodes, and upon the continent in Ionia.

It was not long after that Harpalus fled from Alexander, and came to Athens out of Asia; knowing himself guilty of many misdeeds into which his love of luxury had led him, and fearing the king, who was now grown terrible even to his best friends. Yet this man had no sooner addressed himself to the people, and delivered up his goods, his ships, and himself to their disposal, but the other orators of the town had their eyes quickly fixed upon his money, and came in to his assistance, persuading the Athenians to receive and protect their suppliant. Demosthenes at first gave advice to chase him out of the country, and to beware lest they involved their city in a war upon an unnecessary and unjust occasion. But some few days after, as they were taking an account of the treasure, Harpalus, perceiving how much he was pleased with a cup of Persian manufacture, and how curiously he surveyed the sculpture and fashion of it, desired him to poise it in his hand, and consider the weight of the gold. Demosthenes, being amazed to feel how heavy it was, asked him what weight it *came to*. "To you," said Harpalus, smiling, "it shall *come with* twenty talents." And presently after, when night drew on, he sent him the cup with so many talents.

Harpalus, it seems, was a person of singular skill to discern a man's covetousness by the air of his countenance, and the look and movements of his eyes. For Demosthenes could not resist the temptation, but admitting the present, like an armed garrison, into the citadel of his house, he surrendered himself up to the interest of Harpalus. The next day, he came into the assembly with his neck swathed about with wool and rollers, and when they called on him to rise up and speak, he made signs as if he had lost his voice. But the wits, turning the matter to ridicule, said that certainly the orator had been seized that night with no other than a silver quinsy. And soon after, the people, becoming aware of the bribery, grew angry, and would not suffer him to speak, or make any apology for himself, but ran him down with noise; and one man stood up, and cried out, "What, ye men of Athens, will you not hear the cup-bearer?"

So at length they banished Harpalus out of the city; and fearing lest they should be called to account for the treasure which the orators had purloined, they made a strict inquiry, going from house to house; only Callicles, the son of Arrhenidas, who was newly married, they would not suffer to be searched, out of respect, as Theopompus writes, to the bride, who was within.

Demosthenes resisted the inquisition, and proposed a decree to refer the business to the court of Areopagus, and to punish those whom that court should find guilty. But being himself one of the first whom the court condemned, when he came to the bar, he was fined fifty talents, and committed to prison; where, out of shame of the crime for which he was condemned, and through the weakness of his body, growing incapable of supporting the confinement, he made his escape, by the carelessness of some and by the contrivance of others of the citizens. We are told, at least, that he had not fled far from the city when, finding that he was pursued by some of those who had been his adversaries, he endeavoured to hide himself. But when they called him by his name, and coming up nearer to him, desired he would accept from them some money which they had brought from home as a provision for his journey, and to that purpose only had followed him, when they entreated him to take courage, and to bear up against his misfortune, he burst out into much greater lamentation, saying, "But how is it possible to support myself under so heavy an affliction, since I leave a city in which I have such enemies, while in any other it is not easy to find friends."

He did not show much fortitude in his banishment, spending his time for the most part in Ægina and Trœzen, and, with tears in his eyes, looking towards the country of Attica. And there remain upon record some sayings of his, little resembling those sentiments of generosity and bravery which he used to express when he had the management of the commonwealth. For, as he was departing out of the city, it is reported, he lifted up his hands towards the Acropolis, and said, "O Lady Minerva, how is it that thou takest delight in three such fierce untractable beasts, the owl, the snake, and the people?" The young men that came to visit and converse with him he deterred from meddling with state affairs, telling them that if at first two ways had been proposed to him, the one leading to the speaker's stand and the assembly, the other going direct to destruction, and he could have foreseen the many evils which attend those who deal in public business, such as fears, envies, calumnies, and contentions, he would certainly have taken that which led straight on to his death.

But now happened the death of Alexander, while Demosthenes was in this banishment which we have been speaking of. And the Grecians were once again up in arms, encouraged by the brave attempts of Leosthenes, who was then drawing a circumvallation about Antipater, whom he held close besieged in Lamia. Pytheas, therefore, the orator, and Callimedon, called the Crab, fled from Athens, and taking sides with Antipater, went about with his friends and ambassadors to keep the Grecians from revolting and taking part with the Athenians. But, on the other side, Demosthenes, associating himself with the ambassadors that came from Athens, used his utmost endeavours and gave them his best assistance in persuading the cities to fall unanimously upon the Macedonians, and to drive them out of Greece. Phylarchus says that in Arcadia there happened a rencounter between Pytheas and Demosthenes, which came at last to downright railing, while the one pleaded for the Macedonians, and the other for the Grecians. Pytheas said that as we always suppose there is some disease in the family to which they bring asses' milk, so wherever there comes an embassy from Athens that city must needs be indisposed. And Demosthenes answered him, retorting the comparison: "Asses' milk is brought to restore health and the Athenians come for the safety and recovery of the sick."

With this conduct the people of Athens were so well pleased that they decreed the recall of Demosthenes from banishment. The decree was brought in by Demon the Pæanian, cousin to Demosthenes. So they sent him a ship to Ægina, and he landed at the port of Piræus, where he was met and joyfully received by all the citizens, not so much as an archon or a priest staying behind. And Demetrius, the Magnesian, says that he lifted up his hands towards heaven, and blessed this day of his happy return, as far more honourable than that of Alcibiades; since he was recalled by his countrymen, not through any force or constraint put upon them, but by their own goodwill and free inclinations. There remained only his pecuniary fine, which, according to law, could not be remitted by the people. But they found out a way to elude the law. It was a custom with them to allow a certain quantity of silver to those who were to furnish and adorn the altar for the sacrifice of Jupiter Soter. This office, for that turn, they bestowed on Demosthenes, and for the performance of it ordered him fifty talents, the very sum in which he was condemned.

Yet it was no long time that he enjoyed his country after his return, the attempts of the Greeks being soon all utterly defeated. For the battle of Cranon happened in Metagitnion, in Boëdromion the garrison entered into Munychia, and in the Pyanepsion following died Demosthenes after this manner.

Upon the report that Antipater and Craterus were coming to Athens, Demosthenes with his party took their opportunity to escape privily out of the city; but sentence of death was, upon the motion of Demades, passed upon them by the people. They dispersed themselves, flying some to one place, some to another; and Antipater sent about his soldiers into all quarters to apprehend them. Archias was their captain, and was thence called the Exile-hunter. He was a Thurian born, and is reported to have been an actor of tragedies, and they say that Polus, of Ægina, the best actor of his time, was his scholar; but Hermippus reckons Archias among the disciples of Lacritus, the orator, and Demetrius says he spent some time with Anaximenes. This Archias finding Hyperides, the orator, Aritonicus of Marathon, and Himeræus, the brother of Demetrius the Phalerian, in Ægina, took them by force out of the temple of Æcus, whither they were fled for safety, and sent them to Antipater, then at Cleonæ, where they were all put to death; and Hyperides, they say, had his tongue cut out.

Demosthenes, he heard, had taken sanctuary at the temple of Neptune in Calauria, and, crossing over thither in some light vessels, as soon as he had landed himself, and the Thracian spearmen that came with him, he endeavoured to persuade Demosthenes to accompany him to Antipater, as if he should meet with no hard usage from him. But Demosthenes, in his sleep the night before, had a strange dream. It seemed to him that he was acting a tragedy, and contended with Archias for the victory; and though he acquitted himself well, and gave good satisfaction to the spectators, yet for want of better furniture and provision for the stage, he lost the day. And so, while Archias was discoursing to him with many expressions of kindness, he sate still in the same posture, and looking up steadfastly upon him, "O Archias," said he, "I am as little affected by your promises now as I used formerly to be by your acting." Archias at this beginning to grow angry and to threaten him, "Now," said Demosthenes, "you speak like the genuine Macedonian oracle; before you were but acting a part. Therefore forbear only a little, while I write a word or two home to my family."

Having thus spoken, he withdrew into the temple, and taking a scroll, as if he meant to write, he put the reed into his mouth, and biting it as he was wont to do when he was thoughtful or writing, he held it there some time. Then he bowed down his head and covered it. The soldiers that stood at the door, supposing all this to proceed from want of courage and fear of death, in derision called him effeminate, and faint-hearted, and coward. And Archias drawing near, desired him to rise up, and repeating the same kind of thing he had spoken before, he once more promised to make his peace with Antipater. But Demosthenes, perceiving that now the poison had pierced, and seized his vitals, uncovered his head, and fixing his eyes upon Archias, "Now," said he, "as soon as you please, you may commence the part of Creon in the tragedy, and cast out this body of mine unburied. But, O gracious Neptune, I, for my part, while I am yet alive, will rise up and depart out of this sacred place; though Antipater and the Macedonians have not left so much as thy temple unpolluted." After he had thus spoken and desired to be held up, because already he began to tremble and stagger, as he was going forward, and passing by the altar, he fell down, and with a groan gave up the ghost.

Ariston says that he took the poison out of a reed, as we have shown before. But Pappus, a certain historian whose history was recovered by Hermippus, says that as he fell near the altar, there was found in his scroll this beginning only of a letter, and nothing more, "Demosthenes to Antipater." And that when his sudden death was much wondered at, the Thracians who guarded the doors reported that he took the poison into his hand out of a rag, and put it in his mouth, and that they imagined it had been gold which he swallowed, but the maid that served him, being examined by the followers of Archias, affirmed that he had worn it in a bracelet for a long time, as an amulet. And Eratosthenes also says that he kept the poison in a hollow ring, and that that ring was the bracelet which he wore about his arm.

There are various other statements made by the many authors who have related the story, but there is no need to enter into their discrepancies; yet I must not omit what is said by Demochares, the relation of Demosthenes, who is of opinion it was not by the help of poison that he met with so sudden and so easy a death, but that by the singular favour and providence of the gods he was thus rescued from the cruelty of the Macedonians. He died on the sixteenth of Pyanepsion, the most sad and solemn day of the Thesmophoria, which the women observe by fasting in the temple of the goddess.

Soon after his death, the people of Athens bestowed on him such honours as he had deserved. They erected his statue of brass; they decreed that the eldest of his family should be maintained in the Prytaneum; and on the base of his statue was engraven the famous inscription—

Had you for Greece been strong, as wise you were,
The Macedonian had not conquered her.

But it is simply ridiculous to say, as some have related, that Demosthenes made these verses himself in Calauria, as he was about to take the poison.

A little before he went to Athens, the following incident was said to have happened. A soldier, being summoned to appear before his superior officer, and answer to an accusation brought against him, put that little gold which he had into the hands of Demosthenes's statue. The fingers of this statue were folded one within another, and near it grew a small plane-tree, from which many leaves, either accidentally blown thither by the wind, or placed so on purpose by the man himself, falling together and lying round about the gold, concealed it for a long time. In the end, the soldier returned, and found his treasure entire, and the fame of this incident was spread abroad. And many ingenious persons of the city competed with each other, on this occasion, to vindicate the integrity of Demosthenes in several epigrams which they made on the subject.

As for Demades, he did not long enjoy the new honours he now came in for, divine vengeance for the death of Demosthenes pursuing him into Macedonia, where he was justly put to death by those whom he had basely flattered. They were weary of him before, but at this time the guilt he lay under was manifest and undeniable. For some of his letters were intercepted, in which he had encouraged Perdiccas to fall upon Macedonia, and to save the Grecians, who, he said, hung only by an old rotten thread, meaning Antipater. Of this he was accused by Dinarchus, the Corinthian, and Cassander was so enraged, that he first slew Demades' son in his bosom,

and then gave orders to execute Demades; who might now at last, by his own extreme misfortunes, learn the lesson that traitors who make sale of their country sell themselves first; a truth which Demosthenes had often foretold of him, and he would never believe. Thus, Sosius, you have the life of Demosthenes, from such accounts as we have either read or heard concerning him.

CICERO

106–43 B.C.

IT is generally said, that Helvia, the mother of Cicero, was both well-born and lived a fair life; but of his father nothing is reported but in extremes. For whilst some would have him the son of a fuller, and educated in that trade, others carry back the origin of his family to Tullus Attius, an illustrious king of the Volscians, who waged war not without honour against the Romans. However, he who first of that house was surnamed Cicero seems to have been a person worthy to be remembered; since those who succeeded him not only did not reject, but were fond of that name, though vulgarly made a matter of reproach. For the Latins call a vetch *Cicer,* and a nick or dent at the tip of his nose, which resembled the opening in a vetch, gave him the surname of *Cicero.*

Cicero, whose story I am writing, is said to have replied with spirit to some of his friends, who recommended him to lay aside or change the name when he first stood for office and engaged in politics, that he would make it his endeavour to render the name of Cicero more glorious than that of the Scauri and Catuli. And when he was quæstor in Sicily, and was making an offering of silver plate to the gods, and had inscribed his two names, Marcus and Tullius, instead of the third, he jestingly told the artificer to engrave the figure of a vetch by them. Thus much is told us about his name.

Of his birth it is reported that his mother was delivered, without pain or labour, on the third of the new calends, the same day on which now the magistrates of Rome pray and sacrifice for the emperor. It is said, also, that a vision appeared to his nurse, and foretold the child she then suckled should afterwards

become a great benefit to the Roman states. To such presages, which might in general be thought mere fancies and idle talk, he himself ere long gave the credit of true prophecies. For as soon as he was of an age to begin to have lessons, he became so distinguished for his talent, and got such a name and reputation amongst the boys, that their fathers would often visit the school that they might see young Cicero, and might be able to say that they themselves had witnessed the quickness and readiness in learning for which he was renowned. And the more rude among them used to be angry with their children, to see them, as they walked together, receiving Cicero with respect into the middle place.

And being, as Plato would have the scholar-like and philosophical temper, eager for every kind of learning, and indisposed to no description of knowledge or instruction, he showed, however, a more peculiar propensity to poetry; and there is a poem now extant, made by him when a boy, in tetrameter verse, called Pontius Glaucus. And afterwards, when he applied himself more curiously to these accomplishments, he had the name of being not only the best orator, but also the best poet of Rome. And the glory of his rhetoric still remains, notwithstanding the many new modes in speaking since his time; but his verses are forgotten and out of all repute, so many ingenious poets have followed him.

Leaving his juvenile studies, he became an auditor of Philo the Academic, whom the Romans, above all the other scholars of Clitomachus, admired for his eloquence and loved for his character. He also sought the company of the Mucii, who were eminent statesmen and leaders in the senate, and acquired from them a knowledge of the laws. For some short time he served in arms under Sulla, in the Marsian war. But perceiving the commonwealth running into factions, and from faction all things tending to an absolute monarchy, he betook himself to a retired and contemplative life, and conversing with the learned Greeks, devoted himself to study, till Sulla had obtained the government, and the commonwealth was in some kind of settlement.

At this time, Chrysogonus, Sulla's emancipated slave, having laid an information about an estate belonging to one who was said to have been put to death by proscription, had bought it himself for two thousand drachmas. And when Roscius, the son and heir of the dead, complained, and demonstrated the estate to be worth two hundred and fifty talents, Sulla took it angrily to have his actions questioned, and preferred a process against Roscius for the murder of his father, Chrysogonus managing the evidence. None of the advocates durst assist him, but, fearing the cruelty of Sulla, avoided the cause. The young man, being thus deserted, came for refuge to Cicero. Cicero's friends encouraged him, saying he was not likely ever to have a fairer and more honourable introduction to public life; he therefore undertook the defence, carried the cause, and got much renown for it.

But fearing Sulla, he travelled into Greece, and gave it out that he did so for the benefit of his health. And indeed he was lean and meagre, and had such a weakness in his stomach that he could take nothing but a spare and thin diet, and that not till late in the evening. His voice was loud and good, but so harsh and unmanaged that in vehemence and heat of speaking he always raised it to so high a tone that there seemed to be reason to fear about his health.

When he came to Athens, he was a hearer of Antiochus of Ascalon, with whose fluency and elegance of diction he was much taken, although he did not approve of his innovations in doctrine. For Antiochus had now fallen off from the New Academy, as they call it, and forsaken the sect of Carneades, whether that he was moved by the argument of manifestness and the senses, or, as some say, had been led by feelings of rivalry and opposition to the followers of Clitomachus and Philo to change his opinions, and in most things to embrace the doctrine of the Stoics. But Cicero rather affected and adhered to the doctrines of the New Academy; and purposed with himself, if he should be disappointed of any employment in the commonwealth, to retire hither from pleading and political affairs, and to pass his life with quiet in the study of philosophy.

But after he had received the news of Sulla's death, and his body, strengthened again by exercise, was come to a vigorous habit, his voice managed and rendered sweet and full to the ear and pretty well brought into keeping with his general constitution, his friends at Rome earnestly soliciting him by letters and Antiochus also urging him to return to public affairs, he again prepared for use his orator's instrument of rhetoric, and summoned into action his political faculties, diligently exercising himself in declamations, and attending the most celebrated rhetoricians of the time. He sailed from Athens for Asia and Rhodes. Amongst the Asian masters, he conversed with Xenocles of Adramyttium, Dionysius of Magnesia, and Menippus of Caria; at Rhodes, he studied oratory with Apollonius, the son of Molon, and philosophy with Posidonius.

Apollonius, we are told, not understanding Latin, requested Cicero to declaim in Greek. He complied willingly, thinking that his faults would thus be better pointed out to him. And after he finished, all his other hearers were astonished, and contended who should praise him most, but Apollonius, who had shown no signs of excitement whilst he was hearing him, so also now, when it was over, sate musing for some considerable time, without any remark. And when Cicero was discomposed at this, he said, "You have my praise and admiration, Cicero, and Greece my pity and commiseration, since those arts and that eloquence which are the only glories that remain to her, will now be transferred by you to Rome."

And now when Cicero, full of expectation, was again bent upon political affairs, a certain oracle blunted the edge of his inclination; for consulting the god of Delphi how he should attain most glory, the Pythoness answered, by making his own genius and not the opinion of the people the guide of his life; and therefore at first he passed his time in Rome cautiously, and was very backward in pretending to public offices, so that he was at that time in little esteem, and had got the names, so readily given by low and ignorant people in Rome, of Greek and Scholar. But when his own desire of fame and the eagerness of his father and relations had made him take in earnest to pleading, he made no slow or gentle advance to the first place, but shone out in full lustre at once, and far surpassed all the advocates of the bar.

At first, it is said, he, as well as Demosthenes, was defective in his delivery, and on that account paid much attention to the instructions, sometimes of Roscius the comedian, and sometimes of Æsop the tragedian. They tell of this Æsop, that whilst he was representing on the theatre Atreus deliberating the revenge of Thyestes, he was so transported beyond himself in the heat of action, that he struck with his sceptre one of the servants, who was running across the stage, so violently that he laid him dead upon the place. And such afterwards was Cicero's delivery that it did not a little contribute to render his eloquence persuasive. He used to ridicule loud speakers, saying that they shouted because they could not speak, like lame men who get on horseback because they cannot walk. And his readiness and address in sarcasm, and generally in witty sayings, was thought to suit a pleader very well, and to be highly attractive, but his using it to excess offended many, and gave him the repute of ill-nature.

He was appointed quæstor in a great scarcity of corn, and had Sicily for his province, where, though at first he displeased many, by compelling them to send in their provisions to Rome, yet after they had had experience of his care, justice, and clemency, they honoured him more than ever they did any of their governors before. It happened, also, that some young Romans of good and noble families, charged with neglect of discipline and misconduct in military service, were brought before the prætor in Sicily. Cicero undertook their defence, which he conducted admirably, and got them acquitted.

So returning to Rome with a great opinion of himself for these things, a ludicrous incident befell him, as he tells us himself. Meeting an eminent citizen in Campania, whom he accounted his friend, he asked him what the Romans said and thought of his actions, as if the whole city had been filled with the glory of what he had done. His friend asked him in reply, "Where is it you have been, Cicero?" This for the time utterly mortified and cast him down, to perceive that the report of his actions had sunk into the city of Rome as into an immense ocean, without any

visible effect or result in reputation. And afterwards considering with himself that the glory he contended for was an infinite thing, and that there was no fixed end nor measure in its pursuit, he abated much of his ambitious thoughts. Nevertheless, he was always excessively pleased with his own praise, and continued to the very last to be passionately fond of glory; which often interfered with the prosecution of his wisest resolutions.

On beginning to apply himself more resolutely to public business, he remarked it as an unreasonable and absurd thing that artificers, using vessels and instruments inanimate, should know the name, place, and use of every one of them, and yet the statesman, whose instruments for carrying out public measures are men, should be negligent and careless in the knowledge of persons. And so he not only acquainted himself with the names, but also knew the particular place where every one of the more eminent citizens dwelt, what lands he possessed, the friends he made use of, and those that were of his neighbourhood, and when he travelled on any road in Italy, he could readily name and show the estates and seats of his friends and acquaintance.

Having so small an estate, though a sufficient competency for his own expenses, it was much wondered at that he took neither fees nor gifts from his clients, and more especially that he did not do so when he undertook the prosecution of Verres. This Verres, who had been prætor of Sicily, and stood charged by the Sicilians of many evil practices during his government there, Cicero succeeded in getting condemned, not by speaking, but in a manner by holding his tongue. For the prætors, favouring Verres, had deferred the trial by several adjournments to the last day, in which it was evident there could not be sufficient time for the advocates to be heard, and the cause brought to an issue. Cicero, therefore, came forward, and said there was no need of speeches; and after producing and examining witnesses, he required the judges to proceed to sentence.

However, many witty sayings are on record, as having been used by Cicero on the occasion. When a man named Cæcilius, one of the freed slaves, who was said to be given to Jewish practices, would have put by the Sicilians, and undertaken the prosecution of Verres himself, Cicero asked, "What has a Jew to do with swine?" *verres* being the Roman word for a boar. And when Verres began to reproach Cicero with effeminate living, "You ought," replied he, "to use this language at home, to your sons," Verres having a son who had fallen into disgraceful courses. Hortensius the orator, not daring directly to undertake the defence of Verres, was yet persuaded to appear for him at the laying on of the fine, and received an ivory sphinx for his reward; and when Cicero, in some passage of the speech, obliquely reflected on him, and Hortensius told him he was not skilful in solving riddles, "No," said Cicero, "and yet you have the sphinx in your house!"

Verres was thus convicted; though Cicero, who set the fine at seventy-five myriads, lay under the suspicion of being corrupted by bribery to lessen the sum. But the Sicilians, in testimony of their gratitude, came and brought him all sorts of presents from the island, when he was ædile; of which he made no private profit himself, but used their generosity only to reduce the public price of provisions.

He had a very pleasant seat at Arpi; he had also a farm near Naples, and another about Pompeii, but neither of any great value. The portion of his wife, Terentia, amounted to ten myriads, and he had a bequest valued at nine myriads of denarii; upon these he lived in a liberal but temperate style with the learned Greeks and Romans that were his familiars. He rarely, if at any time, sat down to meat till sunset, and that not so much on account of business, as for his health and the weakness of his stomach. He was otherwise in the care of his body nice and delicate, appointing himself, for example, a set number of walks and rubbings. And after this manner managing the habit of his body, he brought it in time to be healthful, and capable of supporting many great fatigues and trials. His father's house he made over to his brother, living himself near the Palatine hill, that he might not give the trouble of long journeys to those that made suit to him. And, indeed, there were not fewer daily appearing at his door, to do their court to him, than there were that came to Crassus for his riches, or to Pompey for his power amongst the soldiers, these being at that time the two men of the greatest repute and influence in Rome. Nay, even Pompey himself used to pay court to Cicero, and Cicero's public actions did much to establish Pompey's authority and reputation in the state.

Numerous distinguished competitors stood with him for the prætor's office; but he was chosen before them all, and managed the decision of causes with justice and integrity. It is related that Licinius Macer, a man himself of great power in the city, and supported also by the assistance of Crassus, was accused before him of extortion, and that, in confidence of his own influence and the diligence of his friends, whilst the judges were debating about the sentence, he went to his house, where hastily trimming his hair and putting on a clean gown as already acquitted, he was setting off again to go to the Forum; but at his hall door meeting Crassus, who told him that he was condemned by all the votes, he went in again, threw himself upon his bed, and died immediately. This verdict was considered very creditable to Cicero, as showing his careful management of the courts of justice. On another occasion, Vatinius, who had large swellings on his neck, a man of rude manners and often insolent in court to the magistrates, came before his tribunal and made some request, and on Cicero's desiring further time to consider it, told him that he himself would have made no question about it had he been prætor. Cicero, turning quickly upon him, answered, "But I, you see, have not the neck that you have."

When there were but two or three days remaining in his office, Manilius was brought before him, and charged with peculation. Manilius had the good opinion and favour of the common people, and was thought to be prosecuted only for Pompey's sake, whose particular friend he was. And therefore, when he asked a space of time before his trial, and Cicero allowed him but one day, and that the next only, the common people grew highly offended, because it had been the custom of the prætors to allow ten days at least to the accused; and the tribunes of the people, having called him before the people and accused him, he, desiring to be heard, said, that as he had always treated the accused with equity and humanity, as far as the law allowed, so he thought it hard to deny the same to Manilius, and that he had studiously appointed that day of which alone, as prætor, he was master, and that it was not the part of those that were desirous to help him to cast the judgment of his cause upon another prætor. These things being said made a wonderful change in the people, and commending him much for it they desired that he himself would undertake the defence of Manilius; which he willingly consented to, and that principally for the sake of Pompey, who was absent. And, accordingly, taking his place before the people again, he delivered a bold invective against the oligarchical party and on those who were jealous of Pompey.

Yet he was preferred to the consulship no less by the nobles than the common people, for the good of the city; and both parties jointly assisted his promotion, upon the following reasons. The change of government made by Sulla, which at first seemed a senseless one, by time and usage had now come to be considered by the people no unsatisfactory settlement. But there were some that endeavoured to alter and subvert the whole present state of affairs, not from any good motives, but for their own private gain; and Pompey being at this time employed in the wars with the kings of Pontus and Armenia, there was no sufficient force at Rome to suppress any attempts at a revolution.

These people had for their head a man of bold, daring, and restless character, Lucius Catiline, who was accused, besides other great offences, of deflowering his virgin daughter, and killing his own brother; for which latter crime, fearing to be prosecuted at law, he persuaded Sulla to set him down, as though he were yet alive, amongst those that were to be put to death by proscription. This man the profligate citizens choosing for their captain, gave faith to one another, amongst other pledges, by sacrificing a man, and eating of his flesh; and a great part of the young men of the city were corrupted by him, he providing for every one pleasures, drink, and women, and profusely supplying the expense of these debauches. Etruria, moreover, had all been excited to revolt, as well as a great part of Gaul within the Alps. But Rome itself was in the most dangerous inclination to change on account of the unequal distribution of wealth and property, those of highest rank and greatest spirit having impoverished themselves by shows, entertainments, ambition of offices, and sumptuous buildings, and the riches of the city having thus fallen into the hands of mean and low-born persons. So that there wanted but a slight impetus to set all in motion, it being in the power of every daring man to overturn a sickly commonwealth.

Catiline, however, being desirous of procuring a strong position to carry out his designs, stood for the consulship, and had great hopes of success, thinking he should be ap-

pointed, with Caius Antonius as his colleague, who was a man fit to lead neither in a good cause nor in a bad one, but might be a valuable accession to another's power. These things the greatest part of the good and honest citizens apprehending, put Cicero upon standing for the consulship; whom the people readily receiving, Catiline was put by, so that he and Caius Antonius were chosen, although amongst the competitors he was the only man descended from a father of the equestrian and not of the senatorial order.

Though the designs of Catiline were not yet publicly known, yet considerable preliminary troubles immediately followed upon Cicero's entrance upon the consulship. For, on the one side, those who were disqualified by the laws of Sulla from holding any public offices, being neither inconsiderable in power nor in number, came forward as candidates and caressed the people for them; speaking many things truly and justly against the tyranny of Sulla, only that they disturbed the government at an improper and unseasonable time; on the other hand, the tribunes of the people proposed laws to the same purpose, constituting a commission of ten persons, with unlimited powers, in whom as supreme governors should be vested the right of selling the public lands of all Italy and Syria and Pompey's new conquest, of judging and banishing whom they pleased, of planting colonies, of taking moneys out of the treasury, and of levying and paying what soldiers should be thought needful. And several of the nobility favoured this law, but especially Caius Antonius, Cicero's colleague, in hopes of being one of the ten. But what gave the greatest fear to the nobles was, that he was thought privy to the conspiracy of Catiline, and not to dislike it because of his great debts.

Cicero, endeavouring in the first place to provide a remedy against this danger, procured a decree assigning to him the province of Macedonia, he himself declining that of Gaul, which was offered to him. And this piece of favour so completely won over Antonius, that he was ready to second and respond to, like a hired player, whatever Cicero said for the good of the country. And now, having made his colleague thus tame and tractable, he could with greater courage attack the conspirators. And, therefore, in the senate, making an oration against the law of the ten commissioners, he so confounded those who proposed it, that they had nothing to reply.

And when they again endeavoured, and, having prepared things beforehand, had called the consuls before the assembly of the people, Cicero, fearing nothing, went first out, and commanded the senate to follow him, and not only succeeded in throwing out the law, but so entirely overpowered the tribunes by his oratory, that they abandoned all thought of their other projects.

For Cicero, it may be said, was the one man, above all others, who made the Romans feel how great a charm eloquence lends to what is good, and how invincible justice is, if it be well spoken; and that it is necessary for him who would dexterously govern a commonwealth, in action, always to prefer that which is honest before that which is popular, and in speaking, to free the right and useful measure from everything that may occasion offence.

An incident occurred in the theatre, during his consulship, which showed what his speaking could do. For whereas formerly the knights of Rome were mingled in the theatre with the common people, and took their places among them as it happened, Marcus Otho, when he was prætor, was the first who distinguished them from the other citizens, and appointed them a proper seat, which they still enjoy as their special place in the theatre. This the common people took as an indignity done to them, and, therefore, when Otho appeared in the theatre they hissed him; the knights, on the contrary, received him with loud clapping. The people repeated and increased their hissing; the knights continued their clapping. Upon this, turning upon one another, they broke out into insulting words, so that the theatre was in great disorder. Cicero being informed of it, came himself to the theatre, and summoning the people into the temple of Bellona, he so effectually chid and chastised them for it, that again returning into the theatre they received Otho with loud applause, contending with the knights who should give him the greatest demonstrations of honour and respect.

The conspirators with Catiline, at first cowed and disheartened, began presently to take courage again. And assembling themselves together, they exhorted one another boldly to undertake the design before Pompey's return, who, as it was said, was now on his march with his forces for Rome. But the old soldiers of Sulla were Catiline's chief stimulus to action. They had been disbanded all about Italy, but the greatest number and the fiercest of them lay scattered among the cities of Etruria, entertaining themselves with dreams of new plunder and rapine amongst the hoarded riches of Italy. These, having for their leader Manlius, who had served with distinction in the wars under Sulla, joined themselves to Catiline, and came to Rome to assist him with their suffrages at the election. For he again pretended to the consulship, having resolved to kill Cicero in a tumult at the elections. Also, the divine powers seemed to give intimation of the coming troubles, by earthquakes, thunderbolts, and strange appearances. Nor was human evidence wanting, certain enough in itself, though not sufficient for the conviction of the noble and powerful Catiline.

Therefore Cicero, deferring the day of election, summoned Catiline into the senate, and questioned him as to the charges made against him. Catiline, believing there were many in the senate desirous of change, and to give a specimen of himself to the conspirators present, returned an audacious answer, "What harm," said he, "when I see two bodies, the one lean and consumptive with a head, the other great and strong without one, if I put a head to that body which wants one?" This covert representation of the senate and the people excited yet greater apprehensions in Cicero. He put on armour, and was attended from his house by the noble citizens in a body; and a number of the young men went with him into the Plain. Here, designedly letting his tunic slip partly off from his shoulders, he showed his armour underneath, and discovered his danger to the spectators; who, being much moved at it, gathered round about him for his defence. At length, Catiline was by a general suffrage again put by, and Silanus and Murena chosen consuls.

Not long after this, Catiline's soldiers got together in a body in Etruria, and began to form themselves into companies, the day appointed for the design being near at hand. About midnight, some of the principal and most powerful citizens of Rome, Marcus Crassus, Marcus Marcellus, and Scipio Metellus went to Cicero's house, where, knocking at the gate, and calling up the porter, they commanded him to awake Cicero, and tell him they were there. The business was this: Crassus's porter after supper had delivered to him letters brought by an unknown person. Some of them were directed to others, but one to

Crassus, without a name; this only Crassus read, which informed him that there was a great slaughter intended by Catiline, and advised him to leave the city. The others he did not open, but went with them immediately to Cicero, being affrighted at the danger, and to free himself of the suspicion he lay under for his familiarity with Catiline.

Cicero, considering the matter, summoned the senate at break of day. The letters he brought with him, and delivered them to those to whom they were directed, commanding them to read them publicly; they all alike contained an account of the conspiracy. And when Quintus Arrius, a man of prætorian dignity, recounted to them how soldiers were collecting in companies in Etruria, and Manlius stated to be in motion with a large force, hovering about those cities, in expectation of intelligence from Rome, the senate made a decree to place all in the hands of the consuls, who should undertake the conduct of everything, and do their best to save the state. This was not a common thing, but only done by the senate in case of imminent danger.

After Cicero had received this power, he committed all affairs outside to Quintus Metellus, but the management of the city he kept in his own hands. Such a numerous attendance guarded him every day when he went abroad, that the greatest part of the market-place was filled with his train when he entered it. Catiline, impatient of further delay, resolved himself to break forth and go to Manlius, but he commanded Marcius and Cethegus to take their swords, and go early in the morning to Cicero's gates, as if only intending to salute him, and then to fall upon him and slay him. This a noble lady, Fulvia, coming by night, discovered to Cicero, bidding him beware of Cethegus and Marcius. They came by break of day, and being denied entrance, made an outcry and disturbance at the gates, which excited all the more suspicion.

But Cicero, going forth, summoned the senate into the temple of Jupiter Stator, which stands at the end of the Sacred Street, going up to the Palatine. And when Catiline with others of his party also came, as intending to make his defence, none of the senators would sit by him, but all of them left the bench where he had placed himself. And when he began to speak, they interrupted him with outcries. At length Cicero, standing up, commanded him to leave the city, for since one governed the commonwealth with words, the other with arms, it was necessary there should be a wall betwixt them. Catiline, therefore, immediately left the town, with three hundred armed men; and assuming, as if he had been a magistrate, the rods, axes, and military ensigns, he went to Manlius, and having got together a body of near twenty thousand men, with these he marched to the several cities, endeavouring to persuade or force them to revolt. So it being now come to open war, Antonius was sent forth to fight him.

The remainder of those in the city whom he had corrupted, Cornelius Lentulus kept together and encouraged. He had the surname Sura, and was a man of a noble family, but a dissolute liver, who for his debauchery was formerly turned out of the senate, and was now holding the office of prætor for the second time, as the custom is with those who desire to regain the dignity of senator. It is said that he got the surname Sura upon this occasion: being quæstor in the time of Sulla, he had lavished away and consumed a great quantity of the public moneys at which Sulla being provoked, called him to give an account in the senate; he appeared with great coolness and contempt, and said he had no account to give, but they might take this, holding up the calf of his leg, as boys do at ball, when they have missed. Upon which he was surnamed *Sura, sura* being the Roman word for the calf of the leg. Being at another time prosecuted at law, and having bribed some of the judges, he escaped only by two votes, and complained of the needless expense he had gone to in paying for a second, as one would have sufficed to acquit him.

This man, such in his own nature, and now inflamed by Catiline, false prophets and fortune-tellers had also corrupted with vain hopes, quoting to him fictitious verses and oracles, and proving from the Sibylline prophecies that there were three of the name Cornelius designed by fate to be monarchs of Rome; two of whom, Cinna and Sulla, had already fulfilled the decree, and that divine fortune was now advancing with the gift of monarchy for the remaining third Cornelius; and that therefore he ought by all means to accept it, and not lose opportunity by delay, as Catiline had done. He therefore designed no mean or trivial matter, for he had resolved to kill the whole senate, and as many other citizens as he could, to fire the city, and spare nobody, except only Pompey's children, intending to seize and keep them as pledges of his reconciliation with Pompey. For there was then a common and strong report that Pompey was on his way homeward from his great expedition.

The night appointed for the design was one of the Saturnalia; swords, flax, and sulphur they carried and hid in the house of Cethegus; and providing one hundred men, and dividing the city into as many parts, they had allotted to every one singly his proper place, so that in a moment, many kindling the fire, the city might be in a flame all together. Others were appointed to stop up the aqueducts, and to kill those who should endeavour to carry water to put it out. Whilst these plans were preparing, it happened there were two ambassadors from the Allobroges staying in Rome; a nation at that time in a distressed condition, and very uneasy under the Roman government. These Lentulus and his party judging useful instruments to move and seduce Gaul to revolt, admitted into the conspiracy, and they gave them letters to their own magistrates, and letters to Catiline; in those they promised liberty, in these they exhorted Catiline to set all slaves free, and to bring them along with him to Rome. They sent also to accompany them to Catiline, one Titus, a native of Croton, who was to carry those letters to him.

These counsels of inconsidering men, who conversed together over wine and with women, Cicero watched with sober industry and forethought, and with most admirable sagacity, having several emissaries abroad, who observed and traced with him all that was done, and keeping also a secret correspondence with many who pretended to join in the conspiracy. He thus knew all the discourse which passed betwixt them and the strangers; and lying in wait for them by night, he took the Crotonian with his letters, the ambassadors of the Allobroges acting secretly in concert with him.

By break of day, he summoned the senate into the temple of Concord, where he read the letters and examined the informers. Junius Silanus further stated that several persons had heard Cethegus say that three consuls and four prætors were to be slain. Piso, also, a person of consular dignity, testified other matters of the like nature; and Caius Sulpicius, one of the prætors, being sent to Cethegus's house, found there a quantity of darts and of armour, and a still greater number of swords and daggers, all recently whetted. At length, the senate decreeing indemnity to the Crotonian upon his confession of the whole matter, Lentulus was convicted, adjured his office (for he was then

prætor), and put off his robe edged with purple in the senate, changing it for another garment more agreeable to his present circumstances. He thereupon, with the rest of his confederates present, was committed to the charge of the prætors in free custody.

It being evening, and the common people in crowds expecting without, Cicero went forth to them, and told them what was done, and then, attended by them, went to the house of a friend and near neighbour; for his own was taken up by the women, who were celebrating with secret rites the feast of the goddess whom the Romans call the Good, and the Greeks the Women's goddess. For a sacrifice is annually performed to her in the consul's house, either by his wife or mother, in the presence of the vestal virgins. And having got into his friend's house privately, a few only being present, he began to deliberate how he should treat these men. The severest, and the only punishment fit for such heinous crimes, he was somewhat shy and fearful of inflicting, as well from the clemency of his nature, as also lest he should be thought to exercise his authority too insolently, and to treat too harshly men of the noblest birth and most powerful friendships in the city; and yet, if he should use them more mildly, he had a dreadful prospect of danger from them. For there was no likelihood, if they suffered less than death, they would be reconciled, but rather, adding new rage to their former wickedness, they would rush into every kind of audacity, while he himself, whose character for courage already did not stand very high with the multitude, would be thought guilty of the greatest cowardice and want of manliness.

Whilst Cicero was doubting what course to take, a portent happened to the women in their sacrificing. For on the altar, where the fire seemed wholly extinguished, a great and bright flame issued forth from the ashes of the burnt wood; at which others were affrighted, but the holy virgins called to Terentia, Cicero's wife, and bade her haste to her husband, and command him to execute what he had resolved for the good of his country, for the goddess had sent a great light to the increase of his safety and glory. Terentia, therefore, as she was otherwise in her own nature neither tender-hearted nor timorous, but a woman eager for distinction (who, as Cicero himself says, would rather thrust herself into his public affairs, than communicate her domestic matters to him), told him these things, and excited him against the conspirators. So also did Quintus his brother, and Publius Nigidius, one of his philosophical friends, whom he often made use of in his greatest and most weighty affairs of state.

The next day, a debate arising in the senate about the punishment of the men, Silanus, being the first who was asked his opinion, said it was fit they should be all sent to the prison, and there suffer the utmost penalty. To him all consented in order till it came to Caius Cæsar, who was afterwards dictator. He was then but a young man, and only at the outset of his career, but had already directed his hopes and policy to that course by which he afterwards changed the Roman state into a monarchy. Of this others foresaw nothing; but Cicero had seen reason for strong suspicion, though without obtaining any sufficient means of proof. And there were some indeed that said that he was very near being discovered, and only just escaped him; others are of opinion that Cicero voluntarily overlooked and neglected the evidence against him, for fear of his friends and power; for it was very evident to everybody that if Cæsar was to be accused with the conspirators, they were more likely to be saved with him, than he to be punished with them.

When, therefore, it came to Cæsar's turn to give his opinion, he stood up and proposed that the conspirators should not be put to death, but their estates confiscated, and their persons confined in such cities in Italy as Cicero should approve, there to be kept in custody till Catiline was conquered. To this sentence, as it was the most moderate, and he that delivered it a most powerful speaker, Cicero himself gave no small weight, for he stood up and, turning the scale on either side, spoke in favour partly of the former, partly of Cæsar's sentence. And all Cicero's friends, judging Cæsar's sentence most expedient for Cicero, because he would incur the less blame if the conspirators were not put to death, chose rather the latter; so that Silanus, also changing his mind, retracted his opinion, and said he had not declared for capital, but only the utmost punishment, which to a Roman senator is imprisonment.

The first man who spoke against Cæsar's motion was Catulus Lutatius. Cato followed, and so vehemently urged in his speech the strong suspicion against Cæsar himself, and so filled the senate with anger and resolution, that a decree was passed for the execution of the conspirators. But Cæsar opposed the confiscation of their goods, not thinking it fair that those who rejected the mildest part of his sentence should avail themselves of the severest. And when many insisted upon it, he appealed to the tribunes, but they would do nothing; till Cicero himself yielding, remitted that part of the sentence.

After this, Cicero went out with the senate to the conspirators; they were not all together in one place, but the several prætors had them, some one, some another, in custody. And first he took Lentulus from the Palatine, and brought him by the Sacred Street, through the middle of the market-place, a circle of the most eminent citizens encompassing and protecting him. The people, affrighted at what was doing, passed along in silence, especially the young men; as if, with fear and trembling, they were undergoing a rite of initiation into some ancient sacred mysteries of aristocratic power. Thus passing from the market-place, and coming to the gaol, he delivered Lentulus to the officer, and commanded him to execute him; and after him Cethegus, and so all the rest in order, he brought and delivered up to execution. And when he saw many of the conspirators in the market-place, still standing together in companies, ignorant of what was done, and waiting for the night, supposing the men were still alive and in a possibility of being rescued, he called out in a loud voice, and said, *"They did live"*; for so the Romans, to avoid inauspicious language, name those that are dead.

It was now evening, when he returned from the market-place to his own house, the citizens no longer attending him with silence, nor in order, but receiving him, as he passed, with acclamations and applauses, and saluting him as the saviour and founder of his country. A bright light shone through the streets from the lamps and torches set up at the doors, and the women showed lights from the tops of the houses, to honour Cicero, and to behold him returning home with a splendid train of the most principal citizens; amongst whom were many who had conducted great wars, celebrated triumphs, and added to the possessions of the Roman empire, both by sea and land. These, as they passed along with him, acknowledged to one another, that though the Roman people were indebted to several officers and commanders of that age for riches, spoils, and power, yet to Cicero alone they owed the safety and security of all these, for delivering them from so great and imminent a danger. For though it might seem no wonderful thing to prevent the design, and punish the conspirators, yet to defeat the greatest of all conspiracies with so little disturbance, trouble, and commotion, was very extraordinary.

For the greater part of those who had flocked into Catiline, as soon as they heard the fate of Lentulus and Cethegus, left and forsook him, and he himself, with his remaining forces, joining battle with Antonius, was destroyed with his army.

And yet there were some who were very ready both to speak ill of Cicero, and to do him hurt for these actions; and they had for their leaders some of the magistrates of the ensuing year, as Cæsar, who was one of the prætors, and Metellus and Bestia, the tribunes. These, entering upon their office some few days before Cicero's consulate expired, would not permit him to make any address to the people, but throwing the benches before the rostra, hindered his speaking, telling him he might, if he pleased, make the oath of withdrawal from office, and then come down again. Cicero, accordingly, accepting the conditions, came forward to make his withdrawal; and silence being made, he recited his oath, not in the usual, but in a new and peculiar form, namely, that he had saved his country and preserved the empire; the truth of which oath all the people confirmed with theirs. Cæsar and the tribunes, all the more exasperated by this, endeavoured to create him further trouble, and for this purpose proposed a law for calling Pompey home with his army, to put an end to Cicero's usurpation.

But it was a very great advantage for Cicero and the whole commonwealth that Cato was at that time one of the tribunes. For he, being of equal power with the rest, and of greater reputation, could oppose their designs. He easily defeated their other projects, and in an oration to the people so highly extolled Cicero's consulate, that the greatest honours were decreed him, and he was publicly declared the father of his country, which title he seems to have obtained, the first man who did so, when Cato gave it to him in this address to the people.

At this time, therefore, his authority was very great in the city; but he created himself much envy, and offended very many, not by any evil action, but because he was always lauding and magnifying himself. For neither senate, nor assembly of the people, nor court of judicature could meet in which he was not heard to talk of Catiline and Lentulus. Indeed,

he also filled his books and writings with his own praises, to such an excess as to render a style, in itself most pleasant and delightful, nauseous and irksome to his hearers, this ungrateful humour, like a disease, always cleaving to him.

Nevertheless, though he was intemperately fond of his own glory, he was very free from envying others, and was, on the contrary, most liberally profuse in commending both the ancients and his contemporaries, as any one may see in his writings. And many such sayings of his are also remembered; as that he called Aristotle a river of flowing gold, and said of Plato's dialogues, that if Jupiter were to speak, it would be in language like theirs. He used to call Theophrastus his special luxury. And being asked which of Demosthenes's orations he liked best, he answered, the longest. And yet some affected imitators of Demosthenes have complained of some words that occur in one of his letters, to the effect that Demosthenes sometimes falls asleep in his speeches; forgetting the many high encomiums he continually passes upon him, and the compliment he paid him when he named the most elaborate of all his orations, those he wrote against Antony, Philippics.

And as for the eminent men of his own time, either in eloquence or philosophy, there was not one of them whom he did not, by writing or speaking favourably of him, render more illustrious. He obtained of Cæsar, when in power, the Roman citizenship for Cratippus, the Peripatetic, and got the court of Areopagus, by public decree, to request his stay at Athens, for the instruction of their youth and the honour of their city. There are letters extant from Cicero to Herodes, and others to his son, in which he recommends the study of philosophy under Cratippus. There is one in which he blames Gorgias, the rhetorician, for enticing his son into luxury and drinking, and, therefore, forbids him his company. And this, and one other to Pelops, the Byzantine, are the only two of his Greek epistles which seem to be written in anger. In the first, he justly reflects on Gorgias, if he were what he was thought to be, a dissolute and profligate character; but in the other, he rather meanly expostulates and complains with Pelops for neglecting to procure him a decree of certain honours from the Byzantines.

Another illustration of his love of praise is the way in which sometimes, to make his orations more striking, he neglected decorum and dignity. When Munatius, who had escaped conviction by his advocacy, immediately prosecuted his friend Sabinus, he said in the warmth of his resentment, "Do you suppose you were acquitted for your own merits, Munatius, and was it not that I so darkened the case that the court could not see your guilt?"

When from the rostra he had made a eulogy on Marcus Crassus, with much applause, and within a few days after again as publicly reproached him, Crassus called to him, and said, "Did not you yourself two days ago, in this same place, commend me?" "Yes," said Cicero, "I exercised my eloquence in declaiming upon a bad subject." At another time, Crassus had said that no one of his family had ever lived beyond sixty years of age, and afterwards denied it, and asked, "What should put it into my head to say so?" "It was to gain the people's favour," answered Cicero; "you knew how glad they would be to hear it." When Crassus expressed admiration of the Stoic doctrine, that *the good man is always rich,* "Do you not mean," said Cicero, "their doctrine that *all things belong to the wise?*" For Crassus was generally accused of covetousness. One of Crassus's sons, who was thought so exceedingly like a man named Axius as to throw some suspicion on his mother's honour, made a successful speech in the senate. Cicero, on being asked how he liked it, replied with the Greek words, *"Axios Crassou"* (Worthy of Crassus).

When Crassus was about to go into Syria, he desired to leave Cicero rather his friend than his enemy, and, therefore, one day saluting him, told him he would come and sup with him, which the other as courteously received. Within a few days after, on some of Cicero's acquaintances interceding for Vatinius, as desirous of reconciliation and friendship, for he was then his enemy, "What," he replied, "does Vatinius also wish to come and sup with me?" Such was his way with Crassus. When Vatinius, who had swellings in his neck, was pleading a cause, he called him the *tumid* orator; and having been told by some one that Vatinius was dead, on hearing presently after that he was alive, "May the rascal perish," said he, "for his news not being true."

Upon Cæsar's bringing forward a law for the division of the lands in Campania amongst the soldiers, many in the senate opposed it; amongst the rest, Lucius Gellius, one of the oldest men in the house, said it should never pass whilst he lived. "Let us postpone it," said Cicero, "Gellius does not ask us to wait long."

There was a man of the name of Octavius, suspected to be of African descent. He once said, when Cicero was pleading, that he could not hear him: "Yet there are holes," said Cicero, "in your ears." When Metellus Nepos told him that he had ruined more as a witness than he had saved as an advocate, "I admit," said Cicero, "that I have more truth than eloquence." To a young man who was suspected of having given a poisoned cake to his father, and who talked largely of the invectives he meant to deliver against Cicero, "Better these," replied he, "than your cakes." Publius Sextius, having amongst others retained Cicero as his advocate in a certain cause, was yet desirous to say all for himself, and would not allow anybody to speak for him; when he was about to receive his acquittal from the judges, and the ballots were passing, Cicero called to him, "Make haste, Sextius, and use your time; tomorrow you will be nobody."

He cited Publius Cotta to bear testimony in a certain cause, one who affected to be thought a lawyer, though ignorant and unlearned; to whom, when he had said, "I know nothing of the matter," he answered, "You think, perhaps, we ask you about a point of law." To Metellus Nepos, who, in a dispute between them, repeated several times, "Who was your father, Cicero?" he replied, "Your mother has made the answer to such a question in your case more difficult"; Nepos's mother having been of ill-repute. The son, also, was of a giddy, uncertain temper. At one time, he suddenly threw up his office of tribune, and sailed off into Syria to Pompey; and immediately after, with as little reason, came back again. He gave his tutor, Philagrus, a funeral with more than necessary attention, and then set up the stone figure of a crow over his tomb. "This," said Cicero, "is really appropriate; as he did not teach you to speak, but to fly about." When Marcus Appius, in the opening of some speech in a court of justice, said that his friend had desired him to employ industry, eloquence, and fidelity in that cause, Cicero answered, "And how have you had the heart not to accede to any one of his requests?"

To use this sharp raillery against opponents and antagonists in judicial pleading seems allowable rhetoric. But he excited much ill-feeling by his readiness to attack any one for the sake of a jest. A few anecdotes of this kind may be added. Marcus Aquinius, who had two sons-in-law in exile, received from him the name of King Adrastus. Lucius Cotta, an intemperate lover of wine, was censor when Cicero stood for the consulship. Cicero, being thirsty at the election, his friends stood round about him while he was drinking. "You have reason to be afraid," he said, "lest the censor should be angry with me for drinking water."

Meeting one day Voconius with his three very ugly daughters, he quoted the verse—

He reared a race without Apollo's leave.

When Marcus Gellius, who was reputed the son of a slave, had read several letters in the senate with a very shrill and loud voice, "Wonder not," said Cicero, "he comes of the criers." When Faustus Sulla, the son of Sulla the dictator, who had, during his dictatorship, by public bills proscribed and condemned so many citizens, had so far wasted his estate, and got into debt, that he was forced to publish his bills of sale, Cicero told him that he liked these bills much better than those of his father. By this habit he made himself odious with many people.

But Clodius's faction conspired against him upon the following occasion. Clodius was a member of a noble family, in the flower of his youth, and of a bold and resolute temper. He, being in love with Pompeia, Cæsar's wife, got privately into his house in the dress and attire of a music-girl; the women being at that time offering there the sacrifice which must not be seen by men, and there was no man present. Clodius, being a youth and beardless, hoped to get to Pompeia among the women without being taken notice of. But coming into a great house by night, he missed his way in the passages, and a servant belonging to Aurelia, Cæsar's mother, spying him wandering up and down, inquired his name. Thus being necessitated to speak, he told her he was seeking for one of Pompeia's maids, Abra by name; and she, perceiving it not to be a woman's voice, shrieked out, and called in the women; who, shutting the gates, and searching every place, at length found Clodius hidden in the chamber of the maid with whom he had come in. This matter being much talked about, Cæsar put away his wife, Pompeia, and Clodius was prosecuted for profaning the holy rites.

Cicero was at this time his friend, for he had been useful to him in the conspiracy of Catiline, as one of his forwardest assistants and protectors. But when Clodius rested his defence upon this point, that he was not then at Rome, but at a distance in the country, Cicero testified that he had come to his house that day, and conversed with him on several matters; which thing was indeed true, although Cicero was thought to testifiy it not so much for the truth's sake as to preserve his quiet with Terentia his wife. For she bore a grudge against Clodius on account of his sister Clodia's wishing, as it was alleged, to marry Cicero, and having employed for this purpose the intervention of Tullus, a very intimate friend of Cicero's; and his frequent visits to Clodia, who lived in their neighbourhood, and the attentions he paid to her had excited Terentia's suspicions, and, being a woman of a violent temper, and having the ascendant over Cicero, she urged him on to taking a part against Clodius, and delivering his testimony.

Many other good and honest citizens also gave evidence against him, for perjuries, disorders, bribing the people, and debauching women. Lucullus proved, by his women-servants, that he had debauched his youngest sister when she was Lucullus's wife; and there was a general belief that he had done the same with his two other sisters, Tertia, whom Marcius Rex, and Clodia, whom Metellus Celer had married; the latter of whom was called Quadrantia, because one of her lovers had deceived her with a purse of small copper money instead of silver, the smallest copper coin being called a quadrans. Upon this sister's account, in particular, Clodius's character was attacked.

Notwithstanding all this, when the common people united against the accusers and witnesses and the whole party, the judges were affrighted, and a guard was placed about them for their defence; and most of them wrote their sentences on the tablets in such a way that they could not well be read. It was decided, however, that there was a majority for his acquittal, and bribery was reported to have been employed; in reference to which Catulus remarked, when he next met the judges. "You were very right to ask for a guard, to prevent your money being taken from you." And when Clodius upbraided Cicero that the judges had not believed his testimony, "Yes," said he, "five-and-twenty of them trusted me and condemned you, and the other thirty did not trust you, for they did not acquit you till they had got your money."

Cæsar, though cited, did not give his testimony against Clodius, and declared himself not convinced of his wife's adultery, but that he had put her away because it was fit that Cæsar's house should not be only free of the evil fact, but of the fame too.

Clodius, having escaped this danger, and having got himself chosen one of the tribunes, immediately attacked Cicero, heaping up all matters and inciting all persons against him. The common people he gained over with popular laws; to each of the consuls he decreed large provinces, to Piso, Macedonia, and to Gabinius, Syria; he made a strong party among the indigent citizens, to support him in his proceedings, and had always a body of armed slaves about him. Of the three men then in greatest power, Crassus was Cicero's open enemy, Pompey indifferently made advances to both, and Cæsar was going with an army into Gaul. To him, though not his friend (what had occurred in the time of the conspiracy having created suspicions between them), Cicero applied, requesting an appointment as one of his lieutenants in the province. Cæsar accepted him, and Clodius, perceiving that Cicero would thus escape his tribunician authority, professed to be inclinable to a reconciliation, laid the greatest fault upon Terentia, made always a favourable mention of him, and addressed him with kind expressions, as one who felt no hatred or ill-will, but who merely wished to urge his complaints in a moderate and friendly way.

By these artifices, he so freed Cicero of all his fears, that he resigned his appointment to Cæsar, and betook himself again to political affairs. At which Cæsar, being exasperated, joined the party of Clodius against him, and wholly alienated Pompey from him; he also himself declared in a public assembly of the people, that he did not think Lentulus and Cethegus, with their accomplices, were fairly and legally put to death without being brought to trial. And this, indeed, was the crime charged upon Cicero, and this impeachment he was summoned to answer. And so, as an accused man, and in danger for the result, he changed his dress, and went round with his hair untrimmed, in the attire of a suppliant, to beg the people's grace. But Clodius met him in every corner, having a band of abusive and daring fellows about him, who derided Cicero for his change of dress and his humiliation, and often, by throwing dirt and stones at him, interrupted his supplication to the people.

However, first of all, almost the whole equestrian order changed their dress with him, and no less than twenty thousand young gentlemen followed him with their hair untrimmed, and supplicating with him to the people. And then the senate met, to pass a decree that the people should change their dress as in time of public

sorrow. But the consuls opposing it, and Clodius with armed men besetting the senate-house, many of the senators ran out, crying out and tearing their clothes. But this sight moved neither shame nor pity: Cicero must either fly or determine it by the sword with Clodius.

He entreated Pompey to aid him, who was on purpose gone out of the way, and was staying at his country-house in the Alban hills; and first he sent his son-in-law Piso to intercede with him, and afterwards set out to go himself. Of which Pompey being informed, would not stay to see him, being ashamed at the remembrance of the many conflicts in the commonwealth which Cicero had undergone in his behalf, and how much of his policy he had directed for his advantage. But being now Cæsar's son-in-law, at his instance he had set aside all former kindness, and, slipping out at another door, avoided the interview. Thus being forsaken by Pompey, and left alone to himself, he fled to the consuls. Gabinius was rough with him, as usual, but Piso spoke more courteously, desiring him to yield and give place for a while to the fury of Clodius, and to await a change of times, and to be now, as before, his country's saviour from the peril of these troubles and commotions which Clodius was exciting.

Cicero, receiving this answer, consulted with his friends. Lucullus advised him to stay, as being sure to prevail at last; others to fly, because the people would soon desire him again, when they should have enough of the rage and madness of Clodius. This last Cicero approved. But first he took a statue of Minerva, which had been long set up and greatly honoured in his house, and carrying it to the capitol, there dedicated it, with the inscription, "To Minerva, Patroness of Rome." And receiving an escort from his friends, about the middle of the night he left the city, and went by land through Lucania, intending to reach Sicily.

But as soon as it was publicly known that he was fled, Clodius proposed to the people a decree of exile, and by his own order interdicted him fire and water, prohibiting any within five hundred miles in Italy to receive him into their houses. Most people, out of respect for Cicero, paid no regard to this edict, offering him every attention, and escorting him on his way. But at Hipponium, a city of Lucania now called Vibo, one Vibius, a Sicilian by birth, who, amongst many other instances of Cicero's friendship, had been made head of the state engineers when he was consul, would not receive him into his house, sending him word he would appoint a place in the country for his reception. Caius Vergilius, the prætor of Sicily, who had been on the most intimate terms with him, wrote to him to forbear coming into Sicily. At these things Cicero, being disheartened, went to Brundusium, whence putting forth with a prosperous wind, a contrary gale blowing from the sea carried him back to Italy the next day. He put again to sea, and having reached Dyrrachium, on his coming to shore there, it is reported that an earthquake and a convulsion in the sea happened at the same time, signs which the diviners said intimated that his exile would not be long, for these were prognostics of change.

Although many visited him with respect, and the cities of Greece contended which should honour him most, he yet continued disheartened and disconsolate, like an unfortunate lover, often casting his looks back upon Italy; and, indeed, he was become so poor-spirited, so humiliated and dejected by his misfortunes, as none could have expected in a man who had devoted so much of his life to study and learning. And yet he often desired his friends not to call him orator, but philosopher, because he had made philosophy his business, and had only used rhetoric as an instrument for attaining his objects in public life. But the desire of glory has great power in washing the tinctures of philosophy out of the souls of men, and in imprinting the passions of the common people, by custom and conversation, in the minds of those that take a part in governing them, unless the politician be very careful so to engage in public affairs as to interest himself only in the affairs themselves, but not participate in the passions that are consequent to them.

Clodius, having thus driven away Cicero, fell to burning his farms and villas, and afterwards his city house, and built on the site of it a temple to Liberty. The rest of his property he exposed to sale by daily proclamation, but nobody came to buy. By these courses he became formidable to the noble citizens, and being followed by the commonalty, whom he had filled with insolence and licentiousness, he began at last to try his strength against Pompey, some of whose arrangements in the countries he conquered, he attacked. The disgrace of this made Pompey begin to reproach himself for his cowardice in deserting Cicero, and changing his mind, he now wholly set himself with his friends to contrive his return. And when Clo-

dius opposed it, the senate made a vote that no public measure should be ratified or passed by them till Cicero was recalled. But when Lentulus was consul, the commotions grew so high upon this matter, that the tribunes were wounded in the Forum, and Quintus, Cicero's brother, was left as dead, lying unobserved amongst the slain.

The people began to change in their feelings, and Annius Milo, one of their tribunes, was the first who took confidence to summon Clodius to trial for acts of violence. Many of the common people out of the neighbouring cities formed a party with Pompey, and he went with them, and drove Clodius out of the Forum, and summoned the people to pass their vote. And, it is said, the people never passed any suffrage more unanimously than this. The senate, also, striving to outdo the people, sent letters of thanks to those cities which had received Cicero with respect in his exile, and decreed that his house and his country-places, which Clodius had destroyed, should be rebuilt at the public charge.

Thus Cicero returned sixteen months after his exile, and the cities were so glad, and people so zealous to meet him, that what he boasted of afterwards, that Italy had brought him on her shoulders home to Rome, was rather less than the truth. And Crassus himself, who had been his enemy before his exile, went then voluntarily to meet him, and was reconciled, to please his son Publius, as he said, who was Cicero's affectionate admirer.

Cicero had not been long at Rome when, taking the opportunity of Clodius's absence, he went with a great company to the capitol, and there tore and defaced the tribunician tables, in which were recorded the acts done in the time of Clodius. And on Clodius calling him in question for this, he answered that he, being of the patrician order, had obtained the office of tribune against law, and therefore nothing done by him was valid. Cato was displeased at this, and opposed Cicero, not that he commended Clodius, but rather disapproved of his whole administration; yet, he contended, it was an irregular and violent course for the senate to vote the illegality of so many decrees and acts, including those of Cato's own government in Cyprus and at Byzantium. This occasioned a breach between Cato and Cicero, which, though it came not to open enmity, yet made a more reserved friendship between them.

After this, Milo killed Clodius, and, being arraigned for the murder, he procured Cicero as his advocate. The senate, fearing lest the questioning of so eminent and high-spirited a citizen as Milo might disturb the peace of the city, committed the superintendence of this and of the other trials to Pompey, who should undertake to maintain the security alike of the city and of the courts of justice. Pompey, therefore, went in the night, and occupying the high grounds about it, surrounded the Forum with soldiers. Milo, fearing lest Cicero, being disturbed by such an unusual sight, should conduct his cause the less successfully, persuaded him to come in a litter into the Forum, and there repose himself till the judges were set and the court filled. For Cicero, it seems, not only wanted courage in arms, but, in his speaking also, began with timidity, and in many cases scarcely left off trembling and shaking when he had got thoroughly into the current and the substance of his speech. When defending Licinius Murena against the prosecution of Cato, and being eager to outdo Hortensius, who had made his plea with great applause, he took so little rest that night, and was so disordered with thought and overwatching, that he spoke much worse than usual.

And so now, on quitting his litter to commence the cause of Milo, at the sight of Pompey, posted, as it were, and encamped with his troops above, and seeing arms shining round about the Forum, he was so confounded that he could hardly begin his speech for the trembling of his body and hesitance of his tongue; whereas Milo, meantime, was bold and intrepid in his demeanour, disdaining either to let his hair grow or to put on the mourning habit. And this, indeed, seems to have been one principal cause of his condemnation. Cicero, however, was thought not so much to have shown timidity for himself, as anxiety about his friend.

He was made one of the priests, whom the Romans call Augurs, in the room of Crassus the younger, dead in Parthia. Then he was appointed by lot to the province of Cilicia, and set sail thither with twelve thousand foot and two thousand six hundred horse. He had orders to bring back Cappadocia to its allegiance to Ariobarzanes, its king; which settlement he effected very completely without recourse to arms. And perceiving the Cilicians, by the great loss the Romans had suffered in Parthia, and the commotions in Syria, to have become disposed to attempt a revolt, by a gentle course of government he soothed them back into fidelity.

He would accept none of the presents that were offered him by the kings; he remitted the charge of public entertainments, but daily at his own house received the ingenious and accomplished persons of the province, not sumptuously, but liberally. His house had no porter, nor was he ever found in bed by any man, but early in the morning, standing or walking before his door, he received those who came to offer their salutations. He is said never once to have ordered any of those under his command to be beaten with rods, or to have their garments rent. He never gave contumelious language in his anger, nor inflicted punishment with reproach. He detected an embezzlement, to a large amount, in the public money, and thus relieved the cities from their burdens, at the same time that he allowed those who made restitution to retain without further punishment their rights as citizens. He engaged in war, too, so far as to give a defeat to the banditti who infested Mount Amanus, for which he was saluted by his army Imperator. To Cæcilius, the orator, who asked him to send him some panthers from Cilicia, to be exhibited in the theatre at Rome, he wrote, in commendation of his own actions, that there were no panthers in Cilicia, for they were all fled to Caria, in anger that in so general a peace they had become the sole objects of attack.

On leaving his province, he touched at Rhodes, and tarried for some length of time at Athens, longing much to renew his old studies. He visited the eminent men of learning, and saw his former friends and companions; and after receiving in Greece the honours that were due to him, returned to the city, where everything was now just as it were in a flame, breaking out into a civil war.

When the senate would have decreed him a triumph, he told them he had rather, so differences were accommodated, follow the triumphal chariot of Cæsar. In private, he gave advice to both, writing many letters to Cæsar, and personally entreating Pompey; doing his best to soothe and bring to reason both the one and the other. But when matters became incurable, and Cæsar was approaching Rome, and Pompey durst not abide it, but, with many honest citizens, left the city, Cicero as yet did not join in the flight, and was reputed to adhere to Cæsar.

And it is very evident he was in his thoughts much divided, and wavered painfully between both, for he writes in his epistles, "To which side should I turn? Pompey has the fair and honourable plea for war; and Cæsar, on the other hand, has managed his affairs better, and is more able to secure himself and his friends. So that I know whom I should fly, not whom I should fly to." But when Trebatius, one of Cæsar's friends, by letter signified to him that Cæsar thought it was his most desirable course to join his party, and partake his hopes, but if he considered himself too old a man for this, then he should retire into Greece, and stay quietly there, out of the way of either party, Cicero, wondering that Cæsar had not written himself, gave an angry reply, that he should not do anything unbecoming his past life. Such is the account to be collected from his letters.

But as soon as Cæsar was marched into Spain, he immediately sailed away to join Pompey. And he was welcomed by all but Cato; who, taking him privately, chid him for coming to Pompey. As for himself, he said, it had been indecent to forsake that part in the commonwealth which he had chosen from the beginning; but Cicero might have been more useful to his country and friends, if, remaining neuter, he had attended and used his influence to moderate the result, instead of coming hither to make himself, without reason or necessity, an enemy to Cæsar, and a partner in such great dangers.

By this language, partly, Cicero's feelings were altered, and partly, also, because Pompey made no great use of him. Although, indeed, he was himself the cause of it, by his not denying that he was sorry he had come, by his depreciating Pompey's resources, finding fault underhand with his counsels, and continually indulging in jests and sarcastic remarks on his fellow-soldiers. Though he went about in the camp with a gloomy and melancholy face himself, he was always trying to raise a laugh in others, whether they wished it or not. It may not be amiss to mention a few instances. To Domitius, on his preferring to a command one who was no soldier, and saying, in his defence, that he was a modest and prudent person, he replied, "Why did not you keep him for a tutor for your children?"

On hearing Theophanes, the Lesbian, who was master of the engineers in the army, praised for the admirable way in which he had consoled the Rhodians for the loss of their fleet, "What a thing it is," he said, "to have a Greek in command!" When Cæsar had been acting successfully, and in a manner blockading Pompey, Lentulus was saying it was reported that Cæsar's friends were out of heart; "Because," said Cicero, "they do not wish Cæsar well." To one Marcius, who had just come from Italy, and told them that there was a strong report at Rome that Pompey was blocked up, he said, "And you sailed hither to see it with your own eyes." To Nonius, encouraging them after a defeat to be of good hope, because there were seven eagles still left in Pompey's camp, "Good reason for encouragement," said Cicero, "if we were going to fight with jackdaws." Labienus insisted on some prophecies to the effect that Pompey would gain the victory; "Yes," said Cicero; "and the first step in the campaign has been losing our camp."

After the battle of Pharsalia was over, at which he was not present for want of health, and Pompey was fled, Cato, having considerable forces and a great fleet at Dyrrachium, would have had Cicero commander-in-chief, according to law and the precedence of his consular dignity. And on his refusing the command, and wholly declining to take part in their plans for continuing the war, he was in the greatest danger of being killed, young Pompey and his friends calling him traitor, and drawing their swords upon him; only that Cato interposed, and barely rescued and brought him out of the camp.

Afterwards, arriving at Brundusium, he tarried there some time in expectation of Cæsar, who was delayed by his affairs in Asia and Egypt. And when it was told him that he was arrived at Tarentum, and was coming thence by land to Brundusium, he hastened towards him, not altogether without hope, and yet in some fear of making experiment of the temper of an enemy and conqueror in the presence of many witnesses. But there was no necessity for him either to speak or do anything unworthy of himself; for Cæsar, as soon as he saw him coming a good way before the rest of the company, came down to meet him, saluted him, and, leading the way, conversed with him alone for some furlongs. And from that time forward he continued to treat him with honour and respect, so that, when Cicero wrote an oration in praise of Cato, Cæsar in writing an answer to it, took occasion to commend Cicero's own life and eloquence, comparing him to Pericles and Theramenes. Cicero's oration was called "Cato"; Cæsar's, "Anti-Cato."

So also it is related that when Quintus Ligarius was prosecuted for having been in arms against Cæsar, and Cicero had undertaken his defence, Cæsar said to his friends, "Why might we not as well once more hear a speech from

Cicero? Ligarius, there is no question, is a wicked man and an enemy." But when Cicero began to speak, he wonderfully moved him, and proceeded in his speech with such varied pathos, and such a charm of language, that the colour of Cæsar's countenance often changed, and it was evident that all the passions of his soul were in commotion. At length, the orator touching upon the Pharsalian battle, he was so affected that his body trembled, and some of the papers he held dropped out of his hands. And thus he was overpowered, and acquitted Ligarius.

Henceforth, the commonwealth being changed into a monarchy, Cicero withdrew himself from public affairs, and employed his leisure in instructing those young men that would, in philosophy; and by the near intercourse he thus had with some of the noblest and highest in rank, he again began to possess great influence in the city. The work and object to which he set himself was to compose and translate philosophical dialogues and to render logical and physical terms into the Roman idiom. For he it was, as it is said, who first or principally gave Latin names to *phantasia, syncatathesis, epokhe, catalepsis, atamon, ameres, kenon,* and other such technical terms, which, either by metaphors or other means of accommodation, he succeeded in making intelligible and expressible to the Romans. For his recreation, he exercised his dexterity in poetry, and when he was set to it would make five hundred verses in a night.

He spent the greatest part of his time at his country-house near Tusculum. He wrote to his friends that he led the life of Laertes, either jestingly, as his custom was, or rather from a feeling of ambition for public employment, which made him impatient under the present state of affairs. He rarely went to the city, unless to pay his court to Cæsar. He was commonly the first amongst those who voted him honours, and sought out new terms of praise for himself and for his actions. As, for example, what he said of the statues of Pompey, which had been thrown down, and were afterwards by Cæsar's orders set up again; that Cæsar, by this act of humanity, had indeed set up Pompey's statues, but he had fixed and established his own.

He had a design, it is said, of writing the history of his country, combining with it much of that of Greece, and incorporating in it all the stories and legends of the past that he had collected. But his purposes were interfered with by various public and various private unhappy occurrences and misfortunes; for most of which he was himself in fault. For first of all, he put away his wife Terentia, by whom he had been neglected in the time of the war and sent away destitute of necessaries for his journey; neither did he find her kind when he returned into Italy, for she did not join him at Brundusium, where he stayed a long time, nor would allow her young daughter, who undertook so long a journey, decent attendance, or the requisite expenses; besides, she left him a naked and empty house, and yet had involved him in many and great debts.

These were alleged as the fairest reasons for the divorce. But Terentia, who denied them all, had the most unmistakable defence furnished her by her husband himself, who not long after married a young maiden for the love of her beauty, as Terentia upbraided him; or as Tiro, his emancipated slave, has written, for her riches, to discharge his debts. For the young woman was very rich, and Cicero had the custody of her estate, being left guardian in trust; and being indebted many myriads of money, he was persuaded by friends and relations to marry her, notwithstanding his disparity of age, and to use her money to satisfy his creditors. Antony, who mentions this marriage in his answer to the Philippics, reproaches him for putting away a wife with whom he had lived to old age; adding some happy strokes of sarcasm on Cicero's domestic, inactive, unsoldier-like habits. Not long after this marriage, his daughter died in child-bed at Lentulus's house, to whom she had been married after the death of Piso, her former husband. The philosophers from all parts came to comfort Cicero; for his grief was so excessive that he put away his new-married wife, because she seemed to be pleased at the death of Tullia. And thus stood Cicero's domestic affairs at this time.

He had no concern in the design that was now forming against Cæsar, although, in general, he was Brutus's most principal confidant, and one who was as aggrieved at the present, and as desirous of the former state of public affairs, as any other whatsoever. But they feared his temper, as wanting courage, and his old age, in which the most daring dispositions are apt to be timorous.

As soon, therefore, as the act was committed by Brutus and Cassius, and the friends of Cæsar were got together, so that there was fear the city would again be involved in a civil war, Antony, being consul, convened the senate, and made a short address recommending concord. And Cicero following with various remarks such as the occasion called for, persuaded the senate to imitate the Athenians, and decree an amnesty for what had been done in Cæsar's case, and to bestow provinces on Brutus and Cassius. But neither of these things took effect. For as soon as the common people, of themselves inclined to pity, saw the dead body of Cæsar borne through the marketplace, and Antony showing his clothes filled with blood, and pierced through in every part with swords, enraged to a degree of frenzy, they made a search for the murderers, and with firebrands in their hands ran to their houses to burn them. They, however, being forewarned, avoided this danger; and expecting many more and greater to come, they left the city.

Antony on this was at once in exultation, and every one was in alarm with the prospect that he would make himself sole ruler, and Cicero in more alarm than any one. For Antony, seeing his influence reviving in the commonwealth and knowing how closely he was connected with Brutus, was ill-pleased to have him in the city. Besides, there had been some former jealousy between them, occasioned by the difference of their manners. Cicero, fearing the event, was inclined to go as lieutenant with Dolabella into Syria. But Hirtius and Pansa, consuls elect as successors of Antony, good men and lovers of Cicero, entreated him not to leave them, undertaking to put down Antony if he would stay in Rome. And he, neither distrusting wholly, nor trusting them, let Dolabella go without him, promising Hirtius that he would go and spend his summer at Athens, and return again when he entered upon his office.

So he set out on his journey; but some delay occurring in his passage, new intelligence, as often happens, came suddenly from Rome, that Antony had made an astonishing change, and was doing all things and managing all public affairs at the will of the senate, and that there wanted nothing but his presence to bring things to a happy settlement. And therefore, blaming himself for his cowardice, he returned again to Rome, and was not deceived in his hopes at the beginning. For such multitudes flocked out to meet him, that the compliments and civilities which were paid him at the gates, and at his entrance into the city, took up almost one whole day's time.

On the morrow, Antony convened the senate, and summoned Cicero thither. He came not, but kept his bed, pretending to be ill with his journey; but the true reason seemed the fear of some design against him, upon a suspicion and intimation given him on his way to Rome. Antony, however, showed great offence at the affront, and sent soldiers, commanding them to bring him or burn his house; but many interceding and supplicating for him, he was contented to accept sureties. Ever after, when they met, they passed one another with silence, and continued on their guard, till Cæsar, the younger, coming from Apollonia, entered on the first Cæsar's inheritance, and was engaged in a dispute with Antony about two thousand five hundred myriads of money, which Antony detained from the estate.

Upon this, Philippus, who married the mother, and Marcellus, who married the sister of young Cæsar, came with the young man to Cicero, and agreed with him that Cicero should give them the aid of his eloquence and political influence with the senate and people, and Cæsar give Cicero the defence of his riches and arms. For the young man had already a great party of the soldiers of Cæsar about him.

Cicero's readiness to join him was founded, it is said, on some yet stronger motives; for it seems, while Pompey and Cæsar were yet alive, Cicero, in his sleep, had fancied himself engaged in calling some of the sons of the senators into the capitol, Jupiter being about, according to the dream, to declare one of them the chief ruler of Rome. The citizens, running up with curiosity, stood about the temple, and the youths, sitting in their purple-bordered robes, kept silence. On a sudden the doors opened, and the youths, arising one by one in order, passed round the god, who reviewed them all, and, to their sorrow, dismissed them; but when this one was passing by, the god stretched forth his right hand and said, "O ye Romans, this young man, when he shall be lord of Rome, shall put an end to all your civil wars." It is said that Cicero formed from his dream a distinct image of the youth, and retained it afterwards perfectly, but did not know who it was.

The next day, going down into the Campus Martius, he met the boys returning from their gymnastic exercises, and the first was he, just as he had appeared to him in his dream. Being astonished at it, he asked him who were his parents. And it proved to be this young Cæsar, whose father was a man of no great eminence, Octavius, and his mother, Attia, Cæsar's sister's daughter; for which reason, Cæsar, who had no children, made him by will the heir of his house and property. From that time, it is said that Cicero studiously noticed the youth whenever he met him, and he as kindly received the civility; and by fortune he happened to be born when Cicero was consul.

These were the reasons spoken of; but it was principally Cicero's hatred of Antony, and a temper unable to resist honour, which fastened him to Cæsar, with the purpose of getting the support of Cæsar's power for his own public designs. For the young man went so far in his court to him, that he called him Father; at which Brutus was so highly displeased, that, in his epistles to Atticus, he reflected on Cicero saying, it was manifest, by his courting Cæsar for fear of Antony, he did not intend liberty to his country, but an indulgent master to himself. Notwithstanding, Brutus took Cicero's son, then studying philosophy at Athens, gave him a command, and employed him in various ways, with a good result.

Cicero's own power at this time was at the greatest height in the city, and he did whatsoever he pleased; he completely overpowered and drove out Antony, and sent the two consuls, Hirtius and Pansa, with an army, to reduce him; and, on the other hand, persuaded the senate to allow Cæsar the lictors and ensigns of a prætor, as though he were his country's defender. But after Antony was defeated in battle, and the consuls slain, the armies united, and ranged themselves with Cæsar. And the senate, fearing the young man, and his extraordinary fortune, endeavoured, by honours and gifts, to call off the soldiers from him, and to lessen his power; professing there was no further need of arms now Antony was put to flight.

This giving Cæsar an affright, he privately sent some friends to entreat and persuade Cicero to procure the consular dignity for them both together; saying he should manage the affairs as he pleased, should have the supreme power, and govern the young man who was only desirous of name and glory. And Cæsar himself confessed that, in fear of ruin, and in danger of being deserted, he had seasonably made use of Cicero's ambition, persuading him to stand with him, and to accept the offer of his aid and interest for the consulship.

And now, more than at any other time, Cicero let himself be carried away and deceived, though an old man, by the persuasion of a boy. He joined him in soliciting votes, and procured the good-will of the senate, not without blame at the time on the part of his friends; and he, too, soon enough after, saw that he had

ruined himself, and betrayed the liberty of his country. For the young man, once established, and possessed of the office of consul, bade Cicero farewell; and, reconciling himself to Antony and Lepidus, joined his power with theirs, and divided the government, like a piece of property, with them. Thus united, they made a schedule of above two hundred persons who were to be put to death.

But the greatest contention in all their debates was on the question of Cicero's case. Antony would come to no conditions, unless he should be the first man to be killed. Lepidus held with Antony, and Cæsar opposed them both. They met secretly and by themselves, for three days together, near the town of Bononia. The spot was not far from the camp, with a river surrounding it. Cæsar, it is said, contended earnestly for Cicero the first two days; but on the third day he yielded, and gave him up. The terms of their mutual concessions were these: that Cæsar should desert Cicero, Lepidus his brother Paulus, and Antony Lucius Cæsar, his uncle by his mother's side. Thus they let their anger and fury take from them the sense of humanity, and demonstrated that no beast is more savage than man when possessed with power answerable to his rage.

Whilst these things were contriving, Cicero was with his brother at his country-house near Tusculum; whence, hearing of the proscriptions, they determined to pass to Astura, a villa of Cicero's near the sea, and to take shipping from thence for Macedonia to Brutus, of whose strength in that province news had already been heard. They travelled together in their separate litters, overwhelmed with sorrow; and often stopping on the way till their litters came together, condoled with one another. But Quintus was the more disheartened when he reflected on his want of means for his journey; for, as he said, he had brought nothing with him from home. And even Cicero himself had but a slender provision. It was judged, therefore, most expedient that Cicero should make what haste he could to flee and Quintus return home to provide necessaries, and thus resolved, they mutually embraced, and parted with many tears.

Quintus, within a few days after, betrayed by his servants to those who came to search for him, was slain, together with his young son. But Cicero was carried to Astura, where finding a vessel he immediately went on board her, and sailed as far as Circæum with a prosperous gale; but when the pilots resolved immediately to set sail from thence, whether fearing the sea, or not wholly distrusting the faith of Cæsar, he went on shore, and passed by land a hundred furlongs, as if he was going for Rome. But losing resolution and changing his mind, he again returned to the sea, and there spent the night in fearful and perplexed thoughts. Sometimes he resolved to go into Cæsar's house privately, and there kill himself upon the altar of his household gods, to bring divine vengeance upon him; but the fear of torture put him off this course. And after passing through a variety of confused and uncertain counsels, at last he let his servants carry him by sea to Capitæ, where he had a house, an agreeable place to retire to in the heat of summer, when the Etesian winds are so pleasant.

There was at that place a chapel of Apollo, not far from the seaside, from which a flight of crows rose with a great noise, and made towards Cicero's vessel, as it rowed to land, and lighting on both sides of the yard, some croaked, others pecked the ends of the ropes. This was looked upon by all as an ill-omen; and, therefore, Cicero went again ashore, and entering his house, lay down upon his bed to compose himself to rest. Many of the crows settled about the window, making a dismal cawing; but one of them alighted upon the bed where Cicero lay covered up, and with its bill by little and little pecked off the clothes from his face. His servants, seeing this, blamed themselves that they should stay to be spectators of their master's murder, and do nothing in his defence, whilst the brute creatures came to assist and take care of him in his undeserved affliction; and therefore, partly by entreaty, partly by force, they took him up, and carried him in his litter towards the seaside.

But in the meantime the assassins were come with a band of soldiers, Herennius, a centurion, and Popillius, a tribune, whom Cicero had formerly defended when prosecuted for the murder of his father. Finding the doors shut, they broke them open, and Cicero not appearing, and those within saying they knew not where he was, it is stated that a youth, who had been educated by Cicero in the liberal arts and sciences, an emancipated slave of his brother Quintus, Philologus by name, informed the tribune that the litter was on its way to the sea through the close and shady walks. The tribune, taking a few with him, ran to the place where he was to come out. And Cicero,

perceiving Herennius running in the walks, commanded his servants to set down the litter; and stroking his chin, as he used to do, with his left hand, he looked steadfastly upon his murderers, his person covered with dust, his beard and hair untrimmed, and his face worn with his troubles. So that the greatest part of those that stood by covered their faces whilst Herennius slew him. And thus was he murdered, stretching forth his neck out of the litter, being now in his sixty-fourth year. Herennius cut off his head, and, by Antony's command, his hands also, by which his Philippics were written; for so Cicero styled those orations he wrote against Antony, and so they are called to this day.

When these members of Cicero were brought to Rome, Antony was holding an assembly for the choice of public officers; and when he heard it, and saw them, he cried out, "Now let there be an end of our proscriptions." He commanded his head and hands to be fastened up over the rostra, where the orators spoke; a sight which the Roman people shuddered to behold, and they believed they saw there, not the face of Cicero, but the image of Antony's own soul. And yet amidst these actions he did justice in one thing, by delivering up Philologus to Pomponia, the wife of Quintus; who, having got his body into her power, besides other grievous punishments, made him cut off his own flesh by pieces, and roast and eat it; for so some writers have related. But Tiro, Cicero's emancipated slave, has not so much as mentioned the treachery of Philologus.

Some long time after, Cæsar, I have been told, visiting one of his daughter's sons, found him with a book of Cicero's in his hand. The boy for fear endeavoured to hide it under his gown; which Cæsar perceiving, took it from him, and, turning over a great part of the book standing, gave it him again, and said, "My child, this was a learned man, and a lover of his country." And immediately after he had vanquished Antony, being then consul, he made Cicero's son his colleague in the office; and under that consulship the senate took down all the statues of Antony, and abolished all the other honours that had been given him, and decreed that none of that family should thereafter bear the name of Marcus; and thus the final acts of the punishment of Antony were, by the divine powers, devolved upon the family of Cicero.

DEMOSTHENES and CICERO
Compared

THESE are the most memorable circumstances recorded in history of Demosthenes and Cicero which have come to our knowledge. But omitting an exact comparison of their respective faculties in speaking, yet thus much seems fit to be said; that Demosthenes, to make himself a master in rhetoric, applied all the faculties he had, natural or acquired, wholly that way; that he far surpassed in force and strength of eloquence all his contemporaries in political and judicial speaking, in grandeur and majesty all the panegyrical orators, and in accuracy and science all the logicians and rhetoricians of his day; that Cicero was highly educated, and by his diligent study became a most accomplished general scholar in all these branches, having left behind him numerous philosophical treatises of his own on Academic principles; as, indeed, even in his written speeches, both political and judicial, we see him continually trying to show his learning by the way.

And one may discover the different temper of each of them in their speeches. For Demosthenes's oratory was without all embellishment and jesting, wholly composed for real effect and seriousness; not smelling of the lamp, as Pytheas scoffingly said, but of the temperance, thoughtfulness, austerity, and grave earnestness of his temper. Whereas Cicero's love of mockery often ran him into scurrility; and in his love of laughing away serious arguments in judicial cases by jests and facetious remarks, with a view to the advantage of his clients, he paid too little regard to what was decent: saying, for example, in his defence of Cælius, that he had done no absurd thing in such plenty and affluence to indulge himself in pleasures, it being a kind of madness not to enjoy the things we possess, especially since the most eminent philosophers have asserted pleasures to be the chiefest good. So also we are told that when Cicero, being consul, undertook the defence of Murena against Cato's prosecution, by way of bantering Cato, he made a long series of jokes upon the absurd *paradoxes,* as they are called, of the Stoic set; so that a loud laughter passing from the crowd to the judges, Cato, with a quiet smile, said to those that sat next him, "My friends, what an amusing consul we have."

And, indeed, Cicero was by natural temper very much disposed to mirth and pleasantry, and always appeared with a smiling and serene countenance. But Demosthenes had constant care and thoughtfulness in his look, and a serious anxiety, which he seldom, if ever, laid aside; and, therefore, was accounted by his enemies, as he himself confessed, morose and ill-mannered.

Also, it is very evident, out of their several writings, that Demosthenes never touched upon his own praises but decently and without offence when there was need of it, and for some weightier end; but upon other occasions modestly and sparingly. But Cicero's immeasurable boasting of himself in his orations argues him guilty of an uncontrollable appetite for distinction, his cry being evermore that arms should give place to the gown, and the soldier's laurel to the tongue. And at last we find him extolling not only his deeds and actions, but his orations also, as well those that were only spoken, as those that were published; as if he were engaged in a boyish trial of skill, who should speak best, with the rhetoricians, Isocrates and Anaximenes, not as one who could claim the task to guide and instruct the Roman nation, the—

Soldier full-armed, terrific to the foe.

It is necessary, indeed, for a political leader to be an able speaker; but it is an ignoble thing for any man to admire and relish the glory of his own eloquence. And, in this matter, Demosthenes had a more than ordinary gravity and magnificence of mind, accounting his talent in speaking nothing more than a mere accomplishment and matter of practice, the success of which must depend greatly on the good-will and candour of his hearers, and regarding those who pride themselves on such accounts to be men of a low and petty disposition.

The power of persuading and governing the people did, indeed, equally belong to both, so that those who had armies and camps at command stood in need of their assistance; as Charas, Diopithes, and Leosthenes of Demosthenes's, Pompey and young Cæsar of Cicero's, as the latter himself admits in his Memoirs addressed to Agrippa and Mæcenas. But what are thought and commonly said most to demonstrate and try the tempers of men, namely, authority and place, by moving every passion, and discovering every frailty, these are things which Demosthenes never received; nor was he ever in a position to give such proof of himself, having never obtained any eminent office, nor led any of those armies into the field against Philip which he raised by his eloquence.

Cicero, on the other hand, was sent quæstor into Sicily, and proconsul into Cilicia and Cappadocia, at a time when avarice was at the height, and the commanders and governors who were employed abroad, as though they thought it a mean thing to steal, set themselves to seize by open force; so that it seemed no heinous matter to take bribes, but he that did it most moderately was in good esteem. And yet he, at this time, gave the most abundant proofs alike of his contempt of riches and of his humanity and good-nature. And at Rome, when he was created consul in name, but indeed received sovereign and dictatorial authority against Catiline and his conspirators, he attested the truth of Plato's prediction, that then the miseries of states would be at an end when, by a happy fortune, supreme power, wisdom, and justice should be united in one.

It is said, to the reproach of Demosthenes, that his eloquence was mercenary; that he privately made orations for Phormion and Apollodorus, though adversaries in the same cause; that he was charged with moneys received from the King of Persia, and condemned for bribes from Harpalus. And should we grant that all those (and they are not few) who have made these statements against him have spoken what is untrue, yet that Demosthenes was not the character to look without desire on the presents offered him out of respect and gratitude by royal persons, and that one who lent money on maritime usury was likely to be thus indifferent, is what we cannot deny. But that Cicero refused, from the Sicilians when he was quæstor, from the King of Cappadocia

when he was proconsul, and from his friends at Rome when he was in exile, many presents, though urged to receive them, has been said already.

Moreover, Demosthenes's banishment was infamous, upon conviction for bribery; Cicero's very honourable, for ridding his country of a set of villains. Therefore, when Demosthenes fled his country, no man regarded it; for Cicero's sake the senate changed their habit, and put on mourning, and would not be persuaded to make any act before Cicero's return was decreed. Cicero, however, passed his exile idly in Macedonia. But the very exile of Demosthenes made up a great part of the services he did for his country; for he went through the cities of Greece, and everywhere, as we have said, joined in the conflict on behalf of the Grecians, driving out the Macedonian ambassadors, and approving himself a much better citizen than Themistocles and Alcibiades did in the like fortune. And, after his return, he again devoted himself to the same public service, and continued firm to his opposition to Antipater and the Macedonians. Whereas Lælius reproached Cicero in the senate for sitting silent when Cæsar, a beardless youth, asked leave to come forward, contrary to the law, as a candidate for the consulship; and Brutus, in his epistles, charges him with nursing and rearing a greater and more heavy tyranny than that they had removed.

Finally, Cicero's death excites our pity; for an old man to be miserably carried up and down by his servants, flying and hiding himself from that death which was, in the course of nature, so near at hand; and yet at last to be murdered. Demosthenes, though he seemed at first a little to supplicate, yet, by his preparing and keeping the poison by him, demands our admiration; and still more admirable was his using it. When the temple of the god no longer afforded him a sanctuary, he took refuge, as it were, at a mightier altar, freeing himself from arms and soldiers, and laughing to scorn the cruelty of Antipater.

DEMOSTHENES AND CICERO

DEMETRIUS

337?–283 B.C.

INGENIOUS men have long observed a resemblance between the arts and the bodily senses. And they were first led to do so, I think, by noticing the way in which, both in the arts and with our senses, we examine opposites. Judgment once obtained, the use to which we put it differs in the two cases. Our senses are not meant to pick out black rather than white, to prefer sweet to bitter, or soft and yielding to hard and resisting objects; all they have to do is to receive impressions as they occur, and report to the understanding the impressions as received. The arts, on the other hand, which reason institutes expressly to choose and obtain some suitable, and to refuse and get rid of some unsuitable object, have their proper concern in the consideration of the former; though, in a casual and contingent way, they must also, for the very rejection of them, pay attention to the latter.

Medicine, to produce health, has to examine disease, and music, to create harmony, must investigate discord; and the supreme arts of temperance, of justice, and of wisdom, as they are acts of judgment and selection, exercised not on good and just and expedient only, but also on wicked, unjust, and inexpedient objects, do not give their commendations to the mere innocence whose boast is its inexperience of evil, and whose truer name is, by their award, simpleness and ignorance of what all men who live aright should know. The ancient Spartans, at their festivals, used to force their Helots to swallow large quantities of raw wine, and then to expose them at the public tables, to let the young men see what it is to be drunk.

And, though I do not think it consistent with humanity or with civil justice to correct one man's morals by corrupting those of another, yet we may, I think, avail ourselves of the cases of those who have fallen into indiscretions, and have, in high stations, made themselves conspicuous for misconduct; and I shall not do ill to introduce a pair or two of such examples among these biographies, not, assuredly, to amuse and divert my readers, or give variety to my theme, but as Ismenias, the

Theban, used to show his scholars good and bad performers on the flute, and to tell them, "You should play like this man," and, "You should not play like that," and as Antigenidas used to say, young people would take greater pleasure in hearing good playing, if first they were set to hear bad, so, in the same manner, it seems to me likely enough that we shall be all the more zealous and more emulous to read, observe, and imitate the better lives, if we are not left in ignorance of the blameworthy and the bad.

For this reason, the following book contains the lives of Demetrius Poliorcetes and Antonius the Triumvir; two persons who have abundantly justified the words of Plato, that great natures produce great vices as well as virtues. Both alike were amorous and intemperate, warlike and munificent, sumptuous in their way of living and overbearing in their manners. And the likeness of their fortunes carried out the resemblance in their characters. Not only were their lives each a series of great successes and great disasters, mighty acquisitions and tremendous losses of power, sudden overthrows followed by unexpected recoveries, but they died, also, Demetrius in actual captivity to his enemies and Antony on the verge of it.

Antigonus had by his wife, Stratonice, the daughter of Corrhæus, two sons; the one of whom, after the name of his uncle, he called Demetrius, the other had that of his grandfather, Philip, and died young. This is the most general account, although some have related that Demetrius was not the son of Antigonus, but of his brother; and that his own father dying young, and his mother being afterwards married to Antigonus, he was accounted to be his son.

Demetrius had not the height of his father Antigonus, though he was a tall man. But his countenance was one of such singular beauty and expression that no painter or sculptor ever produced a good likeness of him. It combined grace and strength, dignity with boyish bloom, and, in the midst of youthful heat and passion, what was hardest of all to represent was a certain heroic look and air of kingly greatness. Nor did his character belie his looks, as no one was better able to render himself both loved and feared. For as he was the most easy and agreeable of companions, and the most luxurious and delicate of princes in his drinking and banqueting and daily pleasures, so in action there was never any one that showed a more vehement persistence, or a more passionate energy. Bacchus, skilled in the conduct of war, and after war in giving peace its pleasures and joys, seems to have been his pattern among the gods.

He was wonderfully fond of his father Antigonus; and the tenderness he had for his mother led him, for her sake, to redouble attentions, which it was evident were not so much owing to fear or duty as to the more powerful motives of inclination. It is reported that, returning one day from hunting, he went immediately into the apartment of Antigonus, who was conversing with some ambassadors, and after stepping up and kissing his father, he sat down by him, just as he was, still holding in his hand the javelins which he had brought with him. Whereupon Antigonus, who had just dismissed the ambassadors with their answer, called out in a loud voice to them, as they were going, "Mention, also, that this is the way in which we two live together"; as if to imply to them that it was no slender mark of the power and security of his government that there was so perfect good understanding between himself and his son.

Such an unsociable, solitary thing is power, and so much of jealousy and distrust in it, that the first and greatest of the successors of Alexander could make it a thing to glory in that he was not so afraid of his son as to forbid his standing beside him with a weapon in his hand. And, in fact, among all the successors of Alexander, that of Antigonus was the only house which, for many descents, was exempted from crime of this kind; or to state it exactly, Philip was the only one of this family who was guilty of a son's death. All the other families, we may fairly say, afforded frequent examples of fathers who brought their children, husbands their wives, children their mothers, to untimely ends; and that brothers should put brothers to death was assumed, like the postulate of mathematicians, as the common and recognised royal first principle of safety.

Let us here record an example in the early life of Demetrius, showing his natural humane

and kindly disposition. It was an adventure which passed betwixt him and Mithridates, the son of Ariobarzanes, who was about the same age with Demetrius, and lived with him, in attendance on Antigonus; and although nothing was said or could be said to his reproach, he fell under suspicion, in consequence of a dream which Antigonus had. Antigonus thought himself in a fair and spacious field, where he sowed golden seed, and saw presently a golden crop come up; of which, however, looking presently again, he saw nothing remain but the stubble, without the ears. And as he stood by in anger and vexation, he heard some voices saying Mithridates had cut the golden harvest and carried it off into Pontus. Antigonus, much discomposed with his dream, first bound his son by an oath not to speak, and then related it to him, adding that he had resolved, in consequence, to lose no time in ridding himself of Mithridates, and making away with him.

Demetrius was extremely distressed; and when the young man came, as usual, to pass his time with him, to keep his oath he forbore from saying a word, but, drawing him aside little by little from the company, as soon as they were by themselves, without opening his lips, with the point of his javelin he traced before him the words "Fly, Mithridates." Mithridates took the hint, and fled by night into Cappadocia, where Antigonus's dream about him was quickly brought to its due fulfillment; for he got possession of a large and fertile territory; and from him descended the line of the kings of Pontus, which, in the eighth generation, was reduced by the Romans. This may serve for a specimen of the early goodness and love of justice that was part of Demetrius's natural character.

But as in the elements of the world, Empedocles tells us, out of liking and dislike, there spring up contention and warfare, and all the more, the closer the contact, or the nearer the approach of the objects, even so the perpetual hostilities among the successors of Alexander were aggravated and inflamed, in particular cases, by juxtaposition of interests and of territories; as, for example, in the case of Antigonus and Ptolemy. News came to Antigonus that Ptolemy had crossed from Cyprus and invaded Syria, and was ravaging the country and reducing the cities. Remaining, therefore, himself in Phrygia, he sent Demetrius, now twenty-two years old, to make his first essay as sole commander in an important charge.

He, whose youthful heat outran his experience, advancing against an adversary trained in Alexander's school, and practised in many encounters, incurred a great defeat near the town of Gaza, in which eight thousand of his men were taken and five thousand killed. His own tent, also his money, and all his private effects and furniture, were captured. These, however, Ptolemy sent back, together with his friends, accompanying them with the humane and courteous message, that they were not fighting for anything else but honour and dominion. Demetrius accepted the gift, praying only to the gods not to leave him long in Ptolemy's debt, but to let him have an early chance of doing the like to him. He took his disaster, also, with the temper, not of a boy defeated in his attempt, but of an old and long-tried general familiar with reverse of fortune; he busied himself in collecting his men, replenishing his magazines, watching the allegiance of the cities, and drilling his new recruits.

Antigonus received the news of the battle with the remark that Ptolemy had beaten boys and would now have to fight with men. But not to humble the spirit of his son, he acceded to his request, and left him to command on the next occasion.

Not long after, Cilles, Ptolemy's lieutenant, with a powerful army, took the field, and looking upon Demetrius as already defeated by the previous battle, he had in his imagination driven him out of Syria before he saw him. But he quickly found himself deceived; for Demetrius came so unexpectedly upon him that he surprised both the general and his army, making him and seven thousand of the soldiers prisoners of war, and possessing himself of a large amount of treasure. But his joy in the victory was not so much for the prizes he should keep, as for those he could restore; and his thankfulness was less for the wealth and glory than for the means it gave him of requiting his enemy's former generosity. He did not, however, take it into his own hands, but wrote to his father. And on receiving leave to do as he liked, he sent back to Ptolemy Cilles and his friends, loaded with presents. This defeat drove Ptolemy out of Syria, and brought Antigonus from Celænæ to enjoy the victory and the sight of the son who had gained it.

Soon after, Demetrius was sent to bring the Nabathæan Arabs into obedience. And here he got into a district without water, and incurred considerable danger, but by his resolute and composed demeanour he overawed the barbarians, and returned after receiving from them a large amount of booty and seven hundred camels. Not long after, Seleucus, whom Antigonus had formerly chased out of Babylon, but who had afterwards recovered his dominion by his own efforts and maintained himself in it, went with large forces on an expedition to reduce the tribes on the confines of India and the provinces near Mount Caucasus. And Demetrius, conjecturing that he had left Mesopotamia but slenderly guarded in his absence, suddenly passed the Euphrates with his army and made his way into Babylonia unexpectedly, where he succeeded in capturing one of the two citadels, out of which he expelled the garrison of Seleucus, and placed in it seven thousand men of his own. And after allowing his soldiers to enrich themselves with all the spoil they could carry with them out of the country, he retired to the sea, leaving Seleucus more securely master of his dominions than before, as he seemed by this conduct to abandon every claim to a country which he treated like an enemy's. However, by a rapid advance, he rescued Halicarnassus from Ptolemy, who was besieging it.

The glory which this act obtained them inspired both the father and son with a wonderful desire for freeing Greece, which Cassander and Ptolemy had everywhere reduced to slavery. No nobler or juster war was undertaken by any of the kings; the wealth they had gained while humbling, with Greek assistance, the barbarians, being thus employed, for honour's sake and good repute, in helping the Greeks. When the resolution was taken to begin their attempt with Athens, one of his friends told Antigonus, if they captured Athens, they must keep it safe in their own hands, as by this gangway they might step out from their ships into Greece when they pleased. But Antigonus would not hear of it; he did not want a better or a steadier gangway than people's good-will; and from Athens, the beacon of the world, the news of their conduct would soon be handed on to all the world's inhabitants.

So Demetrius, with a sum of five thousand talents, and a fleet of two hundred and fifty ships, set sail for Athens, where Demetrius the Phalerian was governing the city for Cassander, with a garrison lodged in the port of Munychia. By good fortune and skillful management he appeared before Piræus, on the twenty-sixth of Thargelion, before anything had been heard of him. Indeed, when his ships were seen, they were taken for Ptolemy's, and preparations were commenced for receiving them; till at last, the generals, discovering their mistake, hurried down, and all was alarm and confusion, and attempts to push forward preparations to oppose the landing of this hostile force. For Demetrius, having found the entrances of the port undefended, stood in directly, and was by this time safely inside, before the eyes of everybody, and made signals from his ship, requesting a peaceable hearing. And on leave being given, he caused a herald with a loud voice to make proclamation that he was come thither by the command of his father, with no other design than what he prayed the gods to prosper with success, to give the Athenians their liberty, to expel the garrison, and to restore the ancient laws and constitution of the country.

The people, hearing this, at once threw down their shields, and clapping their hands, with loud acclamations entreated Demetrius to land, calling him their deliverer and benefactor. And the Phalerian and his party, who saw that there was nothing for it but to receive the conqueror, whether he should perform his promises or not, sent, however, messengers to beg for his protection; to whom Demetrius gave a kind reception, and sent back with them Aristodemus of Miletus, one of his father's friends. The Phalerian, under the change of government, was more afraid of his fellow-citizens than of the enemy; but Demetrius took precautions for him, and out of respect for his reputation and character, sent him with a safe conduct to Thebes, whither he desired to go. For himself, he declared he would not, in spite of all his curiosity, put his foot in the city till he had completed his deliverance by driving out the garrison. So blockading Munychia with a palisade and trench, he sailed off to attack Megara, where also there was one of Cassander's garrisons.

But, hearing that Cratesipolis, the wife of Alexander, son of Polysperchon, who was famous for her beauty, was well disposed to see him, he left his troops near Megara, and set out with a few light-armed attendants for Patræ, where she was now staying. And, quitting these also, he pitched his tent apart from everybody, that the woman might pay her visit without being seen. This some of the enemy perceived, and suddenly attacked him; and, in his alarm, he was obliged to disguise himself in a shabby cloak, and run for it, narrowly escaping the shame of being made a prisoner, in reward for his foolish passion. And as it was, his tent and money were taken. Megara, however, surrendered, and would have been pillaged by the soldiers, but for the urgent intercession of the Athenians. The garrison was driven out, and the city restored to independence.

While he was occupied in this, he remembered that Stilpo, the philosopher, famous for his choice of a life of tranquillity, was residing here. He, therefore, sent for him, and begged to know whether anything belonging to him had been taken. "No," replied Stilpo, "I have not met with any one to take away knowledge." Pretty nearly all the servants in the city had been stolen away; and so, when Demetrius, renewing his courtesies to Stilpo, on taking leave of him, said, "I leave your city, Stilpo, a city of freemen." "Certainly," replied Stilpo, "there is not one serving man left among us all."

Returning from Megara, he sat down before the citadel of Munychia, which in a few days he took by assault, and caused the fortifications to be demolished; and thus having accomplished his design, upon the request and invitation of the Athenians he made his entrance into the upper city, where, causing the people to be summoned, he publicly announced to them that their ancient constitution was restored, and that they should receive from his father, Antigonus, a present of one hundred and fifty thousand measures of wheat, and such a supply of timber as would enable them to build a hundred galleys. In this manner did the Athenians recover their popular institutions, after the space of fifteen years from the time of the war of Lamia and the battle before Cranon, during which interval of time the government had been administered nominally as an oligarchy, but really by a single man, Demetrius the Phalerian being so powerful.

But the excessive honours which the Athenians bestowed, for these noble and generous acts, upon Demetrius, created offence and disgust. The Athenians were the first who gave Antigonus and Demetrius the title of kings, which hitherto they had made it a point of piety to decline, as the one remaining royal honour still reserved for the lineal descendants of Philip and Alexander, in which none but they could venture to participate. Another name which they received from no people but the Athenians was that of the Tutelar Deities and Deliverers. And to enhance this flattery, by a common vote it was decreed to change the style of the city, and not to have the years named any longer from the annual archon; a priest of the two Tutelary Divinities, who was to be yearly chosen, was to have this honour, and all public acts and instruments were to bear their date by his name.

They decreed, also, that the figures of Antigonus and Demetrius should be woven, with those of the gods, into the pattern of the great robe. They consecrated the spot where Demetrius first alighted from his chariot, and built an altar there, with the name of the Altar of the Descent of Demetrius. They created two new tribes, calling them after the names of these princes, the Antigonid and the Demetriad; and to the Council, which consisted of five hundred persons, fifty being chosen out of every tribe, they added one hundred more to represent these new tribes. But the wildest proposal was one made by Stratocles, the great inventor of all these ingenious and exquisite compliments, enacting that the members of any deputation that the city should send to Demetrius or Antigonus should have the same title as those sent to Delphi or Olympia for the performance of the national sacrifices in behalf of the state at the great Greek festivals.

This Stratocles was, in all respects, an audacious and abandoned character, and seemed to have made it his object to copy, by his buffoonery and impertinence, Cleon's old familiarity with the people. His mistress, Phylacion, one day bringing him a dish of brains and neckbones for his dinner, "Oh," said he, "I am to dine upon the things which we statesmen play at ball with." At another time, when the Athenians received their naval defeat near Amorgos, he hastened home before the news could reach the city, and having a chaplet on his head, came riding through the Ceramicus, announcing that they had won a victory, and moved a vote for thanksgivings to the gods, and a distribution of meat among the people in their tribes. Presently after came those who brought home the wrecks from the battle; and when the people exclaimed at what he had done, he came boldly to face the outcry, and asked what harm there had been in giving them two days' pleasure.

Such was Stratocles. And, "adding flame to fire," as Aristophanes says, there was one who, to outdo Stratocles, proposed that it should be decreed that, whensoever Demetrius should honour their city with his presence, they should treat him with the same show of hos-

pitable entertainment with which Ceres and Bacchus are received; and the citizen who exceeded the rest in the splendour and costliness of his reception should have a sum of money granted him from the public purse to make a sacred offering. Finally, they changed the name of the month of Munychion, and called it Demetrion; they gave the name of the Demetrion to the odd day between the end of the old and the beginning of the new month; and turned the feast of Bacchus, the Dionysia, into the Demetria or feast of Demetrius.

Most of these changes were marked by the divine displeasure. The sacred robe, in which, according to their decree, the figures of Demetrius and Antigonus had been woven with those of Jupiter and Minerva, was caught by a violent gust of wind, while the procession was conveying it through the Ceramicus, and was torn from the top to the bottom. A crop of hemlock, a plant which scarcely grew anywhere, even in the country thereabouts, sprang up in abundance round the altars which they had erected to these new divinities. They had to omit the solemn procession at the feast of Bacchus, as upon the very day of its celebration there was such a severe and rigorous frost, coming quite out of its time, that not only the vines and fig-trees were killed, but almost all the wheat was destroyed in the blade. Accordingly, Philippides, an enemy to Stratocles, attacked him in a comedy, in the following verses:—

He for whom frosts that nipped your vines were
  sent,
And for whose sins the holy robe was rent,
Who grants to men the gods' own honours, he,
Not the poor stage, is now the people's enemy.

Philippides was a great favourite with King Lysimachus, from whom the Athenians received, for his sake, a variety of kindnesses. Lysimachus went so far as to think it a happy omen to meet or see Philippides at the outset of any enterprise or expedition. And, in general, he was well thought of for his own character, as a plain, uninterfering person, with none of the officious, self-important habits of a court. Once, when Lysimachus was solicitous to show him kindness, and asked what he had that he could make him a present of, "Anything," replied Philippides, "but your state secrets." The stage-player, we thought, deserved a place in our narrative quite as well as the public speaker.

But that which exceeded all the former follies and flatteries was the proposal of Dromoclides of Sphettus; who, when there was a debate about sending to the Delphic Oracle to inquire the proper course for the consecration of certain bucklers, moved in the assembly that they should rather send to receive an oracle from Demetrius. I will transcribe the very words of the order, which was in these terms: "May it be happy and propitious. The people of Athens have decreed, that a fit person shall be chosen among the Athenian citizens, who shall be deputed to be sent to the Deliverer; and after he hath duly performed the sacrifices, shall inquire of the Deliverer, in what most religious and decent manner he will please to direct, at the earliest possible time, the consecration of the bucklers; and according to the answer the people shall act." With this befooling they completed the perversion of a mind which even before was not so strong or sound as it should have been.

During his present leisure in Athens, he took to wife Eurydice, a descendant of the ancient Miltiades, who had been married to Opheltas, the ruler of Cyrene, and after his death had come back to Athens. The Athenians took the marriage as a compliment and favour to the city. But Demetrius was very free in these matters, and was the husband of several wives at once; the highest place and honour among all being retained by Phila, who was Antipater's daughter, and had been the wife of Craterus, the one of all the successors of Alexander who left behind him the strongest feelings of attachment among the Macedonians. And for these reasons Antigonus had obliged him to marry her, notwithstanding the disparity of their years, Demetrius being quite a youth, and she much older; and when upon that account he made some difficulty in complying, Antigonus whispered in his ear the maxim from Euripides, broadly substituting a new word for the original, *serve—*

Natural or not,
A man must wed *where profit will be got.*

Any respect, however, which he showed either to Phila or to his other wives did not go so far as to prevent him from consorting with any number of mistresses, and bearing, in this respect, the worst character of all the princes of his time.

A summons now arrived from his father, ordering him to go and fight with Ptolemy in Cyprus, which he was obliged to obey, sorry as he was to abandon Greece. And in quitting this nobler and more glorious enterprise, he sent to Cleonides, Ptolemy's general, who was

holding garrisons in Sicyon and Corinth, offering him money to let the cities be independent. But on his refusal, he set sail hastily, taking additional forces with him, and made for Cyprus; where, immediately upon his arrival, he fell upon Menelaus, the brother of Ptolemy, and gave him a defeat. But when Ptolemy himself came in person, with large forces both on land and sea, for some little time nothing took place beyond an interchange of menaces and lofty talk. Ptolemy bade Demetrius sail off before the whole armament came up, if he did not wish to be trampled under foot; and Demetrius offered to let him retire, on condition of his withdrawing his garrisons from Sicyon and Corinth. And not they alone, but all the other potentates and princes of the time, were in anxiety for the uncertain impending issue of the conflict; as it seemed evident that the conqueror's prize would be, not Cyprus or Syria, but the absolute supremacy.

Ptolemy had brought a hundred and fifty galleys with him, and gave orders to Menelaus to sally, in the heat of the battle, out of the harbour of Salamis, and attack with sixty ships the rear of Demetrius, Demetrius, however, opposing to these sixty ten of his galleys, which were a sufficient number to block up the narrow entrance of the harbour, and drawing out his land forces along all the headlands running out into sea, went into action with a hundred and eighty galleys, and, attacking with the utmost boldness and impetuosity, utterly routed Ptolemy, who fled with eight ships, the sole remnant of his fleet, seventy having been taken with all their men, and the rest destroyed in the battle; while the whole multitude of attendants, friends, and women, that had followed in the ships of burden, all the arms, treasure, and military engines, fell, without exception, into the hands of Demetrius, and were by him collected and brought into the camp.

Among the prisoners was the celebrated Lamia, famed at one time for her skill on the flute, and afterwards renowned as a mistress. And although now upon the wane of her youthful beauty, and though Demetrius was much her junior, she exercised over him so great a charm that all other women seemed to be amorous of Demetrius, but Demetrius amorous only of Lamia.

After this signal victory, Demetrius came before Salamis; and Menelaus, unable to make any resistance, surrendered himself and all his fleet, twelve hundred horse, and twelve thousand foot, together with the place. But that which added more than all to the glory and splendour of the success was the humane and generous conduct of Demetrius to the vanquished. For, after he had given honourable funerals to the dead, he bestowed liberty upon the living; and that he might not forget the Athenians, he sent them, as a present, complete arms for twelve hundred men.

To carry this happy news, Aristodemus of Miletus, the most perfect flatterer belonging to the court, was despatched to Antigonus; and he, to enhance the welcome message, was resolved, it would appear, to make his most successful effort. When he crossed from Cyprus, he bade the galley which conveyed him to come to anchor off the land; and, having ordered all the ship's crew to remain aboard, he took the boat, and was set ashore alone. Thus he proceeded to Antigonus, who, one may well imagine, was in suspense enough about the issue, and suffered all the anxieties natural to men engaged in so perilous a struggle. And when he heard that Aristodemus was coming alone, it put him into yet greater trouble; he could scarcely forbear from going out to meet him himself; he sent messenger on messenger, and friend after friend, to inquire what news.

But Aristodemus, walking gravely and with a settled countenance, without making answer, still proceeded quietly onward; until Antigonus, quite alarmed and no longer able to refrain, got up and met him at the gate, whither he came with a crowd of anxious followers now collected and running after him. As soon as he saw Antigonus within hearing, stretching out his hands, he accosted him with the loud exclamation, "Hail, King Antigonus! We have defeated Ptolemy by sea, and have taken Cyprus and sixteen thousand eight hundred prisoners." "Welcome, Aristodemus," replied Antigonus, "but, as you chose to torture us so long for your good news, you may wait awhile for the reward of it."

Upon this the people around gave Antigonus and Demetrius, for the first time, the title of kings. His friends at once set a diadem on the head of Antigonus; and he sent one presently to his son, with a letter addressed to him as King Demetrius. And when this news was told in Egypt, that they might not seem to be dejected with the late defeat, Ptolemy's followers also took occasion to bestow the style of king upon him; and the rest of the successors of Alexander were quick to follow the example. Lysimachus began to wear the diadem, and Seleucus, who had before received the name in all addresses from the barbarians, now also took it upon him in all business with the Greeks. Cassander still retained his usual superscription in his letters, but others, both in writing and speaking, gave him the royal title.

Nor was this the mere accession of a name, or introduction of a new fashion. The men's own sentiments about themselves were disturbed, and their feelings elevated; a spirit of pomp and arrogance passed into their habits of life and conversation, as a tragic actor on the stage modifies, with a change of dress, his steps, his voice, his motions in sitting down, his manner in addressing another. The punishments they inflicted were more violent after they had thus laid aside that modest style under which they formerly dissembled their power, and the influence of which had often made them gentler and less exacting to their subjects. A single flattering voice effected a revolution in the world.

Antigonus, extremely elevated with the success of his arms in Cyprus, under the conduct of Demetrius, resolved to push on his good fortune, and to lead his forces in person against Ptolemy by land whilst Demetrius should coast with a great fleet along the shore, to assist him by sea. The issue of the contest was intimated in a dream which Medius, a friend to Antigonus, had at this time in his sleep. He thought he saw Antigonus and his whole army running, as if it had been a race; that, in the first part of the course, he went off showing great strength and speed; gradually, however, his pace slackened, and at the end he saw him come lagging up, tired and almost breathless and quite spent. Antigonus himself met with many difficulties by land; and Demetrius, encountering a great storm at sea, was driven, with the loss of many of his ships, upon a dangerous coast without a harbour. So the expedition returned without effecting anything.

Antigonus, now nearly eighty years old, was no longer well able to go through the fatigues of a marching campaign, though rather on account of his great size and corpulence than from loss of strength; and for this reason he left things to his son, whose fortune and experience appeared sufficient for all undertakings, and whose luxury and expense and revelry gave him no concern. For though in peace he vented himself in pleasures, and, when there was nothing to do, ran headlong into any excesses, in war he was as sober and abstemious as the most temperate character.

The story is told that once, after Lamia had gained open supremacy over him, the old man, when Demetrius coming home from abroad began to kiss him with unusual warmth, asked him if he took him for Lamia. At another time, Demetrius, after spending several days in a debauch, excused himself for his absence, by saying he had had a violent flux. "So I heard," replied Antigonus; "was it of Thasian wine, or Chian?" Once he was told his son was ill, and went to see him. At the door he met some young beauty. Going in, he sat down by the bed and took his pulse. "The fever," said Demetrius, "has just left me." "Oh, yes," replied the father, "I met it going out at the door."

Demetrius's great actions made Antigonus treat him thus easily. The Scythians in their drinking-bouts twang their bows, to keep their courage awake amidst the dreams of indulgence; but he would resign his whole being, now to pleasure, and now to action; and though he never let thoughts of the one intrude upon the pursuit of the other, yet when the time came for preparing for war, he showed as much capacity as any man.

And indeed his ability displayed itself even more in preparing for than in conducting a war. He thought he could never be too well supplied for every possible occasion, and took a pleasure, not to be satiated, in great improvements in ship-building and machines. He did not waste his natural genius and power of mechanical research on toys and idle fancies, turning, painting, and playing on the flute, like some kings, Æropus, for example, King of Macedon, who spent his days in making small lamps and tables; or Attalus Philometor, whose amusement was to cultivate poisons, henbane and hellebore, and even hemlock, aconite, and dorycnium, which he used to sow himself in the royal gardens, and made it his business to gather the fruits and collect the juices in their season. The Parthian kings took a pride in whetting and sharpening with their own hands the points of their arrows and javelins.

But when Demetrius played the workman, it was like a king, and there was magnificence in his handicraft. The articles he produced bore marks upon the face of them not of ingenuity only, but of a great mind and a lofty purpose. They were such as a king might not only design and pay for, but use his own hands to make; and while friends might be terrified with their greatness, enemies could be charmed with their beauty; a phrase which is not so pretty to the ear as it is true to the fact. The very people against whom they were to be employed could not forbear running to gaze with admiration upon his galleys of five and six ranges of oars, as they passed along their coasts; and the inhabitants of besieged cities came on their walls to see the spectacles of his famous *City-takers*. Even Lysimachus, of all the kings of his time the greatest enemy of Demetrius, coming to raise the siege of Soli in Cilicia, sent first to desire permission to see his galleys and engines, and, having had his curiosity gratified by a view of them, expressed his admiration and quitted the place. The Rhodians, also, whom he long besieged, begged him, when they concluded a peace, to let them have some of his engines, which they might preserve as a memorial at once of his power and of their own brave resistance.

The quarrel between him and the Rhodians was on account of their being allies to Ptolemy, and in the siege the greatest of all the engines was planted against their walls. The base of it was exactly square, each side containing twenty-four cubits; it rose to a height of thirty-three cubits, growing narrower from the base to the top. Within were several apartments or chambers, which were to be filled with armed men, and in every story the front towards the enemy had windows for discharging missiles of all sorts, the whole being filled with soldiers for every description of fighting. And what was most wonderful was that, notwithstanding its size, when it was moved it never tottered or inclined to one side, but went forward on its base in perfect equilibrium, with a loud noise and great impetus, astounding the minds, and yet at the same time charming the eyes of all the beholders.

Whilst Demetrius was at this same siege, there were brought to him two iron cuirasses from Cyprus, weighing each of them no more than forty pounds, and Zoilus, who had forged them, to show the excellence of their temper, desired that one of them might be tried with a catapult missile, shot out of one of the engines at no greater distance than six-and-twenty paces; and, upon the experiment, it was found that though the dart exactly hit the cuirass, yet it made no greater impression than such a slight scratch as might be made with the point of a style or graver. Demetrius took this for his own wearing, and gave the other to Alcimus the Epirot, the best soldier and strongest man of all his captains, the only one who used to wear armour to the weight of two talents, one talent being the weight which others thought sufficient. He fell during this siege in a battle near the theatre.

The Rhodians made a brave defence, insomuch that Demetrius saw he was making but little progress, and only persisted out of obstinacy and passion; and the rather because the Rhodians, having captured a ship in which some clothes and furniture, with letters from herself, were coming to him from Phila his wife, had sent on everything to Ptolemy, and had not copied the honourable example of the Athenians, who, having surprised an express sent from King Philip, their enemy, opened all the letters he was charged with, excepting only those directed to Queen Olympias, which they returned with the seal unbroken.

Yet, although greatly provoked, Demetrius, into whose power it shortly after came to repay the affront, would not suffer himself to retaliate. Protogenes the Caunian had been making them a painting of the story of Ialysus, which was all but completed, when it was taken by Demetrius in one of the suburbs. The Rhodians sent a herald begging him to be pleased to spare the work and not let it be destroyed; Demetrius's answer to which was that he would rather burn the pictures of his father than a piece of art which had cost so much labour. It is said to have taken Protogenes seven years to paint, and they tell us that Apelles, when he first saw it, was struck dumb with wonder, and called it, on recovering his speech, "a great labour and a wonderful success," adding, however, that it had not the graces which carried his own paintings as it were up to the heavens. This picture, which came with the rest in the general mass to Rome, there perished by fire.

While the Rhodians were thus defending their city to the utmost, Demetrius, who was not sorry for an excuse to retire, found one in the arrival of ambassadors from Athens, by whose mediation terms were made that the Rhodians should bind themselves to aid Antigonus and Demetrius against all enemies, Ptolemy excepted.

The Athenians entreated his help against Cassander, who was besieging the city. So he went thither with a fleet of three hundred and thirty ships, and many soldiers; and not only drove Cassander out of Attica, but pursued him as far as Thermopylæ, routed him and became master of Heraclea, which came over to him voluntarily, and of a body of six thousand Macedonians, which also joined him. Returning hence, he gave their liberty to all the Greeks on this side Thermopylæ, and made alliance with the Bœotians, took Cenchreæ, and reducing the fortresses of Phyle and Panactum, in which were garrisons of Cassander, restored them to the Athenians.

They, in requital, though they had before been so profuse in bestowing honours upon him that one would have thought they had exhausted all the capacities of invention, showed they had still new refinements of adulation to devise for him. They gave him, as his lodging, the back temple in the Parthenon, and here he lived, under the immediate roof, as they meant it to imply, of his hostess, Minerva—no reputable or well-conducted guest to be quartered upon a maiden goddess! When his brother Philip was once put into a house where three young women were living, Antigonus, saying nothing to him, sent for his quartermaster, and told him, in the young man's presence, to find some less crowded lodgings for him.

Demetrius, however, who should, to say the least, have paid the goddess the respect due to an elder sister, for that was the purport of the city's compliment, filled the temple with such pollutions that the place seemed least profaned when his licence confined itself to common women like Chrysis, Lamia, Demo, and Anticyra.

The fair name of the city forbids any further plain particulars; let us only record the severe virtue of the young Damocles, surnamed, and by that surname pointed out to Demetrius, the beautiful; who, to escape importunities, avoided every place of resort, and when at last followed into a private bathing room by Demetrius, seeing none at hand to help or deliver, seized the lid from the cauldron, and, plunging into the boiling water, sought a death untimely and unmerited, but worthy of the country and of the beauty that occasioned it. Not so Cleænetus, the son of Cleomedon, who, to obtain from Demetrius a letter of intercession to the people in behalf of his father, lately condemned in a fine of fifty talents, disgraced himself, and got the city into trouble. In deference to the letter, they remitted the fine, yet they made an edict prohibiting any citizen for the future to bring letters from Demetrius.

But being informed that Demetrius resented this as a great indignity, they not only rescinded in alarm the former order, but put some of the proposers and advisers of it to death and banished others, and furthermore enacted and decreed, that whatsoever King Demetrius should in time to come ordain, should be accounted right towards the gods and just towards men; and when one of the better class of citizens said Stratocles must be mad to use such words, Demochares of Leuconoe observed he would be a fool not to be mad. For Stratocles was well rewarded for his flatteries; and the saying was remembered against Demochares, who was soon after sent into banishment. So fared the Athenians, after being relieved of the foreign garrison, and recovering what was called their liberty.

After this Demetrius marched with his forces into Peloponnesus, where he met with none to oppose him, his enemies fleeing before him, and allowing the cities to join him. He received into friendship all Acte, as it is called, and all Arcadia except Mantinea. He bought the liberty of Argos, Corinth, and Sicyon, by paying a hundred talents to their garrisons to evacuate them. At Argos, during the feast of Juno, which happened at the time, he presided at the games, and, joining in the festivities with the multitude of the Greeks assembled there, he celebrated his marriage with Deidamia, daughter of Æacides, King of the Molossians, and sister of Pyrrhus. At Sicyon he told the people they had put the city just outside of the city, and, persuading them to remove to where they now live, gave their town not only a new site but a new name, Demetrias, after himself.

A general assembly met on the Isthmus, where he was proclaimed, by a great concourse of the people, the Commander of Greece, like Philip and Alexander of old; whose superior he, in the present height of his prosperity and power, was willing enough to consider himself; and certainly, in one respect, he outdid Alexander, who never refused their title to other kings, or took on himself the style of king of kings, though many kings received both their title and their authority as such from him; whereas Demetrius used to ridicule those who gave the name of king to any except himself and his father; and in his entertainments was well pleased when his followers, after drinking to him and his father as kings, went on to drink the healths of Seleucus, with the title of Master of the Elephants; of Ptolemy, by the name of High Admiral; of Lysimachus, with the addition of Treasurer; and of Agathocles, with the style of Governor of the Island of Sicily.

The other kings merely laughed when they were told of this vanity; Lysimachus alone expressed some indignation at being considered a eunuch, such being usually then selected for the office of treasurer. And, in general, there was a more bitter enmity between him and Lysimachus than with any of the others. Once, as a scoff at his passion for Lamia, Lysimachus said he had never before seen a courtesan act a queen's part; to which Demetrius rejoined that his mistress was quite as honest as Lysimachus's own Penelope.

But to proceed. Demetrius being about to return to Athens, signified by letter to the city that he desired immediate admission to the rites of initiation into the mysteries, and wished to go through all the stages of the ceremony, from first to last, without delay. This was absolutely contrary to the rules, and a thing which had never been allowed before; for the lesser mysteries were celebrated in the month of Anthesterion, and the great solemnity in Boëdromion, and none of the novices were finally admitted till they had completed a year after this latter.

Yet all this notwithstanding, when in the public assembly these letters of Demetrius were produced and read, there was not one single person who had the courage to oppose them, except Pythodorus, the torch-bearer. But it signified nothing, for Stratocles at once proposed that the month of Munychion, then current, should by edict be reputed to be the month of Anthesterion; which being voted and done, and Demetrius thereby admitted to the lesser ceremonies, by another vote they turned the same month of Munychion into the other month of Boëdromion; the celebration of the greater mysteries ensued, and Demetrius was fully admitted. These proceedings gave the comedian, Philippides, a new occasion to exercise his wit upon Stratocles—

——whose flattering fear
Into one month hath crowded all the year.

And on the vote that Demetrius should lodge in the Parthenon—

Who turns the temple to a common inn,
And makes the Virgin's house a house of sin.

Of all the disreputable and flagitious acts of which he was guilty in this visit, one that particularly hurt the feelings of the Athenians was that, having given command that they should forthwith raise for his service two hundred and fifty talents, and they to comply with his demands being forced to levy it upon the people with the utmost rigour and severity, when they presented him with the money which they had with such difficulty raised, as if it were a trifling sum, he ordered it to be given to Lamia and the rest of his women, to buy soap. The loss, which was bad enough, was less galling than the shame, and the words more intolerable than the act which they accompanied. Though, indeed, the story is variously reported; and some say it was the Thessalians, and not the Athenians, who were thus treated. Lamia, however, exacted contributions herself to pay for an entertainment she gave to the king, and her banquet was so renowned for its sumptuosity that a description of it was drawn up by the Samian writer, Lynceus. Upon this occasion, one of the comic writers gave Lamia the name of the real *Helepolis;* and Demochares of Soli called Demetrius *Mythus,* because the fable always has its Lamia, and so had he.

And, in truth, his passion for this woman, and the prosperity in which she lived were such as to draw upon him not only the envy and jealousy of all his wives, but the animosity even of his friends. For example, on Lysimachus's showing to some ambassadors from Demetrius the scars of the wounds which he had received upon his thighs and arms by the paws of the lion with which Alexander had shut him up, after hearing his account of the combat, they smiled and answered, that their king, also, was not without his scars, but could show upon his neck the marks of a Lamia, a no less dangerous beast.

It was also matter of wonder that, though he had objected so much to Phila on account of her age, he was yet such a slave to Lamia who was so long past her prime. One evening at supper, when she played the flute, Demetrius asked Demo, whom the men called Madness, what she thought of her. Demo answered she thought her an old woman. And when a quantity of sweetmeats were brought in, and the king said again, "See what presents I get from Lamia!" "My old mother," answered Demo, "will send you more, if you will make her your mistress."

Another story is told of a criticism passed by Lamia on the famous judgment of Bocchoris. A young Egyptian had long made suit to Thonis, the courtesan, offering a sum of gold for her favour. But before it came to pass, he dreamed one night that he had obtained it, and, satisfied with the shadow, felt no more desire for the substance. Thonis upon this brought an action for the sum. Bocchoris, the judge, on hearing the case, ordered the defendant to bring into court the full amount in a vessel, which he was to move to and fro in his hand,

and the shadow of it was to be adjudged to Thonis. The fairness of this sentence Lamia contested, saying the young man's desire might have been satisfied with the dream, but Thonis's desire for the money could not be relieved by the shadow. Thus much for Lamia.

And now the story passes from the comic to the tragic stage in pursuit of the acts and fortunes of its subjects. A general league of the kings, who were now gathering and combining their forces to attack Antigonus, recalled Demetrius from Greece. He was encouraged by finding his father full of a spirit and resolution for the combat that belied his years. Yet it would seem to be true, that if Antigonus could only have borne to make some trifling concessions, and if he had shown any moderation in his passion for empire, he might have maintained for himself till his death and left to his son behind him the first place among the kings. But he was of a violent and haughty spirit; and the insulting words as well as actions which he allowed himself could not be borne by young and powerful princes, and provoked them into combining against him. Though now when he was told of the confederacy, he could not forbear from saying that this flock of birds would soon be scattered by one stone and a single shout.

He took the field at the head of more than seventy thousand foot, and of ten thousand horse, and seventy-five elephants. His enemies had sixty-four thousand foot, five hundred more horse than he, elephants to the number of four hundred, and a hundred and twenty chariots. On their near approach to each other, an alteration began to be observable, not in the purposes, but in the presentiments of Antigonus. For whereas in all former campaigns he had ever shown himself lofty and confident, loud in voice and scornful in speech, often by some joke or mockery on the eve of battle expressing his contempt and displaying his composure, he was now remarked to be thoughtful, silent, and retired. He presented Demetrius to the army, and declared him his successor; and what every one thought stranger than all was that he now conferred alone in his tent with Demetrius; whereas in former time he had never entered into any secret consultations even with him; but had always followed his own advice, made his resolutions, and then given out his commands. Once when Demetrius was a boy and asked him how soon the army would move, he is said to have answered him sharply, "Are you afraid lest you, of all the army, should not hear the trumpet?"

There were now, however, inauspicious signs, which affected his spirits. Demetrius, in a dream, had seen Alexander, completely armed, appear and demand of him what word they intended to give in the time of the battle; and Demetrius answering that he intended the word should be "Jupiter and Victory," "Then," said Alexander, "I will go to your adversaries and find my welcome with them." And on the morning of the combat, as the armies were drawing up, Antigonus, going out of the door of his tent, by some accident or other, stumbled and fell flat upon the ground, hurting himself a good deal. And on recovering his feet, lifting up his hands to heaven, he prayed the gods to grant him, "either victory, or death without knowledge of defeat." When the armies engaged, Demetrius, who commanded the greatest and best part of the cavalry, made a charge on Antiochus, the son of Seleucus, and gloriously routing the enemy, followed the pursuit, in the pride and exultation of success, so eagerly, and so unwisely far, that it fatally lost him the day; for when, perceiving his error, he would have come in to the assistance of his own infantry, he was not able, the enemy with their elephants having cut off his retreat.

On the other hand, Seleucus, observing the main battle of Antigonus left naked of their horse, did not charge, but made a show of charging; and keeping them in alarm and wheeling about and still threatening an attack, he gave opportunity for those who wished it to separate and come over to him; which a large body of them did, the rest taking to flight. But the old King Antigonus still kept his post, and when a strong body of the enemies drew up to charge him, and one of those about him cried out to him, "Sir, they are coming upon you," he only replied, "What else should they do? But Demetrius will come to my rescue." And in this hope he persisted to the last, looking out on every side for his son's approach, until he was borne down by a whole multitude of darts, and fell. His other followers and friends fled, and Thorax of Larissa remained alone by the body.

The battle having been thus decided, the kings who had gained the victory, carving up the whole vast empire that had belonged to Demetrius and Antigonus, like a carcass, into so many portions, added these new gains to their former possessions. As for Demetrius, with five thousand foot and four thousand horse, he fled at his utmost speed to Ephesus, where it was the common opinion he would seize the treasures of the temple to relieve his wants; but he, on the contrary, fearing such an attempt on the part of his soldiers, hastened away, and sailed for Greece, his chief remaining hopes being placed in the fidelity of the Athenians, with whom he had left part of his navy and of his treasures and his wife Deidamia. And in their attachment he had not the least doubt but he should in this his extremity find a safe resource.

Accordingly when, upon reaching the Cyclades, he was met by ambassadors from Athens, requesting him not to proceed to the city, as the people had passed a vote to admit no king whatever within their walls, and had conveyed Deidamia with honourable attendance to Megara, his anger and surprise overpowered him, and the constancy quite failed him which he had hitherto shown in a wonderful degree under his reverses, nothing humiliating or mean-spirited having as yet been seen in him under all his misfortunes. But to be thus disappointed in the Athenians, and to find the friendship he had trusted prove, upon trial, thus empty and unreal, was a great pang to him.

And, in truth, an excessive display of outward honour would seem to be the most uncertain attestation of the real affection of a people for any king or potentate. Such shows lose their whole credit as tokens of affection (which has its virtue in the feelings and moral choice), when we reflect that they may equally proceed from fear. The same decrees are voted upon the latter motive as upon the former. And therefore judicious men do not look so much to statues, paintings, or divine honours that are paid them, as to their own actions and conduct, judging hence whether they shall trust these as a genuine, or discredit them as a forced homage. As in fact nothing is less unusual than for a people, even while offering compliments, to be disgusted with those who accept them greedily, or arrogantly, or without respect to the free-will of the givers.

Demetrius, shamefully used as he thought himself, was in no condition to revenge the affront. He returned a message of gentle expostulation, saying, however, that he expected to have his galleys sent to him, among which was that of thirteen banks of oars. And this being accorded him, he sailed to the Isthmus, and, finding his affairs in very ill condition, his garrisons expelled, and a general secession going on to the enemy, he left Pyrrhus to attend to Greece, and took his course to the Chersonesus, where he ravaged the territories of Lysimachus, and by the booty which he took, maintained and kept together his troops, which were now once more beginning to recover and to show some considerable front. Nor did any of the other princes care to meddle with him on that side; for Lysimachus had quite as little claim to be loved, and was more to be feared for his power.

But not long after Seleucus sent to treat with Demetrius for a marriage betwixt himself and Stratonice, daughter of Demetrius by Phila. Seleucus, indeed, had already, by Apama, the Persian, a son named Antiochus, but he was possessed of territories that might well satisfy more than one successor, and he was the rather induced to this alliance with Demetrius, because Lysimachus had just married himself to one daughter of King Ptolemy, and his son Agathocles to another. Demetrius, who looked upon the offer as an unexpected piece of good fortune, presently embarked with his daughter, and with his whole fleet sailed for Syria. Having during his voyage to touch several times on the coast, among other places he landed in part of Cilicia, which by the apportionment of the kings after the defeat of Antigonus was allotted to Plistarchus, the brother of Cassander. Plistarchus, who took this descent of Demetrius upon his coasts as an infraction of his rights, and was not sorry to have something to complain of, hastened to expostulate in person with Seleucus for entering separately into relations with Demetrius, the common enemy, without consulting the other kings.

Demetrius, receiving information of this, seized the opportunity, and fell upon the city of Quinda, which he surprised, and took in it twelve hundred talents still remaining of the treasure. With this prize, he hastened back to his galleys, embarked, and set sail. At Rhosus, where his wife Phila was now with him, he was met by Seleucus, and their communications with each other at once were put on a frank, unsuspecting, and kingly footing. First, Seleucus gave a banquet to Demetrius in his tent in the camp; then Demetrius received him in the ship of thirteen banks of oars. Meetings for amusements, conferences, and long visits for general intercourse succeeded, all without attendants or arms; until at length Seleucus took his leave, and in great state conducted Stratonice to Antioch. Demetrius meantime possessed himself of Cilicia, and sent Phila to

her brother Cassander, to answer the complaints of Plistarchus. And here his wife Deidamia came by sea out of Greece to meet him, but not long after contracted an illness, of which she died. After her death, Demetrius, by the mediation of Seleucus, became reconciled to Ptolemy, and an agreement was made that he should marry his daughter Ptolemais.

Thus far all was handsomely done on the part of Seleucus. But, shortly after, desiring to have the province of Cilicia from Demetrius for a sum of money, and being refused it, he then angrily demanded of him the cities of Tyre and Sidon, which seemed a mere piece of arbitrary dealing, and, indeed, an outrageous thing, that he, who was possessed of all the vast provinces between India and the Syrian sea, should think himself so poorly off as, for the sake of two cities which he coveted, to disturb the peace of his dear connection, already a sufferer under a severe reverse of fortune. However, he did but justify the saying of Plato, that the only certain way to be truly rich is not to have more property, but fewer desires. For whoever is always grasping at more avows that he is still in want, and must be poor in the midst of affluence.

But Demetrius, whose courage did not sink, resolutely sent him answer, that, though he were to lose ten thousand battles like that of Ipsus, he would pay no price for the good-will of such a son-in-law as Seleucus. He reinforced these cities with sufficient garrisons to enable them to make a defence against Seleucus; and, receiving information that Lachares, taking the opportunity of their civil dissensions, had set up himself as a usurper over the Athenians, he imagined that if he made a sudden attempt upon the city, he might now without difficulty get possession of it. He crossed the sea in safety with a large fleet; but passing along the coast of Attica, was met by a violent storm, and lost the greater number of his ships, and a very considerable body of men on board them. As for him, he escaped, and began to make war in a petty manner with the Athenians, but, finding himself unable to effect his design, he sent back orders for raising another fleet, and, with the troops which he had, marched into Peloponnesus and laid siege to the city of Messena. In attacking which place he was in danger of death; for a missile from an engine struck him in the face, and passed through the cheek into his mouth.

He recovered, however, and, as soon as he was in a condition to take the field, won over divers cities which had revolted from him, and made an incursion into Attica, where he took Eleusis and Rhamnus, and wasted the country thereabout. And that he might straiten the Athenians by cutting off all manner of provision, a vessel laden with corn bound thither falling into his hands, he ordered the master and the supercargo to be immediately hanged, thereby to strike a terror into others, that so they might not venture to supply the city with provisions. By which means they were reduced to such extremities that a bushel of salt sold for forty drachmas, and a peck of wheat for three hundred. Ptolemy had sent to their relief a hundred and fifty galleys, which came so near as to be seen off Ægina; but this brief hope was soon extinguished by the arrival of three hundred ships, which came to reinforce Demetrius from Cyprus, Peloponnesus, and other places; upon which Ptolemy's fleet took to flight, and Lachares, the tyrant, ran away, leaving the city to its fate.

And now the Athenians, who before had made it capital for any person to propose a treaty or accommodation with Demetrius, immediately opened the nearest gates to send ambassadors to him, not so much out of hopes of obtaining any honourable conditions from his clemency as out of necessity, to avoid death by famine. For among many frightful instances of the distress they were reduced to, it is said that a father and son were sitting in a room together, having abandoned every hope, when a dead mouse fell from the ceiling; and for this prize they leaped up and came to blows. In this famine, it is also related, the philosopher Epicurus saved his own life, and the lives of his scholars, by a small quantity of beans, which he distributed to them daily by number.

In this condition was the city when Demetrius made his entrance and issued a proclamation that all the inhabitants should assemble in the theatre; which being done, he drew up his soldiers at the back of the stage, occupied the stage itself with his guards, and, presently coming in himself by the actors' passages, when the people's consternation had risen to its height, with his first words he put an end to it. Without any harshness of tone or bitterness of words, he reprehended them in a gentle and friendly way, and declared himself reconciled, adding a present of a hundred thousand bushels of wheat, and appointing as magistrates persons acceptable to the people. So Dromoclides, the orator, seeing the people at a loss how to express their gratitude by any words or acclamations, and ready for anything that would outdo the verbal encomiums of the public speakers, came forward, and moved a decree for delivering Piræus and Munychia into the hands of King Demetrius. This was passed accordingly, and Demetrius, of his own motion, added a third garrison, which he placed in the Museum, as a precaution against any new restiveness on the part of the people, which might give him the trouble of quitting his other enterprises.

He had not long been master of Athens before he had formed designs against Lacedæmon; of which Archidamus, the king, being advertised, came out and met him, but he was overthrown in a battle near Mantinea; after which Demetrius entered Laconia, and, in a second battle near Sparta itself, defeated him again with the loss of two hundred Lacedæmonians slain, and five hundred taken prisoners. And now it was almost impossible for the city, which hitherto had never been captured, to escape his arms.

But certainly there never was any king upon whom Fortune made such short turns, nor any other life or story so filled with her swift and surprising changes, over and over again, from small things to great, from splendour back to humiliation and from utter weakness once more to power and might. They say in his sadder vicissitudes he used sometimes to apostrophise Fortune in the words of Æschylus—

Thou liftest up, to cast us down again.

And so at this moment, when all things seemed to conspire together to give him his heart's desire of dominion and power, news arrived that Lysimachus had taken all his cities in Asia, that Ptolemy had reduced all Cyprus with the exception of Salamis, and that in Salamis his mother and children were shut up and close besieged; and yet, like the woman in Archilochus—

Water in one deceitful hand she shows,
While burning fire within her other glows.

The same fortune that drew him off with these disastrous tidings from Sparta, in a moment after opened upon him a new and wonderful prospect, of the following kind. Cassander, King of Macedon, dying, and his eldest son, Philip, who succeeded him, not long surviving his father, the two younger brothers fell at variance concerning the succession. And Antipater having murdered his mother Thessalonica, Alexander, the younger brother, call-

748 PLUTARCH'S LIVES

ed in to his assistance Pyrrhus out of Epirus, and Demetrius out of the Peloponnese. Pyrrhus arrived first, and, taking in recompense for his succour a large slice of Macedonia, had made Alexander begin to be aware that he had brought upon himself a dangerous neighbour. And, that he might not run a yet worse hazard from Demetrius, whose power and reputation were so great, the young man hurried away to meet him at Dium, whither he, who on receiving his letter had set out on his march, was now come. And, offering his greetings and grateful acknowledgments, he at the same time informed him that his affairs no longer required the presence of his ally; thereupon he invited him to supper.

There were not wanting some feelings of suspicion on either side already; and when Demetrius was now on his way to the banquet, some one came and told him that in the midst of the drinking he would be killed. Demetrius showed little concern, but, making only a little less haste, he sent to the principal officers of his army commanding them to draw out the soldiers, and make them stand to their arms, and ordered his retinue (more numerous a good deal than that of Alexander) to attend him into the very room of the entertainment, and not to stir from thence till they saw him rise from the table. Thus Alexander's servants, finding themselves overpowered, had not courage to attempt anything. And, indeed, Demetrius gave them no opportunity, for he made a very short visit, and pretending to Alexander that he was not at present in health for drinking wine, left early. And the next day he occupied himself in preparations for departing, telling Alexander he had received intelligence that obliged him to leave, and begging him to excuse so sudden a parting; he would hope to see him further when his affairs allowed him leisure.

Alexander was only too glad, not only that he was going, but that he was doing so of his own motion, without any offence, and proposed to accompany him into Thessaly. But when they came to Larissa, new invitations passed between them, new professions of goodwill, covering new conspiracies; by which Alexander put himself into the power of Demetrius. For as he did not like to use precautions on his own part, for fear Demetrius should take the hint to use them on his, the very thing he meant to do was first done to him. He accepted an invitation, and came to Demetrius's quarters; and when Demetrius,

while they were still supping, rose from the table and went forth, the young man rose also, and followed him to the door, where Demetrius, as he passed through, only said to the guards, "Kill him that follows me," and went on; and Alexander was at once despatched by them, together with such of his friends as endeavoured to come to his rescue, one of whom, before he died, said, "You have been one day too quick for us."

The night following was one, as may be supposed, of disorder and confusion. And with the morning, the Macedonians, still in alarm, and fearful of the forces of Demetrius, on finding no violence offered, but only a message sent from Demetrius desiring an interview and opportunity for explanation of his actions, at last began to feel pretty confident again, and prepared to receive him favourably. And when he came, there was no need of much being said; their hatred of Antipater for his murder of his mother, and the absence of any one better to govern them, soon decided them to proclaim Demetrius King of Macedon. And into Macedonia they at once started and took him. And the Macedonians at home, who had not forgotten or forgiven the wicked deeds committed by Cassander on the family of Alexander, were far from sorry at the change. Any kind recollections that still might subsist of the plain and simple rule of the first Antipater went also to the benefit of Demetrius, whose wife was Phila, his daughter, and his son by her, a boy already old enough to be serving in the army with his father, was the natural successor to the government.

To add to this unexpected good fortune, news arrived that Ptolemy had dismissed his mother and children, bestowing upon them presents and honours; and also that his daughter Stratonice, whom he had married to Seleucus, was remarried to Antiochus, the son of Seleucus, and proclaimed Queen of Upper Asia.

For Antiochus, it appears, had fallen passionately in love with Stratonice, the young queen, who had already made Seleucus the father of a son. He struggled very hard with the beginning of this passion, and at last, resolving with himself that his desires were wholly unlawful, his malady past all cure, and his powers of reason too feeble to act, he determined on death, and thought to bring his life slowly to extinction by neglecting his person and refusing nourishment, under the pretence of being ill.

Erasistratus, the physician who attended him, quickly perceived that love was his distemper, but the difficulty was to discover the object. He therefore waited continually in his chamber, and when any of the beauties of the court made their visit to the sick prince, he observed the emotions and alterations in the countenance of Antiochus, and watched for the changes which he knew to be indicative of the inward passions and inclinations of the soul. He took notice that the presence of other women produced no effect upon him; but when Stratonice came, as she often did, alone, or in company with Seleucus, to see him, he observed in him all Sappho's famous symptoms,—his voice faltered, his face flushed up, his eyes glanced stealthily, a sudden sweat broke out on his skin, the beatings of his heart were irregular and violent, and, unable to support the excess of his passion, he would sink into a state of faintness, prostration, and pallor.

Erasistratus, reasoning upon these symptoms, and, upon the probabilities of things, considering that the king's son would hardly, if the object of his passion had been any other, have persisted to death rather than reveal it, felt, however, the difficulty of making a discovery of this nature to Seleucus. But, trusting to the tenderness of Seleucus for the young man, he put on all the assurances he could, and at last, on some opportunity, spoke out and told him the malady was love, a love impossible to gratify or relieve. The king was extremely surprised, and asked, "Why impossible to relieve?" "The fact is," replied Erasistratus, "he is in love with my wife." "How!" said Seleucus. "And will our friend Erasistratus refuse to bestow his wife upon my son and only successor, when there is no other way to save his life?" "You," replied Erasistratus, "who are his father, would not do so, if he were in love with Stratonice." "Ah, my friend," answered Seleucus, "would to heaven any means, human or divine, could but convert his present passion to that; it would be well for me to part not only with Stratonice, but with my empire, to save Antiochus." This he said with the greatest passion, shedding tears as he spoke; upon which Erasistratus, taking him by the hand, replied, "In that case, you have no need of Erasistratus; for you, who are the husband, the father, and the king, are the proper physician for your own family."

Seleucus, accordingly, summoning a general assembly of his people, declared to them, that he had resolved to make Antiochus king, and Stratonice queen, of all the provinces of Upper Asia, uniting them in marriage; telling them, that he thought he had sufficient power over the prince's will that he should find in him no repugnance to obey his commands; and for Stratonice, he hoped all his friends would endeavour to make her sensible, if she should manifest any reluctance to such a marriage, that she ought to esteem those things just and honourable which had been determined upon by the king as necessary to the general good. In this manner, we are told, was brought about the marriage of Antiochus and Stratonice.

To return to the affairs of Demetrius. Having obtained the crown of Macedon, he presently became master of Thessaly, also. And holding the greatest part of Peloponnesus, and, on this side of the Isthmus, the cities of Megara and Athens, he now turned his arms against the Bœotians. They at first made overtures for an accommodation; but Cleonymus of Sparta having ventured with some troops to their assistance, and having made his way into Thebes, and Pisis, the Thespian, who was their first man in power and reputation, animating them to make a brave resistance, they broke off the treaty. No sooner, however, had Demetrius begun to approach the walls with his engines, but Cleonymus in affright secretly withdrew; and the Bœotians, finding themselves abandoned, made their submission. Demetrius placed a garrison in charge of their towns, and, having raised a large sum of money from them, he placed Hieronymus, the historian, in the office of governor and military commander over them, and was thought on the whole to have shown great clemency, more particularly to Pisis, to whom he did no hurt, but spoke with him courteously and kindly, and made him chief magistrate of Thespiæ.

Not long after, Lysimachus was taken prisoner by Dromichætes, and Demetrius went off instantly in the hopes of possessing himself of Thrace, thus left without a king. Upon this, the Bœotians revolted again, and news also came that Lysimachus had regained his liberty. So Demetrius, turning back quickly and in anger, found on coming up that his son Antigonus had already defeated the Bœotians in battle, and therefore proceeded to lay siege again to Thebes.

But understanding that Pyrrhus had made an incursion into Thessaly, and that he was advanced as far as Thermopylæ, leaving Antigonus to continue the siege, he marched with the rest of his army to oppose this enemy. Pyrrhus, however, made a quick retreat. So, leaving ten thousand foot and a thousand horse for the protection of Thessaly, he returned to the siege of Thebes, and there brought up his famous *City-taker* to the attack, which, however, was so laboriously and so slowly moved on account of its bulk and heaviness, that in two months it did not advance two furlongs.

In the meantime the citizens made a stout defence, and Demetrius, out of heat and contentiousness very often, more than upon any necessity, sent his soldiers into danger; until at last Antigonus, observing how many men were losing their lives, said to him, "Why, my father, do we go on letting the men be wasted in this way without any need of it?" But Demetrius, in a great passion, interrupted him, "And you, good sir, why do you afflict yourself for the matter? Will dead men come to you for rations?" But that the soldiers might see that he valued his own life at no dearer rate than theirs, he exposed himself freely, and was wounded with a javelin through his neck, which put him into great hazard of his life. But, notwithstanding, he continued the siege, and in conclusion took the town again. And after his entrance, when the citizens were in fear and trembling, and expected all the severities which an incensed conqueror could inflict, he only put to death thirteen and banished some few others, pardoning all the rest. Thus the city of Thebes, which had not yet been ten years restored, in that short space was twice besieged and taken.

Shortly after, the festival of the Pythian Apollo was to be celebrated, and the Ætolians having blocked up all the passages to Delphi, Demetrius held the games and celebrated the feast at Athens, alleging there was great reason those honours should be paid in that place, Apollo being the paternal god of the Athenian people, and the reputed first founder of their race.

From thence Demetrius returned to Macedon, and as he not only was of a restless temper himself, but saw also that the Macedonians were ever the best subjects when employed in military expeditions, but turbulent and desirous of change in the idleness of peace, he led them against the Ætolians, and, having wasted their country, he left Pantauchus with a great part of his army to complete the conquest, and with the rest he marched in person to find out Pyrrhus, who in like manner was advancing to encounter him. But so it fell out, that by taking different ways the two armies did not meet; but whilst Demetrius entered Epirus, and laid all waste before him, Pyrrhus fell upon Pantauchus, and in a battle in which the two commanders met in person and wounded each other, he gained the victory, and took five thousand prisoners, besides great numbers slain in the field.

The worst thing, however, for Demetrius was that Pyrrhus had excited less animosity as an enemy than admiration as a brave man. His taking so large a part with his own hand in the battle had gained him the greatest name and glory among the Macedonians. Many among them began to say that this was the only king in whom there was any likeness to be seen of the great Alexander's courage; the other kings, and particularly Demetrius, did nothing but personate him, like actors on a stage, in his pomp and outward majesty. And Demetrius truly was a perfect play and pageant, with his robes and diadems, his gold-edged purple and his hats with double streamers, his very shoes being of the richest purple felt, embroidered over in gold. One robe in particular, a most superb piece of work, was long in the loom in preparation for him, in which was to be wrought the representation of the universe and the celestial bodies. This, left unfinished when his reverse overtook him, not any one of the kings of Macedon, his successors, though divers of them haughty enough, ever presumed to use.

But it was not this theatric pomp alone which disgusted the Macedonians, but his profuse and luxurious way of living; and, above all, the difficulty of speaking with him or of obtaining access to his presence. For either he would not be seen at all, or, if he did give audience, he was violent and overbearing. Thus he made the envoys of the Athenians, to whom yet he was more attentive than to all the other Grecians, wait two whole years before they could obtain a hearing. And when the Lacedæmonians sent a single person on an embassy to him, he held himself insulted, and asked angrily whether it was the fact that the Lacedæmonians had sent but one ambassador. "Yes," was the happy reply he received, "one ambassador to one king."

Once when in some apparent fit of a more popular and acceptable temper he was riding abroad, a number of people came up and presented their written petitions. He courteously received all these, and put them up in the skirt of his cloak, while the poor people were overjoyed, and followed him close. But when he came upon the bridge of the river Axius, shaking out his cloak, he threw all into the river. This excited very bitter resentment among the Macedonians, who felt themselves to be not governed, but insulted. They called to mind what some of them had seen, and others had heard related of King Philip's unambitious and open, accessible manners. One day when an old woman had assailed him several times in the road, and importuned him to hear her after he had told her he had no time, "If so," cried she, "you have no time to be a king." And this reprimand so stung the king that, after thinking of it a while, he went back into the house, and setting all other matters apart, for several days together he did nothing else but receive, beginning with the old woman, the complaints of all that would come. And to do justice, truly enough, might well be called a king's first business.

"Mars," as says Timotheus, "is the tyrant"; but Law, in Pindar's words, the king of all. Homer does not say that kings received at the hands of Jove besieging engines or ships of war, but sentences of justice, to keep and observe; nor is it the most warlike, unjust, and murderous, but the most righteous of kings, that has from him the name of Jupiter's "familiar friend" and scholar. Demetrius's delight was the title most unlike the choice of the king of gods. The divine names were those of the Defender and Keeper, his was that of the Besieger of Cities. The place of virtue was given by him to that which, had he not been as ignorant as he was powerful, he would have known to be vice, and honour by his act was associated with crime.

While he lay dangerously ill at Pella, Pyrrhus pretty nearly overran all Macedon, and advanced as far as the city of Edessa. On recovering his health, he quickly drove him out, and came to terms with him, being desirous not to employ his time in a string of petty local conflicts with a neighbour, when all his thoughts were fixed upon another design. This was no less than to endeavour the recovery of the whole empire which his father had possessed; and his preparations were suitable to his hopes and the greatness of the enterprise. He had arranged for the levying of ninety-eight thousand foot and nearly twelve thousand horse; and he had a fleet of five hundred galleys on the stocks, some building at Athens, others at Corinth and Chalcis, and in the neighbourhood of Pella. And he himself was passing evermore from one to another of these places, to give his directions and his assistance to the plans, while all that saw were amazed, not so much at the number, as at the magnitude of the works. Hitherto, there had never been seen a galley with fifteen or sixteen ranges of oars.

At a later time, Ptolemy Philopator built one of forty rows, which was two hundred and eighty cubits in length and the height of her to the top of her stern, forty-eight cubits; she had four hundred sailors and four thousand rowers, and afforded room besides for very near three thousand soldiers to fight on her decks. But this, after all, was for show, and not for service, scarcely differing from a fixed edifice ashore, and was not to be moved without extreme toil and peril; whereas these galleys of Demetrius were meant quite as much for fighting as for looking at, were not the less serviceable for their magnificence, and were as wonderful for their speed and general performance as for their size.

These mighty preparations against Asia, the like of which had not been made since Alexander first invaded it, united Seleucus, Ptolemy, and Lysimachus in a confederacy for their defence. They also despatched ambassadors to Pyrrhus, to persuade him to make a diversion by attacking Macedonia; he need not think there was any validity in a treaty which Demetrius had concluded, not as an engagement to be at peace with him, but as a means for enabling himself to make war first upon the enemy of his choice. So when Pyrrhus accepted their proposals, Demetrius, still in the midst of his preparations, was encompassed with war on all sides. Ptolemy, with a mighty navy, invaded Greece; Lysimachus entered Macedonia upon the side of Thrace, and Pyrrhus, from the Epirot border, both of them spoiling and wasting the country.

Demetrius, leaving his son to look after Greece, marched to the relief of Macedon, and first of all to oppose Lysimachus. On his way, he received the news that Pyrrhus had taken the city Berœa; and the report quickly getting out among the soldiers, all discipline at once was lost, and the camp was filled with lamentations and tears, anger and execrations on Demetrius; they would stay no longer, they would march off, as they said, to take care of their country, friends, and families; but in reality the intention was to revolt to Lysimachus. Demetrius, therefore, thought it his business to keep them as far away as he could from

Lysimachus, who was their own countryman, and for Alexander's sake kindly looked upon by many; they would be ready to fight with Pyrrhus, a new comer and a foreigner, whom they could hardly prefer to himself.

But he found himself under a great mistake in these conjectures. For when he advanced and pitched his camp near, the old admiration for Pyrrhus's gallantry in arms revived again; and as they had been used from time immemorial to suppose that the best king was he that was the bravest soldier, so now they were also told of his generous usage of his prisoners, and, in short, they were eager to have any one in the place of Demetrius, and well pleased that the man should be Pyrrhus. At first, some straggling parties only deserted, but in a little time the whole army broke out into a universal mutiny, insomuch that at last some of them went up and told him openly that if he consulted his own safety he were best to make haste to be gone, for that the Macedonians were resolved no longer to hazard their lives for the satisfaction of his luxury and pleasure. And this was thought fair and moderate language, compared with the fierceness of the rest. So, withdrawing into his tent, and, like an actor rather than a real king, laying aside his stage-robes of royalty, he put on some common clothes and stole away.

He was no sooner gone but the mutinous army were fighting and quarrelling for the plunder of his tent, but Pyrrhus, coming immediately, took possession of the camp without a blow, after which he, with Lysimachus, parted the realm of Macedon betwixt them, after Demetrius had securely held it just seven years.

As for Demetrius, being thus suddenly despoiled of everything, he retired to Cassandrea. His wife Phila, in the passion of her grief, could not endure to see her hapless husband reduced to the condition of a private and banished man. She refused to entertain any further hope, and resolving to quit a fortune which was never permanent except for calamity, took poison and died. Demetrius, determining still to hold on by the wreck, went off to Greece, and collected his friends and officers there. Menelaus, in the play of Sophocles, to give an image of his vicissitudes of estate, says—

For me, my destiny, alas, is found
Whirling upon the gods' swift wheel around,
And changing still, and as the moon's fair frame
Cannot continue for two nights the same,

But out of shadow first a crescent shows,
Thence into beauty and perfection grows,
And when the form of plenitude it wears,
Dwindles again, and wholly disappears.

The simile is yet truer of Demetrius and the phases of his fortunes, now on the increase, presently on the wane, now filling up and now falling away. And so, at this time of apparent entire obscuration and extinction, his light again shone out, and accessions of strength, little by little, came in to fulfil once more the measure of his hope. At first he showed himself in the garb of a private man, and went about the cities without any of the badges of a king. One who saw him at Thebes applied to him, not inaptly, the lines of Euripides—

Humbled to man, laid by the godhead's pride,
He comes to Dirce and Ismenus's side.

But ere long his expectations had re-entered the royal track, and he began once more to have about him the body and form of empire. The Thebans received back, as his gift, their ancient constitution. The Athenians had deserted him. They displaced Diphilus, who was that year the priest of the two Tutelar Deities, and restored the archons, as of old, to mark the year; and on hearing that Demetrius was not so weak as they had expected, they sent into Macedonia to beg the protection of Pyrrhus. Demetrius, in anger, marched to Athens, and laid close siege to the city. In this distress, they sent out to him Crates the philosopher, a person of authority and reputation, who succeeded so far that, what with his entreaties and the solid reasons which he offered, Demetrius was persuaded to raise the siege; and, collecting all his ships, he embarked a force of eleven thousand men with cavalry, and sailed away to Asia, to Caria and Lydia, to take those provinces from Lysimachus.

Arriving at Miletus, he was met there by Eurydice, the sister of Phila, who brought along with her Ptolemais, one of her daughters by King Ptolemy, who had before been affianced to Demetrius, and with whom he now consummated his marriage. Immediately after, he proceeded to carry out his project, and was so fortunate in the beginning that many cities revolted to him; others, as particularly Sardis, he took by force; and some generals of Lysimachus, also, came over to him with troops and money. But when Agathocles, the son of Lysimachus, arrived with an army, he retreated into Phrygia, with an intention to pass into Armenia, believing that, if he could once plant his foot in Armenia, he might set Media in revolt, and gain a position in Upper Asia, where a fugitive commander might find a hundred ways of evasion and escape.

Agathocles pressed hard upon him, and many skirmishes and conflicts occurred, in which Demetrius had still the advantage; but Agathocles straitened him much in his forage, and his men showed a great dislike to his purpose, which they suspected, of carrying them far away into Armenia and Media. Famine also pressed upon them, and some mistake occurred in their passage of the river Lycus, in consequence of which a large number were swept away and drowned. Still, however, they could pass their jests, and one of them fixed upon Demetrius's tent-door a paper with the first verse, slightly altered, of the *Œdipus*:—

Child of the blind old man, Antigonus,
Into what country are you bringing us?

But at last, pestilence, as is usual when armies are driven to such necessities as to subsist upon any food they can get, began to assail them as well as famine. So that, having lost eight thousand of his men, with the rest he retreated and came to Tarsus, and because that city was within the dominions of Seleucus, he was anxious to prevent any plundering, and wished to give no sort of offence to Seleucus. But when he perceived it was impossible to restrain the soldiers in their extreme necessity, Agathocles also having blocked up all the avenues of Mount Taurus, he wrote a letter to Seleucus, bewailing first all his own sad fortunes, and proceeding with entreaties and supplications for some compassion on his part towards one nearly connected with him, who was fallen into such calamities as might extort tenderness and pity from his very enemies.

These letters so far moved Seleucus, that he gave orders to the governors of those provinces that they should furnish Demetrius with all things suitable to his royal rank, and with sufficient provisions for his troops. But Patrocles, a person whose judgment was greatly valued, and who was a friend highly trusted by Seleucus, pointed out to him that the expense of maintaining such a body of soldiers was the least important consideration, but that it was contrary to all policy to let Demetrius stay in the country, since he, of all the kings of his time, was the most violent, and most addicted to daring enterprises; and he was now in a condition which might tempt persons of the greatest temper and moderation to unlawful and desperate attempts.

Seleucus, excited by this advice, moved with a powerful army towards Cilicia; and Demetrius, astonished at this sudden alteration, betook himself for safety to the most inaccessible places of Mount Taurus; from whence he sent envoys to Seleucus, to request from him that he would permit him the liberty to settle with his army somewhere among the independent barbarian tribes, where he might be able to make himself a petty king, and end his life without further travel and hardship; or, if he refused him this, at any rate to give his troops food during the winter, and not expose him in this distressed and naked condition to the fury of his enemies.

But Seleucus, whose jealousy made him put an ill-construction on all he said, sent him answer, that he would permit him to stay two months and no longer in Cataonia, provided he presently sent him the principal of his friends as hostages for his departure then; and, in the meantime, he fortified all the passages into Syria. So that Demetrius, who saw himself thus, like a wild beast, in the way to be encompassed on all sides in the toils, was driven in desperation to his defence, overran the country, and in several engagements in which Seleucus attacked him, had the advantage of him. Particularly, when he was once assailed by the scythed chariots, he successfully avoided the charge and routed his assailants, and then, expelling the troops that were in guard of the passes, made himself master of the roads leading into Syria. And now, elated himself, and finding his soldiers also animated by these successes, he was resolved to push ahead, and to have one deciding blow for the empire with Seleucus; who indeed was in considerable anxiety and distress, being averse to any assistance from Lysimachus, whom he both mistrusted and feared, and shrinking from a battle with Demetrius, whose desperation he knew, and whose fortune he had so often seen suddenly pass from the lowest to the highest.

But Demetrius, in the meanwhile, was taken with a violent sickness, from which he suffered extremely himself, and which ruined all his prospects. His men deserted to the enemy, or dispersed. At last, after forty days, he began to be so far recovered as to be able to rally his remaining forces, and marched as if he directly designed for Cilicia; but in the night, raising his camp without sound of trumpet, he took a countermarch, and, passing the mountain Amanus, he ravaged all the lower country as far as Cyrrhestica.

Upon this, Seleucus advancing towards him

and encamping at no great distance, Demetrius set his troops in motion to surprise him by night. And almost to the last moment Seleucus knew nothing, and was lying asleep. Some deserter came with the tidings just so soon that he had time to leap, in great consternation, out of bed, and give the alarm to his men. And as he was putting on his boots to mount his horse, he bade the officers about him look well to it, for they had to meet a furious and terrible wild beast. But Demetrius, by the noise he heard in the camp, finding they had taken the alarm, drew off his troops in haste. With the morning's return he found Seleucus pressing hard upon him; so, sending one of his officers against the other wing, he defeated those that were opposed to himself. But Seleucus, lighting from his horse, pulling off his helmet, and taking a target, advanced to the foremost ranks of the mercenary soldiers, and, showing them who he was, bade them come over and join him, telling them that it was for their sakes only that he had so long forborne coming to extremities. And thereupon, without a blow more, they saluted Seleucus as their king and passed over.

Demetrius, who felt that this was his last change of fortune, and that he had no more vicissitudes to expect, fled to the passes of Amanus, where, with a very few friends and followers, he threw himself into a dense forest, and there waited for the night, purposing, if possible, to make his escape towards Caunus, where he hoped to find his shipping ready to transport him. But upon inquiry, finding that they had not provisions even for that one day, he began to think of some other project. Whilst he was yet in doubt, his friend Sosigenes arrived, who had four hundred pieces of gold about him, and, with this relief, he again entertained hopes of being able to reach the coast, and, as soon as it began to be dark, set forward towards the passes.

But, perceiving by the fires that the enemies had occupied them, he gave up all thought of that road, and retreated to his old station in the wood, but not with all his men; for some had deserted, nor were those that remained as willing as they had been. One of them, in fine, ventured to speak out, and say that Demetrius had better give himself up to Seleucus; which Demetrius overhearing, drew out his sword, and would have passed it through his body, but that some of his friends interposed and prevented the attempt, persuading him to do as had been said. So at last he gave way, and sent

to Seleucus, to surrender himself at discretion.

Seleucus, when he was told of it, said it was not Demetrius's good fortune that had found out this means for his safety, but his own, which had added to his other honours the opportunity of showing his clemency and generosity. And forthwith he gave order to his domestic officers to prepare a royal pavilion, and all things suitable to give him a splendid reception and entertainment. There was in the attendance of Seleucus one Apollonides, who formerly had been intimate with Demetrius. He was, therefore, as the fittest person, despatched from the king to meet Demetrius, that he might feel himself more at his ease, and might come with the confidence of being received as a friend and relative. No sooner was this message known, but the courtiers and officers, some few at first, and afterwards almost the whole of them, thinking Demetrius would presently become of great power with the king, hurried off, vying who should be foremost to pay him their respects. The effect of which was that compassion was converted into jealousy, and ill-natured, malicious people could the more easily insinuate to Seleucus that he was giving way to an unwise humanity, the very first sight of Demetrius having been the occasion of a dangerous excitement in the army.

So, whilst Apollonides, in great delight, and after him many others, were relating to Demetrius the kind expressions of Seleucus, and he, after so many troubles and calamities, if indeed he had still any sense of his surrender of himself being a disgrace, had now, in confidence on the good hopes held out to him, entirely forgotten all such thoughts, Pausanias with a guard of a thousand horse and foot came and surrounded him; and, dispersing the rest that were with him, carried him not to the presence of Seleucus, but to the Syrian Chersonese, where he was committed to the safe custody of a strong guard. Sufficient attendance and liberal provisions were here allowed him, space for riding and walking, a park with game for hunting, those of his friends and companions in exile who wished it had permission to see him, and messages of kindness, also, from time to time, were brought him from Seleucus, bidding him fear nothing, and intimating that, as soon as Antiochus and Stratonice should arrive, he would receive his liberty.

Demetrius, however, finding himself in this condition, sent letters to those who were with his son, and to his captains and friends at Athens and Corinth, that they should give no manner of credit to any letters written to them in his name, though they were sealed with his own signet, but that, looking upon him as if he were already dead, they should maintain the cities and whatever was left of his power for Antigonus, as his successor. Antigonus received the news of his father's captivity with great sorrow; he put himself into mourning and wrote letters to the rest of the kings, and to Seleucus himself, making entreaties, and offering not only to surrender whatever they had left, but himself to be a hostage for his father. Many cities also and princes joined in interceding for him; only Lysimachus sent and offered a large sum of money to Seleucus to take away his life. But he, who had always shown his aversion to Lysimachus before, thought him only the greater barbarian and monster for it. Nevertheless, he still protracted the time, reserving the favour, as he professed, for the intercession of Antiochus and Stratonice.

Demetrius, who had sustained the first stroke of his misfortune, in time grew so familiar with it, that, by continuance, it became easy. At first he persevered one way or other in taking exercise, in hunting, so far as he had means, and in riding. Little by little, however, after a while, he let himself grow indolent and indisposed for them, and took to dice and drinking, in which he passed most of his time, whether it were to escape the thoughts of his present condition, with which he was haunted when sober, and to drown reflection in drunkenness, or that he acknowledged to himself that this was the real happy life he had long desired and wished for, and had foolishly let himself be seduced away from it by a senseless and vain ambition, which had only brought trouble to himself and others; that highest good which he had thought to obtain by arms and fleets and soldiers he had now discovered unexpectedly in idleness, leisure, and repose. As, indeed, what other end or period is there of all the wars and dangers which hapless princes run into, whose misery and folly it is, not merely that they make luxury and pleasure, instead of virtue and excellence, the object of their lives, but that they do not so much as know where this luxury and pleasure are to be found?

Having thus continued three years a pris-

oner in Chersonesus, for want of exercise, and by indulging himself in eating and drinking, he fell into a disease, of which he died at the age of fifty-four. Seleucus was ill spoken of, and was himself greatly grieved, that he had yielded so far to his suspicions, and had let himself be so much outdone by the barbarian Dromichætes of Thrace, who had shown so much humanity and such a kingly temper in his treatment of his prisoner Lysimachus.

There was something dramatic and theatrical in the very funeral ceremonies with which Demetrius was honoured. For his son Antigonus, understanding that his remains were coming over from Syria, went with all his fleet to the islands to meet them. They were there presented to him in a golden urn, which he placed in his largest admiral galley. All the cities where they touched in their passage sent chaplets to adorn the urn, and deputed certain of their citizens to follow in mourning, to assist at the funeral solemnity. When the fleet approached the harbour of Corinth, the urn, covered with purple, and a royal diadem upon it, was visible upon the poop, and a troop of young men attended in arms to receive it at landing. Xenophantus, the most famous musician of the day, played on the flute his most solemn measure, to which the rowers, as the ship came in, made loud response, their oars, like the funeral beating of the breast, keeping time with the cadences of the music. But Antigonus, in tears and mourning attire, excited among the spectators gathered on the shore the greatest sorrow and compassion. After crowns and other honours had been offered at Corinth, the remains were conveyed to Demetrias, a city to which Demetrius had given his name, peopled from the inhabitants of the small villages of Iolcus.

Demetrius left no other children by his wife Phila but Antigonus and Stratonice, but he had two other sons, both of his own name, one surnamed the Thin, by an Illyrian mother, and one who ruled in Cyrene, by Ptolemais. He had also, by Deidamia, a son, Alexander, who lived and died in Egypt; and there are some who say that he had a son by Eurydice, named Corrhabus. His family was continued in a succession of kings down to Perseus, the last, from whom the Romans took Macedonia.

And now, the Macedonian drama being ended, let us prepare to see the Roman.

ANTONY

83?-30 B.C.

THE grandfather of Antony was the famous pleader, whom Marius put to death for having taken part with Sulla. His father was Antony, surnamed of Crete, not very famous or distinguished in public life, but a worthy good man, and particularly remarkable for his liberality, as may appear from a single example. He was not very rich, and was for that reason checked in the exercise of his good nature by his wife. A friend that stood in need of money came to borrow of him. Money he had none, but he bade a servant bring him water in a silver basin, with which, when it was brought, he wetted his face, as if he meant to shave, and, sending away the servant upon another errand, gave his friend the basin, desiring him to turn it to his purpose. And when there was, afterwards, a great inquiry for it in the house, and his wife was in a very ill humour, and was going to put the servants one by one to the search, he acknowledged what he had done, and begged her pardon.

His wife was Julia, of the family of the Cæsars, who, for her discretion and fair behaviour, was not inferior to any of her time. Under her, Antony received his education, she being, after the death of his father, remarried to Cornelius Lentulus, who was put to death by Cicero for having been of Catiline's conspiracy. This, probably, was the first ground and occasion of that mortal grudge that Antony bore Cicero. He says, even, that the body of Lentulus was denied burial, till, by application made to Cicero's wife, it was granted to Julia. But this seems to be a manifest error, for none of those that suffered in the consulate of Cicero had the right of burial denied them.

Antony grew up a very beautiful youth, but by the worst of misfortunes, he fell into the acquaintance and friendship of Curio, a man abandoned to his pleasures, who, to make Antony's dependence upon him a matter of greater necessity, plunged him into a life of drinking and dissipation, and led him through a course of such extravagance that he ran, at that early age, into debt to the amount of two hundred and fifty talents. For this sum Curio became his surety; on hearing which, the elder Curio, his father, drove Antony out of his house. After this, for some short time he took part with Clodius, the most insolent and outrageous demagogue of the time, in his course of violence and disorder; but getting weary, before long, of his madness, and apprehensive of the powerful party forming against him, he left Italy and travelled into Greece, where he spent his time in military exercises and in the study of eloquence. He took most to what was called the Asiatic taste in speaking, which was then at its height, and was, in many ways, suitable to his ostentations, vaunting temper, full of empty flourishes and unsteady efforts for glory.

After some stay in Greece, he was invited by Gabinius, who had been consul, to make a campaign with him in Syria, which at first he refused, not being willing to serve in a private character, but receiving a commission to command the horse, he went along with him. His first service was against Aristobulus, who had prevailed with the Jews to rebel. Here he was himself the first man to scale the largest of the works, and beat Aristobulus out of all of them; after which he routed, in a pitched battle, an army many times over the number of his, killed almost all of them and took Aristobulus and his son prisoners. This war ended, Gabinius was solicited by Ptolemy to restore him to his kingdom of Egypt, and a promise made of ten thousand talents reward. Most of the officers were against this enterprise, and Gabinius himself did not much like it, though sorely tempted by the ten thousand talents.

But Antony, desirous of brave actions, and willing to please Ptolemy, joined in persuading Gabinius to go. And whereas all were of opinion that the most dangerous thing before them was the march to Pelusium, in which they would have to pass over a deep sand, where no fresh water was to be hoped for, along the Acregma and the Serbonian marsh (which the Egyptians call Typhon's breathing-hole, and which is, in probability, water left behind by, or making its way through from, the Red Sea, which is here divided from the Mediterranean by a narrow isthmus), Antony, being ordered thither with the horse, not only made himself master of the passes, but won Pelusium itself, a great city, took the garrison prisoners, and by this means rendered the march secure to the army, and the way to victory not difficult for the general to pursue. The enemy also reaped some benefit of his eagerness for honour. For when Ptolemy, after he had entered Pelusium, in his rage and spite against the Egyptians, designed to put them to the sword, Antony withstood him, and hindered the execution.

In all the great and frequent skirmishes and battles he gave continual proofs of his personal valour and military conduct; and once in particular, by wheeling about and attacking the rear of the enemy, he gave the victory to the assailants in the front, and received for this service signal marks of distinction. Nor was his humanity towards the deceased Archelaus less taken notice of. He had been formerly his guest and acquaintance, and, as he was now compelled, he fought him bravely while alive, but on his death, sought out his body and buried it with royal honours. The consequence was that he left behind him a great name among the Alexandrians, and all who were serving in the Roman army looked upon him as a most gallant soldier.

He had also a very good and noble appearance; his beard was well grown, his forehead large, and his nose aquiline, giving him altogether a bold, masculine look that reminded people of the faces of Hercules in paintings and sculptures. It was, moreover, an ancient tradition, that the Antonys were descended from Hercules, by a son of his called Anton; and this opinion he thought to give credit to by the similarity of his person just mentioned, and also by the fashion of his dress. For, whenever he had to appear before large numbers, he wore his tunic girt low about the hips, a broadsword on his side, and over all a large coarse mantle. What might seem to some very insupportable, his vaunting, his raillery, his drinking in public, sitting down by the men as they were taking their food, and eating, as he stood, off the common soldiers' tables, made him the delight and pleasure of the army. In love affairs, also, he was very agreeable: he gained many friends by the assistance he gave them in theirs, and took other people's raillery upon his own with good-humour.

And his generous ways, his open and lavish hand in gifts and favours to his friends and fellow-soldiers, did a great deal for him in his first advance to power, and after he had become great, long maintained his fortunes, when a thousand follies were hastening their overthrow. One instance of his liberality I must relate. He had ordered payment to one of his friends of twenty-five myriads of money or *decies,* as the Romans call it, and his steward, wondering at the extravagance of the sum, laid all the silver in a heap, as he should pass by. Antony, seeing the heap, asked what it meant; his steward replied, "The money you have ordered to be given to your friend." So, perceiving the man's malice, said he, "I thought the *decies* had been much more; 'tis too little; let it be doubled." This, however, was at a later time.

When the Roman state finally broke up into two hostile factions, the aristocratical party joining Pompey, who was in the city, and the popular side seeking help from Cæsar, who was at the head of an army in Gaul, Curio, the friend of Antony, having changed his party and devoted himself to Cæsar, brought over Antony also to his service. And the influence which he gained with the people by his eloquence and by the money which was supplied by Cæsar, enabled him to make Antony, first, tribune of the people, and then, augur.

Antony's accession to office was at once of the greatest advantage to Cæsar. In the first place, he resisted the consul Marcellus, who was putting under Pompey's orders the troops who were already collected, and was giving him power to raise new levies; he, on the other hand, making an order that they should be sent into Syria to reinforce Bibulus, who was making war with the Parthians, and that no one should give in his name to serve under Pompey. Next, when the senators would not suffer Cæsar's letters to be received or read in the senate, by virtue of his office he read them publicly, and succeeded so well, that many were brought to change their mind; Cæsar's demands, as they appeared in what he wrote, being but just and reasonable. At length, two questions being put in the senate, the one, whether Pompey should dismiss his army, the other, if Cæsar his, some were for the former, for the latter all, except some few, when Antony stood up and put the question, if it would be agreeable to them that both Pompey and Cæsar should dismiss their armies. This proposal met with the greatest approval, they gave him loud acclamations, and called for it to be put to the vote.

But when the consuls would not have it so, Cæsar's friends again made some few offers, very fair and equitable, but were strongly opposed by Cato, and Antony himself was commanded to leave the senate by the consul Lentulus. So, leaving them with execrations, and disguising himself in a servant's dress, hiring a carriage with Quintus Cassius, he went straight away to Cæsar, declaring at once, when they reached the camp, that affairs at Rome were conducted without any order or justice, that the privilege of speaking in the senate was denied the tribunes, and that he who spoke for common fair dealing was driven out and in danger of his life.

Upon this, Cæsar set his army in motion, and marched into Italy; and for this reason it is that Cicero writes in his Philippics that Antony was as much the cause of the civil war as Helen was of the Trojan. But this is but a calumny. For Cæsar was not of so slight or weak a temper as to suffer himself to be carried away by the indignation of the moment, into a civil war with his country, upon the sight of Antony and Cassius seeking refuge in his camp meanly dressed and in a hired carriage, without ever having thought of it or taken any such resolution long before. This was to him, who wanted a pretence of declaring war, a fair and plausible occasion; but the true motive that led him was the same that formerly led Alexander and Cyrus against all mankind, the unquenchable thirst of empire, and the distracted ambition of being the greatest man in the world, which was impracticable for him, unless Pompey were put down.

So soon, then, as he had advanced and occupied Rome, and driven Pompey out of Italy, he proposed first to go against the legions that Pompey had in Spain, and then cross over and follow him with the fleet that should be prepared during his absence, in the meantime leaving the government of Rome to Lepidus, as prætor, and the command of the troops and of Italy to Antony, as tribune of the people. Antony was not long in getting the hearts of the soldiers, joining with them in their exercises, and for the most part living amongst them and making them presents to the utmost of his abilities; but with all others he was unpopular enough. He was too lazy to pay attention to the complaints of persons who were injured; he listened impatiently to petitions; and he had an ill name for familiarity with other people's wives. In short, the government of Cæsar (which, so far as he was concerned himself, had the appearance of anything rather than a tyranny) got a bad repute through his friends. And of these friends, Antony, as he had the largest trust, and committed the greatest errors, was thought the most deeply in fault.

Cæsar, however, at his return from Spain, overlooked the charges against him, and had no reason ever to complain, in the employments he gave him in the war, of any want of courage, energy, or military skill. He himself, going aboard at Brundusium, sailed over the Ionian Sea with a few troops and sent back the vessels with orders to Antony and Gabinius to embark the army, and come over with all speed to Macedonia. Gabinius, having no mind to put to sea in the rough, dangerous weather of the winter season, was for marching the army round by the long land route.

Antony, however, being more afraid lest Cæsar might suffer from the number of his enemies, who pressed him hard, beat back Libo, who was watching with a fleet at the mouth of the haven of Brundusium, by attacking his galleys with a number of small boats, and gaining thus an opportunity, put on board twenty thousand foot and eight hundred horse, and so set out to sea. And, being espied by the enemy and pursued, from this danger he was rescued by a strong south wind, which sprang up and raised so high a sea that the enemy's galleys could make little way. But his own ships were driving before it upon a lee shore of cliffs and rocks running sheer to the water, where there was no hope of escape, when all of a sudden the wind turned about to southwest, and blew from land to the main sea, where Antony, now sailing in security, saw the coast all covered with the wreck of the enemy's fleet. For hither the galleys in pursuit had been carried by the gale, and not a few of them dashed to pieces. Many men and much property fell into Antony's hands; he took also the town of Lissus, and, by the seasonable arrival of so large a reinforcement, gave Cæsar great encouragement.

There was not one of the many engagements that now took place one after another in which he did not signalise himself; twice he stopped the army in its full flight, led them back to a charge, and gained the victory. So that not without reason his reputation, next to Cæsar's, was greatest in the army. And what opinion Cæsar himself had of him well appeared when, for the final battle in Pharsalia, which was to determine everything, he himself chose to lead the right wing, committing the charge of the left to Antony, as to the best officer of all that served under him. After the battle, Cæsar, being created dictator, went in pursuit of Pompey, and sent Antony to Rome, with the character of Master of the Horse, who is in office and power next to the dictator, when present, and in his absence the first, and pretty nearly indeed the sole magistrate. For on the appointment of a dictator, with the one exception of the tribunes, all other magistrates cease to exercise any authority in Rome.

Dolabella, however, who was tribune, being a young man and eager for change, was now for bringing in a general measure for cancelling debts, and wanted Antony, who was his friend, and forward enough to promote any popular project, to take part with him in this step. Asinius and Trebellius were of the contrary opinion, and it so happened, at the same time, Antony was crossed by a terrible suspicion that Dolabella was too familiar with his wife; and in great trouble at this, he parted with her (she being his cousin, and daughter to Caius Antonius, colleague of Cicero), and, taking part with Asinius, came to open hostilities with Dolabella, who had seized on the Forum, intending to pass his law by force.

Antony, backed by a vote of the senate that Dolabella should be put down by force of arms, went down and attacked him, killing some of his, and losing some of his own men; and by this action lost his favour with the commonalty, while with the better class and with all well-conducted people his general course of life made him, as Cicero says, absolutely odious, utter disgust being excited by his drinking bouts at all hours, his wild expenses, his gross amours, the day spent in sleeping or walking off his debauches, and the night in banquets and at theatres, and in celebrating the nuptials of some comedian or buffoon. It is related that, drinking all night at the wedding of Hippias, the comedian, on the morning, having to harangue the people, he came forward, overcharged as he was, and vomited before them all, one of his friends holding his gown for him.

Sergius, the player, was one of the friends who could do most with him; also Cytheris, a woman of the same trade, whom he made much of, and who, when he went his progress, accompanied him in a litter, and had her equipage not in anything inferior to his mother's; while every one, moreover, was scandalised at the sight of the golden cups that he took with him, fitter for the ornaments of a procession than the uses of a journey, at his having pavilions set up, and sumptuous morning repasts laid out by river sides and in groves, at his having chariots drawn by lions, and common women and singing girls quartered upon the houses of serious fathers and mothers of families.

It seemed very unreasonable that Cæsar, out of Italy, should lodge in the open field, and, with great fatigue and danger, pursue the remainder of a hazardous war, whilst others, by favour of his authority, should insult the citizens with their impudent luxury. All this appears to have aggravated party quarrels in Rome, and to have encouraged the soldiers in acts of licence and rapacity. And, accordingly, when Cæsar came home, he acquitted Dolabella, and, being created the third time consul, took not Antony, but Lepidus, for his colleague. Pompey's house being offered for sale, Antony bought it, and when the price was demanded of him, loudly complained. This, he tells us himself, and because he thought his former services had not been recompensed as they deserved, made him not follow Cæsar with the army into Libya.

However, Cæsar, by dealing gently with his errors, seems to have succeeded in curing him of a good deal of his folly and extravagance. He gave up his former courses, and took a wife, Fulvia, the widow of Clodius the demagogue, a woman not born for spinning or housewifery, nor one that could be content with ruling a private husband, but prepared to govern a first magistrate, or give orders to a commander-in-chief. So that Cleopatra had great obligations to her for having taught Antony to be so good a servant, he coming to her hands tame and broken into entire obedience to the commands of a mistress. He used to play all sorts of sportive, boyish tricks, to keep Fulvia in good humour. As, for example, when Cæsar, after his victory in Spain, was on his return, Antony, among the rest, went out to meet him; and, a rumour being spread that Cæsar was killed and the enemy marching into Italy, he returned to Rome, and, disguising himself, came to her by night muffled up as a servant that brought letters from Antony. She, with great impatience, before she received the letter, asked if Antony were well, and instead of an answer he gave her the letter; and, as she was opening it, took her about the neck and kissed her.

This little story, of many of the same nature, I give as a specimen.

There was nobody of any rank in Rome that did not go some days' journey to meet Cæsar on his return from Spain; but Antony was the best received of any, admitted to ride the whole journey with him in his carriage, while behind came Brutus Albinus and Octavian, his niece's son, who afterwards bore his name and reigned so long over the Romans. Cæsar being created, the fifth time, consul, without delay chose Antony for his colleague, but designing himself to give up his own consulate to Dolabella, he acquainted the senate with his resolution. But Antony opposed it with all his might, saying much that was bad against Dolabella, and receiving the like language in return, till Cæsar could bear with the indecency no longer, and deferred the matter to another time. Afterwards, when he came before the people to proclaim Dolabella, Antony cried out that the auspices were unfavourable, so that at last Cæsar, much to Dolabella's vexation, yielded and gave it up. And it is credible that Cæsar was about as much disgusted with the one as the other. When some one was accusing them both to him, "It is not," said he, "these well-fed, long-haired men that I fear, but the pale and the hungry-looking"; meaning Brutus and Cassius, by whose conspiracy he afterwards fell.

And the fairest pretext for that conspiracy was furnished, without his meaning it, by Antony himself. The Romans were celebrating their festival, called the Lupercalia, when Cæsar, in his triumphal habit, and seated above the rostra in the marketplace, was a spectator of the sports. The custom is, that many young noblemen and of the magistracy, anointed with oil and having straps of hide in their hands, run about and strike, in sport, at every one they meet. Antony was running with the rest; but, omitting the old ceremony, twining a garland of bay round a diadem, he ran up to the rostra, and, being lifted up by his companions, would have put it upon the head of Cæsar, as if by that ceremony he were declared king. Cæsar seemingly refused, and drew aside to avoid it, and was applauded by the people with great shouts. Again Antony pressed it, and again he declined its acceptance.

And so the dispute between them went on for some time, Antony's solicitations receiving but little encouragement from the shouts of a few friends, and Cæsar's refusal being accompanied with the general applause of the people; a curious thing enough, that they should submit with patience to the fact, and yet at the same time dread the name as the destruction of their liberty. Cæsar, very much discomposed at what had passed, got up from his seat, and, laying bare his neck, said he was ready to receive a stroke, if any one of them desired to give it. The crown was at last put on one of his statues, but was taken down by some of the tribunes, who were followed home by the people with shouts of applause. Cæsar, however, resented it, and deposed them.

These passages gave great encouragement to Brutus and Cassius, who, in making choice of trusty friends for such an enterprise, were thinking to engage Antony. The rest approved, except Trebonius, who told them that Antony and he had lodged and travelled together in the last journey they took to meet Cæsar, and that he had let fall several words, in a cautious way, on purpose to sound him; that Antony very well understood him, but did not encourage it; however, he had said nothing of it to Cæsar, but had kept the secret faithfully. The conspirators then proposed that Antony should die with him, which Brutus would not consent to, insisting that an action undertaken in defence of right and the laws must be maintained unsullied, and pure of injustice. It was settled that Antony, whose bodily strength and high office made him formidable, should, at Cæsar's entrance into the senate, when the deed was to be done, be amused outside by some of the party in a conversation about some pretended business.

So when all was proceeded with, according to their plan, and Cæsar had fallen in the senate-house, Antony, at the first moment, took a servant's dress, and hid himself. But, understanding that the conspirators had assembled in the Capitol, and had no further design upon any one, he persuaded them to come down, giving them his son as a hostage. That night Cassius supped at Antony's house, and Brutus with Lepidus. Antony then convened the senate, and spoke in favour of an act of oblivion, and the appointment of Brutus and Cassius to provinces. These measures the senate passed; and resolved that all Cæsar's acts should remain in force. Thus Antony went out of the senate with the highest possible reputation and esteem; for it was apparent that he had prevented a civil war, and had composed, in the wisest and most statesmanlike way, questions of the greatest difficulty and embarrassment.

But these temperate counsels were soon swept away by the tide of popular applause, and the prospect, if Brutus were overthrown, of being without doubt the ruler-in-chief. As Cæsar's body was conveyed to the tomb, Antony, according to the custom, was making his funeral oration in the market-place, and perceiving the people to be infinitely affected with what he had said, he began to mingle with his praises language of commiseration, and horror at what had happened, and, as he was ending his speech, he took the under-clothes of the dead, and held them up, showing them stains of blood and the holes of the many stabs, calling those that had done this act villains and bloody murderers. All which excited the people to such indignation, that they would not defer the funeral, but, making a pile of tables and forms in the very market-place, set fire to it; and every one, taking a brand, ran to the conspirators' houses to attack them.

Upon this, Brutus and his whole party left the city, and Cæsar's friends joined themselves to Antony. Calpurnia, Cæsar's wife, lodged with him the best part of the property, to the value of four thousand talents; he got also into his hands all Cæsar's papers wherein were contained journals of all he had done, and draughts of what he designed to do, which Antony made good use of; for by this means he appointed what magistrates he pleased, brought whom he would into the senate, recalled some from exile, freed others out of prison, and all this as ordered so by Cæsar. The Romans, in mockery, gave those who were thus benefited the name of Charonites, since, if put to prove their patents, they must have recourse to the papers of the dead. In short, Antony's behaviour in Rome was very absolute, he himself being consul and his two brothers in great place; Caius, the one, being prætor, and Lucius, the other, tribune of the people.

While matters went thus in Rome, the young Cæsar, Cæsar's niece's son, and by testament left his heir, arrived at Rome from Apollonia, where he was when his uncle was killed. The first thing he did was to visit Antony, as his father's friend. He spoke to him concerning the money that was in his hands, and reminded him of the legacy Cæsar had made of seventy-five drachmas to every Roman citizen. Antony, at first, laughing at such discourse from so young a man, told him he wished he were in his health, and that he wanted good counsel and good friends to tell him the burden of being executor to Cæsar would sit very uneasy upon his young shoulders. This was no answer to him; and, when he persisted in demanding the property, Antony went on treating him injuriously both in word and deed, opposed him when he stood for the tribune's office, and, when he was taking steps for the dedication of his father's golden chair, as had been enacted, he threatened to send him to prison if he did not give over soliciting the people. This made the young Cæsar apply himself to Cicero, and all those that hated Antony; by them he was recommended to the senate, while he himself courted the people, and drew together the soldiers from their settlements, till Antony got alarmed, and gave him a meeting in the Capitol, where, after some words, they came to an accommodation.

That night Antony had a very unlucky dream, fancying that his right hand was thunderstruck. And, some few days after, he was informed that Cæsar was plotting to take his life. Cæsar explained, but was not believed, so that the breach was now made as wide as ever; each of them hurried about all through Italy to engage, by great offers, the old soldiers that lay scattered in their settlements, and to be the first to secure the troops that still remained undischarged. Cicero was at this time the man of greatest influence in Rome. He made use of all his art to exasperate the people against Antony, and at length persuaded the senate to declare him a public enemy, to send Cæsar the rods and axes and other marks of honour usually given to prætors, and to issue orders to Hirtius and Pansa, who were the consuls, to drive Antony out of Italy. The armies engaged near Modena, and Cæsar himself was present and took part in the battle. Antony was defeated, but both the consuls were slain. Antony, in his flight, was overtaken by distresses of every kind, and the worst of all of them was famine.

But it was Antony's character in calamities to be better than at any other time. In misfortune, he was most nearly a virtuous man. It is common enough for people, when they fall into great disasters, to discern what is right, and what they ought to do; but there are but few who in such extremities have the strength to obey their judgment, either in doing what it approves or avoiding what it condemns; and a good many are so weak as to give way to their habits all the more, and are incapable of using their minds. Antony, on this occasion, was a most wonderful example to his soldiers. He, who had just quitted so much luxury and sumptuous living, made no difficulty now of drinking foul water and feeding on wild fruits and roots. Nay, it is related they ate the very bark of trees, and, in passing over the Alps, lived upon creatures that no one before had ever been willing to touch.

The design was to join the army on the other side the Alps, commanded by Lepidus, who he imagined would stand his friend, he having done him many good offices with Cæsar. On coming up and encamping near at hand, finding he had no sort of encouragement offered him, he resolved to push his fortune and venture all. His hair was long and disordered, nor had he shaved his beard since his defeat; in this guise, and with a dark coloured cloak flung over him, he came into the trenches of Lepidus, and began to address the army. Some were moved at his habit, others at his words, so that Lepidus, not liking it, ordered the trumpets to sound, that he might be heard no longer. This raised in the soldiers yet a greater pity, so that they resolved to confer secretly with him, and dressed Lælius and Clodius in women's clothes, and sent them to see him. They advised him without delay to attack Lepidus's trenches, assuring him that a strong party would receive him, and, if he wished it, would kill Lepidus.

Antony, however, had no wish for this, but next morning marched his army to pass over the river that parted the two camps. He was himself the first man that stepped in, and, as he went through towards the other bank, he saw Lepidus's soldiers in great numbers reaching out their hands to help him, and beating down the works to make him way. Being entered into the camp, and finding himself absolute master, he nevertheless treated Lepidus with the greatest civility, and gave him the title of Father, when he spoke to him, and though he had everything at his own command, he left him the honour of being called the general. This fair usage brought over to him Munatius Plancus, who was not far off with a considerable force. Thus in great strength he repassed the Alps, leading with him into Italy seventeen legions and ten thousand horse, besides six legions which he left in garrison under the command of Varius, one of his familiar friends and boon companions,

whom they used to call by the nickname of Cotylon.

Cæsar, perceiving that Cicero's wishes were for liberty, had ceased to pay any further regard to him, and was now employing the mediation of his friends to come to a good understanding with Antony. They both met together with Lepidus in a small island, where the conference lasted three days. The empire was soon determined of, it being divided amongst them as if it had been their paternal inheritance. That which gave them all the trouble was to agree who should be put to death, each of them desiring to destroy his enemies and to save his friends. But, in the end, animosity to those they hated carried the day against respect for relations and affection for friends: Cæsar sacrificed Cicero to Antony, Antony gave up his uncle, Lucius Cæsar, and Lepidus received permission to murder his brother Paulus, or, as others say, yielded his brother to them.

I do not believe anything ever took place more truly savage or barbarous than this composition, for, in this exchange of blood for blood, they were equally guilty of the lives they surrendered and of those they took; or, indeed, more guilty in the case of their friends, for whose deaths they had not even the justification of hatred. To complete the reconciliation, the soldiery, coming about them, demanded that confirmation should be given to it by some alliance of marriage: Cæsar should marry Clodia, the daughter of Fulvia, wife to Antony. This also being agreed to, three hundred persons were put to death by proscription.

Antony gave orders to those that were to kill Cicero to cut off his head and right hand, with which he had written his invectives against him; and, when they were brought before him, he regarded them joyfully, actually bursting out more than once into laughter, and, when he had satiated himself with the sight of them, ordered them to be hung up above the speaker's place in the Forum, thinking thus to insult the dead, while in fact he only exposed his own wanton arrogance, and his unworthiness to hold the power that fortune had given him. His uncle, Lucius Cæsar, being closely pursued, took refuge with his sister, who, when the murderers had broken into her house and were pressing into her chamber, met them at the door, and spreading out her hands, cried out several times, "You shall not kill Lucius Cæsar till you first despatch me, who gave your general his birth"; and in this manner she succeeded in getting her brother out of the way, and saving his life.

This triumvirate was very hateful to the Romans, and Antony most of all bore the blame, because he was older than Cæsar, and had greater authority than Lepidus, and withal he was no sooner settled in his affairs, but he turned to his luxurious and dissolute way of living. Besides the ill reputation he gained by his general behaviour, it was some considerable disadvantage to him his living in the house of Pompey the Great, who had been as much admired for his temperance and his sober, citizen-like habits of life, as ever he was for having triumphed three times. They could not without anger see the doors of that house shut against magistrates, officers, and envoys, who were shamefully refused admittance, while it was filled inside with players, jugglers, and drunken flatterers, upon whom were spent the greatest part of the wealth which violence and cruelty procured. For they did not limit themselves to the forfeiture of the estates of such as were proscribed, defrauding the widows and families, nor were they contented with laying on every possible kind of tax and imposition; but hearing that several sums of money were, as well by strangers as citizens of Rome, deposited in the hands of the vestal virgins, they went and took the money away by force.

When it was manifest that nothing would ever be enough for Antony, Cæsar at last called for a division of property. The army was also divided between them, upon their march into Macedonia to make war with Brutus and Cassius, Lepidus being left with the command of the city.

However, after they had crossed the sea and engaged in operations of war, encamping in front of the enemy, Antony opposite Cassius, and Cæsar opposite Brutus, Cæsar did nothing worth relating, and all the success and victory were Antony's. In the first battle, Cæsar was completely routed by Brutus, his camp taken, he himself very narrowly escaping by flight. As he himself writes in his memoirs, he retired before the battle, on account of a dream which one of his friends had. But Antony, on the other hand, defeated Cassius; though some have written that he was not actually present in the engagement, and only joined afterwards in the pursuit. Cassius was killed, at his own entreaty and order, by one of his most trusted freedmen, Pindarus, not being aware of Brutus's victory. After a few days' interval,

they fought another battle, in which Brutus lost the day, and slew himself; and Cæsar being sick, Antony had almost all the honour of the victory.

Standing over Brutus's dead body, he uttered a few words of reproach upon him for the death of his brother Caius, who had been executed by Brutus's order in Macedonia in revenge of Cicero; but, saying presently that Hortensius was most to blame for it, he gave order for his being slain upon his brother's tomb, and, throwing his own scarlet mantle, which was of great value, upon the body of Brutus, he gave charge to one of his own freedmen to take care of his funeral. This man, as Antony came to understand, did not leave the mantle with the corpse, but kept both it and a good part of the money that should have been spent in the funeral for himself; for which he had him put to death.

But Cæsar was conveyed to Rome, no one expecting that he would long survive. Antony, purposing to go to the eastern provinces to lay them under contribution, entered Greece with a large force. The promise had been made that every common soldier should receive for his pay five thousand drachmas; so it was likely there would be need of pretty severe taxing and levying to raise money. However, to the Greeks he showed at first reason and moderation enough; he gratified his love of amusement by hearing the learned men dispute, by seeing the games, and undergoing initiation; and in judicial matters he was equitable, taking pleasure in being styled a lover of Greece, but, above all, in being called a lover of Athens, to which city he made very considerable presents. The people of Megara wished to let him know that they also had something to show him, and invited him to come and see their senate-house. So he went and examined it, and on their asking him how he liked it, told them it was "not very large, but extremely *ruinous*." At the same time, he had a survey made of the temple of the Pythian Apollo as if he had designed to repair it, and indeed he had declared to the senate his intention so to do.

However, leaving Lucius Censorinus in Greece, he crossed over into Asia, and there laid his hands on the stores of accumulated wealth, while kings waited at his door, and queens were rivalling one another, who should make him the greatest presents or appear most charming in his eyes. Thus, whilst Cæsar in Rome was wearing out his strength amidst seditions and wars, Antony, with nothing to do amidst the enjoyments of peace, let his passions carry him easily back to the old course of life that was familiar to him. A set of harpers and pipers, Anaxenor and Xuthus, the dancing-man, Metrodorus, and a whole Bacchic rout of the like Asiatic exhibitors, far outdoing in licence and buffoonery the pests that had followed him out of Italy, came in and possessed the court; the thing was past patience, wealth of all kinds being wasted on objects like these. The whole of Asia was like the city in Sophocles, loaded, at one time—

——with incense in the air,
Jubilant songs, and outcries of despair.

When he made his entry into Ephesus, the women met him dressed up like Bacchantes, and the men and boys like satyrs and fauns, and throughout the town nothing was to be seen but spears wreathed about with ivy, harps, flutes, and psalteries, while Antony in their songs was Bacchus, the Giver of Joy, and the Gentle. And so indeed he was to some, but to far more the Devourer and the Savage; for he would deprive persons of worth and quality of their fortunes to gratify villains and flatterers, who would sometimes beg the estates of men yet living, pretending they were dead, and, obtaining a grant, take possession. He gave his cook the house of a Magnesian citizen, as a reward for a single highly successful supper, and, at last, when he was proceeding to lay a second whole tribute on Asia, Hybreas, speaking on behalf of the cities, took courage, and told him broadly, but aptly enough for Antony's taste, "if you can take two yearly tributes, you can doubtless give us a couple of summers and a double harvest time"; and put it to him in the plainest and boldest way, that Asia had raised two hundred thousand talents for his service: "If this has not been paid to you, ask your collectors for it; if it has, and is all gone, we are ruined men."

These words touched Antony to the quick, who was simply ignorant of most things that were done in his name; not that he was so indolent, as he was prone to trust frankly in all about him. For there was much simplicity in his character; he was slow to see his faults, but when he did see them, was extremely repentant, and ready to ask pardon of those he had injured; prodigal in his acts of reparation, and severe in his punishments, but his generosity was much more extravagant than his severity; his raillery was sharp and insulting, but the edge of it was taken off by his readiness to submit to any kind of repartee; for he was as well contented to be rallied, as he was pleased to rally others. And this freedom of speech was, indeed, the cause of many of his disasters. He never imagined those who used so much liberty in their mirth would flatter or deceive him in business of consequence, not knowing how common it is with parasites to mix their flattery with boldness, as confectioners do their sweetmeats with something biting, to prevent the sense of satiety. Their freedoms and impertinences at table were designed expressly to give to their obsequiousness in council the air of being not complaisance, but conviction.

Such being his temper, the last and crowning mischief that could befall him came in the love of Cleopatra, to awaken and kindle to fury passions that as yet lay still and dormant in his nature, and to stifle and finely corrupt any elements that yet made resistance in him of goodness and a sound judgment. He fell into the snare thus. When making preparation for the Parthian war, he sent to command her to make her personal appearance in Cilicia, to answer an accusation, that she had given great assistance, in the late wars, to Cassius. Dellius, who was sent on this message, had no sooner seen her face, and remarked her adroitness and subtlety in speech, but he felt convinced that Antony would not so much as think of giving any molestation to a woman like this; on the contrary, she would be the first in favour with him. So he set himself at once to pay his court to the Egyptian, and gave her his advice, "to go," in the Homeric style, to Cilicia, "in her best attire," and bade her fear nothing from Antony, the gentlest and kindest of soldiers.

She had some faith in the words of Dellius, but more in her own attractions; which, having formerly recommended her to Cæsar and the young Cnæus Pompey, she did not doubt might prove yet more successful with Antony. Their acquaintance was with her when a girl, young and ignorant of the world, but she was to meet Antony in the time of life when women's beauty is most splendid, and their intellects are in full maturity. She made great preparations for her journey, of money, gifts, and ornaments of value, such as so wealthy a kingdom might afford, but she brought with her her surest hopes in her own magic arts and charms.

She received several letters, both from Antony and from his friends, to summon her, but she took no account of these orders; and at last, as if in mockery of them, she came sailing up the river Cydnus, in a barge with gilded stern and outspread sails of purple, while oars of silver beat time to the music of flutes and fifes and harps. She herself lay all along under a canopy of cloth of gold, dressed as Venus in a picture, and beautiful young boys, like painted Cupids, stood on each side to fan her. Her maids were dressed like sea nymphs and graces, some steering at the rudder, some working at the ropes. The perfumes diffused themselves from the vessel to the shore, which was covered with multitudes, part following the galley up the river on either bank, part running out of the city to see the sight. The market-place was quite emptied, and Antony at last was left alone sitting upon the tribunal; while the word went through all the multitude, that Venus was come to feast with Bacchus, for the common good of Asia.

On her arrival, Antony sent to invite her to supper. She thought it fitter he should come to her; so, willing to show his good-humour and courtesy, he complied, and went. He found the preparations to receive him magnificent beyond expression, but nothing so admirable as the great number of lights; for on a sudden there was let down altogether so great a number of branches with lights in them so ingeniously disposed, some in squares, and some in circles, that the whole thing was a spectacle that has seldom been equalled for beauty. The next day, Antony invited her to supper, and was very desirous to outdo her as well in magnificence as contrivance; but he found he was altogether beaten in both, and was so well convinced of it that he was himself the first to jest and mock at his poverty of wit and his rustic awkwardness. She, perceiving that his raillery was broad and gross, and savoured more of the soldier than the courtier, rejoined in the same taste, and fell into it at once, without any sort of reluctance or reserve.

For her actual beauty, it is said, was not in itself so remarkable that none could be compared with her, or that no one could see her without being struck by it, but the contact of her presence, if you lived with her, was irresistible; the attraction of her person, joining with the charm of her conversation, and the character that attended all she said or did, was something bewitching. It was a pleasure merely to hear the sound of her voice, with which, like an instrument of many strings, she could pass from one language to another; so that there were few of the barbarian nations that she answered by an interpreter; to most of them she spoke herself, as to the Æthiopians, Troglodytes, Hebrews, Arabians, Syrians, Medes, Parthians, and many others, whose language she had learnt; which was all the more surprising because most of the kings, her predecessors, scarcely gave themselves the trouble to acquire the Egyptian tongue, and several of them quite abandoned the Macedonian.

Antony was so captivated by her that, while Fulvia, his wife, maintained his quarrels in Rome against Cæsar by actual force of arms, and the Parthian troops, commanded by Labienus (the king's generals having made him commander-in-chief), were assembled in Mesopotamia, and ready to enter Syria, he could yet suffer himself to be carried away by her to Alexandria, there to keep holiday, like a boy, in play and diversion, squandering and fooling away in enjoyments that most costly, as Antiphon says, of all valuables, time. They had a sort of company, to which they gave a particular name, calling it that of the Inimitable Livers. The members entertained one another daily in turn, with an extravagance of expenditure beyond measure or belief.

Philotas, a physician of Amphissa, who was at that time a student of medicine in Alexandria, used to tell my grandfather Lamprias that, having some acquaintance with one of the royal cooks, he was invited by him, being a young man, to come and see the sumptuous preparations for supper. So he was taken into the kitchen, where he admired the prodigious variety of all things; but particularly, seeing eight wild boars roasting whole, says he, "Surely you have a great number of guests." The cook laughed at his simplicity, and told him there were not above twelve to sup, but that every dish was to be served up just roasted to a turn, and if anything was but one minute ill-timed, it was spoiled. "And," said he, "maybe Antony will sup just now, maybe not this hour, maybe he will call for wine, or begin to talk, and will put it off. So that," he continued, "it is not one, but many suppers must be had in readiness, as it is impossible to guess at his hour."

This was Philotas's story; who related besides, that he afterwards came to be one of the medical attendants of Antony's eldest son by Fulvia, and used to be invited pretty often, among other companions, to his table, when he was not supping with his father. One day another physician had talked loudly, and given great disturbance to the company, whose

PLUTARCH'S LIVES

mouth Philotas stopped with this sophistical syllogism: "In some states of fever the patient should take cold water; every one who has a fever is in some state of fever; therefore, in a fever cold water should always be taken." The man was quite struck dumb, and Antony's son, very much pleased, laughed aloud, and said, "Philotas, I make you a present of all you see there," pointing to a sideboard covered with plate.

Philotas thanked him much, but was far enough from ever imagining that a boy of his age could dispose of things of that value. Soon after, however, the plate was all brought to him, and he was desired to set his mark upon it; and when he put it away from him, and was afraid to accept the present, "What ails the man?" said he that brought it. "Do you know that he who gives you this is Antony's son, who is free to give it, if it were all gold? But if you will be advised by me, I would counsel you to accept of the value in money from us; for there may be amongst the rest some antique or famous piece of workmanship, which Antony would be sorry to part with."

These anecdotes, my grandfather told us, Philotas used frequently to relate.

To return to Cleopatra; Plato admits four sorts of flattery, but she had a thousand. Were Antony serious or disposed to mirth, she had at any moment some new delight or charm to meet his wishes; at every turn she was upon him, and let him escape her neither by day nor by night. She played at dice with him, drank with him, hunted with him; and when he exercised in arms, she was there to see. At night she would go rambling with him to disturb and torment people at their doors and windows, dressed like a servant-woman, for Antony also went in servant's disguise, and from these expeditions he often came home very scurvily answered, and sometimes even beaten severely, though most people guessed who it was. However, the Alexandrians in general liked it all well enough, and joined good-humouredly and kindly in his frolic and play, saying they were much obliged to Antony for acting his tragic parts at Rome, and keeping his comedy for them.

It would be trifling without end to be particular in his follies, but his fishing must not be forgotten. He went out one day to angle with Cleopatra, and, being so unfortunate as to catch nothing in the presence of his mistress, he gave secret orders to the fishermen to dive under water, and put fishes that had been al-ready taken upon his hooks; and these he drew so fast that the Egyptian perceived it. But, feigning great admiration, she told everybody how dexterous Antony was, and invited them next day to come and see him again. So, when a number of them had come on board the fishing-boats, as soon as he had let down his hook, one of her servants was beforehand with his divers, and fixed upon his hook a salted fish from Pontus. Antony, feeling his line give, drew up the prey, and when, as may be imagined, great laughter ensued, "Leave," said Cleopatra, "the fishing-rod, general, to us poor sovereigns of Pharos and Canopus; your game is cities, provinces, and kingdoms."

Whilst he was thus diverting himself and engaged in this boy's play, two despatches arrived; one from Rome, that his brother Lucius and his wife Fulvia, after many quarrels among themselves, had joined in war against Cæsar, and having lost all, had fled out of Italy; the other bringing little better news, that Labienus, at the head of the Parthians, was overrunning Asia, from Euphrates and Syria as far as Lydia and Ionia. So, scarcely at last rousing himself from sleep, and shaking off the fumes of wine, he set out to attack the Parthians, and went as far as Phœnicia; but, upon the receipt of lamentable letters from Fulvia, turned his course with two hundred ships to Italy. And, in his way, receiving such of his friends as fled from Italy, he was given to understand that Fulvia was the sole cause of the war, a woman of a restless spirit and very bold, and withal her hopes were that commotions in Italy would force Antony from Cleopatra.

But it happened that Fulvia, as she was coming to meet her husband, fell sick by the way, and died at Sicyon, so that an accommodation was the more easily made. For when he reached Italy, and Cæsar showed no intention of laying anything to his charge, and he on his part shifted the blame of everything on Fulvia, those that were friends to them would not suffer that the time should be spent in looking narrowly into the plea, but made a reconciliation first, and then a partition of the empire between them, taking as their boundary the Ionian Sea, the eastern provinces falling to Antony, to Cæsar the western, and Africa being left to Lepidus. And an agreement was made that every one in their turn, as they thought fit, should make their friends consuls, when they did not choose to take the office themselves. These terms were well approved of, but yet it was thought some closer tie would be desirable; and for this, fortune offered occasion. Cæsar had an elder sister, not of the whole blood, for Attia was his mother's name, hers Ancharia. This sister, Octavia, he was extremely attached to, as indeed she was, it is said, quite a wonder of a woman. Her husband, Caius Marcellus, had died not long before, and Antony was now a widower by the death of Fulvia; for, though he did not disavow the passion he had for Cleopatra, yet he disowned anything of marriage, reason as yet, upon this point, still maintaining the debate against the charms of the Egyptian. Everybody concurred in promoting this new alliance, fully expecting that with the beauty, honour, and prudence of Octavia, when her company should, as it was certain it would, have engaged his affections, all would be kept in the safe and happy course of friendship. So, both parties being agreed, they went to Rome to celebrate the nuptials, the senate dispensing with the law by which a widow was not permitted to marry till ten months after the death of her husband.

Sextus Pompeius was in possession of Sicily, and with his ships, under the command of Menas, the pirate, and Menecrates, so infested the Italian coast that no vessels durst venture into those seas. Sextus had behaved with much humanity towards Antony, having received his mother when she fled with Fulvia, and it was therefore judged fit that he also should be received into the peace. They met near the promontory of Misenum, by the mole of the port, Pompey having his fleet at anchor close by, and Antony and Cæsar their troops drawn up all along the shore. There it was concluded that Sextus should quietly enjoy the government of Sicily and Sardinia, he conditioning to scour the seas of all pirates, and to send so much corn every year to Rome.

This agreed on, they invited one another to supper, and by lot it fell to Pompey's turn to give the first entertainment, and Antony, asking where it was to be, "There," said he, pointing to the admiral-galley, a ship of six banks of oars, "that is the only house that Pompey is heir to of his father's." And this he said, reflecting upon Antony, who was then in possession of his father's house. Having fixed the ship on her anchors, and formed a bridgeway from the promontory to conduct on board of her, he gave them a cordial welcome. And when they began to grow warm, and jests were passing freely on Antony and Cleopatra's loves,

Menas, the pirate, whispered Pompey, in the ear, "Shall I," said he, "cut the cables, and make you master not of Sicily only and Sardinia, but of the whole Roman empire?" Pompey, having considered a little while, returned him answer, "Menas, this might have been done without acquainting me; now we must rest content; I do not break my word." And so, having been entertained by the other two in their turns, he set sail for Sicily.

After the treaty was completed, Antony despatched Ventidius into Asia, to check the advance of the Parthians, while he, as a compliment to Cæsar, accepted the office of priest to the deceased Cæsar. And in any state affair and matter of consequence, they both behaved themselves with much consideration and friendliness for each other. But it annoyed Antony that in all their amusements, on any trial of skill or fortune, Cæsar should be constantly victorious. He had with him an Egyptian diviner, one of those who calculate nativities, who, either to make his court to Cleopatra, or that by the rules of his art he found it to be so, openly declared to him that though the fortune that attended him was bright and glorious, yet it was overshadowed by Cæsar's; and advised him to keep himself as far distant as he could from that young man; "for your Genius," said he, "dreads his; when absent from him yours is proud and brave, but in his presence unmanly and dejected."

Incidents that occurred appeared to show that the Egyptian spoke truth. For whenever they cast lots for any playful purpose, or threw dice, Antony was still the loser; and repeatedly, when they fought game-cocks or quails, Cæsar's had the victory. This gave Antony a secret displeasure, and made him put the more confidence in the skill of his Egyptian. So, leaving the management of his home affairs to Cæsar, he left Italy, and took Octavia, who had lately borne him a daughter, along with him into Greece.

Here, whilst he wintered in Athens, he received the first news of Ventidius's successes over the Parthians, of his having defeated them in a battle, having slain Labienus and Pharnapates, the best general their king, Hyrodes, possessed. For the celebrating of which he made public feast through Greece, and for the prizes which were contested at Athens he himself acted as steward, and, leaving at home the ensigns that are carried before the general, he made his public appearance in a gown and white shoes, with the steward's wands marching before; and he performed his duty in taking the combatants by the neck, to part them, when they had fought enough.

When the time came for him to set out for the war, he took a garland from the sacred olive, and, in obedience to some oracle, he filled a vessel with the water of the Clepsydra to carry along with him. In this interval, Pacorus, the Parthian king's son, who was marching into Syria with a large army, was met by Ventidius, who gave him battle in the country of Cyrrhestica, slew a large number of his men, and Pacorus among the first. This victory was one of the most renowned achievements of the Romans, and fully avenged their defeats under Crassus, the Parthians being obliged, after the loss of three battles successively, to keep themselves within the bounds of Media and Mesopotamia. Ventidius was not willing to push his good fortune further, for fear of raising some jealousy in Antony, but turning his arms against those that had quitted the Roman interest, he reduced them to their former obedience.

Among the rest, he besieged Antiochus, King of Commagene, in the city of Samosata, who made an offer of a thousand talents for his pardon, and a promise of submission to Antony's commands. But Ventidius told him that he must send to Antony, who was already on his march, and had sent word to Ventidius to make no terms with Antiochus, wishing that at any rate this one exploit might be ascribed to him, and that people might not think that all his successes were won by his lieutenants. The siege, however, was long protracted; for when those within found their offers refused, they defended themselves stoutly, till, at last, Antony, finding he was doing nothing, in shame and regret for having refused the first offer, was glad to make an accommodation with Antiochus for three hundred talents. And, having given some orders for the affairs of Syria, he returned to Athens; and, paying Ventidius the honours he well deserved, dismissed him to receive his triumph.

He is the only man that has ever yet triumphed for victories obtained over the Parthians; he was of obscure birth, but, by means of Antony's friendship, obtained an opportunity of showing his capacity, and doing great things; and his making such glorious use of it gave new credit to the current observation about Cæsar and Antony, that they were more fortunate in what they did by their lieutenants than in their own persons. For Sossius, also,

had great success, and Canidius, whom he left in Armenia, defeated the people there, and also the kings of the Albanians and Iberians, and marched victorious as far as Caucasus, by which means the fame of Antony's arms had become great among the barbarous nations.

He, however, once more, upon some unfavourable stories, taking offence against Cæsar, set sail with three hundred ships for Italy, and, being refused admittance to the port of Brundusium, made for Tarentum. There his wife Octavia, who came from Greece with him, obtained leave to visit her brother, she being then great with child, having already borne her husband a second daughter; and as she was on her way she met Cæsar, with his two friends Agrippa and Mæcenas, and, taking these two aside, with great entreaties and lamentations she told them, that of the most fortunate woman upon earth, she was in danger of becoming the most unhappy; for as yet every one's eyes were fixed upon her as the wife and sister of the two great commanders, but, if rash counsels should prevail, and war ensue, "I shall be miserable," said she, "without redress; for on what side soever victory falls, I shall be sure to be a loser."

Cæsar was overcome by these entreaties, and advanced in a peaceable temper to Tarentum, where those that were present beheld a most stately spectacle; a vast army drawn up by the shore, and as great a fleet in the harbour, all without the occurrence of any act of hostility; nothing but the salutations of friends, and other expressions of joy and kindness, passing from one armament to the other. Antony first entertained Cæsar, this also being a concession on Cæsar's part to his sister; and when at length an agreement was made between them, that Cæsar should give Antony two of his legions to serve him in the Parthian war, and that Antony should in return leave with him a hundred armed galleys, Octavia further obtained of her husband, besides this, twenty light ships for her brother, and of her brother, a thousand foot for her husband. So, having parted good friends, Cæsar went immediately to make war with Pompey to conquer Sicily. And Antony, leaving in Cæsar's charge his wife and children, and his children by his former wife Fulvia, set sail for Asia.

But the mischief that thus long had lain still, the passion for Cleopatra, which better thoughts had seemed to have lulled and charmed into oblivion, upon his approach to Syria gathered strength again, and broke out into a flame.

And, in fine, like Plato's restive and rebellious horse of the human soul, flinging off all good and wholesome counsel, and breaking fairly loose, he sent Fonteius Capito to bring Cleopatra into Syria. To whom at her arrival he made no small or trifling present, Phœnicia, Cœle-Syria, Cyprus, great part of Cilicia, that side of Judæa which produces balm, that part of Arabia—where the Nabathæans extend to the outer sea; profuse gifts which much displeased the Romans. For although he had invested several private persons in great governments and kingdoms, and bereaved many kings of theirs, as Antigonus of Judæa, whose head he caused to be struck off (the first example of that punishment being inflicted on a king), yet nothing stung the Romans like the shame of these honours paid to Cleopatra. Their dissatisfaction was augmented also by his acknowledging as his own the twin children he had by her, giving them the name of Alexander and Cleopatra, and adding, as their surnames, the titles of Sun and Moon.

But he, who knew how to put a good colour on the most dishonest action, would say that the greatness of the Roman empire consisted more in giving than in taking kingdoms, and that the way to carry noble blood through the world was by begetting in every place a new line and series of kings; his own ancestor had thus been born of Hercules; Hercules had not limited his hopes of progeny to a single womb, nor feared any law like Solon's or any audit of procreation, but had freely let nature take her will in the foundation and first commencement of many families.

After Phraates had killed his father, Hyrodes, and taken possession of his kingdom, many of the Parthians left their country; among the rest Monæses, a man of great distinction and authority, sought refuge with Antony, who, looking on his case as similar to that of Themistocles, and likening his own opulence and magnanimity to those of the former Persian kings, gave him three cities, Larissa, Arethusa, and Hierapolis, which was formerly called Bambyce. But when the King of Parthia soon recalled him, giving him his word and honour for his safety, Antony was not unwilling to give him leave to return, hoping thereby to surprise Phraates, who would believe that peace would continue; for he only made the demand of him that he should send back the Roman ensigns which were taken when Crassus was slain, and the prisoners that remained yet alive.

This done, he sent Cleopatra to Egypt, and marched through Arabia and Armenia; and, when his forces came together, and were joined by those of his confederate kings (of whom there were very many, and the most considerable, Artavasdes, King of Armenia, who came at the head of six thousand horse and seven thousand foot), he made a general muster. There appeared sixty thousand Roman foot, ten thousand horse, Spaniards and Gauls, who counted as Romans; and, of other nations, horse and foot thirty thousand. And these great preparations, that put the Indians beyond Bactria into alarm, and made all Asia shake, were all we are told rendered useless to him because of Cleopatra. For, in order to pass the winter with her, the war was pushed on before its due time; and all he did was done without perfect consideration, as by a man who had no power of control over his faculties, who, under the effect of some drug or magic, was still looking back elsewhere, and whose object was much more to hasten his return than to conquer his enemies.

For, first of all, when he should have taken up his winter-quarters in Armenia, to refresh his men, who were tired with long marches, having come at least eight thousand furlongs, and then having taken the advantage in the beginning of the spring to invade Media, before the Parthians were out of winter-quarters, he had not patience to expect his time, but marched into the province of Atropatene, leaving Armenia on the left hand, and laid waste all that country. Secondly, his haste was so great that he left behind the engines absolutely required for any siege, which followed the camp in three hundred waggons, and, among the rest, a ram eighty feet long; none of which was it possible, if lost or damaged, to repair or to make the like, as the provinces of the Upper Asia produce no trees long or hard enough for such uses. Nevertheless, he left them all behind, as a mere impediment to his speed, in the charge of a detachment under the command of Statianus, the waggon officer.

He himself laid siege to Phraata, a principal city of the King of Media, wherein were that king's wife and children. And when actual need proved the greatness of his error, in leaving the siege-train behind him, he had nothing for it but to come up and raise a mound against the walls, with infinite labour and great loss of time. Meantime Phraates, coming down with a large army, and hearing that the waggons were left behind with the battering engines, sent a strong party of horse, by which Statianus was surprised, he himself and ten thousand of his men slain, the engines all broken in pieces, many taken prisoners, and among the rest King Polemon.

This great miscarriage in the opening of the campaign much discouraged Antony's army, and Artavasdes, King of Armenia, deciding that the Roman prospects were bad, withdrew with all his forces from the camp, although he had been the chief promoter of the war. The Parthians, encouraged by their success, came up to the Romans at the siege, and gave them many affronts; upon which Antony, fearing that the despondency and alarm of his soldiers would only grow worse if he let them lie idle, taking all the horse, ten legions, and three prætorian cohorts of heavy infantry, resolved to go out and forage, designing by this means to draw the enemy with more advantage to a battle. To effect this, he marched a day's journey from his camp, and finding the Parthians hovering about, in readiness to attack him while he was in motion, he gave orders for the signal of battle to be hung out in the encampment, but, at the same time, pulled down the tents, as if he meant not to fight, but to lead his men home again; and so he proceeded to lead them past the enemy, who were drawn up in a half-moon, his orders being that the horse should charge as soon as the legions were come up near enough to second them.

The Parthians, standing still while the Romans marched by them, were in great admiration of their army, and of the exact discipline it observed, rank after rank passing on at equal distances in perfect order and silence, their pikes all ready in their hands. But when the signal was given, and the horse turned short upon the Parthians, and with loud cries charged them, they bravely received them, though they were at once too near for bowshot; but the legions coming up with loud shouts and rattling of their arms so frightened their horses and indeed the men themselves, that they kept their ground no longer. Antony pressed them hard, in great hopes that this victory should put an end to the war; the foot had them in pursuit for fifty furlongs, and the horse for thrice that distance, and yet, the advantage summed up, they had but thirty prisoners, and there were but fourscore slain. So that they were all filled with dejection and discouragement, to consider that when they were victorious, their advantages were so small, and that when they were beaten, they lost so great

a number of men as they had done when the carriages were taken.

The next day, having put the baggage in order, they marched back to the camp before Phraata, in the way meeting with some scattering troops of the enemy, and, as they marched further, with greater parties, at length with the body of the enemy's army, fresh and in good order, who defied them to battle, and charged them on every side, and it was not without great difficulty that they reached the camp. There Antony, finding that his men had in a panic deserted the defence of the mound, upon a sally of the Medes, resolved to proceed against them by decimation, as it is called, which is done by dividing the soldiers into tens, and, out of every ten, putting one to death, as it happens by lot. The rest he gave orders should have, instead of wheat, their rations of corn in barley.

The war was now become grievous to both parties, and the prospect of its continuance yet more fearful to Antony, in respect that he was threatened with famine; for he could no longer forage without wounds and slaughter. And Phraates, on the other side, was full of apprehension that if the Romans were to persist in carrying on the siege, the autumnal equinox being past and the air already closing in for cold, he should be deserted by his soldiers, who would suffer anything rather than wintering in open field. To prevent which, he had recourse to the following deceit: he gave orders to those of his men who had made most acquaintance among the Roman soldiers, not to pursue too close when they met them foraging, but to suffer them to carry off some provision; moreover, that they should praise their valour, and declare that it was not without just reason that their king looked upon the Romans as the bravest men in the world.

This done, upon further opportunity, they rode nearer in, and, drawing up their horses by the men, began to revile Antony for his obstinacy; that whereas Phraates desired nothing more than peace, and an occasion to show how ready he was to save the lives of so many brave soldiers, he, on the contrary, gave no opening to any friendly offers, but sat awaiting the arrival of the two fiercest and worst enemies, winter and famine, from whom it would be hard for them to make their escape, even with all the good-will of the Parthians to help them. Antony, having these reports from many hands, began to indulge the hope; nevertheless, he would not send any message to the

Parthian till he had put the question to these friendly talkers, whether what they said was said by order of their king. Receiving answer that it was, together with new encouragement to believe them, he sent some of his friends to demand once more the standards and prisoners, lest if he should ask nothing, he might be supposed to be too thankful to have leave to retreat in quiet.

The Parthian king made answer that, as for the standards and prisoners, he need not trouble himself; but if he thought fit to retreat, he might do it when he pleased, in peace and safety. Some few days, therefore, being spent in collecting the baggage, he set out upon his march. On which occasion, though there was no man of his time like him for addressing a multitude, or for carrying soldiers with him by the force of words, out of shame and sadness he could not find in his heart to speak himself but employed Domitius Ænobarbus. And some of the soldiers resented it, as an undervaluing of them; but the greater number saw the true cause, and pitied it, and thought it rather a reason why they on their side should treat their general with more respect and obedience than ordinary.

Antony had resolved to return by the same way he came, which was through a level country clear of all trees; but a certain Mardian came to him (one that was very conversant with the manners of the Parthians, and whose fidelity to the Romans had been tried at the battle where the machines were lost), and advised him to keep the mountains close on his right hand, and not to expose his men, heavily armed, in a broad, open, riding country, to the attacks of a numerous army of light horse and archers; that Phraates with fair promises had persuaded him from the siege on purpose that he might with more ease cut him off in his retreat; but if so he pleased, he would conduct him by a nearer route, on which, moreover, he should find the necessaries for his army in greater abundance. Antony upon this began to consider what was best to be done; he was unwilling to seem to have any mistrust of the Parthians after their treaty; but, holding it to be really best to march his army the shorter and more inhabited way, he demanded of the Mardian some assurance of his faith, who offered himself to be bound until the army came safe into Armenia.

Two days he conducted the army bound, and, on the third, when Antony had given up all thought of the enemy, and was marching at his ease in no very good order, the Mardian, perceiving the bank of the river broken down, and the water let out and overflowing the road by which they were to pass, saw at once that this was the handiwork of the Parthians, done out of mischief, and to hinder their march; so he advised Antony to be upon his guard, for that the enemy was nigh at hand. And no sooner had he begun to put his men in order, disposing the slingers and dart-men in convenient intervals for sallying out, but the Parthians came pouring in on all sides, fully expecting to encompass them, and throw the whole army into disorder. They were at once attacked by the light troops, whom they galled a good deal with their arrows; but being themselves as warmly entertained with the slings and darts, and many wounded, they made their retreat. Soon after, rallying up afresh, they were beat back by a battalion of Gallic horse, and appeared no more that day.

By their manner of attack Antony, seeing what to do, not only placed the slings and darts as a rear guard, but also lined both flanks with them, and so marched in a square battle, giving order to the horse to charge and beat off the enemy, but not to follow them far as they retired. So that the Parthians, not doing more mischief for the four ensuing days than they received, began to abate in their zeal, and, complaining that the winter season was much advanced, pressed for returning home.

But, on the fifth day, Flavius Gallus, a brave and active officer, who had a considerable command in the army, came to Antony, desiring of him some light infantry out of the rear, and some horse out of the front, with which he would undertake to do some considerable service. Which when he had obtained, he beat the enemy back, not withdrawing, as was usual, at the same time, and retreating upon the mass of the heavy infantry, but maintaining his own ground, and engaging boldly. The officers who commanded in the rear, perceiving how far he was getting from the body of the army, sent to warn him back, but he took no notice of them.

It is said that Titius the quæstor snatched the standards and turned them round, upbraiding Gallus with thus leading so many brave men to destruction. But when he on the other side reviled him again, and commanded the men that were about him to stand firm, Titius made his retreat, and Gallus, charging the enemies in the front, was encompassed by a party that fell upon his rear, which at length perceiving, he sent a messenger to demand suc-cour. But the commanders of the heavy in-fantry, Canidius amongst others, a particular favourite of Antony's, seem here to have com-mitted a great oversight. For, instead of facing about with the whole body, they sent small parties, and, when they were defeated, they still sent out small parties, so that by their bad management the rout would have spread through the whole army, if Antony himself had not marched from the van at the head of the third legion, and, passing this through among the fugitives, faced the enemies, and hindered them from any further pursuit.

In this engagement were killed three thou-sand, five thousand were carried back to the camp wounded, amongst the rest Gallus, shot through the body with four arrows, of which wounds he died. Antony went from tent to tent to visit and comfort the rest of them, and was not able to see his men without tears and a passion of grief. They, however, seized his hand with joyful faces, bidding him go and see to himself and not be concerned about them, calling him their emperor and their general, and saying that if he did well they were safe.

For, in short, never in all these times can history make mention of a general at the head of a more splendid army; whether you consider strength and youth, or patience and sufferance in labours and fatigues; but as for the obedi-ence and affectionate respect they bore their general, and the unanimous feeling amongst small and great alike, officers and common sol-diers, to prefer his good opinion of them to their very lives and being, in this part of mili-tary excellence it was not possible that they could have been surpassed by the very Romans of old. For this devotion, as I have said before, there were many reasons, as the nobility of his family, his eloquence, his frank and open man-ners, his liberal and magnificent habits, his familiarity in talking with everybody, and, at this time particularly, his kindness in visiting and pitying the sick, joining in all their pains, and furnishing them with all things necessary, so that the sick and wounded were even more eager to serve than those that were whole and strong.

Nevertheless, this last victory had so encour-aged the enemy that, instead of their former impatience and weariness, they began soon to feel contempt for the Romans, staying all night near the camp, in expectation of plundering their tents and baggage, which they concluded they must abandon; and in the morning new

forces arrived in large masses, so that their number was grown to be not less, it is said, than forty thousand horse; and the king had sent the very guards that attended upon his own person, as to a sure and unquestioned victory, for he himself was never present in any fight.

Antony, designing to harangue the soldiers, called for a mourning habit that he might move them the more, but was dissuaded by his friends; so he came forward in the general's scarlet cloak, and addressed them, praising those that had gained the victory, and re-proaching those that had fled, the former an-swering him with promises of success, and the latter excusing themselves, and telling him they were ready to undergo decimation, or any other punishment he should please to inflict upon them, only entreating that he would for-get and not discompose himself with their faults. At which he lifted up his hands to heav-en, and prayed the gods that, if to balance the great favours he had received of them any judgment lay in store, they would pour it upon his head alone, and grant his soldiers victory.

The next day they took better order for their march, and the Parthians, who thought they were marching rather to plunder than to fight, were much taken aback, when they came up and were received with a shower of missiles, to find the enemy not disheartened, but fresh and resolute. So that they themselves began to lose courage. But at the descent of a hill where the Romans were obliged to pass, they got to-gether, and let fly their arrows upon them as they moved slowly down. But the full-armed infantry, facing round, received the light troops within; and those in the first rank knelt on one knee, holding their shields before them, the next rank holding theirs over the first, and so again others over these, much like the tiling of a house, or the rows of seats in a theatre, the whole affording sure defence against arrows, which glanced upon them without doing any harm. The Parthians, seeing the Romans down upon their knees, could not imagine but that it must proceed from weariness; so that they laid down their bows, and, taking their spears, made a fierce onset, when the Romans, with a great cry, leaped upon their feet, striking hand to hand with their javelins, slew the foremost, and put the rest to flight.

After this rate it was every day, and the trouble they gave made the marches short; in addition to which famine began to be felt in the camp, for they could get but little corn, and that which they got they were forced to fight for; and, besides this, they were in want of implements to grind it and make bread. For they had left almost all behind, the baggage horses being dead or otherwise employed in carrying the sick and wounded. Provision was so scarce in the army that an Attic quart of wheat sold for fifty drachmas, and barley loaves for their weight in silver. And when they tried vegetables and roots, they found such as are commonly eaten very scarce, so that they were constrained to venture upon any they could get, and, among others, they chanced upon an herb that was mortal, first taking away all sense and understanding. He that had eaten of it remembered nothing in the world, and employed himself only in moving great stones from one place to another, which he did with as much earnestness and industry as if it had been a business of the greatest consequence. Through all the camp there was nothing to be seen but men grubbing upon the ground at stones, which they carried from place to place. But in the end they threw up bile and died, as wine, moreover, which was the one antidote, failed.

When Antony saw them die so fast, and the Parthians still in pursuit, he was heard to exclaim several times over, "O, the Ten Thousand!" as if in admiration of the retreat of the Greeks, with Xenophon, who, when they had a longer journey to make from Babylonia, and a more powerful enemy to deal with, nevertheless came home safe.

The Parthians, finding that they could not divide the Roman army, nor break the order of their battle, and that withal they had been so often worsted, once more began to treat the foragers with professions of humanity; they came up to them with their bows unbent, telling them that they were going home to their houses, that this was the end of their retaliation, and that only some Median troops would follow for two or three days, not with any design to annoy them, but for the defence of some of the villages further on. And, saying this, they saluted them and embraced them with a great show of friendship. This made the Romans full of confidence again, and Antony, on hearing of it, was more disposed to take the road through the level country, being told that no water was to be hoped for on that through the mountains.

But while he was preparing thus to do, Mithridates came into the camp, a cousin to Monæses, of whom we related that he sought refuge with the Romans, and received in gift from Antony three cities. Upon his arrival, he desired somebody might be brought to him that could speak Syriac or Parthian. One Alexander, of Antioch, a friend of Antony's, was brought to him, to whom the stranger, giving his name, and mentioning Monæses as the person who desired to do the kindness, put the question, did he see that high range of hills, pointing at some distance. He told him, yes. "It is there," said he, "the whole Parthian army lie in wait for your passage; for the great plains come immediately up to them, and they expect that, confiding in their promises, you will leave the way of the mountains, and take the level route. It is true that in passing over the mountains you will suffer the want of water, and the fatigue to which you have become familiar, but if you pass through the plains, Antony must expect the fortune of Crassus."

This said, he departed. Antony, in alarm calling his friends in council, sent for the Mardian guide, who was of the same opinion. He told them that, with or without enemies, the want of any certain track in the plain, and the likelihood of their losing their way, were quite objection enough; the other route was rough and without water, but then it was but for a day. Antony, therefore, changing his mind, marched away upon this road that night, commanding that every one should carry water sufficient for his own use; but most of them being unprovided with vessels, they made shift with their helmets, and some with skins. As soon as they started, the news of it was carried to the Parthians, who followed them, contrary to their custom, through the night, and at sunrise attacked the rear, which was tired with marching and want of sleep, and not in condition to make any considerable defence.

For they had got through two hundred and forty furlongs that night, and at the end of such a march to find the enemy at their heels put them out of heart. Besides, having to fight for every step of the way increased their distress from thirst. Those that were in the van came up to a river, the water of which was extremely cool and clear, but brackish and medicinal, and, on being drunk, produced immediate pains in the bowels and a renewed thirst. Of this the Mardian had forewarned them, but they could not forbear, and, beating back those that opposed them, they drank of it. Antony ran from one place to another, begging they would have a little patience, that not far off there was a river of wholesome water, and that the rest of the way was so difficult for the horse that the enemy could pursue them no further; and, saying this, he ordered to sound a retreat to call those back that were engaged, and commanded the tents should be set up, that the soldiers might at any rate refresh themselves in the shade.

But the tents were scarce well put up, and the Parthians beginning, according to their custom, to withdraw, when Mithridates came again to them, and informed Alexander, with whom he had before spoken, that he would do well to advise Antony to stay where he was no longer than needs he must, that, after having refreshed his troops, he should endeavour with all diligence to gain the next river, that the Parthians would not cross it, but so far they were resolved to follow them. Alexander made his report to Antony, who ordered a quantity of gold plate to be carried to Mithridates, who, taking as much as he could well hide under his clothes, went his way.

And, upon this advice, Antony, while it was yet day, broke up his camp, and the whole army marched forward without receiving any molestation from the Parthians, though that night by their own doing was in effect the most wretched and terrible that they passed. For some of the men began to kill and plunder those whom they suspected to have any money, ransacked the baggage, and seized the money there. In the end, they laid hands on Antony's own equipage, and broke all his rich tables and cups, dividing the fragments amongst them. Antony, hearing such a noise and such a stirring to and fro all through the army, the belief prevailing that the enemy had routed and cut off a portion of the troops, called for one of his freedmen, then serving as one of his guards, Rhamnus by name, and made him take an oath that whenever he should give him orders, he would run his sword through his body and cut off his head, that he might not fall alive into the hands of the Parthians, nor, when dead, be recognised as the general.

While he was in this consternation, and all his friends about him in tears, the Mardian came up and gave them all new life. He convinced them, by the coolness and humidity of the air, which they could feel in breathing it, that the river which he had spoken of was now not far off, and the calculation of the time that had been required to reach it came, he said, to the same result, for the night was almost spent. And, at the same time, others came with information that all the confusion in the camp proceeded only from their own violence and robbery among themselves. To compose this tumult, and bring them again into some order after their distraction, he commanded the signal to be given for a halt.

Day began to break, and quiet and regularity were just reappearing, when the Parthian arrows began to fly among the rear, and the light-armed troops were ordered out to battle. And, being seconded by the heavy infantry, who covered one another as before described with their shields, they bravely received the enemy, who did not think convenient to advance any further, while the van of the army, marching forward leisurely in this manner, came in sight of the river, and Antony, drawing up the cavalry on the banks to confront the enemy, first passed over the sick and wounded. And, by this time, even those who were engaged with the enemy had opportunity to drink at their ease; for the Parthians, on seeing the river, unbent their bows, and told the Romans they might pass over freely, and made them great compliments in praise of their valour. Having crossed without molestation, they rested themselves awhile, and presently went forward, not giving perfect credit to the fair words of their enemies.

Six days after this last battle, they arrived at the river Araxes, which divides Media and Armenia, and seemed, both by its deepness and the violence of the current, to be very dangerous to pass. A report, also, had crept in amongst them, that the enemy was in ambush, ready to set upon them as soon as they should be occupied with their passage. But when they were got over on the other side, and found themselves in Armenia, just as if land was now sighted after a storm at sea, they kissed the ground for joy, shedding tears and embracing each other in their delight. But taking their journey through a land that abounded in all sorts of plenty, they ate, after their long want, with that excess of everything they met with that they suffered from dropsies and dysenteries.

Here Antony, making a review of his army, found that he had lost twenty thousand foot and four thousand horse, of which the better half perished, not by the enemy, but by diseases. Their march was of twenty-seven days from Phraata, during which they had beaten the Parthians in eighteen battles, though with little effect or lasting result, because of their being so unable to pursue. By which it is manifest that it was Artavasdes who lost Antony the benefit of the expedition. For had the sixteen thousand horsemen whom he led away, out of Media, armed in the same style as the Parthians, and accustomed to their manner of fight, been there to follow the pursuit when the Romans put them to flight, it is impossible they could have rallied so often after their defeats, and reappeared again as they did to renew their attacks.

For this reason, the whole army was very earnest with Antony to march into Armenia to take revenge. But he, with more reflection, forbore to notice the desertion, and continued all his former courtesies, feeling that the army was wearied out, and in want of all manner of necessaries. Afterwards, however, entering Armenia, with invitations and fair promises he prevailed upon Artavasdes to meet him, when he seized him, bound him, and carried him to Alexandria, and there led him in a triumph; one of the things which most offended the Romans, who felt as if all the honours and solemn observances of their country were, for Cleopatra's sake, handed over to the Egyptians.

This, however, was at an after time. For the present, marching his army in great haste in the depth of winter through continual storms of snow, he lost eight thousand of his men, and came with much diminished numbers to a place called the White Village, between Sidon and Berytus, on the sea-coast, where he waited for the arrival of Cleopatra. And, being impatient of the delay she made, he bethought himself of shortening the time in wine and drunkenness, and yet could not endure the tediousness of a meal, but would start from table and run to see if she were coming. Till at last she came into port, and brought with her clothes and money for the soldiers. Though some say that Antony only received the clothes from her and distributed his own money in her name.

A quarrel presently happened between the King of Media and Phraates of Parthia, beginning, it is said, about the division of the booty that was taken from the Romans, and creating great apprehension in the Median lest he should lose his kingdom. He sent, therefore, ambassadors to Antony, with offers of entering into a confederate war against Phraates. And Antony, full of hopes at being thus asked, as a favour, to accept that one thing, horse and archers, the want of which had hindered his beating the Parthians before, began at once to prepare for a return to Armenia, there to join the Medes on the Araxes, and begin the war afresh.

But Octavia, in Rome, being desirous to see Antony, asked Cæsar's leave to go to him; which he gave her, not so much, say most authors, to gratify his sister, as to obtain a fair pretence to begin the war upon her dishonourable reception. She no sooner arrived at Athens, but by letters from Antony she was informed of his new expedition, and his will that she should await him there. And, though she were much displeased, not being ignorant of the real reason of this usage, yet she wrote to him to know to what place he would be pleased she should send the things she had brought with her for his use; for she had brought clothes for his soldiers, baggage, cattle, money, and presents for his friends and officers, and two thousand chosen soldiers sumptuously armed, to form prætorian cohorts. This message was brought from Octavia to Antony by Niger, one of his friends, who added to it the praises she deserved so well.

Cleopatra, feeling her rival already, as it were, at hand, was seized with fear, lest if to her noble life and her high alliance, she once could add the charm of daily habit and affectionate intercourse, she should become irresistible, and be his absolute mistress forever. So she feigned to be dying for love of Antony, bringing her body down by slender diet; when he entered the room, she fixed her eyes upon him in a rapture, and when he left, seemed to languish and half faint away. She took great pains that he should see her in tears, and, as soon as he noticed it, hastily dried them up and turned away, as if it were her wish that he should know nothing of it. All this was acting while he prepared for Media; and Cleopatra's creatures were not slow to forward the design, upbraiding Antony with his unfeeling, hardhearted temper, thus letting a woman perish whose soul depended upon him and him alone.

Octavia, it was true, was his wife, and had been married to him because it was found convenient for the affairs of her brother that it should be so, and she had the honour of the title; but Cleopatra, the sovereign queen of many nations, had been contented with the name of his mistress, nor did she shun or despise the character whilst she might see him, might live with him, and enjoy him; if she were bereaved of this, she would not survive the loss. In fine, they so melted and unmanned him that, fully believing she would die if he forsook her, he put off the war and returned to Alexandria, deferring his Median expedition until next summer, though news came of the Parthians being all in confusion with intestine disputes. Nevertheless, he did some time after go into that country, and made an alliance with the King of Media, by marriage of a son of his by Cleopatra to the king's daughter, who was yet very young; and so returned, with his thoughts taken up about the civil war.

When Octavia returned from Athens, Cæsar, who considered she had been injuriously treated, commanded her to live in a separate house; but she refused to leave the house of her husband, and entreated him, unless he had already resolved, upon other motives, to make war with Antony, that he would on her account let it alone; it would be intolerable to have it said of the two greatest commanders in the world that they had involved the Roman people in a civil war, the one out of passion for, the other out of resentment about, a woman. And her behaviour proved her words to be sincere. She remained in Antony's house as if he were at home in it, and took the noblest and most generous care, not only of his children by her, but of those by Fulvia also. She received all the friends of Antony that came to Rome to seek office or upon any business, and did her utmost to prefer their requests to Cæsar; yet this her honourable deportment did but, without her meaning it, damage the reputation of Antony; the wrong he did to such a woman made him hated.

Nor was the division he made among his sons at Alexandria less unpopular; it seemed a theatrical piece of insolence and contempt of his country. For assembling the people in the exercise ground, and causing two golden thrones to be placed on a platform of silver, the one for him and the other for Cleopatra, and at their feet lower thrones for their children, he proclaimed Cleopatra Queen of Egypt, Cyprus, Libya, and Cœle-Syria, and with her conjointly Cæsarion, the reputed son of the former Cæsar, who left Cleopatra with child. His own sons by Cleopatra were to have the style of kings of kings; to Alexander he gave Armenia and Media, with Parthia, so soon as it should be overcome; to Ptolemy, Phœnicia, Syria, and Cilicia. Alexander was brought out before the people in Median costume, the tiara and upright peak, and Ptolemy, in boots and mantle and Macedonian cap done about with the diadem; for this was the habit of the successors of Alexander, as the other was of the Medes and Armenians. And as soon as they had saluted their parents, the one was received by a guard of Macedonians, the other by one of Armenians. Cleopatra was then, as at other times when she appeared in public, dressed in the habit of the goddess Isis, and gave audience to the people under the name of the New Isis.

Cæsar, relating these things in the senate, and often complaining to the people, excited men's minds against Antony, and Antony also sent messages of accusation against Cæsar. The principal of his charges were these: first, that he had not made any division with him of Sicily, which was lately taken from Pompey; secondly, that he had retained the ships he had lent him for the war; thirdly, that, after deposing Lepidus, their colleague, he had taken for himself the army, governments, and revenues formerly appropriated to him; and lastly, that he had parcelled out almost all Italy amongst his own soldiers, and left nothing for his. Cæsar's answer was as follows: that he had put Lepidus out of government because of his own misconduct; that what he had got in war he would divide with Antony, so soon as Antony gave him a share of Armenia; that Antony's soldiers had no claims in Italy, being in possession of Media and Parthia, the acquisitions which their brave actions under their general had added to the Roman empire.

Antony was in Armenia when this answer came to him, and immediately sent Canidius with sixteen legions towards the sea; but he, in the company of Cleopatra, went to Ephesus, whither ships were coming in from all quarters to form the navy, consisting, vessels of burden included, of eight hundred vessels, of which Cleopatra furnished two hundred, together with twenty thousand talents, and provision for the whole army during the war. Antony, on the advice of Domitius and some others, bade Cleopatra return into Egypt, there to expect the event of the war; but she, dreading some new reconciliation by Octavia's means, prevailed with Canidius, by a large sum of money, to speak in her favour with Antony, pointing out to him that it was not just that one that bore so great a part in the charge of the war should be robbed of her share of glory in the carrying it on; nor would it be politic to disoblige the Egyptians, who were so considerable a part of his naval forces; nor did he see how she was inferior in prudence to any one of the kings that were serving with him; she had long governed a great kingdom by herself alone, and long lived with him, and gained experience in public affairs.

These arguments (so the fate that destined all to Cæsar would have it) prevailed; and

when all their forces had met, they sailed together to Samos, and held high festivities. For,
as it was ordered that all kings, princes, and
governors, all nations and cities within the
limits of Syria, the Mæotid Lake, Armenia,
and Illyria, should bring or cause to be brought
all munitions necessary for war, so was it also
proclaimed that all stage-players should make
their appearance at Samos; so that, while pretty
nearly the whole world was filled with groans
and lamentations, this one island for some days
resounded with piping and harping, theatres
filling, and choruses playing. Every city sent
an ox as its contribution to the sacrifice, and
the kings that accompanied Antony competed
who should make the most magnificent feasts
and the greatest presents; and men began to
ask themselves, what would be done to celebrate the victory, when they went to such an
expense of festivity at the opening of the war.

This over, he gave Priene to his players for
a habitation, and set sail for Athens, where
fresh sports and play-acting employed him.
Cleopatra, jealous of the honours Octavia had
received at Athens (for Octavia was much beloved by the Athenians), courted the favour of
the people with all sorts of attentions. The
Athenians, in requital, having decreed her
public honours, deputed several of the citizens
to wait upon her at her house; amongst whom
went Antony as one, he being an Athenian
citizen, and he it was that made the speech. He
sent orders to Rome to have Octavia removed
out of his house. She left it, we are told, accompanied by all his children, except the eldest
by Fulvia, who was then with his father, weeping and grieving that she must be looked upon
as one of the causes of the war. But the Romans pitied, not so much her, as Antony himself, and more particularly those who had seen
Cleopatra, whom they could report to have no
way the advantage of Octavia either in youth
or in beauty.

The speed and extent of Antony's preparations alarmed Cæsar, who feared he might be
forced to fight the decisive battle that summer.
For he wanted many necessaries, and the people grudged very much to pay the taxes; freemen being called upon to pay a fourth part of
their incomes, and freed slaves an eighth of
their property, so that there were loud outcries
against him, and disturbances throughout all
Italy. And this is looked upon as one of the
greatest of Antony's oversights, that he did not
then press the war. For he allowed time at once
for Cæsar to make his preparations and for the

commotions to pass over. For while people
were having their money called for, they were
mutinous and violent; but, having paid it, they
held their peace.

Titius and Plancus, men of consular dignity
and friends to Antony, having been ill-used by
Cleopatra, whom they had most resisted in her
design of being present in the war, came over
to Cæsar and gave information of the contents
of Antony's will, with which they were acquainted. It was deposited in the hands of the
vestal virgins, who refused to deliver it up, and
sent Cæsar word, if he pleased, he should come
and seize it himself, which he did. And, reading it over to himself, he noted those places
that were most for his purpose, and, having
summoned the senate, read them publicly.
Many were scandalised at the proceeding,
thinking it out of reason and equity to call a
man to account for what was not to be until
after his death. Cæsar specially pressed what
Antony said in his will about his burial; for he
had ordered that even if he died in the city of
Rome, his body, after being carried in state
through the Forum, should be sent to Cleopatra at Alexandria.

Calvisius, a dependant of Cæsar's, urged
other charges in connection with Cleopatra
against Antony; that he had given her the
library of Pergamus, containing two hundred
thousand distinct volumes; that at a great banquet, in the presence of many guests, he had
risen up and rubbed her feet, to fulfil some
wager or promise; that he had suffered the
Ephesians to salute her as their queen; that he
had frequently at the public audience of kings
and princes received amorous messages written in tablets made of onyx and crystal, and
read them openly on the tribunal; that when
Furnius, a man of great authority and eloquence among the Romans, was pleading,
Cleopatra happening to pass by in her chair,
Antony started up and left them in the middle
of their cause, to follow at her side and attend
her home.

Calvisius, however, was looked upon as the
inventor of most of these stories. Antony's
friends went up and down the city to gain him
credit, and sent one of themselves, Geminius,
to him, to beg him to take heed and not allow
himself to be deprived by vote of his authority,
and proclaimed a public enemy to the Roman
state. But Geminius no sooner arrived in
Greece but he was looked upon as one of Octavia's spies; at their suppers he was made a
continual butt for mockery, and was put to sit

in the least honourable places; all of which he bore very well, seeking only an occasion of speaking with Antony. So at supper, being told to say what business he came about, he answered he would keep the rest for a soberer hour, but one thing he had to say, whether full or fasting, that all would go well if Cleopatra would return to Egypt. And on Antony showing his anger at it, "You have done well, Geminius," said Cleopatra, "to tell your secret without being put to the rack."

So Geminius, after a few days, took occasion to make his escape and go to Rome. Many more of Antony's friends were driven from him by the insolent usage they had from Cleopatra's flatterers, amongst who were Marcus Silanus and Dellius the historian. And Dellius says he was afraid of his life, and that Glaucus, the physician, informed him of Cleopatra's design against him. She was angry with him for having said that Antony's friends were served with sour wine, while at Rome Sarmentus, Cæsar's little page (his *delicia,* as the Romans call it), drank Falernian.

As soon as Cæsar had completed his preparations, he had a decree made declaring war on Cleopatra, and depriving Antony of the authority which he had let a woman exercise in his place. Cæsar added that he had drunk potions that had bereaved him of his senses, and that the generals they would have to fight with would be Mardion the eunuch, Pothinus, Iras, Cleopatra's hair-dressing girl, and Charmion, who were Antony's chief state-councillors.

These prodigies are said to have announced the war. Pisaurum, where Antony had settled a colony, on the Adriatic sea, was swallowed up by an earthquake; sweat ran from one of the marble statues of Antony at Alba for many days together, and though frequently wiped off, did not stop. When he himself was in the city of Patræ, the temple of Hercules was struck by lightning, and, at Athens, the figure of Bacchus was torn by a violent wind out of the Battle of the Giants, and laid flat upon the theatre; with both which deities Antony claimed connection, professing to be descended from Hercules, and from his imitating Bacchus in his way of living having received the name of young Bacchus. The same whirlwind at Athens also brought down, from amongst many others which were not disturbed, the colossal statues of Fumenes and Attalus, which were inscribed with Antony's name. And in Cleopatra's admiral-galley, which was called the Antonias, a most inauspicious omen occurred.

Some swallows had built in the stern of the galley, but other swallows came, beat the first away, and destroyed their nests.

When the armaments gathered for the war, Antony had no less than five hundred ships of war, including numerous galleys of eight and ten banks of oars, as richly ornamented as if they were meant for a triumph. He had a hundred thousand foot and twelve thousand horse. He had vassal kings attending, Bocchus of Libya, Tarcondemus of the Upper Cilicia, Archelaus of Cappadocia, Philadelphus of Paphlagonia, Mithridates of Commagene, and Sadalas of Thrace; all these were with him in person. Out of Pontus Polemon sent him considerable forces, as did also Malchus from Arabia, Herod the Jew, and Amyntus, King of Lycaonia and Galatia; also the Median king sent some troops to join him. Cæsar had two hundred and fifty galleys of war, eighty thousand foot, and horse about equal to the enemy. Antony's empire extended from Euphrates and Armenia to the Ionian sea and the Illyrians; Cæsar's, from Illyria to the westward ocean, and from the ocean all along the Tuscan and Sicilian sea. Of Africa, Cæsar had all the coast opposite to Italy, Gaul, and Spain, as far as the Pillars of Hercules, and Antony the provinces from Cyrene to Æthiopia.

But so wholly was he now the mere appendage to the person of Cleopatra that, although he was much superior to the enemy in land-forces, yet, out of complaisance to his mistress, he wished the victory to be gained by sea, and that, too, when he could not but see how, for want of sailors, his captains, all through unhappy Greece, were pressing every description of men, common travellers and ass-drivers, harvest labourers and boys, and for all this the vessels had not their complements, but remained, most of them, ill-manned and badly rowed. Cæsar, on the other side, had ships that were built not for size or show, but for service, not pompous galleys, but light, swift, and perfectly manned; and from his headquarters at Tarentum and Brundusium he sent messages to Antony not to protract the war, but come out with his forces; he would give him secure roadsteads and ports for his fleet, and, for his land army to disembark and pitch their camp, he would leave him as much ground in Italy, inland from the sea, as a horse could traverse in a single course. Antony, on the other side, with the like bold language, challenged him to a single combat, though he were much the older; and, that being refused, proposed to meet him in the Pharsalian fields, where Cæsar and Pompey had fought before.

But whilst Antony lay with his fleet near Actium, where now stands Nicopolis, Cæsar seized his opportunity and crossed the Ionian sea, securing himself at a place in Epirus called the Ladle. And when those about Antony were much disturbed, their land forces being a good way off, "Indeed," said Cleopatra, in mockery, "we may well be frightened if Cæsar has got hold of the Ladle!"

On the morrow, Antony, seeing the enemy sailing up, and fearing lest his ships might be taken for want of the soldiers to go on board of them, armed all the rowers, and made a show upon the decks of being in readiness to fight; the oars were mounted as if waiting to be put in motion, and the vessels themselves drawn up to face the enemy on either side of the channel of Actium, as though they were properly manned and ready for an engagement. And Cæsar, deceived by this stratagem, retired. He was also thought to have shown considerable skill in cutting off the water from the enemy by some lines of trenches and forts, water not being plentiful anywhere else, nor very good. And again, his conduct to Domitius was generous, much against the will of Cleopatra. For when he had made his escape in a little boat to Cæsar, having then a fever upon him, although Antony could not but resent it highly, yet he sent after him his whole equipage with his friends and servants; and Domitius, as if he would give a testimony to the world how repentant he had become on his desertion and treachery being thus manifest, died soon after. Among the kings, also, Amyntas and Deiotarus went over to Cæsar.

And the fleet was so unfortunate in everything that was undertaken, and so unready on every occasion, that Antony was driven again to put his confidence in the land forces. Canidius, too, who commanded the legions, when he saw how things stood, changed his opinion, and now was of advice that Cleopatra should be sent back, and that, retiring into Thrace or Macedonia, the quarrel should be decided in a land fight. For Dicomes, also, the King of the Getæ, promised to come and join him with a great army, and it would not be any kind of disparagement to him to yield the sea to Cæsar, who, in the Sicilian wars, had had such long practice in ship-fighting; on the contrary, it would be simply ridiculous for Antony, who was by land the most experienced commander living, to make no use of his well-disciplined and numerous infantry, scattering and wasting his forces by parcelling them out in the ships.

But for all this, Cleopatra prevailed that a sea-fight should determine all, having already an eye to flight, and ordering all her affairs, not so as to assist in gaining a victory, but to escape with the greatest safety from the first commencement of a defeat.

There were two long walls, extending from the camp to the station of the ships, between which Antony used to pass to and fro without suspecting any danger. But Cæsar, upon the suggestion of a servant that it would not be difficult to surprise him, laid an ambush, which, rising up somewhat too hastily, seized the man that came just before him, he himself escaping narrowly by flight.

When it was resolved to stand to a fight at sea, they set fire to all the Egyptian ships except sixty; and of these the best and largest, from ten banks down to three, he manned with twenty thousand full-armed men and two thousand archers. Here it is related that a foot captain, one that had fought often under Antony, and had his body all mangled with wounds, exclaimed, "O my general, what have our wounds and swords done to displease you, that you should give your confidence to rotten timbers? Let Egyptians and Phœnicians contend at sea, give us the land, where we know well how to die upon the spot or gain the victory." To which he answered nothing, but, by his look and motion of his hand seeming to bid him be of good courage, passed forwards, having already, it would seem, no very sure hopes, since when the masters proposed leaving the sails behind them, he commanded they should be put aboard, "For we must not," said he, "let one enemy escape."

That day and the three following the sea was so rough they could not engage. But on the fifth there was a calm, and they fought; Antony commanding with Publicola the right, and Cœlius the left squadron, Marcus Octavius and Marcus Insteius the centre. Cæsar gave the charge of the left to Agrippa, commanding in person on the right. As for the land forces, Canidius was general for Antony, Taurus for Cæsar; both armies remained drawn up in order along the shore. Antony in a small boat went from one ship to another, encouraging his soldiers, and bidding them stand firm and fight as steadily on their large ships as if they were on land. The masters he ordered that they should receive the enemy lying still as if they were at anchor, and maintain the entrance of the port, which was a narrow and difficult passage.

Of Cæsar they relate that, leaving his tent and going round, while it was yet dark, to visit the ships, he met a man driving an ass, and asked him his name. He answered him that his own name was "Fortunate, and my ass," says he, "is called Conqueror." And afterwards, when he disposed the beaks of the ships in that place in token of his victory, the statue of this man and his ass in bronze were placed amongst them. After examining the rest of his fleet, he went in a boat to the right wing, and looked with much admiration at the enemy lying perfectly still in the straits, in all appearance as if they had been at anchor. For some considerable length of time he actually thought they were so, and kept his own ships at rest, at a distance of about eight furlongs from them. But about noon a breeze sprang up from the sea, and Antony's men, weary of expecting the enemy so long, and trusting to their large tall vessels, as if they had been invincible, began to advance the left squadron. Cæsar was overjoyed to see them move, and ordered his own right squadron to retire, that he might entice them out to sea as far as he could, his design being to sail round and round, and so with his light and well-manned galleys to attack these huge vessels, which their size and their want of men made slow to move and difficult to manage.

When they engaged, there was no charging or striking of one ship by another, because Antony's, by reason of their great bulk, were incapable of the rapidity required to make the stroke effectual, and on the other side, Cæsar's durst not charge head to head on Antony's, which were all armed with solid masses and spikes of brass; nor did they like even to run in on their sides, which were so strongly built with great squared pieces of timber, fastened together with iron bolts, that their vessels' beaks would easily have been shattered upon them. So that the engagement resembled a land fight, or, to speak yet more properly, the attack and defence of a fortified place; for there were always three or four vessels of Cæsar's about one of Antony's, pressing them with spears, javelins, poles, and several inventions of fire, which they flung among them, Antony's men using catapults also, to pour down missiles from wooden towers. Agrippa drawing out the squadron under his command to out-flank the enemy, Publicola was obliged to observe his motions, and gradually to break off from the middle squadron, where some confusion and alarm ensued, while Arruntius engaged them.

But the fortune of the day was still undecided, and the battle equal, when on a sudden Cleopatra's sixty ships were seen hoisting sail and making out to sea in full flight, right through the ships that were engaged. For they were placed behind the great ships, which, in breaking through, they put into disorder. The enemy was astonished to see them sailing off with a fair wind towards Peloponnesus. Here it was that Antony showed to all the world that he was no longer actuated by the thoughts and motives of a commander or a man, or indeed by his own judgment at all, and what was once said as a jest, that the soul of a lover lives in some one else's body, he proved to be a serious truth. For, as if he had been born part of her, and must move with her wheresoever she went, as soon as he saw her ship sailing away, he abandoned all that were fighting and spending their lives for him, and put himself aboard a galley of five banks of oars, taking with him only Alexander of Syria and Scellias, to follow her that had so well begun his ruin and would hereafter accomplish it.

She, perceiving him to follow, gave the signal to come aboard. So, as soon as he came up with them, he was taken into the ship. But without seeing her or letting himself be seen by her, he went forward by himself, and sat alone, without a word, in the ship's prow, covering his face with his two hands. In the meanwhile, some of Cæsar's light Liburnian ships, that were in pursuit, came in sight. But on Antony's commanding to face about, they all gave back except Eurycles the Laconian, who pressed on, shaking a lance from the deck, as if he meant to hurl it at him. Antony, standing at the prow, demanded of him, "Who is this that pursues Antony," "I am," said he, "Eurycles, the son of Lachares, armed with Cæsar's fortune to revenge my father's death." Lachares had been condemned for a robbery, and beheaded by Antony's orders. However, Eurycles did not attack Antony, but ran with his full force upon the other admiral-galley (for there were two of them), and with the blow turned her round, and took both her and another ship, in which was a quantity of rich plate and furniture.

So soon as Eurycles was gone, Antony returned to his posture and sate silent, and thus he remained for three days, either in anger with Cleopatra, or wishing not to upbraid her, at the end of which they touched at Tænarus. Here the women of their company succeeded first in bringing them to speak, and afterwards to eat and sleep together. And, by this time, several of the ships of burden and some of his friends began to come in to him from the rout, bringing news of his fleet's being quite destroyed, but that the land forces, they thought, still stood firm. So that he sent messengers to Canidius to march the army with all speed through Macedonia into Asia.

And, designing himself to go from Tænarus into Africa, he gave one of the merchant ships, laden with a large sum of money, and vessels of silver and gold of great value, belonging to the royal collections, to his friends, desiring them to share it amongst them, and provide for their own safety. They refusing his kindness with tears in their eyes, he comforted them with all the goodness and humanity imaginable, entreating them to leave them, and wrote letters in their behalf to Theophilus, his steward, at Corinth, that he would provide for their security, and keep them concealed till such time as they could make their peace with Cæsar. This Theophilus was the father of Hipparchus, who had such interest with Antony, who was the first of all his freedmen that went over to Cæsar, and who settled afterwards at Corinth. In this posture were affairs with Antony.

But at Actium, his fleet, after a long resistance to Cæsar, and suffering the most damage from a heavy sea that set in right ahead, scarcely at four in the afternoon, gave up the contest, with the loss of not more than five thousand men killed, but of three hundred ships taken, as Cæsar himself has recorded. Only a few had known of Antony's flight; and those who were told of it could not at first give any belief to so incredible a thing as that a general who had nineteen entire legions and twelve thousand horse upon the seashore, could abandon all and fly away; and he, above all, who had so often experienced both good and evil fortune, and had in a thousand wars and battles been inured to changes. His soldiers, however, would not give up their desires and expectations, still fancying he would appear from some part or other, and showed such a generous fidelity to his service that, when they were thoroughly assured that he was fled in earnest, they kept themselves in a body seven days, making no account of the messages that Cæsar sent to them. But at last, seeing that Canidius himself, who commanded them, was fled from the camp by night, and that all their officers had quite abandoned them, they gave way, and made their submission to the conqueror.

After this, Cæsar set sail for Athens, where he made a settlement with Greece, and distributed what remained of the provision of corn that Antony had made for his army among the cities, which were in a miserable condition, despoiled of their money, their slaves, their horses, and beasts of service. My great-grandfather Nicharchus used to relate that the whole body of the people of our city were put in requisition to carry each one a certain measure of corn upon their shoulders to the seaside near Anticyra, men standing by to quicken them with the lash. They had made one journey of the kind, but when they had just measured out the corn, and were putting it on their backs for a second, news came of Antony's defeat, and so saved Chæronea, for all Antony's purveyors and soldiers fled upon the news, and left them to divide the corn among themselves.

When Antony came into Africa, he sent on Cleopatra from Parætonium into Egypt, and stayed himself in the most entire solitude that he could desire, roaming and wandering about with only two friends, one a Greek, Aristocrates, a rhetorician, and the other a Roman, Lucilius, of whom we have elsewhere spoken, how, at Philippi, to give Brutus time to escape, he suffered himself to be taken by the pursuers, pretending he was Brutus. Antony gave him his life, and on this account he remained true and faithful to him to the last.

But when also the officer who commanded for him in Africa, to whose care he had committed all his forces there, took them over to Cæsar, he resolved to kill himself, but was hindered by his friends. And coming to Alexandria, he found Cleopatra busied in a most bold and wonderful enterprise. Over the small space of land which divides the Red Sea from the sea near Egypt, which may be considered also the boundary between Asia and Africa, and in the narrowest place is not much above three hundred furlongs across, over this neck of land Cleopatra had formed a project of dragging her fleet and setting it afloat in the Arabian Gulf, thus with her soldiers and her treasure to secure herself a home on the other side, where she might live in peace far away from war and slavery. But the first galleys which were carried over being burnt by the Arabians of Petra, and Antony not knowing but that the army before Actium still held together, she desisted from her enterprise, and gave orders for the fortifying of all the approaches to Egypt.

But Antony, leaving the city and the conversation of his friends, built him a dwelling-place in the water, near Pharos, upon a little mole which he cast up in the sea, and there, secluding himself from the company of mankind, said he desired nothing but to live the life of Timon; as indeed, his case was the same, and the ingratitude and injuries which he suffered from those he had esteemed his friends made him hate and distrust all mankind.

This Timon was a citizen of Athens, and lived much about the Peloponnesian war, as may be seen by the comedies of Aristophanes and Plato, in which he is ridiculed as hater and enemy of mankind. He avoided and repelled the approaches of every one, but embraced with kisses and the greatest show of affection Alcibiades, then in his hot youth. And when Apemantus was astonished, and demanded the reason, he replied that he knew this young man would one day do infinite mischief to the Athenians. He never admitted any one into his company, except at times this Apemantus, who was of the same sort of temper, and was an imitator of his way of life. At the celebration of the festival of flagons, these two kept the feast together, and Apemantus, saying to him, "What a pleasant party, Timon!" "It would be," he answered, "if you were away." One day he got up in a full assembly on the speaker's place, and when there was a dead silence and great wonder at so unusual a sight, he said, "Ye men of Athens, I have a little plot of ground, and in it grows a fig-tree, on which many citizens have been pleased to hang themselves; and now, having resolved to build in that place, I wish to announce it publicly, that any of you who may be desirous may go and hang yourselves before I cut it down."

He died and was buried at Halæ, near the sea, where it so happened that, after his burial, a land-slip took place on the point of the shore, and the sea, flowing in, surrounded his tomb, and made it inaccessible to the foot of man. It bore this inscription:—

Here am I laid, my life of misery done,
Ask not my name, I curse you every one.

And this epitaph was made by himself; that more generally known is by Callimachus:—

Timon, the misanthrope, am I below,
Go, and revile me, traveller, only go.

Thus much of Timon, of whom much more might be said.

Canidius now came, and he brought the news in person of the loss of the army before Actium. Then he received news that Herod of Judæa was gone over to Cæsar with some legions and cohorts, and that the other kings and princes were in like manner deserting him, and that, out of Egypt, nothing stood by him. All this, however, seemed not to disturb him, but, as if he were glad to put away all hope, that with it he might be rid of all care, and leaving his habitation by the sea, which he called the Timoneum, he was received by Cleopatra in the palace, and set the whole city into a course of feasting, drinking, and presents. The son of Cæsar and Cleopatra was registered among the youths, and Antyllus, his own son by Fulvia, received the gown without the purple border given to those that are come of age; in honour of which the citizens of Alexandria did nothing but feast and revel for many days.

They themselves broke up the Order of the Inimitable Livers, and constituted another in its place, not inferior in splendour, luxury, and sumptuosity, calling it that of the Diers Together. For all those that said they would die with Antony and Cleopatra gave in their names, for the present passing their time in all manner of pleasures and a regular succession of banquets. But Cleopatra was busied in making a collection of all varieties of poisonous drugs, and, in order to see which of them were the least painful in the operation, she had them tried upon prisoners condemned to die. But, finding that the quick poisons always worked with sharp pains, and that the less painful were slow, she next tried venomous animals, and watched with her own eyes whilst they were applied, one creature to the body of another. This was her daily practice, and she pretty well satisfied herself that nothing was comparable to the bite of the asp, which, without convulsion or groaning, brought on a heavy drowsiness and lethargy, with a gentle sweat on the face, the senses being stupefied by degrees; the patient, in appearance, being sensible of no pain, but rather troubled to be disturbed or awakened like those that are in a profound natural sleep.

At the same time, they sent ambassadors to Cæsar into Asia, Cleopatra asking for the kingdom of Egypt for her children, and Antony, that he might have leave to live as a private man in Egypt, or, if that were thought too much, that he might retire to Athens. In lack of friends, so many having deserted, and others not being trusted, Euphronius, his son's tutor, was sent on this embassy. For Alexas of Laodicea, who, by the recommendation of Timagenes, became acquainted with Antony at Rome, and had been more powerful with him than any Greek, and was, of all the instruments which Cleopatra made use of to persuade Antony, the most violent, and the chief subverter of any good thoughts that from time to time might rise in his mind in Octavia's favour, had been sent before to dissuade Herod from desertion; but betraying his master, stayed with him and, confiding in Herod's interest, had the boldness to come into Cæsar's presence. Herod, however, was not able to help him, for he was immediately put in chains and sent into his own country, where, by Cæsar's orders, he was put to death. This reward of his treason Alexas received while Antony was yet alive.

Cæsar would not listen to any proposals for Antony, but he made answer to Cleopatra that there was no reasonable favour which she might not expect, if she put Antony to death, or expelled him from Egypt. He sent back with the ambassadors his own freedman, Thyrsus, a man of understanding, and not at all ill-qualified for conveying the messages of a youthful general to a woman so proud of her charms and possessed with the opinion of the power of her beauty. But by the long audiences he received from her, and the special honours which she paid him, Antony's jealousy began to be awakened; he had him seized, whipped, and sent back; writing Cæsar word that the man's busy, impertinent ways had provoked him; in his circumstances he could not be expected to be very patient: "But if it offend you," he added, "you have got my freedman, Hipparchus, with you; hang him up and scourge him to make us even."

But Cleopatra, after this, to clear herself, and to allay his jealousies, paid him all the attentions imaginable. When her own birthday came, she kept it as was suitable to their fallen fortunes; but his was observed with the utmost prodigality of splendour and magnificence, so that many of the guests sat down in want, and went home wealthy men. Meantime, continual letters came to Cæsar from Agrippa, telling him his presence was extremely required at Rome.

And so the war was deferred for a season. But, the winter being over, he began his march; he himself by Syria, and his captains through Africa. Pelusium being taken, there went a report as if it had been delivered up to

Cæsar by Seleucus, not without the consent of Cleopatra; but she, to justify herself, gave up into Antony's hands the wife and children of Seleucus to be put to death.

She had caused to be built, joining to the temple of Isis, several tombs and monuments of wonderful height, and very remarkable for the workmanship; thither she removed her treasure, her gold, silver, emeralds, pearls, ebony, ivory, cinnamon, and, after all, a great quantity of torchwood and tow. Upon which Cæsar began to fear lest she should, in a desperate fit, set all these riches on fire; and, therefore, while he was marching towards the city with his army, he omitted no occasion of giving her new assurances of his good intentions. He took up his position in the Hippodrome, where Antony made a fierce sally upon him, routed the horse, and beat them back into their trenches, and so returned with great satisfaction to the palace, where, meeting Cleopatra, armed as he was, he kissed her, and commended to her favour one of his men, who had most signalised himself in the fight, to whom she made a present of a breastplate and helmet of gold; which he having received went that very night and deserted to Cæsar.

After this, Antony sent a new challenge to Cæsar to fight him hand-to-hand; who made him answer that he might find several other ways to end his life; and he, considering with himself that he could not die more honourably than in battle, resolved to make an effort both by land and sea. At supper, it is said, he bade his servants help him freely, and pour him out wine plentifully, since to-morrow, perhaps, they should not do the same, but be servants to a new master, whilst he should lie on the ground, a dead corpse, and nothing. His friends that were about him wept to hear him talk so; which he perceiving, told them he would not lead them to a battle in which he expected rather an honourable death than either safety or victory.

That night, it is related, about the middle of it, when the whole city was in a deep silence and general sadness, expecting the event of the next day, on a sudden was heard the sound of all sorts of instruments, and voices singing in tune, and the cry of a crowd of people shouting and dancing, like a troop of bacchanals on its way. This tumultuous procession seemed to take its course right through the middle of the city to the gate nearest the enemy; here it became the loudest, and suddenly passed out. People who reflected considered this to signify that Bacchus, the god whom Antony had always made it his study to copy and imitate, had now forsaken him.

As soon as it was light, he marched his infantry out of the city, and posted them upon a rising ground, from whence he saw his fleet make up to the enemy. There he stood in expectation of the event; but as soon as the fleets came near to one another, his men saluted Cæsar's with their oars; and on their responding, the whole body of the ships, forming into a single fleet, rowed up direct to the city. Antony had no sooner seen this, but the horse deserted him, and went over to Cæsar; and his foot being defeated, he retired into the city, crying out that Cleopatra had betrayed him to the enemies he had made for her sake. She, being afraid lest in his fury and despair he might do her a mischief, fled to her monument, and letting down the falling doors, which were strong with bars and bolts, she sent messengers who should tell Antony she was dead. He, believing it, cried out, "Now, Antony, why delay longer? Fate has snatched away the only pretext for which you could say you desired yet to live."

Going into his chamber, and there loosening and opening his coat of armour, "I am not," said he, "troubled, Cleopatra, to be at present bereaved of you, for I shall soon be with you; but it distresses me that so great a general should be found of a tardier courage than a woman." He had a faithful servant, whose name was Eros; he had engaged him formerly to kill him when he should think it necessary, and now he put him to his promise. Eros drew his sword, as designing to kill him, but, suddenly turning round, he slew himself. And as he fell dead at his feet, "It is well done, Eros," said Antony; "you show your master how to do what you had not the heart to do yourself;" and so he ran himself into the belly, and laid himself upon the couch. The wound, however, was not immediately mortal; and the flow of blood ceasing when he lay down, presently he came to himself, and entreated those that were about him to put him out of his pain; but they all fled out of the chamber, and left him crying out and struggling, until Diomede, Cleopatra's secretary, came to him, having orders from her to bring him into the monument.

When he understood she was alive, he eagerly gave order to the servants to take him up, and in their arms was carried to the door of the building. Cleopatra would not open the door, but, looking from a sort of window, she let down ropes and cords, to which Antony was fastened; and she and her two women, the only persons she had allowed to enter the monument, drew him up. Those that were present say that nothing was ever more sad than this spectacle, to see Antony, covered all over with blood and just expiring, thus drawn up, still holding up his hands to her, and lifting up his body with the little force he had left. As, indeed, it was no easy task for the women; and Cleopatra, with all her force, clinging to the rope, and straining with her head to the ground, with difficulty pulled him up, while those below encouraged her with their cries, and joined in all her efforts and anxiety.

When she had got him up, she laid him on the bed, tearing all her clothes, which she spread upon him; and, beating her breast with her hands, lacerating herself, and disfiguring her own face with the blood from his wounds, she called him her lord, her husband, her emperor, and seemed to have pretty nearly forgotten all her own evils, she was so intent upon his misfortunes. Antony, stopping her lamentations as well as he could, called for wine to drink, either that he was thirsty, or that he imagined that it might put him the sooner out of pain. When he had drunk, he advised her to bring her own affairs, so far as might be honourably done, to a safe conclusion, and that, among all the friends of Cæsar, she should rely on Proculeius; that she should not pity him in this last turn of fate, but rather rejoice for him in remembrance of his past happiness, who had been of all men the most illustrious and powerful, and in the end had fallen not ignobly, a Roman by a Roman overcome.

Just as he breathed his last, Proculeius arrived from Cæsar; for when Antony gave himself his wound, and was carried into Cleopatra, one of his guards, Dercetæus, took up Antony's sword and hid it; and, when he saw his opportunity, stole away to Cæsar, and brought him the first news of Antony's death, and withal showed him the bloody sword. Cæsar, upon this, retired into the inner part of his tent, and giving some tears to the death of one that had been nearly allied to him in marriage, his colleague in empire, and companion in so many wars and dangers, he came out to his friends, and, bringing with him many letters, he read to them with how much reason and moderation he had always addressed himself to Antony, and in return what overbearing and arrogant answers he received.

Then he sent Proculeius to use his utmost

endeavours to get Cleopatra alive into his power; for he was afraid of losing a great treasure, and, besides, she would be no small addition to the glory of his triumph. She, however, was careful not to put herself in Proculeius's power; but from within her monument, he standing on the outside of a door, on the level of the ground, which was strongly barred, but so that they might well enough hear one another's voice, she held a conference with him; she demanding that her kingdom might be given to her children, and he binding her to be of good courage, and trust Cæsar in everything.

Having taken particular notice of the place, he returned to Cæsar, and Gallius was sent to parley with her the second time; who, being come to the door, on purpose prolonged the conference, while Proculeius fixed his scaling-ladders in the window through which the women had pulled up Antony. And so entering, with two men to follow him, he went straight down to the door where Cleopatra was discoursing with Gallius. One of the two women who were shut up in the monument with her cried out, "Miserable Cleopatra, you are taken prisoner!" Upon which she turned quick, and, looking at Proculeius, drew out her dagger which she had with her to stab herself. But Proculeius ran up quickly, and seizing her with both his hands, "For shame," said he, "Cleopatra; you wrong yourself and Cæsar much, who would rob him of so fair an occasion of showing his clemency, and would make the world believe the most gentle of commanders to be a faithless and implacable enemy." And so, taking the dagger out of her hand, he also shook her dress to see if there were any poison hid in it. After this, Cæsar sent Epaphroditus, one of his freedmen, with orders to treat her with all the gentleness and civility possible, but to take the strictest precautions to keep her alive.

In the meanwhile, Cæsar made his entry into Alexandria, with Areius the philosopher at his side, holding him by the hand and talking with him; desiring that all his fellow-citizens should see what honour was paid to him, and should look up to him accordingly from the very first moment. Then, entering the exercise ground, he mounted a platform erected for the purpose, and from thence commanded the citizens (who, in great fear and consternation, fell prostrate at his feet) to stand up, and told them that he freely acquitted the people of all blame; first, for the sake of Alexander,

who built their city; then for the city's sake itself, which was so large and beautiful; and, thirdly, to gratify his friend Areius.

Such great honour did Areius receive from Cæsar; and by his intercession many lives were saved, amongst the rest that of Philostratus, a man, of all the professors of logic that ever were, the most ready in extempore speaking, but quite destitute of any right to call himself one of the philosophers of the Academy. Cæsar, out of disgust at his character, refused all attention to his entreaties. So, growing a long white beard, and dressing himself in black, he followed behind Areius, shouting out the verse,

The wise, if they are wise, will save the wise.

Which Cæsar hearing, gave him his pardon, to prevent rather any odium that might attach to Areius, than any harm that Philostratus might suffer.

Of Antony's children, Antyllus, his son by Fulvia, being betrayed by his tutor, Theodorus, was put to death; and while the soldiers were cutting off his head, his tutor contrived to steal a precious jewel which he wore about his neck, and put it in his pocket, and afterwards denied the fact, but was convicted and crucified. Cleopatra's children, with their attendants, had a guard set on them, and were treated very honourably. Cæsarion, who was reputed to be the son of Cæsar the Dictator, was sent by his mother, with a great sum of money, through Æthiopia, to pass into India; but his tutor, a man named Rhodon, about as honest as Theodorus, persuaded him to turn back, for that Cæsar designed to make him king. Cæsar consulting what was best to be done with him, Areius, we are told, said:

Too many Cæsars are not well.

So, afterwards, when Cleopatra was dead he was killed.

Many kings and great commanders made petition to Cæsar for the body of Antony, to give him his funeral rites; but he would not take away his corpse from Cleopatra, by whose hands he was buried with royal splendour and magnificence, it being granted to her to employ what she pleased on his funeral. In this extremity of grief and sorrow, and having inflamed and ulcerated her breasts with beating them, she fell into a high fever, and was very glad of the occasion, hoping, under this pretext, to abstain from food, and so to die in quiet without interference. She had her own physician, Olympus, to whom she told the truth, and asked his advice and help to put an end to herself, as Olympus himself has told us, in a narrative which he wrote of these events. But Cæsar, suspecting her purpose, took to menacing language about her children, and excited her fears for them, before which engines her purpose shook and gave way, so that she suffered those about her to give her what meat or medicine they pleased.

Some few days after, Cæsar himself came to make her a visit and comfort her. She lay then upon her pallet-bed in undress, and, on his entering, sprang up from off her bed, having nothing on but the one garment next her body, and flung herself at his feet, her hair and face looking wild and disfigured, her voice quivering, and her eyes sunk in her head. The marks of the blows she had given herself were visible about her bosom, and altogether her whole person seemed no less afflicted than her soul. But, for all this, her old charm, and the boldness of her youthful beauty, had not wholly left her, and, in spite of her present condition, still sparkled from within, and let itself appear in all the movements of her countenance. Cæsar, desiring her to repose herself, sat down by her; and, on this opportunity, she said something to justify her actions, attributing what she had done to the necessity she was under, and to her fear of Antony; and when Cæsar, on each point, made his objections, and she found herself confuted, she broke off at once into language of entreaty and deprecation, as if she desired nothing more than to prolong her life.

And at last, having by her a list of her treasure, she gave it into his hands; and when Seleucus, one of her stewards, who was by, pointed out that various articles were omitted, and charged her with secreting them, she flew up and caught him by the hair, and struck him several blows on the face. Cæsar smiling and withholding her, "Is it not very hard, Cæsar," said she, "when you do me the honour to visit me in this condition I am in, that I should be accused by one of my own servants of laying by some women's toys, not meant to adorn, be sure, my unhappy self, but that I might have some little present by me to make your Octavia and your Livia, that by their intercession I might hope to find you in some measure disposed to mercy?" Cæsar was pleased to hear her talk thus, being now assured that she was desirous to live. And, therefore, letting her know that the things she had laid by she might dispose of as she pleased, and his usage of her should be honourable above her expectation, he went away, well satisfied that

he had overreached her, but, in fact, was himself deceived.

There was a young man of distinction among Cæsar's companions named Cornelius Dolabella. He was not without a certain tenderness for Cleopatra, and sent her word privately, as she had besought him to do, that Cæsar was about to return through Syria, and that she and her children were to be sent on within three days. When she understood this, she made her request to Cæsar that he would be pleased to permit her to make oblations to the departed Antony; which being granted, she ordered herself to be carried to the place where he was buried, and there, accompanied by her women, she embraced his tomb with tears in her eyes, and spoke in this manner: "O, dearest Antony," said she, "it is not long since that with these hands I buried you; then they were free, now I am a captive, and pay these last duties to you with a guard upon me, for fear that my just griefs and sorrows should impair my servile body, and make it less fit to appear in their triumph over you. No further offerings or libations expect from me; these are the last honours that Cleopatra can pay your memory, for she is to be hurried away far from you. Nothing could part us whilst we lived, but death seems to threaten to divide us. You, a Roman born, have found a grave in Egypt; I, an Egyptian, am to seek that favour, and none but that, in your country. But if the gods below, with whom you now are, either can or will do anything (since those above have betrayed us), suffer not your living wife to be abandoned; let me not be led in triumph to your shame, but hide me and bury me here with you, since, amongst all my bitter misfortunes, nothing has afflicted me like this brief time that I have lived away from you."

Having made these lamentations, crowning the tomb with garlands and kissing it, she gave orders to prepare her a bath, and, coming out of the bath, she lay down and made a sumptuous meal. And a country fellow brought her a little basket, which the guards intercepting and asking what it was, the fellow put the leaves which lay uppermost aside, and showed them it was full of figs; and on their admiring the largeness and beauty of the figs, he laughed, and invited them to take some, which they refused, and, suspecting nothing, bade him carry them in. After her repast, Cleopatra sent to Cæsar a letter which she had written and sealed; and, putting everybody out of the monument but her two women, she shut the doors.

Cæsar, opening her letter, and finding pathetic prayers and entreaties that she might be buried in the same tomb with Antony, soon guessed what was doing. At first he was going himself in all haste, but, changing his mind, he sent others to see. The thing had been quickly done. The messengers came at full speed, and found the guards apprehensive of nothing; but on opening the doors they saw her stone-dead, lying upon a bed of gold, set out in all her royal ornaments. Iras, one of her women, lay dying at her feet, and Charmion, just ready to fall, scarce able to hold up her head, was adjusting her mistress's diadem. And when one that came in said angrily, "Was this well done of your lady, Charmion," "Extremely well," she answered, "and as became the descendant of so many kings;" and as she said this, she fell down dead by the bedside.

Some relate that an asp was brought in amongst those figs and covered with the leaves, and that Cleopatra had arranged that it might settle on her before she knew, but, when she took away some of the figs and saw it, she said, "So here it is," and held out her bare arm to be bitten. Others say that it was kept in a vase, and that she vexed and pricked it with a golden spindle till it seized her arm. But what really took place is known to no one, since it was also said that she carried poison in a hollow bodkin, about which she wound her hair; yet there was not so much as a spot found, or any symptom of poison upon her body, nor was the asp seen within the monument; only something like the trail of it was said to have been noticed on the sand by the sea, on the part towards which the building faced and where the windows were. Some relate that two faint puncture-marks were found on Cleopatra's arm, and to this account Cæsar seems to have given credit; for in his triumph there was carried a figure of Cleopatra, with an asp clinging to her. Such are the various accounts.

But Cæsar, though much disappointed by her death, yet could not but admire the greatness of her spirit, and gave order that her body should be buried by Antony with royal splendour and magnificence. Her women, also, received honourable burial by his directions. Cleopatra had lived nine-and-thirty years, during twenty-two of which she had reigned as queen, and for fourteen had been Antony's partner in his empire. Antony, according to some authorities, was fifty-three, according to others, fifty-six years old. His statues were all thrown down, but those of Cleopatra were left untouched; for Archibius, one of her friends, gave Cæsar two thousand talents to save them from the fate of Antony's.

Antony left by his three wives seven children, of whom only Antyllus, the eldest, was put to death by Cæsar; Octavia took the rest, and brought them up with her own. Cleopatra, his daughter by Cleopatra, was given in marriage to Juba, the most accomplished of kings; and Antony, his son by Fulvia, attained such high favour that, whereas Agrippa was considered to hold the first place with Cæsar, and the sons of Livia the second, the third, without dispute, was possessed by Antony. Octavia, also, having had by her first husband, Marcellus, two daughters, and one son named Marcellus, this son Cæsar adopted, and gave him his daughter in marriage; as did Octavia one of the daughters to Agrippa. But Marcellus dying almost immediately after his marriage, she, perceiving that her brother was at a loss to find elsewhere any sure friend to be his son-in-law, was the first to recommend that Agrippa should put away her daughter and marry Julia. To this Cæsar first, and then Agrippa himself, gave assent; so Agrippa married Julia, and Octavia, receiving her daughter, married her to the young Antony.

Of the two daughters whom Octavia had borne to Antony, the one was married to Domitius Ahenobarbus; and the other, Antonia, famous for her beauty and discretion, was married to Drusus, the son of Livia, and stepson to Cæsar. Of these parents were born Germanicus and Claudius. Claudius reigned later; and of the children of Germanicus, Caius, after a reign of distinction, was killed with his wife and child; Agrippina, after bearing a son Lucius Domitius, to Ahenobarbus, was married to Claudius Cæsar, who adopted Domitius, giving him the name of Nero Germanicus. He was emperor in our time, and put his mother to death, and with his madness and folly came not far from ruining the Roman empire, being Antony's descendant in the fifth generation.

ANTONY and DEMETRIUS
Compared

As BOTH are great examples of the vicissitudes of fortune, let us first consider in what way they attained their power and glory. Demetrius hired a kingdom already won for him by Antigonus, the most powerful of the successors, who, before Demetrius grew to be a man, traversed with his armies and subdued the greater part of Asia. Antony's father was well enough in other respects, but was no warrior, and could bequeath no great legacy of reputation to his son, who had the boldness, nevertheless, to take upon him the government, to which birth gave him no claim, which had been held by Cæsar, and became the inheritor of his great labours. And such power did he attain, with only himself to thank for it, that, in a division of the whole empire into two portions, he took and received the nobler one; and, absent himself, by his mere subalterns and lieutenants often defeated the Parthians, and drove the barbarous nations of the Caucasus back to the Caspian Sea. Those very things that procured him ill-repute bear witness to his greatness. Antigonus considered Antipater's daughter Phila, in spite of the disparity of her years, an advantageous match for Demetrius. Antony was thought disgraced by his marriage with Cleopatra, a queen superior in power and glory to all, except Arsaces, who were kings in her time. Antony was so great as to be thought by others worthy of higher things than his own desires.

As regards the right and justice of their aims at empire, Demetrius need not be blamed for seeking to rule a people that had always had a king to rule them. Antony, who enslaved the Roman people, just liberated from the rule of Cæsar, followed a cruel and tyrannical object. His greatest and most illustrious work, his successful war with Brutus and Cassius, was done to crush the liberties of his country and of his fellow-citizens. Demetrius, till he was driven to extremity, went on, without intermission, maintaining liberty in Greece, and expelling the foreign garrisons from the cities; not like Antony, whose boast was to have slain in Macedonia those who had set up liberty in Rome. As for the profusion and magnificence of his gifts, one point for which Antony is lauded, Demetrius so far outdid them that what he gave to his enemies was far more than Antony ever gave to his friends. Antony was renowned for giving Brutus honourable burial; Demetrius did so to all the enemy's dead, and sent the prisoners back to Ptolemy with money and presents.

Both were insolent in prosperity, and abandoned themselves to luxuries and enjoyments. Yet it cannot be said that Demetrius, in his revellings and dissipations, ever let slip the time for action; pleasures with him attended only the superabundance of his ease, and his Lamia, like that of the fable, belonged only to his playful, half-waking, half-sleeping hours. When war demanded his attention, his spear was not wreathed with ivy, nor his helmet redolent of unguents; he did not come out to battle from the women's chamber, but, hushing the bacchanal shouts and putting an end to the orgies, he became at once, as Euripides calls it, "the minister of the unpriestly Mars"; and, in short, he never once incurred disaster through indolence or self-indulgence. Whereas Antony, like Hercules in the picture where Omphale is seen removing his club and stripping him of his lion's skin, was over and over again disarmed by Cleopatra, and beguiled away, while great actions and enterprises of the first necessity fell, as it were, from his hands, to go with her to the seashore of Canopus and Taphosiris, and play about. And in the end, like another Paris he left the battle to fly to her arms; or rather, to say the truth, Paris fled when he was already beaten; Antony fled first, and, following Cleopatra, abandoned his victory.

There was no law to prevent Demetrius from marrying several wives; from the time of Philip and Alexander it had become usual with Macedonian kings, and he did no more than was done by Lysimachus and Ptolemy. And those he married he treated honourably. But Antony, first of all, in marrying two wives at once, did a thing which no Roman had ever allowed himself; and then he drove away his lawful Roman wife to please the foreign and unlawful woman. And so Demetrius incurred no harm at all; Antony procured his ruin by his marriage. On the other hand, no licentious act of Antony's can be charged with that impiety which marks those of Demetrius. Historical writers tell us that the very dogs are excluded from the whole Acropolis because of their gross, uncleanly habits. The very Parthenon itself saw Demetrius consorting with harlots and debauching free women of Athens. The vice of cruelty, also, remote as it seems from the indulgence of voluptuous desires, must be attributed to him, who, in the pursuit of his pleasures, allowed or, to say more truly, compelled the death of the most beautiful and most chaste of the Athenians, who found no way but this to escape his violence. In one word, Antony himself suffered by his excesses, and other people by those of Demetrius.

In his conduct to his parents, Demetrius was irreproachable. Antony gave up his mother's brother, in order that he might have leave to kill Cicero, this itself being so cruel and shocking an act that Antony would hardly be forgiven if Cicero's death had been the price of this uncle's safety. In respect of breaches of oaths and treaties, the seizure of Artabazes, and the assassination of Alexander, Antony may urge the plea which no one denies to be true, that Artabazes first abandoned and betrayed him in Media; Demetrius is alleged by many to have invented false pretexts for his act, and not to have retaliated for injuries, but to have accused one whom he injured himself.

The achievements of Demetrius are all his own work. Antony's noblest and greatest victories were won in his absence by his lieutenants. For their final disasters they have both only to thank themselves; not, however, in an equal degree. Demetrius was deserted, the Macedonians revolted from him; Antony deserted others, and ran away while men were fighting for him at the risk of their lives. The fault to be found with the one is that he had thus entirely alienated the affections of his soldiers; the other's condemnation is that he abandoned so much love and faith as he still possessed. We cannot admire the death of either, but that of Demetrius excites our greater contempt. He let himself become a prisoner, and was thankful to gain a three years' accession of life in captivity. He was tamed like a wild beast by his belly, and by wine; Antony took himself out of the world in a cowardly, pitiful, and ignoble manner, but still in time to prevent the enemy having his person in their power.

DION

408?–353 B.C.

If it be true, Sosius Senecio, that, as Simonides tells us—

Of the Corinthians Troy does not complain

for having taken part with the Achæans in the siege, because the Trojans also had Corinthians (Glaucus, who sprang from Corinth) fighting bravely on their side, so also it may be fairly said that neither Romans nor Greeks can quarrel with the Academy, each nation being equally represented in the following pair of lives, which will give an account of Brutus and of Dion—Dion, who was Plato's own hearer, and Brutus, who was brought up in his philosophy. They came from one and the self-same school, where they had been trained alike to run the race of honour; nor need we wonder that in the performance of actions often most nearly allied and akin, they both bore evidence to the truth of what their guide and teacher said, that, without the concurrence of power and success, with justice and prudence, public actions do not attain their proper, great, and noble character.

For as Hippomachus the wrestling-master affirmed, he could distinguish his scholars at a distance, though they were but carrying meat from the shambles, so it is very probable that the principles of those who have had the same good education should appear with a resemblance in all their actions, creating in them a certain harmony and proportion, at once agreeable and becoming.

We may also draw a close parallel of the lives of the two men from their fortunes, wherein chance, even more than their own designs, made them nearly alike. For they were both cut off by an untimely death, not being able to accomplish those ends which through many risks and difficulties they aimed at. But, above all, this is most wonderful; that by preternatural interposition both of them had notice given of their approaching death by an unpropitious form, which visibly appeared to them. And yet there are people who utterly deny any such thing, and say that no man in his right senses ever yet saw any supernatural phantom or apparition, but that children only, and silly women, or men disordered by sickness, in some aberration of the mind or distemperature of the body, have had empty and extravagant imaginations, whilst the real evil genius, superstition, was in themselves.

Yet if Dion and Brutus, men of solid understanding, and philosophers, not to be easily deluded by fancy or discomposed by any sudden apprehension, were thus affected by visions that they forthwith declared to their friends what they had seen, I know not how we can avoid admitting again the utterly exploded opinion of the oldest times, that evil and beguiling spirits, out of envy to good men, and a desire of impeding their good deeds, make efforts to excite in them feelings of terror and distraction, to make them shake and totter in their virtue, lest by a steady and unbiassed perseverance they should obtain a happier condition than these beings after death.

But I shall leave these things for another opportunity, and, in this twelfth book of the lives of great men compared one with another, begin with his who was the elder.

Dionysius the First, having possessed himself of the government, at once took to wife the daughter of Hermocrates, the Syracusan. She, in an outbreak which the citizens made before the new power was well settled, was abused in such a barbarous and outrageous manner that for shame she put an end to her own life. But Dionysius, when he was re-established and confirmed in his supremacy, married two wives together, one named Doris, of Locri, the other Aristomache, a native of Sicily, and daughter of Hipparinus, a man of the first quality in Syracuse, and colleague with Dionysius when he was first chosen general with unlimited powers for the war. It is said he married them both in one day, and no one ever knew which of the two he first made his wife; and ever after he divided his kindness equally between them, both accompanying him together at his table, and in his bed by turns.

Indeed, the Syracusans were urgent that their own countrywoman might be preferred before the stranger; but Doris, to compensate her for her foreign extraction, had the good fortune to be the mother of the son and heir of the family, whilst Aristomache continued a long time without issue, though Dionysius was very desirous to have children by her, and, indeed, caused Doris's mother to be put to death, laying to her charge that she had given drugs to Aristomache to prevent her being with child.

Dion, Aristomache's brother, at first found an honourable reception for his sister's sake; but his own worth and parts soon procured him a nearer place in his brother-in-law's affection, who, among other favours, gave special command to his treasurers to furnish Dion with whatever money he demanded, only telling him on the same day what they had delivered out. Now, though Dion was before reputed a person of lofty character, of a noble mind, and daring courage, yet these excellent qualifications all received a great development from the happy chance which conducted Plato into Sicily; not assuredly by any human device or calculation, but some supernatural power, designing that this remote cause should hereafter occasion the recovery of the Sicilians' lost liberty and the subversion of the tyrannical government, brought the philosopher out of Italy to Syracuse, and made acquaintance between him and Dion.

Dion was, indeed, at this time extremely young in years, but of all the scholars that attended Plato he was the quickest and aptest to learn, and the most prompt and eager to practise the lessons of virtue, as Plato himself reports of him and his own actions sufficiently testify. For though he had been bred up under a tyrant in habits of submission, accustomed to a life on the one hand of servility and intimidation, and yet on the other of vulgar display and luxury, the mistaken happiness of people that knew no better thing than pleasure and self-indulgence, yet, at the first taste of reason and a philosophy that demands obedience to virtue, his soul was set in a flame, and in the simple innocence of youth, concluding, from his own disposition, that the same reason would work the same effects upon Dionysius, he made it his business, and at length obtained the favour of him, at a leisure hour, to hear Plato.

At this their meeting, the subject-matter of their discourse in general was human virtue, but, more particularly, they disputed concerning fortitude, which Plato proved tyrants, of all men, had the least pretence to; and thence proceeding to treat of justice, asserted the happy estate of the just and the miserable condition of the unjust: arguments which Dionysius would not hear out, but, feeling himself, as it were, convicted by his words, and much displeased to see the rest of the auditors full of admiration for the speaker and captivated with his doctrine, at last, exceedingly exasperated, he asked the philosopher in a rage, what business he had in Sicily. To which Plato answered, "I came to seek a virtuous man." "It seems, then," replied Dionysius, "you have lost your labour."

Dion, supposing that this was all, and that nothing further could come of his anger, at Plato's request conveyed him aboard a galley, which was conveying Pollis, the Spartan, into Greece. But Dionysius privately dealt with Pollis, by all means to kill Plato in the voyage; if not, to be sure to sell him for a slave: he would, of course, take no harm of it, being the same just man as before; he would enjoy that happiness, though he lost his liberty. Pollis, therefore, it is stated, carried Plato to Ægina, and there sold him; the Æginetans, then at war with Athens, having made a decree that whatever Athenian was taken on their coasts should forthwith be exposed to sale.

Notwithstanding, Dion was not in less favour and credit with Dionysius than formerly, but was intrusted with the most considerable employments, and sent on important embassies to Carthage, in the management of which he gained very great reputation. Besides, the usurper bore with the liberty he took to speak his mind freely, he being the only man who, upon any occasion, durst boldly say what he thought, as, for example, in the rebuke he gave him about Gelon. Dionysius was ridiculing Gelon's government, and, alluding to his name, said he had been the laughing-stock of Sicily. While others seemed to admire and applaud the quibble, Dion very warmly replied, "Nevertheless, it is certain that you are sole governor here, because you were trusted for Gelon's sake; but for your sake no man will ever hereafter be trusted again." For, indeed, Gelon had made a monarchy appear the best, whereas Dionysius had convinced men that it was the worst of governments.

Dionysius had three children by Doris, and by Aristomache four, two of which were daughters, Sophrosyne and Arete. Sophrosyne was married to his son Dionysius; Arete, to his brother Thearides, after whose death Dion received his niece Arete to wife. Now when Dionysius was sick and like to die, Dion endeavoured to speak with him in behalf of the children he had by Aristomache, but was still prevented by the physicians, who wanted to ingratiate themselves with the next successor, who also, as Timæus reports, gave him a sleeping potion which he asked for, which produced an insensibility only followed by his death.

Nevertheless, at the first council which the young Dionysius held with his friends, Dion discoursed so well of the present state of affairs that he made all the rest appear in their politics but children, and in their votes rather slaves than counsellors, who timorously and disingenuously advised what would please the young man, rather than what would advance his interest. But that which startled them most was the proposal he made to avert the imminent danger they feared of a war with the Carthaginians, undertaking, if Dionysius wanted peace, to sail immediately over into Africa, and conclude it there upon honourable terms; but, if he rather preferred war, then he would fit out and maintain at his own cost and charges fifty galleys ready for the service.

Dionysius wondered much at his greatness of mind, and received his offer with satisfaction. But the other courtiers, thinking his generosity reflected upon them, and jealous of being lessened by his greatness, from hence took all occasions by private slanders to render him obnoxious, to the young man's displeasure; as if he designed, by his power at sea, to surprise the government, and by the help of those naval forces confer the supreme authority upon his sister Aristomache's children.

But, indeed, the most apparent and the strongest grounds for dislike and hostility existed already in the difference of his habits, and his reserved and separate way of living. For they, who, from the beginning by flatteries and all unworthy artifices, courted the favour and familiarity of the prince, youthful and voluptuously bred, ministered to his pleasures, and sought how to find him daily some new amours and occupy him in vain amusements, with wine or with women, and in other dissipations; by which means, the tyranny, like iron softened in the fire, seemed, indeed, to the subject, to be more moderate and gentle, and to abate somewhat of its extreme severity; the edge of it being blunted, not by the clemency, but rather the sloth and degeneracy of the sovereign, whose dissoluteness, gaining ground daily, and growing upon him, soon weakened and broke those "adamantine chains," with which his father, Dionysius, said he had left the monarchy fastened and secured. It is reported of him that, having begun a drunken debauch, he continued it ninety days without intermission; in all which time no person on business was allowed to appear, nor was any serious conversation heard at court, but drinking, singing, dancing, and buffoonery reigned there without control.

It is likely then they had little kindness for Dion, who never indulged himself in any youthful pleasure or diversion. And so his very virtues were the matter of their calumnies, and were represented under one or other plausible name as vices; they called his gravity pride, his plain-dealing self-will, the good advice he gave was all construed into reprimand, and he was censured for neglecting and scorning those in whose misdemeanours he declined to participate.

And to say the truth, there was in his natural character something stately, austere, reserved, and unsociable in conversation, which made his company unpleasant and disagreeable not only to the young tyrant, whose ears had been corrupted by flatteries; many also of Dion's own intimate friends, though they loved the integrity and generosity of his temper, yet blamed his manner, and thought he treated those with whom he had to do less courteously and affably than became a man engaged in civil business. Of which Plato also afterwards wrote to him; and, as it were, prophetically advised him carefully to avoid an arbitrary temper, whose proper helpmate was a solitary life. And, indeed, at this very time, though circumstances made him so important, and in the danger of the tottering government he was recognised as the only or the ablest support of it, yet he well understood that he owed not his high position to any good-will or kindness, but to the mere necessities of the usurper.

And, supposing the cause of this to be ignorance and want of education, he endeavoured to induce the young man into a course of liberal studies, and to give him some knowledge of moral truths and reasonings, hoping he might thus lose his fear of virtuous living, and learn to take pleasure in laudable actions. Dionysius, in his own nature, was not one of the worst kind of tyrants, but his father, fearing that if he should come to understand himself better, and converse with wise and reasonable men, he might enter into some design against him, and dispossess him of his power, kept him closely shut up at home; where, for want of other company, and ignorant how to spend his time better, he busied himself in making little chariots, candlesticks, stools, tables, and other things of wood.

For the elder Dionysius was so diffident and suspicious, and so continually on his guard

against all men, that he would not so much as let his hair be trimmed with any barber's or hair-cutter's instruments, but made one of his artificers singe him with a live coal. Neither were his brother or his son allowed to come into his apartment in the dress they wore, but they, as all others, were stript to their skins by some of the guard, and, after being seen naked, put on other clothes before they were admitted into his presence. When his brother Leptines was once describing the situation of a place, and took a javelin from one of the guard to draw the plan of it, he was extremely angry with him, and had the soldier who gave him the weapon put to death. He declared the more judicious his friends were the more he suspected them; because he knew that, were it in their choice, they would rather be tyrants themselves than the subjects of a tyrant. He slew Marsyas, one of his captains whom he had preferred to a considerable command, for dreaming that he killed him: without some previous waking thought and purpose of the kind, he could not, he supposed, have had that fancy in his sleep. So timorous was he, and so miserable a slave to his fears, yet very angry with Plato, because he would not allow him to be the valiantest man alive.

Dion, as we said before, seeing the son thus deformed and spoilt in character for want of teaching, exhorted him to study, and to use all his entreaties to persuade Plato, the first of philosophers, to visit him in Sicily, and when he came, to submit himself to his direction and advice; by whose instructions he might conform his nature to the truths of virtue, and, living after the likeness of the divine and glorious model of Being, out of obedience to whose control the general confusion is changed into the beautiful order of the universe, so he in like manner might be the cause of great happiness to himself and to all his subjects, who, obliged by his justice and moderation, would then willingly pay him obedience as their father, which now grudgingly, and upon necessity, they were forced to yield him as their master. Their usurping tyrant he would then no longer be, but their lawful king.

For fear and force, a great navy and standing army of ten thousand hired barbarians are not, as his father had said, the adamantine chains which secure the regal power, but the love, zeal, and affection inspired by clemency and justice; which, though they seem more pliant than the stiff and hard bonds of severity, are nevertheless the strongest and most durable ties to sustain a lasting government. Moreover, it is mean and dishonourable that a ruler, while careful to be splendid in his dress, and luxurious and magnificent in his habitation, should, in reason and power of speech, make no better show than the commonest of his subjects, nor have the princely palace of his mind adorned according to his royal dignity.

Dion frequently entertaining the king upon this subject, and, as occasion offered, repeating some of the philosopher's sayings, Dionysius grew impatiently desirous to have Plato's company, and to hear him discourse. Forthwith, therefore, he sent letter upon letter to him to Athens, to which Dion added his entreaties; also several philosophers of the Pythagorean sect from Italy sent their recommendations, urging him to come and obtain a hold upon this pliant, youthful soul, which his solid and weighty reasonings might steady, as it were, upon the seas of absolute power and authority. Plato, as he tells us himself, out of shame more than any other feeling, lest it should seem that he was all mere theory, and that of his own good-will he would never venture into action, hoping withal, that if he could work a cure upon one man, the head and guide of the rest, he might remedy the distempers of the whole island of Sicily, yielded to their requests.

But Dion's enemies, fearing an alteration in Dionysius, persuaded him to recall from banishment Philistus, a man of learned education, and at the same time of great experience in the ways of tyrants, and who might serve as a counterpoise to Plato and his philosophy. For Philistus from the beginning had been a great instrument in establishing the tyranny, and for a long time had held the office of captain of the citadel. There was a report that he had been intimate with the mother of Dionysius the First, and not without his privity. And when Leptines, having two daughters by a married woman whom he had debauched, gave one of them in marriage to Philistus, without acquainting Dionysius, he, in great anger, put Leptine's mistress in prison, and banished Philistus from Sicily. Whereupon, he fled to some of his friends on the Adriatic coast, in which retirement and leisure it is probable he wrote the greatest part of his history; for he returned not into his country during the reign of that Dionysius.

But after his death, as is just related, Dion's enemies occasioned him to be recalled home, as fitted for their purpose, and a firm friend to the arbitrary government. And this, indeed,

immediately upon his return he set himself to maintain; and at the same time various calumnies and accusations against Dion were by others brought to the king: as that he held correspondence with Theodotes and Heraclides, to subvert the government; as, doubtless, it is likely enough, that Dion had entertained hopes, by the coming of Plato, to mitigate the rigid and despotic severity of the tyranny, and to give Dionysius the character of a fair and lawful governor; and had determined, if he should continue averse to that, and were not to be reclaimed, to depose him, and restore the commonwealth to the Syracusans; not that he approved a democratic government, but thought it altogether preferable to a tyranny, when a sound and good aristocracy could not be procured.

This was the state of affairs when Plato came into Sicily, who, at his first arrival, was received with wonderful demonstration of kindness and respect. For one of the royal chariots, richly ornamented, was in attendance to receive him when he came on shore; Dionysius himself sacrificed to the gods in thankful acknowledgment for the great happiness which had befallen his government. The citizens, also, began to entertain marvellous hopes of a speedy reformation, when they observed the modesty which now ruled in the banquets, and the general decorum which prevailed in all the court, their tyrant himself also behaving with gentleness and humanity in all their matters of business that came before him. There was a general passion for reasoning and philosophy, insomuch that the very palace, it is reported, was filled with dust by the concourse of the students in mathematics who were working their problems there.

Some few days after, it was the time of one of the Syracusan sacrifices, and when the priest, as he was wont, prayed for the long and safe continuance of the tyranny, Dionysius, it is said, as he stood by, cried out, "Leave off praying for evil upon us." This sensibly vexed Philistus and his party, who conjectured, that if Plato, upon such brief acquaintance, had so far transformed and altered the young man's mind, longer converse and greater intimacy would give him such influence and authority that it would be impossible to withstand him.

Therefore, no longer privately and apart, but jointly and in public, all of them, they began to slander Dion, noising it about that he had charmed and bewitched Dionysius by Plato's sophistry, to the end that when he was persuaded voluntarily to part with his power, and lay down his authority, Dion might take it up, and settle it upon his sister Aristomache's children. Others professed to be indignant that the Athenians, who formerly had come to Sicily with a great fleet and a numerous land army, and perished miserably without being able to take the city of Syracuse, should now, by means of one sophister, overturn the sovereignty of Dionysius; inveighing him to cashier his guard of ten thousand lances, dismiss a navy of four hundred galleys, disband an army of ten thousand horse and many times over that number of foot, and go seek in the schools an unknown and imaginary bliss, and learn by mathematics how to be happy; while, in the meantime, the substantial enjoyments of absolute power, riches, and pleasure would be handed over to Dion and his sister's children.

By these means, Dion began to incur at first suspicion, and by degrees more apparent displeasure and hostility. A letter, also, was intercepted and brought to the young prince which Dion had written to the Carthaginian agents, advising them that, when they treated with Dionysius concerning the peace, they should not come to their audience without communicating with him: they would not fail to obtain by this means all that they wanted. When Dionysius had shown this to Philistus, and consulted with him, as Timæus relates, about it, he overreached Dion by a feigned reconciliation, professing, after some fair and reasonable expression of his feelings, that he was at friends with him, and thus, leading him alone to the seaside, under the castle wall, he showed him the letter, and taxed him with conspiring with the Carthaginians against him. And when Dion essayed to speak in his own defence, Dionysius suffered him not; but immediately forced him aboard a boat, which lay there for that purpose, and commanded the sailors to set him ashore on the coast of Italy.

When this was publicly known, and was thought very hard usage, there was much lamentation in the tyrant's own household on the part of the women, but the citizens of Syracuse encouraged themselves, expecting that for his sake some disturbance would ensue; which, together with the mistrust others would now feel, might occasion a general change and revolution in the state. Dionysius seeing this, took alarm, and endeavoured to pacify the women and others of Dion's kindred and friends, assuring them that he had not banished, but only

sent him out of the way for a time, for fear of his own passion, which might be provoked some day by Dion's self-will into some act which he should be sorry for. He gave also two ships to his relations, with liberty to send into Peloponnesus for him whatever of his property or servants they thought fit.

Dion was very rich, and had his house furnished with little less than royal splendour and magnificence. These valuables his friends packed up and conveyed to him, besides many rich presents which were sent him by the women and his adherents. So that, so far as wealth and riches went, he made a noble appearance among the Greeks, and they might judge, by the affluence of the exile, what was the power of the tyrant.

Dionysius immediately removed Plato into the castle, designing, under colour of an honourable and kind reception, to set a guard upon him, lest he should follow Dion, and declare to the world, in his behalf, how injuriously he had been dealt with. And, moreover, time and conversation (as wild beasts by use grow tame and tractable) had brought Dionysius to endure Plato's company and discourse, so that he began to love the philosopher, but with such an affection as had something of the tyrant in it, requiring of Plato that he should, in return of his kindness, love him only, and attend to him above all other men; being ready to permit to his care the chief management of affairs, and even the government, too, upon condition that he would not prefer Dion's friendship before his. This extravagant affection was a great trouble to Plato, for it was accompanied with petulant and jealous humours, like the fond passions of those that are desperately in love; frequently he was angry and fell out with him, and presently begged and entreated to be friends again. He was beyond measure desirous to be Plato's scholar, and to proceed in the study of philosophy, and yet he was ashamed of it with those who spoke against it and professed to think it would ruin him.

But a war about this time breaking out, he sent Plato away, promising him in the summer to recall Dion, though in this he broke his word at once; nevertheless, he remitted to him his revenues, desiring Plato to excuse him as to the time appointed, because of the war, but, as soon as he had settled a peace, he would immediately send for Dion, requiring him in the interim to be quiet, and not raise any disturbance, nor speak ill of him among the Grecians. This Plato endeavoured to effect, by keeping Dion with him in the Academy, and busying him in philosophical studies.

Dion sojourned in the Upper Town of Athens, with Callippus, one of his acquaintance; but for his pleasure he bought a seat in the country, which afterwards, when he went into Sicily, he gave to Speusippus, who had been his most frequent companion while he was at Athens, Plato so arranging it, with the hope that Dion's austere temper might be softened by agreeable company, with an occasional mixture of seasonable mirth. For Speusippus was of the character to afford him this; we find him spoken of in Timon's *Silli*, as "good at a jest." And Plato himself, as it happened, being called upon to furnish a chorus of boys, Dion took upon him the ordering and management of it, and defrayed the whole expense, Plato giving him this opportunity to oblige the Athenians, which was likely to procure his friend more kindness than himself credit. Dion went also to see several other cities, visiting the noblest and most statesmanlike persons in Greece, and joining in their recreations and entertainments in their times of festival.

In all which, no sort of vulgar ignorance, or tyrannic assumption, or luxuriousness was remarked in him; but, on the contrary, a great deal of temperance, generosity, and courage, and a well-becoming taste for reasoning and philosophic discourses. By which means he gained the love and admiration of all men, and in many cities had public honours decreed him; the Lacedæmonians making him a citizen of Sparta, without regard to the displeasure of Dionysius, though at that time he was aiding them in their wars against the Thebans.

It is related that once, upon invitation, he went to pay a visit to Ptœodorus, the Megarian, a man, it would seem, of wealth and importance; and when, on account of the concourse of people about his door, and the press of business, it was very troublesome and difficult to get access to him, turning about to his friends, who seemed concerned and angry at it, "What reason," said he, "have we to blame Ptœodorus, when we ourselves used to do no better when we were at Syracuse?"

After some little time, Dionysius, envying Dion, and jealous of the favour and interest he had among the Grecians, put a stop upon his incomes, and no longer sent him his revenues, making his own commissioners trustees of the estate. But, endeavouring to obviate the ill-will and discredit which, upon Plato's account, might accrue to him among the philosophers,

he collected in his court many reputed learned men; and ambitiously desiring to surpass them in their debates, he was forced to make use, often incorrectly, of arguments he had picked up from Plato. And now he wished for his company again, repenting he had not made better use of it when he had it, and had given no greater heed to his admirable lessons. Like a tyrant, therefore, inconsiderate in his desires, headstrong and violent in whatever he took a will to, on a sudden he was eagerly set on the design of recalling him, and left no stone unturned, but addressed himself to Archytas, the Pythagorean (his acquaintance and friendly relations with whom owed their origin to Plato), and persuaded him to stand as surety for his engagements, and to request Plato to revisit Sicily.

Archytas, therefore, sent Archedemus and Dionysius some galleys, with divers friends, to entreat his return; moreover, he wrote to him himself expressly and in plain terms, that Dion must never look for any favour or kindness if Plato would not be prevailed with to come into Sicily; but if Plato did come Dion should be assured of whatever he desired. Dion also received letters full of solicitations from his sister and his wife, urging him to beg Plato to gratify Dionysius in this request, and not give him an excuse for further ill-doing. So that, as Plato says himself, the third time he set sail for the Strait of Scylla—

Venturing again Charybdis's dangerous gulf.

This arrival brought great joy to Dionysius, and no less hopes to the Sicilians, who were earnest in their prayers and good wishes that Plato might get the better of Philistus, and philosophy triumph over tyranny. Neither was he unbefriended by the women, who studied to oblige him; and he had with Dionysius that peculiar credit which no man else ever obtained, namely, liberty to come into his presence without being examined or searched. When he would have given him a considerable sum of money, and, on several repeated occasions made fresh offers, which Plato as often declined, Aristippus, the Cyrenæan, then present, said that Dionysius was very safe in his munificence, he gave little to those who were ready to take all they could get, and a great deal to Plato, who would accept of nothing.

After the first compliments of kindness were over, when Plato began to discourse of Dion, he was at first diverted by excuses for delay, followed soon after by complaints and disgusts, though not as yet observable to others, Dionysius endeavouring to conceal them, and, by other civilities and honourable usage, to draw him off from his affection to Dion. And for some time Plato himself was careful not to let anything of this dishonesty and breach of promise appear, but bore with it, and dissembled his annoyance. While matters stood thus between them, and, as they thought, they were unobserved and undiscovered, Helicon, the Cyzicenian, one of Plato's followers, foretold an eclipse of the sun, which happened according to his prediction; for which he was much admired by the tyrant, and rewarded with a talent of silver; whereupon Aristippus, jesting with some others of the philosophers, told them, he also could predict something extraordinary; and on their entreating him to declare it, "I foretell," said he, "that before long there will be a quarrel between Dionysius and Plato."

At length, Dionysius made sale of Dion's estate, and converted the money to his own use, and removed Plato from an apartment he had in the gardens of the palace to lodgings among the guards he kept in pay, who from the first had hated Plato, and sought opportunity to make away with him, supposing he advised Dionysius to lay down the government and disband his soldiers.

When Archytas understood the danger he was in, he immediately sent a galley with messengers to demand him of Dionysius; alleging that he stood engaged for his safety, upon the confidence of which Plato had come to Sicily. Dionysius, to palliate his secret hatred, before Plato came away, treated him with great entertainments and all seeming demonstrations of kindness, but could not forbear breaking out one day into the expression, "No doubt, Plato, when you are at home among the philosophers, your companions, you will complain of me, and reckon up a great many of my faults." To which Plato answered with a smile, "The Academy will never, I trust, be at such a loss for subjects to discuss as to seek one in you." Thus, they say, Plato was dismissed; but his own writings do not altogether agree with this account.

Dion was angry at all this, and not long after declared open enmity to Dionysius, on hearing what had been done with his wife; on which matter Plato, also, had had some confidential correspondence with Dionysius. Thus it was. After Dion's banishment, Dionysius, when he sent Plato back, had desired him to ask Dion privately, if he would be averse to his wife's marrying another man. For there went a report, whether true, or raised by Dion's enemies, that his marriage was not pleasing to him, and that he lived with his wife on uneasy terms. When Plato therefore came to Athens, and had mentioned the subject to Dion, he wrote a letter to Dionysius speaking of other matters openly, but on this in language expressly designed to be understood by him alone, to the effect that he had talked with Dion about the business, and that it was evident he would highly resent the affront, if it should be put into execution. At that time, therefore, while there were yet great hopes of an accommodation, he took no new steps with his sister, suffering her to live with Dion's child.

But when things were come to that pass, that no reconciliation could be expected, and Plato, after his second visit, was again sent away in displeasure, he then forced Arete, against her will, to marry Timocrates, one of his favourites, in this action coming short even of his father's justice and lenity; for he, when Polyxenus, the husband of his sister, Theste, became his enemy, and fled in alarm out of Sicily, sent for his sister, and taxed her, that, being privy to her husband's flight, she had not declared it to him. But the lady, confident and fearless, made him this reply: "Do you believe me, brother, so bad a wife, or so timorous a woman, that, having known my husband's flight, I would not have borne his company, and shared his fortunes? I knew nothing of it; since otherwise it had been my better lot to be called the wife of the exile Polyxenus than the sister of the tyrant Dionysius." It is said, he admired her free and ready answer, as did the Syracusans also her courage and virtue, insomuch that she retained her dignity and princely retinue after the dissolution of the tyranny, and when she died, the citizens, by public decree, attended the solemnity of her funeral. And the story, though a digression from the present purpose, was well worth the telling.

From this time, Dion set his mind upon warlike measures; with which Plato, out of respect for past hospitalities, and because of his age, would have nothing to do. But Speusippus and the rest of his friends assisted and encouraged him, bidding him deliver Sicily, which with lift-up hands implored his help, and with open arms was ready to receive him. For when Plato was staying at Syracuse, Speusippus, being oftener than he in company with the citizens, had more thoroughly made out how they were inclined; and though at first they had been on their guard, suspecting his bold language, as though he had been set on by the tyrant to trepan them, yet at length they trusted him. There was but one mind and one wish or prayer among them all, that Dion would undertake the design, and come, though without either navy, men, horse, or arms; that he would simply put himself aboard any ship, and lend the Sicilians his person and name against Dionysius.

This information from Speusippus encouraged Dion, who, concealing his real purpose, employed his friends privately to raise what men they could; and many statesmen and philosophers were assisting him, as, for instance, Eudemus the Cyprian, on whose death Aristotle wrote his dialogue *On the Soul,* and Timonides the Leucadian. They also engaged on his side Miltas the Thessalian, who was a prophet, and had studied in the Academy. But of all that were banished by Dionysius, who were not fewer than a thousand, five and twenty only joined in the enterprise; the rest were afraid, and abandoned it. The rendezvous was in the island Zacynthus, where a small force of not quite eight hundred men came together, all of them, however, persons already distinguished in plenty of previous hard service, their bodies well trained and practised, and their experience and courage amply sufficient to animate and embolden to action the numbers whom Dion expected to join him in Sicily.

Yet these men, when they first understood the expedition was against Dionysius, were troubled and disheartened, blaming Dion, that, hurried on like a madman by mere passion and despair, he rashly threw both himself and them into certain ruin. Nor were they less angry with their commanders and mustermasters that they had not in the beginning let them know the design. But when Dion in his address to them had set forth the unsafe and weak condition of arbitrary government, and declared that he carried them rather for commanders than soldiers, the citizens of Syracuse and the rest of the Sicilians having been long ready for a revolt, and when, after him, Alcimenes, an Achæan of the highest birth and reputation, who accompanied the expedition, harangued them to the same effect, they were contented.

It was now the middle of summer, and the Etesian winds blowing steadily on the seas, the moon was at the full, when Dion prepared a magnificent sacrifice to Apollo, and with great solemnity marched his soldiers to the temple in all their arms and accoutrements. And after the sacrifice, he feasted them all in the racecourse of the Zacynthians, where he had made provision for their entertainment. And when here they beheld with wonder the quantity and the richness of the gold and silver plate, and the tables laid to entertain them, all far exceeding the fortunes of a private man, they concluded with themselves that a man now past the prime of life, who was master of so much treasure, would not engage himself in so hazardous an enterprise without good reason of hope, and certain and sufficient assurances of aid from friends over there.

Just after the libations were made, and the accompanying prayers offered, the moon was eclipsed; which was no wonder to Dion, who understood the revolutions of eclipses, and the way in which the moon is overshadowed and the earth interposed between her and the sun. But because it was necessary that the soldiers, who were surprised and troubled at it, should be satisfied and encouraged, Miltas the diviner, standing up in the midst of the assembly, bade them be of good cheer, and expect all happy success, for that the divine powers foreshowed that something at present glorious and resplendent should be eclipsed and obscured; nothing at this time being more splendid than the sovereignty of Dionysius, their arrival in Sicily should dim this glory, and extinguish this brightness. Thus Miltas, in public descanted upon the incident. But concerning a swarm of bees which settled on the poop of Dion's ship, he privately told him and his friends that he feared the great actions they were like to perform, though for a time they should thrive and flourish, would be of short continuance, and soon suffer a decay.

It is reported, also, that many prodigies happened to Dionysius at that time. An eagle, snatching a javelin from one of the guard, carried it aloft, and from thence let it fall into the sea. The water of the sea that washed the castle walls was for a whole day sweet and potable, as many that tasted it experienced. Pigs were farrowed perfect in all their other parts, but without ears. This the diviners declared to portend revolt and rebellion, for that the subjects would no longer give ear to the commands of their superiors. They expounded the sweetness of the water to signify to the Syracusans a change from hard and grievous times into easier and more happy circumstances. The eagle being the bird of Jupiter, and the spear an emblem of power and command, this prodigy was to denote that the chief of the gods designed the end and dissolution of the present government. These things Theopompus relates in his history.

Two ships of burden carried all Dion's men; a third vessel, of no great size, and two galleys of thirty oars attended them. In addition to his soldiers' own arms, he carried two thousand shields, a very great number of darts and lances, and abundant stores of all manner of provisions, that there might be no want of anything in their voyage; their purpose being to keep out at sea during the whole voyage, and use the winds, since all the land was hostile to them, and Philistus, they had been told, was in Iapygia with a fleet, looking out for them. Twelve days they sailed with a fresh and gentle breeze; on the thirteenth, they made Pachynus, the Sicilian cape. There Protus, the chief pilot, advised them to land at once and without delay, for if they were forced again from the shore, and did not take advantage of the headland, they might ride out at sea many nights and days, waiting for a southerly wind in the summer season. But Dion, fearing a descent too near his enemies, and desirous to begin at a greater distance, and further on in the country, sailed on past Pachynus.

They had not gone far, before stress of weather, the wind blowing hard at north, drove the fleet from the coast; and it being now about the time that Arcturus rises, a violent storm of wind and rain came on, with thunder and lightning; the mariners were at their wits' end, and ignorant what course they ran, until on a sudden they found they were driving with the sea on Cercina, the island on the coast of Africa, just where it is most craggy and dangerous to run upon. Upon the cliffs there they escaped narrowly being forced and staved to pieces; but, labouring hard at their oars, with much difficulty they kept clear until the storm ceased. Then, lighting by chance upon a vessel, they understood they were upon the Heads, as it is called, of the Great Syrtis; and when they were now again disheartened by a sudden calm, and beating to and fro without making any way, a soft air began to blow from the land, when they expected anything rather than wind from the south, and scarce believed the happy change of their fortune. The gale gradually increasing, and beginning to blow fresh, they clapped on all their sails, and, praying to the gods, put out again into the open seas, steering right from Africa for Sicily.

And, running steady before the wind, the fifth day they arrived at Minoa, a little town of Sicily, in the dominion of the Carthaginians, of which Synalus, an acquaintance and friend of Dion's, happened at that time to be governor; who, not knowing it was Dion and his fleet, endeavoured to hinder his men from landing; but they rushed on shore with their swords in their hands, not slaying any of their opponents (for this Dion had forbidden, because of his friendship with the Carthaginians), but forced them to retreat, and, following close, pressed in a body with them into the place, and took it. As soon as the two commanders met, they mutually saluted each other; Dion delivered up the place again to Synalus, without the least damage done to any one therein, and Synalus quartered and entertained the soldiers, and supplied Dion with what he wanted.

They were most of all encouraged by the happy accident of Dionysius's absence at this nick of time; for it appeared that he was lately gone with eighty sail of ships to Italy. Therefore, when Dion was desirous that the soldiers should refresh themselves there, after their tedious and troublesome voyage, they would not be prevailed with, but earnest to make the best use of that opportunity, they urged Dion to lead them straight on to Syracuse. Leaving, therefore, their baggage, and the arms they did not use, Dion desired Synalus to convey them to him as he had occasion, and marched directly to Syracuse.

The first that came in to him upon his march were two hundred horse of the Agrigentines who were settled near Ecnomum, and, after them, the Geloans. But the news soon flying to Syracuse, Timocrates, who had married Dion's wife, the sister of Dionysius, and was the principal man among his friends now remaining in the city, immediately despatched a courier to Dionysius, with letters announcing Dion's arrival; while he himself took all possible care to prevent any stir or tumult in the city, where all were in great excitement, but as yet continued quiet, fearing to give too much credit to what was reported.

A very strange accident happened to the messenger who was sent with the letters; for being arrived in Italy, as he travelled through the land of Rhegium, hastening to Dionysius at Caulonia, he met one of his acquaintance, who was carrying home part of a sacrifice. He accepted a piece of the flesh, which his friend offered him, and proceeded on his journey with all speed; having travelled a good part of the night, and being, through weariness, forced to take a little rest, he laid himself down in the next convenient place he came to, which was in a wood near the road. A wolf, scenting the flesh, came and seized it as it lay fastened to the letter-bag, and with the flesh carried away the bag also, in which were the letters to Dionysius. The man, awaking and missing his bag, sought for it up and down a great while, and, not finding it, resolved not to go to the king without his letters, but to conceal himself, and keep out of the way.

Dionysius, therefore, came to hear of the war in Sicily from other hands, and that a good while after. In the meantime, as Dion proceeded in his march, the Camarineans joined his forces, and the country people in the territory of Syracuse rose and joined him in a large body. The Leontines and Campanians, who, with Timocrates, guarded the Epipolæ, receiving a false alarm which was spread on purpose by Dion, as if he intended to attack their cities first, left Timocrates, and hastened off to carry succour to their own homes. News of which being brought to Dion, where he lay near Macræ, he raised his camp by night, and came to the river Anapus which is distant from the city about ten furlongs; there he made a halt, and sacrificed by the river, offering vows to the rising sun. The soothsayers declared that the gods promised him victory; and they that were present, seeing him assisting at the sacrifice with a garland on his head, one and all crowned themselves with garlands. There were about five thousand that had joined his forces in their march; who, though but ill-provided, with such weapons as came next to hand, made up by zeal and courage for the want of better arms; and when once they were told to advance, as if Dion were already conqueror, they ran forward with shouts and acclamations, encouraging each other with the hopes of liberty.

The most considerable men and better sort of the citizens of Syracuse, clad all in white, met him at the gates. The populace set upon all that were of Dionysius's party, and principally searched for those they called setters or informers, a number of wicked and hateful wretches, who made it their business to go up and down the city, thrusting themselves into all companies, that they might inform Diony-

sius what men said, and how they stood affected. These were the first that suffered, being beaten to death by the crowd.

Timocrates, not being able to force his way to the garrison that kept the castle, took horse, and fled out of the city, filling all the places where he came with fear and confusion, magnifying the amount of Dion's forces that he might not be supposed to have deserted his charge without good reason for it. By this time, Dion was come up, and appeared in the sight of the people; he marched first in a rich suit of arms, and by him on one hand his brother, Megacles, on the other, Callippus the Athenian, crowned with garlands. Of the foreign soldiers, a hundred followed as his guard, and their several officers led the rest in good order; the Syracusans looking on and welcoming them, as if they believed the whole to be a sacred and religious procession, to celebrate the solemn entrance, after an absence of forty-eight years, of liberty and popular government.

Dion entered by the Menitid gate, and, having by sound of trumpet quieted the noise of the people, he caused proclamation to be made, that Dion and Megacles, who were come to overthrow the tyrannical government, did declare the Syracusans and all other Sicilians to be free from the tyrant. But, being desirous to harangue the people himself, he went up through the Achradina. The citizens on each side the way brought victims for sacrifice, set out their tables and goblets, and as he passed by each door threw flowers and ornaments upon him, with vows and acclamations, honouring him as a god.

There was under the castle and the Pentapyla a lofty and conspicuous sun-dial, which Dionysius had set up. Getting up upon the top of that, he made an oration to the people, calling upon them to maintain and defend their liberty; who, with great expressions of joy and acknowledgment, created Dion and Megacles generals, with plenary powers, joining in commission with them, at their desire and entreaty, twenty colleagues, of whom half were of those that had returned with them out of banishment. It seemed also to the diviners a most happy omen that Dion, when he made his address to the people, had under his feet the stately monument which Dionysius had been at such pains to erect; but because it was a sun-dial on which he stood when he was made general, they expressed some fears that the great actions he had performed might be subject to change, and admit some rapid turn and declination of fortune.

After this, Dion, taking the Epipolæ, released the citizens who were imprisoned there, and then raised a wall to invest the castle. Seven days after, Dionysius arrived by sea, and got into the citadel, and about the same time came carriages, bringing the arms and ammunition which Dion had left with Synalus. These he distributed among the citizens; and the rest that wanted furnished themselves as well as they could, and put themselves in the condition of zealous and serviceable men-at-arms.

Dionysius sent agents, at first privately, to Dion, to try what terms they could make with him. But he declaring that any overtures they had to make must be made in public to the Syracusans as a free people, envoys now went and came between the tyrant and the people, with fair proposals, and assurances that they should have abatements of their tributes and taxes, and freedom from the burdens of military expeditions, all which should be made according to their own approbation and consent with him. The Syracusans laughed at these offers, and Dion returned answer to the envoys, that Dionysius must not think to treat with them upon any other terms but resigning the government; which if he would actually do, he would not forget how nearly he was related to him, or be wanting to assist him in procuring oblivion for the past, and whatever else was reasonable and just. Dionysius seemed to consent to this, and sent his agents again, desiring some of the Syracusans to come into the citadel and discuss with him in person the terms to which on each side they might be willing, after fair debate, to consent. There were, therefore, some deputed, such as Dion approved of; and the general rumour from the castle was, that Dionysius would voluntarily resign his authority, and rather do it himself as his own good deed than let it be the act of Dion.

But this profession was a mere trick to amuse the Syracusans. For he put the deputies that were sent to him in custody, and by break of day, having first to encourage his men made them drink plentifully of raw wine, he sent the garrison of mercenaries out to make a sudden sally against Dion's works. The attack was quite unexpected, and the barbarians set to work boldly with loud cries to pull down the cross-wall, and assailed the Syracusans so furiously that they were not able to maintain their post. Only a party of Dion's hired soldiers, on first taking the alarm, advanced to the rescue; neither did they at first know what to do, or how to employ the aid they brought, not being able to hear the commands of their officers, amidst the noise and confusion of the Syracusans, who fled from the enemy and ran in among them, breaking through their ranks, until Dion, seeing none of his orders could be heard, resolved to let them see by example what they ought to do, and charged into the thickest of the enemy.

The fight about him was fierce and bloody, he being as well known by the enemy as by his own party, and all running with loud cries to the quarters where he fought. Though his time of life was no longer that of the bodily strength and agility for such a combat, still his determination and courage were sufficient to maintain him against all that attacked him; but, while bravely driving them back, he was wounded in the hand with a lance, his body armour also had been much battered, and was scarcely any longer serviceable to protect him, either against missiles or blows hand-to-hand. Many spears and javelins had passed into it through the shield, and, on these being broken back, he fell to the ground, but was immediately rescued, and carried off by his soldiers. The command-in-chief he left to Timonides, and, mounting a horse, rode about the city, rallying the Syracusans that fled; and ordering up a detachment of the foreign soldiers out of Achradina, where they were posted on guard, he brought them as a fresh reserve, eager for battle, upon the tired and failing enemy, who were already well inclined to give up their design.

For having hoped at their first sally to take the whole city, when beyond their expectation they found themselves engaged with bold and practised fighters, they fell back towards the castle. As soon as they gave ground, the Greek soldiers pressed the harder upon them, till they turned and fled within the walls. There were lost in this action seventy-four of Dion's men, and a very great number of the enemy. This being a signal victory, and principally obtained by the valour of the foreign soldiers, the Syracusans rewarded them in honour of it with a hundred minæ, and the soldiers on their part presented Dion with a crown of gold.

Soon after, there came heralds from Dionysius bringing Dion letters from the women of his family, and one addressed outside, "To his father, from Hipparinus"; this was the name of Dion's son, though Timæus says he was, from his mother Arete's name, called Aretæus; but I think credit is rather to be given to Timonides's report, who was his father's fellow-soldier and confidant. The rest of the letters were read publicly, containing many solicitations and humble requests of the women; that professing to be from his son, the heralds would not have them open publicly, but Dion, putting force upon them, broke the seal.

It was from Dionysius, written in the terms of it to Dion, but in effect to the Syracusans, and so worded that, under a plausible justification of himself and entreaty to him, means were taken for rendering him suspected by the people. It reminded him of the good service he had formerly done the usurping government, it added threats to his dearest relations, his sister, son, and wife, if he did not comply with the contents, also passionate demands mingled with lamentations, and, most to the purpose of all, urgent recommendations to him not to destroy the government, and put the power into the hands of men who always hated him, and would never forget their old piques and quarrels; let him take the sovereignty himself, and so secure the safety of his family and his friends.

When this letter was read, the Syracusans were not, as they should have been, transported with admiration at the unmovable constancy and magnanimity of Dion, who withstood all his dearest interests to be true to virtue and justice, but, on the contrary, they saw in this their reason for fearing and suspecting that he lay under an invincible necessity to be favourable to Dionysius; and they began, therefore, to look out for other leaders, and the rather because to their great joy they received the news that Heraclides was on his way.

This Heraclides was one of those whom Dionysius had banished, a very good soldier, and well known for the commands he had formerly had under the tyrant; yet a man of no constant purpose, of a fickle temper, and least of all to be relied upon when he had to act with a colleague in any honourable command. He had had a difference formerly with Dion in Peloponnesus, and had resolved, upon his own means, with what ships and soldiers he had, to make an attack upon Dionysius. When he arrived at Syracuse, with seven galleys and three small vessels, he found Dionysius already close besieged, and the Syracusans high

and proud of their victories. Forthwith, therefore, he endeavoured by all ways to make himself popular; and, indeed, he had in him naturally something that was very insinuating and taking with a populace that loves to be courted. He gained his end, also, the easier, and drew the people over to his side, because of the dislike they had taken to Dion's grave and stately manner, which they thought overbearing and assuming; their successes having made them so careless and confident that they expected popular arts and flatteries from their leaders before they had in reality secured a popular government.

Getting, therefore, together in an irregular assembly, they chose Heraclides their admiral; but when Dion came forward, and told them that conferring this trust upon Heraclides was in effect to withdraw that which they had granted him, for he was no longer their generalissimo if another had the command of the navy, they repealed their order, and, though much against their wills, cancelled the new appointment. When this business was over, Dion invited Heraclides to his house, and pointed out to him, in gentle terms, that he had not acted wisely or well to quarrel with him upon a punctilio of honour, at a time when the least false step might be the ruin of all; and then, calling a fresh assembly of the people, he there named Heraclides admiral, and prevailed with the citizens to allow him a life-guard, as he himself had.

Heraclides openly professed the highest respect for Dion, and made him great acknowledgments for this favour, attending him with all deference, as ready to receive his commands; but underhand he kept up his dealings with the populace and the unrulier citizens, unsettling their minds and disturbing them with his complaints, and putting Dion into the utmost perplexity and disquiet. For if he advised to give Dionysius leave to quit the castle, he would be exposed to the imputation of sparing and protecting him; if, to avoid giving offence or suspicion, he simply continued the siege, they would say he protracted the war to keep his office of general the longer and overawe the citizens.

There was one Sosis, notorious in the city for his bad conduct and his impudence, yet a favourite with the people, for the very reason that they liked to see it made a part of popular privileges to carry free speech to this excess of licence. This man, out of a design against Dion, stood up one day in an assembly, and, having sufficiently railed at the citizens as a set of fools that could not see how they had made an exchange of a dissolute and drunken for a sober and watchful despotism, and thus having publicly declared himself Dion's enemy, took his leave. The next day he was seen running through the streets, as if he fled from some that pursued him, almost naked, wounded in the head, and bloody all over. In this condition, getting people about him in the market-place, he told them that he had been assaulted by Dion's men; and, to confirm what he said, showed them the wounds he had received in his head. And a good many took his part, exclaiming loudly against Dion for his cruel and tyrannical conduct, stopping the mouths of the people by bloodshed and peril of life.

Just as an assembly was gathering in this unsettled and tumultuous state of mind, Dion came before them, and made it appear how this Sosis was brother to one of Dionysius's guard, and that he was set on by him to embroil the city in tumult and confusion; Dionysius having now no way left for his security but to make his advantage of their dissensions and distractions. The surgeons, also, having searched the wound, found it was rather raised than cut with a downright blow; for the wounds made with a sword are, from their mere weight, most commonly deepest in the middle, but this was very slight, and all along of an equal depth; and it was not one continued wound, as if cut at once, but several incisions, in all probability made at several times, as he was able to endure the pain. There were credible persons, also, who brought a razor, and showed it in the assembly, stating that they met Sosis, running in the street, all bloody, who told them that he was fleeing from Dion's soldiers, who had just attacked and wounded him; they ran at once to look after them, and met no one, but spied this razor lying under a hollow stone near the place from which they observed he came.

Sosis was now likely to come by the worst of it. But, when to back all this, his own servants came in, and gave evidence that he had left his house alone before break of day, with the razor in his hand, Dion's accusers withdrew themselves, and the people by a general vote condemned Sosis to die, being once again well satisfied with Dion and his proceedings.

Yet they were still as jealous as before of his soldiers, and the rather because the war was now carried on principally by sea; Philistus be-

ing come from Iapygia with a great fleet to Dionysius's assistance. They supposed, therefore, that there would be no longer need of the soldiers, who were all landsmen and armed accordingly; these were rather, indeed, they thought, in a condition to be protected by themselves, who were seamen, and had their power in their shipping.

Their good opinion of themselves was also much enhanced by an advantage they got in an engagement by sea, in which they took Philistus prisoner, and used him in a barbarous and cruel manner. Ephorus relates that when he saw his ship was taken, he slew himself. But Timonides, who was with Dion from the very first, and was present at all the events as they occurred, writing to Speusippus the philosopher, relates the story thus: that Philistus's galley running aground, he was taken prisoner alive, and first disarmed, then stripped of his corselet, and exposed naked, being now an old man, to every kind of contumely; after which they cut off his head, and gave his body to the boys of the town, bidding them drag it through the Achradina, and then throw it into the Quarries. Timæus, to increase the mockery, adds further, that the boys tied him by his lame leg, and so drew him through the streets, while the Syracusans stood by laughing and jesting at the sight of that very man thus tied and dragged about by the leg, who had told Dionysius that, so far from fleeing on horseback from Syracuse, he ought to wait until he should be dragged out by the heels. Philistus, however, has stated that this was said to Dionysius by another, and not by himself.

Timæus avails himself of this advantage, which Philistus truly enough affords against himself in his zealous and constant adherence to the tyranny, to vent his own spleen and malice against him. They, indeed, who were injured by him at the time, are perhaps excusable, if they carried their resentment to the length of indignities to his dead body; but they who write history afterwards, and were noways wronged by him in his lifetime, and have received assistance from his writings, in honour should not with opprobrious and scurrilous language upbraid him for those misfortunes which may well enough befall even the best of men. On the other side, Ephorus is as much out of the way in his encomiums. For, however ingenious he is in supplying unjust acts and wicked conduct with fair and worthy motives, and in selecting decorous and honourable terms, yet when he does his best, he does not himself stand clear of the charge of being the greatest lover of tyrants, and the fondest admirer of luxury and power and rich estates and alliances of marriage with absolute princes. He that neither praises Philistus for his conduct, nor insults over his misfortunes, seems to me to take the fittest course.

After Philistus's death, Dionysius sent to Dion, offering to surrender the castle, all the arms, provisions, and garrison soldiers, with full pay for them for five months, demanding in return that he might have safe conduct to go unmolested into Italy, and there to continue, and also to enjoy the revenues of Gyarta, a large and fruitful territory belonging to Syracuse, reaching from the seaside to the middle of the country. Dion rejected these proposals, and referred him to the Syracusans. They, hoping in a short time to take Dionysius alive, dismissed his ambassadors summarily. But he, leaving his eldest son, Apollocrates, to defend the castle, and putting on board his ships the persons and the property that he set most value upon, took the opportunity of a fair wind, and made his escape, undiscovered by the admiral, Heraclides, and his fleet.

The citizens loudly exclaimed against Heraclides for this neglect; but he got one of their public speakers, Hippo by name, to go among them, and make proposals to the assembly for a redivision of lands, alleging that the first beginning of liberty was equality, and that poverty and slavery were inseparable companions. In support of this, Heraclides spoke, and used the faction in favour of it to overpower Dion, who opposed it; and in fine, he persuaded the people to ratify it by their vote, and further to decree that the foreign soldiers should receive no pay, and that they would elect new commanders, and so be rid of Dion's oppression.

The people, attempting, as it were, after their long sickness of despotism, all at once to stand on their legs, and to do their part, for which they were yet unfit, of freemen, stumbled in all their actions; and yet hated Dion, who, like a good physician, endeavoured to keep the city to a strict and temperate regimen.

When they met in the assembly to choose their commanders, about the middle of summer, unusual and terrible thunders, with other inauspicious appearances, for fifteen days together, dispersed the people, deterring them, on grounds of religious fear, from creating new generals. But, at last, the popular leaders, having found a fair and clear day, and, having got their party together, were proceeding to an election, when a draught-ox, who was used to the crowd and noise of the streets, but for some reason or other grew unruly to his driver, breaking from his yoke, ran furiously into the theatre where they were assembled, and set the people flying and running in all directions before him in the greatest disorder and confusion; and from thence went on, leaping and rushing about, over all that part of the city which the enemies afterwards made themselves masters of.

However, the Syracusans, not regarding all this, elected five-and-twenty captains, and, among the rest, Heraclides, and underhand tampered with Dion's men, promising, if they would desert him, and enlist themselves in their service, to make them citizens of Syracuse, with all the privileges of natives. But they would not hear the proposals, but, to show their fidelity and courage, with their swords in their hands, placing Dion for his security in the midst of their battalion, conveyed him out of the city, not offering violence to any one, but upbraiding those they met with their baseness and ingratitude. The citizens, seeing they were but few, and did not offer any violence, despised them; and, supposing that with their large numbers they might with ease overpower and cut them off before they got out of the city, fell upon them in the rear.

Here Dion was in a great strait, being necessitated either to fight against his own countrymen or tamely suffer himself and his faithful soldiers to be cut in pieces. He used many entreaties to the Syracusans, stretching out his hands towards the castle that was full of their enemies, and showing them the soldiers, who in great numbers appeared on the walls and watched what was doing. But when no persuasions could divert the impulse of the multitude, and the whole mass, like the sea in a storm, seemed to be driven before the breath of the demagogues, he commanded his men, not to charge them, but to advance with shouts and clashing of their arms; which being done, not a man of them stood his ground; all fled at once through the streets, though none pursued them. For Dion immediately commanded his men to face about, and led them towards the city of the Leontines.

The very women laughed at the new captains for this retreat; so, to redeem their credit, they bid the citizens arm themselves again, and followed after Dion, and came up with him as he was passing a river. Some of the light-horse rode up and began to skirmish. But when they saw Dion no more tame and calm, and no signs in his face of any fatherly tenderness towards his countrymen, but with an angry countenance, as resolved not to suffer their indignities any longer, bidding his men face round and form in their ranks for the onset, they presently turned their backs more basely than before, and fled to the city, with the loss of some few of their men.

The Leontines received Dion very honourably, gave money to his men, and made them free of their city; sending envoys to the Syracusans, to require them to do the soldiers justice, who, in return, sent back other agents to accuse Dion. But when a general meeting of the confederates met in the town of the Leontines, and the matter was heard and debated, the Syracusans were held to be in fault. They, however, refused to stand to the award of their allies, following their own conceit, and making it their pride to listen to no one, and not to have any commanders but those who would fear and obey the people.

About this time, Dionysius sent in a fleet, under the command of Nypsius the Neapolitan, with provisions and pay for the garrison. The Syracusans fought him, had the better, and took four of his ships; but they made very ill use of their good success, and for want of good discipline, fell in their joy to drinking and feasting in an extravagant manner, with so little regard to their main interest that, when they thought themselves sure of taking the castle, they actually lost their city. Nypsius, seeing the citizens in this general disorder, spending day and night in their drunken singing and revelling, and their commanders well pleased with the frolic, or at least not daring to try and give any orders to men in their drink, took advantage of this opportunity, made a sally, and stormed their works; and having made his way through these, let his barbarians loose upon the city, giving up it and all that were in it to their pleasure.

The Syracusans quickly saw their folly and misfortune, but could not, in the distraction they were in, so soon redress it. The city was in actual process of being sacked, the enemy putting the men to the sword, demolishing the fortifications, and dragging the women and children, with lamentable shrieks and cries, prisoners into the castle. The commanders, giving all for lost, were not able to put the citizens in any tolerable posture of defence, finding them confusedly mixed up and scattered among the enemy. While they were in

this condition, and the Achradina in danger to be taken, every one was sensible who he was in whom all their remaining hopes rested, but no man for shame durst name Dion, whom they had so ungratefully and foolishly dealt with. Necessity at last forcing them, some of the auxiliary troops and horsemen cried out, "Send for Dion and his Peloponnesians from the Leontines."

No sooner was the venture made and the name heard among the people, but they gave a shout for joy, and, with tears in their eyes, wished him there, that they might once again see that leader at the head of them whose courage and bravery in the worst of dangers they well remembered, calling to mind not only with what an undaunted spirit he always behaved himself, but also with what courage and confidence he inspired them when he led them against the enemy. They immediately, therefore, despatched Archonides and Telesides of the confederate troops and of the horsemen, Hellanicus and four others. These, traversing the road between at their horses' full speed, reached the town of the Leontines in the evening. The first thing they did was to leap from their horses and fall at Dion's feet, relating with tears the sad condition the Syracusans were in. Many of the Leontines and Peloponnesians began to throng about them, guessing by their speed and the manner of their address that something extraordinary had occurred.

Dion at once led the way to the assembly, and the people being gathered together in a very little time, Archonides and Hellanicus and the others came in among them, and in short declared the misery and distress of the Syracusans, begging the foreign soldiers to forget the injuries they had received, and assist the afflicted, who had suffered more for the wrong they had done than they themselves who received it would (had it been in their power) have inflicted upon them. When they had made an end, there was a profound silence in the theatre; Dion then stood up, and began to speak, but tears stopped his words; his soldiers were troubled at his grief, but bade him take good courage and proceed.

When he had recovered himself a little, therefore, "Men of Peloponnesus," he said, "and of the confederacy, I asked for your presence here, that you might consider your own interests. For myself, I have no interests to consult while Syracuse is perishing, and though I may not save it from destruction, I will nevertheless hasten thither, and be buried in the ruins of my country. Yet if you can find in your hearts to assist us, the most inconsiderate and unfortunate of men, you may to your eternal honour again retrieve this unhappy city. But if the Syracusans can obtain no more pity nor relief from you, may the gods reward you for what you have formerly valiantly done for them, and for your kindness to Dion, of whom speak hereafter as one who deserted you not when you were injured and abused, nor afterwards forsook his fellow-citizens in their afflictions and misfortunes."

Before he had yet ended his speech, the soldiers leapt up, and with a great shout testified their readiness for the service, crying out to march immediately to the relief of the city. The Syracusan messengers hugged and embraced them, praying the gods to send down blessings upon Dion and the Peloponnesians. When the noise was pretty well over, Dion gave orders that all should go to their quarters to prepare for their march, and having refreshed themselves, come ready armed to their rendezvous in the place where they now were, resolving that very night to attempt the rescue.

Now at Syracuse, Dionysius's soldiers, as long as day continued, ransacked the city, and did all the mischief they could; but when night came on, they retired into the castle, having lost some few of their number. At which the factious ringleaders taking heart, and hoping the enemy would rest content with what they had done and make no further attempt upon them, persuaded the people again to reject Dion, and, if he came with the foreign soldiers, not to admit him; advising them not to yield, as inferior to them in point of honour and courage, but to save their city and defend their liberties and properties themselves. The populace, therefore, and their leaders, sent messengers to Dion to forbid him to advance, while the noble citizens and the horse sent others to him to desire him to hasten his march; for which reason he slacked his pace, yet did not remit his advance. And in the course of the night, the faction that was against him set a guard upon the gates of the city to hinder him from coming in.

But Nypsius made another sally out of the castle with a far greater number of men, and those far more bold and eager than before, who quite ruined what of the rampart was left standing, and fell in, pell-mell, to sack and ravage the city. The slaughter was now very great, not only of the men, but of the women,

also, and children; for they desired not so much to plunder, as to destroy and kill all they met. For Dionysius, despairing to regain the kingdom, and mortally hating the Syracusans, resolved to bury his lost sovereignty in the ruin and desolation of Syracuse. The soldiers, therefore, to anticipate Dion's succours, resolved upon the most complete and ready way of destruction, to lay the city in ashes, firing all at hand with torches and lamps, and at distance with flaming arrows, shot from their bows. The citizens fled every way before them; they who, to avoid the fire, forsook their houses, were taken in the streets and put to the sword; they who betook themselves for refuge into the houses were forced out again by the flames, many buildings being now in a blaze, and many falling in ruins upon them as they fled past.

This fresh misfortune by general consent opened the gates for Dion. He had given up his rapid advance, when he received advice that the enemies were retreated into the castle, but, in the morning, some horse brought him the news of another assault, and, soon after, some of those who before opposed his coming fled now to him, to entreat him he would hasten his relief. The pressure increasing, Heraclides sent his brother, and after him his uncle, Theodotes, to beg him to help them; for that now they were not able to resist any longer; he himself was wounded, and the greatest part of the city either in ruins or in flames.

When Dion met this sad news, he was about sixty furlongs distant from the city. When he had acquainted the soldiers with the exigency, and exhorted them to behave themselves like men, the army no longer marched but ran forwards, and by the way were met by messengers upon messengers entreating them to make haste. By the wonderful eagerness of the soldiers, and their extraordinary speed, Dion quickly came to the city, and entered what is called the Hecatompedon, sending his light-armed men at once to charge the enemy, that, seeing them, the Syracusans might take courage. In the meantime, he drew up in good order his full-armed men and all the citizens that came in and joined him; forming his battalions deep, and distributing his officers in many separate commands, that he might be able to attack from many quarters at once, and so be more alarming to the enemy.

So, having made his arrangements and offered vows to the gods, when he was seen in the streets advancing at the head of his men to engage the enemy, a confused noise of shouts, congratulations, vows, and prayers was raised by the Syracusans, who now called Dion their deliverer and Tutelar Deity, and his soldiers their friends, brethren, and fellow-citizens. And, indeed, at that moment, none seemed to regard themselves, or value their safeties, but to be concerned more for Dion's life than for all their own together, as he marched at the head of them to meet the danger, through blood and fire and over heaps of dead bodies that lay in his way.

And indeed the posture of the enemy was in appearance terrible; for they were flushed and ferocious with victory, and had posted themselves very advantageously along the demolished works, which made the access to them very hazardous and difficult. Yet that which disturbed Dion's soldiers most was the apprehension they were in of the fire, which made their march very troublesome and difficult; for the houses being in flames on all sides, they were met everywhere with the blaze, and, treading upon burning ruins and every minute in danger of being overwhelmed with falling houses, through clouds of ashes and smoke they laboured hard to keep their order and maintain their ranks. When they came near to the enemy, the approach was so narrow and uneven that but few of them could engage at a time; but at length, with loud cheers and much zeal on the part of the Syracusans, encouraging them and joining with them, they beat off Nypsius's men, and put them to flight. Most of them escaped into the castle, which was near at hand; all that could not get in were pursued and picked up here and there by the soldiers, and put to the sword.

The present exigency, however, did not suffer the citizens to take immediate benefit of their victory in such mutual congratulations and embraces as became so great a success; for now all were busily employed to save what houses were left standing, labouring hard all night, and scarcely so could master the fire.

The next day, not one of the popular haranguers durst stay in the city, but all of them, knowing their own guilt, by their flight confessed it, and secured their lives. Only Heraclides and Theodotes went voluntarily and surrendered themselves to Dion, acknowledging that they had wronged him, and begging he would be kinder to them than they had been just to him; adding how much it would become him who was master of so many excel-

lent accomplishments to moderate his anger and be generously compassionate to ungrateful men, who were here before him, making their confession that, in all the matter of their former enmity and rivalry against him they were now absolutely overcome by his virtue. Though they thus humbly addressed him, his friends advised him not to pardon these turbulent and ill-conditioned men, but to yield them to the desires of his soldiers, and utterly root out of the commonwealth the ambitious affectation of popularity, a disease as pestilent and pernicious as the passion for tyranny itself.

Dion endeavoured to satisfy them, telling them that other generals exercised and trained themselves for the most part in the practices of war and arms; but that he had long studied in the Academy how to conquer anger, and not let emulation and envy conquer him; that to do this it is not sufficient that a man be obliging and kind to his friends, and those that have deserved well of him, but, rather, gentle and ready to forgive in the case of those who do wrong; that he wished to let the world see that he valued not himself so much upon excelling Heraclides in ability and conduct, as he did in outdoing him in justice and clemency; herein to have the advantage is to excel indeed; whereas the honour of success in war is never entire; fortune will be sure to dispute it, though no man should pretend to have a claim. What if Heraclides be perfidious, malicious, and base, must Dion therefore sully or injure his virtue by passionate concern for it? For, though the laws determine it juster to revenge an injury than to do an injury, yet it is evident that both, in the nature of things, originally proceed from the same deficiency and weakness. The malicious humour of men, though perverse and refractory, is not so savage and invincible but it may be wrought upon by kindness, and altered by repeated obligations.

Dion, making use of these arguments, pardoned and dismissed Heraclides and Theodotes.

And now, resolving to repair the blockade about the castle, he commanded all the Syracusans to cut each man a stake and bring it to the works; and then, dismissing them to refresh themselves, and take their rest, he employed his own men all night, and by morning had finished his line of palisade; so that both the enemy and the citizens wondered, when day returned, to see the work so far advanced in so short a time. Burying, therefore, the dead and redeeming the prisoners, who were near two thousand, he called a public assembly, where Heraclides made a motion that Dion should be declared general, with full powers at land and sea. The better citizens approved well of it, and called on the people to vote it so. But the mob of sailors and handicraftsmen would not yield that Heraclides should lose his command of the navy; believing him, if otherwise an ill man, at any rate to be more citizen-like than Dion, and readier to comply with the people. Dion, therefore, submitted to them in this, and consented that Heraclides should continue admiral.

But when they began to press the project of the redistribution of lands and houses, he not only opposed it, but repealed all the votes they had formerly made upon that account, which sensibly vexed them. Heraclides, therefore, took a new advantage of him, and, being at Messene, harangued the soldiers and ships' crews that sailed with him, accusing Dion that he had a design to make himself absolute. And yet at the same time he held private correspondence for a treaty with Dionysius by means of Pharax the Spartan. Which, when the noble citizens of Syracuse had intimation of, there arose a sedition in the army, and the city was in great distress and want of provisions; and Dion now knew not what course to take, being also blamed by all his friends for having thus fortified against himself such a perverse and jealous and utterly corrupted man as Heraclides was.

Pharax at this time lay encamped at Neapolis, in the territory of Agrigentum. Dion, therefore, led out the Syracusans, but with an intent not to engage him till he saw a fit opportunity. But Heraclides and his seamen exclaimed against him, that he had delayed fighting on purpose that he might the longer continue his command; so that, much against his will, he was forced to an engagement and was beaten, his loss, however, being inconsiderable, and that occasioned chiefly by the dissension that was in the army. He rallied his men, and, having put them in good order and encouraged them to redeem their credit, resolved upon a second battle. But in the evening, he received advice that Heraclides with his fleet was on his way to Syracuse, with the purpose to possess himself of the city and keep him and his army out. Instantly, therefore, taking with him some of the strongest and most active of his men, he rode off in the dark, and about nine the next morning was at the gates, having ridden seven hundred furlongs that night.

Heraclides, though he strove to make all the speed he could, yet, coming too late, tacked and stood out again to sea; and, being unresolved what course to steer, accidentally he met Gæsylus the Spartan, who told him he was come from Lacedæmon to head the Sicilians, as Gylippus had formerly done. Heraclides was only too glad to get hold of him, and fastening him as it might be a sort of amulet to himself, he showed him to the confederates, and sent a herald to Syracuse to summon them to accept the Spartan general. Dion returned answer that they had generals enough, and, if they wanted a Spartan to command them, he could supply that office, being himself a citizen of Sparta. When Gæsylus saw this, he gave up all pretensions, and sailed in to Dion, and reconciled Heraclides to him, making Heraclides swear the most solemn oaths to perform what he engaged, Gæsylus himself also undertaking to maintain Dion's right and inflict chastisement on Heraclides if he broke his faith.

The Syracusans then laid up their navy, which was at present a great charge and of little use to them, but an occasion of differences and dissensions among the generals, and pressed on the siege, finishing the wall of blockade with which they invested the castle. The besieged, seeing no hopes of succour and their provisions failing, began to mutiny; so that the son of Dionysius, in despair of holding out longer for his father, capitulated, and articled with Dion to deliver up the castle with all the garrison soldiers and ammunition; and so, taking his mother and sisters and manning five galleys, he set out to go to his father, Dion seeing him safely out, and scarce a man in all the city not being there to behold the sight, as indeed they called even on those that were not present, out of pity, that they could not be there to see this happy day and the sun shining on a free Syracuse. And as this expulsion of Dionysius is even now always cited as one of the greatest and most remarkable examples of fortune's vicissitudes, how extraordinary may we imagine their joy to have been, and how entire their satisfaction, who had totally subverted the most potent tyranny that ever was by very slight and inconsiderable means!

When Apollocrates was gone, and Dion coming to take possession of the castle, the women could not stay while he made his entry, but ran to meet him at the gate. Aristomache led Dion's son, and Arete followed after weeping, fearful and dubious how to salute or address her husband, after living with another man. Dion first embraced his sister, then his son; when Aristomache bringing Arete to him, "O Dion," said she, "your banishment made us all equally miserable; your return and victory has cancelled all sorrows, excepting this poor sufferer's, whom I, unhappy, was compelled to see another's while you were yet alive. Fortune has now given you the sole disposal of us. How will you determine concerning her hard fate? In what relation must she salute you, as her uncle, or as her husband?" This speech of Aristomache's brought tears from Dion, who with great affection embraced his wife, gave her his son, and desired her to retire to his own house, where he continued to reside when he had delivered up the castle to the Syracusans.

For though all things had now succeeded to his wish, yet he desired not to enjoy any present advantage of his good fortune, except to gratify his friends, reward his allies, and bestow upon his companions of former time in Athens, and the soldiers that had served him, some special mark of kindness and honour, striving herein to outdo his very means in his generosity. As for himself, he was content with a very frugal and moderate competency, and was indeed the wonder of all men, that when not only Sicily and Carthage, but all Greece looked to him as in the height of prosperity, and no man living greater than he, no general more renowned, for valour and success, yet in his guard, his attendance, his table, he seemed as if he rather commoned with Plato in the Academy than lived among hired captains and paid soldiers, whose solace of their toils and dangers it is to eat and drink their fill, and enjoy themselves plentifully every day.

Plato indeed wrote to him that the eyes of all the world were now upon him; but it is evident that he himself had fixed his eye upon one place in one city, the Academy, and considered that the spectators and judges there regarded not great actions, courage, or fortune, but watched to see how temperately and wisely he could use his prosperity, how evenly he could behave himself in the high condition he now was in. Neither did he remit anything of his wonted stateliness in conversation or serious charge to the people; he made it rather a point to maintain it, notwithstanding that a little condescension and obliging civility were very necessary for his present affairs; and Plato, as we said before, rebuked him, and wrote to tell him that self-will keeps house with solitude. But certainly his natural temperament was one

that could not bend to complaisance; and, besides, he wished to work the Syracusans back the other way, out of their present excess of license and caprice.

Heraclides began again to set up against him, and, being invited by Dion to make one of the council, refused to come, saying he would give his opinion as a private citizen in the public assembly. Next he complained of Dion because he had not demolished the citadel, and because he had hindered the people from throwing down Dionysius's tomb and doing despite to the dead; moreover, he accused him for sending to Corinth for counsellors and assistants in the government, thereby neglecting and slighting his fellow-citizens. And indeed he had sent messages for some Corinthians to come to him, hoping by their means and presence the better to settle that constitution he intended, for he designed to suppress the unlimited democratic government, which indeed is not a government, but, as Plato calls it, a market-place of governments, and to introduce and establish a mixed polity, on the Spartan and Cretan model, between a commonwealth and a monarchy, wherein an aristocratic body should preside, and determine all matters of greatest consequence; for he saw also that the Corinthians were chiefly governed by something like an oligarchy, and the people but little concerned in public business.

Now knowing that Heraclides would be his most considerable adversary, and that in all ways he was a turbulent, fickle, and factious man, he gave way to some whom formerly he hindered when they designed to kill him, who, breaking in, murdered Heraclides in his own house. His death was much resented by the citizens. Nevertheless, when Dion made him a splendid funeral, followed the dead body with all his soldiers, and then addressed them, they understood that it would have been impossible to have kept the city quiet, as long as Dion and Heraclides were competitors in the government.

Dion had a friend called Callippus, an Athenian, who, Plato says, first made acquaintance and afterwards obtained familiarity with him, not from any connection with his philosophic studies, but on occasions afforded by the celebration of the mysteries, and in the way of ordinary society. This man went with him in all his military service, and was in great honour and esteem; being the first of his friends who marched by his side into Syracuse, wearing a garland upon his head, having behaved himself very well in all the battles, and made himself remarkable for his gallantry.

He, finding that Dion's principal and most considerable friends were cut off in the war, Heraclides now dead, and the people without a leader, and that the soldiers had a great kindness for him, like a perfidious and wicked villain, in hopes to get the chief command of Sicily as his reward for the ruin of his friend and benefactor, and, as some say, being also bribed by the enemy with twenty talents to destroy Dion, inveigled and engaged several of the soldiers in a conspiracy against him, taking this cunning and wicked occasion for his plot. He daily informed Dion of what he heard or what he feigned the soldiers said against him; whereby he gained that credit and confidence, that he was allowed by Dion to consort privately with whom he would, and talk freely against him in any company, that he might discover who were his secret and factious maligners. By this means, Callippus in a short time got together a cabal of all the seditious malcontents in the city; and if any one who would be drawn in advised Dion that he was tampered with, he was not troubled or concerned at it, believing Callippus did it in compliance with his directions.

While this conspiracy was afoot, a strange and dreadful apparition was seen by Dion. As he sat one evening in a gallery in his house, alone and thoughtful, hearing a sudden noise he turned about, and saw at the end of the colonnade, by clear daylight, a tall woman, in her countenance and garb like one of the tragical Furies, with a broom in her hand, sweeping the floor. Being amazed and extremely affrighted, he sent for some of his friends, and told them what he had seen, entreating them to stay with him and keep him company all night; for he was excessively discomposed and alarmed, fearing that if he were left alone the spectre would again appear to him. He saw it no more. But a few days after, his only son, being almost grown up to man's estate, upon some displeasure and pet he had taken upon a childish and frivolous occasion, threw himself headlong from the top of the house and broke his neck.

While Dion was under this affliction, Callippus drove on his conspiracy, and spread a rumour among the Syracusans that Dion, being now childless, was resolved to send for Dionysius's son, Apollocrates, who was his wife's nephew and sister's grandson, and make him his heir and successor. By this time, Dion and his wife and sister began to suspect what was

doing, and from all hands information came to them of the plot. Dion being troubled, it is probable, for Heraclides's murder, which was like to be a blot and stain upon his life and actions, in continual weariness and vexation, he had rather die a thousand times, and open his breast himself to the assassin, than live not only in fear of his enemies but suspicion of his friends.

But Callippus, seeing the women very inquisitive to search to the bottom of the business, took alarm, and came to them, utterly denying it with tears in his eyes, and offering to give them whatever assurances of his fidelity they desired. They required that he should take the Great Oath, which was after this manner. The juror went into the sanctuary of Ceres and Proserpine, where, after the performance of some ceremonies, he was clad in the purple vestment of the goddess, and, holding a lighted torch in his hand, took his oath. Callippus did as they required, and forswore the fact. And indeed he so little valued the goddesses that he stayed but till the very festival of Proserpine, by whom he had sworn, and on that very day committed his intended murder; as truly he might well enough disregard the day, since he must at any other time as impiously offend her, when he who had acted as her initiating priest should shed the blood of her worshipper.

There were a great many in the conspiracy; and as Dion was at home with several of his friends in a room with tables for entertainment in it, some of the conspirators beset the house around, others secured the doors and windows. The actual intended murderers were some Zacynthians, who went inside in their underdresses without swords. Those outside shut the doors upon them and kept them fast. The murderers fell on Dion, endeavouring to stifle and crush him; then, finding they were doing nothing, they called for a sword, but none durst open the door. There were a great many within with Dion, but every one was for securing himself, supposing that by letting him lose his life he should save his own, and therefore no man ventured to assist him. When they had waited a good while, at length Lycon the Syracusan reached a short sword in at the window to one of the Zacynthians, and thus, like a victim at a sacrifice, this long time in their power and trembling for the blow, they killed him. His sister, and wife big with child, they hurried to prison, who, poor lady, in her unfortunate condition was there brought to bed of a son, which, by the consent of the keepers, they intended to bring up, the rather because Callippus began already to be embroiled in troubles.

After the murder of Dion, he was in great glory, and had the sole government of Syracuse in his hands; and to that effect wrote to Athens, a place which, next the immortal gods, being guilty of such an abominable crime, he ought to have regarded with shame and fear. But true it is, what is said of that city, that the good men she breeds are the most excellent, and the bad the most notorious; as their country also produces the most delicious honey and the most deadly hemlock.

Callippus, however, did not long continue to scandalise fortune and upbraid the gods with his prosperity, as though they connived at and bore with the wretched man, while he purchased riches and power by heinous impieties, but quickly received the punishment he deserved. For, going to take Catana, he lost Syracuse; whereupon they report he said, he had lost a city and got a bauble. Then attempting Messene, he had most of his men cut off, and, among the rest, Dion's murderers. When no city in Sicily would admit him, but all hated and abhorred him, he went into Italy and took Rhegium; and there, being in distress and not able to maintain his soldiers, he was killed by Leptines and Polysperchon, and, as fortune would have it, with the same sword by which Dion was murdered, which was known by the size, being but short, as the Spartan swords, and the workmanship of it very curious and artificial. Thus Callippus received the reward of his villainies.

When Aristomache and Arete were released out of prison, Hicetes, one of Dion's friends, took them to his house, and seemed to intend to entertain them well and like a faithful friend. Afterwards, being persuaded by Dion's enemies, he provided a ship and pretended to send them into Peloponnesus, but commanded the sailors, when they came out to sea, to kill them and throw them overboard. Others say that they and the little boy were thrown alive into the sea. This man also escaped not the due recompense of his wickedness, for he was taken by Timoleon and put to death, and the Syracusans, to revenge Dion, slew his two daughters: of all which I have given a more particular account in the life of Timoleon.

MARCUS BRUTUS

85?–42 B.C.

MARCUS BRUTUS was descended from that Junius Brutus to whom the ancient Romans erected a statue of brass in the capitol among the images of their kings with a drawn sword in his hand, in remembrance of his courage and resolution in expelling the Tarquins and destroying the monarchy. But that ancient Brutus was of a severe and inflexible nature, like steel of too hard a temper, and having never had his character softened by study and thought, he let himself be so far transported with his rage and hatred against tyrants that, for conspiring with them, he proceeded to the execution even of his own sons. But this Brutus, whose life we now write, having to the goodness of his disposition added the improvements of learning and the study of philosophy, and having stirred up his natural parts, of themselves grave and gentle, by applying himself to business and public affairs, seems to have been of a temper exactly framed for virtue; insomuch that they who were most his enemies upon account of his conspiracy against Cæsar, if in that whole affair there was any honourable or generous part, referred it wholly to Brutus, and laid whatever was barbarous and cruel to the charge of Cassius, Brutus's connection and familiar friend, but not his equal in honesty and pureness of purpose.

His mother, Servilia, was of the family of Servilius Ahala, who when Spurius Mælius worked the people into a rebellion and designed to make himself king, taking a dagger under his arm, went forth into the market-place, and upon pretense of having some private business with him, came up close to him, and, as he bent his head to hear what he had to say, struck him with his dagger and slew him. And thus much, as concerns his descent by the mother's side, is confessed by all; but as for his father's family, they who for Cæsar's murder bore any hatred or ill-will to Brutus say that he came not from that Brutus who expelled the

Tarquins, there being none of his race left after the execution of his two sons; but that his ancestor was a plebeian, son of one Brutus, a steward, and only rose in the latest times to office or dignity in the commonwealth. But Posidonius the philosopher writes that it is true indeed what the history relates, that two of the sons of Brutus who were of men's estate were put to death, but that a third, yet an infant, was left alive, from whom the family was propagated down to Marcus Brutus; and further, that there were several famous persons of this house in his time whose looks very much resembled the statue of Junius Brutus. But of this subject enough.

Cato the philosopher was brother to Servilia, the mother of Brutus, and he it was whom of all the Romans his nephew most admired and studied to imitate, and he afterwards married his daughter Porcia. Of all the sects of the Greek philosophers, though there was none of which he had not been a hearer, and in which he had not made some proficiency, yet he chiefly esteemed the Platonists; and not much approving of the modern and middle Academy, as it is called, he applied himself to the study of the ancient. He was all his lifetime a great admirer of Antiochus of the city of Ascalon, and took his brother Aristus into his own house for his friend and companion, a man for his learning inferior indeed to many of the philosophers, but for the evenness of his temper and steadiness of his conduct equal to the best. As for Empylus, of whom he himself and his friends often make mention in their epistles, as one that lived with Brutus, he was a rhetorician, and has left behind him a short but well-written history of the death of Cæsar, entitled *Brutus*.

In Latin, he had by exercise attained a sufficient skill to be able to make public addresses and to plead a cause; but in Greek, he must be noted for affecting the sententious and short Laconic way of speaking in sundry passages of his epistles; as when, in the beginning of the war, he wrote thus to the Pergamenians: "I hear you have given Dolabella money; if willingly, you must own you have injured me; if unwillingly, show it by giving willingly to me." And another time to the Samians: "Your counsels are remiss and your performances slow; what think ye will be the end?" And of the Patareans thus: "The Xanthians, suspecting my kindness, have made their country the grave of their despair; the Patareans, trusting themselves to me, enjoy in all points their former liberty; it is in your power to choose the judgment of the Patareans or the fortune of the Xanthians." And this is the style for which some of his letters are to be noted.

When he was but a very young man, he accompanied his uncle Cato to Cyprus, when he was sent there against Ptolemy. But when Ptolemy killed himself, Cato, being by some necessary business detained in the isle of Rhodes, had already sent one of his friends, named Canidius, to take into his care and keeping the treasure of the king; but presently, not feeling sure of his honesty, he wrote to Brutus to sail immediately for Cyprus out of Pamphylia, where he then was staying to refresh himself, being but just recovered of a fit of sickness. He obeyed his orders, but with a great deal of unwillingness, as well out of respect to Canidius, who was thrown out of this employment by Cato with so much disgrace, as also because he esteemed such a commission mean and unsuitable to him, who was in the prime of his youth, and given to books and study. Nevertheless, applying himself to the business, he behaved himself so well in it that he was highly commended by Cato, and having turned all the goods of Ptolemy into ready money, he sailed with the greatest part of it in his own ship to Rome.

But upon the general separation into two factions, when, Pompey and Cæsar taking up arms against one another, the whole empire was turned into confusion, it was commonly believed that he would take Cæsar's side; for his father in past time had been put to death by Pompey. But he, thinking it his duty to prefer the interest of the public to his own private feelings, and judging Pompey's to be the better cause, took part with him; though formerly he used not so much as to salute or take any notice of Pompey, if he happened to meet him, esteeming it a pollution to have the least conversation with the murderer of his father. But now, looking upon him as the general of his country, he placed himself under his command, and set sail for Cilicia in quality of lieutenant to Sestius, who had the government of that province.

But finding no opportunity there of doing any great service, and hearing that Pompey and Cæsar were now near one another and preparing for the battle upon which all depended, he came of his own accord to Macedonia to partake in the danger. At his coming it is said that Pompey was so surprised and so pleased that, rising from his chair in the sight of all who were about him, he saluted and embraced him, as one of the chiefest of his party. All the time that he was in the camp, excepting that which he spent in Pompey's company, he employed in reading and in study, which he did not neglect even the day before the great battle. It was the middle of summer, and the heat was very great, the camp having been pitched near some marshy ground, and the people that carried Brutus's tent were a long while before they came. Yet though upon these accounts he was extremely harassed and out of order, having scarcely by the middle of the day anointed himself and eaten a sparing meal, whilst most others were either laid to sleep or taken up with the thoughts and apprehensions of what would be the issue of the fight, he spent his time until the evening in writing an epitome of Polybius.

It is said that Cæsar had so great a regard for him that he ordered his commanders by no means to kill Brutus in the battle, but to spare him if possible, and bring him safe to him, if he would willingly surrender himself; but if he made any resistance, to suffer him to escape rather than do him any violence. And this he is believed to have done out of a tenderness to Servilia, the mother of Brutus; for Cæsar had, it seems, in his youth been very intimate with her, and she passionately in love with him; and, considering that Brutus was born about that time in which their loves were at the highest, Cæsar had a belief that he was his own child.

The story is told that, when the great question of the conspiracy of Catiline, which had like to have been the destruction of the commonwealth, was debated in the senate, Cato and Cæsar were both standing up, contending together on the decision to be come to; at which time a little note was delivered to Cæsar from without, which he took and read silently to himself. Upon this, Cato cried out aloud, and accused Cæsar of holding correspondence with and receiving letters from the enemies of the commonwealth; and when many other senators exclaimed against it, Cæsar delivered the note as he had received it to Cato, who reading it found it to be a love-letter from his own sister Servilia, and threw it back again to Cæsar with the words, "Keep it, you drunkard," and returned to the subject of the debate. So public and notorious was Servilia's love to Cæsar.

After the great overthrow at Pharsalia, Pompey himself having made his escape to the sea,

and Cæsar's army storming the camp, Brutus stole privately out by one of the gates leading to marshy ground full of water and covered with reeds, and travelling through the night, got safe to Larissa. From Larissa he wrote to Cæsar who expressed a great deal of joy to hear that he was safe, and, bidding him come, not only forgave him freely, but honoured and esteemed him among his chiefest friends. Now when nobody could give any certain account which way Pompey had fled, Cæsar took a little journey along with Brutus, and tried what was his opinion herein, and after some discussion which passed between them, believing that Brutus's conjecture was the right one, laying aside all other thoughts, he set out directly to pursue him towards Egypt. But Pompey, having reached Egypt, as Brutus guessed his design was to do, there met his fate.

Brutus in the meantime gained Cæsar's forgiveness for his friend Cassius; and pleading also in defence of the king of the Libyans, though he was overwhelmed with the greatness of the crimes alleged against him, yet by his entreaties and deprecations to Cæsar in his behalf, he preserved to him a great part of his kingdom. It is reported that Cæsar, when he first heard Brutus speak in public, said to his friends, "I know not what this young man intends, but, whatever he intends, he intends vehemently." For his natural firmness of mind, not easily yielding, or complying in favour of every one that entreated his kindness, once set into action upon motives of right reason and deliberate moral choice, whatever direction it thus took, it was pretty sure to take effectively, and to work in such a way as not to fail in its object. No flattery could ever prevail with him to listen to unjust petitions, and he held that to be overcome by the importunities of shameless and fawning entreaties, though some compliment it with the name of modesty and bashfulness, was the worst disgrace a great man could suffer. And he used to say that he always felt as if they who could deny nothing could not have behaved well in the flower of their youth.

Cæsar, being about to make his expedition into Africa against Cato and Scipio, committed to Brutus the government of Cisalpine Gaul, to the great happiness and advantage of that province. For while people in other provinces were in distress with the violence and avarice of their governors, and suffered as much oppression as if they had been slaves and captives of war, Brutus, by his easy government, actually made them amends for their calamities under former rulers, directing moreover all their gratitude for his good deeds to Cæsar himself; insomuch that it was a most welcome and pleasant spectacle to Cæsar, when in his return he passed through Italy, to see the cities that were under Brutus's command, and Brutus himself increasing his honour and joining agreeably in his progress.

Now several prætorships being vacant, it was all men's opinions that that of the chiefest dignity, which is called the prætorship of the city, would be conferred either upon Brutus or Cassius; and some say that, there having been some little difference upon former accounts between them, this competition set them much more at variance, though they were connected in their families, Cassius having married Junia, the sister of Brutus. Others say that the contention was raised between them by Cæsar's doing, who had privately given each of them such hopes of his favour as led them on, and provoked them at last into this open competition and trial of their interests. Brutus had only the reputation of his honour and virtue to oppose to the many and gallant actions performed by Cassius against the Parthians.

But Cæsar, having heard each side, deliberating about the matter among his friends, said, "Cassius has the stronger plea, but we must let Brutus be first prætor." So another prætorship was given to Cassius; the gaining of which could not so much oblige him, as he was incensed for the loss of the other. And in all other things Brutus was partaker of Cæsar's power as much as he desired: for he might, if he had pleased, have been the chief of all his friends, and had authority and command beyond them all, but Cassius and the company he met with him drew him off from Cæsar. Indeed, he was not yet wholly reconciled to Cassius, since that competition which was between them; but yet he gave ear to Cassius's friends, who were perpetually advising him not to be so blind as to suffer himself to be softened and won over by Cæsar, but to shun the kindness and favours of a tyrant, which they intimated that Cæsar showed him, not to express any honour to his merit or virtue, but to unbend his strength, and undermine his vigour of purpose.

Neither was Cæsar wholly without suspicion of him, nor wanted informers that accused Brutus to him; but he feared, indeed, the high spirit and the great character and the friends that he had, but thought himself secure in his

moral disposition. When it was told him that Antony and Dolabella designed some disturbance, "It is not," said he, "the fat and the long-haired men that I fear, but the pale and the lean," meaning Brutus and Cassius. And when some maligned Brutus to him, and advised him to beware of him, taking hold of his flesh with his hand, "What," he said, "do you think that Brutus will not wait out the time of this little body?" as if he thought none so fit to succeed him in his power as Brutus. And indeed it seems to be without doubt that Brutus might have been the first man in the commonwealth, if he had had patience but a little time to be second to Cæsar, and would have suffered his power to decline after it was come to its highest pitch, and the fame of his great actions to die away by degrees.

But Cassius, a man of a fierce disposition, and one that out of private malice, rather than love of the public, hated Cæsar, not the tyrant, continually fired and stirred him up. Brutus felt the rule an oppression, but Cassius hated the ruler; and, among other reasons on which he grounded his quarrel against Cæsar, the loss of his lions which he had procured when he was ædile elect was one; for Cæsar, finding these in Megara, when that city was taken by Calenus, seized them to himself. These beasts, they say, were a great calamity to the Megarians; for, when their city was just taken, they broke open the lions' dens, and pulled off their chains and let them loose that they might run upon the enemy that was entering the city; but the lions turned upon them themselves, and tore to pieces a great many unarmed persons running about, so that it was a miserable spectacle even to their enemies to behold.

And this, some say, was the chief provocation that stirred up Cassius to conspire against Cæsar; but they are much in the wrong. For Cassius had from his youth a natural hatred and rancour against the whole race of tyrants, which he showed when he was but a boy, and went to the same school with Faustus, the son of Sulla; for, on his boasting himself amongst the boys, and extolling the sovereign power of his father, Cassius rose up and struck him two or three boxes on the ear; which when the guardians and relations of Faustus designed to inquire into and to prosecute, Pompey forbade them, and, sending for both the boys together, examined the matter himself. And Cassius is then reported to have said thus, "Come, then, Faustus, dare to speak here those words that provoked me, that I may strike you again as I did before." Such was the disposition of Cassius.

But Brutus was roused up and pushed on to the undertaking by many persuasions of his familiar friends, and letters and invitations from unknown citizens. For under the statue of his ancestor Brutus, that overthrew the kingly government, they wrote the words, "O that we had a Brutus now!" and, "O that Brutus were alive!" And Brutus's own tribunal, on which he sat as prætor, was filled each morning with writings such as these: "You are asleep, Brutus," and, "You are not a true Brutus." Now the flatterers of Cæsar were the occasion of all this, who, among other invidious honours which they strove to fasten upon Cæsar, crowned his statues by night with diadems, wishing to incite the people to salute him king instead of dictator. But quite the contrary came to pass, as I have more particularly related in the life of Cæsar.

When Cassius went about soliciting friends to engage in this design against Cæsar, all whom he tried readily consented, if Brutus would be head of it; for their opinion was that the enterprise wanted not hands or resolution, but the reputation and authority of a man such as he was, to give, as it were, the first religious sanction, and by his presence, if by nothing else, to justify the undertaking; that without him they should go about this action with less heart, and should lie under greater suspicions when they had done it; for if their cause had been just and honourable, people would be sure that Brutus would not have refused it. Cassius, having considered these things with himself, went to Brutus and made him the first visit after their falling out; and after the compliments of reconciliation had passed, and former kindnesses were renewed between them, he asked him if he designed to be present on the calends of March, for it was discoursed, he said, that Cæsar's friends intended then to move that he might be made king.

When Brutus answered, that he would not be there, "But what," says Cassius, "if they should send for us?" "It will be my business, then," replied Brutus, "not to hold my peace, but to stand up boldly, and die for the liberty of my country." To which Cassius with some emotion answered, "But what Roman will suffer you to die? What, do you not know yourself, Brutus? Or do you think that those writings that you find upon your prætor's seat were put there by weavers and shopkeepers, and not by the first and most powerful men of Rome?

From other prætors, indeed, they expect largesses and shows and gladiators, but from you they claim, as an hereditary debt, the extirpation of tyranny; they are all ready to suffer anything on your account, if you will but show yourself such as they think you are and expect you should be." Which said, he fell upon Brutus, and embraced him; and after this, they parted each to try their several friends.

Among the friends of Pompey there was one Caius Ligarius, whom Cæsar had pardoned, though accused for having been in arms against him. This man, not feeling so thankful for having been forgiven as he felt oppressed by that power which made him need a pardon, hated Cæsar, and was one of Brutus's most intimate friends. Him Brutus visited, and finding him sick, "O Ligarius," says he, "what a time you have found out to be sick in!" At which words Ligarius, raising himself and leaning on his elbow, took Brutus by the hand, and said, "But, O Brutus, if you are on any design worthy of yourself, I am well."

From this time they tried the inclinations of all their acquaintances that they durst trust, and communicated the secret to them, and took into the design not only their familiar friends, but as many as they believed bold and brave and despisers of death. For which reason they concealed the plot from Cicero, though he was very much trusted and as well beloved by them all, lest, to his own disposition, which was naturally timorous, adding now the weariness and caution of old age, by his weighing, as he would do, every particular, that he might not make one step without the greatest security, he should blunt the edge of their forwardness and resolution in a business which required all the despatch imaginable.

As indeed there were also two others that were companions of Brutus, Statilius the Epicurean, and Favonius, the admirer of Cato, whom he left out for this reason: as he was conversing one day with them, trying them at a distance, and proposing some such question to be disputed of as among philosophers, to see what opinion they were of, Favonius declared his judgment to be that a civil war was worse than the most illegal monarchy; and Statilius held, that to bring himself into troubles and danger upon the account of evil or foolish men did not become a man that had any wisdom or discretion. But Labeo, who was present, contradicted them both; and Brutus, as if it had been an intricate dispute, and difficult to be decided, held his peace for that time, but afterwards discovered the whole design to Labeo, who readily undertook it.

The next thing that was thought convenient was to gain the other Brutus, surnamed Albinus, a man of himself of no great bravery or courage, but considerable for the number of gladiators that he was maintaining for a public show, and the great confidence that Cæsar put in him. When Cassius and Labeo spoke with him concerning the matter, he gave them no answer; but, seeking an interview with Brutus himself alone, and finding that he was their captain, he readily consented to partake in the action. And among the others, also, the most and best were gained by the name of Brutus. And, though they neither gave nor took any oath of secrecy, nor used any other sacred rite to assure their fidelity to each other, yet all kept their design so close, were so wary, and held it so silently among themselves that, though by prophecies and apparitions and signs in the sacrifices the gods gave warning of it, yet could it not be believed.

Now Brutus, feeling that the noblest spirits of Rome for virtue, birth, or courage were depending upon him, and surveying with himself all the circumstances of the dangers they were to encounter, strove indeed, as much as possible, when abroad, to keep his uneasiness of mind to himself, and to compose his thoughts; but at home, and especially at night, he was not the same man, but sometimes against his will his working care would make him start out of his sleep, and other times he was taken up with further reflection and consideration of his difficulties, so that his wife that lay with him could not choose but take notice that he was full of unusual trouble, and had in agitation some dangerous and perplexing question.

Porcia, as was said before, was the daughter of Cato, and Brutus, her cousin german, had married her very young, though not a maid, but after the death of her former husband, by whom she had one son, that was named Bibuius; and there is a little book, a memoir of Brutus, written by him, yet extant. This Porcia, being addicted to philosophy, a great lover of her husband, and full of an understanding courage, resolved not to inquire into Brutus's secrets before she had made this trial of herself. She turned all her attendants out of her chamber, and taking a little knife, such as they use to cut nails with, she gave herself a deep gash in the thigh; upon which followed a great flow of blood, and soon after, violent pains and a shivering fever, occasioned by the wound.

Now when Brutus was extremely anxious and afflicted for her, she, in the height of all her pain, spoke thus to him: "I, Brutus, being the daughter of Cato, was given to you in marriage, not like a concubine, to partake only in the common intercourse of bed and board, but to bear a part in all your good and all your evil fortunes; and for your part, as regards your care for me, I find no reason to complain; but from me, what evidence of my love, what satisfaction can you receive, if I may not share with you in bearing your hidden griefs, nor to be admitted to any of your counsels that require secrecy and trust? I know very well that women seem to be of too weak a nature to be trusted with secrets; but certainly, Brutus, a virtuous birth and education, and the company of the good and honourable, are of some force to the forming of our manners; and I can boast that I am the daughter of Cato, and the wife of Brutus, in which two titles though before I put less confidence, yet now I have tried myself, and find that I can bid defiance to pain."

Which words having spoken, she showed him her wound, and related to him the trial that she had made of her constancy; at which he being astonished, lifted up his hands to heaven, and begged the assistance of the gods in his enterprise, that he might show himself a husband worthy of such a wife as Porcia. So then he comforted his wife.

But a meeting of the senate being appointed, at which it was believed that Cæsar would be present, they agreed to make use of that opportunity; for then they might appear all together without suspicion; and, besides, they hoped that all the noblest and leading men of the commonwealth, being then assembled, as soon as the great deed was done, would immediately stand forward and assert the common liberty. The very place, too, where the senate was to meet seemed to be by divine appointment favourable to their purpose. It was a portico, one of those joining the theatre, with a large recess, in which there stood a statue of Pompey, erected to him by the commonwealth, when he adorned that part of the city with the porticos and the theatre. To this place it was that the senate was summoned for the middle of March (the Ides of March is the Roman name for the day); as if some more than human power were leading the man thither, there to meet his punishment for the death of Pompey.

As soon as it was day, Brutus, taking with

him a dagger, which none but his wife knew of, went out. The rest met together at Cassius's house, and brought forth his son that was that day to put on the manly gown, as it is called, into the Forum; and from thence, going all to Pompey's porch, stayed there, expecting Cæsar to come without delay to the senate. Here it was chiefly that any one who had known what they had purposed, would have admired the unconcerned temper and the steady resolution of these men in their most dangerous undertaking; for many of them, being prætors, and called upon by their office to judge and determine causes, did not only hear calmly all that made application to them and pleaded against each other before them, as if they were free from all other thoughts, but decided causes with as much accuracy and judgment as they had heard them with attention and patience. And when one person refused to stand to the award of Brutus, and with great clamour and many attestations appealed to Cæsar, Brutus, looking round about him upon those that were present, said, "Cæsar does not hinder me, nor will he hinder me, from doing according to the laws."

Yet there were many unusual accidents that disturbed them and by mere chance were thrown in their way. The first and chiefest was the long stay of Cæsar, though the day was spent, and he being detained at home by his wife, and forbidden by the soothsayers to go forth, upon some defect that appeared in his sacrifice. Another was this: There came a man up to Casca, one of the company, and, taking him by the hand, "You concealed," said he, "the secret from us, but Brutus has told me all." At which words when Casca was surprised, the other said laughing, "How came you to be so rich of a sudden, that you should stand to be chosen ædile?" So near was Casca to let out the secret, upon the mere ambiguity of the other's expression. Then Popilius Lænas, a senator, having saluted Brutus and Cassius more earnestly than usual, whispered them softly in the ear, and said, "My wishes are with you, that you may accomplish what you design, and I advise you to make no delay, for the thing is now no secret." This said, he departed, and left them in great suspicion that the design had taken wind. In the meanwhile, there came one in haste from Brutus's house and brought him news that his wife was dying.

For Porcia, being extremely disturbed with expectation of the event, and not able to bear the greatness of her anxiety, could scarce keep herself within doors; and at every little noise or voice she heard, starting up suddenly, like those possessed with the bacchic frenzy, she asked every one that came in from the Forum what Brutus was doing, and sent one messenger after another to inquire. At last, after long expectation and waiting, the strength of her constitution could hold out no longer; her mind was overcome with her doubts and fears, and she lost the control of herself, and began to faint away. She had not time to betake herself to her chamber, but, sitting as she was amongst her women, a sudden swoon and a great stupor seized her, and her colour changed, and her speech was quite lost. At this sight her women made a loud cry, and many of the neighbours running to Brutus's door to know what was the matter, the report was soon spread about that Porcia was dead; though with her women's help she recovered in a little while, and came to herself again. When Brutus received this news, he was extremely troubled, not without reason, yet was not so carried away by his private grief as to quit his public purpose.

For now news was brought that Cæsar was coming, carried in a litter. For, being discouraged by the ill-omens that attended his sacrifice, he had determined to undertake no affairs of any great importance that day, but to defer them till another time, excusing himself that he was sick.

As soon as he came out of his litter, Popilius Lænas, he who but a little before had wished Brutus good success in his undertaking, coming up to him, conversed a great while with him, Cæsar standing still all the while, and seeming to be very attentive. The conspirators (to give them this name), not being able to hear what he said, but guessing by what themselves were conscious of that this conference was the discovery of their treason, were again disheartened, and, looking upon one another, agreed from each other's countenances that they should not stay to be taken, but should all kill themselves. And now when Cassius and some others were laying hands upon their daggers under their robes, and were drawing them out, Brutus, viewing narrowly the looks and gesture of Lænas, and finding that he was earnestly petitioning and not accusing, said nothing, because there were many strangers to the conspiracy mingled amongst them, but by a cheerful countenance encouraged Cassius. And after a little while, Lænas, having kissed Cæsar's hand, went away, showing plainly that all his discourse was about some particular business relating to himself.

Now when the senate was gone in before to the chamber where they were to sit, the rest of the company placed themselves close about Cæsar's chair, as if they had some suit to make to him, and Cassius, turning his face to Pompey's statue, is said to have invoked it, as if it had been sensible of his prayers. Trebonius, in the meanwhile, engaged Antony's attention at the door, and kept him in talk outside. When Cæsar entered, the whole senate rose up to him. As soon as he was sat down, the men all crowded round about him, and set Tullius Cimber, one of their own number, to intercede in behalf of his brother that was banished; they all joined their prayers with his, and took Cæsar by the hand, and kissed his head and his breast.

But he putting aside at first their supplications, and afterwards, when he saw they would not desist, violently rising up, Tullius with both hands caught hold of his robe and pulled it off from his shoulders, and Casca, that stood behind him, drawing his dagger, gave him the first, but a slight wound, about the shoulder. Cæsar snatching hold of the handle of the dagger, and crying out aloud in Latin, "Villain Casca, what do you?" he, calling in Greek to his brother, bade him come and help. And by this time, finding himself struck by a great many hands, and looking around about him to see if he could force his way out, when he saw Brutus with his dagger drawn against him, he let go Casca's hand, that he had hold of, and covering his head with his robe, gave up his body to their blows. And they so eagerly pressed towards the body, and so many daggers were hacking together, that they cut one another; Brutus, particularly, received a wound in his hand, and all of them were besmeared with the blood.

Cæsar being thus slain, Brutus, stepping forth into the midst, intended to have made a speech, and called back and encouraged the senators to stay; but they all affrighted ran away in great disorder, and there was a great confusion and press at the door, though none pursued or followed. For they had come to an express resolution to kill nobody beside Cæsar, but to call and invite all the rest to liberty.

It was indeed the opinion of all the others, when they consulted about the execution of their design, that it was necessary to cut off Antony with Cæsar, looking upon him as an insolent man, an affecter of monarchy, and one that, by his familiar intercourse, had gained a powerful interest with the soldiers. And this they urged the rather, because at that time to the natural loftiness and ambition of his temper there was added the dignity of being consul and colleague to Cæsar. But Brutus opposed this counsel, insisting first upon the injustice of it, and afterwards giving them hopes that a change might be worked in Antony. For he did not despair but that so highly gifted and honourable a man, and such a lover of glory as Antony, stirred up with emulation of their great attempt, might, if Cæsar were once removed, lay hold of the occasion to be joint restorer with them of the liberty of his country. Thus did Brutus save Antony's life. He, in the general consternation, put himself into a plebeian habit, and fled.

But Brutus and his party marched up to the capitol, on their way showing their hands all bloody, and their naked swords, and proclaiming liberty to the people. At first all places were filled with cries and shouts; and the wild running to and fro, occasioned by the sudden surprise and passion that every one was in, increased the tumult in the city. But no other bloodshed following, and no plundering of the goods in the streets, the senators and many of the people took courage and went up to the men in the capitol; and a multitude being gathered together, Brutus made an oration to them, very popular, and proper for the state that affairs were then in. Therefore, when they applauded his speech, and cried out to him to come down, they all took confidence and descended into the Forum; the rest promiscuously mingled with one another, but many of the most eminent persons, attending Brutus, conducted him in the midst of them with great honour from the capitol, and placed him in the rostra.

At the sight of Brutus, the crowd, though consisting of a confused mixture and all disposed to make a tumult, were struck with reverence, and expected what he would say with order and with silence, and, when he began to speak, heard him with quiet and attention. But that all were not pleased with this action they plainly showed when, Cinna beginning to speak and accuse Cæsar, they broke out into a sudden rage, and railed at him in such language that the whole party thought fit again to withdraw to the capitol. And there Brutus, expecting to be besieged, dismissed the most eminent of those that had accompanied them thither, not thinking it just that they who were not partakers of the fact should share in the danger.

But the next day, the senate being assembled in the temple of the Earth, and Antony and Plancus and Cicero having made orations recommending concord in general and an act of oblivion, it was decreed that the men should not only be put out of all fear or danger, but that the consuls should see what honours and dignities were proper to be conferred upon them. After which done, the senate broke up; and, Antony having sent his son as an hostage to the capitol, Brutus and his company came down, and mutual salutes and invitations passed amongst them, the whole of them being gathered together. Antony invited and entertained Cassius, Lepidus did the same to Brutus, and the rest were invited and entertained by others, as each of them had acquaintance or friends. And as soon as it was day, the senate met again, and voted thanks to Antony for having stifled the beginning of a civil war; afterwards Brutus and his associates that were present received encomiums; and had provinces assigned and distributed among them. Crete was allotted to Brutus, Africa to Cassius, Asia to Trebonius, Bithynia to Cimber, and to the other Brutus Gaul about the Po.

After these things, they began to consider of Cæsar's will, and the ordering of his funeral. Antony desired that the will might be read, and that the body should not have a private or dishonourable interment, lest that should further exasperate the people. This Cassius violently opposed, but Brutus yielded to it, and gave leave; in which he seems to have a second time committed a fault. For as before in sparing the life of Antony he could not be without some blame from his party, as thereby setting up against the conspiracy a dangerous and difficult enemy, so now, in suffering him to have the ordering of the funeral, he fell into a total and irrevocable error. For first, it appearing by the will that Cæsar had bequeathed to the Roman people seventy-five drachmas a man, and given to the public his gardens beyond Tiber (where now the temple of Fortune stands), the whole city was fired with a wonderful affection for him, and a passionate sense of the loss of him.

And when the body was brought forth into the Forum, Antony, as the custom was, making a funeral oration in the praise of Cæsar, and finding the multitude moved with his speech, passing into the pathetic tone, unfolded the bloody garment of Cæsar, showed them in how

many places it was pierced, and the number of his wounds. Now there was nothing to be seen but confusion; some cried out to kill the murderers, others (as was formerly done when Clodius led the people) tore away the benches and tables out of the shops round about, and, heaping them altogether, built a great funeral pile, and having put the body of Cæsar upon it, set it on fire, the spot where this was done being moreover surrounded with a great many temples and other consecrated places, so that they seemed to burn the body in a kind of sacred solemnity. As soon as the fire flamed out, the multitude, flocking in some from one part and some from another, snatched the brands that were half burnt out of the pile, and ran about the city to fire the houses of the murderers of Cæsar. But they, having beforehand well fortified themselves, repelled this danger.

There was, however, a kind of poet, one Cinna, not at all concerned in the guilt of the conspiracy, but on the contrary one of Cæsar's friends. This man dreamed that he was invited to supper by Cæsar, and that he declined to go, but that Cœsar entreated and pressed him to it very earnestly; and at last, taking him by the hand, led him into a very deep and dark place, whither he was forced against his will to follow in great consternation and amazement. After this vision, he had a fever the most part of the night; nevertheless in the morning, hearing that the body of Cæsar was to be carried forth to be interred, he was ashamed not to be present at the solemnity, and came abroad and joined the people, when they were already infuriated by the speech of Antony. And perceiving him, and taking him not for that Cinna who indeed he was, but for him that a little before in a speech to the people had reproached and inveighed against Cæsar, they fell upon him and tore him to pieces.

This action chiefly, and the alteration that Antony had wrought, so alarmed Brutus and his party that for their safety they retired from the city. The first stay they made was at Antium, with a design to return again as soon as the fury of the people had spent itself and was abated, which they expected would soon and easily come to pass in an unsettled multitude, apt to be carried away with any sudden and impetuous passion, especially since they had the senate favourable to them; which, though it took no notice of those that had torn Cinna to pieces, yet made a strict search and apprehended in order to punishment those that had assaulted the houses of the friends of Brutus and Cassius. By this time, also, the people began to be dissatisfied with Antony, who they perceived was setting up a kind of monarchy for himself; they longed for the return of Brutus, whose presence they expected and hoped for at the games and spectacles which he, as prætor, was to exhibit to the public.

But he, having intelligence that many of the old soldiers that had borne arms under Cæsar, by whom they had had lands and cities given them, lay in wait for them, and by small parties at a time had stolen into the city, would not venture to come himself; however, in his absence there were most magnificent and costly shows exhibited to the people; for, having brought up a great number of all sorts of wild beasts, he gave order that not any of them should be returned or saved, but that all should be spent freely at the public spectacles. He himself made a journey to Naples to procure a considerable number of players, and hearing of one Canutius that was very much praised for his acting upon the stage, he wrote to his friends to use all their entreaties to bring him to Rome (for, being a Grecian, he could not be compelled); he wrote also to Cicero, begging him by no means to omit being present at the shows.

This was the posture of affairs when another sudden alteration was made upon the young Cæsar's coming to Rome. He was son to the niece of Cæsar, who adopted him, and left him his heir by his will. At the time when Cæsar was killed, he was following his studies at Apollonia, where he was expecting also to meet Cæsar on his way to the expedition which he had determined on against the Parthians; but, hearing of his death, he immediately came to Rome, and to ingratiate himself with the people, taking upon himself the name of Cæsar, and punctually distributing among the citizens the money that was left them by the will, he soon got the better of Antony; and by money and largesses, which he liberally dispersed amongst the soldiers, he gathered together and brought over to his party a great number of those that had served under Cæsar.

Cicero himself, out of the hatred which he bore to Antony, sided with young Cæsar; which Brutus took so ill that he treated with him very sharply in his letters, telling him that he perceived Cicero could well enough endure a tyrant, but feared only that he who hated him should be the man; that in writing and speaking so well of Cæsar, he showed that his aim

was to have an easy slavery. "But our forefathers," said Brutus, "could not brook even gentle masters." Further, he added that for his own part he had not as yet fully resolved whether he should make war or peace; but that as to one point he was fixed and settled, which was, never to be a slave; that he wondered Cicero should fear the dangers of a civil war, and not be much more afraid of a dishonourable and infamous peace; that the very reward that was to be given him for subverting Antony's tyranny was the privilege of establishing Cæsar as tyrant in his place. This is the tone of Brutus's first letters to Cicero.

The city being now divided into two factions, some betaking themselves to Cæsar and others to Antony, the soldiers selling themselves, as it were, by public outcry, and going over to him that would give them most, Brutus began to despair of any good event of such proceedings, and, resolving to leave Italy, passed by land through Lucania and came to Elea by the seaside. From hence it was thought convenient that Porcia should return to Rome. She was overcome with grief to part from Brutus, but strove as much as was possible to conceal it; but, in spite of all her constancy, a picture which she found there accidentally betrayed it. It was a Greek subject, Hector parting from Andromache when he went to engage the Greeks, giving his young son Astyanax into her arms, and she fixing her eyes upon him. When she looked at this piece, the resemblance it bore to her own condition made her burst into tears, and several times a day she went to see the picture, and wept before it.

Upon this occasion, when Acilius, one of Brutus's friends, repeated out of Homer the verses, where Andromache speaks to Hector:—

But Hector, you
To me are father and are mother too,
My brother, and my loving husband true,

Brutus, smiling, replied, "But I must not answer Porcia, as Hector did Andromache:—
Mind you your loom, and to your maids give law,
"For though the natural weakness of her body hinders her from doing what only the strength of men can perform, yet she has a mind as valiant and as active for the good of her country as the best of us."

This narrative is in the memoirs of Brutus written by Bibulus, Porcia's son.

Brutus took ship from thence, and sailed to Athens, where he was received by the people with great demonstrations of kindness, expressed in their acclamation and the honours that were decreed him. He lived there with a private friend, and was a constant auditor of Theomnestus, the Academic, and Cratippus, the Peripatetic, with whom he so engaged in philosophical pursuits that he seemed to have laid aside all thoughts of public business, and to be wholly at leisure for study. But all this while, being unsuspected, he was secretly making preparations for war; in order to which he sent Herostratus into Macedonia to secure the commanders there to his side, and he himself won over and kept at his disposal all the young Romans that were then students at Athens. Of this number was Cicero's son, whom he everywhere highly extols, and says that whether sleeping or waking he could not choose but admire a young man of so great a spirit and such a hater of tyranny.

At length he began to act openly, and to appear in public business, and, being informed that there were several Roman ships full of treasure that in their course from Asia were to come that way, and that they were commanded by one of his friends, he went to meet him about Carystus. Finding him there, and having persuaded him to deliver up the ships, he made a more than usually splendid entertainment, for it happened also to be his birthday. Now when they came to drink, and were filling their cups with hopes for victory to Brutus and liberty to Rome, Brutus, to animate them the more, called for a larger bowl, and holding it in his hand, on a sudden, upon no occasion or forethought, pronounced aloud this verse:—

But fate my death and Leto's son have wrought.
And some writers add that in the last battle which he fought at Philippi, the word that he gave to his soldiers was "Apollo," and from thence conclude that this sudden unaccountable exclamation of his was a presage of the overthrow that he suffered there.

Antistius, the commander of these ships, at his parting, gave him fifty thousand myriads of the money that he was conveying to Italy; and all the soldiers yet remaining of Pompey's army, who after their general's defeat wandered about Thessaly, readily and joyfully flocked together to join him. Besides this, he took from Cinna five hundred horse that he was carrying to Dolabella into Asia. After that, he sailed to Demetrias, and there seized a great quantity of arms that had been provided by the command of the deceased Cæsar for the Parthian war, and were now to be sent to Antony. Then Macedonia was put into his

hands and delivered up by Hortensius, the prætor, and all the kings and potentates round about came and offered their services. So when news was brought that Caius, the brother of Antony, having passed over from Italy, was marching on directly to join the forces that Vatinius commanded in Dyrrhachium and Apollonia, Brutus resolved to anticipate him, and to seize them first, and in all haste moved forwards with those that he had about him. His march was very difficult, through rugged places and in a great snow, but so swift that he left those that were to bring his provisions for the morning meal a great way behind.

And now, being very near to Dyrrhachium, with fatigue and cold he fell into the distemper called *bulimia*. This is a disease that seizes both men and cattle after much labour, and especially in a great snow; whether it is caused by the natural heat when the body is seized with cold, being forced all inwards, and consuming at once all the nourishment laid in, or whether the sharp and subtle vapour which comes from the snow as it dissolves cuts the body, as it were, and destroys the heat which issues through the pores; for the sweatings seem to arise from the heat meeting with the cold, and being quenched by it on the surface of the body. But this I have in another place discussed more at large.

Brutus growing very faint, and there being none in the whole army that had anything for him to eat, his servants were forced to have recourse to the enemy, and, going as far as to the gates of the city, begged bread of the sentinels that were upon duty. As soon as they heard of the condition of Brutus, they came themselves, and brought both meat and drink along with them; in return for which Brutus, when he took the city, showed the greatest kindness, not to them only, but to all the inhabitants, for their sakes.

Caius Antonius, in the meantime, coming to Apollonia, summoned all the soldiers that were near that city to join him there; but finding that they nevertheless went all to Brutus, and suspecting that even those of Apollonia were inclined to the same party, he quitted that city, and came to Buthrotum, having first lost three cohorts of his men, that in their march thither were cut to pieces by Brutus. After this, attempting to make himself master of some strong places about Byllis which the enemy had first seized, he was overcome in a set battle by young Cicero, to whom Brutus gave the command, and whose conduct he made use of often and with much success. Caius himself was surprised in a marshy place, at a distance from his support; and Brutus having him in his power would not suffer his soldiers to attack, but manœuvring about the enemy with his horse, gave command that none of them should be killed, for that in a little time they would all be of his side; which accordingly came to pass, for they surrendered both themselves and their general. So that Brutus had by this time a very great and considerable army.

He showed all marks of honour and esteem to Caius for a long time, and left him the use of the ensigns of his office, though, as some report, he had several letters from Rome, and particularly from Cicero, advising him to put him to death. But at last, perceiving that he began to corrupt his officers, and was trying to raise a mutiny amongst the soldiers, he put him aboard a ship and kept him close prisoner. In the meantime, the soldiers that had been corrupted by Caius retired to Apollonia, and sent word to Brutus, desiring him to come to them thither. He answered that this was not the custom of the Romans, but that it became those who had offended to come themselves to their general and beg forgiveness for their offences; which they did, and accordingly received his pardon.

As he was preparing to pass into Asia, tidings reached him of the alteration that had happened at Rome; where the young Cæsar, assisted by the senate, in opposition to Antony, and having driven his competitor out of Italy, had begun himself to be very formidable, suing for the consulship contrary to law, and maintaining large bodies of troops of which the commonwealth had no manner of need. And then, perceiving that the senate, dissatisfied with the proceedings, began to cast their eyes abroad upon Brutus, and decreed and confirmed the government of several provinces to him, he had taken the alarm. Therefore, despatching messengers to Antony, he desired that there might be a reconciliation, and a friendship between them. Then, drawing all his forces about the city, he made himself to be chosen consul, though he was but a boy, being scarce twenty years old, as he himself writes in his memoirs.

At the first entry upon the consulship he immediately ordered a judicial process to be issued out against Brutus and his accomplices for having murdered a principal man of the city, holding the highest magistracies of Rome, without being heard or condemned; and appointed Lucius Cornificus to accuse Brutus, and Marcus Agrippa to accuse Cassius. None appearing to the accusation, the judges were forced to pass sentence and condemn them both. It is reported that when the crier from the tribunal, as the custom was, with a loud voice cried Brutus to appear, the people groaned audibly, and the noble citizens hung down their heads for grief. Publicus Silicius was seen to burst out into tears, which was the reason that not long after he was put down in the list of those that were proscribed. After this, the three men, Cæsar, Antony, and Lepidus, being perfectly reconciled, shared the provinces among themselves, and made up the catalogue of proscription, wherein were set those that were designed for slaughter, amounting to two hundred men, in which number Cicero was slain.

The news being brought to Brutus in Macedonia, he was under a compulsion, and sent orders to Hortensius that he should kill Caius Antonius in revenge of the death of Cicero his friend, and Brutus his kinsman, who also was proscribed and slain. Upon this account it was that Antony, having afterwards taken Hortensius in the battle of Philippi, slew him upon his brother's tomb. But Brutus expresses himself as more ashamed for the cause of Cicero's death than grieved for the misfortune of it, and says he cannot help accusing his friends at Rome, that they were slaves more through their own doing than that of those who now were their tyrants; they could be present and see and yet suffer those things which even to hear related ought to them to have been insufferable.

Having made his army, that was already very considerable, pass into Asia, he ordered a fleet to be prepared in Bithynia and about Cyzicus. But going himself through the country by land, he made it his business to settle and confirm all the cities, and gave audience to the princes of the parts through which he passed. And he sent orders into Syria to Cassius to come to him, and leave his intended journey into Egypt; letting him understand that it was not to gain an empire for themselves, but to free their country, that they went thus wandering about and had got an army together whose business it was to destroy the tyrants; that therefore, if they remembered and resolved to persevere in their first purpose, they ought not to be too far from Italy, but make what haste they could thither, and endeavour to relieve their fellow-citizens from oppression.

Cassius obeyed his summons, and returned, and Brutus went to meet him; and at Smyrna they met, which was the first time they had seen one another since they parted at the Piræus in Athens, one for Syria, and the other for Macedonia. They were both extremely joyful and had great confidence of their success at the sight of the forces that each of them had got together, since they who had fled from Italy, like the most despicable exiles, without money, without arms, without a ship or a soldier or a city to rely on, in a little time after had met together so well furnished with shipping and money, and an army both of horse and foot, that they were in a condition to contend for the empire of Rome.

Cassius was desirous to show no less respect and honour to Brutus than Brutus did to him; but Brutus was still beforehand with him, coming for the most part to him, both because he was the elder man, and of a weaker constitution than himself. Men generally reckoned Cassius a very expert soldier, but of a harsh and angry nature, and one that desired to command rather by fear than love, though, on the other side, among his familiar acquaintance he would easily give way to jesting and play the buffoon. But Brutus, for his virtue, was esteemed by the people, beloved by his friends, admired by the best men, and hated not by his enemies themselves. For he was a man of a singularly gentle nature, of a great spirit, insensible of the passions of anger or pleasure or covetousness, steady and inflexible to maintain his purpose for what he thought right and honest.

And that which gained him the greatest affection and reputation was the entire faith in his intentions. For it had not ever been supposed that Pompey the Great himself, if he had overcome Cæsar, would have submitted his power to the laws, instead of taking the management of the state upon himself, soothing the people with the specious name of consul or dictator, or some other milder title than king. And they were well persuaded that Cassius, being a man governed by anger and passion, and carried often, for his interest's sake, beyond the bounds of justice, endured all these hardships of war and travel and danger most assuredly to obtain dominion to himself, and not liberty to the people. And as for the former disturbers of the peace of Rome, whether a Cinna, a Marius, or a Carbo, it is manifest that they, having set their country as a stake for him that should win, did almost own in express terms

that they fought for empire. But even the enemies of Brutus did not, they tell us, lay this accusation to his charge; nay, many heard Antony himself say that Brutus was the only man that conspired against Cæsar out of a sense of the glory and the apparent justice of the action, but that all the rest rose up against the man, himself, from private envy and malice of their own.

And it is plain by what he writes himself, that Brutus did not so much rely upon his forces, as upon his own virtue. For thus he speaks in a letter to Atticus, shortly before he was to engage with the enemy: that his affairs were in the best state of fortune that he could wish; for that either he should overcome, and restore liberty to the people of Rome, or die, and be himself out of the reach of slavery; that other things being certain and beyond all hazard, one thing was yet in doubt, whether they should live or die free men. He adds further, that Mark Antony had received a just punishment for his folly, who, when he might have been numbered with Brutus and Cassius and Cato, would join himself to Octavius; that though they should not now be both overcome, they soon would fight between themselves. And in this he seems to have been no ill prophet.

Now when they were at Smyrna, Brutus desired of Cassius that he might have part of the great treasure that he had heaped up, because all his own was expended in furnishing out such a fleet of ships as was sufficient to keep the whole interior sea in their power. But Cassius's friends dissuaded him from this; "for," said they, "it is not just that the money which you with so much parsimony keep, and with so much envy have got, should be given to him to be disposed of in making himself popular, and gaining the favour of the soldiers." Notwithstanding this, Cassius gave him a third part of all that he had; and then they parted each to their several commands. Cassius, having taken Rhodes, behaved himself there with no clemency; though at his first entry, when some had called him lord and king, he answered that he was neither king nor lord, but the destroyer and punisher of a king and lord. Brutus, on the other part, sent to the Lycians to demand from them a supply of money and men, but Laucrates, their popular leader, persuaded the cities to resist, and they occupied several little mountains and hills with a design to hinder Brutus's passage.

Brutus at first sent out a party of horse which, surprising them as they were eating, killed six hundred of them, and afterward, having taken all their small towns and villages round about, he set all his prisoners free without ransom, hoping to win the whole nation by good-will. But they continued obstinate, taking in anger what they had suffered, and despising his goodness and humanity; until, having forced the most warlike of them into the city of Xanthus, he besieged them there. They endeavoured to make their escape by swimming and diving through the river that flows by the town, but were taken by nets let down for that purpose in the channel, which had little bells at the top, which gave present notice of any that were taken in them. After that, they made a sally in the night, and seizing several of the battering engines, set them on fire; but being perceived by the Romans, were beaten back to their walls, and there being a strong wind, it carried the flames to the battlements of the city with such fierceness that several of the adjoining houses took fire. Brutus, fearing lest the whole city should be destroyed, commanded his own soldiers to assist and quench the fire.

But the Lycians were on a sudden possessed with a strange and incredible desperation; such a frenzy as cannot be better expressed than by calling it a violent appetite to die, for both women and children, the bondmen and the free, those of all ages and of all conditions strove to force away the soldiers that came in to their assistance from the walls; and themselves gathering together reeds and wood, and whatever combustible matter they found, spread the fire over the whole city, feeding it with whatever fuel they could, and by all possible means exciting its fury, so that the flame, having dispersed itself and encircled the whole city, blazed out in so terrible a manner that Brutus, extremely afflicted at their calamity, got on horseback and rode round the walls, earnestly desirous to preserve the city, and stretching forth his hands to the Xanthians, begged of them that they would spare themselves and save the town.

Yet none regarded his entreaties, but, by all manner of ways, strove to destroy themselves; not only men and women, but even boys and little children, with a hideous outcry, leaped some into the fire, others from the walls, others fell upon their parents' swords, baring their throats and desiring to be struck. After the destruction of the city, there was found a woman who had hanged herself with her young child hanging from her neck, and the torch in her hand with which she had fired her own house.

It was so tragical a sight that Brutus could not endure to see it, but wept at the very relation of it and proclaimed a reward to any soldier that could save a Xanthian. And it is said that an hundred and fifty only were found, to have their lives saved against their wills. Thus the Xanthians after a long space of years, the fated period of their destruction having, as it were, run its course, repeated by their desperate deed the former calamity of their forefathers, who after the very same manner in the Persian war had fired their city and destroyed themselves.

Brutus, after this, finding the Patareans resolved to make resistance and hold out their city against him, was very unwilling to besiege it, and was in great perplexity lest the same frenzy might seize them too. But having in his power some of their women, who were his prisoners, he dismissed them all without any ransom; who, returning and giving an account to their husbands and fathers, who were of the greatest rank, what an excellent man Brutus was, how temperate and how just, persuaded them to yield themselves and put their city into his hands. From this time all the cities round about came into his power, submitting themselves to him, and found him good and merciful even beyond their hopes. For though Cassius at the same time had compelled the Rhodians to bring in all the silver and gold that each of them privately was possessed of, by which he raised a sum of eight thousand talents, and besides this had condemned the public to pay the sum of five hundred talents more, Brutus, not having taken above a hundred and fifty talents from the Lycians, and having done them no other manner of injury, parted from thence with his army to go into Ionia.

Through the whole course of this expedition, Brutus did many memorable acts of justice in dispensing rewards and punishments to such as had deserved either; but one in particular I will relate, because he himself, and all the noblest Romans, were gratified with it above all the rest. When Pompey the Great, being overthrown from his great power by Cæsar, had fled to Egypt, and landed near Pelusium, the protectors of the young king consulted among themselves what was fit to be done on that occasion, nor could they all agree in the same opinion, some being for receiving him, others for driving him from Egypt.

But Theodotus, a Chian by birth, and then attending upon the king as a paid teacher of rhetoric, and for want of better men admitted into the council, undertook to prove to them that both parties were in the wrong, those that counselled to receive Pompey, and those that advised to send him away; that in their present case one thing only was truly expedient, to seize him and to kill him; and ended his argument with the proverb, that "dead men don't bite." The council agreed to his opinion, and Pompey the Great (an example of incredible and unforeseen events) was slain, as the sophister himself had the impudence to boast, through the rhetoric and cleverness of Theodotus. Not long after, when Cæsar came to Egypt, some of the murderers received their just reward and suffered the evil death they deserved. But Theodotus, though he had borrowed from fortune a little further time for a poor, despicable, and wandering life, yet did not lie hid from Brutus as he passed through Asia; but being seized by him and executed, had his death made more memorable than was his life.

About this time, Brutus sent to Cassius to come to him at the city of Sardis, and, when he was on his journey, went forth with his friends to meet him; and the whole army in array saluted each of them with the name of Imperator. Now (as it usually happens in business of great concern, and where many friends and many commanders are engaged), several jealousies of each other and matters of private accusation having passed between Brutus and Cassius, they resolved, before they entered upon any other business, immediately to withdraw into some apartment; where, the door being shut and they two alone, they began first to expostulate, then to dispute hotly, and accuse each other; and finally were so transported into passion as to fall to hard words, and at last burst out into tears. Their friends who stood without were amazed, hearing them loud and angry, and feared lest some mischief might follow, but yet durst not interrupt them, being commanded not to enter the room.

However, Marcus Favonius, who had been an ardent admirer of Cato, and, not so much by his learning or wisdom as by his wild, vehement manner, maintained the character of a philosopher, was rushing in upon them, but was hindered by the attendants. But it was a hard matter to stop Favonius, wherever his wildness hurried him; for he was fierce in all his behaviour, and ready to do anything to get his will. And though he was a senator, yet, thinking that one of the least of his excellences, he valued himself more upon a sort of cynical

liberty of speaking what he pleased, which sometimes, indeed, did away with the rudeness and unseasonableness of his addresses with those that would interpret it in jest. This Favonius, breaking by force through those that kept the doors, entered into the chamber, and with a set voice declaimed the verses that Homer makes Nestor use—

Be ruled, for I am older than ye both.

At this Cassius laughed; but Brutus thrust him out, calling him impudent dog and counterfeit Cynic; but yet for the present they let it put an end to their dispute, and parted. Cassius made a supper that night, and Brutus invited the guests; and when they were set down, Favonius, having bathed, came in among them. Brutus called out aloud and told him he was not invited, and bade him go to the upper couch; but he violently thrust himself in, and lay down on the middle one; and the entertainment passed in sportive talk, not wanting either wit or philosophy.

The next day after, upon the accusation of the Sardians, Brutus publicly disgraced and condemned Lucius Pella, one that had been censor of Rome, and employed in offices of trust by himself, for having embezzled the public money. This action did not a little vex Cassius; for but a few days before, two of his own friends being accused of the same crime, he only admonished them in private, but in public absolved them, and continued them in his service; and upon this occasion he accused Brutus of too much rigour and severity of justice in a time which required them to use more policy and favour. But Brutus bade him remember the Ides of March, the day when they killed Cæsar, who himself neither plundered nor pillaged mankind, but was only the support and strength of those that did; and bade him consider that if there was any colour for justice to be neglected, it had been better to suffer the injustice of Cæsar's friends than to give impunity to their own; "for then," said he, "we would have been accused of cowardice only; whereas now we are liable to the accusation of injustice, after all our pain and dangers which we endure." By which we may perceive what was Brutus's purpose, and the rule of his actions.

About the time that they were going to pass out of Asia into Europe, it is said that a wonderful sign was seen by Brutus. He was naturally given to much watching, and by practice and moderation in his diet had reduced his allowance of sleep to a very small amount of time. He never slept in the daytime, and in the night then only when all his business was finished, and when, every one else being gone to rest, he had nobody to discourse with him. But at this time, the war being begun, having the whole state of it to consider, and being solicitous of the event, after his first sleep, which he let himself take after his supper, he spent all the rest of the night in settling his most urgent affairs; which if he could despatch early and so make a saving of any leisure, he employed himself in reading until the third watch, at which time the centurions and tribunes were used to come to him for orders.

Thus one night before he passed out of Asia, he was very late all alone in his tent, with a dim light burning by him, all the rest of the camp being hushed and silent; and reasoning about something with himself and very thoughtful, he fancied some one came in, and, looking up towards the door, he saw a terrible and strange appearance of an unnatural and frightful body standing by him without speaking. Brutus boldly asked it, "What are you, of men or gods, and upon what business come to me?" The figure answered, "I am your evil genius, Brutus; you shall see me at Philippi." To which Brutus, not at all disturbed, replied, "Then I shall see you."

As soon as the apparition vanished, he called his servants to him, who all told him that they had neither heard any voice nor seen any vision. So then he continued watching till the morning, when he went to Cassius, and told him of what he had seen. He, who followed the principles of Epicurus's philosophy, and often used to dispute with Brutus concerning matters of this nature, spoke to him thus upon this occasion: "It is the opinion of our sect, Brutus, that not all that we feel or see is real and true; but that the sense is a most slippery and deceitful thing, and the mind yet more quick and subtle to put the sense in motion and affect it with every kind of change upon no real occasion of fact; just as an impression is made upon wax; and the soul of man, which has in itself both what imprints, and what is imprinted on, may most easily, by its own operations, produce and assume every variety of shape and figure. This is evident from the sudden changes of our dreams; in which the imaginative principle, once started by any trifling matter, goes through a whole series of most diverse emotions and appearances. It is its nature to be ever in motion, and its motion is fantasy or conception.

"But besides all this, in your case, the body, being tired and distressed with continual toil, naturally works upon the mind and keeps it in an excited and unusual condition. But that there should be any such thing as supernatural beings, or, if there were, that they should have human shape or voice or power that can reach to us, there is no reason for believing; though I confess I could wish that there were such beings, that we might not rely upon our arms only, and our horses and our navy, all which are so numerous and powerful, but might be confident of the assistance of gods also, in this our most sacred and honourable attempt."

With such discourses as these Cassius soothed the mind of Brutus. But just as the troops were going on board, two eagles flew and lighted on the first two ensigns, and crossed over the water with them, and never ceased following the soldiers and being fed by them till they came to Philippi, and there, but one day before the fight, they both flew away.

Brutus had already reduced most of the places and people of these parts; but they now marched on as far as to the coast opposite Thasos, and, if there were any city or man of power that yet stood out, brought them all to subjection. At this point Norbanus was encamped, in a place called the Straits, near Symbolum. Him they surrounded in such sort that they forced him to dislodge and quit the place; and Norbanus narrowly escaped losing his whole army, Cæsar by reason of sickness being too far behind; only Antony came to his relief with such wonderful swiftness that Brutus and those with him did not believe when they heard he was come. Cæsar came up ten days after, and encamped over against Brutus, and Antony over against Cassius.

The space between the two armies is called by the Romans the Campi Philippi. Never had two such large Roman armies come together to engage each other. That of Brutus was somewhat less in number than that of Cæsar, but in the splendidness of the men's arms and richness of their equipage it wonderfully exceeded; for most of their arms were of gold and silver, which Brutus had lavishly bestowed among them. For though in other things he had accustomed his commanders to use all frugality and self-control, yet he thought that the riches which soldiers carried about them in their hands and on their bodies would add something of spirit to those that were desirous of glory, and would make those that were covetous and lovers of gain fight the more valiantly to preserve the arms which were their estate.

Cæsar made a view and lustration of his army within his trenches, and distributed only a little corn and but five drachmas to each soldier for the sacrifice they were to make. But Brutus, either pitying this poverty, or disdaining this meanness of spirit in Cæsar, first, as the custom was, made a general muster and lustration of the army in the open field, and then distributed a great number of beasts for sacrifice to every regiment, and fifty drachmas to every soldier; so that in the love of his soldiers and their readiness to fight for him Brutus had much the advantage.

But at the time of lustration it is reported that an unlucky omen happened to Cassius; for his lictor, presenting him with a garland that he was to wear at sacrifice, gave it him the wrong way up. Further, it is said that some time before, at a certain solemn procession, a golden image of Victory, which was carried before Cassius, fell down by a slip of him that carried it. Besides this there appeared many birds of prey daily about the camp, and swarms of bees were seen in a place within the trenches, which place the soothsayers ordered shut out from the camp, to remove the superstition which insensibly began to infect even Cassius himself and shake him in his Epicurean philosophy, and had wholly seized and subdued the soldiers; from whence it was that Cassius was reluctant to put all to the hazard of a present battle, but advised rather to draw out the war until further time, considering that they were stronger in money and provisions, but in numbers of men and arms inferior.

But Brutus, on the contrary, was still, as formerly, desirous to come with all speed to the decision of a battle; that so he might either restore his country to her liberty, or else deliver from their misery all those numbers of people whom they harassed with the expenses and the service and exactions of the war. And finding also his light-horse in several skirmishes still to have had the better, he was the more encouraged and resolved; and some of the soldiers having deserted and gone to the enemy, and others beginning to accuse and suspect one another, many of Cassius's friends in the council changed their opinions to that of Brutus. But there was one of Brutus's party, named Attellius, who opposed his resolution, advising rather that they should tarry over the winter. And when Brutus asked him in how much better a condition he hoped to be a year after,

his answer was, "If I gain nothing else, yet I shall live so much the longer." Cassius was much displeased at this answer; and among the rest, Attellius was held in much disesteem for it. And so it was presently resolved to give battle the next day.

Brutus that night at supper showed himself very cheerful and full of hope, and reasoned on subjects of philosophy with his friends, and afterwards went to his rest. But Messala says that Cassius supped privately with a few of his nearest acquaintance, and appeared thoughtful and silent, contrary to his temper and custom; that after supper he took him earnestly by the hand, and speaking to him, as his manner was when he wished to show affection, in Greek, said, "Bear witness for me, Messala, that I am brought into the same necessity as Pompey the Great was before me, of hazarding the liberty of my country upon one battle; yet ought we to be of courage, relying on our good fortune, which it were unfair to mistrust, though we take evil counsels." These, Messala says, were the last words that Cassius spoke before he bade him farewell; and that he was invited to sup with him the next night, being his birthday.

As soon as it was morning, the signal of battle, the scarlet coat, was set out in Brutus's and Cassius's camps, and they themselves met in the middle space between their two armies. There Cassius spoke thus to Brutus: "Be it as we hope, O Brutus, that this day we may overcome, and all the rest of our time may live a happy life together; but since the greatest of human concerns are the most uncertain, and since it may be difficult for us ever to see one another again, if the battle should go against us, tell me, what is your resolution concerning flight and death?"

Brutus answered, "When I was young, Cassius, and unskilful in affairs, I was led, I know not how, into uttering a bold sentence in philosophy, and blamed Cato for killing himself, as thinking it an irreligious act, and not a valiant one among men, to try to evade the divine course of things, and not fearlessly to receive and undergo the evil that shall happen, but run away from it. But now in my own fortunes I am of another mind; for if Providence shall not dispose what we now undertake according to our wishes, I resolve to put no further hopes or warlike preparations to the proof, but will die contented with my fortune. For I already have given up my life to my country on the Ides of March; and have lived since then a second life for her sake, with liberty and honour."

Cassius at these words smiled, and, embracing Brutus, said, "With these resolutions let us go on upon the enemy; for either we ourselves shall conquer, or have no cause to fear those that do." After this they discoursed among their friends about the ordering of the battle; and Brutus desired of Cassius that he might command the right wing, though it was thought that this was more fit for Cassius, in regard both of his age and his experience. Yet even in this Cassius complied with Brutus, and placed Messala with the valiantest of all his legions in the same wing, so Brutus immediately drew out his horse, excellently well equipped, and was not long in bringing up his foot after them.

Antony's soldiers were casting trenches from the marsh by which they were encamped across the plain, to cut off Cassius's communications with the sea. Cæsar was to be at hand with his troops to support them, but he was not able to be present himself, by reason of his sickness; and his soldiers, not much expecting that the enemy would come to a set battle, but only make some excursions with their darts and light arms to disturb the men at work in the trenches, and not taking notice of the troops drawn up against them ready to give battle, were amazed when they heard the confused and great outcry that came from the trenches.

In the meanwhile Brutus had sent his tickets, in which was the word of battle, to the officers; and himself riding about to all the troops, encouraged the soldiers; but there were but few of them that understood the word before they engaged; the most of them, not staying to have it delivered to them, with one impulse and cry ran upon the enemy. This disorder caused an unevenness in the line, and the legions got severed and divided one from another; that of Messala first, and afterwards the other adjoining, went beyond the left wing of Cæsar; and having just touched the extremity, without slaughtering any great number, passing around that wing, fell directly into Cæsar's camp. Cæsar himself, as his own memoirs tell us, had but just before been conveyed away, Marcus Artorius, one of his friends, having had a dream bidding Cæsar be carried out of the camp. And it was believed that he was slain; for the soldiers had pierced his litter, which was left empty, in many places with their darts and pikes. There was a great slaughter in the camp that was taken; and two

thousand Lacedæmonians that were newly come to the assistance of Cæsar were all cut off together.

The rest of the army, that had not gone round, but had engaged the front, easily overthrew them, finding them in great disorder, and slew upon the place three legions; and being carried on with the stream of victory, pursuing those that fled, fell into the camp with them, Brutus himself being there. But they that were conquered took the advantage in their extremity of what the conquerors did not consider. For they fell upon that part of the main body which had been left exposed and separated, where the right wing had broke off from them and hurried away in the pursuit; yet they could not break into the midst of their battle, but were received with strong resistance and obstinacy.

Yet they put to flight the left wing, where Cassius commanded, being in great disorder, and ignorant of what had passed on the other wing; and pursuing them to their camp, they pillaged and destroyed it, neither of their generals being present; for Antony, they say, to avoid the fury of the first onset, had retired into the marsh that was hard by; and Cæsar was nowhere to be found after his being conveyed out of the tents; though some of the soldiers showed Brutus their swords bloody, and declared that they had killed him, describing his person and his age. By this time also the centre of Brutus's battle had driven back their opponents with great slaughter; and Brutus was everywhere plainly conqueror, as on the other side Cassius was conquered. And this one mistake was the ruin of their affairs, that Brutus did not come to the relief of Cassius, thinking that he, as well as himself, was conqueror; and that Cassius did not expect the relief of Brutus, thinking that he, too, was overcome.

For as a proof that the victory was on Brutus's side, Messala urges his taking three eagles and many ensigns of the enemy without losing any of his own. But now, returning from the pursuit after having plundered Cæsar's camp, Brutus wondered that he could not see Cassius's tent standing high, as it was wont, and appearing above the rest, nor other things appearing as they had been; for they had been immediately pulled down and pillaged by the enemy upon their first falling into the camp. But some that had a quicker and longer sight than the rest acquainted Brutus that they saw a great deal of shining armour and silver targets moving to and fro in Cassius's camp, and that they thought, by their number and the fashion of their armour, they could not be those that they left to guard the camp; but yet that there did not appear so great a number of dead bodies thereabouts as it was probable there would have been after the actual defeat of so many legions. This first made Brutus suspect Cassius's misfortune, and, leaving a guard in the enemy's camp, he called back those that were in the pursuit, and rallied them together to lead them to the relief of Cassius, whose fortune had been as follows.

First, he had been angry at the onset that Brutus's soldiers made, without the word of battle or command to charge. Then, after they had overcome, he was as much displeased to see them rush on to the plunder and spoil, and neglect to surround and encompass the rest of the enemy. Besides this, letting himself act by delay and expectation, rather than command, boldly and with a clear purpose, he got hemmed in by the right wing of the enemy, and, his horse making with all haste their escape and flying towards the sea, the foot also began to give way, which he perceiving laboured as much as ever he could to hinder their flight and bring them back; and, snatching an ensign out of the hand of one that fled, he stuck it at his feet, though he could hardly keep even his own personal guard together. So that at last he was forced to fly with a few about him to a little hill that overlooked the plain.

But he himself, being weak-sighted, discovered nothing, only the destruction of his camp, and that with difficulty. But they that were with him saw a great body of horse moving towards him, the same whom Brutus had sent. Cassius believed these were enemies, and in pursuit of him; however, he sent away Titinius, one of those that were with him, to learn what they were. As soon as Brutus's horse saw him coming, and knew him to be a friend and a faithful servant of Cassius, those of them that were his more familiar acquaintance, shouting out for joy and alighting from their horses, shook hands and embraced him, and the rest rode round about him singing and shouting, through their excess of gladness at the sight of him. But this was the occasion of the greatest mischief that could be. For Cassius really thought that Titinius had been taken by the enemy, and cried out, "Through too much fondness of life, I have lived to endure the sight of my friend taken by the enemy before my face."

After which words he retired into an empty tent, taking along with him only Pindarus, one of his freemen, whom he had reserved for such an occasion ever since the disasters in the expedition against the Parthians, when Crassus was slain. From the Parthians he came away in safety; but now, pulling up his mantle over his head, he made his neck bare, and held it forth to Pindarus, commanding him to strike. The head was certainly found lying severed from the body. But no man ever saw Pindarus after, from which some suspected that he had killed his master without his command. Soon after they perceived who the horsemen were, and saw Titinius, crowned with garlands, making what haste he could towards Cassius. But as soon as he understood by the cries and lamentations of his afflicted friends the unfortunate error and death of his general, he drew his sword, and having very much accused and upbraided his own long stay, that had caused it, he slew himself.

Brutus, as soon as he was assured of the defeat of Cassius, made haste to him; but heard nothing of his death till he came near his camp. Then having lamented over his body, calling him "the last of the Romans," it being impossible that the city should ever produce another man of so great a spirit, he sent away the body to be buried at Thasos, lest celebrating his funeral within the camp might breed some disorder. He then gathered the soldiers together and comforted them; and, seeing them destitute of all things necessary, he promised to every man two thousand drachmas in recompense of what he had lost. They at these words took courage, and were astonished at the magnificence of the gift; and waited upon him at his parting with shouts and praises, magnifying him for the only general of all the four who was not overcome in the battle. And indeed the action itself testified that it was not without reason he believed he should conquer; for with a few legions he overthrew all that resisted him; and if all his soldiers had fought, and the most of them had not passed beyond the enemy in pursuit of the plunder, it is very likely that he had utterly defeated every part of them.

There fell of his side eight thousand men, reckoning the servants of the army, whom Brutus calls Briges; and on the other side, Messala says his opinion is that there were slain about twice that number. For which reason they were more out of heart than Brutus, until a servant of Cassius, named Demetrius, came in the evening to Antony, and brought to him the garment which he had taken from the dead body, and his sword; at the sight of which they were so encouraged, that, as soon as it was morning, they drew out their whole force into the field, and stood in battle array.

But Brutus found both his camps wavering and in disorder; for his own, being filled with prisoners, required a guard more strict than ordinary over them; and that of Cassius was uneasy at the change of general, besides some envy and rancour, which those that were conquered bore to that part of the army which had been conquerors. Wherefore he thought it convenient to put his army in array, but to abstain from fighting. All the slaves that were taken prisoners, of whom there was a great number that were mixed up, not without suspicion, among the soldiers, he commanded to be slain; but of the freemen and citizens, some he dismissed, saying that among the enemy they were rather prisoners than with him, for with them they were captives and slaves, but with him freemen and citizens of Rome. But he was forced to hide and help them to escape privately, perceiving that his friends and officers were bent upon revenge against them.

Among the captives there was one Volumnius, a player, and Sacculio, a buffoon; of these Brutus took no manner of notice, but his friends brought them before him and accused them that even then in that condition they did not refrain from their jests and scurrilous language. Brutus, having his mind taken up with other affairs, said nothing to their accusation; but the judgment of Messala Corvinus was that they should be whipped publicly upon a stage, and so sent naked to the captains of the enemy, to show them what sort of fellow drinkers and companions they took with them on their campaigns. At this some that were present laughed; and Publius Casca, he that gave the first wound to Cæsar, said, "We do ill to jest and make merry at the funeral of Cassius. But you, O Brutus," he added, "will show what esteem you have for the memory of that general, according as you punish or preserve alive those who will scoff and speak shamefully of him." To this Brutus, in great discomposure, replied, "Why then, Casca, do you ask me about it, and not do yourselves what you think fitting?" This answer of Brutus was taken for his consent to the death of these wretched men; so they were carried away and slain.

After this he gave the soldiers the reward that he had promised them; and having slightly reproved them for having fallen upon the enemy in disorder without the word of battle or command, he promised them, that if they behaved themselves bravely in the next engagement, he would give them up two cities to spoil and plunder, Thessalonica and Lacedæmon. This is the one indefensible thing of all that is found fault with in the life of Brutus; though true it may be that Antony and Cæsar were much more cruel in the rewards that they gave their soldiers after victory; for they drove out, one might almost say, all the old inhabitants of Italy, to put their soldiers in possession of other men's lands and cities. But indeed their only design and end in undertaking the war was to obtain dominion and empire, whereas Brutus, for the reputation of his virtue, could not be permitted either to overcome or save himself but with justice and honour, especially after the death of Cassius, who was generally accused of having been his adviser to some things that he had done with less clemency.

But now, as in a ship, when the rudder is broken by a storm, the mariners fit and nail on some other piece of wood instead of it, striving against the danger not well, but as well as in that necessity they can, so Brutus, being at the head of so great an army, in a time of such uncertainty, having no commander equal to his need, was forced to make use of those that he had, and to do and to say many things according to their advice; which was, in effect, whatever might conduce to the bringing of Cassius's soldiers into better order. For they were very headstrong and intractable, bold and insolent in the camp for want of their general, but in the field cowardly and fearful, remembering that they had been beaten.

Neither were the affairs of Cæsar and Antony in any better posture; for they were straitened for provision, and, the camp being in a low ground, they expected to pass a very hard winter. For being driven close upon the marshes, and a great quantity of rain, as is usual in autumn, having fallen after the battle, their tents were all filled with mire and water, which through the coldness of the weather immediately froze.

And while they were in this condition, there was news brought to them of their loss at sea. For Brutus's fleet fell upon their ships, which were bringing a great supply of soldiers out of Italy, and so entirely defeated them, that but very few of the men escaped being slain, and they too were forced by famine to feed upon the sails and tackle of the ship. As soon as they heard this, they made what haste they could to come to the decision of a battle, before Brutus should have notice of his good success. For it had so happened that the fight both by sea and land was on the same day, but by some misfortune, rather than the fault of his commanders, Brutus knew not of his victory twenty days after. For had he been informed of this, he would not have been brought to a second battle, since he had sufficient provisions for his army for a long time, and was very advantageously posted, his camp being well sheltered from the cold weather, and almost inaccessible to the enemy, and his being absolute master of the sea, and having at land overcome on that side wherein he himself was engaged, would have made him full of hope and confidence.

But it seems the state of Rome not enduring any longer to be governed by many, but necessarily requiring a monarchy, the divine power, that it might remove out of the way the only man that was able to resist him that could control the empire, cut off his good fortune from coming to the ears of Brutus; though it came but a very little too late, for the very evening before the fight, Clodius, a deserter from the enemy, came and announced that Cæsar had received advice of the loss of his fleet, and for that reason was in such haste to come to a battle. But his story met with no credit, nor was he so much as seen by Brutus, being simply set down as one that had no good information, or invented lies to bring himself into favour.

The same night, they say, the vision appeared again to Brutus, in the same shape that it did before, but vanished without speaking. But Publius Volumnius, a philosopher, and one that had from the beginning borne arms with Brutus, makes no mention of this apparition, but says that the first eagle was covered with a swarm of bees, and that there was one of the captains whose arm of itself sweated oil of roses, and, though they often dried and wiped it, yet it would not cease; and that immediately before the battle, two eagles falling upon each other fought in the space between the two armies, that the whole field kept incredible silence and all were intent upon the spectacle, until at last that which was on Brutus's side yielded and fled. But the story of the Ethiopian is very famous, who, meeting the standard-bearer at the opening of the gate of the camp, was cut to pieces by the soldiers, that took it for an ill omen.

Brutus, having brought his army into the field and set them in array against the enemy, paused a long while before he would fight; for as he was reviewing the troops, suspicions were excited and informations laid against some of them. Besides, he saw his horse not very eager to begin the action, and waiting to see what the foot would do. Then suddenly Camulatus, a very good soldier, and one whom for his valour he highly esteemed, riding hard by Brutus himself, went over to the enemy, the sight of which grieved Brutus exceedingly. So that partly out of anger, and partly out of fear of some greater treason and desertion, he immediately drew on his forces upon the enemy, the sun now declining, about three of the clock in the afternoon. Brutus on his side had the better, and pressed hard on the left wing, which gave way and retreated; and the horse too fell in together with the foot, when they saw the enemy in disorder.

But the other wing, when the officers extended the line to avoid its being encompassed, the numbers being inferior, got drawn out too thin in the centre, and was so weak here that they could not withstand the charge, but at the first onset fled. After defeating these, the enemy at once took Brutus in the rear, who all the while did all that was possible for an expert general and valiant soldier, doing everything in the peril, by counsel and by hand, that might recover the victory. But that which had been his superiority in the first fight was to his prejudice in the second. For in the first, that part of the enemy which was beaten was killed on the spot; but of Cassius's soldiers that fled, few had been slain, and those that escaped, daunted with their defeat, infected the other and larger part of the army with their want of spirit and their disorder. Here Marcus, the son of Cato, was slain, fighting and behaving himself with great bravery in the midst of the youth of the highest rank and greatest valour. He would neither flee nor give the least ground, but still fighting and declaring who he was and naming his father's name, he fell upon a heap of dead bodies of the enemy. And of the rest, the bravest were slain in defending Brutus.

There was in the field one Lucilius, an excellent man and a friend of Brutus, who, seeing some barbarian horse taking no notice of any other in the pursuit, but galloping at full speed after Brutus, resolved to stop them, though with the hazard of his life; and, letting himself fall a little behind, he told them that he was Brutus. They believed him the rather, because he prayed to be carried to Antony, as if he feared Cæsar, but durst trust him. They, over-joyed with their prey, and thinking themselves wonderfully fortunate, carried him along with them in the night, having first sent messengers to Antony of their coming. He was much pleased, and came to meet them; and all the rest that heard that Brutus was taken and brought alive flocked together to see him, some pitying his fortune, others accusing him of a meanness unbecoming his former glory, that out of too much love of life he would be a prey to barbarians.

When they came near together, Antony stood still, considering with himself in what manner he should receive Brutus; but Lucilius, being brought up to him, with great confidence said: "Be assured, Antony, that no enemy either has taken or ever shall take Marcus Brutus alive (forbid it, heaven, that fortune should ever so much prevail above virtue!), but he shall be found, alive or dead, as becomes himself. As for me, I am come hither by a cheat that I put upon your soldiers, and am ready, upon this occasion, to suffer any severities you will inflict."

All were amazed to hear Lucilius speak these words. But Antony, turning himself to those that brought him, said: "I perceive, my fellow-soldiers, that you are concerned, and take it ill that you have been thus deceived, and think yourselves abused and injured by it; but know that you have met with a booty better than that you sought. For you were in search of an enemy, but you have brought me here a friend. For indeed I am uncertain how I should have used Brutus, if you had brought him alive; but of this I am sure, that it is better to have such men as Lucilius our friends than our enemies." Having said this, he embraced Lucilius, and for the present commended him to the care of one of his friends, and ever after found him a steady and a faithful friend.

Brutus had now passed a little brook, running among trees and under steep rocks, and, it being night, would go no further, but sat down in a hollow place with a great rock projecting before it, with a few of his officers and friends about him. At first, looking up to heaven, that was then full of stars, he repeated two verses, one of which, Volumnius writes, was this:—

Punish, great Jove, the author of these ills.

The other he says he has forgot. Soon after, naming severally all his friends that had been slain before his face in the battle, he groaned heavily, especially at the mentioning of Flavius

and Labeo, the latter his lieutenant, and the other chief officer of his engineers. In the meantime, one of his companions, that was very thirsty and saw Brutus in the same condition, took his helmet and ran to the brook for water, when a noise being heard from the other side of the river, Volumnius, taking Dardanus, Brutus's armour-bearer, with him, went out to see what it was. They returned in a short space, and inquired about the water. Brutus, smiling with much meaning, said to Volumnius, "It is all drunk; but you shall have some more fetched." But he that had brought the first water, being sent again, was in great danger of being taken by the enemy, and having received a wound, with much difficulty escaped.

Now Brutus guessing that not many of his men were slain in the fight, Statyllius undertook to dash through the enemy (for there was no other way), and to see what was become of their camp; and promised, if he found all things there safe, to hold up a torch for a signal, and then return. The torch was held up, Statyllius got safe to the camp; but when after a long time he did not return, Brutus said, "If Statyllius be alive, he will come back." But it happened that in his return he fell into the enemy's hands, and was slain.

The night now being far spent, Brutus, as he was sitting, leaned his head towards his servant Clitus, and spoke to him; he answered him not, but fell a-weeping. After that he drew aside his armour-bearer, Dardanus, and had some discourse with him in private. At last, speaking to Volumnius in Greek, he reminded him of their common studies and former discipline and begged that he would take hold of his sword with him, and help him to thrust it through him. Volumnius put away his request, and several others did the like; and some one saying, that there was no staying there, but they needs must fly, Brutus, rising up, said, "Yes, indeed, we must fly, but not with our feet, but with our hands."

Then giving each of them his right hand, with a countenance full of pleasure, he said that he found an infinite satisfaction in this, that none of his friends had been false to him; that as for fortune, he was angry with that only for his country's sake; as for himself, he thought himself much more happy than they who had overcome, not only as he had been a little time ago, but even now in his present condition; since he was leaving behind him such a reputation of his virtue as none of the conquerors with all their arms and riches should ever be able to acquire, no more than they could hinder posterity from believing and saying, that being unjust and wicked men, they had destroyed the just and the good, and usurped a power to which they had no right.

After this, having exhorted and entreated all about him to provide for their own safety, he withdrew from them with two or three only of his peculiar friends; Strato was one of these, with whom he had contracted an acquaintance when they studied rhetoric together. Him he placed next to himself, and, taking hold of the hilt of his sword and directing it with both his hands, fell upon it, and killed himself. But others say, that not he himself, but Strato, at the earnest entreaty of Brutus, turning aside his head, held the sword, upon which he violently throwing himself, it pierced his breast, and he immediately died.

This same Strato, Messala, a friend of Brutus, being after reconciled to Cæsar, brought to him once at his leisure, and with tears in his eyes said, "This, O Cæsar, is the man that did the last friendly office to my beloved Brutus." Upon which Cæsar received him kindly; and had good use of him in his labours and his battles at Actium, being one of the Greeks

that proved their bravery in his service. It is reported of Messala himself, that, when Cæsar once gave him this commendation, that though he was his fiercest enemy at Philippi in the cause of Brutus, yet he had shown himself his most entire friend in the fight of Actium, he answered, "You have always found me, Cæsar, on the best and justest side."

Brutus's dead body was found by Antony, who commanded the richest purple mantle that he had to be thrown over it, and afterwards the mantle being stolen, he found the thief, and had him put to death. He sent the ashes of Brutus to his mother Servilia. As for Porcia his wife, Nicolaus the philosopher and Valerius Maximus write, that, being desirous to die, but being hindered by her friends, who continually watched her, she snatched some burning charcoal out of the fire, and, shutting it close in her mouth, stifled herself, and died. Though there is a letter current from Brutus to his friends, in which he laments the death of Porcia, and accuses them for neglecting her so that she desired to die rather than languish with her disease. So that it seems Nicolaus was mistaken in the time; for this epistle (if it indeed is authentic and truly Brutus's) gives us to understand the malady and love of Porcia, and the way in which her death occurred.

BRUTUS and DION
Compared

THERE are noble points in abundance in the characters of these two men, and one to be first mentioned is their attaining such a height of greatness upon such inconsiderable means; and on this score Dion has by war the advantage. For he had no partner to contest his glory, as Brutus had in Cassius, who was not, indeed, his equal in proved virtue and honour, yet contributed quite as much to the service of the war by his boldness, skill, and activity; and some there be who impute to him the rise and beginning of the whole enterprise, saying that it was he who roused Brutus, till then indisposed to stir, into action against Cæsar. Whereas Dion seems of himself to have provided not only arms, ships, and soldiers, but likewise friends and partners for the enterprise. Neither did he, as Brutus, collect money and forces from the war itself, but, on the contrary, laid out of his own substance, and employed the very means of his private sustenance in exile for the liberty of his country.

Besides this, Brutus and Cassius, when they fled to Rome, could not live safe or quiet, being condemned to death and pursued, and were thus of necessity forced to take arms and hazard their lives in their own defence, to save themselves, rather than their country. On the other hand, Dion enjoyed more ease, was more safe, and his life more pleasant in his banishment, than was the tyrant's who had banished him, when he flew to action, and ran the risk of all to save Sicily.

Take notice, too, that it was not the same thing for the Sicilians to be freed from Dionysius, and for the Romans to be freed from Cæsar. The former owned himself a tyrant, and vexed Sicily with a thousand oppressions; whereas Cæsar's supremacy, certainly, in the process for attaining it, had inflicted no trouble on its opponents, but, once established and victorious, it had indeed the name and appearance, but fact that was cruel or tyrannical there was none. On the contrary, in the mal-

ady of the times and the need of a monarchical government, he might be thought to have
been sent as the gentlest physician, by no other
than a divine intervention. And thus the
common people instantly regretted Cæsar, and
grew enraged and implacable against those
that killed him. Whereas Dion's chief offence
in the eyes of his fellow-citizens was his having let Dionysius escape, and not having demolished the former tyrant's tomb.

In the actual conduct of war, Dion was a
commander without fault, improving to the
utmost those counsels which he himself gave,
and where others led him into disaster correcting and turning everything to the best. But
Brutus seems to have shown little wisdom in
engaging in the final battle, which was to decide everything, and when he failed not to have
done his business in seeking a remedy; he gave
all up, and abandoned his hopes, not venturing against fortune even as far as Pompey did,
when he had still means enough to rely on in
his troops, and was clearly master of all the
seas with his ships.

The greatest thing charged on Brutus is, that
he, being saved by Cæsar's kindness, having
saved all the friends whom he chose to ask for,
he moreover accounted a friend, and preferred
above many, did yet lay violent hands upon his
preserver. Nothing like this could be objected
against Dion; quite the contrary; whilst he
was of Dionysius's family and his friend, he
did good service and was useful to him; but
driven from his country, wronged in his wife,
and his estate lost, he openly entered upon a
war just and lawful.

Does not, however, the matter turn the other
way? For the chief glory of both was their
hatred of tyranny, and abhorrence of wickedness. This was unmixed and sincere in Brutus;
for he had no private quarrel with Cæsar, but
went into the risk singly for the liberty of his
country. The other, had he not been privately
injured, had not fought. This is plain from
Plato's epistles, where it is shown that he was
turned out, and did not forsake the court to
wage war upon Dionysius. Moreover, the public good made Brutus Pompey's friend (instead
of his enemy as he had been) and Cæsar's enemy; since he proposed for his hatred and his
friendship no other end and standard but justice. Dion was very serviceable to Dionysius
whilst in favour; when no longer trusted, he
grew angry and fell to arms. And, for this reason, not even were his own friends all of them
satisfied with his undertaking, or quite as-

sured that, having overcome Dionysius, he
might not settle the government on himself,
deceiving his fellow-citizens by some less obnoxious name than tyranny. But the very enemies of Brutus would say that he had no other
end or aim, from first to last, save only to restore to the Roman people their ancient government.

And apart from what has just been said, the
adventure against Dionysius was nothing
equal with that against Cæsar. For none that
was familiarly conversant with Dionysius but
scorned him for his life of idle amusement with
wine, women, and dice; whereas it required an
heroic soul and a truly intrepid and unquailing
spirit so much as to entertain the thought of
crushing Cæsar, so formidable for his ability,
his power, and his fortune, whose very name
disturbed the slumbers of the Parthian and Indian kings. Dion was no sooner seen in Sicily
but thousands ran in to him and joined him
against Dionysius; whereas the renown of
Cæsar, even when dead, gave strength to his
friends; and his very name so heightened the
person that took it, that from a simple boy he
presently became the chief of the Romans;
and he could use it for a spell against the enmity and power of Antony.

If any object that it cost Dion great trouble
and difficulties to overcome the tyrant, whereas
Brutus slew Cæsar naked and unprovided, yet
this itself was the result of the most consummate policy and conduct, to bring it about that
a man so guarded around, and so fortified at
all points, should be taken naked and unprovided. For it was not on the sudden, nor alone,
nor with a few, that he fell upon and killed
Cæsar; but after long concerting the plot, and
placing confidence in a great many men, not
one of whom deceived him. For he either at
once discerned the best men, or by confiding
in them made them good. But Dion, either
making a wrong judgment, trusted himself
with ill men, or else by his employing them
made ill men of good; either of the two would
be a reflection on a wise man. Plato also is
severe upon him, for choosing such for friends
as betrayed him.

Besides, when Dion was killed, none appeared to revenge his death. Whereas Brutus,
even amongst his enemies, had Antony that
buried him splendidly; and Cæsar also took
care his honours should be preserved. There
stood at Milan in Gaul, within the Alps, a
brazen statue, which Cæsar in aftertimes noticed (being a real likeness, and a fine work of

art), and passing by it presently stopped short, and in the hearing of many commanded the magistrates to come before him. He told them their town had broken their league, harbouring an enemy. The magistrates at first simply denied the thing, and, not knowing what he meant, looked one upon another, when Cæsar, turning towards the statue and gathering his brows, said, "Pray is not that our enemy who stands there?" They were all in confusion, and had nothing to answer; but he, smiling, much commended the Gauls, as who had been firm to their friends, though in adversity, and ordered that the statue should remain standing as he found it.

ARATUS

271–213 B.C.

THE Philosopher, Chrysippus, O Polycrates, quotes an ancient proverb, not as really it should be, apprehending, I suppose, that it sounded too harshly, but so as he thought it would run best, in these words:—

Who praise their fathers but the generous sons?

But Dionysodorus, the Trœzenian, proves him to be wrong, and restores the true reading, which is thus:—

Who praise their fathers but degenerate sons?

telling us that the proverb is meant to stop the mouth of those who, having no merit of their own, take refuge in the virtues of their ancestors, and make their advantage of praising them. But, as Pindar hath it—

> *He that by nature doth inherit*
> *From ancestors a noble spirit,*

as you do, who made your life the copy of the fairest originals of your family,—such, I say, may take great satisfaction in being reminded, both by hearing others speak and speaking themselves, of the best of their progenitors. For they assume not the glory of praises earned by others out of any want of worth of their own, but affiliating their own deeds to those of their ancestors, give them honour as the authors both of their descent and manners.

Therefore, I have sent to you the life which I have written of your fellow-citizen and forefather, Aratus, to whom you are no discredit in point either of reputation or of authority, not as though you had not been most diligently careful to inform yourself from the beginning concerning his actions, but that your sons, Polycrates and Pythocles, may both by hearing and reading become familiar with those family examples which it behooves them to follow and imitate. It is a piece of self-love, and not of the love of virtue, to imagine one has already attained to what is best.

The city of Sicyon, from the time that it first fell off from the pure and Doric aristocracy (its harmony being destroyed, and a mere series of seditions and personal contests of popular leaders ensuing) continued to be distempered and unsettled, changing from one tyrant to another, until, Cleon being slain, Timoclides and Clinias, men of the most repute and power amongst the citizens, were chosen to the magistracy. And the commonwealth now seemed to be in a pretty settled condition. Timoclides died, and Abantidas, the son of Paseas, to possess himself of the tyranny, killed Clinias, and, of his kindred and friends, slew some and banished others. He sought also to kill his son Aratus, whom he left behind him, being but seven years old. This boy in the general disorder getting out of the house with those that fled, and wandering about the city helpless and in great fear, by chance got undiscovered into the house of a woman who was Abantidas's sister, but married to Prophantus, the brother of Clinias, her name being Soso. She, being of a generous temper, and believing the boy had by some supernatural guidance fled to her for shelter, hid him in the house, and at night sent him away to Argos.

Aratus, being thus delivered and secured from this danger, conceived from the first and ever after nourished a vehement and burning hatred against tyrants, which strengthened with his years. Being therefore bred up amongst his father's acquaintance and friends at Argos with a liberal education, and perceiving his body to promise good health and stature, he addicted himself to the exercises of the palæstra, to that degree that he competed in the five games, and gained some crowns; and indeed in his statues one may observe a certain kind of athletic cast, and the sagacity and majesty of his countenance does not dissemble his full diet and the use of the hoe. Whence it came to pass that he less studied eloquence than perhaps became a statesman, and yet he was more accomplished in speaking than many believe, judging by the commentaries which he left behind him, written carelessly and, by the way, as fast as he could do it, and in such words as first came to his mind.

In the course of time, Dinias and Aristotle the logician killed Abantidas, who used to be present in the market-place at their discussions, and to make one in them; till they taking the occasion, insensibly accustomed him to the practice, and so had opportunity to contrive and execute a plot against him. After him Paseas, the father of Abantidas, taking upon him the government, was assassinated by Nicocles, who set himself up for tyrant. Of him it is related that he was strikingly like Periander, the son of Cypselus, just as it is said that Orontes, the Persian, bore a great resemblance to Alcmæon, the son of Amphiaraus, and that Lacedæmonian youth, whom Myrsilus relates to have been trodden to pieces by the crowd of those that came to see him upon that report, to Hector.

This Nicocles governed four months, in which, after he had done all kinds of mischief to the city, he very nearly let it fall into the hands of the Ætolians. By this time Aratus, being grown a youth, was in much esteem, both for his noble birth, and his spirit and disposition, which, while neither insignificant nor wanting in energy, were solid, and tempered with a steadiness of judgment beyond his years. For which reason the exiles had their eyes most upon him, nor did Nicocles less observe his motions, but secretly spied and watched him, not out of apprehension of any such considerable or utterly audacious attempt, but suspecting he held correspondence with the kings, who were his father's friends and acquaintance. And, indeed, Aratus first attempted this way; but, finding that Antigonus, who had promised fair, neglected him and delayed the time, and that his hopes from Egypt and Ptolemy were long to wait for, he determined to cut off the tyrant by himself.

And first he broke his mind to Aristomachus and Ecdelus, the one an exile of Sicyon, the other, Ecdelus, an Arcadian of Megalopolis, a philosopher, and a man of action, having been the familiar friend of Arcesilaus the Academic at Athens. These readily consenting, he communicated with the other exiles, whereof some few, being ashamed to seem to despair of success, engaged in the design; but most of them endeavoured to divert him from his purpose, as one that for want of experience was too rash and daring.

Whilst he was consulting to seize upon some post in Sicyonia, from whence he might make war upon the tyrant, there came to Argos a certain Sicyonian, newly escaped out of prison, brother to Xenocles, one of the exiles, who, being by him presented to Aratus, informed him that that part of the wall over which he escaped was, inside, almost level with the ground, adjoining a rocky and elevated place, and that from the outside it might be scaled with ladders. Aratus, hearing this, despatched away Xenocles with two of his own servants, Seuthas and Technon, to view the wall, resolving, if possible, secretly and with one risk to hazard all on a single trial, rather than carry on a contest as a private man against a tyrant by long war and open force. Xenocles, therefore, with his companions, returning, having taken the height of the wall, and declaring the place not to be impossible or indeed difficult to get over, but that it was not easy to approach it undiscovered by reason of some small but uncommonly savage and noisy dogs belonging to a gardener hard by, he immediately undertook the business.

Now the preparation of arms gave no jealousy, because robberies and petty forays were at that time common everywhere between one set of people and another; and for the ladders, Euphranor, the machine-maker, made them openly, his trade rendering him unsuspected, though one of the exiles. As for men, each of his friends in Argos furnished him with ten apiece out of those few they had, and he armed thirty of his own servants, and hired some few soldiers of Xenophilus, the chief of the robber captains, to whom it was given out that they were to march into the territory of Sicyon to seize the king's stud; most of them were sent before, in small parties, to the tower of Polygnotus, with orders to wait there; Caphisias also was despatched beforehand lightly armed, with four others, who were, as soon as it was dark, to come to the gardener's house, pretending to be travellers, and procuring their lodging there, to shut up him and his dogs; for there was no other way to getting past. And for the ladders, they had been made to take in pieces, and were put into chests, and sent before, hidden upon waggons.

In the meantime, some of the spies of Nicocles appearing in Argos, and being said to go privately about watching Aratus, he came early in the morning into the market-place, showing himself openly and conversing with his friends; then he anointed himself in the exercise ground, and, taking with him thence some of the young men that used to drink and spend their time with him, he went home; and presently after several of his servants were seen about the market-place, one carrying garlands, another buying flambeaux, and a third speaking to the women that used to sing and play at banquets, all of which things the spies observing were deceived, and said, laughing to one another, "Certainly nothing can be more timorous than a tyrant, if Nicocles, being master of so great a city and so numerous a force, stands in fear of a youth that spends what he has to subsist upon in his banishment in pleasures and day-debauches"; and being thus imposed upon, they returned home.

But Aratus, departing immediately after his morning meal, and coming to his soldiers at Polygnotus's tower, led them to Nemea; where he disclosed to most of them, for the first time, his true design, making them large promises and fair speeches, and marched towards the city, giving for the word "Apollo Victorious," proportioning his march to the motion of the moon, so as to have the benefit of her light upon the way, and to be in the garden, which was close to the wall, just as she was setting. Here Caphisias came to him, who had not secured the dogs, which had run away before he could catch them, but had only made sure of the gardener.

Upon which most of the company being out of heart and desiring to retreat, Aratus encouraged them to go on, promising to retire in case the dogs were too troublesome; at the same time sending forward those that carried the ladders, conducted by Ecdelus and Mnasitheus, he followed them himself leisurely, the dogs already barking very loud and following the steps of Ecdelus and his companion. However, they got to the wall, and reared the ladders with safety. But as the foremost men were mounting them, the captain of the watch that was to be relieved by the morning guard passed on his way with the bell; and there were many lights, and a noise of people coming up. Hearing which, they clapt themselves close to the ladders, and so were unobserved; but as the

other watch also was coming up to meet this, they were in extreme danger of being discovered. But when this also went by without observing them, immediately Mnasitheus and Ecdelus got upon the wall, and, possessing themselves of the approaches inside and out, sent away Technon to Aratus, desiring him to make all the haste he could.

Now there was no great distance from the garden to the wall and to the tower in which latter a large hound was kept. The hound did not hear their steps of himself, whether that he were naturally drowsy, or overwearied the day before, but, the gardener's curs awaking him, he first began to growl and grumble in response, and then as they passed by to bark out aloud. And the barking was now so great, that the sentinel opposite shouted out to the dog's keeper to know why the dog kept such a barking, and whether anything was the matter; who answered, that it was nothing but only that his dog had been set barking by the lights of the watch and the noise of the bell. This reply much encouraged Aratus's soldiers, who thought the dog's keeper was privy to their design, and wished to conceal what was passing, and that many others in the city were of the conspiracy. But when they came to scale the wall, the attempt then appeared both to require time and to be full of danger, for the ladders shook and tottered extremely unless they mounted them leisurely and one by one, and time pressed, for the cocks began to crow, and the country people that used to bring things to the market would be coming to the town directly.

Therefore Aratus made haste to get up himself, forty only of the company being already upon the wall, and, staying but for a few more of those that were below, he made straight to the tyrant's house and the general's office, where the mercenary soldiers passed the night, and, coming suddenly upon them, and taking them prisoners without killing any one of them, he immediately sent to all his friends in their houses to desire them to come to him, which they did from all quarters. By this time the day began to break, and the theatre was filled with a multitude that were held in suspense by uncertain reports and knew nothing distinctly of what had happened, until a public crier came forward and proclaimed that Aratus, the son of Clinias, invited the citizens to recover their liberty.

Then at last assured that what they had so long looked for was come to pass, they pressed in throngs to the tyrant's gates to set them on fire. And such a flame was kindled, the whole house catching fire, that it was seen as far as Corinth; so that the Corinthians, wondering what the matter could be, were upon the point of coming to their assistance. Nicocles fled away secretly out of the city by means of certain underground passages, and the soldiers helping the Sicyonians to quench the fire, plundered the house. This Aratus hindered not, but divided also the rest of the riches of the tyrant amongst the citizens.

In this exploit, not one of these engaged in it was slain, nor any of the contrary party, fortune so ordering the action as to be clear and free from civil bloodshed. He restored eighty exiles who had been expelled by Nicocles, and no less than five hundred who had been driven out by former tyrants and had endured a long banishment, pretty nearly, by this time, of fifty years' duration. These returning, most of them very poor, were impatient to enter upon their former possessions, and, proceeding to their several farms and houses, gave great perplexity to Aratus, who considered that the city without was envied for its liberty and aimed at by Antigonus, and within was full of disorder and sedition.

Wherefore, as things stood, he thought it best to associate it to the Achæan community, and so, although Dorians, they of their own will took upon them the name and citizenship of the Achæans, who at that time had neither great repute nor much power. For the most of them lived in small towns, and their territory was neither large nor fruitful, and the neighbouring sea was almost wholly without a harbour, breaking direct upon a rocky shore. But yet these above others made it appear that the Grecian courage was invincible, whensoever it could only have order and concord within itself and a prudent general to direct it. For though they had scarcely been counted as any part of the ancient Grecian power, and at this time it did not equal the strength of one ordinary city, yet by prudence and unanimity, and because they knew not how to envy and malign, but to obey and follow him amongst them that was most eminent for virtue, they not only preserved their own liberty in the midst of so many great cities, military powers, and monarchies, but went on steadily saving and delivering from slavery great numbers of the Greeks.

As for Aratus, he was in his behaviour a true statesman, high-minded, and more intent upon the public than his private concerns, a bitter hater of tyrants, making the common good the rule and law of his friendships and enmities. So that indeed he seems not to have been so faithful a friend, as he was a reasonable and gentle enemy, ready, according to the needs of the state, to suit himself on occasion to either side; concord between nations, brotherhood between cities, the council and the assembly unanimous in their votes, being the objects above all other blessings to which he was passionately devoted; backward, indeed, and diffident in the use of arms and open force, but in effecting a purpose underhand, and outwitting cities and potentates without observation, most politic and dexterous. Therefore, though he succeeded beyond hope in many enterprises which he undertook, yet he seems to have left quite as many unattempted, though feasible enough, for want of assurance.

For it should seem, that as the sight of certain beasts is strong in the night but dim by day, the tenderness of the humours of their eyes not bearing the contact of the light, so there is also one kind of human skill and sagacity which is easily daunted and disturbed in actions done in the open day and before the world, and recovers all its self-possession in secret and covert enterprises; which inequality is occasioned in noble minds for want of philosophy, a mere wild and uncultivated fruit of a virtue without true knowledge coming up; as might be made out by examples.

Aratus, therefore, having associated himself and his city to the Achæans, served in the cavalry, and made himself much beloved by his commanding officers for his exact obedience; for though he had made so large an addition to the common strength as that of his own credit and the power of his country, yet he was as ready as the most ordinary person to be commanded by the Achæan general of the time being, whether he were a man of Dynæ, or of Tritæa, or any yet meaner town than these. Having also a present of five-and-twenty talents sent him from the king, he took them, but gave them all to his fellow-citizens, who wanted money, amongst other purposes, for the redemption of those who had been taken prisoners.

But the exiles being insatiable, disturbing continually those that were in possession of their estates, Sicyon was in great danger of falling into perfect desolation; so that, having no hope left but in the kindness of Ptolemy, he resolved to sail to him, and to beg so much money of him as might reconcile all parties. So he set sail from Mothone beyond Malea, designing to make the direct passage. But the pilot not being able to keep the vessel up against a strong wind and high waves that came in from the open sea, he was driven from his course, and with much ado got to shore in Andras, an enemy's land, possessed by Antigonus, who had a garrison there. To avoid which he immediately landed, and, leaving the ship, went up into the country a good way from the sea, having along with him only one friend, called Timanthes; and throwing themselves into some ground thickly covered with wood, they had but an ill night's rest of it.

Not long after, the commander of the troops came, and, inquiring for Aratus, was deceived by his servants, who had been instructed to say that he had fled at once over into the island of Euboea. However, he declared the ship, the property on board of her, and the servants, to be lawful prize, and detained them accordingly. As for Aratus, after some few days in his extremity, by good fortune a Roman ship happened to put in just at the spot in which he made his abode, sometimes peeping out to seek his opportunity, sometimes keeping close. She was bound for Syria; but going aboard, he agreed with the master to land him in Caria. In which voyage he met with no less danger on the sea than before.

From Caria being after much time arrived in Egypt, he immediately went to the king, who had a great kindness for him, and had received from him many presents of drawings and paintings out of Greece. Aratus had a very good judgment in them, and always took care to collect and send him the most curious and finished works, especially those of Pamphilus and Melanthus. For the Sicyonian pieces were still in the height of their reputation, as being the only ones whose colours were lasting; so that Apelles himself, even after he had become well known and admired, went thither, and gave a talent to be admitted into the society of the painters there, not so much to partake of their skill, which he wanted not, but of their credit.

And accordingly Aratus, when he freed the city, immediately took down the representations of the rest of the tyrants, but demurred a long time about that of Aristratus, who flourished in the time of Philip. For this Aristratus was painted by Melanthus and his scholars, standing by a chariot, in which a figure of Victory was carried, Apelles himself having had a hand in it, as Polemon the geographer reports. It was an extraordinary piece, and therefore Aratus was fain to spare it for the workmanship, and yet, instigated by the hatred he bore the tyrants, commanded it to be taken down. But Neacles the painter, one of Aratus's friends, entreated him, it is said, with tears in his eyes, to spare it, and finding he did not prevail with him, told him at last he should carry on his war with the tyrants, but with the tyrants alone: "Let therefore the chariot and the Victory stand, and I will take means for the removal of Aristratus"; to which Aratus consenting, Neacles blotted out Aristratus, and in his place painted a palm-tree, not daring to add anything else of his own invention. The feet of the defaced figure of Aristratus are said to have escaped notice, and to be hid under the chariot.

By these means Aratus got favour with the king, who, after he was more fully acquainted with him, loved him so much the more, and gave him for the relief of his city one hundred and fifty talents; forty of which he immediately carried away with him, when he sailed to Peloponnesus, but the rest the king divided into instalments, and sent them to him afterwards at different times.

Assuredly it was a great thing to procure for his fellow-citizens a sum of money, a small portion of which had been sufficient, when presented by a king to other captains and popular leaders, to induce them to turn dishonest, and betray and give away their native countries to him. But it was a much greater, that by means of this money he effected a reconciliation and good understanding between the rich and poor, and created quiet and security for the whole people. His moderation, also, amidst so great power was very admirable. For being declared sole arbitrator and plenipotentiary for settling the questions of property in the case of the exiles, he would not accept the commission alone, but, associating with himself fifteen of the citizens, with great pains and trouble he succeeded in adjusting matters, and established peace and good-will in the city, for which good service, not only all the citizens in general bestowed extraordinary honours upon him, but the exiles, apart by themselves, erecting his statue in brass, inscribed on it these elegiac verses:—

Your counsels, deeds, and skill for Greece in war
Known beyond Hercules's pillars are;
But we this image, O Aratus, gave,
Of you who saved us, to the gods who save,
By you from exile to our homes restored,

That virtue and that justice to record,
To which the blessing Sicyon owes this day
Of wealth that's shared alike, and laws that all
* obey.*

By his success in effecting these things, Aratus secured himself from the envy of his fellow-citizens, on account of the benefits they felt he had done them; but King Antigonus being troubled in his mind about him, and designing either wholly to bring him over to his party, or else to make him suspected by Ptolemy, besides other marks of his favour shown to him, who had little mind to receive them, added this too, that, sacrificing to the gods in Corinth, he sent portions to Aratus at Sicyon, and at the feast, where were many guests, he said openly, "I thought this Sicyonian youth had been only a lover of liberty and of his fellow-citizens, but now I look upon him as a good judge of the manners and actions of kings. For formerly he despised us, and, placing his hopes further off, admired the Egyptian riches, hearing so much of their elephants, fleets, and palaces. But after seeing all these at a nearer distance, perceiving them to be but mere stage show and pageantry, he is now come over to us. And for my part I willingly receive him, and, resolving to make great use of him myself, command you to look upon him as a friend."

These words were soon taken hold of by those that envied and maligned him, who strove which of them should, in their letters to Ptolemy, attack him with the worst calumnies, so that Ptolemy sent to expostulate the matter with him; so much envy and ill-will did there always attend the so much contended for, and so ardently and passionately aspired to, friendships of princes and great men.

But Aratus, being now for the first time chosen general of the Achæans, ravaged the country of Locris and Calydon, just over against Achæa, and then went to assist the Bœotians with ten thousand soldiers, but came not up to them until after the battle near Chæronea had been fought, in which they were beaten by the Ætolians, with the loss of Abœocritus the Bœotarch, and a thousand men besides. A year after, being again elected general, he resolved to attempt the capture of the Acro-Corinthus, not so much for the advantage of the Sicyonians or Achæans, as considering that by expelling the Macedonian garrison he should free all Greece alike from a tyranny which oppressed every part of her. Chares, the Athenian, having the good fortune to get the better,

in a certain battle, of the king's generals, wrote to the people of Athens that this victory was "sister to that at Marathon."

And so may this action be very safely termed sister to those of Pelopidas the Theban and Thrasybulus the Athenian, in which they slew the tyrants; except, perhaps, it exceed them upon this account, that it was not against natural Grecians, but against a foreign and stranger domination.

The Isthmus, rising like a bank between the seas, collects into a single spot and compresses together the whole continent of Greece; and Acro-Corinthus, being a high mountain springing up out of the very middle of what here is Greece, whensoever it is held with a garrison, stands in the way and cuts off all Peloponnesus from intercourse of every kind, free passage of men and arms, and all traffic by sea and land, and makes him lord of all that is master of it. Wherefore the younger Philip did not jest, but said very true, when he called the city of Corinth "the fetters of Greece." So that this post was always much contended for, especially by the kings and tyrants; and so vehemently was it longed for by Antigonus, that his passion for it came little short of that of frantic love; he was continually occupied with devising how to take it by surprise from those that were then masters of it, since he despaired to do it by open force.

Therefore Alexander, who held the place, being dead, poisoned by him, as is reported, and his wife Nicæa succeeding in the government and the possession of Acro-Corinthus, he immediately made use of his son, Demetrius, and, giving her pleasing hopes of a royal marriage and of a happy life with a youth, whom a woman now growing old might well find agreeable, with this lure of his son he succeeded in taking her; but the place itself she did not deliver up, but continued to hold it with a very strong garrison, of which he seeming to take no notice, celebrated the wedding in Corinth, entertaining them with shows and banquets every day, as one that had nothing else in his mind but to give himself up for a while to indulgence in pleasure and mirth. But when the moment came, and Amœbeus began to sing in the theatre, he waited himself upon Nicæa to the play, she being carried in a royally decorated chair, extremely pleased with her new honour, not dreaming of what was intended. As soon, therefore, as they were come to the turning which led up to the citadel, he desired her to go on before him to the theatre, but for himself, bidding farewell to the music, farewell to the wedding, he went on faster than one would have thought his age would have admitted to the Acro-Corinthus, and, finding the gate shut, knocked with his staff, commanding them to open, which they within, being amazed, did.

And having thus made himself master of the place, he could not contain himself for joy; but, though an old man, and one that had seen so many turns of fortune, he must needs revel in the open streets and in the midst of the market-place, crowned with garlands and attended with flute-women, inviting everybody he met to partake in his festivity. So much more does joy without discretion transport and agitate the mind than either fear or sorrow. Antigonus, therefore, having in this manner possessed himself of Acro-Corinthus, put a garrison into it of those he trusted most, making Persæus the philosopher governor.

Now Aratus, even in the lifetime of Alexander, had made an attempt, but, a confederacy being made between Alexander and the Achæans, he desisted. But now he started afresh, with a new plan of effecting the thing, which was this: there were in Corinth four brothers, Syrians born, one of whom, called Diocles, served as a soldier in the garrison, but the three others, having stolen some gold of the king's, came to Sicyon, to one Ægias, a banker, whom Aratus made use of in his business. To him they immediately sold part of their gold, and the rest, one of them, called Erginus, coming often thither, exchanged by parcels. Becoming, by this means, familiarly acquainted with Ægias, and being by him led into discourses concerning the fortress, he told him that in going up to his brother he had observed, in the face of the rock, a side cleft, leading to that part of the wall of the castle which was lower than the rest. At which Ægias joking with him and saying, "So, you wise man, for the sake of a little gold you have broken into the king's treasure; when you might, if you chose, get money in abundance for a single hour's work, burglary, you know, and treason being punished with the same death."

Erginus laughed and told him then, he would break the thing to Diocles (for he did not altogether trust his older brothers), and, returning within a few days, he bargained to conduct Aratus to that part of the wall where it was no more than fifteen feet high, and to do what else should be necessary, together with his brother Diocles.

Aratus, therefore, agreed to give them sixty talents if he succeeded, but if he failed in his enterprise, and yet he and they came off safe, then he would give each of them a house and a talent. Now the threescore talents having to be deposited in the hands of Ægias for Erginus and his partners, and Aratus neither having so much by him, nor willing, by borrowing it from others, to give any one a suspicion of his design, he pawned his plate and his wife's golden ornaments to Ægias for the money. For so high was his temper, and so strong his passion for noble actions, that, even as he had heard that Phocion and Epaminondas were the best and justest of the Greeks, because they refused the greatest presents, and would not surrender their duty for money, so he now chose to be at the expense of this enterprise privately, and to advance all the cost out of his own property, taking the whole hazard on himself for the sake of the rest that did not so much as know what was doing. And who indeed can withhold, even now, his admiration for, and his sympathy with, the generous mind of one who paid so largely to purchase so great a risk, and lent out his richest possessions to have an opportunity to expose his own life, by entering among his enemies in the dead of the night, without desiring any other security for them than the hope of a noble success.

Now the enterprise, though dangerous enough in itself, was made much more so by an error happening through mistake in the very beginning. For Technon, one of Aratus's servants, was sent away to Diocles, that they might together view the wall. Now he had never seen Diocles, but made no question of knowing him by the marks Erginus had given him of him; namely, that he had curly hair, a swarthy complexion, and no beard. Being come, therefore, to the appointed place, he stayed waiting for Erginus and Diocles outside the town, in front of the place called Ornis. In the meantime, Dionysius, elder brother to Erginus and Diocles, who knew nothing at all of the matter, but much resembled Diocles, happened to pass by. Technon, upon this likeness, all being in accordance with what he had been told, asked him if he knew Erginus; and on his replying that he was his brother, taking it for granted that he was speaking with Diocles, not so much as asking his name or staying for any other token, he gave him his hand, and began to discourse with him and ask him questions about matters agreed upon with Erginus.

Dionysius, cunningly taking the advantage

of his mistake, seemed to understand him very well, and returning towards the city, led him on, still talking, without any suspicion. And being now near the gate, he was just about to seize on him, when by chance again Erginus met them, and, apprehending the cheat and the danger, beckoned to Technon to make his escape, and immediately both of them, betaking themselves to their heels, ran away as fast as they could to Aratus, who for all this despaired not, but immediately sent away Erginus to Dionysius to bribe him to hold his tongue. And he not only effected that, but also brought him along with him to Aratus. But when they had him, they no longer left him at liberty, but binding him, they kept him close shut up in a room, whilst they prepared for executing their design.

All things being now ready, he commanded the rest of his forces to pass the night by their arms, and taking with him four hundred chosen men, few of whom knew what they were going about, he led them to the gates by the temple of Juno. It was the midst of summer, and the moon was at full, and the night so clear without any clouds that there was danger lest the arms glistening in the moonlight should discover them. But as the foremost of them came near the city, a mist came off from the sea, and darkened the city itself and the outskirts about it. Then the rest of them, sitting down, put off their shoes, because men both make less noise and also climb surer if they go up ladders barefooted, but Erginus, taking with him seven young men dressed like travellers, got unobserved to the gate, and killed the sentry with the other guards. And at the same time the ladders were clapped to the walls, and Aratus, having in great haste got up a hundred men, commanded the rest to follow as they could, and immediately drawing up his ladders after him, he marched through the city with his hundred men towards the castle, being already overjoyed that he was undiscovered, and not doubting of the success.

But while still they were some way off, a watch of four men came with a light, who did not see them, because they were still in the shade of the moon, but were seen plainly enough themselves as they came on directly towards them. So withdrawing a little way amongst some walls and plots for houses, they lay in wait for them; and three of them they killed. But the fourth, being wounded in the head with a sword, fled, crying out that the enemy was in the city. And immediately the trumpets sounded, and all the city was in an uproar at what had happened, and the streets were full of people running up and down, and many lights were seen shining both below in the town, and above in the castle, and a confused noise was to be heard in all parts.

In the meantime, Aratus was hard at work struggling to get up the rocks, at first slowly and with much difficulty, straying continually from the path, which lay deep, and was overshadowed with the crags, leading to the wall with many windings and turnings; but the moon immediately, and as if by miracle, it is said, dispersing the clouds, shone out and gave light to the most difficult part of the way, until he got to that part of the wall he desired, and there she overshadowed and hid him, the clouds coming together again.

Those soldiers whom Aratus had left outside the gate, near Juno's temple, to the number of three hundred, entering the town, now full of tumult and lights, and not knowing the way by which the former had gone, and finding no track of them, slunk aside, and crowded together in one body under a flank of the cliff that cast a strong shadow, and there stood and waited in great distress and perplexity. For, by this time, those that had gone with Aratus were attacked with missiles from the citadel, and were busy fighting, and a sound of cries of battle came down from above, and a loud noise echoed back and back from the mountain sides, and therefore confused and uncertain whence it proceeded, was heard on all sides. They being thus in doubt which way to turn themselves, Archelaus, the commander of Antigonus's troops, having a great number of soldiers with him, made up towards the castle with great shouts and noise of trumpets to fall upon Aratus's people, and passed by the three hundred, who, as if they had risen out of an ambush, immediately charged him, killing the first they encountered, and so affrighted the rest, together with Archelaus, that they put them to flight and pursued them until they had quite broken and dispersed them about the city.

No sooner were these defeated, but Erginus came to them from those that were fighting above, to acquaint them that Aratus was engaged with the enemy, who defended themselves very stoutly, and there was a fierce conflict at the very wall, and need of speedy help. They therefore desired him to lead them on without delay, and, marching up, by their shouts made their friends understand who they were, and encouraged them; and the full moon, shining on their arms, made them, in the long line by which they advanced, appear more in number to the enemy than they were; and the echo of the night multiplied their shouts. In short, falling on with the rest, they made the enemy give way, and were masters of the castle and garrison, day now beginning to be bright, and the rising sun shining out upon their success. By this time, also, the rest of his army came up to Aratus from Sicyon, the Corinthians joyfully receiving them at the gates and helping them to secure the king's party.

And now, having put all things into a safe posture, he came down from the castle to the theatre, an infinite number of people crowding thither to see him and to hear what he would say to the Corinthians. Therefore, drawing up the Achæans on each side of the stage-passages, he came forward himself upon the stage, with his corselet still on, and his face showing the effects of all his hard work and want of sleep, so that his natural exultation and joyfulness of mind were overborne by the weariness of his body. The people, as soon as he came forth, breaking out into great applauses and congratulations, he took his spear in his right hand, and, resting his body upon it with his knee a little bent, stood a good while in that posture, silently receiving their shouts and acclamations, while they extolled his valour and wondered at his fortune; which being over, standing up, he began an oration in the name of the Achæans, suitable to the late action, persuading the Corinthians to associate themselves to the Achæans, and withal delivered up to them the keys of their gates, which had never been in their power since the time of King Philip. Of the captains of Antigonus, he dismissed Archelaus, whom he had taken prisoner, and Theophrastus, who refused to quit his post, he put to death.

As for Persæus, when he saw the castle was lost, he had got away to Cenchreæ, where, some time after, discoursing with one that said to him that the wise man only is a true general, "Indeed," he replied, "none of Zeno's maxims once pleased me better than this, but I have been converted to another opinion by the young man of Sicyon." This is told by many of Persæus.

Aratus immediately after made himself master of the temple of Juno and haven of Lechæum, seized upon five-and-twenty of the king's ships, together with five hundred horses and four hundred Syrians: these he sold. The Achæans kept guard in the Acro-Corinthus with a body of four hundred soldiers, and fifty dogs with as many keepers.

The Romans, extolling Philopœmen, called him the last of the Grecians, as if no great man had ever since his time been bred amongst them. But I should call this capture of the Acro-Corinthus the last of the Grecian exploits, being comparable to the best of them, both for the daringness of it, and the success, as was presently seen by the consequences. For the Megarians, revolting from Antigonus, joined Aratus, and the Trœzenians and Epidaurians enrolled themselves in the Achæan community, and issuing forth for the first time, he entered Attica, and passing over into Salamis, he plundered the island, turning the Achæan force every way, as if it were just let loose out of prison and set at liberty. All freemen whom he took he sent back to the Athenians without ransom, as a sort of first invitation to them to come over to the league. He made Ptolemy become a confederate of the Achæans, with the privilege of command both by sea and land.

And so great was his power with them, that since he could not by law be chosen their general every year, yet every other year he was, and by his counsels and actions was in effect always so. For they perceived that neither riches nor reputation, nor the friendship of kings, nor the private interest of his own country, nor anything else was so dear to him as the increase of the Achæans' power and greatness. For he believed that the cities, weak individually, could be preserved by nothing else but a mutual assistance under the closest bond of the common interest, and, as the members of the body live and breathe by the union of all in a single natural growth, and on the dissolution of this, when once they separate, pine away and putrify, in the same manner are cities ruined by being dissevered, as well as preserved when, as the members of one great body, they enjoy the benefit of that province and counsel that govern the whole.

Now being distressed to see that, whereas the chief neighbouring cities enjoyed their own laws and liberties, the Argives were in bondage, he took counsel for destroying their tyrant, Aristomachus, being very desirous both to pay his debt of gratitude to the city where he had been bred up, by restoring it its liberty, and to add so considerable a town to the Achæans. Nor were there some wanting who had the courage to undertake the thing, of whom Æschylus and Charimenes the soothsayer were the chief. But they wanted swords; for the tyrant had prohibited the keeping of any under a great penalty. Therefore Aratus, having provided some small daggers at Corinth and hidden them in the pack-saddles of some pack-horses that carried ordinary ware, sent them to Argos. But Charimenes letting another person into the design, Æschylus and his partners were angry at it, and henceforth would have no more to do with him, and took their measures by themselves, and Charimenes, on finding this, went, out of anger, and informed against them, just as they were on their way to attack the tyrant; however, the most of them made a shift to escape out of the marketplace, and fled to Corinth.

Not long after, Aristomachus was slain by some slaves, and Aristippus, a worse tyrant than he, seized the government. Upon this, Aratus, mustering all the Achæans present that were of age, hurried away to the aid of the city, believing that he should find the people ready to join with him. But the greater number being by this time habituated to slavery and content to submit, and no one coming to join him, he was obliged to retire, having moreover exposed the Achæans to the charge of committing acts of hostility in the midst of peace; upon which account they were sued before the Mantineans, and, Aratus not making his appearance, Aristippus gained the cause, and had damages allowed him to the value of thirty minæ. And now hating and fearing Aratus, he sought means to kill him, having the assistance herein of King Antigonus; so that Aratus was perpetually dogged and watched by those that waited for an opportunity to do this service.

But there is no such safeguard of a ruler as the sincere and steady good-will of his subjects, for where both the common people and the principal citizens have their fears not of, but for, their governor, he sees with many eyes and hears with many ears whatsoever is doing. Therefore I cannot but here stop short a little in the course of my narrative to describe the manner of life which the so much envied arbitrary power and the so much celebrated and admired pomp and pride of absolute government obliged Aristippus to lead.

For though Antigonus was his friend and ally, and though he maintained numerous soldiers to act as his body-guard, and had not left one enemy of his alive in the city, yet he was forced to make his guards encamp in the colonnade about his house; and for his servants, he turned them all out immediately after supper, and then shutting the doors upon them, he crept up into a small upper chamber, together with his mistress, through a trap-door, upon which he placed his bed, and there slept after such a fashion, as one in his condition can be supposed to sleep, that is, interruptedly and in fear. The ladder was taken away by the woman's mother, and locked up in another room; in the morning she brought it again, and putting it to, called up this brave and wonderful tyrant, who came crawling out like some creeping thing out of its hole.

Whereas Aratus, not by force of arms, but lawfully and by his virtue, lived in possession of a firmly settled command, wearing the ordinary coat and cloak, being the common and declared enemy of all tyrants, and has left behind him a noble race of descendants surviving among the Grecians to this day; while those occupiers of citadels and maintainers of body-guards, who made all this use of arms and gates and bolts to protect their lives, in some few cases perhaps escaped like the hare from the hunters; but in no instance have we either house or family, or so much as a tomb to which any respect is shown, remaining to preserve the memory of any one of them.

Against this Aristippus, therefore, Aratus made many open and many secret attempts, whilst he endeavoured to take Argos, though without success; once, particularly, clapping scaling ladders in the night to the walls, he desperately got up upon it with a few of his soldiers, and killed the guards that opposed him. But the day appearing, the tyrant set upon him on all hands, whilst the Argives, as if it had not been their liberty that was contended for, but some Nemean game going on for which it was their privilege to assign the prize, like fair and impartial judges, sat looking on in great quietness. Aratus, fighting bravely, was run through the thigh with a lance, yet he maintained his ground against the enemy till night, and, had he been able to go on and hold out that night also, he had gained his point; for the tyrant thought of nothing but fleeing, and had already shipped most of his goods. But Aratus, having no intelligence of this, and wanting water, being disabled himself by his wound, retreated with his soldiers.

Despairing henceforth to do any good this way, he fell openly with his army into Argolis, and plundered it, and in a fierce battle with Aristippus near the river Chares, he was accused of having withdrawn out of the fight, and thereby abandoned the victory. For whereas one part of his army had unmistakably got the better, and was pursuing the enemy at a good distance from him, he yet retreated in confusion into his camp, not so much because he was overpressed by those with whom he was engaged, as out of mistrust of success and through a panic fear. But when the other wing, returning from the pursuit, showed themselves extremely vexed, that though they had put the enemy to flight and killed many more of his men than they had lost, yet those that were in a manner conquered should erect a trophy as conquerors, being much ashamed he resolved to fight them again about the trophy, and the next day but one drew up his army to give them battle. But, perceiving that they were reinforced with fresh troops, and came on with better courage than before, he durst not hazard a fight, but retired and sent to request a truce to bury his dead.

However, by his dexterity in dealing personally with men and managing political affairs, and by his general favour, he excused and obliterated this fault, and brought in Cleonæ to the Achæan association, and celebrated the Nemean games at Cleonæ, as the proper and more ancient place for them. The games were also celebrated by the Argives at the same time, which gave the first occasion to the violation of the privilege of safe conduct and immunity always granted to those that came to compete for the prizes, the Achæans at that time selling as enemies all those they caught going through their country after joining in the games at Argos. So vehement and implacable a hater was he of the tyrants.

Not long after, having notice that Aristippus had a design upon Cleonæ, but was afraid of him, because he then was staying in Corinth, he assembled an army by public proclamation, and commanding them to take along with them provisions for several days, he marched to Cenchreæ, hoping by this stratagem to entice Aristippus to fall upon Cleonæ, when he supposed him far enough off. And so it happened, for he immediately brought his forces against it from Argos. But Aratus, returning from Cenchreæ to Corinth in the dusk of the evening, and setting posts of his troops in all the roads, led on the Achæans, who followed in such good order and with so much speed and alacrity, that they were undiscovered by Aristippus, not only whilst upon their march,

but even when they got, still in the night, into Cleonæ, and drew up in order of battle. As soon as it was morning, the gates being opened and the trumpets sounding, he fell upon the enemy with great cries and fury, routed them at once, and kept close in pursuit, following the course which he most imagined Aristippus would choose, there being many turns that might be taken. And so the chase lasted as far as Mycenæ, where the tyrant was slain by a certain Cretan called Tragiscus, as Dinias reports. Of the common soldiers, there fell above fifteen hundred.

Yet though Aratus had obtained so great a victory and that, too, without the loss of a man, he could not make himself master of Argos, nor set it at liberty, because Agias and the younger Aristomachus got into the town with some of the king's forces, and seized upon the government. However, by this exploit he spoiled the scoffs and jests of those that flattered the tyrants, and in their raillery would say that the Achæan general was usually troubled with a looseness when he was to fight a battle, that the sound of a trumpet struck him with a drowsiness and a giddiness, and that when he had drawn up his army and given the word, he used to ask his lieutenants and officers whether there was any further need of his presence now the die was cast, and then went aloof, to await the result at a distance. For indeed these stories were so generally listened to, that, when the philosophers disputed whether to have one's heart beat and to change colour upon any apparent danger be an argument of fear, or rather of some distemperature and chilliness of bodily constitution, Aratus was always quoted as a good general who was always thus affected in time of battle.

Having thus despatched Aristippus, he advised with himself how to overthrow Lydiades, the Megalopolitan, who held usurped power over his country. This person was naturally of a generous temper, and not insensible of true honour, and had been led into this wickedness, not by the ordinary motives of other tyrants, licentiousness and rapacity, but being young, and stimulated with the desire of glory, he had let his mind be unwarily prepossessed with the vain and false applauses given to tyranny, as some happy and glorious thing. But he no sooner seized the government, than he grew weary of the pomp and burden of it. And at once emulating the tranquillity and fearing the policy of Aratus, he took the best resolutions, first, to free himself from hatred and fear, from soldiers and guards, and, secondly, to be the public benefactor of his country. And sending for Aratus, he resigned the government, and incorporated his city into the Achæan community.

The Achæans, applauding this generous action, chose him their general; upon which, desiring to outdo Aratus in glory, amongst many other uncalled-for things, he declared war against the Lacedæmonians; which Aratus opposing was thought to do so out of envy; and Lydiades was the second time chosen general, though Aratus acted openly against him, and laboured to have the office conferred upon another. For Aratus himself had the command every other year, as has been said. Lydiades, however, succeeded so well in his pretensions, that he was thrice chosen general, governing alternately, as did Aratus; but at last, declaring himself his professed enemy, and accusing him frequently to the Achæans, he was rejected, and fell into contempt, people now seeing that it was a contest between a counterfeit and a true, unadulterated virtue, and, as Æsop tells us that the cuckoo once, asking the little birds why they flew away from her, was answered, because they feared she would one day prove a hawk, so Lydiades's former tyranny still cast a doubt upon the reality of his change.

But Aratus gained new honour in the Ætolian war. For the Achæans resolving to fall upon the Ætolians on the Megarian confines, and Agis also, the Lacedæmonian king, who came to their assistance with an army, encouraging them to fight, Aratus opposed this determination. And patiently enduring many reproaches, many scoffs and jeerings at his soft and cowardly temper, he would not, for any appearance of disgrace, abandon what he judged to be true common advantage, and suffered the enemy to pass over Geranea into Peloponnesus without a battle.

But when, after they passed by, news came that they had suddenly captured Pellene, he was no longer the same man, nor would he hear of any delay, or wait to draw together his whole force, but marched towards the enemy, with such as he had about him, to fall upon them, as they were indeed now much less formidable through the intemperances and disorders committed in their success. For as soon as they entered the city, the common soldiers dispersed and went hither and thither into the houses, quarrelling and fighting with one another about the plunder, and the officers and commanders were running about after the

wives and daughters of the Pellenians, on whose heads they put their own helmets, to mark each man his prize, and prevent another from seizing it. And in this posture were they when news came that Aratus was ready to fall upon them. And in the midst of the consternation likely to ensue in the confusion they were in before all of them heard of the danger, the outmost of them, engaging at the gates and in the suburbs with the Achæans, were already beaten and put to flight, and as they came headlong back, filled with their panic those who had taken her and put his crested helmet assistance.

In this confusion, one of the captives, daughter of Epigethes, a citizen of repute, being extremely handsome and tall, happened to be sitting in the temple of Diana, placed there by the commander of the band of chosen men, who had taken her and put his crested helmet upon her. She, hearing the noise, and running out to see what was the matter, stood in the temple gates, looking down from above upon those that fought, having the helmet upon her head; in which posture she seemed to the citizens to be something more than human, and struck fear and dread into the enemy, who believed it to be a divine apparition; so that they lost all courage to defend themselves. But the Pellenians tell us that the image of Diana stands usually untouched, and when the priestess happens at any time to remove it to some other place, nobody dares look upon it, but all turn their faces from it; for not only is the sight of it terrible and hurtful to mankind, but it makes even the trees, by which it happens to be carried, become barren and cast fruit. This image, therefore, they say, the priestess produced at that time, and holding it directly in the faces of the Ætolians, made them lose their reason and judgment.

But Aratus mentions no such thing in his commentaries, but saying that having put to flight the Ætolians, and falling in pell-mell with them into the city, he drove them out by main force, and killed seven hundred of them. And the action was extolled as one of the most famous exploits, and Timanthes, the painter, made a picture of the battle, giving by his composition a most lively representation of it.

But many great nations and potentates combining against the Achæans, Aratus immediately treated for friendly arrangements with the Ætolians, and, making use of the assistance of Pantaleon, the most powerful man amongst them, he not only made a peace, but an alliance between them and the Achæans. But being desirous to free the Athenians, he got into disgrace and ill-repute among the Achæans, because, notwithstanding the truce and suspension of arms made between them and the Macedonians, he had attempted to take the Piræus. He denies this fact in his commentaries, and lays the blame on Erginus, by whose assistance he took Acro-Corinthus, alleging that he upon his own private account attacked the Piræus, and his ladders happening to break, being hotly pursued, he called out upon Aratus, as if present, by which means deceiving the enemy he got safely off.

This excuse, however, sounds very improbable; for it is not in any way likely that Erginus, a private man and a Syrian stranger, should conceive in his mind so great an attempt, without Aratus at his back, to tell him how and when to make it, and to supply him with the means. Nor was it twice or thrice, but very often, that, like an obstinate lover, he repeated his attempts on the Piræus, and was so far from being discouraged by his disappointments, that his missing his hopes but narrowly was an incentive to him to proceed the more boldly in a new trial. One time amongst the rest, in making his escape through the Thrasian plain, he put his leg out of joint, and was forced to submit to many operations with the knife before he was cured, so that for a long time he was carried in a litter to the wars.

And when Antigonus was dead, and Demetrius succeeded him in the kingdom, he was more bent than ever upon Athens, and in general quite despised the Macedonians. And so, being overthrown in battle near Phylacia by Bithys, Demetrius's general, and there being a very strong report that he was either taken or slain, Diogenes, the governor of the Piræus, sent letters to Corinth, commanding the Achæans to quit that city, seeing Aratus was dead. When these letters came to Corinth, Aratus happened to be there in person, so that Diogenes's messengers being sufficiently mocked and derided, were forced to return to their master. King Demetrius himself also sent a ship, wherein Aratus was to be brought to him in chains. And the Athenians, exceeding all possible fickleness of flattery to the Macedonians, crowned themselves with garlands upon the first news of his death. And so in anger he went at once and invaded Attica, and penetrated as far as the Academy, but then suffer-

ing himself to be pacified he did no further act of hostility.

And the Athenians afterwards, coming to a due sense of his virtue when upon the death of Demetrius they attempted to recover their liberty, called him to their assistance; although at that time another person was general of the Achæans, and he himself had long kept his bed with a sickness, yet rather than fail the city in a time of need, he was carried thither in a litter, and helped to persuade Diogenes the governor to deliver up the Piræus, Munychia, Salamis, and Sunium to the Athenians in consideration of a hundred and fifty talents, of which Aratus himself contributed twenty to the city. Upon this, the Æginetans and the Hermionians immediately joined the Achæans, and the greatest part of Arcadia entered their confederacy; and the Macedonians being occupied with various wars upon their own confines and with their neighbours, the Achæan power, the Ætolians also being in alliance with them, rose to great height.

But Aratus, still bent on effecting his old project, and impatient that tyranny should maintain itself in so near a city as Argos, sent to Aristomachus to persuade him to restore liberty to that city, and to associate it to the Achæans, and that, following Lydiades's example, he should rather choose to be the general of a great nation, with esteem and honour, than the tyrant of one city, with continual hatred and danger. Aristomachus slighted not the message, but desired Aratus to send him fifty talents, with which he might pay off the soldiers. In the meantime, whilst the money was providing, Lydiades, being then general, and extremely ambitious that this advantage might seem to be of his procuring for the Achæans, accused Aratus to Aristomachus, as one that bore an irreconcilable hatred to the tyrants, and, persuading him to commit the affair to his management, he presented him to the Achæans.

But there the Achæan council gave a manifest proof of the great credit Aratus had with them and the good-will they bore him. For when he, in anger, spoke against Aristomachus's being admitted into the association, they rejected the proposal, but when he was afterwards pacified and came himself and spoke in its favour, they voted everything cheerfully and readily, and decreed that the Argives and Phliasians should be incorporated into their commonwealth, and the next year they chose Aristomachus general. He, being in good credit with the Achæans, was very desirous to invade Laconia, and for that purpose sent for Aratus from Athens. Aratus wrote to him to dissuade him as far as he could from that expedition, being very unwilling the Achæans should be engaged in a quarrel with Cleomenes, who was a daring man, and making extraordinary advances to power. But Aristomachus resolving to go on, he obeyed and served in person, on which occasion he hindered Aristomachus from fighting a battle when Cleomenes came upon them at Pallantium; and for this act was accused by Lydiades, and, coming to an open conflict with him in a contest for the office of general, he carried it by the show of hands, and was chosen general the twelfth time.

This year, being routed by Cleomenes, near the Lycæum, he fled, and, wandering out of the way in the night, was believed to be slain; and once more it was confidently reported so throughout all Greece. He, however, having escaped this danger and rallied his forces, was not content to march off in safety, but making a happy use of the present conjuncture, when nobody dreamed of any such thing, he fell suddenly upon the Mantineans, allies of Cleomenes, and, taking the city, put a garrison into it, and made the stranger inhabitants free of the city; procuring, by this means, those advantages for the beaten Achæans, which being conquerors, they would not easily have obtained. The Lacedæmonians again invading the Megalopolitan territories, he marched to the assistance of the city, but refused to give Cleomenes, who did all he could to provoke him to it, any opportunity of engaging him in a battle, nor could be prevailed upon by the Megalopolitans, who urged him to it extremely. For besides that by nature he was ill-suited for set battles, he was then much inferior in numbers, and was to deal with a daring leader, still in the heat of youth, while he himself, now past the prime of courage and come to a chastised ambition, felt it his business to maintain by prudence the glory which he had obtained, and the other was only aspiring to by forwardness and daring.

So that though the light-armed soldiers had sallied out and driven the Lacedæmonians as far as their camp, and had come even to their tents, yet would not Aratus lead his men forward, but, posting himself in a hollow water-course in the way thither, stopped and prevented the citizens from crossing this. Lydiades, extremely vexed at what was going on, and loading Aratus with reproaches, entreated

the horse that, together with him, they would second them that had the enemy in chase, and not let a certain victory slip out of their hands, nor forsake him that was going to venture his life for his country. And being reinforced with many brave men that turned after him, he charged the enemy's right wing, and routing it followed the pursuit without measure or discretion, letting his eagerness and hopes of glory tempt him on into broken ground, full of planted fruit-trees and cut up with broad ditches, where, being engaged by Cleomenes, he fell, fighting gallantly the noblest of battles, at the gate of his country. The rest, flying back to their main body and troubling the ranks of the full-armed infantry, put the whole army to the rout.

Aratus was extremely blamed, being suspected to have betrayed Lydiades, and was constrained by the Achæans, who withdrew in great anger, to accompany them to Ægium, where they called a council, and decreed that he should no longer be furnished with money, nor have any more soldiers hired for him, but that, if he would make war, he should pay them himself.

This affront he resented so far as to resolve to give up the seal and lay down the office of general; but upon second thoughts he found it best to have patience, and presently marched with the Achæans to Orchomenus and fought a battle with Megistonus, the stepfather of Cleomenes, where he got the victory, killing three hundred men and taking Megistonus prisoner. But whereas he used to be chosen general every other year, when his turn came and he was called to take upon him that charge, he declined it, and Timoxenus was chosen in his stead; the true cause of which was not the pique he was alleged to have taken at the people, but the ill circumstances of the Achæan affairs. For Cleomenes did not now invade them gently and tenderly as hitherto, as one controlled by the civil authorities, but having killed the ephors, divided the lands, and made many of the stranger residents free of the city, he was responsible to no one in his government; and therefore fell in good earnest upon the Achæans, and put forward his claim to the supreme military command.

Wherefore Aratus is much blamed, that in a stormy and tempestuous time, like a cowardly pilot, he should forsake the helm when it was even perhaps his duty to have insisted, whether they would or no, on saving them; or if he thought the Achæan affairs desperate, to have yielded all up to Cleomenes, and not to have let Peloponnesus fall once again into barbarism with Macedonian garrisons, and Acro-Corinthus be occupied with Illyric and Gaulish soldiers, and, under the specious name of confederates, to have made those masters of the cities whom he had held it his business by arms and by policy to baffle and defeat, and, in the memoirs he left behind him, loaded with reproaches and insults. And say that Cleomenes was arbitrary and tyrannical, yet was he descended from the Heraclidæ, and Sparta was his country, the obscurest citizens of which deserved to be preferred to the generalship before the best of the Macedonians by those that had any regard to the honour of Grecian birth. Besides, Cleomenes sued for that command over the Achæans as one that would return the honour of that title with real kindnesses to the cities; whereas Antigonus, being declared absolute general by sea and land, would not accept the office unless Acro-Corinthus were by special agreement put into his hands, following the example of Æsop's hunter; for he would not get up and ride the Achæans, who desired him so to do, and offered their backs to him by embassies and popular decrees, till, by a garrison and hostages, they had allowed him to bit and bridle them.

Aratus exhausts all his powers of speech to show the necessity that was upon him. But Polybius writes, that long before this, and before there was any necessity, apprehending the daring temper of Cleomenes, he communicated secretly with Antigonus, and that he had beforehand prevailed with the Megalopolitans to press the Achæans to crave aid from Antigonus. For they were the most harassed by the war, Cleomenes continually plundering and ransacking their country. And so writes also Phylarchus, who, unless seconded by the testimony of Polybius, would not be altogether credited; for he is seized with enthusiasm when he so much as speaks a word of Cleomenes, and as if he were pleading, not writing a history, goes on throughout defending the one and accusing the other.

The Achæans, therefore, lost Mantinea, which was recovered by Cleomenes, and being beaten in a great fight near Hecatombæum, so general was the consternation that they immediately sent to Cleomenes to desire him to come to Argos and take the command upon himself. Aratus, as soon as he understood that he was coming, and was got as far as Lerna with his troops, fearing the result, sent ambassadors to him to request him to come accompanied with three hundred only, as to friends and confederates, and, if he mistrusted anything, he should receive hostages. Upon which Cleomenes, saying this was mere mockery and affront, went away, sending a letter to the Achæans full of reproaches and accusation against Aratus. And Aratus also wrote letters against Cleomenes; and bitter revilings and railleries were current on both hands, not sparing even their marriages and wives.

Hereupon Cleomenes sent a herald to declare war against the Achæans, and in the meantime missed very narrowly taking Sicyon by treachery. Turning off at a little distance, he attacked and took Pellene which the Achæan general abandoned, and not long after took also Pheneus and Penteleum. Then immediately the Argives voluntarily joined with him, and the Phliasians received a garrison, and in short nothing among all their new acquisitions held firm to the Achæans. Aratus was encompassed on every side with clamour and confusion; he saw the whole of Peloponnesus shaking hands around him, and the cities everywhere set in revolt by men desirous of innovations.

Indeed no place remained quiet or satisfied with the present condition; even amongst the Sicyonians and Corinthians themselves, many were well known to have had private conferences with Cleomenes, who long since, out of desire to make themselves masters of their several cities, had been discontented with the present order of things. Aratus, having absolute power given him to bring these to condign punishment, executed as many of them as he could find at Sicyon, but going about to find them out and punish them at Corinth also, he irritated the people, already unsound in feeling and weary of the Achæan government. So collecting tumultuously in the temple of Apollo, they sent for Aratus, having determined to take or kill him before they broke out into open revolt. He came, accordingly, leading his horse in his hand, as if he suspected nothing. Then several leaping up and accusing and reproaching him, with mild words and a settled countenance he bade them sit down, and not stand crying out upon him in a disorderly manner, desiring also, that those that were about the door might be let in, and saying so, he stepped out quietly, as if he would give his horse to somebody.

Clearing himself thus of the crowd, and speaking without discomposure to the Corinthians that he met, commanding them to go to

Apollo's temple, and being now, before they were aware, got near to the citadel, he leaped upon his horse, and commanding Cleopater, the governor of the garrison, to have a special care of his charge, he galloped to Sicyon, followed by thirty of his soldiers, the rest leaving him and shifting for themselves. And not long after, it being known that he was fled, the Corinthians pursued him; but not overtaking him, they immediately sent for Cleomenes and delivered up the city to him, who, however, thought nothing they could give was so great a gain as was the loss of their having let Aratus get away. Nevertheless, being strengthened by the accession of the people of the Acte, as it is called, who put their towns into his hands, he proceeded to carry a palisade and lines of circumvallation around the Acro-Corinthus.

But Aratus being arrived at Sicyon, the body of the Achæans there flocked to him, and, in an assembly there held, he was chosen general with absolute power, and he took about him a guard of his own citizens, it being now three-and-thirty years since he first took a part in public affairs among the Achæans, having in that time been the chief man in credit and power of all Greece; but he was now deserted on all hands, helpless and overpowered, drifting about amidst the waves and danger on the shattered hulk of his native city. For the Ætolians, whom he applied to, declined to assist him in his distress, and the Athenians who were well affected to him were diverted from lending him any succour by the authority of Euclides and Micion.

Now whereas he had a house and property in Corinth, Cleomenes meddled not with it, nor suffered anybody else to do so, but calling for his friends and agents, he bade them hold themselves responsible to Aratus for everything, as to him they would have to render their account; and privately he sent to him Tripylus, and afterwards Megistonus, his own stepfather, to offer him, besides several other things, a yearly pension of twelve talents, which was twice as much as Ptolemy allowed him, for he gave him six; and all that he demanded was to be declared commander of the Achæans, and together with them to have the keeping of the citadel of Corinth. To which Aratus returning answer that affairs were not so properly in his power as he was in the power of them, Cleomenes, believing this a mere evasion, immediately entered the country of Sicyon, destroying all with fire and sword, and besieged the city three months, whilst Aratus held firm,

and was in dispute with himself whether he should call in Antigonus upon condition of delivering up the citadel of Corinth to him; for he would not lend him assistance upon any other terms.

In the meantime, the Achæans assembled at Ægium, and called for Aratus; but it was very hazardous for him to pass thither, while Cleomenes was encamped before Sicyon; besides, the citizens endeavoured to stop him by their entreaties, protesting that they would not suffer him to expose himself to so evident danger, the enemy being so near; the women, also, and children hung about him, weeping and embracing him as their common father and defender. But he, having comforted and encouraged them as well as he could, got on horseback, and being accompanied with ten of his friends and his son, then a youth, got away to the seaside, and finding vessels there waiting off the shore, went on board them and sailed to Ægium to the assembly; in which it was decreed that Antigonus should be called in to their aid, and should have the Acro-Corinthus delivered to him. Aratus also sent his son to him with the other hostages. The Corinthians, extremely angry at this proceeding, now plundered his property, and gave his house as a present to Cleomenes.

Antigonus being now near at hand with his army, consisting of twenty thousand Macedonian foot and one thousand three hundred horse, Aratus, with the members of council, went to meet him by sea, and got, unobserved by the enemy, to Pegæ, having no great confidence either in Antigonus or the Macedonians. For he was very sensible that his own greatness had been made out of the losses he had caused them, and that the first great principle of his public conduct had been hostility to the former Antigonus. But perceiving the necessity that was now upon him, and the pressure of the time, that lord and master of those we call rulers to be inexorable, he resolved to put all to the venture. So soon, therefore, as Antigonus was told that Aratus was coming up to him, he saluted the rest of the company after the ordinary manner, but him he received at the very first approach with especial honour, and finding him afterwards to be both good and wise, admitted him to his nearer familiarity. For Aratus was not only useful to him in the management of great affairs, but singularly agreeable also as the private companion of a king in his recreations. And therefore, though Antigonus was young, yet as soon as he observed the temper of the man to be proper for a prince's friendship, he made more use of him than of any other, not only of the Achæans, but also of the Macedonians that were about him.

So that the thing fell out to him just as the god had foreshown in a sacrifice. For it is related that, as Aratus was not long before offering sacrifice, there were found in the liver two gall-bags inclosed in the same caul of fat; whereupon the soothsayer told him that there should very soon be the strictest friendship imaginable between him and his greatest and most mortal enemies; which prediction he at that time slighted, having in general no great faith in soothsayings and prognostications, but depending most upon rational deliberation. At an after time, however, when, things succeeding well in the war, Antigonus made a great feast at Corinth, to which he invited a great number of guests, and placed Aratus next above him, and presently calling for a coverlet, asked him if he did not find it cold, and on Aratus's answering, "Yes, extremely cold," bade him come nearer, so that when the servants brought the coverlet, they threw it over them both, then Aratus, remembering the sacrifice, fell a-laughing, and told the king the sign which had happened to him, and the interpretation of it. But this fell out a good while after.

So Aratus and the king, plighting their faith to each other at Pegæ, immediately marched toward the enemy, with whom they had frequent engagements near the city, Cleomenes maintaining a strong position, and the Corinthians making a very brisk defence. In the meantime, Aristotle the Argive, Aratus's friend, sent privately to him to let him know that he would cause Argos to revolt if he would come thither in person with some soldiers. Aratus acquainted Antigonus, and taking fifteen hundred men with him, sailed in boats along the shore as quickly as he could from the Isthmus to Epidaurus. But the Argives had not patience till he could arrive, but, making a sudden insurrection, fell upon Cleomenes's soldiers, and drove them into the citadel. Cleomenes having news of this, and fearing lest, if the enemy should possess themselves of Argos, they might cut off his retreat home, left the Acro-Corinthus and marched away by night to help his men. He got thither first, and beat off the enemy, but Aratus appearing not long after, and the king approaching with his forces, he retreated to Mantinea, upon

which all the cities again came over to the Achæans, and Antigonus took possession of the Acro-Corinthus.

Aratus, being chosen general by the Argives, persuaded them to make a present to Antigonus of the property of the tyrants and the traitors. As for Aristomachus, after having put him to the rack in the town of Cenchreæ, they drowned him in the sea; for which, more than anything else, Aratus was reproached, that he could suffer a man to be so lawlessly put to death, who was no bad man, had been one of his long acquaintance, and at his persuasion had abdicated his power and annexed the city to the Achæans.

And already the blame of the other things that were done began to be laid to his account; as that they so lightly gave up Corinth to Antigonus, as if it had been an inconsiderable village; that they had suffered him, after first sacking Orchomenus, then to put into it a Macedonian garrison; that they made a decree that no letters nor embassy should be sent to any other king without the consent of Antigonus, that they were forced to furnish pay and provision for the Macedonian soldiers, and celebrated sacrifices, processions, and games in honour of Antigonus, Aratus's citizens setting the example and receiving Antigonus, who was lodged and entertained at Aratus's house. All these things they treated as his fault, not knowing that having once put the reins into Antigonus's hands and let himself be borne by the impetus of regal power, he was no longer master of anything but one single voice, the liberty of which it was not so very safe for him to use.

For it was very plain that Aratus was much troubled at several things, as appeared by the business about the statues. For Antigonus replaced the statues of the tyrants of Argos that had been thrown down, and on the contrary threw down the statues of all those that had taken the Acro-Corinthus, except that of Aratus, nor could Aratus, by all his entreaties, dissuade him. Also, the usage of the Mantineans by the Achæans seemed not in accordance with the Grecian feelings and manners. For being master of their city by the help of Antigonus, they put to death the chief and most noted men amongst them; and of the rest, some they sold, others they sent, bound in fetters, into Macedonia, and made slaves of their wives and children; and of the money thus raised, a third part they divided among themselves, and the other two-thirds were distributed among the

Macedonians. And this might seem to have been justified by the law of retaliation; for although it be a barbarous thing for men of the same nation and blood thus to deal with one another in their fury, yet necessity makes it, as Simonides says, sweet and something excusable, being the proper thing, in the mind's painful and inflamed condition, to give alleviation and relief.

But for what was afterwards done to that city, Aratus cannot be defended on any ground either of reason or necessity. For the Argives having had the city bestowed on them by Antigonus, and resolving to people it, he being then chosen as the new founder, and being general at that time, decreed that it should no longer be called Mantinea, but Antigonea, which name it still bears. So that he may be said to have been the cause that the old memory of the "beautiful Mantinea" has been wholly extinguished and the city to this day has the name of the destroyer and slayer of its citizens.

After this, Cleomenes, being overthrown in a great battle near Sellasia, forsook Sparta and fled into Egypt, and Antigonus, having shown all manner of kindness and fair-dealing to Aratus, retired into Macedonia. There, falling sick, he sent Philip, the heir of the kingdom, into Peloponnesus, being yet scarce a youth, commanding him to follow above all the counsel of Aratus, to communicate with the cities through him, and through him to make acquaintance with the Achæans; and Aratus, receiving him accordingly, so managed him as to send him back to Macedon both well affected to himself and full of desire and ambition to take an honourable part in the affairs of Greece.

When Antigonus was dead, the Ætolians, despising the sloth and negligence of the Achæans, who having learnt to be defended by other men's valour and to shelter themselves under the Macedonian arms, lived in ease and without any discipline, now attempted to interfere in Peloponnesus. And plundering the land of Patræ and Dyme in their way, they invaded Messene and ravaged it; at which Aratus being indignant, and finding that Timoxenus, then general, was hesitating and letting the time go by, being now on the point of laying down his office, in which he himself was chosen to succeed him, he anticipated the proper term by five days, that he might bring relief to the Messenians. And mustering the Achæans, who were both in their persons unexercised in arms

and in their minds relaxed and averse to war, he met with a defeat at Caphyæ.

Having thus begun the war, as it seemed, with too much heat and passion, he then ran into the other extreme, cooling again and desponding so much that he let pass and overlooked many fair opportunities of advantage given by the Ætolians, and allowed them to run riot, as it were, throughout all Peloponnesus, with all manner of insolence and licentiousness. Wherefore, holding forth their hands once more to the Macedonians, they invited and drew in Philip to intermeddle in the affairs of Greece, chiefly hoping, because of the affection and trust that he felt for Aratus, they should find him easy-tempered, and ready to be managed as they pleased.

But the king, being now persuaded by Apelles, Megaleas, and other courtiers, that endeavoured to ruin the credit Aratus had with him, took the side of the contrary faction and joined them in canvassing to have Eperatus chosen general by the Achæans. But he being altogether scorned by the Achæans, and, for the want of Aratus to help, all things going wrong, Philip saw he had quite mistaken his part, and, turning about and reconciling himself to Aratus, he was wholly his; and his affairs, now going on favourably both for his power and reputation, he depended upon him altogether as the author of all his gains in both respects; Aratus hereby giving a proof to the world that he was as good a nursing father of a kingdom as he had been of a democracy, for the actions of the king had in them the touch and colour of his judgment and character.

The moderation which the young man showed to the Lacedæmonians, who had incurred his displeasure, and his affability to the Cretans, by which in a few days he brought over the whole island to his obedience, and his expedition against the Ætolians, so wonderfully successful, brought Philip reputation for hearkening to good advice, and to Aratus for giving it; for which things the king's followers envying him more than ever and finding they could not prevail against him by their secret practices, began openly to abuse and affront him at the banquets and over their wine with every kind of petulance and impudence; so that once they threw stones at him as he was going back from supper to his tent. At which Philip being much offended, immediately fined them twenty talents, and finding afterwards that they still went on disturbing matters and doing mischief in his affairs, he put them to death.

But with his run of good success, prosperity began to puff him up, and various extravagant desires began to spring and show themselves in his mind; and his natural bad inclinations breaking through the artificial restraints he had put upon them, in a little time laid open and discovered his true and proper character. In the first place, he privately injured the younger Aratus in his wife, which was not known for a good while, because he was lodged and entertained at their house; then he began to be more rough and untractable in the domestic politics of Greece, and showed plainly that he was wishing to shake himself loose of Aratus. This the Messenian affairs first gave occasion to suspect. For they falling into sedition, and Aratus being just too late with his succours, Philip, who got into the city one day before him, at once blew up the flame of contention amongst them, asking privately, on the one hand, the Messenian generals, if they had not laws whereby to suppress the insolence of the common people, and on the other, the leaders of the people, whether they had not hands to help themselves against their oppressors. Upon which gathering courage, the officers attempted to lay hands on the heads of the people, and they on the other side, coming upon the officers with the multitude, killed them, and very near two hundred persons with them.

Philip having committed this wickedness, and doing his best to set the Messenians by the ears together more than before, Aratus arrived there, and both showed plainly that he took it ill himself, and also he suffered his son bitterly to reproach and revile him. It should seem that the young man had an attachment for Philip, and so at this time one of his expressions to him was that he no longer appeared to him the handsomest, but the most deformed of all men, after so foul an action. To all which Philip gave him no answer, though he seemed so angry as to make it expected he would, and though several times he cried out aloud while the young man was speaking.

But as for the elder Aratus, seeming to take all that he said in good part, and as if he were by nature a politic character and had a good command of himself, he gave him his hand and led him out of the theatre, and carried him with him to the Ithomatas, to sacrifice there to Jupiter, and take a view of the place, for it is a post as fortifiable as the Acro-Corinthus, and, with a garrison in it, quite as strong and as impregnable to the attacks of all around it. Philip therefore went up thither, and having offered sacrifice, receiving the entrails of the ox with both his hands from the priest, he showed them to Aratus and Demetrius the Pharian presenting them sometimes to the one and sometimes to the other, asking them what they judged, by the tokens in the sacrifice, was to be done with the fort; was he to keep it for himself, or restore it to the Messenians? Demetrius laughed and answered, "If you have in you the soul of a soothsayer, you will restore it, but if of a prince you will hold the ox by both the horns," meaning to refer to Peloponnesus, which would be wholly in his power and at his disposal if he added the Ithomatas to the Acro-Corinthus.

Aratus said not a word for a good while; but Philip entreating him to declare his opinion, he said: "Many and great hills are there in Crete, and many rocks in Bœotia and Phocis, and many remarkable strongholds both near the sea and in the midland in Acarnania, and yet all these people obey your orders, though you have not possessed yourself of any one of those places. Robbers nest themselves in rocks and precipices; but the strongest fort a king can have is confidence and affection. These have opened to you the Cretan sea; these make you master of Peloponnesus, and by the help of these, young as you are, are you become captain of the one, and lord of the other." While he was still speaking, Philip returned the entrails to the priest, and drawing Aratus to him by the hand, "Come, then," said he, "let us follow the same course"; as if he felt himself forced by him, and obliged to give up the town.

From this time Aratus began to withdraw from court, and retired by degrees from Philip's company; when he was preparing to march into Epirus, and desired him that he would accompany him thither, he excused himself and stayed at home, apprehending that he should get nothing but discredit by having anything to do with his actions. But then, afterwards, having shamefully lost his fleet against the Romans and miscarried in all his designs, he returned into Peloponnesus, where he tried once more to beguile the Messenians by his artifices, and failing in this, began openly to attack them and to ravage their country. Then Aratus fell out with him downright, and utterly renounced his friendship; for he had begun then to be fully aware of the injuries done to his son in his wife, which vexed him greatly, though he concealed them from his son, as he could but know he had been abused, without having any means to revenge himself. For indeed, Philip seems to have been an instance of the greatest and strangest alteration of character; after being a mild king and modest and chaste youth, he became a lascivious man and most cruel tyrant; though in reality this was not a change of his nature, but a bold unmasking, when safe opportunity came, of the evil inclinations which his fear had for a long time made him dissemble.

For that the respect he at the beginning bore to Aratus had a great alloy of fear and awe appears evident from what he did to him at last. For being desirous to put him to death, not thinking himself, whilst he was alive, to be properly free as a man, much less at liberty to do his pleasure as king or tyrant, he durst not attempt to do it by open force, but commanded Taurion, one of his captains and familiars, to make him away secretly by poison, if possible, in his absence. Taurion, therefore, made himself intimate with Aratus, and gave him a dose not of your strong and violent poisons, but such as cause gentle, feverish heats at first, and a dull cough, and so by degrees bring on certain death. Aratus perceived what was done to him, but, knowing that it was in vain to make any words of it, bore it patiently and with silence, as if it had been some common and usual distemper. Only once, a friend of his being with him in his chamber, he spat some blood, which his friend observing and wondering at, "These, O Cephalon," said he, "are the wages of a king's love."

Thus died he in Ægium, in his seventeenth generalship. The Achæans were very desirous that he should be buried there with a funeral and monument suitable to his life, but the Sicyonians treated it as a calamity to them if he were interred anywhere but in their city, and prevailed with the Achæans to grant them the disposal of the body.

But there being an ancient law that no person should be buried within the walls of their city, and besides the law also a strong religious feeling about it, they sent to Delphi to ask counsel of the Pythoness, who returned this answer:—

Sicyon, whom oft he rescued, "Where," you say,
"Shall we the relics of Aratus lay?"
The soil that would not lightly o'er him rest,
Or to be under him would feel opprest,
Were in the sight of earth and seas and skies
unblest

This oracle being brought, all the Achæans were well pleased at it, but especially the Sicyonians, who, changing their mourning into public joy, immediately fetched the body from Ægium, and in a kind of solemn procession brought it into the city, being crowned with garlands, and arrayed in white garments, with singing and dancing, and, choosing a conspicuous place, they buried him there, as the founder and saviour of their city. The place is to this day called Aratium, and there they yearly make two solemn sacrifices to him, the one on the day he delivered the city from tyranny, being the fifth of the month Dæsius, which the Athenians call Anthesterion, and this sacrifice they call Soteria; the other in the month of his birth, which is still remembered.

Now the first of these was performed by the priest of Jupiter Soter, the second by the priest of Aratus, wearing a band around his head, not pure white, but mingled with purple. Hymns were sung to the harp by the singers of the feasts of Bacchus; the procession was led up by the president of the public exercises, with the boys and young men; these were followed by the councillors wearing garlands, and other citizens such as pleased. Of these observances, some small traces it is still made a point of religion not to omit on the appointed days; but the greatest part of the ceremonies have through time and other intervening accidents been disused.

And such, as history tells us, was the life and manners of the elder Aratus. And as for the younger, his son, Philip, abominably wicked by nature and a savage abuser of his power, gave him such baneful medicines that though they did not kill him indeed, yet made him lose his senses, and run into wild and absurd attempts and desire to do actions and satisfy appetites that were ridiculous and shameful. So that his death, which happened to him while he was yet young and in the flower of his age, cannot be so much esteemed a misfortune as a deliverance and end of his misery.

However Philip paid dearly, all through the rest of his life, for these impious violations of friendship and hospitality. For, being overcome by the Romans, he was forced to put himself wholly into their hands, and, being deprived of his other dominions and surrendering all his ships except five, he had also to pay a fine of a thousand talents, and to give his son for hostage, and only out of mere pity he was suffered to keep Macedonia and its dependencies; where continually putting to death the noblest of his subjects and the nearest relations he had, he filled the whole kingdom with horror and hatred of him. And whereas amidst so many misfortunes he had but one good chance, which was the having a son of great virtue and merit, him, through jealousy and envy at the honour the Romans had for him, he caused to be murdered, and left his kingdom to Perseus, who, as some say, was not his own child, but supposititious, born of a sempstress, Gnathænion. This was he whom Paulus Æmilius led in trumph, and in whom ended the succession of Antigonus's line and kingdom. But the posterity of Aratus continued still in our days at Sicyon and Pellene.

ARTAXERXES

C. 437-359 B.C.

THE first Artaxerxes, among all the kings of Persia the most remarkable for a gentle and noble spirit, was surnamed the Long-handed, his right hand being longer than his left, and was the son of Xerxes. The second, whose story I am now writing, who had the surname of the Mindful, was the grandson of the former, by his daughter Parysatis, who brought Darius four sons, the eldest Artaxerxes, the next Cyrus, and two younger than these, Ostanes and Oxathres. Cyrus took his name of the ancient Cyrus, as he, they say, had his from the sun, which, in the Persian language, is called Cyrus. Artaxerxes was at first called Arsicas; Dinon says Oarses; but it is utterly improbable that Ctesias (however otherwise he may have filled his books with a perfect farrago of incredible and senseless fables) should be ignorant of the name of the king with whom he lived as his physician, attending upon himself, his wife, his mother, and his children.

Cyrus, from his earliest youth, showed something of a headstrong and vehement character; Artaxerxes, on the other side, was gentler in everything, and of a nature more yielding and soft in its action. He married a beautiful and virtuous wife, at the desire of his parents, but kept her as expressly against their wishes. For King Darius, having put her brother to death, was purposing likewise to destroy her. But Arsicas, throwing himself at his mother's feet, by many tears, at last, with much ado, persuaded her that they should neither put her to death nor divorce her from him. However, Cyrus was his mother's favourite, and the son whom she most desired to settle in the throne. And therefore, his father Darius now lying ill, he, being sent for from the sea to the court, set out thence with full hopes that by her means he was to be declared the successor to the kingdom. For Parysatis had the specious plea in his behalf, which Xerxes on the advice of Demaratus had of old made use of, that she had borne him Arsicas when he was a subject, but Cyrus, when a king. Notwithstanding, she prevailed not with Darius, but the eldest son, Arsicas, was proclaimed king, his name being changed into Artaxerxes; and Cyrus remained satrap of Lydia, and commander in the maritime provinces.

It was not long after the decease of Darius that the king, his successor, went to Pasargadæ, to have the ceremony of his inauguration consummated by the Persian priests. There is a temple dedicated to a warlike goddess, whom one might liken to Minerva, into which when the royal person to be initiated has passed, he must strip himself of his own robe, and put on that which Cyrus the first wore before he was king; then, having devoured a frail of figs, he must eat turpentine, and drink a cup of sour milk. To which if they superadd any other rites, it is unknown to any but those that are present at them. Now Artaxerxes being about to address himself to this solemnity, Tisaphernes came to him, bringing a certain priest, who, having trained up Cyrus in his youth in the established discipline of Persia, and having taught him the Magian philosophy, was likely to be as much disappointed as any man that his pupil did not succeed to the throne. And for that reason his veracity was the less questioned when he charged Cyrus as though he had been about to lie in wait for the king in the temple, and to assault and assassinate him as he was putting off his garment.

Some affirm that he was apprehended upon this impeachment, others that he had entered the temple and was pointed out there, as he lay lurking by the priest. But as he was on the point of being put to death, his mother clasped him in her arms, and entwining him with the tresses of her hair, joined his neck close to her own, and by her bitter lamentation and intercession to Artaxerxes for him, succeeded in saving his life; and sent him away again to the sea and to his former province. This, however, could no longer content him; nor did he so well remember his delivery as his arrest, his resentment for which made him more eagerly desirous of the kingdom than before.

Some say that he revolted from his brother, because he had not a revenue allowed him sufficient for his daily meals; but this is on the face of it absurd. For had he had nothing else, yet he had a mother ready to supply him with whatever he could desire out of her own means. But the great number of soldiers who were hired from all quarters and maintained, as Xenophon informs us, for his service, by his friends and connections, is in itself a sufficient proof of his riches. He did not assemble them together in a body, desiring as yet to conceal his enterprise; but he had agents everywhere, enlisting foreign soldiers upon various pretences; and, in the meantime, Parysatis, who was with the king, did her best to put aside all suspicions, and Cyrus himself always wrote in a humble and dutiful manner to him, sometimes soliciting favour, sometimes making countercharges against Tisaphernes, as if his jealousy and contest had been wholly with him. Moreover, there was a certain natural dilatoriness in the king, which was taken by many for clemency. And, indeed, in the beginning of his reign, he did seem really to emulate the gentleness of the first Artaxerxes, being very accessible in his person, and liberal to a fault in the distribution of honours and favours.

Even in his punishments, no contumely or vindictive pleasure could be seen; and those who offered him presents were as much pleased with his manner of accepting, as were those who received gifts from him with his graciousness and amiability in giving them. Nor truly was there anything, however inconsiderable, given him, which he did not deign kindly to accept of; insomuch that when one Omises had presented him with a very large pomegranate, "By Mithras," said he, "this man, were he intrusted with it, would turn a small city into a great one."

Once when some were offering him one thing, some another, as he was on a progress, a certain poor labourer, having got nothing at hand to bring him, ran to the river side, and,

taking up water in his hands, offered it to him; with which Artaxerxes was so well pleased that he sent him a goblet of gold and a thousand darics. To Euclidas, the Lacedæmonian, who had made a number of bold and arrogant speeches to him, he sent word by one of his officers, "You have leave to say what you please to me, and I, you should remember, may both say and do what I please to you."

Teribazus once, when they were hunting, came up and pointed out to the king that his royal robe was torn; the king asked him what he wished him to do; and when Teribazus replied, "May it please you to put on another and give me that," the king did so, saying withal, "I give it you, Teribazus, but I charge you not to wear it." He, little regarding the injunction, being not a bad, but a lightheaded, thoughtless man, immediately the king took it off, put it on, and bedecked himself further with royal golden necklaces and women's ornaments, to the great scandal of everybody, the thing being quite unlawful. But the king laughed and told him, "You have my leave to wear the trinkets as a woman, and the robe of state as a fool."

And whereas none usually sat down to eat with the king, besides his mother and his wedded wife, the former being placed above, the other below him, Artaxerxes invited also to his table his two younger brothers, Ostanes and Oxathres. But what was the most popular thing of all among the Persians was the sight of his wife Statira's chariot, which always appeared with its curtains down, allowing her country-women to salute and approach her, which made the queen a great favourite with the people.

Yet busy, factious men, that delighted in change, professed it to be their opinion that the times needed Cyrus, a man of great spirit, an excellent warrior, and a lover of his friends, and that the largeness of their empire absolutely required a bold and enterprising prince. Cyrus, then, not only relying upon those of his own province near the sea, but upon many of those in the upper countries near the king, commenced the war against him.

He wrote to the Lacedæmonians, bidding them come to his assistance and supply him with men, assuring them that to those who came to him on foot he would give horses, and to the horsemen chariots; that upon those who had farms he would bestow villages, and those who were lords of villages he would make so of cities; and that those who would be his soldiers should receive their pay, not by count, but by weight. And among many other high praises of himself, he said he had the stronger soul; was more a philosopher and a better Magian; and could drink and bear more wine than his brother, who, as he averred, was such a coward and so little like a man, that he could neither sit his horse in hunting nor his throne in time of danger. The Lacedæmonians, his letter being read, sent a staff to Clearchus, commanding him to obey Cyrus in all things.

So Cyrus marched towards the king, having under his conduct a numerous host of barbarians, and but little less than thirteen thousand stipendiary Grecians; alleging first one cause, then another, for his expedition. Yet the true reason lay not long concealed, but Tisaphernes went to the king in person to declare it. Thereupon, the court was all in an uproar and tumult, the queen-mother bearing almost the whole blame of the enterprise, and her retainers being suspected and accused. Above all, Statira angered her by bewailing the war and passionately demanding where were now the pledges and the intercession which saved the life of him that conspired against his brother; "to the end," she said, "that he might plunge us all into war and trouble." For which words Parysatis hating Statira, and being naturally implacable and savage in her anger and revenge, consulted how she might destroy her.

But since Dinon tells us that her purpose took effect in the time of the war, and Ctesias says it was after it, I shall keep the story for the place to which the latter assigns it, as it is very unlikely that he, who was actually present, should not know the time when it happened, and there was no motive to induce him designedly to misplace its date in his narrative of it, though it is not infrequent with him in his history to make excursions from truth into mere fiction and romance.

As Cyrus was upon the march, rumours and reports were brought him, as though the king still deliberated, and were not minded to fight and presently to join battle with him; but to wait in the heart of his kingdom until his forces should have come in thither from all parts of his dominions. He had cut a trench through the plain ten fathoms in breadth, and as many in depth, the length of it being no less than four hundred furlongs. Yet he allowed Cyrus to pass across it, and to advance almost to the city of Babylon. Then Teribazus, as the report goes, was the first that had the boldness to tell the king that he ought not to avoid the conflict, nor to abandon Media, Babylon, and even Susa, and hide himself in Persis, when all the while he had an army many times over more numerous than his enemies, and an infinite company of governors and captains that were better soldiers and politicians than Cyrus. So at last he resolved to fight, as soon as it was possible for him.

Making, therefore, his first appearance, all on a sudden, at the head of nine hundred thousand well-marshalled men, he so startled and surprised the enemy, who with the confidence of contempt were marching on their way in no order, and with their arms not ready for use, that Cyrus, in the midst of such noise and tumult, was scarcely able to form them for battle. Moreover, the very manner in which he led on his men, silently and slowly, made the Grecians stand amazed at his good discipline; who had expected irregular shouting and leaping, much confusion and separation between one body of men and another, in so vast a multitude of troops. He also placed the choicest of his armed chariots in the front of his own phalanx over against the Grecian troops, that a violent charge with these might cut open their ranks before they closed with them.

But as this battle is described by many historians, and Xenophon in particular as good as shows it us by eyesight, not as a past event, but as a present action, and by his vivid account makes his hearers feel all the passions and join in all the dangers of it, it would be folly in me to give any larger account of it than barely to mention any things omitted by him which yet deserve to be recorded. The place, then, in which the two armies were drawn out is called Cunaxa, being about five hundred furlongs distant from Babylon. And here Clearchus beseeching Cyrus before the fight to retire behind the combatants, and not expose himself to hazard, they say he replied, "What is this, Clearchus? Would you have me, who aspire to empire, show myself unworthy of it?"

But if Cyrus committed a great fault in entering headlong into the midst of danger, and not paying any regard to his own safety, Clearchus was as much to blame, if not more, in refusing to lead the Greeks against the main body of the enemy, where the king stood, and in keeping his right wing close to the river, for fear of being surrounded. For if he wanted, above all other things, to be safe, and considered it his first object to sleep in a whole skin, it had been his best way not to have stirred from home. But, after marching in arms ten thousand furlongs from the sea-coast, simply on his choosing, for the purpose of placing Cyrus on the throne, to look about and select a position which would enable him, not to preserve him under whose pay and conduct he was, but himself to engage with more ease and security, seemed much like one that through fear of present dangers had abandoned the purpose of his actions, and been false to the design of his expedition.

For it is evident from the very event of the battle that none of those who were in array around the king's person could have stood the shock of the Grecian charge; and had they been beaten out of the field, and Artaxerxes either fled or fallen, Cyrus would have gained by the victory, not only safety, but a crown. And, therefore, Clearchus by his caution must be considered more to blame for the result in the destruction of the life and fortune of Cyrus, than he by his heat and rashness. For had the king made it his business to discover a place, where having posted the Grecians he might encounter them with the least hazard, he would never have found out any other but that which was most remote from himself and those near him; of his defeat in which he was insensible, and, though Clearchus had the victory, yet Cyrus could not know of it, and could take no advantage of it before his fall. Cyrus knew well enough what was expedient to be done, and commanded Clearchus with his men to take their place in the centre. Clearchus replied that he would take care to have all arranged as was best, and then spoiled all.

For the Grecians, where they were, defeated the barbarians till they were weary, and chased them successfully a very great way. But Cyrus being mounted upon a noble but a headstrong and hard-mouthed horse, bearing the name, as Ctesias tells us, of Pasacas, Artagerses, the leader of the Cadusians, galloped up to him, crying aloud, "O most unjust and senseless of men, who are the disgrace of the honoured name of Cyrus, are you come here leading the wicked Greeks on a wicked journey, to plunder the good things of the Persians, and this with the intent of slaying your lord and brother, the master of ten thousand times ten thousand servants that are better men than you? As you shall see this instant; for you shall lose your head here, before you look upon the face of the king." Which when he had said, he cast his javelin at him. But his coat of mail stoutly repelled it, and Cyrus was not wounded; yet the stroke falling heavy upon him, he reeled

under it. Then Artagerses turning his horse, Cyrus threw his weapon, and sent the head of it through his neck near the shoulder bone. So that it is almost universally agreed to by all the authors that Artagerses was slain by him.

But as to the death of Cyrus, since Xenophon, as being himself no eye-witness of it, has stated it simply and in few words, it may not be amiss perhaps to run over on the one hand what Dinon, and on the other, what Ctesias had said of it.

Dinon then affirms that, after the death of Artagerses, Cyrus, furiously attacking the guard of Artaxerxes, wounded the king's horse, and so dismounted him, and when Teribazus had quickly lifted him up upon another, and said to him, "O king, remember this day, which is not one to be forgotten," Cyrus, again spurring up his horse, struck down Artaxerxes. But at the third assault the king being enraged and saying to those near him that death was better, rode out against Cyrus, who furiously and blindly rushed in the face of the weapons opposed to him. So the king struck him with a javelin, as likewise did those that were about him. And thus Cyrus fell, as some say, by the hand of the king; as others, by the dart of a Carian, to whom Artaxerxes for a reward of his achievement gave the privilege of carrying ever after a golden cock upon his spear before the first ranks of the army in all expeditions. For the Persians call the men of Caria cocks, because of the crests with which they adorn their helmets.

But the account of Ctesias, to put it shortly, omitting many details, is as follows: Cyrus, after the death of Artagerses, rode up against the king, as he did against him, neither exchanging a word with the other. But Ariæus, Cyrus's friend, was beforehand with him, and darted first at the king, yet wounded him not. Then the king cast his lance at his brother, but missed him, though he both hit and slew Satiphernes, a noble man and a faithful friend to Cyrus. Then Cyrus directed his lance against the king, and pierced his breast with it quite through his armour, two inches deep, so that he fell from his horse with the stroke. At which those that attended him being put to flight and disorder, he, rising with a few, among whom was Ctesias, and making his way to a little hill not far off, rested himself. But Cyrus, in the thick of the enemy, was carried off a great way by the wildness of his horse, the darkness which was now coming on making it hard for them to know him, and for his followers to find him. However, being made elate with victory, and full of confidence and force, he passed through them, crying out, and that more than once, in the Persian language, "Clear the way, villains, clear the way"; which they indeed did, throwing themselves down at his feet. But his tiara dropped off his head, and a young Persian, by name Mithridates, running by, struck a dart into one of his temples near his eye, not knowing who he was; out of which wound much blood gushed, so that Cyrus, swooning and senseless, fell off his horse. The horse escaped, and ran about the field; but the companion of Mithridates took the trappings which fell off, soaked with blood. And as Cyrus slowly began to come to himself, some eunuchs who were there tried to put him on another horse, and so convey him safe away. And when he was not able to ride, and desired to walk on his feet, they led and supported him, being indeed dizzy in the head and reeling, but convinced of his being victorious, hearing, as he went, the fugitives saluting Cyrus as king, and praying for grace and mercy.

In the meantime, some wretched, poverty-stricken Caunians, who in some pitiful employment as camp followers had accompanied the king's army, by chance joined these attendants of Cyrus, supposing them to be of their own party. But when, after a while, they made out that their coats over their breastplates were red, whereas all the king's people wore white ones, they knew that they were enemies. One of them, therefore, not dreaming that it was Cyrus, ventured to strike him behind with a dart. The vein under the knee was cut open, and Cyrus fell, and at the same time struck his wounded temple against a stone, and so died. Thus runs Ctesias's account, tardily, with the slowness of a blunt weapon effecting the victim's death.

When he was now dead, Artasyras, the king's eye, passed by on horseback, and, having observed the eunuchs lamenting, he asked the most trusty of them, "Who is this, Pariscas, whom you sit here deploring?" He replied, "Do not you see, O Artasyras, that it is my master, Cyrus?" Then Artasyras wondering, bade the eunuch be of good cheer, and keep the dead body safe. And going in all haste to Artaxerxes, who had now given up all hope of his affairs, and was in great suffering also with his thirst and his wound, he with much joy assured him that he had seen Cyrus dead. Upon this, at first, he set out to go in person to the place, and commanded Artasyras to conduct

him where he lay. But when there was a great noise made about the Greeks, who were said to be in full pursuit, conquering and carrying all before them, he thought it best to send a number of persons to see; and accordingly thirty men went with torches in their hands.

Meantime, as he seemed to be almost at the point of dying from thirst, his eunuch Satibarzanes ran about seeking drink for him; for the place had no water in it and he was at a good distance from his camp. After a long search he at last met one of those poor Caunian camp-followers, who had in a wretched skin about four pints of foul and stinking water, which he took and gave to the king; and when he had drunk all off, he asked him if he did not dislike the water; but he declared by all the gods that he never so much relished either wine, or water out of the lightest or purest stream. "And therefore," said he, "if I fail myself to discover and reward him who gave it to you, I beg of heaven to make him rich and prosperous."

Just after this, came back the thirty messengers, with joy and triumph in their looks, bringing him the tidings of his unexpected fortune. And now he was also encouraged by the number of soldiers that again began to flock in and gather about him; so that he presently descended into the plain with many lights and flambeaux round about him. And when he had come near the dead body, and, according to a certain law of the Persians, the right hand and head had been lopped off from the trunk, he gave orders that the latter should be brought to him, and, grasping the hair of it, which was long and bushy, he showed it to those who were still uncertain and disposed to fly. They were amazed at it, and did him homage; so that there were presently seventy thousand of them got about him, and entered the camp again with him. He had led out to the fight, as Ctesias affirms, four hundred thousand men. But Dinon and Xenophon aver that there were many more than forty myriads actually engaged. As to the number of the slain, as the catalogue of them was given up to Artaxerxes, Ctesias says, they were nine thousand, but that they appeared to him no fewer than twenty thousand. Thus far there is something to be said on both sides.

But it is a flagrant untruth on the part of Ctesias to say that he was sent along with Phalinus the Zacynthian and some others to the Grecians. For Xenophon knew well enough that Ctesias was resident at court; for he makes mention of him, and had evidently met with his writings. And, therefore, had he come, and been deputed the interpreter of such momentous words, Xenophon surely would not have struck his name out of the embassy to mention only Phalinus. But Ctesias, as is evident, being excessively vainglorious and no less a favourer of the Lacedæmonians and Clearchus, never fails to assume to himself some province in his narrative, taking opportunity, in these situations, to introduce abundant high praise of Clearchus and Sparta.

When the battle was over, Artaxerxes sent goodly and magnificent gifts to the son of Artagerses, whom Cyrus slew. He conferred likewise high honours upon Ctesias and others, and, having found out the Caunian who gave him the bottle of water, he made him—a poor, obscure man—a rich and an honourable person. As for the punishments he inflicted upon delinquents, there was a kind of harmony betwixt them and the crimes. He gave order that one Arbaces, a Mede, that had fled in the fight to Cyrus and again at his fall had come back, should, as a mark that he was considered a dastardly and effeminate, not a dangerous or treasonable man, have a common harlot set upon his back, and carry her about for a whole day in the market-place. Another, besides that he had deserted to them, having falsely vaunted that he had killed two of the rebels, he decreed that three needles should be struck through his tongue. And both supposing that with his own hand he had cut off Cyrus, and being willing that all men should think and say so, he sent rich presents to Mithridates, who first wounded him, and charged those by whom he conveyed the gifts to him to say to him: "The king has honoured you with these his favours, because you found and brought him the horse-trappings of Cyrus."

The Carian, also, from whose wound in the ham Cyrus died, suing for his reward, he commanded those that brought it him to declare: "The king presents you with this as a second remuneration for the good news told him; for first Artasyras, and, next to him, you assured him of the decease of Cyrus." Mithridates retired without complaint, though not without resentment. But the unfortunate Carian was fool enough to give way to a natural infirmity. For being ravished with the sight of the princely gifts that were before him, and being tempted thereupon to challenge and aspire to things above him, he deigned not to accept the king's present as a reward for good news, but

indignantly crying out and appealing to witnesses, he protested that he, and none but he, had killed Cyrus, and that he was unjustly deprived of the glory. These words, when they came to his ear, much offended the king, so that forthwith he sentenced him to be beheaded.

But the queen mother, being in the king's presence, said, "Let not the king so lightly discharge this pernicious Carian; let him receive from me the fitting punishment of what he dares to say." So when the king had consigned him over to Parysatis, she charged the executioners to take up the man, and stretch him upon the rack for ten days, then, tearing out his eyes, to drop molten brass into his ears till he expired.

Mithridates, also, within a short time after, miserably perished by the like folly; for being invited to a feast where were the eunuchs both of the king and of the queen mother, he came arrayed in the dress and the golden ornaments which he had received from the king. After they began to drink, the eunuch that was the greatest in power with Parysatis thus spoke to him: "A magnificent dress, indeed, O Mithridates, is this which the king has given you; the chains and bracelets are glorious, and your scymetar of invaluable worth; how happy has he made you, the object of every eye!" To whom he, being a little overcome with the wine, replied, "What are these things, Sparamizes? Sure I am, I showed myself to the king in that day of trial to be one deserving greater and costlier gifts than these." At which Sparamizes smiling, said, "I do not grudge them to you, Mithridates; but since the Grecians tell us that wine and truth go together, let me hear now, my friend, what glorious or mighty matter was it to find some trappings that had slipped off a horse, and to bring them to the king?"

And this he spoke, not as ignorant of the truth, but desiring to unbosom him to the company, irritating the vanity of the man, whom drink had now made eager to talk and incapable of controlling himself. So he forbore nothing, but said out, "Talk you what you please of horse-trappings and such trifles; I tell you plainly, that this hand was the death of Cyrus. For I threw not my darts as Artagerses did, in vain and to no purpose, but only just missing his eye, and hitting him right on the temple, and piercing him through, I brought him to the ground; and of that wound he died." The rest of the company, who saw the end and the hapless fate of Mithridates as if it were already completed, bowed their heads to the ground; and he who entertained them said, "Mithridates, my friend, let us eat and drink now, revering the fortune of our prince, and let us waive discourse which is too weighty for us."

Presently after, Sparamizes told Parysatis what he said, and she told the king, who was greatly enraged at it, as having the lie given him, and being in danger to forfeit the most glorious and most pleasant circumstance of his victory. For it was his desire that every one, whether Greek or barbarian, should believe that in the mutual assaults and conflicts between him and his brother, he, giving and receiving a blow, was himself indeed wounded, but that the other lost his life. And, therefore, he decreed that Mithridates should be put to death in boats; which execution is after the following manner:

Taking two boats framed exactly to fit and answer each other, they lay down in one of them the malefactor that suffers, upon his back; then, covering it with the other, and so setting them together that the head, hands, and feet of him are left outside, and the rest of his body lies shut up within, they offer him food, and if he refuse to eat it, they force him to do it by pricking his eyes; then, after he has eaten, they drench him with a mixture of milk and honey, pouring it not only into his mouth, but all over his face. They then keep his face continually turned towards the sun: and it becomes completely covered up and hidden by the multitude of flies that settle on it. And as within the boats he does what those that eat and drink must needs do, creeping things and vermin spring out of the corruption and rottenness of the excrement, and these entering into the bowels of him, his body is consumed. When the man is manifestly dead, the uppermost boat being taken off, they find his flesh devoured, and swarms of such noisome creatures preying upon and, as it were, growing to his inwards.

In this way Mithridates, after suffering for seventeen days, at last expired.

Masabates, the king's eunuch, who had cut off the hand and head of Cyrus, remained still as a mark for Parysatis's vengeance. Whereas, therefore, he was so circumspect, that he gave her no advantage against him, she framed this kind of snare for him. She was a very ingenious woman in other ways, and was an excellent player at dice, and, before the war, had

often played with the king. After the war, too, when she had been reconciled to him, she joined readily in all amusements with him, played at dice with him, was his confidant in his love matters, and in every way did her best to leave him as little as possible in the company of Statira, both because she hated her more than any other person, and because she wished to have no one so powerful as herself. And so once when Artaxerxes was at leisure, and inclined to divert himself, she challenged him to play at dice with her for a thousand darics, and purposely let him win them, and paid him down in gold.

Yet, pretending to be concerned for her loss, and that she would gladly have her revenge for it, she pressed him to begin a new game for a eunuch; to which he consented. But first they agreed that each of them might except five of their most trusty eunuchs, and that out of the rest of them the loser should yield up any the winner should make choice of. Upon these conditions they played. Thus being bent upon her design, and thoroughly in earnest with her game, and the dice also running luckily for her, when she had got the game, she demanded Masabates, who was not in the number of the five excepted. And before the king could suspect the matter, having delivered him up to the tormentors, she enjoined them to flay him alive, to set his body upon three stakes, and to stretch his skin upon stakes separately from it.

These things being done, and the king taking them ill, and being incensed against her, she with raillery and laughter told him, "You are a comfortable and happy man indeed, if you are so much disturbed for the sake of an old rascally eunuch, when I, though I have thrown away a thousand darics, hold my peace and acquiesce in my fortune." So the king, vexed with himself for having been thus deluded, hushed up all. But Statira both in other matters openly opposed her, and was angry with her for thus, against all law and humanity, sacrificing to the memory of Cyrus the king's faithful friend and eunuch.

Now after that Tisaphernes had circumvented and by a false oath had betrayed Clearchus and the other commanders, and, taking them, had sent them bound in chains to the king, Ctesias says that he was asked by Clearchus to supply him with a comb; and that when he had it, and had combed his head with it, he was much pleased with this good office, and gave him a ring, which might be a token of the obligation to his relatives and friends in Sparta; and that the engraving upon this signet was a set of Caryatides dancing. He tells us that the soldiers, his fellow-captives, used to purloin a part of the allowance of food sent to Clearchus, giving him but little of it; which thing Ctesias says he rectified, causing a better allowance to be conveyed to him, and that a separate share should be distributed to the soldiers by themselves; adding that he ministered to and supplied him thus by the interest and at the instance of Parysatis. And there being a portion of ham sent daily with his other food to Clearchus, she, he says, advised and instructed him, that he ought to bury a small knife in the meat, and thus send it to his friend, and not leave his fate to be determined by the king's cruelty; which he, however, he says, was afraid to do.

However, Artaxerxes consented to the entreaties of his mother, and promised her with an oath that he would spare Clearchus; but afterwards, at the instigation of Statira, he put every one of them to death except Menon. And thenceforth, he says, Parysatis watched her advantage against Statira and made up poison for her, not a very probable story, or a very likely motive to account for her conduct, if indeed he means that out of respect to Clearchus she dared to attempt the life of the lawful queen, that was mother of those who were heirs of the empire.

But it is evident enough, that this part of his history is a sort of funeral exhibition in honour of Clearchus. For he would have us believe that, when the generals were executed, the rest of them were torn in pieces by dogs and birds; but as for the remains of Clearchus, that a violent gust of wind, bearing before it a vast heap of earth, raised a mound to cover his body, upon which, after a short time, some dates having fallen there, a beautiful grove of trees grew up and overshadowed the place, so that the king himself declared his sorrow, concluding that in Clearchus he put to death a man beloved of the gods.

Parysatis, therefore, having from the first entertained a secret hatred and jealousy against Statira, seeing that the power she herself had with Artaxerxes was founded upon feelings of honour and respect for her, but that Statira's influence was firmly and strongly based upon love and confidence, was resolved to contrive her ruin, playing at hazard, as she thought, for the greatest stake in the world. Among her attendant women there was one that was trusty

and in the highest esteem with her, whose name was Gigis; who, as Dinon avers, assisted in making up the poison. Ctesias allows her only to have been conscious of it, and that against her will; charging Belitaras with actually giving the drug, whereas Dinon says it was Melantas.

The two women had begun again to visit each other and to eat together; but though they had thus far relaxed their former habits of jealousy and variance, still, out of fear and as a matter of caution, they always ate of the same dishes and of the same parts of them. Now there is a small Persian bird, in the inside of which no excrement is found, only a mass of fat, so that they suppose the little creature lives upon air and dew. It is called *rhyntaces*. Ctesias affirms, that Parysatis, cutting a bird of this kind into two pieces with a knife one side of which had been smeared with the drug, the other side being clear of it, ate the untouched and wholesome part herself, and gave Statira that which was thus infected; but Dinon will not have it to be Parysatis, but Melantas, that cut up the bird and presented the envenomed part of it to Statira; who, dying with dreadful agonies and convulsions, was herself sensible of what had happened to her, and aroused in the king's mind suspicion of his mother, whose savage and implacable temper he knew.

And therefore proceeding instantly to an inquest, he seized upon his mother's domestic servants that attended at her table and put them upon the rack. Parysatis kept Gigis at home with her a long time, and though the king commanded her, she would not produce her. But she, at last herself desiring that she might be dismissed to her own home by night, Artaxerxes had intimation of it, and lying in wait for her, hurried her away, and adjudged her to death. Now poisoners in Persia suffer thus by law. There is a broad stone, on which they place the head of the culprit, and then with another stone beat and press it, until the face and the head itself are all pounded to pieces; which was the punishment Gigis lost her life by. But to his mother, Artaxerxes neither said nor did any other hurt, save that he banished and confined her, not much against her will, to Babylon, protesting that while she lived he would not come near that city. Such was the condition of the king's affairs in his own house.

But when all his attempts to capture the Greeks that had come with Cyrus, though he desired to do so no less than he had desired to overcome Cyrus and maintain his throne, proved unlucky, and they, though they had lost both Cyrus and their own generals, nevertheless escaped, as it were, out of his very palace, making it plain to all men that the Persian king and his empire were mighty indeed in gold and luxury and women, but otherwise were a mere show and vain display, upon this all Greece took courage and despised the barbarians; and especially the Lacedæmonians thought it strange if they should not now deliver their countrymen that dwelt in Asia from their subjection to the Persians, nor put an end to the contumelious usage of them.

And first having an army under the conduct of Thimbron, then under Dercyllidas, but doing nothing memorable, they at last committed the war to the management of their King Agesilaus, who, when he had arrived with his men in Asia, as soon as he had landed them, fell actively to work, and got himself great renown. He defeated Tisaphernes in a pitched battle, and set many cities in revolt. Upon this, Artaxerxes, perceiving what was his wisest way of waging the war, sent Timocrates the Rhodian into Greece, with large sums of gold, commanding him by a free distribution of it to corrupt the leading men in the cities, and to excite a Greek war against Sparta. So Timocrates following his instructions, the most considerable cities conspiring together, and Peloponnesus being in disorder, the ephors remanded Agesilaus from Asia. At which time, they say, as he was upon his return, he told his friends that Artaxerxes had driven him out of Asia with thirty thousand archers; the Persian coin having an archer stamped upon it.

Artaxerxes scoured the seas, too, of the Lacedæmonians, Conon the Athenian and Pharnabazus being his admirals. For Conon, after the battle of Ægospotami, resided in Cyprus; not that he consulted his own mere security, but looking for a vicissitude of affairs with no less hope than men wait for a change of wind at sea. And perceiving that his skill wanted power, and that the king's power wanted a wise man to guide it, he sent him an account of his projects, and charged the bearer to hand it to the king, if possible, by the mediation of Zeno the Cretan, or Polycritus the Mendæan, (the former being a dancing-master, the latter a physician), or, in the absence of them both, by Ctesias; who is said to have taken Conon's letter, and foisted into the contents of it a request that the king would also be pleased to send over Ctesias to him, who was likely to be of use on the sea-coast. Ctesias, however, declares that the king, of his accord, deputed him to his service.

Artaxerxes, however, defeating the Lacedæmonians in a sea-fight at Cnidos, under the conduct of Pharnabazus and Conon, after he had stripped them of their sovereignty by sea, at the same time brought, so to say, the whole of Greece over to him, so that upon his own terms he dictated the celebrated peace among them, styled the peace of Antalcidas. This Antalcidas was a Spartan, the son of one Leon, who, acting for the king's interest, induced the Lacedæmonians to covenant to let all the Greek cities in Asia and the islands adjacent to it become subject and tributary to him, peace being upon these conditions established among the Greeks, if indeed the honourable name of peace can fairly be given to what was in fact the disgrace and betrayal of Greece, a treaty more inglorious than had ever been the result of any war to those defeated in it.

And therefore Artaxerxes, though always abominating other Spartans, and looking upon them, as Dinon says, to be the most impudent men living, gave wonderful honour to Antalcidas when he came to him into Persia; so much so that one day, taking a garland of flowers and dipping it in the most precious ointment, he sent it to him after supper, a favour which all were amazed at. Indeed he was a person fit to be thus delicately treated, and to have such a crown, who had among the Persians thus made fools of Leonidas and Callicratidas. Agesilaus, it seems, on some one having said, "O the deplorable fate of Greece, now that the Spartans turn Medes!" replied, "Nay, rather it is the Medes who become Spartans."

But the subtilty of the repartee did not wipe off the infamy of the action. The Lacedæmonians soon after lost their sovereignty in Greece by their defeat at Leuctra; but they had already lost their honour by this treaty. So long then as Sparta continued to be the first state in Greece, Artaxerxes continued to Antalcidas the honour of being called his friend and his guest; but when, routed and humbled at the battle of Leuctra, being under great distress for money, they had despatched Agesilaus into Egypt, and Antalcidas went up to Artaxerxes, beseeching him to supply their necessities, he so despised, slighted, and rejected him, that finding himself, on his return, mocked and insulted by his enemies, and fearing also the ephors, he starved himself to death. Ismenias, also, the Theban, and Pelopidas, who had already gained the victory at Leuctra, arrived at the Persian court; where the latter did nothing unworthy of himself. But Ismenias, being commanded to do obeisance to the king, dropped his ring before him upon the ground, and so, stooping to take it up, made a show of doing him homage.

Artaxerxes was so gratified with some secret intelligence which Timagoras the Athenian sent in to him by the hand of his secretary, Beluris, that he bestowed upon him ten thousand darics, and because he was ordered, on account of some sickness, to drink cow's milk, there were fourscore milch kine driven after him; also, he sent him a bed, furniture, and servants for it, the Grecians not having skill enough to make it, as also chairmen to carry him, being infirm in body, to the seaside. Not to mention the feast made for him at court, which was so princely and splendid that Ostanes, the king's brother, said to him, "O Timagoras, do not forget the sumptuous table you have sat at here; it was not put before you for nothing"; which was indeed rather a reflection upon his treason than to remind him of the king's bounty. And indeed the Athenians condemned Timagoras to death for taking bribes.

But Artaxerxes gratified the Grecians in one thing in lieu of the many wherewith he plagued them, and that was by taking off Tisaphernes, their most hated and malicious enemy, whom he put to death, Parysatis adding her influence to the charges made against him.

For the king did not persist long in his wrath with his mother, but was reconciled to her, and sent for her, being assured that she had wisdom and courage fit for royal power, and there being now no cause discernible but that they might converse together without suspicion or offence. And from thenceforward humouring the king in all things according to his heart's desire, and finding fault with nothing that he did, she obtained great power with him, and was gratified in all her requests. She perceived he was desperately in love with Atossa, one of his own two daughters, and that he concealed and checked his passion chiefly for fear of herself, though, if we may believe some writers, he had privately given way to it with the young girl already. As soon as Parysatis suspected it, she displayed a greater fondness for the young girl than before, and extolled both her virtue and beauty to him, as being truly imperial and majestic. In fine, she persuaded him to marry her and

declare her to be his lawful wife, over-riding all the principles and the laws by which the Greeks hold themselves bound, and regarding himself as divinely appointed for a law to the Persians, and the supreme arbitrator of good and evil.

Some historians further affirm, in which number is Heraclides of Cuma, that Artaxerxes married not only this one, but a second daughter also, Amestris, of whom we shall speak by and by. But he so loved Atossa when she became his consort, that when leprosy had run through her whole body, he was not in the least offended at it; but putting up his prayers to Juno for her, to this one alone of all the deities he made obeisance, by laying his hands upon the earth; and his satraps and favourites made such offerings to the goddess by his direction, that all along for sixteen furlongs betwixt the court and her temple, the road was filled up with gold and silver, purple and horses, devoted to her.

He waged war out of his own kingdom with the Egyptians, under the conduct of Pharnabazus and Iphicrates, but was unsuccessful by reason of their dissensions. In his expedition against the Cadusians, he went himself in person with three hundred thousand footmen and ten thousand horse, and making an incursion into their country, which was so mountainous as scarcely to be passable, and withal very misty, producing no sort of harvest of corn or the like, but with pears, apples, and other tree-fruits feeding a war-like and valiant breed of men, he unawares fell into great distresses and dangers. For there was nothing to be got, fit for his men to eat, of the growth of that place, nor could anything be imported from any other. All they could do was to kill their beasts of burden, and thus an ass's head could scarcely be bought for sixty drachmas. In short, the king's own table failed; and there were but few horses left; the rest they had spent for food.

Then Teribazus, a man often in great favour with his prince for his valour and as often out of it for his buffoonery, and particularly at that time in humble estate and neglected, was the deliverer of the king and his army. There being two kings amongst the Cadusians, and each of them encamping separately, Teribazus, after he had made his application to Artaxerxes and imparted his design to him, went to one of the princes, and sent away his son privately to the other. So each of them deceived his man, assuring him that the other prince had deputed an ambassador to Artaxerxes, suing for friendship and alliance for himself alone; and, therefore, if he were wise, he told him, he must apply himself to his master before he had decreed anything, and he, he said, would lend him his assistance in all things. Both of them gave credit to these words, and because they supposed they were each intrigued against by the other, they both sent their envoys, one along with Teribazus, and the other with his son. All this taking some time to transact, fresh surmises and suspicions of Teribazus were expressed to the king, who began to be out of heart, sorry that he had confided in him, and ready to give ear to his rivals who impeached him. But at last he came, and so did his son, bringing the Cadusian agents along with them, and so there was a cessation of arms and a peace signed with both the princes.

And Teribazus, in great honour and distinction, set out homewards in the company of the king; who, indeed, upon this journey made it appear plainly that cowardice and effeminacy are the effects, not of delicate and sumptuous living, as many suppose, but of a base and vicious nature, actuated by false and bad opinions. For notwithstanding his golden ornaments, his robe of state, and the rest of that costly attire, worth no less than twelve thousand talents, with which the royal person was constantly clad, his labours and toils were not a whit inferior to those of the meanest persons in his army. With his quiver by his side and his shield on his arm, he led them on foot, quitting his horse, through craggy and steep ways, insomuch that the sight of his cheerfulness and unwearied strength gave wings to the soldiers, and so lightened the journey that they made daily marches of above two hundred furlongs.

After they had arrived at one of his own mansions, which had beautiful ornamented parks in the midst of a region naked and without trees, the weather being very cold, he gave full commission to his soldiers to provide themselves with wood by cutting down any, without exception, even the pine and cypress. And when they hesitated and were for sparing them, being large and goodly trees, he, taking up an axe himself, felled the greatest and most beautiful of them. After which his men used their hatchets, and piling up many fires, passed away the night at their ease. Nevertheless, he returned not without the loss of many and valiant subjects, and of almost all his horses. And supposing that his misfortunes and the ill-success of his expedition made him despised in the eyes of his people, he looked jealously on his nobles, many of whom he slew in anger, and yet more out of fear. As, indeed, fear is the bloodiest passion in princes; confidence, on the other hand, being merciful, gentle, and unsuspicious. So we see among wild beasts, the intractable and least tamable are the most timorous and most easily startled; the nobler creatures, whose courage makes them trustful, are ready to respond to the advances of men.

Artaxerxes, now being an old man, perceived that his sons were in controversy about his kingdom, and that they made parties among his favourites and peers. Those that were equitable among them thought it fit that as he had received it, so he should bequeath it, by right of age, to Darius. The younger brother, Ochus, who was hot and violent, had indeed a considerable number of the courtiers that espoused his interest, but his chief hope was that by Atossa's means he should win his father. For he flattered her with the thoughts of being his wife and partner in the kingdom after the death of Artaxerxes. And truly it was rumoured that already Ochus maintained a too intimate correspondence with her. This, however, was quite unknown to the king; who, being willing to put down in good time his son Ochus's hopes, lest, by his attempting the same things his uncle Cyrus did, wars and contentions might again afflict his kingdom, proclaimed Darius, then twenty-five years old, his successor, and gave him leave to wear the upright hat, as they called it.

It was a rule and usage of Persia, that the heir apparent to the crown should beg a boon, and that he that declared him so should give whatever he asked, provided it were within the sphere of his power. Darius therefore requested Aspasia, in former time the most prized of the concubines of Cyrus, and now belonging to the king. She was by birth a Phocæan, of Ionia, born of free parents, and well educated. Once when Cyrus was at supper, she was led in to him with other women, who, when they were sat down by him, and he began to sport and dally and talk jestingly with them, gave way freely to his advances. But she stood by in silence, refusing to come when Cyrus called her, and when his chamberlains were going to force her towards him, said, "Whosoever lays hands on me shall rue it"; so that she seemed to the company a sullen and rude-mannered person. However, Cyrus was well pleased, and laughed, saying to the man that brought the women, "Do you not see to a certainty that this woman alone of all that came with you is truly noble and pure in character?" After which time he began to regard her, and loved her, above all of her sex, and called her the Wise. But Cyrus being slain in the fight, she was taken among the spoils of his camp.

Darius, in demanding her, no doubt much offended his father, for the barbarian people keep a very jealous and watchful eye over their carnal pleasures, so that it is death for a man not only to come near and touch any concubine of his prince, but likewise on a journey to ride forward and pass by the carriages in which they are conveyed. And though, to gratify his passion, he had against all law married his daughter Atossa, and had besides her no less than three hundred and sixty concubines selected for their beauty, yet being importuned for that one by Darius, he urged that she was a free-woman, and allowed him to take her, if she had an inclination to go with him, but by no means to force her away against it.

Aspasia, therefore, being sent for, and, contrary to the king's expectation, making choice of Darius, he gave him her indeed, being constrained by law, but when he had done so, a little after he took her from him. For he consecrated her priestess to Diana of Ecbatana, whom they name Anaitis, that she might spend the remainder of her days in strict chastity, thinking thus to punish his son, not rigorously, but with moderation, by a revenge checkered with jest and earnest. But he took it heinously, either that he was passionately fond of Aspasia, or because he looked upon himself as affronted and scorned by his father.

Teribazus, perceiving him thus minded, did his best to exasperate him yet further, seeing in his injuries a representation of his own, of which the following is the account: Artaxerxes, having many daughters, promised to give Apama to Pharnabazus to wife, Rhodogune to Orontes, and Amestris to Teribazus; whom alone of the three he disappointed, by marrying Amestris himself. However, to make him amends, he betrothed his youngest daughter Atossa to him. But after he had, being enamoured of her too, as has been said, married her, Teribazus entertained an irreconcilable enmity against him. As indeed he was seldom at any other time steady in his temper, but uneven and inconsiderate; so that whether he were in the number of the choicest favourites of his prince, or whether he were offensive and odious to him, he demeaned himself in neither

condition with moderation, but if he was advanced he was intolerably insolent, and in his degradation not submissive and peaceable in his deportment, but fierce and haughty.

And therefore Teribazus was to the young prince flame added upon flame, ever urging him, and saying, that in vain those wear their hats upright who consult not the real success of their affairs, and that he was ill-befriended of reason if he imagined, whilst he had a brother, who, through the women's apartments, was seeking a way to the supremacy, and a father of so rash and fickle a humour, that he should by succession infallibly step up into the throne. For he that out of fondness to an Ionian girl has eluded a law sacred and inviolable among the Persians is not likely to be faithful in the performance of the most important promises. He added, too, that it was not all one for Ochus not to attain to, and for him to be put by his crown; since Ochus as a subject might live happily, and nobody could hinder him; but he, being proclaimed king, must either take up his sceptre or lay down his life.

These words presently inflamed Darius: what Sophocles says being indeed generally true:—

Quick travels the persuasion to what's wrong.

For the path is smooth, and upon an easy descent, that leads us to our own will; and the most part of us desire what is evil through our strangeness to and ignorance of good. And in this case, no doubt, the greatness of the empire and the jealousy Darius had of Ochus furnished Teribazus with material for his persuasions. Nor was Venus wholly unconcerned in the matter, in regard, namely, of his loss of Aspasia.

Darius, therefore, resigned himself up to the dictates of Teribazus; and many now conspiring with them, a eunuch gave information to the king of their scheme and the way it was to be managed, having discovered the certainty of it, that they had resolved to break into his bed-chamber by night, and there to kill him as he lay. After Artaxerxes had been thus advertised, he did not think fit, by disregarding the discovery, to despise so great a danger, nor to believe it when there was little or no proof of it. Thus then he did: he charged the eunuch constantly to attend and accompany the conspirators wherever they were; in the meanwhile, he broke down the party-wall of the chamber behind his bed, and placed a door in it to open and shut, which he covered up with tapestry; so the hour approaching, and the eunuch having told him the precise time in which the traitors designed to assassinate him, he waited for them in his bed, and rose not up till he had seen the faces of his assailants and recognised every man of them.

As soon as he saw them with their swords drawn and coming up to him, throwing up the hanging, he made his retreat into the inner chamber, and, bolting the door, raised a cry. Thus when the murderers had been seen by him, and had attempted him in vain, they with speed went back through the same doors they came in by; enjoining Teribazus and his friends to flee, as their plot had been certainly detected. They, therefore, made their escape different ways; but Teribazus was seized by the king's guards, and after slaying many, while they were laying hold on him, at length being struck through with a dart at a distance, fell.

As for Darius, who was brought to trial with his children, the king appointed the royal judges to sit over him, and because he was not himself present, but accused Darius by proxy, he commanded his scribes to write down the opinion of every one of the judges, and show it to him. And after they had given their sentences, all as one man, and condemned Darius to death, the officers seized on him, and hurried him to a chamber not far off. To which place the executioner, when summoned, came with a razor in his hand, with which men of his employment cut off the heads of offenders. But when he saw that Darius was the person thus to be punished he was appalled and started back, offering to go out, as one that had neither power nor courage enough to behead a king; yet at the threats and commands of the judges who stood at the prison door, he returned and grasping the hair of his head and bringing his face to the ground with one hand, he cut through his neck with the razor he had in the other.

Some affirm that sentence was passed in the presence of Artaxerxes; that Darius, after he had been convicted by clear evidence, falling prostrate before him, did humbly beg his pardon; that instead of giving it, he rising up in rage and drawing his scymetar, smote him till he had killed him; and then, going forth into the court, he worshipped the sun, and said, "Depart in peace, ye Persians, and declare to your fellow-subjects how the mighty Oromas-

des hath dealt out vengeance to the contrivers of unjust and unlawful things."

Such, then, was the issue of this conspiracy. And now Ochus was high in his hopes, being confident in the influence of Atossa; but yet was afraid of Ariaspes, the only male surviving, besides himself, of the legitimate offspring of his father, and of Arsames, one of his natural sons. For indeed Ariaspes was already claimed as their prince by the wishes of the Persians, not because he was the elder brother, but because he excelled Ochus in gentleness, plain dealing, and good-nature; and on the other hand Arsames appeared, by his wisdom, fitted for the throne, and that he was dear to his father Ochus well knew.

So he laid snares for them both, and being no less treacherous than bloody, he made use of the cruelty of his nature against Arsames, and of his craft and wiliness against Ariaspes. For he suborned the king's eunuchs and favourites to convey to him menacing and harsh expressions from his father, as though he had decreed to put him to a cruel and ignominious death. When they daily communicated these things as secrets, and told him at one time that the king would do so to him ere long, and at another, that the blow was actually close impending, they so alarmed the young man, struck such a terror into him, and cast such a confusion and anxiety upon his thoughts, that, having prepared some poisonous drugs, he drank them, that he might be delivered from his life.

The king, on hearing what kind of death he died, heartily lamented him, and was not without a suspicion of the cause of it. But being disabled by his age to search into and prove it, he was, after the loss of this son, more affectionate than before to Arsames, did manifestly place his greatest confidence in him, and made him privy to his counsels. Whereupon Ochus had no longer patience to defer the execution of his purpose, but having procured Arpates, Teribazus's son, for the undertaking, he killed Arsames by his hand. Artaxerxes at that time had but a little hold on life, by reason of his extreme age, and so, when he heard of the fate of Arsames, he could not sustain it at all, but sinking at once under the weight of his grief and distress, expired, after a life of ninety-four years, and a reign of sixty-two. And then he seemed a moderate and gracious governor, more especially as compared to his son Ochus, who outdid all his predecessors in blood-thirstiness and cruelty.

GALBA

5 B.C.?–A.D. 69

IPHICRATES the Athenian used to say that it is best to have a mercenary soldier fond of money and of pleasures, for thus he will fight the more boldly, to procure the means to gratify his desires. But most have been of opinion that the body of an army, as well as the natural one, when in its healthy condition, should make no efforts apart, but in compliance with its head. Wherefore they tell us that Paulus Æmilius, on taking command of the forces in Macedonia, and finding them talkative and impertinently busy, as though they were all commanders, issued out his orders that they should have only ready hands and keen swords, and leave the rest to him. And Plato, who can discern no use of a good ruler or general if his men are not on their part obedient and comfortable (the virtue of obeying, as of ruling, being, in his opinion, one that does not exist without first a noble nature, and then a philosophic education, where the eager and active powers are allayed with the gentler and humaner sentiments), may claim in confirmation of his doctrine sundry mournful instances elsewhere, and, in particular, the events that followed among the Romans upon the death of Nero, in which plain proofs were given that nothing is more terrible than a military force moving about in an empire upon uninstructed and unreasoning impulses.

Demuades, after the death of Alexander, compared the Macedonian army to the Cyclops after his eye was out, seeing their many disorderly and unsteady motions. But the calamities of the Roman government might be likened to the motions of the giants that assailed heaven, convulsed as it was, and distracted, and from every side recoiling, as it were, upon itself, not so much by the ambition of those who were proclaimed emperors, as by the covetousness and licence of the soldiery, who drove commander after commander out, like nails one upon another.

Dionysius, in raillery, said of the Pheræan who enjoyed the government of Thessaly only ten months, that he had been a tragedy-king, but the Cæsars' house in Rome, the Palatium, received in a shorter space of time no less than four emperors, passing, as it were, across the stage, and one making room for another to enter.

This was the only satisfaction of the distressed, that they need not require any other justice on their oppressors, seeing them thus murder each other, and first of all, and that most justly, the one that ensnared them first, and taught them to expect such happy results from a change of emperors, sullying a good word by the pay he gave for its being done and turning revolt against Nero into nothing better than treason.

For, as already related, Nymphidius Sabinus, captain of the guards, together with Tigellinus, after Nero's circumstances were now desperate, and it was perceived that he designed to flee into Egypt, persuaded the troops to declare Galba emperor, as if Nero had been already gone, promising to all the court and prætorian soldiers, as they are called, seven thousand five hundred drachmas apiece, and to those in service abroad twelve hundred and fifty drachmas each; so vast a sum for a largess as it was impossible any one could raise, but he must be infinitely more exacting and oppressive than ever Nero was. This quickly brought Nero to his grave, and soon after Galba, too; they murdered the first in expectation of the promised gift, and not long after the other because they did not obtain it from him; and then, seeking about to find some one who would purchase at such a rate, they consumed themselves in a succession of treacheries and rebellions before they obtained their demands. But to give a particular relation of all that passed would require a history in full form; I have only to notice what is properly to my purpose, namely what the Cæsars did and suffered.

Sulpicius Galba is owned by all to have been the richest private person that ever came to the imperial seat. And besides the additional honour of being of the Servii, he valued himself more especially for his relationship to Catulus, the most eminent citizen of his time both for virtue and renown, however he may have voluntarily yielded to others as regards power and authority. Galba was also akin to Livia, the wife of Augustus, by whose interest he was preferred to the consulship by the emperor. It is said of him that he commanded the troops well in Germany, and, being made proconsul in Libya, gained a reputation that few ever had. But his quiet manner of living and his sparingness in expenses and his disregard of appearances gave him, when he became emperor, an ill-name for meanness, being, in fact, his worn-out credit for regularity and moderation. He was entrusted by Nero with the government of Spain, before Nero had yet learned to be apprehensive of men of great repute. To the opinion, moreover, entertained of his mild natural temper, his old age added a belief that he would never act incautiously.

There while Nero's iniquitous agents savagely and cruelly harassed the provinces under Nero's authority, he could afford no succour, but merely offer this only ease and consolation, that he seemed plainly to sympathise, as a fellow-sufferer, with those who were condemned upon suits and sold. And when lampoons were made upon Nero and circulated and sung everywhere about, he neither prohibited them, nor showed any indignation on behalf of the emperor's agents, and for this was the more beloved; as also that he was now well acquainted with them, having been in chief power there eight years at the time when Junius Vindex, general of the forces in Gaul, began his insurrection against Nero. And it is reported that letters came to Galba before it fully broke out into an open rebellion, which he neither seemed to give credit to, nor on the other hand to take means to let Nero know as other officers did, sending to him the letters which came to them, and so spoiled the design, as much as in them lay, who yet afterwards shared in the conspiracy, and confessed they had been treacherous to themselves as well as him.

At last Vindex, plainly declaring war, wrote to Galba, encouraging him to take the government upon him, and give a head to this strong body, the Gaulish provinces, which could already count a hundred thousand men in arms, and were able to arm a yet greater number if necessary. Galba then laid the matter before his friends, some of whom thought it fit to wait, and see what movement there might be and what inclinations displayed at Rome for the revolution. But Titus Vinius, captain of his

prætorian guard, spoke thus: "Galba, what means this inquiry? To question whether we shall continue faithful to Nero is, in itself, to cease to be faithful. Nero is our enemy, and we must by no means decline the help of Vindex; or else we must at once denounce him, and march to attack him, because he wishes you to be the governor of the Romans, rather than Nero their tyrant."

Thereupon Galba, by an edict, appointed a day when he would receive manumissions, and general rumour and talk beforehand about his purpose brought together a great crowd of men so ready for a change, that he scarcely appeared, stepping up to the tribunal, but they with one consent saluted him emperor. That title he refused at present to take upon him; but after he had a while inveighed against Nero, and bemoaned the loss of the more conspicuous of those that had been destroyed by him, he offered himself and service to his country, not by the titles of Cæsar or emperor, but as the lieutenant of the Roman senate and people.

Now that Vindex did wisely in inviting Galba to the empire, Nero himself bore testimony; who, though he seemed to despise Vindex and altogether to slight the Gauls and their concerns, yet when he heard of Galba (as by chance he had just bathed and sat down to his morning meal), at this news he overturned the table. But the senate having voted Galba an enemy, presently, to make his jest, and likewise to personate a confidence among his friends, "This is a very happy opportunity," he said, "for me, who sadly want such a booty as that of the Gauls, which must all fall in as lawful prize; and Galba's estate I can use or sell at once, he being now an open enemy." And accordingly he had Galba's property exposed to sale, which when Galba heard of, he sequestered all that was Nero's in Spain, and found far readier bidders.

Many now began to revolt from Nero, and pretty nearly all adhered to Galba; only Clodius Macer in Africa, and Virginius Rufus, commander of the German forces in Gaul, followed counsel of their own; yet these two were not of one and the same advice, for Clodius, being sensible of the rapines and murders to which he had been led by cruelty and covetousness, was in perplexity, and felt it was not safe for him either to retain or quit his command. But Virginius, who had the command of the strongest legions, by whom he was many repeated times saluted emperor and pressed to take the title upon him, declared that he neither would assume that honour himself, nor see it given to any other than whom the senate should elect.

These things at first did not a little disturb Galba, but when presently Virginius and Vindex were in a manner forced by their armies, having got the reins, as it were, out of their hands, to a great encounter and battle, in which Vindex, having seen twenty thousand of the Gauls destroyed, died by his own hand, and when the report straight spread abroad that all desired Virginius, after this great victory, to take the empire upon him, or else they would return to Nero again, Galba, in great alarm at this, wrote to Virginius, exhorting him to join with him for the preservation of the empire and the liberty of the Romans, and so retiring with his friends into Clunia, a town in Spain, he passed away his time, rather repenting his former rashness, and wishing for his wonted ease and privacy, than setting about what was fit to be done.

It was now summer, when on a sudden, a little before dusk, comes a freedman, Icelus by name, having arrived in seven days from Rome; and being informed where Galba was reposing himself in private, he went straight on, and pushing by the servants of the chamber, opened the door and entered the room, and told him that Nero being yet alive but not appearing, first the army, and then the people and senate, declared Galba emperor; not long after, it was reported that Nero was dead; "but I," said he, "not giving credit to common fame, went myself to the body and saw him lying dead, and only then set out to bring you word." This news at once made Galba great again, and a crowd of people came hastening to the door, all very confident of the truth of his tidings, though the speed of the man was almost incredible. Two days after came Titus Vinius with sundry others from the camp, who gave an account in detail of the orders of the senate, and for this service was considerably advanced. On the freedman, Galba conferred the honour of the gold ring, and Icelus, as he had been before, now taking the name of Marcianus, held the first place of the freedmen.

But at Rome, Nymphidius Sabinus, not gently, and little by little, but at once, and without exception, engrossed all power to himself; Galba, being an old man (seventy-three years of age), would scarcely, he thought, live long enough to be carried in a litter to Rome; and the troops in the city were from old time attached to him, and now bound by the vastness of the promised gift, for which they regarded him as their benefactor, and Galba as their debtor. Thus presuming on his interest, he straightway commanded Tigellinus, who was in joint commission with himself, to lay down his sword; and giving entertainments, he invited the former consuls and commanders, making use of Galba's name for the invitation; but at the same time prepared many in the camp to propose that a request should be sent to Galba that he should appoint Nymphidius sole prefect for life without a colleague.

And the modes which the senate took to show him honour and increase his power, styling him their benefactor, and attending daily at his gates, and giving him the compliment of heading with his own name and confirming all their acts, carried him on to a yet greater degree of arrogance, so that in a short time he became an object, not only of dislike, but of terror, to those that sought his favour. When the consuls themselves had despatched their couriers with the decrees of the senate to the emperor, together with the sealed diplomas, which the authorities in all the towns where horses or carriages are changed look at, and on that certificate hasten the couriers forward with all their means, he was highly displeased that his seal had not been used, and none of his soldiers employed on the errand. Nay, he even deliberated what course to take with the consuls themselves, but upon their submission and apology he was at last pacified.

To gratify the people, he did not interfere with their beating to death any that fell into their hands of Nero's party. Amongst others, Spiclus, the gladiator, was killed in the Forum by being thrown under Nero's statues, which they dragged about the place over his body. Aponius, one of those who had been concerned in accusations, they knocked to the ground, and drove carts loaded with stones over him. And many others they tore in pieces, some of them no way guilty, insomuch that Mauriscus, a person of great account and character, told the senate that he feared, in a short time, they might wish for Nero again.

Nymphidius, now advancing towards the consummation of his hopes, did not refuse to let it be said that he was the son of Caius Cæsar, Tiberius's successor; who, it is told, was well acquainted with his mother in his early youth, a woman indeed handsome enough, the offspring of Callistus, one of Cæsar's freedmen, and a certain sempstress. But it is plain that Caius's familiarity with his mother was of too late date to give him any pretensions, and it was suspected he might, if he pleased, claim a father in Martianus, the gladiator, whom his mother, Nymphidia, took a passion for, being a famous man in his way, whom also he much more resembled. However, though he certainly owned Nymphidia for his mother, he ascribed meantime the downfall of Nero to himself alone, and thought he was not sufficiently rewarded with the honours and riches he enjoyed (nay, though to all was added the company of Sporus, whom he immediately sent for while Nero's body was yet burning on the pile, and treated as his consort with the name of Poppæa), but he must also aspire to the empire. And at Rome he had friends who took measures for him secretly, as well as some women and some members of the senate also, who worked underhand to assist him. And into Spain he despatched one of his friends, named Gellianus, to view the posture of affairs.

But all things succeeded well with Galba after Nero's death; only Virginius Rufus, still standing doubtful, gave him some anxiety, lest he should listen to the suggestions of some who encouraged him to take the government upon him, having, at present, besides the command of a large and warlike army, the new honours of the defeat of Vindex and the subjugation of one considerable part of the Roman empire, namely, the entire Gaul, which had seemed shaking about upon the verge of open revolt. Nor had any man indeed a greater name and reputation than Virginius, who had taken a part of so much consequence in the deliverance of the empire at once from a cruel tyranny and a Gallic war. But he, standing to his first resolves, reserved to the senate the power of electing an emperor.

Yet when it was now manifest that Nero was dead, the soldiers pressed him hard to it, and one of the tribunes, entering his tent with his drawn sword, bade him either take the government or that. But after Fabius Valens, having the command of one legion, had first sworn fealty to Galba, and letters from Rome came with tidings of the resolves of the senate, at last with much ado he persuaded the army to declare Galba emperor. And when Flaccus Hordeonius came by Galba's commission as his successor, he handed over to him his forces, and went himself to meet Galba on his way, and having met him turned back to attend him; in all which no apparent displeasure nor yet honour was shown him. Galba's feelings of respect for him prevented the former; the latter was checked by the envy of his friends, and particularly of Titus Vinius, who, acting in the desire of hindering Virginius's promotion, unwittingly aided his happy genius in rescuing him from those hazards and hardships which other commanders were involved in, and securing him the safe enjoyment of a quiet life and peaceable old age.

Near Narbo, a city in Gaul, the deputation of the senate met Galba, and after they had delivered their compliments, begged him to make what haste he could to appear to the people that impatiently expected him. He discoursed with them courteously and unassumingly, and in his entertainment, though Nymphidius had sent him royal furniture and attendance of Nero's, he put all aside, and made use of nothing but his own, for which he was well spoken of, as one who had a great mind, and was superior to little vanities. But in a short time, Vinius, by declaring to him that these noble, unpompous, citizen-like ways were a mere affectation of popularity and a petty bashfulness at assuming his proper greatness, induced him to make use of Nero's supplies, and in his entertainments not to be afraid of a regal sumptuosity. And in more than one way the old man let it gradually appear that he had put himself under Vinius's disposal.

Vinius was a person of an excessive covetousness, and not quite free from blame in respect to women. For being a young man, newly entered into the service under Calvisius Sabinus, upon his first campaign, he brought his commander's wife, a licentious woman, in a soldier's dress, by night into the camp, and was found with her in the very general's quarters, the *principia,* as the Romans call them. For which insolence Caius Cæsar cast him into prison, from whence he was fortunately delivered by Caius's death. Afterwards, being invited by Claudius Cæsar to supper, he privily conveyed away a silver cup, which Cæsar hearing of, invited him again the next day, and gave order to his servants to set before him no silver plate, but only earthenware. And this offence, through the comic mildness of Cæsar's reprimand, was treated rather as a subject of jest than as a crime. But the acts to which now, when Galba was in his hands and his power was so extensive, his covetous temper led him were the causes, in part, and in part the provocation, of tragical and fatal mischiefs.

Nymphidius became very uneasy upon the return out of Spain of Gellianus, whom he had sent to pry into Galba's actions, understanding that Cornelius Laco was appointed commander of the court guards, and that Vinius was the great favourite, and that Gellianus had not been able so much as to come nigh, much less have any opportunity to offer any words in private, so narrowly had he been watched and observed. Nymphidius, therefore, called together the officers of the troops, and declared to them that Galba of himself was a good, well-meaning old man, but did not act by his own counsel, and was ill-guided by Vinius and Laco; and lest, before they were aware, they should engross the authority Tigellinus had with the troops, he proposed to them to send deputies from the camp, acquainting him that if he pleased to remove only these two from his counsel and presence, he would be much more welcome to all at his arrival.

Wherein, when he saw he did not prevail (it seeming absurd and unmannerly to give rules to an old commander what friends to retain or displace, as if he had been a youth newly taking the reins of authority into his hands), adopting another course, he wrote himself to Galba letters in alarming terms, one time as if the city were unsettled, and had not yet recovered its tranquillity; then that Clodius Macer withheld the corn-ships from Africa; that the legions in Germany began to be mutinous, and that he heard the like of those in Syria and Judæa. But Galba not minding him much or giving credit to his stories, he resolved to make his attempt beforehand, though Clodius Celsus, a native of Antioch, a person of sense, and friendly and faithful to Nymphidius, told him he was wrong, saying he did not believe one single street in Rome would ever give him the title of Cæsar. Nevertheless many also derided Galba, amongst the rest Mithridates of Pontus, saying, that as soon as this wrinkled, baldheaded man should be seen publicly at Rome, they would think it an utter disgrace even to have had such a Cæsar.

At last it was resolved, about midnight, to bring Nymphidius into the camp, and declare him emperor. But Antonius Honoratus, who was first among the tribunes, summoning together in the evening those under his command, charged himself and them severely with their many and unreasonable turns and alterations, made without any purpose or regard to merit, simply as if some evil genius hurried them from one reason to another. "What though Nero's miscarriages," said he, "gave some colour to your former acts, can you say you have any plea for betraying Galba in the death of a mother, the blood of a wife, or the degradation of the imperial power upon the stage and amongst players? Neither did we desert Nero for all this, until Nymphidius had persuaded us that he had first left us and fled into Egypt. Shall we, therefore, send Galba after, to appease Nero's shade, and, for the sake of making the son of Nymphidia emperor, take off one of Livia's family, as we have already the son of Agrippina? Rather, doing justice on him, let us revenge Nero's death, and show ourselves true and faithful by preserving Galba."

The tribune having ended his harangue, the soldiers assented, and encouraged all they met with to persist in their fidelity to the emperor, and, indeed, brought over the greatest part. But presently hearing a great shout, Nymphidius, imagining, as some say, that the soldiers called for him, or hastening to be in time to check any opposition and gain the doubtful, came on with many lights, carrying in his hand a speech in writing, made by Cingonius Varro, which he had got by heart, to deliver to the soldiers. But seeing the gates of the camp shut up, and large numbers standing armed about the walls, he began to be afraid. Yet drawing nearer he demanded what they meant, and by whose orders they were then in arms; but hearing a general acclamation, all with one consent crying out that Galba was their emperor, advancing towards them, he joined in the cry, and likewise commanded those that followed him to do the same. The guard notwithstanding permitted him to enter the camp only with a few, where he was presently struck with a dart, which Septimius, being before him, received on his shield; others, however, assaulted him with their naked swords, and on his fleeing, pursued him into a soldier's cabin, where they slew him. And dragging his body thence, they placed a railing about it, and exposed it next day to public view.

When Galba heard of the end which Nymphidius had thus come to, he commanded that all his confederates who had not at once killed themselves should immediately be despatched; amongst whom were Cingonius, who made his oration, and Mithridates, formerly mentioned. It was, however, regarded as arbitrary and illegal, and though it might be just, yet by no means popular, to take off men of their rank and equality without a hearing. For every one expected another scheme of government, being deceived, as is usual, by the first plausible pretences; and the death of Petronius Turpilianus, who was of consular dignity, and had remained faithful to Nero, was yet more keenly resented. Indeed, the taking off of Macer in Africa by Trebonius, and Fonteius by Valens in Germany, had a fair pretence, they being dreaded as armed commanders, having their soldiers at their bidding; but why refuse Turpilianus, an old man and unarmed, permission to try to clear himself, if any part of the moderation and equity at first promised were really to come to a performance? Such were the comments to which these actions exposed Galba.

When he came within five-and-twenty furlongs or thereabouts of the city, he happened to light on a disorderly rabble of the seamen, who beset him as he passed. These were they whom Nero made soldiers, forming them into a legion. They so rudely crowded to have their commission confirmed that they did not let Galba either be seen or heard by those that had come out to meet their new emperor; but tumultuously pressed on with loud shouts to have colours to their legion, and quarters assigned them. Galba put them off until another time, which they interpreted as a denial, grew more insolent and mutinous, following and crying out, some with their drawn swords in their hands. Upon seeing which, Galba commanded the horse to ride over them, when they were soon routed, not a man standing his ground, and many of them were slain, both there and in the pursuit; an ill-omen, that Galba should make his first entry through so much blood and among dead bodies. And now he was looked upon with terror and alarm by any one who had entertained contempt of him at the sight of his age and apparent infirmities.

But when he desired presently to let it appear what a change would be made from Nero's profuseness and sumptuosity in giving presents, he much missed his aim, and fell so short of magnificence, that he scarcely came within the limits of decency. When Canus, who was a famous musician, played at supper for him, he expressed his approbation, and bade the bag be brought to him; and taking a few gold pieces, put them in with this remark, that it was out of his own purse, and not on the public account. He ordered the largesses which Nero had made to actors and wrestlers and such like to be strictly required again, allowing only the tenth part to be retained; though it turned to very small account, most of those persons expending their daily income as fast as they received it, being rude, improvident livers; upon which he had further inquiry made

as to those who had bought or received from them, and called upon these people to refund.

The trouble was infinite, the exactions being prosecuted far, touching a great number of persons, bringing disrepute on Galba and general hatred on Vinius, who made the emperor appear base-hearted and mean to the world, whilst he himself was spending profusely, taking whatever he could get, and selling to any buyer. Hesiod tells us to drink without stinting of—

The end and the beginning of the cask.
And Vinius, seeing his patron old and decaying, made the most of what he considered to be at once the first of his fortune and the last of it.

Thus the aged man suffered in two ways, first, through the evil deeds which Vinius did himself, and, next, by his preventing or bringing into disgrace those just acts which he himself designed. Such was the punishing of Nero's adherents. When he destroyed the bad, amongst whom were Helius, Polycletus, Petinus, and Patrobius, the peoples mightily applauded the act, crying out, as they were dragged through the Forum, that it was a goodly sight, grateful to the gods themselves, adding, however, that the gods and men alike demanded justice on Tigellinus, the very tutor and prompter of all the tyranny. This good man, however, had taken his measures beforehand, in the shape of a present and a promise to Vinius. Turpilianus could not be allowed to escape with life, though his one and only crime had been that he had not betrayed or shown hatred to such a ruler as Nero.

But he who had made Nero what he became, and afterwards deserted and betrayed him whom he had so corrupted, was allowed to survive as an instance that Vinius could do anything, and an advertisement that those that had money to give him need despair of nothing. The people, however, were so possessed with the desire of seeing Tigellinus dragged to execution that they never ceased to require it at the theatre and in the race-course, till they were checked by an edict from the emperor, himself, announcing that Tigellinus could not live long, being wasted with a consumption, and requesting them not to seek to make his government appear cruel and tyrannical. So the dissatisfied populace were laughed at, and Tigellinus made a splendid feast, and sacrificed in thanksgiving for his deliverance; and after supper, Vinius, rising from the emperor's table, went to revel with Tigellinus, taking his daughter, a widow, with him; to whom Tigellinus presented his compliments, with a gift of twenty-five myriads of money, and bade the superintendent of his concubines take off a rich necklace from her own neck and tie it about hers, the value of it being estimated at fifteen myriads.

After this, even reasonable acts were censured; as, for example, the treatment of the Gauls who had been in the conspiracy with Vindex. For people looked upon their abatement of tribute and admission of citizenship as a piece, not of clemency on the part of Galba, but of money-making on that of Vinius. And thus the mass of the people began to look with dislike upon the government. The soldiers were kept on a while in expectation of the promised donative, supposing that if they did not receive the full, yet they should have at least as much as Nero gave them. But when Galba, on hearing they began to complain, declared greatly, and like a general, that he was used to enlist and not to buy his soldiers,—when they heard of this, they conceived an implacable hatred against him; for he did not seem to defraud them merely himself in their present expectations, but to give an ill precedent, and instruct his successors to do the like.

This heart-burning, however, was as yet at Rome a thing undeclared, and a certain respect for Galba's personal presence somewhat retarded their motions, and took off their edge, and their having no obvious occasion for beginning a revolution curbed and kept under, more or less, their resentments. But those forces that had been formerly under Virginius, and now were under Flaccus in Germany, valuing themselves much upon the battle they had fought with Vindex, and finding now no advantage of it, grew very refractory and intractable towards their officers; and Flaccus they wholly disregarded, being incapacitated in body by unintermitted gout, and, besides, a man of little experience in affairs. So at one of their festivals, when it was customary for the officers of the army to wish all health and happiness to the emperor, the common soldiers began to murmur loudly, and on their officers persisting in the ceremony, responded with the words, "If he deserves it."

When some similar insolence was committed by the legions under Vitellius, frequent letters with the information came to Galba from his agents; and taking alarm at this, and fearing that he might be despised not only for his old age, but also for want of issue, he determined to adopt some young man of distinction, and declare him his successor.

There was at this time in the city Marcus Otho, a person of fair extraction, but from his childhood one of the few most debauched, voluptuous, and luxurious livers in Rome. And as Homer gives Paris in several places the title "of fair Helen's love," making a woman's name the glory and addition to his, as if he had nothing else to distinguish him, so Otho was renowned in Rome for nothing more than his marriage with Poppæa, whom Nero had a passion for when she was Crispinus's wife. But being as yet respectful to his own wife, and standing in awe of his mother, he engaged Otho underhand to solicit her. For Nero lived familiarly with Otho, whose prodigality won his favour, and he was well pleased when he took the freedom to jest upon him as mean and penurious. Thus when Nero one day perfumed himself with some rich essence and favoured Otho with a sprinkle of it, he, entertaining Nero next day, ordered gold and silver pipes to disperse the like on a sudden freely, like water, throughout the room.

As to Poppæa, he was beforehand with Nero, and first seducing her himself, then, with the hope of Nero's favour, he prevailed with her to part with her husband, and brought her to his own house as his wife, and was not content afterwards to have a share in her, but grudged to have Nero for a claimant, Poppæa herself, they say, being rather pleased than otherwise with this jealousy; she sometimes excluded Nero, even when Otho was not present, either to prevent his getting tired with her, or, as some say, not liking the prospect of an imperial marriage, though willing enough to have the emperor as her lover. So that Otho ran the risk of his life, and strange it was he escaped, when Nero, for this very marriage, killed his wife and sister. But he was beholden to Seneca's friendship, by whose persuasions and entreaty Nero was prevailed with to despatch him as prætor into Lusitania, on the shores of the Ocean; where he behaved himself very agreeably and indulgently to those he had to govern, well knowing this command was but to colour and disguise his banishment.

When Galba revolted from Nero, Otho was the first governor of any of the provinces that came over to him, bringing all the gold and silver he possessed in the shape of cups and tables, to be coined into money, and also what servants he had fitly qualified to wait upon a prince. In all other points, too, he was faithful to him, and gave him sufficient proof that he was inferior to none in managing public business. And he so far ingratiated himself that he rode in the same carriage with him during the whole journey, several days together. And in this journey and familiar companionship he won over Vinius also, both by his conversation and presents, but especially by conceding to him the first place, securing the second, by his interest, for himself. And he had the advantage of him in avoiding all odium and jealousy, assisting all petitioners, without asking for any reward, and appearing courteous and of easy access towards all, especially to the military men, for many of whom he obtained commands, some immediately from the emperor, others by Vinius's means, and by the assistance of the two favourite freedmen, Icelus and Asiaticus, these being the men in chief power in the court. As often as he entertained Galba, Otho gave the cohort on duty, in addition to their pay, a piece of gold for every man there, upon pretence of respect to the emperor, while really he undermined him, and stole away his popularity with the soldiers.

So Galba consulting about a successor, Vinius introduced Otho, yet not even this gratis, but upon promise that he would marry his daughter if Galba should make him his adopted son and successor to the empire. But Galba, in all his actions, showed clearly that he preferred the public good before his own private interest, not aiming so much to pleasure himself as to advantage the Romans by his selection. Indeed he does not seem to have been so much as inclined to make choice of Otho had it been but to inherit his own private fortune, knowing his extravagant and luxurious character, and that he was already plunged in debt five thousand myriads deep. So he listened to Vinius, and made no reply, but mildly suspended his determination. Only he appointed himself consul, and Vinius his colleague, and it was the general expectation that he would declare his successor at the beginning of the new year. And the soldiers desired nothing more than that Otho should be the person.

But the forces in Germany broke out into their mutiny whilst he was yet deliberating, and anticipated his design. All the soldiers in general felt much resentment against Galba for not having given them their expected largess, but these troops made a pretence of a more particular concern, that Virginius Rufus was cast off dishonourably, and that the Gauls who had fought with them were well rewarded, while those who had refused to take part with Vindex were punished; and Galba's thanks seemed all to be for him, to whose memory he had done honour after his death with public solemnities as though he had been made emperor by his means only. Whilst these discourses passed openly throughout the army, on the first day of the first month of the year, the calends, as they call it, of January, Flaccus summoning them to take the usual anniversary oath of fealty to the emperor, they overturned and pulled down Galba's statues, and having sworn in the name of the senate and people of Rome, departed.

But the officers now feared anarchy and confusion, as much as rebellion; and one of them came forward and said: "What will become of us, my fellow-soldiers, if we neither set up another general, nor retain the present one? This will be not so much to desert from Galba as to decline all subjection and command. It is useless to try and maintain Flaccus Hordeonius, who is but a mere shadow and image of Galba. But Vitellius, commander of the other Germany, is but one day's march distant, whose father was censor and thrice consul, and in a manner co-emperor with Claudius Cæsar; and he himself has the best proof to show of his bounty and largeness of mind, in the poverty with which some reproach him. Him let us make choice of, that all may see we know how to choose an emperor better than either Spaniards or Lusitanians."

Which motion whilst some assented to, and others gainsaid, a certain standard-bearer slipped out and carried the news to Vitellius, who was entertaining much company by night. This, taking air, soon passed through the troops, and Fabius Valens, who commanded one legion, riding up next day with a large body of horse, saluted Vitellius emperor. He had hitherto seemed to decline it, professing a dread he had to undertake the weight of the government; but on this day, being fortified, they say, by wine and a plentiful noon-day repast, he began to yield, and submitted to take on him the title of Germanicus they gave him, but desired to be excused as to that of Cæsar. And immediately the army under Flaccus also, putting away their fine and popular oaths in the name of the senate, swore obedience to Vitellius as emperor, to observe whatever he commanded.

Thus Vitellius was publicly proclaimed emperor in Germany; which news coming to Galba's ear, he no longer deferred his adoption; yet knowing that some of his friends were using their interest for Dolabella, and the greatest number of them for Otho, neither of whom he approved of, on a sudden, without any one's privity, he sent for Piso, the son of Crassus and Scribonia, whom Nero slew, a young man in general of excellent disposition for virtue, but his most eminent qualities those of steadiness and austere gravity. And so he set out to go to the camp to declare him Cæsar and successor to the empire.

But at his very first going forth many signs appeared in the heavens, and when he began to make a speech to the soldiers, partly extempore, and partly reading it, the frequent claps of thunder and flashes of lightning, and the violent storm of rain that burst on both the camp and the city, were plain discoveries that the divine powers did not look with favour or satisfaction on this act of adoption that would come to no good result. The soldiers, also, showed symptoms of hidden discontent, and wore sullen looks, no distribution of money being even now made to them. However, those that were present and observed Piso's countenance and voice could not but feel admiration to see him so little overcome by so great a favour, of the magnitude of which at the same time he seemed not at all insensible. Otho's aspect, on the other hand, did not fail to let many marks appear of his bitterness and anger at his disappointment; since to have been the first man thought of for it, and to have come to the very point of being chosen, and now to be put by, was in his feelings a sign of the displeasure and ill-will of Galba towards him.

This filled him with fears and apprehensions, and sent him home with a mind full of various passions, whilst he dreaded Piso, hated Galba, and was full of wrath and indignation against Vinius. And the Chaldeans and soothsayers about him would not permit him to lay aside his hopes or quit his design, chiefly Ptolemæus, insisting much on a prediction he had made, that Nero should not murder Otho, but he himself should die first, and Otho succeed as emperor; for the first proving true, he thought he could not distrust the rest. But none perhaps stimulated him more than those that professed privately to pity his hard fate and compassionate him for being thus ungratefully dealt with by Galba; especially Nymphidius's and Tigellinus's creatures, who, being now cast off and reduced to low estate, were eager to put themselves upon him, exclaiming at the indignity he had suffered, and provoking him to revenge himself.

Amongst these were Veturius and Barbius, the one an *optio,* the other a *tesserarius* (these are men who have the duties of messengers and scouts), with whom Onomastus, one of Otho's freedmen, went to the camp to tamper with the army, and brought over some with money, others with fair promises, which was no hard matter, they being already corrupted, and only wanting a fair pretence. It had been otherwise more than the work of four days (which elapsed between the adoption and murder), so completely to infect them as to cause a general revolt. On the sixth day ensuing, the eighteenth, as the Romans call it, before the calends of February, the murder was done. On that day, in the morning, Galba sacrificed in the Palatium in the presence of his friends, when Umbricius, the priest, taking up the entrails, and speaking not ambiguously, but in plain words, said that there were signs of great troubles ensuing, and dangerous snares laid for the life of the emperor.

Thus Otho had even been discovered by the finger of the god, being there just behind Galba, hearing all that was said, and seeing what was pointed out to them by Umbricius. His countenance changed to every colour in his fear, and he was betraying no small discomposure, when Onomastus, his freedman, came up and acquainted him that the master builders had come, and were waiting for him at home. Now that was the signal for Otho to meet the soldiers. Pretending then that he had purchased an old house, and was going to show the defects to those that had sold it to him, he departed; and passing through what is called Tiberius's house, he went on into the Forum, near the spot where a golden pillar stands, at which all the several roads through Italy terminate.

Here, it is related, no more than twenty-three received and saluted him emperor; so that, although he was not in mind as in body enervated with soft living and effeminacy, being in his nature bold and fearless enough in danger, nevertheless, he was afraid to go on. But the soldiers that were present would not suffer him to recede, but came with their swords drawn around his chair, commanding the bearers to take him up, whom he hastened on, saying several times over to himself, "I am a lost man." Several persons overheard the words, who stood by wondering, rather than alarmed, because of the small number that attempted such an enterprise. But as they marched on through the Forum, about as many more met him, and here and there three or four at a time joined in. Thus returning towards the camp, with their bare swords in their hands, they saluted him as Cæsar; whereupon Martial-ias, the tribune in charge of the watch, who was, they say, noways privy to it, but was simply surprised at the unexpectedness of the thing, and afraid to refuse, permitted him entrance. And after this, no man made any resistance; for they that knew nothing of the design, being purposely encompassed by the conspirators as they were straggling here and there, first submitted for fear, and afterwards were persuaded into compliance.

Tidings came immediately to Galba in the Palatium, whilst the priests were still present and the sacrifices at hand, so that persons who were most entirely incredulous about such things, and most positive in their neglect of them, were astonished, and began to marvel at the divine event. A multitude of all sorts of people now began to run together out of the Forum; Vinius and Laco and some of Galba's freedmen drew their swords and placed themselves beside him; Piso went forth and addressed himself to the guards on duty in the court; and Marius Celsus, a brave man, was despatched to the Illyrian legion, stationed in what is called the Vipsanian chamber, to secure them.

Galba now consulting whether he should go out, Vinius dissuaded him, but Celsus and Laco encouraged him by all means to do so, and sharply reprimanded Vinius. But on a sudden a rumour came hot that Otho was slain in the camp; and presently appeared one Julius Atticus, a man of some distinction in the guards, running up with his drawn sword, crying out that he had slain Cæsar's enemy; and pressing through the crowd that stood in his way, he presented himself before Galba with his bloody weapon, who, looking on him, demanded, "Who gave you your orders?" And on his answering that it had been his duty and the obligation of the oath he had taken, the people applauded, giving loud acclamations, and Galba got into his chair and was carried out to sacrifice to Jupiter, and so to show himself publicly. But coming into the Forum, there met him there, like a turn of wind, the opposite story, that Otho had made himself master of the camp. And as usual in a crowd of such a size, some called to him to return back, others to move forwards; some encouraged him to be bold and fear nothing, others bade him to be cautious and distrust. And thus whilst his chair was tossed to and fro, as it were on the waves, often tottering, there appeared first horse, and straightway heavy-armed foot, coming through Paulus's court, and all with one accord crying out, "Down with this private man."

Upon this, the crowd of people set off running, not to flee and disperse, but to possess themselves of the colonnades and elevated places of the Forum, as it might be to get places to see a spectacle. And as soon as Atillius Vergilio knocked down one of Galba's statues, this was taken as the declaration of war, and they sent a discharge of darts upon Galba's litter, and missing their aim, came up and attacked him nearer at hand with their naked swords. No man resisted or offered to stand up in his defence, save one only, a centurion, Sempronius Densus, the single man among so many thousands that the sun beheld that day act worthily of the Roman empire, who, though he had never received any favour from Galba, yet out of bravery and allegiance endeavoured to defend the litter. First, lifting up his switch of vine, with which the centurions correct the soldiers when disorderly, he called aloud to the aggressors, charging them not to touch their emperor. And when they came upon him hand-to-hand, he drew his sword, and made a defence for a long time, until at last he was cut under the knees and brought to the ground.

Galba's chair was upset at the spot called the Lacus Curtius, where they ran up and struck at him as he lay in his corselet. He, however, offered his throat, bidding them, "Strike, if it be for the Romans' good." He received several wounds on his legs and arms, and at last was struck in the throat, as most say, by one Camurius, a soldier of the fifteenth legion. Some name Terentius, others Lecanius; and there are others that say it was Fabius Fabulus, who it is reported cut off the head and carried it away in the skirt of his coat, the baldness making it a difficult thing to take hold of. But those that were with him would not allow him to keep it covered up, but bade him let every one see the brave deed he had done; so that after a while he stuck upon the lance the head of the aged man that had been their grave and temperate ruler, their supreme priest and consul, and, tossing it up in the air, ran like a bacchanal, twirling and flourishing with it, while the blood ran down the spear.

But when they brought the head to Otho, "Fellow-soldiers," he cried out, "this is nothing, unless you show me Piso's too," which was presented him not long after. The young man, retreating upon a wound received, was pursued by one Murcus, and slain at the temple of Vesta. Titus Vinius was also despatched, avowing himself to have been privy to the conspiracy against Galba by calling out that they were killing him contrary to Otho's pleasure. However, they cut off his head, and Laco's too, and brought them to Otho, requesting a boon.

And as Archilochus says—

When six or seven lie breathless on the ground,
'Twas I, 'twas I, say thousands, gave the wound.

Thus many that had no share in the murder wetted their hands and swords in blood, and came and showed them to Otho, presenting memorials suing for a gratuity. Not less than one hundred and twenty were identified afterwards from their written petitions; all of whom Vitellius sought out and put to death. There came also into the camp Marius Celsus, and was accused by many voices of encouraging the soldiers to assist Galba, and was demanded to death by the multitude. Otho had no desire for this, yet, fearing an absolute denial, he professed that he did not wish to take him off so soon, having many matters yet to learn from him; and so committed him safe to the custody of those he most confided in.

Forthwith a senate was convened, and as if they were not the same men, or had other gods to swear by, they took that oath in Otho's name which he himself had taken in Galba's and had broken; and withal conferred on him the titles of Cæsar and Augustus; whilst the dead carcasses of the slain lay yet in their consular robes in the market-place. As for their heads, when they could make no other use of them, Vinius's they sold to his daughter for two thousand five hundred drachmas; Piso's was begged by his wife, Verania; Galba's they gave to Patrobius's servants; who when they had it, after all sorts of abuse and indignities, tumbled it into the place where those that suffer death by the emperor's orders are usually cast, called Sessorium. Galba's body was conveyed away by Priscus Helvidius by Otho's permission, and buried in the night by Argius, his freedman.

Thus you have the history of Galba, a person inferior to few Romans, either for birth or riches, rather exceeding all of his time in both, having lived in great honour and reputation in the reigns of five emperors, insomuch that he overthrew Nero rather by his fame and repute in the world than by actual force and power. Of all the others that joined in Nero's deposition, some were by general consent regarded as unworthy, others had only themselves to vote them deserving of the empire. To him the title was offered, and by him it was accepted; and simply lending his name to Vindex's attempt, he gave to what had been called rebellion before, the name of a civil war, by the presence of one that was accounted fit to govern.

And therefore, as he considered that he had not so much sought the position as the position had sought him, he proposed to command those whom Nymphidius and Tigellinus had wheedled into obedience no otherwise than Scipio formerly and Fabricius and Camillus had commanded the Romans of their times. But being now overcome with age, he was indeed among the troops and legions an upright ruler upon the antique model; but for the rest, giving himself up to Vinius, Laco, and his freedmen, who make their gain of all things, no otherwise than Nero had done to his insatiate favourites, he left none behind him to wish him still in power, though many to compassionate his death.

OTHO

A.D. 32–69

THE new emperor went early in the morning to the capitol, and sacrificed; and, having commanded Marius Celsus to be brought, he saluted him, and with obliging language desired him rather to forget his accusation than remember his acquittal; to which Celsus answered neither meanly nor ungratefully, that his very crime ought to recommend his integrity, since his guilt had been his fidelity to Galba, from whom he had never received any personal obligations. Upon which they were both of them admired by those that were present, and applauded by the soldiers.

In the senate, Otho said much in a gentle

and popular strain. He was to have been consul for part of that year himself, but he gave the office to Virginius Rufus, and displaced none that had been named for the consulship by either Nero or Galba. Those that were remarkable for their age and dignity he promoted to the priesthoods; and restored the remains of their fortunes, that had not yet been sold, to all those senators that were banished by Nero, and recalled by Galba. So that the nobility and chief of the people, who were at first apprehensive that no human creature, but some supernatural, or penal vindictive power had seized the empire, began now to flatter themselves with hopes of a government that smiled upon them thus early.

Besides, nothing gratified or gained the whole Roman people more than his justice in relation to Tigellinus. It was not seen how he was in fact already suffering punishment, not only by the very terror of retribution which he saw the whole city requiring as a just debt, but with several incurable diseases also; not to mention those unhallowed frightful excesses among impure and prostitute women, to which, at the very close of life, his lewd nature clung, and in them gasped out, as it were, its last; these, in the opinion of all reasonable men, being themselves the extremest punishment, and equal to many deaths. But it was felt like a grievance by people in general that he continued yet to see the light of day, who had been the occasion of the loss of it to so many persons, and such persons, as had died by his means. Wherefore Otho ordered him to be sent for, just as he was contriving his escape by means of some vessels that lay ready for him on the coast near where he lived, in the neighbourhood of Sinuessa. At first he endeavoured to corrupt the messenger, by a large sum of money, to favour his design; but when he found this was to no purpose, he made him as considerable a present as if he had really connived at it, only entreating him to stay till he had shaved; and so took that opportunity, and with his razor despatched himself.

And while giving the people this most righteous satisfaction of their desires, for himself he seemed to have no sort of regard for any private injuries of his own. And at first, to please the populace, he did not refuse to be called Nero in the theatre, and did not interfere when some persons displayed Nero's statues to public view. And Cluvius Rufus says, imperial letters, such as are sent with couriers, went into Spain with the name of Nero affixed

adoptively to that of Otho; but as soon as he perceived this gave offence to the chief and most distinguished citizens, it was omitted.

After he had begun to model the government in this manner, the paid soldiers began to murmur, and endeavoured to make him suspect and chastise the nobility, either really out of a concern for his safety, or wishing, upon this pretence, to stir up trouble and warfare. Thus, whilst Crispinus, whom he had ordered to bring him the seventeenth cohort from Ostia, began to collect what he wanted after it was dark, and was putting the arms upon the waggons, some of the most turbulent cried out that Crispinus was disaffected, that the senate was practising something against the emperor, and that those arms were to be employed against Cæsar, and not for him. When this report was once set afoot, it got the belief and excited the passions of many; they broke out into violence; some seized the waggons, and others slew Crispinus and two centurions that opposed them; and the whole number of them, arraying themselves in their arms, and encouraging one another to stand by Cæsar, marched to Rome. And hearing there that eighty of the senators were at supper with Otho, they flew into the palace, and declared it was a fair opportunity to take off Cæsar's enemies at one stroke.

A general alarm ensued of an immediate coming sack of the city. All were in confusion about the palace, and Otho himself in no small consternation, being not only concerned for the senators (some of whom had brought their wives to supper thither), but also feeling himself to be an object of alarm and suspicion to them, whose eyes he saw fixed on him in silence and terror. Therefore he gave orders to the prefects to address the soldiers and do their best to pacify them, while he bade the guests rise, and leave by another door. They had only just made their way out, when the soldiers rushed into the room, and called out, "Where are Cæsar's enemies?"

Then Otho, standing up on his couch, made use both of arguments and entreaties, and by actual tears at last, with great difficulty, persuaded them to desist. The next day he went to the camp, and distributed a bounty of twelve hundred and fifty drachmas a man amongst them; then commended them for the regard and zeal they had for his safety, but told them that there were some who were intriguing among them, who not only accused his own clemency, but had also misrepresented their loyalty; and, therefore, he desired their assistance in doing justice upon them. To which, when they all consented, he was satisfied with the execution of two only, whose deaths he knew would be regretted by no one man in the whole army.

Such conduct, so little expected from him, was regarded by some with gratitude and confidence; others looked upon his behaviour as a course to which necessity drove him, to gain the people to the support of the war. For now there were certain tidings that Vitellius had assumed the sovereign title and authority, and frequent expresses brought accounts of new accessions to him; others, however, came, announcing that the Pannonian, Dalmatian, and Mœsian legions, with their officers, adhered to Otho. Ere long also came favourable letters from Mucianus and Vespasian, generals of two formidable armies, the one in Syria, the other in Judæa, to assure him of their firmness to his interest: in confidence whereof he was so exalted, that he wrote to Vitellius not to attempt anything beyond his post; and offered him large sums of money and a city, where he might live his time out in pleasure and ease.

These overtures at first were responded to by Vitellius with equivocating civilities; which soon, however, turned into an interchange of angry words; and letters passed between the two, conveying bitter and shameful terms of reproach, which were not false indeed, for that matter, only it was senseless and ridiculous for each to assail the other with accusations to which both alike must plead guilty. For it were hard to determine which of the two had been most profuse, most effeminate, which was most a novice in military affairs, and most involved in debt through previous want of means.

As to the prodigies and apparitions that happened about this time, there were many reported which none could answer for, or which were told in different ways; but one which everybody actually saw with their eyes, was the statue, in the capitol, of Victory carried in a chariot, with the reins dropped out of her hands, as if she were grown too weak to hold them any longer; and a second, that Caius Cæsar's statue in the island of Tiber, without any earthquake or wind to account for it, turned round from west to east; and this, they say, happened about the time when Vespasian and his party first openly began to put themselves forward. Another incident, which the people in general thought an evil sign, was the inundation of the Tiber; for though it happened at a time when rivers are usually at their fullest, yet such height of water and so tremendous a flood had never been known before, nor such a destruction of property, great part of the city being under water, and especially the corn market, so that it occasioned a great dearth for several days.

But when news was now brought that Cæcina and Valens, commanding for Vitellius, had possessed themselves of the Alps, Otho sent Dolabella (a patrician, who was suspected by the soldiery of some evil purpose), for whatever reason, whether it were fear of him or of any one else, to the town of Aquinum, to give encouragement there; and proceeding then to choose which of the magistrates should go with him to the war, he named amongst the rest Lucius, Vitellius's brother, without distinguishing him by any new marks either of his favour or displeasure. He also took the greatest precautions for Vitellius's wife and mother, that they might be safe, and free from all apprehension for themselves. He made Flavius Sabinus, Vespasian's brother, governor of Rome, either in honour to the memory of Nero, who had advanced him formerly to that command, which Galba had taken away, or else to show his confidence in Vespasian by his favour to his brother.

After he came to Brixillum, a town of Italy near the Po, he stayed behind himself, and ordered the army to march under the conduct of Marius Celsus, Suetonius Paulinus, Gallus, and Spurina, all men of experience and reputation, but unable to carry their own plans and purposes into effect, by reason of the ungovernable temper of the army, which would take orders from none but the emperor whom they themselves had made their master. Nor was the enemy under much better discipline, the soldiers there also being haughty and disobedient upon the same account, but they were more experienced and used to hard work; whereas Otho's men were soft from their long easy living and lack of service, having spent most of their time in the theatres and at state shows and on the stage; while moreover they tried to cover their deficiencies by arrogance and vain display, pretending to decline their duty, not because they were unable to do the thing commanded, but because they thought themselves above it. So that Spurina had like to have been cut in pieces for attempting to force them to their work; they assailed him with insolent language, accusing him of a design to betray and ruin Cæsar's interest; nay, some of them that were in drink forced his tent in the night, and demanded money for the expenses of their journey, which they must at once take, they said, to the emperor, to complain of him.

However, the contemptuous treatment they met with at Placentia did for the present good service to Spurina, and to the cause of Otho. For Vitellius's men marched up to the walls, and upbraided Otho's upon the ramparts, calling them players, dancers, idle spectators of Pythian and Olympic games, but novices in the art of war, who never so much as looked on at a battle; mean souls, that triumphed in the beheading of Galba, an old man unarmed, but had no desire to look real enemies in the face. Which reproaches so inflamed them that they kneeled at Spurina's feet, entreated him to give his orders, and assured him no danger or toil should be too great or too difficult for them. Whereupon when Vitellius's forces made a vigorous attack on the town, and brought up numerous engines against the walls, the besieged bravely repulsed them, and, repelling the enemy with great slaughter, secured the safety of a noble city, one of the most flourishing places in Italy.

Besides, it was observed that Otho's officers were much more inoffensive, both towards the public and to private men, than those of Vitellius; among whom was Cæcina, who used neither the language nor the apparel of a citizen, an overbearing, foreign-seeming man, of gigantic stature, and always dressed in trews and sleeves, after the manner of the Gauls, whilst he conversed with Roman officials and magistrates. His wife, too, travelled along with him, riding in splendid attire on horseback, with a chosen body of cavalry to escort her. And Fabius Valens, the other general, was so rapacious that neither what he plundered from enemies, nor what he stole or got as gifts and bribes from his friends and allies, could satisfy his wishes. And it was said that it was in order to have time to raise money that he had marched so slowly that he was not present at the former attack. But some lay the blame on Cæcina, saying, that out of a desire to gain the victory by himself before Fabius joined him, he committed sundry other errors of lesser consequence, and by engaging unseasonably and when he could not do so thoroughly, he very nearly brought all to ruin.

When he found himself beat off at Placentia, he set off to attack Cremona, another large and rich city. In the meantime, Annius Gallus marched to join Spurina at Placentia; but having intelligence that the siege was raised, and that Cremona was in danger, he turned to its relief, and encamped just by the enemy, where he was daily reinforced by other officers. Cæcina placed a strong ambush of heavy infantry in some rough and woody country, and gave orders to his horse to advance, and if the enemy should charge them, then to make a slow retreat, and draw them into the snare. But his stratagem was discovered by some deserters to Celsus, who attacked with a good body of horse, but followed the pursuit cautiously, and succeeded in surrounding and routing the troops in the ambuscade; and if the infantry which he ordered up from the camp had come soon enough to sustain the horse, Cæcina's whole army, in all appearance, had been totally routed.

But Paulinus, moving too slowly, was accused of acting with a degree of needless caution not to have been expected from one of his reputation. So that the soldiers incensed Otho against him, accused him of treachery, and boasted loudly that the victory had been in their power, and that if it was not complete, it was owing to the mismanagement of their generals; all which Otho did not so much believe as he was willing to appear not to disbelieve. He therefore sent his brother Titianus, with Proculus, the prefect of the guards, to the army, where the latter was general in reality, and the former in appearance. Celsus and Paulinus had the title of friends and counsellors, but not the least authority or power. At the same time, there was nothing but quarrel and disturbance amongst the enemy, especially where Valens commanded; for the soldiers here, being informed of what had happened at the ambuscade, were enraged because they had not been permitted to be present to strike a blow in defence of the lives of so many men that had died in that action; Valens, with much difficulty, quieted their fury, after they had now begun to throw missiles at him, and quitting his camp, joined Cæcina.

About this time, Otho came to Bedriacum, a little town near Cremona, to the camp, and called a council of war; where Proculus and Titianus declared for giving battle, while the soldiers were flushed with their late success, saying they ought not to lose their time and opportunity and present height of strength, and wait for Vitellius to arrive out of Gaul. But Paulinus told them that the enemy's whole force was present, and that there was no body of reserve behind; but that Otho, if he would not be too precipitate, and chose the enemy's time, instead of his own, for the battle, might expect reinforcements out of Mœsia and Pannonia, not inferior in numbers to the troops that were already present. He thought it probable, too, that the soldiers, who were then in heart before they were joined, would not be less so when the forces were all come up. Besides, the deferring battle could not be inconvenient to them that were sufficiently provided with all necessaries; but the others, being in an enemy's country, must needs be exceedingly straitened in a little time. Marius Celsus was of Paulinus's opinion; Annius Gallus, being absent and under the surgeon's hands through a fall from his horse, was consulted by letter, and advised Otho to stay for those legions that were marching from Mœsia. But after all he did not follow the advice; and the opinion of those that declared for a battle prevailed.

There are several reasons given for this determination, but the most apparent is this; that the prætorian soldiers, as they are called, who serve as guards, not relishing the military discipline which they now had begun a little more to experience, and longing for their amusements and unwarlike life among the shows of Rome, would not be commanded, but were eager for a battle, imagining that upon the first onset they should carry all before them. Otho also himself seems not to have shown the proper fortitude in bearing up against the uncertainty, and, out of effeminacy and want of use, had not patience for the calculations of danger, and was so uneasy at the apprehension of it that he shut his eyes, and like one going to leap from a precipice, left everything to fortune.

This is the account Secundus the rhetorician, who was his secretary, gave of the matter. But others would tell you that there were many movements in both armies for acting in concert; and if it were possible for them to agree, then they should proceed to choose one of their most experienced officers that were present; if not, they should convene the senate, and invest it with the power of election. And it is not improbable that, neither of the emperors then bearing the title having really any reputation, such purposes were really entertained among the genuine, serviceable, and sober-minded part of the soldiers. For what could be more odious and unreasonable than that the evils which the Roman citizens had formerly thought it so lamentable to inflict upon each other for the sake of a Sulla or a Marius, a Cæ-

sar or a Pompey, should now be undergone anew, for the object of letting the empire pay the expenses of the gluttony and intemperance of Vitellius, or the looseness and effeminacy of Otho? It is thought that Celsus, upon such reflections, protracted the time in order to effect a possible accommodation; and that Otho pushed on things to an extremity to prevent it.

He himself returned to Brixillum, which was another false step, both because he withdrew from the combatants all the motives of respect and desire to gain his favour which his presence would have supplied, and because he weakened the army by detaching some of his best and most faithful troops for his horse and foot guards.

About the same time also happened a skirmish on the Po. As Cæcina was laying a bridge over it, Otho's men attacked him, and tried to prevent it. And when they did not succeed, on their putting into their boats torchwood, with a quantity of sulphur and pitch, the wind on the river suddenly caught their material that they had prepared against the enemy, and blew it into a light. First came smoke, and then a clear flame, and the men, getting into great confusion and jumping overboard, upset the boats, and put themselves ludicrously at the mercy of their enemies. Also the Germans attacked Otho's gladiators upon a small island in the river, routed them, and killed a good many.

All which made the soldiers at Bedriacum full of anger, and eagerness to be led to battle. So Proculus led them out of Bedriacum to a place fifty furlongs off, where he pitched his camp so ignorantly and with such a ridiculous want of foresight that the soldiers suffered extremely for want of water, though it was the spring time, and the plains all around were full of running streams and rivers that never dried up. The next day he proposed to attack the enemy, first making a march of not less than a hundred furlongs; but to this Paulinus objected, saying they ought to wait, and not immediately after a journey engage men who would have been standing in their arms and arranging themselves for battle at their leisure, whilst they were making a long march, with all their beasts of burden and their camp followers to encumber them. As the generals were arguing about this matter, a Numidian courier came from Otho with orders to lose no time, but give battle. Accordingly they consented, and moved. As soon as Cæcina had notice, he was much surprised, and quitted his post on the river to hasten to the camp. In the meantime, the men had armed themselves mostly, and were receiving the word from Valens; so while the legions took up their position, they sent out the best of their horse in advance.

Otho's foremost troops, upon some groundless rumour, took up the notion that the commanders on the other side would come over; and accordingly, upon their first approach, they saluted them with the friendly title of fellow-soldiers. But the others returned the compliment with anger and disdainful words; which not only disheartened those that had given the salutation, but excited suspicions of their fidelity amongst the others on their side, who had not. This caused a confusion at the very first onset. And nothing else that followed was done upon any plan; the baggage-carriers, mingling up with the fighting men, created great disorder and division; as well as the nature of the ground, the ditches and pits in which were so many that they were forced to break their ranks to avoid and go round them, and so to fight without order, and in small parties.

There were but two legions, one of Vitellius's, called The Ravenous, and another of Otho's, called The Assistant, that got out into the open out-spread level and engaged in proper form, fighting, one main body against the other, for some length of time. Otho's men were strong and bold, but had never been in battle before; Vitellius's had seen many wars, but were old and past their strength. So Otho's legion charged boldly, drove back their opponents, and took the eagle, killing pretty nearly every man in the first rank, till the others, full of rage and shame, returned the charge, slew Orfidius, the commander of the legion, and took several standards. Varus Alfenus, with his Batavians, who are the natives of an island of the Rhine, and are esteemed the best of the German horse, fell upon the gladiators, who had a reputation both for valour and skill in fighting. Some few of these did their duty, but the greatest part of them made towards the river, and, falling in with some cohorts stationed there, were cut off. But none behaved so ill as the prætorians, who, without ever so much as meeting the enemy, ran away, broke through their own body that stood, and put them into disorder. Notwithstanding this, many of Otho's men routed those that were opposed to them, broke right into them, and forced their way to the camp through the very middle of their conquerors.

As for their commanders, neither Proculus nor Paulinus ventured to re-enter with the troops; they turned aside, and avoided the soldiers, who had already charged the miscarriage upon their officers. Annius Gallus received into the town and rallied the scattered parties, and encouraged them with an assurance that the battle was a drawn one and the victory had in many parts been theirs. Marius Celsus, collecting the officers, urged the public interest; Otho himself, if he were a brave man, would not, after such an expense of Roman blood, attempt anything further; especially since even Cato and Scipio, though the liberty of Rome was then at stake, had been accused of being too prodigal of so many brave men's lives as were lost in Africa, rather than submit to Cæsar after the battle of Pharsalia had gone against them. For though all persons are equally subject to the caprice of fortune, yet all good men have one advantage she cannot deny, which is this, to act reasonably under misfortunes.

This language was well accepted amongst the officers, who sounded the private soldiers, and found them desirous of peace; and Titianus also gave directions that envoys be sent in order to make a treaty. And accordingly it was agreed that the conference should be between Celsus and Gallus on one part, and Valens with Cæcina on the other. As the two first were upon their journey, they met some centurions, who told them the troops were already in motion, marching for Bedriacum, but that they themselves were deputed by their generals to carry proposals for an accommodation. Celsus and Gallus expressed their approval, and requested them to turn back and carry them to Cæcina. However, Celsus, upon his approach, was in danger from the vanguard, who happened to be some of the horse that had suffered at the ambush. For as soon as they saw him, they hallooed, and were coming down upon him; but the centurions came forward to protect him, and the other officers crying out and bidding them desist, Cæcina came up to inform himself of the tumult, which he quieted, and giving a friendly greeting to Celsus, took him in his company and proceeded towards Bedriacum.

Titianus, meantime, had repented of having sent the messengers; and placed those of the soldiers who were more confident upon the walls once again, bidding the others also go and support them. But when Cæcina rode up on his horse and held out his hand, no one did or said to the contrary; those on the walls greeted his men with salutations, others opened the gates and went out, and mingled freely with those they met; and instead of acts of hostility, there was nothing but mutual shaking of hands and congratulations, every one taking the oaths and submitting to Vitellius.

This is the account which the most of those that were present at the battle give of it, yet own that the disorder they were in, and the absence of any unity of action, would not give them leave to be certain as to particulars. And when I myself travelled afterwards over the field of battle, Mestrius Florus, a man of consular degree, one of those who had been, not willingly, but by command, in attendance on Otho at the time, pointed out to me an ancient temple, and told me, that as he went that way after the battle, he observed a heap of bodies piled up there to such a height that those on the top of it touched the pinnacles of the roof. How it came to be so, he could neither discover himself nor learn from any other person; as indeed, he said, in civil wars it generally happens that greater numbers are killed when an army is routed, quarter not being given, because captives are of no advantage to the conquerors; but why the carcasses should be heaped up after that manner is not easy to determine.

Otho, at first, as it frequently happens, received some uncertain rumours of the issue of the battle. But when some of the wounded that returned from the field informed him rightly of it, it is not, indeed, so much to be wondered at that his friends should bid him not give all up as lost or let his courage sink; but the feeling shown by the soldiers is something that exceeds all belief. There was not one of them would either go over to the conqueror or show any disposition to make terms for himself, as if their leader's cause was desperate; on the contrary, they crowded his gates, called out to him the title of emperor, and as soon as he appeared, cried out and intreated him, catching hold of his hand, and throwing themselves upon the ground, and with all the moving language of tears and persuasion, besought him to stand by them, not abandon them to their enemies, but employ in his service their lives and persons, which would not cease to be his so long as they had breath; so urgent was their zealous and universal importunity. And one obscure and private soldier, after he had drawn his sword, addressed himself to Otho: "By this, Cæsar, judge our fidelity; there is not a man

amongst us but would strike thus to serve you"; and so stabbed himself.

Notwithstanding this, Otho stood serene and unshaken, and, with a face full of constancy and composure, turned himself about and looked at them, replying thus: "This day, my fellow-soldiers, which gives me such proofs of your affection, is preferable even to that on which you saluted me emperor; deny me not, therefore, the yet higher satisfaction of laying down my life for the preservation of so many brave men; in this, at least, let me be worthy of the empire, that is, to die for it. I am of opinion the enemy has neither gained an entire nor a decisive victory; I have advice that the Mœsian army is not many days' journey distant, on its march to the Adriatic; Asia, Syria, and Egypt, and the legions that are serving against the Jews, declare for us; the senate is also with us, and the wives and children of our opponents are in our power; but alas, it is not in defence of Italy against Hannibal or Pyrrhus or the Cimbri that we fight; Romans combat here against Romans, and, whether we conquer or are defeated our country suffers and we commit a crime: victory, to whichever it fall, is gained at her expense. Believe it many times over, I can die with more honour than I can reign. For I cannot see at all how I should do any such great good to my country by gaining the victory, as I shall by dying to establish peace and unanimity and to save Italy from such another unhappy day."

As soon as he had done, he was resolute against all manner of argument or persuasion, and taking leave of his friends and the senators that were present, he bade them depart, and wrote to those that were absent, and sent letters to the towns, that they might have every honour and facility in their journey. Then he sent for Cocceius, his brother's son, who was yet a boy, and bade him be in no apprehension of Vitellius, whose mother and wife and family he had treated with the same tenderness as his own; and also told him that this had been his reason for delaying to adopt him, which he had meant to do as his son; he had desired that he might share his power, if he conquered, but not be involved in his ruin if he failed. "Take notice," he added, "my boy, of these my last words, that you neither too negligently forget, nor too zealously remember, that Cæsar was your uncle." By and by he heard a tumult amongst the soldiers at the door, who were treating the senators with menaces for preparing to withdraw; upon which, out of regard to their safety, he showed himself once more in public, but not with a gentle aspect and in a persuading manner as before; on the contrary, with a countenance that discovered indignation and authority, he commanded such as were disorderly to leave the place, and was not disobeyed.

It was now evening, and feeling thirsty, he drank some water, and then took two daggers that belonged to him, and when he had carefully examined their edges, he laid one of them down, and put the other in his robe, under his arm, then called his servants, and distributed some money amongst them, but not inconsiderately, nor like one too lavish of what was not his own; for to some he gave more, to others less, all strictly in moderation, and distinguishing every one's particular merit. When this was done, he dismissed them, and passed the rest of the night in so sound a sleep that the officers of his bed-chamber heard him snore. In the morning, he called for one of his freedmen, who had assisted him in arranging about the senators, and bade him bring him an account if they were safe. Being informed they were all well and wanted nothing, "Go then," said he, "and show yourself to the soldiers, lest they should cut you to pieces for being accessory to my death."

As soon as he was gone, he held his sword upright under him with both his hands, and falling upon it expired with no more than one single groan to express his sense of the pang, or to inform those that waited without. When his servants, therefore, raised their exclamations of grief, the whole camp and city were at once filled with lamentation; the soldiers immediately broke in at the doors with a loud cry, in passionate distress, and accusing themselves that they had been so negligent in looking after that life which was laid down to preserve theirs. Nor would a man of them quit the body to secure his own safety with the approaching enemy; but having raised a funeral pile, and attired the body, they bore it thither, arrayed in their arms, those among them greatly exulting who succeeded in getting first under the bier and becoming its bearers. Of the others, some threw themselves down before the body and kissed his wound, others grasped his hand, and others that were at a distance knelt down to do him obeisance. There were some who, after putting their torches to the pile, slew themselves, though they had not, so far as appeared, either any particular obligations to the dead, or reason to apprehend ill usage from the victor.

Simply, it would seem, no king, legal or illegal, had ever been possessed with so extreme and vehement a passion to command others, as was that of these men to obey Otho. Nor did their love of him cease with his death; it survived and changed ere long into a mortal hatred to his successor, as will be shown in its proper place.

They placed the remains of Otho in the earth, and raised over them a monument which neither by its size nor the pomp of its inscription might excite hostility. I myself have seen it, at Brixillum; a plain structure, and the epitaph only this: "To the memory of Marcus Otho. He died in his thirty-eighth year, after a short reign of about three months, his death being as much applauded as his life was censured; for if he lived not better than Nero, he died more nobly."

The soldiers were displeased with Pollio, one of their two prefects, who bade them immediately swear allegiance to Vitellius; and when they understood that some of the senators were still upon the spot, they made no opposition to the departure of the rest, but only disturbed the tranquillity of Virginius Rufus with an offer of the government, and moving in one body to his house in arms, they first entreated him, and then demanded of him to accept of the empire, or at least to be their mediator. But he, that refused to command them when conquerors, thought it ridiculous to pretend to it now they were beat, and was unwilling to go as their envoy to the Germans, whom in past time he had compelled to do various things that they had not liked; and for these reasons he slipped away through a private door. As soon as the soldiers perceived this, they owned Vitellius, and so got their pardon, and served under Cæcina.

INDEX

PRINTED IN THE U. S. A.

THE GREAT IDEAS, *Volumes 2 and 3*

••	FAMILY
ANGEL	FATE
ANIMAL	FORM
ARISTOCRACY	GOD
ART	GOOD AND EVIL
ASTRONOMY	GOVERNMENT
BEAUTY	HABIT
BEING	HAPPINESS
CAUSE	HISTORY
CHANCE	HONOR
CHANGE	HYPOTHESIS
CITIZEN	IDEA
CONSTITUTION	IMMORTALITY
COURAGE	INDUCTION
CUSTOM AND	INFINITY
CONVENTION	JUDGMENT
DEFINITION	JUSTICE
DEMOCRACY	KNOWLEDGE
DESIRE	LABOR
DIALECTIC	LANGUAGE
DUTY	LAW
EDUCATION	LIBERTY
ELEMENT	LIFE AND DEATH
EMOTION	LOGIC
ETERNITY	LOVE
EVOLUTION	MAN
EXPERIENCE	MATHEMATICS